DICTIONARY
OF THE
REFORMATION

THE ENCYCLOPEDIA OF THEOLOGY AND CHURCH

A Theological Reference Libracy
based on the third edition of the
LEXIKON FÜR THEOLOGIE UND KIRCHE

Michael Buchberger
Series founder

Edited by
Walter Kasper
Konrad Baumgartner
Horst Bürkle
Klaus Ganzer
Karl Kertelge
Wilhelm Korff
Peter Walter

DICTIONARY
of the
REFORMATION

Edited by
KLAUS GANZER AND BRUNO STEIMER

Translated by
BRIAN McNEIL

A Herder and Herder Book
The Crossroad Publishing Company
New York

The Crossroad Publishing Company
481 Eighth Avenue, New York, NY 10001

Originally published in German under the title
Lexikon der Reformationszeit
© 2002 by Verlag Herder, Freiburg im Breisgau

English copyright © 2004 by the Crossroad Publishing Company

Printed in the United States of America

Library of Congress Cataloging-in-Publication Data

Lexikon der Reformationszeit. English.
   Dictionary of the Reformation / edited by Klaus Ganzer and Bruno Steimer ;
translated by Brian McNeil.
      p. cm.
   Includes bibliographical references and index.
   ISBN 0-8245-2119-6 (hardcover)
      1. Reformation – Dictionaries. I. Title: At head of title: Encyclopedia of
theology and church. II. Ganzer, Klaus. III. Steimer, Bruno. IV. Title.
BR302.8.L4913 2004
270.6′03 – dc22

                                                                    2004018930

1   2   3   4   5   6   7   8   9   10   08   07   06   05   04

CONTENTS

Frequently Cited Reference Works

ACO	*Acta Conciliorum Oecumenicorum,* ed. E. Schwartz. 1st series, 4 vols. Berlin, 1914–84; 2nd series, 1984–.
ADB	*Allgemeine Deutsche Biographie.* 55 vols. Leipzig, 1875–1920; index volume, 1912.
AHC	*Annuarium historiae conciliorum.* Paderborn, 1969–.
AHP	*Archivum historiae pontificiae.* Rome, 1963– (containing *Bibliographia historiae pontificiae.*
ARCEG	*Acta reformationis catholicae ecclesiam Germaniae concernentia saeculi X VI,* ed. G. Pfeilschifter. 6 vols. Regensburg, 1959–74.
ARG	*Archiv für Reformationsgeschichte.* Vols. 1–41. Leipzig, 1903–50; vol. 42, Göttingen, 1951, includes bibliography.
BBKL	*Biographisch-bibliographisches Kirchenlexikon,* ed. F. W. Bautz. Hamm, 1975–.
BDG	*Bibliographie zur deutschen Geschichte im Zeitalter der Glaubensspaltung 1517–85,* ed. K. Schottenloher. 6 vols. Leipzig, 1933–40; 2d ed., 7 vols., 1956–66.
BiDi	*Bibliotheca dissidentium: répertoire des non-conformistes religieux des seizième et dix-septième siècles,* ed. A. Séguenny. Baden-Baden, 1980–.
BSLK	*Die Bekenntnisschriften der evangelisch-lutherischen Kirche,* ed. Deutschen Evangelischen Kirchenausschuss. 11th ed. Göttingen, 1992; 12th ed. 1998.
CATH	*Catholicisme: Hier—Aujourd'hui—Demain,* ed. G. Jacquemet et al., 15 vols. Paris, 1948–2000.
CCath	Corpus Catholicorum, J. Greving, founding editor. Münster, 1919–.
CCG	Corpus Christianorum. Series Graeca. Turnhout, 1974–.
CCL	Corpus Christianorum. Series Latina. Turnhout, 1953–.
CCM	Corpus Christianorum. Continuatio medievalis. Turnhout, 1966–.
CEras	*Contemporaries of Erasmus. A Biographical Register of the Renaissance and Reformation,* ed. P. G. Bietenholz and T. B. Deutscher. 3 vols. Toronto, 1985–87.
ChH	*Church History.* Chicago, 1932–.
CHR	*The Catholic Historical Review.* Washington, 1915–.
COD	*Conciliorum oecumenicorum decreta,* ed. G. Alberigo et al. 3d ed., Bologna, 1974; 4th ed., 1991.
CR	Corpus Reformatorum. Vols. 1–28 (Melanchthon), ed. G. Bretschneider et al. Halle, 1834–60; reprint, New York, 1963; vols. 29–87 (Calvin), ed. J. W. Braun et al. Braunschweig, 1863–1900; reprint, 1964; vols. 88ff. (Zwingli), ed. E. Egli et al. Berlin/Leipzig, 1905–.
CrS	*Cristianesimo nella storia.* Bologna, 1980–.
CT	*Concilium Tridentinum. Diariorum, Actorum, Epistularum, Tractatuum nova Collectio,* ed. Görres-Gesellschaft. 13 vols. Freiburg, 1901–2001.
DBF	*Dictionnaire de biographie française.* Paris 1929–.

DBI	*Dizionario biografico degli Italiani.* Rome, 1960–.
DH	H. Denzinger, *Enchiridion symbolorum, definitionum et declarationum de rebus fidei et morum,* 37th ed. with German trans. by P. Hünermann. Freiburg, 1991.
DHEE	*Diccionario de historia eclesiástica de Espana,* 4 vols. Madrid, 1972–75. Supplement volume. Madrid, 1987.
DHGE	*Dictionnaire d'histoire et de géographie ecclésiastiques,* ed. A. Baudrillart et al. Paris, 1912–.
DizEc	*Dizionario ecclesiastico,* ed. A. Mercati and A. Pelzer. 3 vols. Turin 1953–58.
DNB	*The Dictionary of National Biography,* ed. L. Stephen and S. Lee. 63 vols. London, 1885–1901. New editions and supplements through 1990. To be published in 2004 as *Oxford Dictionary of National Biography.*
DS	H. Denzinger and A. Schönmetzer, *Enchiridion symbolorum, definitionum et declarationum de rebus fidei et morum.* 36th ed., Freiburg, 1976.
DSp	*Dictionnaire de spiritualité, Ascétique et Mystique: Doctrine et historie,* ed. M. Viller, 16 vols., index vol. Paris, 1932–95.
DThC	*Dictionnaire de théologie catholique,* ed. A. Vacant and E. Mangenot, continued by E. Amann, 15 vols. Paris, 1903–50; 3 index vols., 1951–72.
DtLit	*Die deutsche Literatur. Biographisches und bibliographisches Lexikon,* ed. H.-G. Roloff. Reihe 1ff., Abteilung A (Autorenlexikon), Abteilung B (Forschungsliteratur), vol. 1ff. Bern, 1985–.
EC	*Enciclopedia Cattolica,* 13 vols. Rome, 1949–69.
EKL	*Evangelisches Kirchenlexikon,* 3d ed., 5 vols. Göttingen, 1986–97.
EKO	*Evangelische Kirchenordnungen des XVI. Jh.,* ed. E. Sehling. 5 vols. Leipzig, 1902–13; vol. 6/1ff. ed. Institut für evangelisches Kirchenrecht der EKD. Tübingen, 1955–.
GCh	*Geschichte des Christentums,* 14 vols. Freiburg, 1991–.
HCMA	*Hierachia Catholica medii (et recentioris) aevi,* founded by K. Eubel: vols. 1–3, ed. L. Schmitz-Kallenberg. Münster, 1898–1910; 2nd ed. 1913–23. Vol. 4, ed. C. Gauchat. Münster, 1935. Vols. 5–8, ed. V. Ritzler. Padua, 1952–79.
HDThG	*Handbuch der Dogmen- und Theologiegeschichte,* ed. C. Andresen. 3 vols. Gottingen, 1980–84; 2nd ed., 1998–99.
HJ	*Historisches Jahrbuch der Görres-Gesellschaft.* Cologne, 1880–.
HKG	*Handbuch der Kirchengeschichte,* ed. H. Jedin, 7 vols. Freiburg, 1962–79.
Inst	J. Calvin, *Christianae Religionis Institutio: Opera selecta,* 5 vols. ed. R. Barth et al. Munich, 1926–39; 2nd ed. vols. 3–5, 1957–62.
Jedin	H. Jedin, *Geschichte des Konzils von Trient.* 3rd ed., vol. 1, Freiburg, 1977; 2nd ed., vol. 2, 1978; vols. 4/1 and 4/1, 1976.
JEH	*The Journal of Ecclesiastical History.* London, 1950–.
Klaiber	*Katholische Kontroverstheologen und Reformer des 16. Jh.,* ed. W. Klaiber. Münster, 1978.
KLK	*Katholisches Leben und Kirchenreform* (to 1966: Kämpfen) *im Zeitalter der Glaubensspaltung.* Münster, 1927–.
Köhler BF	H.-J. Köhler, *Bibliographie der Flugschriften des 16.Jh.,* part 1ff., vol. 1ff., Tübingen, 1991–.

KThR	*Katholische Theologen der Reformationszeit,* ed. E. Iserloh. 5 vols. Münster, 1984–88; 2nd ed., 1991–.
LMA	*Lexikon des Mittelalters,* 9 vols. Munich/Zurich, 1980–98; study ed., Stuttgart, 1999.
LThK	*Lexikon für Theologie und Kirche,* ed. M. Buchberger. 10 vols. Freiburg, 1930–38; 2nd ed., ed. J. Höfer and K. Rahner, 10 vols. and index vol. Freiburg, 1957–67; 3rd ed., ed. W. Kasper et al., 10 vols. and supplement/index vol., Freiburg, 1993–2001.
NBD	*Nuntiaturberichte aus Deutschland nebst ergänzenden Aktenstücken,* I., III., und IV. Abteilung ed. Deutsches Historisches Institut in Rom, II. Abteilung ed. Österreichisches Historisches Institut in Rom. I. Abteilung (1533–59): vols. 1–12 (Gotha/Berlin, 1892–1912; reprint Frankfurt a.M., 1968); vols. 13ff. (Tübingen, 1959–); additional vols. 1–2 (1530–31 and 1532) (Tübingen, 1963–69). II. Abteilung (1560–72): vols. 1–8 (Vienna/Leipzig, 1897–1939; Graz/Cologne, 1952–67). III. Abteilung (1572–85): vols. 1–5 (Berlin, 1892–1909; reprint Turin, 1972); vols. 6ff. (Tübingen, 1982–). IV. Abteilung (17th cent.): 3 unnumbered vols. (Berlin, 1895–1913; reprint Turin, 1973). Further vols. in preparation.
NBD(G)	*Nuntiaturberichte aus Deutschland nebst ergänzenden Aktenstücken,* ed. Görres-Gesellschaft (no continuous numbering of vols.). I. Abteilung: *Die Kölner Nuntiatur,* vols. 1 and 2/1 (1585[84]–90) (Paderborn, 1895–99; reprint 1969); vols. 2/2ff. (1590–1630); (Munich et al., 1969–). II. Abteilung: *Die Nuntiatur am Kaiserhofe,* 3 vols. (1585[84]–92) (Paderborn, 1905–19).
NCE	*New Catholic Encyclopedia,* ed. W. J. MacDonald et al., 15 vols. New York, 1967.
NDB	*Neue Deutsche Biographie,* ed. Historischen Kommission bei der Bayerischen Akademie der Wissenschaften. Berlin, 1953–.
OER	*The Oxford Encyclopedia of the Reformation,* ed. H. J. Hillerbrand. 4 vols. New York, 1996.
PG	*Patrologia Graeca,* ed. J. P. Migne, 167 vols., Paris, 1857–66.
PL	*Patrologia Latina,* ed. J. P. Migne, 217 vols., 4 index vols. Paris, 1841–64.
PLS	*Patrologia Latina,* suppl. vols. 1–5, ed. A. Hamman. Paris, 1958–70.
QFIAB	*Quellen und Forschungen aus italienischen Archiven und Bibliotheken.* Rome, 1897–.
RE	*Realencyklopädie für protestantische Theologie und Kirche,* founded by J. J. Herzog; ed. A. Hauck. 3rd ed., 24 vols., Leipzig, 1896-1913.
RGG	*Die Religion in Geschichte und Gegenwart.* Tübingen, 1909–13; 2nd ed., 1927–32; 3rd ed., 1956–62; index vol. 1965; 4th ed., 1998–.
RGST	*Reformationsgeschichtliche Studien und Texte,* founded by J. Greyling. Münster, 1906–.
RHE	*Revue d'histoire ecclésiastique.* Leuven, 1900–.
RHEF	*Revue d'histoire de l'Eglise de France.* Paris, 1910–.
RSCI	*Rivista di storia della Chiesa in Italia.* Rome, 1947–.
RQ	*Römische Quartalschrift für christliche Altertumskunde und Kirchengeschichte.* Freiburg, 1887–.
SCJ	*The Sixteenth Century Journal.* St. Charles, 1970–.
TRE	*Theologische Realenzyklopädie,* ed. G. Krause and G. Müller. Berlin/New York, 1976–.

TRZRK	*Die Territorien des Reichs im Zeitalter der Reformation und Konfessionalisierung,* ed. A. Schindling. 7 vols. Münster, 1989–97.
VD 16	*Verzeichnis der im deutschen Sprachbereich erschienenen Drucke des XVI. Jh.,* ed. Bayerischen Staatsbibliothek in München in Verbindung mit der Herzog-August-Bibliothek in Wolfenbuttel, bearbeitet von I. Bezzel. 25 vols. Stuttgart, 1983–2000.
WA	M. Luther, *Werke. Kritische Gesamtausgabe* "Weimarer Ausgabe." Weimar, 1883ff.
WA.BR	— Briefwechsel
WA.TR	— Tischreden
WA.DB	— Deutsche Bibel
ZBKG	*Zeitschrift für bayerische Kirchengeschichte.* Nuremberg, 1926–.
ZHF	*Zeitschrift für historische Forschung.* Berlin, 1974–.
ZKG	*Zeitschrift für Kirchengeschichte.* Stuttgart, 1877–.
ZSRG.K	*Zeitschrift der Savigny-Stiftung für Rechtsgeschichte. Kanonistische Abteilung.* Weimar, 1911–.

A

Acontius (Acontio, Aconcio, Contio, Contio), *Jacobus*. Italian Protestant humanist, lawyer, and theologian, born in Ossana (Val di Sole) or Trent before 1515, died c. 1567 in London. From 1540 to 1549, he was a notary in Ossana and Trent; later, he worked primarily at the imperial court. In 1556, he became secretary to Cristoforo → Madruzzo, governor of Trent. He fled for reasons of faith to Switzerland in 1557, and arrived in England in 1559, where he served the queen as castle engineer until his death. He wrote many works, especially on methodological and religious questions. In his major work, *Stratagemata Satanae* (Basle, 1565, republished Florence, 1846), he attempted to distinguish those elements in the Christian faith that were necessary for salvation from less important matters. In his view, the → fundamental articles of the faith are explicitly mentioned in sacred scripture, and the term "heresy" can be properly applied only to error in those doctrines that are necessary for salvation. The French wars of religion made a profound impression on him and led him to oppose confessional coercion and the persecution of heretics. He criticized the formation of dogmas and emphasized that sanctification through orientation to scripture was more important than orthodoxy in the dogmatic and confessional sense.

■ **Literature:** *TRE* 1:402–7; *DtLit* II A 1:99–110.—L. Girard, "L'itinéraire intellectuel de Giacomo Aconcio," *Revue des sciences philosophiques et théologiques* 67 (1983) 531–52.

MICHAEL BECHT

■ **Additional Bibliography:** *BiDi* 16:55–117.—J. Freudiger, "Methodus resolutiva. Antikes und Neuzeitliches in Jacopo A.s Methodenschrift," *Freiburger Zeitschrift für Philosophie und Theologie* 45 (1998) 407–46.

Adelmann von Adelmannsfelden (1), *Bernhard*. Humanist, born 1457/1459, died December 16, 1523 in Eichstätt. He studied in Heidelberg (1472), Basle (1476), Ferrara and Rome (1481/1482). He was a canon of the collegiate church in Ellwangen in 1486/1487 and was appointed cathedral canon and provost in Augsburg in 1498. Here, he became a member of the "Sodality of Letters" (Conrad → Peutinger, Jakob → Fugger) and exchanged letters with → Erasmus of Rotterdam, Johannes → Reuchlin, Nikolaus → Ellenbog, and Willibald → Pirckheimer. So great was his enthusiasm for Martin Luther that Johannes → Eck observed in 1519 that scarcely anyone in Augsburg took Luther's side any more, apart from a few "ignorant canons." This was an allusion to the Adelmann brothers, who replied by commissioning Johannes → Oecolampadius, the cathedral preacher, to write his sarcastic response *Canonicorum indoctorum responsio ad Eccium* ("Reply of the ignorant canons to Eck"). Eck got his revenge in 1520, when he added Adelmann's name in his own writing to the bull → *Exsurge Domine* with its threat of excommunication. Adelmann, however, obtained an absolution from this excommunication in the same year and remained an adherent of the Roman church.

(2) *Konrad*. Humanist, born September 8, 1462, died February 6, 1547 in Holzheim near Dillingen on the Danube. He was the brother of Bernhard (1 above). As a student, he was already a canon of Eichstätt cathedral; he was educated in Heidelberg (1473), Basle (1476), Ferrara (1481), Tübingen (1483), and Ingolstadt (1486). In 1486, he was appointed a canon of the collegiate church in Ellwangen and canon of the cathedral in Augsburg in 1502; he became cathedral treasurer in Augsburg in 1517, where he was a member of the humanist circle and had contacts with Johannes Reuchlin (whose part he took in the conflict with the Dominicans in Cologne), with Kilian → Leib, Johannes → Aventinus, and Bohuslav von Lobkowitz zu Hassenstein. In the period after 1520, Adelmann was an adherent of the old church, and the introduction of the Reformation to Augsburg forced him to go into exile in Dillingen at the beginning of 1537.

■ **Literature:** H. A. Lier, "Der Augsburger Humanistenkreis mit besonderer Berücksichtigung B. A.s," *Zeitschrift des Historischen Vereins für Schwaben* 7 (1880) 68–108; F. X. Thumhofer, *Bernhard A.* (Freiburg, 1900); J. Zeller, "Die Brüder B., K. und Kaspar A. als Stiftsherren in Ellwangen," *Ellwanger Jahrbuch* 1922/23,

75–85; G. S. Graf Adelmann von Adelmannsfelden, *Das Geschlecht der A.* (Tübingen, 1948); F. Zoepfl, *Lebensbilder aus dem Bayerischen Schwaben,* vol. 11 (Weissenhorn, 1976) 39–45; H. Immenkötter, *Geschichte der Stadt Augsburg* (Stuttgart, ²1985) 391–412; K. Kosel, *Der Augsburger Domkreuzgang und seine Denkmäler* (Sigmaringen, 1991).

HERBERT IMMENKÖTTER

Adiaphora controversy. This controversy was born of the various reactions of the Protestants to the Interim of → Augsburg or Leipzig (1548). The policy of Charles V aimed at reunification by means of a far-reaching recatholicization of the Protestant churches (reintroduction of the seven sacraments, of the Mass, and of the veneration of images (→ Art and Reformation), of the feast of Corpus Christi, and of episcopal jurisdiction; purgatory and → indulgences were not mentioned in his program), and this prompted discussion of the value of these *adiaphora* ("intermediate matters"). The question was not whether a neutral concept of adiaphora could exist, but rather under what precise circumstances intermediate matters could take on a directly confessional significance. Philipp Melanchthon and his followers (Georg → Major, Justus → Menius, Johann → Pfeffinger, etc.) were willing to accept Catholic rites, if this price had to be paid to ensure the right to preach freely in accord with the gospel; but he was opposed by the → Gnesiolutherans (Nikolaus → Amsdorf, Nikolaus → Gallus, Kaspar Aquila, etc.) under Matthias → Flacius, who affirmed: "When the confession is at stake and scandal is involved, there is no such thing as an adiaphoron." Article 10 of the Formula of → Concord confirms that the value of intermediate matters changes when their observance is imposed by force: in a situation of persecution, one may not yield even on such minor issues.

■ **Literature:** *HDThG* 2:108–13.—W. Preger, *Matthias Flacius Illyricus und seine Zeit,* 2 vols. (Erlangen, 1859–61; reprint Hildesheim—Nieuwkoop, 1964); idem, "Flacius von den Kirchlichen Mitteldingen," *Zeitschrift für Protestantismus und Kirche* Neue Serie (1858) 165–86; O. Ritschl, *Dogmengeschichte des Protestantismus,* vol. 2 (Leipzig, 1912) 325ff.; Ch. von Hase, *Die Gestalt der Kirche Luthers. Der casus confessionis im Kampf des Matthias Flacius gegen das Interim von 1548* (Göttingen, 1940).

FRIEDHELM KRÜGER

■ **Additional Bibliography:** G. Wartenberg, "Philipp Melanchthon und die sächsisch-albertinische Interimspolitik," *Lutherisches Jahrbuch* 55 (1988) 60–82.

Agricola, *Johann* (Islebius, Eislebius, Schnitter, Schneyder). Protestant theologian and reformer, born 1492 or 1494 probably in Eisleben, died September 22, 1566 in Berlin. He studied in Leipzig (1509/1510) and Wittenberg (1515/1516). He strongly influenced the early theology of Martin Luther, and his humanism influenced Philipp Melanchthon. He held lectures in exegesis and dialectics and engaged in catechetical work in Wittenberg; after 1521 he was increasingly critical of Thomas → Müntzer and later composed several treatises against him. In 1525, he became rector of the Latin school in Eisleben, where he engaged in controversies with Georg → Witzel from 1533 onwards; he returned to Wittenberg in 1536. He disagreed with Melanchthon in 1527 about the preaching of the law and with Luther too from 1537 onward (→ Antinomian controversy about the relationship between law—gospel—penance—rebirth [→ Law and Gospel]). Agricola denied that the process of penance necessarily required the preaching of the law, and emphasized the gospel and the working of the Holy Spirit. In mid-August, 1540, he was in Berlin, where he became court preacher to → Joachim II of Brandenburg, General Superintendent, and Visitor. He collaborated in the → Augsburg Interim (1548), promoting the policy of the Elector of Brandenburg; he expressed criticism of Andreas → Osiander and Philippism. He was catechist, exegete, and preacher, and wrote many theological works. He also composed church hymns, published an important collection of proverbs (from 1529 onwards), and made translations.

■ **Literature:** *NDB* 1:100f.; *RGG*³ 1:187f.; *BBKL* 1:57–59; *VD 16* 1:138–48; *TRE* 2:110–18; *DtLit* II A 1:453–96; Köhler *BF* 1:20–28.—G. Kawerau, *J. A.* (Berlin, 1881); J. Rogge, *J. A.s Lutherverständnis. Unter Berücksichtigung des Antinomismus* (Berlin, 1960); S. L. Gilman, "The Hymns of J. A. of Eisleben. A Literary Reappraisal," *Modern Language Review* 67 (1972) 364–89; M. U. Edwards, Jr., *Luther and the False Brethren* (Stanford, Calif., 1975); S. Hausammann, *Buße als Umkehr und Erneuerung von Mensch und Gesellschaft* (Zurich, 1975); S. L. Gilman, "J. A. of Eisleben's Proverb Collection (1529)," *SCJ* 8 (1977) 77–84; S. Kjeldgaard-Pedersen, *Gesetz, Evangelium und Buße. Theologiegeschichtliche*

Studien zum Verhältnis zwischen dem jungen A. (Eisleben) und Martin Luther (Leiden, 1983); J. Rogge, *Innerlutherische Streitigkeiten um Gesetz und Evangelium, Rechtfertigung und Heiligung: Leben und Werk Martin Luthers von 1526 bis 1546,* ed. H. Junghans (Göttingen, 1983) 187–204; E. Koch, *J. A. neben Lutherischer Schülerschaft und theologischer Eigenart: Lutheriana,* ed. G. Hammer and K.-H. zur Mühlen (Cologne-Vienna, 1984) 131–50; R. Mau, *Bekenntnis und Machtwort. Die Stellung Joachims II. im Streit um die Notwendigkeit der guten Werke: 450 Jahre Evangelische Theologie in Berlin,* ed. G. Besier and Ch. Gestrich (Göttingen, 1989) 39–64.

HERIBERT SMOLINSKY

■ **Additional Bibliography:** *RGG*⁴ 1:191.—T. J. Wengert, *Law and Gospel. Philip Melanchton's Debate with J. A. of Eisleben over Poenitentia* (Carlisle, 1997); idem, "Gesetz und Buße. Philipp Melanchthons erster Streit mit J. A.," in *Der Theologe Melanchthon* (Stuttgart, 2000) 375–92.

Agricola, *Mikael.* Finnish reformer and founder of the Finnish literary language and literature, born c. 1509 in Pernaja, died April 9, 1557 in Uusikirkko, while returning from a political mission. He became acquainted with Reformation teachings at an early age. Martin Skytte, the first Protestant bishop in Finland, made Agricola his secretary and sent him to study at Wittenberg from 1536 to 1539. He headed the cathedral school in Åbo and became Skytte's coadjutor in 1548 and bishop of Åbo in 1550. He was ordained bishop in 1554 and governed the see until his death. He composed a primer with catechism in Finnish (1543), a prayer book (1544), translations of the New Testament (1548) and parts of the Old Testament (1551–1552), a catechism, and an Order of the Mass (1549).
■ **Works:** *M. Agricolan teokset (Die Werke M. A.s),* 3 vols. (Helsinki, 1931, ²1987).
■ **Literature:** *DHGE* 17:217–31; *TRE* 11:185–92.— J. Gummerus, *M. A., der Reformator Finnlands* (Helsinki, 1941); idem, *M. A. rukouskirja ja sen lähteet (Das Gebetbuch M. A.s und seine Quellen),* 3 vols. (Helsinki, 1941–1955); K. Antel, "M. A. släkt," *Historisk Tidskrift för Finland* 39 (1954) 7–15; G. Johannesson, *Die Kirchenreformation in den nordischen Ländern* (Göteborg, 1960) 48–83; G. Schwaiger, *Die Reformation in den nordischen Ländern* (Munich, 1962); idem, "Bischofsweihen und Apostolische Sukzession der schwedischen Kirche im 16.Jh.," *Würzburger Diözesangeschichtsblätter* 35/36 (1974) 367–80; P. G. Lindhardt, *Skandinavische Kirchengeschichte seit dem 16.Jh.* (Göttingen, 1982).

GEORG SCHWAIGER

Agricola (K[C]astenbauer, also called Boius), *Stephan* the Elder. Protestant theologian, born c. 1491 in Abensberg, died April 10/11, 1547 in Eisleben. He studied in Vienna and in Italy and worked as pastor in Vienna c. 1515. He took his doctorate in theology in 1519 and joined the Order of Augustinian Hermits (Vienna, Regensburg; prior in Rattenberg am Inn). In 1522, Cardinal Matthäus → Lang ordered his arrest, but he managed to escape. In 1525, he was active as a Lutheran preacher in Augsburg. He was a resolute opponent of Huldrich Zwingli's teachings about the Lord's Supper. He was pastor in Hof (c. 1541), Sulzbach (1543), and Eisleben (1545). He was one of the signatories of the Articles of Marburg (1529) and of → Schmalkald (1537). He translated Johannes → Bugenhagen's *Contra novum errorem de sacramento* into German in 1525 and the *Syngramma suevicum* in the following year. His son, Stephan the Younger (c. 1526–1562), who is often confused with him, was a more productive writer than his father.
■ **Literature:** *NDB* 1:104f.; *RGG*³ 1:188f.; *BBKL* 1:62; *ARCEG* 1; *VD 16* 4:72; Köhler *BF* 1/1:28f.; *DtLit* II A 1:759–63, 764–75.—M. Simon, "Zur Lebensgeschichte des S. A. und zur Person des A. Boius," *ZBKG* 30 (1961) 168–74; J. Pflug, *Correspondance,* ed. J. V. Pollet, vol. 5/2 (Leiden, 1982); M. Brecht and H. Ehmer, *Südwestdeutsche Reformationsgeschichte* (Stuttgart, 1984); M. Brecht, *Martin Luther,* vols. 2–3 (Stuttgart, 1986–87).

HERIBERT SMOLINSKY

■ **Additional Bibliography:** B. Moeller, "Sterbekunst in der Reformation. Der 'köstliche, gute, notwendige Sermon vom Sterben' des Augustiner-Eremiten Stefan Kastenbauer," in *Vita religiosa im Mittelalter.* Festschrift K. Elm (Berlin, 1999) 739–65; M. Lommer, "Der altbayerische Frühlutheraner Dr. S. Kastenbauer," *ZBKG* 69 (2000) 227–30.

Alba, *Fernando Álvarez de Toledo.* Third duke of Alba, Spanish statesman and general, born October 29, 1507 in Piedrahita (Ávila) of an ancient noble family, died December 11, 1582 in Tomar near Lisbon. His military career began during the campaign against the Turks (1530–1533). He became the chief military adviser of → Charles V in 1536. He gave proof of his qualities as general during the → Schmalkald War (battle of Mühlberg, 1547). As viceroy of Naples (1556), he was drawn into the war against Pope → Paul IV, which ended in 1577 with a peace treaty favorable to Spain. → Philip II sent him to the Netherlands in 1567 to crush the revolt against Spain. His harsh actions against the rebels, including the setting up of the "Council for the Troubles" (also known as the "Council of Blood"), and the taxes that he introduced made him the embodiment in the Netherlands of the hated Spanish rule. He returned to Spain in 1573, where he was a member of the council of state until he fell from Philip's favor in 1579 and was exiled. He was rehabilitated one year later and led the conquest of Portugal. He was regent of Portugal until July, 1582.

■ **Literature:** W. Kirchner, *A., Spaniens eiserner Herzog* (Göttingen, 1963); M. Dierickx, "Nieuwe gegevens over het bestuur van de hertog van A. in de Nederlanden," *Tijdschrift voor geschiedenis* 77 (1964) 167–92; G. Janssens, "Het oordeel van tijdgenoten en historici over A.'s bestuur in de Nederlanden," *Revue belge de philologie et d'histoire* 54 (1976) 474–88; G. Parker, *The Dutch Revolt* (London, 1977); F. H. M. Grapperhaus, *A. en de tiende penning* (Zutphen, 1982); W. S. Maltby, *A. A Biography of Fernando Álvarez de Toledo. Third Duke of A.* (Berkeley, Calif., 1983).

PETER J. A. NISSEN

Alber, *Matthäus.* Reformer of Reutlingen, born there December 12, 1495, died in Blaubeuren December 1, 1570. He became parish priest of Reutlingen in 1521, and he and the town council introduced the Reformation in 1524. He defended the Reformation before the imperial government in Esslingen in 1525. Although Huldrych Zwingli attempted to win Alber over to his doctrine of the Lord's Supper, he remained faithful to the Lutheran position. When Reutlingen accepted the → Augsburg Interim, he was expelled; the duke of Württemberg appointed him preacher of the collegiate church in Stuttgart and General Superintendent in 1549. Alber became one of the most influential men in the church of Württemberg, alongside Johannes → Brenz. In 1563, he became the first Protestant abbot of the monastery of Blaubeuren.

■ **Literature:** *TRE* 2:170–77; *DtLit* II A 1:983–93.—H. Ströle, "M. A.," *Schwäbische Lebensbilder* 4 (1950) 26–59.

MICHAEL BECHT

■ **Additional Bibliography:** *RGG*[4] 1:266f.

Albrecht V of Bavaria ruled as duke from 1550 to 1579 and was the founder of the confessional state of Bavaria in the early modern period. He was born on February 29, 1528 in Munich, where he died on October 24, 1579. Under Albrecht and his chancellor Simon Thaddäus Eck, the endeavors to preserve the Catholic Church abandoned their predominantly passive character and took a positive direction (recall of the Jesuits, 1555; chalice for the laity, 1556/1564). Albrecht reformed state administration (Court Chamber, 1550; constitutional decree, 1553), and his interventions in church politics took an ever clearer form, once he had outmaneuvered a faction of Protestant nobles in 1563–1564. The high point came with the visitation, "mandate of faith," and decree about schools in 1569, and the establishment of the Spiritual Council in 1570; the concession of the chalice was revoked. Significant victories of the external confessional politics were the recatholicization of enclaves within Bavaria, the role of guardian, which Albrecht assumed in Protestant Baden, and above all the election of his son → Ernest as bishop of Freising (1566) and Hildesheim (1573), which laid the foundations of subsequent success in Cologne (1583; the War of Cologne). Albrecht was also a prominent patron of the arts (court chapel, museum of antiquities, library), and this makes his reign a classic example of government in the period of confessionalization.

■ **Literature:** *NDB* 1:158ff.—M. Mayer, *Quellen zur Behördengeschichte Bayerns* (Bamberg, 1890); A. Knöpfler, *Die Kelchbewegung in Bayern unter Herzog A. V.* (Munich, 1891); S. Riezler, "Zur Würdigung Herzog A.s V. von Bayern und seiner inneren Regierung," *Abhandlungen der historischen Klasse der bayerischen Akademie der Wissenschaften* 21 (1898) 65–132; W. Goetz, *Beiträge zur Geschichte Herzog A.s V. und des Landsberger Bundes 1556–98* (Munich, 1898); W. Goetz and L. Theobald, *Beiträge zur Geschichte Herzog A.s V. und der sogenannten Adelsverschwörung von 1563* (Leipzig, 1913); R. Bauerreiss, *Kirchengeschichte Bayerns,* vol. 6 (Augsburg, 1965); M. Lanzinner, *Fürst, Räte und Landstände. Die Entstehung der Zentralbehörden in Bayern 1511–98* (Göttingen, 1980); S. Weinfurter, "Herzog, Adel und Reformation. Bayern im Übergang vom Mittelalter zur Neuzeit," *ZHF* 10 (1983) 1–39; *Handbuch der bayerischen Geschichte,* ed. A. Kraus, vol. 2 (Munich, [2]1988) 373–92; *Handbuch der Bayerischen Kirchengeschichte,* ed. W. Brandmüller et al., vol. 2 (Augsburg, 1993).

WALTER ZIEGLER

■ **Additional Bibliography:** D. Heil, *Die Reichspolitik Bayerns unter der Regierung Herzog Albrechts V.* (Göttingen, 1998)

Albrecht of Brandenburg. Bishop of Halberstadt and archbishop of Magdeburg (both 1513), archbishop and elector of Mainz (1514), cardinal (1518), born June 28, 1490 in Cölln (Berlin), died September 24, 1545 in Mainz. He was the son of elector Johann (1486–1499) and founded the university of Frankfurt on the Oder with his brother, elector → Joachim I. He received a humanist education and supported → humanism throughout his life. In the course of the expansionist territorial politics of his brother, he was promoted to high ecclesiastical positions at a very early age. When he was made archbishop of Magdeburg, he was required to pay the pallium fees, which were exceptionally high because the see had been vacant a number of times. Albrecht reached an agreement with the pope that an → indulgence should be proclaimed and that half the money raised in this way would accrue to the see of Mainz to help pay the pallium fees. Albrecht published the indulgence in his dioceses and in the electorate of Brandenburg, thereby contributing directly to the outbreak of the Reformation. Unlike his brother Joachim I, he maintained a conciliatory attitude toward the Reformation, while, however, defending the cause of the old church in the spheres of ecclesiastical and imperial politics, and he participated in the League of → Dessau. Initially, he supported the idea of a peaceful reconciliation among the religious parties that were taking shape within the empire, and this allowed the new teaching to spread in part of his territories in central Germany (Erfurt, Magdeburg). He became a fierce opponent of the innovations only when the Reformation achieved a breakthrough in his favorite residence of Halle on the Saale (1541, Treaty of Calb). Taking with him the relics of the new collegiate church, which he himself had founded, he moved his residence to Mainz, where he now resolutely endeavored to ensure the maintenance or restoration of the old church. The Jesuit Petrus → Faber encouraged him in this aim.

Among the German princes, Albrecht was the leading patron of humanism and of Renaissance art. From the very beginning of his episcopate, he surrounded himself with celebrated authors. He was close in intellectual terms to → Erasmus of Rotterdam, who honored him with the dedication of his *Ratio verae theologiae* (1518). He supported Johannes → Reuchlin and had close contact with men such as Ulrich von → Hutten and Wolfgang

→ Capito, who later became leading Reformers. In his last period, he opened his doors in Mainz to humanist defenders of the old church, such as Johannes → Cochlaeus, Michael → Helding, Georg → Witzel, and Friedrich → Nausea. Although the Reformation won the day in his central German dioceses, he was largely successful in his efforts to maintain the old church in the electoral territories of Mainz. He bequeathed these lands to his successors in conditions which made it possible for later bishops to give a new stability to considerable remnants of Catholicism in the struggles of the 16th and 17th centuries.

■ **Literature:** *NDB* 1:166f.; *TRE* 2:184f.; *TRZRK* 2:68–86; 4:60–97.—F. Schrader, "Kardinal A. von . . . im Spannungsfeld zwischen alter und neuer Kirche," *Von Konstanz nach Trient.* Festschrift A. Franzen (Paderborn, 1972); W. Delius, *Die Reformationsgeschichte der Stadt Halle* (Berlin, 1953); *Martin Luther und die Reformation. Ausstellungskatalog des Germanischen Nationalmuseums.* (Frankfurt/Main, 1983) 78 132f., 142; F. Jürgensmeier, *Das Bistum Mainz* (Frankfurt/ Main, 1988) 174–91; H. Rabe, *Deutsche Geschichte 1500–1600* (Munich, 1991) 212f.

ERNST WALTER ZEEDEN

■ **Additional Bibliography:** H. Reber, *A. von Brandenburg* (Mainz, 1990); F. Jürgensmeier, ed., *Erzbischof A. von Brandenburg* (Frankfurt/Main, 1991); S. Fastert, "Wahrhaftige Abbildung der Person? A. von Brandenburg im Spiegel der zeitgenössischen Bildpropaganda," *RQ* 97 (2002) 284–300.

Albrecht of Brandenburg-Ansbach the Elder. High Master of the Teutonic Order (1511-1525), duke in Prussia (from 1525), born May 17, 1490 in Ansbach, died March 20, 1568 in Tapiau. Thanks to the sermons of Andreas → Osiander in Nuremberg (1522), Albrecht developed a sympathy with Martin Luther's movement and visited him secretly in 1523. In the following period, he allowed Georg von → Polentz, bishop of Samland, to permit Lutheran preachers to work in Königsberg. In 1525, Albrecht received the territory of the Teutonic Order as a secular principality in vassalage to King Sigismund of Poland—a political decision influenced by religious factors and motivations. Thereafter, Albrecht himself introduced the Reformation into his duchy, while retaining its episcopal constitution, and he supported the Lutherans in Poland-Lithuania, in Livonia, and in the part of Prussia that was subject to the king of

Poland. He founded the University of Königsberg in 1544. The prayers that he composed bear witness to his genuine piety, and he displayed independent theological insights and knowledge when a conflict broke out in Königsberg about Osiander's doctrine of justification. Although Albrecht took Osiander's side, the states of the realm opposed him on both religious and political grounds and humiliated him by their successful insistence on the condemnation of Osiander's teaching and adherents in 1566–1567. Albrecht was married twice, to Dorothea of Denmark (1526-1547) and to Anna of Brunswick-Calenberg (1550).

■ **Literature:** J. R. Fligge, "Herzog A. von Preussen und der Osiandrismus 1522–68" (dissertation, Bonn, 1972); U. Arnold, "Luther und die Reformation im Preussenland," in U. Hutter, ed., *Martin Luther und die Reformation in Ostdeutschland und Südosteuropa* (Sigmaringen, 1991) 27–44.

ERNST MANFRED WERMTER

■ **Additional Bibliography:** K. Kressel, "A. Markgraf zu Brandenburg-Ansbach, Herzog in Preussen," *Lutherische Kirche in der Welt* 39 (1992) 83–102.

Aleander, *Hieronymus.* Humanist and papal diplomat, born February 13, 1480 in Motta (Friuli), died February 1, 1542 in Rome. After a period in Padua and Venice (1501–1508), he worked in Paris and Orleans from 1508 to 1513 and then in Liège until 1516. He moved to Rome and rose swiftly to high positions: he was appointed papal librarian in 1519, and nuncio to → Charles V in the following year. It was Aleander who was charged to publish the bull → *Exsurge Domine,* which threatened Martin Luther with excommunication; and he composed the Edict of Worms (→ Reformation). He became archbishop of Brindisi in 1524 and was nuncio in France until 1525, then once again papal emissary in Germany from 1531 to 1532 and nuncio in Venice from 1533 to 1535. He was created cardinal *in petto* in 1536 and published in 1538. He was appointed papal legate to the council that was summoned to meet at Vicenza and returned to central Europe again in 1538–1539. He drew on his expert knowledge of Germany when he wrote the Instruction for Gasparo → Contarini at the imperial parliament of 1541. He was active as a diplomat in the highest political circles and was also important as

a collector of documents illustrating the history of his own times.

■ **Sources:** NBD I, 3–4 (betreffend 1538/39), Ergänzungs-Bd. 1. und 2. (Tübingen, 1963–69).
■ **Literature:** *TRE* 2:227–31.—F. Gaeta, *Un nunzio pontificio a Venezia nel Cinquecento* (Venice—Rome, 1960).

GERHARD MÜLLER

■ **Additional Bibliography:** *RGG*⁴ 1:278f.

Allen, *William* (Gulielmus Alanus; Allyn). English cardinal, born 1532 in Rossal (Lancashire), died October 16, 1594 in Rome. He began his studies in Oxford in 1547, taking the degree of master of arts in 1554. He became principal of St. Mary's Hall in 1556, proctor of the university in 1556/1557, and canon of York in 1558. His recatholicizing endeavors led to his expulsion to Flanders in 1561. He was ordained priest in Mechlin and founded an English college at the University of → Douai in 1568 to train Catholic missionaries for England and to diffuse publications intended to defend Catholicism in England. Allen was one of the founders of the colleges in Rome (1579) and in Valladolid (1589). In 1580, he organized the first Jesuit mission in England. He moved to Rome in 1585 and took part in political efforts for the recatholicization of England, with the support of Philip II. He was created cardinal in 1587; he was appointed archbishop of Mechlin by Philip II in 1589, but the pope did not confirm this. He became prefect of the Vatican Library in 1591 and took part in the Douai translation of the Bible and in the revision of the Vulgate.

■ **Works:** *Certain Brief Reasons Concerning Catholic Faith* (1564); *A Defense and Declaration of the Catholike Churchies Doctrine touching Purgatory* (1565); *A Treatise Made in Defense of the Lawful Power of Priesthood to Remit Sins* (1567); *Tractatus de sacramentis* (1576); *An Apology for the English Colleges at Reims and Rome* (1581); *Apologia* (1583); *A True and Modest Defense of the English Catholics* (1584).

■ **Literature:** *A Literary and Biographical History or Bibliographical Dictionary of the English Catholics from the Breach with Rome in 1534 to the Present Time,* ed. J. Gillow, vol. 1 (reprint, New York, 1968) 14–24; *DNB* 1:314–22; *Dictionary of Catholic Biography,* ed. J. J. Delanay and J. E. Tobin (London, 1962) 38f.—B. Camm, *Cardinal W. A.* (New York, 1909); Ph. Hughes, *The Reformation in England,* vol. 3 (London, 1954) 281–396; G. Mattingly, "W. A. and the Catholic Propaganda in England," in G. Berthous et al., eds., *Aspects de la propagande religieuse* (Geneva, 1957) 325–39;

P. Guilday, *The English Catholic Refugees on the Continent 1558–1795*, vol. 1 (New York, 1974); A. Morey, *The Catholic Subjects of Elizabeth I* (London, 1978); A. Pritchard, *Catholic Loyalism in Elizabethan England* (London, 1979); P. Holmes, *Resistance and Compromise* (Cambridge, 1982).

REINHOLD RIEGER

Altenburg Religious Dialogue from October 21, 1568 to March 9, 1569 between theologians of the electorate of Saxony (Paul → Eber, Heinrich Salmuth, Caspar → Cruciger, etc.) and of the duchy of Saxony (Johann → Wigand, etc.). After a difficult preliminary phase, this dialogue sought to reestablish unity between the positions of the Philippists and the → Gnesiolutherans on justification and good works; Duke Johann Wilhelm attended some of the conversations. The dialogue was unsuccessful and led only to increased opposition between the two parties.

■ **Literature:** H. Heppe, *Geschichte des deutschen Protestantismus in den Jahren 1555–81*, vol. 2 (Marburg, 1853) 206–27; M. Hollerbach, *Das Religionsgespräch als Mittel der konfessionellen und politischen Auseinandersetzung im Deutschland des 16.Jh.* (Frankfurt/Main, 1982) 236–42; E. Koch, *Der kursächsische Philippismus und seine Krise in den 1560er und 1570er Jahren: Die reformierte Konfessionalisierung in Deutschland—Das Problem der "Zweiten Reformation,"* ed. H. Schilling (Gütersloh, 1986) 64f.; H. Junghans, ed., *Das Jahrhundert der Reformation in Sachsen* (Berlin, 1989); E. Koch, "Auseinandersetzungen um die Autorität von Philipp Melanchthon und Martin Luther in Kursachsen im Vorfeld der Konkordienformel von 1577," *Luther-Jahrbuch* 59 (1992) 129f.

HERIBERT SMOLINSKY

Altham(m)er (also Palaeosphyra), *Andreas.* Protestant theologian, born in Brenz (Württemberg) before 1500, died c. 1539 in Neumark or Ansbach. After studies in Leipzig and Tübingen (1516–1520), he was assistant schoolmaster in Halle on the Saale and in Ulm; in 1524, he became curate in Schwäbisch Gmünd but was expelled in the following year because of his adherence to the Reformation. He then studied in Wittenberg and became pastor in Eltersdorf near Erlangen in 1527, deacon at St. Sebald's church in Nuremberg in 1528, and pastor in Ansbach later in the same year. He took part in the visitation in the county of Brandenburg-Ansbach/Kulmbach (1528–1529) and in the composition of the → Church Order of Brandenburg-Nuremberg (1533), which was to have a lasting effect. He was active as a reformer in

Neumark in 1537. He composed a catechism with Johann Rurer, published at Nuremberg in 1528; he was the first to use this title for a book providing instruction in the faith. He also produced other theological and historical-humanist writings.

■ **Literature:** *NDB* 1:219; *RGG*³ 1:293; *BBKL* 1:129f.; *VD 16* 1:287–91; Köhler *BF* 1/1:40ff.; *DtLit* II A 2:319–44.—Th. Kolde, *A. A.* (Erlangen, 1895; reprinted Nieuwkoop, 1967); H. Ehmer, "A. A. und die gescheiterte Reformation in Schwäbisch Gmünd," *Blätter für württembergische Kirchengeschichte* 78 (1978) 46–72; G. Müller, "Die Reformation im Fürstentum Brandenburg-Ansbach/Kulmbach," *ZBKG* 48 (1979) 1–18; *Andreas-Osiander-Gesamtausgabe*, ed. G. Müller and G. Seebass, vols. 2–5 (Gütersloh, 1977–1983).

HERIBERT SMOLINSKY

■ **Additional Bibliography:** B. C. Schneider, "A. A. und sein Vierfrontenkrieg," *ZBKG* 71 (2002) 48–68.

Alveldt, *Augustin von.* Franciscan controversial theologian, born perhaps in Alfeld near Hildesheim, died c. 1535. Documentary evidence from 1520 identifies him as a member of the Saxon province of the Franciscan Observants and lector in the *Studium Generale* at Leipzig. In 1522, he moderated a disputation in Weimar about the monastic life; in 1524, he became Guardian in Halle and had contacts with Princess Margarete of Anhalt. He was provincial of his province from 1529 to 1532. From 1520 on, he opposed Martin Luther and composed numerous writings against him, supported by Duke → George of Saxony. In 1528, he published the second edition of the translation of the New Testament by Hieronymus → Emser and of the duke's pamphlet *To the Christians at Halle, against Luther's consolation.*

■ **Works:** *Erklärung der Klarissenregel für das Klarissenkloster in Eger* (Latin, 1534; German 1535); *Erklärung der Franziskanerregel* (Codex Guelf., 1905 Helmst. der Herzog-August-Bibliothek in Wolfenbüttel); *Loci communes* (Stadtbibliothek Dessau, Georg HS 113.40).

■ **Literature:** *RGG*³ 1:301; *BBKL* 1:135f.; *VD 16* 1:300–303; Klaiber nos. 69–83; Köhler *BF* 1/1:42–51; *KThR* 1²:47–55; *DtLit* II A 2:379–90.—H. Smolinsky, *A. von A. und Hieronymus Emser* (Münster, 1983); E. Koch, "Handschriftliche Überlieferungen aus der Reformationszeit in der Stadtbibliothek Dessau," *ARG* 78 (1987) 321–45; K. Hammann, *Ecclesia spiritualis. Luthers Kirchenverständnis in den Kontroversen mit A. von A. und Ambrosius Catharinus* (Göttingen, 1989); D. V. N. Bagchi, *Luther's Earliest Opponents. Catholic Controversialists, 1518–1525* (Minneapolis, 1991).

HERIBERT SMOLINSKY

Ambrosius Catharinus Politus (Lancellotto de' Politi). Dominican controversial theologian, born 1484 in Siena, died November 8(?), 1553 in Naples. He taught civil law, first in Siena, then from 1514 at the Sapienza University in Rome; he became an advocate in the papal consistory in 1515 and was led by reading Girolamo Savonarola to the "doctrine of Christ," becoming a Dominican at San Marco in Florence on April 5, 1517. He published an *Apologia* (CCath 27) against Martin Luther in 1520, followed by the *Excusatio disputationis contra Martinum* in 1521. He was in Siena from 1527 to 1532; he was deposed as prior in 1530 because he had celebrated the feast of the Immaculate Conception of Mary and was forbidden to preach. In 1532, he opposed the official teaching of his Order (Thomas → Cajetan de Vio) in his *Disputatio pro veritate Immaculatae Conceptionis Beatae Virginis Mariae*. He was in France from 1532 to 1537 and again from 1540 to 1543 (Lyons, Paris, Toulouse); in 1535, he published his *Annotationes* against Cajetan, → Erasmus of Rotterdam, and Luther (this book sees Jerome as an unquestionable authority and supports the literal meaning of scripture). He was in Rome 1538-39 and 1543-45. Here, he joined the reform party of Gasparo → Contarini. He was a member of Vittoria Colonna's circle and worked on exegesis of the letters of Paul; he also criticized abuses in the clergy and in current theology. He composed treatises against Bernardino → Ochino and others. He took part in the Council of Trent from 1545 to 1548, where he engaged in controversies with Bartolomé → Carranza (arguing that bishops were not obliged by divine law to reside in their dioceses) and Domingo de → Soto (about the certainty of salvation). He also wrote against Savonarola, on the doctrine of justification and of the sacraments, and against Niccolò Macchiavelli, and composed scriptural commentaries (Genesis 1–5, New Testament epistles). Although he was accused of holding erroneous views, he was appointed bishop of Minori in 1546 and archbishop of Conza in 1552.

■ **Literature:** *Marien-Lexikon*, ed. L. Scheffczyk and R. Bäumer, vol. 1 (St. Ottilien, 1988) 125; *DSp* 12:1844–58; *KThR* 2²:104–14.—J. Schweizer, *A. Catharinus Politus* (Münster, 1910); V. Criscuolo, *Ambrogio Catarino Politi* (Rome, 1985); U. Horst, *Zwischen Konziliarismus und Reformation* (Rome, 1985) 162–68; *Lehrverurteilungen—kirchentrennend?* vol. 3, ed. W. Pannenberg (Freiburg, 1990) 171–76.

VINZENZ PFNÜR

■ **Additional Bibliography:** L. Faldi, "Una conversione savonaroliana: Ambrogio Catarino Politi," *Vivens homo* 5 (1994) 553–74; G. Bedouelle, "L'introduction à l'Ecriture sainte du dominicain Ambrosio Catharino Politi (1543)," *Protestantesimo* 54 (1999) 273–84; P. Preston, "A. C.'s Commentary on the General Epistle of St Jude," *Reformation and Renaissance Review* 4 (2002) 217–29.

Amerbach, *Bonifatius*. Youngest son of Johann Amerbach, humanist and legal scholar, born October 11, 1495 in Basle, died there April 24/25, 1562. He studied in his native city (master of arts, 1512), in Freiburg (under Ulrich → Zasius), and in Avignon (under Andrea Alciati); he became doctor in civil and canon law in 1520 and professor of jurisprudence in Basle in 1530. He attempted to create a bridge between the humanistic understanding of law held by his teachers (the *mos gallicus*) and the traditional understanding (*mos italicus*). After Basle accepted the Reformation (1529), he maintained his own standpoint on the question of the Eucharist. He was a friend and executor of → Erasmus of Rotterdam.

■ **Literature:** *Lexikon des gesamten Buchwesens*, vol. 1 (Stuttgart, ²1987) 76; *CEras* 1:42–47.—A. Hartmann and B. R. Jenny, eds., *Die A.-Korrespondenz* (Basle, 1942ff.).

PETER WALTER

■ **Additional Bibliography:** H. Jaco-Friesen, *B. A.* (Basel, 1995); H.-R. Hagemann, *Die Rechtsgutachten des B. A.* (Basle, 2001).

Amerbach (Amerpachius; his real name was Trolmann), *Veit*. Scholar and humanist, born 1503 in Wemding (near Amerbach in Bavarian Swabia), died September 13, 1557 in Ingolstadt. He studied at Ingolstadt (1517), Freiburg (1521), and Wittenberg (1522), and became a schoolmaster in Eisleben in 1526, on Martin Luther's recommendation. He became a professor at the faculty of arts in Wittenberg in 1530. He sympathized with the Reformation until c. 1540. In the late 1530s, he engaged in literary controversy with Philipp Melanchthon; in November, 1543, he became professor at the faculty of arts in Ingolstadt. He produced numerous philosophical texts and commentaries on classic texts.

■ **Literature:** *RGG*³ 1:310; *NDB* 1:248f.; *BBKL* 1:144f.; *VD 16* 1:321–24.—L. Fischer, *Veit Trolmann von Wemding genannt Vitus Amerpachius als Professor in*

Wittenberg 1530–43 (Freiburg, 1926); *Melanchthons Briefwechsel,* compiled by H. Scheible, vols. 1 und 3 (Stuttgart, 1977–79) nos. 629, 2949; J. Pflug, *Correspondance,* ed. J. V. Pollet, vol. 5/1 (Leiden, 1982).

HERIBERT SMOLINSKY

■ **Additional Bibliography:** G. Frank, *V. A.: Melanchthon in seinen Schülern* (Wiesbaden, 1997) 103–28.

Amman (Ammon), *Kaspar.* Augustinian hermit, humanist, and Hebraist, born c. 1450 in Hasselt near Liège, died 1524 in Lauingen. He studied in Italy and was appointed lector in 1484. He was prior in Lauingen from 1485 to 1524 (with some pauses). He studied at Freiburg from 1497 to 1500 and took his doctorate in theology; he was provincial from 1500 to 1503 and from 1513 to 1518. He studied Hebrew under Johannes Böschenstein in Ingolstadt from 1505 to 1510. He sympathized with Martin Luther and preached against the bull → *Exsurge Domine* (which threatened Luther with excommunication) and against the Edict of Worms. He was arrested but released six months later. He probably remained faithful to the church and to his Order. He had contacts with contemporary humanists. He attempted to interpret scripture on the basis of the Hebrew language, translating existing texts back into Hebrew.

■ **Principal Work:** *Grammatica Hebrea latine conscripta (Autograph)* (Bern, Burger-Bibliothek Ms 198, Folium 295).

■ **Literature:** *BDG* 1, n. 18; *NDB* 1:250f.—A. Zumkeller, *Manuskripte von Werken der Autoren des Augustinereremitenordens in mitteleuropäischen Bibliotheken* (Würzburg, 1966) 101 n. 207f.; 575 n. 206a; A. Kunzelmann, *Geschichte der deutschen Augustinereremiten,* vol. 2: *Die rheinisch-schwäbische Provinz bis zum Ende des Mittelalters* (Würzburg, 1970) 37, 156f., 160f.; E. Gindele, *Bibliographie zur Geschichte und Theologie des Augustinereremitenordens bis zum Beginn der Reformation* (Berlin and New York, 1977) 182f.

WILLIGIS ECKERMANN

Amsdorf, *Nikolaus von.* Lutheran theologian, born December 3, 1483 in Torgau, died May 14, 1565 in Eisenach. He studied at Leipzig (1500) and Wittenberg (1502) and was an adherent of Martin Luther from 1516. Between 1524 and 1539, he actively promoted the Reformation in Magdeburg, Goslar, Einbeck, and Meissen. Luther ordained him first Protestant bishop of Naumburg in 1542. He was one of the founders of the University of Jena and one of the editors of the Jena edition of Luther's works. He was one of Luther's closest collaborators and fought uncompromisingly to maintain the purity of Luther's teaching against the → Augsburg Interim and Andreas → Osiander, and in the controversy with Georg → Major.

■ **Literature:** *TRE* 2:487–97.—R. Kolb, *N. von A.* (Nieuwkoop, 1978).

MICHAEL BECHT

■ **Additional Bibliography:** *RGG*[4] 1:421.—R. Kolb, "Kollege und Schüler. N. von A.," *Lutherische Theologie und Kirche* 22 (1998) 137–50; D. Whitford: "The Duty to Resist Tyranny: The Magdeburg 'Confession' and the Reframing of Romans 13," *Caritas and Reformation. Festschrift for Cater Lindberg* (Saint Louis, 2002) 89–101.

Andersson, *Lars* (Laurentius Andreae). Swedish Lutheran reformer and church politician, born c. 1470 in Strängnäs, where he died on April 14, 1552. A talented and ambitious man, Andersson became cathedral canon in Strängnäs after his studies in Sweden and in Germany and visited Rome three times. In 1520, he became a member of the court before King Christian II's "Bloodbath of Stockholm"; in the same year he was appointed archdeacon and head of the diocese of Strängnäs. He supported the Lutheran preaching of Olaus → Petri. In 1524, he became archdeacon of the archdiocese of Uppsala. He was secretary and chancellor of King → Gustav Vasa from 1523 to 1531; he advised the king on matters of church politics and won him over to the Reformation. After the parliament of Strängnäs in 1523, it was the king, Petri, and Andersson who determined the history of the Swedish Reformation. Under the leadership of Andersson, aided by Petri, the Bible was translated into Swedish (New Testament 1526, later the complete edition in the Gustav Vasa Bible). Andersson made an important contribution to the decision by the Swedish parliament at Västerås in 1529 to adopt the Reformation. Andersson and Petri lost the king's favor and were condemned to death for high treason in 1540; they were subsequently pardoned, but Andersson died in utter poverty.

■ **Literature:** H. Holmquist, *Die schwedische Reformation 1523–31* (Leipzig, 1925); idem, *Handbok i Svensk Kyrkohistoria,* vol. 2 (Stockholm, 1940); G. Schwaiger, *Die Reformation in den nordischen Ländern*

(Munich, 1962); B. Gustavsson, *Svensk Kyrkohistoria* (Stockholm, ²1963); S. Kjöllerström, *Kräkla och mitra* (Lund, 1965); G. Schwaiger, "Bischofsweihen und Apostolische Sukzession der schwedischen Kirche im 16.Jh.," *Würzburger Diözesangeschichtsblätter* 35/36 (1974) 367–80; P. G. Lindhardt, *Skandinavische Kirchengeschichte seit dem 16.Jh.* (Göttingen, 1982); G. Behre, L.-O. Larsson, and E. Österberg, *Sveriges historia 1521–1809* (Stockholm, 1985).

GEORG SCHWAIGER

Andreae, *Jakob.* Lutheran theologian, born March 25, 1528 in Waiblingen (Württemberg), died January, 7, 1590 in Tübingen. He began his studies in Tübingen in 1540 and was appointed deacon in Stuttgart in 1548. As a result of the → Augsburg Interim, he lost this position. He was pastor and special superintendent in Göppingen in 1552. In 1553, he took his doctorate in theology at Tübingen and was appointed general superintendent. From 1562 until his death, he was provost of the collegiate church, chancellor and professor at Tübingen. From 1555 onward, he was given the task of organizing church structures and of overseeing the Reformation in the territories outside Württemberg; he participated in numerous parliamentary sessions and religious dialogues. His most important achievement was the unification of the Protestant churches in the empire, which he had pursued since 1568. His work led to the Formula of → Concord in 1577 and the Book of Concord in 1580. Nothing came of the exchange of letters with the patriarch of Constantinople, which he began in 1573 in the hope of achieving reconciliation, and the attempt to make contact with the Ethiopian church was likewise unsuccessful. In theological terms, Andreae looked to Johannes → Brenz as his teacher; he was primarily concerned with practical church issues and had a gift for expressing theological questions in an easily understood way. He composed more than 250 works, especially occasional pamphlets, sermons, disputations, and contributions to current controversies.

■ **Literature:** *TRE* 2:672–80.—H. Gürsching, "J. A. und seine Zeit," *Blätter für württembergische Kirchengeschichte* 54 (1954) 123–56; R. Müller-Streisand, *Theologie und Kirchenpolitik bei J. A. bis zum Jahr 1568* (Stuttgart, 1960/61) 224–395; H. Ehmer, ed., *Leben des J. A.,... von ihm selbst... beschrieben...* (Stuttgart, 1991).

HERMANN EHMER

■ **Additional Bibliography:** *RGG*⁴ 1:470.—M. D. Tranvik, "Jacob A.'s Defense of the Lutheran Doctrine of Baptism at Montbéliard," *Lutheran Quarterly* 6 (1992) 425–45; H. Neumaier, " J. A. im Streit mit Cyriakus Spangenberg," *Blätter für württembergische Kirchengeschichte* 95 (1995) 49–88; W. Klän, "Luther, Melanchthon und ihre Schüler," *Lutherische Theologie und Kirche* 21 (1997) 152–67.

Anglican Articles. Brief doctrinal and confessional affirmations in the form of articles played a central role in the clarification and definition of the doctrinal positions in the 16th-century reform movements in the Church of → England. As early as 1536, → Henry VIII attempted a rapprochement among diverse theological schools by means of ten articles. → Edward VI published the celebrated 42 articles in 1533 as the official doctrinal basis of the church; this was the fruit of many years of preliminary work by Archbishop Thomas → Cranmer (including a conference with Lutherans). The articles did not claim to be a comprehensive presentation of the doctrine that was to be believed but sought to respond to the particular challenges of that time. The influence both of the → Confessio Augustana and of Calvinism is unmistakable.

Under Elizabeth I, the → *Book of Common Prayer* was initially the decisive doctrinal basis. On his own authority, Archbishop Matthew → Parker composed 11 articles and revised the existing 42, which acquired their definitive form and legal force in 1571 as the *Thirty-Nine* [Anglican] *Articles.* Until 1571, only members of the synod had been required to assent to the articles; after that date, all clergy had to assent to the 39.

■ **Literature:** E. J. Bicknell and H. J. Carpenter, *A Theological Introduction to the Thirty-Nine Articles of the Church of England* (London and New York, ¹1919, ³1955, often reprinted); J. E. Neale, *English Historical Review* 67 (1952) 510–21.

ALOYS KLEIN

■ **Additional Bibliography:** O. O'Donovan, *On the Thirty-nine Articles* (Exeter, 1986).

Antinomian controversy. The term "antinomian" is applied to interpretations of the Christian existence that deny that this is in any way determined by a "law" (Greek: *nomos*). The name "Antinomian controversy" is given to the debates in Wittenberg (1537–1540) about the manner in which the Old Testament (ethical) law might still be held valid for Christians; these debates continued in different circumstances among Lutheran theologians, especially in the electoral principality of Saxony, between 1556 and 1577. Martin Luther called his opponents in these disputes *antinomi* and described their views as *positiones antinomicae*. This has led to a wider application of these terms to all theological positions that are critical of the law—but this usage is incorrect, since those views have nothing, either historically or substantially, to do with the debates within Lutheranism.

The starting point of all antinomian views since the beginning of church history has been misunderstandings and manipulations of Paul's theology of the law and of his proclamation of Christian freedom. The following consequence was drawn: since the ethical law is no longer required as a condition for attaining salvation, it has lost its validity.

The Wittenberg debates were not about whether one is still bound by the ethical law: all the disputants agreed that penitence was necessary, since the gospel is not a cheap word of consolation; they agreed that good works were necessary, since faith in the gospel cannot remain without ethical consequences; they agreed that the gospel too leads to knowledge of sin, since the cross is the harshest accusation leveled against human wickedness; they agreed that every kind of "righteousness by works" must be excluded, since precisely this is the quintessence of the gospel; and they agreed that one must take measures in civil society to limit evil, since not all human persons (indeed, not even those in the church) are true Christians who would not require such external measures. The question in Wittenberg was: How, precisely, is the human being brought to repentance?

Luther himself had replied to this question by means of the distinction between → law and gospel, which he had clarified no later than 1519 in his short commentary on Galatians: it is the "office" of the law to convict the human person of sin, for otherwise he cannot understand what is promised him in the gospel. And since the human being as such remains a sinner all his life, law and gospel remain valid for him, as the one antithetical word of God. Here we have a life-long existential dialectic, which makes the preaching both of the law and of the gospel dependent on the specific personal experience and situation of the hearers—one will not preach the law to someone who is depressive!

In his proposed text for directives to those charged with the visitation in 1527, Philipp Melanchthon dissolves this dialectic into a chronological sequence: first comes the preaching of the law, then the preaching of the gospel. Johannes → Agricola, a pupil and friend of Luther since 1515/1516, countered with the thesis that it is not the law, but the sight of the crucified Christ, the impression produced by the "violation of the Son," that brings about a Christian's repentance, since true repentance is not a presupposition of faith but rather a fruit of faith. Agricola appealed to important affirmations by Luther that took a similar line; but Luther had not intended these in an exclusive sense. The controversy, which had not been genuinely resolved in 1527, escalated when Agricola returned from Eisleben to Wittenberg in 1537 and found many who accepted his view. It was these followers (not Agricola himself) who summarized their position against Luther and Melanchthon in 18 theses.

Luther published these and replied in theses of his own, which were discussed in the first "Antinomian disputation." Three further such disputations followed between 1538 and 1540. Agricola feared that an independent preaching of the law might obscure the pure character of God's word as grace. Luther's answer was the final terminological clarification of the "double use of the law." In its first "use," God's law serves externally to set limits to evil and to establish "justice in society"—and this too is God's good and life-giving gift to human beings. In the "second use," the "proper, convicting, theological" function, the law serves to convince the human person that there is no way out of his sin, driving him into that salvific state of desperation before God that makes him yearn for the gospel that acquits him. There was no compromise, still less any reconciliation with Agricola and his adherents.

This dispute flared up anew, in the context of other controversies within → Lutheranism, in the period leading up to the Formula of → Concord in 1577. Where the earlier debate had concerned the meaning of the law for repentance, the second phase concerned the continuing significance of the law as an orientation for Christians' ethical living. Under the influence of Melanchthon's theology, there developed the doctrine that in addition to the two functions of the law that Luther had distinguished, there was a "third use of the law."

The parties agreed that believers live in a new obedience to God's commandment, which they must put into practice, and it was clear to all that the substance of the law corresponds to the obligatory will of God. The only question was whether one should speak of a "use" of the law when a Christian consults a text such as the Ten Commandments in his search for orientation for his conduct and observes these commandments out of a new delight and joy in God's will.

In his response to Agricola, Luther had defined the concept of "law" entirely on the basis of its function: that which convicts us of sin is the law, and the repentance generated by looking upon the "violation of the Son" is nothing other than an intensified effect of the law (WA 39/1:384f.). The joyful fulfillment of God's will by the believer cannot be the effect of the law; similarly, repentance cannot be the fruit of the gospel as such (as was taught by the later Melanchthon and by his adherents, the Philippists). Those who rejected the idea of a "third use of the law" found vigorous spokesmen in Andreas Poach (1515–1585), Anton Otto (Otho, c. 1505–1583), Michael → Neander, and Andreas → Musculus, who argued that one must maintain this position, because otherwise there would no longer be a clear distinction between the law and the gospel. Their opponents, especially Matthias → Flacius and Joachim → Mörlin, were successful in their defense of the "third use": the Formula of Concord adopted the formula of a "third use of the law" (*BSLK* 793:1; 962:1). Scholars are divided up to the present day about whether Luther himself would have accepted the "third use"—or, if not the actual term, at any rate the substance which it implies.

Even many in Luther's own circle felt that Luther had reacted too harshly and implacably to Agricola's person and his theology. It must, however, be borne in mind that Luther could not tolerate any suspicion—however unjustified—that he had adopted an ethical libertinism.

■ *LThK*[3] 1:762–66 (unabridged version).

■ **Literature:** *DThC* 1:1391ff.; *LThK*[2] 1:642–46; *Historisches Wörterbuch der Philosophie*, ed. J. Ritter et al., vol. 1 (Basle, 1971) 406; *HDThG* 2:39–45, 117–21.— R. Bring, *Gesetz und Evangelium und der Dritte Gebrauch des Gesetzes in der lutherischen Theologie* (Helsinki, 1943); J. Rogge, *Johann Agricolas Lutherverständnis unter besonderer Berücksichtigung des Antinomismus* (Berlin, 1960); G. Ebeling, "Zur Lehre vom triplex usus legis in der reformatorischen

Theologie," in idem, *Wort und Glaube*, vol. 1 (Tübingen, 1962) 50–68; H. E. Eisenhut, *Luther und der Antinomismus* (Berlin, 1963) 18–44; W. Joest, *Gesetz und Freiheit. Das Problem des tertius usus legis bei Luther und die neutestamentliche Paränese* (1951) (Göttingen, [4]1964); S. Kjeldgaard-Pedersen, *Gesetz, Evangelium und Buße. Theologiegeschichtliche Studien zum Verhältnis zwischen dem jungen Johann Agricola (Eisleben) und Martin Luther* (Leiden, 1983); E. Koch, "Johann Agricola neben Luther," *Archiv zur WA*, vol. 5 (Cologne, 1983) 131–50; R. Schwarz, *Die Kirche in ihrer Geschichte*, ed. B. Moeller, vol. 3/1 (Göttingen, 1986) 201ff.; M. Brecht, *Martin Luther*, vol. 3 (Stuttgart, 1987) 158–73.

OTTO HERMANN PESCH

■ **Additional Bibliography:** M. Richter, *Gesetz und Heil* (Göttingen, 1996); G. G. Krodel, "Luther—An Antinomian?" *Luther-Jahrbuch* 63 (1996) 69–101; F. Buzzi, "Lutero contro l'antinomismo," *Annali di scienze religiose* 2 (1997) 81–106; T. J. Wengert, *Law and Gospel. Philip Melanchton's Debate with J. A. of Eisleben over Poenitentia* (Carlisle, 1997); idem, *Gesetz und Buße. Philipp Melanchthons erster Streit mit Johannes Agricola: Der Theologe Melanchthon* (Stuttgart, 2000) 375–92.

Antitrinitarians. This term applies to all who deny the trinitarian dogma, whether the Monarchians in the early church or movements in the Reformation period at the beginning of the modern age. This polemical term has been bestowed on the latter movements—the new "Arians" and "Sabellians"—since the 17th century.

These groups had a variety of origins: we find a radical antidogmatism critical of the Bible, as well as influence from Baptist movements, humanism, and nominalism. The "antitrinitarian" par excellence of his century was Michael → Servet, philosopher of religion and doctor, who presented a systematic critique of trinitarian doctrine in his chef d'oeuvre *Christianismi restitutio* (Lyons, 1553); although he escaped condemnation to death by the Lyons inquisition at Vienne, Jean Calvin had him burned as a heretic in Geneva in 1553.

Antitrinitarian ideas from Italy spread in humanistic and spiritualistic circles in Switzerland, but their proponents were soon expelled (e.g., Bernardino → Ochino in 1563) or else killed (Giovanni Valentino → Gentile in 1566). Antitrinitarian parishes came into being in the Reformed churches of Poland and Transylvania. When they were excluded from the Consensus of Sandomir between Lutherans, Calvinists, and →

Baptists (1570) and designated as an *ecclesia minor,* Rakow near Sandomir became their spiritual center. In Transylvania, the "Unitarian Church" (a name used since 1598) was accorded the same rights as the other confessions.

Fausto Sozzini (1539–1604) is regarded as the true founder of the antitrinitarian church, and the "Polish Brethren" are also known as → "Socinians." Their standard confessional document was the "Catechism of Rakow" (Polish 1605, German 1608, Latin 1609), which transforms Christianity, on the basis of a rational biblicism, into a doctrine about morality and virtues. In the course of the → Counter-Reformation, the antitrinitarian parishes and schools in Poland were closed down.

■ **Literature:** *TRE* 3:168–74.—E. M. Wilbur, *A History of Unitarianism. Socinianism and its Antecedents* (Cambridge, Mass., 1947); B. Stasiewski, *Reformation und Gegenreformation in Polen* (Münster, 1960); P. Wrzecionko, ed., *Reformation und Frühaufklärung in Polen* (Göttingen, 1977).

LOTHAR ULLRICH

■ **Additional Bibliography:** *RGG*[4] 1:574f.—R. Dán, *Antitrinitarianism in the Second Half of the 16th century* (Budapest, 1982); M. Balázs, *Early Transylvanian Antitrinitarianism (1566–71)* (Baden-Baden, 1996); R. Kolb, "The Formula of Concord and Contemporary Anabaptists, Spirituals, and Anti-trinitarians," *Lutheran Quarterly* 15 (2001) 453–82.

Arcimboldi, *Giovannangelo.* Born September 27, 1485 in Milan, where he died on April 6, 1555; nephew of Cardinal Giovanni Arcimboldi, archbishop of Milan. In 1514, he was appointed nuncio and commissioner for indulgences in Germany and the Scandinavian countries, with Johannes → Tetzel as his subcommissioner for Meissen. Political intrigues in Denmark led to grave accusations against him, but Arcimboldi escaped arrest by flight. He was in Rome in 1520; in 1526, he was appointed bishop of Novara, and archbishop of Milan in 1550. He was an easygoing man, but endeavored to promote renewal in Milan.

■ **Works:** *Autobiographie,* ed. C. Marcora, *Memorie storiche della diocesi di Milano,* vol. 1 (Milan, 1954) 153–61; *Ordinationes pro clero et sua dioecesi* (Milan, 1550); *Catalogus Haereticorum* (Milan, 1554).

■ **Literature:** *DBI* 3:773–76.—A. Rimoldi, *La prima metà del Cinquecento: Diocesi di Milano,* ed. A. Caprioli et al. (Brescia, 1990) 579.

JOSEF GELMI

Armagnac, *Georges d'.* Cardinal (1544), born c. 1500, died in Avignon in 1585. He was the son of Pierre and Fleurette de Luppé and was raised at the court of Margaret of Angoulême. He was appointed bishop of Rodez in 1530 and was French ambassador in Venice from 1536 to 1538, then in Rome from 1540 to 1545, where he defended the policy of → Francis I against → Charles V. He invited artists and writers to his residence. He was again ambassador in Rome from 1547 to 1549. In 1562, he became archbishop of Toulouse and royal vicegerent in Languedoc, where he fought against the → Huguenots. In 1565, he received the legation of Avignon and was appointed archbishop of this Roman enclave on French territory in 1577. Here, he endeavored to preserve Catholicism, which was under threat; he also sought to extend French influence. In 1584, he became archbishop of Toulouse for a second time. He baptized the future → Henry IV in Tau. He had copies of Greek and Latin manuscripts made for his library, one of the most extensive in France. His correspondence with prominent Frenchmen and Italians provides important contributions to 16th-century French history, as do his diplomatic reports.

■ **Literature:** *DHGE* 4:263–67; *Cath* 1:879.—P. Tamizey, "Briefe," *Revue historique* 2 (1876) 516–65; 5 (1877) 317–47.

CLAUDE MULLER

Arnold of Tongern (Tungern; Arnoldus Luyde von Tongern, von Luyde, Lude). Augustinian canon regular and theologian; born in Tongern, died August 28, 1540 in Liège. He studied in Cologne, where he took his licentiate in 1489. He became regent of the Laurentian college in 1494, and was professor of theology from 1509 and dean of the theological faculty in Cologne in 1510/1511. He was canon of the collegiate church of St. Mariengraden in Cologne and cathedral canon in Liège. He supported Albertinism and published commentaries in keeping with this position. He wrote against Johannes → Reuchlin in 1512 and was attacked in the *Epistolae obscurorum virorum* (→ Obscure Men, Letters of). He was involved in the reform of the university in 1525. He composed a Latin work on the veneration of the saints in 1536, which Johannes → Cochlaeus published in German. Arnold had contacts with the Carthusians in Cologne (Peter → Blomevenna).

13

■ **Literature:** J. Hartzheim, *Bibliotheca Coloniensis* (Cologne, 1747) 25; *NDB* 1:381; *BBKL* 1:235f.; *VD 16* 1:553ff.; Klaiber nos. 163–66; Köhler *BF* 1/1:64f.—N. Paulus, *Die deutschen Dominikaner im Kampfe gegen Luther* (Freiburg, 1903); E. Meuthen, *Kölner Universitätsgeschichte,* vol. 1: *Die alte Universität* (Cologne and Vienna, 1988).

HERIBERT SMOLINSKY

Arnoldi, *Bartholomäus* (von Usingen). Augustinian hermit (1512), philosopher, and theologian, born c. 1464 in Usingen, died September 9, 1532 in Würzburg (tomb in the Augustinian church). He began his studies at the University of Erfurt in 1484 and became master of arts in 1491. Martin Luther studied philosophy under Arnoldi from 1501 to 1505. In 1514, he took his doctorate in theology and was appointed preacher in the Augustinian church. In 1518, he held fast to the old faith and opposed the innovators. He became cathedral preacher in 1522 and defended Catholic doctrine. He was obliged to leave Erfurt in 1525 and was welcomed in the Augustinian monastery in Würzburg, where he defended the Catholic faith with tongue and pen—although he also attacked the abuses in the church. He was a counselor of Konrad von Thüngen, bishop of Würzburg. He was appointed visitor of monasteries. He took part in the parliament of Augsburg, where he contributed to a refutation of the → Confessio Augustana; later, he wrote a *Responsio* against Philipp Melanchthon's apologia for the Confessio. Arnoldi's writings on logic, natural philosophy, and pedagogy show him to be an Aristotelian who was open to the thinking of William of Ockham and of the Augustinian Gregory of Rimini. His controversial writings bear witness to his knowledge of scripture and of patristic teaching.

■ **Literature:** *KThR* 2:27–37.—A. Kunzelmann, *Geschichte der deutschen Augustinereremiten,* vol. 5 (Würzburg, 1974) 477f., 518f.

WILLIGIS ECKERMANN

■ **Additional Bibliography:** *RGG⁴* 1:1141f.—A. Zumkeller, "Ein Manuskript des Bartholomäus von Usingen OSA . . . ," *Analecta Augustiniana* 58 (1995) 5–43; S. Lalla, *Secundum viam modernam: ontologischer Nominalismus bei Arnoldi von Usingen* (Würzburg, 2002).

Arnoldi, *Franz.* Catholic controversial theologian, born in Leisnig, died c. 1535. He was parish priest

in Cölln on the Elbe and composed polemic works against Martin Luther. The text he published in 1531, *Against Luther's Warning Addressed to the Germans,* like the manuscript outline of an anti-Lutheran work from the year 1533 (Dresden municipal archive, loc. 10300), was written by → George of Saxony.

■ **Literature:** *NDB* 1:389f.; *VD 16* 1:551; Klaiber nos. 167–70.—H. Becker, "Herzog Georg von Sachsen als kirchlicher und theologischer Schriftsteller," *ARG* 24 (1927) 161–269; H. Smolinsky, *Augustin von Alveldt und Hieronymus Emser* (Münster, 1983); M. U. Edwards, Jr., *Luther's Last Battles* (Leiden, 1983).

HERIBERT SMOLINSKY

Art and Reformation
1. Initial situation

Until well into the 20th century, the debates among the Reformers about the legitimacy and possibility of a sacred art, especially the representation of Christ and the saints, were treated by historians of church and of art as a peripheral topic; this changed in the second half of the century, since the question of images took on a central importance and many new aspects came to light. Scholars recognized that it was insufficient to trace a trajectory from the controversies about images in late antiquity and the early Middle Ages to the early modern period, and that—if justice was to be done to the actual course of history—a univocal concept of "iconoclasm" was an inadequate tool for understanding the Reformation controversies; violent iconoclasm was in fact rare. In addition to the traditional disputes about images, we must also analyze the role of artists in the events of the Reformation and the effect of the Reformation on the arts as a whole.

2. Veneration and Criticism of Images
   before the Reformation

Thanks to the acknowledgment of religious images by Pope Gregory I (died 604) as "images of the laity" and to the decisions of early medieval synods in favor of images, sacred art was able to develop in the West virtually undisturbed, although this development was almost continuously accompanied by iconoclastic tendencies (Bernard of Clairvaux, the Wyclifites, the Hussites). The Renaissance reached its apogee in Italy c. 1500; a few decades later, it had triumphed north of the Alps too. Its program entailed a conscious recourse to classical antiquity, but Renaissance art retained its Christian framework. Archbishop Antoninus of Florence (1389–1459) described the tasks of painting in his *Summa theologica* (3.8.4.11) as follows: the painter had a higher status than the craftsman, and beauty was the goal of art; whatever was incorrect from a dogmatic point of view, unbiblical and apocryphal motifs, and additions which did not promote devotion, should be avoided. Fifty years later, Girolamo Savonarola, the great preacher of repentance in Florence, demanded in similar terms that church art should be morally irreproachable. The demands formulated by Antoninus and Savonarola were echoed frequently in the late Middle Ages and were renewed by the Council of Trent (*COD* 751f.).

In northern Europe, disputes about images were more frequent, and many treatises on this subject were composed. We may take → Erasmus of Rotterdam as a representative on the highest level of the criticism of images. He insisted on spiritual worship and a genuine following of Christ and rejected all external forms such as pilgrimages or the veneration of images. Most of the Reformers were familiar with Erasmus's writings.

3. The Reformers
Martin Luther

Andreas → Karlstadt in Wittenberg initiated the Reformed attacks on images when he published his polemical treatise "On the Abolition of Images" in January, 1522; he was one of the leaders of the actual physical onslaught on images in Wittenberg in the following month. Karlstadt argued that the Bible as a whole rejected images in churches; one must abandon the doctrine that images were the books of the laity, since as long as the "idols in oil paint" were displayed in the churches, they would lead to idolatry. Luther replied in the third and fourth of his *Invocavit* sermons that the Christian is free either to have images or not, since the alleged principal danger—viz., idolatry—cannot be regarded as grave. The images must be torn out of people's hearts; and one must reject the donation of images to churches as a "good work." Where this insight has been attained, Luther wishes people to have biblical and other pictures on the walls of their homes "to promote remembrance and a better understanding" (WA 18:22.27f.). He did not object to

an orderly removal of images, but he did not accept the use of force. Luther himself saw to the illustration of his writings with pictures and planned a complete Bible in pictures. He was a master of the medium of print.

Huldrych Zwingli

An onslaught on images took place in Zurich too, in 1523. Zwingli came to the following conclusion: the first commandment remains valid for the church today. The sacramental images seduced people into idolatry, and a neutral use of images was impossible. Nor were images useful for teaching the laity. Zwingli and the council agreed on an orderly process for the removal of images from churches; this did not affect the private possession of pictures.

Jean Calvin

Of all the Reformers, Calvin was the harshest opponent of the pictorial representation of God. Since God transcends every human concept, the attempt to fashion an image of God insults his honor. The only "images" acceptable in churches were the sacraments, which made God's action visible; but Calvin also recommended historical pictures as teaching aids.

4. Images of the Unseen

It is clear that Luther is familiar with the basic concepts of the contemporary theory of art: he defines sculpture as "the art of elimination," he demands that artists both imitate and beautify nature, and he makes use of the *Ars poetica* of Horace. Luther's theory of the imagination deserves particular attention. Since our thinking proceeds by means of images, it is inevitable that we will form images of the things in our consciousness: "When I hear the name of Christ, there is formed in my heart the image of a man who hangs on the cross" (WA 18:83). Luther presupposes the Aristotelian teaching that it is the imagination which evokes sensuous images, including those images which accompany our thought (cf. Aristotle, *De anima* 3.8; Augustine, *Epistula* 7). Zwingli rejected this understanding of imaginative images, while Johannes → Eck affirmed it.

5. Iconoclasm

The physical onslaught on images in the Reformation period was not due to some incomprehensible destructiveness, nor was it a question of faith. Rather, the bodily removal of images which had once been venerated was an unparalleled opportunity for Protestants to experience at first hand what religious liberation meant; the only analogous experience of liberation was the new doctrine about the Lord's Supper in southern Germany and Switzerland.

This iconoclasm was not one single event, in either geographical or chronological terms. Luther, in agreement with the government of electoral Saxony, was able to put an end to the attack on images unleashed by Karlstadt in Wittenberg (1522), and Zwingli too succeeded in the following year in bringing the attack on images in Zurich under the control of the city council. The usual resolution of this crisis in the empire was a directive by the civil authorities that images were to be removed from the churches; an exception was the rule of the → Baptists in Münster (1533–35). Iconoclasm took on much vaster dimensions in western Europe: in England under → Henry VIII, most images were removed under pressure "from above," and the mutilation or destruction of images and statues was a routine activity by the → Huguenots during the French wars of religion.

6. Artists and the Reformation

Many artists accepted the Reformation or at least sympathized with it in the early stages before Protestant churches were fully formed; here we may mention names such as Albrecht Dürer, Lukas Cranach the Elder and the Younger, Hans Baldung Grien, and probably also Matthias Grünewald and Wolf Huber, as well as many lesser artists. A decision in favor of Protestant doctrine did not necessarily lead at once to a noticeable change in the artist's work, since what counted was not his intention but the wishes of his patron. One exception was Dürer's "Four Apostles" (1526), which he dedicated to the city of Nuremberg with the exhortation to remain faithful to the gospel. Lukas Cranach the Elder was appointed court painter in electoral Saxony as early as 1504/1505, and he built up a large workshop in Wittenberg. He was a friend of Luther, and he became "the Reformation artist" par excellence with his paintings and prints. Nevertheless, he and his workshop accepted two large commissions for Cardinal Albrecht of Mainz between 1520 and 1540.

The introduction of the Reformation entailed considerable financial losses for artists and craftsmen, since although there were more than enough church buildings, there was a great reduction in new commissions for religious images. Some painters approved of the abolition of images and abandoned their profession (Niklaus Manuel Deutsch in Bern; Jörg Breu the Elder in Augsburg), while others made a successful transition to work as craftsmen. In the second half of the 16th century, however, new commissions increased, since new churches had to be built in confessionally mixed regions where existing church buildings belonged to only one group. In addition to pulpits and altars, the creation of epitaphs became an important task.

7. The Catholic Response

From the outset of the Reformation, theologians who remained faithful to the old church put up an obstinate defense of images and their ecclesial function. The controversy found its official closure in the Tridentine decree "On the Invocation, Veneration, and Relics of the saints and on Sacred Images" (December 3, 1563; DH 1821–25), which basically confirms the medieval teaching about images: the images of Christ, Mary, and the saints do not contain any "divinity or power," and the honor shown to them is paid to the "prototypes." The main concern, however, is the instructive and edifying effect of images (*COD* 751.15-25; DH 1824). The most important thematic cycle for images is the biblical history (*COD* 26f., 39f.). "The people must be taught explicitly that portrayals of God in biblical images do not mean that God has a visible form. All superstition must be overcome, and artists must avoid anything lascivious" (*COD* 751.36-52; DH 1825). The decree takes up the demands that reforming theologians had made since the 15th century; it doubtless succeeded in warding off the worst misunderstandings and abuses, and that was the most that could be hoped for at the end of the 16th century. The flowering of baroque art shows what artistic vigor still lay hidden in Catholicism.

■ **Literature:** O. Christin, *Une revolution symbolique* (Paris, 1991); A. Tacke, *Der katholische Cranach* (Mainz, 1992); J. Harasimowicz, *Kunst als Glaubensbekenntnis* (Baden-Baden, 1996); *Imagination und Wirklichkeit,* ed. K. Krüger and A. Nova (Mainz, 2000).

GERHARD MAY

■ **Additional Literature:** J. T. Moger, "Pamphlets, Preaching, and Politics: The Image-controversy in Reformation Wittenberg, Zürich and Strassburg," *Mennonite Quarterly Review* 75 (2001) 325–54; N. R. Leroux, "'In the Christian City of Wittenberg'. Karlstadt's Tract on Images and Begging," *SCJ* 34 (2003) 73–105.

Articulus stantis et cadentis ecclesiae ("article of faith by which the church stands or falls"). From Martin Luther's days onward, the doctrine of → justification has been considered such an article of faith: the term indicates that it is the center and criterion of his theology, and indeed of all Reformation theology. The term itself, which later became standard, is not found in Luther's works, but some expressions come very close (above all WA 40:3.352, 3: "If this article stands, the church stands; if it collapses, the church collapses"); in any case, he never tires of insisting on the substantial point, e.g., in the Articles of → Schmalkald (1536), where he calls the doctrine of justification the "first main article" (WA 50:199.22; *BSLK* 415:21). Although Luther was not the first theologian to discuss the "justification of the unrighteous"—following the theological systematization of Peter Lombard, this was primarily treated in the context of the doctrine of the sacraments—the absolute priority which Luther attributes to justification is without precedent in the history of theology. This central article is not simply one topic alongside others; rather, it is the synthesis of the entire proclamation of Christ. This is why the church "stands or falls" along with this article.

■ **Literature:** F. Loofs, "Der A.," *Theologische Studien und Kritiken* 90 (1917) 323–420; E. Wolf, "Die Rechtfertigungslehre als Mitte und Grenze reformatorischer Theologie," *Evangelische Theologie* 9 (1949/50) 298–308.

HARALD WAGNER

■ **Additional Bibliography:** *RGG*[4] 1:799f.

Auger, *Edmond.* Jesuit (1550), the "French Canisius," born 1530 near Troyes, died January 31, 1592 in Como. He was received into the novitiate at Rome by → Ignatius Loyola. After his priestly ordination, he worked in several French cities as preacher and helped found numerous colleges. He became provincial of Aquitaine in 1564 and was confessor to → Henry III from 1583 to 1587. He moved to Lombardy in 1589. In order to counter the Reformation, which was spreading in the south of France, Auger published in 1563 his *Catéchisme et sommaire de la doctrine chrétienne*, followed at a later date by other catechisms. In order to refute Jean Calvin's catechism, he adopted its structure, i.e., faith, law, prayer, sacraments. His handbook quickly became a bestseller. It is particularly noteworthy for its conceptuality and its didactic qualities.

■ **Literature:** J. Dorigny, *La vie du père E. A.* (Avignon, 1828 [1716]); J. Brand, *Die Katechismen des Edmundus Augerius, S.J., in historischer, dogmatisch-moralischer und katechetischer Bearbeitung* (Freiburg, 1917); J. C. Dhôtel, *Les origines du catéchisme moderne d'après les premiers manuels imprimés en France* (Paris, 1967).

STANISLAS LALANNE

■ **Additional Bibliography:** M. Pernot, "L'univers spirituel du père E. A., S.J.," *RHEF* 75 (1989) 103–14.

Augsburg Interim. → Charles V gave a commission of dogmatically moderate Protestant and Catholic theologians the task of elaborating this "Declaration on how religion is to be ordered in the Holy Roman Empire" until a council could reach a final decision; → Paul III was compelled to tolerate it, and it was published on May 25, 1548. It was intended to serve as the basis for the reunion of the Protestants with the Catholics. It acquired the character of imperial law when a resolution of the imperial parliament adopted it on June 30 of the same year. This so-called imperial intermediate religion was based on fundamental Catholic positions but made concessions to the Protestants on such questions as the → chalice for the laity, the Mass, clerical marriage (→ celibacy), and church possessions. Its authors included Johannes → Agricola, Julius → Pflug, Eberhard → Billick, Michael → Helding, and Pedro de → Soto. The Interim was at once printed.

It satisfied none of the contending religious parties. In southern Germany, under pressure from the emperor, it was adopted in the imperial cities, and it was accepted in modified form in the electorate of Saxony ("Leipzig Interim"), but it was widely rejected in northern Germany. It generated vigorous political and theological debates, and many polemical pamphlets were written. Even where it was accepted, it did not long remain in force. The treaty of → Passau in 1552 made it basically irrelevant, and the Religious Peace of →

Augsburg in 1555 removed it from imperial law. As a consequence of the Augsburg Interim, small groups remained faithful to the Catholic Church in numerous imperial cities (Ulm, and especially Augsburg itself) and in small territories in southern Germany.

■ **Text:** *BDG* 38259a; *ARCEG* 6:308–48.
■ **Literature:** *TRE* 16:230–34, 236f.—H. Rabe, *Reichsbund und Interim* (Cologne and Vienna, 1974); E. W. Zeeden, *Martin Luther . . . Ausstellung zum 500. Geburtstag* (Frankfurt/Main, 1983) 454–59; H. Rabe, *Deutsche Geschichte 1500–1600* (Munich, 1991) 416–24.

ERNST WALTER ZEEDEN

■ **Additional Bibliography:** R. Kastner, ed., *Der Kampf um das AI: Quellen zur Reformation* (Darmstadt, 1994) 447–86; J. Mehlhausen, *Das AI* (Neukirchen-Vluyn, ²1996); R. Kolb, ed., "The Augsburg Interim," in *Sources and Contexts of the Book of Concord* (Minneapolis, 2001) 144–82; N. B. Rein, "Faith and Empire: Conflicting Visions of Religion in a Late Reformation Controversy: The Augsburg 'Interim' and Its Opponents, 1548–50," *Journal of the American Academy of Religion* 71 (2003) 45–74.

Augsburg, Religious Peace of. This brought a conclusion on September 29, 1555 to thirty-five years' endeavor (both peaceful and military) on the part of Emperor Charles V to bring the Lutherans back to the Catholic Church. The Religious Peace of Augsburg called a temporary halt to the decades of religious and constitutional struggles in the empire and gave → Lutheranism—though not → Zwinglianism, → Calvinism, the → Baptist groups, and all the Protestant sects—the status of a confession enjoying the same recognition in imperial law as Catholicism.

The political ground was prepared by the revolt of the princes and the treaty of Passau (1552); favorable factors were the death of Charles's most important opponent in Germany, the electoral prince → Moritz of Saxony, in 1553, and by the increased desire for peace in the imperial parliament. Above all, the Religious Peace was born of the realization by princes on both the Catholic side (including the emperor's brother, → Ferdinand I) and the Protestant side that they had common interests; they saw it as an urgent priority to establish a lasting *modus vivendi* for the peaceful cohabitation of two confessions in the political sphere of the empire, and this led them to abandon Charles's goal (based on his own religious convictions) of maintaining the religious unity of the empire on the basis of the Catholic profession of faith. They did indeed hold religious unity to be desirable, but they left it to the future to bring this about (cf. preamble). They deprived the emperor of the right to determine the confession of his subjects (→ *Cuius regio, eius et religio*), but claimed this right for themselves. They also gave themselves the right to establish a specific religious unity within their own territories (with the exception of the cities). This right of confessional coercion, the so-called → *Ius reformandi*, gave those territories that were immediately subordinate to the empire a status of far-reaching political independence ("liberty," a step in the direction of "sovereignty"), since it was now virtually impossible for the emperor to dictate to the princes on religious and ecclesiastical matters.

This so-called dispensation made a number of special regulations necessary. A free choice of religion was available only to princes, counts, and knights who were immediately subordinate to the empire, and (in principle) to the citizens of imperial cities. The choice of confession meant that the bishops lost the so-called spiritual jurisdiction which they had hitherto exercised over Protestant territories; this was now assumed by the political rulers of these territories, as the so-called *summi episcopi* (Religious Peace, §20). Spiritual imperial princes (bishops, abbots, etc.) lost their territories if they converted to Protestantism (→ ecclesiastical reservation), since the Catholic confession was the presupposition for their political lordship. Other special clauses concerned freedom of confession for regional parliamentary assemblies in spiritual territories; confessional parity in some imperial cities; the prohibition (which was not unanimously accepted) of secularizing monasteries after 1552 where these belonged indirectly to the Catholic Church; and the conditional right of subjects to emigrate from their lord's territory.

Although unclarities in the text of the Religious Peace of Augsburg caused many complications, the principle that imperial law should guarantee religious peace between the confessions was firmly established for the future; it was confirmed in 1648 as a basic law of the empire and remained a determinative element of German history until 1803/1806. By linking confession to territory, it set the seal on the divisions in belief, ensured that Germany would be the home of more than one confession, promoted the development of the individual imperial territories to a greater autonomy as states, and gave the confessions a relative freedom for dogmatic and institutional development within specific states, so that they could give birth to appropriate forms of religious, intellectual, and cultural life.

■ **Text:** K. Zeumer, *Quellensammlung . . .* (Tübingen, ²1913; critical edition by K. Brandi, Göttingen, ²1927).

■ **Literature:** *TRE* 3:639–45.—E. W. Zeeden, "Deutschland der Mitte des 16.Jh. bis zum Westfälischen Frieden," in Th. Schieder, ed., *Handbuch der europäischen Geschichte,* vol. 3 (Stuttgart, 1971) 536–48; B. Moeller, *Deutschland im Zeitalter der Reformation* (Göttingen, 1977) 172–84; H. Rabe, *Deutsche Geschichte 1500–1600* (Munich, 1991) 445–58; E. W. Zeeden, *Hegemonialkriege und Glaubenskämpfe* (Frankfurt [Main] and Berlin, ²1992) 9–33.

ERNST WALTER ZEEDEN

■ **Additional Bibliography:** *RGG*⁴ 1:957f.—H. Rabe, *Der AR: Die frühe Neuzeit,* ed. P. Burgard (Munich, 1997) 84–90; Ch. A. Stumpf, "Die Bedeutung der Reichsgrundgesetze für die konfessionellen Wiedervereinigungsversuche," *ZKG* 111 (2000) 342–55; E. Laubach, *Ferdinand I. als Kaiser* (Münster, 2001) 29–139; H. Jesse, "Die Entwicklung zum Religionsfrieden von Augsburg 1555," *Jahrbuch des Vereins für Augsburger Bistumsgeschichte* 35 (2001) 20–57; J. Wagner, *Der A. R.* (Preetz, 2003).

Augustine of Piedmont (dei Mainardi, Pedemontanus). Born 1482 in Caraglio (Cuneo), died July 31, 1563 in Chiavenna (Veltlin); first an Augustinian hermit, then a Lutheran. He took his doctorate in theology in 1513, was appointed preacher and director of studies in Rome in 1519, in Siena in 1521, and in Florence in 1523. Girolamo → Seripando, subsequently general of the Order, was his student; the two were sent to → Paul III as emissaries of the general chapter of Verona in 1538. He was accused of heresy because of some affirmations in his Lenten sermons at Asti but was rehabilitated by Paul III. When → Ignatius of Loyola voiced the same suspicions in Rome in 1538, Augustine did not succeed in clearing his name, so that the governor of Milan intervened in 1541. Augustine escaped from the trial that threatened him by converting to the Lutherans with Bernardino → Ochino. In 1542, Seripando expelled his former teacher from the Order. After this date, Augustine developed his fundamentally Augustinian views in a decidedly Lutheran sense.

■ **Works:** *Confessione della Chiesa di Chiavenna* (1548); *Dell'Eucaristia* (1552); *Dell unica e perfetta satisfazione di Cristo* (1561); *Sermone della Grazia di Dio* (1562).

■ **Literature:** G. Gonnet, "Les débuts de la Réforme en Italie," *Revue de l'histoire des religions* 199 (1982) 37–65; H. Jedin, *Girolamo Seripando* (Würzburg, ²1984; reprint of 1937 edition), vol. 1, 263 et al.; vol. 2, 254, 311, 556–59; *Registra Priorum Generalium: Aegidius Viterbiensis,* vols. 1–2 (Rome, 1984–88); *Hieronymus Seripando,* vols. 1–5 (Rome, 1982–88); *Christophorus Patavinus,* vol. 2 (Rome, 1989).

WILLIGIS ECKERMANN

Aurifaber, (1) *Andreas.* Doctor and like-minded friend of Andreas → Osiander, born 1514 in Breslau, died December 12, 1559 in Königsberg. He began his studies at Wittenberg in 1527 and entered the philosophical faculty there in 1537. He became rector of the school at Danzig in 1539 and in Elbing in 1541; he then studied medicine for three years in Germany and Italy. In 1543, he became dean of the philosophical faculty in Wittenberg. In 1546, he became personal physician to Duke → Albrecht of Brandenburg and professor of physics and medicine in Königsberg. He attempted to win support for the disputed ideas of Osiander, who was his father-in-law.

■ **Literature:** RE³ 2, 287f.; 23, 139; *BBKL* 1:302f.—E. D. Schnaase, "A. A. und seine Schola Dantiscana," *Altpreußische Monatsschrift* 11 (1874) 304–25, 456–80; G. von Selle, *Geschichte der Albertus-Universität zu Königsberg in Preußen* (Würzburg, ²1956); M. Stupperich, *Osiander in Preußen 1549–1552* (Berlin and New York, 1973); *Andreas Osiander der Ältere. Gesamtausgabe,* vol. 9 (Gütersloh, 1993).

(2) *Johann.* Born January 30, 1517 in Breslau; died there, October 19, 1568; brother of Andreas. He began his studies at Wittenberg in 1534 and entered the philosophical faculty in 1540, becoming its dean in 1545. In 1547, he became rector in Breslau and professor of theology at Rostock in 1550. He was the principal author of the Mecklenburg church order (1551/1552). From 1554, he was president of the diocese of Samland and was one of the authors of the Prussian church order of 1558. He returned to Breslau in 1567. He exchanged letters with Philipp Melanchthon.

■ **Literature:** RE³ 2, 288ff.; 23, 139; *EKO* 4:22–25; 5:132–36, 161–219; *BBKL* 1:303.—*Melanchthons Briefwechsel. Kritische und kommentierte Gesamtausgabe,* ed. H. Scheible, *Regesten,* vol. 4 (Stuttgart-Bad Cannstatt, 1983) n. 4529–.

IRENE DINGEL

Aurifaber (Goldschmied), *Johann*. Lutheran theologian, born 1519 in Weimar, died November 18, 1575 in Erfurt. After studies at Wittenberg from 1537 to 1540, he became a teacher and preacher to soldiers. From 1545, he was Martin Luther's last *famulus* in Wittenberg. In 1550, he was appointed preacher at the court of Weimar. When the court broke with the → Gnesiolutherans in 1561, Aurifaber's strictly Lutheran views meant that he lost this position. In 1566, he was appointed pastor of the Preachers' Church in Erfurt, and he was Senior in the Erfurt ministry from 1572. His historical importance is as collector and transmitter of Luther's works. He wanted Luther's teaching to survive, and so he collected and published his statements from 1540 onward. He played a major role in the Jena edition of Luther's writings from 1553 on; he published two volumes of Luther's letters (1556, 1565) and two supplementary volumes of works by Luther (1564, 1565). His best-known publication is the German edition of the "Table Talk" (1566). Aurifaber's influence on editions of Luther's letters, sermons, and table talk lasted well into the 19th century; his arbitrary redactional activity left a deep imprint on the popular image of Luther.
- **Literature:** *VD 16* 1:44; *TRE* 4:752–55.

MICHAEL BECHT

Aurogallus (Goldhahn), *Matthäus*. Hebraist, born c. 1490 in Komotau (Bohemia), died November 10, 1543 in Wittenberg. He came into contact with Philipp Melanchthon after 1519 and became professor of Hebrew at the University of Wittenberg in 1521 and rector in 1542. He developed Hebrew studies into a university discipline; Martin Luther called on his advice while he was translating the Old Testament. His *Grammatica hebraicae-chaldaicae linguae* appeared in 1525 (2nd ed., 1539), and his lexicon *De Hebraeis urbium, locorum, populorumque nominibus e Veteri Instrumento congestis . . . Libellus* in 1526 (2nd ed., 1539; 3rd ed., 1543).
- **Literature:** *NDB* 1:457.—O. Eissfeldt, "Des Matthäus Aurigallus hebräische Grammatik von 1523," in idem, *Kleine Schriften*, vol. 3 (Tübingen, 1966) 200–204; idem, *Ein Lexikon der altpalästinensischen und altorientalischen Geographie aus den Anfängen der Universität Wittenberg* (Tübingen) 184–99; H. H. Holfelder, "M. A.," *ZKG* 85 (1974) 383–88.

MICHAEL BECHT

Avenarius (Habermann), *Johannes*. Lutheran theologian, born August 10, 1516 in Eger, died December 5, 1590 in Zeitz. He was active as a preacher in electoral Saxony from 1542 and became professor of theology at Wittenberg in 1574. He was appointed superintendent in Naumburg-Zeitz in 1576. In addition to linguistic studies of Hebrew, he published a prayer book which was widely read and translated into several languages. This book largely succeeded in integrating the Protestant and the Catholic traditions of prayer.
- **Works:** *Christliche Gebeth für allerley Not und Stende der gantzen Christenheit außgetheilet auf alle Tage in der Woche zu sprechen* (Wittenberg, 1567).
- **Literature:** *NDB* 1:467; *RGG*³ 3:7.

MICHAEL BECHT

- **Additional Bibliography:** *RGG*⁴ 3:1364.—T. Koch, *Johann Habermanns "Betbüchlein" im Zusammenhang seiner Theologie* (Tübingen, 2001).

Aventinus (Turmair), *Johannes*. Bavarian historian, born July 4, 1477 in Abensberg, died January 9, 1534 in Regensburg. During his studies in Ingolstadt and Vienna, he came into contact with the great German humanist Konrad Celtis. He studied in Krakow and Paris and was appointed tutor of the princes at the ducal court in Munich in 1509. He was appointed the first historiographer of the land of Bavaria in 1517, and his main works are the *Annales ducum Boiariae* and the *Bayerische Chronik*. These are milestones in the development of historical methodology, thanks to their systematic and critical evaluation of a wide range of source material, including archives, and physical evidence such as monuments. Their outstanding literary quality was another contributory factor to their influence on the historiography of the following centuries—a success unparalleled by any other work of German humanism. Aventinus was not able to complete the plan he had drawn up for the *Germania illustrata*. He took an intermediary position in the confessional conflicts that broke out in his lifetime, but this did not prevent him from being imprisoned for a time in 1528. This experience led him to spend the last years of his life in the imperial city of Regensburg.
- **Works:** *J. Turmair's, genannt A., Sämmtliche Werke*, 6 vols. (Munich, 1881–1908).
- **Literature:** *BDG* 721a–792, 52515–521; R. Vom Bruch and R. A. Müller, *Historikerlexikon* (Munich,

1991) 16f. — G. Strauss, *Historian in an Age of Crisis. The Life and Work of J. A. 1477–1534* (Cambridge, Mass., 1963).

ALOIS SCHMID

■ **Additional Bibliography:** A. Schmid, *J. A.: Berühmte Regensburger* (Regensburg, 1997) 109–19.

B

Baden Disputation. A Swiss debate about the faith, organized by the Catholic towns in Zurich from May 21 to June 8, 1526. This was the last attempt by Catholics to preserve the religious unity of Switzerland under the aegis of the Catholic Church, but it failed when Basle and Berne took the line of Zurich—which wanted to demote Huldrych Zwingli and bring the Catholic towns and Berne back to the Catholic Church, by force if necessary. The subject of the Disputation was seven theses of Johannes → Eck, most of which concerned the Mass. The participants included prominent Catholics (Eck, Johannes → Fabri, Thomas → Murner) and Protestants (Johannes → Oecolampadius, Berchtold → Haller). The outcome was not unification but rather a hardening of the divisions, and religious wars (between country areas and the city cantons) and religious division became a real threat; Zwingli considered using political and military means to further the Reformation cause.
■ **Literature:** F. Büsser, *Huldrych Zwingli* (Göttingen, 1973); G. W. Locher, *Die Zwinglische Reformation . . .* (Göttingen, 1979).

ERNST WALTER ZEEDEN

Badia, *Tommaso* (de Abbatiis de Mutina). Dominican theologian and cardinal (1542), born November 10, 1483 in Modena, died September 6, 1547 in Rome. He taught philosophy and theology at Ferrara, Venice, and Bologna, and became master of the sacred palace in 1529. He defended the orthodoxy of some Augustinian hermits (including → Augustine of Piedmont) who were suspected of being Lutherans because they held Augustinian positions on justification and predestination. He censured the first edition of Jacopo → Sadoleto's commentary on Romans in 1535, and the *Problemata* of Francesco Zorzi in the fol-

lowing year; in 1539, he approved the *Summa Instituti* of the Jesuits. He belonged to the circle around Gasparo → Contarini and Hieronymus → Aleander (whose confessor he was) and prepared a proposal for church reform which was presented to Paul III in 1537. He took part in the religious debates in Worms and Regensburg (1540–1541) and joined Contarini in supporting the consensus reached on the doctrine of justification. He became a member of the Congregation of the Holy Office in 1542. Although he was appointed legate to the Council of Trent, he remained in Rome as the pope's theological adviser.
■ **Works:** (handwritten, up to 1808 in S. Marco, Florence) *Quaestiones physicae et metaphysicae; Liber de anima; Tractatus III: 1. De intensione formarum, 2. De analogia entis, 3. De pluralitate intelligentiarum iuxta Aristotelem; Tractatus II: 1. De immortalitate animae, 2. De opinantes; De providentia divina; De pugna duorum Angelorum homini astantium, ad Gabrielem Ferrarium; Tractatus adversus Lutheranorum errores (?).*
■ **Literature:** *DBI* 5:74ff.

VINZENZ PFNÜR

Bajus (De Bay), *Michael*. Theologian at Louvain, born 1513 in Meslin l'Evêque (Hennegau), died 1589 in Louvain; ordained priest in 1542.

1. Life and Teachings

He was professor of philosophy from 1544 to 1550 and thereafter doctor and professor of theology; he was president of the college of Pope → Hadrian VI, and often served as dean of his faculty. He published *De libero arbitrio, De iustitia et iustificatione, De sacrificio* (1563; 2nd ed., 1566, including also *De peccato originis, De charitate, De indulgentiis, De oratione pro defunctis*), and *De meritis operum, De prima hominis iustitia, De virtutibus impiorum, De sacramentis, De forma baptismi* (1564). The theological methodology of Bajus and of his colleague Jan → Hessels is influenced by humanism (a return to the sources) and by the struggle against Protestantism. Bajus seeks to expound church doctrine on the basis of scripture and of the fathers, especially Augustine, bypassing the doctrinal developments in scholasticism. He does not indeed interpret the condition of the human person in paradise as *natura pura,* but he affirms that Adam was created to enjoy heavenly bliss and that his original righteousness—his perfect knowledge of God's law, the complete submission of his body to his spirit, his lack of desire—is one of the requirements of intact nature (*debitum naturae*). Thanks to the fall, however, human nature is corrupt. → Original sin consists in blindness to divine realities, in love of worldly things, and in the inclination to sin. Concupiscence makes our desires (even those that are involuntary) sinful; the same is true of the works of unbelievers, and their virtues are in fact vices, since the goal at which they aim is not God himself. Does this then entail the abolition of freedom? Bajus replies by making a distinction between freedom from external coercion—the possibility of willing or not willing to do something—and freedom from internal necessity: the lack of external coercion is sufficient to ensure human freedom and responsibility. However, human nature need not remain in its sinful state: the Redeemer has made it possible for us through grace to follow the divine law and hence to perform good deeds. Although the righteous remain in servitude to the "flesh," the indwelling of the Holy Spirit means that concupiscence no longer overpowers them. The will experiences a conversion to God, and sins are forgiven in the sacraments. The human person is justified through love (*caritas*), i.e., the intentional act of loving God and loving one's neighbor in God; but there are different levels in *caritas,* ascending from the initial desire for that which is good up to the perfect fulfillment of the law. This means that → justification is continuous progress in the exercise of the virtues, accompanied by progress in the forgiveness of sins.

2. Condemnation

In 1560, the Sorbonne condemned eighteen propositions in Bajus's teaching which had been diffused by students from the Franciscan Order. Bajus defended these propositions in his commentary on this censure. At the request of Antoine Perrenot de → Granvella and the cardinal legate Giovanni Francesco Commendone, Rome enjoined silence on both parties until the Council of Trent should have decided this issue. In 1563, Bajus, Hessels, and Cornelius Jansenius went to the council; but thanks to the intervention of Balduinus → Rythovius, the council took no decision. Bajus's colleague Josse → Ravesteyn sent a number of propositions from his second work—once again, formulated in language that deviated from Thomistic terminology and in a sharp

tone—to → Philip II, who had them condemned by the Universities of Alcalá and Salamanca (March 31 and August 8, 1565); and on July 20, 1567, the University of Alcalá pronounced a second condemnation, citing propositions from the second, enlarged printing of Bajus's first work. These Spanish condemnations were followed by the bull *Ex omnibus afflictionibus* of Pius V (October 1, 1567), in which he condemned 76 (or, following a different textual division, 69) propositions. Since, however, many of Bajus's propositions merely reproduced what Augustine had said, Rome was cautious: the text of the papal bull was not merely vague but downright ambiguous, taking the form of a general condemnation with a central passage which was punctuated in such a way ("Pius's comma," the *comma Pianum*) that it could be interpreted to mean *either* that all the propositions were rejected in the sense intended by Bajus *or* that a number of the propositions could be maintained precisely in the sense intended by Bajus! Most of Bajus's contemporaries followed the latter interpretation. Another problem was that the bull was not printed; only the faculty in Louvain was meant to have access to it. Naturally enough, its contents became known, and the debate continued, despite a letter of Pius V (May 13, 1569), which Bajus signed. Urged by Philip II, → Gregory XIII published the bull *Provisionis nostrae,* repeating the contents of the bull of Pius V but without clarifying the text that condemned Bajus's propositions. The uncertainty remained, and the debate refused to die down. In order to put an end to it, the faculty had to draw up a *corpus doctrinae* on the basis of the condemned propositions (1586), and it is probable that Bajus himself was one of the signatories. In the meantime, Bajus had awakened renewed controversy because of a lecture in which he affirmed that bishops received their jurisdictional authority directly from God, not from the pope; besides this, he was accused of failing to defend with sufficient vigor the authority of the church and the pope in his debate with Philipp Marnix of St. Adelgundis about the church and the Eucharist (1577-1581). Finally, when Louvain and → Douai expressed a negative judgment about the teaching of Leonardus Lessius and Jean Hamelius about grace, freedom, and justification, some suspected—probably wrongly—that this condemnation was meant to include Bajus too.

■ *LThK*[3] 1:1360ff. (unabridged version).

■ **Editions:** *Michaelis Baii opera, studio A.P. Theologi* [= G. Gerberon] (Cologne [= Amsterdam], 1696; part 1: Works; part 2: Documents).

■ **Literature:** *DThC* 2:38–111; *DHGE* 6:274–78; *Nationaal Biografisch Woordenboek*, vol. 1 (Brussels, 1964) 114–29.—A. Kaiser, *Natur und Gnade im Urstand. Eine Untersuchung der Kontroverse zwischen M. B. und Johannes Martínez de Ripalda* (Munich, 1965); G. Colombo, "Bellarmino contro Baio sulla questione del soprannaturale," *Scuola cattolica* 95 (1967) 307–38; V. Grossi, *Baio e Bellarmino interpreti di S. Agostino nelle questioni del soprannaturale* (Rome, 1968); J. A. G. Tans, *Quesnel et Jansénius: L'image de Jansénius jusqu'à la fin du XVIIIᵉ siècle*, ed. E. J. M. van Eijl (Louvain, 1987) 137–49.

JOSEPH A. G. TANS

■ **Additional Bibliography:** L. Ceyssens, "Nivelles contre Louvain? Étrange episode de l'histoire du baianisme," *Augustiniana* 47 (1997) 377–98; T. Quaghebeur, "'Sed illud intactum reliquerit': une virgule mal biffée: le 'comma pianum', la bulle 'Ex omnibus afflictionibus' du St-Office et la lecture du cardinal de Lugo," *RHE* 98 (2003) 61–79.

Baptists

1. Concept

The "Baptists" of the Reformation period included many religious groups who rejected infant baptism and practiced adult baptism from 1525 onward. An imperial law of 1529 threatened the "anabaptists" (i.e., those who "repeated baptism") with the sentence of death; this renewed the imperial law of late antiquity, which was directed against the Donatists in the 5th century and was later codified under Emperor Justinian I (527-565). The concept of "re-baptizers" retains its defamatory ring even today. The Baptists themselves employed designations such as "Christian brothers and sisters." Modern scholars agree on using "Baptists" as a collective term for all who adhered to the practice of adult baptism.

2. History

The Baptist movement arose in three regions: in 1525, in Zurich and Switzerland; in 1526, in Thuringia and Franconia; and in 1530, in the Netherlands. The first adult baptism—the baptism of the priest Jörg Blaurock († 1529) by the young Zurich patrician Konrad → Grebel on January 21, 1525 in Zurich—was administered in the context of the debates generated by Huldrych Zwingli's Reformation. Persecution by the city council soon led to the formation of the first Baptist community in Zollikon, very close to Zurich. The swift spread of the Baptist movement in Switzerland was connected with the → Peasants' War. Continuing persecution resulted in a wider dispersion of the Baptists in southern Germany and Austria. This experience of suffering led the Swiss Baptist movement to develop its characteristic separatism ("Schleitheim Confession," 1527).

The Baptist movement in central Germany, generated by the activity of the bookseller Hans Hut (c. 1490-1527), also spread in southern Germany and Austria. It took a different path from the Swiss movement, since it acquired a strong eschatological momentum through its reception of the teachings of Thomas → Müntzer.

Under the leadership of Jakob Hutter (died 1536), the Swiss Baptists who had emigrated to Austria settled in Moravia, where they became known as the → Hutterite Brethren. Here too, they took the path of pacifist separatism.

The mission of the lay preacher Melchior → Hoffman in the Netherlands (the so-called Melchiorites) began from Strasbourg, which initially tolerated the Baptist movement. Dutch Baptists initiated adult baptism in Münster, where the Baptist movement took over the city government in 1534/1535: under the prophet and king Jan van Leiden (Jan Beuckels, Beuckelson, Bockelson, Johannes of Leiden; 1509-1536), the Reformation of the city of Münster (Bernhard → Rothmann) and the Melchiorite expectation of the sovereign rule of Christ developed into a revolutionary Baptist praxis. The city was besieged by Prince Bishop Franz von → Waldeck, and then conquered by imperial troops on June 25, 1535. After 1536, the former priest → Menno Simons established lasting community structures for the Dutch Baptists, and their movement spread into the Baltic area (so-called Mennonites).

3. Doctrine

Despite considerable divergences of points of detail, all Baptists agreed in demanding that those who received believer's baptism must thereby express their willingness to lead a new, Christian way of life. Their hopes of fundamental societal change were disappointed, and they experienced suffering: some reacted by a withdrawal into the fellowship of the "true Christians," others by a

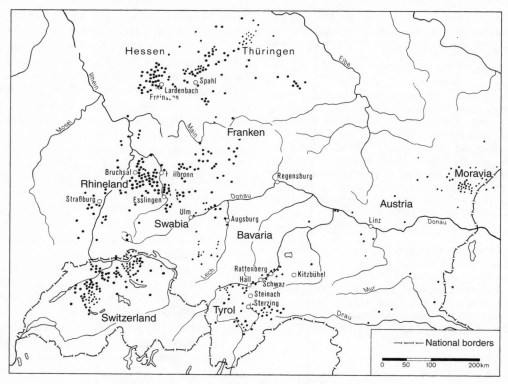

Baptists in Southern Germany, Austria, and Switzerland, c. 1540

keener expectation of the kingdom of God on earth. The Baptist movement had adherents of both sexes; initially, its leaders were former priests and members of the upper and middle classes, lower social classes later joined the movement in some regions. Catholic theologians looked on the Baptist movement as one of the consequences of the Reformation against which they were fighting; they paid little attention to it, sometimes dismissing the Baptists as "Abecedarians," i.e., persons with little scholarly learning. Protestant theologians, on the other hand, attempted to reintegrate the Baptists into the official church. The imperial law against the "anabaptists" was enforced with rigor by most of the Catholic rulers, but Protestant rulers took a milder line.

■ **Bibliography:** (T.=Täufer, Baptists) H. J. Hillerbrand, *Anabaptist Bibliography 1520–1630* (St. Louis, Mo., 1991).

■ **Sources:** *Quellen zur Geschichte der (Wieder-)T.,* 16 vols. (Leipzig—Gütersloh, 1930–88); *Quellen zur Geschichte der T. in der Schweiz,* 4 vols. (Zurich, 1952–74); *Documenta Anabaptistica Neerlandica,* 7 vols. (Leiden, 1975–95).

■ **Literature:** *GCh* 8:122–90.—*Täufertum und radikale*

Reformation im 16.Jh., ed. J.-G. Rott and S. L. Verheus (Baden-Baden, 1987); H.-J. Goertz, *Die T.* (Munich, [2]1988; English, London, 1996); R. Klötzer, *Die T.-Herrschaft von Münster* (Münster, 1992); H.-J. Goertz, *Religiöse Bewegungen in der Frühen Neuzeit* (Munich, 1993); W. O. Packull, *Hutterite Beginnings* (Baltimore and London, 1995); G. H. Williams, *The Radical Reformation,* 2 vols. (Kirksville, Mo., [3]2000).

RALF KLÖTZER

■ **Additional Bibliography:** E. Wolgast, "Melanchthon und die T.," *Mennonitische Geschichtsblätter* 54 (1997) 31–51; M. Mattern, *Leben im Abseits. Frauen und Männer im Täufertum (1525–50).* (Frankfurt/Main, 1998); H.-G. Tanneberger, *Die Vorstellung der T. von der Rechtfertigung des Menschen* (Stuttgart, 1999); O. Kuhr, "Johannes Oekolampad und die T.," *Freikirchen-forschung* 9 (1999) 78–95; C. Baecher, *Anabaptimes naissants (1525–1535) et millénarismes: Formes du millénarisme en Europe à l'aube des temps modernes* (Paris, 2001) 37–74; C. A. Snyder, *Anabaptist History and Theology* (Kitchener, 2002).

Barlow, *William.* Augustinian canon regular, died 1568 or 1569; under → Henry VIII, → Edward VI, and → Elizabeth I, he was successively bishop of several dioceses, finally becoming bishop of Chichester in 1559. Since he was one of the four bishops who ordained Matthew → Parker as the first Protestant archbishop of Canterbury in 1559, but the validity of his own consecration is dubious, Barlow has played a certain role in the discussion of the validity of Anglican orders; however, his importance here should not be exaggerated.

■ **Literature:** *DHGE* 6:845; *DThC* 2:416; *NCE* 2:101.— C. Jenkins, *Bishop B.'s Consecration and Archbishop Parker's Register* (London, 1935).

BURKHARD NEUMANN

Barnes, *Robert.* English Augustinian hermit, born 1495, died July 30, 1540. He was imprisoned several times because of his Lutheran views, but fled in 1528 to Germany, where he became a close associate of Martin Luther. In 1531, under the pseudonym "Antonius Anglus," he published an apologia for Lutheran teachings. He then returned to England, but → Henry VIII sent him back to Germany with the mission of winning support for the king's divorce. In 1540, he fell from the king's favor and was burnt without trial as a recidivist heretic. Luther wrote a foreword to Barnes's history of the popes, which was published in 1536.

■ **Works:** *Führnehmlich Artickel der Christlichen Kirchen* (Nuremberg, 1531); *Vitae Romanorum Pontificum* (Wittenberg, 1536).
■ **Literature:** H. Thieme, *Die Ehescheidung Heinrichs VIII. und die europäischen Universitäten* (Karlsruhe, 1957) 17–21; M. L. Loane, *Pioneers of the Reformation in England* (London, 1964) 47–89; J. P. Lusardi, "The Career of R. B.," in *The Complete Works of St. Thomas More*, vol. 8, pt. 3 (New Haven and London, 1973) 1365–1415; R. Bäumer, *Martin Luther und der Papst* (Münster, ⁵1987) 89f.

FRANZ-BERNHARD STAMMKÖTTER

■ **Additional Bibliography:** J. E. McGoldrick, *Luther's English Connection: The Reformation Thought of R. B. and William Tyndale* (Milwaukee, Wisc., 1979); C. R. Trueman, "'The Saxons Be Sore on the Affirmative': R. B. on the Lord's Supper," in *The Bible, the Reformation and the Church.* Festschrift J. Atkinson (Sheffield, 1995) 290–307.

Bartholomew, Night of Saint (also called the "Bloody marriage of Paris"). The night from August 23-24, 1572. In the aftermath of the Edict of St-Germain-en-Laye (August 8, 1570) which guaranteed four places of secure refuge for the →

Huguenots, → Charles IX sought to bring about reconciliation between Catholics and Huguenots through the marriage of his sister, Margaret of Valois, to Henry of Navarre (→ Henry IV) on August 18, 1572. Admiral Gaspard → Coligny, the Huguenot leader, came to exercise an ever stronger influence on Charles IX, and prompted him to go to war against Spain in favor of the Protestants in the Spanish Netherlands. The queen mother, Catharine de → Medici, who disapproved of this policy and risked losing her influence at court, sought to remove Coligny from power. Four days after the wedding of her daughter Margaret, which had been attended by many Huguenot nobles, she organized an attack on Coligny, who was wounded but escaped. The king ordered an investigation into the instigators of this attack, which threatened to expose the queen mother; she therefore resolved to kill Coligny and the leaders of the Huguenots, with the sole exception of the princes of Navarre, who were of royal blood, and prince Henri de Condé—on condition that they returned to the Catholic Church (a condition they accepted). The king hesitated, but Catharine pressured him into consenting to her plan. The massacre was carried out by servants of the Guise household on St. Bartholomew's night; in Paris alone, between three and four thousand persons were killed, and the slaughter continued subsequently in the French provinces. Altogether, between five and ten thousand persons died. These events had nothing to do with religious motives, but were born of an unscrupulous lust for power; however, misleading reports led Gregory XIII to see St. Bartholomew's night as the crushing of a treasonable attack on the king and as a victory over Calvinism.

■ **Literature:** S. L. England, *The Massacre of St. Bartholomew* (London, 1938); Ph. Erlanger, *Le massacre de la Saint-Barthélemy* (Paris, 1960, ²1981).

KLAUS GANZER

■ **Additional Bibliography:** *RGG*⁴ 1:1142f.—R. M. Kingdon, *Myths about the St. Bartholomew's Day Massacres 1572–76* (Cambridge, Mass., 1988); K. Crawford, "Catherine de Medici and the Performance of Political Motherhood," *SCJ* 31 (2000) 643–73.

Bauduin (Balduin), *François.* Humanist and lawyer, born January 1, 1520 in Arras, died October 24, 1573 in Paris. He was professor of canon and civil law in Bourges (1548-1555), Strasbourg (1555), and Heidelberg (1556-1561); after an interlude of activity in church politics, he was professor in Angers from 1569. He was an adherent of Jean Calvin from c. 1545, but he was later attacked by Calvin and Theodor → Beza because of his irenical attitude; he returned to the Catholic Church in 1563. Like Georg → Cassander, he sought a reconciliation between the confessions on the basis of scripture and the early church. His significance lies primarily in his researches into Roman law and early Christianity, as well as in the elaboration of a methodology for the study of the history of law.

■ **Works:** *Constantinus Magnus sive de Constantini imperatoris legibus ecclesiasticis atque civilibus* (Basle, 1556); *Ad edicta veterum principum Romanorum de christianis* (Basle, 1557); *De institutione historiae universae et eius cum iurisprudentia coniunctione* (Paris, 1561); *Historia Carthaginensis collationis sive disputationis de ecclesia* (Paris, 1566; reprinted in *PL* 11:1439–1506).— *Edited works: Minucius Felix, Octavius* (Heidelberg, 1560); *Optatus von Mileve, Libri sex de schismate Donatistarum* (Paris, 1563).

■ **Literature:** D. R. Kelley, *Foundations of Modern Historical Scholarship* (New York, 1970) 116–48; M. Erbe, *F. B. Biographie eines Humanisten* (Gütersloh, 1978); M. Turchetti, *Concordia o tolleranza? F. B. e i "moyenneurs"* (Geneva, 1984).

PETER WALTER

Beatus Rhenanus (Beat Bild). Humanist, born August 22, 1485 in Schlettstadt, died July 20, 1547 in Strasbourg. He studied in Paris from 1503 to 1507, where one of his professors was → Faber Stapulensis. He was in Schlettstadt and Strasbourg from 1507 to 1511, and published works by contemporary Italian humanists. From 1511, he worked in Basle as editor of classical and patristic texts (including the *editio princeps* of Tertullian in 1521); he was a collaborator of → Erasmus of Rotterdam, whose text-critical methodology he perfected. Initially, he supported the Reformation, but the victory of the Reformers in Basle led him to return to Schlettstadt in 1528. He had already written a commentary on the *Germania* of Tacitus (Basle, 1519), and now he turned to the study of early German history (*Rerum germanicarum libri tres,* Basle, 1531).

■ **Works:** *Briefwechsel des B.,* ed. A. Horawitz and K. Hartfelder (Leipzig, 1886; reprinted Hildesheim, 1966;

partly new edition: *Un grand humaniste alsacien et son époque. B.,* ed. R. Walter (Strasbourg, 1986).

■ **Literature:** *CEras* 1:104–9.—*Annuaire de la Société des Amis de la Bibliothèque Humaniste de Sélestat* 35 (1985) (Gedenkschrift zum 500. Geburtstag); J. F. D'Amico, *Theory and Practice in Renaissance Textual Criticism* (Berkeley, 1988); U. Muhlack, "B.," in P. G. Schmidt, ed., *Humanismus im deutschen Südwesten* (Sigmaringen, 1993) 195–220.

PETER WALTER

■ **Additional Bibliography:** R. Walter, *Trois profiles de B.* (Sélestat, 1997); "B. Lecteur et editeur des textes anciens," *Actes du colloque International tenu à Strasbourg et à Sélestat, 13–15 novembre 1998* (Turnhout, 2000).

Beccadelli, *Ludovico.* Diplomat, born January 29, 1501 in Bologna, died October 17, 1572 in Prato. He had contacts with groups involved in a humanistic religious revival; he was secretary to Gasparo → Contarini and Reginald → Pole, whose biographies he wrote, and was later in the service of Marcello Cervini (→ Marcellus II). He became bishop of Ravello in 1549; he was nuncio in Venice from 1550 to 1554, and became archbishop of Ragusa in 1555. He accompanied Contarini and Giovanni → Morone on their legations. He took an active part in the third period of the Council of Trent. He resigned as archbishop of Ragusa in 1564.

■ **Works:** *Monumenti di varia letteratura tratti dai manoscritti originali di mons. L. B. arcivescovo di Ragusa,* 2 vols. (Bologna, 1797–1804).—Numerous mss. in Biblioteca Palatina, Parma, and Biblioteca Apostolica Vaticana.

■ **Literature:** *DBI* 7:407–13.—F. Dittrich, *Gasparo Contarini* (Braunsberg, 1885) passim; P. Paschini, "L'inquisizione a Venezia e il nunzio L. B.," *Archivio della Società Romana di Storia Patria* 65 (1942) 61–152; H. Jedin, *Das Bischofsideal der Katholischen Reformation: Kirche des Glaubens, Kirche der Geschichte,* vol. 2 (Freiburg, 1966) 91–97.

KLAUS GANZER

Beda, *Noel.* Theologian, born c. 1470 in Mont-Saint-Michel, died there January 8, 1537. He headed the Collège de Montaigu in Paris from 1504 to 1535; he took his doctorate in theology in 1508 and was Syndicus of the theological faculty from 1520 to 1533. He was a bitter foe of the exegesis and theology of Jacob → Faber Stapulensis, Josse → Clichtove, and → Erasmus of Rotterdam.

The increasing divergence of views between Beda and King → Francis I culminated in his official demotion from office in 1535.

■ **Works:** *Annotationum Natalis Bede . . . in Jacobum Fabrum Stapulensem libri duo, et in Desiderium Erasmum Roterodamum liber unus* (Paris, 1526); *Apologia . . . adversus clandestinos Lutheranos* (Paris, 1529).

■ **Literature:** J. K. Farge, *Biographical Register of Paris Doctors of Theology, 1500–36* (Toronto, 1989) 31–36; *CEras* 1:116ff.—F. Renaudet, *Études Érasmiennes (1521–29)* (Paris, 1939); W. Bense, "N. B. and the Humanist Reformation at Paris, 1504–34" (Ph.D. diss., Harvard, 1967); F. Higman, *Censorship and the Sorbonne* (Geneva, 1979); J. K. Farge, *Orthodoxy and Reform in Early Reformation France* (Leiden, 1985); E. Rummel, *Erasmus and His Catholic Critics*, vol. 2 (Nieuwkoop, 1989) 29–59; J. K. Farge, ed., *Registre des procès-verbaux de la Faculté de Théologie de l'Université de Paris de janvier 1524 à novembre 1533* (Paris, 1990); idem, *Le parti conservateur au XVIᵉ siècle* (Paris, 1992).

PETER WALTER

Bembo, *Pietro*. Humanist, born May 20, 1470 in Venice, died January 18, 1547 in Rome. After studies in Messina (1492-1494), Padua (1494-1495), and Ferrara (1497-1499), he was active as publisher of Italian authors (Petrarch, 1501; Dante, 1502) and as a writer (*Gli Asolani*, 1505); he attempted in vain to start a diplomatic career. He worked at the court of Urbino from 1506 to 1512. He became secretary to → Leo X in 1513 (working with Jacopo → Sadoleto). He taught privately in Padua from 1521, where he completed his *Prose della volgar lingua* (1525), a work of decisive importance for the development of Italian as a literary language. Although he lived together with a woman and had three children in this relationship, he made his religious profession as a Canon of the Holy Sepulcher in 1522. In 1530, he was appointed official historian of the republic of Venice (*Historiae Venetae libri XII*, 1531). He was created cardinal *in petto* in 1538, and publicly in 1539; he was then ordained priest. He became bishop of Gubbio in 1541, but resided there only for a short period; in 1544, he was transferred to Bergamo, where a coadjutor represented him. He had contacts with the reform-minded circles around Gasparo → Contarini, and attempted in vain to win support in Rome for Contarini's endeavors at the religious dialogue in → Regensburg (1541).

■ **Works:** *Opere*, 4 vols. (Venice, 1729; 12 vols. Milan, 1808–10).—Partial editions: *Opere in volgare*, ed. M. Marti (Florence, 1961); *Prose e Rime*, ed. C. Dionisotti (Turin, ²1966); *Lettere*, ed. E. Travi, 4 vols. (Bologna, 1987–93); *Carmina* (Turin, 1990); *Gli Asolani*, ed. G. Dilemmi (Florence, 1991); *Asolaner Gespräche*, ed. and trans. M. Rumpf (Heidelberg, 1992); *Sacra*, ed. O. Schönberger (Würzburg, 1994).

■ **Literature:** *DBI* 8:133–51; *CEras* 1:120–23.—P. Simoncelli, "P. B. e l'evangelismo italiano," *Critica storica* 15 (1978) 1–63; D. Perocco, "Rassegna di studi bembiani (1964–85)," *Lettere italiane* 37 (1985) 512–40; P. Simoncelli, "Vom Humanismus zur Gegenreformation," in E. Neuss and J. V. Pollet, eds., *Pflugiana* (Münster, 1990) 93–114.

PETER WALTER

■ **Additional Bibliography:** Ch. Raffini, *Marsilio Ficino, P. B., Baldassare Castiglione* (New York, 1998); M. Prada, *La lingua dell'epistolario volgare di P. B.*, 2 vols. (Genoa, 2000–2002).

Benedictus Deus. Bull issued by Pius IV on January 26, 1564 and published on June 30 of that year, confirming the reforming decrees of the Council of Trent and requiring these to be accepted and put into practice. Every interpretation made "without Our authority" is sharply rejected, since the pope alone is competent to interpret the decrees. This bull was promulgated despite opposition on the part of curial circles who feared that the reforms (especially the bishops' obligation to reside in their dioceses) would mean the "ruin of the Roman curia."

■ **Text:** DH 1847–50.

■ **Literature:** Jedin 4/2:223–33.

GISBERT GRESHAKE

Berquin, *Louis de*. Humanist, born c. 1490, died April 17, 1529 in Paris. After studying law in Orleans, he served at the French court. Berquin's translations of writings by the Reformers and Erasmus led to accusations of heresy, with Noel → Beda as the prime mover; King → Francis I was able to save him from execution in 1523 and 1526, but not in 1529.

■ **Works:** *Erasmus-Übersetzungen (1525)*, ed. E. V. Telle, *Déclamation des louanges de mariage* (Geneva, 1976); *La Complainte de la paix* (Geneva, 1978); *Brefve admonition de la manière de prier. Le Symbole des Apostres de Jesuchrist* (Geneva, 1979).

■ **Literature:** *CEras* 1:135–40.—M. Mann Phillips, *Érasme et les débuts de la réforme française* (Paris, 1934)

113–49; J. K. Farge, *Orthodoxy and Reform in Early Reformation France* (Leiden, 1985).

PETER WALTER

Bertano, *Pietro.* Dominican (1516), cardinal (1551), theologian, and nuncio, born November 4, 1501 in Nonantola (Modena), died March 8, 1558 in Rome. He studied theology in Bologna; after taking his doctorate, he taught in Bologna, Ferrara, and Venice. In 1537, he became lector in Mantua, where he worked closely with Cardinal Ercole → Gonzaga. He was appointed bishop of Fano in 1537, and was theological counselor to the conciliar legates in Trent from 1545 to 1547. He spoke in favor of the importance of scripture and tradition, the revision of the Vulgate, and the obligation of bishops to reside in their sees. He was nuncio at the imperial court from 1548 to 1550 and in 1551; he was a candidate for the papacy at the second conclave in 1555. Bertano was an important conciliar theologian and church reformer, and his personal life was irreproachable.

■ **Literature:** *DBI* 9:467–71.—*Nuntiatur des Bischofs P. B. von Fano 1548–49,* ed. W. Friedensburg (Gotha, 1910); idem, "Der Briefwechsel Gasparo Contarinis mit Ercole Gonzaga," *QFIAB* 2 (1899) 174–81; *Nuntiaturen des P. B. und Pietro Camaiani 1550–52,* ed. G. Kupke (Gotha, 1901); F. Lauchert, *Die italienischen Gegner Luthers* (Freiburg, 1912) 671; C. Erdmann, "Unbekannte Briefe des Kardinals Farnese an den Nuntius B.," *QFIAB* 21 (1929–30) 293–304; C. Richard, *Concile de Trente,* vol. 1 (Paris, 1930) passim; A. Walz, *I cardinali domenicani al Concilio di Trento* (Florence, 1959) passim; G. Müller, "Die Kandidatur Giovanni Salviatis im Konklave 1549/50," *QFIAB* 42–43 (1963) 435–52; Jedin 2², passim.

KLAUS JAITNER

Berthold of Chiemsee (Berthold Pürstinger). Theological writer, born 1465 in Salzburg, died July 16, 1543 in Saalfelden (Pinzgau). After studying law in Perugia, he was ordained priest in 1490, and became parish priest of Schnaitsee and an official of the prince bishop of Salzburg in 1493. He became bishop of Chiemsee and auxiliary bishop of Salzburg in 1508. He mediated in the societal and political tensions between the prince bishop, the citizens, and the peasants in 1511 and 1525. He resigned his diocese in 1526 and withdrew to Raitenhaslach near Burghausen, and in 1528-1529 to Saalfelden. His *Tewtsche Theologey* (1528, reprint 1852; Latin edition, Augsburg,

1531) is a vernacular exposition of the doctrine of the faith, encompassing redemption, justification, faith, the sacraments and works; it was useful both in instruction and in resisting the Reformation. His *Tewtsch Rational* and *Das Keligpuchel* ("Pamphlet on the chalice"), both published at Augsburg in 1535, are also responses to the Reformation. If he is the author of the *Onus Ecclesiae* (Landshut, 1524), which deals with reform in an apocalyptic and prophetic tone, then we may affirm that he was keenly aware of the critical situation of his own day.

■ **Works and Sources:** *VD 16* 16:25ff.; Klaiber nos. 275–78; *ARCEG* 1–3.

■ **Literature:** *DSp* 12:2611–14; *KThR* 3:65–75.—J. Schmuck, *Die Prophetie "Onus Ecclesiae"* (Vienna, 1973); *Bavaria Sancta,* vol. 3 (Regensburg, 1973) 293–302; G. Marx, *Glaube, Werke und Sakramente im Dienste der Rechtfertigung in den Schriften von B. Pürstinger* (Leipzig, 1982); E. W. Zeeden, "B. Pürstinger," *Rottenburger Jahrbuch für Kirchengeschichte* 5 (1986) 177–212.

HERIBERT SMOLINSKY

■ **Additional Bibliography:** P. J. Langsfeld, *Theology-for-Piety in Early Reformation Era. B. Pürstinger's Tewtsche Theology* (Rome, 1993); M. Milway, "Apocalyptic Reform and Forerunners of the End: B. Pürstinger, Bishop of Chiemsee († 1543)," *Zeitsprünge* 3 (1999) 316–27.

Ber(us) (Bär), *Ludwig.* Theologian, born May 24, 1479 in Basle, died April 14, 1554 in Freiburg. He studied in Paris from 1496 (master of arts, 1499; doctor of theology, 1512) and became professor of theology in Basle in 1513. He was rector of the university in 1514 and 1520; he was president of the → Baden Disputation. He became a member of the cathedral chapter in Basle in 1526, and moved with the other canons to Freiburg in 1529, after the consolidation of the Reformation. He became head of the cathedral school in 1535. He advised → Erasmus of Rotterdam on theological questions.

■ **Works:** *Septem psalmorum poenitentialium . . . explanatio* (Basle, 1545); *Pro salutari hominis ad felicem mortem praeparatione* (Basle, 1551).

■ **Literature:** J. K. Farge, *Biographical Register of Paris Doctors of Theology 1500–36* (Toronto, 1980) 22–26; *CEras* 1:84ff.—P. G. Bietenholz, "L. B., Erasmus and the Tradition of the 'Ars bene moriendi,'" *Revue de littérature comparée* 52 (1978) 155–70.

PETER WALTER

Beza (de Bèze), *Theodor.* Collaborator and successor of Jean Calvin, born June 24, 1519 in Vézelay, died October 13, 1605 in Geneva. He came to Orleans in 1528 and lived in the household of the humanist Melchior Vollmar, who educated Beza and took him with him to Bourges in 1530. After Vollmar emigrated, Beza studied law in Orleans from 1535 to 1539; humanistic studies in Paris followed. He emigrated to Switzerland in 1548. After ten years as professor of Greek in Lausanne, where he wrote humanistic and polemical treatises, as well as the vernacular play *Abraham sacrifiant,* Beza moved to Geneva, where he worked as clergyman, city councilor, and rector of the academy. He and Calvin alternated as theological lecturers. In the following period, and especially after Calvin's death in 1564, he took on further ecclesiastical and academic tasks and devoted all his energy to the maintenance and consolidation of the church of Geneva. He was also the spiritual leader of the Reformed Church in France and adviser to its political leadership; he made statements on a large number of controversial issues. Most of his writings deal with controversial points of theology; only his humanistic works and his late sermons are untouched by the confessional conflict. His achievements in biblical scholarship included five editions of the New Testament; he also collaborated in the preparation of the Geneva Bible (1588), for which he wrote the preface. Beza himself collected his writings in three volumes (*Tractationum theologicarum,* Geneva, 1570-1582); the *Confessio fidei christianae* in the first volume (originally published in French, Geneva, 1558; Latin, 1559) offers the best synthesis of his theology. In the *De haereticis a civili magistratu puniendis* (Geneva, 1554), he defended the actions taken by Calvin against Jérôme → Bolsec and Michael → Servet.

■ **Literature:** *TRE* 5:765–74.—F. Gardy, *Bibliographie des œuvres . . . de Théodore de Béze* (Geneva, 1960); P.-F. Geisendorf, *Théodore de Béze* (Geneva, ²1967); G. Bedouelle, *Le temps des réformes et la Bible* (Paris, 1989) 431–43, 641–46.

FERNANDO DOMÍNGUEZ

■ **Additional Bibliography:** M. Jinkins, "T. B.: Continuity and Regression in the Reformed Tradition," *Evangelical Quarterly* 64 (1992) 131–54; C. van Sliedregt, *Calvijns opvolger Th. B.* (Leiden, 1996); R. Bodenmann, "Die wiederaufgefundene Kampfschrift Th. B.s und seiner Kollegen gegen die Konkordienformel (1578)," *Lutherische Theologie und Kirche* 21 (1997) 59–98; S. M. Manetsch, *Th. B. and the Quest for Peace in France 1572–98* (Leiden, 2000); G. M. Thomas, "Constructing and Clarifying the Doctrine of Predestination," *Reformation and Renaissance Review* 2 (2000) 7–28; S. M. Manetsch, "Psalms before Sonnets. T. B. and the 'Studia Humanitatis,'" in *Continuity and Change. Festschrift H. A. Oberman* (Leiden, 2000) 400–416.

Biandrata (Blandrata), *Giorgio.* Doctor, antitrinitarian, born 1516 in Saluzzo (Piedmont), died 1588 in Alba Julia. He was influenced by the antitrinitarian Matteo Gribaldi. After working as a doctor in Poland and Transylvania, he came to Geneva in 1557, but left the city in the following year because of disagreements with Jean Calvin. After a lengthy stay in Poland, he came to Transylvania in 1563 as personal physician to prince Johann Sigismund Zápolya. Here he joined the court preacher Franz Dávid in combating the trinitarian dogma (Disputation of Alba Julia, 1568; → Antitrinitarians), but they parted company on the issue of the adoration of Christ, which Dávid rejected.

■ **Literature:** *DBI* 10:257–64; *TRE* 5:777–81.—D. Cantimori, *Italienische Häretiker der Spätrenaissance* (Basle, 1949); A. Rotondò, *Studi e ricerche di storia ereticale italiana del Cinquecento,* vol. 1 (Turin, 1974) 161–223; J. M. Tylenda, "Warning That Went Unheeded: John Calvin on G. B.," *Calvin Theological Journal* 12 (1977) 24–62; R. Dán and A. Pirnát, eds., *Antitrinitarianism in the Second Half of the 16th Century* (Budapest and Leiden, 1982) esp. 157–90, 231–41.

ROBERT ROTH

■ **Additional Bibliography:** S. Carletto, *La trinità e l'anticristo: G. B. tra eresia e diplomazia* (Cuneo, 2001).

Bibliander (Buchmann), *Theodor.* Reformed Hebraist, born c. 1504 in Bischofszell (Thurgau), died September 26, 1564 in Zurich. He studied under Konrad → Pellikan and Johannes → Oecolampadius; in 1531, he succeeded Huldrych Zwingli as professor of Old Testament. He worked on the Zurich Latin translation of the Bible (*Biblia sacrosancta Testamenti Veteris et Novi,* 1543) and published a Latin translation of the Qur'an (Basle, 1543). His criticism of the Calvinist doctrine of predestination led to his removal from office in 1560.

■ **Principal Works:** *Institutionum grammaticarum de lingua hebraea liber unus* (Zurich, 1535); *De ratione communi omnium linguarum et literarum commentarius*

(Zurich, 1548); *De ratione temporum* (Basle, 1551); *Temporum supputatio partitioque exactior* (Basle, 1551; chronology); *De legitima vindicatione Christianismi* (Basle, 1553; against the papacy and Trent).

■ **Literature:** K. Maeder, *Die Via Media in der Schweizerischen Reformation* (Zurich, 1970) 236–42; V. Segesvary, *L'Islam et la Réforme* (Lausanne, 1977) 161–99; F. Büsser, *In Defence of Zwingli: Prophet, Pastor, Protestant*, ed. E. I. Furcha and H. W. Pipkin (Allison Park, Pa., 1984) 1–21; H. Clark, "The Publication of the Koran in Latin," *SCJ* 15 (1984) 3–12; H. Bobzin, "Zur Anzahl der Drucke von B.s Koranauszug von 1543," *Basler Zeitschrift für Geschichte und Altertumskunde* 85 (1985) 213–19; G. Bedouelle, *Les temps des réformes et la Bible* (Paris, 1989) with index.

ROBERT ROTH

■ **Additional Bibliography:** R. S. Armour, "Th. B.'s 'Alcoran' of 1543/50," *Perspectives in Religious Studies* 24 (1997) 101–15.

Biel, *Gabriel.* Theologian, born c. 1408 in Speyer, died December 7, 1495 in Einsiedel near Tübingen. He began his studies in Heidelberg in 1432 and took the bachelor's degree in 1438 and the licentiate and master's degree in 1438. He was in Erfurt in 1451, and in 1453 came to Cologne, where he took the bachelor's degree in theology. He returned to Erfurt in 1455, where he took the licentiate in theology. From 1457 to 1466, he was preacher in the cathedral of Mainz; during the conflict among the cathedral clergy in 1462, he supported the papal candidate, Adolf of Nassau, against Diether of Isenburg. He promoted the → *devotio moderna* and helped found houses of Brethren in Marienthal (Rheingau, 1463), Königstein (Taunus, 1467), Butzbach (where he was the first rector, 1468), Urach (at the request of Count Eberhard the Bearded of Württemberg, 1477), and Rome (1482). In 1484, he became professor at the university of Tübingen (founded in 1477), as a representative of the *Via moderna.* He was rector in 1485/1486 and 1489, and retired in 1491. In 1492, he founded a house of the Brethren at St. Peter's in Einsiedel, where he was provost until his death. In his commentary on the *Sentences,* the *Collectorium,* Biel presents himself as an interpreter of William of Ockham, but the confrontation with other intellectual approaches and their elaboration (e.g., in Duns Scotus) leads him often to find independent solutions to problems on an Ockhamite basis; these solutions indicate a way to reconcile the positions of the various theological schools. His *Collectorium* was commented upon in a number of European universities (e.g., Salamanca and Coimbra) in the 16th century. Biel influenced both Martin Luther (who studied his theology intensively) and the Council of Trent.

■ **Works:** *Sacri Canonis Misse Expositio* (Reutlingen 1488), ed. H. A. Oberman and W. J. Courtenay, 4 vols. (Wiesbaden, 1963–67); *Dispositio et conspectus materiae cum indice conceptuum et rerum,* curavit W. Werbeck (Wiesbaden, 1976); *Collectorium circa quattuor libros Sententiarum* (Tübingen, 1501), ed. W. Werbeck and U. Hofmann, 5 vols. (Tübingen, 1973–84), with indexes prepared by W. Werbeck (Tübingen, 1992); *Passionis dominicae sermo historialis* (Reutlingen, 1489, often reprinted) (anonymous); *Sermones,* ed. W. Steinbach, 4 vols. (Tübingen, 1499–1500); *Defensorium oboedientiae apostolicae* (1462), ed. and trans. (English) H. A. Oberman, D. E. Zerfoss, and W. J. Courtenay (Cambridge, Mass., 1968); *De communi vita clericorum,* ed. W. M. Landeen, in "B.'s Tractate of the Common Life," *Research Studies* 28 (1960) 79–95.

■ **Literature:** *TRE* 6:488–91.—L. Grane, *Contra Gabrielem. Luthers Auseinandersetzung mit G. B. in der Disputatio Contra Scholasticam Theologiam 1517* (Copenhagen, 1962); H. A. Oberman, *Spätscholastik und Reformation,* vol. 1 (Zurich, 1965); W. Ernst, *Gott und Mensch am Vorabend der Reformation* (Leipzig, 1972); F. J. Burkard, *Philosophische Lehrgehalte in G. B.s Sentenzenkommentar* (Meisenheim, 1974); M. Schrama, *G. B. en zijn leer over de Allerheiligste Drievuldigheid* (Munich, 1981); W. G. Bayerer, *Gabrielis Biel Gratiarum actio: Berichte und Arbeiten aus der Universitätsbibliothek Gießen 39* (1985); J. L. Farthing, *Thomas Aquinas and G. B.* (Durham and London, 1988).

FRANZ-JOSEF BURKARD

■ **Additional Bibliography:** U. Köpf, ed., *G. B. und die Brüder vom gemeinsamen Leben* (Stuttgart, 1998); M. Basse, "Gott— der Heilige Geist: Tröster und Bewahrer," in *Relationen. Studien zum Übergang vom Spätmittelalter zur Reformation.* Festschrift K.-H. zur Mühlen (Münster, 2000) 217–32; Ch. Morerod, "La manque de clarté de G. B. et son impact sur la Réforme," *Nova et vetera* 75 (2000) 15–32; D. Metz, *G. B. und die Mystik* (Stuttgart, 2001); P. J. van Geest, "The Interiorisation of the Spirituality of the Modern Devotion by G. B. (d. 1495)," *Augustiniana* 51 (2001) 243–83.

Billicanus (Gerlacher), *Theobald* (Diepold). Theologian, born 1490 (1495/1496?) in Billigheim (Palatinate), died August 8, 1554 in Marburg. He began his studies at Heidelberg in 1510, where he met Philipp Melanchthon and studied Greek under Johannes → Oecolampadius. He took the degree of master of arts in 1513, and then studied medicine; prompted by Martin Luther, he began theological studies in 1518. He was appointed preacher in Weil der Stadt in 1522, and subsequently in Nördlingen, where his *Renovatio Ecclesiae Nordlingiacensis* (1525) created a church order which followed Luther's thinking on many points. He was involved in the controversy about the Lord's → Supper from 1525 onwards; initially, he sought an intermediate position, but his study of the church fathers and of → Erasmus of Rotterdam led him to accept the faith of the Catholic Church, and he made the Catholic profession of faith in Augsburg in 1530. He continued to work as a married preacher until 1535 in Nördlingen, where he did not reverse all the changes which had been introduced by the Reformers. He returned to Heidelberg for studies in 1534, and took the licentiate in civil and canon law in 1542. In 1544, he moved to the university of Marburg, where he took his doctorate in civil and canon law in 1546. He lectured in jurisprudence and in rhetoric from 1548, and was rector of the university in 1548/1549. In addition to theological writings (which reflect the fluid situation in the first years of the Reformation), he was interested in teaching, and wrote a number of school textbooks.

■ **Works and Sources:** Klaiber nos. 280–95; *VD 16* 7:583ff.; Köhler *BF* 122–25.—*Andreas Osiander. Gesamtausgabe*, vol. 2, ed. G. Müller (Gütersloh, 1977); E. Sehling, ed., *Die evangelischen Kirchenordnungen des 16.Jh.*, vol. 12/2 (Tübingen, 1963) 289–306.
■ **Literature:** G. A. Benrath, "Th. B.," *Pfälzer Lebensbilder* 3 (1977) 31–63; G. Simon, *Humanismus und Konfession. Th. B.—Leben und Werk* (Berlin and New York, 1980); idem, "Die Nördlinger Reformation unter Th. B.," *Luther* 52 (1981) 131–37; H.-Ch. Rublack, *Eine bürgerliche Reformation: Nördlingen.* (Gütersloh, 1982); M. Brecht and H. Ehmer, *Südwestdeutsche Reformationsgeschichte* (Stuttgart, 1984).

HERIBERT SMOLINSKY

Billick (Steinberger, Lapicida), *Eberhard.* Carmelite (1513), theologian in favor of church reform, born 1499/1500 in Cologne, where he died on January 12, 1557. He became lector in his Order in 1528, and began his studies at the university of Cologne, where he took the doctorate in theology in 1540. He was appointed prior in Cologne in 1536, and became provincial of the Lower German province in 1542; he was vicar general of the Upper German province for a short

period in 1546/1547. He represented the archbishop of Cologne at the religious dialogue in → Worms (1540) and the emperor at the dialogue in → Regensburg (1541, 1546); in the controversy about the "Reformation of Cologne" introduced by Archbishop Hermann von → Wied in 1543, Billick and Johann → Gropper were the principal opponents of Martin → Bucer, Philipp Melanchthon and Johannes → Oldendorp. Billick and Gropper attended the Council of Trent in 1551/1552. Billick took part in the negotiations about the → Augsburg Interim at the Augsburg parliament in 1548, and it was he who oversaw the formulation of the imperial *Formula Reformationis.* He criticized the Religious Peace of → Augsburg (1555). He was appointed auxiliary bishop of Cologne on December 22, 1556, but died before he could take up this office.

■ **Works:** Klaiber nos. 296–302; *VD 16* 2:765.
■ **Sources:** *ARCEG* 1 and 4–6; Johann Gropper, *Briefwechsel*, ed. R. Braunisch, vol. 1 (Münster, 1977); Julius Pflug, *Correspondance*, ed. J.V. Pollet, vol. 2–3 (Leiden, 1973–77).
■ **Literature:** *KThR* 5:97–116.—A. Postina, *Der Karmelit E. B.* (Freiburg, 1901); J. Meier: *Der priesterliche Dienst nach Johannes Gropper* (Münster, 1976); E. Meuthen, *Kölner Universitätsgeschichte*, vol. 1: *Die alte Universität* (Cologne and Vienna, 1977); F.-B. Lickteig, *The German Carmelites at the Medieval Universities* (Rome, 1981) 266–76; J. V. Pollet, *Martin Bucer*, 2 vols. (Leiden, 1985).

HERIBERT SMOLINSKY

Bilney, *Thomas.* Theologian and reformer, born 1495 in East Bilney or Norfolk, died August 19, 1531 in Norwich. He studied law in Cambridge and was ordained priest in 1519. He was won over to Martin Luther's reforming ideas at an early date, and he supported these publicly. He was imprisoned in the Tower of London for heresy in 1528/1529, and distanced himself from Luther. After his release, he defied the prohibition which had been imposed on him, supporting the Reformation in his sermons to the people. He was once again imprisoned for spreading heresy, and was burnt at the stake in 1531. It was thanks to Bilney that Robert → Barnes, Hugh → Latimer, and Matthew → Parker were won over to the Reformation cause.

■ **Literature:** *DNB* 2:502–5; *DHGE* 8:1491; *The Oxford Dictionary of the Christian Church* (London ²1974)

174f.—K. Carey, ed., *The Historic Episcopate in the Fullness of the Church* (London, 1954).

HEINZ SCHÜTTE

■ **Additional Bibliography:** *RGG*⁴ 1:1598f.—G. Walker, "Saint or Schemer? The 1527 Heresy Trial of T. B. Reconsidered," *JEH* 40 (1989) 219–38.

Blankenfeld, *Johannes.* An important figure in the history of the Reformation in Livonia, born c. 1471 as the son of the mayor of Berlin, died September 9, 1527 in Torquemada (Spain). He worked as a lawyer in Leipzig and Frankfurt on the Oder; he was procurator of the Teutonic Order in Rome, and became bishop of Reval in 1514, and additionally of Dorpat in 1518. He became coadjutor to the archbishop of Riga in 1523, and succeeded him in the following year. He fought vigorously against the Reformation. When he formed an alliance with the Grand Prince of Moscow, the Master of the Teutonic Order in Livonia, Wolter von → Plettenburg, had him imprisoned. On his release in 1526, he went to → Charles V to ask him to intervene.
■ **Literature:** *LMA* 2:262f.—W. Schnöring, *J. B.* (Halle, 1905); L. Arbusow, *Die Einführung der Reformation in Liv-, Est- und Kurland* (Leipzig, 1921); O. Pohrt, *Reformationsgeschichte Livlands* (Halle, 1928); H. Quednau, *Livland im politischen Wollen Herzog Albrechts von Preußen* (Leipzig, 1939).

MARTIN HELLMANN

Blarer, (1) *Ambrosius.* Reformer, born probably April 4, 1492 in Constance, died December 6, 1564 in Winterthur. He was the son of a patrician family in Constance, and studied in Tübingen, where he became master of arts in 1512. He was a Benedictine in Alpersbach (profession 1510, prior· 1521). He accepted the Reformation in 1522 and became a protagonist of southern German Protestantism. He was active as preacher in Constance, and organized the development of Reformed Church structures in other imperial cities and in the duchy of Württemberg from 1534 to 1538. He worked in Switzerland after 1548, and was pastor in Biel from 1551 to 1559. He was also a prominent author of hymns, some of which are still in use today.

(2) *Thomas,* brother of (1). Reformer, born c. 1501 in Constance, died March 19, 1567 in Gyrsberg (Thurgau). He studied arts, law, and theology in Freiburg and Wittenberg. After 1524, he was a leading politician in the Reformed city of Constance, serving as mayor and delegate of the emperor from 1537 to 1548; he moved to Switzerland in 1548.
■ **Literature:** *TRE* 6:711–15.—T. Schiess, *Briefwechsel der Brüder A. und Thomas B.,* 3 vols. (Freiburg, 1908–12); B. Moeller, *Der Konstanzer Reformator A. B.* (Constance, 1964).
■ **Literature:** J. Vögeli, *Schriften zur Reformation in Constance 1519–38,* ed. A. Vögeli (Tübingen et al., 1972–73), vol. 2/2, 1065–71; W. Dobras, *Ratsregiment, Sittenpolizei und Kirchenzucht in . . . Konstanz 1531–1548* (Gütersloh, 1993).

BERND MOELLER

Blomevenna, *Peter.* Carthusian (1489), born March 29, 1466 in Leiden, died September 30, 1536 in Cologne. After his studies in Cologne, he entered the charterhouse in that city and was prior from 1507 to 1536. He led his monastery in the attempt to resist the Reformation in its early days, through his own works (*Candela evangelica, Assertatio purgatorii*) and through his support of the printing of the writings of Denys the Carthusian. The first of Blomevenna's mystical-contemplative writings was the Latin translation of Heinrich Herp's *Spieghel der volcomenheit* in 1509; the last was *De bonitate divina* (1538), which is considered a "summa" of his thinking.
■ **Literature:** M. Bernards, "Zur Kartäusertheologie des 16.Jh.," in *Von Konstanz nach Trient. Festschrift A. Franzen* (Paderborn, 1972) 447–79; J. Hogg, *Die Kartause, Köln und Europa: Die Kölner Kartause um 1500* (Cologne, 1991) 169–91.

HEINRICH RÜTHING

Bohemian Brethren (Unitas Fratrum)
1. History
About 1458, a Reform-minded group left Prague and founded a "community of brethren" (the *fratres legis Christi*) in Kunvald in eastern Bohemia, under the leadership of an utraquist priest. A conflict arose in the first decades between the "little ones" (or "Amosites") and the "great party" about the appropriate relationship to the world (including the question whether one might hold public office), and especially to the civil authorities; this led to the separation of the Amosite party in 1494. In 1480, the German

Waldensians from the county of Brandenburg under Michael Weisse joined the Bohemian Brethren, who had c. 100,000 members at the beginning of the 16th century. Bishop → Luke of Prague laid the theological and liturgical foundations of the community. He warded off the threat of isolation from the world and emphasized a structure of states of life "in keeping with the grace each one has received," and a life which imitated Christ. He retained seven sacraments, and his thinking gave indirect encouragement to the introduction of Protestant confirmation. Under his successor, Jan Roh/Horn (c. 1490-1547), the Bohemian Brethren began to accept Martin Luther's Reformation; Jan Augusta (1500-1572) aimed at union with the → Utraquists, and found inspiration in Calvin's Reformation. In 1535, the Brethren published their own confession of faith (Latin text, 1538). In 1538, they rejected rebaptism. They suffered harsh persecution after the war of → Schmalkald (1547), and this led to the foundation of communities in Poland, Prussia, and Hungary; Augusta himself was imprisoned for sixteen years in the fortress of Pürglitz. The Utraquists and the Brethren united in 1575, on the basis of the *Confessio Bohemica* (a text drawn up on the model of the Confessio Augustana), which the Brethren adopted in the same year; it rejects the position of the Spiritualizers and professes the true (*vere*) presence of Christ in the Lord's Supper. This period was the golden age of literary production among the Brethren. Their theologians translated the Bible into Czech (the so-called Bible of Kralitz) between 1578 and 1593; they retained Jerome's canon.

2. Church Order

The Bohemian Brethren made a distinction between things essential (the Trinity, faith, hope, and love), things which were useful (Word and sacrament), and "arbitrary" things (church constitution); nevertheless, they esteemed their church order highly. They retained a vivid idea of the unity of the church, as is seen in their later endeavors to ensure that their office bearers were in the apostolic succession. The Brethren as a whole were led by the "Close Council," consisting of four bishops, and by synods; a differentiated structure of ministries distributed responsibility among many persons. Four grades of the ecclesiastical ministry existed: *senior, minister, diaconus,*

acoluthus. The priests lived in the house of the Brethren, and celibacy was recommended (especially in the early years of the movement). The laity in the community formed a council for pastoral questions, which had judicial functions. They rejected the position of Martin → Bucer, and sought to enforce church discipline without the intervention of the civil authorities; they replaced the principle of → *cuius regio, eius religio* by the principle of tolerance. The spiritual life of the communities is reflected in the hymns of the Bohemian Brethren (first printed hymnal, 1501; luxury edition, 1576).

■ *LThK*[3] 2:553ff. (unabridged version).

■ **Literature:** *On 1:* J.Ch. Köchler, ed., *Die drey Glaubensbekenntnisse* (Frankfurt/Main, 1741); J. Müller, *Geschichte der BB,* 3 vols. (Herrnhut, 1922–31); R. Říčan, *Die BB* (Berlin, 1958); Lukas von Prag, "Abendmahlsformular," in I. Pahl, ed., *Coena Domini* (Freiburg, 1983) 543–61.—*On 2:* J. A. Comenius, *Ratio disciplinae: Veškeré spisy J. A. Komenského,* vol. 17 (Brünn, 1912) 15–137.

JOSEF SMOLÍK

■ **Additional Bibliography:** *RGG*[4] 2:1789ff.—R. Říčan, *The History of the Unity of Brethren* (Bethlehem, Pa., 1992); D. R. Holeton, "Church or Sect? The Jednota Bratrská and the Growth of Dissent from Mainline Utraquism," *Communio viatorum* 38 (1996) 5–35; Z. V. David, "Pavel Bydzovsky and Czech Utraquism's Encounter with Luther," *Communio viatorum* 38 (1996) 36–63; Z. V. David, "Utraquists, Lutherans, and the Bohemian Confession of 1575," *ChH* 68 (1999) 294–336; L. Broz, *Justification and Sanctification in the Czech Reformation: Justification and sanctification in the traditions of the Reformation,* ed. WARC (Geneva, 1999) 38–43; P. Filipi, "Der singende Gefangene auf Pürglitz. Zum pastoraltheologischen Werk Jan Augustas," in *Vertraut den neuen Wegen.* Festschrift K.-P. Hertzsch (Leipzig, 2000) 23–31; J. Halama, "The Crisis of the Union of Czech Brethren in the Years Prior to the Thirty Years War," *Communio viatorum* 44 (2002) 51–68.

Bolsec, *Jérôme.* Theologian and doctor, born in Paris, died c. 1584 in Annecy. He was a Carmelite in Paris, but accepted the Reformation and moved to Ferrara. In 1551, he moved with his wife to Chablais near Geneva, where he worked as a doctor. His disagreements with Jean Calvin about the doctrine of predestination led to his arrest and exile from Geneva in 1551; subsequently, he was also exiled from Berne. Bolsec returned to the Catholic faith and worked as a doctor in Autun and Lyons. His biographies of Calvin (Lyons,

1577; German, Cologne, 1581) and Theodor → Beza (Paris, 1582) played a role in polemics against Calvinism until the 19th century. Bolsec dedicated to → Charles IX his *Le miroir envoyé de vérité,* a book about the religious war (published without indication of place, 1562).

■ **Literature:** *Bibliotheca Carmelitana,* ed. C. de Villiers a S. Stephano, vol. 1 (Orléans, 1752) 637ff.; *DHGE* 9:676–79.—F. Pfeilschifter, *Das Calvinbild bei B.* (Augsburg, 1983); P. C. Holtrop, *The B. Controversy on Predestination, from 1551 to 1555,* 2 vols. (Lewiston, N.Y., 1993).

ROBERT ROTH

■ **Additional Bibliography:** G. M. Thomas, "Constructing and Clarifying the Doctrine of Predestination," *Reformation and Renaissance Review* 2 (2000) 7–28.

Bonner, *Edmund.* Last Catholic bishop of London, born c. 1500 in Davenham (Cheshire), died September 5, 1569 in London. He was a supporter of King → Henry VIII, who nominated him bishop in 1540. Later, he opposed the governmental policies of → Edward VI, and was dismissed from office in 1549; → Mary I restored him to his diocese in 1553, and he played a central role in the Catholic restoration, which the queen vigorously propagated. Under Queen → Elizabeth I, he was once again deposed, and died in prison. Most modern historians agree that his reputation as a persecutor of Protestants has been exaggerated.
■ **Literature:** *DNB* 5:356–60.—G. Alexander, "B. and the Marian Persecutions," *History* 60 (1975) 374–91; idem, "Bishop B. and the Parliament of 1559," *Bulletin of the Institute of Historical Research* 56 (1983) 164–79; A. M. Jagger, "B.'s Episcopal Visitation of London 1554," *Bulletin of the Institute of Historical Research* 45 (1972) 306–11.

SUSAN HARDMAN MOORE

Bonnus, *Hermann.* Reformer, born 1504 in Quakenbrück, died February 2, 1548 in Lübeck. He studied in Wittenberg from 1523 to 1525, and was influenced by Martin Luther, Philipp Melanchthon and Johannes → Bugenhagen. Thanks to Greifswald and Gottorf (responsible for the education of the princes at the Danish court), Bonnus became rector of the newly founded St. Catharine's school in Lübeck in 1531; shortly afterwards, on Bugenhagen's proposal, he became Superintendent of the Lübeck church, a position he held until his death. At the invitation of Prince

Bishop Franz von → Waldeck, he drew up a church order for the city and the region that introduced the Reformation into Osnabrück. Bonnus was prominent as a writer of practical-theological texts (lectures, books of sermons to be read at domestic worship, catechism prayer book, etc.), hymns, and church orders.
■ **Literature:** B. Spiegel, *H. B.* (Göttingen, ²1892); W. D. Hauschild, *Leben und Werk des Reformators H. B.,* ed. H.-R. Jarck (Quakenbrück, 1985) 298–318; P. Savvidis, *H. B.* (Lübeck, 1992); K. G. Kaster and G. Steinwascher, *450 Jahre Reformation in Osnabrück* (Bramsche, 1993).

FRIEDHELM KRÜGER

Bora, *Katharina von.* Wife of Martin Luther, born January 29, 1499 in Lippendorf, died December 20, 1552 in Torgau. She was born in an impoverished noble Saxon family and lived in the Cistercian convent of Nimbschen near Grimma, where she made her religious profession in 1515; in 1522, she was one of the twelve nuns whom Luther helped escape from the convent. He married the former nun on June 13, 1525. This marriage provoked sharp criticism from the Catholic party (in particular, the negative portrait by Johann → Cochlaeus was to color the Catholic image of Luther for a long time to come); but among Protestants, it became the paradigm for pastors' marriages. Despite all the hostilities from without, the marriage was harmonious, and the couple had six children. Katharina Luther governed her growing household in the former Augustinian monastery in Wittenberg with prudence and great skill, and her organizational capacity and her energetic character sometimes led Luther to call her "Mr. Käthe" in his letters. At the same time, he clearly expressed his love for his "morning star from Wittenberg."
■ **Literature:** C. L. Deutler, *Katherine Luther of the Wittenberg Parsonage* (Philadelphia, 1924); H. Boehmer, "Luthers Ehe," *Luther-Jahrbuch* 7 (1925) 40–76; G. Müller, "Käthe und Martin Luther," *Zeitwende* 47 (1976) 150–64; E. Kroker, *K. von B.* (Berlin, ¹⁵1980); H. Junghans, *Luther in Wittenberg. Leben und Werk Martin Luthers von 1526 bis 1546,* ed. H. Junghans, 2 vols. (Wittenberg, 1983) 11–37, 723–32; M. Brecht, *Martin Luther* (Stuttgart, vol. 2, 1986, 194–203; vol. 3, 1987, 234–39); I. M. Winter, *K. von B.* (Düsseldorf, 1990).

UTE GAUSE

■ **Additional Bibliography:** J. C. Smith, "K. von B. through Five Centuries," *SCJ* 30 (1999) 745–74; M. Treu, "Die Frau an Luthers Seite: K. von B. Leben und

Werk," *Luther* 70 (1999) 10–29; U. Hahn, ed., *K. von B.* (Stuttgart, 1999); M. Treu, "K. von B., the Woman at Luther's Side," *Lutheran Quarterly* 13 (1999) 157–78 (this quotation replaces the German version of the same article!); K. Stjerna, "Katie Luther: A Mirror to the Promises and Failures of the Reformation," in *Caritas et Reformatio. Festschrift* C. Lindberg (Saint Louis, 2002) 27–39; R. K. Markwald, *K. von B.: A Reformation Life* (Saint Louis, 2002).

Borrhaus (Bur[r]ess, Cellarius), *Martin.* Radical Reformer, born 1499 in Stuttgart, died October 11, 1564 in Basle. He studied in Tübingen, Ingolstadt and Wittenberg; he was forced to leave Wittenberg in 1522 because of his Baptist views. After spending time in Austria, Poland, Switzerland, and Prussia, he returned to Wittenberg in 1526, but he could not come to any accord with Martin Luther, and left for Strasbourg. From 1536, he lived in Basle, becoming professor of rhetoric in 1541 and of Old Testament in 1544; he was rector of the university in 1546/1547 and 1553/1554. Borrhaus denied the eternal divine sonship of Christ and maintained a symbolic sacramental theology. His chef d'oeuvre, *De operibus Dei* (Strasbourg, 1527), has a chiliastic character.

■ **Literature:** I. Backus, *M. B. (Cellarius)* (Baden-Baden, 1981); R. L. Williams, "M. Cellarius and the Reformation in Strasbourg," *JEH* 32 (1981) 477–97; A. Seifert, "Reformation und Chiliasmus," *ARG* 77 (1986) 226–64.

PETER WALTER

■ **Additional Bibliography:** L. Felici, *Tra riforma ed eresia. La giovinezza di M. B.* (Florence, 1995).

Borromeo, *Charles.* Saint (canonized 1610; feast November 4), born October 2, 1538 in Arona, died November 3, 1584 in Milan. He was destined for a church career at an early age, and finished his studies at the university of Pavia in 1559 with the doctorate in civil and canon law. Cardinal Gian Angelo Medici, his maternal uncle, was elected pope on December 25, 1559, taking the name of → Pius IV. He created Borromeo cardinal on January 21, 1560, appointed him administrator of the diocese of Milan on February 2 of the same year, and made him his closest collaborator. As "cardinal nephew," Borromeo had the oversight of correspondence with the papal emissaries to foreign courts, with the external organs of the papal administration, and with the cardinal legates to

the Council of Trent from 1561 to 1563. This made him familiar with the political and religious problems of his age. There is, however, reason to doubt whether he did in fact influence the papal decisions which he was charged to communicate to his correspondents.

The spiritual crisis provoked by the early death of his brother Federico in 1562 was the turning point in Borromeo's life. Hitherto, he had only been a deacon; he was ordained priest on June 17, 1563 and sought to lead an ascetic life, improving his theological knowledge, holding his first sermons, and spending more time in prayer and meditation. Borromeo had conversations in autumn 1563 in Rome with Bartolomeu dos Mártires, archbishop of Braga, who gave him the unpublished manuscript of his *Stimulus pastorum.* This was of decisive importance for Borromeo, who now resolved to dedicate himself to pastoral work; this encounter probably prompted his decision to accept episcopal ordination on December 7, 1563.

After his uncle's death, he was a prominent supporter of the candidature of Pius V in the ensuing conclave. He moved to Milan in April, 1566, and began an intensive pastoral activity which concentrated on the systematic implementation of the Tridentine decrees. During his episcopate, which lasted for almost twenty years, he visited all the c. 800 parishes of his huge diocese; indeed, he visited some parishes more than once. He made provisions for the education of the clergy, founded the Collegio Borromeo in Pavia, the seminary, and the Swiss College (for seminarians from Switzerland); he was also involved in the foundation of the Jesuit college of Brera. He held six provincial synods and eleven diocesan synods, and endeavored to improve the religious instruction of the people by means of sermons and teaching the Christian faith. While this reform work made good progress, his growing prestige led to tensions with the Spanish governors, and Borromeo excommunicated one of them, Luis de Requeséns, in 1573. The tensions were resolved when Borromeo sent an emissary to Spain who succeeded in convincing → Philip II of the archbishop's honest intentions.

Borromeo died in 1584 with a reputation for holiness, which had spread with particular strength after some rebellious members of the dissolved Order of Humiliati attacked him in 1569, and had become even stronger thanks to the material and spiritual help which he organized for the victims of the plague epidemic of 1576/1577.

His contemporaries regarded him as the model Tridentine bishop; evidence of their esteem is the wide diffusion of all the documents from his period in office, which were collected and published in 1582 under the title *Acta Ecclesiae Mediolanensis.*

■ **Literature:** *Bibliographies:* C. Bascapè, *De vita et rebus gestis Caroli S.R.E. Cardinalis tituli S. Praxedis, archiepiscopi Mediolani libri septem* (Milan, 1983) 971–1009; A. Rimoldi, "Bibliografia de San Carlo Borromeo (1984–89)," *Studia Borromaica* 3 (1989) 259–84.—*San Carlo e il suo tempo. Atti del convegno internazionale del IV centenario della morte (Milano, 21–26 maggio 1984),* 2 vols. (Rome, 1986); *San Carlo Borromeo. Catholic Reform and Ecclesiastical Politics in the Second Half of the Sixteenth Century,* ed. J. M. Headley and J. B. Tomaro (Washington et al., 1988).

AGOSTINO BORROMEO

■ **Additional Bibliography:** *KLK* 55; F. Buzzi, ed., *Carlo Borromeo e l'opera della "Grande Riforma"* (Milan, 1997); F. A. Rossi, *Carlo Borromeo* (Milan, 1999); J. I. Tellechea Idigoras, "Los conflictis de Milan (1567–70)," *Scriptorium Victoriense* 47 (2000) 47–127; W. T. de Boer, "Calvin and B.," in *Early Modern Catholicism.* Festschrift J. W. O'Malley (Toronto, 2001) 84–96; B. W. Westervelt, "The Prodigal Son at Santa Justina: The Homily in the Borromean Reform of Pastoral Preaching," *SCJ* 32 (2001) 109–26.

Botzhelm (Botzemus, Abstemius), *Johann von.* Humanist, born c. 1480 in Sasbach near Achern, died March 24 or 29, 1535 in Überlingen. He studied in Heidelberg from 1496 to 1500, and in Bonn from 1500 to 1504, taking the doctorate in civil and canon law. He became cathedral canon in Strasbourg in 1510, and in Constance in 1510. He headed the humanist circle in Constance. His support for Martin Luther led to a summons to Rome in 1524. After the Reformation was consolidated in Constance, he joined the cathedral chapter in their move to Überlingen in 1527.

■ **Literature:** *NDB* 2:490f.; *CEras* 1:177f.—*Schriften zur Reformation in Konstanz 1519–1538,* ed. A. Vögeli, vol. 2/2 (Tübingen and Basle, 1973) 873–81.

PETER WALTER

Brant, *Sebastian.* Lawyer and writer; born 1457 in Strasbourg, where he died May 10, 1521. He began his legal studies in Basle in 1475, taking his doc-

torate in 1489 and becoming professor in 1496. He returned to Strasbourg in 1500 and was appointed town lawyer in 1501 and town clerk in 1503. His many writings include legal, historical-geographical, and poetical works in Latin and German, pamphlets, and editions and translations of classical and medieval authors; these reveal his close contacts with the humanistic circles in the Upper Rhine area, men who were skeptical about the aims promoted by the Reformation. Brant's literary activity bears witness to his good knowledge of the tradition of classical antiquity, patristic literature, and Renaissance poetry. This is particularly true of his poems, which are modeled on classical meter and rhetoric (*In laudem gloriose virginis Mariae multorumque sanctorum varii generis carmina,* 1494; *Varia carmina,* 1498), and of his most celebrated work, the moral satire *Das Narrenschiff* (1494), which attacks the vices of his times and calls to repentance. Each of the 112 chapters of this work is illustrated by a woodcut.

■ **Editions:** *Flugblätter,* ed. P. Heitz (Strasbourg, 1915); *Das Narrenschiff,* ed. M. Lemmer (Tübingen, ²1968); *Tugent Spyl,* ed. H.-G. Roloff (Berlin, 1968); *Fabeln,* ed. B. Schneider (Stuttgart-Bad Cannstatt, 1999).

■ **Literature:** *Die deutsche Literatur des Mittelalters. Verfasserlexikon,* ed. K. Ruh et al., vol. 1 (Berlin, ²1978) 992–1005; *Literaturlexikon. Autoren und Werke deutscher Sprache,* ed. W. Killy, vol. 2. (Gütersloh and Munich) 162–65.—J. Knape and D. Wuttke, *S.-B.-Bibliographie* (Tübingen, 1990); T. Wilhelmi, *S.-B.-Bibliographie* (Berne), 1990.

SILVIA SERENA TSCHOPP

■ **Additional Bibliography:** J. Knape, *Dichtung, Recht und Freiheit. Studien zu Leben und Werk S. B.s.* (Baden-Baden, 1992); G. L. Fink, ed., "S. B., seine Zeit und das 'Narrenschiff.'" in *Actes du colloque international, Strasbourg 10–11 mars, 1994* (Strasbourg, 1995); T. Wilhelmi, ed., *S. B.* (Basel, 2002).

Braun, *Konrad.* Lawyer and theological disputant; born 1491/1495 in Kirchheim (Neckar), died June 20, 1563 in Munich. He studied at the university of Tübingen, taking his doctorate in civil and canon law, and taught there. He was counselor and chancellor of the bishop of Würzburg from 1526 to 1536. He was appointed assessor of the chancellery in the imperial supreme court in 1533, and head of this office in 1540. He was chancellor in Bavaria and chancellor to the bishop of Augsburg, Cardinal Otto Truschsess von → Waldburg, whose protest against the Religious Peace of → Augsburg (1555) Braun composed. He was an early supporter of confessional politics, and cooperated with the endeavors of the local civil rulers to reform the church. He wrote pamphlets against the Truce of → Frankfurt and the Centuriators of → Magdeburg, as well as legal treatises and a catechism. His private library survives intact.

■ **Literature:** *NDB* 2:556.—M. B. Rössner, *K. B.* (Salzburg, 1991); R. Bäumer, "K. B. und der Augsburger Religionsfriede," in *Fides et ius.* Festschrift G. May (Regensburg, 1991) 283–301.

MARIA BARBARA RÖSSNER-RICHARZ

■ **Additional Bibliography:** M. B. Rössner-Richarz, "K. B. und seine Bibliothek," *Bibliotheksforum Bayern* 21 (1993) 44–61; M. de Kroon, "Bucers conflict met K. B.," in *Om de Kerk.* Festschrift W. van't Spijker (Leiden, 1997) 158–75.

Bredenbach (Brempke, Breidbach), *Matthias.* Catholic theological disputant, teacher, and humanist, born 1499 in Kierspe near Altena, died June 5, 1569 in Emmerich. He began his studies at the university of Cologne in 1521, and took the degree of master of arts in 1524. He became a teacher, and was rector of the grammar school in Emmerich from 1533/1534. He had contacts with the Jesuits in Cologne, and wrote numerous works against the Reformation, as well as the *Introductiuncula in Graecas litteras iuxta Erasmi Roterdami sententiam,* and commentaries on the Psalms and Matthew's Gospel (published by his sons Tilmann and Dietrich).

■ **Works:** Klaiber nos. 378–85; *VD 16* 3:244f.
■ **Literature:** *LThK*² 2:664.—H. Ulrich, *M. B.* (Emmerich, 1984).

HERIBERT SMOLINSKY

Brendel von Homburg, *Daniel.* Electoral prince and arch-chancellor of Mainz, born March 22, 1522 in Aschaffenburg, where he died March 22, 1582. He was cathedral schoolmaster in Speyer from 1545 to 1555, and became canon of the cathedral of Mainz in 1548. He was civil governor of the territory of the Speyer diocese in 1552/1553. He became archbishop of Mainz in 1555 and received episcopal ordination in 1557; the election of Brendel (instead of Palatine Count Richard von Simmern) as archbishop determined the confessional orientation of the archbishopric and of the

electoral state of Mainz for a long time to come. Brendel consistently promoted Catholic reform: the Jesuit grammar school in Mainz was opened in 1561, and he published a new breviary in 1570, made the Tridentine confession of faith obligatory in the cathedral chapter, and recatholicized the Eichsfeld region. He acquired possession of the county of Rieneck in 1559, and the county of Königstein in 1581.

■ **Literature:** A. Dölle, "Erzbischof Daniel und die Gegenreformation auf dem Eichsfeld," *Universitas.* Festschrift Bischof A. Stohr, vol. 2 (Munich, 1958) 110–25; F. Jürgensmeier, *Das Bistum Mainz. Von der Römerzeit bis zum II. Vatikanischen Konzil* (Frankfurt/ Main, ²1989) 198–205.

FRIEDHELM JÜRGENSMEIER

Brenz, *Johannes.* Reformer, born June 24, 1499 in Weil der Stadt, died September 11, 1570 in Stuttgart. He began his studies at Heidelberg in 1514, and was profoundly influenced by Martin Luther at the Heidelberg Disputation of 1518. He was appointed preacher in Schwäbisch Hall in 1522, and introduced the Reformation there (church orders of 1527 and 1543; catechisms, 1527 and 1535; school reform). He was involved in the controversy about the Lord's → Supper, and was theological and judicial counselor in several territories where the Reformation was introduced. He was expelled from Hall in 1548 because of his opposition to the → Augsburg Interim. From 1553 onwards, he consolidated an exemplary Reformation structure in Württemberg, working with Duke Christopher. In 1551, he composed the → *Confessio Virtembergica* for the Council of Trent (including an *apologia* for this text, directed against Pedro de → Soto), and played a major role in drawing up the *Great Church Order* of 1559, which set the standard in many territories. Beginning with the religious debates of Marburg (1529) and Augsburg (1530), Brenz took part in almost all the important debates and decisions of the Lutheran Church in his age, and he has continued to exercise influence down to the present day, thanks to his catechism of 1535 (with more than 500 editions in several languages), his exegetical writings on almost all the books of the Bible, and his sermons (*Postillen,* 1550 and 1556).

■ **Works:** *Opera,* 8 vols. (Tübingen, 1576–90); *Werke (Studienausgabe),* ed. M. Brecht and G. Schäfer

(Tübingen, 1970ff.); *Anecdota Brentiana,* ed. Th. Pressel (Tübingen, 1868).

■ **Literature:** *TRE* 7:170–81.—I. Hartmann and K. Jäger, *Johann B.,* 2 vols. (Hamburg, 1840–42); W. Köhler, *Bibliographia Brentiana* (Berlin, 1904); M. Brecht, *Die frühe Theologie des J. B.* (Tübingen, 1966); H.-M. Maurer and K. Ulshöfer, *J. B. und die Reformation in Württemberg* (Stuttgart and Aalen, 1974); J. M. Estes, *Christian Magistrate and State Church: The Reforming Career of J. B.* (Toronto, 1982); H. C. Brandy, *Die späte Christologie des J. B.* (Tübingen, 1991); Ch. Weismann, *Die Katechismen des J. B.,* 3 vols. (Berlin, 1990–92).

CHRISTOPH WEISMANN

■ **Additional Bibliography:** I. Fehle, ed., *J. B. Ausstellungskatalog* (Schwäbisch Hall, 1999); G. Kraft, *J. B. und seine Zeit* (Stuttgart, 1999); H. C. Brandy, "Zwischen Festigkeit und Verständigung. J. B. als Bekenner und Ökumeniker," *Luther* 70 (1999) 127–45; J. M. Estes, "B. and the Office of Christian Magistrate," *Blätter für württembergische Kirchengeschichte* 100 (2000) 186–214; J. M. Estes, "J. B. and the German Reformation," *Lutheran Quarterly* 16 (2002) 373–414.

Brès, *Guy de* (Guido de Bray). Reformer in the southern Netherlands, born c. 1522 in Mons, died May 31, 1567 in Valenciennes. He was educated as a Catholic and became a painter of images on glass; he accepted the Reformation at an early age, and fled to England in 1548. On his return in 1552, he worked in Rijsel (Lille) as a lay preacher. He fled in 1556 via Frankfurt am Main (where he took part in a public disputation with the → Baptists) to Geneva and Lausanne, where he studied theology. From 1557 onwards, he was a preacher in Doornik (Tournai), Amiens, Sedan, Antwerp, and Valenciennes; after the siege of the last city, he was captured and hanged. His *Confession de foy* (Rouen, 1561; often reprinted) was an *apologia* addressed to → Philip II of Spain; this work, influenced by Calvinism, was soon adopted by the Reformed churches in the Netherlands as the so-called *Confessio Belgica.*

■ **Works:** E. Braekman and J. F. Gilmont, "Les écrits de G. de B.," *Annales Société d'histoire du protestantisme belge* 5/8 (1971) 265–76; *A Collection of Writings on the Reformation,* ed. E. Braekman (Leiden, 1995).

■ **Literature:** *TRE* 7:181ff.; *Biografisch Lexicon voor de Geschiedenis van het Nederlandse Protestantisme,* vol. 2 (Kampen, 1983) 97–100.—E. Braekman, *G. de B.* (Brussels, 1960); J. N. Bakhuizen van den Brink, *De Nederlandse Belijdenisgeschriften* (Amsterdam, ²1976) 1–27, 59–146.

PETER J. A. NISSEN

■ **Additional Bibliography:** E. Braekman, *Le protestantisme belge au 16ᵉ siécle* (Carrières, 1999); N. H. Gootjes, "The Earliest Report on the Author of the Belgic Confession (1561)," *Nederlands Archief voor Kerkgeschiedenis* 82 (2002) 86–94.

Briçonnet, *Guillaume.* Bishop and church reformer, son of Cardinal Guillaume Briçonnet, born c. 1470, died January 24, 1534 in Esmans (Seine-et-Marne). While still a student, he was appointed bishop of Lodève in 1489; additionally, he succeeded his father as commendatory abbot of St-Germain-des-Prés in 1507, and became bishop of Meaux in 1515. His diplomatic services for Louis XII included an embassy to Julius II in 1507 and participation in the Council of Pisa in 1511; he also negotiated the concordat of Bologna (1516) on behalf of → Francis I. He gathered humanistic reformers such as Jakobus → Faber Stapulensis around himself, and endeavored to reform the diocese of Meaux by means of visitations and diocesan synods, laying particular emphasis on the duty of priests to reside and preach in their parishes. From 1521 onwards, he was spiritual counselor of the sister of Francis I, Margaret of Angoulême (later queen of Navarre). The "Meaux group," which included Guillaume → Farel and Franciscus → Vatablus, was accused of agitating in favor of the Reformation, and broke up after 1525.

■ **Sources:** *G. B./Marguerite d'Angoulême: Correspondance (1521–24),* ed. C. Martineau and M. Veissière, 2 vols. (Geneva, 1975–79).

■ **Literature:** *TRE* 7:187–90; *CEras* 1:198f.—M. Veissière, *L'évêque G. B.* (Provins, 1986); J.-C. Margolin, "Érasme, G. B. et les débuts de la réforme en France," *RHEF* 77 (1991) 13–28; M. Veissière, *Autour de G. B.* (Provins, 1993); idem, "G. B. et l'évangile selon St. Jean," *Revue des sciences philosophiques et théologiques* 79 (1995) 431–37; J.-F. Pernot, ed., *Jacques Lefèvre d'Etaples* (Paris, 1995).

PETER WALTER

■ **Additional Bibliography:** H. M. Vose, "A Sixteenth-century Assessment of the French Church in the Years 1521–4 by Bishop G. B. of Meaux," *JEH* 39 (1988) 509–19.

Briesmann, *Johannes.* Reformer of Königsberg, born December 31, 1488 in Cottbus, died October

1, 1549 in Königsberg. He took his doctorate of theology at Wittenberg in 1522; on Martin Luther's recommendation, → Albrecht of Brandenburg-Ansbach invited him to Königsberg in 1523, and his position as Albrecht's counselor gave him a decisive influence on the Reformation in Prussia. He was appointed preacher of the cathedral in Riga in 1527, where he collaborated in the introduction of the Reformation in Livonia. He returned to Königsberg as cathedral preacher in 1531. Here, he wrote extensively and played a central role in the development of the university. He was president of the diocese of Samland from 1546 to 1549. In the struggle against the followers of → Schwenckfeld and against Andreas → Osiander, he attempted to preserve the unity of the church.

■ **Works:** *Kurze Ordnung des Kirchendiensts, samt einer Vorrede von Ceremonien (1530)*, ed. E. Sehling, *Die Evangelischen Kirchenordnungen des 16.Jh.*, vol. 5 (Leipzig, 1913) 11–17; *Flosculi de homine interiore et exteriore, fide et operibus (1523)*, ed. P. Tschackert (Gotha, 1887).
■ **Literature:** *NDB* 2:612f.; *RGG*[4] 1:1764.—R. Stupperich, "J. B.s reformatorische Anfänge," *Jahrbuch für brandenburgische Kirchengeschichte* 34 (1939) 3–21; idem, *Die Reformation im Ordensland Preußen 1523/24* (Ulm, 1966).

MICHAEL BECHT

Brück, *Gregor* (Gregorius Pontanus; his real name was Heintz[e]). Lawyer and politician in electoral Saxony; born 1485/1486 in Brück near Potsdam, died February 2, 1557 in Jena. → Frederick III (the "Wise") of Saxony appointed him counselor in 1519 and made him chancellor of Duke Johann the "Steadfast"; in 1529, he was appointed "counselor for life," and his influence reached its peak in the years from 1529 to 1546. He promoted the foundation of the League of → Schmalkald and left his mark on the consistorial constitution of the local church. He lived in Jena in the last ten years of his life and made an important contribution to the foundation of the university there.

■ **Literature:** E. Fabian, *Dr. G. B.* (Tübingen, 1957); idem, *Die Entstehung des Schmalkaldischen Bundes und seiner Verfassung* (Tübingen, ²1962.)

IRMGARD HÖSS

■ **Additional Bibliography:** *RGG*[4] 1:1778.—U. von Brück, *Im Dienste der Reformation. Ein Lebensbild des kursächsischen Kanzlers G. B.* (Berlin, 1985).

Brus von Müglitz, *Anton.* Archbishop of Prague (1561), born February 13, 1518 in Müglitz (Moravia), died May 27, 1580 in Prague. After his studies, he joined the Order of the Holy Cross in Prague and was ordained priest in 1540. He was military chaplain in the Turkish war, then parish priest; in 1552, he became high master of his Order. He was appointed bishop of Vienna in 1558 and formally confirmed by the pope in 1560. He was the spokesman of Emperor → Ferdinand I at the Council of Trent in 1562-1563, and was a vigorous proponent of the emperor's wishes for church reform. He collaborated in the reform of the Index. After the council, he failed to secure the permission of Maximilian II to promulgate the conciliar decrees at a provincial synod, but he endeavored to put church reform into practice in Bohemia.

■ **Literature:** Th. Sickel, *Zur Geschichte des Konzils von Trient* (Vienna, 1872) (council reports); *Briefe des Prager Erzbischofs A. B.*, ed. S. Steinherz (Prague, 1907); idem, "Eine Denkschrift des Prager Erzbischofs A. B. über die Herstellung der Glaubenseinheit in Böhmen," *Mitteilungen des Vereins für Geschichte der Deutschen in Böhmen* 45 (1906) 162–77; Jedin vol. 4/1–2.

KLAUS GANZER

Bucer (Butzer), *Martin.* Reformer, born November 11, 1491 in Schlettstadt, died February 28, 1551 in Cambridge. He joined the Dominican Order in his hometown in 1507. In the *Studium Generale* in Heidelberg, he was influenced by → Erasmus of Rotterdam, and the encounter with Martin Luther in 1518 at the Heidelberg Disputation left a deep and lasting mark on Bucer. After several years of wandering from town to town, he arrived in Strasbourg as a refugee at the beginning of May, 1523. Here he outlined his theological program in *Das ym selbs niemant, sonder anderen leben;* the main concern is the sanctification of the individual and of the community, on the basis of the principles of → *sola scriptura, solus Christus,* and → *sola fide.* In his endeavor to overcome the political and theological isolation of Strasbourg after the death of Huldrych Zwingli in 1531, Bucer sought a consensus with Luther on the question of the Lord's Supper. He reached an agreement with Philipp Melanchthon in 1534, and the Concord of → Wittenberg was concluded in May, 1536—a genuine consensus, though on a Lutheran basis. Most towns in southern Germany accepted the

Concord, but not the Swiss Protestants. In this period, Bucer was active as ecclesiastical counselor and organizer in many territories and cities of southern Germany. He had particularly close contacts with → Philip of Hessen and reorganized church life and ecclesiastical discipline in Hessen, introducing → confirmation for the first time; this made it possible for a group of → Baptists to return to the church. Bucer also played an important role in arranging Philip's double marriage in 1539-1540.

Bucer wrote his great work, *Von der waren Seelsorge* (1539), a treatise of pastoral theology, in connection with the reorganization of the church in Strasbourg, which began in 1533. Here he elaborates his understanding of the → church (*Gemeinde*) as a community of believing Christians who are willing to bear responsibility for one another; this ecclesiology makes it necessary to establish various ministries and to enforce church discipline. Bucer's influence attained its peak in the religious debates between 1539 and 1541; he and Johannes Gropper wrote the → Regensburg Book. However, his plans for a national council came to nothing, and he failed in his attempt to introduce the Reformation in the archdiocese of Cologne. After the emperor's victory over the → Schmalkaldic League, Bucer's bitter struggle against the introduction of the → Augsburg Interim in Strasbourg meant that he had to emigrate to England at the beginning of 1549. A professorship in Cambridge allowed him to complete his great book about theological and social-political reform, *De regno Christi*, in 1550.

■ **Works:** *M. B.s Deutsche Schriften* (Gütersloh, 1960ff.); *Martini Buceri Opera latina.* (Paris, 1955; Leiden, 1982ff.); *Correspondance de M. B.* (Leiden, 1979ff.); *Bibliographia Bucerana*, ed. R. Stupperich (Gütersloh, 1952).
■ **Literature:** *TRE* 7:258–70.—H. Eells, *M. B.* (New Haven, 1931; reprinted New York, 1971); M. Greschat, *M. B. Ein Reformer und seine Zeit* (Munich, 1990).

MARTIN GRESCHAT

■ **Additional Bibliography:** *RGG*[4] 1:1810ff.—H. Joisten, *der Grenzgänger M. B.* (Speyer, 1991); M. de Kroon, *M. B. und Johannes Calvin* (Göttingen, 1991); D. F. Wright, ed., *M. B. Reforming Church and Community* (Cambridge, 1994); W. van't Spijker, *The Ecclesiastical Offices in the Thought of M. B.* (Leiden, 1996); G. Seebass, "B.-Forschung seit dem Jubiläumsjahr 1991," *Theologische Rundschau* 62 (1997) 271–300; V. Ortmann, *Reformation und Einheit der Kirche. M. B.s*

Einigungsbemühungen bei den Religionsgesprächen . . . (Mainz, 2001); A. Gäumann, *Reich Christi und Obrigkeit. Eine Studie zum reformatorischen Denken und Handeln M. B.s.* (Berne, 2001); . Puchta, "Aspects of B.'s Thought with Particular Reference to His Correspondance of 1530," *Reformation and Renaissance Review* 3 (2001) 167–76; S. E. Buckwalter, "M. B. deutsche Schriften: Current Work, Future Projects," *Reformation and Renaissance Review* 3 (2001) 177–87; M. Greschat, *M. B.: Un réformateur et son temps* (Paris, 2002); N. S. Amos, "The Alsatian among the Athenians: M. B., Mid-Tudor Cambridge and the Edwardian Reformation," *Reformation and Renaissance Review* 4 (2002) 94–124; G. Seebass, "B.'s Views on Ecclesiastical Property in the Light of Civil and Canon Law," *Reformation and Renaissance Review* 4 (2002) 152–67.

Buchstab, *Johannes.* Catholic theologian, born c. 1499 in Winterthur, died August 29, 1528 in Fribourg. He was curate in Herisau (1522), then Latin teacher and canon in Bremgarten (1523) and in Zofingen (1524). He was appointed teacher in Fribourg in 1528. He supported the Catholic position at the Berne Disputation in 1528 (Berchtold → Haller), and composed writings on controversial points of theology in the last two years of his life.
■ **Works:** *VD 16* 3:478f.; Klaiber nos. 434–43; Köhler *BF* 173–78.
■ **Literature:** G. W. Locher, "Die Berner Disputation 1528," *Zwingliana* 14 (1974–78) 542–64; I. Backus, *The Disputations of Baden, 1526, and Berne, 1528* (Princeton, N.J., 1993).

HERIBERT SMOLINSKY

Budé (Budaeus), *Guillaume.* Humanist, born January 26, 1468 in Paris, where he died August 22, 1540. He studied law in Orleans from 1483 to 1486; he pursued self-taught humanistic studies from 1491. He was secretary to the king from 1497 to 1502, and was later entrusted with diplomatic tasks at various periods. He held official posts from 1522, and was one of the initiators of the legal school of France with its philological-historical orientation (the *mos gallicus*). His *Annotationes* to the *Pandects* of Justinian (Paris, 1508) put knowledge of Roman law on a completely new foundation. His *De Asse* (Paris, 1515) shed light on ancient measures and coinage—and also on the economic and social circumstances of his own day. In *De studio literarum* and *De philologia* (Paris, 1532), he makes philology (not philosophy) the basis of all the sciences; but he also warns against a relapse into paganism in *De transitu hellenismi ad christianismum* (Paris, 1535). Although his thinking agreed on many points with Reformation ideas, he supported the anti-Reformation attitude of King → Francis I. Jean Calvin was influenced by Budé.

■ **Works:** *Opera omnia,* 4 vols. (Basle, 1557); *De transitu hellenismi ad christianismum,* ed. M. Lebel (Sherbrooke, 1973); *Correspondance,* ed. G. Lavoie and R. Galibois (Sherbrooke, 1977); *De studio literarum recte et commode instituendo,* ed. M.-M. de la Garanderie (Paris, 1988).

■ **Literature:** *TRE* 7:335–38; *CEras* 1:212–17.—L. Delaruelle, *G. B.* (Paris, 1907); J. Plattard, *G. B. et les origines de l'humanisme français* (Paris, 1923); J. Bohatec, *B. und Calvin* (Graz, 1950); D. F. Penham, *De transitu Hellenismi ad Christianismum* (New York, 1954); D. O. McNeil, *G. B. and Humanism in the Reign of Francis I* (Geneva, 1975); M.-M. de la Garanderie, *Christianisme et lettres profanes (1515–35)* (Paris, 1995).

PETER WALTER

■ **Additional Bibliography:** M. M. de La Garanderie, "G. B., a Philosopher of Culture," *SCJ* 19 (1988) 379–87; G. Gadoffre, *La révolution culturelle dans la France des humanistes. G. B. et François Ier* (Geneva, 1997); M. J. Ahn, "The Influence on Calvin's Hermeneutics and the Development of His Method," *Hervormde Teologiese Studies* 55 (1999) 228–39.

Bugenhagen (Pomeranus), *Johannes.* Protestant theologian, born June 24, 1485 in Wollin, died April 20, 1558 in Wittenberg. He was appointed lector in scripture in the monastery of Belbuck in 1517. He came to Wittenberg in 1521, and gave lectures in exegesis from 1522 onwards; he became parish priest of the main church in 1523, and professor in 1533. He was Martin Luther's friend and spiritual advisor. Bugenhagen's particular gifts lay in the field of practical organization. He promoted the spread of the Reformation by means of numerous journeys in northern Germany and Scandinavia; he drew up church orders for the cities of Braunschweig (1528), Hamburg (1529), Lübeck (1531), and Hildesheim (1542-1544), as well as for the territories of Pomerania (1535), Denmark (1537), Holstein (1542), and Braunschweig-Wolfenbüttel (1543). He reduced his activities after Luther's death. Bugenhagen was an important contributor to the translation of the Bible into Lower German. He composed a number of exegetical writings, and wrote the first history of Pomerania in 1518 (*Pomerania,* first printed 1728).

■ **Literature:** *NDB* 3:9f.; *TRE* 7:354–63.—O. Vogt, *Dr. J. B.s Briefwechsel* (Stettin, 1888; Hildesheim, ²1966, with suppls.); G. Geisenhof, *Bibliotheca Bugenhagiana* (Leipzig, 1908); H.-G. Leder, ed., *J. B. Gestalt und Wirkung* (Berlin, 1984); K. Stoll, ed., *Kirchenreform als Gottesdienst. Der Reformator J. B.* (Hannover, 1985); E. Wolgast, "J. B.s Beziehungen zur Politik nach Luthers Tod," in *Gedenkschrift für R. Olesch* (Cologne, 1990) 115–38; A. Bieber, *J. B. zwischen Reform und Reformation.* (Göttingen, 1993); V. Gummelt, *Lex et Evangelium* (Berlin, 1994).

EIKE WOLGAST

■ **Additional Bibliography:** *RGG*⁴ 1:1852f.—R. Kötter, *J. B.s Rechtfertigungslehre und der römische Katholizismus* (Göttingen, 1994); H.-G. Leder, ed., *J. B. Pomeranus—vom Reformer zum Reformator* (Frankfurt/Main, 2002); Y. Brunk, *Die Tauftheologie J. B.s* (Hannover, 2003).

Bullinger, *Heinrich.* Swiss Reformer, born July 18, 1504 in Bremgarten, died September 17, 1575 in Zurich; son of Heinrich Bullinger, who was parish priest and dean. During his studies in Emmerich and Cologne, he became acquainted with the writings of the humanists and Reformers, and became a convinced follower of Huldrych Zwingli during his time as teacher in the monastery of Kappel (1523) and as parish priest in Bremgarten (1529). He was elected to succeed Zwingli on December 9, 1531, and left his stamp on the church in Zurich and its relationship to the civil authorities (ordinance for preachers and the synod, 1532). His extensive correspondence—c. 12,000 of his letters survive—soon gave him considerable influence on the Reformed Christians throughout Europe (→ Zwinglianism), and his writings were equally effective. His biblical commentaries, collections of sermons, and controversial works were often reprinted and translated, and found a wide readership. He took a position clearly distinct from both → Baptists and Catholics, and sought a reconciliation within Protestantism. He did not succeed in achieving a consensus with Martin Luther on the question of the Lord's → Supper, but he did reach agreement with Jean Calvin in 1549 (the → *Consensus Tigurinus*). His *Confessio Helvetica posterior* (1566) furnished the doctrinal foundations for numerous Reformed churches in Europe. His study of covenant theology (*De Testa-*

mento seu foedere Dei unico et aeterno, 1534) made a particularly long-lasting impact, and his historical studies of the history of the Reformation and of Switzerland ("Chronicle of Zurich") were also important.

■ **Works:** *H. B. Werke* (Zurich, 1972ff.).

■ **Literature:** *TRE* 7:375–87.—J. Staedtke, *Die Theologie des jungen B.* (Zurich, 1962); S. Hausammann, *Römerbriefauslegung zwischen Humanismus und Reformation* (Zurich, 1970); U. Gäbler and E. Herkenrath, eds., *H. B.,* 2 vols. (Zurich, 1975); H. U. Bächtold, *H. B. vor dem Rat, 1531–75* (Berne, 1982); F. Blanke and I. Leuschner, *H. B.* (Zurich, 1990); P. Biel, *Doorkeepers at the House of Righteousness. H. B. and the Zurich Clergy 1535–1575* (Berne, 1991); C. S. McCoy and J. W. Baker, *Fountainhead of Federalism. H.B. and the Covenantal Tradition* (Louisville, Ky., 1991).

HANS ULRICH BÄCHTOLD

■ **Additional Bibliography:** A. A. García Archilla, *The Theology of History and Apologetic Historiography in H. B.* (San Francisco, 1992); J. W. Baker, "H. B., the Covenant, and the Reformed Tradition in Retrospect," *SCJ* 29 (1998) 359–76; A. W. Raath and S. A. de Freitas, "Theologico-political Federalism: The Office of Magistracy and the Legacy of H. B.," *Westminster Theological Journal* 63 (2001) 285–304; A. Mühling, *H. B.s europäische Kirchenpolitik* (Berne, 2001); C. P. Venema, *H. B. and the Doctrine of Predestination* (Grand Rapids, Mich., 2002); P. Stephens, "B.'s Defence of Infant Baptism in Debate with the Anabaptists," *Reformation and Renaissance Review* 4 (2002) 168–89.

Bürki (also Steiger), *Barnabas.* Benedictine, reforming abbot of Engelberg, born c. 1473/1474 in Altstätten (canton of St. Gallen), died December 29, 1546. He studied in Paris from 1495 to 1503, and was one of the reform-minded theologians in the circle of → Faber Stapulensis. He took the degree of master of arts in 1503, and joined the monastery in the same year; he became abbot before July 13, 1505. He remained in contact with the humanists (Oswald → Myconius). Under his leadership, the abbey of Engelberg remained loyal to the old faith. He was the first president of the → Baden Disputation in 1526, and was active in support of the Catholic faith in the uplands around Berne in 1528. He sought to improve the economic situation of his monastery, and proved a wise legislator in the little monastic state.

■ **Literature:** A. Weiss, *Das Kloster Engelberg unter Abt B. B. 1505–46* (*Zeitschrift für Schweizer Kirchengeschichte,* Beiheft 16) (Fribourg, 1956).

URBAN HODEL

Buschius (von Büschen, von dem Busche; Pasiphilus), *Hermannus.* Humanist, born c. 1468 in Sassenberg castle near Warendorf, died 1534 in Dülmen. He studied *inter alia* in Heidelberg, Tübingen, Rome, and Bologna, and taught rhetoric and poetics in Cologne from 1494 to 1498, 1508 to 1515, and 1518 to 1523; in the intervals, he taught in various other places. He was involved in the Reuchlin affair, and collaborated in the "Letters of Obscure Men." From 1523 to 1526, he was professor of Roman literature in Heidelberg; from 1527 to 1533, he was professor of history and rhetoric in Marburg. He became an adherent of Martin Luther at a very early date, and disputed in Münster in 1533 with the Baptist Bernhard → Rothmann. In his chef d'oeuvre, *Vallum humanitatis* (Cologne, 1518), Buschius defends humanistic studies and explains how they are useful to theology.

■ **Literature:** *LMA* 2:1116f.; *CEras* 1:233f.—H. J. Liessem, *H. von dem Busche: Programm des Kaiser-Wilhelm-Gymnasiums zu Köln 1884–89, 1904–08* (reprint, Nieuwkoop, 1965); A. Bömer, *Westfälische Lebensbilder* 1 (1930) 50–67; *Die Schriften der Münsterischen Täufer und ihrer Gegner,* ed. R. Stupperich, vol. 1 (Münster, 1970) 94–119; J. H. Overfield, *Humanism and Scholasticism in Late Medieval Germany* (Princeton, N.J., 1984); *Kölner Universitätsgeschichte,* vol. 1 (Cologne, 1988) 223ff.; J. V. Mehl, "H. von dem Busches "Vallum humanitatis" (1518)," *Renaissance Quarterly* 42 (1989) 480–506.

PETER WALTER

■ **Additional Bibliography:** J. V. Mehl, "Hermann von dem Busche's Poem in Honor of Erasmus' Arrival in Cologne in 1516," in *In laudem Caroli.* Festschrift Ch. G. Nauert (Kirksville, Mo., 1998) 65–73.

C

Cajetan, *Thomas* (baptismal name: Jacobus) *de Vio.* Dominican (1484), born February 20, 1469 in Gaëta, died August 10, 1534 in Rome (tomb in Santa Maria sopra Minerva). He took the degree of master of theology in Padua in 1494, and taught in Padua, Brescia, and Pavia; then he taught at the Sapienza university in Rome from 1500 to 1507. He became master general of his Order in 1508, and was created cardinal of San Sisto in 1517. He was appointed archbishop of Palermo in 1518, and bishop of his hometown Gaëta in 1519. He was legate in Germany (1518-1519) and Hungary (1523-1524), and was a reform-minded counselor to the papal curia.

Cajetan's earliest scholarly works were philosophical commentaries on Aristotle (*Praedicamenta; De anima*), Porphyry (*Eisagogē*), and Thomas Aquinas (*De ente et essentia*). He wrote against Averroism and against the univocal concept of Being in Scotism. The key to his metaphysics is his doctrine of analogy (*De nominum analogia,* 1498), which gives the analogy of proportionality precedence over the analogy of attribution. His contemporaries (like many scholars up to the present day) found it difficult to understand the differentiation between theology and philosophy that is adumbrated in Cajetan's works—a differentiation which is in keeping with the spirit of the early modern period. Cajetan held the mysteries of faith (Trinity, incarnation, resurrection of the flesh) to be logically inderivable, but he maintained the possibility of proving the immortality of the soul by philosophical means.

His theological chef d'oeuvre is his commentary on Thomas's *Summa theologiae* (the first complete commentary to be published): vol. I was published in 1507, I-II in 1511, II-II in 1516, and III in 1522. This work left its mark on the methodology and contents of the reception of Thomas, and did much to ensure that the *Summa theologiae* replaced the *Sentences* of Peter Lombard as the standard theological textbook.

Cajetan was an outstanding protagonist of reform in his Order and in the church as a whole. He was a deeply pious man who led a modest and strict life; as master general, he emphasized the importance of life in community, poverty, and studies. Even before he had read Martin Luther's theses on indulgences, his own treatise *De indulgentiis* (December 8, 1517) had taken a critical position on this question. After the death of Leo X, Cajetan was a supporter of the reforming pope Hadrian VI. The report he drew up on communion from the → chalice for the laity and on the marriage of priests (→ celibacy) took the Reformers' concerns seriously.

Cajetan's position on questions of moral theology and social ethics helped make moral theology an autonomous discipline. His *Summula peccatorum* (1523) discusses contemporary pastoral problems, including economic and societal questions such as interest, usury, simony, booty of war, etc.

Leo X entrusted the *causa Lutheri* to Cajetan, who met the Reformer at the parliament of Augsburg in 1518. 15 *Opuscula* (October 9-29, 1518) document Cajetan's position on the disputed questions. He considered Luther's doctrine that the certainty of one's own → justification was a constitutive element of this justification as schismatic: "This amounts to building a new church" (*Opuscula* 111a).

Cajetan detaches ecclesiology from the study of canon law and makes it a branch of dogmatic theology. His doctrine of the → church, based on the Bible and on Christology, came into play above all in his rejection of conciliarist tendencies (Council of Pisa, 1511-1512; and at the fifth Lateran council, 1512-1517) and in his defense of papal primacy against the Reformers.

Cajetan devoted the last decade of his life to the exposition of scripture (1524-1529: New Testament, with the exception of Acts; 1530-1534: Old Testament as far as Isaiah). His approach begins with the literal sense of the texts; he follows Jerome on the question of the canon, and displays courage in presenting a "new meaning" which goes against the "current of the doctors." All this led to controversies with the Dominican → Ambrosius Catharinus and with the Sorbonne.

The scholastic vocabulary of his work, and the anti-Reformation cast of post-Tridentine theology prevented the reception and elaboration of his pioneering theology.

■ **Works:** *Opuscula omnia* (Paris, 1530, often reprinted; Lyons, 1562); *Opera omnia quotquot in Sacrae Scripturae expositionem reperiuntur,* 5 vols. (Lyons, 1639); *Kommentar zur Summa theologiae in der Editio Leonina der Werke des Thomas von Aquin,* vols. 4–12 (Rome, 1888–1906); vol. 14: indexes (Rome, 1948); *De comparatione auctoritatis Papae et concilii* (1511), ed. V.-M. Pollet (Rome, 1936); *De divina institutione pontificatus Romani Pontificis* (1521), ed. F. Lauchert (Münster, 1925); *Summula peccatorum* (1523) (Paris, 1526).

■ **Literature:** J. F. Groner, *Kardinal C.* (Fribourg and Louvain, 1951); R. Bauer, *Gotteserkenntnis und Gottesbeweise bei Cardinal C.* (Regensburg, 1955); G. Hennig, *C. und Luther* (Stuttgart, 1966); A. Bodem, *Das Wesen der Kirche nach Kardinal C.* (Trier, 1971); H. de Lubac, *Die Freiheit der Gnade* (Paris, 1965; 2 vols., Einsiedeln, 1971); J. Wicks, *C. und die Anfänge der Reformation* (Münster, 1983); B. Hallensleben, *Communicatio. Anthropologie und Gnadenlehre bei Thomas de Vio C.* (Münster, 1985); idem, "Das heisst eine neue Kirche bauen," *Catholica. Vierteljahresschrift für Ökumenische Theologie* 39 (1985) 217–39; *Rationalisme analogique et* *humanisme théologique. La culture de Thomas de Vio "Il Gaetano,"* ed. B. Pinchard and S. Ricci (Naples, 1993).

BARBARA HALLENSLEBEN

■ **Additional Bibliography:** Ch. Morerod, *C. et Luther en 1518,* 2 vols. (Fribourg, 1994); M. Nieden, *Organum Deitatis. Die Christologie des Th. de Vio C* (Leiden, 1997); B. A. R. Felmberg, *Die Ablaßtheorie Kardinal C.s.* (Leiden, 1998); T. M. Izbicki, "C.'s Attack on Parallels between Church and State," *CrS* 20 (1999) 81–89; A. Krause, *Zur Analogie bei C. und Thomas von Aquin* (Halle [Saale], 1999).

Cajetan of Thiene (Gaetano da Thiene). Saint (canonized 1678; feast August 7), founder of a religious order, born 1480 in Vicenza, died August 7, 1547 in Naples (tomb in San Paolo Maggiore). After studying law, he worked at the papal curia under Julius II. He was ordained priest in 1516. Influenced by reform circles in northern Italy, he and three companions (including Giampietro Carafa, later Pope → Paul IV) founded in 1524 the first Order of Clerks Regular ("Theatines") to promote the work of church reform. Cajetan worked in Rome, Venice, and Naples.

■ **Literature:** *Bibliotheca Sanctorum,* ed. Istituto Giovanni XXIII, vol. 5 (Rome, 1972) 1345–49.—F. Andreu, "Le Lettere di San Gaetano," *Studi e Testi* 177 (1954); G. Llompart, *Gaetano da Thiene, 1480–1547* (Wiesbaden, 1969).

KARL SUSO FRANK

■ **Additional Bibliography:** M. J. Hufnagel, *St. Cajetan, ein wenig bekannter Schutzpatron Bayerns* (St. Ottilien, 1992).

Calini, *Muzio.* Italian Latinist, born 1525 in Brescia, died April 22, 1570 in Terni. After humanistic studies, he was in Cyprus in 1544, and later in Malta; he became a Knight of St. John in 1549. He had contact with reform-minded groups in Rome, and was appointed archbishop of Zara in 1555. He took an active part in the Council of Trent from 1561 to 1563, and the 233 letters that he sent from Trent to Cardinal Alvise Cornaro are an important source for the history of this council. He was appointed bishop of Terni in 1566.

■ **Editions:** M. C., *Lettere conciliari* (1561–63), ed. A. Marani (Brescia, 1963); *Lettere postconciliari di M. C.,* ed. A. Marani (Florence, 1979); *Monumenti di varia letteratura,* ed. G. B. Morandi, vol. 3 (Bologna, 1804) 69–155.

■ **Literature:** *DBI* 16:725ff.—L. Castano, "Mons. M. C. . . . al concilio di Trento," *Concilio di Trento, Rivista commemorativa del IV centenario* 2 (1943) 123–38.

KLAUS GANZER

Calvin, *Jean,* theologian and Reformer

1. Life

Calvin was born July 10, 1509 in Noyon (Picardy) and died May 27, 1564 in Geneva. His father was administrator of the property of the cathedral chapter; his mother, a woman deeply attached to popular piety, died when Jean was young. He came to Paris in 1523 and began his education at the Collège de la Marche under Mathurin Cordier; subsequently, he studied the liberal arts at the Collège Montaigu.

After a dispute with the cathedral chapter, his father urged him to study law instead of theology, and Jean did so in Orleans and Bourges. Under the influence of humanists who, to some extent, already adhered to the ideas of Martin Luther, Calvin began to read the Bible and the church fathers. After the death of his father, he returned to Paris in order to improve his knowledge of the biblical languages and of classical and Christian antiquity at the Collège Royal, an academy which worked in the spirit of → Erasmus of Rotterdam and → Faber Stapulensis, in contrast to the inquisitorial spirit of the Sorbonne theological faculty. Calvin's first work was a commentary on Seneca's *De Clementia,* which exhorts rulers to exercise tolerance. He became acquainted with Luther's ideas thanks to the reforming circle around Bishop Guillaume → Briçonnet of Meaux.

The Sorbonne soon began to suspect him of the Lutheran heresy, and Calvin felt obliged to flee from Paris to Basle at the end of 1533; it was in this city that he first became a decided adherent of the Reformation. It remains a matter of dispute whether this happened as a "sudden conversion to instruction" by the gospel, as he himself wrote twenty-five years later (CR 59:21); contemporary evidence tends rather to suggest a gradual transition, which was expressed in the theological manual *Christianae Religionis Institutio* (Basle, 1536). Calvin's principal sources are Luther's two catechisms and such works as "The Freedom of a Christian Man" and "The Babylonian Captivity"; he draws on Martin → Bucer, Philipp Melanchthon and Huldrych Zwingli only for clarification of individual questions.

The great success of his *Institutio* encouraged the 27-year-old lay theologian to continue his studies in the Protestant city of Strasbourg, but this did not happen at once: Guillaume → Farel, who experienced considerable difficulties in introducing the Reformation into Geneva, appealed to Calvin to help him (cf. CR 59:23). Calvin became "lector of sacred scripture" in Geneva, where he also composed a church order that envisaged an ecclesiastical discipline supported by the threat of excommunication from the monthly celebration of the Lord's Supper; he also wrote a catechism and a profession of faith "which all citizens bind themselves by oath [...] to follow and observe" (CR 22:85).

The city council, as *minister Dei,* was to oversee the promotion of "pure religion." However, they objected to the excessive zeal of the pastors, and expelled Farel and Calvin in the spring of 1538. Calvin accepted Bucer's invitation to come to Strasbourg, where he became pastor of the French-speaking parish and published an expanded version of the *Institutio* in Latin (1539) and in French (1541). He took part in the religious dialogues in Frankfurt, Hagenau, Worms, and Regensburg, where he met Melanchthon; he never met Luther in person. In the negotiations, Calvin displayed openness even toward the "Roman" party, and he accepted the Regensburg consensus on justification, which unfortunately made no lasting impact (→ Regensburg Book). He married Idelette de Bure, the widow of a Baptist; their only child died shortly after birth.

The attempt by Cardinal Jacopo → Sadoleto, bishop of Carpentras in Provence, to recatholicize Geneva demanded a response from Calvin (cf. CR 5:382ff.), and the confused citizens themselves asked him to intervene. His answer once again takes up the theme of the "true church" which is based, not (as Sadoleto held) on a centuries-old consensus of human traditions, but on God's Word alone (CR 5:392). The Holy Spirit continually calls prophets to serve this Word (CR 5:393f.). Today, the Roman church has moved so far from this ideal form that it needs a radical renewal, without any schism or doctrinal innovations (ibid., 412). The Genevans recalled Calvin in 1541, and this time, the council gave its approval to his church order, which envisaged four ministries.

First, "pastors" were ordained by the laying-on of hands to serve the Word through preaching and sacraments. They formed the college of "Compagnie des Pasteurs," meeting regularly for Bible study, pastoral consultations, censure of morals, and the cooptation of new members. (Calvin himself was not ordained, as far as we know; scholars attribute this to his conception of himself as prophet.) Second, "teachers" were entrusted with the charge of religious education in schools and at the theological level. Third, the "elders" had the task of overseeing the conduct of people's lives; as representatives of the laity, they met with the pastors in the "consistory" to deal with political business. Fourth, the "deacons" were in charge of social care: their service of the poor and the sick was seen as a proclamation of the gospel in praxis and was the reason why they helped distribute the bread and wine in the Lord's Supper.

In his new catechism, Calvin maintained a more positive understanding of the law than Luther: it not only reveals our sinfulness, but also serves as a stimulus to ethical progress and as a "covenantal ordering." This is the context in which we should see the disciplinary trials about doctrine in Geneva—against Sebastian → Castellio, Jérôme → Bolsec, and especially Michel → Servet, who proposed a modalistic doctrine of the Trinity (→ Antitrinitarians). When Servet came to Geneva, Calvin denounced him to the court, which condemned him to death at the stake. The reformed communities in Basle, Berne, Schaffhausen, and Zurich, and later Melanchthon, consented to this procedure, which resembled that of the Inquisition. Calvin showed greater patience with Reformed theologians from Switzerland and Germany in the controversy about the Lord's → Supper. He signed the *Confessio Augustana variata,* which affirms that the body and blood of Christ are truly administered "with" the bread and wine (*BSLK* 65). He negotiated the → Consensus Tigurinus with Heinrich → Bullinger, Zwingli's successor, achieving a common doctrine of the Lord's Supper (1549). In Geneva itself, however, Calvin never succeeded in fully enforcing his church order. The "patriots" resisted him for a period because of his demand that the "consistory" should inspect people's private lives. Outside Switzerland, Calvin's Geneva long acted as a model city. Calvin exchanged many letters with persecuted brethren in the faith in France, as well as with governments in Poland and England. Many future pastors from northern and central Europe studied at the academy founded in Geneva in 1559. Its library contained many exegetical, patristic, and systematic books, including works of Roman scholasticism.

Calvin's health suffered under the enormous burden of work, and he died before his 55th birthday. At his own wish, he was buried at an unknown place, without witnesses or burial service .

2. *Works*

Calvin composed (a) the *Institutio* in continuously expanding editions (1536, 1539, 1543, 1559). The first French translation (1541) is his own work; another scholar translated the last French edition (1564). (b) He wrote commentaries on almost all the books of scripture; (c) sermons; (d) treatises, small monographs, and occasional and polemical works; (e) letters.

3. *Theology*

Calvin's systematics can be considered a synthesis of wisdom and scholarship. In keeping with the sapiential tradition, it seeks to let God address both mind and heart, individual and fellowship, calling to salvation; as a work of scholarship, it employs knowledge of scripture and classical antiquity, as well as the instruments made available by logic and dialectics. A typical statement of his hermeneutical approach is the affirmation that "The sum total of our wisdom" consists "in the knowledge of God and of our own self" (*Inst.* [1559] 1.1.1). Anthropology must have a theological orientation, and the doctrine about God must show how the human person and the world can attain wholeness, to the glory of God.

Initially, the *human person* bore the likeness of God "in his spirit and in his heart," and his body too was illuminated thereby (1.15.3). He possessed "free will" until "his spirit fell into perdition" (1.15.8) and incurred "guilt before the judgment of God" (2.1.8). Since then, reason is liable to error, though "not wholly destroyed" (2.2.12); only the Holy Spirit can overcome this situation, by means of scripture and of the gift of enlightenment (1.6.1). It is the Spirit who brings about → justification and the renewal of God's image in the human person.

God is one (1.10.2), and hence triune. In his loving mercy towards sinners, he reveals himself as the fellowship of Father, Son, and Holy Spirit in love (3.1.2). Consequently, the divine characteristics cannot be understood in a static manner, but as *virtutes* which are active in history (1.10.2), creative and revelatory (1.11.1). As creator, God determines everything "beforehand," and his predestination includes Christ, at least as far as election is concerned: election to damnation or to salvation depends on Christ.

Christ brings salvation as the absolute "image of the one who is invisible" (Col 1:15; 2.6.4). Calvin shows a preference for the Johannine Christology of incarnation. He infers, from the fact that the Logos has become flesh, that the relationship between God and human beings has a consistently verbal character: gospel, scripture, preaching, and sacramental verbal action. The Word is heard, believed, and followed where the inner testimony of the divine Spirit makes this possible (1.6.2). The Son of God humbled himself in order to become "like us in all things except sin" (CR 74:225). "Although he governed all things," he prayed as our brother (CR 73:4441). When Jesus took death upon himself, the omnipotence of the Son remained "as it were hidden" (CR 73:104), and his resurrection and exaltation to heaven were the fruit of such lowliness. "He ascended in order that he might fill all things (Eph 4:10)" (2.16.4) and intercede for human beings (cf. CR 76:617f.). As king and priest, he is eternally active as the mediator of our salvation (cf. CR 55:29).

His *Spirit* translates the *justification* which Christ merited once and for all into a progressive sanctification: for we cannot "be justified as a gift by faith alone, if we do not also lead a holy life" (CR 77:331). Like Luther, Calvin teaches that the righteousness of Christ is "reckoned" to the sinner (CR 51:692); he goes beyond Luther in emphasizing the necessity of a process of sanctification which takes concrete form in ethical behavior. The grace of the Spirit of Christ, which "brings about the desire and the fulfillment" in us (CR 68:248), is absolutely necessary for salvation.

The *church* and the two *sacraments* are "external aids" in this process. With Cyprian, Calvin affirms: "He who has God as Father, must also have the church as mother" (4.1.1). "Outside her bosom, one cannot hope for any forgiveness of sins" (4.1.4). This idea leads Calvin to speak of the educative function of the church's teaching office: no one should read scripture "on his own" like the "enthusiasts" (4.1.5), neglecting the exposition of the Bible by tradition and preaching (cf. 4.1.6). The church is the "faithful guardian" of God's truth (4.1.10). Baptism and the Lord's Supper mediate Christ *in ecclesia,* and it is Christ who is "the substance of all sacraments" (4.14.16). Through baptism we are "taken up into the fellowship of the church" and "grafted onto Christ" (4.15.1). In communion, Christ is "truly given" to us "through the signs of bread and wine [...], in order that we may grow into one body together with him" (4.17.11). Calvin maintains a dynamic theory of the real presence and consecration: the elements, marked by God's Word, become something "that they were not beforehand" (4.14.18). "We declare that Christ descends to us both in the outward symbol and in his Spirit, in order to make our souls truly alive with the substance of his flesh and blood" (4.17.24). Calvin sees in both sacraments processes of communication whereby God "accommodates" himself and allows his "spiritual goods" to be experienced by physical intermediaries (4.14.3).

The *ministry* is indispensable for the church, which cannot remain without leadership—provided of course that this leadership is exercised as a *ministerium evangelii.* The apostles served "God and Christ" well, for the glory of the Lord and "the salvation" of human beings (CR 80:95). They did so as *collegae et socii* equal in rank (CR 79:198), and hence as "God's fellow-workers" (CR 77:352). Unlike Luther, Calvin does not make the "common priesthood" the basis of his doctrine of ministry. He acknowledges the presbyterate and the episcopate as a pastoral ministry attested in scripture and exercised in the individual communities (CR 29:185); at that early period, there was only a difference in degree between bishop and priest, since the *episcopus* was the elected president of a college of presbyters (4.4.2). The same applies to "archbishops" and "patriarchs" with their authority to convoke regional synods (4.4.1). Calvin writes that the deacons of the early church had responsibility for social care (4.4.1). The "consent of the entire people" is required when office-bearers are to be elected (4.4.10). In his endeavor to give the Reformed Church a new structure in keeping with this model, Calvin retains ordination by the laying-on of hands, and he is willing to

acknowledge this as the "third sacrament," provided that it is administered in accordance with scripture (4.19.28 and 31).

On the disputed *issue of primacy,* two things are important to Calvin: first, the recognition of a functional precedence of Peter within the apostolic college (cf. 4.6.4 and 7) and, by analogy, the appropriateness of the first seat for the Roman patriarchate within the *communio ecclesiarum* (cf. 4.7.1 and 5); second, the strict refusal of the claim that the pope is the monarchic head of the entire church (4.2.6). There is a contradiction between the Petrine ministry and the desire to exalt oneself over the gospel—only in the Antichrist do these two coincide (4.7.24). When the primacy takes the concrete form of service of unity in doctrine and fellowship, the Reformation does not exclude this: "God wanted this" form of the succession to Peter "to endure up to the present day. We would be happy to give it the honor which it deserved" (CR 35:611).

Calvin's theology has also a notable *societal orientation.* It contains reflections on work and specific jobs, as well as a doctrine of the state which sees the *politica administratio* as one of the *media salutis* (4.20.4). The state is the fruit of God's creative, redemptive, and perfecting will—provided that it avoids tyranny and anarchy. Secular legislation must obey the principal commandment of love. The Christian must obey civil authorities, even when they behave unjustly (4.20.22 and 29ff.), but he must resist when they demand something repugnant to God (4.20.32). Calvin holds that the best possible societal form is an oligarchy tempered by democratic elements (4.20.8).

■ **Works:** *Calvini Opera,* ed. G. Baum, E. Cunitz, and E. Reuss: CR vols. 29–87; *Institutio Christianae Religionis,* 1559 edition: *Joannis Calvini Opera selecta,* ed. P. Barth and W. Niesel (Munich, vol. 3 ²1957; vol. 4 ²1959; vol. 5 ²1962; German by O. Weber: *Unterricht in der christlichen Religion,* Neukirchen-Vluyn ²1963); *Ioannis Calvini Opera omnia denuo recognita et adnotatione critica instructa notisque illustrata,* ed. B. G. Armstrong et al., series I and II (Geneva, 1992ff.); M. Bihary, *Bibliographia Calviniana. C.s Werke und ihre Übersetzungen 1850–1997* (Prague, 2000).

■ **Literature:** *On 1 und 2:* E. Doumergue, *J. C. Les hommes et les choses de son temps,* 7 vols. (Paris and Lausanne, 1899–1927); P. Imbart de la Tour, *C.* (Munich, 1936); W. F. Dankbaar, *C. Sein Weg und sein Werk* (Neukirchen-Vluyn, 1959); A. Ganoczy, *Le jeune C.* (Wiesbaden, 1966); F. Wendel, *C. Ursprung und Entwicklung seiner Theologie* (Neukirchen-Vluyn, 1968);

T. H. L. Parker, *John C.* (London, [2]1987); J. Bouwsma, *C. A Sixteenth Century Portrait* (New York, 1988); R. S. Wallace, *C., Geneva and the Reformation* (Edinburgh, 1988).—*On 3.:* W. Niesel, *Die Theologie C.s* (Munich, [2]1957); W. Krusche, *Das Wirken des Heiligen Geistes nach C.* (Göttingen, 1957); E. D. Willis, *C.'s Catholic Christology* (Leiden, 1966); A. Ganoczy, *Ecclesia ministrans. Dienende Kirche und kirchlicher Dienst bei C.* (Freiburg, 1968); R. Stauffer, *Dieu, la création et la Providence dans la prédication de C.* (Berne et al., 1978); T. F. Torrance, *The Hermeneutics of John C.* (Edinburgh, 1988).—*Bibliographies:* W. Niesel (Munich, 1961); D. A. Erichson (Nieuwkoop, 1965); D. Kempff (Leiden, 1975); continued in "C.," *Theological Journal* 1 (Grand Rapids, Mich., 1975).

ALEXANDRE GANOCZY

■ **Additional Bibliography:** *RGG*[4] 2:16–36.—A. E. MacGrath, *J. C.* (Zurich, 1991); W. van't Spijker, ed., *C. Festschrift W. H. Neuser* (Kampen, 1991); W. de Greef, *The Writings of John C.* (Grand Rapids, Mich., 1993); P. Opitz, *C.s theologische Hermeneutik* (Neukirchen-Vluyn, 1994); W. G. Naphy, *C. and the Consolidation of the Genevan Reformation* (Manchester, 1994); B. Cottret, *C.* (Stuttgart, 1998); D. Crouzet, *J. C.* (Paris, 2000); R. A. Muller, *The Unaccommodated C.* (Oxford, 2000); P. Chung, *Spirituality and Social Ethics in John C.* (Lanham, 2000); G. H. Tavard, *The Starting Point of C.'s Theology* (Grand Rapids, 2000); C.-A. Keller, *C. mystique* (Geneva, 2001); W. van't Spijker, *C.: Die Kirche in ihrer Geschichte,* vol. 2 (Göttingen, 2001) 102–236; M. de Kroon, *The Honour of God and Human Salvation* (Edinburgh, 2001); D. H. Compier, *John C.'s Rhetorical Doctrine of Sin* (Lewiston, 2002); P. Opitz, ed., *C. im Kontext der Schweizer Reformation* (Zurich, 2003); H. A. Oberman (D. Weinstein, ed.), *The Two Reformations* (New Haven, 2003).

Calvinism

1. Concept

"Calvinism" came into being as a polemical designation of the Protestant community, which would never have thought of calling itself after a "founder," since it understood itself as "the church reformed in keeping with God's Word" (cf. CR 48:76f.). So-called Calvinism was generated by a phenomenon in ecclesiastical, intellectual, and social history marked not only by Jean Calvin (1509-1564), but also by Martin → Bucer, Huldrych Zwingli, Heinrich → Bullinger, Theodor → Beza, and the → "Puritans."

2. Diffusion

Calvinism was brought to *France* largely by theologians who had studied in Geneva, and it spread among the aristocracy (de Condé, Coligny). It formed a political party, which was attacked as such by the Catholic civil authorities (→ Huguenots) until → Henry IV issued the edict of tolerance at Nantes in 1598. The French Calvinists had adopted the *Confessio Gallicana* with a corresponding church order as early as 1559.

In the *Netherlands,* Calvinism took the form of a national movement (→ Geusen) for liberation from the Spaniards. The Reformer Guy de → Brès was the principal author of the *Confessio Belgica.* The terror unleashed by the duke of → Alba drove c. 100,000 Reformed Christians to seek exile in England and Germany. The proclamation of Religious Peace in 1578 led to the separation of the Reformed North from the Catholic South.

In *Germany,* Wallonian, Flemish, and French refugees founded Calvinist communities. They drew up a church order at the Synod of Emden in 1571. In the Electoral Palatinate, → Frederick III saw them as proponents of the "second Reformation" and gave them his support. The → Heidelberg catechism of 1563 summarized Reformed doctrine in a way that all could understand. The Reformed Christians spread above all in Nassau, Bremen, Lippe, Anhalt, Hessen-Kassel, and Brandenburg. The academy of Herborn was the first important educational institute for theologians. The Prussian state imposed a union between Reformed and Lutheran Christians in 1817.

In *Hungary* and Transylvania, Calvinism worked as a catalyst of national independence vis-à-vis the Catholic Habsburgs. A *Confessio Christianae fidei* was adopted in 1562/1563. Prominent representatives of the Hungarian-speaking Reformed groups were Georg Szikszai, Szegedi (István Kis), Peter → Melius, and Gáspár Károlyi.

Scotland's Reformer was John → Knox (died 1572). The "Reformation parliament" of 1560 abolished papal jurisdiction over Scotland and approved the → *Confessio Scotica,* which was complemented by a "Book of Discipline." The ecclesiastical provinces were headed by superintendents, and the annual "kirk session" was the highest authority. A new university was founded in Edinburgh. Knox's successor, Andrew Melville (1545-1622), overcame the resistance of the episcopal church and won the day for a Presbyterianism characterized by a strong involvement on the part of the laity.

3. Doctrine

Calvin is the main source of the doctrine of the "church reformed in accordance with God's Word." Its historical development was guided for more than a century by the idea of "orthodoxy," understood as a scholastic dogmatics which emphasized the ecclesial character of theology, its methodology, and systematics (the *loci communes*). The exchange of views between Beza and Petrus Ramus shows that Calvinism from the outset employed philosophical tools derived ultimately from Aristotle.

The doctrine of double → predestination was the doctrinal center. This was interpreted in opposite directions by two theologians in Leiden, Jakob Arminius (1560-1609) and Franciscus Gomarius (1563-1641). Arminius and his school (Moyse Amyraut, Josué de la Place [1596-1655/1656] in Saumur) taught the so-called "infralapsarianism," i.e., that divine election occurred only after the fall of Adam and Eve; Gomarius and his adherents (Pierre du Moulin and Samuel Desmaret in Sedan) taught "supralapsarianism," i.e., that election had already taken place before the fall. The → Heidelberg catechism is basically the work of Zacharias → Ursinus (1534-1582). This quickly won international acknowledgment as a precise and universally comprehensible summary of Reformed doctrine. We already see in Ursinus and his Heidelberg colleague Caspar → Olevian the beginnings of the federal theology which broke with the metaphysical-speculative interests of earlier "orthodoxy" and tended to think in historical terms.

■ *LThK*³ 2:900–904 (unabridged version).
■ **Literature:** J. McNeill, *The History and Character of Calvinism* (Oxford, 1954); M. Bucsay, *Geschichte des Protestantismus in Ungarn* (Stuttgart, 1959); W. Hollweg, *Der Augsburger Reichstag von 1566 und seine Bedeutung für die Entstehung der Reformierten Kirche und ihres Bekenntnisses* (Neukirchen-Vluyn, 1964); M. Schaab, *Territorialstaat und C.* (Stuttgart, 1993); E. A. Pettegree, *Calvinism in Europe 1540–1620* (Cambridge, 1994); Ch. Link, "Calvin und der C.," in *Hilfreiches Erbe.* Festschrift. H. Scholl (Bovenden, 1995) 97–119; E. Wolgast, *Reformierte Konfession und Politik im 16.Jh.* (Heidelberg, 1998); M. Freudenberg, "Das Verhältnis von Kirche und Staat nach den reformierten Bekenntnissen des 16.Jh.," *Communio viatorum* 40 (1998) 228–55; idem, ed., *Profile des reformierten Protestantismus aus vier Jahrhunderten* (Wuppertal, 1999); B. Nischan, *Lutherans and Calvinists in the Age of Confessionalism* (Aldershot, 1999); J.-M. Berthoud,

Calvin et la France (Lausanne, 1999); S. Bildheim, *Calvinistische Staatstheorien* (Frankfurt/Main, 2001).

ALEXANDRE GANOCZY

■ **Additional Bibliography:** C. Elwood, *The Body Broken: The Calvinist Doctrine of the Eucharist and the Symbolization of Power in Sixteenth-century France* (New York, 1999); P. Benedict, *Christ's Churches Purely Reformed. A Social History of Calvinism* (New Haven, 2002).

Camaiani, *Pietro.* Nuncio, born June 1, 1519 in Arezzo, died July 27, 1579 in Ascoli Piceno. He entered the service of Duke Cosimo I of Florence in 1539, and represented him in Trent and Bologna from 1546 to 1549, where he wrote precise and reliable reports. He was Cosimo's agent in Venice for a short period in 1549. He was sent to Ottavio Farnese at the beginning of 1551, with a commission from Julius III to prevent the formation of a league with France directed against the emperor and the pope, and he was nuncio to the imperial court from 1551 to 1553. He was appointed bishop of Fiesole in 1552, and was nuncio in Naples from 1554 to 1555. He took part in the third session of the Council of Trent from 1561 onwards. Here he joined the opposition under Charles de → Guise, cardinal of Lorraine, and turned a deaf ear to Duke Cosimo's demand that he change his position. Pius V sent Camaiani as special nuncio to Spain in 1566-1567, with the tasks of charging Philip II to wage war in a decisive manner in the Netherlands, to bring Archbishop Bartolomé → Carranza from Toledo to Rome, and to protest against the infringements of ecclesiastical jurisdiction. He was appointed bishop of Ascoli Piceno in 1566, and endeavored to reform the clergy by means of visitations and synods. He founded a seminary in 1571.

■ **Literature:** *DHGE* 11:504–9; *DBI* 17:72–76.—G. de Leva, "La guerra di papa Giulio III contro Ottavio Farnese," *Rivista storica italiana* 1 (1884) 663f.; *Nuntiaturen des Pietro Bertano und P. C. 1550–52,* ed. G. Kupke (Gotha, 1901); *Correspondéncia diplomática entre España y la Santa Sede durante el pontificado de Pío V,* ed. L. Serrano, 2 vols. (Madrid, 1914); H. Jedin, *Girolamo Seripando. Sein Leben und Denken im Geisteskampf des 16.Jh.,* vol. 2 (Würzburg, 1937) 596ff.; idem, "La politica conciliare di Cosimo I," *Rivista storica italiana* 62 (1950) 345–74, 477–96; G. Fabiani, "Sinodi e visite pastorali ad Ascoli dopo il Concilio," *RSCI* 6 (1952) 265–79; idem, *Ascoli nel Cinquecento,* vol. 1 (Ascoli Piceno, 1957); *Nuntiaturen des P. C. und Achille* *de Grassi. Legation des Girolamo Dandini 1552–53,* ed. H. Lutz (Tübingen, 1959).

KLAUS JAITNER

■ **Additional Bibliography:** G. Raspini, *P. C.* (Fiesole, 1983).

Camerarius (Kammermeister), *Joachim.* Lutheran humanist, born April 12, 1500 in Bamberg, died April 17, 1574 in Leipzig. He studied in Leipzig and Erfurt, where he was a member of the humanist circle around Conradus → Mutianus, → Crotus Rubeanus, and Eobanus Hessus. He began his studies in Wittenberg in 1521, and became a close friend of Philipp Melanchthon, who recommended him for the position of rector of the grammar school which was founded in Nuremberg in 1526. In 1535, he became professor at the university of Tübingen, and it was he who directed the process of reorganization there. In 1541, he became professor in Leipzig; here too, he reorganized the university, which became one of the most important academic institutes in Germany under his rectorship. He endeavored to reduce the confessional hostilities, and supported Melanchthon in the composition of the *Confessio Augustana* in 1530; he collaborated in the Religious Peace of → Augsburg (1555) and the resolution of the conflict about Andreas → Osiander in the following year. In 1568, he advised Emperor → Maximilian II about the possibilities of religious unity. Camerarius was one of the leading philologists of his age. He wrote many books in a variety of fields, and also edited and translated classical works; in addition to numerous philological, pedagogical, and historical treatises, his biographical studies deserve special mention. His extensive correspondence is an important contemporary historical source.

■ **Works:** *Symbola et emblemata (naturae),* ed. H. Reinitzer, 2 vols. (Graz, 1986–88).
■ **Literature:** *CEras* 1:247f.—I. Mayerhöfer, *J. C. und seine Eklogendichtung. Philosophische Dissertation* (Vienna, 1970); G. Pfeiffer, *J. C. der Ältere: Fränkische Lebensbilder,* vol. 7 (Neustadt, 1977) 97–108; F. Baron, ed., *J. C. (1500–1574). Beiträge zur Geschichte des Humanismus im Zeitalter der Reformation* (Munich, 1978).

MICHAEL BECHT

■ **Additional Bibliography:** C. A. Staswick, *J. C. and the Republic of Letters in the Age of the Reformation* (Berkeley, 1992); S. Kunkler, *Zwischen Humanismus*

und Reformation. Der Humanist J. C. (Hildesheim, 2000); J. Hamm, "Persönliches Schicksal in bukolischer Verhüllung. Die Eklogen des J. C.," in *Servilia bella.* (Wiesbaden, 2001) 263–77; C. A. Staswick, *J. C. and the Republic of Letters in the Age of the Reformation* (Berkeley, 1992); R. Kössling, ed., *J. C.* (Tübingen, 2003).

Campanus, *Johannes.* Spiritualist, born c. 1500 in Maaseik, died after 1574. He studied in Cologne, and was at Wittenberg in 1527/1528. He came into conflict with Martin Luther in the subsequent period, and had links to the → Baptist movement in 1531/1532, probably in Strasbourg. His pamphlet *Göttlicher und heiliger Schrift Restitution* attacked Luther and Philipp Melanchthon, and displayed ideas close to the Spiritualism of Kaspar von → Schwenckfeld and Sebastian → Franck. Campanus was a proponent of ditheism. His apocalyptic preaching led to social unrest, and he was imprisoned for life by the duke of Kleve in 1553.

■ **Works:** *Carmen Timanni Cameneri cantilenae respondens* (Wittenberg, 1526); *Göttlicher und heiliger Schrift Restitution* (1532).
■ **Literature:** *BiDi* 1:13–35; *BBKL* 1:897; *TRE* 7:601–4.—K. Rembert, *Die Wiedertäufer im Herzogtum Jülich* (Berlin, 1899) 161–342; Ch. MacCormick, *The Restitution of John C.* (Cambridge, Mass., 1959); G. H. Williams, *The Radical Reformation* (Philadelphia, 1962) 272f., 309ff.; H. Weigelt, "Luthers Beziehungen zu Kaspar von Schwenckfeld, J. C., und Michael Stiefel," in *Leben und Werk Martin Luthers von 1526–46,* ed. H. Junghans (Göttingen, 1983) 473–80.

PETER J. A. NISSEN

Campeggi, (1) *Lorenzo.* Lawyer and cardinal (1517), born 1474 in Milan, died July 25, 1539 in Rome. After legal studies in Rome, he became lector in Padua in 1493, and professor in Bologna in 1499. After the death of his wife in 1509, he began an ecclesiastical career. He became auditor to the Rota in 1511 and was sent as papal envoy to Maximilian I, with the aim of detaching him from his league with Louis XII and from the "Conciliabulum" in Pisa. He became bishop of Feltre in 1512 (he resigned this see in favor of his brother Tommaso in 1520). He was at the imperial court once again between 1514 and 1517, endeavoring to promote a league against Turkey and peace with Venice. He was legate in England in 1518-1519 and 1528-1529: negotiations here concerned the Turkish war, peace with France, and consultations about the divorce of → Henry VIII, and he became Protector of England at the curia in 1523. He became a member of the Signatura Iustitiae court in 1520, and composed a memorandum about church reform for → Hadrian VI. He was papal legate to the second imperial parliament in Nuremberg in 1524. Although he could not prevent the proclamation of a national council, he did succeed in establishing an alliance among reform-minded princes in southern Germany. He attended the imperial parliaments in Augsburg and Regensburg in 1530-1532. It proved impossible to achieve unity with the Lutherans, and Campeggi held a violent resolution of the confessional question to be unavoidable. Despite his grave illness, he was appointed legate in 1538 to the council which was to be held in Vicenza. Alongside Hieronymus → Aleander, Campeggi was the most important curial diplomat at the beginning of the 16th century.

■ **Literature:** *DHGE* 11:633–40; *DBI* 17:454–62.—C. Sigonio, *De vita Laurentii Campegii cardinalis* (Bologna, 1581); G. Fantuzzi, *Notizie degli scrittori bolognesi,* vol. 3 (Bologna, 1783) 47–61; *Römische Dokumente zur Geschichte der Ehescheidung Heinrichs VIII. von England,* ed. S. Ehses (Paderborn, 1893); idem, "Berichte vom Augsburger Reichstag," *RQ* 17 (1903) 583–606; 18 (1904) 358–84; E. V. Cardinal, *Cardinal Lorenzo Campeggi* (Boston, 1955); *ARCEG* 1; *Legation L. C.s 1530–31 und Nuntiatur Girolamo Aleandros 1531,* ed. G. Müller (Tübingen, 1963); *Legation L. C.s 1532 und Nuntiatur Girolamo Aleandros 1532,* ed. G. Müller (Tübingen, 1969); idem, *Die römische Kurie und die Reform, 1523–34* (Gütersloh, 1969); Jedin vol. 1³.

(2) *Tommaso,* brother of (1). Born 1483 in Pavia, died January 21, 1564 in Rome. After studying philosophy and law in Padua and Bologna, he was professor of philosophy in Bologna in 1505/1506. He took his doctorate in civil and canon law in 1512, and became internuncio in Milan in 1513, where he assisted his brother Lorenzo in the administration of Parma and Piacenza. He accompanied him to England in 1518-1519. In 1519, he was appointed notary to both Signatura courts, and bishop of Feltre in 1520. He was nuncio in Venice from 1523 to 1526, charged with reconciling the republic with the emperor and persuading Venice to join the league against the Turks. He was ordained priest and bishop in 1526, and pursued the work of church reform in the diocese of Feltre between 1528 and 1530. He accompanied Lorenzo to the imperial parliaments in Germany from 1530 to 1532; in 1531, he encouraged the composition of anti-Protestant treatises and pamphlets about the reform of the curia. He was regent of the Apostolic Chancellery from 1540 to 1550. He attended the Religious Dialogue of → Worms in 1540 as nuncio, accompanying Giovanni → Morone; he was present at the imperial parliament in Regensburg in 1541; he attended the Council of Trent in 1542-1543, 1545-1548, and 1551-1552. He drew up curial memoranda for → Paul IV and → Pius IV. As a conservative representative of the curial praxis and a moderate reformer, Campeggi influenced the course of the council.

■ **Works:** *De coelibatu sacerdotum* (Venice, 1554); *De auctoritate et potestate Romani Pontificis et alia opuscola* (Venice, 1555); *De auctoritate sacrorum conciliorum* (Venice, 1561); *CT* 4, 12 und 13/1.

■ **Literature:** *DBI* 17:472ff.—E. Tolomei, "La nunziatura di Venezia nel pontificato di Clemente VII.," *Rivista storica italiano* 9 (1892) 577–628; *Gesandtschaft C.s, Nuntiaturen Morones und Poggios 1540–41,* ed. L. Cardauns (Gotha, 1910); *Festgabe J. Lortz,* ed. E. Iserloh and P. Manns, 2 vols. (Baden-Baden, 1957) 405–17; H. Jedin, *T. C. Tridentinische Reform und Kuriale Tradition* (Münster, 1958); G. Alberigo, *I vescovi italiani al Concilio di Trento* (Florence, 1959) 169–73; E. Nasalli Rocca, "Prime esperienze di T. C. vescovo di Feltre," *Atti e memorie della Deputazione di storia patria di Romagna Neue Serie* 15–16 (1963–65).

KLAUS JAITNER

■ **Additional Bibliography:** U. Mazzone, "I libri di T. e Marco C.," *CrS* 10 (1989) 509–52.

Candidus (Blanckart), *Alexander.* Carmelite (c. 1520), theologian; born in Ghent, died December 31, 1555 in Cologne. He studied in Cologne and was lector in Geldern, Trier, and Utrecht. He became prior in Utrecht in 1541, and master of students in Cologne in 1545. He took his doctorate in theology at Cologne in 1550 and became university professor; he became dean of the theological faculty in 1554. He was an active opponent of the Reformation. He took part in the Religious Dialogue of → Regensburg in 1546, and in the Council of Trent in 1551. He translated the Vulgate into Dutch (Cologne, 1547) and wrote the *Judicium Johannis Calvini de Sanctorum reliquiis* (Cologne, 1551).

■ **Literature:** *Bibliotheca Carmelitana,* ed. C. de Villiers a S. Stephano, vol. 1 (Orléans, 1752) 27f.—G. a Virgine

Carmeli, "Die Karmeliten auf dem Konzil von Trient," *Ephemerides Carmeliticae* 4 (1950) 321f.; F.-B. Lickteig, *The German Carmelites at the Medieval Universities* (Rome, 1981) 268ff.; E. Meuthen, *Die alte Universität (Kölner Universitätsgeschichte 1)* (Cologne and Vienna, 1988) 272f.

KLEMENS RACZEK

Canisius, *Peter.* Jesuit (1543), saint (feast December 21), and doctor of the church; born May 8, 1521 in Nijmegen, died December 21, 1597 in Fribourg. He began his studies in Cologne in 1535, becoming master of arts in 1540 and bachelor in biblical studies in 1545. Here, he had links to the Charterhouse in Cologne and to the circle around Maria von Oisterwijk. After making the "Spiritual Exercises" with Petrus → Faber in Mainz in April, 1543, he entered the Society of Jesus on May 8, using his inheritance from his father to finance the Jesuit house which was founded in Cologne the following year. Prompted by the clergy and the university of Cologne, he appealed in 1545 to → Charles V against the Protestant archbishop Hermann von → Wied. He was ordained priest in 1546, and took part in the session of the Council of Trent that met in Bologna in 1547, as theologian to Cardinal Otto Truchsess von → Waldburg. → Ignatius Loyola summoned him to Rome and sent him as tutor to Messina. In 1549, he was the eighth Jesuit to make solemn profession; in the same year, he took his doctorate in theology at Bologna. He was professor of theology and preacher in Ingolstadt from 1549 to 1552, and in Vienna from 1552 to 1556; he was also administrator of the diocese of Vienna in 1554-1555. In 1556, he founded the Jesuit college in Prague, and was first Jesuit provincial of southern Germany (1556-1569). He took part in the imperial parliament in Regensburg and the Religious Dialogue in → Worms in 1556-1557. In 1558, he attended the general congregation of the Society of Jesus in Rome, and then accompanied the papal nuncio Camillo Mentuato to Poland, where he attended the parliament of Petrikau. He attended the imperial parliament in Augsburg in 1559. He was cathedral preacher in Augsburg from 1559 to 1566. He attended the Council of Trent briefly in 1562, and then acted as counselor to Emperor → Ferdinand in Innsbruck, helping to resolve the differences between the emperor and the conciliar legate Giovanni → Morone. In 1565, he was again in Rome for a general congregation of the Jesuits.

In the following period, he traveled extensively through western and northern Germany, transmitting the decrees of Trent to the Catholic princes and bishops and promoting the acceptance of the council. From 1580 until his death, he worked to consolidate a Jesuit college in Fribourg. His tomb is in St. Michael's church.

His activity as counselor in matters of church politics and his correspondence with leading persons of his age show that Canisius played a central role in the reconstruction of the Catholic Church in Germany. His writings made a particularly important contribution, especially his catechisms. His first works were editions of patristic texts (works of Cyril of Alexandria and Leo the Great, Cologne, 1546; letters of Jerome, Dillingen, 1562). He published his *Summa doctrinae christianae,* later known as the *Catechismus maior,* in Vienna in 1555; this was revised in 1566, in the light of the Tridentine decrees. His *Catechismus minimus* was published in Ingolstadt in 1556, and the *Catechismus minor* in Cologne in 1558; this last work was translated into many languages during Canisius's lifetime, and went through more than 200 editions in Germany and Austria. In 1568, → Pius V commissioned Canisius to refute the → "Magdeburg Centuries" of Matthias → Flacius Illyricus; under the general heading *De corruptelis verbi Dei,* he published two volumes, on John the Baptist (Dillingen, 1571) and on Mary (Ingolstadt, 1577), but did not complete the third volume, on Peter. He also wrote explanations of scripture and legends about the saints.

Canisius's enduring significance is due to his foundation of numerous colleges, which made a decisive contribution to the renewal of the church, and to his catechisms. His ecclesiology, with its christological orientation, and his loyalty to his ecclesiastical superiors generated a new awareness of what it meant to belong to the church.

■ **Works:** Critical editions: *Beati Petri Canisii epistulae et acta,* ed. O. Braunsberger, 8 vols. (Freiburg, 1896–1923); *Sancti Petri Canisii Doctoris Ecclesiae Catechismi latini et germanici,* ed. F. Streicher, 2 vols. (Rome and Munich, 1933–36); *Meditationes seu Notae in Evangelicas Lectiones,* ed. F. Streicher, 3 vols. (Freiburg, 1939–55; Munich, 1961).—Catalogue: C. Sommervogel, *Bibliothèque de Compagnie de Jésus* (Louvain, ³1960) vol. 2, 617–88; vol. 8, 1974–83; vol. 12, 988; F. Streicher, *Catechismi* (see above) 1, 29*–37*.—Selected works (German): *Briefe,* ed. B. Schneider (Salzburg, 1959); *Briefe,* ed. S. Seifert (Leipzig, 1983).

■ **Literature:** *BDG* 1:106–11, 5:44f.; 7:41f.; L. Polgár,

Bibliographie sur l'histoire de la Compagnie de Jésus 1901–80, vol. 3/1 (Rome, 1990) 425–53.—*TRE* 7:611–14.—J. Brodrick, *Saint P. C.* (London, 1935); *Bavaria Sacra*, vol. 1 (Regensburg, 1970) 327–48; J. Krasenbrink, *Die Congregatio Germanica und die katholische Reform in Deutschland nach dem Tridentinum* (Münster, 1972); E. M. Buxbaum, *P. C. und die kirchliche Erneuerung des Herzogtums Bayern 1549–56* (Rome, 1973); J. Bruhin, ed., *P. Kanisius* (Fribourg, 1980); K. Diez, *Christus und seine Kirche. Zum Kirchenverständnis des P. C.* (Paderborn, 1987); Bayrisches Hauptstaatsarchiv, ed., *Die Jesuiten in Bayern 1549–1773* (Weissenhorn, 1991); M. Weitlauff, "Die Anfänge der Gesellschaft Jesu in Süddeutschland," *Jahrbuch des Historischen Vereins Dillingen* 94 (1992) 15–66.

ENGELBERT MAXIMILIAN BUXBAUM

■ **Additional Bibliography:** J. Oswald, ed., *P. C. Reformer der Kirche. Festschrift zum 400. Todestag des zweiten Apostels Deutschlands* (Augsburg, [2]1997); J. Brodrick, *Saint P. C.* (Chicago, 1998); R. Berndt, ed., *P. C. SJ. Humanist und Europäer* (Berlin, 2000) (includes a bibliography); T. M. Lucas, "P. C.: Jesuit Urban Strategist," *P. C. SJ*, ed. R. Berndt (Berlin, 2000) 275–91.

Cano, *Melchior.* Dominican (1523), born c. 1509 in Tarancón or Pastraña, died September 30, 1560 in Toledo. He studied in Salamanca from 1527 to 1531, where his professor, Francisco de → Vitoria, put him in touch with the contemporary renaissance of interest in France in Thomas Aquinas; he pursued his studies at his Order's academy in Valladolid. He was a celebrated teacher at Valladolid from 1533 to 1541, professor of theology at the university of Alcalá from 1543 to 1546, and succeeded Vitoria as professor of theology in Salamanca in 1546. → Charles V appointed him theologian to the Council of Trent, and he played an important part in the discussions of the sacrament of penance, the Eucharist and the sacrifice of the Mass in 1551/1552. → Julius III appointed him bishop of the Canary Isles, at the emperor's suggestion, in 1552, but he renounced the diocese in 1554, without ever having taken up office as bishop. In 1554, he became rector of San Gregorio college in Valladolid, and prior of San Esteban in Salamanca in 1557. He was elected provincial of his Order in 1557, but despite the emperor's support, this did not receive papal confirmation; he was elected again in 1559, but this was confirmed only in 1560 (after the death of → Paul IV).

Cano is considered the outstanding representative of the school of Salamanca. His chef d'oeuvre was the *De locis theologicis* (printed after his death, in 1563, without books 13 and 14; reprinted more than thirty times, most recently by T.M. Cucchi in 1890, with the *Relectiones;* the university of Navarra is preparing a new edition). This work opened up new paths in theological epistemology and methodology. Cano was a passionate contributor to the political, ecclesiastical, and theological debates of his age. He was counselor to Charles V and → Philip II; in 1556, he told the emperor that he was allowed to wage war on the pope, considered in the latter's capacity as temporal sovereign. He also fought against the Jesuits and against the privileges of the cathedral chapters. For twenty-five years, he was locked in a conflict with his confrère and rival, Bartolomé → Carranza, and he did his utmost to ensure that Carranza was condemned by the Inquisition.

Apart from his main work, the *Relectio de poenitentia* and *Relectio de sacramentis* have both been printed (first of many editions, 1550), while his commentaries on the *Sentences* of Peter Lombard and on the *Summa theologiae* of Thomas Aquinas exist only in manuscript form. Parts of the latter work have been printed: on I 1.1-10: C. Pozo, *Fuentes para la historia del método teológico en la Escuela de Salamanca*, I (Granada, 1962); on I 1.8: J. Belda-Plans, *Los lugares teológicos de Melchor Cano en los comentarios a la Suma* (Pamplona, 1982); on II-II 1.1-5: F. Casado, "En torno a la génesis del De locis theologicis de Melchor Cano," *Revista española de teología* 32 (1972) 55-81.

The main (though not always reliable) source for Cano's biography and activities is F. Caballero, *Vida de illmo Melchor Cano* (1871), which is based on A. Pellicer and on studies of Dominican history by Quétif-Echard and A. Touron. According to Lang, Beltrán de Heredia offers the best corrections and amplifications of Caballero's book; the state of research is documented (with source texts) by Sanz y Sanz (1959).

■ **Literature:** *BBKL* 1:914f.—A. Lang, *Die loci theologici des M. C. und die Methode des dogmatischen Beweises* (Munich, 1925); V. Beltrán de Heredia, *Los manuscritos del Maestro Fray Francisco de Vitoria* (Madrid, 1928); idem, "Los manuscritos de los teólogos de la Escuela Salmantina," *Ciencia tomista* 42 (1930) 327–49; idem, "M. C. en la Universidad de Salamanca," *Ciencia tomista* 48 (1933) 178–208; J. Sanz y Sanz, *M. C. Cuestiones fundamentales de crítica histórica sobre su vida y sus escritos* (Madrid, 1959); M. Seckler, *Die ekklesiologische Bedeutung des Systems der loci theologici* (Freiburg, 1988)

79–104; B. Körner, *M. C., De locis theologicis. Ein Beitrag zur theologischen Erkenntnislehre* (Graz, 1994).

BERNHARD KÖRNER

■ **Additional Bibliography:** H. J. Sander, "Das Aussen des Glaubens—eine Autorität der Theologie. Das Differenzprinzip in den Loci theologici des M. C.," in *Das Volk Gottes—ein Ort der Befreiung. Festschrift E. Klinger* (Würzburg, 1998) 240–58; B. Körner, "Die Geschichte als 'locus theologicus' bei M. C.," *Rivista teologica di Lugano* 5 (2000) 257–69.

Capito (Köpfel), *Wolfgang.* Humanist and Reformer, born probably 1481 in Hagenau, died November 3, 1541 in Strasbourg. He studied in Ingolstadt, Heidelberg, and Freiburg, where he took his doctorate in theology in 1515. He was preacher at the collegiate church in Bruchsal from 1512 to 1515, at the cathedral in Basle from 1515 to 1520, and at the cathedral in Mainz in 1520. During part of his period in Basle, he was a close friend of → Erasmus of Rotterdam. After he had given decisive support to Martin Luther's cause both in Basle and as counselor of Archbishop Albrecht of Mainz, he made the definitive transition to the Reformation in 1523, as provost of the collegiate church of St. Thomas in Strasbourg. He became one of the most prominent Reformers in southern Germany. As theologian and churchman, he left his imprint (along with Martin → Bucer) on Protestantism in Strasbourg, but he was also active in the empire (*Confessio Tetrapolitana,* 1530 [→ Confessional documents]; religious dialogues, 1540/1541) and in Switzerland (synod of Berne, 1532). His most important writings include a Hebrew grammar and commentaries on books of the Old Testament.

■ **Works:** *Correspondance de W. C.,* ed. O. Millet (Strasbourg, 1982).
■ **Literature:** *TRE* 7:636–40.—B. Stierle, *C. als Humanist* (Gütersloh, 1974); J. K. Kittelson, *W. C., from Humanist to Reformer* (Leiden, 1975); H. Scheible, *Melanchthons Pforzheimer Schulzeit: Pforzheim in der frühen Neuzeit,* ed. H.-P. Becht (Sigmaringen, 1989) 13ff.; B. Moeller, *Die Reformation und das Mittelalter* (Göttingen, 1991) 151–60, 321–27; Th. Kaufmann, *Die Abendmahlstheologie der Straßburger Reformatoren bis 1528* (Tübingen, 1992).

BERND MOELLER

■ **Additional Bibliography:** *RGG*⁴ 2:59f.—Th. Kaufmann, "C. als heimlicher Propagandist der frühen Wittenberger Theologie," *ZKG* 103 (1992) 81–86.

Caracciolo, *Galeazzo.* Born 1517 in Naples, died May 7, 1586 in Geneva; nephew of → Paul IV. The encounter with Petrus → Vermigli led him at an early age to adopt Protestant doctrine. He took part in the religious dialogue about papal primacy at the imperial parliament in Regensburg in 1542, the year in which the Roman Inquisition was set up. Its activities led him to emigrate, initially to Augsburg; then, after becoming acquainted with John Calvin, he founded an Italian Protestant church in Geneva, serving as its deacon. He divorced his Catholic wife, Donna Vittoria Carafa, the heiress to the duchy of Nocera, and married the wealthy Anne de Framéry from Rouen, his fellow-refugee in Geneva.

■ **Literature:** *DBI* 19:363–66; *BBKL* 1:924f.; *RGG*⁴ 2:62.

MICHAEL F. FELDKAMP

Carafa, *Carlo.* Nephew of → Paul IV, born 1519 (1517?), died March 5, 1561. He began a military career, but his uncle created him cardinal in 1555 and gave him absolution from all his past crimes (which included murder). He exploited his position as "cardinal nephew" in an outrageous manner, enriching himself. He encouraged Paul IV in his anti-Habsburg policy. When the pope became aware of Carlo's scandalous way of life, he was dismissed from his posts and exiled along with the other nephews of the pope. After a criminal trial, he was condemned to death and executed.

■ **Literature:** *DHGE* 11:986ff.; *DBI* 19:497–509.—G. Duruy, *Le cardinal C. C.* (Paris, 1882); R. Ancel, "La question de Sienne et la politique du cardinal C. C. (1536–57)," *Revue bénédictine* 22 (1905) 15–49, 206–31, 398–428; idem, "La disgrâce et le procès C. (1559–67)," *Revue bénédictine* 22 (1905) 525–35; 24 (1907) 224–53; 479–509; 25 (1908) 194–224; 26 (1909) 52–80; 189–220, 301–24; R. Cantagalli, *La guerra di Siena (1552–59)* (Siena, 1962); H. Lutz, *Christianitas afflicta. Europa, das Reich und die päpstliche Politik im Niedergang der Hegemonie Kaiser Karls V. (1552–56).* (Göttingen, 1964).

KLAUS GANZER

■ **Additional Bibliography:** D. Chiomenti Vassalli, *Paolo IV e il processo C.* (Milan, 1993).

Carlowitz (Karlowitz), *Christoph von.* Saxon state counselor, born December 13, 1507 in Hermsdorf, died January 8, 1578 in Rothenhaus (Bohemia). His most important place of study was

Leipzig, from 1520. He was influenced by → Erasmus of Rotterdam and took the "Erasmian" position in favor of religious reconciliation. He was counselor to Duke → George of Saxony and was an influential diplomat in the service of Duke (later Elector) → Moritz of Saxony, who sent him on numerous missions; he represented his sovereign in several imperial parliaments. He was involved in the treaty of Regensburg (1546), which allied Moritz with → Charles V and was one factor which made the Schmalkaldic war possible (→ Schmalkald, League). His participation in the negotiations about the Saxon Interim in 1549 led the opponents of the Interim to hate him. After 1555, Carlowitz served the Habsburgs.

■ **Literature:** *NDB* 3:145f.; *LThK*² 2:951; *CEras* 1:269f.—J. Pflug, *Correspondance,* ed. J. V. Pollet, 5 vols. (Leiden, 1969–82); E. Brandenburg, J. Herrmann, and G. Wartenberg, eds., *Politische Korrespondenz des Herzogs und Kurfürsten Moritz von Sachsen,* 4 vols. (Leipzig, 1900–4; Berlin, 1982–92); G. Wartenberg, *Landesherrschaft und Reformation. Moritz von Sachsen und die albertinische Kirchenpolitik* (Weimar, 1988).

HERIBERT SMOLINSKY

Carnesecchi, *Pietro.* Humanist, born December 24, 1508 in Florence, died October 1, 1566 in Rome. Initially, he pursued a successful career in the service of the popes; he was an apostolic protonotary and received many benefices. He was profoundly impressed by the preaching of Bernardino → Ochino, and Juan de → Valdés left a decisive mark upon him in Naples. He became a resolute defender of justification by faith, and was one of the "spiritual" circle around Cardinal Reginald → Pole in Viterbo. He made a thorough study of the works of Philipp Melanchthon and Jean Calvin, and accepted Reformation ideas. Proceedings before the Inquisition led to his acquittal in 1546 and 1561. → Pius V ordered the case to be reopened. After repeated tortures, Carnesecchi professed his allegiance to Reformed doctrines. He was condemned and executed on the Campo de' Fiori in Rome.

■ **Literature:** *DBI* 20:466–76.—"Estratto del processo di P. C.," ed. G. Manzoni, *Miscellanea di storia italiana* 10 (1870) 187–573; O. Ortolani, *Per la storia della vita religiosa italiana nel Cinquecento. P. C.* (Florence, 1963); D. Fenlon, *Heresy and Obedience in Tridentine Italy. Cardinal Pole and the Counter Reformation* (Cambridge, 1972) 93–99; M. Firpo, *Tra Alumbrados e "Spirituali"*

(Florence, 1990) 24–43; idem, *Inquisizione Romana e Controriforma* (Bologna, 1992) 359–82.

KLAUS GANZER

■ **Additional Bibliography:** *I Processi inquisitoriali di P. C. (1557–67),* ed. M. Firpo, *Editio critica,* vol. 1ff. (Vatican City, 1998ff.).

Carranza, *Bartolomé.* Dominican (1520) theologian, born 1503 in Miranda de Arga (Navarre), died May 2, 1576 in Rome. He studied in Alcalá, Salamanca, and Valladolid, and taught in the convent of San Gregorio de Artes in Valladolid in 1530; he began to teach theology in 1533. In 1539, he became master of theology in Rome. He took part in the Council of Trent as an imperial theologian from 1545 to 1547 and from 1551 to 1552. He accompanied → Philip II to England in 1553 and to Flanders in 1557. In 1558, he was appointed archbishop of Toledo. As a consequence of the anti-Protestant atmosphere which followed the show-trials of Seville and Valladolid (1558), the general inquisitor, Fernando de Valdés, had Carranza arrested in 1559; after Melchior → Cano and others had attacked his work *Comentarios del Catechismo christiano* (Antwerp, 1558; ed. J. I. Tellechea Idígoras, 2 vols., Madrid, 1972) and had rejected his spiritual theology with its vocabulary which deviated from scholasticism. The trial was transferred from Spain to Rome in 1567. Shortly before his death, Carranza was condemned by Gregory XIII and was obliged to renounce sixteen propositions (April 14, 1576).

■ **Works:** *Summa conciliorum, Quatuor controversiae (De auctoritate ecclesiae, scripturae, concilii et papae)* (Venice, 1546); *De necessaria residentia episcoporum* (Venice, 1547).

■ **Literature:** *DHEE* 1:358–61.—H. Jedin, "Die C.-Tragödie in neuer Beleuchtung," in *Die Einheit der Kirche.* Festschrift P. Meinhold (Wiesbaden, 1977) 255–70; J. I. Tellechea Idígoras, *B. C. Mis treinta años de investigación* (Salamanca, 1984); G. Díaz Díaz, *Hombres y Documentos de la Filosofía Española,* vol. 2 (Madrid, 1983) 160–67; K. Reinhardt, *Bibelkommentare spanischer Autoren,* vol. 1 (Madrid, 1990) 96ff.

FERNANDO DOMÍNGUEZ

■ **Additional Bibliography:** J. I. Tellechea Idígoras, *El proceso romano del arzobispo C.* (Rome, 1994); I. Jerico Bermejo, "Sobre la possibilidad de juzgar al Papa. En los comentários de B. C. sobre la justicia," *Studium* 38 (1998) 325–39.

Cassander (Kadzander, van Cadsant), *Georg.* Humanist Catholic theologian, born August 28, 1513 (1515?) in Pitthem near Bruges, died February 3, 1566 in Cologne. He studied arts in Louvain, matriculating in Cologne in 1544 and in Heidelberg in 1546. He published monographs on church history (in defense of infant baptism and of the chalice for the laity) and studies which aimed at restoring church unity. His *De officio pii ac publicae tranquillitatis vere amantis viri in hoc religionis dissidio* (Basle, 1561), which was presented at the Religious Dialogue of → Poissy in 1561 by François Bauduin, met with both agreement (Julius → Pflug, Georg → Witzel) and disapproval (Jean Calvin, Wilhelm → Lindanus). In his *Traditionum Veteris Ecclesiae et SS. Patrum defensio* (1564), Cassander defended the ancient church against Calvin's attacks, and he also used patristic ideas as the basis of his evaluation of the → Confessio Augustana, which he undertook at the request of → Ferdinand I (*De articulis religionis inter catholicos et protestantes controversis consultatio*, 1564/1565, printed at Cologne, 1577). This patristic perspective helps to explain the ecumenical character of these works. Cassander's mediatory attitude, as seen for example in the dialogue with the Baptists in Duisburg, was appreciated by the emperor and by Duke William V of Jülich-Kleve-Berg, and his ideas continued to be influential, especially among Protestant theologians such as Georg Calixt.

■ **Works:** *Opera omnia* (Paris, 1616); Klaiber nos. 598–616; *VD 16* vol. 4.
■ **Literature:** *BBKL* 1:949f.—R. Stauffer, *Autour du Colloque de Poissy: Actes du Colloque L'Amiral de Coligny et son temps* (Paris, 1974) 135–71; A. Stegmann, *G. C., victime des orthodoxies: Aspects du libertinisme au XVIᵉ siècle* (Paris, 1974) 199–214; M. Erbe, "François Bauduin und G. C. Dokumente einer Humanistenfreundschaft," *Bibliothèque d'humanisme et renaissance* 40 (1978) 537–60; G. H. M. Posthumus Meyjes, "Charles Perrot (1541–1608). His Opinion on a Writing of G. C.," in *Humanism and reform . . . Festschrift J. K. Cameron* (Oxford, 1991) 221–36 (continued in: *Nederlands archief voor kerkgeschiedenis* 72 [1992] 72–91).

BARBARA HENZE

■ **Additional Bibliography:** *RGG*⁴ 2:78f.

Castellio, *Sebastian* (S. Chât[e]illon; pseudonym: Martinus Bellius). Philologist and translator of the Bible, born in 1515 in St-Martin-du-Fresne (department of Ain), died December 29, 1563 in Basle. He met Jean Calvin in Strasbourg, and was summoned to Geneva by Calvin in 1541 to assume the position of rector of the school. Disagreements about criticism of the canon and about the exegesis of the Song of Songs led to his departure from Geneva; he moved to Basle in 1545 and became professor of Greek in that city in 1553. Further difficulties arose because of controversies with Calvin and Theodor → Beza about hermeneutical questions, the Trinity, and predestination, as well as his criticism of the burning of Michael → Servet. Castellio's writings about tolerance had a long-lasting effect.

■ **Principal Works:** *Biblia sacra latina* (Basle, 1551, often reprinted); *La Bible nouvellement translatée avec annotations.* (Basle, 1555); *De haereticis, an sint persequendi* (1554), ed. S. van der Woude (Geneva, 1954); *De l'impunité des hérétiques. De haereticis non puniendis,* ed. B. Becker and M. F. Valkhoff (Geneva, 1971); *Conseil à la France désolée* (1562), ed. M. F. Valkhoff (Geneva, 1967); *De arte dubitandi,* ed. E. Feist Hirsch (Leiden, 1981).
■ **Literature:** *TRE* 7:663ff.—H. R. Guggisberg: *S. C. im Urteil seiner Nachwelt vom Späthumanismus bis zur Aufklärung* (Basle and Stuttgart, 1956); G. Gallicet Calvetti, *S. C., il reformato umanista contro il riformatore Calvino . . . Dialoghi IV postumi di C.* (Milan, 1989); G. Bedouelle, *Les temps des réformes et la Bible* (Paris, 1989); A. Berchtold, *Bâle et l'Europe,* vol. 2 (Lausanne, 1990) 547–77; H. R. Guggisberg, "C. auf dem Index (1551–96)," *ARG* 83 (1992) 112–29.

ROBERT ROTH

■ **Additional Bibliography:** C. Gilly, "Die Zensur von C.s 'Dialogi quatuor' durch die Basler Theologen (1578)," in *Querdenken.* Festschrift H. R. Guggisberg (Mannheim, 1996) 169–92; idem, "S. C. und der politische Widerstand gegen Philipp II. von Spanien," *Nederlands archief voor kerkgeschiedenis* 77 (1997) 23–40; G. T. Park, "Le problème de la liberté de conscience chez Calvin et C.," *Chongshin Theological Journal* 5 (2000) 202–32; J. Roubaud, "'Traduire pour les »idiots«'. Sébastien Châteillon et la Bible," *Recherches de science religieuse* 89 (2001) 353–76.

Castro, *Alfonso de.* Franciscan (c. 1510) theologian and preacher, born 1495 in Zamora, died February 2, 1588 in Brussels. He studied in Salamanca and Alcalá, and became instructor in theology in the monastery in Salamanca in 1512. In 1530, he accompanied → Charles V to his coronation as emperor in Bologna. He was active as preacher in the Netherlands, Germany, and

France between 1532 and 1535. He took part in the Council of Trent as theologian to Cardinal Pedro Pacheco (1545-1547) and subsequently to the emperor (1551-1552). In 1553, he was appointed court chaplain to prince → Philip II, whom he accompanied to England in 1554. Thereafter, he returned to Flanders, where he died shortly after being appointed bishop of Santiago.

■ **Works:** *Adversus omnes haereses* (Paris, 1534, often reprinted); *De iusta haereticorum punitione* (Salamanca, 1547); *De potestate legis poenalis* (Salamanca, 1550).
■ **Literature:** *DHEE* 1:381f.—G. Díaz Díaz, *Hombres y Documentos de la Filosofía Española,* vol. 2 (Madrid, 1983) 255–61; K. Reinhardt, *Bibelkommentare spanischer Autoren,* vol. 1 (Madrid, 1990) 107f.

FERNANDO DOMÍNGUEZ

Catechismus Romanus (CR, Roman Catechism). This has been the customary abbreviation designating the catechism for parish priests which was published in Rome in 1566 under the title *Catechismus ex decreto Concilii Tridentini ad parochos Pii V Pont. Max. iussu editus* ("catechism according to the decree of the Council of Trent, for the use of parish priests, published on the orders of Pope Pius V"). The adjective "Roman" has been common since the edition at Dillingen in 1567.

The origins of CR go back to the first session of the Council of Trent (1545-1548), but its composition began only in the third session (1562-1563), so that the last session of the council asked the pope to finish the task (Sessio XXV *de reformatione*), placing in his hands the material which had been collected up to that point. In January, 1564, → Pius IV entrusted an editorial commission under the leadership of Charles → Borromeo with the task of completing the work which Trent had begun; the members of this commission were Muzio → Calini, Leonardo de Marinis, Egidio → Foscarari, and Francisco Foreiro, all of whom had taken part in the council. This editorial work, involving two revisions, lasted from February, 1564 to December, 1565, and culminated in the *textus emendatus.* → Pius V, who succeeded Pius IV in January, 1566, appointed a new revising commission under Guglielmo → Sirleto, and the third and fourth revisions followed between February and September of that year, until the *textus definitivus* emerged, which formed the manuscript basis of the *editio princeps.* The original manuscripts of the two commissions (Codex Vati-

canus latinus 4994, *pars* I *et* II), which have recently been rediscovered, as well as the six reports by Sirleto and Marius Victorius on the proposals of the commission, allow an exact reconstruction of the various phases of the genesis of the text between 1564 and 1566.

The CR presents the Catholic teaching on faith and morals in the context of the four catechetical "main points": faith, with the creed (13 chapters); sacraments (8 chapters); God's commandments, with the decalogue (10 chapters); and prayer, with the Our Father (17 chapters); the catechism teaches these in 1,014 numbered doctrinal paragraphs. After the first bilingual edition (Bordeaux, 1578), many subsequent editions included an appendix ("Praxis") in which the parochial clergy were helped to prepare their catechetical sermons by means of a distribution of the contents of CR among all the Sundays of the year.

■ *LThK*³ 2:976f. (unabridged version).
■ **Sources:** P. Rodríguez et al., ed., *CR seu catechismus ex decreto . . .* (Vatican City, 1989).
■ **Literature:** *TRE* 7:665–68; *EKL*³ 1:638f.—G.-J. Bellinger, *Der CR und die Reformation* (Paderborn, 1970); R. Donghi, *"Credo la Santa Chiesa cattolica." Dibattiti pretridentini e tridentini sulla Chiesa e formulazione dell'articulo nel catechismo romano* (Rome, 1980); P. Rodríguez and R. Lanzetti, *El Catecismo Romano. Fuentes e historia del texto y de la redacción* (Pamplona, 1982); G.-J. Bellinger, *Bibliographie des CR 1566–1978* (Baden-Baden, 1983); P. Rodríguez and R. Lanzetti, *El manuscrito original del Catecismo Romano* (Pamplona, 1985); R. I. Bradley, *The Roman Catechism in the Catechetical Tradition of the Church* (Lanham, Md., 1990); G.-J. Bellinger, "Der CR, seine Geschichte und bleibende Bedeutung für Theologie und Kirche," in *Katechismus der Welt—Weltkatechismus,* ed. M. Buschkühl (Eichstätt, 1993) 41–64 132–43.

GERHARD J. BELLINGER

■ **Additional Bibliography:** R. I. Bradley, *The Roman Catechism in the Catechetical Tradition of the Church* (Lanham, 1990); G. J. Bellinger, "Der CR des Trienter Konzils," *Rottenburger Jahrbuch für Kirchengeschichte* 16 (1997) 23–40.

Celibacy. Denial of the sacrament of Orders led to a questioning of celibacy, which was the subject of harsh controversies in the Reformation period. The imperial parliament at Nuremberg (1522-1523) refused to take action against the married clergy; a different position was taken by some of the Catholic Estates in Regensburg in 1524 and by

the Imperial Resolution of Augsburg in 1530. →
Ferdinand I and other princes made an appeal in
favor of celibacy during the Council of Trent, and
endeavored in vain to secure exceptions to canon
law for their own domains after the council
decided to retain clerical celibacy, affirming that
those in major orders cannot marry (DH 1809).
No explicit decision was taken on the question
whether clerical celibacy is based on an ecclesiastical law or on a vow, but when the text mentions
the "law or vow" which obligates priests or religious to celibacy, this indicates that priestly
celibacy is based on church law. In the case of
minor orders, Trent tolerated the older custom of
admitting married men to these ministries (Session XXIII c. 6 and 17).

■ *LThK*[2] 10:1395–98 (unabridged version).
■ **Literature:** S. Burghartz, "Das starke Geschlecht und
das schwache Fleisch. Erasmus und Zwingli zur
Priesterehe," in *Querdenken*. Festschrift H. R. Guggisberg (Mannheim, 1996) 89–106; W. Keller, "Zölibat
und Priesterehe als reformatorische Anliegen auf dem
Reichstag zu Augsburg 1530," *Würzburger Diözesangeschichtsblätter* 58 (1996) 153–69; R. Mau, "Die
leidende und bittende Kirche. Stationen des Bekennens
im Konflikt um die Priesterehe (CA, Apologie und CA
variata)," in *Wege zum Einverständnis*. Festschrift Ch.
Demke (Leipzig, 1997) 190–202; S. E. Buckwalter, *Die
Priesterehe in Flugschriften der frühen Reformation*
(Gütersloh, 1998); H. L. Parish, *Clerical Marriage and
the English Reformation* (Aldershot, 2000).

KLAUS MÖRSDORF

Chalice for laity. In his early period, Martin
Luther declared that the Hussites were unjustified
in separating from the church because of the lay
chalice, but later he himself demanded communion "under both kinds" (*sub utraque specie*) as
the form which was in keeping with scripture.
Since this demand was employed by the Protestants as a weapon against the old church, Catholic
princes (e.g., in Bavaria and the house of Habsburg) and theologians (e.g., Johannes → Cochlaeus, Julius → Pflug, and Georg → Witzel) saw
the concession of the lay chalice as a way to stop
(at least to some extent) people from leaving the
old church. In a report which he presented to the
pope, Cardinal Thomas → Cajetan de Vio supported this concession. Emperor → Charles V
granted the lay chalice to the German Protestants
in the → Augsburg Interim of 1548, until the
council should decide this question; Session XXII

of Trent referred this decision to the pope on September 17, 1562, and → Pius IV yielded to the
insistence of Emperor → Ferdinand I and Duke
→ Albrecht V of Bavaria, granting the lay chalice
in an indult of April 16, 1564 to Germany, Austria,
Bohemia (Prague), and Hungary (Esztergom).
There was little enthusiasm for the application of
this indult, which met with concerted opposition
in Bavaria, Austria, and Tyrol: the division into
separate confessions had already gone too far.
Albrecht abolished the lay chalice in Bavaria in
1571, and Austria followed this example in 1584.
In the same year, → Gregory XIII revoked the
indult.

■ *LThK*[3] 6:611f. (unabridged version).
■ **Literature:** A. Knöpfler, *Die Kelchbewegung in Bayern
unter Herzog Albrecht V* (Munich, 1891); G. Constant,
*Concession à l'Allemagne de la communion sous les deux
espèces*, 2 vols. (Paris, 1923); H. Lutz, "Bayern und der
Laienkelch," *QFIAB* 34 (1954) 203–35; A. Franzen, *Die
Kelchbewegung am Niederrhein im 16.Jh.* (Münster,
1955); R. Damerau, *Der Laienkelch* (Giessen, 1964); J.
Sopta, *Die Teilnehmer aus den kroatischen Diözesen an
der 3. Tagungsperiode des Tridentinums und die Frage des
Laienkelch* (Freiburg, 1987).

KLAUS GANZER

■ **Additional Bibliography:** H. Krmíčková, *Studie a
texty k počátkům kalicha v Čechách* (Brünn, 1997); K.
Schatz, "Zwischen Rombindung und landesherrlichem
Interesse," in *Petrus Canisius SJ*, ed. H. Berndt (Berlin,
2000) 385–97.

Charles V. Emperor (1519-1556; Charles I as king
of Spain), born February 2, 1500 in Ghent, the son
of Philip the Fair of Burgundy and Joanna the
Mad of Spain, grandson of Emperor Maximilian I
and the Catholic sovereigns Isabella of Castile and
Ferdinand II of Aragon, died September 21, 1558
in the monastery of San Yuste (Extremadura). He
was educated in the Netherlands as heir to an
immense array of territories: Burgundy with the
Netherlands, Austria, Castile with its colonies in
America, and Aragon with Naples and Sicily.

His mentor, William of Croy (Chièvres), who
leaned towards France, was able to pave the way
for Charles to become ruler of Spain in 1516, but
Maximilian's strategy, which aimed to see Charles
succeed him as emperor, led from 1517 onwards
to dissension with the king of France, → Francis I,
who sought to make his country a superpower in
Europe. Pope → Leo X opposed Charles's candi-

dature as emperor, but Habsburg financial power and German imperial patriotism led the electoral princes to elect Charles in 1519, after Maximilian's death. In the electoral capitulation, Charles was obliged to maintain the German constitution, which had been given a more compact form by means of imperial reform measures.

An important influence on Charles's understanding of his role as emperor was the grand chancellor, Mercurino Gattinara, who interpreted the imperial office in terms of Roman law and in keeping with the tradition of the Italian Ghibellines. The struggle for hegemony in Italy led Gattinara to intensify the conflict with France, and Charles fought five wars with Kings Francis I and → Henry II (1521-1526, 1526-1529, 1536-1538, 1542-1544, 1552-1559). These conflicts between the houses of Habsburg and Valois resulted in Habsburg hegemony in Italy (Milan) and the "encirclement" of France, but this perennial struggle was to prove in subsequent years a heavy burden on the relations between the European states.

The shadow of this political entanglement fell on Charles' actions in the religious crisis. The emperor and the reformer met at the imperial parliament in Worms in 1521. Charles saw it as a duty of his office to reject Luther's position, but the wars with France and Charles' lengthy absences from the empire (1521-1530, 1532-1540) meant that the Edict of Worms against Luther was not put into practice. This gave the Reformation time to spread, and its main supporters organized themselves within the framework of the opposition of the imperial Estates to the house of Habsburg (→ Schmalkaldic League, 1531). After the resolution of the conflict with Pope → Clement VII, who had taken the side of France (→ Sack of Rome, 1527), Charles was crowned emperor in Bologna in 1530, and he attempted to bring the two confessional parties to the concord which he desired.

Charles' endeavors took the form of negotiations for a compromise at the imperial parliaments in Augsburg in 1530 (→ Confessio Augustana) and in Regensburg in 1541; his promise of a council; and preliminary truces (the Truces of → Frankfurt and Nuremberg, 1532). His plans failed, owing to the depth of the theological divisions, the scanty willingness of the imperial bishops to accept reform, and the Roman curia's fear of a council.

The war against the Turks in Hungary and in the Mediterranean cast further shadows over the question of religious doctrine. After Charles's military victory over the Schmalkaldic League, these difficulties continued to make it impossible to overcome the confessional division—despite the convocation of the Council of Trent (1545-1548, 1551-1552) and some concessions to the Protestants (→ Augsburg Interim, 1548).

Catholic and Protestant Estates in the empire united in their opposition to Charles' far-reaching plans for political restructuring (the imperial league; the succession of his son → Philip II as emperor). When the rebellion of the "warring princes" (electoral Saxony, Hessen) in 1552 put an end to Charles's political and religious aims and unleashed a new war with France, Charles's brother, → Ferdinand I, negotiated the treaty of → Passau, which became the basis for the recognition of the Lutheran Reformation in imperial law in 1555, in the Religious Peace of → Augsburg.

After spending ten years in the empire, Charles now withdrew to the Netherlands in 1553; the awareness of his defeat prompted him to abdicate by stages. After dividing his inheritance between Philip (Spain, Burgundy, Italy) and Ferdinand (the imperial office, Austria), Charles moved to Spain in 1556 and spent his last years there. Many historians have studied this man who ruled so many territories; however, it is impossible to evaluate his reign, with its epochal character in European history, from the perspective of one national tradition alone.

■ **Literature:** *NDB* 11:191–211; *TRE* 17:635–44.—K. Brandi, *Kaiser Karl V.*, vol. 1 (Frankfurt/Main, [8]1986), vol. 2 (Munich, 1941); H. Lutz, *Christianitas afflicta* (Göttingen, 1964); H. Rabe, *Reichsbund und Interim* (Cologne, 1971); V. Press, *Kaiser Karl V., König Ferdinand und die Entstehung der Reichsritterschaft* (Wiesbaden, [2]1980); A. Kohler, *Antihabsburgische Politik in der Epoche Karls V.* (Göttingen, 1982); H. Lutz, ed., *Das römisch-deutsche Reich im politischen System Karls V.* (Munich, 1982); H. Lutz and A. Kohler, eds., *Aus der Arbeit an den Reichstagen unter Kaiser Karl V.* (Göttingen, 1986); A. Schindling and W. Ziegler, eds., *Die Kaiser der Neuzeit* (Munich, 1990) 33–54.

ANTON SCHINDLING

■ **Additional Bibliography:** F. Seibt, *K. V. und die Reformation* (Berlin, 1990); H. Schilling, "Veni, vidi, Deus vixit. Karl V. zwischen Religionskrieg und Religionsfrieden," *ARG* 89 (1998) 144–66; E. Schulin, *Kaiser Karl V. Geschichte eines übergroßen Wirkungsbereiches* (Stuttgart, 1999); P. Chaunu and M. Escamilla,

Charles Quint (Paris, 2000); L. Schorn-Schütte, *Karl V.* (Munich, 2000); W. Blockmans, *Emperor Charles V, 1500–1558* (London, 2002); J. D. Tracy, *Emperor Charles V, Impresario of War* (Cambridge, 2002); W. S. Maltby, *The Reign of Charles V* (Basingstoke, 2002).

Charles IX of France (king 1560-1574). Born June 27, 1550 in St-Germain-en-Laye, died May 30, 1574 in Vincennes. This intelligent but reserved king never emerged from the influence of his mother, Catherine de → Medici. While Catholics and → Huguenots fought for control of the state, he dreamed a humanist dream of a kingdom where unity ruled (Edict of St-Germain-en-Laye, 1570). In 1571, he was won over to Gaspard → Coligny and his anti-Spanish politics. The murder of Coligny and the Night of St. → Bartholomew, for which the king accepted ultimate responsibility, burst the bubble of his dream of unity, and have cast a shadow up to the present day on the image of this king.
■ Literature: J. Boutier, A. Dewerpe, and D. Nordman, *Un Tour de France royal: le voyage de Charles IX (1564–66)* (Paris, 1984); D. Crouzet, *La Nuit de la Saint-Barthélemy. Un rêve perdu de la Renaissance* (Paris, 1994); M. Simonin, *Charles IX* (Paris, 1995).

GERALD CHAIX

■ Additional Bibliography: J.-L. Bourgeon, *Charles IX devant la Saint-Barthélemy* (Geneva, 1995).

Chemnitz, *Martin.* "The outstanding theologian of our age" in the view of the following generation, one of Philipp Melanchthon's most important pupils, principal author of the Formula of → Concord (1577) and father of early Lutheran orthodoxy; born November 9, 1522 in Treuenbrietzen, died April 8, 1586 in Braunschweig. After schooling in Magdeburg and university studies in Frankfurt on the Oder and Wittenberg, he worked as librarian in Königsberg. He was appointed lecturer in Wittenberg in 1553, where he gave courses on Melanchthon's *Loci communes.* From 1567, he worked as reformer in the duchy of Braunschweig-Wolfenbüttel, first under Joachim → Mörlin, then on his own. Various disappointments and conflicts led him to give up this office in 1584.

The main emphasis of his theology, which follows central Reformation insights, is soteriology, and its structure is determined by the distinction between → law and gospel. His most important

works are the posthumously published *Loci theologici* (1591/1592) and his controversial monograph *Examen Concilii Tridentini* (1566-1573), which contains both polemic against the council and a positive exposition of Protestant doctrine. He also composed works on the doctrine of the Lord's Supper and on Christology.
■ Literature: *TRE* 7:714–21.

HARALD WAGNER

■ Additional Bibliography: *RGG⁴* 2:127f.—J. A. Preus, *The second Martin. The life and theology of M.Ch.* (Saint Louis, Mo., 1994); R. Kolb, "Preaching the Christian Life: Ethical Instruction in the Postils of M. C.," *Lutheran Quarterly* 16 (2002) 274–301.

Chiericati, *Francesco.* Diplomat and reform-minded member of the curia, born 1478 in Vicenza, died December 5, 1539 in Bologna. He studied law in Padua, Bologna, and Siena and came to Rome in 1512 as notary and secretary to Cardinal Matthäus → Schiner. He took part in an embassy to England, and was nuncio in England (1515-1517), Spain (1518-1519), and Portugal (1520-1521). In 1522, he was appointed bishop of Teramo and nuncio to the imperial parliament that met in Nuremberg to discuss the war against the Turks and to carry out the Edict of Worms. This mission was a failure, and his admission of the great inadequacies at the Roman curia was interpreted wrongly, so that → Clement VII and → Paul III no longer employed him for diplomatic tasks.
■ Sources: *Bibliotheca Apostolica Vaticana,* Codex Barbarinus latinus 4907: *Notizie della famiglia Chieregati;* Codex Barbarinus latinus 4912: *Memorie della vita di F. C.*
■ Literature: *DHGE* 12:676ff.; *DBI* 24:674–81.—B. Morsolin, *F. C. vescovo e diplomatico del secolo XVI* (Vicenza, 1873); *Deutsche Reichstagsakten,* earlier series, vol. 3 (Gotha) 383–452; *Korrespondenzen und Akten zur Geschichte des Kardinals Matthäus Schiner,* ed. A. Büchi, vol. 1 (Basle, 1920) 133f.; K. Hofmann, "Die Konzilsfrage auf den deutschen Reichstagen 1521–24" (dissertation, Heidelberg, 1932) 34–66; P. Paschini, "Tre illustri prelati del Rinascimento," *Lateranum* 23 (1957) 1–4.

KLAUS JAITNER

Christian III of Denmark. Born August 12, 1503 in Gottorf, died January 1, 1559 in Koldinghus (Jutland), duke of Schleswig and Holstein (1553-1559), king of Denmark and Norway (1537-

1559). He was viceroy of the duchies and real ruler of the domains of his father, Frederick I, from 1523 to 1533. He supported the new teachings in his period as viceroy (Confessio Hafnica, 1530); as king, he sought to win over the nobles, most of whom had Catholic sentiments, by means of concessions. In 1536, he imprisoned all the Catholic bishops and confiscated their goods. He allowed the collegiate chapters to continue in existence as Protestant institutions, but he closed the Catholic monasteries, whose wealth went to the state coffers. He summoned Martin Luther's closest collaborator, Johannes → Bugenhagen, the organizer of four local churches in northern Germany, to Denmark for two years, and later to Schleswig-Holstein, in order to transform the Catholic Church into a Protestant church. It was Bugenhagen who crowned Christian king.

■ **Literature:** *NDB* 3:233f.—O. Brandt, *Geschichte Schleswig-Holsteins* (Kiel, [3]1938); E. Feddersen, *Kirchengeschichte Schleswig-Holsteins* (Kiel, 1938); E. H. Dungley, *The Reformation in Denmark* (London, 1948); G. Schwaiger, *Die Reformation in den nordischen Ländern* (Munich, 1962).

ERNST WALTER ZEEDEN

■ **Additional Bibliography:** L. Grane, *Reformationsstudien. Beiträge zu Luther und zur dänischen Reformation* (Mainz, 1999).

Christopher of Württemberg (duke from 1550). Born May 12, 1515 in Urach, died December 28, 1568 in Stuttgart. After the Swabian league expelled his father → Ulrich and occupied Württemberg in 1519, Christopher was brought up at the court of → Charles V. When the emperor wished to take him with him to Spain, Christopher fled to his uncle, Duke → William of Bavaria. When he returned after the battle of Lauffen in 1534, Duke Ulrich sent his son for further education to the court of → Francis I of France. The treaty of Reichenweiher (1542) ensured that Christopher would be the only heir in Württemberg and would exercise sovereignty over the county of Montbéliard, while he committed himself to maintain the Protestant confession in the country. It seems that Christopher definitively accepted the Lutheran faith during the following period, when he was viceroy in Montbéliard. On February 24, 1544, he married Anna-Maria, daughter of Marquis → George of Brandenburg-Ansbach, a resolute proponent of the new faith.

After his father's death, Christopher took over the government of Württemberg on November 6, 1550. Since his father had fought against Charles V in the Schmalkaldic war (league of → Schmalkald), King → Ferdinand began criminal proceedings on a charge of felony, and Christopher risked the loss of his sovereignty. This led him to accept being represented at the second session of the Council of Trent, where his envoys (who included Johannes → Brenz) presented the → Confessio Virtembirgica on January 24, 1552; however, the "princely rebellion" of → Moritz of Saxony prevented the discussion of this formula and of other open questions (e.g., the standing order of the council). Christopher himself was neutral during this rebellion, but its outcome, which went against the interests of the emperor, made it possible for him to get rid of the → Augsburg Interim in Württemberg and to reorganize the church system, with an ecclesiastical council as the highest governing body (under the duke himself) and the establishment of a central treasury which was to help finance pastoral work, schools, and care for the poor. The thirteen monasteries of men in Württemberg remained autonomous legal bodies, and the Catholic abbots were replaced on their death by Protestants. The main purpose of these monasteries was now to prepare future clergymen in their schools for the subsequent study of theology in Tübingen. The Great Church Order of 1559 codified the reorganization of church life and of the school sector in the duchy of Württemberg.

■ **Literature:** *NDB* 3:248f.; *LThK*[2] 2:1166; *TRE* 8:68–71.—*Briefwechsel des Herzogs Ch. von Württemberg*, ed. V. Ernst, 4 vols. (Stuttgart, 1899–1907); *Confessio Virtembergica. Das württembergische Bekenntnis von 1551*, ed. M. Bizer (Stuttgart, 1952); Jedin 3, passim; H.-M. Maurer, "Herzog Ch. (1550–1568)," in *900 Jahre Haus Württemberg. Leben und Leistung für Land und Volk*, ed. R. Uhland (Stuttgart, 1984) 136–62.

RUDOLF REINHARDT

■ **Additional Bibliography:** *RGG*[4] 322f.—F. Brendle, *Dynastie, Reich und Reformation. Die württembergischen Herzöge Ulrich und Ch., die Habsburger und Frankreich* (Tübingen, 1997).

Church

1. Reformers

For *Martin Luther,* the church is not primarily or properly speaking an institution, but the people of God gathered together in the Holy Spirit, a people which receives its very existence and its holiness "from the Word of God" (the church as *creatura Verbi:* WA 6:550; cf. also WA 50:629). In addition to the proclamation of the Word, Luther acknowledges other divine institutions which give life to the church: baptism, the Lord's Supper, and ministries. These are also *notae* or *notae ecclesiae,* "identifying signs" which permit us to recognize the existence of the church; in terms of its spiritual essence, the church is hidden (and the true church is hidden under the false church—i.e., at that period, the church of the pope).

In the course of the development of *Philipp Melanchthon's* thinking, the emphasis in the concept of "church" shifts, reflecting the difference between Luther's period and the growing establishment of a specifically Protestant church body. The ministry of proclamation of the Word and the ministry of the sacraments, and hence the institutional character of the church, move into the foreground. Indeed, the late Melanchthon can compare the church to a *coetus scholasticus* (Study ed., 2/2:480:31; 481:6) consisting of teachers and students; in theological terms, he describes the church as a visible fellowship of those called by God (*coetus vocatorum*).

Both these concepts have left their mark on the → confessional documents which set the doctrinal standard in the Lutheran churches. The church is defined as *congregatio sanctorum, in qua evangelium pure docetur et recte administrantur sacramenta* ("congregation of the saints, in which the gospel is taught in its purity and the sacraments are ministered aright," CA 7); here, the "saints," i.e., those justified in faith, represent the spiritual, hidden element in a definition which otherwise tends to use institutional language. Consequently, the ApolCA (art. 7) distinguishes between an *ecclesia proprie dicta* ("church in the proper sense of the term")—viz., the fellowship of those who are sanctified by the Spirit in their hearts—and an *ecclesiae late dicta* ("church in the broad sense of the term"), viz. the society of all those who are baptized and gather together in worship to hear the Word and receive the Lord's Supper. This tension in the concept of church, which goes back to Augustine, can be seen throughout the history of Protestant ecclesiology in all its variants up to the present.

This tension is also found in *Jean Calvin's* concept of the church. In terms of its spiritual essence,

the church is the invisible fellowship of those chosen from all eternity in Christ; but his main interest is the external and visible church, since membership in this church is (so to speak) the precondition if one is to be a member of the real church. The visible church must be structured as a true church in terms of doctrine and life, with the help of four ministries mentioned in scripture (pastor, teacher, elder, deacon); in this task, the church discipline administered by the elders plays a particularly important role. This is why a certain ethical rigorism is typical of the Calvinist form of church, e.g., in Geneva or in Scotland.

■ *LThK*[3] 5:1474ff. (unabridged version).

■ **Literature:** *TRE* 18:262–317.—M. Doerne, "Gottes Volk und Gottes Wort," *Luther-Jahrbuch* 14 (1932) 61–98 (on Luther); E. Hirsch, *Geschichte der neuern evangelischen Theologie,* vol. 5 (Gütersloh, [3]1964), chap. 49: "Der Streit um den Kirche-Begriff"; O. Weber, "Calvins Lehre von der Kirche," in idem, *Die Treue Gottes in der Geschichte der Kirche* (Neukirchen-Vluyn, 1968) 19–104; E. Herms, *Erfahrbare K. Beiträge zur Ekklesiologie* (Tübingen, 1990); U. Kühn, *Kirche* (Gütersloh, [2]1990); W. Hüffmeier, ed., *Die Kirche Jesu Christi. Der reformatorische Beitrag zum ökumenischen Dialog über die kirchliche Einheit* (Frankfurt/Main, 1995).

ULRICH KÜHN

■ **Additional Bibliography:** *RGG*[4] 4:1006ff.—G. Müller, "Die reformatorische Ekklesiologie und ihre ökumenischen Herausforderungen," in *In der Wahrheit bleiben.* Festschrift R. Slenczka (Göttingen, 1996) 137–55; M. Brecht, *Die reformatorische Kirche in Melanchthons ekklesiologischen Reden: Humanismus und Wittenberger Reformation* (Leipzig, 1996) 297–312; R. Keen, "Political Authority and Ecclesiology in Melanchthon's 'De Ecclesiae Autoritate'," *ChH* 65 (1996) 1–14; G. Neebe, *Apostolische Kirche. Grundunterscheidungen an Luthers Kirche-Begriff unter besonderer Berücksichtigung seiner Lehre von den notae ecclesiae* (Berlin, 1997); U. Kühn, "Bedingungen von Kirche-Gemeinschaft aufgrund von Luthers Kirche-Verständnis," *Lutherische Kirche in der Welt* 44 (1997) 59–73; O. E. Lee, "L'ecclésiologie de Calvin," *Korean Journal of Systematic Theology* 3 (1999) 314–29; D. S. Yeago, "Ecclesia sancta, ecclesia peccatrix. The Holiness of the Church in Martin Luther's Theology," *Pro ecclesia* 9 (2000) 331–54; E. K. Kim, "John Calvin's Ecclesiology," *Chongshin Theological Journal* 7 (2002) 3–19; J. M. Kittelson, "Leading the Least of These Astray: 'Evangelical Catholic' Ecclesiology and Luther," in *Caritas et reformatio.* Festschrift C. Lindberg (St. Louis, 2002) 245–60;

2. The *process of confessionalization,* viewed in the context of ecclesiology, primarily concerned

the question of the possibility of discerning the existence of the true church: what were the essential characteristics of this church? It was not the question of the church, but the question of salvation, that was the central issue in the Reformation (see 1., above), but the breach of unity is rooted ultimately not in the doctrine of → justification, but in ecclesiology, and more precisely, in the question whether the church in its specific form, with its essential institutional structures, was theologically essential—and this meant: necessary for salvation.

While not simply forgetting the mystical dimension of the church, the *Catholic controversial theologians* (Peter → Canisius, Thomas → Stapleton, Konrad → Schatzgeyer, John → Fisher, Johannes → Driedo, Jacobus → Latomus, Albert → Pigge, Nikolaus → Ferber, Stanislaus → Hosius, Michael → Vehe, etc.) emphasized above all the possibility of discerning the church, and the visible structure of this church as a hierarchical fellowship under the authority of the pope. One original counterweight to this reduction of ecclesiology to papal authority can be seen in the *loci theologici* of Melchior → Cano, if these are read in the light of modern interpretations as "the expression of a way of building up the church, not merely as aspects of theological methodology" (Seckler, p. 101).

Fear of conciliarist tendencies led the *Council of Trent* to speak only indirectly of ecclesiological questions. De facto, however, the council provided the stimulus for a wide-ranging reform which was promoted by new lay movements and Orders, especially the Jesuits. The new ecclesiastical self-awareness with its triumphalistic traits found visible expression in Baroque church buildings, as well as in a strengthening of church centralism and in the development of an ecclesiology conceived in juridical terms as a doctrine of the church hierarchy.

■ *LThK*[3] 5:1458–65 (unabridged version).
■ Literature: G. Alberigo, "L'ecclesiologia del concilio di Trento," *RSCI* 18 (1964) 227–42; Y. Congar, *Handbuch der Dogmengeschichte*, vol. 3/3d (Freiburg, 1971) 40–62; M. Midali, *Rivelazione, Chiesa, scrittura e tradizione alla quarta sessione del concilio di Trento* (Rome, 1973); E. Klinger, *Ekklesiologie der Neuzeit* (Freiburg, 1978); M. Seckler, "Die ekklesiologische Bedeutung der 'loci theologici,'" in idem, *Die schiefen Wände des Lehrhauses* (Freiburg, 1988) 79–104; K. Diez, "Das Verhältnis von Rechtfertigungslehre und Ekklesiologie im Denken

Reginald Poles (1550–58)," in *Ecclesia tertii millennii advenientis 1997. Festschrift A. Anton* (Casale Monferrato, 1997) 372–90; K. Ganzer, "Gesamtkirche und Ortskirche auf dem Konzil von Trient," *RQ* 95 (2000) 167–78.

WALTER KASPER/JOACHIM DRUMM

Church order. Martin Luther's fear that canon law might once more take hold of the church and his faith in the mighty power of God's Word alone were not able to prevent the development of a Protestant canon law, which took the form of "church orders." Everything in the Protestant churches was to be done with honesty and due order (1 Cor 14:40). Written directives were required in the territories, cities, and towns which adopted the Reformation, and these replaced Catholic canon law. In the towns, the elaboration of a church order was often preceded by social-political and anticlerical popular movements in favor of Reformation teachings, by disputations among theologians, and by a resolution by the council or by council and citizens together; in the territories, church orders were composed in connection with visitations. Their authors were famous theologians, some of whom (e.g., Johannes → Bugenhagen, Antonius → Corvinus, Urbanus → Rhegius, etc.) took Catholic canon law as a reference point, sometimes in order to take a contradictory position, but sometimes using it as a subsidiary legal source. This demonstrated the desire to take up the inheritance of the ancient church (e.g., by quotations from patristic authors) and to integrate the church orders into imperial law.

The central point of the Protestant church orders was the *ius divinum*. To the extent that a church order translated this into legal terms, its regulations automatically had binding legal force; these acquired the force of law in human terms when they were accepted or ordained by the ruler; the constitution of the cities might also require a resolution by the citizens. Since they were written by the same authors, and commercial or dynastic relationships also played a role in their composition, the church orders are often very similar, sometimes borrowing lengthy passages from earlier texts. When Bugenhagen elaborated his later church orders, he drew on his fundamental church order for the city of Braunschweig (1528), as can be seen in his texts for Hamburg (1529), Lübeck (1531), the duchy of Pomerania (1534-1535), the kingdom of Denmark (1537), Schleswig-Holstein (1542), Braunschweig-Wolfenbüttel (1543), and Hildesheim (1544); Braunschweig itself preferred Philipp Melanchthon's "Visitation Directives." Bugenhagen's church orders in turn became the model for East Frisia (1529), Wittenberg (1533), Osnabrück (1543, Hermann Bonus), and others; and the church order for the county of Brandenburg and the imperial city of Nuremberg (1533) had wide-reaching influence; this had a catechetical perspective and contained catechism sermons by Andreas → Osiander which were also included in the church order for the electoral principality of Brandenburg (1540). The latter church order then transmitted these sermons to the church orders for the principality of Calenberg-Göttingen (1542, Corvinus) and for the duchy of Pfalz-Neuburg (1543, Osiander). The Württemberg church order of 1553 (Johannes → Brenz) also enjoyed a wide influence in the Lutheran sphere. Related texts are the church orders for Mecklenburg (1552), the principality of Lüneburg (1564), Braunschweig-Wolfenbüttel (1569), Lippe-Spiegelberg-Pyrmont (1571), Hoyas (1581), the church territory of Verden (1606), etc.

Influenced by Martin → Bucer, Jean Calvin composed the *Ordonnances ecclésiastiques* for Geneva in 1541; these were the model for the "Discipline ecclésiastique" of the Reformed general synod in Paris in 1559 and the church order of the Reformed synod of refugees in Emden in 1571. The church order of the electoral Palatinate (1563) drew on that of the Reformed Dutchmen in London (1554), in addition to models from Zurich, Geneva, and other places.

The church orders contain instruction in Reformation theology; orders of service for worship, celebrations of the Lord's Supper, baptism, weddings, funerals, prayers or cycles of prayers; church law concerning the ministries of superintendent, parish pastor, preacher, elder, deacon, etc.; church discipline, regulations for visitations, marriage law, school regulations, directives for the care of the poor, regulations for the salaries of church employees, etc.

Some of the Reformation church orders went through many editions; they continued to enjoy validity long after the Reformation period itself.

■ **Literature:** *EKO; TRE* 18:670–703.—A. L. Richter, ed., *Die evangelischen Kirchen des 16.Jh.* (Weimar, 1846); R. H. Helmholz, ed., *Canon Law in Protestant Lands* (Berlin, 1992); K. Sichelschmidt, *Recht aus christlicher Liebe oder obrigkeitlichem Gesetzesbefehl?* (Tübingen, 1995); A. Sprengler-Ruppenthal, "Die Bremer Kirchenordnung von 1534," *ZSRG.K* 113 (1996) 107–269; 114 (1997) 449–528.

ANNELIESE SPRENGLER-RUPPENTHAL

■ **Additional Bibliography:** B. Roussel, "La Discipline des Églises reformées de France en 1559," in *De l'humanisme aux lumières, Bayle et le protestantisme.* Festschrift E. Labrousse (Paris, 1996) 169–91; G. Seebass, "Die Augsburger Kirchenordnung von 1537 in ihrem historischen und theologischen Zusammenhang," in *Die Reformation und ihre Außenseiter*, ed. I. Dingel (Göttingen, 1997) 125–48; G. Seebass, "Evangelische Kirchenordnung im Spannungsfeld von Theologie, Recht und Politik," in *Recht und Reich im Zeitalter der Reformation*, ed. Ch. Roll (Frankfurt/Main, [2]1997) 231–73; J. M. Estes, ed., *Godly Magistrates and Church Order: Johannes Brenz and the Establishment of the Lutheran Territorial Church in Germany 1525–1559* (Toronto, 2001).

Chytraeus (Kochhafe), *David.* Lutheran theologian, born February 26, 1530 in Ingelfingen (Württemberg), died June 25, 1600 in Rostock. He began his studies in Tübingen in 1539(!), and took his master's degree in 1544; thereafter, he went to Wittenberg and became a table companion of Philipp Melanchthon. He was appointed to a position in the "Paedagogium" at Rostock in 1550, and was a central figure in the reorganization of the university, the establishment of a consistory, and the elaboration of regulations for the church superintendent. He was active on a wide scale, organizing Protestant church life in Mecklenburg, Austria, Scandinavia, and Antwerp. His fame rested primarily on his historical studies, but he also wrote works of theological instruction. He maintained a moderate Lutheranism and was an important representative of the link between the Reformation and the humanist ideal of academic work.

■ **Literature:** *TRE* 8:88ff.—J. Ebel, "Die Herkunft des Konzeptes der Konkordienformel," *ZKG* 91 (1980) 237–82; "D. und Nathan Ch.," in *Humanismus im konfessionellen Zeitalter*, ed. K.-H. Glaser (Ubstadt-Weiher, 1993).

MICHAEL BECHT

■ **Additional Bibliography:** *RGG*[4] 2:377f.—G. Händler, "Der Rostocker Theologe D. Ch. in neueren Büchern,"

Theologische Literaturzeitung 121 (1996) 3–16; K.-H. Glaser, ed., *D.Ch. Norddeutscher Humanismus in Europa* (Ubstadt-Weiher, 2000).

Clarenbach, *Adolf.* Martyr and symbolic figure in Protestantism in the Rhine area; born c. 1495 near Lennep, died September 28, 1529 in Cologne. After schooling in Lennep and Münster, he attended the faculty of arts and took his master's degree in Cologne in 1517. He taught in Münster (1521-1523) and in Wesel (1523-1525), but he came under suspicion of holding Lutheran views, and was expelled from both towns. He was in Büderich in 1525, and in Osnabrück in 1526, but was expelled from the latter city in spring 1527. When Lennep expelled him, Clarenbach replied with a defense of his theological positions. He was arrested in Cologne on April 3, 1528, and the trial for heresy ended with his burning (together with Peter Fliesteden).

■ **Literature:** W. Rotscheidt, "A. C.-Bibliographie (1529–1929)," *Monatsheft für Rheinische Kirchengeschichte* 23 (1929) 257–84; H. Klugkist Hesse, ed., "Die Bekenntnisschrift A. C.s vom Jahre 1527," *Beiträge zur Gemeindegeschichte* 1 (1930) 3–30; idem, *A. C.* (Neuwied, 1929).

HANSGEORG MOLITOR

Clement VII. Pope (November 19, 1523–September 25, 1534), previously *Giulio de' Medici,* born May 26, 1478 in Florence as the illegitimate son of the city ruler, Guiliano de' Medici. His cousin, → Leo X, appointed him archbishop of Florence and cardinal in 1513. He was the candidate of the imperial party in the conclave which elected him to succeed Hadrian VI. In the gravest crisis of church history, Clement acted like a Renaissance prince: his priority was the church state and the Medici family, and he employed the methods of an underhanded and untrustworthy diplomacy in every sphere. His attempt to limit the emperor's hegemony in Italy by means of the Holy League of Cognac (1526) with the French king → Francis I (who was conspiring with the Turks against Emperor → Charles V) and with Venice led in 1527 to the → Sack of Rome; Clement himself was taken prisoner. His subsequent reconciliation with the emperor (Peace of Barcelona, 1529; imperial coronation in Bologna, 1530) did not mean that the pope provided any help in the con-fusions of the German Reformation—for Clement consistently evaded demands for a council. The weakness of his character was also revealed in the dragging treatment of the question of → Henry VIII's marriage and in his relations with the Scandinavian kingdoms. During his pontificate, one third of western Christendom separated from the church (large areas of Germany, England, Scandinavia, etc.). This is why Leopold von Ranke rightly called him "the most disastrous of all the popes." This judgment is not watered down by the fact that he consolidated the hierarchy in America and was a prominent patron of the arts.

■ **Literature:** *DHGE* 12:1175–1224; *HKG* 4:246–50, 693; *DBI* 26:237–59.—S. Ehses, "Die Politik des Papstes C. VII. bis zur Schlacht von Pavia," *HJ* 6 (1885) 557–603; 7 (1886) 553–93; J. Fraikin, *Nonciatures de France. Clément VII,* 2 vols. (Paris, 1906–26); T. Pandolfi, "G. M. Giberti e l'ultima difesa della libertà d'Italia negli anni 1521–25," *Archivio della Società Romana di Storia Patria* 34 (1911) 131–237; L. von Pastor, *Geschichte der Päpste seit dem Ausgang des Mittelalters,* vol. 4/1 and 4/2 (Freiburg, 1906–7); *HCMA* 3:18–22; E. Rodocanachi, *Les pontificats d'Adrien VI et de Clément VII* (Paris, 1933.

GEORG SCHWAIGER

■ **Additional Bibliography:** *TRE* 8:98–101; *Vatikanlexikon,* ed. N. Del Re (Augsburg, 1998) 129ff.— S. E. Reiss, *Cardinal Giulio de' Medici as a Patron of Art (1513–23).* (Princeton, N.J., 1992).

Cles, *Bernhard von.* Cardinal, born March 11, 1485 in Cles (Trent), died July 30, 1539 in Bologna. After studies in civil and canon law in Bologna, he was appointed bishop of his native city in 1514, and began a distinguished political career as confidant of the ruler of Tyrol, Emperor Maximilian I, who entrusted him with the government of Verona. He continued to consolidate his position at the Habsburg court, where he exercised crucial influence from 1522 (and even more from 1528, as supreme chancellor) on the entire politics of King → Ferdinand. Cles took a very active part in all the negotiations about the German Reformation. He resolutely maintained that a council was the solution. He was made cardinal in 1530, on the occasion of the coronation of → Charles V. At the conclave in 1534, the Austrian court endeavored to secure his election as pope. As bishop and prince of Trent, Cles enjoyed unique importance; diocesan synods and visitations bear witness to his activity as reformer. As local ruler, he transformed the outward appearance of his capital and extended the Castello del Buonconsiglio, his splendid residence, which opened its doors to important artists and humanists. Cles gave up his political offices in 1539 and became administrator of the cathedral chapter of Brixen.

■ **Literature:** *DBI* 26:406–11.—*Bernardo Clesio e il suo tempo,* ed. P. Prodi, 2 vols. (Rome, 1987); C. Walsh, "La nòmina di Bernardo Clesio a protonotario apostolico," *Studi Trentini di Scienze Storiche, Sezione 1a,* 66 (1987) 3–13; G. Cristoforetti, *La visita pastorale del cardinale Bernardo Clesio alla diocesi di Trento 1537–38* (Trent, 1989).

IGINIO ROGGER

■ **Additional Bibliography:** *BBKL* 16:122f.

Clichtove, *Josse* (Jodocus Clichtoveus). Humanist and theologian, born 1472/1473 in Nieuport (Flanders), died September 22, 1543 in Chartres. He took the degrees of master of arts in Paris 1492, and doctor of theology in 1506. He was a student and colleague of → Faber Stapulensis until 1520; after this period, he was an opponent of Martin Luther and his adherents. He became canon theologian of Chartres in 1528. He elaborated the ideal image of a priest, as the Catholic reformers saw it, and defended priestly → celibacy.

■ **Principal Works:** *Editions and Commentaries: Divi Bernardi opera* (Paris, 1513); *Theologia Damasceni* (Paris, 1513); *Theologia vivificans . . . Dionysii (Areopagitae)* (Paris, 1515).—Ascetical Writings: *De laude monasticae religionis* (Paris, 1513); *Elucidatorium ecclesiasticum* (Paris, 1516); *De vita et moribus sacerdotum* (Paris, 1519); *Sermones.* (Paris, 1534).—Controversial theology: *Antilutherus* (Paris, 1524); *Propugnaculum Ecclesiae* (Paris, 1526); *De sacramento Eucharistiae contra Œcolampadium* (Paris, 1527).

■ **Literature:** *DThC* 3:236–43; *CEras* 1:317–20.—J.-P. Massaut, *J. C., l'humanisme et la réforme du clergé,* 2 vols. (Paris, 1968); idem, *Critique et tradition à la veille de la Réforme en France* (Paris, 1974); idem, "Thèmes ecclésiologiques dans les controverses antiluthériennes de J. C.," in *Les Réformes,* ed. B. Chevalier and R. Sauzet (Paris, 1985) 327–35; J. K. Farge, *Biographical Register of the Paris Doctors of Theology, 1500–36* (Toronto, 1980) 90–104; idem, *Orthodoxy and Reform in Early Reformation France* (Leiden, 1980); P. Fabisch, "J. C.," in *Katholische Theologen der Reformationzeit,* ed. E. Iserloh, vol. 2 (Münster, 1985) 82–91.

JEAN-PIERRE MASSAUT

■ **Additional Bibliography:** H. Smolinsky, "Humanistische römisch-katholische Gegner Luthers. Das Beispiel Jodocus Clichtoveus," in *Humanismus und Wittenberger Reformation. Festgabe anläßlich des 500. Geburtstages des Praeceptor Germaniae Philipp Melanchthon* (Leipzig, 1996) 73–87; N. Lemaître, "Le prêtre mis à part ou le triomphe d'une idéologie sacerdotale au XVIᵉ siècle," *RHEF* 85 (1999) 275–99.

Clinge (Klinge, Cling), *Conrad.* Franciscan, born 1483/1484 in Nordhausen (?), died March 10, 1556 in Erfurt. He took the degree of doctor of theology in Erfurt in 1520; he was custodian of Thuringia, guardian of the Franciscan monastery, and cathedral preacher in Erfurt from 1530. He was a vigorous defender of the Catholic party. His teaching on justification was a cautious attempt to integrate into Catholic doctrine insights that were important to the Reformers.

■ **Works:** Klaiber nos. 726–29.

■ **Literature:** *BBKL* 4:60f.—J. Beumer, "Ein Beispiel katholischer Zusammenarbeit während der Reformationszeit," *Franziskanische Studien* 49 (1967) 373–83; H.-Ch. Rickauer, *Rechtfertigung und Heil. Die Vermittlung von Glaube und Heilshandeln in der Auseinandersetzung mit der reformatorischen Lehre bei K. Klinge (1483/84–1556)* (Leipzig, 1986); idem, "Glaube und Heilshandeln. Zur theologischen Auseinandersetzung des Erfurter Franziskaners K. Klinge mit der reformatorischen Lehre," in *Denkender Glaube in Geschichte und Gegenwart,* ed. W. Ernst and K. Feiereis (Leipzig, 1992) 55–70.

BARBARA HENZE

Cochlaeus (Dobeneck), *Johannes.* Humanist and theologian, born 1479 in Rabersried near Wendelstein (central Franconia), died January 10/11, 1552 in Breslau. After studies in Cologne and Bologna, he took his doctorate in theology at Ferrara in 1517 and was ordained priest in Rome in 1518. He became dean of the chapter of St. Mary's (Liebfrauenstift) in Frankfurt am Main in 1519. He had initially been favorably inclined towards Martin Luther, but became his resolute opponent after Luther published *De captivitate Babylonica ecclesiae* in 1520. He attempted to persuade Luther to recant at Worms in 1521. He took part, with Lorenzo → Campeggi, in the imperial parliament at Worms and the dialogue at Regensburg in 1524. After the death of Hieronymus → Emser, he became court chaplain to → George of Saxony in

1527, and accompanied him in 1530 to the imperial parliament at Augsburg, where he helped draw up the *Confutatio confessionis Augustanae*. After the Reformation was introduced into Saxony, Cochlaeus went to Breslau in 1539. In 1540 and 1541, he took part in the religious debates in → Hagenau, → Worms, and → Regensburg; he participated in the second religious debate in Regensburg in 1546, and in the provincial synod at Mainz in 1549.

Cochlaeus endeavored to uphold the Catholic faith, and defended the old church in more than 200 publications. His theology was influenced by Thomas Aquinas, by fifteenth-century theology, and by humanism; it can be taken as a representative witness to the views of 16th-century pre-Tridentine theology with regard to ecclesiology, the Eucharist, the priesthood, justification, the freedom of the will, and Mariology. It left a deep imprint on later theologians, including Peter → Canisius and Robert Bellarmine. His *Commentaria de actis et scriptis M. Lutheri* (1548) is one of the most important sources for Reformation history, and the first attempt at a complete presentation of Luther's life and work. It left a lasting mark on the Catholic picture of Luther.

■ **Catalogue of Works:** M. Spahn, *J. C.* (Berlin, 1898; reprinted Nieuwkoop, 1964) 341–72.

■ **Literature:** *TRE* 8:140–46; *KThR* 1²:72–81.—H. Jedin, *Des J. C. Streitschrift "De libero arbitrio hominis"* (Breslau, 1927); A. Herte, *Die Lutherkommentare des J. C.* (Münster, 1935); idem, *Das katholische Lutherbild im Bann der Lutherkommentare des J. C.*, 3 vols. (Münster, 1943); F. Machilek, "J. C.." *Fränkische Lebensbilder* 8 (1978) 51–69; R. Bäumer, *J. C.* (Münster, 1980); idem, "J. C. und die Reform der Kirche," in *Reformatio Ecclesiae*. Festschrift E. Iserloh (Paderborn, 1980) 333–54; idem, "Die Religionspolitik Karls V. im Urteil der Lutherkommentare des J. C.," in *Politik und Konfession*. Festschrift K. Repgen (Berlin, 1983) 31–47; Ch. Dittrich, *Die vortridentinische katholische Kontroverstheologie und die Täufer* (Frankfurt/Main, 1991) 1–106, 269–360; R. Keen, "The Arguments and Audiences of C.'s 'Philippica VII,'" *CHR* 88 (1992) 371–94; M. Samuel-Scheyder, *J. C., humaniste et adversaire de Luther* (Nancy, 1993).

REMIGIUS BÄUMER

■ **Additional Bibliography:** A. Laube, "Das Gespann C./Dietenberger im Kampf gegen Luther," *ARG* 87 (1996) 119–35; A. Thiem, "Freier Wille bei Calvin und C.," *Archiv für schlesische Kirchengeschichte* 57 (1999) 101–44; B. Peter, "J. C.," *Archiv für schlesische Kirchengeschichte* 58 (2000) 185–215.

Coligny

(1) *Odet*. Known as cardinal de Châtillon, born July 10, 1517 in castle Châtillon-sur-Loing (department of Loiret), died February 2, 1571 in Hampton Court (London). He was created cardinal deacon of SS Sergius & Bacchus at the age of ten; at eleven, he was appointed archbishop of Toulouse in succession to Gabriel von Gramont, under whom the Reformed doctrines had won increasing acceptance. He was appointed prince bishop of Beauvais in 1535. Coligny renounced Catholicism and professed his allegiance to Reformed doctrine in 1561; Pius IV deposed him from his dignities and benefices in 1563, and he married Isabelle de Hauteville ("Madame la Cardinale") in 1564. In 1568, he left France for the court of Queen → Elizabeth I in England.

■ **Literature:** *DHGE* 13:250f.—J. Delaborde, *O. de C.* (Paris, 1879); L. Merlet, *O. de C.* (Paris, 1885); *Revue des questions historiques* 76 (1904) 61–108.

(2) *Gaspard*. Lord of Châtillon, born February 16, 1519 in castle Châtillon-sur-Loing (department of Loiret), died August 24, 1572 in Paris; brother of (1). He became admiral in 1552 and governor of Picardy in 1555. He was taken prisoner after the battle of St-Quentin in 1557, and kept captive in the Netherlands, where he was won over to the Reformation. He converted to Calvinism in 1560 and soon after became the leader of the → Huguenots in the four first wars of religion in France. Through the Peace of St-Germain-en-Laye (1570), he was granted free exercise of religion and four stable places of residence for the Reformed Christians. He was readmitted to court as a royal counselor in 1571, and gained considerable influence on → Charles IX. He had, however, bitter enemies, and Catherine de Medici had him murdered on St. → Bartholomew's Night.

■ **Literature:** *RE* 4, 219–28; *DHGE* 13:247f.; *RGG*³ 1:1849f.—J. Delaborde, *G. de C.*, 3 vols. (Paris, 1879–82); E. Bersier, *C. avant les guerres de religion* (Paris, 1883); A. W. Whitehead, *G. de C. Admiral of France* (London, 1904); W. Besant, *G. de C.* (London, 1905); L. von Pastor, *Geschichte der Päpste seit dem Ausgang des Mittelalters* (Freiburg, vol. 7, 1920, 397, 400f., 408, 420, 432; vol. 8, 1920, passim); J. Héritier, *Catherine de Médicis* (Paris, 1941); K. Kupisch, *C.* (Berlin, ²1951).

JOSEPH JORDAN

■ **Additional Bibliography:** *RGG*⁴ 2:420.—L. Crété, *C.* (Paris, 1985); J.-L. Bourgeon, *L'assasinat d'C.* (Geneva, 1992); "C., les protestants et la mer," in *Actes du colloque* *organisé à Rochefort et La Rochelle les 3 et 4 octobre 1996* (Paris, 1997).

Common Prayer, Book of. With the → Anglican articles and the *Ordinal*, the *Book of Common Prayer* is the traditional doctrinal foundation of the Church of → England (which is the oldest part of today's Anglican Communion). This Book regulates the entire course of the church year, with regular and occasional services of worship. It goes back to Thomas → Cranmer, whom → Henry VIII appointed archbishop of Canterbury in 1533, the first to hold this office after the break with Rome. A complete revision appeared in 1549; the second revised edition appeared in 1552.

■ *LThK*[3] 2:590 (unabridged version).
■ **Literature:** *RGG*[4] 1:1691–94.—E. C. Whitaker, *Martin Bucer and the B.* (Great Wakering, 1974); J. D. Maltby, *Prayer Book and People in Elizabethan and Early Stuart England* (Cambridge, 2000).

CARSTEN PETER THIEDE

■ **Additional Bibliography:** R. Targoff, *Common Prayer: The Language of Public Devotion in Early Modern England* (Chicago, 2001); R. Beckwith, "'For the More Explanation' and 'for the More Perfection': Cranmer's Second Prayer Book," *Churchman* 116 (2002) 259–66; G. Wiedermann, "The First Latin 'B.,'" *Reformation and Renaissance Review* 4 (2002) 190–216.

Communion/Lord's Supper.

1. Concept

Abendmahl (literally, "evening meal"; "Lord's Supper" is the usual English term) has been the most popular term among Protestants since 1522, when Martin Luther used it as a designation for that act of worship on the part of the Christian community which is explicitly derived from the last meal which Jesus ate with his disciples. From a Roman Catholic and Orthodox perspective, this term is considered inappropriate, because "meal" reduces the significance of what happens in the service, and "evening" seems to tie down the time of celebration too specifically; besides this, the term can misleadingly suggest that the Lord's Supper is the representation only of Jesus' last meal on earth.

HERBERT VORGRIMLER

2. The heart of the Lutheran-Catholic controversy about the sacrament of the altar in the Reformation period is the question whether the

Lord's Supper is a work of the church, rather than a gift of God to the church. In 1520, Martin Luther seeks to free the Mass from the "captivity" of a sacrifice which must be offered by the priest (*De captivitate Babylonica*), and in 1537 (articles of → Schmalkald), he still sees the Mass, understood as "sacrifice and work," as the "greatest and most terrible horror" which is opposed to the "main article" of → justification by faith (CA 24 speaks in similar terms). Nevertheless, Luther can also describe the Lord's Supper as a "sacrifice of praise" on the part of the community, thereby certainly acknowledging its eucharistic character (WA 30.2:603ff.; likewise ApolCA 24).

On the question of the real presence of Christ in the Lord's Supper, however, there is a substantial closeness between Luther and Catholic doctrine, despite his rejection of the theory of transubstantiation and of eucharistic veneration outside the celebration of the Mass. In his new liturgical order for the Lord's Supper (*Formula Missae*, 1523; German Mass, 1526), Luther retained the elevation of the elements, but deleted both the offertory and the eucharistic prayer which framed the words of institution. The celebration of the Lord's Supper concentrated on the recitation of the words of institution and on the reception of the elements by the communicants.

The Reformed tradition (especially Huldrych Zwingli) emphasizes more strongly the idea that the Lord's Supper confesses and recalls Christ. The Reformed understanding of the sacrament is marked by the debate with the Lutheran theology of the real presence: Jean Calvin goes beyond Zwingli by teaching that there is a presence of Christ for faith, transmitted by the Spirit, parallel to the eating and drinking of bread and wine (*Inst* 4:17; cf. Heidelberg catechism, questions 78-79). Calvinism agrees with Lutheranism in the complete rejection of the view that the Mass is an expiatory sacrifice that must be offered by the priest (ibid., question 80; cf. Calvin, *Inst* 4:18).

Although the Church of → England likewise rejected the understanding of the Lord's Supper as an expiatory sacrifice, it retained more elements of the traditional rite in the *Book of* → *Common Prayer* (e.g., epiclesis and anamnesis), and even has a prayer in which the church offers itself.

■ *LThK*[3] 3:953ff. (unabridged version).
■ **Literature:** *RGG*[4] 1:24–40.—H. Grass, *Die Abendmahl-Lehre bei Luther und Calvin* (Gütersloh, [2]1954); J.

Diestelmann, *Actio sacramentalis* (Gross Ösingen, 1996); Th. J. Davis: "'The Truth of the Divine Words.' Luther's Sermons on the Eucharist, 1521–28, and the Structure of Eucharist Meaning," *SCJ* 30 (1999) 323–42.

ULRICH KÜHN

■ **Additional Bibliography:** Y. H. Lee, "Calvin's Doctrine of the Lord's Supper," *Yonsei Journal of Theology* 5 (2000) 73–92; M. Tinker, "Language, Symbols and Sacraments: Was Calvin's View of the Lord's Supper Right?," *The Churchman* 112 (1998) 131–49; T. J. Wengert, "Luther's Catechisms and the Lord's Supper," *Word and World* 17 (1997) 54–60.

Concord, Formula and Book. Neither the → Frankfurt Recess of 1558 (*BSLK* 744) nor the assembly of the princes at → Naumburg in 1561 (with a new signing of the → Confessio Augustana) nor the religious dialogue at → Altenburg in 1568-1569 succeeded in overcoming the tensions within Lutheranism.

The Torgau Book was produced by the assembly in Torgau from May 27 to June 7, 1576, on the basis of the Swabian Concord which had been proposed by Jakob → Andreae in 1574. The assembly listened to the views of Nikolaus → Selnecker, Wolfgang → Musculus, and Christoph Cornerus; it also drew on expert evaluations of the Swabian-Saxon Concord by David → Chytraeus and Martin → Chemnitz in northern Germany, and took account of the Maulbronn formula proposed by Lukas → Osiander. Andreae, Chemnitz, and Selnecker wrote reports on the Torgau Book in the monastery of Berge near Magdeburg (March 1-14, 1577), and collaborated with Chytraeus, Musculus, and Cornerus on the final revision (May 19-28). The outcome was the Formula of Concord ("Berge Book") with *Solida Declaratio* and *Epitome,* the "summary excerpts" compiled by Andreae and signed by all six theologians on May 29, 1577.

The formula does not intend to put forward a new creed, but to "repeat and explain" a number of disputed articles (*a*) in the Confessio Augustana, which are now compared with one another in accordance with the directives of scripture, which is "the one single rule and criterion," (*b*) in the creeds of the early church, which are central texts of the "unanimous, universal Christian faith," and (*c*) in the "first, unaltered Confession of Augsburg" with the Apology, the articles of →

Schmalkald, and Martin Luther's Great and Small Catechisms, in which "our Christian faith and creed are explained." Extreme positions on both sides are rejected, disputed concepts are set forward with greater nuances, and a distinction is made between the positions taken by academic theologians and the profession of faith itself.

The articles deal with the following subjects. (1) On → original sin (not "the substance of the corrupt human being"; Victorinus → Strigel against Matthias → Flacius); (2) on the free will (which cannot "on the basis of its own natural powers do that which is in accord with grace"— but the reborn will collaborates); (3) on the righteousness of faith (the whole Christ, in both his natures, not only considered in terms of his divinity, Andreas → Osiander); (4) on good works ("due obedience," which is however neither "necessary" nor "detrimental to salvation," Nikolaus von → Amsdorf; the loss of faith "through deliberate sin"); (5) on → law and gospel; (6) on the third use of the law (preaching of the law—as God's unchangeable will—even to those already reborn; (7) on the holy Lord's Supper of Christ (*manducatio impiorum;* the rite [*usus*] in its entirety: consecration, distribution, and reception); (8) on the person of Christ (*communicatio idiomatum*); (9) on the descent of Christ into hell (Johannes Aepinus); (10) on church customs (freedom of the church to make use of things indifferent); (11) on eternal providence and election (" … one should not investigate the hidden counsel of God" [cf. Luther's *Deus absconditus*], but should investigate the revealed Word; Girolamo → Zanchi; Johannes → Marbach, Cyriakus Spangenberg); (12) on other flocks and sects which never profess their allegiance to the Confession of Augsburg (→ Baptists, Schwenkfeldians [Kaspar → Schwenckfeld], new Arians, and → Antitrinitarians).

Taken as a whole, the Formula of Concord is the expression of confessional consolidation. In positive terms, this means the attainment of a clear profession of faith on the lines of general Christian credal tradition (cf. the appendix to the Book of Concord, a *Catalogus testimoniorum* intended to demonstrate that it "has not departed from the ancient pure church and from the fathers"). Extreme positions are rejected, and exaggerated positions of academic theologians are corrected and relativized. In negative terms, polemical images are used to draw boundary lines: the text speaks of "papistical errors and idolatries," and calls Calvinists "sacramentarists."

The Book of Concord was published on June 25, 1580 with more than 8,000 signatures. It consists of the creeds of the early church and writings connected with the Confessio Augustana (see above; these include the *Tractatus de potestate papae*), and the Formula of Concord. Although the goal of uniting all Lutherans was not achieved, this book remains the most important Lutheran → Corpus doctrinae up to the present day.

■ **Literature:** (K.= Konkordienformel/Konkordienbuch) *OER* 1:193f.; 2, 117–21.—W. Lohff and L. W. Spitz, ed., *Widerspruch, Dialog und Einigung* (Stuttgart, 1977); S. Napiórkowski, *Solus Christus* (Lublin, 1978); J. Schöne, ed., *Bekenntnis zur Wahrheit* (Erlangen, 1978); M. Brecht and R. Schwarz, ed., *Bekenntnis und Einheit der Kirche* (Stuttgart, 1980); E. Koch, *Vom Dissensus zum Konsensus* (Hamburg, 1980); J. Ch. Ebel, *Wort und Geist bei den Verfassern der K.* (Munich, 1981); E. Koch, *Aufbruch und Weg* (Stuttgart, 1983); D. P. Daniel and Ch. P. Arand, *A Bibliography of the Lutheran Confessions* (St. Louis, Mo., 1988); R. Kolb, *Confessing the Faith: Reformers Define the Church, 1530–80* (St. Louis, Mo., 1991); H.-Ch. Rublack, ed., *Die lutherische Konfessionalisierung in Deutschland* (Gütersloh, 1992); I. Mager, *Die K. im Fürstentum Braunschweig-Wolfenbüttel* (Göttingen, 1993); I. Dingel, *Concordia controversa* (Gütersloh, 1996); H. G. Pöhlmann, T. Austad, and F. Krüger, *Theologie der Lutherischen Bekenntnisschriften* (Munich, 1996); G. Wenz, *Theologie der Bekenntnisschriften der evangelisch-lutherischen Kirche*, vol. 1 (Berlin and New York, 1996).

VINZENZ PFNÜR

■ **Additional Bibliography:** *RGG*[4] 4:1603–06.—R. Bodenmann, "Die wiederaufgefundene Kampfschrift Theodor Bezas und seiner Kollegen gegen die K. (1578)," *Lutherische Theologie und Kirche* 21 (1997) 59–98; G. Martens, "Die Adiaphora als theologisches Problem. Ansätze zu einer Hermeneutik von FC X," *Lutherische Beiträge* 5 (2000) 117–27; I. Dingel, "The Preface of the 'Book of Concord' as a Reflection of Sixteenth-century Confessional Development," *Lutheran Quarterly* 15 (2001) 373–95; R. Kolb, "The Formula of Concord and Contemporary Anabaptists, Spiritualists, and Antitrinitarians," *Lutheran Quarterly* 15 (2001) 453–82.

Confessio Augustana, Confutatio and Apology.

1. Confessio Augustana (Confession of Augsburg; CA).

This text was presented by Lutheran princes and cities at the imperial parliament in Augsburg on June 26, 1530. Its main author was Philipp Melanchthon, and it went through several revisions; the *editio princeps* was published in 1531. It supplied the confessional basis for the league of → Schmalkald and was the basic text for religious dialogues. It was the basis for the tolerance accorded in the Religious Peace of → Augsburg in 1555. Those taking doctorates or being ordained were obliged to observe its doctrine. It is the fundamental confessional document of the Lutheran churches, and in the version of 1540 (Variata) it is also a confessional text in Reformed churches.

2. History

After the Peace of Barcelona and Cambrai (June 29 and August 3, 1529), → Charles V convoked on January 21, 1530 an imperial parliament to meet at Augsburg. It was to discuss resistance to the danger that threatened from the Turks (who had besieged Vienna in 1529) and find a solution to the religious question (Edict of Worms, Protestation in Speyer on April 15, 1529). Before the arrival of the delegation of electoral Saxony on May 2 (Martin Luther remained on Coburg), Johannes → Eck presented for disputation before the emperor 404 "articles" which attacked exaggerated versions of propositions of the Reformers; the "devilish" alternative which faced the Reformers was either to defend these propositions or to concede victory. Melanchthon countered by setting forth "that which is taught and preached unanimously in the electoral principality of Saxony" (MSA 7/2:149). This "apologia," which embraces almost all the articles of faith, was presented as their profession of faith by electoral Prince Johann, his son Duke → Johann Friedrich of Saxony, Marquis → George of Brandenburg-Ansbach, Dukes Ernst and Franz of Lüneburg, Prince Wolf of Anhalt, and the imperial cities of Nuremberg and Reutlingen.

3. Contents

The first part, the basic "articles of faith and of doctrine" (CA 1-21), is an outline of salvation history, with the accent on Christology (cf. CA 3): Trinity and Creator (CA 1), Christ (CA 3), Spirit (CA 5; see the version of May 1530 in the Nuremberg copy, Na 4), church (CA 7 and 8), sacraments: baptism (CA 9), Lord's Supper (CA 10), confession, penance (CA 11 and 12), the use of the sacraments (CA 13), church ordination (CA 14;

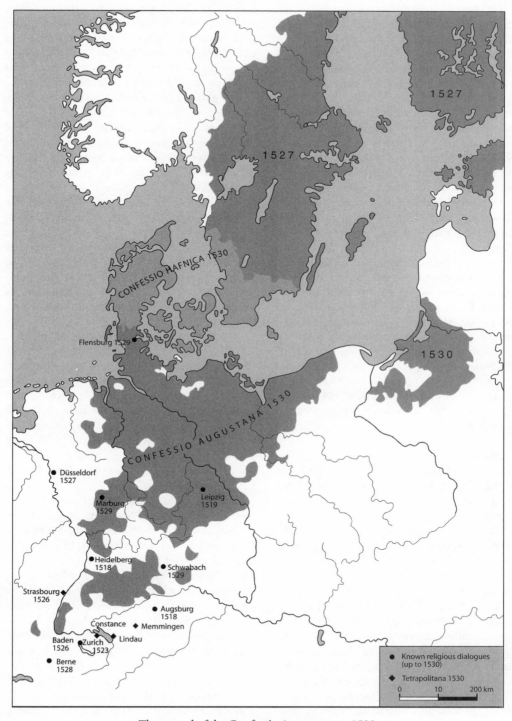

The spread of the Confessio Augustana, c. 1530.

CA Variata: . . . *presbyteros constituat*), and Christ's return in judgment (CA 17). CA 15 and 16 (ecclesiastical regulations, politics) were inserted into this outline (Schwabach articles). CA 2 (original sin) forms the salvation-historical link between CA 1 and CA 3. CA 6 emphasizes the fruits of that faith which is brought about by the Spirit. Justification by faith (CA 4) has its foundations in Christ's atoning sacrifice (CA 3) and in the working of the Spirit, who is communicated by means of ministry, Word, and sacraments, and who brings about faith (CA 5); this is developed further in CA 7-14. CA 18 and 19 were added only in the last editorial phase, in response to Eck; CA 20 (faith and good works) and CA 21 (veneration of the saints) became doctrinal articles (articles of → Torgau).

The second part, in which the "articles about which there is dissension, and the abuses which are to be changed, are set out," includes the articles which had been prepared beforehand (Förstemann 1:68ff.) in order to justify the new order of worship and the → church order which had been introduced: on the sacrament of the altar under both species (CA 22), on the marriage of priests (CA 23), on the Mass (CA 24), on confession (CA 25), on distinctions among foods (CA 26), on monastic vows (CA 27), and on the authority of bishops (CA 28).

4. Evaluation

The CA must be seen not only in the context of imperial politics, but especially in the broader context of the new organization of church communities in the territories which had become Lutheran (instruction for visitation, 1528; Luther's Great and Small Catechisms, 1529), of the demarcation against → Enthusiasts, → Baptists, and Huldrych Zwingli (Luther: *Vom Abendmahl Christi*; profession of faith, 1528; → Schwabach articles, 1529; religious dialogue in → Marburg, Marburg articles), and of the clarification and differentiation of the Lutheran doctrinal position (Johann → Agricola; Melanchthon's lectures on Colossians). Making the local ruler the supreme visitor of the church was a compromise solution. The CA seeks to resolve this question by means of the bishops, whose ministry it is to regulate church life and who have *iure divino* the right to forgive sins, to reject teaching which does not agree with the gospel, and to exclude from the fellowship of the church godless persons whose wickedness is manifestly known (CA 28, 21); the CA is ready to acknowledge the jurisdiction of the Catholic bishops, provided that these concede the → chalice for the laity, marriage of priests (→ celibacy), and the preaching of the pure doctrine of the gospel (CA 28:69f.; Förstemann, 1:196; MSA 7/2:164, 176, 246, 277; CR 2:282).

Against the "rebaptizers," CA rejects the propositions that the Holy Spirit is imparted without the external Word which is communicated in the church (CA 5), that infant baptism is wrong (CA 9), that it is unchristian to accept political office (CA 16), and that hell has an end (CA 17). Against Zwingli, CA 10 teaches "that the true body and blood of Christ are truly present under the form of bread" (*vere* [*et substantialiter*, Apology 10:1] *adsint*). Like Luther (WA 26:500-505), CA appeals against old and new heretics to the doctrinal tradition of the church: "One must believe the decision of the Council of Nicaea without any doubt" (CA 1; for CA 3, cf. DH 1337f.).

Clarification and correction are supplied by CA 18, on free will (1521: everything happens out of absolute necessity), and by CA 19, on the cause of evil (1521: evil, the betrayal by Judas, is God's own work). Against those who "preach ... faith without penance" (CR 26:9; Agricola, 1527), CA 12 emphasizes the two parts of penance: repentance, or horror in the face of sin, and faith in the gospel; this should (*debent*) be followed by an improved life and good works (cf. MSA 1:242-47; CR 26:11 and 20).

The polemic against a → justification by one's own power (CA 18 *editio princeps*; CA 2:4.12) or *ex opere operato*, without any stirring to the good in the person who is justified (CA 13 *editio princeps*; CA 24—but note CA 8, which affirms that the sacraments are efficacious even when they are administered by bad priests), is directed against Gabriel → Biel and the tradition which he transmitted (going back to John Duns Scotus).

Hateful articles, e.g., those that call the pope Antichrist, "belong in the school, rather than in sermons in the churches" (CR 2:182f.), and we do not find such texts in CA, which understands itself as the expression of the teaching of churches (CA 1: *Ecclesiae apud nos docent*) which "do not deviate in any article of faith from the Catholic Church" (*BSLK* 84, cf. 83c.d; MSA 7/2:196, 21f.). When this claim by CA was taken seriously, a new impetus was given to Catholic-Lutheran dialogue in our own days.

- **Sources:** *BSLK*; J. Lorz, ed., *Das Ausburger Bekenntnis. Studienausgabe.* (Göttingen, 1980); CR 26; *Melanchthons Werke in Auswahl*, ed. R. Stupperich, vol. 1–7/2 (Gütersloh, 1951–75) (= MSA), vol. 6, 12–79; W. H. Neuser, *Bibliographie der CA und Apologie 1530–80* (Nieukoop, 1987).

- **Literature:** *TRE* 4:616–28; *HDThG* 81–94.—V. Pfnür, *Einig in der Rechtfertigungslehre?* (Wiesbaden, 1970); H. Meyer et al., eds., *Katholische Anerkennung des Augsburger Bekenntnisses* (Frankfurt/Main, 1977); W. Maurer, *Historischer Kommentar zur CA* (Gütersloh, 1978); E. Iserloh, ed., *CA und Confutatio* (Münster, 1980); H. Meyer et al., ed., *CA. Bekenntnis des einen Glaubens* (Paderborn and Frankfurt/Main, 1980); P. Gauly, *Katholisches Ja zum Augsburger Bekenntnis?* (Freiburg, 1980); M. Cassese, *Augusta 1530* (Milan, 1981); H. Neuhaus, "Der Augsburger Reichstag des Jahres 1530. Ein Forschungsbericht," *ZHF* 9 (1982) 167–211; B. Dittrich, *Das Traditionsverständnis in der CA und in der Confutatio* (Leipzig, 1983); *Lehrverurteilungen kirchentrennend?*, vol. 2, ed. K. Lehmann (Freiburg and Göttingen, 1989) 191–209; M. Brecht, ed., *Martin Luther und das Bischofsamt* (Stuttgart, 1990); K. Koch, *Gelähmte Ökumene* (Freiburg, 1991).

VINZENZ PFNÜR

- **Additional Bibliography:** J. P. Meyer, *Studies in the Augsburg Confession* (Milwaukee, Wisc., 1995); L. Grane, *Die CA.* (Göttingen, ⁵1996); C. Lindberg, "Augsburg 1530 to Augsburg 1555," in *The European Reformations* (Oxford, 1996) 229–48; H. Immenkötter and G. Wenz, eds., *Im Schatten der CA* (Münster, 1997); G. Seebass, *Apologie und Confessio: Die Reformation und ihre Außenseiter* (Göttingen, 1997) 31–43; R. Decot, *Vermittlungsversuch auf dem Augsburger Reichstag. Melanchthon und die CA: 500 Jahre Philipp Melanchthon* (Wiesbaden, 1998) 48–72; E. W. Gritsch, "Reflections on Melanchthon as Theologian of the Augsburg Confession," *Lutheran Quarterly* 12 (1998) 445–52; Ch. Peters, "Reformatorische Doppelstrategie. Melanchthon und das Augsburger Bekenntnis," in *Der Theologe Melanchthon* (Stuttgart, 2000) 169–93.

2. Confutatio

About twenty Catholic theologians (Johannes → Cochlaeus, Johann → Dietenberger, Johannes → Eck, Johannes → Fabri, Julius → Pflug, Bartholomäus → Arnoldi, Konrad → Wimpina, et al.) elaborated a "Response" or "Refutation" of CA. This went through various stages: (*a*) the *Responsio Theologorum* (of which arts. 1-4 survive: CFR 27:85-97), which was much too long; (*b*) the *Catholica Responsio* (Ficker 1-140), which was dis-

cussed under the chairmanship of Fabri and was completed on July 12, 1530; this met with the approval of the papal legate, Lorenzo → Campeggi, but not of the imperial court; (*c*) the *Confutatio Confessionis Augustanae* (Immenkötter, *Confutatio*, 74-207), which closely followed the text of CA, both emphasizing the shared doctrinal convictions (in arts. 1-3, 5, 8-14, 16-18, and 20) and justifying (with reference to scripture, the church fathers, and the early councils) the different positions taken by the Catholic side (especially on the doctrines of original sin, justification, good works, *sola fide*, the existence of seven sacraments, the intercession of the saints, and the so-called abuses mentioned in part 2 of CA). In the preface and the epilog, Charles V underlines that this version claims the character of imperial law.

When the various sheets of paper were put together to form the text to be read on March 8, a complete section was left out by mistake. This is why the conclusion to art. 24 and arts. 25 and 26 are missing in the German original, though not in the Latin text which was made for the emperor. The imperial court forbade the text to be communicated to the Lutheran Estates. From that time, the Protestant evaluation of the *Confutatio* has been characterized by polemical positions—all the more so, since the text was soon considered obsolete (despite some half-hearted attempts at revision), and was then forgotten.

- **Sources:** J. Ficker, *Die Konfutation des Augsburgischen Bekenntnisses* (Leipzig, 1891); CR 27:1–243; H. Immenkötter, *Die Confutatio der CA* (Münster, ²1981).

- **Literature** (see also bibliography to 1) K. E. Förstemann, ed., *Urkundenbuch zu der Geschichte des Reichstages zu Augsburg im Jahre 1530*, 2 vols. (Halle, 1833–35, reprinted Hildesheim, 1966); Th. Brieger, "Beiträge zur Geschichte des Augsburger Reichstags," *ZKG* 12 (1891) 123–87; S. Ehses, "Kardinal Lorenzo Campeg(g)io auf dem Reichstag zu Augsburg 1530," *RQ* 17 (1903) 383–406; 18 (1904) 358–84; 19 (1905) II 129–52; 20 (1906) II 54–80; 21 (1907) II 114–39; *Protokoll des Augsburger Reichstages 1530*, ed. H. Grundmann (Gütersloh, 1958); K. Rischar, *Johannes Eck auf dem Reichstag zu Augsburg 1530* (Münster, 1968); H. Immenkötter, *Um die Einheit im Glauben* (Münster, ²1974); E. Iserloh, ed., *CA und Confutatio* (Münster, 1980); W. Reinhard, ed., *Bekenntnis und Geschichte* (Munich, 1981); H. Immenkötter, *Der Augsburger Reichstag und die Confutatio* (Münster, ²1981); M. Cassese, ed., *Augusta 1530* (Milan, 1981); idem, "La Scuola Cattolica," *Varese* 110 (1982) 272–88; H. J. Urban, *Theologische Revue* 77 (1981) 441–58; M. Marcocchi, *Aevum* 56 (1982) 395–406; B. Dittrich, *Das*

Traditionsverständnis in der CA und in der Confutatio
(Leipzig, 1983); E. Honée, *Der Libell des Hieronymus
Vehus zum Augsburger Reichstag 1530* (Münster, 1988);
R. Decot, ed., *Vermittlungsversuch auf dem Augsburger
Reichstag 1530* (Stuttgart, 1989).

3. *Apology*

Melanchthon and others began work in
August, 1530 on a "Discourse of Defense or Apology," and an early draft was ready on Oct. 22.
However, the Turkish threat prompted Archduke
Ferdinand to prevent the imperial court from
accepting it. Thereafter, attention concentrated
primarily on the doctrine of justification, which
takes up more than half of the *editio princeps*
(April, 1531). The opposition to the doctrine of
the "old faith" is formulated more precisely,
sometimes in a polemic tone, and the *Confutatio* is
rejected. Originally a private initiative of
Melanchthon, the Apology (like the CA itself) was
made the doctrinal basis of the Schmalkaldic
League as early as 1531, and has formed part of the
Lutheran confessional documents since that date.
- **Sources:** H. G. Pöhlmann, ed., *Apologia Confessionis
Augustanae* (Gütersloh, 1967); *BSLK* 141–404.
- **Literature** (see also bibliographies to 1 and 2): G.
Plitt, *Die Apologie* (Erlangen, 1873); E. Schlink,
Theologie der Bekenntnisschriften (Munich, ³1948); H.
Fagerberg, *Theologie der Bekenntnisschriften von 1529–
37* (Göttingen, 1965); V. Pfnür, *Einig in der Recht-
fertigungslehre?* (Wiesbaden, 1970); M. Brecht and K.
Schwarz, eds., *Bekenntnis und Einheit der Kirche*
(Stuttgart, 1980); G. Wenz, *Theologie der Bekenntnis-
schriften* (Darmstadt, 1993).

HERBERT IMMENKÖTTER

- **Additional Bibliography:** A. E. Buchrucker,
"Melanchthons Apologie der Augustana als Beitrag zu
einträchtiger Lehre in der evangelisch-lutherischen
Kirche," in *Einträchtig lehren*. Festschrift J. Schöne
(Gross Ösingen, 1997) 69–94.

Confessio Scotica (Scottish Confession). The confessional document of the Scottish Reformation
was composed and accepted by parliament in
1560 but was ratified only in 1567, under James VI
(later James I of England). This remained the fundamental doctrinal text of the Protestant church
in Scotland until it was superseded by the Westminster Confession. It was drawn up at the
request of parliament in only four days, by a
group of theologians (John → Knox and five colleagues) of varying theological backgrounds); this

explains its formal deficiencies and a certain lack
of theological balance. Although strongly orientated to Jean Calvin's theology, it is not "purely
Calvinistic," but is also influenced by Martin →
Bucer, Huldrych Zwingli, Johannes → Oecolampadius, and Heinrich → Bullinger. Its 25 articles
treat of such themes as sanctification, rebirth, and
good works as gifts of grace, the church, scripture,
and sacraments, as well as the rights and obligations of the secular government. Relatively
unusual features are the link between systematic
and biblical theology, the emphasis on ecclesiology, and the explicit treatment of Christian ethics.
- **Literature:** *Dictionary of Scottish Church History and
Theology* (Edinburgh, 1993) 751f.; *OER* 4:33–36.—
W. I. P. Hazlet, "The Scots Confession. Context,
Complexion and Critique," *ARG* 78 (1987) 287–320.

GEORG HINTZEN

- **Additional Bibliography:** J. M. Owen, "The Angel of
the Great Counsel of God and the Christology of the
'Scots Confession' of 1560," *Scottish Journal of Theology*
55 (2002) 303–24.

Confessio Virtembirgica (Württemberg Confession; CV). In order to get rid of the temporary
solution laid down in the → Augsburg Interim,
the Protestant duke → Christopher of Württemberg had to agree to send representatives to the
Council of → Trent. For this purpose, CV was
drawn up under the supervision of Johannes →
Brenz; it was the only Protestant confession to be
presented to the council, in 1552. A reply was
promised, but never materialized. Nevertheless,
CV is important not only as a Protestant → confessional document, but also because it unites theological openness and firmness vis-à-vis the
Catholic party.
- **Sources:** *CV. Das Württembergische Bekenntnis von
1551*, ed. E. Bizer (Stuttgart, 1952); *CV. Das
Württembergische Bekenntnis von 1552*, ed. M. Brecht
and H. Ehmer (Holzgerlingen, 1999).
- **Literature:** M. Brecht, "Abgrenzung oder Verständigung. Was wollten die Protestanten in Trient?," in
Concilium Tridentinum, ed. R. Bäumer (Darmstadt,
1979) 161–95.

MARTIN BRECHT

Confessional documents

1. The elaboration of Protestant confessional
statements was seen as an expression of the Chris-

tian obligation to confess the faith (Rom 10:10), in continuity with the preceding history of the formation of confessional documents in the church, especially in the earliest centuries. Protestant statements are indeed analogous to these, but have their own characteristics, so that we can speak of a specific genre here: these are documents of ecclesiastical teaching, most of which elaborate the totality (or *summa*) of God's revelation in Christ as this is fundamentally attested in sacred scripture in its most important elements. They demarcate this *summa* from erroneous interpretations and claim that the preaching and doctrine of their church fellowship have a binding and normative character.

The original intention of the Reformation confessional documents was to attest the universal (Catholic) apostolic faith within the whole church; only in the course of history did they become doctrinal norms for confessional churches. This obscures, but does not remove, their original aim.

Since the Reformers were convinced that the → church does not have the autonomous authority to posit any articles of faith, all their confessional documents derive their theological-dogmatic binding character from the claim that they are expositions of scripture, which remains the highest norm—even when the confessional documents themselves are used for the exegesis of the Bible. In this sense, the confessional documents understand themselves as *norma normata*—there is a tension between their claim to be normative and the reserve entailed by the position that only scripture is normative. They are legally binding because they have a firm place in the constitutions of most churches, and those ordained to the ministry of public preaching are obligated to maintain the doctrine set out in the confessional statements; there are however differences on this point among the various Protestant churches.

The first clear indications of the elaboration of Reformation confessional documents are found in 1528 (the Zwinglian Berne theses) and 1529 (the Lutheran → Schwabach articles). Like the formation of confessions in general, the formulation of Protestant confessional documents is the result of specific historical occasions: they provide orientation for ecclesial reform in doctrine and praxis, they ward off acute dangers or establish church fellowship, they give an account of the faith and doctrine to political or church authorities, or they provide instruction for pastors, parishes, and families.

Accordingly, there is a considerable number and variety of Reformation confessional documents, linked directly or indirectly to one another. Some have local validity, others regional or even wider authority. Some take the form of catechisms, but the great majority present their instruction in the form of an orderly list of short doctrinal statements (often formulated as theses). These, however, can be expanded to form tractates, so that there is great variety in the length of the confessional documents. This greatly reduces the element of confession and doxology, and makes them unsuitable for use in the liturgy.

2. Despite all their formal and substantial similarities, we can make a clear distinction between Lutheran and Reformed confessional documents, in terms both of their status and of their use in the church.

It is characteristic of *Lutheranism* that the confessional documents retain their validity and binding character beyond the place and time of their composition. The documents originating in the milieu of the Wittenberg Reformation either possess *a priori* a more than regional character, or else are received in other local churches inside and outside Germany. Some regional confessional documents do indeed emerge, but their importance is short-lived and disappears in favor of the larger confessional fellowship which finds expression in the acknowledgment of one and the same confessional document. This development reaches its conclusion in the Book of → Concord (1580), a collection of the Lutheran confessional documents which includes the three "ecumenical" creeds from the early church.

In the *Reformed churches,* however, there always existed a large number of local or regional confessional documents, whose validity remained geographically limited.

The articles of faith of the Church of → England and (deriving from these) of the Methodist Church in North America are historically linked to the formation of the Lutheran confession and share the Lutheran urge to have one single confessional document. Nevertheless, they come much closer (especially today) to the Reformed position, since they relativize the validity of their doctrinal articles in an historical sense; besides this, neither of these churches accords the centrality to a formulated doctrinal agreement which we find in Lutheranism. The same holds true *a fortiori* of Congregationalists and Baptists.

3. Individual Documents

Lutheran Confessional Documents

In the period prior to the imperial parliament at Augsburg in 1555, the following documents with a supra-regional status had been drawn up: the → Confessio Augustana (CA), which was presented to the emperor in 1530 and was given the status of imperial law in 1555; the *Apologia for the CA* (1531), drawn up by Philipp Melanchthon, which was given the formal status of a confessional document in 1537; Luther's *Schmalkaldic articles,* composed at the request of the electoral prince of Saxony, in view of the council which Paul III had convoked; Melanchthon's *Tractatus de potestate et primatu papae,* conceived as an addition to CA; finally, Luther's *Great and Small Catechisms* (1529). These confessional documents were included in the *Book of* → *Concord* in 1580 and have abiding validity within Lutheranism. In addition, we should mention a number of regional doctrinal and confessional documents, e.g., Melanchthon's *Instructions for Visitors* (1528) and his *Examen ordinandorum* (1552), the → *Confessio Virtembirgica,* composed for the Council of Trent, and the *Confessio Saxonica* (1551).

From c. 1560, a number of → Corpora Doctrinae were drawn up, with a binding character only for particular territorial churches. These reflect doctrinal differences within Lutheranism, since each such text includes only some of the confessional documents mentioned above. In order to resolve these doctrinal conflicts, the Formula of Concord (1577) was composed after lengthy negotiations. It took the double form of the more detailed *Solida Declaratio* and the briefer *Epitome.* It saw itself as a "repetition and explanation" of CA, and was included in the Book of Concord (1580) together with the three patristic creeds and the supra-regional confessional documents mentioned above. This basically brought the development of the Lutheran confession to its close. Although the Book of Concord itself is not authoritative in all the Lutheran churches, CA and Luther's Small Catechism do have this status.

Reformed Confessional Documents

These are many in number, and form two groups, pre- and post-Calvin. The first group includes, e.g., the *Berne theses* (1528); Huldrych Zwingli's *Fidei ratio* (1530), which he sent to → Charles V; the *Confessio Tetrapolitana* of the cities of Strasbourg, Memmingen, Lindau, and Constance, composed for the imperial parliament at Augsburg (1530); the *Confessio Basilensis* (1534); and the *Confessio Helvetica Prior* (1536).

Swiss confessional documents from the time of Calvin onwards include the *Genevan Catechism* (Calvin, 1545) and the *Confessio Helvetica Posterior* (Heinrich Bullinger, 1562), which was signed by the Reformed churches of other countries too (Scotland, Hungary, Bohemia, Poland, Holland).

Confessional documents from the West include the *Confessio Gallicana* (La Rochelle, 1559) for the French communities and the *Confessio Belgica* (1561) for the Dutch communities, the → *Confessio Scotica* (John Knox, 1560), and German documents such as the *Confession of the Foreign Community in Frankfurt* (1554), the *Emden Catechism* (1554), and especially the widely diffused → *Heidelberg Catechism* (1563).

Anglican Communion

In the *Anglican Communion,* the *Thirty-Nine Articles of Religion* (→ Anglican articles) have authoritative status in the version drawn up in 1563/1571, which goes back to earlier texts, some of which were influenced by Lutheranism.

■ **Literature:** *TRE* 5:487–511.—Ph. Schaff, ed., *The Creeds of Christendom,* 3 vols. (New York, 1877; Grand Rapids, Mich., ⁵1977/78); E. F. K. Müller, ed., *Die Bekenntnisschriften der reformierten Kirche* (Leipzig, 1903); P. Tschackert, *Die Entstehung der lutherischen und reformierten Kirchenlehre* (Göttingen, 1910); W. Niesel, ed., *Bekenntnisschriften und Kirchenordnungen der nach Gottes Wort reformierten Kirchen* (Zurich, 1938); E. Schlink, *Theologie der lutherischen Bekenntnisschriften* (Munich, ³1948); F. Brunstäd, *Theologie der lutherischen Bekenntnisschriften* (Gütersloh, 1951); E. J. Bicknell, *A Theological Introduction to the 39 Articles* (London ²1955); *Die Bekenntnisschriften der evangelisch-lutherischen Kirche* (Göttingen, ³1956); P. Jakobs, *Theologie reformierter Bekenntnisschriften in Grundzügen* (Neukirchen-Vluyn, 1959); V. Vajta and H. Weissgerber, eds., *Das Bekenntnis im Leben der (lutherischen) Kirche* (Berlin and Hamburg, 1963); F. Mildenberger, *Theologie der lutherischen Bekenntnisschriften* (Stuttgart, 1983).

HARDING MEYER

■ **Additional Bibliography:** *RGG*[4] 1:1270–74.—M. A. Noll, *Confessions and Catechisms of the Reformation* (Grand Rapids, Mich., 1991); G. Seebass, "Die reformatorischen Bekenntnisse vor der Confessio Augustana," in *Die Reformation und ihre Außenseiter,* ed. I. Dingel (Göttingen, 1997) 11–30; G. Wenz, *Theologie der Bekenntnisschriften der evangelisch-lutherischen Kirche,* 2 vols. (Berlin, 1996–98); E. F. K. Müller, ed., *Die Bekenntnisschriften der reformierten Kirche,* 2 vols. (Waltrop, 1999); R. Kolb, "Sources and Contexts of the Lutheran Confessional Writings," *Lutheran Quarterly* 15 (2001) 125–41; S. H. Hendrix, "Luther und die lutherischen B. in der englischsprachighen Forschung seit 1983," *Lutherjahrbuch* 68 (2001) 115–36; E. F. Klug, "The Lutheran Confessions: Luther's role," *Concordia Theological Quarterly* 65 (2001) 246–54; D. G. Truemper, "The Role and Authority of the Lutheran Confessional Writings," *Mennonite Quarterly Review* 76 (2002) 299–313; J. Webster, "Confession and Confessions," *Toronto Journal of Theology* 18 (2002) 167–79.

Confessionalization. Older scholarship spoke of the age of Reformation and Counter-Reformation, but Hubert Jedin picked up the concept of "Catholic Reformation," coined by Wilhelm Maurenbrecher in 1880, and pleaded for a triadic division: Reformation, Catholic → Reform, → Counter-Reformation. This found a generally positive echo. Drawing on Ernst Walter Zeeden's researches into "the formation of confessions," Wolfgang Reinhard and Heinz Schilling have recently elaborated the concept of "confessionalization" and applied it to the whole period of the 16th and early 17th centuries. The paradigm is broadly similar for the Catholic, Lutheran, and Calvinist confessions; it is the contents that differ in each case.

Confessionalization designates a "fundamental process of change in social history, including ecclesiastical, religious, cultural, civil, political and social transformations, as well as changes in mentality" (Reinhard and Schilling, p. 4). Confessionalization involves religious innovations promoted by a clear and specific creed, demarcation vis-à-vis the other confession, the monopolization of education, emphasis on the rites which consolidate confessional differentiation, new or renewed forms of institutional church organization, specific confessional schools and colleges, a system of control, and a symbiosis with the civil authority. The consequences of confessionalization included an unintentional contribution to the growth of state power and to the modernization of state and society (cf. ibid., 426f.).

The process of confessionalization includes the emergence and development of the Reformation movements, impulses to reform within Catholicism, and Counter-Reformation actions. Although this paradigm has met with some criticism, its methodological approach has won wide international recognition. At any rate, this paradigm is better suited to grasp the complex events of the formation of confessions in the 16th and 17th centuries than an isolated study of the Reformation on the one hand and Catholic reform and the Counter-Reformation on the other.

■ **Literature:** W. Reinhard, "Zwang zur Konfessionalisierung? Prolegomena zu einer Theorie des konfessionellen Zeitalters," *ZHF* 10 (1983) 257–77; E. W. Zeeden, *Konfessionsbildung* (Stuttgart, 1985); H. Schilling, ed., *Die reformierte Konfessionalisierung in Deutschland—Das Problem der "Zweiten Reformation."* (Gütersloh, 1986); W. Reinhard, "Reformation, Counter-Reformation, and the Early Modern State, A Reassessment," *CHR* 75 (1989) 383–404; H.-Ch. Rublack, ed., *Die lutherische Konfessionalisierung in Deutschland* (Gütersloh, 1992); H. Schilling, "Konfessionelle und politische Identität," *Nationale und ethnische Minderheiten und regionale Identitäten in Mittelalter und Neuzeit,* ed. A. Czacharowski (Thorn, 1994) 103–23; W. Reinhard and H. Schilling, eds., *Die katholische Konfessionalisierung* (Münster and Gütersloh, 1995).

KLAUS GANZER

■ **Additional Bibliography:** Th. Kaufmann, "Die Konfessionalisierung von Kirche und Gesellschaft," *Theologische Literaturzeitung* 121 (1996) 1008–25; J. Bahlcke and A. Strohmeyer, eds., *Konfessionalisierung in Ostmitteleuropa* (Stuttgart, 1999) 21 essays; E. Rummel, *The confessionalization of humanism in Reformation Germany* (Oxford, 2000); A. Lexutt, "Konfessionalisierung—neuer Schlauch für alten Wein?," *Verkündigung und Forschung* 45 (2000) 3–24 (report on literature); N. Blough, "'The Uncovering of the Babylonian Whore': Confessionalization and Politics Seen from the Underside," *Mennonite Quarterly Review* 75 (2001) 35–55; R. Pörtner, "Confessionalization and Ethnicity: The Slovenian Reformation and Counter-Reformation in the 16th and 17th centuries," *ARG* 93 (2002) 239–77; S. Rau, *Geschichte und Konfession* (Hamburg, 2002); G. Sebass, "Confessionalization and Tolerance," in *Caritas et reformatio.* Festschrift C. Lindberg (St. Louis, 2002) 59–71; J. R. Farr, "Confessionalization and Social Discipline in France, 1530–1685," *ARG* 94 (2003) 276–93; A. M. Poska, "Confessionalization and Social Discipline in the Iberian World," *ARG* 94 (2003) 308–19.

Confirmation. The Reformation abolished confirmation by bishops on the grounds that this is not a sacrament based in the New Testament and that it degrades baptism by making it an incomplete action. Nevertheless, a Protestant *confirmatio* developed in the 16th century, consisting of instruction, confession, and an examination in the catechism (an annual or once-only *interrogatio seu exploratio* on the subject of the Lord's Supper: Martin Luther, *Formula missae,* 1523; *Christiana catechesis:* Jean Calvin, *Institutiones,* 1536), and this won universal acceptance thanks to Pietism and the Enlightenment; the last places to accept it were Lübeck (1817) and Hamburg (1832). Confirmation has been interpreted in various ways up to the present: as the conclusion of the catechumenate, as a remembrance of baptism, as the personal ratification of the church's profession of faith, as intercession on the part of the community for the one confirmed, as a blessing, as admission to the Lord's Supper, as the bestowal of ecclesiastical rights, or as imposing obligations.

In order to help enforce church discipline, Martin → Bucer introduced in Hessen a "sacramental ceremony" with examination in the catechism, a vow, intercessory prayer, and the laying-on of hands which was interpreted in the following "exhibitory" words: "Receive the Holy Spirit, a shield and protection from all harm, and strength and help to do all that is good, from the loving hand of God . . ." (Disciplinary order of Ziegenhain, 1538/1539, Kassel, 1539). The Cologne Reformation of 1543 transmitted this confirmation ceremony to the 1540 Anglican *Book of* → *Common Prayer,* where it is an action performed by the bishop with a "deprecative" form of words; it is later found in Waldeck (1556), Austria (1571), Niedersachsen (1585), Gotha (1682), Speyer (1700), Friedberg (1704), and Stuttgart (1790). Lutheran confirmation goes back to Martin → Chemnitz (*Examen Concilii Tridentini,* vol. 2 [1566], 3) and has a more strongly catechetical character; it is found, e.g., in Pomerania (1563) and Braunschweig-Wolfenbüttel (1569).

■ *LThK*[3] 6:241f. (unabridged version).
■ **Literature:** *EKL*[3] 2:1370–77; *TRE* 19:437–51; H.-Ch. Schmidt-Lauber and K.-H. Bieritz, eds., *Handbuch der Liturgik* (Leipzig and Göttingen, 1995) 333–53, 925–36.—G. Rietschel and P. Graff, *Lehrbuch der Liturgik,* vol. 2 (Göttingen, [2]1952) 621–75; L. Vischer, *Geschichte der Konfirmation* (Zollikon, 1958); B. Hareide, *Konfirmation in der Reformationszeit* (Göttingen, 1971); R.

Bornet, "La confirmation dans le Protestantisme et dans l'Anglicanisme," *La Maison-Dieu* 168 (1986) 77–105.

HANS–CHRISTOPH SCHMIDT-LAUBER

■ **Additional Literature:** B. Steinberg, "What Is Confirmation?," *One in Christ* 32 (1996) 53–63.

Consensus Tigurinus (Consensus of Zurich; CT). The CT was a response to theological tensions between Geneva and Zurich or Berne in a number of questions about dogma, liturgy, and practical church order (Text: P. Barth and D. Scheuner, eds., *Joannis Calvini Opera selecta,* vol. 2 [Munich, 1952] 241-58). The CT is an agreement between Jean Calvin and the Protestant clergy in Zurich about the doctrine of the Lord's Supper, two pages in length, drawn up under the leadership of Zwingli's successor, Heinrich → Bullinger, against the background of political developments in the empire, in France, and in Geneva.

In terms of its substance, the CT is a compromise. The Zurich party concedes that the Lord's Supper promotes the memory of Christ and strengthens the *fides historica,* while Calvin limits the reception of the sacramental gift to those chosen by God. Other disputed questions remained unresolved. The CT restored mutual confidence between Zurich and Calvin, but failed in its aim of reducing the tensions in the immediate sphere of conflict, viz., Wadtland, the French-speaking territory which was subject to Berne. After it was printed in 1551, the CT helped widen the gulf between the Swiss and the Wittenberg Reformation (→ eucharistic controversy with Joachim → Westphal).

■ **Literature:** *TRE* 8:189–92.—U. Gäbler, "Das Zustandekommen des CT im Jahre 1549," *Theologische Literaturzeitung* 104 (1979) 321–32.

ERNST KOCH

Contarini, *Gasparo.* Catholic reformer, born October 16, 1483 in Venice, son of a patrician family, died August 24, 1542 in Bologna. He studied philosophy and mathematics in Padua, where Pietro Pomponazzi was one of his teachers, and he formed friendships with Tommaso Giustiniani and Vincenzo Quirini, who entered the monastery of Camaldoli. After doubts and an experience of interior grace on Holy Saturday, 1511, Contarini decided to remain in the world and dedicated himself with greater zeal to theological studies. In 1518, he began his career in the public service of the republic of Venice, and he took part in the imperial parliament at Worms in 1521 as the Venetian ambassador to → Charles V, though he did not meet Martin Luther in person. He was the Venetian envoy to → Clement VII from 1528 to 1530.

In 1535, as a layman, he was created cardinal by → Paul III and soon became a key figure in endeavors to promote church reform in Rome. A commission set up by Paul III, with Contarini as its spokesman, presented the *Consilium de emendanda ecclesia* in March, 1537. He had received the bishopric of Belluno on October 23, 1536, but basically entrusted the care of this diocese to vicars general. On January 10, 1541, he was appointed papal legate to the imperial parliament in Regensburg and the religious dialogue which was to be held there. Thanks to his initiative, a compromise formula on the doctrine of → justification was accepted in Regensburg. This went a long way to meet the Lutheran position of double righteousness, but was rejected both by Luther and by Rome; no agreement was reached in this dialogue about other disputed points, above all transubstantiation. The compromise formula of Regensburg led to suspicion in Rome that Contarini's faith was not orthodox; he defended himself on May 25, 1541 in the *Epistola de iustificatione*. After his return from Germany, Paul III entrusted him in March 1542 with the legation in Bologna, and he retained this office until his death. His tomb is in S. Maria dell'Orto in Venice.

Contarini was an important representative of the forces of religious renewal in Italy which are designated by the name "Spirituals." The "Spirituals" included Reginald → Pole and Vittoria Colonna, who were personal friends of Contarini. His position on justification was determined by his experience on Holy Saturday of 1511, an experience which took on an ever deeper significance for him. He had become certain that no one could justify himself through his works: one must take refuge in the grace of God, which one receives through faith in Jesus Christ. This explains his promotion of the Regensburg formula. In his teaching about the sacraments and in his ecclesiology, Contarini is rooted in the standard Catholic doctrinal tradition. His studies made him primarily a philosopher with a strong Aristotelian orien-

tation; apart from his doctrine of justification, there is little originality in his theological writings. His importance in church history is primarily due to his activity as a reformer.

■ **Sources:** "Vita von L. Beccadelli," in *Monumenti di varia letteratura*, ed. G. Morandi, vol. 1/2 (Bologna 1799) 9–59; L. Beccadelli, "Lettere del Cardinal G. C.," in *Monumenti di varia letteratura*, 61–216; F. Dittrich, *Regesten und Briefe des Cardinals G. C.* (Braunsberg, 1881); W. Friedensburg, "Der Briefwechsel G. C.s mit Ercole Gonzaga," *QFIAB* 2 (1899) 161–222; L. Pastor, "Die Correspondenz des Cardinals C. während seiner deutschen Legation 1541," *HJ* 1 (1880) 321–92, 473–501; H. Jedin, *C. und Camaldoli* (Rome, 1953) (30 letters 1510–23).

■ **Works:** *G. C. Opera* (Paris 1571; Venice, 1578, 1589); F. Hünermann, *G. C. Gegenreformatorische Schriften* (Münster, 1923).—The most important writings are: *De officio episcopi* (1517); *De immortalitate animae* (1518); *De magistratibus et republica Venetorum* (1524–34); *Confutatio articulorum seu questionum Lutheranorum* (1530); *De potestate pontificis* (1534); *De sacramentis christianae legis et catholicae ecclesiae* (1539/40); *De iustificatione* (1541); *De praedestinatione* (1537).

■ **Literature:** *DBI* 28:172–92; *TRE* 8:202–6.—F. Dittrich, *G. C.* (Braunsberg, 1885); H. Rückert, *Die theologische Entwicklung G. C.s.* (Bonn, 1926); H. Hackert, *Die Staatsschrift C.s und die politischen Verhältnisse Venedigs im 16.Jh.* (Heidelberg, 1940); H. Jedin, *Kardinal C. als Kontroverstheologe* (Münster, 1949); idem, "Ein 'Turmerlebnis' des jungen C.," *HJ* 70 (1951) 115–30; idem, "G. C. e il contributo veneziano alla riforma cattolica," in *La civiltà veneziana del Rinascimento* (Florence, 1958) 103–24; H. Mackensen, "The Diplomatic Role of G. Cardinal C. at the Colloquy of Ratisbon in 1541," *ARG* 51 (1960) 36–57; P. Matheson, *Cardinal C. at Regensburg* (Oxford, 1972); K. Ganzer, "Zum Kirchenverständnis G. C.s," *Würzburger Diözesangeschichtsblätter* 35/36 (1974) 241–60; P. Simoncelli, *Evangelismo italiano del Cinquecento* (Rome, 1979); G. Fragnito, *G. C. Un magistrato veneziano al servizio della cristianità* (Florence, 1988); *G. C. e il suo tempo*, ed. F. Cavazzana Romanelli (Venice, 1988); E. G. Gleason, *G. C. Venice, Rome, and Reform* (Berkeley, 1993).

KLAUS GANZER

■ **Additional Bibliography:** V. DeBoni, "Il cardinale G. C.," *RSCI* 51 (1997) 463–92; . Furey, "The Communication of Friendship: G. C.'s Letters to Hermits at Camaldoli," *ChH* 72 (2003) 71–191.

Controversial theology

1. Concept

In the broadest sense, this term refers to every theological debate with those who hold different beliefs and with those within the church who hold divergent views on questions of doctrine and ethics which either allegedly or *de facto* split the church. In the narrower sense, it refers to the theological controversies which developed from the 16th century onwards between Roman Catholic and Protestant theologians, or between the Protestant confessions themselves.

2. History

The decisive factor for the development of controversial theology in the narrower sense was the → Reformation. This theology was not elaborated as a completely coherent and morphologically unified system, but followed the developments and ramifications of the Reformation, debating these both in written texts and through other means of communication. Since it too was a part of politics, controversial theology was not completely detached from the specific demands made by the political situation in which the authors wrote.

In the earliest phase, central topics of controversial theology (Sylvester → Prierias, 1518; → Leipzig disputation, 1519) were → indulgences, → penance, and salvation, as well as the question of papal authority (and hence ecclesiology). But new problems continually emerged, e.g., the doctrine of → justification, the Mass (→ Communion), the → chalice for the laity, the → sacraments, and the veneration of the → saints and of Mary: and these became the new themes of controversial theology. Thomas → Cajetan discussed the question of the individual certainty of faith in the process of salvation; Johannes → Eck and Augustin von → Alveldt debated papal authority with Martin Luther; the Reformation principle of *sola scriptura* prompted Hieronymus → Emser to produce works on scripture and tradition, and on → law and gospel, in 1521. The veneration of images became the object of dispute from 1522 onwards (→ Art and Reformation), and problems connected with the Lord's Supper and baptism were a central theme from 1525/1526 onwards, not only in Roman Catholic theology, but also among Lutherans and Zwinglians (→ eucharistic controversy). A similar development can be seen among the "Spiritualists," who in turn were attacked by both the Reformation and the Catholic parties (e.g., Kaspar → Schwenckfeld). The polemics between the Protestant groups

(→ Lutheranism, → Zwinglianism, → Calvinism, Church of → England) influenced not only their Roman Catholic opponents, but also the Protestant churches themselves, and these polemics became ever clearer and sharper in the second half of the 16th century; numerous Catholic controversial theologians followed Johannes → Cochlaeus in utilizing the resulting dissonance as an argument against the Reformation. The growing number of → confessional documents on the Lutheran, Zwinglian, and Calvinist side helped give controversial theology a clearer structure. Its spectrum went from a decided drawing of boundary lines to a middle path which appealed to the figure of → Erasmus of Rotterdam and aimed at reform and church unity (this is found in some of Philipp Melanchthon's writings, and is the path consciously chosen by Georg → Witzel, Georg → Cassander, and Claude d'→ Espence). Although Erasmus himself had written against Luther, he remained to some extent a mediating figure between the solidifying lines of battle.

There was no methodological unity in the first decades of the Reformation. We find among the opponents of the Reformation both an argumentation drawing on scholasticism (e.g., Jacob → Hoogstraeten) and an argumentation strongly orientated to scripture (e.g., Kaspar → Schatzgeyer), sometimes with a philological-humanistic orientation (Johannes → Fabri [died 1541]). Melanchthon's *Loci* (1521) quickly provided a model for numerous works which offered summaries of controversial theology; the most successful of these books was the Catholic Eck's *Enchiridion locorum communium* (1525, often reprinted).

From the 1530s onwards, theologians in Louvain such as Johannes → Driedo and Albert → Pigge improved the methodological quality by seeking to establish a more inherently appropriate link between scripture, the church fathers, and scholasticism; they attached great importance to the patristic evidence (*consensus patrum*). By the end of the 16th century, all the great confessions sought to claim the fathers as their own. The form of controversial theology was also influenced by the Thomism which was developed in Spain (Salamanca) and further elaborated by the Jesuits, as well as by the recourse in Protestantism to Aristotle and scholasticism. Melchior → Cano's *Loci* (1563) laid down the subsequent path for Roman

Catholic controversial theology, by making available and evaluating the available arsenal of arguments.

The Council of Trent, which was attended by a number of controversial theologians (→ Ambrosius Catharinus, Domingo de → Soto, Stanislaus → Hosius, etc.), gave Catholic controversial theology a new basis; but Trent itself had to be defended against Protestant attacks (Martin → Chemnitz). As a result of Trent, the decisive point of controversy in Protestant eyes became scripture and tradition; in the aftermath of the council, the Catholic side increasingly emphasized the role of the church and the pope as guaranteeing the faith. Robert Bellarmine's *Disputationes de controversiis* (1586-1593) can be considered a preliminary summing-up of controversial theology from the Roman Catholic perspective.

Controversial theology was given a place in academic structures by the foundation of professorships (e.g., at the Roman College in 1561, in Freiburg in 1595, in Ingolstadt in 1605). The Jesuit regulations for studies (1599) laid down that not all students were to attend lectures in controversial theology, but only those destined for work in confessionally mixed areas. Controversial theology was also included in many Protestant regulations for studies. At the end of the 16th and beginning of the 17th centuries, controversial theology stimulated the development of positive theology, but it also sharpened the divisions between the confessions.

■ *LThK*[3] 6:333ff. (unabridged version).

■ **Literature:** *DThC* 3:1694–1748; *Sacramentum mundi*, ed. K. Rahner et al., vol. 3 (Freiburg, 1969) 31–39; *EKL*[2] 2:927ff.; *EKL*[3] 2:1422.—Klaiber; R. Köster, "Zur Theorie der Kontroverstheologie," *Zeitschrift für Katholische Theologie* 88 (1966) 121–62; M. Péronnet, ed., *La controverse religieuse (XVIe – XIXe siècles),* 2 vols. (Montpellier, 1981); D. Birch, *Early Reformation English Polemics* (Salzburg, 1983); L. Desgraves, *Répertoire des ouvrages de controverse entre Catholiques et Protestants en France (1598–1685),* 2 vols. (Geneva, 1984–85); A. Mancia, "La controversia con i Protestanti e i programmi degli studi teologici nella Compagnia di Gesù 1547–99," *Archivum historicum Societatis Jesu* 54 (1985) 3–43; idem, "L'Opera del Bellarmino nella riorganizzazione degli studi filosofici e teologici," *R. Bellarmino, arcivescovo di Capua, teologo e pastore della riforma cattolica,* ed. G. Galeota (Capua, 1990) 271–81; *GCh* 7:844–55; 8:309–55; M. Basse, "Theologiegeschichtsschreibung und Kontroverstheologie," *ZKG* 107 (1996) 50–71.

HERIBERT SMOLINSKY

■ **Additional Bibliography:** A. Lexutt, "Glaube im Gespräch," *Monatshefte für evangelische Kirchengeschichte des Rheinlandes* 45/46 (1996/97) 1–47; K. Diez, *Ecclesia—non est civitas Platonica* (Frankfurt/Main, 1997); J. Wicks, "Argumentative Legitimation in 16th Century Catholic Theology," in *Ecclesia tertii millennii advenientis.* Festschrift A. Anton (Casale Monferrato, 1997) 888–897; S. J. Barnett, "'Where Was Your Church before Luther?': Claims for the Antiquity of Protestantism Examined," *ChH* 68 (1999) 14–41; H. Smolinsky, *Deutungen der Zeit im Streit der Konfessionen* (Heidelberg, 2000); H. V. Bonavita, "Key to Christendom: The 1565 Siege of Malta, Its Histories, and Their Use in Reformation Polemic," *SCJ* 33 (2002) 1021–43; M. U. Edwards, "Luther on His Opponents," *Lutheran Quarterly* 16 (2002) 329–48; T. A. Fudge, "Incest and Lust in Luther's Marriage," *SCJ* 34 (2003) 319–45.

Cordatus (Hertz), *Conrad.* Lutheran theologian, born 1480 in Leombach near Wels, died March 25, 1546 on a journey near Spandau. He studied in Vienna and Ferrara and came to Ofen in 1510; here, he was later imprisoned for preaching Reformation doctrine. He was in Wittenberg in 1524. In 1527, Cordatus worked for a short time as a teacher at the academy in Liegnitz. After the failure of a new attempt to spread the Reformation in Hungary, he became preacher in Zwickau and pastor in Niemegk and Eisleben; in 1540, he became superintendent of Stendal. Cordatus achieved fame as the collector of Martin Luther's table talk. He had a violent disagreement with Philipp Melanchthon and Caspar → Cruciger on the question whether → justification involved any presuppositions.

■ **Literature:** *NDB* 3:356f.—A. Molnar, "The Riddle of C. C.," *Communio Viatorum* 30 (1987) 23–31.

MICHAEL BECHT

Corpus doctrinae (or: Corpora doctrinae; CD). A technical term for collections of ancient and more recent creeds and → confessional documents during one particular phase of the confessional consolidation in the Lutheran territorial churches, especially between 1560 and 1580. These collections attest the relevance and the continuity of the Lutheran profession of faith, and were often included in territorial → church orders. They were intended as a doctrinal law which would guarantee the preservation of the Lutheran confession in territories in northern, central and eastern Germany. This phase reached its conclusion with the Book of → Concord (1580), which could be called a "CD for all of Lutheranism," although the text itself avoids this concept. Since a significant minority refused to accept the Book of Concord (because of the Formula of Concord), regional *corpora doctrinae* remained in force, e.g., the *Corpus Juli(an)um* in Braunschweig-Wolfenbüttel.

The concept of CD goes back to Philipp Melanchthon, who employs it in the statutes of the university of Wittenberg in 1533 (*integrum corpus . . . doctrinae ecclesiasticae,* viz., doctrinal points in the Letter to the Romans and the doctrine of the Trinity in John's Gospel) and includes it in the → Frankfurt Recess of 1558 (CR 9:494) to designate a body of doctrinal statements in which the *incorrupta Evangelii doctrina* is presented in its entirety. Melanchthon was the first to produce a collection of doctrinal texts, in the *CD Christianae,* published privately in 1560, after his death; this was received as the *CD Philippicum* in Pomerania (1561), in electoral Saxony (as *CD Misnicum,* 1566), and in Bremen (1572). It met with sympathy in Anhalt and Schleswig-Holstein, but also provoked anti-Melanchthonian, emphatically Lutheran *Corpora doctrinae:* the Hamburg confessional book and the *Formula consensus* in Lübeck (1569), the CD of the city of Braunschweig (1563; this is the first work to employ the term in its title), the *CD christianae Pomeranicum* (1564), the CD of the city of Göttingen (1568), the *CD christianae Thuringicum* (1570), the *CD Brandenburgicum* (1572), the *CD Wilhelminum* for Braunschweig-Lüneburg, and the *CD Juli(an)um* for Braunschweig-Wolfenbüttel (1576). Independently of these codified *Corpora doctrinae,* antecedently or at the same period, other confessional formulae and doctrinal texts were included as *credenda* in the church orders.

■ **Literature:** *TRE* 5:499ff.; *EKL*[3] 1:771ff.—W. D. Hauschild, "Corpus doctrinae und Bekenntnisschriften," in *Bekenntnis und Einheit der Kirche,* ed. M. Brecht and R. Schwarz (Stuttgart, 1980) 235–52.

LOTHAR ULLRICH

Corro, *Antonio del.* Spanish Protestant, born 1527 in Seville, died March 30, 1591 in London; a student of Juan → Gil. Corro fled to Geneva in 1557 with Casiodoro de → Reina, Cipriano de →

Valera, and others. In 1558-1559, he studied under Theodor → Beza in Lausanne, working subsequently as a preacher in Bordeaux and Toulouse. He came to the French Reformed community in Antwerp in 1566, but disagreements led him to flee to London in 1569; he became a teacher in Oxford in 1577. Corro was an independent thinker. He admired Sebastian → Castellio and fought for religious tolerance. Against the Calvinist doctrine of predestination, Corro maintained that all are called to salvation.

■ **Works:** *Lettre envoyée à la Maiesté du Roy des Espagnes* (1567); *Dialogus theologicus, quo epistola divi Pauli apostoli ad Romanos explanatur . . .* (London, 1574, often reprinted); *Sapientissimi regis Salomonis concio de summo hominis bono, quam Hebraei Cohelet, graeci et latini Ecclesiasten vocant . . .* (London, 1579); *The Spanish Grammar with certeine rules teaching both the spanish and franch tongues . . .* (London, 1590; Span. trans. Madrid, 1988).

■ **Literature:** P. J. Hauben, *Three Spanish Heretics and the Reformation* (Geneva, 1967); G. Díaz Díaz, *Hombres y Documentos de la Filosofía Española,* vol. 2 (Madrid, 1983) 419ff.; C. Gilly, *Spanien und der Basler Buchdruck bis 1600* (Basle and Frankfurt/Main, 1985) passim; *BiDi* 6:121–76; K. Reinhardt, *Bibelkommentare spanischer Autoren (1500–1700),* vol. 1 (Madrid, 1990) 127ff.

FERNANDO DOMÍNGUEZ

■ **Additional Bibliography:** A. G. Kinder, "Obras teologicas de A. del C.," *Dialogo ecumenico* 30 (1995) 311–40.

Cortese, *Gregorio.* Benedictine, cardinal (1542), born between 1480 and 1483 in Modena or Venice, died September 21, 1547 in Rome. After studies, culminating in the doctorate in law, he became a Benedictine, and was abbot in several monasteries, including S. Giorgio Maggiore in Venice. He was well versed in scripture and the church fathers and promoted monastic reform. He was a close associate of Gasparo → Contarini, Reginald → Pole, and other supporters of religious renewal; he was a member of a papal reform commission in 1536-1537. He became bishop of Urbino in 1542, and was a member of the Roman Inquisition.

■ **Works:** *Opera* (Padua, 1774).

■ **Literature:** *DBI* 29:733–40.—G. Fragnito, "Il cardinal G. C. nella crisi religiosa del Cinquecento," *Benedictina* 30 (1983) 129–71, 417–59; 31 (1984) 79–134.

KLAUS GANZER

■ **Additional Bibliography:** F. C. Cesareo, *Humanism and Catholic Reform. The Life and Work of G. C.* (New York, 1990).

Corvinus (Rabe), *Antonius.* Lutheran theologian, born April 11, 1501 in Wartburg, died April 5, 1553 in Hanover. As an adherent of Martin Luther, Corvinus was expelled from the monastery of Ridaggshausen in 1523. He was preacher in Goslar in 1528, and pastor in Witzenhausen in 1529. He accompanied → Philip of Hessen as his theological adviser to the religious dialogues in → Hagenau, → Worms, and → Regensburg, and to the negotiations in Schmalkalden. Corvinus helped introduce the Reformation in Northeim, Lippe, Hildesheim, and Braunschweig. From 1542, he was in the service of Duchess Elizabeth of Braunschweig and guided the consolidation of the Protestant church in Calenberg-Göttingen as superintendent. His resolute opposition to the → Augsburg Interim led to his imprisonment (1549-1552).

■ **Literature:** *NDB* 3:371f.; *TRE* 8:216ff.; *CEras* 1:347f.— R. Stupperich, "A. C.," *Westfälische Lebensbilder* 7 (1959) 20–39.

MICHAEL BECHT

■ **Additional Bibliography:** I. Mager, "'Gott erhalte uns Philippum.' A. Corvins Mahnbrief an Philipp Melanchthon wegen des Leipziger Interims," *Jahrbuch der Gesellschaft für Niedersächsische Kirchengeschichte* 89 (1991) 89–104.

Coster, *Frans.* Jesuit (1552), controversial theologian, born June 16, 1532 in Mechlin, died December 6, 1619 in Brussels. He studied philosophy in Louvain and theology in Rome (1553-1556) and Cologne. He was teacher, master of novices, rector, and provincial. He composed a widely diffused handbook for the many Marian congregations which he founded. He engaged in debate with theologians such as Lukas → Osiander and Martin → Chemnitz.

■ **Works:** *Libellus sodalitatis* (Antwerp, 1586) (first draft with another title, Cologne, 1576); *Enchiridion controversiarum praecipuarum nostri temporis* (Cologne, 1585, often reprinted).

■ **Literature:** C. Sommervogel, *Bibliothèque de la Compagnie de Jésus* (Louvain, ³1960; vol. 2, 1510–34; vol. 9, 128–37; vol. 11, 1977; *DSp* 2:2416–19; *Nationaal biografisch Woordenboek,* vol. 1 (Brussels, 1964) 333–41;

L. Polgár, *Bibliographie sur l'histoire de la Compagnie de Jésus,* vol. 3/1 (Rome, 1990) 528.—L. Châtellier, *L'Europe des dévots* (Paris, 1987) passim; E. Meuthen, *Kölner Universitätsgeschichte,* vol. 1 (Cologne, 1988) with index; *Les Jésuites belges 1542–1992* (Brussels, 1992) 66, 89.

SILVEER DE SMET

Counter-Reformation (CR)

1. The *concept* of CR was first employed in 1776 by the Göttingen lawyer Johann S. Pütter, who made a distinction between the "Protestant Reformation" and the "Catholic Counter-Reformations"; initially, this concept was used in the plural to designate individual actions intended to recatholicize by force territories which had gone over to Protestantism. Leopold von Ranke uses the concept as the name of an epoch in his *Deutsche Geschichte im Zeitalter der Reformation,* 5 vols. (Berlin, 1839-1847): the epoch of the → Reformation is followed by the CR. Moritz Ritter's *Deutsche Geschichte im Zeitalter der Gegenreformation und des Dreißigjährigen Krieges (1555-1648),* 3 vols. (Stuttgart, 1889-1907) helped make this a standard concept, and the word was adopted in other European languages too (e.g., Italian *controriforma*).

Wilhelm Maurenbrecher identified the roots of the CR in a number of Catholic reform movements prior to the Reformation, and coined the term "Catholic Reformation" in the first volume of his *Geschichte der katholischen Reformation* (Nördlingen, 1880; → Reformation, Catholic). Hubert Jedin suggested that the two concepts were related as follows: "The Catholic Reformation is the church's reflection on itself and on the ideal of Catholic life by means of inner renewal; the CR is the church's self-assertion in the struggle against Protestantism" (*Katholische Reformation oder Gegenreformation?,* 38). Jedin's definition has won wide acceptance but has been criticized by Karl Eder as a one-sided concentration on the internal life of the church.

The concept of CR has played an important role in recent scholarly discussion. Reinhard (*CHR*) rejects a chronological sequence of Reformation and CR, as well as an inherent antithesis between these two movements, since they are generated by a common root. Church reform movements emerged again and again from the late Middle Ages on, and the Protestant movement of

Martin Luther and the reform movements in the Catholic sphere belong to this chain of endeavors for reform. Both the Protestant movement and the Catholic reform movements lead however to the process of → confessionalization, and this gives the Catholic reform a new quality, since it is marked in part by a strong confessional tendency to draw boundary lines vis-à-vis the Protestant confessions. Consequently, the so-called "CR actions" must be seen in the context of the confessionalization process. This would make the concept of CR meaningless.

The concept of *controriforma* is widespread in recent Italian historiography, where it designates primarily measures taken by an intransigent wing of the Catholic reform, or else the mentality of those involved, e.g., the Inquisition and Popes → Paul IV and → Pius V, who drew boundary lines and enacted repressive measures not only against Protestant groups, but also against a more open tendency of the Catholic Reform which was influenced by humanist thinking or by a theological Augustinianism (here, we can mention Gasparo → Contarini, Reginald → Pole, Giovanni → Morone, the "Spirituals" and → Evangelism in general). It is undeniable that the process of demarcation vis-à-vis Protestantism was accompanied in the theological sphere by a narrowing-down in comparison to the theological plurality of the late Middle Ages.

2. Characteristics

One central element in the CR—as in → Lutheranism and → Calvinism—is the importance of the secular rulers, who take a much stronger hold of church life (in both the Catholic and the Protestant spheres) than had been the case in the late Middle Ages; this applies in particular to the houses of Habsburg and Wittelsbach, but also to the French kings. Even the piety cultivated by the ruling dynasty becomes standard in their territory (the *Pietas Austriaca* and *Pietas Bavarica*). Some rulers extended their dynastic politics to the bishoprics; this is especially true of the Wittelsbachs (→ Ernest of Bavaria and the subsequent development of a secundogeniture in Cologne). Generally speaking, CR measures on the part of the bishops were possible only where they themselves were the local rulers. It was the local princes, not the papacy, that promoted CR policies; political, military, and legal means were employed to

secure the victory of the prince's confession (cf. the War of Cologne). At the same time, there is a tendency at work here to cut back the power of the Estates in Austria and France. The Religious Peace of → Augsburg (1555) provided the basis in imperial law for CR measures.

Apart from the local rulers and the bishops, it was the new Orders—the Capuchins and especially the Jesuits—who promoted the CR. While the Capuchins were active primarily in pastoral work, the Jesuits were also heavily committed to educational work in universities and colleges. The educational sector made great advances in the CR: many new universities and colleges were founded, especially under Jesuit leadership. The Jesuit theater in their colleges was another instrument of confessional propaganda.

Preaching took on particular importance in pastoral work and piety. Pilgrimages and processions were revitalized, frequently as a demonstration against Protestants; and those forms of piety which were rejected by the Protestants were now emphasized strongly, e.g., eucharistic piety. The sacrament of confession increased in importance, and the veneration of the → saints took on a new intensity (e.g., thanks to Charles → Borromeo as archbishop of Milan).

CR religion was spread by means of catechisms (in Germany, the catechisms of Peter → Canisius were especially important) and of a specific literature: viz. theological treatises, devotional and edifying books, and spiritual narratives. Some church hymns used in the liturgy functioned as propaganda. The "Index of forbidden books" developed as an instrument of literary surveillance (first Index under Paul IV in 1559; Tridentine Index under → Pius IV in 1564; Congregation of the Index founded in 1571). General surveillance of the faith and the persecution of deviants were incumbent upon the Inquisition, whose central Roman body was set up in 1542 (Gianpietro Carafa, later Pope Paul IV) and which sometimes had recourse to measures of the utmost severity, including many executions. Earlier scholarship tended to see the CR as a whole as reactionary and backward-looking, in contrast to modern Protestantism. Today, its unintentional contribution to the modernization of societal and political life and to education (Jesuit pedagogy) is assessed as higher than that of the other confessions (Reinhard: ARG).

3. Phases of the CR

The first political and legal measures against the Reformation movement were taken as early as the Edict of Worms in 1521. Later, political confessional alliances were founded both among Catholics and among Protestants (→ Regensburg Convent, League of → Dessau [Catholic]; League of Gotha-Torgau, → Schmalkaldic League [Protestant]). The religious strife in Switzerland led to the second War of Kappel in 1531. The Schmalkaldic War in 1546-1547 was a further stage in the military confrontations.

The potential which the Religious Peace of Augsburg opened up for the CR in the sphere of imperial law was increasingly exploited in the last decades of the 16th and the beginning of the 17th centuries; a correspondingly militant politics on the part of German Protestants under the leadership of the Palatinate led to a closer collaboration between the emperor and the Estates. Ferdinand II followed a strictly CR policy. In France, the first ruthless persecutions of the → Huguenots took place, and there were violent clashes in the Spanish Netherlands too. The kings of Poland and the Habsburgs (as kings of Hungary) attacked the Protestant forces.

These political actions were accompanied in the period after Trent by an intensification of the CR mentality: theological uniformity was promoted through an emphasis on scholasticism, disciplinary action was taken against those who held deviant views, and church life was subjected to control and discipline. Powerful reforming impulses were also at work: an improvement of pastoral care and the raising of priestly competence through the foundation of numerous theological faculties, seminaries, and colleges (which must be seen against the background of the general raising of educational standards in this period). Many of the reforms demanded by Trent failed to materialize in Germany, however, thanks to the institution of the imperial church, where the bishops were imperial princes and the aristocracy held the monopoly of nominations to the cathedral chapters.

Evaluation.

The CR must not be seen in isolation, but in the context of the → confessionalization process, and its evaluation remains ambivalent. On the one hand, it certainly contributed to the moderniza-tion of the state in the early modern period, in societal, political, and educational terms, and it gave valuable and lasting impulses to ecclesiastical renewal in the Catholic sphere. On the other hand, the tendencies to draw boundary lines led in the ecclesial and theological fields to a confessionalist narrowing-down. The fact that the state gave powerful support to the CR meant that the CR in its turn greatly helped consolidate the state-church structures in the Catholic monarchies in the 17th and 18th centuries.

■ **Literature:** *TRZRK.*—H. Jedin, *Katholische Reformation oder Gegenreformation?* (Lucerne, 1946); K. Eder, *Die Kirche im Zeitalter des konfessionellen Absolutismus (1555–1648)* (Freiburg, 1949); D. Cantimori, *Italien. Häretiker der Spätrenaissance* (Basle, 1949); M. Heckel, "Autonomia et Pacis Compositio. Der Augsburger Religionsfriede in der Deutung der Gegenreformation," *ZSRG.K* 76 (1959) 141–248; R. Garcia Villoslada, "La contrareforma. Su nombre y su concepto histórico," in *Miscellanea historiae pontificiae* 21 (1959) 189–242; B. Stasiewski, *Reformation und Gegenreformation in Polen* (Münster, 1960); E. Hassinger, *Das Werden des neuzeitlichen Europa 1300–1600* (Braunschweig, ²1966); H. O. Evenett, *The Spirit of the Counter-Reformation,* ed. J. Bossy (Cambridge, 1968); A. Prosperi, *Tra Evangelismo e Controriforma: G.M. Giberti* (Rome, 1969); E. W. Zeeden, "Das Zeitalter der Glaubenskämpfe (1555–1648)," in B. Gebhardt, *Handbuch der deutschen Geschichte,* vol. 2 (Stuttgart, ⁹1970) 118–239; W. Reinhard, "Katholische Reform und Gegenreformation in der Kölner Nuntiatur 1584–1621," *RQ* 66 (1971) 8–65; E. W. Zeeden, ed., *Gegenreformation* (Darmstadt, 1973); K. D. Schmidt, *Die Katholische Reform und die Gegenreformation* (Göttingen, 1975); J. Delumeau, *Rome au XVIᵉ siècle* (Paris, 1975); W. Brückner, "Geistliche Erzählliteratur der G. im Rheinland," *Rheinische Vierteljahrsblätter* 40 (1976) 150–69; W. Reinhard, "Gegenreformation als Modernisierung?" *ARG* 68 (1977) 226–52; E. W. Zeeden, *Das Zeitalter der Gegenreformation* (Munich, 1979); J. M. Valentin, ed., *Gegenreformation und Literatur* (Amsterdam, 1979); K. Brandi, *Deutsche Geschichte im Zeitalter der Reformation und Gegenreformation* (Frankfurt/Main, ⁵1979); R. Birley, *Religion and Politics in the Age of the Counterreformation* (Chapel Hill, N.C., 1981); D.-R. Moser, *Verkündigung durch Volksgesang. Studien zur Liedpropaganda und -katechese der Gegenreformation* (Berlin and Munich, 1981); A. D. Wright, *The Counter-Reformation* (London, 1982); A. Coreth, *Pietas Austriaca. Österreichische Frömmigkeit im Barock* (Vienna, ²1982); M. Heckel, *Deutschland im konfessionellen Zeitalter* (Göttingen, 1983); *Kirche und Visitation,* ed. E. W. Zeeden and P. Th. Lang (Stuttgart, 1984); *Forme di disciplinamento sociale nella prima età moderna* (Bologna, 1984); W. Reinhard, "Reformation, Counter-Reformation, and the Early Modern State," *CHR* 75

(1989) 383–404; W. Seibrich, *Gegenreformation als Restauration. Die restaurativen Bemühungen der alten Orden im Deutschen Reich von 1580–1648* (Münster, 1991); M. Firpo, *Inquisizione Romana e Controriforma* (Bologna, 1992); H. Lutz, *Reformation und Gegenreformation* (Munich, [4]1997).

KLAUS GANZER

■ **Additional Bibliography:** *Historical Dictionary of the Reformation and Counter-reformation* (Lanham, Md., 2000).—M. D. Jones, *The Counter Reformation* (Cambridge, 1995); R. P. Hsia, *G. Die Welt der katholischen Erneuerung* (Frankfurt/Main, 1998); R. Bireley, *The Refashioning of Catholicism* (Washington, D.C., 1999); M. A. Mullett, *The Catholic Reformation* (London, 1999); A. Herzig, *Der Zwang zum wahren Glauben. Rekatholisierung vom 16. bis zum 18.Jh.* (Göttingen, 2000); E. Bonora, *La controriforma* (Rome, 2001). → Reformation, Catholic; → Confessionalization; K. M. Comerford, ed., *Early Modern Catholicism*. Festschrift J. W. O'Malley (Toronto, 2001).

Covenant theology. An important element in Reformed Protestantism in the 16th and 17th centuries. The biblical concept of covenant was employed as the key both to the relationship between God and the human person and to the continuity of salvation history in the Old and New Testaments. It is first found in Heinrich → Bullinger's defense of infant baptism (*De testamento aeterno seu foedere Dei unico et aeterno*, Zurich, 1534), and the covenantal system was elaborated by Zacharias → Ursinus and Caspar → Olevian (Heidelberg catechism, 1563). A *foedus operum* is established at creation, while a *foedus gratiae* is God's answer to the fall of Adam; this is comparable to the Lutheran antithesis between → law and gospel. Further theological development spoke of a *foedus redemptionis* between the Father and the Son (Johannes Cocceius, *Summa doctrinae de foedere et testamento dei*, Franeker, 1648). Covenantal theology had an important influence on the political theories of the early modern period, especially in northern America (cf. the idea that society is based on a social contract).
■ **Literature:** *TRE* 11:246–52.—C. McCoy and J. W. Baker, *Fountainhead of Federalism. Heinrich Bullinger and the Covenantal Tradition* (Louisville, Ky., 1991); J. F. G. Goeters, "Die reformierte F. und ihre rechtsgeschichtlichen Aspekte," in *Liechtenstein, Politische Schriften* 19 (1994) 83–95.

ALASDAIR I. C. HERON

■ **Additional Bibliography:** D. N. Poole, *Stages of Religious Faith in the Classical Reformation Tradition.*

The Covenant Approach to the Ordo Salutis (Lewiston, 1995); P. A. Lillback, *The Binding of God. Calvin's Role in the Development of Covenant Theology* (Carlisle, 2001).

Coverdale, *Miles.* Biblical translator, born 1487/1488 in York (?), died January 20, 1569 in London. He studied philosophy and theology in Cambridge. He left the Augustinian Order in 1528, after Robert → Barnes had communicated Martin Luther's teachings to him. Coverdale worked to spread the Reformation in England, then translated the Pentateuch in Hamburg together with William → Tyndale. He produced his own translation of the Bible in Antwerp in 1534-1535, following Luther and the Zurich Bible, and he wrote a concordance to the English New Testament in 1535. After his return to England, he produced the Great Bible in 1539. He fled to the Continent in 1540 and was pastor in Bergzabern from 1543 to 1547. He returned to England in 1548, and was bishop of Exeter from 1551 to 1553, when he was deposed and again obliged to flee; he resumed the post of pastor in Bergzabern from 1555 to 1559, returning in that year to England. Because of his Puritan tendencies, he lost his post at St. Magnus' church in London in 1566-1567. Coverdale translated → Erasmus of Rotterdam and some of Luther's shorter works, and compiled the first Reformation hymnal in England.
■ **Works:** *Writings*, ed. G. Pearson (Cambridge, 1844); *Remains of M. C.*, ed. G. Pearson (Cambridge, 1846).
■ **Literature:** *NCE* 4:407; *DNB* 12:364–72; *BBKL* 1:1145.—G. F. Swearingen, *Die englische Schriftsprache bei C.* (Weimar, 1904); J. F. Mozley, *C. and His Bibles* (London, 1953); R. A. Leaver, "A Newly-discovered Fragment of C.'s Ghostly Psalms," *Jahrbuch für Liturgik und Hymnologie* 26 (1982) 136–50; E. W. Cleveland, *A study of Tindale's Genesis compared with the Genesis of C.* (1911; reprint, Hamden, Conn., 1972).

REINHOLD RIEGER

■ **Additional Bibliography:** G. Latré, "The 1535 C. Bible and Its Antwerp Origins," in *The Bible as Book*, ed. O. O'Sullivan (London, 2000) 89–102.

Cranmer, *Thomas* (1489-1556). Archbishop of Canterbury from 1533-1556 and principal martyr of the English Reformation. Cranmer was born in 1489 at Aslockton, Nottinghamshire, the second son of minor gentry. He began his education at

Jesus College, Cambridge, in 1503 but would forfeit his fellowship there in order to marry. Soon after marrying, however, his wife, Joan, died in childbirth, and Cranmer regained his fellowship at Jesus College. He was ordained to the priesthood around 1520 and earned a doctorate in divinity there in 1526. At Cambridge he was exposed to the subtleties of scholastic theology (including the writings of Scotus) and to the textualism of Erasmus. As an examiner at Cambridge, he was known as one of the first proponents of an "orthodoxy of a moderate humanist with an enthusiasm for the biblical text" (Diarmaid MacCulloch). A focus on scriptural, patristic, and liturgical texts was to mark his work throughout his career, which not only brought him in line with Renaissance learning but also made it easier for him to embrace the ideas of the European Reformation.

Cranmer's academic career changed directions radically when in 1529 he suggested to two of Henry VIII's advisers that European faculties of canon law should determine the king's suit for the annulment of his marriage to Catherine of Aragon. The king liked Cranmer's proposal and subsequently commissioned him to write an opinion and present the case at Cambridge—and eventually on the Continent to Charles V, the Holy Roman Emperor. While representing Henry abroad, Cranmer met and secretly married his second wife, Margaret, niece of the noted Lutheran theologian Andreas Osiander. This rejection of his clerical vow of celibacy was indicative of his growing sympathies with reformist religious views.

In late 1532, Cranmer was recalled to England by the king as his surprise choice to succeed William Warham as archbishop of Canterbury. Cranmer reluctantly accepted the honor but delayed his return, so that he was not consecrated until March 30, 1533. In light of his delay, he was not informed of Henry's secret marriage to Anne Boleyn in January 1533 until after the event; nevertheless, he pronounced Henry's divorce from Catherine of Aragon and presided over Anne's coronation in late May 1533. As archbishop, Cranmer was dutifully loyal to Henry's wishes, including granting him two further divorces—from Anne Boleyn in 1536 and from Anne of Cleves in 1540.

While respecting and serving the wishes of the king constituted what Cranmer perceived as his role as archbishop, his passion continued to be the reform of the English church. In 1534, for example, he initiated a project of translating the Bible into English. While traditionalist-leaning bishops attempted to stall his efforts, by 1537 Cranmer persuaded Henry to sponsor what would be called the Matthew Bible. Cranmer wrote the preface and dedicated the translation to Henry, and despite restrictions on its use later, in the ensuing religious struggles in England, it remained the most significant precursor to the Elizabethan Bishops' Bible and the authorized King James Version of 1611.

With Henry's death early in 1547 and the accession of the young Edward VI to the throne, Cranmer became increasingly aggressive in his push for reform. Arguably his greatest achievement was the central role he played in writing and editing the two versions of the *Book of Common Prayer* (1549 and 1552). Among his lasting liturgical innovations were the establishment of a twofold pattern of Matins and Evensong as offices for regular congregational worship and devotion and, in the 1549 marriage service, the introduction of the idea of "the mutual society, help, and comfort that the one ought to have of the other" as a liturgically expressed justification for marriage. Throughout, Cranmer displayed his true genius by combining reforming and traditional elements of the liturgy even when his reforms were quite radical (as in the cases of baptism and Eucharist). With slight changes, the 1552 edition eventually became the basis for the abiding 1662 prayer book and thus shaped Anglican liturgical life and, through its liturgical repetition, the development of the English language for centuries.

Moreover, as a companion to the *Book of Common Prayer*, he oversaw the publication of the *Book of Homilies* (1547), a collection of official sermons to which he contributed, writing on such topics as scripture, faith and good works, and death. To aid in the right conduct of worship and expounding of true belief, Cranmer helped draft the *Ordinal* of 1550 and the *Forty-Two Articles* (1553), the latter of which formed the basis of the famous statement of Tudor faith—the *Thirty-Nine Articles* (1563). In addition to his writing and editing, he also encouraged leading Continental theologians, including Martin Bucer and Peter

Martyr Vermigli, to take refuge in England, continuing his long-standing tradition of personal hospitality to foreign scholars. Thus he helped transmit the radical theological ideas of the European continent to the English church in ways that, suitably adapted, proved crucial to the ultimate survival of English Protestantism.

Theologically, Cranmer argued against papal supremacy (and the jurisdictional claims of authority that come with it), private masses, and the idea of purgatory. But central to his reformist theological vision was his deep commitment to the doctrine of justification by faith, for from it, he argued, flowed the substance of Christian belief. As a true humanist, Cranmer embraced the early creeds and the importance of patristic theological insight, but this "catholic" sentiment was balanced by his profound sense of the authority of the Bible and his ultimately non-Catholic view of the Eucharist. And therein lies the difficulty of reconstructing his theology. On the one hand, he sought to bring the best of the Catholic tradition to bear on the current interpretation and authority of the Bible, which were of great concern to sixteenth-century Protestant thought. On the other hand, over the course of his theological career his mind changed on central doctrines such as the Eucharist—the very doctrines that were the greatest sources of contention between Roman Catholics and Protestants.

Cranmer was also a complex and perhaps embattled person, torn between loyalties to sovereign and to church. For while he, along with other bishops, submitted to large-scale losses of diocesan estates at Henry's order, nevertheless, he could stand up to Henry on other issues, such as Henry's treatment of Anne Boleyn and Henry's lack of appreciation of the centrality of justification by faith. Moreover, Cranmer's commitment to genuine reform was at times called into question by his practice of authority as archbishop. For example, in response to *The Six Articles* (1539) which, among other things, enforced clergy celibacy, he concealed his own marriage for fifteen years by sending his wife to live on the European continent; during this time, he complied with the disciplining of other married clergy in England.

When Edward died in July 1553, Mary Tudor's accession to the English throne abruptly halted the reforming movement of the church. Cranmer had reluctantly acquiesced to the duke of Northumberland's ultimately unsuccessful attempt to put Lady Jane Grey on the throne in place of Mary. Once Mary secured the throne, however, those who had opposed her were arrested, and many were executed. Cranmer remained free until September 1553, and was then arrested only after he publicly criticized her efforts at restoring the Mass in English church worship. He was convicted of high treason on November 13, 1553; though he was not pardoned, he was spared a traitor's death by Mary so that his theological views, particularly on the Eucharist, could be examined. His subsequent trial at Oxford for heresy in September 1555 provided the formal evidence for a condemnation by Rome the following December.

Dejected by his nearly three-year imprisonment, Cranmer was under unrelenting pressure to recant his views. Moreover, his deep commitment to the divine right of the sovereign—a belief that earlier had made it easier for him to accept Henry's often deadly and destructive actions—made it difficult for him to accept his own rejection of Mary, even when he felt that the queen was misusing it to restore England to papal obedience. Subsequently, under this pressure and guilt, he signed six recantations in February and March 1556, but was still condemned to burn at the stake at Oxford. Quite unexpectedly, at the service before his execution on March 21, 1556, he made a final confession of his Protestant faith. At the stake, instead of reading the public recantation, he dramatically renounced it by thrusting his right hand (the one he had used to sign the recanting documents) into the flames, to emphasize his rejection of the recantations.

Cranmer's life seemingly ended in failure, for Mary overturned his reformist policies and, through persecution, effectively squelched any enthusiasm for continued reform. Nevertheless, Cranmer's legacy endured long after Mary's reign came to its quick end, and the subsequent Elizabethan Settlement secured the Protestant vision of Cranmer by advocating an English Bible, reintroducing the *Articles of Religion* (i.e., the *Thirty-Nine Articles*), and ultimately restoring Cranmer's masterpiece—*The Book of Common Prayer*.

■ **Works:** *The Works of Th. C.,* 2 vols., ed. J. E. Cox (Cambridge, 1844, 1846).

■ **Literature:** Paul Ayris and David Selwyn, eds., *Thomas Cranmer: Churchman and Scholar* (Rochester, 1993);

Geoffrey Bromiley, *Thomas Cranmer, Theologian* (London, 1956); Peter Newman Brooks, *Cranmer in Context: Documents from the English Reformation* (Minneapolis, 1989); idem, *Thomas Cranmer's Doctrine of the Eucharist*, 2nd ed. (London, 1992); idem, "Thomas Cranmer" in *The Reformation Theologians: An Introduction to Theology in the Early Modern Period*, Carter Lindberg, ed. (Oxford, 2002) 239-52; Diarmaid MacCulloch, *Thomas Cranmer* (New Haven, 1996); C. H., Smyth, *Thomas Cranmer and the Reformation under Edward VI* (Cambridge, 1926).

JEFFREY HENSLEY

■ **Additional Bibliography:** P. Ayris, "The Correspondance of T. C., Archbishop of Canterbury, and Its English Audience 1533–54," *Reformation and Renaissance Review* 2 (2000) 9–33; P. Ayris, "The Public Career of T. C.," *Reformation and Renaissance Review* 2 (2000) 75–125.

Crespin, Jean. Lawyer and printer, born c. 1520 in Arras, died April 12, 1572 in Geneva. After gaining the licentiate in civil and canon law in Louvain in 1541, he worked in Paris. He escaped condemnation as a heretic in 1545 by fleeing to Geneva, where he opened a printing works in 1548. This helped spread the Calvinist Reformation in the French-speaking lands; c. 250 works were published in his lifetime. Crespin's own works include a martyrology (*Le livre des Martyrs* [Geneva, 1554]).
■ **Literature:** J.-F. Gilmont, *J. C.* (Geneva, 1981); idem, *Bibliographie des éditions de J. C.*, 2 vols. (Verviers, 1981).

JEAN-FRANÇOIS GILMONT

■ **Additional Bibliography:** J. E. Olson, "J. C., Humanist Printer among Reformation Martyrologists," in *The Harvest of Humanism in Central Europe*. Festschrift L. W. Spitz (St. Louis, 1992) 317–40.

Cromwell, Thomas. English statesman, born 1485 (?) in Putney, died July 28, 1540 in London. Little is known about his early years. Although he probably had no formal education, he worked as a lawyer and was one of Cardinal Thomas Wolsey's collaborators from 1516 onwards. He became a member of parliament in 1523. He survived Wolsey's fall (1529) and his parliamentary career was very successful: by the end of 1531, he held an influential position in the council of King → Henry VIII. Scholars disagree about his influence on the English Reformation. In Elton's view, the juridical processes by which England broke its relations with Rome and by which the style of Tudor government was radically altered were the fruit of Cromwell's insight and strategy, but other historians question this interpretation of Cromwell as a great political thinker and initiator in matters of state.

In 1535, he became vicar general of the king, with responsibility for religious questions. Although he was a layman, this gave him a higher position than Thomas → Cranmer. He survived the king's dismissal of Anne Boleyn (1536) but could not prevent Henry's politics from taking an increasingly conservative turn in the last years of that decade. After the failure of the marriage between Henry and Anne of Cleves, which Cromwell had negotiated, he was found guilty (without any trial) of high treason and heresy, and was executed.
■ **Literature:** W. G. Zeeveld, *Foundations of Tudor Policy* (Cambridge, Mass., 1948); G. R. Elton, *The Tudor Revolution in Government* (Cambridge, 1953); A. G. Dickens, *Th. C. and the English Reformation* (London, 1959); S. Lehmberg, *The Reformation Parliament, 1529–36* (London, 1970); G. R. Elton, *Policy and Police: The Enforcement of the Reformation in the Age of Th. C.* (London, 1972); idem, *Reform and Renewal: Th. C. and the Common Weal* (Cambridge, 1973); idem, *Studies in Tudor and Stuart Politics,* 3 vols. (Cambridge, 1974–83); J. S. Block, "Th. C.'s Patronage of Preaching," *SCJ* 8 (1977) 37–50; G. R. Elton, *Reform and Reformation. England 1509–58* (London, 1977); S. E. Lehmberg, *The Later Parliaments of Henry VIII 1536–47* (Cambridge, 1977); B. W. Beckingsale, *Th. C., Tudor Minister* (London, 1978); W. Ullmann, "This Realm of England Is an Empire," *JEH* 30 (1979) 175–203; S. Brigden, "Popular Disturbance and the Fall of Th. C. and the Reformers, 1539–40," *Historical Journal* 24 (1981) 257–78; G. R. Elton, *The Tudor Constitution* (Cambridge, ²1982); J. Guy, "Henry VIII and the Praemunire Manoeuvres of 1530–31," *English Historical Review* 97 (1982) 481–503; C. Coleman and D. R. Starkey, ed., *Revolution Reassessed* (Oxford, 1986); A. Fox and J. Guy, *Reassessing the Henrician Age* (Oxford, 1986); G. Nicholson, "The Act of Appeals and the English Reformation," in C. Cross et al., eds., *Law and Government under the Tudors* (Cambridge, 1988); T. F. Mayer, *Thomas Starkey and the Commonweal* (Cambridge, 1989); A. J. Slavin, "Defining the Divorce," *SCJ* 20 (1989) 105–11.

SUSAN HARDMAN MOORE

■ **Additional Bibliography:** *RGG*⁴ 2:498f.—J. S. Block, *Factional Politics and the English Reformation* (Woodbridge, 1993) D. A. Wilson, *In the Lion's Court:*

Power, Ambition and Sudden Death in the Court of Henry VIII (London, 2001).

Crotus Rubeanus (real name *Johannes Jäger*). Humanist, born 1480 in Dornheim near Arnstadt (Thüringen), died c. 1540. He studied in Erfurt (for part of the time as a companion of Martin Luther) and in Cologne, with Ulrich von → Hutten, in 1505-1506; he took the degree of master of arts in 1507 and became head of the monastic school in Fulda in 1509. He was the principal author of the first part of the *Letters of → Obscure Men* (1515). He was in Italy from 1517 to 1520, and took the degree of doctor of theology in Bologna; he was rector of the university of Erfurt in 1520-1521 and greeted Luther on the latter's journey to the imperial parliament at Worms. Thereafter, he returned to Fulda, and was at the court of Albrecht of Prussia (→ Albrecht of Brandenburg-Ansbach) in Königsberg from 1524 to 1530. After renouncing Lutheranism, he served → Albrecht of Brandenburg from 1531, defending him against Lutheran polemic. He was canon of the New Church in Halle.
■ **Works:** *Epistolae obscurorum virorum,* ed. A. Bömer, 2 vols. (Heidelberg, 1924); *Apologia qua respondetur temeritati calumniatorum non verentium confictis criminibus in populare odium protrahere reverendissimum . . . Albertum* (Leipzig, 1531).
■ **Literature:** *NDB* 3:424f.; *CEras* 1:362f.—G. Knod, *Deutsche Studenten in Bologna* (Berlin, 1899) 463f.; P. Redlich, *Kardinal Albrecht von Brandenburg und das Neue Stift zu Halle* (Munich, 1900) 55–69; *Erzbischof Albrecht von Brandenburg,* ed. F. Jürgensmeier (Frankfurt/Main, 1991); E. Kleineidam, *Universitas Studii Erffordiensis,* vol. 2 (Leipzig, ²1992).

PETER WALTER

Cruciger
(1) *Caspar* the Elder. Assistant and collaborator of Martin Luther, born January 1, 1504 in Leipzig, died November 16, 1548 in Wittenberg. He was rector of the school in Magdeburg in 1525, and became professor at the university and preacher at the castle church in Wittenberg in 1528. He took part in the Reformation of Leipzig (1539) and in the religious dialogues in → Hagenau, → Worms, and → Regensburg (1540-1541), accompanying Philipp Melanchthon; through Melanchthon, he became acquainted with Jean Calvin. Theologically, he was close to Melanch-

thon, and this led Conrad → Cordatus, a stricter adherent of Luther, to attack him for so-called synergistic doctrinal views (which affected the question of sanctification by works). Cruciger helped Luther in the revision of his biblical translation, especially of the Psalms, and he published the first volumes of the Wittenberg edition of Luther's works (from 1539). He died young, and Melanchthon preached at his funeral.
■ **Literature:** RE 4, 843f.; *NDB* 3:427f.; *RGG*³ 1:1886f.—H. Petrich, *C. C.* (Hamburg, 1904).

ERNST WALTER ZEEDEN

■ **Additional Bibliography:** *RGG*⁴ 2:501.—T. J. Wengert, "C. C.," *SCJ* 20 (1989) 417–41; idem, "C. C. Sr.'s 1546 'Enarratio' on John's Gospel," *ChH* 61 (1992) 60–150.

(2) *Caspar* the Younger. Protestant theologian in the first generation after Luther, son of (1); born March 19, 1535 in Wittenberg, died April 16, 1597 in Kassel. The typical marks of his generation were doctrinal disputes and confessional consolidation, and both can be seen in Cruciger's biography. He succeeded Melanchthon in his professorship at Wittenberg, but was accused of → Crypto-Calvinism as the leader of the so-called Philippistic tendency, and was expelled from electoral Saxony in 1576. He died as consistorial president in Hessen-Kassel, which at that period was sympathetic to Calvinism.

ERNST WALTER ZEEDEN

Crypto-Calvinism (i.e., concealed or secret Calvinism). A polemic term applied to endeavors within → Lutheranism to accept Calvinist views on eucharistic doctrine and Christology, thereby achieving a reconciliation within Protestantism. This entailed *inter alia* calling into question the *manducatio oralis,* the *manducatio impiorum,* and the doctrine of → ubiquity. In the context of the → eucharistic controversy (→ Consensus Tigurinus), Crypto-Calvinism was maintained especially by adherents of the mediating theology of Philipp Melanchthon (the Philippists) and led to vigorous controversies in Bremen (Albert → Hardenberg), electoral Palatinate (adoption of Calvinism), Silesia, Denmark (Niels → Hemmingsen), and especially in electoral Saxony (Caspar → Peucer; Christoph → Pezel). It was forcibly suppressed in Saxony in 1574 by electoral Prince

August I (1553-1586), but revived under Christian I (1586-1591) and was definitively overcome with the beheading of chancellor Nikolaus → Krell in 1601. These debates made an important contribution to the consolidation of Lutheran doctrine and to the formation of a Lutheran confession.

■ **Literature:** I. Mager, *Die Konkordienformel im Fürstentum Braunschweig-Wolfenbüttel* (Göttingen, 1993) 126–41; M. Schaab, ed., *Territorialstaat und Calvinismus* (Stuttgart, 1993) 137–48.

GEORG HINTZEN

■ **Additional Bibliography:** *RGG*[4] 4:1793.—I. Mager, "Das Ringen um Wahrheit und Eintracht im Consensus Dresdensis vom 10.10.1571," in *Praxis pietatis.* Festschrift W. Sommer (Stuttgart, 1999) 103–18; I. Dingel, "Die Torgauer Artikel (1574) als Vermittlungsversuch zwischen der Theologie Luthers und der Melanchthons," in *Praxis pietatis,* 119–34; H. Klüting, "'Wittenberger Katechismus' (1571) und 'Wittenberger Fragstücke' (1571). Christoph Petzel und die Wittenberger Theologie," *ZKG* 112 (2001) 1–43.

Crypto-Protestantism (i.e., concealed or secret Protestantism). Designates the attempt to maintain secretly Lutheran or Reformed Church praxis in areas which had been recatholicized; we have evidence of this in the Habsburg territories. It differed in strength from one region to another, since it depended on the various Protestant groups which had previously given open support to the Reformation. For example, the Lutheran aristocracy in Inner Austria helped secure the borders against the Turks, and they received concessions in the "Pamphlet of Bruck" in 1578; no force was used against them until after 1600. → Maximilian II tolerated all the varieties of Protestantism in his territories, including the → Bohemian Brethren in Transylvania and Moravia. At a later date, Crypto-Protestantism in Hungary, Bohemia, and Moravia was able to make use of the prayer books and hymnals which were composed and translated into the vernacular during this period. Such was the cultural dominance of Protestantism that the destruction of these books (e.g., in the burnings of books in Inner Austria in 1600) could mean that an entire culture was destroyed (as in Slovenia).

The ruthless measures taken against those who did not openly confess the Catholic faith led many to go underground. This meant that, with the increasing success of the Counter-Reformation, the main support for Crypto-Protestantism was found among rural farmers, who did not want to risk expulsion; in regions which remained inaccessible to the Visitors or to members of the new religious Orders which were brought into the land, they celebrated worship in their houses, concealed Protestant literature, and taught their own children until the edict of tolerance by Joseph II in 1781.

■ **Literature:** G. Reingrabner, "Über die Eigenart der burgenländischen Protestantengeschichte," *Jahrbuch für die Geschichte des Protestantismus in Österreich* 97 (1981) 147–72; P. F. Barton, *Evangelisch in Österreich* (Vienna et al., 1987); I. Burian, "Die Gegenreformation in den tschechischen Ländern," *Jahrbuch für die Geschichte des Protestantismus in Österreich* 106 (1990) 19–61.

BARBARA HENZE

■ **Additional Bibliography:** L. Ferrari, "Riforma cattolica e controriforma nei territori austriaci," *CrS* 17 (1996) 611–29; O. Chaline, *La reconquête catholique de l'Europe centrale (XVIᵉ –XVIIIᵉ siècle)* (Paris, 1998).

Cuius regio, eius religio. This formula was coined by the lawyer Joachim Stephan at the beginning of the 17th century as a summary of the regulation imposed by the Religious Peace of Augsburg, which gave the imperial Estates the freedom to choose between Catholicism and Lutheranism, but made this choice binding on their subjects. This sovereignty of the territorial states in matters of religion set the final seal on a territorial church government which had its roots in the period before the Reformation, and was practiced by both Catholic and Protestant princes. The Peace of Westphalia put a limit on this regulation by guaranteeing the confessions in keeping with the status quo in the "normal year" of 1624.

■ **Literature:** *TRZRK.*—M. Heckel, *Deutschland im konfessionellen Zeitalter* (Göttingen, 1983); A. Schindling, "Reichskirche und Reformation," *ZHF* Beiheft 3 (1987) 81–112.

ANTON SCHINDLING

D

Daneau, *Lambert.* Reformed theologian, born c. 1530 in Beaugency (Loire), died November 11, 1595 in Castres (department of Tarn). He took his doctorate in law in 1559 and converted to the

Reformed Church. In the following year, he emigrated to Geneva, where he studied theology under Jean Calvin. He was pastor in Gien (Loire), Jussy, and Vendoeuvre from 1561 to 1574; from 1574 to 1581, he was pastor and professor of theology in Geneva. From 1581, he worked in Leiden, Ghent, Orthez (department of Basses-Pyrénées), and Castres. Apart from works of controversial theology (against Senebier, Gilbert Genebrard, Andreas → Osiander, and Robert Bellarmine), his voluminous literary production includes commentaries on scripture and on Augustine, Cyprian, and Peter Lombard. He was a rigorous proponent of a Puritan lifestyle, and composed a Reformed moral theology (*Christianae Ethices Libri III,* Geneva, 1577). He is one of the most important Reformed theologians in the 16th century, and his books display great analytical skill and an encyclopedic learning. New perspectives were opened up by his biblical hermeneutics and his methodology, which was based on the dialectic of the *via compendiaria* (which goes back to Melanchthon, or even further, to Aristotle and Cicero).

■ **Literature:** *DBF* 10:88f.—O. Fatio, *Méthode et Théologie. L. D. et les débuts de la scolastique réformée* (Geneva, 1976).

MICHAEL BECHT

■ **Additional Bibliography:** Ch. Strohm, *Ethik im frühen Calvinismus* (Berlin, 1996); idem, "Zur Eigenart der frühen calvinistischen Ethik," *ARG* 90 (1999) 230–54.

Decet Romanum Pontificem. Leo X's bull of excommunication against Martin Luther (January 3, 1521). Luther had not revoked his position within the sixty days granted him by the bull → *Exsurge Domine* (June 15, 1520), which had threatened him with excommunication; on December 10, 1520, he burned this bull in public in Wittenberg and defended the 41 propositions that *Exsurge Domine* attacked. The ensuing bull excommunicated Luther and his adherents. Ecclesiastical excommunication was followed by the sentence of outlawry within the empire, pronounced in the Edict of Worms (May 26, 1521). → Reformation.

■ **Source:** CCath 42:457–67.
■ **Literature:** R. Bäumer, *Lutherprozeß und Lutherbann* (*KLK* 32) (Münster, 1972); P. Fabisch, "J. Eck und die Publikation der Bullen 'Exsurge Domine' und 'D.,'"

RGST 127 (1988) 74–107; H. Feld, "Wurde Martin Luther 1521 in effigie in Rom verbrannt?," *Luther-Jahrbuch* 63 (1996) 11–18; V. Pfnür, "Excommunicatio und amicorum colloquium. Das Religionsgespräch auf dem Reichstag zu Augsburg 1530 auf dem Hintergrund der Frage des Lutherbannes," in *Unterwegs zum einen Glauben.* Festschrift L. Ullrich (Leipzig, 1997) 448–60.

BRUNO STEIMER

Delfino (Dolfino), *Zaccaria,* papal diplomat, born May 30, 1527 in Venice, died January 9, 1584 in Rome. After studies in Venice and Padua, he entered the service of the Roman curia. He was bishop of Lesina from 1553 to 1574. He was nuncio to Emperor → Ferdinand I from 1553 to 1556, and was created cardinal in 1565, at the prompting of the imperial court; he was deputy protector of the German nation. He was ambitious, a plotter (including espionage for the imperial court against Venice), and a man who accepted bribes. As a diplomat, he acted with opportunism and cunning, but he was also capable of adapting to the difficult situation in Germany.

■ **Literature:** *DBI* 40:576–88.—*NBD* II, 1, 3 and 4, ed. S. Steinherz (Vienna, 1897–1914); II, 5 and 6, ed. I. P. Dengel (Vienna and Leipzig, 1926–39); II, 7, ed. H. Kramer (Graz and Cologne, 1952); II, 8, ed. J. Rainer (Graz and Cologne, 1967); L. von Pastor, *Geschichte des Papsttums seit dem Ausgang des Mittelalters,* vols. 6–9 (Freiburg, 1913–23) passim; B. G. Dolfin, *I Dolfin . . .* (Milan, ²1924).

KLAUS GANZER

■ **Additional Bibliography:** *BBKL* 17:256ff.—D. Squicciarini, *Die Apostolischen Nuntien in Wien* (Vatican City, 1999) 61–65.

Delphius (Delfius, Delphinus; his real name was Brants), *Johannes.* Auxiliary bishop in Strasbourg, born March 6, 1524 in Delft, died July 14, 1582 in Strasbourg. He began his studies at the university of Cologne in 1539, where he met Peter → Canisius; he took his licentiate in theology in 1549 and entered the service of the archbishop of Trier in the same year, accompanying him as his theologian to the Council of Trent (1551-1552). He became auxiliary bishop of Strasbourg in 1553 (public proclamation in Rome, 1556), and was cathedral preacher in Strasbourg until 1559. He took part in the religious dialogue in → Worms in 1557. It remains unclear to what extent he collaborated in the *Statuta et decreta* (Mainz, 1566) of the Strasbourg diocesan synod.

■ **Works:** *De potestate pontificis et notis ecclesiae* (Cologne, 1580); *Concio . . . in Evangelium* (Strasbourg, 1581); *Quaestiones proponendae ordinandis in maioribus* (Cologne, 1581); *VD 16* 5:192.

■ **Literature:** *NDB* 3:589; *DHGE* 14:187ff.; *Encyclopédie de l'Alsace,* vol. 4 (Strasbourg, 1983) 2306f.; B B. von Bundschuh, *Das Wormser Religionsgespräch* (Münster, 1988).

HERIBERT SMOLINSKY

Denck, Hans. Baptist, born c. 1500 in Heybach, died 1527 in Basle. He had a humanistic education in Ingolstadt, and spent brief periods as domestic tutor or "corrector" in Augsburg, Donauwörth, Regensburg, and Basle (1518-1523). On the recommendation of Johannes → Oecolampadius, he became rector of the school in Nuremberg in 1525. He was already influenced by mystical traditions, and this was intensified by encounters with Thomas → Müntzer and Andreas → Karlstadt. His spiritualistic criticism of the Reformation led to his expulsion from Augsburg and Strasbourg, where he became a Baptist; nevertheless, his most important writings were published in Worms. (He and Ludwig → Hätzer were called the "prophets of Worms.") He found no place in southwest Germany that would accept him, but Oecolampadius tolerated him in Basle. In his so-called Revocation, Denck bade farewell to the Baptist movement, but not to Spiritualism. His writings were transmitted by the Hutterites and in the appendix to the → *Theologia Deutsch,* and were widely read until the following century.

■ **Literature:** *TRE* 8:488ff.—C. Baumann, *The Spiritual Legacy of H. D.* (Leiden, 1991).

GOTTFRIED SEEBASS

■ **Additional Bibliography:** M. Gockel, "A Reformer's Dissent from Lutheranism. Reconsidering the Theology of H. D.," *ARG* 91 (2000) 127–48; J. Beck, "The Anabaptists and the Jews," *Mennonite Quarterly Review* 75 (2001) 407–27; *Selected Writings of H. D. 1500–1527,* ed. E. J. Furcha (Lewiston, 1989).

Dessau, League of. This designates an agreement between the electoral Princes → Joachim I of Brandenburg and Albrecht of Mainz (→ Albrecht of Brandenburg) and Dukes → George of Saxony and → Henry II, the Younger, of Braunschweig-

Wolfenbüttel on July 15, 1525 with the aim of taking political action in common against the spread of Lutheranism. It was a north German parallel to the convent of → Regensburg (1524). Neither league had any great historical significance, but they are noteworthy as symptoms of the beginnings of a political reaction to Lutheranism, which itself was developing into a political territorial power.

ERNST WALTER ZEEDEN

Devotio moderna. A reform movement (c. 1375-1500) initiated by Geert Grote in Deventer, with roots in the religious women's movement, the mysticism of Brabant and the Rhine area, and Carthusian spirituality; it belongs to the European network of related reform movements. The *devotio moderna* emphasized for every Christian the ideal of the *vita communis* of the early church (shared property, an apostolic life), concrete piety, and personal discipleship of Christ in poverty and humility. It took shape initially in the semi-monastic urban milieu (Brothers and Sisters of the Common Life; men and women tertiaries), and took monastic form in 1387 with the foundation of a monastery of its own in Windesheim (Augustinian canons). The congregation of Windesheim, founded in 1395, grew by 1511 to encompass 97 monasteries in the Netherlands, Belgium, and Germany; many independent women's monasteries also lived under the influence of the *devotio moderna.*

The *devotio* promoted literary culture (copying of books, libraries), the Christian inheritance (church fathers, monasticism), the development of literature in the vernacular (biographies of Sisters of the Common Life and of nuns, the breviary), the revival of dialogues about scripture ("collations"), the Christian reform of schools (Johannes Cele), the pastoral care of boys in schools (system of boarding schools), and the reform of the religious life (Johannes Busch, Johannes Mauburnus). We should also mention the following supporters and authors of the *devotio moderna*: Jan van Ruusbroec (with whom Groote stayed for a long period), Florentius Radewijns, Gerhard of Zutphen, Gerlach Petersz, Heinrich Mande, and Thomas Hemerken (à Kempis), often identified as the author of the *Imitation of Christ.*

■ *LThK*[3] 3:173f. (unabridged version).

■ **Literature:** R. Post, *The Modern Devotion* (Leiden, 1968); G. Epiney-Burgard, *Gérard Grote (1340–84) et les débuts de la Dévotion moderne* (Wiesbaden, 1970); *Monasticon Windeshemense,* ed. W. Kohl et al., 3 vols. (Brussels, 1976–80); *Monasticon Fratrum Vitae Communis,* ed. W. Leesch et al., 2 vols. (Brussels, 1977–79); *Geert Grote & Moderne Devotie,* ed. J. Andriessen et al., *Ons Geestelijk Erf* 59 (1985) 111–505; G. Rehm, *Die Schwestern vom gemeinsamen Leben im nordwestlichen Deutschland* (Berlin, 1985); N. Staubach, "Pragmatische Schriftlichkeit im Bereich der D.," *Frühmittelalterliche Studien* 25 (1991) 418–61; R. van Dijk, "Die Frage einer nördlichen Variante der D.," in *Wessel Gansfort and Northern Humanism* (Groningen, 1993) 157–69.

RUDOLF TH. M. VAN DIJK

■ **Additional Bibliography:** R. Fuller, *The Brotherhood of the Common Life and Its Influence* (Albany, N.Y., 1994); Th. Kock, *Die Buchkultur der D.* (Frankfurt/Main, 1999).

Diaz, *Juan.* Spanish humanist, born 1510 in Cuenca, died March 27, 1546 in Neuburg on the Danube. He studied theology, Greek, and Hebrew in Paris, where Spanish and French Erasmians acquainted him with Paul's doctrine of justification. In 1545, he visited Jean Calvin in Geneva and Martin → Bucer in Strasbourg. He accompanied Bucer to the religious dialogue in → Regensburg in the following year. He then went to Neuburg, where he published his *Christianae Religionis Summa* (1546). His brother Alfonso, a legal consultor at the papal court of law, attempted to convert him to Catholicism, but when this failed, he had him murdered in Neuburg.

■ **Literature:** *RGG*[3] 2:180.—C. de Senarcleus, *Historia vera de morte sancti viri Ioannis Diazij Hispani . . . cum praefatione D. Martini Buceri* (Basle, 1546) (Spanish edition, Madrid, 1865, reprinted Barcelona, 1983); M. Bataillon, *Erasme et l'Espagne* (Paris, 1937) 551f.; G. L. Pinette, "Die Spanier und Spanien im Urteil des deutschen Volkes zur Zeit der Reformation," *ARG* 48 (1957) 182–91.

MICHAEL BECHT

Dick (Dickius; in the Greek form, Pachis), *Leopold.* Legal scholar, born at the close of the 15th century in Babenhausen, died after 1570. He studied in Padua and took his doctorate in civil and canon law in Turin. From 1527, he worked at the imperial supreme court in Speyer (he was Adolf → Clarenbach's advocate in 1528-1529, and

was attorney general for Gerwig Blarer from 1548 on). He was ennobled in 1532. He praised → Erasmus of Rotterdam as the intellectual leader of the age (*Oratio ad Carolum Romanum Imperatorem,* published without indication of place, 1521) and Martin Luther as the one who had restored Christian kindness to its proper place (*Gnad frid und barmhertzigkait* [Augsburg, 1522]). But he also praised Johannes → Eck as one who defended Christian freedom: Dick refused to be anyone's defense counsel or prosecutor (*Paraclesis* [Augsburg, 1523]). Dick laments both those human statutes which have obscured the gospel and the lack of piety seen in the lives of those who call themselves "evangelical" (*Ad Christum sponsum ecclesiae sponsae epistola* [Augsburg, 1523]). He castigates greed and usury as the reason why the clergy and the aristocracy oppress the poor, widows, and orphans; the rebellious peasants nominated Dick as their arbitrator. He defended the Catholic doctrine of the Eucharist (*De mysterio venerabili sacramenti eucharistiae* [Augsburg, 1525]) and of infant baptism (*Adversus impios Anabaptistarum errores* [Hagenau, 1530]), and exhorted the German Estates to make peace (*Ad universos Germaniae proceres, status et principes adhortatio* [Augsburg, 1535]). His meditation on the Lord's Prayer (*Paraphrastica meditatio in sacrosanctam precationem Dominicam* [Mainz, 1543]) was put on the Louvain Index in 1546, and the Roman Index of 1559 classified Dick as a heretic of the first class. He published a manual on the work of judges (*Oikonomia* [Basle, 1562]), and a methodological introduction for students and compendium of Christian and societal living (*De optima studiorum ratione; Christianae et civilis vitae compendium* [Basle, 1564]).

■ **Works:** Klaiber nos. 77f.; *VD 16* 5:325f.

■ **Literature:** *DSp* 3:859f.; *DHGE* 14:394.

VINZENZ PFNÜR

Dietenberger, *Johannes.* Dominican (1501) controversial theologian, born 1475 in Frankfurt am Main, died September 4, 1537 in Mainz. He studied in Cologne and Heidelberg from 1511 to 1514; he took his licentiate in 1514 and his doctorate of theology in Mainz in 1515. He became prior in Frankfurt in 1517, and regent of studies in Trier in 1518, devoting himself to the study of Thomas. He became prior in Coblenz in 1519, and was again prior in Frankfurt in 1520. He was in Coblenz in 1526, and worked as inquisitor in Cologne and Mainz. He was one of the authors of the *Confutatio* at the imperial parliament in Augsburg in 1530 (→ Confessio Augustana). At the request of the Trier legate, Johann von Metzenhausen, Dietenberger composed 15 theological treatises (*Phimostomus scripturariorum* [Cologne, 1532]; critical edition in CCath 38). He became professor of theology and canon of St. Mary's in Mainz in 1532, and worked as a commentator of Peter Lombard. He published the biblical translation of Hieronymus → Emser (1529-1532); his own German translation of the Bible was published at Mainz in 1534.

■ **Works:** *Obe die Christen mügen durch iere guten werck das hymelreich verdienen* (Strasbourg, 1523, often reprinted); *Contra temerarium M. Lutheri de votis monasticis iudicium* (Cologne, 1524, often reprinted); *Wider das unchristlich Buch Martini Lutheri von dem mißbrauch der Mess* (Frankfurt/Main, 1524, often reprinted); *Fragstuck an alle Christglaubigen* (Frankfurt/Main, 1529); *Catechismus* (Mainz, 1537, often reprinted).

■ **Literature:** *KThR* 1:82–89.—H. Wedewer, *J. D.* (Freiburg, 1888); N. Paulus, *Die deutschen Dominikaner im Kampfe gegen Luther* (Frankfurt/Main, 1903) 186–89; P. H. Vogel, "Die Bibelübersetzungen von D. und Ulenberg," *Gutenberg-Jahrbuch 1964,* 227–33; U. Horst, "Das Verhältnis von Heiliger Schrift und Kirche nach J. D.," *Theologie und Philosophie* 46 (1971) 223–47; C. E. Maxcey, "Why Do Good?" *ARG* 75 (1984) 93–112.

PETER FABISCH

■ **Additional Bibliography:** R. Hütter, "Martin Luther and J. D. on 'Good Works,'" *Lutheran Quarterly* 6 (1992) 127–52: A. Laube, "Das Gespann Cochläus/D. im Kampf gegen Luther," *ARG* 87 (1996) 119–35.

Dietrich, *Veit.* Lutheran theologian, born December 8, 1506 in Nuremberg, died there March 25, 1549. He began his studies in Wittenberg in 1522. He was a protégé of Philipp Melanchthon, and became confidential secretary to Martin Luther, whom he accompanied to the religious dialogue in → Marburg in 1529; he was with Luther in the Coburg fortress during the imperial parliament in Augsburg in 1530. In 1535, he was appointed preacher in St. Sebald's church in Nuremberg. He took part in the religious dialogue in → Regensburg in 1546, and opposed the Interim of → Augsburg in 1548. He played an important role in the transmission of Luther's teachings thanks to

his transcription of Luther's domestic sermons, which he published in his *Hauspostille* (1530-1534).

■ **Works:** *Etliche Schrifften fuer den gemeine man von unterricht Christlicher lehr,* ed. O. Reichmann (Assen, 1972).

■ **Literature:** *NDB* 3:699.—B. Klaus, *V. D. Leben und Werk* (Nuremberg, 1958); idem, "V. D.," *Fränkische Lebensbilder,* vol. 3 (Würzburg, 1969) 141–57; U. M. Schwob, *Kulturelle Beziehungen zwischen Nürnberg und den Deutschen im Südosten im 14. bis 16.Jh.* (Munich, 1969).

MICHAEL BECHT

■ **Additional Bibliography:** *RGG*[4] 2:848.—B. Klaus, *V. D.* (Nuremberg, 1996); idem, "V. D.s Gutachten über heimliche Eheschliessungen 'Von den Wickeleen bedencken,'" *ZBKG* 68 (1999) 1–11.

Doppenn (Doppen, Dappen), *Bernhard.* Franciscan, born in Dorsten. He was lector in the Franciscan monastery in Jüterborg in 1519, in Leipzig in 1526, and in Stadthagen in 1530. Academic studies and sermons survive in 19 manuscripts (1526-1532), covering such topics as sacramental doctrine, marriage law, controversial questions, and the spirituality of the religious life; he continually quotes from scripture and from Augustine. On May 4/5, 1519, → Albrecht of Brandenburg asked Johannes → Eck for an expert evaluation of two letters by Doppenn. Eck published his text in Ingolstadt under the title: *Articuli per fratres minores de observantia propositi reverendissimo domino episcopo Brandenburgensi contra Lutheranos.* In these letters, Doppenn describes the debate in Jüterborg at Easter 1519 between the Franciscans and the preachers "of the new doctrine" who had been appointed by the city council, viz., Franz Günther (cf. WA 1:221ff.) and Thomas → Müntzer. Martin Luther defended the theses of Günther which are described in this text, both vis-à-vis the monastery in Jüterborg (WA, Correspondence 1, nr. 174) and in reply to Eck (WA 2:621-654). Eck's response was entitled: *Ad criminatricem Martini Ludes Vittenbergen. offensionem super iudicio iustissimo facto ad articulos quosdam per minoritas de observantia Rev. Ep. Brandenburg. oblatos Eckiana responsio* (Paris and Ingolstadt, 1519).

■ **Literature:** *Die Helmstedter Handschriften, beschrieben von O. von Heinemann,* vol. 3 (Frankfurt/Main, 1965) 51f.; M. Bensing and W. Trillitzsch, "B. D.s 'Articuli . . .

contra Lutheranos,'" *Jahrbuch für Regionalgeschichte* (Weimar) 2 (1961) 113–47; G. Hammer, WA 59, 628 n. 84.

VINZENZ PFNÜR

Doré, *Pierre* (Petrus Auratus). Dominican (1514), controversial theologian and spiritual writer, born c. 1500 probably in Orleans, died May 19, 1569 in Paris. He took his doctorate in theology at Paris in 1532, and worked as teacher and superior in Dominican houses in Paris, Blois, Reims, and Châlons-sur-Marne. He was a close associate of the duke of → Guise, Claude de Lorraine, and of his family. He wrote about thirty books, mostly in French, which found a wide readership.
■ **Works:** *Les voies de paradis* (Lyons, 1537, often reprinted); *Les allumettes du feu divin* (Paris, 1538, often reprinted); *Le cerf spirituel* (Paris, 1544); *Conserve de grâce* (Paris, 1548); *L'arche de l'alliance nouvelle* (Paris, 1549); *Anti-Calvin* (Paris, 1551).
■ **Literature:** *DSp* 3:1641–45; *DHGE* 14:680f.; *DBF* 11:566f.—J. K. Farge, *Biographical Register of Paris Doctors of Theology, 1500–1536* (Toronto, 1980) 137–42.

VIOLA TENGE-WOLF

■ **Additional Bibliography:** J. Langlois, "P. D., écrivain spirituel et théologien des laïcs," *Mémoire Dominicaine* 12 (1998) 39–47.

Douai. Former university, founded 1559-1560 by → Philip II of Spain and opened in 1562. The most important of the colleges was founded in 1568 by William → Allen, intended to replace the universities of Oxford and Cambridge, since it was no longer possible—thanks to the restrictive religious policies of → Elizabeth I—for the English Catholic clergy to be trained there. Apart from Allen, Robert Bristow (1538-1581), Richard Smith (1566-1655), and Owen Lewis (1572-1633) came to Douai from Oxford. Under the influence of the Jesuits, the English college became a center of attempts to recatholicize England. It was transferred to Reims from 1578 to 1593; there, and later in Douai, Allen, Bristow, Gregory Martin (c. 1540-1582), and Thomas Worthington (1549-1627) translated the Bible from the Vulgate text. The "Douai-Reims Bible" played an important role in English Catholicism (New Testament: Reims, 1582; Old Testament: Douai, 1609).
■ *LThK*[3] 3:352 (unabridged version).
■ **Sources:** Th. F. Knox, ed., *The First and Second Diaries of the English College, D.* (London, 1878); E. H. Burton

and T. L. Williams, ed., *The D. Diaries 1598–1654,* 2 vols. (London, 1911); E. H. Burton and E. Nolan, ed., *The D. Diaries 1715–78* (London, 1928); P. R. Harris, ed., *D. College Documents 1639–1794* (St. Alban's, 1972).
■ **Literature:** G. Anstruther, *The Seminary Priests,* vol. 1: *Elizabethan* (Durham, 1969); J. Bossy, *The English Catholic Community 1570–1850* (London, 1975); A. Morey, *The Catholic Subjects of Elizabeth I* (London, 1978) 105–14; A. Dures, *English Catholicism 1558–1642* (Harlow, 1983); E. Norman, *Roman Catholicism in England* (Oxford, 1985).

REINHOLD RIEGER

■ **Additional Bibliography:** J. A. Loewe, "Richard Smyth and the Foundation of the University of D.," *Nederlands archief voor kerkgeschiedenis* 79 (1999) 142–69; J. A. Löwe, "'Facite, quod fieri': Biblical Exegesis at D. in the Mid-sixteenth Century," *Reformation and Renaissance Review* 3 (2001) 9–35.

Draconites (Drach), *Johannes.* Lutheran theologian, born 1494 in Karlstadt (Main), died April 18, 1566 in Wittenberg. He began his studies in 1509 in Erfurt, where he belonged to the humanist circle around Eobanus → Hessus. In 1522, he became Lutheran pastor in Miltenberg (Main). He took his doctorate in theology in Wittenberg in 1523. He was pastor in Waltershausen near Gotha from 1526 to 1528, and became professor in Marburg (Lahn) in 1534. He was one of the signatories of the → Schmalkaldic articles in 1537, and took part in the imperial parliament in Regensburg in 1541. He became professor in Rostock in 1551, and was president of the diocese of Pomerania from 1560 to 1564. In his final years, he devoted all his energies to his life's work, a *Biblia pentapla*. Only fragments of this polyglot Bible were printed.
■ **Literature:** *NDB* 4:95; *CEras* 1:404f.—E. O. Kiefer, *Die Theologie des J. D.* (Heidelberg, 1938); H. von Hintzenstern, "J. D.," in *Des Herren Name steht uns bei,* ed. K. Brinkel (Berlin, 1961) 25–34.

MICHAEL BECHT

■ **Additional Bibliography:** E. Bernstein, *Der Erfurter Humanistenkreis am Schnittpunkt von Humanismus und Reformation: Der polnische Humanismus und die europäischen Sodalitäten,* ed. S. Füssel (Wiesbaden, 1997) 137–65; H. Scheible, "J. D.," *ZBKG* 71 (2002) 29–47.

Drašković de Trakosčan, *Juraj* (Georg Draaskovics), bishop and statesman, born in a Croatian-

Hungarian aristocratic family February 5, 1525 in Biline castle (southern Croatia), died January 13, 1587 in Vienna. After studies in Krakow, Vienna, Bologna, and Rome, he was ordained priest in Rome in 1539 and held numerous ecclesiastical benefices in Hungary. He was appointed apostolic protonotary in 1537, bishop of Pécs in 1538, and bishop of Zagreb in 1563; from 1573, he was also archbishop of Kalocsa, but only nominally, since this diocese was under Turkish rule. He became bishop of Raab in 1578, and was created cardinal in 1585. He was Banus (viceroy) of Croatia and Dalmatia from 1567 to 1578, and royal governor and imperial chancellor in Hungary from 1578 to 1585. As orator of King → Ferdinand I and bishop, he took part in the Council of Trent from 1561 onwards, supporting the church reform which the king desired, viz., the → chalice for the laity and priestly marriage (→ celibacy). On his return to Zagreb, he introduced the conciliar decrees into his diocese, and ensured that the Reformation gained no foothold in Croatia. As Banus, he resisted both the Turkish attacks and rebellions by the peasants. By means of the synods which he held in Zagreb (1570, 1574) and Raab (1579), he restored clerical discipline. He founded seminaries for the education of priests, spread Catholic literature, and encouraged Jesuit foundations. His pioneer work for Catholic renewal in his diocese also included patronage of the arts and literary composition.

■ **Works:** A. Dudith, *Orationes quinque in Conc. Trid. habitae cum appendice orationum duarum G. Draskowith*, ed. L. Samuelfy (Halle, 1743); *Igen szép könyv minden eretnekség ujságai ellen* (Vienna, 1561); *Übersetzung des Commonitoriums des Vinzenz von Lérins ins Ungarische;* also edited some writings of Lactantius.

■ **Literature:** *Magyar Életrajzi Lexikon* (Hungarian biographical lexicon), vol. 1 (Budapest, 1967) 397.—A. Horányi, *Memoria Hungarorum*, vol. 1 (Vienna, 1775) 532; S. Katona, *Hist. Metrop. Calocens. eccl.*, vol. 2 (Kalocsa, 1800) 38–55; J. Koller: *Hist. Episc. Quinque-eccl.*, vol. 6 (Pressburg, 1806) 1–266; *Felsö-Magyarországi Minerva* I (1829); II (1834); I. Nagy, *Magyarország családai*, vol. 2 (Pest, 1858) 389–95; V. Frankl, *A magyar főpapok a trienti zsinaton* (Hungarian prelates at the Council of Trent) (Esztergom, 1863); V. Klaić, *Geschichte der Kroaten*, vol. 3/1 (Zagreb, 1911) 276–318; P. Brezanóczy, "Ungarische Bischöfe auf dem Konzil von Trient" (dissertation, Innsbruck, 1935); G. Adriányi, "Die ungarischen Synoden," *AHC* 8 (1976) 541–75, esp. 551.

GABRIEL ADRIÁNYI

Driedo(ens), *Johannes* (Johan Nys). Controversial theologian, born c. 1480 in Darisdonck near Turnhout, died August 4, 1535 in Louvain. He began the study of arts at the Collège du Faucon in Louvain in 1491, and took the degrees of master of arts in 1499, *baccalaureatus formatus* in 1511, and doctor of theology in 1512. He was ordained priest in 1515 and became dean of the theological faculty (re-elected to this post in 1518, 1523, 1528, 1531); he was rector of the university in 1518 and 1533. Driedoens did not get involved in the conflict between the Louvain theologians and humanism (→ Erasmus of Rotterdam; Collegium trilingue); while he remained faithful to the tradition of scholasticism, he was also open to a reform of studies, especially through the inclusion of the biblical languages. He maintained a moderate Augustinianism, which made him the ideal theological dialogue partner for Protestants. He made striking attempts to meet his theological opponents halfway.

■ **Works:** *Opera omnia*, ed. B. Gravius, 2 vols. (Louvain, 1547–50, often reprinted); *De ecclesiasticis scripturis et dogmatibus* (Louvain, 1533); *De captivitate et redemptione humani generis* (Louvain, 1534); *De concordia liberi arbitrii et praedestinationis divinae* (Louvain, 1537); *De gratia et libero arbitrio* (Louvain, 1537); *De libertate christiana* (Louvain, 1540) (against Luther's "Von der Freiheit eines Christenmenschen").

■ **Literature:** *DHGE* 14:795f.; *CEras* 1:405f.; *KThR* 3:33–47.—J. Etienne, *Spiritualisme érasmien et théologiens louvanistes* (Louvain and Gembloux, 1956) 103–60; J. Murphy, *The Notion of Tradition in J. D.* (Milwaukee, Wisc., 1959); M. Gielis, "L'augustinisme anti-érasmien des premiers controversistes de Louvain," in *L'augustinisme à l'ancienne faculté de théologie à Louvain*, ed. M. Lamberigts (Louvain, 1994) 19–61.

PETER FABISCH

■ **Additional Bibliography:** M. Kreuzer, *"Und das Wort ist Fleisch geworden." Zur Bedeutung des Menschseins Jesu bei J. D. und Martin Luther* (Paderborn, 1998).

Du Bellay, *Guillaume*. Humanist and industrious French diplomat in the service of → Francis I, born 1491 in Glatigny (department of Loir-et-Cher), died January 9, 1543 in St-Symphorien-de-Lay. He took part in the negotiations for the Peace of Cambrai (1529) between Francis I and → Charles V, and he was the architect of the League of Scheyer (1532) which united Bavaria, the Protestant imperial princes, and France in the endeavor to keep the Habsburgs out of Württemberg (→ Ulrich of Württemberg). He negotiated with the Protestant princes in 1535, seeking their acceptance of the convocation of a council, and he ensured French support for → Henry VIII in the matter of his divorce. He was governor of Turin in 1537 and of Piedmont from 1539 to 1542.

■ **Literature:** *DBF* 11:889ff.—V. L. Bourrilly, *G. D. Seigneur de Langey 1491–1543* (Paris, 1905); K. J. Seidel, *Frankreich und die deutschen Protestanten* (Münster, 1970).

BRUNO STEIMER

Dudith (Dudich), *András*. Humanist and polyhistorian, born February 16, 1533 in Ofen (Buda) of Croatian-Italian stock, died February 23, 1589 in Breslau. He studied in Breslau, Verona, Padua, and Paris. He accompanied Cardinal Reginald → Pole, the papal legate, to England and Scotland. He was ordained priest in 1557 and received many ecclesiastical benefices in Hungary. He represented the Hungarian bishops at the Council of Trent in 1561, where he sought to further the emperor's program of church reform. He was sent as conciliar legate to Vienna. → Ferdinand I sent him three times on diplomatic missions to Poland, and nominated him bishop of Csanád in 1562 and bishop of Pécs in the following year. In 1565, the emperor sent him to the Polish court at Vilnius, where he married a lady-in-waiting of the queen in 1567. He was excommunicated by the pope and stripped of all his offices by the Consistorial congregation. He became a Protestant, and later joined the → Antitrinitarians. He wrote extensively while in Poland, but was expelled from the country because of his involvement in political intrigues. Most of his correspondence with important contemporaries is still unpublished.

■ **Works:** *Orationes quinque in Conc. Trid. habitae . . . ,* ed. L. Samuelfy (Halle, 1743); *Dionysii Halicarnassei de Thucydidis Historia judicium* (Venice, 1560); *Vita Reginaldi Poldi* (Venice, 1563; London, 1690); *Commentariolus de Cometarum significatione* (Basle, 1579); A. Berndorfer, ed., "Die medizinischen Briefe des ungarischen Humanisten A. D.," in *Communicationes ex Bibl. Hist. Med. Hung.* (Budapest, 1956) n. 2, 46–71.

■ **Literature:** B. Stoll, I. Varga, and S. V. Kovács, *A magyar irodalomtörténet bibliográfiája 1772-ig* (Bibliography of Hungarian literature up to 1772) (Budapest, 1972) 301f.—K. B. Stieff, *Versuch einer . . . Geschichte von Leben und Glaubensmeynungen A. D.s.* (Breslau, 1756); E. Engelhardt, *Leben des A. D.* (Bielefeld, 1864); E. Lutteri, "Della vita di A. D.," in *Atti dell' Accademia degli Agiati di Rovereto,* vol. 2 (Rovereto, 1884) 65–112;

J. Faludy, *A. D. et les humanistes français* (Szeged, 1927); P. Costil, *A. D. humaniste hongrois. Sa vie, son œuvre, et ses manuscrits grecs* (Paris, 1935); K. Juhász, "A. D. Ein Beitrag zur Geschichte des Humanismus," *HJ* 55 (1935) 55–74.

GABRIEL ADRIÁNYI

■ **Additional Bibliography:** J. Jankovics, *A. D.'s Library* (Szeged, 1993); L. Ronchi, "L'epistolario di Andrea D. Sbardellati," *Protestantismo* 55 (2000) 128–35.

Dumoulin, *Charles* (Carolus Molinaeus). Lawyer, born 1500 in Paris, where he died December 27, 1566. He studied in Paris, Poitiers, and Orleans. He was an opponent of the Council of Trent, and changed his confessional allegiance several times. In 1552, he fled to Germany and Switzerland. He held lectures on civil law in Tübingen in 1553-1554, then in Dôle and Besançon. He oversaw a critical edition of the *Corpus iuris canonici* (Lyons, 1554).

■ **Editions:** *Molinaei Caroli Opera omnia,* ed. J. Brodeau, 5 vols. (Paris, 1681).

■ **Literature:** *Dictionnaire de droit canonique,* vol. 5, 41–67.—J. F. von Schulte, *Geschichte der Quellen und der Literatur des kanonischen Rechts,* vol. 3/2 (Stuttgart, 1880) 251f.; G. Meyer, *Ch. D.* (Nuremberg, 1956); J.-L. Thireau, *Ch. du Moulin* (Geneva, 1980).

MICHAEL BENZ

■ **Additional Bibliography:** Th. Wanegffelen, "Le 'plat-pays de la croyance.' Frontière confessionnelle et sensibilité religieuse en France au XVIᵉ siècle," *RHEF* 81 (1995) 391–411.

Dungershei(y)m (Ochsenfart), *Hieronymus*. Controversial theologian, born April 22, 1465 in Ochensfurt (Main), died March 2, 1540 in Leipzig. He began his studies in Leipzig in 1504, continuing in Cologne, and took his doctorate in theology at Siena in 1504. He was professor of theology in Leipzig from 1506 to 1540, and cathedral canon in Zeitz. He was frequently active as preacher (Chemnitz, Zwickau, Mühlhausen in 1525) and visitor (Meissen 1522, Merseburg 1524). As a theologian, he was profoundly influenced by Thomism; he composed textbooks and wrote against the → Bohemian Brethren in 1514-1515. He began the debate with Martin Luther and other Reformers in 1520, first in letters and then in print.

■ **Works:** Klaiber nos. 866–80; *VD 16* 5:553–57; Köhler *BF* I/1:332ff.; CCath 39.

■ **Literature:** *CEras* 1:412; *KThR* 2:38–48.—E. Peschke, *Kirche und Welt in der Theologie der Böhmischen Brüder* (Berlin, 1981) 179–84; Th. Freudenberger, *H. D. von Ochsenfurt* (Münster, 1988); D. V. N. Bagchi, *Luther's Earliest Opponents* (Minneapolis, 1991).

HERIBERT SMOLINSKY

■ **Additional Bibliography:** S. Bräuer, "'Ich begere lauttern vnd reinen wein | so vormischt er mirn mith wasser': der Flugschriftenstreit zwischen dem Eilenburger Schuhmacher Georg Schönichen und dem Leipziger Theologen H. D.," in *Reformation und Katholizismus. FS G. Maron* (Hannover, 2003) 97–140.

Duplessis-Mornay, *Philippe.* French Reformed theologian, born November 5, 1549 in Buhy-en-Vexin, died November 11, 1623 in La-Forêt-sur-Sèvre. After pursuing academic studies from 1568 to 1572, he fled from Paris before St. → Bartholomew's Eve. He fought against the League, supported the claim of → Henry of Navarre to the throne, and took part in the negotiations which led to the Edict of → Nantes. He became governor of Saumur in 1589, where he founded the celebrated Protestant university; he was deposed from office by Louis XIII in May, 1621. In the political sphere, he promoted tolerance by his actions and by his theoretical reflections. As a theologian, he engaged in vigorous controversy against the Catholic party. His desire was to see the various Reformation churches draw closer to one another on the basis of the → Fundamental articles.

■ **Principal Works:** *De la vérité de la religion chrétienne* (Antwerp, 1581); *Institution, usage et doctrine du saint sacrement de l'Eucharistie en l'Eglise ancienne* (La Rochelle, 1598); *Traitté de l'Eglise* (La Rochelle, 1599); *Le mystère d'iniquité* (Saumur, 1611).

■ **Literature:** R. Patry, *Ph. D. Un Huguenot homme d'Etat* (Paris, 1922); F. Laplanche, *L'évidence du Dieu chrétien* (Strasbourg, 1983); J. Solé, *Le débat entre protestants et catholiques français de 1598 à 1685*, 4 vols. (Paris, 1985); F. Laplanche, *L'Écriture, le sacré et l'histoire* (Amsterdam, 1986).

FRANÇOIS LAPLANCHE

■ **Additional Bibliography:** A. L. Herman, "Protestant Churches in a Catholic Kingdom," *SCJ* 21 (1990) 543–58; H. Daussy, "Au cœur des négociations pur l'édit de Nantes. Le rôle de Ph. D.," *Bulletin de la Société de l'Histoire du Protestantisme Français* 144 (1998) 207–52; O. Fatio, "La vérité menacée. L'apologétique de Ph. D.," *Bulletin de la Société de l'Histoire du Protestantisme*

Français 144 (1998) 253–64; H. Daussy, *Les Huguenots et le roi: le combat politique de P.D. (1572–1600)* (Geneva, 2002).

Duprat (Du Prat), *Antoine-Bohier* (Antonius a Prato). Chancellor of France and cardinal (1527), born January 17, 1463 in Issoire (Auvergen), son of a merchant and city counselor, died July 9, 1535 in Nantrouillet near Meaux. After studying law, he became governor of the protectorate of Montferrand in 1490, advocate general in the parliament of Toulouse in 1495, secretary in the council of state in 1503, president of the parliament of Paris in 1508, and chancellor in 1515. He accompanied → Francis I of France on his military expedition in Italy, and negotiated with → Leo X about the concordat of Bologna (1516); he succeeded in getting this treaty ratified, despite the opposition of parliament and of the university. His wife died in 1508; he was ordained in 1516, but did not give up his political activity. He was involved in the king's financial reforms in 1523-1524 (especially the recognition that offices of state were open to purchase). In 1525, he became archbishop of Sens and abbot of St-Benoît-sur-Loire. In 1528, he summoned a provincial council which enacted strict measures against the Lutherans. He also became administrator of the dioceses of Albi (1528) and Meaux (1530), and papal legate in 1530. He died in his castle of Nantrouillet—rich, respected, and hated.

■ **Literature:** *DHGE* 14:1144ff.; *DBF* 12:503ff.; J.-M. Bizière and J. Solé, *Dictionnaire des biographies*, vol. 3 (Paris, 1993) 93f.—A. Buisson, *Le chancelier A. D.* (Paris, 1935).

GÉRALD CHAIX

Duranti, *Jean-Etienne.* Lawyer, president of the senate of Toulouse, born 1534, died February 10, 1589. A resolute Catholic, he was involved for a long period in Reformation struggles against the → Huguenots; his fidelity to the king led to his murder during a revolt. His literary fame is due primarily to his explanation of the liturgy, *De ritibus Ecclesiae catholicae libri tres* (published posthumously [Rome, 1591 and Cologne, 1592]; often reprinted), a work which has no serious rivals in the 16th century. Here he discusses church buildings and furniture (including sacramental celebrations), the Mass, and the liturgy of the Hours. Methodologically speaking, he remains somewhat close to the *Rationale* of Durandus of Mende (died 1296), but Duranti presents a richer selection of patristic and medieval sources, and his tone is less allegorical; to some extent, his work is directed against the Reformation.

■ **Literature:** *Cath* 3:1199; *DBF* 12:721f.—R. A. Mentzer, "Calvinist Propaganda and the Parliament of Toulouse," *ARG* 68 (1977) 268–83.

MARTIN KLÖCKENER

E

Eber, *Paul.* Lutheran theologian and hymn-writer, born November 8, 1511 in Kitzingen (Lower Franconia), died December 10, 1569 in Wittenberg. He was severely handicapped but highly gifted, and studied from 1532 in Wittenberg, where he became a close collaborator of Philipp Melanchthon (*Repertorium Philippi*). In 1541, he became professor of Latin in Wittenberg; in 1544, professor of physics; and in 1557 professor of Old Testament and court preacher. He took part in the religious dialogue of → Worms. In 1558, he succeeded Johannes → Bugenhagen as pastor of the city church and general superintendent of the electoral principality. He followed Melanchthon in teaching a mild Lutheran doctrine, and sought to mediate in the theological conflicts which arose in German Lutheranism after Martin Luther's death, especially in the controversy about the Lord's Supper. He was an effective preacher, and some of his hymns are still sung today (especially *Wenn wir in höchsten Nöten sein*).

■ **Works:** *Contexta populi Judaici historia* (Wittenberg, 1548, often reprinted) (with German and French translations); *Calendarium historicum* (Wittenberg, 1550, often reprinted) (with German and French translations); *Vom heiligen Sakrament des Leibs und Bluts [. . .] Christi* (Wittenberg, 1562).—Prepared the Old Testament in Biblia germanico-latina (Wittenberg, 1565, often reprinted).—Editions: Ph. Wackernagel, *Das deutsche Kirchenlied von der ältesten Zeit bis zu Anfang des 17.Jh.* (Leipzig, vol. 4, 1874, 1–8; vol. 5, 1877, 1367f.)—Bibliography: *VD* 16 5:10–72.

■ **Literature:** Ch. H. Sixt, *P. E.* (Heidelberg, 1843); idem, *P. E. (1532–69)* (Ansbach, 1857); G. Buchwald, *P. E.* (Leipzig, 1897); W. Thüringer, "P. E.," in *Melanchthon*

in seinen Schülern, ed. H. Scheible (Wiesbaden, 1997) 219–35.

WERNER RAUPP

■ **Additional Bibliography:** W. Janse, "Wittenberg 'Calvinizans,'" in *Ordenlich und fruchtbar.* FS W. van't Spijker (Leiden, 1997) 53–67.

Eberlin von Günzburg, *Johann.* Humanist and Lutheran preacher, born 1465/1470 in Kleinkötz near Günzburg, died 1533 in Leutershausen near Ansbach. He began his studies in Basle in 1489, moving to Freiburg in 1493. He became a Franciscan in Tübingen in 1519 and was preacher in Ulm, where he preached a formal farewell sermon on June 29, 1521 which marked his definitive adherence to Martin Luther. His first religious and social-critical pamphlets grew out of sermons which he delivered in Aargau and Lauingen (*Die 15 Bundesgenossen* [Basle, 1521]). He was in Wittenberg from 1522 to 1524, and in Erfurt in 1524-1525 (he preached his first sermon there on May 1, 1524). He married Martha von Aurach, a former nun. He was court preacher and superintendent in Wertheim from 1525 to 1530; it was here that he drew up his Lutheran Church order and translated Tacitus's *Germania.* After the death of Count George II, he moved to Leutershausen, where he looked after the parish until his death.

■ **Literature:** E. Deuerlein, "J. E.," in *Lebensbilder aus dem Bayerischen Schwaben,* vol. 5 (Munich, 1956) 70–92; R. Adamcyk, "Die Flugschriften des J. E. von Günzburg" (diss., Vienna, 1981); M. Brecht, *Wertheimer Jahrbuch 1983,* 47–54; H. Ehmer, *Wertheimer Jahrbuch 1983,* 55–71; E. Langguth, *Wertheimer Jahrbuch 1983,* 73–102; L. Noack, "J. E. von Günzburg und seine Flugschriften" (diss., Leipzig, 1983); G. Heger, *J. E. von Günzburg und seine Vorstellungen über eine Reform in Reich und Kirche* (Berlin, 1985); U. Petry, in *Sprache in Vergangenheit und Gegenwart,* ed. W. Brandt (Marburg, 1988) 65–90; M. Rössing-Hager, in *Sprache in Vergangenheit und Gegenwart,* 47–64; idem, *Deutscher Wortschatz,* ed. H. Haider Munske (Berlin, 1988) 279–320; M. Bujnáková, *Philosophica pragensia* 31 (1988) 184–94; Ch. Peters, "'Der Teufel sieht mich hier nicht gern . . .' Die 12 Briefe J. E.s von Günzburg aus seiner Zeit als Pfarrverweser in Leutershausen," *ZBKG* 59 (1990) 23–68; idem, "Franziskanischer Reformer, Humanist und konservativer Reformator" (diss., Münster, 1990); A. Masser, in Festschrift J. Erben (Frankfurt/Main, 1990) 227–38; Ch. Peters, *J. E. von Günzburg* (Gütersloh, 1994).

HERBERT IMMENKÖTTER

■ **Additional Bibliography:** H.-C. Rublack, "Anticlericalism in German Reformation Pamphlets," in *Anticlericalism in Late Medieval and Early Modern Europe*, ed. P. A. Dykema (Leiden, 1993) 461–89; E. Wolgast, "Die Neuordnung von Kirche und Welt in deutschen Utopien der Frühreformation," in *Festschrift M. Hengel* (Tübingen, 1999) 659–79.

Ecclesiastical reservation. The Religious Peace of → Augsburg (Zeumer §18) specified that if the clerical ruler of a territory directly subject to the emperor converted to the Protestant faith, he must abdicate from government. At the same time, a Catholic candidate could be elected as the new territorial ruler. The intention of this regulation was to ensure that these territories with their clerical rulers remained in the hands of the Catholic party. Like most of the regulations in the Peace of Augsburg, this too was an interim measure until a new rule should be laid down. It was not easy to win acceptance for this law; the Protestants extracted the *Declaratio Ferdinandea* (→ Ferdinand I) as compensation. In the ensuing period up to the outbreak of the Thirty Years' War, the conflict about the ecclesiastical reservation occupied, directly or indirectly, the center stage in imperial history. It was not possible to enforce the ecclesiastical reservation in the spiritual territories of northern Germany between the Weser and the Oder (with the exception of Breslau and Hildesheim) and in some southern and western German lands (Hessen, Württemberg, Ansbach-Kulmbach), but this regulation proved an important buttress of Catholicism in the area of the Rhine and Main rivers, in Westphalia, and in Bavaria. Through the Peace of Westphalia (1648), the ecclesiastical reservation acquired legal validity until the end of the old empire (1806) for all those territories with spiritual rulers which had belonged in 1624 (the "normal year") to the Catholic confession; an exception was made for Osnabrück. The conflicts about the ecclesiastical reservation (including the controversy about the Session in Magdeburg, the chapter controversy in Strasbourg, and especially the War of Cologne) were a great disturbance to the structure of the empire and hampered the functioning of the imperial constitution.

■ **Text:** K. Zeumer, *Quellensammlung zur Geschichte der deutschen Reichsverfassung in Mittelalter und Neuzeit* (Tübingen, ²1913); *Der Augsburger Religionsfriede*, ed. K. Brandi (Göttingen, ²1927).
■ **Literature:** M. Ritter, *Deutsche Geschichte im Zeitalter der Gegenreformation und des Dreißigjährigen Krieges*, 3 vols. (Stuttgart, 1889–1908) passim; M. Heckel, *Deutschland im konfessionellen Zeitalter* (Göttingen, 1983) esp. 72ff., 198ff.; H. Rabe, *Deutsche Geschichte 1500–1600* (Munich, 1991) 449–55.

ERNST WALTER ZEEDEN

Eck, *Johannes* (real name: Johannes Maier or Mayer). Controversial theologian, born November 13, 1486 in Egg (Eck) on the river Günz, died February 10, 1543 in Ingolstadt. He began his studies at the university of Heidelberg in 1498 and continued at Tübingen (where he took the degree of master of arts in 1501) and Cologne; he moved to Freiburg in 1502 and was a member of the Peacock Hostel, with its nominalistic orientation, from 1503. His first printed work, *Bursa pavonis. Logices exercitamenta* (Strasbourg, 1507), was based on lectures he held. He also pursued legal studies under Ulrich Zasius and humanistic studies (Greek and Hebrew) under Gregor Reisch, and later under Johannes → Reuchlin. He became bachelor of biblical studies in 1505 and commentator on the *Sentences* in 1506. He was ordained priest in Strasbourg in 1508, and took his licentiate in theology the following year and his doctorate of theology in Freiburg in 1510. In the same year, he became professor of theology and vicechancellor of the university in Ingolstadt, on the recommendation of Conrad → Peutinger; he was made a canon of Eichstätt. In 1514, he published his first large-scale work, the *Chrysopassus,* on predestination and grace. From 1515, he played a central role in university reform, thanks to the textbooks he wrote on logic (1516-1517) and his commentaries on Aristotle (1517-1520), which simplified the text in keeping with the "selfreform of scholasticism" (Seifert). In 1515, he held a public disputation in Bologna on economic ethics, and pleaded for a moderate interest rate of 5 percent.

Until 1518-1519, Eck's primary academic interests were philosophy and theology—the study of Cusanus and Augustine, and a commentary on the mystical theology of Ps.-Dionysius the Areopagite (1519)—but from 1518, he developed into a controversial theologian who played a central role in Bavarian church politics and was in turn influenced by political events. Eck's earliest contacts with Martin Luther were controversial. The first debate arose as a result of manuscript observations by Eck (*Annotationes* or *Obelisci*, printed in 1545) on the 95 theses on indulgences, to which Luther replied in *Asterisci*, while Andreas → Karlstadt drew up a list of theses of his own. This conflict led to the disputation of → Leipzig in 1519 and generated numerous controversial writings. Eck contributed in Rome to the formulation of the bull → *Exsurge Domine* which threatened Luther with excommunication (1520), and he published it in Germany along with Hieronymus → Aleander. He was again in Rome in 1523-1524, charged by the Bavarian dukes to draw up reform proposals of a conservative character. For the imperial parliament which met at Augsburg in 1530, Eck elaborated a catalogue of heresy in 404 articles; he was one of the authors of the refutations of the → Confessio Augustana (*Catholica Responsio* and *Confutatio*), and took part in negotiations for a reconciliation. He was even more open to compromise when he participated as Bavaria's representative in the religious dialogue in → Worms (1540-1541). In → Regensburg, however, in keeping with Bavarian policy, he increasingly took a position against the emperor's policy of reconciliation and rejected the "Book of Regensburg."

The most influential of Eck's many controversial theological writings was his *Enchiridion* (first printed in 1525; critical edition by P. Fraenkel in CCath 34), a discussion of the most important points of dispute, which he frequently expanded; it went through 121 editions and was translated into German, French, and Flemish. He discussed the ecclesiology which was the object of dispute in Leipzig in *De primatu Petri* (Paris, 1521), which he presented to the pope in 1520; this work takes the papalist line. In the 1520s, Eck wrote works on the veneration of images (→ Art and Reformation), purgatory, penance, and the Mass. From 1523-1524 onwards, he engaged in debates with Huldrych Zwingli and the Swiss Reformation, and he took part in the → Baden disputation (1526) which had a positive outcome for the Catholic side. Eck was the first Catholic theologian to engage in literary argument with the → Baptists (from 1526 on). Later writings are occasional works connected with the religious dialogues. In *Ains Judenbuechlins Verlegung* (1541), Eck drew

on medieval anti-Jewish texts in his controversy with Andreas → Osiander.

The controversial theology of the 1530s sought to promote church reform, not merely to engage in polemics. This is the context in which Eck published five volumes of sermons (Ingolstadt, 1530-1539; he was parish priest of St. Moritz from 1519 to 1525, and of Our Lady's church in Ingolstadt from 1525 to 1532 and 1538 to 1540), a translation of the Bible (Ingolstadt, 1537), printed versions of his exegetical lectures on Psalm 20 and Haggai, as well as proposals (from the end of the 1530s on) for a simplification of theological studies.

Since all these controversies made great demands on his energy, Eck was unable to develop a coherent theological system that would have looked to the future, although he frequently adumbrated reforms and was receptive to modern developments (e.g., in the question of interest). Although he made use of his knowledge of the biblical languages in lectures and publications, this did not lead him to draw any significant consequences for his theology. The decisive point remained for him the church as the source of the authoritative interpretation of scripture, with the ecclesiastical tradition and the hierarchy. The fact that his work served the Bavarian rulers in their government of church life was also very important to him. As the disputation in Leipzig showed, the concerns of the Reformers largely remained a closed book for Eck.

■ **Works:** CCath 1f., 6, 13f., 34ff., 41f.; J. Metzler, CCath 16:LXXI–CXXXI (list of works); W. Gussmann, *Des J. E. 404 Artikel* (Kassel, 1930); ARCEG 1–4; P. O. Kristeller, *Iter Italicum. A Finding List of Uncatalogued or Incompletely Catalogued Humanistic Manuscripts of the Renaissance*, vols. 1–3 and 5 (London, and Leiden, 1963–90); W. L. Moore, Jr., ed., *In primum librum Sententiarum Annotatiunculae D. J. Eckio Praelectore* (Leiden, 1976); VD 16 5:618–41; Ch.H. Lohr, *Latin Aristotle Commentaries*, vol. 2 (Florence, 1988); Köhler BF 1/1:353–73.

■ **Literature:** NDB 4:273ff.; LThK² 3:642ff.; BBKL 1:1452ff.; TRE 9:249–58; KThR² 1:65–72.—Th. Wiedemann, *Dr. J. E.* (Regensburg, 1865); G. Épiney-Burgard, "J. E. et le Commentaire de la Théologie mystique du pseudo-Denys," *Bibliothèque d'humanisme et renaissance* 34 (1972) 7–29; A. Seifert, *Logik zwischen Scholastik und Humanismus. Das Kommentarwerk J. E.s* (Munich, 1978); *Gestalten der Kirchengeschichte*, ed. M. Greschat, vol. 5 (Stuttgart et al., 1981) 247–70; idem, *J. E.* (Münster, 1981); W. Klaiber, "Ecclesia militans," *Studien zu den Festtagspredigten des J. E.* (Münster,

1982); R. Bäumer, "J. E. und Freiburg," *Freiburger Diözesan-Archiv* 106 (1986) 21–41; H. Smolinsky, "Der Humanismus an Theologischen Fakultäten des katholischen Deutschland," in *Der Humanismus und die oberen Fakultäten*, ed. G. Keil et al. (Weinheim, 1987) 21–42; E. Iserloh, ed., *J. E. im Streit der Jahrhunderte* (Münster, 1988); H. Smolinsky, "Reform der Theologie? Beobachtungen zu J. E.s exegetischen Vorlesungen," in *Papst und Kirchenreform*. Festschrift G. Schwaiger (St. Ottilien, 1990) 333–49; D. V. N. Bagchi, *Luther's Earliest Opponents* (Minneapolis, 1991); B. Hägler, *Die Christen und die "Judenfrage." Am Beispiel der Schriften Osianders und E.s zum Ritualmordvorwurf* (Erlangen, 1992); J. Wicks, *Luther's Reform* (Mainz, 1992); K.-V. Selge, "Kirchenväter auf der Leipziger Disputation," in *Auctoritas Patrum*, ed. L. Grane et al. (Mainz, 1993) 197–212; J. P. Wurm, *J. E. und der oberdeutsche Zinsstreit 1513–15* (Münster, 1997).

HERIBERT SMOLINSKY

■ **Additional Bibliography:** G. R. Tewes, "Luthergegner der ersten Stunde," *QFIAB* 75 (1995) 256–365; Th. Fuchs, "Die Disputation zwischen E. und Melanchthon in Worms," in *Konfession und Gespräch* (Cologne, 1995) 409–22; M. Schulze, "J. E. im Kampf gegen Martin Luther," *Luther-Jahrbuch* 63 (1996) 39–68; R. Schwarz, "Wie weit reicht der Konsens zwischen E. und Melanchthon in der theologischen Anthropologie?" in *Im Schatten der Confessio Augustana*, ed. H. Immenkötter (Münster, 1997) 169–84; J. Wicks and M. J. Haemig, "The Other John in John: Luther and E. on John the Baptist," *Word and World* 21 (2001) 377–84; R. Kolb, ed., "J. E.'s Four Hundred and Four Articles for the Imperial Diet at Augsburg," in *Sources and Contexts of the Book of Concord* (Minneapolis, 2001) 31–82.

Ecken (de Acie, Eckius, von der Eck, von Eck, Eck), *Johannes von der*. Born in a middle-class family in Trier, died December 2, 1524 in Esslingen. After studies in Bologna and Siena, he became professor at the legal faculty of the university of Trier in 1506; he became rector of the university in 1514 and dean in 1523. From 1515 (1512?), he was a curial official of Archbishop Richard von Greiffenklau in Trier. At the imperial parliament in Worms on April 17-18, 1521, as the emperor's representative, he presided at the interrogation of Martin Luther, and he was present with Johannes → Cochlaeus at the secret conversation between the archbishop and Luther on 24 April. His career and lifestyle belong to the late gothic period; he had scarcely any training in theology, but he was an astute lawyer.

■ **Literature:** *Deutsche Reichstagsakten*, earlier series, vol. 2 (Gotha, ²1896); *BDG* 5245ff.; *NDB* 4:277.—P. Kalkoff,

Der Wormser Reichstag (Munich and Berlin, 1922) with index; E. Zenz, *Die Trierer Universität* (Trier, 1949) 30f.; *Der Reichstag zu Worms von 1521*, ed. F. Reuter (Worms, 1971) with index; Jedin 1:163.

JOSEF STEINRUCK

Edward VI of England (1547-1553). Born October 12, 1537 at Hampton Court, son of King → Henry VIII and Jane Seymour, died July 6, 1553 at Greenwich. His father had him educated by teachers who were convinced Protestants. He was a clever child, attracted by the study of ancient languages and of theology. He succeeded his father on the throne in 1547. The regency which ruled in his name was dominated first by the duke of Somerset, and from 1549 by the duke of Northumberland. Under the influence of Thomas → Cranmer and of foreign counselors, and with the consent of the king, who was filled with religious zeal, the English church in this period opened its doors to Calvinism (Book of Homilies, 1547; first and second *Book of* → *Common Prayer* and catechism, 1549, with a more strongly Calvinist text in 1552; 42 → Anglican articles, 1553; destruction of altars and removal of side-chapels in the cathedrals . . .). Edward's attempt in 1553, together with Northumberland, to exclude his half-sisters → Mary and → Elizabeth from succession to the throne was a failure.

■ **Literature:** *DNB* 62:502–8.—J. G. Nichols, *Literary Remains of King Edward VI*, 2 vols. (London, 1857); H. W. Chapman, *The Last Tudor King* (London, 1958); J. Ridley, *Thomas Cranmer* (Oxford, 1962); W. K. Jordan, *Edward VI*, 2 vols. (London, 1968–70).

KARL SCHNITH

■ **Additional Bibliography:** D. G. Selwyn, "The 'Book of Doctrine,' the Lords' Debate and the First Prayer Book of Edward VI," *Journal of Theological Studies* 40 (1989) 446–80; N. Heard, *Edward VI and Mary* (London, ³1992); J. Loach, *Edward VI* (New Haven, Conn., 1999); P. Ayris, "Review Article: The Edwardian Reformation," *Reformation and Renaissance Review* 3 (2001) 188–207; C. Davies, *A Religion of the Word: The Defence of the Reformation in the Reign of Edward VI* (Manchester, 2002); S. Alford, *Kingship and Politics in the Reign of Edward VI* (Cambridge, 2002).

Eisengrein, *Martin*. Controversial theologian, born December 28, 1535 in Stuttgart, died May 4, 1578 in Ingolstadt. He studied in Tübingen, Vienna, and Ingolstadt, and became professor in

Vienna in 1557. He converted to Catholicism in 1558/1559 and was ordained priest in 1560. He became parish priest of St. Moritz in Ingolstadt in 1562, and doctor of theology and professor in Ingolstadt in 1564; he founded the university library. As inspector of the university (1570-1578), he sought to mediate in the conflict between secular priests and Jesuits. He supported the → chalice for the laity in a memorandum commissioned by the Bavarian duke in 1563 and took part in several negotiations about religion. He was involved in reforming and Counter-Reformation measures. He held numerous ecclesiastical benefices; he was provost of the pilgrimage sanctuary of Altötting, which he endeavored to reform. His writings display an interest in pastoral theology and anti-Protestant polemics; he produced many sermons and treatises.

■ **Catalogue of Works:** Pfleger (see under Literature); Klaiber nos. 915–50; *VD 16* 5:697–706.

■ **Literature:** *NDB* 4:412f.; *DHGE* 15:102–5; *Handbuch der Bayerischen Kirchengeschichte*, ed. W. Brandmüller et al., vol. 2 (St. Ottilien, 1993).—L. Pfleger, *M. E.* (Freiburg, 1908); A. Seifert, *Die Universität Ingolstadt im 15. und 16.Jh.* (Berlin, 1973); W. Kausch, *Geschichte der Theologischen Fakultät Ingolstadt im 15. und 16.Jh.* (Berlin, 1977); A. Seifert, *Weltlicher Staat und Kirchenreform* (Münster, 1978).

HERIBERT SMOLINSKY

Elgard, *Nicolaus.* Supporter of Catholic reform, born c. 1538 in Arlon (Luxembourg), died August 11, 1587 in Erfurt. He was a priest of the diocese of Trier and studied, after a period of pastoral work, at the German college in Rome from 1569 to 1572. He was visitor in Augsburg in 1572-1573 and accompanied the nuncio Kaspar → Gropper on his journey through Germany from 1573 to 1576; as subdelegate, he was given the charge of carrying out some visitations himself, e.g., in Mainz, Fulda, Würzburg, and Bamberg. He encouraged students to attend the German college, and urged the bishops to found seminaries under Jesuit leadership. He was appointed auxiliary bishop of Mainz in 1578, with responsibility for Thüringen; his residence was in Erfurt. He did not see the realization of his hopes that Erfurt, or even Saxony as a whole, might be recatholicized; but he was able to bring many priests with a Tridentine mentality to Erfurt and to take the first steps towards the foundation of a Jesuit house.

■ **Sources:** W. E. Schwarz, *Die Nuntiaturkorrespondenz K. Groppers* (Paderborn, 1898) LXX–XCII.

■ **Literature:** L. Drehmann, *N. E.* (Leipzig, 1958); Ch. Grebner, *K. Gropper und N. E.* (Münster, 1982) 175–352.

CHRISTIAN GREBNER

■ **Additional Bibliography:** Ch. Grebner, "Der Mainzer Weihbischof N. E.," in *Weihbischöfe und Stifte*, ed. F. Jürgensmeier (Frankfurt/Main, 1995) 122–29.

Elizabeth I of England (queen 1558-1603). Born September 7, 1533 at Greenwich, died March 24, 1603 in Richmond. She was the daughter of King → Henry VIII and his second wife, Anne Boleyn (beheaded 1536); her right of succession to the throne was based on the will Henry made in 1540, which acquired exclusive validity through a statute of the "king in parliament." After she became queen on November 17, 1558, Elizabeth summoned parliament for January 25, 1559 and dissolved it on May 8, after it had collaborated with the crown in laying down the legal foundations of the "Church of → England," the "Elizabethan settlement"; the church Convocation, which met in Canterbury at the same time and held fast to the papal primacy, was not invited to join in this task. The Act of Supremacy did not style Elizabeth "head" of the episcopal church, but only "supreme governor." The Act of → Uniformity demanded that office-bearers take an oath, but accepted a merely external conformity (i.e., attendance at worship). Parliament also laid down the form of piety to be followed in the Church of England by means of a new version of the *Book of → Common Prayer* (1559). Later, in 1563, the *Thirty-Nine Articles* (→ Anglican articles) formulated by the Convocations were given the rank of "statute law" by parliament.

Elizabeth favored a pragmatic policy which aimed at reconciliation, and she claimed the right to instruct parliament and to issue a veto. She supported the "covenant" of the Scottish lords against the Stuarts, who were allied with France; this allowed the establishment of the Scottish Presbyterian church in 1560. In the treaty of Berwick (1586), she went so far as to acknowledge the Protestant religions in Scotland and Germany as equal branches on the tree of Christ's foundation. The return to the Scottish throne of the widowed queen Mary Stuart of France in 1561 ended, after many intrigues, with her flight to England in 1568; since she was a rival to Elizabeth's throne, she was kept a prisoner. → Pius V's bull *Regnans in excelsis*, which excommunicated Elizabeth (1570), brought a terrible persecution upon the English Catholics, who hitherto had been tolerated as "recusants," provided that they paid their fines. Now, "popery" was declared a capital crime, but Elizabeth saved the Catholics by means of her veto, so that the new penal laws were applied only to persons who entered England from abroad. No Catholic was burned as a heretic, but c. 250 were executed for "treason."

■ **Literature:** W. MacCaffrey, *The Shaping of the Elizabethan Regime* (Princeton, N.J., 1968; Paderborn, 1994); G. R. Elton, *England under the Tudors* (London, 1974); G. Lottes, *E. I. Eine politische Biographie* (Göttingen, 1981).

KURT KLUXEN

■ **Additional Bibliography:** S. Doran, *Elizabeth I and Religion* (London, 1994); C. Erickson, *The First Elizabeth* (New York, 1997); K. MacMillan, "Zurich Reform and the Elizabethan Settlement of 1559," *Anglican and Episcopal History* 68 (1999) 285–311; S. Doran, "Elizabeth I's Religion," *JEH* 51 (2000) 699–720; Ch. Haigh, *Elizabeth I* (Harlow, 2001); S. Doran, *Queen Elizabeth I* (New York, 2003).

Ellenbog (Cubitensis, Cubitus), *Nikolaus.* Benedictine (1504), humanist, born March 18, 1481 in Biberach (Württemberg), died June 6, 1543 in Ottobeuren. He began his studies in 1497, attending the universities of Heidelberg, Krakow, and Montpellier. He entered the Benedictine monastery of Ottobeuren in 1504 and was ordained priest in 1506. He held the offices of prior, bursar, master of novices, and head of the monastery's printing works. He was a man of many interests (astronomy, astrology, medicine, mathematics), with leanings to humanism, and he extended the monastic library. He welcomed the (short-lived) Benedictine university which opened in Ottobeuren in 1543. He exchanged many letters with such men as → Erasmus of Rotterdam, Johannes → Reuchlin, and Johannes → Eck. The *Passio septem fratrum filiorum s. Foelicitatis* (Ottobeuren, 1511) was the only one of his many works to be printed (the others include *Enarrationes in regulam s. Patris Benedicti* and sermons about saints). He rejected the Reformation and composed numerous tractates against it, which survive in manuscripts.

■ **Works:** CCath 19/21 (correspondence); P. O. Kristeller, *Iter Italicum. A Finding List of Uncatalogued or Incompletely Catalogued Humanistic Manuscripts of the Renaissance,* vol. 3 (London and Leiden, 1983) (manuscripts and letters); VD 16 5:734.
■ **Literature:** *NDB* 4:454; *DSp* 4:597ff.; *DHGE* 15:236f.; *CEras* 1:428.—A. Bigelmair, *Lebensbilder aus dem Bayerischen Schwaben,* vol. 5 (Munich, 1956) 112–39; A. Kolb, ed., *Ottobeuren* (Kempten, 1986) 88–91.

HERIBERT SMOLINSKY

Eltz, *Jakob III von.* Archbishop of Trier (1567), born 1510 in castle Eltz, died June 4, 1581 in Trier. He became cathedral dean in 1547 and was ordained priest in 1569. He was the first German ecclesiastical prince to submit himself to the informative process, and he promoted church reform in keeping with the ideals of Trent in a more decisive manner than his predecessor. He formed alliances with others to promote the Counter-Reformation. He had a general visitation carried out in 1569-1570 and supported the Jesuit houses in Trier and Coblenz. In 1576, he achieved the unification of the abbey of Prüm with the archiepiscopal territory of Trier; in 1580, he definitively established the sovereignty of the archbishops as rulers of the city of Trier.

■ **Literature:** V. Conzemius, *J. III. von Eltz* (Wiesbaden, 1956); B. Caspar, *Das Erzbistum Trier im Zeitalter der Glaubensspaltung* (Münster, 1965); H. G. Molitor, *Kirchliche Reformversuche der Kurfürsten und Erzbischöfe von Trier im Zeitalter der Gegenreformation* (Wiesbaden, 1967).

VICTOR CONZEMIUS

Emser, *Hieronymus.* Humanist and controversial theologian, born March 26 (or 16), 1478 in Weidenstetten near Ulm, died November 8, 1527 in Dresden. He began his studies in 1493 and attended Tübingen, Basle, and Leipzig, taking the degree of bachelor of theology and the licentiate in canon law in Leipzig in 1505. He was secretary and court chaplain to Duke → George of Saxony in Dresden from 1505 to 1511. He had humanistic and literary interests; from 1519 onwards, he developed into a controversial theologian who promoted the religious policy of the duke—in favor of church reform, but decidedly opposed to the Reformation. The main themes in Emser's writings are the → Leipzig disputation, veneration of images (→ Art and Reformation) and of the →

saints, the Mass, and the exegesis of the New Testament. Emser edited and translated works by → Erasmus of Rotterdam and → Henry VIII of England. He published the New Testament in Dresden in 1527 in what he saw as a corrected and more critical version of Luther's translation.

■ **Works:** L. Enders, *Luther und E.*, 2 vols. (Halle, 1890–92); *RGST* 3 and 40; *CCath* 4 and 28; Klaiber nos. 957–1002; *VD 16* 5:745–53; Köhler *BF* I/1:378–91.

■ **Literature:** *NDB* 4:488f.; *LThK*[2] 3:855f.; *KThR* 2:37–46; *CEras* 1:429f.; *TRE* 9:576–80—H. Smolinsky, "Reformation und Bildersturm," in *Reformatio Ecclesiae*. Festschrift E. Iserloh (Paderborn, 1980) 427–40; H. Bluhm, *Luther Translator of Paul* (New York et al., 1984); H. Smolinsky, *Augustin von Alvedt und H. E.* (Münster, 1984); idem, "Streit um die Exegese? Die Funktion des Schriftarguments in der Kontroverstheologie des H. E.," in *Zum Gedenken an J. Lortz*, ed. R. Decot and R. Vinke (Stuttgart, 1989) 358–75; H. Gelhaus, *Der Streit um Luthers Bibelverdeutschung im 16. und 17.Jh.*, 2 Teile (Tübingen, 1989–90); D. V. N. Bagchi, *Luther's Earliest Opponents* (Minneapolis, 1991).

HERIBERT SMOLINSKY

■ **Additional Bibliography:** G. L. Dipple, "Luther, E. and the Development of Reformation Anticlericalism," *ARG* 87 (1996) 38–56; B. Peter, *Der Streit um das kirchliche Amt. Die theologischen Positionen der Gegner Luthers* (Mainz, 1997).

England, Church of (CofE)

1. Concept

When Henry VIII laid claim to the title "supreme head on earth of the Church of England" in the Act of → Supremacy (November 3, 1534), he used the name which the English church itself had used in the many centuries during which it was dependent on Rome. By means of this Act, the king claimed nothing less than the papal *plenitudo potestatis*. This was the birth of the CofE as a confessional church. The concept "Anglican" designates a fellowship of churches which trace their roots back to the CofE.

BRUNO STEIMER

2. History

The causes of the English Reformation lie on three levels: the movements of protest and criticism which were widespread in the late 15th century; the humanist scholars who were influenced by the writings of Martin Luther; and the tensions that had marked relations between the Catholic Church (especially the papacy) and England since the Middle Ages. The refusal of → Clement VII to annul the marriage between → Henry VIII and Catharine of Aragon led Henry's court to search the Bible and canon law for another possibility of satisfying the king's wish. In 1532, Henry appointed Thomas → Cranmer archbishop of Canterbury; Cranmer was to help achieve the divorce and to transfer the highest government of the CofE to the king himself. The necessary laws (especially the Act of → Supremacy) were promulgated in 1533-1534, resulting in a reformed Catholic Church detached from the papacy. Henry was excommunicated. The principal instruments of the Reform in this period were the unscrupulous dissolution of the monasteries (1535-1540), the spread of the Bible in English, and developments in the direction of a vernacular liturgy; but the Protestant confession of faith continued to be subject to harsh penalties. Apart from the English Bible, the strongest influence on the nascent CofE was its Prayer Books, especially the *Book of* → *Common Prayer* (1549). The Prayer Book and the → Anglican articles were recognizably influenced by the continental Reformers, especially Martin → Bucer, but the ecclesiastical hierarchy was retained and its pastoral character strengthened. Thus, Anglican theologians taught that the bishops, whose office derived by divine decree from the ministry of the apostles, were the spiritual leaders of the nation and that they were united under the monarch, who had been installed in office by God.

STEPHEN SYKES

■ **Literature:** A. G. Dickens, *The English Reformation* (London, 1968); P. E. Hughes, *Theology of the English Reformers* (Abington, [2]1997); D. MacCulloch, *Die zweite Phase der englischen Reformation (1547–1603) und die Geburt der Anglikanischen Via Media* (Münster, 1998); A. A. Chibi, "'Had I But Served God with Half the Zeal . . .' The Service Records of the Men Who Became Henry VIII's Bishops," *Reformation* 3 (1998) 75–136; C. Litzenberger, "Defining the ChE," in *Belief and Practice in Reformation England*. Festschrift P. Collinson (Aldershot, 1998) 137–53; N. S. Amos, "'It is fallow ground here.' Martin Bucer as Critic of the English Reformation," *Westminster Theological Journal* 61 (1999) 41–52.

■ **Additional Literature:** J. P. Richardson, "The Neglected Reformer: Martin Luther through Anglican Eyes," *Churchman* 110 (1996) 140–55; G. Bray, ed., *Tudor Church Reform* (Woodbridge, 2000); L.

Wooding, *Rethinking Catholicism in Reformation England* (Oxford, 2000), C. Pendrill, *The English Reformation* (Oxford, 2000); K. Carleton, *Bishops and Reform in the English Church* (Woodbridge, 2001); E. H. Shagan, *Popular Politics and the English Reformation* (Cambridge, 2003).

Enthusiasts. Martin Luther coined this term (*Schwärmer*) as a polemical designation of those who led violent onslaughts and wandered around without any fixed goal. In the 16th and 17th centuries, it was applied above all to Andreas → Karlstadt, Thomas → Müntzer, Huldrych Zwingli, Luther himself, the → Baptists, the Calvinists, Kaspar von → Schwenckfeld, Andreas → Osiander, Nikolaus → Amsdorf, the Quakers, and the Pietists. Since the 18th century, it has been used in general for Christians who employ violent means or pursue fantastic goals; today, it tends to indicate an "alternative" way of thinking.

Although Luther was not always fair towards his opponents, his rejection of "enthusiasm connected with the sacrament, images, and baptism" (WA 15:393f.) became an important guideline for the self-understanding of the Lutheran Reformation.

Ultimately, this concerns the question of the validity of scripture alone. How is one to deal with matters which cannot be explicitly demonstrated from scripture (cf. Karlstadt's opposition to canon law, vestments, singing and the use of Latin in worship, infant baptism, etc.)? What of scriptural statements such as the prohibition of images in the decalogue (the Wittenberg church order of 1522 demands the removal of images; WA 18:17.13; → Art and Reformation) or the command to destroy the godless (cf. Deut 7:16; 13; 17; Müntzer)? How is one to deal with a controversial interpretation of scripture (→ eucharistic controversy)? What of those who appeal against the literal meaning of scripture to their own private revelations (Müntzer)? This also involves the principle of *sola fide* in the definition of the relationship between faith and the sacrament (cf. *BSLK* 10th ed., 701–4, 710f., 979, 1008) and of the relationship between faith and sin (cf. ibid., 448).

■ **Literature:** (Sch.=Schwärmer, Enthusiasts) G. Mühlpfordt, "Luther und die 'Linken'—Eine Untersuchung seiner Sch.-Terminologie," in *M. Luther. Leben, Werk und Wirkung,* ed. G. Vogler (Berlin, 1983) 325–45; *Wegscheiden der Reformation. Alternatives Denken vom 16. bis zum 18.Jh.,* ed. G. Vogler (Weimar, 1994); *Aussenseiter zwischen Mittelalter und Neuzeit.* Festschrift H.-J. Goertz, ed. N. Fischer and M. Kobelt-Groch (Leiden, 1997); A. M. Haas, *Der Kampf um den Heiligen Geist – Luther und die Schwärmer* (Fribourg, 1997).

VINZENZ PFNÜR

■ **Additional Bibliography:** D. Fauth, *Träume bei religiösen Dissidenten in der frühen Reformation: Religiöse Devianz in christlich geprägten Gesellschaften* (Würzburg, 1999) 69–105.

Enzinas (known as Dryander), *Francisco de.* Spanish Protestant, born November 1, 1518 in Burgos, died December 30, 1552 in Strasbourg. He began his studies in Louvain in 1539, and came to Wittenberg in 1541, where he translated the New Testament into Spanish in Philipp Melanchthon's house. When he presented the printed version to → Charles V, he was imprisoned in Brussels, but succeeded in fleeing in 1545, before his trial. He returned to Wittenberg, and went to England in 1546 via Strasbourg, Zurich, St. Gallen, Constance, and Basle, where he met Martin → Bucer, Heinrich → Bullinger, Joachim → Vadian, and Ambrosius → Blarer. He was made professor of Greek at Cambridge University. He returned to Germany in 1549.

■ **Principal Works:** *El Nuevo Testamento de nuestro Redemptor y Salvador Jesucristo* (Antwerp 1543). *Epistolario,* ed. I. J. García Pinilla (Geneva, 1995).
■ **Literature:** DHGE 15:512–15.—A. Hoermann, *F. de Enzinas und sein Kreis* (Berlin, 1902); B. A. Vermaseren, "Autour de l'Edition de l' 'Histoire de l'Estat du Pais Bas et de la religion d'Espagne' par F. de E. dit Dryander (1558)," *Bibliothèque d'humanisme et renaissance* 27 (1965) 463–94.

MICHAEL BECHT

■ **Additional Bibliography:** J. L. Nelson, "'Solo Saluador' Printing the 1543 New Testament of F. de E.," *JEH* 50 (1999) 94–116.

Erasmus of Rotterdam (Desiderius Erasmus). Humanist, born October 28, 1466/1467 in Rotterdam, the son of a priest, died July 12, 1536 in Basle. He entered the monastery of the Augustinian canons regular in Steyn near Gouda in 1487 (he was dispensed from his vows in 1517); he was ordained priest in 1492 and became secretary to the bishop of Cambrai in 1493. He studied theology in Paris from 1495 to 1499, and was in England in 1499-1500, 1505-1506, and 1509-1514, where John Colet and Thomas → More became his friends; in the intervening years, he was in Paris and the Netherlands (1500-1505), and in Italy (1506-1509). He took his doctorate in theology in Turin in 1506, and came to know the leading Roman humanists. He was in Basle from 1514 to 1516, and began his collaboration with the printer Johannes Froben. He was appointed imperial counselor in 1516. He was in Louvain from 1517 to 1521. He returned to Basle in 1521, but moved to Freiburg after the victory of the Reformation; he returned to Basle in 1535.

Within the framework of his general humanist orientation, a number of different emphases can be discerned in Erasmus's work. (*a*) Philological-rhetorical and pedagogical writings. These begin with the collection and commentary on classical proverbs (*Adagia*, Paris, 1500; often reprinted) and include books intended for use in schools (e.g., *Colloquia familiaria* [Basle, 1518]; often reprinted), as well as a critique of the humanist Latin which was too one-sidedly Ciceronian (*Dialogus Ciceronianus* [Basle, 1528]).—(*b*) Spiritual and moral-philosophical writings: *Enchiridion militis Christiani* (Antwerp, 1504; often reprinted), *Moriae encomium sive stultitiae laus* (Paris, 1511; often reprinted), *Institutio principis christiani* (Basle, 1516), *Querela pacis* (Basle, 1517; often reprinted).—(*c*) Editions of the New Testament (*Novum instrumentum* [Basle, 1516; often reprinted]) and of important church fathers (Jerome, 1516; Cyprian, 1520; Arnobius, 1522; Hilary, 1523; Chrysostom, 1525-1533; Irenaeus, 1526; Origen, 1527 and 1533; Ambrose, 1527; Augustine, 1528/1529).—(*d*) Writings on biblical hermeneutics: the introductions to his edition of the New Testament, especially the *Ratio verae theologiae*, which was published separately at Louvain in 1518; the paraphrases on the New Testament; and commentaries on the Psalms.—(*e*) Catechetical and homiletic writings: *Explanatio symboli apostolorum* (Basle, 1533); *Ecclesiastes* (Basle, 1535).—(*f*) Controversial theology: *De libero arbitrio diatribe*, a critique of Martin Luther (Basle, 1524), and *Hyperaspistes* (Basle, 1526-1527), polemical writings against Swiss Reformers and Catholics who opposed Erasmus's views.—(*g*) Letters.

Until Luther appeared on the scene, Erasmus was considered the leading scholar of his age. He criticized scholasticism and endeavored to initiate a reform of theology based on the biblical and patristic sources (*philosophia Christi*) and a renewal of the church—which must begin, not with the institution as such, but with the conversion of individual Christians. After the outbreak of the Reformation, he continued to be seen as its forerunner, but both Protestants and Catholics accused him of half-heartedness. Erasmus had a lasting influence not only in the sphere of humanistic, biblical, and patristic philology, but also (despite the fact that his works were placed on the Index) on reform movements within Catholicism.

■ **Works:** *Opera omnia,* ed. J. LeClerc, 10 vols. (Leiden 1703–6, reprint, Hildesheim, 1961–62); *Erasmi opuscula,* ed. W. K. Ferguson (The Hague, 1933, reprint, Hildesheim, 1978); *Ausgewählte Werke,* ed. A. and H. Holborn (Munich, 1933, ²1964); *Opera omnia D. Erasmi Roterodami* (Amsterdam, 1969ff.); *Opus epistolarum D. Erasmi Roterodami,* ed. P.S. Allen et al., 12 vols. (Oxford, 1906–58).—Translations: *Ausgewählte Schriften, lateinisch und deutsch,* ed. W. Welzig, 8 vols. (Darmstadt, 1967–80); *Collected Works of E.* (Toronto, 1974ff.).—Bibliographies: J.-C. Margolin, *Douze années de bibliographie Erasmienne* (Paris, 1963); idem, *Quatorze années . . .* (Paris, 1969); idem, *Neuf années . . .* (Paris and Toronto, 1977); idem, *Cinq années . . .* (Paris, 1997).

■ **Literature:** TRE 10:2–18.—J. Huizinga, E. (Basle, 1928; new edition Reinbek, 1993); M. Bataillon, *E. et l'Espagne* (Paris, 1937; new edition, Geneva, 1991); A. Auer, *Die vollkommene Frömmigkeit des Christen* (Düsseldorf, 1954); R. Padberg, *E. als Katechet* (Freiburg, 1956); K. H. Oelrich, *Der späte E. und die Reformation* (Münster, 1961); E.-W. Kohls, *Die Theologie des E.,* 2 vols. (Basle, 1966); C. Béné, *E. et s. Augustin* (Geneva, 1969); J. B. Payne, *E. His Theology of the Sacraments.* (n.p., 1970); G. Chantraine, *"Mystère" et "Philosophie du Christ" selon E.* (Namur, 1971); M. Hoffmann, *Erkenntnis und Verwirklichung der wahren Theologie nach E. von Rotterdam* (Tübingen, 1972); A. Rabil, *E. and the New Testament* (San Antonio, Tex., 1972; new edition Lanham, Md., 1993); J. D. Tracy, *the Growth of a Mind* (Geneva, 1972); W. Hentze, *Kirche und kirchliche Einheit bei Desiderius E. von Rotterdam* (Paderborn, 1974); G. B. Winkler, *E. von Rotterdam und die Einleitungsschriften zum Neuen Testament* (Münster, 1974); H. Holeczek, *Humanistische Bibelphilologie als Reformproblem bei E. von Rotterdam, Thomas More und William Tyndale* (Leiden, 1975); D. Kerlen, *Assertio* (Wiesbaden, 1976); R. Stupperich, *E. von Rotterdam und seine Welt* (Berlin, 1977); M. O'Rourke Boyle, *E. on Language and Method in Theology* (Toronto, 1977); J. D. Tracy, *The Politics of E.* (Toronto, 1978); B. Mansfield, *Phoenix of His Age* (Toronto, 1979); M. O'Rourke Boyle,

Christening Pagan Mysteries (Toronto, 1981); G. Chantraine, *E. et Luther* (Paris, 1981); J. Chomarat, *Grammaire et rhétorique chez E.* (Paris, 1981); A. Godin, *E. lecteur d'Origène* (Geneva, 1982); H. Holeczek, *E. deutsch,* vol. 1 (Stuttgart-Bad Cannstatt, 1983); M. O'Rourke Boyle, *Rhetoric and Reform* (Cambridge, Mass., 1983); E. Rummel, *E. as a Translator of the Classics* (Toronto, 1985); C. Augustijn, *E. von Rotterdam* (Munich, 1986); F. Krüger, *Humanistische Evangelienauslegung* (Tübingen, 1986); E. Rummel, *E.' Annotations on the New Testament.* (Toronto, 1986); idem, *E. and His Catholic Critics,* 2 vols. (Nieuwkoop, 1989); G. Bedouelle, *Le temps des réformes et la Bible* (Paris, 1989); L.-E. Halkin, *E. von Rotterdam* (Zurich, 1989); R. J. Schoeck, *E. of Europe,* 2 vols. (Edinburgh, 1990–93); L. d'Ascia, *Erasmo e l'Umanesimo romano* (Florence, 1991); P. Walter, *Theologie aus dem Geist der Rhetorik* (Mainz, 1991); R. Coogan, *E., Lee and the Correction of the Vulgate* (Geneva, 1992); B. Mansfield, *Interpretations of E.* (Toronto, 1992); S. Seidel Menchi, *E. als Ketzer* (Leiden, 1992); C. Asso, *La teologia e la grammatica* (Florence, 1993); M. Hoffmann, *Rhetoric and Theology* (Toronto, 1994).
■ Additional Bibliography: A. G. Dickens and W. R. D. Jones, *E. the Reformer* (London, 1994); C. Augustijn, *E.—der Humanist als Theologe und Kirchenreformer* (Leiden, 1996); M. E. H. N. Mout et al., eds., *Erasmianism* (Amsterdam, 1997); H. M. Pabel, *Conversing with God. Prayer in E.' Pastoral Writings* (Toronto, 1997); M. Becht, *Pium consensum tueri. Studien zum Begriff consensus im Werk von E. von Rotterdam, Philipp Melanchthon und Johannes Calvin* (Amsterdam, 2000); R. Torzini, *I labirinti del libero arbitrio* (Florence, 2000); I. P. Bejczy, *E. and the Middle Ages* (Leiden, 2001); F. de'Michelis Pintacuda, *Tra Erasmo e Lutero* (Rome, 2001).

PETER WALTER

Erastus, *Thomas* (real name: Lieber, Liebler, Lüber). Reformed theologian, doctor and church politician, born September 7, 1524 in Baden (Switzerland), died December 31, 1583 in Basle. He became professor of medicine in Heidelberg and personal physician to the electoral prince of the Palatinate in 1558. All his life, he remained an adherent of the Zurich Reformation, and was a friend of its leader, Heinrich → Bullinger. He aided electoral Prince → Frederick III in the introduction of Calvinism into his land, which had been Lutheran since 1556. Later, he mounted a sustained opposition to the stricter Genevan line within Calvinism (the so-called Disciplinist line) which was taken by Caspar → Olevian. The Lutheran restoration in the Palatinate led him to move to Basle in 1580. Here, he became professor

of ethics; as doctor and natural philosopher, he opposed → Paracelsus. His support for the state-church system makes him, along with Huldrych Zwingli, one of the earliest Reformed theologians to engage in specific reflection on the state.
■ Literature: R. Wesel-Roth, *Th. E.* (Lahr, 1954).

ERNST WALTER ZEEDEN

■ Additional Bibliography: *RGG*[4] 2:1384.—R. C. Walton, "Der Streit zwischen Th. E. und Caspar Olevian über die Kirchenzucht in der Kurpfalz in seiner Bedeutung für die internationale reformierte Bewegung," *Monatshefte für evangelische Kirchengeschichte des Rheinlandes* 37/38 (1988/89) 205–46; J. Shackelford, "Early Reception of Paracelsian Theory," *SCJ* 26 (1995) 123–36; J. W. Baker, "Erastianism in England," in *Die Züricher Reformation,* ed. A. Schindler (Frankfurt/Main, 2001) 327–49.

Ernest of Bavaria. Archbishop and electoral prince of Cologne (1583), born December 17, 1554 in Munich, the youngest child of Duke → Albrecht V, died February 17, 1612 in Arnsberg. He began his studies in Ingolstadt in 1563, and acquired numerous cathedral benefices. Thanks to the importance of Bavaria in the endeavors to preserve Catholicism, he received one archdiocese, four dioceses, and two imperial abbeys: Freising (1566), Hildesheim (1573), Liège, Stablo, and Malmédy (1581), Cologne (1583), and Münster (1585). Cologne, the seat of a reforming nunciature since 1584, had to be reconquered in the War of Cologne (1583-1589) against his predecessor, Gebhard von → Waldburg, who had been stripped of office. The financial situation posed an insoluble problem, and Ferdinand of Bavaria was made his coadjutor in 1596. Ernest, who was ordained priest in 1577, never led a life in keeping with his church office. As ruler of several territories, he mostly limited himself to the coordination of the various governing bodies. He supported church reform (visitations, foundations of Jesuit houses, seminaries for the training of priests, central spiritual councils).
■ Sources: *NDB(G)* I, 1, 2/1, 2/2–5/1.
■ Literature: E. Gatz, ed., *Die Bischöfe des Heiligen Römischen Reiches 1448–1648* (Berlin, 1996).

FRANZ BOSBACH

Espence (Espencaeus), *Claude d'.* Controversial theologian, born 1511 in Châlons-sur-Marne, died October 4/5, 1571 in Paris. He studied theology at the College of Navarre in Paris, taking his doctorate in theology in 1542. He was tutor to Charles de Lorraine (→ Guise) and a celebrated preacher. In 1543, the theological faculty in Paris demanded that he make a public revocation after his Lenten sermons were accused of propagating Erasmian, if not indeed Lutheran, views. In 1545, → Francis I nominated him to a commission in Melun which did preparatory work for the Council of Trent. Henry II sent him to the conference of Bologna in 1547, but he played no particular role in this meeting. Instead, he wrote a treatise on predestination (*Traicté contre l'erreur vieil et renouvellé des predestinez* [Lyons, 1548]) and an *Oraison pour la paix de l'Eglise* (appendix to *Paraphrase ou Méditation sur l'oraison dominicale* [Lyons, 1547]). On his journey home, he debated with Jean Calvin in Geneva (1548). He took an active part in the king's endeavors to promote religious reconciliation from 1560 onwards. He took a mediating position in the meetings of the Estates General in Orleans, and especially at the religious dialogue of → Poissy; he defended this position in his *Apologie* (Paris, 1569). However, he refused to go to Trent in 1562. In his christocentric will, drawn up in 1571, there are no provisions for the celebration of Masses; instead, he makes donations to the needy. Espence was one of the most interesting representatives of Erasmian thinking in France; the precise position he took is still a matter of scholarly debate.

■ **Editions:** *Opera omnia*, ed. G. Génébrard (Paris, 1619).

■ **Literature:** *DSp* 4:1206f.; *DBF* 12:1503f.—H. O. Evennett, "C. d'E. et son 'Discours du Colloque de Poissy,'" *Revue historique* 164 (1930) 40–78; M. Venard, *L'abjuration de C. d'E.* (1543) M. Lienhard, ed., *Les dissidents du XVIe siècle entre l'humanisme et le catholicisme* (Baden-Baden, 1983) 111–26; M. Turchetti, *Concordia o tolleranza?* (Geneva, 1984).

MARC VENARD

■ **Additional Bibliography:** P. Walter, *Schriftauslegung und Väterrezeption im Erasmianismus am Beispiel von C. d'E.: Erasmianism*, ed. M. Mout et al. (Amsterdam, 1997) 139–53.

Esschen, *Johannes van (den),* Augustinian Hermit, born c. 1500 in 's-Hertogenbosch, died July 1, 1523 in Brussels. An adherent of the Reformation, he was imprisoned in 1522 and burnt at the stake with his confrère Henricus Vo[e]s after a trial in which Jakob van → Hoogstraeten took part. This execution prompted the composition of many pamphlets: Martin Luther wrote *Eyn brieff an die Christen ym Nidderland* (WA 12:73-80) and the hymn *Eyn newes Lied wir heben an* (Archive to WA 4:217-222).

■ **Sources:** P. Fredericq, *Corpus documentorum inquisitionis haereticae pravitatis neerlandicae,* vol. 4 (Ghent, 1900) 191–214, 223–28, 250ff.; *Bibliotheca reformatoria neerlandica,* ed. F. Pijper, vol. 8 (The Hague, 1911) 1–114.

■ **Literature:** *Biografisch Lexicon voor de Geschiedenis van het Nederlandse Protestantisme,* vol. 1 (Kampen, 1983) 77, 411f.; *CEras* 1:444. J. Böhmer, "Die Beschaffenheit der Quellenschriften zu H. Voes und J. van den E.," *ARG* 28 (1931) 112–33.

PETER WALTER

■ **Additional Bibliography:** M. Gielis, "Augustijnergeloof en predikherengeloof," *Luther-Bulletin* 6 (1997) 46–57.

Eucharistic controversy. In the late Middle Ages, many theologians still followed William of Ockham in holding that consubstantiation (i.e., the coexistence of the unchanged substance of bread and wine along with the Body and Blood of Christ after the consecration) was not only tenable, but actually more plausible and less encumbered with difficulties than transubstantiation (i.e., the complete change of the substance of bread and wine into the Body and Blood of Christ). Nevertheless, they accepted the decision of the church and upheld the doctrine of transubstantiation; one example is Peter d'Ailly, to whom Martin Luther appeals.

John Wyclif absolutely rejected transubstantiation, especially in the very common explanation of this doctrine (following Ockham) as the destruction (*annihilatio*) of the substance of bread and wine and their replacement (under the accidents, which continued to exist, but without any subject) by the substance of the Body and Blood of Christ (*substitutio/adductio*). He maintained the real presence of the humanity of Christ, but in the sense of coexistence or concomitance with the substance of bread and wine. However, he emphatically affirms that this is not a local, spatial form of presence: it is a sacramental mode of existence, with a spiritual significance. The language he uses—calling the sacrament *signum/figura effi-*

cax ("efficacious sign/image")—clearly reveals Augustinian influence. He rejects both a total identification of the sacrament with the Lord's Body and the theory of "impanation" (i.e., that Christ becomes bread, on analogy to the doctrine of incarnation). Although Jan Hus was strongly influenced by Wyclif, he did not share his rejection of transubstantiation, as he made clear at the Council of Constance when he was accused of holding such views. It is, however, only among the Reformers that we can speak of a genuine eucharistic controversy.

The first great debate took place between Luther and Huldrych Zwingli from 1525 to 1529. Luther rejected transubstantiation; but the words of institution themselves led him to maintain consistently the real presence of the Body and Blood of Christ, understood in terms of consubstantiation. Luther had already emphasized the real presence prior to this controversy, in his theological demarcation vis-à-vis the → Bohemian Brethren and especially in his polemic against Cornelius → Hoen's "significationist" doctrine of the sacrament. Now, the real presence became ever more central in Luther's understanding, and he underlined (against Andreas → Karlstadt) the significance of the Lord's Supper as a means of grace. Zwingli, on the other hand, followed Hoen in maintaining a symbolic-significationist interpretation. He explicitly denied the real presence of the human nature of Christ in the sacrament, which is a *signum* attesting God's salvific action, but does not itself communicate any grace. The Swiss Reformers appealed in support of this view to → Erasmus of Rotterdam, but he himself dismissed this appeal as unjustified.

In the course of this debate, conducted polemically by both sides, Luther elaborated the doctrine of the → ubiquity of the human nature of Christ, not as a demonstration of the possibility of the real presence, but as an aid to understanding. For Luther, the litmus test of the profession of faith in the real presence is the position taken on the questions of *manducatio oralis* (physical eating of the Body of Christ) and *manducatio impiorum* (reception of the sacrament by godless persons, independently of faith). On this point, it proved impossible to resolve the dogmatic antithesis between Luther and Zwingli. This accounts for the failure of the religious dialogue in → Marburg (October, 1529); nor did the → Wittenberg Con-

cord of 1536 achieve a truly viable agreement between the Lutherans and the Reformed cities in Upper Germany. Hence, it was the question of the real presence that caused the breakdown of Protestant unity.

This is obvious in the second great debate about the Eucharist, between the Lutheran theologian Joachim → Westphal in Hamburg and Jean Calvin. Calvin rejected not only Luther's doctrine of ubiquity, but also the bodily presence of Christ in the elements of the Lord's Supper, and the *manducatio oralis* and *impiorum*. Calvin himself proposed a dynamic understanding of the eucharistic presence; the concept of "virtual presence" does not do justice to his position, which is more adequately described as the "spiritual presence" of the person and work of Christ, bestowed effectively by the Holy Spirit on those who receive the sacrament with faith. In this sense, Calvin can speak of a substantial presence (*vere, realiter, substantialiter*) and of a communication of the substance of Christ to the believer. This debate found no resolution; ultimately, the condemnation in the Formula of Concord of the Reformed doctrine of the Lord's Supper (*Solida declaratio* 7; *BSLK* 975f.) set the seal for centuries on the ecclesial split within Protestantism.

■ **Literature:** *TRE* 1:89–142.—E. Iserloh, *Gnade und Eucharistie in der philosophischen Theologie des Wilhelm von Ockham* (Wiesbaden, 1956); J. Rogge, *Virtus und Res. Um die Abendmahlswirklichkeit bei Calvin* (Stuttgart, 1965); K. McDonnell, *John Calvin, the Church, and the Eucharist* (Princeton, N.J., 1967); S. N. Bosshard, *Zwingli, Erasmus, Cajetan. Die Eucharistie als Zeichen der Einheit* (Wiesbaden, 1978).

HANS JORISSEN

■ **Additional Bibliography:** *RGG*⁴ 1:24–28.—B. A. Gerrish, "Discerning the Body: Sign and Reality in Luther's Controversy with the Swiss," *The Journal of Religion* 68 (1988) 377–95; Th. Kaufmann, *Die Abendmahlstheologie der Straßburger Reformatoren bis 1528* (Tübingen, 1992).

Evangelism. This concept (*évangélisme*) was coined by Imbart de la Tour in 1914 and applied to certain phases of the history of the Reformation in France. According to Bataillon, an Erasmian Evangelism existed in Spain from c. 1525, including men such as Bartolomé → Carranza. Modern scholarship tends to apply this concept above all to some of the Italian religious movements in the

16th century. Jung sees Italian Evangelism as a transitional phenomenon, an undogmatic and aristocratic Catholic reform movement in the period before Trent (520); more recent scholars see Evangelism as a generic concept for a broad spectrum of religious ideas which found various expressions in different social groups throughout almost the whole of the 16th century. The primary concern of Evangelism was the spiritual and moral renewal of the individual Christian who encountered the Word of God in sacred scripture; in this process, the writings of Paul had particular importance. The question of → justification was central. Some groups saw no conflict between the doctrine of the Catholic Church and the view that the human being is justified by faith alone, without works; others, however, perceived this as an irreconcilable conflict. The most eloquent and widely read text of Italian Evangelism is the short book *Beneficio di Cristo,* probably written by Benedetto Fontanini (1543).

One important group within Italian Evangelism was the circle of reformers around Cardinals Gasparo → Contarini and Reginald → Pole, often called "Spirituals." After Contarini was created cardinal in 1535 and other members of this group, mostly linked by friendship, were given high offices in the curia, Evangelism became an influential force in the central Roman bodies. These men also attempted to win the day for institutional reforms.

In view of the variety and diversity of Evangelism, it is inappropriate to speak of a "right" and a "left" wing; nor can one call Evangelism a "political group" (Simoncelli). The Inquisition, especially after it took on organized form in Rome in 1542, was suspicious of Evangelism and persecuted it because it seemed to make too many concessions to Protestantism. Nevertheless, Evangelism continued to exist even in the second half of the 16th century.

■ **Literature:** P. Imbart de la Tour, *Les origines de la Réforme,* vol. 3: *L'Évangélisme* (Paris, 1914); M. Bataillon, *Érasme et l'Espagne* (Paris, 1937; new edition, 3 vols., Geneva, 1991); E. M. Jung, "On the Nature of Evangelism in Sixteenth-Century Italy," *Journal of the History of Ideas* 14 (1953) 511–27; E. G. Gleason, "On the Nature of Sixteenth-Century Italian Evangelism," *SCJ* 9 (1978) 3–25; P. Simoncelli, *Evangelismo italiano del Cinquecento* (Rome, 1979); M. Firpo, *Tra alumbrados e "Spirituali". Studi su Juan de Valdés e il Valdesianesimo nella crisi religiosa del '500 italiano*

(Florence, 1990); E. G. Gleason: *Gasparo Contarini, Venice, Rome, and Reform* (Berkeley, 1993) passim, esp. 190–93.

KLAUS GANZER

Exsurge Domine. The bull of June 15, 1520 (DH 1451-1492) in which Leo X threatens Martin Luther and his adherents with excommunication; the text was the result of preparatory work by three commissions, beginning in January of that year, and the third commission (Pietro Accolti, Thomas → Cajetan de Vio, Doctor Hispanus, and Johannes → Eck) drew up the final version, based on the memorandum of Louvain (November 7, 1519) and a letter sent by Adrian of Utrecht (later Pope → Hadrian VI) on December 4, 1519 which demanded that Luther's works be quoted literally. Johannes Eck had selected 38 (and subsequently 41) propositions from Luther's writings, but the bull did not include the individual quotation and condemnation of these texts, as had originally been envisaged. The bull follows a concept suggested by Jakob von → Hoogstraeten (*Destructio Cabale prologus*). Luther is given the space of sixty days to recant; otherwise, he will be subject to excommunication and interdict, and his books will be burnt. The bull was published in the empire by Hieronymus → Aleander the Elder and Eck.

■ **Sources:** Three original parchments are preserved: Vienna (Haus-, Hof- und Staatsarchiv), Stuttgart (Hauptstaatsarchiv) und Dresden (Sächsisches Landeshauptarchiv); "Registereintrag Rom," *Registrum Vaticanum 1160,* 251–59 (first printing, Rome, J. Mazochius, 1520); H. Roos, "Die Quellen der Bulle 'ED' (15.6.1520)," in *Theologie und Geschichte*. Festschrift M. Schmaus (Munich, 1957) 909–26; CCath 42 (1991) 317–412.

■ **Literature:** K. Müller, "Luthers römischer Prozess," *ZKG* 24 (1903) 46–85; A. Schulte, "Zu den römischen Verhandlungen über Luther," *QFIAB* 6 (1904) 32–52 174ff., 374–78; P. Kalkoff, "Zu Luthers römischem Prozess," *ZKG* 25 (1904) 90–147, 273–90, 399–459, 503–603; 31 (1910) 48–65, 368–414; 32 (1911) 1–67, 199–258, 408–56, 572–95; 33 (1912) 1–72; 35 (1914) 166–203; idem, "Die Bulle 'ED,'" *ZKG* 37 (1917/18) 89–174; idem, "Die Bulle 'ED.' Ihre Vollziehung durch die Bischöfe von Eichstätt, Augsburg, Regensburg und Vienna," *ZKG* 39 (1921) 1–44, 134–39; idem, "Ein neugefundenes Original der Bulle 'ED,'" *ZKG* 44 (1925) 213–25; R. Bäumer, *Lutherprozeß und Lutherbann (KLK 32)* (Münster, 1972); P. Fabisch, "J. Eck und die Publikation der Bullen 'ED' und 'Decet Romanum Pontificem,'" *RGST* 127 (1988) 74–107.

PETER FABISCH

Eyb, *Gabriel von.* Prince bishop of Eichstätt, born September 29, 1455 in Arberg, died December 1, 1535 in Eichstätt. He became a cathedral canon in Bamberg in 1467 and cathedral custodian in 1492. He was candidate for a canonry in Würzburg in 1473. He studied in Erfurt, Ingolstadt, and Pavia, where he took the degree of doctor of decrees; then he was counselor to Wilhelm von Reichenau, bishop of Eichstätt. He was elected bishop of Eichstätt on December 5, 1496 in preference to his rival Bernhard → Adelmann von Adelmannsfelden, and was consecrated on April 16, 1497. He supported the imperial and church policies of the emperor. He maintained a neutral position in the Landshut War of Succession (1504). He fought unsuccessfully to secure the position of coadjutor for the house of Wittelsbach in the person of Duke Ernest of Bavaria (from 1519 onwards) and for electoral prince Ludwig V of the Palatinate (from 1529). Eyb was a resolute opponent of the Reformation movement, along with his friend prior Kilian → Leib of Rebdorf. After 1522, he tried in vain to prevent the introduction of the Reformation in the county of Ansbach and the imperial cities of Nuremberg and Weissenburg. He put down the peasants' rebellions in 1524-1525. As patron of the arts, Eyb supported Master Loy Hering (monument to St. Willibald in Eichstätt cathedral, an epoch-making work in the field of sepulcher statuary) and above all Lukas Cranach the Elder. He had the Eichstätt breviary (1497, new edition 1525) and the Eichstätt missal (1517) printed.

■ **Literature:** Th. Neuhofer, *G. von E. Fürstbischof von Eichstätt* (Eichstätt, 1934); E. von Eyb, *Das reichsritterliche Geschlecht der Freiherren von E.* (Neustadt [Aisch], 1984); M. Fink-Lang, *Untersuchungen zum Eichstätter Geistesleben im Zeitalter des Humanismus* (Regensburg, 1985); E. von Eyb and A. Wendehorst, "G. E. (1455–1535)," *Fränkische Lebensbilder* 12 (1986) 42–55; S. Weinfurter et al., "Die Viten der Eichstätter Bischöfe im 'Pontifikale Gundekarianum,'" in *Das Pontifikale Gundekarianum,* ed. A. Bauch and E. Reiter (Wiesbaden, 1987) 111–47; H. Flachenecker, *Eine geistliche Stadt. Eichstätt vom 13. bis zum 16.Jh.* (Regensburg, 1988).

KONSTANTIN MAIER

F

Faber, *Johannes.* Dominican theologian, born c. 1470 in Augsburg, died 1530. He took the degree of doctor of theology in Padua in 1507 and became prior in Augsburg, where he built the monastic church. From 1511-1524, he also held the position of vicar general of the Upper German conventual congregation. In 1515, he became imperial counselor and court preacher to Maximilian I. He planned a humanistically orientated course of studies for his Order in Augsburg. In the *Consilium,* which he wrote together with → Erasmus of Rotterdam (1520/1521), he proposed that a council be held to resolve the controversy about Luther. His opposition to the Reformation led to his expulsion from Augsburg in 1525.

■ **Principal Works:** *Consilium cuiusdam ex animo cupientis esse consultum et Romani Pontificis dignitati et Christianae religionis tranquillitati* (n.p., 1521), ed. W. K. Ferguson, in *Erasmi Opuscula* (The Hague, 1933) 338–61.

■ **Literature:** *CEras* 2:4f.—N. Paulus, *Die deutschen Dominikaner im Kampfe gegen Luther* (Freiburg, 1903) 292–313; P. Kalkoff, "Die Vermittlungspolitik des Erasmus und sein Anteil an den Flugschriften der ersten Reformationszeit," *ARG* 1 (1903) 1–83; P. Siemer, *Geschichte des Dominikanerklosters St. Magdalena in Augsburg* (Vechta, 1936); B. Hübscher, *Die deutsche Predigerkongregation 1517–20* (Fribourg, 1953); T. A. Dillis, *J. F.: Lebensbilder aus dem Bayerischen Schwaben,* vol. 5 (Munich, 1956) 93–111.

PETER WALTER

Faber, *Petrus* (Pierre Favre, also Lefèvre). Jesuit, one of the first seven companions of → Ignatius Loyola, Blessed (1872, feast August 2), born April 13, 1506 in Villaret (Savoy), died August 1, 1546 in Rome. He began his studies in Paris in 1525 and met Ignatius in 1529. In 1534, he celebrated the Mass in Montmartre during which Ignatius and the others made their vows, thus laying the foundations of the subsequent Society of Jesus. Initially, he was active as a preacher in Rome. The pope charged him to accompany Cardinal Ennio Filonardi to Parma in 1539; he also accompanied the imperial chargé d'affaires Pedro Ortiz to Spain and Germany in 1540, and the papal legate Cardinal Giovanni → Morone to imperial parliaments and religious dialogues in 1542-1543. In 1543, he went via the Netherlands to Spain and Portugal, and returned to Rome in 1546. He urged gentleness and tolerance vis-à-vis the Protestants, and supported renewal within the church, especially by means of his sermons and the retreats he gave. It was thanks to Faber that Peter → Canisius entered the Order in 1543. His *Memoriale* reveals something of his spirituality and profound inner piety.

■ **Works:** *Memoriale* (Monumenta Hispaniae sacra 15), 1914, [2]1973; German translation by P. Henrici (Trier, [2]1989).

■ **Literature:** L. Koch, *Jesuitenlexikon* (Paderborn, 1934) 1413f.; C. Sommervogel, *Bibliothèque de la Compagnie de Jésus* (Louvain, [3]1960), vol. 4, 1657f.; *DSp* 12:1573–82; L. Polgár, *Bibliographie sur l'histoire de la Compagnie de Jésus 1901–80*, vol. 3 (Rome, 1990) nn. 6645–6707.— G. Guitton, *L'âme du Bienheureux P. F.* (Paris, 1934, [2]1959); W. J. Read, "The Industry in Prayer of Blessed P. F." (diss., Rome, 1950); M. J. Purcell, "The Quiet Companion," *Archivum historicum Societatis Jesu* 42 (1973) 333ff.; G. Goulet, "Deux compagnons: Bienheureux P. F., St. Pierre Canisius," *Cahiers de Spiritualité Ignatienne* 15 (1991) 5–29.

JOHANNES WRBA

■ **Additional Bibliography:** J. W. Koterski, "Discerning the More Fruitful Paths to Reform. P. F. and the Lutheran Reformation," *Heythrop Journal* 31 (1990) 488–504; K. Schatz, "Deutschland und die Reformation in der Sicht P. F.s," *Geist und Leben* 69 (1996) 259–72.

Faber Stapulensis, *Jakob* (Jacques Lefèvre d'Etaples). French reforming humanist and exegete, born c. 1450 or 1455 in Etaples (Picardy), died 1536 in Nérac (department of Lot-et-Garonne). He studied theology and philosophy in Italy and Paris, and taught at the Sorbonne. In 1523, he became vicar general of Cardinal Guillaume → Briçonnet in Meaux. Faber Stapulensis translated the Bible into French (edition of the whole Bible [Antwerp, 1530]) and wrote commentaries in Latin on the Pauline letters, the catholic epistles, and the Gospels, as well as commentaries on Aristotle. He published the first complete edition of the works of Nicholas Cusanus (Paris, 1514), whose positions he himself followed. He endeavored to achieve a synthesis of the philosophies of Plato and Aristotle, united with mystical elements. His exegetical writings led to controversies with the Sorbonne and were placed on the Index. He inclined to Reformation views, but did not break with the Catholic Church.

■ **Literature:** *BBKL* 1:1582ff.; *Enzyklopädie Philosophie und Wissenschaftstheorie*, ed. J. Mittelstrass, vol. 1 (Mannheim, 1980) 629.—S. Meier-Oeser, *Die Präsenz des Vergessenen. Zur Rezeption der Philosophie des Nicolaus Cusanus vom 15. bis zum 18.Jh.* (Münster, 1989).

CHRISTOPH KANN

■ **Additional Bibliography:** *RGG*[4] 3:1f.—Ph. E. Hughes, *Lefèvre* (Grand Rapids, Mich., 1984); J.-F. Pernot, ed., *Jacques Lefèvre d'Etaples. Actes du colloque les 7 et 8 novembre 1992* (Paris, 1995).

Fabri (known as Faber), *Johannes.* Catholic controversial theologian, bishop of Vienna (1530), born 1478 in Leutkirch (Allgäu), died August 21, 1541 in Vienna. He began the study of civil and canon law, theology, and classical languages in Tübingen in 1505, and moved in 1509 to Freiburg, where he took his doctorate in civil and canon law under Ulrich → Zasius. Papal indults permitted him to acquire many ecclesiastical benefices: he was episcopal official in Basle (1513), parish priest in Leutkirch, Lindau, and Wain, vicar general in Constance (1518), cathedral canon in Basle, Constance, Mainz, Breslau, and Prague, provost in Ofen, Ölenberg, and Leitmeritz, dean in Gross-Glogau, coadjutor in Wiener Neustadt (1524), etc. From 1523-1524, he was counselor and confessor to Archduke → Ferdinand. He took part in the religious dialogues in Zurich (1523) and → Baden (1526), in the Convent of → Regensburg (1524), and in the imperial parliaments in Nuremberg (1524), Speyer (1526 and 1529), Augsburg (1530, where he led the work on the *Confutatio*), and → Regensburg (1532). After lengthy hesitation, he finally parted company with the ideas of Martin Luther at the end of 1521 (*Malleus*). His theological writings—sermons, disputations, and memoranda in German and Latin—have an irenical tone, but they are heavy with learning, and they did not find a wide readership.

■ **Principal Works:** *Malleus in haeresim Lutheranam* (Rome, 1522; Cologne [2]1524 [= CCath 23–26]); *Summarium* (Mainz, 1526); *Antilogiae* (Augsburg, 1530); *Praeparatoria futuri . . . concilii* (1536) (manuscript, edition: *CT* 4:10–23); his handwritten literary remains can be found in the Austrian national library.

■ **Literature:** Klaiber nos. 100–103; *TRE* 10:784–88; *KThR* 1:90–97.—L. Helbling, *J. F.* (Münster, 1941); Ch. Radey, "J. F.," Diss., Vienna, 1976; A. Angst, "Heigerlin oder Schmid?" *Rottenburger Jahrbuch für Kirchengeschichte* 3 (1984) 197– 205; K. D. Lewis, "Ulrich von Hutten, Johann Faber, and Das Gyren Rupffen," *ARG* 78 (1987) 124–46; E. Junod, *La Dispute de Lausanne (1536)* (Lausanne, 1988); K. Maier, *Die Bischöfe von Konstanz*, ed. E. L. Kuhn et al., vol. 1 (Friedrichshafen, 1988) 85– 89; Ch. Dittrich, "Katholische Kontroverstheologie im Kampf gegen Reformation und Täufertum," *Mennonitische Geschichtsblätter* 47/48 (1990/91) 71–88; idem, *Die vortridentinische* *katholische Kontroverstheologie und die Täufer* (Frankfurt/Main, 1991) 208–58.

HERBERT IMMENKÖTTER

■ **Additional Bibliography:** W. Dobras, "J. Faber: Pfarrer von Lindau, Bischof von Wien," *Jahrbuch des Landkreises Lindau* 13 (1998) 89–93.

Fabri, *Johannes.* Dominican (c. 1520), Catholic controversial theologian, born 1504 in Heilbronn, died February 27, 1558 in Augsburg. He studied in Cologne (1534-1535) and Freiburg (1539). He became city preacher in Colmar in 1540, and prior in Schlettstadt in 1545. At the urging of Cardinal Otto Truchsess von → Waldburg, he was appointed cathedral preacher in Augsburg, which at that period was 90 percent Protestant; for this position, a doctoral title was necessary, and he took this degree in Ingolstadt in 1552; in addition to his other duties, he taught in Ingolstadt until 1554-1555. He was the most important polemical writer for the publishing house of S. Mayer, which Truchsess founded and which produced 31 titles between 1550 and 1600; in particular, his booklet on confession and his treatise on the Mass were standard works in southern Germany for decades. In 1559, Peter → Canisius succeeded Fabri as cathedral preacher in Augsburg.

■ **Principal Works:** *Ein nutzlich Beychtbüchlin* (Augsburg, 1551); *Ain christenlicher Catechismus* (Augsburg, 1551); *Der recht Weg* (Dillingen, 1553); *Was die Evangelisch Meß sey* (Dillingen, 1555); *Christenliche underricht* (Dillingen, 1556).

■ **Literature:** *DThC* 5:2055–60; Klaiber 98ff.—N. Paulus, *Die deutschen Dominikaner im Kampf gegen Luther* (Freiburg, 1903) 232–66; F. Roth, *Augsburgs Reformationsgeschichte,* 4 vols. (Munich, [2]1911); E. M. Buxbaum, "Der Augsburger Domprediger J. F. OP von Heilbronn," *Jahrbuch des Vereins für Augsburger Bistumsgeschichte* 2 (1968) 47– 61; F. Zoepfl, *Das Bistum Augsburg und seine Bischöfe im Reformationsjahrhundert* (Munich, 1969).

HERBERT IMMENKÖTTER

Farel, *Guillaume.* Reformer of western Switzerland, born 1489 in Les Fareaux near Gap (Dauphiné), died September 13, 1565 in Neuchâtel. During his studies in Paris, he came under the influence of Jakob → Faber Stapulensis. He embraced the Reformation in 1521, and fled in 1523 to Johannes → Oecolampadius in Basle. He was expelled from this city in 1524 after a violent controversy with → Erasmus of Rotterdam. He wandered from one city to another, spending time in Montbéliard, Metz, Strasbourg, and other towns; from 1528, he was employed by the Reformed city of Berne to promote the Reformation in western Switzerland. He was in Aigle from 1526 to 1530, and in Murten from 1530 to 1534, propagating the new teaching in Biel, Neuchâtel, Avenches, and Grandson. From 1534 to 1538, he was in Geneva under the protection of Berne; here, he led the Reformation to victory and imposed the new church order together with Jean Calvin. He took part in the disputation of Lausanne in 1536. After he was expelled from Geneva, Farel organized the Reformed Church in Neuchâtel and sought to establish the Reformation in Franche-Comté and the prince bishopric of Basle too. He was a passionate public speaker. In 1529, he wrote the *Sommaire,* the first presentation of Protestant doctrine in French.

■ **Literature:** L. Aubert et al., *G. F. Biographie nouvelle* (Neuchâtel, 1930); *Actes du Colloque G. F.* (Neuchâtel, 1980), ed. P. Barthel et al. (Geneva et al., 1983).

PIERRE LOUIS SURCHAT

■ **Additional Bibliography:** H. Heyer, *G. F.* (Lewiston et al., 1990); H. H. Esser, "Die Stellung des 'Summaire' von G. F. innerhalb der frühen reformierten Bekenntnisschriften," *Zwingliana* 19 (1991/ 1992) 93–114; H. A. Oberman, "Calvin and F.," *Reformation and Renaissance Review* 1 (1999) 7–40; F. P. van Stam, "F.s und Calvins Ausweisung aus Genf am 23.4.1538," *ZKG* 110 (1999) 209–28; idem, "Die Genfer 'Artikel' vom Januar 1537: aus Calvins oder F.s Feder?," *Zwingliana* 27 (2000) 87–101.

Ferber, *Nikolaus.* Franciscan (known in his Order as Nikolaus of Herborn, and in the Danish diaspora as Stagefyr, "blazing torch"), controversial theologian, born c. 1483 in Herborn, died April 15, 1535 in Toulouse. He studied in Cologne (1512) and became guardian in Marburg in 1520. He engaged in debate with Franz Lambert of Avignon (synod of → Homberg, 1526). He became guardian in Brühl in 1527, and was cathedral preacher in Cologne. Invited to attend the parliament in Copenhagen in 1530, he composed an *Apology* for King Frederick I. From 1532 to 1535, he was general commissioner for the provinces of his Order north of the Alps.

■ **Works:** *Locorum communium adversus huius temporis haereses Enchiridion* (Cologne, 1528; Cologne, 1529 =

CCath 12); *Epitome convertendi gentes Indiarum ad fidem Christi* (Cologne, 1532) (in *Collectanea Franciscana Neerlandica* 2 [1931] 395–425).
■ **Literature:** *ADB* 12:42–45; *NDB* 5:80f.; *DThC* 6:2205ff.; Klaiber 106; *KThR* 5:32–49.

PETER FABISCH

Ferdinand I (emperor 1558-1564). Born March 10, 1503 in Alcalá, died July 25, 1564 in Vienna. He was brother of Emperor → Charles V, who entrusted him with the government of the German and Habsburg hereditary territories, and made him his viceroy in the empire for a period. He became king of Hungary and Bohemia in 1526, king of Rome in 1531, and emperor in 1558. In imperial politics, he was a loyal helper of his brother, but unlike Charles, he was open to a reconciliation with the Protestant princes in the empire, and he succeeded in achieving this in the treaty of → Passau (1552) and the Religious Peace of → Augsburg (1555) in which Ferdinand permitted the imperial Estates to profess the Lutheran faith, renouncing the principle that the Protestants must return to the Catholic Church. At the same time, however, he salvaged for the Catholic Church, by means of the → Ecclesiastical reservation, what could still be saved: viz., many imperial bishoprics and abbeys. The *Declaratio Ferdinandea*, conceived as a compensation for the Protestants (though without the force of imperial law), allowed the Lutherans confessional freedom in those principalities where the ruler was a Catholic cleric. In his own domains, Ferdinand supported the Catholic Church, but the abuses and the shortage of priests meant that he was unable to do much to prevent the growth of Protestantism, which enjoyed the support of the local Estates and cities. His endeavors to promote the restoration of Catholicism can be seen in his decrees on questions of church politics, in the foundation of numerous Jesuit colleges, in the invitations issued to able Jesuits (especially Peter → Canisius), and in the publication and introduction of the catechisms which Canisius wrote at Ferdinand's request. His reforming statute of 1562 made the concessions of priestly marriage (→ celibacy) and the → chalice for the laity, but this did little to halt the progress of Protestantism. By accepting compromises on points of church politics, Ferdinand made it possible to bring the Council of Trent to a conclusion.

■ **Literature:** F. von Buchholz, *Geschichte der Regesten F.s I.* (Graz, 1968–71); A. Kohler, *Antihabsburgische Politik in der Epoche Karls V. Die reichsständische Opposition gegen die Wahl F.s zum römischen König . . .* (Göttingen, 1982); G. Rill and Ch. Thomas, *Bernhard Cles als Politiker . . .* (Graz, 1987); P. Sutter-Fichtner, *F. I. Wider Türken und Glaubensspaltung* (Vienna et al., 1986); H. Rabe, *Reich und Glaubensspaltung, Deutschland 1500–1600* (Munich, 1989) passim; idem, *Deutsche Geschichte 1500–1600* (Munich, 1991).

ERNST WALTER ZEEDEN

■ **Additional Bibliography:** E. Laubach, *F. I. als Kaiser* (Münster, 2001); Z. Csepregi, " Konfessionsbildung und Einheitsbestrebungen im Königreich Ungarn zur Regoierungszeit F.s I.," *ARG* 94 (2003) 243–275; A. Kohler, *Ferdinand I.* (Munich, 2003).

Fisher, *John.* Saint (1935; feast June 22), bishop, humanist, martyr, born 1469 in Beverley (Yorkshire), died June 22, 1535 in London. He entered Michaelhouse College in Cambridge in 1483, and took the degrees of bachelor (1488), master of arts (1491, the year in which he was ordained priest), and doctor of theology (1501). He became vice-chancellor in 1501, professor of theology in 1502, and chancellor of the university of Cambridge in 1504; he was reelected for life to this office in 1514. He did much to promote the expansion of his university. As confessor to Lady Margaret Beaufort, the mother of King → Henry VIII, he persuaded her to found a chair of theology as well as Christ's College (1505) and St. John's College (1511). Fisher was well versed in the theological tradition and open to the intellectual movements of his days. He felt a particular obligation to pursue the ideals of Christian humanism. He exchanged letters with Johannes → Reuchlin, and he played a central role in making it possible for → Erasmus of Rotterdam to stay in Cambridge from 1511 to 1514; Fisher was a personal friend of Erasmus, whose works inspired him. From 1516 onwards, he encouraged the study of the biblical languages at St. John's College. Fisher had become bishop of Rochester (Kent) in 1504, and he devoted considerable energy to the exemplary administration of his diocese, paying particular attention to the reform of preaching and of the clergy. The emergence of the Reformation compelled him to take a clear position; he became one of the sharpest literary opponents of Martin Luther, and wrote a number of anti-Reformation books (including

Assertionis Lutheranae Confutatio [Antwerp, 1523]; *Sacri Sacerdotii Defensio* [Cologne, 1525]; *De Veritate Corporis et Sanguinis Christi in Eucharistia* [Cologne, 1527]). The style and the substance of these works are outstanding, and the Council of Trent made extensive use of them. He fell out of favor with King Henry VIII during the controversy about the king's planned divorce, which Fisher resolutely rejected. He was imprisoned in April, 1534, after he had refused to confirm by oath the declaration of invalidity of the king's marriage with Catharine of Aragon. He likewise rejected the Act of → Supremacy (1534), whereby parliament made the king the head of the English church. When Pope → Paul III created Fisher a cardinal on May 20, 1535, his fate was sealed: he was formally arraigned on June 17, declared guilty of high treason, and beheaded.

■ **Works:** *Opera, quae hactenus inveniri potuerunt omnia* (Würzburg, 1597); *The English Works of J. F.*, ed. J. E. B. Mayor (London, 1876, ²1935); Klaiber 109ff.

■ **Literature:** *TRE* 11:204ff.—B. Bradshaw and E. Duffy, eds., *Humanism, Reform and the Reformation: The Career of Bishop J. F.* (Cambridge, 1989); R. Rex, *The Theology of J. F.* (Cambridge, 1991).

MICHAEL BECHT

■ **Additional Bibliography:** J. Wicks, "Argumentative Legitimation in 16th Century Catholic Theology," in *Ecclesia tertii millennii advenientis.* Festschrift A. Anton (Casale Monferrato, 1997) 888–97; M. Dowling, *Fisher of Men. A Life of J. F.* (Basingstoke et al., 1999).

Flacius (Vlaci?), **Matthias.** Lutheran theologian, born March 3, 1520 in Albona (today Labin in Istria, hence his name Illyricus Albonensis), died March 11, 1575 in Frankfurt am Main. After humanist studies in Venice, Basle, and Tübingen, he was in Wittenberg from 1541, where he made the acquaintance of Martin Luther. He took his master's degree in 1543 and became professor of Hebrew in Wittenberg in 1544. After the defeat of the Schmalkaldic forces, Flacius, a strict opponent of all accommodations (→ Augsburg Interim), had a sharp disagreement with the "Philippists," the adherents of Philipp Melanchthon (→ Adiaphora controversy; → Gnesiolutherans), and left Wittenberg in 1549. He lived in Magdeburg from 1551. As the theological leader of the Gnesiolutherans, Flacius launched the struggle for the "pure doctrine" of Luther in Germany, and endeavored to spread the Reformation in his own native land. He wrote the first Protestant work in Croatian in 1555, and published a children's Bible, *Otrocja biblija,* with his pupil Sebastian Krelj in the five most important languages of Illyria (Tübingen, 1566). Thanks to his studies in biblical exegesis, Flacius is considered the founder of modern hermeneutics, and his rejection of the annalistic method makes him the first church historian of the modern period. In Magdeburg, he worked with a large group of collaborators on the *Catalogus testium veritatis* (Basle, 1556) and began the *Historia ecclesiastica* (→ Magdeburg Centuriators), the most important historical work of the 16th century. He became professor of New Testament in Jena in 1557, and organized the Protestant church in Thüringen. After a church governing body was set up by the duke in 1561, he was dismissed from office, and went to Regensburg (1562-1566), but did not succeed in his plans to found Protestant universities in that city and in Klagenfurt, to coordinate the printing of literature in the southern Slavic languages, and to organize a synod for all the Protestant churches. He was head of the Lutheran community in Antwerp in 1566-1567, and then went to Strasbourg. He engaged in bitter polemics against Jakob → Andreae's "policy of reconciliation." In the disputation of Weimar (1560), where Victorinus → Strigel called original sin an "accident," Flacius maintained the opposite position, viz., that original sin was the *forma substantialis* of the fallen human being; he continued to defend this position after the doctrinal letter of Tilemann → Heshusius (1568), and this led to a breach between the majority of the Gnesiolutherans and the "Flacians" who held this particular doctrine. His insistence on his doctrine of original sin led to Flacius's almost total isolation and to his expulsion from Strasbourg in 1573. He ended his life as a private teacher in Frankfurt.

■ **Works:** *De vocabulo fidei* (Wittenberg, 1549); expanded new edition: *De voce et re fidei* (Basle, 1555); *Clavis scripturae s[acrae],* 2 vols. (Basle, 1567) (Tract. I, 1–4: M. F. Illyricus, *De ratione cognoscendi sacras literas, lateinisch-deutsch,* ed. L. Geldsetzer [Düsseldorf, 1968]); *Glossa compendiaria in Novum Testamentum* (Basle, 1570).

■ **Literature:** *TRE* 11:206–14.—J. Preger, *M. F. Illyricus und seine Zeit,* 2 vols. (Erlangen, 1859–61, reprinted 1964); L. Haikola, *Gesetz und Evangelium bei M. F. Illyricus* (Lund, 1952); M. Mirković, *Matija Vlacić Ilirik* (Zagreb, 1959); J. Scheible, *Die Entstehung der Magdeburger Zenturien* (Gütersloh, 1966); *Gestalten der Kirchengeschichte,* ed. M. Greschat, vol. 6 (Stuttgart,

1981) 277–92; G. Bedouelle, *Le temps des réformes et la Bible* (Paris, 1989) 258–61; R. Keller, *Der Schlüssel zur Schrift* (Hamburg, 1984); *M. F. Illyricus. Leben und Werk. Internationales Symposium Mannheim, Februar 1991*, ed. J. Matešić (Munich, 1993); A. Bernard, "La Réforme et le livre slovène," *Bulletin de la Société de l'Histoire du Protestanisme français* 141 (1995) 5–26.

PETER F. BARTON

■ **Additional Bibliography:** O. K. Olson, *M. F. and the Survival of Luther's Reform* (Wiesbaden, 2000); M. Hartmann, "Humanismus und Kirchenkritik," in *M. F. Illyricus als Erforscher des Mittelalters* (Stuttgart, 2001); O. K. Olson, "M. F. Faces the Netherlands Revolt," in *Caritas et reformatio*. FS C. Lindberg (New York, 2002) 103–12; O. K. Olson, *M. F. and the Survival of Luther's Reform* (Wiesbaden, 2002).

Foscarari, *Egidio.* Dominican (1526), theologian and bishop, born January 27, 1512 in Bologna, died December 23, 1564 in Rome. He taught theology in Bologna, and was conciliar theologian in Trent and Master of the Sacred Palace. He was appointed bishop of Modena in 1550, and took part in the Council of Trent in 1551-1552. Under → Paul IV, he was accused of heresy and imprisoned in Castel Sant'Angelo in January, 1558; he was released in August of that year, and officially declared innocent in 1560. He took part again in the Council of Trent in 1562-1563 and played an important role there. He participated in the elaboration of the → *Catechismus Romanus* and in the reform of the breviary and the missal.
■ **Literature:** *CT* 1–11; *DHGE* 17:1198f.—A. Walz, *I domenicani al Concilio di Trento* (Rome, 1961); Jedin vols. 3[2] and 4; M. Firpo and D. Marcatto, *Il processo inquisitoriale del cardinal Giovanni Morone*, vol. 1–5 (Rome, 1981–89); M. Firpo, *Inquisizione Romana e Controriforma* (Bologna, 1992).

KLAUS GANZER

■ **Additional Bibliography:** M. M. Fontaine, "For the Good of the City. The Bishop and the Ruling Elite in the Tridentine Modena," *SCJ* 28 (1997) 29–43.

Francis I of France (king 1515-1547). Born September 12, 1494 in Cognac, died March 31, 1547 in Rambouillet. He succeeded Louis XII in 1515; in the same year, in the struggle for the duchy of Milan, he defeated the Swiss near Marignano, and concluded the concordat of Bologna with → Leo X in 1516. As inheritor of the French policies vis-à-vis Italy and of the French claims to the duchy of Burgundy, he was the perpetual enemy of → Charles V. After his defeat at Pavia (1525), he was taken prisoner, but regained his freedom of action through the sham Peace of Milan (1526). Francis was a splendid Renaissance prince, a patron of arts, and a supporter of French humanism. His attitude to the great religious controversies of his age was primarily determined by political considerations. He made treaties with Turks and Protestants, but in France itself, after initial hesitation, he became a resolute opponent of the spread of the new teachings after 1534 ("affair of the posters").
■ **Literature:** *DBF* 14:1005–11; *TRE* 11:385–89.— *Catalogue des actes de François Ier*, 7 vols. (Paris, 1887–97); G. F. Mänzer, *F. I. und die Anfänge der französischen Reformation* (Freiburg, 1935); C. Terrasse, *François Ier. Le roi et le règne*, 3 vols. (Paris, 1945–70); K. J. Seidel, *Frankreich und die deutschen Protestanten 1534/35.* (Münster, 1970); S. Skalweit, "Die 'affaire des placards' und ihr reformationsgeschichtlicher Hintergrund," in *Gestalten und Probleme der frühen Neuzeit* (Berlin, 1987) 44–63.

STEPHAN SKALWEIT

■ **Additional Bibliography:** G. Treffer, *F. I. von Frankreich* (Regensburg, 1993); J. Jacquard, *François Ier* (Paris, 1994); F. M. Higman, "De l'affaire des placards aux Nicodemites. Le mouvement évangelique français sous François Ier," *Etudes théologiques et religieuses* 70 (1995) 359–66; G. Gadoffre, *La révolution culturelle dans la France des humanistes. Guillaume Budé et François Ier* (Geneva, 1997).

Franck, *Kaspar.* Catholic theologian, born November 2, 1543 in Ortrand (Pulsnitz), died March 12, 1584 in Ingolstadt. He was the son of Kaspar Franck (died 1578; preacher in Joachimsthal from 1546, pastor there from 1565). After studies in Wittenberg from 1561-1565 (taking his master's degree in 1564), Franck was a Lutheran preacher in the county of Haag in 1565-1566. Impressed by Martin → Eisengrein, he followed him to Ingolstadt. He converted publicly to Catholicism and was ordained priest in 1568. Duke → Albrecht V of Bavaria invited him to Haag, which had been recatholicized, appointing him subsequently court preacher and spiritual counselor in 1570. From 1572, he was a parish priest, and (from 1578) additionally professor of exegesis in Ingolstadt; he took his doctorate in theology at Siena in 1575. He wrote many works of piety and controversial theology (against Jacob → Andreae, Johann Friedrich Cölestin, Georg Nigrinus, Martin → Chemnitz, and other Lutheran theologians).

■ **Catalogue of Works:** N. Paulus, "C. F.," *Historisch-politische Blätter für das katholische Deutschland* 124 (1899) 545–57, 617–27; *VD 16* 7:131–34.

■ **Literature:** *ADB* 7:272f.; *DThC* 6:720f.—J. B. Götz, "Die Grabsteine der Moritzkirche in Ingolstadt," *Sammelblatt des Historischen Vereins Ingolstadt* 45 (1926) 26; idem, "St. Moritz in Ingolstadt. Kirche und Pfarrei," *Sammelblatt des Historischen Vereins Ingolstadt* 47 (1928) 66; A. Eckert, *Die deutschen evangelischen Pfarrer der Reformationszeit in Westböhmen* (Bad Rappenau, 1974–76) 48; W. Kausch, *Geschichte der theologischen Fakultät Ingolstadt im 15. und 16.Jh.* (Berlin, 1977) with index.

BRUN APPEL

Franck, *Sebastian.* Representative of 16th-century "Spiritualism," born c. 1500 in Donauwörth, died end of October, 1542 in Basle. After studies in Ingolstadt and Heidelberg, he became a Catholic priest of the diocese of Augsburg, then a Lutheran preacher. After periods in a number of cities (Nuremberg, Strasbourg, Esslingen, Geislingen, Ulm), he ended his life as an independent writer and publisher in Basle. His religious philosophy seeks to make it possible for the human person, supported by direct contact with God, to grasp the absolute dimension of the world by means of intellectual endeavor; this radicalization of ideas of Cusanus and Erasmus influenced modern religious philosophy (Wilhelm Dilthey, Ernst Troeltsch).

■ **Works:** *Sämtliche Werke,* ed. H.-G. Roloff (Berne, 1992ff.); K. Kaczerowsky, *S. F. Bibliographie* (Wiesbaden, 1976); *BiDi* 7:39–119.

■ **Literature:** *TRE* 11:307–12; *CEras* 2:53f.—H. Weigelt, *S. F. und die lutherische Reformation* (Gütersloh, 1972); S. Wollgast, *Der deutsche Pantheismus im 16.Jh.* (Berlin, 1972); A. Séguenny, *Spiritualistische Philosophie als Antwort auf die religiöse Frage des 16.Jh.* (Wiesbaden, 1978); C. Dejung, *Wahrheit und Häresie* (Zurich, 1980); J.-D. Müller, ed., *S. F.* (Wiesbaden, 1993); B. Quast, *S. F.s "Kriegbüchlin des Frides"* (Tübingen and Basle, 1993).

ANDRÉ SÉGUENNY

■ **Additional Bibliography:** P.-M. Hayden-Roy, *The Inner Word and the Outer World. A Biography of S. F.* (New York, 1994); S. Waldhoff, "Der Evangelist des gewappneten Moses. S. F.s Auseinandersetzung mit Martin Bucers Obrigkeitsverständnis," *ZKG* 107 (1996) 327–54; H. Weigelt, "S. F. und Caspar Schwenckfeld in ihren Beziehungen zueinander," in *Von Schwenckfeld bis Löhe. Festschrift H. Weigelt* (Neustadt [Aisch], 1999) 21–38; *Beiträge zum 500. Geburtstag von S. F.,* ed. S. Wollgast (Berlin, 1999); J.-C. Colbus, "Die Vorrede vom Adler oder die verschiedenen Stufen einer satirisch-überzeitlichen Zeitkritik," *Simpliciana* 22 (2000) 31–56.

Frankfurt, Truce of. From 1538 onwards, the two emperors → Charles V and → Ferdinand I attempted a reconciliation with the Protestants (Truce of Nice; danger from the Turks), mediated by the electors of Brandenburg and the Palatinate. The negotiations in Frankfurt am Main, under the chairmanship of Johann von Weeze, archbishop of Lund, led to the "Truce" of April 19, 1539 which granted all those who adhered to confessions related to the → Confessio Augustana a temporary religious peace; all trials before the supreme court were to be adjourned. This peace was to last for fifteen months, provided that no further secularizations of church property took place and that the League of → Schmalkald did not admit any new members. Help in the struggle against the Turks was announced, as was a religious dialogue with the aim of achieving unity in the faith.

■ **Literature:** A. P. *Luttenberger, Glaubenseinheit und Reichsfriede* (Göttingen, 1982); H. Rabe, *Reich und Glaubensspaltung* (Munich, 1989). → Reformation.

ANTON SCHINDLING

Frankfurt, Recess of. This was the first (unsuccessful) attempt on March 18, 1558 to bring religious and political peace to the Lutheran churches. After Martin Luther's death in 1546, and in the aftermath of the → Augsburg Interim of 1548, antithetical doctrinal positions developed within Lutheranism about the interpretation of the doctrine of justification (the conflict about → Osiander), the role of good works, the role played by the strength of the human person's own will in the process of redemption (Majoristic or synergistic conflict; Georg → Major), and the interpretation of the bodily presence of Christ in the elements of the Lord's Supper. This conflict, known as the Interimistic or → Adiaphora controversy, raged between Philipp Melanchthon and his adherents on the one side (the so-called Philippists) and a group of theologians led by Matthias → Flacius, Nikolaus → Amsdorf, and Johann → Wigand on the other, who claimed to uphold Luther's genuine positions (the so-called → Gnesiolutherans). Since the Catholic side (Peter → Canisius) had exploited the debates within Protestantism during the last "interconfessional" religious dialogue in the Reformation period, at → Worms (1557), concord was clearly necessary, if Lutheranism was to survive in political terms. During the imperial parliament that was held on the occasion of the proclamation of → Ferdinand I as emperor, the electoral Palatinate, electoral Saxony, electoral Brandenburg, Württemberg, Hessen, and Zweibrücken conducted negotiations, concentrating on a memorandum drawn up by Melanchthon which became the basis of the Recess of Frankfurt, the text approved by these six Estates. The aim of the Recess was to demonstrate the viability of the → Confessio Augustana (which had been recognized in imperial law since 1555) against the Catholic charge that the Protestants were "quarrelers, erroneous and divided in their confession." The Recess should be read as an exposition and updating of the Confessio Augustana (1530). Although it was rejected, the Recess launched a tradition of confessional formulation within Lutheranism which reached its goal in the Formula of → Concord in 1577: this tradition presents the dogmatic position of the Lutheran confession as an interpretation of the Confessio Augustana against the background of contemporary controversies. On the question of → justification, the Recess maintained, against Andreas Osiander, the *justificatio imputativa propter Christum*. It teaches a *necessitas causae et effectus* of good works. On the question of the Lord's Supper, it links the presence of the Body of Christ to the act of eating, not to the elements themselves (→ Eucharistic controversy). It was above all the eucharistic doctrine of the Recess of Frankfurt—which excludes a *manducatio* on the part of unbelievers, and could therefore be interpreted as supporting a Calvinist position—and the "presumption" of the princes to judge doctrinal matters that provoked some Gnesiolutherans to oppose this text, and prevented it from being received by the church and having any effect on subsequent history. The struggle against the Recess of Frankfurt was led by the theologians of Johann Friedrich II of Saxony (who belonged to

the Ernestine line) at the newly founded university of Jena; these scholars wrote the Weimer Book of Confutation in 1558.

■ **Literature:** RE[3] 6, 169–72; CR 9:489–507.—H. Heppe, *Geschichte des deutschen Protestantismus in den Jahren 1555–81*, vol. 1 (Marburg, 1852) 266ff.; G. Wolf, *Die Geschichte der deutschen Protestanten* (Berlin, 1888) 110–53, 376–407; M. Brecht and R. Schwarz, eds., *Bekenntnis und Einheit der Kirche* (Stuttgart, 1980); E. Koch, *Aufbruch und Weg. Studien zur lutherischen Bekenntnisbildung im 16.Jh.* (Berlin, 1983); B. von Bundschuh, *Das Wormser Religionsgespräch von 1557* (Münster, 1988).

THOMAS KAUFMANN

Frederick III of the Palatinate ("the Pious"). Born February 14, 1515 in Simmern, died October 26, 1576 in Heidelberg. He became Count Palatinate of Simmern in 1557, and electoral prince of the Palatinate in 1559. Initially, his wife, Maria of Brandenburg-Ansbach, won him over to Lutheranism, but personal Bible study later led him to embrace → Calvinism, and he resolved to introduce this into his electoral principality. He summoned important theologians to Heidelberg (Caspar → Olevian, Zacharias → Ursinus, Thomas → Erastus). In order to restructure the church in his territories in keeping with Reformed ideas, Frederick and Olevian exchanged letters with Jean Calvin. He set up the so-called church council to exercise surveillance of the local church (a measure which proved unsuccessful), and he charged Olevian and Ursinus to compose the catechism of → Heidelberg, which set out the faith of the Calvinist confession and was the favorite basic introduction to the Reformed understanding of the faith among German-speaking European Calvinists. Frederick made the university of Heidelberg the most important educational establishment of German Calvinism. On the level of imperial politics, he became the most resolute opponent of the emperor and the Catholic imperial princes, but he also opposed the leader of the Protestants in imperial politics, the Lutheran electoral prince of Saxony—thereby contributing in no little measure to weakening the position of German Protestantism (which would otherwise have been powerful) in imperial political debates. In his own territory, he acted with rigor against Catholics and Lutherans, Baptists and members of sects. In the Upper Palatinate, his policy of enforced confessionalization failed to overcome the resistance of the local Estates, who were convinced Lutherans; in the Rhineland Palatinate, however, he expelled the Lutheran pastors, theologians, and university teachers.

■ Literature: *NDB* 5:529–33; B. Gebhardt, *Handbuch der deutschen Geschichte,* vol. 2 (Stuttgart, ⁹1974) 235ff.—A. Kluckhohn, ed., *Briefe F.s des Frommen,* 2 vols. (Braunschweig, 1867–72); M. Ritter, *Deutsche Geschichte im Zeitalter der Gegenreformation und des Dreißigjährigen Krieges,* 3 vols. (Stuttgart, 1889–1908); R. Lossen, "Die Glaubensspaltung in Kurpfalz," *Freiburger Diözesan-Archiv* 45 (1917) 208–310; J. B. Götz, *Die erste Einführung des Calvinismus in der Oberpfalz* (Münster, 1933); idem, *Die religiösen Wirren in der Oberpfalz 1576–1620* (Münster, 1937); A. A. van Schelven, "Der Generalstab des politischen Calvinismus in Zentraleuropa . . . ," *ARG* 36 (1939) 123f.; F. H. Schubert, "Die pfälzische Exilregierung im Dreissigjährigen Krieg," *Zeitschrift für die Geschichte des Oberrheins* 102 (1954) 575–680; P. Güss, *Das Verhalten der kurpfälzischen Regierung zum Täufertum* (Stuttgart, 1961); V. Press, *Kriege und Krisen. Deutsche Geschichte 1600–1715* (Munich, 1991) 193–200.

ERNST WALTER ZEEDEN

Frederick III of Saxony ("the Wise"). Electoral prince of the Ernestine line, born January 14, 1463 in Torgau, died May 5, 1525 in Lochau. A typical medieval local prince, thinking in legal categories, Frederick consistently supported the semi-sovereign rights of the princes after Berthold of Henneberg initiated his endeavors to achieve reform within the empire. In 1502, Frederick founded the university of Wittenberg, entrusting to the Augustinian Hermits a number of professorships in philosophy and theology. From 1517 on, he was Martin Luther's protector (not his adherent). He successfully resisted attempts to have Luther sent to Rome, insisting that Luther be interrogated on German soil by the papal legate, Thomas → Cajetan de Vio (1518). He also ensured that, before any ecclesiastical steps were taken against Luther, he would be able to speak about his doctrine before the emperor and the imperial Estates (Worms, 1521). After Luther was declared an outlaw, the prince took the precautionary measure of imprisoning him in Wartburg in electoral Saxony, thereby protecting him from potential dangers. In religious terms, he was completely conservative (cf. his collection of relics in Wittenberg), but his conscientiousness and sense of justice led him to

act to ward off any legal or imperial-political steps against Luther. In practice, he allowed Luther to act freely; hence, Frederick indirectly made a very decisive contribution to the spread of the Reformation. He maintained Catholic worship in the "castle church" of All Saints in Wittenberg until 1524; before his death, he received the sacrament under both kinds. His biography and his conduct in church politics show that it was possible for late-medieval piety and openness to reforms to flow unproblematically into Luther's Reformation movement.

■ Literature: *NDB* 5:568–72; *TRE* 11:666–69.—P. Münch, "F. der Weise als Landesfürst" (diss., Jena, 1922); P. Kirn, *F. der Weise und die Kirche* (Leipzig, 1926); I. Höss, *Georg Spalatin* (Weimar, 1956); I. Ludophy, *F. der Weise, Kurfürst von Sachsen* (Göttingen, 1984).

ERNST WALTER ZEEDEN

■ **Additional Bibliography:** *RGG*⁴ 3:380.—M. Schulze, "F. der Weise. Politik und Reformation," in *Relationen.* Festschrift K.-H. zur Mühlen (Münster, 2000) 335–55.

Frecht (Frächt, Frech[t]us, Phrecht), *Martin.* Professor of theology, reformer of Ulm, born 1419 in Ulm, died September 14, 1566 in Tübingen. He began his studies in Heidelberg in 1514 and took the degree of master of arts in 1517; he took the licentiate in theology no later than 1529. He was dean in 1524 and 1526-1527, and rector of the university in 1525 and 1530-1531. He was lector in sacred scripture in Heidelberg from 1529 to 1531, and in Ulm from 1531 to 1548. He became "principal preacher" in Ulm in 1537, with responsibility for building up the structures of church life. Despite conflicts with the authoritarian church government of the city council, and despite invitations to become pastor or professor in Switzerland, Tübingen, or Heidelberg, Frecht remained in Ulm. The unclarity of the confessional situation compelled him to take part in the colloquium with Ambrosius → Blarer and Martin → Bucer in Tübingen about Kaspar von → Schwenckfeld (1535); he endeavored to have the → Wittenberg Concord recognized by the city in 1536. In 1539, a religious dialogue between Frecht and Schwenckfeld took place before the assembled city council; a similar debate was held in 1543 between Frecht and Archbishop Gasparo d'Avalos of Santiago de Compostela and Pedro de → Soto on the question of images (→ Art and Reformation), ceremonies, the authority of the pope, and the position taken by → Erasmus of Rotterdam. He was the official representative and adviser of Ulm in the religious dialogues in → Hagenau and → Worms (1540), and in → Regensburg (1541, 1546). In the aftermath of the → Augsburg Interim, he was expelled from Ulm, and entered the service of the church in Württemberg in November, 1550. He was head of the Tübingen college, professor at the theological faculty (from June 1552), and rector of the university (1555-1556).

He was acquainted with Martin Luther's thinking from 1518 onwards (Heidelberg disputation). In the → eucharistic controversy, he took the side of Andreas → Karlstadt, Martin Bucer and Johannes → Oecolampadius against Luther and Johannes → Brenz. His spirit was irenic, and he was disturbed by the increasing rigidity of theological positions. His correspondence was extensive (above all with Bucer and Blarer). Few of his writings (biblical commentaries, sermons, lectures, memoranda) have been published; the scattered manuscripts still await a critical edition. His fame as an historian is due to his collection of chronicles of German history from the 10th to the 15th centuries (*Witichindi Saxonis Rerum ab Henrico et Ottone I. Impp. Gestarum Libri III* [Basle, 1532]).

■ **Literature:** *NDB* 5:384; *DHGE* 18:1137f.; *TRE* 11:482ff.—W.-U. Deetjen, "Licentiat M. F., Professor und Prädikant (1494–1556)," in *Die Einführung der Reformation in Ulm,* ed. H. E. Specker and G. Weig (Ulm, 1981) 269–321.

BARBARA HENZE

Frith, *John.* English Protestant theologian, martyr, born c. 1503 in Westerham, died July 7, 1533 in Smithfield. He studied at Eton and Cambridge. Thanks to Cardinal Thomas → Wolsey, Frith came to Oxford in 1525, and was imprisoned there for heresy in 1528. He fled to Marburg, and helped William → Tyndale in his translation of the Bible. On his return to England in 1532, he was arrested. His doctrine of the Eucharist, which was opposed by Thomas → More and others, led to his execution.

■ **Works:** *The Whole Works of W. Tyndale, J. F. and Dr Barnes,* ed. J. Foxe (London, 1573, new edition London,

1831); *The Work of J. F.,* ed. N. T. Wright (Oxford, 1983).

■ **Literature:** RE 6, 286–89; *DNB* 20:278ff.; *The Oxford Dictionary of the Christian Church* (London, ²1974) 539.

WOLFGANG PALAVER

■ **Additional Bibliography:** *RGG*⁴ 3:384.

Fritzhans (Fritzehans), *Johannes.* Franciscan Observant friar for a period, born in Frauenreuth, died 1540 in Magdeburg. As a member of the monastery in Leipzig, he defended his teacher, Augustin von → Alveldt, in 1520 against Johannes Feldkirch (Bernardi, died 1534) and Andreas → Karlstadt. While in the monastery in Magdeburg, he embraced the Reformation, and left his Order in 1523. He became Lutheran pastor in Magdeburg in 1524 and made a significant contribution to the consolidation of the Protestant church. In 1526/1527, he and Eberhard Weidensee (died 1547) wrote against the prior of the Dominican monastery, Johannes → Mensing.

■ **Works:** *VD 16* 7:3032–47.

■ **Literature:** *NDB* 5:635; *DHGE* 19:1197; *BBKL* 2:133f.—H. Smolinsky, *Augustin von Alveldt und Hieronymus Emser* (Münster, 1983) 58–61, 72–78.

BARBARA HENZE

Frundsberg, *Georg von.* Lord of the territory of Mindelheim (Lower Allgäu), born September (?) 24, 1473 in Mindelburg, where he died August 20, 1528. He was the son of the military captain Ulrich von Frundsberg, who came from a noble family in Tyrol and became governor of the city of Mindelheim in 1467. Frundsberg was in the service of the Swabian League and of Emperors Maximilian I and → Charles V from 1492. His central role in the victories of Bicocca (1522) and Pavia (1525), thanks to the troops of lansquenets whom he equipped and led, made him a hero among the people. The alleged meeting with Martin Luther at the imperial parliament in Worms in 1521 is probably not historical; but Frundsberg sympathized with the Reformation in the period between 1522 and 1526. In 1523, he sent his son Melchior to the university of Wittenberg, and permitted Johannes → Wanner, formerly parish priest in Mindelheim and Zwinglian clergyman in Constance since 1521, to preach in Mindelheim. This was most likely due to the influence of his second wife, Anna von Lodron, who was receptive to the new teaching. Frundsberg did not however convert to the Augsburg confession. As imperial general, he led the campaign against → Clement VII and the city of Rome, but he was reconciled with the pope in Ferrara during his last illness (1527-1528).

■ **Literature:** *LMA* 4:1001; *Handbuch der bayerischen Kirchengeschichte,* ed. W. Brandmüller, vol. 2 (St. Ottilien, 1993) 93.—R. Baumann, *G. von F., der Vater der Landsknechte und Feldhauptmann von Tirol* (Munich, ²1991).

PETER RUMMEL

Fugger. One of the leading merchant houses in Augsburg, along with the Wels and Höchstetter families, which played an important role in the economic, ecclesiastical, and cultural history of the 16th century. The Fuggers began as weavers and traders in textiles, but their capital in the early modern period was derived from the silver, copper, and mercury which were employed for coinage and in industrial production, as well as from financial transactions and banking. Two heads ("governors") of the firm, Jakob the Rich (1459-1525) and Anton (1493-1560), were players on the stage of world history. They made available in advance the money needed to cover the election costs of Maximilian I and → Charles V and the wars these emperors waged; in this period, they provided money for the imperial court and had a network of trading posts for the exchange of information across the whole of Europe. They followed the Habsburgs to Spain, where they exploited the territories which had once belonged to the Spanish military Orders, especially the mercury in Almadén, thanks to the lease they took on Maestrazgo. Subsequent withdrawal to their castles and domains in Swabia, where they possessed extensive properties and forests, has ensured the continued existence of this aristocratic house until the present day.

In terms of church history, the Fuggers were opponents of the Wittenberg Reformation thanks to their Roman bank (founded in 1495), which provided technical aid in servicing money connected with indulgences, and especially thanks to the debate in Germany about usury and monopolies. While Johannes → Eck, with an eye on Augsburg, supplied theological legitimation for the early-modern credit system, and Conrad →

Peutinger defended the usefulness of trading companies in the political sphere, Martin Luther used biblical and popular arguments to mount a vigorous attack on the "damned Fuggers." The Fuggers' piety was directed to reforms in the Augsburg parishes, to charitable foundations (e.g., the provision of social dwellings in the "Fuggerei," which the family still supports today), and to artistic commissions (e.g., the first Renaissance church in Germany, the Fugger chapel at St. Anne's in Augsburg). With the exception of Ulrich II the Younger (1526-1584), who was a Protestant, the Fuggers promoted the Counter-Reformation in a discreet manner typical of humanistic circles in the imperial cities. In particular, they supported Peter → Canisius and the Jesuit college which was founded in 1581. Marx Fugger ("governor" from 1560 to 1597) translated one volume of Caesar Baronius's church history. One general of the League came from this family (Ottheinrich, 1592-1644), as well as one bishop of Constance (Jakob, 1567-1626) and two bishops of Regensburg (Sigmund Friedrich, 1542-1600, and Anton Ignaz, 1711-1787). They supported Renaissance music, the arts, and sciences over a long period.

■ **Literature:** *Fuggerorum et Fuggerarum Imagines* (Augsburg, 1618); *F.-Archiv Dillingen und Studien zur F.-Geschichte,* 36 vols. to date (Dillingen, 1907ff.); G. von Pölnitz, *Jakob F.,* 2 vols. (Tübingen, 1949–51); N. Lieb, *Die F. und die Kunst,* 2 vols. (Munich, 1952–58); G. von Pölnitz, *Anton F.,* 3 vols. (Tübingen, 1958–86); G. Lutz, "Marx F. und die Annales Ecclesiastici des Baronius," in *Baronico Storico e la Controriforma* (Sora, 1982) 423–545; G. von Pölnitz, *Die F.* (Tübingen, ⁵1990); H. Kellenbenz, *Die F. in Spanien und Portugal,* 2 vols. (Munich, 1990); B. Bushart, *Die F.-Kapelle bei St. Anna in Augsburg* (Munich, 1994); *Anton F. (1493–1560). Das 500jährige Jubiläum,* ed. J. Burkhardt (Weissenhorn, 1994).

JOHANNES BURKHARDT

■ **Additional Bibliography:** F. Thoma, "Jakob F.," in *Bayerische Profile,* ed. P. Gauweiler (Munich, 1995) 27–47; *Augsburger Handelshäuser im Wandel des historischen Urteils,* ed. J. Burkhardt (Berlin, 1996) (additional studies); F. Herre, *The Age of the F.s* (Augsburg, 2002).

Fundamental Articles. This concept first appears in 16th-century Protestantism, but similar expressions are found in contemporary Catholic theologians too, and it has clear roots in the Catholic tradition. Various Protestant authors have been identified as the first to discuss this subject:

Jacobus → Acontius (*Stratagemata Satanae,* 1565), Matthias Hafenreffer (*Loci theologici,* 1600), or Jean Calvin (*Institutio,* 1556); the origins of the doctrine of fundamental articles have also been discerned in the *Loci theologici* of Johann Gerhard (1610-1622).

This concept makes a differentiation among the "articles" or "individual doctrines" within the doctrine of faith as a whole: not all have equal importance. Scholasticism had taught that the faith of simple persons, provided that it was attached to the church, shared in the totality of the faith (as *fides implicita*), and the 16th-century theologians assumed the existence of a basic "stock" of faith which covered everything necessary for salvation. The soteriological perspective is in the foreground here: in order to be saved, it is not necessary that the Christian should know all the truths of the faith, still less that one confess them all explicitly. As in earlier centuries, these theologians were convinced that there is an inherent structure in the faith which not only makes it possible, but actually necessary, to demonstrate that the center of everything is God in Christ Jesus. During the Reformation period and afterwards, the reference to the fundamental articles was intended to ensure that the basic truths of the faith (*articuli fidei fundamentales*) were indeed preserved in one's own confession, and at the same time to demonstrate that a basis existed for the unification of Christendom. This makes the question of church unity a guiding principle in the elaboration of this doctrine, first from a purely apologetic perspective, but later from a genuinely ecumenical position.

■ *LThK*³ 4:223 (unabridged version).
■ **Literature:** H. Meyer, "Überlegungen zum Gedanken und zur Lehre von den 'F.,'" in *In Verantwortung für den Glauben.* Festschrift H. Fries (Freiburg, 1992) 267–77.

HARALD WAGNER

■ **Additional Bibliography:** *RGG*⁴ 3:412ff.

G

Gallus (Gall, Hahn), *Nikolaus.* Lutheran theologian, reformer of Regensburg, born 1516 in Köthen (Anhalt), died 1570 in Bad Liebenzell. He began his studies in Wittenberg in 1530, taking the

degree of master of arts in 1537. He became head of the municipal school in Mansfeld in 1540, and was deacon in Regensburg from 1543 to 1548, until he was obliged to leave the city because of the → Augsburg Interim. He moved to Magdeburg, where he became an adherent of Matthias → Flacius. He was appointed superintendent in Regensburg in 1553, and supported Protestantism in the Habsburg territories. As a → Gnesio-lutheran, he attacked Philipp Melanchthon and the Philippists, Georg Major, the Interim (→ Adiaphora controversy), and participation in the third conciliar period in Trent.

■ **Works:** *VD 16* 7:250–317.
■ **Literature:** *NDB* 6:55f.; *DHGE* 19:900f.; *TRE* 12:21ff.—H. Vogt, *N. G.* (Neustadt [Aisch], 1977); R. Kolb, "The German Lutheran Reaction to the Third Period of the Council of Trent," *Luther-Jahrbuch* 51 (1984) 63–95.

BARBARA HENZE

■ **Additional Bibliography:** P. Schmid, "N. G.: der Organisator der lutherischen Gemeinde Regensburg," in *Berühmte Regensburger,* ed. K. Dietz and G. H. Waldherr (Regensburg, 1997) 132–41; R. Kolb, "N. G.'s Critique of Philip Melanchthon's Teaching on the Freedom of the Will," *ARG* 91 (2000) 87–110.

Gardiner, *Stephen.* Canon lawyer and Greek scholar, born c. 1483, died November 12, 1555 in Whitehall. He taught at the university of Cambridge from 1525 onwards, and became bishop of Winchester in 1531. In keeping with the ideas of → Henry VIII, Gardiner supported the royal supremacy over the church (*De vera obedientia,* 1535). His rejection of Protestantism led to his imprisonment under → Edward VI. Under Queen → Mary I, he was lord chancellor and took part in negotiations for reconciliation with Rome.

■ **Works:** *Three Political Tracts by S. G.,* ed. P. Janelle (Cambridge 1930; reprint, New York, 1968); *The Letters of S. G.,* ed. J. A. Muller (Cambridge, 1933; reprint, Westport, Conn., 1970).
■ **Literature:** *The Oxford Dictionary of the Christian Church* (London, ²1974) 549.—J. A. Muller, *S. G. and the Tudor Reaction* (London, 1926; reprint, New York, 1970); G. Redworth, *In Defence of the Church Catholic. The Life of S. G.* (Oxford, 1990).

WOLFGANG PALAVER

■ **Additional Literature:** J. B. Bates, "S. G.'s 'Explication' and the Identity of the Church," *Anglican and Episcopal History* 72 (2003) 22–54.

Gebwiler, *Hieronymus*. Humanist, educational reformer, historian, born 1473 in Kaysersberg, died June 21, 1545 in Hagenau. He studied in Basle and Paris, where he took the degree of master of arts in 1495, and was the head of excellent schools in the Upper Rhineland in decisively important decades: Breisach (1498-1501), Schlettstadt (1501-1509), the cathedral school in Strasbourg (1509-1524), and St. George's school in Hagenau (from 1525). He was a friend of Johann → Geiler von Kaysersberg and Jakob → Wimpfeling, and published classical and contemporary works for use in schools. His interests as a historian were local and Habsburg history. He wrote against the Reformation, and translated → Erasmus of Rotterdam.

■ **Works:** *Die Straßburger Chronik des elsässischen Humanisten H. G.,* ed. K. Stenzel (Berlin and Leipzig, 1926).—Catalogue: F. Ritter, Répertoire bibliographique des livres imprimés en Alsace aux XVe et XVIe siècles (Strasbourg, 1937–60), vol. 2 nos. 940–45, vol. 4 nos. 1823–31; *VD 16* 7:593–604.

■ **Literature:** *ADB* 8:846f.; *DHGE* 20:235f.; *CEras* 2:81f.; *Literaturlexikon. Autoren und Werke deutscher Sprache,* ed. W. Killy, vol. 4 (Gütersloh and Munich, 1989) 94f.; *BDG* n. 6938–42; *Nouveau Dictionnaire de biographie alsacienne,* vol. 2 (Strasbourg, 1987) 1132f.—Ch. Schmidt, *Histoire littéraire d'Alsace,* vol. 2 (Paris, 1879, reprint, Hildesheim, 1966) 159–73 407–11; J. Knepper, *Jakob Wimpfeling* (Freiburg, 1902); idem, *Das Schul- und Unterrichtswesen im Elsaß* (Strasbourg, 1905); *Die Amerbachkorrespondenz,* ed. A. Hartmann, vol. 1 (Basle, 1942); E. Kleinschmidt, *Herrscherdarstellung* (Berne and Munich, 1974); H. Holeczek, *Erasmus deutsch,* vol. 1 (Stuttgart-Bad Cannstatt, 1983); Jakob Wimpfeling, *Briefwechsel,* ed. O. Herding and D. Mertens (Munich, 1990).

DIETER MERTENS

Geiler von Kaysersberg, *Johannes*. Preacher, born March 16, 1445 in Schaffhausen, died March 10, 1510 in Strasbourg. He studied in Freiburg (master of arts, 1463-1464) and Basle (doctor of theology, 1475). He became professor of theology in Freiburg in 1476 and was preacher in the Strasbourg Minster from 1478 to 1510. All his surviving works come from his period as preacher; only a few, such as his translation of Jean Gerson, were published by Geiler von Kaysersberg himself. The great collections of sermons, a high point in late medieval homiletic literature, were published between 1508 and 1522 (i.e., before the Reformation was introduced in Strasbourg), based partly

on his own Latin notes (edited by Jakob → Otter and others) and partly on notes taken in German by his hearers (edited by Johannes Pauli and others). Following Gerson, he appeals for a church reform based primarily on the secular clergy and the bishops, involving instruction, synods, and visitations. The clear moral-pedagogical impulse which directs his criticism of his age links him with fellow campaigners such as Jakob → Wimpfeling and Sebastian → Brant. → Paul IV placed his works on the Index in 1559.

■ **Works:** L. Dacheux, *Les plus anciens écrits de Geiler de Kaysersberg* (Colmar, 1882; German trans. Freiburg, 1882, reprinted Amsterdam, 1965); J. G., *Sämtliche Werke,* vol. 1ff., ed. G. Bauer (Berlin, 1989ff.)—Catalogue: F. Ritter, *Répertoire bibliographique des livres imprimés en Alsace aux XVe et XVIe siècles* (Strasbourg, 1937–60), vol. 1 no. 177, vol. 2 nos. 947–86, vol. 3 nos. 284–86, vol. 4 nos. 1010, 1832–59; *VD 16* 7:712–826.

■ **Literature:** *ADB* 8:509–18; *RGG*³ 2:1266f.; *NDB* 6:150f.; *DSp* 6:174–79; *Die deutsche Literatur des Mittelalters. Verfasserlexikon,* vol. 2, ed. W. Stammler (Berlin and Leipzig, 1936) 1141–52; *DHGE* 20:251–56; *TRE* 12:159–62; *Literaturlexikon. Autoren und Werke in deutscher Sprache,* ed. W. Killy, vol. 4 (Gütersloh and Munich, 1989) 100f.; *LMA* 4:1174f.; *Nouveau Dictionnaire de biographie alsacienne,* vol. 2 (Strasbourg, 1987) 1136–39.—E. J. Dempsey Douglass, *Justification in Late Medieval Preaching* (Leiden, 1966); Jakob Wimpfeling/Beatus Rhenanus, *Das Leben des J. G.,* ed. O. Herding (Munich, 1970); F. Rapp, *Réformes et réformation à Strasbourg* (Paris, 1974); H. Kraume, *Die Gerson-Übersetzung G.s* (Munich, 1980); Jakob Wimpfeling, *Briefwechsel,* ed. O Herding and D. Mertens (Munich, 1990).

DIETER MERTENS

■ **Additional Bibliography:** *RGG*⁴ 3:554.—U. Israel, *J. G. Der Straßburger Münsterprediger als Rechtsreformer* (Berlin, 1997); B. Hamm, "Between Severity and Mercy: Three Models of Pre-Reformation Urban Preaching," in *Continuity and Change,* Festschrift H. Oberman (Leiden, 2000) 321–58.

Geneva Catechism. Written by Jean Calvin in 1541, this appeared in French in 1542, and in Latin three years later with a new dedication by Calvin to the pastors of East Frisia. It contains 373 questions and answers in four main sections: On faith (§§ 1-130), On the law (§§ 131-232), On prayer (§§ 233-295), and On the sacraments (§§ 296-373). It was further subdivided in 1548 into 55 chapters, so that it could be worked through in its entirety, week for week, in the course of a year. The order of the first two main sections reverses the sequence of law and faith which Calvin had adopted from Martin Luther in the first version of his *Institutio* (1536); here he follows Martin → Bucer. This developed into the Reformed emphasis on the *tertius usus legis* (*usus in renatis*), while Lutheranism gave priority to the *usus primus* (*usus elenchticus;* → law and gospel). This catechism was widely diffused during Calvin's own lifetime, thanks to translations into Italian, Spanish, Greek, Hebrew, English, and German, but it was only in French-speaking areas that it became *the* Reformed catechism. It is, however, a classic Reformed → confessional document and an excellent synthesis of Calvin's doctrine.

■ **Editions:** *Bekenntnisschriften und Kirchenordnungen der nach Gottes Wort reformierten Kirche,* ed. W. Niesel (Zurich, n.d.; French trans., ³1938); *Calvini Opera Selecta,* vol. 2, ed. P. Barth and W. Niesel (Munich, 1952) 59–151 (Latin); *Reformierte Bekenntnisschriften und Kirchenordnungen in deutscher Übersetzung,* ed. P. Jacobs (Neukirchen-Vluyn, 1949) 11–71.
■ **Literature:** E. Saxer, "Der Genfer Katechismus von 1545," in *Calvin, Studienausgabe,* vol. 2, ed. E. Busch et al. (introduction and major parts 1 and 2, Latin and German) (Neukirchen-Vluyn, 1997).

ALASDAIR I. C. HERON

■ **Additional Bibliography:** *RGG*⁴ 3:671.—I. J. Hesselink, *Calvin's First Catechism* (Louisville, Ky., 1997).

Gentile, *Giovanni Valentino.* Italian humanist and antitrinitarian, born c. 1530 in Cosenza (Calabria), died September 10, 1566 in Berne. He fled in 1556 or 1557 to Geneva, where he joined the Italian refugee community and came under the influence of Matteo Gribaldi. His rejection of the scholastic concept of "substance" led him to a subordinationist understanding of the Trinity; this provoked conflict with Genevan orthodoxy. After he had been arrested several times, Gentile worked in Poland from 1563 on, but was obliged to leave the country as a consequence of the Edict of Parczów (1564). He went to Berne, where he was condemned for blaspheming against the Trinity and beheaded.

■ **Literature:** *HDThG* 3:58; *DHGE* 20:512f.—L. Hein, *Italienische Protestanten und ihr Einfluß auf die Reformation in Polen während der beiden Jahrzehnte vor dem Sandomirer Konsens* (1570) (Leiden, 1974) 169–84.

MICHAEL BECHT

George III of Anhalt-Dessau ("the saintly"). Born August 15, 1507 in Dessau, where he died October 17, 1553. He studied canon law in Leipzig, and was an autodidact in theological studies. He became cathedral canon in Merseburg in 1518 and was ordained priest in 1524, becoming cathedral provost in Magdeburg and archdeacon of the territory of Köthen. In 1544, he became coadjutor in spiritual matters to the secular administrator of the diocese of Merseburg, Duke August of Saxony; Martin Luther ordained him bishop in 1545. The Reformation of the cathedral chapter was his work. After the cathedral chapter yielded to the insistence of Emperor → Charles V and elected Michael → Helding as bishop, George withdrew in 1550 to Warmsdorf castle in Anhalt. He exchanged letters with Luther, but the influence of Philipp Melanchthon and the → Confessio Augustana was more lasting. In his ideas about the church (cf. his synodal rules, the twelfth of which is by Caspar → Cruciger), he developed reflections by Melanchthon; his own theology is that of the Leipzig Interim.

■ **Literature:** *RE*³ 6, 521f.; *NDB* 6:197; *RGG*³ 2:1394f.; *BBKL* 2:210f.; *DHGE* 20:589f.—E. Sehling, *Die Kirchengesetzgebung unter Moritz von Sachsen 1544–49 und G. III. von Anhalt* (Leipzig, 1899); N. Müller, "Beziehungen zwischen den Kurfürsten Joachim I. und II. von Brandenburg und G. III. von Anhalt in den Jahren 1534–40," *Jahrbuch für Brandenburgische Kirchengeschichte* 4 (1907); idem, *Fürst G.s III. des Gottseligen von Anhalt schriftstellerische Tätigkeit 1530–38, ungedruckte Quellenschriften zur Geschichte des 16.Jh.* (Leipzig and New York, 1907); F. Westphal, *Fürst G. der Gottselige von Anhalt* (Dessau, 1907; Leipzig, ²1922); J. Herrmann, "Augsburg, Leipzig, Passau. Das Leipziger Interim nach Akten des Landeshauptarchivs Dresden 1547–52" (diss., Leipzig, 1952); F. Lau, "G. III. von Anhalt," *Wissenschaftliche Zeitschrift der Karl-Marx-Universität Leipzig,* 3 (1953/54) 139–52.

RUDOLF JOPPEN

■ **Additional Bibliography:** *RGG*⁴ 3:693.—*Reformation in Anhalt. Melanchthon—Fürst G. III.,* ed. der Evangelischen Landeskirche Anhalts (Dessau, 1997); T. J. Wengert, "Certificate of Ordination (1545) for G. von Anhalt, Coadjutor Bishop of Merseburg," *Lutheran Quarterly* 16 (2002) 229–33.

George of Brandenburg-Ansbach and Kulmbach ("the Pious"). Marquis 1515-1543, born March 4, 1484 in Ansbach, died December 27, 1543. He ruled jointly with his brother, Marquis Kasimir, from 1515 to 1527. He purchased the principalities of Jägerndorf, Ratibor, and Oppeln in Upper Silesia in 1523, and introduced the Reformation there at once; he had to wait in Ansbach-Kulmbach until 1528, soon after he became the sole ruler. In imperial politics, he was a champion of the Lutheran Reformation. In 1529, he was a signatory of the celebrated protest in Speyer, and he signed the → Confessio Augustana in Augsburg in 1530. His promulgation (together with Nuremberg) of the church order for Brandenburg and Nuremberg established the basis for the Lutheran Church in Franconia; this church order had immense influence, and became the prototype of liturgically, pastorally, and constitutionally conservative Lutheran Church orders in the rest of the 16th century. (Its influence can be demonstrated on the church orders in Württemberg, Baden, Palatinate-Neuburg, the electoral Palatinate, electoral Brandenburg, East Prussia, etc.) In his capacity as local ruler, George did not have images and altars destroyed, but he made it impossible for Catholic institutions and monasteries to continue in existence. He ruthlessly seized church property, partly in order to pay the debts incurred by members of his family.

■ Literature: *NDB* 6:204f.; *DHGE* 20:599ff.—K. Schornbaum, *Zur Politik des Markgrafen G. von Brandenburg* (Munich, 1906); J. B. Götz, *Die Glaubensspaltung in der Markgrafschaft Ansbach-Kulmbach* (Freiburg, 1907); K. Schornbaum, *Aktenstücke zur ersten Brandenburgischen Kirchenvisitation* (Munich, 1928).

ERNST WALTER ZEEDEN

■ **Additional Bibliography:** I. Gundermann, "Markgraf G. der Fromme von Ansbach," *Jahrbuch für schlesische Kirchengeschichte* 73 (1994) 205–54.

George III of Saxony ("the Bearded").

Born August 27, 1471, the son of Albrecht the Brave and Sidonia Podiebrad, died April 17, 1539. He was duke and sole ruler of Albertine Saxony from 1500, and reorganized the administration with great care and success. He promoted economic growth and attempted many times to reform the university of Leipzig. He was initially opposed to Johann → Tetzel's sermons about indulgences, and supported the disputation of → Leipzig in 1519, but the theologically educated Duke developed from the end of 1519 into a vigorous opponent of Martin Luther and the Reformation, which he fought with both governmental measures and literary works—pamphlets which he himself wrote against Luther, and books by Johannes → Cochlaeus, Hieronymus → Emser, Augustin von → Alveldt, etc. This made Leipzig an important center of anti-Reformation publishing until 1539. George corresponded with → Erasmus of Rotterdam and was a committed church reformer. From 1535 onwards, he attempted by means of visitations of monasteries by the territorial government and with the aid of reform projects drawn up by humanist counselors and theologians to ensure that the Reformation could not be introduced into Albertine Saxony after his own death; but in this he was unsuccessful.

■ Works: *VD 16* 7:551f.; Köhler *BF* I/1:552–58.

■ Literature: *TRE* 12:385–89; *DHGE* 20:661ff.; *CEras* 3:205–8; *TRZRK* 2³:8–32.—F. Gess, ed., *Akten und Briefe zur Kirchenpolitik Herzog G.s von Sachsen,* 2 vols. (Leipzig, 1905–17, reprinted 1985); J. Pflug, *Correspondance,* ed. J. V. Pollet, vol. 1–5 (Leiden, 1969–82); H. Smolinsky, *A. von Alveldt und H. Emser* (Münster, 1983); G. Wartenberg, "Zum 'Erasmianismus' am Dresdener Hof G.s des Bärtigen," *Nederlands Archief voor Kerkgeschiedenis* 66 (1986) 2–16; H. Junghans, ed., *Das Jahrhundert der Reformation in Sachsen* (Berlin, 1989); H. Smolinsky, "Aspekte altgläubiger Theologie im albertinischen Sachsen in der Reformationszeit bis 1542," *Herbergen der Christenheit. Jahrbuch für deutsche Kirchengeschichte* 18 (1993/1994) 29–43.

HERIBERT SMOLINSKY

Gerbel, *Nikolaus* (known as Musophilus).

Humanist, born c. 1485 in Pforzheim, died January 20, 1560 in Strasbourg. After studies in Vienna, Cologne (where he took the degree of master of arts in 1508), Tübingen, and Bologna (where he became doctor of canon law in 1514), he began work as a lawyer in the service of the church in Strasbourg in 1515. He also edited and published humanist writings. As an adherent of Martin Luther, Gerbel was not on good terms with Wolfgang → Capito and Martin → Bucer; they diverged especially on the doctrine of the Lord's Supper. He was professor of history at the grammar school in Strasbourg from 1541 to 1543.

■ **Principal Works:** *In descriptionem Graeciae Sophiani praefatio* (Basle, 1545 [commentary on the maps of Greece of Nikolaos Sophianos]; expanded edition: *Pro declaratione picturae siue descriptionis Graeciae Sophiani libri septem* [Basle, 1550]).

■ **Literature:** *CEras* 2:90f.; *Nouveau dictionnaire de*

biographie alsacienne 12 (Strasbourg, 1988) 1153ff.—J. Rott, "L'humaniste N. G. et son diaire 1522–29," in idem, *Investigationes historicae*, vol. 2 (Strasbourg, 1986) 313–22; T. Kaufmann, *Die Abendmahlstheologie der Straßburger Reformatoren bis 1528* (Tübingen, 1992).

PETER WALTER

Gerstmann, *Martin von.* Bishop of Breslau (1574), born March 8, 1527 in Bunzlau, died May 23, 1585 in Neisse. He was brought up as a Lutheran, but converted to Catholicism between 1556 and 1561. He was made cathedral custodian in Breslau in 1561, cathedral canon and chancellor in Olmütz in 1565, counselor and secretary to Emperor → Maximilian II in 1569, and cathedral dean in Breslau in 1571. During his time as bishop, Gerstmann energetically promoted the enforcement of the decisions of the Council of Trent.

■ Literature: *NDB* 6:328.—E. Brzoska, *975-Jahr-Feier des Fürstbistums und der Erzdiözese Breslau* (Wiesbaden, 1977) 33; W. Marschall, *Geschichte des Bistums Breslau* (Stuttgart, 1980) 72f., 102; *Geschichte Schlesiens,* vol. 2 (Sigmaringen, 1988) 30, 34f.; *Archiv für schlesische Kirchengeschichte* 15 (1957) 175–88; 37 (1979) 198; 38 (1980) 258, 268; 39 (1981) 99, 284; 40 (1982) 121; 44 (1986) 9, 82; 46 (1988) 78, 82, 88; 50 (1992) 181.

PAUL MAI

Geusen. (From the French *gueux,* "beggar"), originally a mocking nickname, later the self-designation of the party of Dutch noblemen who opposed the violent rule and the religious policies of Spain in the Netherlands. The name is said to have originated on April 5, 1566, when a petition was presented to the vicereine, → Margaret of Parma, asking for the abolition of the Inquisition, and one of her counselors remarked contemptuously: "What a fine collection of beggars!" The name was immediately adopted as a war cry in the rebellion against Spain. The "Wilhelmus" song (now the Dutch national anthem) is one of the battle songs known as the "Geusen songs." During the German occupation (1940-1945), resistance groups took up the name "Geusen" anew.

■ Literature: *RGG*[3] 2:1541; *DHGE* 22:744ff.; *TRZRK* 3:200–35.—J. D. M. Cornelissen, *Waarom zij geuzen werden genoemd* (Tilburg, 1936); J. C. A. de Meij, *De Watergeuzen en de Nederlanden 1568–72* (Amsterdam and London, 1972).

PETER J. A. NISSEN

Giberti, *Gian Matteo.* Bishop of Verona, pre-Tridentine reformer, born September 20, 1495 in Palermo, died December 29, 1543 in Verona. Little is known about his studies. He became secretary to Cardinal Giulio de' Medici (later → Clement VII). Under → Leo X, he received influential curial offices and numerous ecclesiastical benefices. Clement VII appointed him datary, and he became bishop of Verona on August 8, 1524. Giberti was Clement's special confidant and had a decisive influence on the anti-imperial policy of this pope; but after the collapse of this policy in the → Sack of Rome (1527), Giberti withdrew to his diocese, where he pursued an active reform course. He conducted pastoral visitations, took measures to promote instruction and a general deepening of the religious life of the people, reformed the monasteries, and dedicated particular intention to raising the spiritual and pastoral level of the clergy. This required the strengthening of his episcopal authority against tough resistance, especially on the part of the cathedral chapter. Education and continuing study were his favored instrument in the creation of a suitable clergy. He was not motivated by the idea of a return to the past; on the contrary, he was influenced by the ideas of Italian → Evangelism (which emphasized the Bible and the patristic writings), and he had personal contacts with a number of important representatives of this movement. In 1536, → Paul III made him a member of the reform commission which elaborated the *Consilium de emendanda ecclesia* (1537).

■ Works: *Opera,* ed. P. und G. Ballerini (Verona 1733; editio altera, Hostilia, 1740).

■ Literature: *DHGE* 20:1241–46.—G. B. Pighi, *G. M. G.* (Verona, 1900, [2]1924); P. Paschini, *S. Gaetano Thiene* (Rome, 1926) passim; A. Grazioli, *G. M. G.* (Verona, 1955); H. Jedin, "Das Bischofsideal der Katholischen Reformation," in *Kirche des Glaubens, Kirche der Geschichte,* vol. 2 (Freiburg, 1966) 87–91; A. Prosperi, *Tra Evangelismo e Controriforma: G. M. G.* (Rome, 1969); Jedin 1[3], passim; C. Dionisotti, *Machiavellerie* (Turin, 1980); A. Fasani, ed., *Riforma pretridentina della diocesi di Verona,* vol. 1: *Visite pastorali del Vescovo G. M. G.* (Vicenza, 1989).

KLAUS GANZER

Giese, *Tiedemann.* Irenic theologian in Ermland, born June 1, 1480 in Danzig, died October 23, 1550 in Heilsberg. He studied in Leipzig from 1492 to 1499, taking the degree of master of arts, and became cathedral canon in Ermland in 1507. He acquired experience in the administration of the diocese of Ermland and in the politics of Prussia; he was a friend of Nicolaus Copernicus. He was bishop of Kulm from 1538 to 1549, and bishop of Ermland from 1549 to 1550. He composed the *Antilogikon flosculorum Lutheranorum* (Krakow, 1525), an irenic refutation of the Lutheran doctrine of justification as put forward by Johannes → Briesmann. He sympathized with the Christian humanism of → Erasmus of Rotterdam. As bishop, he took action against the Protestants, but he used moderation and attempted to persuade them, since he hoped that the unity of the church might be restored.

■ **Literature:** T. Borawska, *T. G. (1480–1550) w życiu wewnętrznym Warmii i Prus Królewskich* (Olsztyn, 1984), German summary on pp. 391–98.

ERNST MANFRED WERMTER

Gil (Egidio), *Juan.* Preacher and alleged founder of the Protestant parish in Seville, born c. 1500 in Olvés near Saragossa, died November 22, 1555 in Seville. He studied theology under Domingo de → Soto in Alcalá from 1525 to 1531, and became professor of theology at the same university in 1531. He became cathedral canon in Seville in 1537, dedicating himself exclusively to his office of preacher. He belonged to the circle of humanists who sympathized with the Reformation. His pupils included the Protestants Antonio del → Corro, Cipriano de → Valera, and Casiodoro de → Reina. Immediately after his appointment as bishop of Tortosa (1549), he and Constantino → Ponce de la Fuente were delated to the Inquisition. Since Gil revoked a number of theses, he escaped with a mild sentence. After his death, this sentence was revised, and Gil was condemned as a heretic; his corpse was exhumed and burned at the stake. No writings survive.

■ **Literature:** *DHEE* supplement vol. 1:363–66.—M. Menéndez Pelayo, *Historia de los heterodoxos españoles,* vol. 4 (Santander, 1947) 77–82; V. Beltrán de Heredia, *Domingo de Soto* (Madrid, 1961) 415–32, 645–55; M. Bataillon, *Erasmo y España* (México, 1966) passim; K. Reinhardt, *Bibelkommentare spanischer Autoren,* vol. 1 (Madrid, 1990) 183f.; J. C. Nieto, *El Renacimiento y la otra España* (Geneva, 1997) 189–216.

FERNANDO DOMÍNGUEZ

■ **Additional Literature:** R. C. Spach, "J. G. and Sixteenth-Century Spanish Protestantism," *SCJ* 26 (1995) 857–79.

Gnesiolutherans and Philippists. After Martin Luther's death, it was above all Philipp Melanchthon who determined the course of the Reformation. The Interim of → Augsburg (or of Leipzig), concluded between the emperor and the Protestant Estates in 1548, led to doctrinal conflicts within Protestantism. One group of theologians, especially Matthias → Flacius (after whom the group as a whole were sometimes called "Flacians"), Nikolaus von → Amsdorf, Nikolaus → Gallus, Johann → Wigand, Matthäus Judex, Kaspar Aquila, Joachim → Mörlin, Timotheus Kirchner, and Tilemann → Heshusius, called themselves "Lutherans," but have been given the additional qualification of "genuine" (*gnēsios* in Greek) "Lutherans" since the 17th century. They opposed Melanchthon's position ("Philippism") on six points:

1. *Adiaphora controversy.* Melanchthon had said that one could take an "indifferent" position vis-à-vis the hierarchy and customs of the Catholic Church, but the Gnesiolutherans maintained that there was no such thing as an *adiaphoron* in questions of the profession of faith.—2. *Majorist controversy,* called after Georg → Major, who had taught that good works were necessary for eternal beatitude; the Gnesiolutherans saw this as a denial of → justification by faith alone.—3. → *Antinomistic controversy.* Linked with the second point of conflict was the question about the validity and significance of the law (*nomos* in Greek) in the life of those reborn; here, the Gnesiolutherans held a variety of views.— 4. *Synergistic controversy.* Johannes → Pfeffinger and Victorinus → Strigel followed Melanchthon in holding that the human will collaborates (*synergeia*) in conversion, but the Gnesiolutherans insisted that the natural human being can do nothing with respect to his salvation.—5. *Osiandrist controversy,* called after Andreas → Osiander, who affirmed the "essential righteousness" of the new human being; here, the Gnesiolutherans and the Philippists both emphasized "imputed righteousness."—6. In the so-called *second* → *eucharistic controversy,* the Gnesiolutherans defended the real presence against what they saw as the → Crypto-Calvinism of the Philippists. It was only with the agreement on the Formula of → Concord in 1577 that the doctrinal disputes were to some extent resolved.

MICHAEL WITTIG

129

■ **Literature:** *RGG*[4] 3:1043.—S. Sterhle, "Imputatio iustitiae. Its Origins in Melanchthon, Its Opposition in Osiander," *Theologische Zeitschrift* 50 (1994) 201–19; J. Diestelmann, *Actio Sacramentalis* (Gross Oesingen, 1996); M. Richter, *Gesetz und Heil* (Göttingen, 1996); F. Buzzi, "Lutero contro l'antinomismo," *Annali di scienze religiose* 2 (1997) 81–106; P. T. Ferry, "Confessionalization and Popular Preaching. Sermons against Synergism in Reformation Saxony," *SCJ* 28 (1997) 1143–66; T. J. Wengert, "Georg Major Defender of Wittenberg's Faith and Melanchthonian Exegete," in *Melanchthon in seinen Schülern* (Wiesbaden, 1997) 129–55; I. Dingel, "Flacius als Schüler Luthers und Melanchthons," in *Vestigia pietatis*. Festschrift E. Koch (Leipzig, 2000) 77–92; P. F. Barton, "Heiliger Geist, Evangelium und Amt. Marginalien zum Gnesioluthertum," *Wiener Jahrbuch für Theologie* 3 (2000) 51–63; G. Martens, "Die Adiaphora als theologisches Problem," *Lutherische Beiträge* 5 (2000) 117–27.

■ **Additional Literature:** R. Kolb, "Altering the Agenda, Shifting the Strategy: The 'Grundfest' of 1571 as Philippist Programm for Lutheran Concord," *SCJ* 30 (1999) 705–26; D. M. Whitford, *Tyranny and Resistance: The Magdeburg Confession and the Lutheran Tradition* (St. Louis, 2001).

Góis (Goes), *Damião de*. Humanist and historian, born 1502 in Alenquer, died January 30, 1574 in Lisbon. He became a page at the royal court in 1511, and headed the Portuguese settlement in Antwerp from 1523. He traveled to central, northern, and eastern Europe, studying in Louvain, Freiburg, and Padua. He returned to Louvain in 1538 and took part in the defense of the city against the French in 1542. He was taken prisoner, and was kept at the court of → Francis I. He returned to Portugal in 1545, and worked as tutor to the princes, as archivist and as chronicler. His contacts with Philipp Melanchthon and → Erasmus of Rotterdam led the Inquisition to take proceedings against him in 1571; this ended in a mild sentence.

■ **Works:** *Pro Hispania adversus Munsterum defensio: Rerum Hispanicarum scriptores,* vol. 3 (Frankfurt/Main, 1579) 1243; *Fides, religio moresque Aethiopum* (Louvain 1540; German trans. Wiesbaden, 1994); *Chronica do Principe Dom Joam* (Lisbon, 1567), ed. G. Almeida Rodrigues (Lisbon, 1977); *Chronica do Felicissimo Rei Dom Emanuel,* 4 vols. (Lisbon, 1566–67; reprint, Coimbra, 1949– 55); *De captivitate sua,* ed. S. Schard, *Historicum opus,* vol. 4 (Basle, 1574) 1869–82.

■ **Literature:** *CEras* 2:113–17.—M. Bataillon, "Le cosmopolitanisme de D. de G.," in *Études sur le Portugal au temps de l'humanisme* (Coimbra, 1962) 149–96; E.

Feist Hirsch, *D. de G.* (The Hague, 1967); J. Veríssimo Serrão, *D. de G., historiador* (Lisbon, 1976); J. Alves Osório, "Em torno do humanismo de D. de G.," *Annali—Sezione Romanza dell'Istituto Universitario Orientale di Napoli* 18/2 (1976) 297–342; A. Torres, ed., *Noese e crise na epistolografia latina Goisiana,* 2 vols. (Paris, 1982).

FERNANDO DOMÍNGUEZ

■ **Additional Bibliography:** A. Novinsky, "Political Xionism in the Portuguese Renaissance (D. de G.)," in *Hesed ve-emet*. Festschrift E. S. Frerichs (Atlanta, Ga., 1998) 419–29; J. F. Tavares, *D. de G.* (Lisbon, 1999).

Gonzaga, (1) *Ercole*. Cardinal (1527), second son of Marquis Francesco Gonzaga and Isabella d'Este, born November 23, 1505 in Mantua, died March 3, 1563 in Trent. Through the abdication of his uncle Sigismondo in 1521, he became bishop of Mantua, but was ordained priest only in 1556 (and bishop in 1561). He began his humanistic studies in Bologna under Pietro Pomponazzi and Lazzaro Buonamici in 1522, receiving a good classical formation but with little knowledge of theology or canon law. He was a friend of Gasparo → Contarini and Jacopo → Sadoleto; he had contacts with the reforming bishop of Verona, Giovanni Matteo → Giberti, with Giovanni Pietro Carafa (later Pope → Paul IV), and with Reginald → Pole. During most of the pontificate of → Paul III, he was in Mantua, where he carried out church reform and studied theology under the Dominican Pietro → Bertano. He took part in five conclaves; in 1559, objections by Spain were put to his candidacy for the papal throne. From 1540 to 1561, he exercised the regency in Mantua for his nephews Francesco and Guglielmo, who were still minors. He promoted the traditional pro-imperial foreign policy of his dynasty, introduced rigorous measures to save money, and developed the Mantuan economy. Despite his reluctant protests, he was appointed legate to the Council of Trent in 1561, and prepared the work of the third period with Girolamo → Seripando (beginning on January 18, 1562). The question of the obligation of bishops to reside in their sees led to a crisis between the reformers and the curia, and the situation remained unresolved until after the deaths of Gonzaga and Seripando.

■ **Works:** *Catecismo overo instruttione delle cose pertinenti alla salute delle anime di commissione del Rev.mo et Ill.mo Card. di Mantova composto et pubblicato* *per la Città et Diocesi sua da Mons. Leonardo De Marini vescovo di Laodicea suo suffraganeo.* (Mantua, 1555); *Breve ricordo di mons. Ill.mo et Rev.mo Mons. Hercole G., card. di Mantova delle cose spettanti alla vita de' chierici, al governo delle chiese et alla cura delle anime di questo vescovato di Mantova* (Mantua, 1561).

(2) *Giulia.* Born 1513 in Gazzuolo, died April 16, 1566 in Naples, daughter of Ludovico Gonzaga-Sabbioneta and Francesca Fieschi. She married Vespasiano Colonna in August, 1526, becoming countess of Fondi and duchess of Trajetta; she was widowed in 1528. She was celebrated for her beauty and her intellectual gifts, and gathered a circle of artists and scholars around her in Fondi (Ludovico Ariosto, Torquato Tasso, Sebastiano Piombo, Titian, etc.). After 1537, she had contacts in Naples with Catholic reformers (Girolamo → Seripando, Reginald → Pole, Ercole Gonzaga [see (1) above], Vittoria Colonna), but also to Bernardino → Ochino, Juan de → Valdés, Marc Antonio Flaminio and Pietro → Carnesecchi, who sympathized with the Reformation; although she aroused the suspicion of the Inquisition, she was left in peace.

(3) *Ludovico* (Louis de Gonzague). Duke of Nevers, third son of Federico II, born September 18, 1539 in Mantua, died October 23, 1595 in Nesle. He was at the French court from 1549, and inherited the properties of his grandmother, Anne d'Alençon; he became a naturalized Frenchman in 1550. Through his marriage to Henriette de Clèves in 1565, he became duke of Nevers and Rethel, and Pair de France in 1566. He was counselor to Catharine de → Medici and to the duke of Anjou, and shared responsibility for St. → Bartholomew's Eve. He was involved in the revival of the Catholic League in 1585, but soon dissociated himself from the policy of the → Guise family. He was governor of Picardy and Champagne in 1588-1589. Initially, he was neutral vis-à-vis → Henry IV of Navarre, but supported him from 1590. At the end of 1593, he went to Rome in order to receive absolution for Henry IV from Clement VIII, thereby paving the way for reconciliation between the pope and the king.

■ *LThK*³ 4:833–836 (unabridged version).
■ **Literature:** *On 1:* W. Friedensburg, "Der Briefwechsel Gasparo Contarinis mit E. G.," *QFIAB* 2 (1899) 161–222; G. Drei, "Per la storia del Concilio di Trento. Lettere inedite del segretario Camillo Olivo (1562),"

Archivio storico italiano 74 (1916) 246–87; idem, "La politica di Pio IV e del card. E. G.," *Archivio della Società di Storia Patria* 40 (1917) 65–115; idem, "Il card. E. G. alla presidenza del Concilio di Trento," *Archivio della Società di Storia Patria* 40 (1917) 205–45; 41 (1918) 171–222; idem, "La corrispondenza del card. E. G. presidente del concilio di Trento (1562–63)," *Archivio storico per le provincie Parmensi* 17 (1917) 185–242; 18 (1918) 29–143; J. F. Montesinos, *Cartas inéditas de Juan de Valdés al Card. G.* (Madrid, 1931); A. Cocconcelli, *La rivalità dei G. coi Farnese e la riconciliazione voluta da Pio IV a mezzo di San Carlo Borromeo e del Card. di Mantova* (Reggio Emilia, 1937); H. Jedin, "Il figlio di Isabella d'Este: il card. E. G.," *Humanitas* 3 (1946) 370–80; German in *Kirche des Glaubens—Kirche der Geschichte,* vol. 1 (Freiburg, 1966) 195–205; M. Mazzocchi, "Aspetti della vita religiosa a Mantova nel carteggio fra il card. E. G. e il vescovo ausiliare (1561–63)," *Aevum* 33 (1959) 382–403.—*On 2:* B. Amante, *G. G., contessa di Fondi, ed il movimento religioso femminile nel secolo XVI* (Bologna, 1896); Ch. Hare, *Men and Women of the Italian Reformation* (London, 1914); Dominicus a S. Teresa, *Juan de Valdés* (Rome, 1957) 104–23, 404–9.—*On 3:* Marin Le Roy de Gomberville, *Mémoires du duc de Nevers* (Paris 1665); F.-H. Turpin (pseudonym: Henriques Pangrapho), *Histoire de Louis de Gonzague, duc de Nevers, pair de France* (Paris, 1788); J. Berger de Xivrey, *Lettres inédites de Henri IV au duc et à la duchesse de Nevers, 1589–95* (Nogent-le-Rotrou, 1900); E. Brambilla, *L. G., duca di Nevers, 1539–95* (Udine, 1906); *Die Hauptinstruktionen Clemens' VIII. für die Nuntien und Legaten an den europäischen Fürstenhöfen, 1592–1605,* vol. 1 (Tübingen, 1984) CCXXXVIf., 150–55.

KLAUS JAITNER

■ **Additional Bibliography:** *On 1:* R. Rezzaghi, *Il "Catecismo" di Leonardo de Marini: nel contesto della reforma pastorale del Card. E. G.* (Rome, 1986); L. Pescasio, *Cardinale E. G.* (Suzzara, 1999); P. V. Murphy, "A Worldly Reform. Honor and Pastoral Practice in the Career of Cardinal E. G.," *SCJ* 31 (2000) 399–418; P. V. Murphy, "Between 'Spirituali' and 'Intransigenti': Cardinal E. G. and Patrician Reform in Sixteenth-century Italy," *Catholic Historical Review* 88 (2002) 446–69.—*On 2:* Ch. Hare, *A Princess of the Italian Reformation: G. G.* (London, 1912); M. Oliva, *G. G. Colonna. Tra Rinascimento e Controriforma* (Milan, 1985).—*On 3:* A. Boltanski, "Réconcilier les catholiques et l'Etat: Louis de Gonzague et les dilemmes de la pacification du royaume à la fin du XVIᵉ siècle," in *Paix aux armes, paix des âmes* (Paris, 2000) 89–101.

Grace

1. According to the *Lutheran-Reformed understanding,* grace is an essential element in → justification, since salvation is bestowed on the human

person *sola gratia* ("by grace alone"). This so-called *particula exclusiva*—like the similar expressions → *sola fide* and → *sola scriptura*—indicates that the Reformation understanding of grace took shape in the context of controversial theology. The Reformation concept understands grace in a strictly personal sense, as God's loving "disposition" which leads him to turn "graciously" to the human person. Luther makes a fundamental differentiation in his book against Jacobus → Latomus (1521) when he distinguishes between *gratia* and *donum,* so that *gratia* designates God's love for us, not a quality of our soul (WA 8:106, 10), while *donum* is the gift of the renewing power of the Holy Spirit. This *donum* makes sin "mastered sin," but it cannot be considered the basis or reason for justification (in the sense of the verdict by which God's grace acquits us). The → Confessio Augustana expresses this fundamental differentiation between grace and the gift whereby the human person is renewed, and the mutual orientation of these two, when it defines justification, which is bestowed *gratis,* as *in gratiam recipi,* "being received into grace" (Art. IV). This position leaves no place for works in the event of justification (ApolCA, Art. 4); and this is the reason why the Formula of → Concord strictly refuses to include renewal by the Holy Spirit in the article about justification (*Solida Declaratio* 3:24f., 28). The Reformation formula *simul iustus et peccator* expresses the tension involved here: it signifies that the one who has received complete righteousness through God's gracious judgment continues to be sinful (the so-called "total aspect"), and also expresses the continuing sanctification of the one who nevertheless must struggle against sin throughout his life (the so-called "particular aspect").—In *Jean Calvin,* the transforming power of grace has a more central role (we find the term "grace" at *Inst* 3:9:6 and other texts).

ULRICH KÜHN

2. The *Council of Trent* goes some way to address the concern of the Reformers when it emphasizes the necessity of grace and subordinates the doctrine of grace to the doctrine of justification, without however reducing it to this dimension alone (DH 1520-1583). When the council speaks of the grace which awakens and helps the human person (DH 1525), the intention is to ensure the absolute priority of God's grace

before all human activity; at the same time, the council maintains the freedom of the human person (DH 1521, 1554f.) and the possibility of meritorious collaboration with grace (DH 1545-1549, 1582). The boundary drawn vis-à-vis the Reformation understanding of faith and the certainty of salvation (DH 1531f., 1562, 1533f., 1563-1566) corresponds to the polemical situation at that period; viewed from today's perspective, these demarcations tend rather to attest a substantial agreement. In the following period, the effects of grace in and on the human person (*gratia creata*) were emphasized (DH 1524, 1528-1531, 1561), in response to the suspicion that the Reformation viewed justification as changing nothing at all in the human person. This shift of emphasis was very influential, leading the Counter-Reformation theology of grace to concentrate on the anthropological aspect of grace, viz., on "created grace" and the ethical consequences of justification.

GISBERT GRESHAKE/EVA-MARIA FABER

■ *LThK*[3] 4:785ff. (1); 772–79 (2) (unabridged version).
■ **Literature:** E. Iserloh, "Gratia und Donum," in *Studien zur Geschichte und Theologie der Reformation.* Festschrift E. Bizer (Neukirchen-Vluyn, 1969) 141–56; O. H. Pesch and A. Peters, *Einführung in die Lehre von G. und Rechtfertigung* (Darmstadt, 1981, [3]1994); Th. Dieter, "L'origine de la controverse. Luther aux prises avec la doctrine du salut du Haut Moyen Age," *Positions luthériennes* 48 (2000) 359–72; J. Couenhoven, "Grace as Pardon and Power," *Journal of Religious Ethics* 28 (2000) 63–88.

■ **Additional Literature:** D. A. Campbell, "A Reformational Slogan on Ministry and Paul's Gospel of Grace," in *The Call to Serve* (Sheffield, 1996) 51–72; J. Wicks, "God and His Grace according to Luther 1509–1517," *Luther-Bulletin* 10 (2001) 83–107.

Granvella (Granvelle), (1) *Nicolas Perrenot de.* Statesman, born 1484 or 1486 in Ornans, died August 27, 1550 in Augsburg. He was the first state counselor of → Charles V, with responsibility for Burgundy, the Netherlands, and the empire. He enjoyed the confidence of the emperor, who appointed him his commissioner for the imperial parliament of Worms in 1540, which he opened. He presided at the religious dialogue in Worms and at the imperial parliament in Regensburg (1541), drawing up its conclusions. He took part in the opening session of the Council of Trent, and attempted in vain to persuade the Protestants to join in the Habsburg line of defense against the Turks and → Francis I of France.

■ **Literature:** *Biographie nationale,* ed. der Academie de Belgique, vol. 8, 185–97; *Nationaal Biografisch Woordenboek,* vol. 1, 572–76.—M. van Durme, "N.P. van G. en het protestantisme in Duitschland, 1530–1550," *Miscellanea Historica L. van der Essen,* vol. 1 (Brussels, 1947) 649–55; Jedin 2², passim.

BURKHARD ROBERG

■ **Additional Bibliography:** see 2 below.

(2) *Antoine Perrenot de.* Cardinal (1561) and statesman, son of (1), born August 26, 1517 in Besançon, died September 21, 1586 in Vallecas near Madrid. He was educated by Jean Sachet in the humanist spirit, and was a gifted linguist. He studied in Louvain and Padua. He became papal protonotary in 1529, and bishop of Arras in 1538; he was ordained priest in 1540, and bishop in 1543. After the death of his father, he became the most important counselor of Emperor → Charles V; in this capacity, he led many legations and strongly influenced the emperor's policy with regard to the council during the second period of Trent. As confidant of → Philip II of Spain in the Netherlands, he supported the vicereine, Margaret of Parma, and fought to prevent heterodox doctrines from entering the country (1555-1559). He supported the reorganization of the dioceses in the Netherlands (1559-1570), which was initiated by → Pius IV with the help of the king, and he exchanged the rich see of Arras for the metropolitan see of Mechelin, which had much poorer endowments. After he had made many enemies, the Spanish king advised him to move from Brussels to Besançon in 1564. From 1566, he was Philip's influential representative at the curia, and played a central role in the measures taken by the pope against Michael → Bajus. Granvella organized the alliance against the Turks; as papal legate, he dispatched the League's fleet under Don John of Austria from Naples to Lepanto in 1571. He was viceroy of Naples from 1571 to 1577, and often upheld the authority of the state against the archbishop and the nuncio. He took part as cardinal in the election of → Gregory XIII in 1572, but refused the new pope's offer of the position of grand penitentiary. He spent the last seven years of his life at the Spanish court, and was archbishop of his native city of Besançon in 1583-1584.

Granvella upheld the principles of the state government of the church vis-à-vis the curia and the hierarchy, and was a politician, rather than the embodiment of the Tridentine episcopal ideal. His accumulation of benefices has often been criticized but must seen against the background of the times; and the wealth acquired from this source allowed him to act, in the spirit of humanism, as a benefactor of education (university of → Douai; Platin's printing house) and patron of the arts.

■ **Sources:** Ch. Weiss, *Papiers d'état du Card. de G.,* 9 vols. (Paris, 1841–52); E. Poullet and Ch. Piot, *Correspondance du Card. de G.,* 12 vols. (Brussels, 1877–96); H. O. Evennett, "The Manuscripts of the Vargas-Granvelle Correspondence 1551–52," *JEH* 11 (1960) 219–24; M. van Durme, "Lettres inédits du Card. de G. à Ch. Plantin," *Gutenberg-Jahrbuch 1962,* 280–86; C. Gutiérrez, "Nueva documentación tridentina (1551–52)," *AHP* 1 (1963) 179f.; idem, *Trento: Un Concilio para la Unión (1550–1552).* (Madrid, 1981).

■ **Literature:** *Nationaal Biografisch Woordenboek,* 1:566–72; *DHGE* 21:1175–88.—L. Courchetet, *Histoire du card. de G.* (Paris, 1751); M. Philippson, *Ein Ministerium unter Philipp II. Kard. G. am spanischen Hofe (1579–86)* (Berlin, 1895); M. Dierickx, *De oprichting der nieuwe bisdommen in de Nederlanden onder Filips II, 1559–70* (Antwerp and Utrecht, 1950); M. van Durme, *Antoon Perrenot, bisschop van Atrecht, kardinaal van G., minister van Karel V en van Filips II, 1517–86* (Brussels, 1953); idem, *El card. G. (1517–86). Imperio y revolución bajo Carlos V y Felipe II* (Barcelona, 1957); H. Lutz, *Christianitas afflicta. Europa, das Reich und die päpstliche Politik im Niedergang der Hegemonie Karls V. (1552–56)* (Göttingen, 1964); Jedin 3² und 4, passim (index, s.v. Arras, Granvella); A. Puaux, *Madama fille de Charles-Quint (Marguerite de Parma), régente des Pays-Bas* (Paris, 1987); G. Jonnekin, *Le Card. de G. Un destin européen au XVIᵉ siècle* (Versailles, 1989); P. Postma, "Nieuw licht op een oude zaak. De oprichting van de nieuwe bisdommen in 1559," *Tijdschrift voor geschiedenis* 103 (1990) 10–27.

BURKHARD ROBERG

■ **Additional Bibliography:** *Le Granvelle et l'Italie au XVIᵉ siècle,* ed. J. Brunet (Besançon, 1996); C. Banz, *Höfisches Mäzenatentum in Brüssel* (Berlin, 2000); K. de Jonge, *Les Granvelles et les anciens Pays-Bas* (Louvain, 2000).

Gratius (van Graes), *Ortwinus.* Humanist, born c. 1480 in Holtwick (Westphalia), died May 22, 1542 in Cologne. He began his studies in Cologne in 1501, taking the degree of master of arts in 1506; from 1507, he taught at the faculty of arts there, and worked as corrector for the printing house of the Quentell brothers. He was ordained priest in 1514. He was a supported of Johannes → Pfefferkorn and became involved in his controversy with Johannes Reuchlin; the Letters of → Obscure Men were aimed chiefly at Gratius. His collection of writings on church reform, *Fasciculus rerum expetendarum ac fugiendarum* (Cologne, 1535), was placed on the Index in 1554.

■ **Works:** *Orationes quodlibeticae* (Cologne, 1508); *Lamentationes obscurorum virorum* (Cologne, 1518); *Epistola apologetica* (Cologne, 1518).

■ **Literature:** *DHGE* 21:1249; *CEras* 2:124f.—D. Reichling, *O. G.* (Heiligenstadt, 1884, reprinted Nieuwkoop, 1963 [bibliography]); K. G. Fellerer, "Zur 'Oratio de laudibus musicae disciplinae' des O. G.," *Kirchenmusikalisches Jahrbuch* 37 (1953) 43–47; J. Chomarat, "Les hommes obscurs et la poésie," in *L'humanisme allemand* (Paris and Munich, 1979) 261–83; J. V. Mehl, "O. G.' 'Orationes quodlibeticae,'" *Journal of Medieval and Renaissance Studies* 11 (1981) 57–69; J. H. Overfield, *Humanism and Scholasticism in Late Medieval Germany* (Princeton, N.J., 1984); J. V. Mehl, "O. G., Conciliarism, and the Call for Church Reform," *ARG* 76 (1985) 169–94; G. Chaix, "Le 'Fasciculus rerum expetendarum ac fugiendarum' d'O. G. et l'esprit reformateur à Cologne en 1535," in *Les réformes, enracinement socio-culturel* (Paris, 1985) 387–92; J. V. Mehl, "The First Printed Editions of the History of Church Councils," *AHC* 18 (1986) 128–43; G.-R. Tewes, *Die Bursen der Kölner Artistenfakultät bis zur Mitte des 16.Jh.* (Cologne, 1993).

PETER WALTER

Gravamina. The *Gravamina nationis germanicae* (a title first used in 1456) are the "complaints" of the empire and the imperial church against the pope and the curia. On the basis of the concordat of Vienna (1448), a distinction is made between *gravamina* by the clergy, the cities, and official imperial parliaments. These complaints were leveled above all at Roman administrative and taxation praxis, as well as against the procedures entailed by ecclesiastical trials. The first official *gravamen*, the Pamphlet of Mainz in 1451, was followed by others: in 1455 (at the provincial synod of Mainz in Aschaffenburg, 13 articles); the twelve *avisamenta* of Frankfurt in 1456; the *gravamina* of the imperial parliament at Frankfurt in 1458; the 26 *gravamina* of the united clergy of the three Rhineland church provinces at Coblenz; the *gravamina* of the humanist Jakob → Wimpfeling in 1510; and the 102 complaints by the imperial parliament of Worms in 1521, which are not

directly connected with Martin Luther's appearance before this parliament, but were subsequently linked to the demands he made. The dynamic of the Reformation gave new impetus to the discussion of the status of *gravamina*, but they lost their significance in the aftermath of the Council of Trent. The electoral archbishops of Rhineland presented complaints in 1673 and 1769 (the 31 *gravamina* of Coblenz), and the imperial electoral capitulation of 1711 (art. 14) and the Emser Punctation of 1786 likewise took up the tradition of the pre-Reformation *gravamina*.

■ **Literature:** B. Gebhardt, *Die G. der deutschen Nation gegen den römischen Hof* (Breslau, ²1895); W. Michel, "Das Wiener Konkordat von 1448 und die nachfolgenden G. des Primarklerus der Mainzer Kirchenprovinz" (diss., Heidelberg, 1929); H. Cellarius, *Die Reichsstadt Frankfurt und die G. der deutschen Nation* (Leipzig, 1938); H. Raab, *Die Concordata nationis Germanicae in der kanonistischen Diskussion des 17. – 19.Jh.* (Wiesbaden, 1956); H. Scheible, "Die G., Luther und der Wormser Reichstag von 1521," *Blätter für Pfälzische Kirchengeschichte und religiöse Volkskunde* 39 (1972) 167–83.

MANFRED RUDERSDORF

Grebel, *Konrad.* One of the founders of the Zurich → Baptist movement, born c. 1498 in Zurich, died July/August, 1526 in Maienfeld. After humanist studies in Basle, Vienna, Paris, and other cities, he returned to Zurich in 1520 and became an adherent of Huldrych Zwingli, but had serious disagreements with him from 1523 on. He accused Zwingli of a willingness to accept false compromises in the work of church renewal. The definitive breach came with the first "believer's baptism" on January 21, 1525; the movement spread rapidly, thanks to extensive preaching by Grebel and others. Weakened by persecution, Grebel died of the plague.

■ **Literature:** C. J. Dyck, ed., *Mennonite Encyclopedia,* vol. 5 (Scottdale, 1990) 354ff.—H. Bender, *K. G.* (Scottdale, 1950); H. Fast, "K. G.," in *Radikale Reformatoren,* ed. H. Goertz (Munich, 1978) 103–14; G. W. Locher, *Die Zwinglische Reformation im Rahmen der europäischen Kirchengeschichte* (Göttingen, 1979); M. Baumgartner, *Die Täufer und Zwingli* (Zurich, 1993).

HANSPETER JECKER

■ **Additional Bibliography:** P. I. Kaufman, "Social History, Psychohistory, and the Prehistory of Swiss Anabaptism," *Journal of Religion* 68 (1988) 527–544; W.

de Greef, "The Origin and Development of the Doctrine of the Covenant," in *Calvin's Books.* Festschrift P. De Klerk (Heerenveen, 1997) 337–56; H.-J. Goertz, *K. G.— Kritiker des frommen Scheins* (Hamburg, 1998); D. G. Lichdi, *K. G. und die frühe Täuferbewegung* (Lage, 1998).

Gregory XIII. Pope (May 13, 1572–April 10, 1585), formerly *Ugo Boncompagni,* born January 1, 1502, at Bologna, the son of a merchant. He studied in Bologna and taught law there from 1531 to 1539. He entered the service of the curia at Rome in 1539. The curia sent him to the Council of Trent in 1546 and from 1561 to 1563, where he was largely responsible for the formulation of the reform decrees; in the intervening period, he carried out diplomatic tasks in France (1556) and Brussels (1557). He was made bishop of Viesti in 1558. He was created cardinal in 1565 and sent as legate to Spain, where he won the confidence of King → Philip II. Gregory's election as pope, in an unusually brief conclave, was due above all to the influence of Philip and of Cardinal Antoine Perenot de → Granvella.

Although Gregory had grown up in the atmosphere of the Renaissance, his life as pope remained modest. As a trained lawyer with administrative experience, he expedited the most important business in person. His rule was mild, but he was a decisive promoter of the Catholic → reform and the → Counter-Reformation, employing harsh and sometimes dubious methods. He supported → Henry III of France against the → Huguenots and held a public celebration in Rome of the St. → Bartholomew's Day massacre, although he had not been involved in its preparation. He supported the revolt of the Irish and the buildup of Spanish arms against → Elizabeth I of England; similarly, he supported the Spanish Counter-Reformation in the Netherlands. While the Catholic Church in Poland was able to regain strength and renew itself decisively, the recatholicization of Sweden failed. The nuncio Antonio Possevino did not succeed in forging either a union or a closer relationship to the Russia of Ivan IV, and the endeavors to create a grand alliance against the Turks were unsuccessful. Gregory devoted particular attention to German matters, setting up a "German" congregation of cardinals in 1573 and establishing new permanent nunciatures in Cologne, Graz, and Lucerne. His most important church-political intervention here was

the retention of the imperial electorate of Cologne for the Catholic Church after Archbishop Gebhard II Truchsess von → Waldburg became a Protestant in 1583; this ensured both that the imperial church in Lower Germany remained Catholic (despite the grave risks to which it was exposed), and that the imperial throne would continue to be occupied by Catholics.

As a friend of the sciences, church education, and the Jesuit Order, Gregory played a decisive role in the foundation of seminaries in all the Catholic countries. In Rome, he founded the English, Hungarian, Greek, Armenian, and Maronite colleges, ensured the survival of the German college by means of a rich endowment, and refounded the Roman College. He promoted the missions, especially in India and Japan. He drew up the official edition of the *Corpus Iuris Canonici,* as desired by the Council of Trent, and carried out the reform of the Julian calendar (so that the day following October 4, 1582 was October 15). He began the reform of the liturgical chants and reorganized the Congregation of the Index. In 1580, Gregory repeated the condemnation of Michael → Bajus, who submitted.

Gregory was one of the great reforming popes of the post-Tridentine period, who established the Catholic reform on the basis of the council and sought to regain lost territory. The immense expenditure on education, colleges, and diplomatic tasks, and the extension of Rome and splendid buildings caused very serious financial problems, which led to unrest. Rome and the papal states suffered greatly, especially in the final years of his reign, from a plague of bandits, who were often supported by the aristocracy. The aged pope, who was all too inclined toward caution, could not restore order, and this became the most urgent task for his successor, → Sixtus V.

■ **Literature:** L. von Pastor, *Geschichte der Päpste seit dem Ausgang des Mittelalters,* vol. 9 (Freiburg, 1923); J. Krüger, "Das ursprüngliche Grabmal G.s XIII. in St. Peter zu Rom," *Korrespondenzblatt des Collegium Germanicum* 95 (1986) 41–59; G. Schwaiger, "Die Päpste der Katholischen Reform und Gegenreformation," in *Gestalten der Kirchengeschichte,* ed. M. Greschat, vol. 12 (Stuttgart et al., 1985) 79–102; F. M. De' Reguardati, "Il fenomeno del banditismo sotto Gregorio XIII e Sisto V," *Rivista araldica* 85 (1987) 198–207; S. Vareschi, *La legazione del card. Ludovico Madruzzo alla dieta imperiale di Augusta 1582. Chiesa, Papato e Impero nella seconda metà del sec. XVI* (Trent, 1990); V. Peri, "Roma e l'idea del patriarcato di Mosca all'epoca di Gregorio XIII," in *IV Centenario dell'istituzione de Patriarcato in Russia* (Trent, 1991) 177–205; A. Fernández Collado, *Gregorio XIII y Felipe II en la nunciatura de Felipe Sega (1577–87)* (Toledo, 1991).

GEORG SCHWAIGER

■ **Additional Bibliography:** *Vatikanlexikon,* ed. N. Del Re (Augsburg, 1998) 282ff.; *RGG*[4] 3:1261.—E. Olivares, "La bula 'Ascendente Domino,' 1584, y los teológicos posttridentinos," *Archivo teológico Granadino* 62 (1999) 5–75; M. Freiberg, "Going Gregorian, 1582–1752. A Summary View," *CHR* 86 (2000) 1–19; J. P. Donelly, "Antonio Possevino, S.J. as Papal Mediator between Emperor Rudolf II and King Stephan Báthory," *Archivum historicum Societatis Jesu* 69 (2000) 3–56.

Gregory XIV. Pope (December 4, 1590–October 16, 1591), formerly *Niccolò Sfondrati,* born February 11, 1535 in Somma Lombardo (Varese). He became bishop of Cremona in 1560 and was created cardinal in 1583. He was a friend of Charles → Borromeo and Philip Neri. Since his health was always poor and he lacked political experience, he entrusted business to his cardinal nephew, Paolo Camillo Sfondrati, who was unsuited to this task and pursued an unsuccessful anti-French policy under Spanish influence, supporting the Holy League in France with money and troops and renewing the sentence of excommunication against King → Henry IV.

■ **Literature:** M. Facini, *Il pontificato di Gregorio XIV* (Rome, 1911); *HCMA* 3:53f., 181; L. von Pastor, *Geschichte der Päpste seit dem Ausgang des Mittelalters,* vol. 10 (Freiburg, 1926) 531–73; L. Castano, *N. Sfondrati vescovo di Cremona al Concilio di Trento 1561–63* (Turin, 1939); idem, *Gregorio XIV* (Turin, 1957).

GEORG SCHWAIGER

■ **Additional Bibliography:** *Vatikanlexikon,* ed. N. Del Re (Augsburg, 1998) 284f.

Gropper, (1) *Johann.* Cathedral canon in Cologne, theologian and church politician, born February 24, 1503 in Soest, died March 13, 1559 in Rome. He studied philosophy and civil and canon law in Cologne, becoming doctor of law in 1525. He was influenced by Erasmian thinking, and promoted administrative reforms in the archdiocese of Cologne. His interests turned to theology in 1530. At the provincial council in 1536, Gropper presented pioneering reform statutes. His *Enchiridion christianae institutionis* appeared in 1538. This was an unpolemical discussion of the questions raised by the Reformers, showing the author's desire for reconciliation. He took part in the religious dialogues of → Worms and → Regensburg in 1540-1541. When Archbishop Hermann von → Wied wished to have Martin → Bucer introduce the Reformation into Cologne (1542-1548), Gropper headed the resistance, which was ultimately successful. After this, he worked under Archbishops Adolf and Anton von → Schaumburg for the religious renewal of the church in Cologne. He took an active part in the Council of Trent in 1551-1552. He was designated cardinal in 1555 and moved to Rome in 1558. His theological concepts and practical ideas about church reform found a wide echo in Italy, France, and Spain until well into the 1560s.

■ **Works:** *Canones Concilii Provincialis Coloniensis/ Enchiridion christianae institutionis* (Cologne, 1538); *Antididagma seu Christianae et Catholicae religionis propugnatio* (Cologne, 1544); *Capita Institutionis ad pietatem* (Cologne, 1546); *Institutio Catholica* (Cologne, 1550); *Vonn warer, wesenlicher und pleibender Gegenwertigkeit des Leybs und Blůts Christi* (Cologne, 1556).

■ **Sources:** *J. G. Briefwechsel,* vol. 1: 1529–47, ed. R. Braunisch (Münster, 1977).

■ **Literature:** *KThR* 1:116–24.—W. Lipgens, *Kardinal J. G. und die Anfänge der katholischen Reform in Deutschland* (Münster, 1951); R. Braunisch, *Die Theologie der Rechtfertigung im "Enchiridion" (1538) des J. G.* (Münster, 1974); J. Meier, "Das 'Enchiridion christianae institutionis' (1538) von J. G. Geschichte seiner Entstehung, Verbreitung und Nachwirkung," *ZKG* 86 (1975) 289–328; idem, *Der priesterliche Dienst nach J. G. (1503–59)* (Münster, 1977); J. I. Tellechea Idigoras, "J. G. expurgado por la inquisición española," *Scriptorium Victoriense. Revista cuatrimestral de investigación teológica* 24 (1977) 197–218; K. Repgen, "J. G.s Oktoberartikel von 1546," in *Ecclesia militans.* Festschrift R. Bäumer, vol. 2 (Paderborn, 1988) 363–94; A. Willsch, *Das Verständnis der Ehe im "Enchiridion" des J. G.* (St. Ottilien, 1991).

JOHANNES MEIER

■ **Additional Bibliography:** H. Filser, *Ekklesiologie und Sakramentenlehre des Kardinals J. G.* (Münster, 1995); H. Finger, *Der Kölner Seelsorger und Theologe Kardinal J.G.* Catalogue of an Exhibition (Cologne, 2003).

(2) *Kaspar.* Nuncio, brother of (1), born c. 1514 in Soest, died March 9, 1594 in Cologne. His brother was a decisive influence on his choice of

career. Kaspar became dean of St. Patroclus in Soest in 1542, dean of St. Victor's in Xanten in 1550, episcopal official in 1550, and cathedral canon in Cologne in 1552. He went to Rome in 1558 and became auditor at the Rota. He was provost of Bonn from 1560 to 1594. In 1573, he was sent as nuncio to Augsburg, Würzburg, Mainz, Cologne, Münster, and Jülich-Kleve, with the task of insisting on the enforcement of the decisions of Trent. He was supported by Nicolaus → Elgard in this work. He resigned as nuncio in 1576, a hurt and probably also mentally ill man.

■ **Sources:** W. E. Schwarz, *Die Nuntiaturkorrespondenz K. G.s.* (Paderborn, 1898).

■ **Literature:** C. Grebner, *K. G. und N. Elgard* (Münster, 1982).

CHRISTIAN GREBNER

Grumbach, *Argula von.* Née von Stauff, Reformer, born 1492, died probably 1568. She came from one of the oldest Bavarian dynasties and was brought up at the court of Duke Albrecht IV in Munich. After the death of her father, Bernhardin von Stauff, in 1509, she was given a German Bible, and this became the center of her life. She married Friedrich von Grumbach in 1514 or 1515 and bore four children. Although her husband remained Catholic, she studied the new Reformation doctrine intensively and defended Arsacius Seehofer before the university of Ingolstadt in 1523. Her first public appearance as a Reformer led to the dismissal of her husband from the office of curator in Dietfurt. Despite increasing pressure from his family, she remained until her death an eloquent and courageous defender of the new teachings. She was in contact with Martin Luther and other Reformers. Luther himself saw in her "a special instrument of Christ" and a great warrior on behalf of the Reformation movement.

■ **Literature:** M. Heinsius, *Das Bekenntnis der Frau A. von G.* (Munich, 1936); S. Halbach, *A. von G. als Verfasserin reformatorischer Flugschriften* (Frankfurt/Main, 1992); H. Spachmüller, *A. von G. – selbst ist die Frau* (Schwabach, 1992); P. Matheson, *A. von G.—A Woman's Voice in the Reformation* (Edinburgh, 1995); M. Vogt-Lüerssen, *40 Frauenschicksale aus dem 15. und 16.Jh.* (Mainz, 2001) 119–23.

MAIKE VOGT-LÜERSSEN

■ **Additional Literature:** P. Matheson, "A Reformation for Women?: Sin, Grace and Gender in the Writings of A. von G.," *Scottish Journal of Theology* 49 (1996) 39–55.

Grynäus (Gryner), (1) *Simon.* Humanist and Reformed theologian, born 1493 in Vehringen (Hohenzollern), died August 1, 1541 in Basle. He studied in Pforzheim and Vienna, where he took the degree of master of arts. He became professor of Greek in Heidelberg in 1524 and additionally professor of Latin in 1526; in 1529, he became professor of Greek in Basle. He visited England in 1531. He took part in the reorganization of the university of Tübingen on a Reformed basis in 1534-1535 and returned to Basle in 1536, where he was rector in 1540-1541. He was one of the authors of the *Confessio Helvetica Prior* (1536) and took part in the negotiations about the Concord of → Wittenberg (1536) and in the religious dialogue of → Worms (1540).

■ **Literature:** *BBKL* 2:377.—Ch.H. Lohr, *Latin Aristotle Commentaries* II: *Renaissance Authors* (Florence, 1988) 175f.; idem, *Aristotelica helvetica* (Fribourg, 1994).

(2) *Johann Jakob.* Reformed theologian, son of Thomas Grynäus (1512-1564) and nephew of (1), born October 1, 1540 in Berne, died August 30, 1617 in Basle. He studied in Basle and Tübingen from 1551 to 1564, taking his doctorate in theology in the latter year. He became superintendent in Röteln in 1565 and was professor of Old Testament in Basle from 1575 to 1584. He reformed the university of Heidelberg on a Calvinist basis from 1584 to 1586. He became Antistes and professor of New Testament in Basle in 1586. Grynäus halted the convergence between the Basle church and Lutheranism, and gave the church in Basle its Calvinist character.

■ **Literature:** *BBKL* 2:376.

CHARLES H. LOHR

■ **Additional Bibliography:** A. Szábo, *J. J. G. magyar kapscolatai* (Szeged, 1989) (with a German summary and Latin letters); H. Jecker, *Ketzer, Rebellen, Heilige. Das Basler Täufertum von 1580 bis 1700* (Liestal, 1998) esp. 484ff.; A. N. Burnett, "Controlling the Clergy. The Oversight of Basel's Rural Pastors in the 16th Century," *Zwingliana* 25 (1998) 129–42.

Guerrero, *Pedro.* Theologian, born December 11, 1501 in Leza del Rio Leza (La Rioja), died April 2, 1576 in Granada. He studied in Sigüenza and Alcalá and taught at the faculty of arts in Salamanca from 1529. He took the degree of master of theology in 1534 and became professor of theology in Sigüenza in 1535. He was appointed archbishop of Granada in 1546. Guerrero was the most important Spanish representative during the second and third periods of the Council of Trent.

■ Literature: *DHEE* 2:1065f.; *OER* 2:201.—C. Gutiérrez, *Españoles en Trento* (Valladolid, 1951) 946–62; Jedin 4/2, passim; A. Marín Ocete, *El arzobispo Don P. G. y la política conciliar española en el siglo XVI*, 2 vols. (Madrid, 1970); J. López Martín, "Don P. G.," in *Epistolario y documentación* (Rome, 1974).

FERNANDO DOMÍNGUEZ

Guise. Ducal dynasty in France, younger collateral line of the house of Lorraine.

The founder of the house was *Claude* (October 20, 1496–April 12, 1550), who was related to the French royal house of Valois through his marriage to Antoinette of Bourbon-Vendôme.

His first son, *François* (December 17, 1519–February 24, 1563), won renown under → Francis I and → Henry II in the wars against → Charles V. He was the de facto ruler of the kingdom (with his brother Charles; see below) during the brief reign of Francis II (1559-1560). In 1560, he suppressed the conspiracy of Amboise (an attempt by → Huguenots to kidnap Francis II). The violent action he took against the Huguenots in his property of Wassy in Champagne (Massacre of Wassy, March 1, 1562) gave the signal for the outbreak of the French Wars of Religion. He was murdered near Orleans by a Huguenot.

STEPHAN SKALWEIT

Charles. Second son of Duke Claude (February 17, 1525–December 26, 1574), known as the cardinal de Lorraine, he was destined for an ecclesiastical career. He was well educated, intelligent, and a good speaker. He ceaselessly collected church benefices (including Toul and Verdun), drawing on their revenues to finance an enlightened patronage of the arts. He had a great influence on King Francis II and played an important role in church politics both in France (religious dialogue of → Poissy, September, 1561; meeting with Duke → Christopher of Württemberg and his theologian Johannes → Brenz, February, 1562) and at the Council of Trent, where he led the French delegation during the third period and defended Gallican theses (November, 1562). He was the founder of the universities of Reims (1548) and Pont-à-Mousson (1572). He supported the Jesuits and undertook a visitation of the diocese of Reims.

GÉRALD CHAIX

The sons of François. Henri (December 31, 1550–December 23, 1588). Known as "Le Balafré," he became under → Charles IX a champion of the French Catholics against the → Huguenots. He was one of those chiefly responsible for St. → Bartholomew's Eve in 1572 and became the head of the League in 1576; its double character as a religious movement among the people and as a regional reaction by the Estates to the royal claims to power inevitably caused a clash between the duke of Guise and the king, who had him and his brother *Louis,* cardinal and archbishop of Lyons (July 6, 1555–December 24, 1588), murdered in the castle of Blois. The third brother, *Charles de Mayenne* (March 26, 1554–October 4, 1611), became leader of the League and submitted to → Henry IV only in 1595. One indication of the leading role played by this dynasty in 16th-century France is their prominence in the church: members of the family occupied almost continuously the important bishoprics of Metz, Reims, and Lyons.

STEPHAN SKALWEIT

■ Literature: *DBF* 17:325–32; *DHGE* 22:1118–25.—H. O. Evennett, *The Cardinal of Lorraine and the Council of Trent* (Cambridge, 1930); J.-M. Coustant, *Les G.* (Paris, 1984); E. Bourassin, *L'assassinat du duc de G.* (Paris, 1991); Th. E. Taylor, *Charles, Second Cardinal of Lorraine* (Charlottesville, Va., 1995); Y. Bellenger, ed., *Le mécénat et l'influence des Guises. Actes du colloque, Joinville 31 mai au 4 juin 1994* (Paris, 1997); S. Carroll, *Noble Power during the French Wars of Religion* (Cambridge, 1998).

Gustav I Vasa of Sweden (king 1523). Founder of the modern Swedish state, born May 12, 1496/1497 (?) in Rydboholm, died September 29, 1560. A member of the Swedish aristocracy, he was taken captive in the War of Sten Sture the Younger in 1518 and brought to Denmark; however, he managed to make his way back to Sweden, where he heard of the "Stockholm Bloodbath," in which Christian II, king of the united Scandinavian monarchy, had ruthlessly disposed of all genuine and supposed opposition. Gustav put himself at the head of a resistance movement, and he succeeded in expelling the Danes and setting up a national kingdom. Since Archbishop Gustav Trolle of Uppsala was seen as one of those responsible for the Bloodbath of 1520, a conflict with the church was inevitable. In 1527, at the parliament of Västerås, Gustav deliberately smashed the political and economic power of the Catholic Church. He supported the activity of the Swedish Reformers, at first cautiously, but then more and more unambiguously; the ordination of Laurentius → Petri as archbishop in 1531 set the seal on the breach with Rome. Gustav's plundering of churches provoked resistance movements, which were crushed with a harsh hand. On his death, Sweden was a hereditary kingdom and on its way to becoming a state in which only the Lutheran confession was accepted.

■ **Literature:** G. Schwaiger, *Die Reformation in den nordischen Ländern* (Munich, 1962); M. Roberts, *The Early Vasas* (Cambridge, 1968).

LARS CAVALLIN

■ **Additional Bibliography:** A. Åberg, *G. Vasa* (Stockholm, 1996); M. Nyman, *Förlorarnas historia* (Uppsala, 1997).

H

Hadrian VI. Pope (January 9, 1522–September 14, 1523), formerly *Adrian Florensz Boeyens*, born March 2, 1459 in Utrecht, the son of a carpenter; his tomb is in Santa Maria dell'Anima. He was a pupil of the Brethren of the Common Life and studied at the university of Louvain, where he taught theology from 1491 to 1507. He was influenced by late scholasticism, and his principal interests lay in the fields of canon law and casuistic moral theology. Emperor Maximilian I appointed him tutor of his grandson, later Emperor → Charles V, in 1507. Boeyens ensured that Charles retained the full right of inheritance in the Spanish monarchy. From 1516 onward, he and Cardinal Francisco Jiménez Cisneros governed Spain; after the cardinal's death, Boeyens ruled alone. He became bishop of Tortosa in 1516, and inquisitor and cardinal in 1517. While Charles V was absent for the imperial election, Boeyens was once again regent in Spain and played a part in subduing the revolt in Castille (1520-1522). In the conclave that followed the death of → Leo X, which was lacerated by political rivalries, he was elected pope *in absentia*, thanks to his position in Spain, to his close links to Emperor Charles V, and to his exemplary life.

The pious and severely ascetic Hadrian encountered hostility and rejection on the part of the worldly curia and the Roman populace as soon as he entered Rome on August 29, 1522, taking the sea route to emphasize his political neutrality. He saw his principal task as the checking of the Reformation which Martin Luther had unleashed and the achieving of a common front of the Christian powers against the Turks (Belgrade had fallen in 1521, and Rhodes in 1522). He earned resentment by his policy of thrift (in contrast to his predecessor, who had piled up debts) and by his serious intention to carry out reform; he was also disliked as a foreigner. Hadrian was isolated, supported only by a few Spanish and Dutch associates, such as Cardinal Willem van Enkevoirt.

He sent Francesco → Chiericati as nuncio to the imperial parliament at Nuremberg in 1523. In the instructions he gave Chiericati, Hadrian spoke of the abuses in the curia and expressed his will to bring about reforms. He was unsuccessful in his attempt to have the Edict of Worms applied to Luther. He was similarly unsuccessful in his mediation between Charles V and King → Francis I of France; when France applied sanctions to him, Hadrian saw no other course than to enter an alliance against France with Charles V, England, and Venice. Other areas of concern in Hadrian's pontificate were Switzerland, Poland, Hungary, and the Scandinavian kingdoms.

■ **Literature:** *DHGE* 22:1487ff.; 24:379f. (s.v. Hezius [Thierry] secrétaire d'Adrien VI); *TRE* 14:309f.—L. von Pastor, *Geschichte der Päpste seit dem Ausgang des Mittelalters*, vol. 4/2 (Freiburg, 1893); A. Mercati, *Diarii di concistori del pontificato di Adrino VI* (Rome, 1951); *Ephemerides theologicae Lovanienses* 35 (1959) 513–629; J. Posner, *Der deutsche Papst Adrian VI* (Recklinghausen, 1962);R.-E. McNally, "Pope Adrian VI and Church Reform," *AHP* 7 (1969) 253–85); P. Berglar, "Die kirchliche und politische Bedeutung des Pontifikats H.s VI.," *Archiv für Kulturgeschichte* 54 (1972) 97–112; K. H. Ducke, *Handeln zum Heil. Eine Untersuchung zur Morallehre H.s VI* (Leipzig, 1976); J. Bijloos, *Adrianus VI. De Nederlandse Paus* (Haarlem, 1980).

GEORG SCHWAIGER

■ **Additional Bibliography:** *RGG*[4] 3:1370f.—K. Mittermaier, *Die deutschen Päpste* (Graz, 1991); R. B. Hein, *"Gewissen" bei Adrian von Utrecht (H. VI.), Erasmus von Rotterdam und Thomas More* (Münster, 2000); P. Nissen, *Adrianus VI. Een biografie* (Amsterdam, 2000); M. Graulich, "Adriano VI e la richiesta di perdono," *Salesianum* 62 (2000) 741–55.

Hagenau, religious dialogue. After political Protestantism had grown in strength thanks to the → Schmalkaldic League, the curia succeeded in delaying the convocation of a council. Meanwhile, the empire was under threat from both → Francis I of France and the Turks, and → Charles V issued a decree in Frankfurt on April 19, 1539, summoning a national religious dialogue to meet in Nuremberg. Thanks to the opposition of the curia, this convened more than a year later, from June 18 to July 28, 1540, in Hagenau, under the chairmanship of King → Ferdinand. The negotiators were the electoral princes of the Palatinate and of Trier (who was replaced by the electoral prince of Mainz on July 23), the duke of Bavaria, and the bishop of Strasbourg. They discussed the procedure and the basis of the religious dialogue. The Hagenau Resolution of July 28 stipulated (*a*) that invitations would be issued to a further religious dialogue which would meet in → Worms on October 28, 1540; (*b*) that each party would have eleven votes to cast on the disputed religious questions; and (*c*) that the basis of negotiations would be the → Confessio Augustana and its Apology. This laid the foundations of the religious dialogue in Worms from October 28, 1540 to January 18, 1541, and of the dialogue in → Regensburg from April 27 to May 22, 1541.

■ **Sources:** CR vol. 3; *NBD* I/5; *ARCEG* 3.
■ **Literature:** C. Augustijn, *De Godsdienstgesprekken tussen Rooms-Katholieken en Protestanten van 1538 to 1541* (Haarlem, 1967); W. Neuser, *Die Vorbereitung der Religionsgespräche von Worms und Regensburg 1540/41* (Neukirchen-Vluyn, 1974); M. Hollerbach, *Das Religionsgespräch als Mittel der konfessionellen und politischen Auseinandersetzung im Deutschland des 16.Jh.* (Frankfurt/Main, 1982); E. Honée, "Über das Vorhaben und Scheitern eines Religionsgesprächs," *ZKG* 76 (1985) 196–216; K.-H. zur Mühlen, "Die Edition der Akten und Berichte der Religionsgespräche von Hagenau und Worms 1540/41," in *Standfester Glaube.* Festschrift J. F. G. Goeters (Cologne, 1991) 47–82.

KARL-HEINZ ZUR MÜHLEN

■ **Additional Bibliography:** *Akten der deutschen Reichsreligionsgespräche im 16.Jh.*, vol. 1, 1 and 2, ed. K. Ganzer (Göttingen, 2000).

Haldrein (Halderen, Haldrenius) von Wesel, *Arnold.* Humanist, died October 30, 1534 in Cologne. He began his studies at the university of Cologne in 1501 and took the degree of master of arts in 1504. He was a member of the faculty of arts from 1516 to 1527, and dean in 1518. He took his licentiate in theology in 1522, and held one of the university benefices in St. Severin's church. He became cathedral canon in Cologne in 1531, and was professor of Greek and Hebrew. He edited works of classical authors. He was entrusted with the refutation of the → Confessio Augustana at the imperial parliament in Augsburg in 1530, and he is the probable author of the *Brevis responsio.*
■ **Works:** *VD 16* 8:293–317.
■ **Literature:** E. Meuthen, *Kölner Universitätsgeschichte* (Cologne and Vienna, 1988) 1:214ff.

BARBARA HENZE

Haller, *Berchtold.* Reformer of Berne, born 1492 in Aldingen near Rottweil, died February 25, 1536 in Berne. He took the degree of master of arts at the university of Cologne in 1512, and became curate in Berne in 1513. He was influenced by the Reformation ideas of Thomas → Wyttenbach (1472-1526), whom he succeeded as pastor of souls in 1519, and as canon in 1520. He was a friend of Philipp Melanchthon; he became a friend of Huldrych Zwingli in 1521, and later of Johannes → Oecolampadius too. In Berne, he was the center of a circle of church leaders with Protestant views. After the order of scriptural readings in church was abandoned, he ceased celebrating Mass after Christmas, 1525. He was sent by the council to the disputation in → Baden in 1526. Tensions in Switzerland helped the consolidation of the Reformation in Berne, where the Reformed party held the majority in the city council from 1527 onwards; the disputation of Berne in 1528, for which Haller and his collaborator Franz Kolb (1465-1535) had composed ten theses, brought the victory of the Protestants. The General Reformation edict of Berne (February 7, 1528) was drawn up by Haller, and the Lord's Supper was officially celebrated in the city for the first time at Easter of that year. He attempted in vain to introduce the Reformation in Solothurn in 1530. The Berne church order of 1532 (Berne *Synodus*) was composed by Wolfgang → Capito. As a theologian, Haller was not important, but it was his persistence and flexibility, with the aid of his friends, that made him the Reformer of Berne.
■ **Literature:** *BBKL* 2:485–93; *RGG*⁴ 3:1395.

ALBERT PORTMANN-TINGUELY

Haller, *Leonhard.* Auxiliary bishop and theologian, born 1500 in Denkendorf near Eichstätt, died March 25, 1570 in Eichstätt. He studied in Ingolstadt from 1518 to 1530, taking the degree of master of arts. He was curate in Ingolstadt in 1528, preacher in Aichach in 1530, curate in Munich in 1533, parish priest in Augsburg in 1534, and became presbyteral canon of Eichstätt cathedral in June, 1536. He was appointed titular bishop of Philadelphia and auxiliary bishop in Eichstätt in 1540, and consecrated in 1541; he became a canon of the choir of St. Willibald, renouncing his presbyteral canonry. He traveled to Rome in 1550-1551 (without taking part in the Council of Trent), but took part in the council from July, 1562 to October, 1563, as representative of Eichstätt and Würzburg. He was a resolute defender of the rights of auxiliary bishops and procurators, and an opponent of the concession of the → chalice for the laity. He was a zealous pastor of souls and preacher, and a reliable helper of his bishop. He owned a large collection of theological works, both manuscripts and printed books.

■ **Catalogue of Works:** L. Ott (see below) 67 (1974) 92–109 and 69 (1976) 117–40.

■ **Literature:** *CT* vols. 3/1, 8 and 9; F. X. Buchner, "Das Bistum Eichstätt und das Konzil von Trient," in *Das Weltkonzil von Trient, sein Werden und Wirken,* ed. G. Schreiber, vol. 2 (Freiburg, 1951) 94–103; Th. Freudenberger, *L.H. von Eichstätt im Streit um die Ehre der Weihbischöfe im Konzil von Trient. Festschrift J. Kardinal Döpfner* (Würzburg, 1973) 141–97; Jedin 4 (index); L. Ott, "Leben und Schrifttum (und Bibliothek) des Eichstätter Weihbischofs L.H.," *Sammelblatt des Historischen Vereins Eichstätt* 67 (1974) 83–131; 68 (1975) 7–29; 69 (1976) 91–159; idem, *L.H.s Bericht über das Predigtverbot in Augsburg im Jahre 1534.* Festschrift A. Brems (Regensburg, 1981) 217–28; idem, "Ein bisher unbekannter Brief des Ingolstädter Professors Georg Hauer an L.H.," *Sammelblatt des Historischen Vereins Ingolstadt* 89 (1980) 109–14; E. Gatz, ed., *Die Bischöfe des Heiligen Römischen Reiches 1448–1648* (Berlin, 1996).

ERNST REITER

Hamelmann, *Hermann.* Lutheran theologian and historian, born 1526 in Osnabruck, died June 26, 1595 in Oldenburg. After humanistic and theological studies, he was ordained priest in Münster in 1550. In 1553, he became a Protestant in Kamen, and worked as a preacher in Bielefeld, Lemgo, Antwerp, Essen, and Gandersheim. From 1573 onward, he was superintendent of the county of

Oldenburg (-Delmenhorst-Jever), where he organized the Lutheran state church, issuing a church-order, carrying out visitations, and introducing the Formula of Concord. He wrote works of controversial theology against Catholics, Reformed Protestants, and Baptists, as well as historical monographs, including a history of the Reformation in Westphalia and a chronicle of Oldenburg.

■ **Works:** *H.H.s geschichtliche Werke,* ed. H. Detmer et al., 3 vols. (Münster, 1902–40).

■ **Literature:** A. Schröer, *Die Reformation in Westfalen,* 2 vols. (Münster, 1979–83); A. Eckhardt and H. Schmidt, eds., *Geschichte des Landes Oldenburg* (Oldenburg, 1987); *Biographisches Handbuch zur Geschichte des Landes Oldenburg* (Oldenburg, 1992).

ANTON SCHINDLING

■ **Additional Literature:** R. Schäfer, "H. und die Anfänge der oldenburgischen Reformation," *Jahrbuch der Gesellschaft für Niedersächsische Kirchengeschichte* 99 (2001) 69–99.

Hamilton, (1) *Patrick.* Scottish Reformer, born c. 1504 in a noble Scottish family, died February 29, 1528 in St. Andrews. He became commendatory abbot of Ferne in 1517. He studied in Paris (where he took the degree of master in 1520) and probably also in Louvain; from 1523, he was at the university of St. Andrews. When he was accused of holding Lutheran views, he moved in spring 1527 to Wittenberg and then attended the Protestant university of Marburg, where he wrote his only work, the *Loci communes.* After his return to Scotland, the investigation of his doctrine by Archbishop Beaton led to his condemnation for heresy. He was burnt at the stake, and is counted as the first martyr of the Scottish Reformation.

■ **Literature:** *DNB* 24:201ff.; *The Oxford Dictionary of the Christian Church* (London, ²1974) 616f.; *BBKL* 2:508f.; *DHGE* 23:243f.—P. Lorimer, *P.H. the First Preacher and Martyr of the Scottish Reformation* (Edinburgh, 1867); *P.H., First Scottish Martyr of the Reformation,* ed. A. Cameron (Edinburgh, 1929); I. R. Torrance, "P. H. and John Knox: A Study in the Doctrine of Justification by Faith," *ARG* 65 (1974) 171–85; J. E. McGoldrick, "P.H., Luther's Scottish Disciple," *SCJ* 18 (1987) 81–88.

DIETER J. WEISS

■ **Additional Bibliography:** *RGG*⁴ 3:1402f.—N. Jones, *Through a Glass Darkely. The Life of P.H.* (London, 1991); S. French, *P.H.* (London, 1993); R. Haas, "P.'s places: die erste theologische Abhandlung an der

Universität Marburg 1527," *Jahrbuch der Hessischen Kirchengeschichtlichen Vereinigung* 53 (2002) 97–144.

(2) *John.* Archbishop of St. Andrews, half-brother of (1), born c. 1511, died April 6, 1571 in Stirling. He was educated by Benedictines and became commendatory abbot of Paisley in 1525. He studied from 1540 to 1543 in Paris, where he was ordained priest. On his return to Scotland, he was an adherent of the Catholic party and became keeper of the Great Seal in 1543, bishop of Dunkeld in 1545, and archbishop of St. Andrews in 1546. He summoned synods to fight against the Protestant movement (1548, 1549, 1552, 1559); the fruit of these synods was his important catechism. Although his own lifestyle was dubious, he defended the doctrine of the church against the → Confessio Scotica of John → Knox. This led to his imprisonment in 1563. He was freed by Queen → Mary Stuart and became a member of her council. He baptized her son, James VI (James I of England), in 1566, and made it possible for her to marry James Bothwell. As a member of the queen's party, he was embroiled in the struggles of the following years. He was hanged in his pontifical vestments on the market square in Stirling in 1571, allegedly because of his involvement in political murders, but in fact because of his fidelity to the Catholic Church.

■ **Literature:** *DNB* 24:190ff.; *The Oxford Dictionary of the Christian Church* (London, ²1974) 616; *BBKL* 2:508; *DHGE* 23:239–42.—*The Catechism of J.H. 1552,* ed. Th. G. Law (Oxford, 1884); I. B. Cowan, *The Scottish Reformation, Church and Society in 16th-century Scotland* (London, 1982).

DIETER J. WEISS

Haner, *Johannes.* Catholic theologian, born 1480 (?) in Nuremberg, died 1545 (?) in Bamberg. He studied in Ingolstadt, and in Freiburg (from 1507). He returned to Nuremberg in 1513 and was parish priest of several churches. Willibald → Pirckheimer counted him in 1517 among the representatives of a new theology; Haner was initially sympathetic to Martin Luther's concerns, but parted company with him in 1532. He was advisor to → Philip of Hessen at the imperial parliament in Speyer in 1526 and began a correspondence with Johannes → Oecolampadius and Huldrych Zwingli. The introduction of the Reformation forced him to leave Nuremberg in 1535; an inter-vention by King → Ferdinand secured him the post of cathedral curate in Bamberg, and he was cathedral preacher from 1541 to 1544. Haner had contacts with men such as Johannes → Cochlaeus, → Erasmus of Rotterdam, Duke → George of Saxony, Julius von → Pflug, and Georg → Witzel. His theology has not yet been the object of thorough research.

■ **Works:** "Briefe und Aufsätze von H. und Wizel," *Beiträge zur politischen, kirchlichen und Culturgeschichte der sechs letzten Jahrhunderte,* vol. 3, ed. J. J. I. von Döllinger (Vienna, 1882) 105–43; J. V. Pollet, ed., *Julius Pflug. Correspondance* II (Leiden, 1973); *VD 16* 8:511ff.
■ **Literature:** *BBKL* 2:513; *CEras* 2:161ff.; *DHGE* 23:271f.

BARBARA HENZE

Hardenberg, *Albert* (Rizaeus). Protestant theology, born c. 1510 in Hardenberg (Overijssel, Netherlands), died May 18, 1574 in Emden. He was educated by the Brethren of the Common Life in Groningen, and was in the monastery of Aduard from 1527 to 1532. He studied in Louvain and Mainz, taking his doctorate in theology in the latter city in 1539. It was here that he made the acquaintance of Jan → Łaski the Younger. His Protestant views led to his expulsion from Louvain, and he was once again in Aduard in 1540. He came to Wittenberg in 1542, and became a sympathizer of Philipp Melanchthon. He accompanied Archbishop Hermann von → Wied of Cologne to the imperial parliament in Speyer in 1544. He met Martin → Bucer in Strasbourg and translated Bucer's revision of Hermann von Wied's *Einfältiges Bedenken* into Latin. After journeys to Basle and Zurich (where he met Heinrich → Bullinger), he moved to Bonn, becoming pastor in Linz (Rhine) and then in Kempen. After a forcible end was put to the attempted introduction of the Reformation into Cologne, he became cathedral preacher in Bremen in 1547, and married. He was involved in controversies with the Lutheran clergy, especially about the Lord's Supper, and he was expelled from Bremen in 1561. He lived for a period in the monastery of Rastede. He became pastor in Sengwarden in 1565, then in Emden in 1567; his library has been preserved in Emden, and his epitaph can be seen there. Hardenberg always refused to sign the → Confessio Augustana. Theologically, Bucer profoundly influenced him. Hardenberg "unites the Reformation spirit of the Netherlands with Zwingli's reform" (Molt-mann). His opposition to Lutheran orthodoxy paved the way for Reformed Church life.

■ **Literature:** B. Spiegel, *D. A. Rizäus H.* (Bremen, 1869); J. Moltmann, *Christoph Pesch und der Calvinismus in Bremen* (Bremen, 1958); V. Pollert, *Martin Bucer* (Leiden, 1985), vol. 1, 263–79, vol. 2, 185–202 (catalogue of letters).

HANSGEORG MOLITOR

■ **Additional Bibliography:** W. Janse, *A. H. als Theologe* (Leiden, 1994); idem, "A. Lasco und A. H.," in *Johannes a Lasco,* ed. Ch. Strohm (Tübingen, 2000) 261–82.

Hätzer, *Ludwig.* Swiss "Spiritualist" and antitrinitarian, born c. 1500 in Bischofszell, died February 4, 1529 in Constance (beheaded for bigamy). He was priest in Wädenswil (until his deposition in 1523) and in Zurich. His writings supported the attack on images in Zurich in 1523 (→ Art and Reformation), and he was expelled from the city along with the → Baptists in 1525. Thereafter, he led an unstable life as an itinerant missionary in southern Germany and Switzerland. He organized translations of the works of Johannes → Oecolampadius, as well as the translation of the so-called prophets of Worms, with his friend Johann → Denck (1527). He was one of the few members of the early Baptist movement who wrote books, and one of the first German → antitrinitarians in the Reformation period; he was an extreme "Spiritualist."

■ **Literature:** *BBKL* 2:453–56.

ALBERT PORTMANN-TINGUELY

■ **Additional Bibliography:** *RGG*[4] 3:1471.—J. F. G. Goeters, *L.H.* (Gütersloh, 1957); J. Beck, "The Anabaptist and the Jews," *Mennonite Quarterly Review* 75 (2001) 407–27.

Haydlauf (Haidlauf[f]), *Sebastian.* Born April 4, 1539 in Messkirch, died September 18, 1580 in Freising. He studied in Ingolstadt, taking the degree of master of arts in 1562. He was ordained priest and took his licentiate in theology in 1563. He was parish priest in Ingolstadt in 1567 and rector of the university in 1568-1569. He was appointed auxiliary bishop in Freising in 1569. In five books published after that date, Haydlauf contrasts the unity of the Catholic Church with the divisions among Protestants. His polemic is directed primarily against Jakob → Andreae.

■ **Works:** *VD 16* 8:847–54.

■ **Literature:** *DHGE* 23:648.—F. Lauchert, "Der Freisinger Weihbischof S.H. und seine Schriften," *HJ* 26 (1905) 19–42.

BARBARA HENZE

Hedio(n) (Seiler), *Caspar.* Protestant theologian, historian, and translator, born 1494/1495 in Ettlingen near Karlsruhe, died October 17, 1552 in Strasbourg. He took his doctorate in theology in Mainz in 1523 and became principal preacher at the Strasbourg Minster. He was president of the Strasbourg church convention from 1549 onward. His character was irenic, and he disliked theological speculations; he became known above all through his numerous translations into German of patristic, medieval, and contemporary texts, e.g., the works of Josephus (Strasbourg, 1531), the *Ecclesiastical History* of Eusebius and the *Historia Tripartita* (Strasbourg, 1530), the biblical commentaries of Smaragdus (Strasbourg, 1536), the Chronicle of Ursperg (which he brought up to date), Platina's history of the popes, and the irenical book *Unio dissidentium* by Hermann Bodius (Strasbourg, 1538).

■ **Literature:** *Nouveau dictionnaire de biographie alsacienne,* no. 16 (Strasbourg, 1990) 1470–73.—Ch. Spindler, *H.* (Strasbourg, 1864); V. Himmelheber, *C.H.* (Karlsruhe, 1881); J. Adam, "Versuch einer Bibliographie Kaspar H.s," *Zeitschrift für die Geschichte des Oberrheins* 31 (1916) 424–29; H. Keute, *Reformation und Geschichte. Kaspar H. als Historiograph* (Göttingen, 1980); H. Ehmer, "Reformatorische Geschichtsschreibung am Oberrhein," in *Historiographie am Oberrhein im Späten Mittelalter und in der Frühen Neuzeit,* ed. K. Andermann (Sigmaringen, 1988) 227–45; R. Bodenmann, "Pour tenter d'en finir avec le G.H. des légendes," *Revue d'histoire et de philosophie religieuses* 70 (1990) 311–34; idem, "Martin Bucer et Gaspar Hédion," in *M. Bucer and Sixteenth Century Europe,* ed. Ch. Krieger and M. Lienhard, vol. 1 (Leiden, 1993) 297–315.

REINHARD BODENMANN

■ **Additional Bibliography:** *RGG*[4] 3:1501.

Heerbrand, *Jakob.* Lutheran theologian, born August 12, 1521 in Giengen (Brenz), died May 22, 1600 in Tübingen. He attended the Latin school in Ulm and began his studies in Wittenberg in 1538. He became deacon in Tübingen in 1548, but was dismissed from office in the aftermath of the →

Augsburg Interim. He became pastor and super-intendent in Herrenberg in 1551, and took his doctorate in theology in the same year. He became professor of theology in Tübingen in 1557, and additionally superintendent in the city in 1561; in 1590, he became chancellor of the university, provost of the main city church, and counselor to the duke. He was one of the signatories of the → Confessio Virtembergica, and a member of the Württemberg delegation to the Council of Trent in 1552. He took part in the controversies about Andreas → Osiander and was an opponent of Pedro de → Soto and the Jesuits. He is considered one of the founders of Lutheran orthodoxy. He is the author of numerous disputations, sermons, polemical pamphlets, funeral and memorial addresses; his textbook *Compendium theologiae* (Tübingen, 1573; revised edition, 1578; often reprinted) found a wide readership.

■ **Works:** *VD 16* 8:472–89.
■ **Literature:** *NDB* 8:194f.; *TRE* 14:524ff.—W. Anger-bauer, *Das Kanzleramt an der Universität Tübingen* (Tübingen, 1972); F. Seck et al., *Bibliographie zur Geschichte der Universität Tübingen* (Tübingen, 1980) with index.

CHRISTOPH WEISMANN

■ **Additional Literature:** C. Methuen, "Time Human or Time Divine? Theological Aspects in the Opposition of the Gregorian Calendar Reform," *Reformation and Renaissance Review* 3 (2001) 36–50.

Heidelberg Catechism. This work (1563), still in use today in many Reformed churches, counts alongside the Confessio Helvetica Posterior (1566) and the English Westminster Confession (1647) as one of the most influential classical con-fessions of the Reformed faith. Its main author is generally held to be Zacharias → Ursinus. The polemical question 80 (still a matter of dispute today), according to which the Roman Catholic Mass is an "accursed act of idolatry," was included only in the 4th printed edition of 1563; in this form, the catechism was included in the Palatinate church order of the same year. In more recent edi-tions, a more nuanced note tones down the sub-stance of question 80.—The 129 questions of the catechism combine Calvinist, Lutheran, and Melanchthonist elements, and are divided into three sections: On the human person (§§ 3-11), On human redemption (§§ 12-85, including faith and the sacraments), and On gratitude (§§ 86-129, including law and prayer). This "analytical" structure is established in the famous first two questions.

■ **Editions:** *Bekenntnisschriften der nach Gottes Wort reformierten Kirche,* ed. W. Niesel (Zurich, n.d.; ³1938) 149–81; *Bekenntnisse der Kirche,* ed. H. Steubing et al. (Wuppertal, 1985) 133–54.
■ **Literature:** *TRE* 14:582–86.

ALASDAIR I. C. HERON

■ **Additional Bibliography:** *RGG*⁴ 3:1514f.—M. Beintker, "Glaubensgewissheit nach dem Heidelberger Katechismus," in *Certitudo salutis. Symposion für H.H. Esser* (Münster, 1996) 55–69; W. Verboom, *De theologie van de Heidelbergse Catechismus* (Zoetermeer, 1996); A. Rauhaus, *Den Glauben verstehen* (Wuppertal, 2003).

Henry II, the Younger, of Braunschweig-Wolfen-büttel (reigning duke 1514–1568). Born Novem-ber 10, 1489 in Wolfenbüttel, where he died June 11, 1568. He was the last important Catholic lay prince in northern Germany. His actions in for-eign and domestic politics were typical of a sover-eign in the early modern period—he acquired territory as a result of the feud with the chapter of Hildesheim (1519-1523) and took possession of Goslar in pledge; he introduced the system of pri-mogeniture in 1535, and set up a chancellery in 1548. He acted with violence and a lack of moral scruples. In the religious question, he followed the emperor's position; he was the political leader of the League of Nuremberg in 1538, and he exer-cised church leadership in place of the bishopric of Hildesheim, which had been weakened. A war conducted by means of polemical pamphlets (Martin Luther, *Wider Hans Worst,* 1541) led to his expulsion by the Schmalkalders in 1542 and the forcible introduction of the Reformation. After his return to power in 1547, he was only par-tially successful in reversing this, since his third son and successor, Julius, gave up the Catholic faith.

■ **Literature:** *NDB* 8:351f.; *TRE* 7:142f.; *TRZRK* 3:8–43.—F. Koldewey, *Heinz von Wolfenbüttel* (Halle, 1883); H. Reller, *Vorreformatorische und reformatorische Kirchenverfassung im Fürstentum Braunschweig-Wolfen-büttel* (Göttingen, 1959); F. Petri, "Herzog H. der Jüngere von Braunschweig-Wolfenbüttel," *ARG* 72 (1981) 122–58; H. Patze, ed., *Geschichte Niedersachsens,* vol. 3/2 (Hildesheim, 1983) 37ff.

WALTER ZIEGLER

■ **Additional Bibliography:** D. Demandt, "Die Auseinandersetzungen des Schmalkaldischen Bundes mit Herzog H. d.J. von Braunschweig-Wolfenbüttel im Briefwechsel des St. Gallener Reformators Vadian," *Zwingliana* 22 (1995) 45–66.

Henry II of France (king 1547-1559). Enemy of the house of Habsburg and of the French Protestants, renewer of the administrative structures in France, born March 31, 1519 in St-Germain-en-Laye, died July 10, 1559 in Paris from injuries sustained during a tournament. He was the second son of King → Francis I, and succeeded to the throne on March 31, 1547 because the Dauphin Francis had died in 1536. He married Catharine de → Medici on October 28, 1533. He conducted an anti-Habsburg policy, for which he sought the support of the Protestant Estates in the empire; political and military defeats and problems within France forced him to conclude the Peace of Cateau-Cambrésis in 1559, which meant that France renounced its ambitions to be the dominating power in the European political system of states, yielding this position to the house of Habsburg. Henry could not prevent the spread of Protestantism in France. He was successful in developing French institutions. Scholars differ widely in their assessment of his life and his achievements.

■ **Literature:** I. Cloulas, *Henri II* (Paris, 1985); F. J. Baumgartner, *Henry II, King of France* (London, 1988); R. Babel, "H. II.," in *Französische Könige und Kaiser der Neuzeit,* ed. P. C. Hartmann (Munich, 1994) 71–90.

KLAUS MALETTKE

■ **Additional Bibliography:** M. Wintroub, "Civilizing the Savage and Making a King. The Royal Entry Festival of Henri II (Rouen, 1550)," *SCJ* 29 (1998) 465–94.

Henry III of France (king 1574-1589). The last of the Valois, born September 19, 1551 in Fontainebleau, died August 2, 1589 in St-Cloud after being attacked by an assassin the previous day. He became dauphin in 1560, and was king of Poland from 1573 to 1574. Earlier scholars were probably incorrect to assume that Henry shared in planning the murders of Huguenots (St. → Bartholomew's Eve), which began on the morning of August 24, 1572. During the civil wars, which grew in intensity after 1576 and embroiled the French crown in the greatest crisis of its history

hitherto in 1588, he attempted to use all means (even dubious methods) to stabilize his country and give it peace, and things began to take a turn for the better in summer of 1589. This positive turn of events was halted by his assassination.

■ **Sources:** *Lettres de Henri III,* ed. M. François, 4 vols. (Paris, 1959–84).

■ **Literature:** P. Champion, *La jeunesse de Henri III. 1551–71,* 2 vols. (Paris, 1941–42); idem, *Henri II roi de Pologne* (Paris, 1943); P. Chevallier, *Henri III* (Paris, 1985); *Henri III et son temps,* ed. R. Sauzet (Tours, 1992).

KLAUS MALETTKE

■ **Additional Bibliography:** J.-F. Solnon, *Henri III* (Paris, 2001).

Henry IV of France (king 1589-1610). Born December 13, 1553 in Pau, died May 14, 1610 in Paris, murdered by the lay brother François de Ravaillac (1578-1610). He became king of Navarre in 1572, and became direct heir to the French throne in 1584. He converted to the Catholic faith on July 25, 1593, and was anointed in Chartres on February 27, 1594. In his childhood and youth, he was deeply marked by the antithetical personalities of his mother, Jeanne d'Albert (a staunch adherent of Calvinism), and his father, Antoine de Bourbon (who returned to the old faith), as well as by a lengthy period at the French court. Henry changed his religious confession six times in the course of his life. Under the impact of the civil war, which intensified in character after St. → Bartholomew's Eve (1572), Henry became the leader of the Protestant party, but he kept open the alternative of a reconciliation with the court.

When → Henry III died childless in 1589, the Valois dynasty came to an end. In keeping with the rules laid down in the ancient Salic law, the throne passed to Henry of Navarre, a Bourbon. This had dramatic effects on developments within France—and not only because he was a Calvinist. It was only after a long struggle, in which his military and diplomatic skills stood him in good stead, and after his definitive embrace of Catholicism, that he was universally acknowledged as king. His great merits include the internal pacification of France, the enforcement of the Edict of Nantes (April 13, 1598), which ensured the peaceful coexistence of both confessions, and the reconstruction of the country. He also laid the foundations of the absolute monarchy and made France count once more as a European power.

■ **Sources:** *Recueil des Lettres missives de Henri IV,* ed. J. Berger de Xivrey and J. Guadet, 7 vols. and 2 supp. vols. (Paris, 1843–76).

■ **Literature:** Y. Cazaux, *Henri IV ou la Grande victoire* (Paris, 1977); J.-P. Babelon, *Henri IV* (Paris, 1982); Y. Cazaux, *Henri IV. Les horizons du règne* (Paris, 1986).

KLAUS MALETTKE

■ **Additional Bibliography:** M. Greengrass, *France in the Age of Henri IV* (London, 1995); Ch. Biet, *Henri IV* (Paris, 2000).

Henry VIII of England (king 1509-1547). Son of Henry VII, born June 28, 1491 in Greenwich, died January 28, 1547 in Westminster. He came to power at the age of 18, but soon entrusted government business to Cardinal Thomas → Wolsey, who developed the system whereby the state controlled the church. In 1519, Henry was an unsuccessful candidate for the imperial crown. He had studied theology, and wrote in 1521 the *Assertio septem sacramentorum* in defense of Catholic sacramental doctrine against Martin Luther; → Leo X rewarded him for this book with the title "Defender of the Faith." After the fruitless attempt to have Rome declare invalid his marriage with Catharine of Aragon, which had initially been made possible by a dispensation of Julius II, and had lasted seventeen years, he obtained from Thomas → Cranmer, archbishop of Canterbury, the declaration of nullity and permission to marry Anne Boleyn (1533). The synod of Canterbury proclaimed Henry head of the Church of England in 1531; supported by the "Reformation parliament" (1529-1536), Henry attacked the authority and jurisdiction of the pope. The clergy submitted in 1532; rights of appeal to Rome were limited in 1533; the Act of → Supremacy was passed in 1534; and the monasteries were secularized between 1535 and 1540. Although Henry was excommunicated in 1535, negotiations with Rome continued. Most of the bishops, clergy, and laity submitted to Henry; in 1535, he had Thomas → More and Cardinal John → Fisher executed for their refusal to swear the oath of supremacy. In 1536, Henry married Anne of Cleves, in order to consolidate his alliance with electoral Saxony. However, Protestant tendencies were repressed by the Catholic six articles of June 2, 1539 (the "Bloody Act"), which

cost Thomas → Cromwell his life. The royal supremacy did not lead to the immediate introduction of Protestant teachings and rites, since Henry had no sympathy with these (Church of → England). His theological position depended on the state of his political relationships to → Charles V and the German Protestant princes. His book *A Necessary Doctrine* (1543) took an intermediary course between Catholic and Protestant doctrine. The great changes during his reign came about through decisions of parliament. Henry was an English version of the typical Renaissance prince: learned but ruthless.

■ **Literature:** *DNB* 26:76–94; *HKG* 4:341–51; *Encyclopaedia Britannica* 11:439f.; *The Oxford Dictionary of the Christian Church* (London, 1957) 623f.—*Letters and Papers of the Reign of Henry VIII,* ed. J. S. Brewer et al., 21 vols. (London, 1861–1910); G. R. Elton, *Reform and Reformation* (London, 1977); J. Ridley, *H. VIII* (Zurich, 1990); J. J. Scarisbrick, *Henry VIII* (New Haven, Conn., 1997); K. Kluxen, *Geschichte Englands* (Stuttgart, [5]2001).—Bibliographies: *The Bibliography of the Reform 1540–1648,* ed. D. Baker (Oxford, 1979) (up to 1970); U. Baumann, *Henry VIII in History, Historiography and Literature* (Frankfurt/ Main, 1992).

DIETER J. WEISS

■ **Additional Bibliography:** *Assertio septem sacramentorum,* ed. and with an intro. by P. Fränkel (Münster, 1992); R. Rex, *Henry VIII and the English Reformation* (Basingstoke, 1993); D. G. Newcombe, *Henry VIII and the English Reformation* (London, 1995); A. Weir, *Henry VIII* (London, 2001); A. Ryrie, "The Strange Death of Lutheran England," *JEH* 53 (2002) 64–92; idem, "Divine Kingship and Royal Theology in H. VIII's Reformation," *Reformation* 7 (2002) 49–77; R. McEntegart, *Henry VIII, the League of Schmalkalden and the English Reformation* (London, 2002); A. Graves, *Henry VIII* (London, 2003).

Henry of Zutphen. Augustinian Hermit, born 1488 or 1489 in Zutphen (Netherlands), died December 10, 1524 in Heide (Holstein). He began his studies at Wittenberg in 1508. He became subprior in Cologne in 1514, and was later prior in Dordrecht. He returned to Wittenberg in 1520, where he had close contacts with Martin Luther and Philipp Melanchthon. He became prior of the Augustinian monastery in Antwerp in 1522. He was forced to flee to Bremen because of his Protestant sermons, and he introduced the Reformation into this city. After a sermon in Meldorf (Dithmarschen), he was condemned to be burnt at the stake. Henry, whose theology influenced not only Luther, but also → Erasmus of Rotterdam and Andreas → Karlstadt, was one of the first martyrs for the Protestant faith.

■ **Literature:** *ADB* 11:642f.; *RE* 21:737–42; *Nieuw Nederlandsch Biografisch Woordenboek,* vol. 5, 1179ff.; *RGG*³ 3:205; *NDB* 8:431; *BBKL* 2:685f.; *RGG*⁴ 3:1602. – J. F. Iken, *H. von Zutphen* (Halle, 1886); W. Seegrün, "H. von Zutphen—seine Ideen, sein Feuertod und Dithmarschens Weg einer Gemeindereform," *Beiträge und Mitteilungen des Vereins für katholische Kirchengeschichte in Hamburg und Schleswig-Holstein* 3 (1990) 105–23.

HANS-GEORG ASCHOFF

Held, *Matthias* (raised to the imperial nobility 1536). Lawyer, imperial vice-chancellor under → Charles V, born in Arlon (Belgian province of Luxembourg), died 1563 in Cologne. He became secretary to the imperial supreme court in 1527, and endeavored to preserve the old faith and to preserve the rights of the emperor. He was appointed imperial vice-chancellor in 1531, and was an important adviser to the emperor. In 1536, he undertook a delicate mission in the empire, furnished with two instructions (concerning aid against the Turks, a council, and religious trials); scholars disagree in their evaluation of this mission. Convinced that he was acting in keeping with the emperor's own views, he encouraged the foundation of the so-called Catholic (Nuremberg) Alliance in 1538, but its exaggerated confessional character was a hindrance to the imperial policy, which aimed at achieving an overall balance between the confessions; it was ratified by the emperor only on May 20, 1539. He was dismissed from office as vice-chancellor in 1541 and withdrew to Cologne, where he led a private life.

■ **Literature:** *ADB* 11:680; *NDB* 8:464.—V. Press, "Die Bundespläne Kaiser Karls V.," in *Das römisch-deutsche Reich im politischen System Karls V.,* ed. H. Lutz (Munich and Vienna, 1982) 55–106.

IRMGARD HÖSS

Helding, *Michael.* Catholic theologian, born 1506 in Langenenslingen (Hohenzollern), died September 30, 1561 in Vienna. He studied in Tübingen and took the degree of master of arts in the academic year 1528-1529. He taught at the cathedral school in Mainz in 1531 and became parish priest at the cathedral in 1533. He took his doctorate in theology in 1543. In 1537, he was appointed titular bishop of Sidon and auxiliary bishop in Mainz; he was a leading member of the diocesan (1548) and provincial (1549) synods in Mainz. He took part in the religious dialogues in → Worms in 1540 and 1557, and in the Council of Trent in 1545-1546. Along with Julius von → Pflug, he drew up a "formula of comparison," which influenced the → Augsburg Interim of 1548. The sermons about the Mass, which he delivered at the imperial parliament in Augsburg in 1547-1548 and published in 1548, led to controversies with Matthias → Flacius. He was elected bishop of Merseburg in 1549, but renounced the government of this diocese in 1558, becoming a member of the imperial supreme court in Speyer, and then president of the imperial court council in Vienna in 1561. He was open to church reform in the spirit of biblical studies and humanism, published collections of sermons and catechetical writings, and composed a *Formula Reformationis* in 1557 which influenced the improved formula of reform proposed by the emperor in 1559.

■ **Works:** Feifel (see below) (catalogue); Klaiber nos. 1467–85; *VD 16* 8:556–64.

■ **Literature:** *NDB* 8:486f.; *DSp* 7:138ff.; *KThR* 2:124–36; *TRE* 15:15f.; *DHGE* 23:863f.—E. Feifel, *Grundzüge einer Theologie des Gottesdienstes. Motive und Konzeption der Glaubensverkündigung M.H.s.* (Freiburg, 1960); J. Pflug, *Correspondance,* ed. J. V. Pollet, vols. 2–5 (Leiden, 1973–82); B. von Bundschuh, *Das Wormser Religionsgespräch von 1557* (Münster, 1988); F. Jürgensmeier, ed., *Erzbischof Albrecht von Brandenburg* (Frankfurt/Main, 1991).

HERIBERT SMOLINSKY

Helgesen, *Poul* (Paulus Helle). Carmelite, Danish Catholic theologian, born c. 1485 in Varberg (province of Halland, today in Sweden), died c. 1535 (place of death unknown). In 1519, he took the degree of bachelor of theology and became regent of the newly founded Carmelite house of studies in Copenhagen, where he also held theological lectures at the university; he became provincial of his Order in 1522. He was influenced by → Erasmus of Rotterdam, and initially welcomed Martin Luther; but unlike many of his students, he did not himself embrace the Reformation. He composed numerous works of controversial theology and a chronicle of Denmark from 1448-1534 (the so-called Chronicle of Skiby).

■ **Works:** *Skrifter af P.H.,* ed. P. Severinsen, *M. Kristensen and N.K. Andersen,* 7 vols. (Copenhagen, 1932–48).

■ **Literature:** *DHGE* 15:198–201; *Dansk Biografisk Leksikon,* 3. Auflage, vol. 6, 210ff.—J. O. Andersen, *P.H.,* vol. 1 (Copenhagen, 1936); N. K. Andersen, "Det teologiske Fakultet 1479–1597," in *København Universitet 1479–1979,* ed. L. Grane, vol. 5 (Copenhagen, 1980) 1–92; L. Grane, "Studia humanitatis und Theologie an den Universitäten Wittenberg und Kopenhagen im 16.Jh.," in *Der Humanismus und die oberen Fakultäten,* ed. G. Keil, B. Möller, and W. Trusen (Weinheim, 1987) 65–82; L. Grane and K. Hørby, eds., *Die dänische Reformation vor ihrem internationalen Hintergrund* (Göttingen, 1990) passim.

JØRGEN STENBÆK

Hemmingsen, *Niels* (Nicolaus Hemming[ius]). Danish Lutheran theologian, born May or June, 1513 on the island of Lolland, died May 23, 1600 in Roskilde. He studied under Philipp Melanchthon in Wittenberg from 1537 to 1542. He taught Greek in Copenhagen from 1543, dialectic and Hebrew from 1545, and theology from 1553. He took his doctorate in theology in 1557, and became vice-chancellor of the university in 1572. Despite his great influence in theology and church politics, he was dismissed from office in 1579 because of his teaching on the Lord's Supper, which was suspected of → Crypto-Calvinism. He ended his life as cathedral canon in Roskilde.

■ **Works:** *De methodis* (Rostock, 1555, often reprinted); *Enchiridion theologicum* (Wittenberg, 1557, often reprinted); *Postilla seu enarratio evangeliorum* (Copenhagen, 1561, often reprinted); *De lege naturae apodictica methodus* (Wittenberg, 1562, often reprinted); *Pastor sive pastoris optimus vivendi agendique modus* (Copenhagen, 1562, often reprinted); *Commentaria in omnes epistolas apostolicas* (Strasbourg, 1572, often reprinted); *Syntagma institutionum Christianarum* (Copenhagen, 1574, often reprinted); *Libellus de coniugio, repudio et divortio* (Leipzig, 1576, often reprinted); *Commentarii in evangelium Johannis,* 2 vols. (Basle, 1590/91); *Tractatus de gratia universali* (Copenhagen, 1591).— Partial collection: *Opuscula theologica* (Geneva, 1586).

■ **Literature:** *Dansk Biografisk Leksikon,* 3. Auflage, vol. 6, 247ff.; *DHGE* 23:994f.—K. Barnekow, *N. H.s teologiska åskådning* (Lund, 1940); E. Munch Madsen, *N.H.s Ethik* (Copenhagen, 1946); O. Fatio, *Méthode et théologie* (Geneva, 1976); J. Glebe-Møller, "Socialetiske aspekter af N.H.s forfatterskab," *Kirkehistoriske Samlinger* 17 (1979) 7–56; N. K. Andersen, "Det teologiske Fakultet 1479–1597," in *Københavns*

Universitet 1479–1979, vol. 5, ed. L. Grane (Copenhagen, 1980) 1–92.

JØRGEN STENBÆK

Hervet, *Gentien.* humanist and controversial theologian, born 1499 in Olivet near Orleans, died September 12, 1594 in Reims. He took part in all three periods of the Council of Trent. As a collaborator of Cardinal Marcello Cervini (later Pope → Marcellus II), he contributed patristic material to the conciliar texts. He was ordained priest in 1556. He wrote several works against Calvinism. He became canon in Reims in 1562, and was conciliar theologian to Cardinal Charles de → Guise in Trent in 1562-1563. He also produced outstanding translations of classical writers and church fathers.

■ **Sources:** J. Le Plat, *Monumentorum ad historiam Concilii Tridentini spectantium collectio 5* (Louvain, 1785) 777–89; *CT* 5:566–69; 12:530–36.

■ **Literature:** *DThC* 6:2315–20; *Cath* 5:693–97; Jedin vol. 2; 3; 4/2.

KLAUS GANZER

Heshusius (van Heshusen), *Tilemann.* Lutheran theologian, born November 3, 1527 in Wesel, died September 25, 1588 in Helmstedt. He began his studies in Wittenberg in 1546, and taught there from 1552. He became superintendent in Goslar in 1553, and took his doctorate in theology the same year. He became a collaborator of Matthias → Flacius in Magdeburg in 1556, and attempted in vain to mediate between Flacius and his teacher, Philipp Melanchthon. In the same year, he became professor of theology in Rostock. In 1558-1559, he was general superintendent of the electoral Palatinate and professor in Heidelberg, where he resisted the adoption of the Reformed confession. He became pastor in Magdeburg in 1560, and superintendent there the following year. After a short period in Wesel, he became superintendent and court preacher in Neuburg on the Danube in 1565. He became professor in Jena in 1569, and bishop of Samland in Königsberg in 1573. In 1578, he became professor in Helmstedt. Both in theology and in church politics, Heshusius opposed Calvinist influence on the Lutheran confession (→ Gnesiolutherans), but he maintained independent positions of his own on the Lord's Supper (against the doctrine of → ubiquity) and on original sin (against Flacius).

■ **Principal Works:** *Examen theologicum* (Jena, 1571).—
Catalogue: *VD 16* 9:66–89.
■ **Literature:** *TRE* 15,:256–60.—P. F. Barton, *Um
Luthers Erbe* (Witten, 1972).

PETER FRIEDRICH BARTON

Hess (Hesse), *Johann.* Reformer of Breslau, born
September 23 (?), 1490 in Nuremberg, died January 1, 1547 in Breslau. He studied in Leipzig
(1505-1510) and in Wittenberg (1510-1512; master of arts, 1511), where he had contacts with
Johann → Lang, Martin Luther, and Georg →
Spalatin. In 1513, he became secretary to Johann
V. Thurzo, bishop of Breslau, in Neisse, and
received canonries in Neisse, Brieg, and in the
church of the Holy Cross in Breslau. In 1517, he
continued his studies in Erfurt and in Italy,
encountering Eobanus Hessus and → Crotus
Rubeanus. He took his doctorate in theology in
1519, perhaps in Ferrara. He had conversations in
Wittenberg with Luther and Philipp Melanchthon
at the end of 1519 and beginning of 1520. He was
ordained priest in Breslau on June 2, 1520, and
worked as cathedral preacher for a short period;
from the end of 1520, he was court theologian to
the duke of Münsterberg in Oels. His sermons
both here and in Nuremberg in 1522 proposed
Lutheran ideas. The council in Breslau summoned
him to the office of preacher in St. Mary Magda-
lene's parish church in 1523; Bishop Johann von
Salza agreed initially to this, but pressure from the
cathedral chapter, the pope, and the Polish king
led him to refuse the investiture. After the religious dialogue in Breslau from April 20 to 22,
1524, which Hess had initiated, cautious reforms
were introduced into the liturgy. In his further
work, Hess collaborated closely with Ambrosius
Moibanus, and made it clear that he did not share
the ideas of Kaspar → Schwenckfeld.
■ **Literature:** *NDB* 9:7f.; *TRE* 15:260–63; *BBKL* 2:784ff.;
DHGE 24:276f.; *TRZRK* 2:102–38, esp. 114f.—N.
Holzberg, *W. Pirckheimer* (Munich, 1981) index.

FRANZ MACHILEK

■ **Additional Bibliography:** *OER* 2:234f.; *RGG*[4] 3:1704.

Hessels, *Jan* (Johannes a Lovanio). Controversial
theologian, born 1522 in Louvain, where he died
November 7, 1566. He studied theology at the
university of Louvain, where he was professor of

theology from 1554 to 1556. He and Michael →
Bajus were sent to the Council of Trent by →
Philip II. His theology rejected the methodology
of scholasticism, and he promoted a new tendency
that was open to fundamental methodological
demands of the Reformers. Bajus supported this
tendency, and its opponents called this
"Bajanism." At his death, he left many controversial writings in manuscript form, some of them
incomplete (especially writings on the Eucharist,
against Georg → Cassander, Johannes → Monheim, etc.), and commentaries on the New Testament (Matthew, 1 Timothy, 1 Peter, 1-3 John)
which were cleansed from "Bajanist" passages by
Henricus Gravius and published at Louvain in
1568.
■ **Literature:** *Dictionnaire de la Bible,* ed. F. Vigouroux,
vol. 3/1 (Paris, 1912) 665; *DThC* 6:2321–24.—P.
Polman, *L'Élément historique dans la Controverse
religieuse du XVIe siècle* (Gembloux, 1932) passim; H. de
Vocht, *History of the Foundation and the Rise of the
Collegium Trilingue Lovaniense,* vol. 4 (Louvain, 1955)
158–62; M. Lamberigts, "The Place of Augustine in the
First and the Second Books of Hessels' Catechismus," in
idem, ed., *L'Augustinisme à l'ancienne Faculté de
Théologie de Louvain* (Louvain, 1994) 99–122.

FERNANDO DOMÍNGUEZ

Hochwart, *Lorenz.* Catholic theologian and historian, born c. 1500 in Tirschenreuth, died February
20, 1570 in Regensburg. He became cathedral
preacher in Regensburg in 1534, and took part in
the Council of Trent in 1552 as procurator of the
bishop of Regensburg. He was a staunch defender
of Catholic doctrine, both in his published sermons and in his work as canon lawyer. His historical works *Catalogus episcoporum Ratisponensium*
(ed. A. F. von Oefele [Augsburg, 1763]) and *Chro-
nographia* (only in manuscript) give Hochwart a
place among the leading representatives of
humanist historiography.
■ **Works:** (manuscripts) *Annotationes in evangelio;
Monotessaron divisum; Bellum Luthericum; Historia
Turcarum; Catalogus episcoporum Salisburgensium.*
■ **Literature:** *ADB* 12:529f.—H. Wurster, "L.H.," in
Lebensbilder aus der Geschichte des Bistums Regensburg
(Regensburg, 1989) 245–56.

MANFRED KNEDLIK

■ **Additional Bibliography:** M. Knedlik, "Poetisches
Tagebuch. Zwei Grabschriften für L.H. und Philipp
Dobereiner," *Heimat Landkreis Tirschenreuth* 11 (1999)
63–69.

Hoen (Hoon, Ho[n]ius), *Cornelis Henricxzoon.* Lawyer, died 1524 (?) in The Hague. He was a lawyer at the Dutch court in The Hague. Under the influence of Wessel Gansfort, he rejected the doctrine of transubstantiation and interpreted the verb *est* ("this is my body") in the words of institution as *significat* ("this signifies my body"). He set out this view in a letter of 1521 which reached Germany and Switzerland. Whereas Martin Luther rejected it outright, Huldrych Zwingli saw it as confirming his own position (→ eucharistic controversy); but it was not Zwingli himself (as earlier scholarship supposed) who printed the letter without indicating its author (*Epistola christiana admodum,* published at Strasbourg without indication of place in 1525, and often reprinted; ed. G. Finsler, *Huldreich Zwinglis Sämtliche Werke,* vol. 4 [Leipzig, 1927], 509-19), but rather Martin → Bucer, who also published a translation into German (*Von dem brot und weyn des Herren* [Strasbourg 1525, often reprinted]). Hoen was imprisoned from February to October, 1523 under suspicion of heresy.

■ **Literature:** *RGG*[3] 3:411; *DHGE* 24:741ff.—J. Staedtke, "Voraussetzungen der Schweizer Abendmahlslehre," *Theologische Zeitschrift* 16 (1960) 19–32; T. Kaufmann, *Die Abendmahlstheologie der Straßburger Reformatoren bis 1528* (Tübingen, 1992) 292–302.

PETER WALTER

■ **Additional Bibliography:** B. J. Spruyt, "Cornelius Henrici H. (Honius) and His Epistle on the Eucharist (1525)" (diss., Leiden, 1996).

Hoffäus, *Paulus.* Jesuit (1554), born c. 1530 (or 1523) in Münster near Bingen, died December 17, 1608 in Ingolstadt. Together with Peter → Canisius, he played a central role in building up the Society of Jesus in Germany as rector (Prague, Vienna, Ingolstadt, Munich), vice-provincial (1567-1569) and provincial (1569-1581) of the Upper German province, German assistant (1581-1591), and visitor (1594-1597). Hoffäus argued against the → chalice for the laity, and supported a relaxation of the prohibition of interest on loans. He produced the first German translation of the → Catechismus Romanus (Dillingen, 1568).

■ **Literature:** *DSp* 7:580ff.; *NDB* 9:388; *Helvetia Sacra,* ed. R. Henggeler, vol. 7 (Berne, 1976) 82f.—C. Sommervogel, *Bibliothèque de la Compagnie de Jésus,* vol. 4 (Paris, 1893) 422f.; 9, 494; B. Duhr, *Geschichte der Jesuiten in den Ländern deutscher Zunge,* vol. 1

(Freiburg, 1907) 780–98; B. Schneider, *P. H.* (Rome, 1956); P. Rodríguez, *El Catecismo Romano* (Pamplona, 1982) 228–34; L. Polgár, *Bibliographie sur l'histoire de la Compagnie de Jésus,* vol. 3/2 (Rome, 1990) 143.

ALFONS KNOLL

Hoffman, *Melchior.* Lay preacher and Baptist leader, born c. 1500 in Schwäbisch Hall, died 1543 in Strasbourg. A furrier by trade, he worked to promote the Reformation above all in Livonia and in Kiel. He turned his back on Lutheranism in 1529 and went to East Frisia, then to Strasbourg. He founded the Baptist movement (the Melchiorites) in the Netherlands in the 1530s; he was imprisoned in Strasbourg from 1533 onward. He set out his doctrine in numerous writings. In the context of his eschatological ideas, which he developed early on in his life, he believed that the Catholic and Lutheran powers would be overcome by Protestant imperial cities under the leadership of Strasbourg.

■ **Literature:** *TRE* 15:470–73.—K. Deppermann, *M. H.* (Edinburgh, 1987).

RALF KLÖTZER

■ **Additional Bibliography:** *RGG*[4] 3:1819.—R. G. Bailey, "M. H. Proto-anabaptist and Printer in Kiel," *ChH* 59 (1990) 175–90; J. Derksen, "Melchiorites after M. H. in Strasbourg," *Mennonite Quarterly Review* 68 (1994) 351–66.

Homberg Synod. An assembly of the spiritual and lay Estates in Homberg (Efze) from October 21 to 23, 1526, convoked by Marquis → Philip of Hessen after the imperial parliament at Speyer in the same year, with the aim of guaranteeing the introduction of the Reformation into his territory. The lawyers disputed whether the assembly in Homberg was a synod, a local parliament, or a learned disputation. Philip's adviser here was Franz → Lambert of Avignon, whose *Paradoxa* (138 theses on reform) formed the basis of discussion. Nikolaus → Ferber, who headed the Catholic party, argued against the growing trend among Protestants whereby the local sovereign governed the church: he denied that the marquis had the authority to summon church assemblies and promulgate → church orders. The assembly took no decisions and dissolved without reaching any results. Subsequently, under Lambert's chairmanship, a commission of thirteen scholars formulated the *Reformatio Ecclesiarum Hassiae*. Although this was the programmatic starting point for the ensuing history of the Reformation in Hessen, Martin Luther's reservations about the text meant that it never became formal church law in Hessen.

■ **Sources:** *Francisci Lamberti Avenionensis ad Colonienses epistula (Marburg 15.2. 1527)* (Erfurt, 1527); G. Franz, *Urkundliche Quellen zur hessischen Reformationsgeschichte*, vol. 2 (Marburg, 1954); E. Sehling, *Die evangelischen Kirchenordnungen des XVI. Jh.*, vol. 8/1: *Hessen: Die gemeinsamen Ordnungen*, ed. H. Jahr (Tübingen, 1965).

■ **Literature:** W. Sohm, *Territorium und Reformation in der hessischen Geschichte* (Marburg, 1915); W. Schmitt, *Die Synode zu Homberg und ihre Vorgeschichte* (Homberg, 1926); G. Müller, *Franz Lambert von Avignon und die Reformation in Hessen* (Marburg, 1958); W. Zeller, *Frömmigkeit in Hessen* (Marburg, 1970); M. Rudersdorf, *Ludwig IV. Landgraf von Hessen-Marburg. Landesteilung und Luthertum in Hessen.* (Wiesbaden, 1991).

MANFRED RUDERSDORF

■ **Additional Literature:** H. Kemler, "'Ein Haufen Gesetze' und was dahinter steht. Luthers Nein zum Ergebnis der Homberger Synode von 1526," *Jahrbuch der Hessischen Kirchengeschichtlichen Vereinigung* 52 (2001) 77–84.

Honterus, *Johannes.* Humanist, pioneer of Lutheranism in Transylvania, born 1498 in Kronstadt (Transylvania), where he died January 23, 1579. He studied in Vienna from 1515 to 1525, lived in Basle and Krakow from 1529 to 1533, and returned to Kronstadt in 1533. Here, he helped the Lutheran Reformation attain its breakthrough among the Transylvanian Saxons ten years later. He became pastor of the main church in Kronstadt in 1544.

■ **Principal Works:** *Cosmographia* (Krakow, 1541/ 1542); *Reformatio Ecclesiae Coronensis* (Kronstadt, 1543).

■ **Literature:** *TRE* 15:578ff.—E. Roth, *Die Reformation in Siebenbürgen*, 2 vols. (Cologne, 1962–64); O. Wittstock, *J.H., der Siebenbürger Humanist und Reformator* (Stuttgart, 1970); K. Reinerth, *Die Gründung der evangelischen Kirche in Siebenbürgen* (Cologne, 1979); G. Engelmann, *J.H. als Geograph* (Cologne, 1982).

REMIGIUS BÄUMER

■ **Additional Bibliography:** *RGG*[4] 3:1896f.—L. Binder, *J. H. Schriften, Briefe, Zeugnisse* (Bucharest, 1996); G. Nussbächer, *J.H.* (Kronstadt, 1997); *Die H.-Schule in Kronstadt*, ed. H. von Killyen (Munich, 1998); H. Zimmermann: *J.H.* (Bonn, 1998).

Hoogstraeten (Hochstraten), *Jacob.* Dominican, born c. 1460 in Hoogstraeten (Brabant), died January 27, 1527 in Cologne. He took the degree of master of arts at the university of Louvain in 1485 and entered the Dominican Order soon afterwards, probably in Cologne. He took the degree of bachelor of biblical studies at the university of Cologne in 1496. He took his theological doctorate and became professor theology in Cologne in 1504, combining this position in 1505 and 1509 with the regency of the *studium generale* of the Dominican Order. He was prior of the monastery in Cologne from 1508, as well as inquisitor in the ecclesiastical province of Cologne, Mainz, and Trier.

He took his duties seriously and was personally modest, but he maintained his convictions in a harsh and unyielding manner. He reacted to new ways of thinking with suspicion or outright rejection. He defended the rights of the mendicant Orders to hear confessions and to bury the dead. In a memorandum which he drew up for the archbishop of Cologne, he threatened the penalty of burning at the stake for those who turned to magicians for help against the machinations of witches, and he himself had Herman van Rijswijk, a doctor, burned at the stake in 1512 for returning to heretical views that he had previously recanted.

He was anti-Jewish and supported the measures taken by the convert Johannes → Pfefferkorn against the books of the Jews; he approved of the confiscation of the Talmud, and delated the lawyer Johannes → Reuchlin to the tribunal of the Inquisition in Mainz because his *Augenspiegel* had confirmed the rights of the Jews to possess their books, including the Talmud. When Reuchlin was acquitted in Mainz and Speyer, Hoogstraeten appealed to the pope, and persuaded him to open a new trial; he was in Rome from 1514 to 1517. When Reuchlin was acquitted yet again, this time in Rome, Hoogstraeten persuaded → Leo X to issue a *mandatum de supersedendo*, postponing the final sentence indefinitely. Many humanists, who saw Hoogstraeten as a threat to the freedom of academic research and teaching, took the side of Reuchlin, and the Letters of → Obscure Men poured scorn on Hoogstraeten, who defended his position in two *apologias* (1518-1519). In his *Destructio Cabale* (1519), he also rejected Reuchlin's plea for a Christian kabbala, arguing that since the Jews had cast Christ aside, they possessed no genuine knowledge of God, and anyone who recommended the study of Jewish writings would be doing harm to the Christian faith. The provincial chapter of 1520 dismissed Hoogstraeten as prior, but not as inquisitor, and the university of Cologne supported him.

The rapid spread of the Reformation caused Rome to change its mind: in 1520, the *Augenspiegel* was condemned and Hoogstraeten rehabilitated. He played a major role in the formulation of the memoranda of the theological faculties of the universities of Cologne and Louvain against Martin Luther. He attempted to draw on his own knowledge of Augustine to refute the doctrine of grace and justification put forward by Luther, who himself appealed to the very same Augustine. In his *Colloquia* (1521-1522), he presented Luther's understanding of original sin and concupiscence as the kernel of the new teaching. Hoogstraeten also defended the ecclesial praxis of veneration of the saints. In his last writings, he sought to defend good works and the freedom of the human will.

Hoogstraeten fiercely attacked not only Luther and the Lutherans, but also those theologians who sought a mediating position. Although his writings had no direct influence on the Council of Trent, Hoogstraeten contributed, through his pupils, to the clear boundary lines that the council drew vis-à-vis the positions of the Reformers.

■ **Works:** *Defensorium fratrum mendicantium contra curatos* (Cologne, 1507); *Contra quaerentes auxilium a maleficis* (Cologne, 1510); *Erronee assertiones in Oculari Speculo J. Reuchlin* (Rome, 1517); *Acta Judiciorum inter J.H. et J. Reuchlin* (Hagenau, 1518); *Apologia Ia* (Cologne, 1518); *Apologia IIa* (Cologne, 1519); *Destructio Cabale* (Cologne, 1519); *Margarita moralis philosophiae* (Cologne, 1521); *Cum Divo Augustino colloquia contra enormes atque perversos M. Lutheri errores,* 2 Teile (Cologne, 1521–22); *Dialogus de veneratione et invocatione sanctorum* (Cologne, 1524); *Epitome de fide et operibus catholicae aliquot disputationes contra Lutheranos* (Cologne, 1526).

■ **Literature:** KThR 4:7–14.—J. Quétif and J. Echard, *Scriptores Ordinis Praedicatorum,* vol. 2 (Paris, 1721) 67–72; N. Paulus, *Die deutschen Dominikaner im Kampfe gegen Luther* (Freiburg, 1903) 87–107; *BDG* 1, n. 8436–39; 5, n. 46832–836; H. Jedin, *Des Johannes Cochlaeus Streitschrift "de libero arbitrio hominis" 1525* (Breslau, 1927) 17–47; Jedin 1:153 et al.; 2:120 et al.; U. Hofmann, "Via compendiosa in salutem. Studien zu J. von H.s letzten kontroverstheologischen Schriften (1525–26)" (diss., Tübingen, 1981); E. Meuthen, *Cologneer Universitätsgeschichte,* vol. 1: *Die alte Universität* (Cologne, 1988) 158; J. M. Peterse, "Humanismus und Judentum in den Schriften des Kölner Dominikaners J.H.," *Geschichte in Köln* 27 (1990) 27–41.

WILLEHAD PAUL ECKERT

■ **Additional Bibliography:** S. Ickert, "Defending and Defining the Ordo Salutis: J. von H. vs. Martin Luther," *ARG* 78 (1987) 81–97; H. Peterse, *Jacobus H. gegen Johannes Reuchlin* (Mainz, 1995).

Hosius, *Stanislaus.* Catholic controversial theologian, cardinal (1561), born May 5, 1504 in Krakow, son of the Krakow burgher Ulrich Hose from Pforzheim, died August 5, 1579 in Capranica near Rome. He studied the liberal arts in Krakow in 1519-1520, and was private tutor to the sons of rich magnates from 1521 to 1529. He was a member of the Krakow circle that sympathized with → Erasmus of Rotterdam. He studied in Padua and Bologna from 1530 to 1534, taking his doctorate in law in 1534. He worked in the royal Polish chancellery from 1534 to 1549, becoming general secretary in 1543. He was ordained priest in 1543. In 1549, he was appointed bishop of Kulm and royal envoy to King → Ferdinand in Prague and Vienna and to Emperor → Charles V in Brussels; he became bishop of Ermland in 1551. He was in Rome from 1558 to 1560, and was nuncio in Vienna in 1560-1561. He was papal legate to the Council of Trent from 1561 to 1563, and returned to Poland in 1564, where he devoted particular attention to the struggle against Protestantism and to pastoral work in his diocese of Ermland. He carried out a visitation and held a synod in 1565, and founded the Jesuit college and seminary in Braunsberg. From 1569, he was once again in Rome, where he supported efforts to put the Tridentine reform into practice, especially in his capacity as member of the Congregation of the Council and Grand Penitentiary (from 1573). He supported the Catholic missions in Sweden. He gave his support to Henry of Valois as king of Poland (1572-1573; → Henry III of France), and opposed the Warsaw Confederation of 1573; he also founded the Polish hospice in Rome.

The main characteristics of Hosius's theology can already be seen in his early years. *See also* under the influence of Erasmus's thought, he emphasizes the value of the patristic tradition in the struggle against Lutheranism. After 1540, his thinking was enriched by the study of Augustine's theology. He developed his own methodology for teaching the Christian faith, with both a positive theological and a controversial orientation. These elements are found in his great work, *Confessio catholicae fidei christiana,* an extensive Latin catechism composed at the request of the synod of Piotrków (1551) and first printed in Krakow in 1553, and in other polemical works directed against Jan → Łaski, Pietro Paolo → Vergerio, Johannes → Brenz, and others, as well as in the historical polemical work *De actis cum diversis haereticis,* and in his voluminous correspondence (c. 10,000 letters). His theology is christocentric and ecclesiocentric, concentrating on the defense of the unity of the church and of the societal structures of the Middle Ages.

■ Editions and Sources: *Opera,* 2 vols. (Cologne, 1584); *Die deutschen Predigten und Katechesen der ermländischen Bischöfe H. und Kromer,* ed. F. Hipler (Cologne, 1888); *Stanislai H. epistulae,* vols. 1–2, ed. F. Hipler and V. Zarkzewski (Krakow, 1879–88); vol. 3/1, ed. H. D. Wojtyska (Olsztyn, 1980); vols. 5–6, ed. A. Szorc (Olsztyn, 1976–78).—*NBD* II, 1, compiled by S. Steinherz (Vienna, 1897); *Die römische Kurie und das Konzil von Trient,* ed. J. Šusta (Vienna, 1909); *CT* passim; *Kardinal S. H., Bischof von Ermland, und Herzog Albrecht von Preussen. Ihr Briefwechsel,* ed. E. M. Wermter (Münster, 1957); *Poezje (Carmina),* ed. A. Kamieńska (Olsztyn, 1980).—Klaiber nos. 1598–1615.

■ Literature: *KThR* 5:137–52.—A. Eichhorn, *Der ermländische Bischof und Cardinal S. H.,* 2 vols. (Mainz, 1854–55); J. Lortz, *Kardinal S. H.* (Braunsberg, 1931); L. Bernacki, *La doctrine de l'Église chez le cardinal H.* (Paris, 1936); F. Zdrodowski, *The Concept of Heresy according to Cardinal H.* (Washington, 1947); E. M. Wermter, "Herzog Albrecht von Preussen und die Bischöfe von Ermland," *Zeitschrift für die Geschichte und Altertumskunde Ermlands* 29 (1957) 264–307; H. D. Wojtyska, *Cardinal H., Legate to the Council of Trent* (Rome, 1967); idem, *Studia Warmińskie* 7 (1970) 35–88; H. Fokciński, *Studia Warmińskie* 18 (1981) 21–98.

HENRYK D. WOJTYSKA

Host, *Johannes.* Dominican (c. 1496), theologian and editor, born c. 1480 in Hof Romberg near Kierspe (Westphalia) and hence often called Johannes Romberg (Romberch), died at the end of 1532 or beginning of 1553, probably in Cologne. He was preacher in Cologne from 1505 to 1514, and represented Jacob → Hoogstraeten in the trial of Johannes → Reuchlin in Speyer and Rome. He studied in Rome from 1514 to 1516, and in Bologna from 1516 to 1519. He was parish

priest of the German community in Venice in 1519-1520, and returned in the latter year to Cologne, where he became professor in 1523. He edited works by Albert the Great, → Erasmus, Johannes → Fabri (known as Faber), Johannes → Eck, Konrad → Wimpina, and others. He was a resolute opponent of the Reformation.

■ Literature: *NDB* 9:653f.; Klaiber 151ff.; *BBKL* 2:1078f.; *DHGE* 24:1237ff.—N. Paulus, *Die deutschen Dominikaner im Kampf gegen Luther* (Freiburg, 1903) 134–53.

VIOLA TENGE-WOLF

Hoya, *Count Johann von.* Prince bishop of Osnabrück (1553), Münster (1566), and Paderborn (1568), born April 18, 1529 in Vyborg (Finland), the nephew of → Gustav I of Sweden, died April 5, 1575 in Ahaus castle near Münster. He studied in Tallinn, Paris, and Rome. He became a member of the imperial supreme court in 1552 and was its president in 1556-1557; he was ordained bishop on October 5, 1567. He modernized the administration of finances, the judicial system, and the curia in his three dioceses. He was elected bishop in the hope that he could prevent war; in keeping with his own convictions, as well as with the perilous situation of his dioceses, he signed the confession of faith of the Council of Trent in 1566, and had its decrees and catechism printed (along with a translation by Georg Eder). Although he officially recommended these decrees, he did not promulgate them as law; rather, he sought to introduce the appropriate reforms by means of synods, visitations, pastoral letters, and by encouraging candidates for the priesthood to study in Rome. His work in Paderborn met with opposition by the aristocracy and suffered under a conflict with the cathedral chapter.

■ Literature: *NDB* 10:508f.; *TRZRK* 3:108–29 (Münster) 130–46 (Osnabrück) 148–61 (Paderborn).—L. Keller, *Die Gegenreformation in Westfalen und am Niederrhein,* vol. 1 (Leipzig, 1881); W. E. Schwarz, ed., *Die Akten der Visitation des Bistums Münster aus der Zeit J.s von H.* (Münster, 1913); W. Kohl, *Westfälische Lebensbilder* 10 (1970) 1–18; G. May, *Die deutschen Bischöfe angesichts der Glaubensspaltung des 16.Jh.* (Vienna, 1983) 140ff., 154ff., 318f.; H.-J. Brandt and K. Hengst, *Die Bischöfe und Erzbischöfe von Paderborn* (Paderborn, 1984) 206–10; Ch. van den Heuvel, *Beamtenschaft und Territorialstaat ... im Hochstift Osnabrück 1550–1800.* (Osnabrück, 1984) 62–70; A. Schröer, *Die Kirche in Westfalen im Zeichen der Erneuerung,* vol. 1 (Münster, 1986) 74–101,

134–54, 278–343; H. Molitor, "Die untridentinische Reform," in *Ecclesia Militans*. Festschrift R. Bäumer, vol. 1 (Paderborn, 1988) 399–431, esp. 419–23; W.-D. Mohrmann, "Osnabrücks Geschichte in der Europäischen Dimension," *Osnabrücker Mitteilungen* 96 (1991) 11–25, esp. 16–18; B. U. Hucker, *Die Grafen von H.* (Bielefeld, 1993) 97–104; A. Schröer (compiler), *Vatikanische Dokumente zur Geschichte der Reformation und der katholischen Erneuerung in Westfalen* (Münster, 1993); idem, "Die Bischöfe von Münster," in W. Thissen, ed., *Das Bistum Münster* (Münster, 1993) 197–200; W. Seegrün, "Um den Weg der Mitte," *Osnabrücker Mitteilungen* 98 (1993) 11–37; E. Gatz, ed., *Die Bischöfe des Heiligen Römischen Reiches 1448–1648* (Berlin, 1996).

WOLFGANG SEEGRÜN

Hubmaier (Hiebmair), known as Friedberger (Pacimontanus), *Balthasar*. Baptist theologian, born c. 1485 in Friedberg near Augsburg, died March 10, 1528 in Vienna. He studied theology under Johannes → Eck in Freiburg in 1503-1512, taking his doctorate in theology in Ingolstadt in 1512. He was professor and pro-rector of the university. He was appointed cathedral preacher in Regensburg in 1516, and played a central role in the expulsion of the Jews from the city in 1519; the synagogue, which was badly damaged, became a Marian pilgrimage chapel, where Hubmaier himself attracted large numbers of pilgrims. He became parish priest of Waldshut (Hochrhein) in 1521. He had contacts with humanism and read the writings of Martin Luther; his sympathy with Huldrych Zwingli and the Zurich Baptists led him to join the → Baptist movement, and the Baptist Reformation was introduced into Waldshut at Easter 1525. Hubmaier wrote many theological works (e.g., *Von der christlichen Taufe der Gläubigen*, 1525, against infant baptism). Unlike other Baptists, he did not teach a doctrine of non-resistance; indeed, he supported the rebellious peasants. At the end of 1525, Ferdinand of Austria conquered and recatholicized Waldshut. Hubmaier and his wife, Elsbeth Hügline, fled to Zurich. After a period of harsh imprisonment, he recanted, escaped to Nikolsburg in Moravia, and introduced the Baptist Reformation there too. He was burnt at the stake in Vienna as a heretic and rebel, and his wife was drowned in the Danube.

■ **Sources:** *H.s Schriften*, ed. G. Westin and T. Bergsten (Gütersloh, 1962); *B. H. Theologian of Anabaptism*, ed. H. W. Pipkin and J. H. Yoder (Scottdale, 1989).

■ **Literature:** T. Bergsten, *B. H.* (Kassel, 1961); Ch. Windhorst, *Täuferisches Taufverständnis* (Leiden, 1976); H.-J. Goertz, *Die Täufer* (Munich, 80).

CHRISTOF WINDHORST

■ **Additional Bibliography:** J. D. Rempel, *The Lord's Supper in Anabaptism. A Study in the Christology of B. H., Pilgram Marpeck, and Dirk Philips* (Waterloo [Ontario], 1993); H. Schwarz, "B. H. Toleranz in einer intoleranten Zeit," in *Reformation und Reichsstadt*, ed. H. Schwarz (Regensburg, 1994) 89–99; E. L. Mabry, *B. H.'s Doctrine of the Church* (Lanham, 1994); H. Roser, "B. H. Schüler Ecks—Gefolgsmann Luthers," in *Altbayern und Luther*, ed. H. Roser (Munich, 1996) 61–67; E. L. Mabry, *B. H.'s Understanding of Faith* (Lanham, 1998).

Huguenots. This contemptuous nickname was coined c. 1560 as a designation of the "allegedly reformed religion" or "the so-called reformed faith," and indicates the close links between the French movement and the Genevan Reformation: the French word *huguenauds* is derived from *aignos*, i.e., members of the Swiss confederation. Despite ruthless persecution by the French king → Henry II (1547-1559), the Protestants managed to hold the first national synod of the Reformed Church in Paris in 1559. In the same period, the spirit of opposition grew more intense among the highest noblemen, many of whom had embraced the new teaching, while the power of the crown was waning. The religious dialogue of → Poissy in 1561 was a failure; nevertheless, the January Edict of St-Germain (1562) granted the Huguenots the free exercise of religion outside the cities, and gave them an initial basis in law.

The massacre of Wassy on March 1, 1562, in which Protestants were murdered by the followers of Duke François de → Guise, prompted the outbreak of the first Religious (or Huguenot) War. Many Protestants fled; they lost most of their battles until 1585, but they found support abroad, while the French government drew closer to Spain. This meant that the Protestant rebellion took on a national impetus, as an expression of hostility to Spain. After the third Religious War, the Edict of St-Germain-en-Laye (1570) strengthened the political position of the Huguenots: for the first time, they were guaranteed four safe places of refuge (La Rochelle, Cognac, La Charité-sur-Loire, and Montauban). Catherine de → Medici planned the assassination of the Huguenot leader, Gaspard de → Coligny; the failure of this attack led to the bloodbath of St. → Batholomew's Eve on August 23-24, 1572. The Pacification Edict of Beaulieu (1576) showed that the hope of Christian unity was not yet dead, but the political and religious situation became ever more tense under pressure from the "Holy Alliance of French Catholics" under the leadership of Henri de → Guise. King → Henry III was murdered on August 1, 1589. When the legitimacy of → Henry IV was confirmed by his conversion (1593) and coronation (1594)—and not least by his military victories—he was able not merely to proclaim peace but also to enforce it. The Edict of → Nantes (April 13, 1598) granted the Huguenots freedom of conscience and the right to hold public worship in specific places; private worship services were permitted in the homes of higher magistrates who were Protestants. The Huguenots were given access to all the offices of state, and they received military guarantees.

Towards the end of the 16th century, there were 274,000 Protestant families (c. 1.25 million persons, roughly 8 percent of the population), concentrated in Languedoc, Poitou, and Charentes, the Loire valley, and in the Dauphiné (the *cultes de possession*). The Edict of Nantes made it possible for them to grow in strength in the other French regions too (the *cultes de concession*). No Protestant worship was allowed in Paris itself, but a Protestant church was built in Charenton in 1606.

■ *LThK*³ 5:301ff. (unabridged version).
■ **Literature:** *TRE* 15:618ff.—J. Condy, ed., *Die H. in Augenzeugenberichten* (Darmstadt, 1965; Munich, 1980); R. Mandrou, ed., *Histoire des protestants en France* (Toulouse, 1977); J. Garrisson-Estèbe, *Protestants du Midi 1559–98* (Toulouse, 1980); N. M. Sutherland, *The Huguenot Struggle for Recognition* (New Haven–London, 1980); R. Gagg, *H. Profil ihres Glaubens* (Basle, 1984); *Les Huguenots* (Paris, 1985); A. Steffe, *Die H. Reformation und Glaubenskriege in Frankreich* (Gernsbach, 1988); M. Greengras, *The French Reformation* (Oxford, 1987); A. Steffe, *Die H. Macht des Geistes gegen den Geist der Macht* (Tübingen, 1989); D. Crouzet, *Les guerriers de Dieu. La violence au temps des troubles de religion vers 1525—vers 1610* (Paris, 1990); P. Benedict, *The Huguenot Population in France* (Philadelphia, 1991).

GÉRALD CHAIX

■ **Additional Bibliography:** *Coexister dans l'intolérance: L'édit de Nantes (1598)*, ed. M. Grandjean (Paris, 1998); Ph. Bénédict, "Les vicissitudes des églises reformées de France jusqu'en 1598," *Bulletin de la Société de l'Histoire du Protestantisme Français* 144 (1998) 53–73; F.

Léstringant, "Minorité et martyre. Les Huguenots en France au temps des guerres de religion," *Études théologiques et religieuses* 74 (1999) 21–34; "The Adventure of Religious Pluralism in Early Modern France, " *Papers from the Exeter Conference, April 1999*, ed. K. Cameron (Oxford, 2000); M. Yardeni, *Repenser l'histoire. Aspects de l'historiographie huguenote des guerres de religion à la Révolution française* (Paris, 2000).—Bibliographies: *Bulletin de la Société de l'Histoire du Protestantisme Français* 1 (1852ff.); A. Pettegree, "Recent Writings on the French Wars of Religion," *Reformation* 4 (1999) 231–50; H. Davies, *French Huguenots in English-speaking Lands* (New York, 2000); R. A. Mentzer, *Society and Culture in the Huguenot World* (Cambridge, 2002).

Huguenot Psalter (Genevan Metrical Psalm Book). The most important collection of French psalms and hymns of the Reformation period, begun by Clément Marot as a new creation aiming at simplicity, and completed by Theodor → Beza in 1562. Loys Bourgeois composed most of the 125 melodies for these metrical psalms, and Claude Goudimel arranged them for several voices. This Psalter spread quickly, and its texts were translated into numerous languages, while preserving the original melodies. The most successful German version was the Metrical Psalm Book of Ambrosius Lobwasser (Leipzig, 1573; the Catholic counterpart was Kaspar Ulenberg's Metrical Psalm Book, Cologne, 1582). → Music and Reformation.

■ **Literature:** *TRE* 18:602–29.—Ph. Harnoncourt, *Gesamtkirchliche und teilkirchliche Liturgie* (Freiburg, 1974).

ECKHARD JASCHINSKI

■ **Additional Literature:** R. Weeda, "La vie du Psautier Huguenot entre 1551 et 1598," *Positions luthériennes* 49 (2001) 17–63.

Humanism

1. Concept

In the late Middle Ages, the citizens of the independent city-states of central and northern Italy came to embrace an intellectual tendency that subsequently spread over the whole of Europe, orientated to the educational ideal of *studia humanitatis* ("the humanities") which they adopted from classical Rome. The representatives of this tendency who taught at the universities were called *[h]umanista*—on the analogy of terms such as *iurista* and *canonista*. Since the *studia humanitatis* entailed a relatively stable canon of subjects (grammar, rhetoric, poetry, moral philosophy, and history), which were taught with reference to the authors of classical antiquity, we can define more precisely the contents of Renaissance humanism: it is an intellectual tendency with a primarily literary character, seeking ethical and aesthetical orientation (above all in questions concerning the conduct of life) in those classical works which were now for the first time collected and edited in a complete and systematic manner. This did not in the least involve a contradiction of the Christian faith or the church, although particular phenomena—scholastic theology, the veneration of relics and of the → saints, monasticism, etc.—were sometimes the object of severe criticism, and humanism as a whole meant that a raising of the position of the laity, since it no longer considered education a privilege exclusively reserved to the clergy.

2. Humanism and Academic Studies

By making available a large number of sources which hitherto had been known only in fragments (or not at all), but were now made accessible by improved philological methods and quickly and widely diffused by the new technology of printing, humanism brought about a profound transformation of the basis of education and academic work. This became obvious above all in the *artes,* wherever educational institutions opened their doors to this field of study. The formal training in logic ("dialectics") gave way to a study of grammar that was more strongly philological in character, and no longer limited to the Latin language alone, while questions of ethics and the conduct of life occupied the central position previously reserved for metaphysical problems. History was not considered only as a quarry for *exempla*—there was a keener awareness of the distance between the past and the present, and this not only brought with it a deeper understanding of history and of historicity than had existed in the Middle Ages but also prompted scholars to engage in their own original historical research.

In the higher faculties (theology, jurisprudence, medicine), humanism made its impact primarily by making classical texts available. In the case of theology, these were for the most part critical editions of scripture and of the church fathers

in the original languages, as well as translations into Latin and the vernacular. Pioneering achievements of humanistic philological study of the Bible are the *editio princeps* of the New Testament that → Erasmus of Rotterdam published on the basis of preliminary work by Lorenzo Valla (Basle, 1516) and the Complutensian Polyglot of the entire Bible (Alcalá, 1514-1517, published 1520). Humanistic theological editorial work was not limited to the Bible and the fathers but also included texts of medieval mysticism, e.g., in Jakob Faber → Stapulensis' editions of Hildegard of Bingen, Elizabeth of Schönau, Mechthild of Hackeborn, Raymond Lull, etc.

3. Humanism and Theology

Although many humanists made pronouncements on theologically relevant topics such as free will (Francesco Petrarca, Coluccio Salutati, Valla, Erasmus), human dignity (Giannozzo Manetti, Giovanni Pico della Mirandola), and the immortality of the soul (Pietro Pomponazzi), humanism as a whole was not much interested in theology. Naturally, one can discern many indirect influences on theology and the church, such as the genesis of a critical spirit which did not spare the church, and the attribution of a higher dignity to the laity.

We can however also speak of a specifically humanist theology, in that scholars such as Lorenzo Valla attempted to replace the traditional scholasticism—which they saw as the inappropriate penetration of the sphere of revelation by philosophical thinking—by a theology based on different linguistic-philosophical presuppositions. Instead of an ontological, abstract mode of thought, they sought to take due account of the historical character of biblical language. The paradigm of this humanist theology was not Aristotelian metaphysics but classical rhetoric as synthesized by Quintilian. After ensuring that the text of scripture was critically secure, they attempted to use the rules of rhetoric to understand it and expound it as testimony to God's self-manifestation ("rhetorical theology," to use Trinkaus's phrase). The humanists did not completely reject the traditional exegesis in terms of the four "senses" of scripture, but their philological work paved the way for historical-critical exegesis. The outstanding example of this school of thought is the sapiential theology of Erasmus, drawn from the sources of scripture and the church fathers, and aiming at Christian praxis rather than at systematic reflection.

Despite humanist criticism, university theology continued to follow the contents and methodology of scholasticism. One oddity is the commentary on the *Sentences* by Paolo Cortesi (1465-1510), which translated scholastic terminology into the language of Cicero; but serious attempts to unite scholasticism and humanism—e.g., by Giles of Viterbo and Thomas → Cajetan in his last years, or by representatives of the school of Salamanca such as Francisco de → Vitoria and Melchior → Cano—met in general with no success. At the end of the 16th century, both Catholic and Protestant systematic theology continued along the path of scholasticism; the positive theology which the humanists had encouraged was often domesticated by reducing it to nothing more than a source of *dicta probantia*. Nevertheless, the critical impulses supplied by humanism were at work not only in new research in exegesis, patristics, and church history but also in the endeavors of academic theology to address more directly questions of Christian praxis; this led to the development of dogmatics and moral theology as specific disciplines. Last but not least, the numerous catechisms of the 16th century are the fruit of humanist endeavors to renew lay piety, even when the contents of such catechisms lack a directly humanist orientation.

4. Humanism and the Reformation

Although humanism was certainly not the only cause of the Reformation, it provided decisive stimuli: the critical work of the humanists supplied criteria for the evaluation of the religious situation, and their recourse to scripture and to the early church indicated alternatives to the state of affairs that they criticized. All the new confessional parties included adherents of that humanism, which was especially linked with the name of Erasmus, and many of them sought to mediate (→ mediating theology, irenicism, → controversial theology); however, the tendency towards → confessionalization proved too strong. In Italy and Spain, where Erasmianism found a particular echo (→ Evangelism), it was extirpated in the mid-16th century by the Inquisition.

Humanism was often regarded officially as theologically unreliable. But neither the Protestant school system nor the Jesuit pedagogy, which soon acquired an exemplary character within the framework of the Catholic → reform, is conceivable without the influence of humanism.

■ **Literature and Supplements:** *DSp* 7:989–1028; *TRE* 15:639–61.—P. Polman, *L'élément historique dans la controverse religieuse du XVIᵉ siècle* (Gembloux, 1932); A. Renaudet, *Préréforme et humanisme à Paris pendant les premières guerres d'Italie (1494–1517)* (Paris, ²1953); L. W. Spitz, *The Religious Renaissance of the German Humanists* (Cambridge, Mass., 1963); C. Trinkaus, *In Our Image and Likeness*, 2 vols. (Chicago, 1970); idem and H. A. Oberman, eds., *The Pursuit of Holiness in Late Medieval and Renaissance Religion* (Leiden, 1974); P. O. Kristeller, *H. und Renaissance*, 2 vols. (Munich, 1974–76); O. Fatio and P. Fraenkel, eds., *Histoire de l'exégèse au XVIᵉ siècle* (Geneva, 1978); L. W. Spitz et al., eds., *H. und Reformation als kulturelle Kräfte in der deutschen Geschichte* (Berlin and New York, 1981); J. F. D'Amico, *Renaissance Humanism in Papal Rome* (Baltimore, 1983); J. H. Bentley, *Humanists and Holy Writ* (Princeton, 1983); A. Buck, ed., *Renaissance—Reformation* (Wiesbaden, 1984); J. H. Overfield, *Humanism and Scholasticism in Late Medieval Germany* (Princeton, 1984); A. Buck, *H.* (Freiburg and Munich, 1987); H. Smolinsky, "Der H. an Theologischen Fakultäten des katholischen Deutschland," in G. Keil et al., eds., *Der H. und die oberen Fakultäten* (Weinheim, 1987); A. Rabil, Jr., ed., *Renaissance Humanism*, 3 vols. (Philadelphia, 1988); G. Bedouelle and B. Roussel, eds., *Le temps des Réformes et la Bible* (Paris, 1989); I. Backus, ed., *Théorie et pratique de l'exégèse* (Geneva, 1990); L. Grane et al., eds., *Auctoritas Patrum. Zur Rezeption der Kirchenväter im 15. und 16.Jh.* (Mainz, 1993); H. Kerner, ed., *H. und Theologie in der frühen Neuzeit* (Nuremberg, 1993); J. W. O'Malley et al., eds., *Humanity and Divinity in Renaissance and Reformation* (Leiden, 1993); G. D'Onofrio, ed., *Storia della teologia*, vol. 3 (Casale Monferrato, 1995); *Humanismus und Wittenberger Reformation* (Leipzig, 1996); I. Kraye, ed., *The Cambridge Companion to Renaissance Humanism* (Cambridge, 1996); L. Grane et al., eds., *Auctoritas Patrum II. Neue Beiträge zur Rezeption der Kirchenväter im 15. und 16.Jh.* (Mainz, 1998); M. H. Jung and P. Walter, eds., *Theologen des 16.Jh.* (Darmstadt, 2002).

PETER WALTER

■ **Additional Literature:** E. Rummel, *The Confessionalization of Humanism in Reformation Germany* (Oxford, 2000); R. Mokrosch, ed., *Humanismus und Reformation* (Münster, 2001); A. Levi, *Renaissance and Reformation* (New Haven, 2002); B. Cummings, *The Literary Culture of the Reformation* (Oxford, 2002).

Hutten, Franconian dynasty of knights

(1) *Ulrich von,* imperial knight and humanist, born April 21, 1488 in Steckelberg castle (Rhön),

died August 29, 1523 on the island of Ufenau (Lake Zurich). He entered the cathedral school in Fulda in 1499 as candidate for a canonry, and went to the university of Erfurt in 1503. He wandered aimlessly from one university to another (Cologne, Frankfurt on the Oder, Leipzig, Greifswald, Wittenberg). In 1511, attracted by the fame of the school headed by Konrad Celtis, he went to Vienna. In 1514, at the court of the electoral prince in Mainz, he met → Erasmus of Rotterdam, who encouraged his humanist interests. He served in the imperial army in Italy in 1512-1513, and returned to Germany in 1514, taking the side of Johannes → Reuchlin against the Cologne Dominicans in the literary conflict (Letters of → Obscure Men). In five discourses held between 1515 and 1519, he sharply attacked Duke → Ulrich of Württemberg, who had murdered his cousin Hans. He studied law in Italy from 1515 to 1517, and followed the excesses of the worldly Renaissance papacy with a critical eye. He was crowned *poeta laureatus* by Maximilian I in 1517, and then entered the service of → Albrecht of Brandenburg at his court. He joined Franz von → Sickingen in the expulsion of Duke Ulrich in 1519. After the → Leipzig disputation, he became sympathetic to the ideas of Martin Luther, and his agitation against Rome took the form of a violent attack on the pope and the curia in 1519-1520; in the latter year, he sought in vain to win Archduke → Ferdinand in Brussels for Luther's cause. When Albrecht dismissed him from his service in Mainz, he found refuge in 1520 with Sickingen in Ebernburg, where he continued his literary fight (mostly in German) against Rome and against the extension of princely government. Attempts by the imperial diplomacy to make use of the services of Hutten came to nothing during the imperial parliament in Worms in 1521. Hutten went to ground, and got involved in a "war against the priests" in the style of a robber baron. After Sickingen's defeat in the "skirmish of Trier" in autumn 1522, Hutten, who had been infected with syphilis as a young man, sought refuge in Basle with Erasmus, who refused to give him shelter; his last writing, *Expostulatio cum Erasmo* (1523), is an attempt at revenge. Thanks to Huldrych Zwingli, Hutten found a home with pastor Johannes Klarer, who was skilled in medicine, in Ufenau. Here he died at the age of 35, penniless and alone.

The determinative factor in Hutten's life was his membership in one particular societal grouping, viz., the imperial knights, who were in conflict with the much stronger imperial princes. His thought and action were dominated by humanism and the ethos appropriate to his social rank, by imperial patriotism, and by a radical critique of the church. This combination of knightly status, humanism, and a national spirit makes him unique. In politics he was a failure; in literary terms, he was very influential. He had little real sympathy with Luther's reforming concerns.

■ **Works:** *Gesamtausgabe,* ed. E. Böcking, 7 vols. (Leipzig, 1859–69; new printing, Aalen, 1963); *Deutsche Schriften,* ed. S. Szamatólski (Strasbourg, 1891).

■ **Literature:** *TRE* 15:747–52.—D. F. Strauss, *U. von H.,* 3 parts (Leipzig, 1858–60); P. Kalkoff, *U. von H. und die Reformation* (Leipzig, 1920); P. Held, *U. von H., seine religiös-geistige Auseinandersetzung mit Katholizismus, Humanismus und Reformation* (Leipzig, 1928); H. Holborn, *U. von H. and the German Reformation* (New Haven, 1937); J. Benzing, *U. von H. und seine Drucker* (Wiesbaden, 1956); H. Grimm, *U. von H.* (Göttingen, 1971); V. Press, "U. von H., Reichsritter und Humanist," *Nassauische Annalen* 85 (1974) 71–86; G. Schmidt, "U. von H., der Adel und das Reich um 1500," in *U. von H. in seiner Zeit* (Kassel, 1988) 19–34; *U. von H., Ritter, Humanist, Publizist 1488–1523. Ausstellungskatalog* (Kassel, 1988).

MANFRED RUDERSDORF

■ **Additional Bibliography:** *RGG*[4] 3:1966f.—*U. von H. 1488–1988,* ed. S. Füssel (Munich, 1989); H. Kornfeld, "U. von H.s Stellung zu Martin Luther," *Blätter für pfälzische Kirchengeschichte und religiöse Volkskunde* 56 (1989) 231–54; A. Schäfer, "U.s von H. publizistischer Kampf um die Reform des Reiches, *Blätter für pfälzische Kirchengeschichte und religiöse Volkskunde* 61 (1994) 279–304; M. Treu, *H., Melanchthon und der nationale Humanismus: Humanismus und Wittenberger Reformation* (Leipzig, 1996) 353–66.

(2) *Moritz von.* Prince bishop of Eichstätt (1539), cousin of (1), born November 25, 1503 in Arnstein (Lower Franconia), died December 6, 1552 in Eichstätt. He became cathedral canon in Eichstätt in 1512 and vicar capitular in 1532; he became cathedral canon in Würzburg in 1516 and vicar capitular in 1530. He studied between 1518 and 1530 in Leipzig, Ingolstadt, Padua, Basle, and Freiburg. He became cathedral provost in Würzburg in 1536. He was a zealous bishop and a supporter of the Jesuits. He endeavored to reform the clergy, and visited Trent in 1543. He presided

at the religious dialogue in → Regensburg in 1543, and held a diocesan synod in 1548. He was in contact with men such as Johannes → Eck, Kilian → Leib, Johannes → Cochlaeus, and Julius von → Pflug. He was tolerant in relation to Protestants outside the territory where he himself ruled.

■ **Literature:** *NDB* 8:98; *DHGE* 24:465f.—*ARCEG* 3 and 4; J. V. Pollet, ed., *Julius Pflug. Correspondance,* vols. 2, 3 and 5/1 (Leiden, 1973–82); K. Ried, *M. von H., Fürstbischof von Eichstätt, und die Glaubensspaltung* (Münster, 1925).

ERNST REITER

■ **Additional Bibliography:** *Die Bischöfe des Heiligen Römischen Reiches 1448–1648,* ed. E. Gatz (Berlin, 1996) 323f.

Hutterite Brethren. The oldest community of → Baptists in existence today. The first community settled in Haushaben (later known as Bruderhof) in Austerlitz/Slavkov in Moravia, based on absolute non-resistance and the fellowship of goods. Between 1533 and 1535, a fraternal-communist community order was introduced at the directives of the Tyrolean Baptist leader Jakob Hut(t)er, who was burnt at the stake in Innsbruck in 1536. The golden age, with up to 70,000 members, was from 1564 to 1592. The Brethren were expelled from Moravia in 1622, and a remnant emigrated to Slovakia and Transylvania.

■ *LThK*³ 5:347 (unabridged version).
■ **Sources:** *Geschicht-Buch der Hutterischen Brüder.* (Vienna, 1923).
■ **Literature:** R. Friedmann, *Die Habaner in der Slowakei* (Vienna, 1927); J. A. Hostetler, *Hutterite Society* (Baltimore and London, 1974); M. Holzach, *Das vergessene Volk* (Hamburg, 1980); K. A. Peter, *The Dynamics of Hutterite Society* (Edmonton [Alberta], 1987); Th. von Stieglitz, "Kirche als Bruderschaft" (diss., Paderborn, 1990).

THOMAS VON STIEGLITZ

■ **Additional Bibliography:** W. O. Packull, *Hutterite Beginnings* (Baltimore, 1995); A. von Schlachta, "'Searching through the Nations.' Tasks and Problems of Sixteenth Century Hutterian Mission," *Mennonite Quarterly Review* 74 (2000) 27–49; M. Rothkegel, "The Hutterian Brethren and the Printed Book," *Mennonite Quarterly Review* 74 (2000) 51–85; W. O. Packull, "Anabaptist-Hutterite Confessions," in *Reformation und Recht.* Festschrift G. Sebass (Gütersloh, 2002) 58–72; A. von Schlachta, *Hutterische Konfession und Tradition (1578–1619)* (Mainz, 2003).

Hyperius (real name Gheeraerdts, Gerhard), *Andreas.* Protestant theologian, born May 16, 1511 in Ypres, died February 1, 1564 in Marburg. After humanist studies in France and England, he became professor of theology in Marburg in 1541, and supported the reorganization of the church in Hessen according to Protestant principles; he was one of the authors of the church order of 1566. He also supported the reform of the university of Marburg. His program, which recalls that of → Erasmus of Rotterdam, sought to mediate between the mutually hostile wings of the Reformation. His combination of theological and juridical argumentation locates him at the point of transition to orthodoxy. His primary interests were the education of future pastors, preaching, and the care of the poor.

■ **Works:** *De recte formando theologiae studio* (Basle, 1556, often reprinted); *Briefe 1530–63,* ed. G. Krause (Tübingen, 1981).
■ **Literature:** *TRE* 15:778–81. G. Krause, *A. G. H.* (Tübingen, 1977); W. van't Spijker, *Principe, methode en functie van de theologie bij A. H.* (Kampen, 1990).

GERHARD RAU

■ **Additional Literature:** W. W. Meissner, *The Greater Glory* (Milwaukee, Wisc., 1999).

I

Ignatius of Loyola (Iñigo López de Loyola). Saint (feast, July 31), founder of an Order, born 1491 in Loyola castle near Azpeitia (Basque province of Guipúzcoa), died July 31, 1556 in Rome. He was given a courtly education in Arévalo from 1506 (?) to 1517, and entered the service of the viceroy of Navarre in the latter year. He was gravely wounded in the defense of Pamplona on May 20, 1521, and experienced a conversion while reconvalescing in Loyola, when he read the *Life of Christ* by Ludolf of Saxony and legends about the saints (the *Legenda aurea*) by James of Voragine. At the end of 1522, Ignatius went to the monastery of Montserrat, where he made a general confession of the sins of his life and probably became acquainted with the *Ejercitatorio* of García Jiménez de Cisneros. From March 1522 to February of the following year, he lived a life of penitence in Manresa, close to Montserrat, experiencing both interior crises and mystical illuminations; these experiences form the basis of his *Exercises*. After a pilgrimage to the Holy Land (June, 1523–January, 1524), Ignatius returned to Spain and began to study "in order to help souls." He studied Latin in Alcalá (1524-1526) and philosophy in Salamanca (1526-1527); his initial attempts at pastoral work caused him to be suspected of being an *alumbrado*. From 1528 to 1535, he was in Paris, studying philosophy (and taking his master's degree) and theology; it was here that he first called himself "Ignatius."

On August 15, 1534, on Montmartre near Paris, Ignatius and six companions took the vows of poverty and chastity, as well as a vow to undertake missionary work in the Holy Land—and if this should prove impossible, then they would make themselves available to the pope. It did in fact prove impossible to travel to the Holy Land. Ignatius was ordained priest in Venice on June 24, 1537, and went to Rome in November of that year; one year later, in November 1538, the pope accepted the offer made by the group. Ignatius resolved in 1539 to found an Order, which was confirmed by → Paul III on September 27, 1540 in the bull *Regimini militantis Ecclesiae*. Ignatius was elected first general superior in 1541, and his main activity now consisted in guiding the Order, elaborating its constitutions, and conducting a voluminous correspondence.

Although he was not really a "writer," Ignatius left many writings with a practical orientation, above all the *Exercises,* the constitutions, fragments of his spiritual journal, autobiographical texts (the so-called *Narrative of a Pilgrim*), and more than 6,800 letters.—It was only after all the sources became accessible that it became possible to free our picture of Ignatius from the painting-over by Baroque hagiography and from psychological misunderstandings. His view of the world and the goal of his prayer ("to find God in all things") must be understood on the basis of his trinitarian mysticism. His Christ-mysticism leads him to become a follower of the Jesus who became poor for our sakes, and to serve in the church. In order to discern the "choice" or "election" of God's will in an existential decision, "discernment of spirits" is needed. For Ignatius, the Spirit and the church can never be separated. His thinking is characterized by the dialectic between mysticism and asceticism, contemplation and action, obedi-ence and freedom—a dialectic that can never be resolved in favor of one side only. Through the *Spiritual Exercises* and his Order, Ignatius had a great influence on the Catholic → reform.

■ **Works:** *Monumenta Ignatiana* (part of the *Monumenta Historica Societatis Jesu*) 26 vols. (Madrid and Rome, 1903–77); *Geistliche Übungen und erläuternde Texte,* trans. P. Knauer (Graz, [3]1988); *Der Bericht des Pilgers,* trans. B. Schneider (Freiburg, [7]1991); *Briefe und Unterweisungen,* trans. P. Knauer (Würzburg, 1993).

■ **Literature:** *DSp* 7:1266–1318; *TRE* 16:45–55.—F. Wulf, ed., *I. von Loyola. Seine geistliche Gestalt und sein Vermächtnis* (Würzburg, 1956); H. Rahner, *I. von Loyola als Mensch und Theologe* (Freiburg, 1964); L. Polgár, *Bibliographie sur l'histoire de la Compagnie de Jésus,* vol. 1 (Rome, 1981) 101–234; A. Ravier, *I. von Loyola gründet die Gesellschaft Jesu* (Würzburg, 1982); R. García-Villoslada, *San I. de Loyola. Nueva Biografía* (Madrid, 1986); C. de Dalmases, *I. von Loyola* (Munich, 1989); M. Sievernich and G. Switek, eds., *Ignatianisch. Eigenart und Methode der Gesellschaft Jesu* (Freiburg, 1990); I. Tellechea, *I. von Loyola. "Allein und zu Fuss."* (Zurich, 1991).

GÜNTER SWITEK

■ **Additional Bibliography:** D. C. Steinmetz, "Luther and Loyola," *Interpretation* 47 (1993) 5–14; H. Schilling, "Luther, Loyola, Calvin und die europäische Neuzeit," *ARG* 85 (1994) 5–31; A. Henkel, *Geistliche Erfahrung und geistliche Übungen bei I. von Loyola und Martin Luther* (Frankfurt/Main, 1995); W. W. Meissner, *I. von Loyola* (Freiburg, 1997); S. Kiechle, *I. von Loyola* (Freiburg, 2001); G. Maron, *I. von Loyola* (Göttingen, 2001).

Ilanz, religious dialogue. The influence of the Zurich Reformation reached the Three Leagues (the canon of Graubünden) by 1525, and the complaint by the bishop of Chur to the parliament in Graubünden, that the Protestant preachers in the Three Leagues were heretics and sectarians, led to a public disputation, which the Catholic party frequently tried to prevent. It was held under tumultuous circumstances on January 7-8, 1526 in Ilanz near Chur and ended with the dismissal of the bishop's complaint and conversions to the new confession. The religious dialogue in Ilanz was the beginning of the success of the Reformation in the Three Leagues.

■ **Sources:** *Eidgenössische Abschiede,* 4 vols. (Berne, 1861–72) 4.820.

■ **Literature:** E. Camenisch, *Bündnerische Reformationsgeschichte* (Chur, 1920) 36–59; *HKG* 5:171.

SAMUEL SCHÜPBACH-GUGGENBÜHL

Indulgences. This term designates the "remission of a temporal penalty by God for sins, where the guilt of these sins has already been forgiven" (Paul VI, *Indulgentiarum doctrina,* 12); it was only in the Latin tradition that the church came to deal in this specific manner with repentant sinners, since the Eastern churches never knew this development. In the West, the controversy about indulgences occasioned the split of the church in the 16th century. Protestant criticism attacked not only the fiscal abuse involved, but also what the Reformers saw as a quantitative, objectified understanding and mediation of grace, as well as the presumption on the part of the church's ministry that it could impart salvation—something that depended on God's mercy alone.

The church's magisterium has never put forward a complete theory of indulgences, but some doctrinal elements were specified when theological and pastoral doubts were raised about the praxis of indulgences (which indeed was often questionable) by Jan Hus and John Wyclif (cf. DH 1192, 1266-1268), and by Martin Luther (cf. DH 1447f., 1467-1472). The custom and praxis of the church were defended, and the essence, mode of action, effects, usefulness, and conditions for receiving indulgences were explained. The doctrine of the "treasury of the church" as the basis of indulgences was first proposed in the jubilee bull *Unigenitus Dei Filius* of January 27, 1343 by Clement VI (DH 1025-1027). In the bull *Salvator noster* (August 3, 1476; DH 1398), amplified in the encyclical *Romano Pontifici provida* (November 27, 1477; DH 1405-1407, cf. 1416), Sixtus IV explained how indulgences worked in favor of the dead. → Leo X responded in the decree *Cum postquam* (addressed to Cardinal Thomas → Cajetan on November 9, 1518; DH 1447-1449) and in the bull → *Exsurge Domine* which threatened the Reformer with excommunication (June 15, 1520; DH 1467-1472) for Luther's criticism that indulgences were a pious fraud which lulled people into a false security and seduced them into a neglect of good works. Leo's summary of doctrine and praxis up to that point was confirmed by the Council of → Trent in *Sessio XXV*, in the decree on indulgences (December 4, 1563; *COD,* 4th ed., 796f.; DH 1835, cf. 1867, 2537): Christ has entrusted the church with the authority to grant indulgences, which are rich in blessings and therefore must be retained. The anathema is pronounced only on those who declare indulgences to be useless and who deny that the church has the right to impart them. The council urges moderation in the use of indulgences, in order that ecclesial discipline may not suffer; abuses must be abolished.

■ **Literature:** (A.=Ablass, indulgences) *TRE* 1:347–64.—N. Paulus, *Geschichte des A. im Mittelalter. Vom Ursprung bis zur Mitte des 14.Jh.,* 2 vols. (Paderborn, 1922–23); idem, *Geschichte des A. am Ausgang des Mittelalters* (Paderborn, 1923); B. Poschmann, *Der A. im Licht der Bussgeschichte* (Berlin, 1948); J. A. Jungmann, *Die lateinischen Bussriten in ihrer geschichtlichen Entwicklung* (Innsbruck, 1932); W. Köhler, *Dokumente zum A.-Streit von 1517* (Tübingen, ²1934); M. Lackmann, "Thesaurus sanctorum. Ein vergessener Beitrag Luthers zur Hagiologie," in *Reformation,* vol. 1. Festgabe für J. Lortz (Baden-Baden, 1957) 135–71; G. Muschalek, H. Echternach, and M. Lackmann, "Gespräch über den A. Graz et al." (1965); P. E. Perrson, "Der wahre Schatz der Kirche," *Lutherische Rundschau* 17 (1967) 315–27.

GERHARD LUDWIG MÜLLER

■ **Additional Bibliography:** I. Dingel, "Theorie und Praxis des A.-Wesens im Mittelalter und am Vorabend der Reformation," *Der Evangelische Erzieher* 48 (1996) 361–72; B. A. R. Felmberg, *Die A.-Theorie Kardinal Cajetans* (Leiden, 1998); W. E. Winterhagen, "A.-Kritik als Indikator historischen Wandels vor 1517," *ARG* 90 (1999) 6–71.

Ius reformandi. In keeping with principle that the sovereign determined the religion of his subjects (→ "cuius regio, eius religio"), the *ius reformandi* designated the right to embrace one of the two religions, Catholic or Lutheran (from 1648 onward, also Reformed) and to impose this religion on the ruler's subjects. This right was initially granted to the princes and imperial cities by the imperial parliament in Speyer (1526), and was definitively confirmed by the Religious Peace of → Augsburg in 1555.

■ **Literature:** H. Conrad, *Deutsche Rechtsgeschichte,* vol. 2 (Karlsruhe, 1966) 18.

JOSEPH LISTL

■ **Additional Bibliography:** B. Ch. Schneider, *I. Die Entwicklung eines Staatskirchenrechts von seinen Anfängen bis zum Ende des alten Reichs* (Tübingen, 2001); M. Heckel, "Ius reformandi: auf dem Weg zum 'modernen' Staatskirchenrecht im konfessionellen Zeitalter," in *Reformation und Recht.* Festschrift G. Seebass (Göttingen, 2002) 75–126.

J

Jewel, *John.* Anglican theologian and bishop, born May 24, 1522 in Buden near Ilfracombe (Devonshire), died September 23, 1571 in Monkton Fairleigh (Wiltshire). He studied at Merton and Corpus Christi Colleges in Oxford, and took the degree of master of arts in 1545. He came under the influence of Pietro Martire → Vermigli from 1547, and was ordained in 1551. Under Queen → Mary Tudor, he put his signature to statements of Catholic doctrine, but soon afterwards recanted; he fled in 1555 to Frankfurt am Main, Strasbourg, and Zurich. He returned to London in 1559, and became bishop of Salisbury in 1560. His *Apologia pro Ecclesia Anglicana,* one of the most important Anglican controversial works directed against the Roman Catholic Church, appeared in London in 1562 (English translation, London, 1564). He was influenced by humanism and sought to prove the conformity of the Anglican church with the early church, and to justify the royal supremacy. His book generated a tremendous controversy, especially with Thomas Harding and Thomas → Stapleton.

■ **Works:** *The Works of J. J.,* ed. J. Ayre, 4 vols. (Cambridge 1845–50); *An Apology of the Church of England,* ed. J. E. Booty (Charlottesville, 1974); *VD 16* 10:103.
■ **Literature:** *RGG*³ 3:664; *Cath* 6:872f.; *NCE* 7:971f.; *HDThG* 2:375ff.—W. M. Southgate, *J. J. and the Problem of Doctrinal Authority* (Cambridge, Mass., 1962); J. E. Booty, *J. J. as Apologist of the Church of England* (London, 1963); idem, "The Bishop Confronts the Queen, J. J. and the Failure of the English Reformation," in F. Church and Th. George, eds., *Continuity and Discontinuity in Church History* (Leiden, 1979) 215–31; A. G. Dickens, *The English Reformation* (London, ²1989).

HERIBERT SMOLINSKY

■ **Additional Bibliography:** M. Pasquarello, "J. J.," *Anglican and Episcopal History* 69 (2000) 276–94; P. I. Kaufman, "J. on the Eucharist," in *Anglican and Episcopal History* 69 (2000) 421–42; S. A. Wenig, "The Ecclesiastical Vision of the Reformed Bishops under Elizabeth I, 1559–1570," *Anglican and Episcopal History* 70 (2001) 270–301.

Joachim I Nestor of Brandenburg (electoral prince 1499-1535). Born February 21, 1484 in Stendal, died July 11, 1535 in Cölln. He had a gift for languages and was given a humanistic educa-

tion. He succeeded his father while still a minor, and married Elizabeth of Denmark in 1502. He ruled jointly with his brother → Albrecht until 1513, and the two princes opened the university in Frankfurt on the Oder, which had been planned by Bishop Dietrich von Bülow since 1493. In order to enforce his sovereignty over his territory, Joachim disciplined the quarrelsome nobles, forced the territorial Estates to submit to his authority, and improved the administration of justice, setting up the supreme court in 1518. Extensive political action in favor of his dynasty helped Albrecht to secure the bishoprics of Magdeburg, Halberstadt, and Mainz. At the imperial election in 1519, Joachim voted first for → Francis I of France, and ultimately for the Habsburg → Charles V; despite disappointments, he remained loyal to Charles. This was closely connected with Joachim's church politics. On the one hand, he tightened his control over the dioceses of Brandenburg, Havelberg, and Lebus in his own domains; on the other hand, he opposed Martin Luther and his innovations from the outset, because he himself profited from the sale of indulgences in his brother's ecclesiastical province. Theologians in Frankfurt on the Oder (Konrad → Wimpina) supplied the arguments against Luther, whom Joachim met at the imperial parliament in Worms in 1521. He was a resolute supporter of the Edict of Worms (May 25) and sought to have it enforced against Luther's adherents. His close relations with the Habsburgs and his membership in the Catholic Leagues of → Dessau (1525) and Halle (1533), like the measures he took in his own territories, helped ward off the Reformation, which made no breakthrough there until 1535. Joachim was unable to prevent the secret conversion and flight of the electoral princess to electoral Saxony in 1528; his marriage had in fact already broken down, thanks to his relationship with the sister of Johannes von → Blankenfeld, bishop of Dorpat and Riga, who lived in Berlin. His last will sought in vain to obligate his sons, → Joachim II and Johann (of Küstrin, 1513-1571), to maintain the old Catholic faith.
■ **Literature:** → Joachim II. Hector von Brandenburg.

PETER BAUMGART

Joachim II Hector of Brandenburg. Born January 13, 1505 in Cölln, died January 3, 1571 in

Köpenick. Like his father, → Joachim I, he received a humanistic education and was interested in theology, corresponding with Martin Luther from 1532. He loved pomp and led a life of luxury. After his territories were divided, he ruled only over Kurmark. His brother Johann introduced the Reformation into Neumark from 1537 onward and joined the League of → Schmalkald, but Joachim long pursued an ambivalent "policy between the confessions." He aligned himself with the emperor and mediated between the confessional parties (religious dialogues in → Worms and → Regensburg); he remained neutral even during the War of → Schmalkald, and accepted the imperial → Augsburg Interim in 1548. On the one hand, he bestowed rich gifts on the cathedral chapter in Cölln in 1536; on the other, he and his nobles received communion under both kinds on November 1, 1539 from the hands of Matthias von Jagow, bishop of Brandenburg. The church order which he promulgated in 1540 was the fruit of a theology of compromise and retained important Catholic elements. The construction of a Protestant local church with church visitations and secularizations began slowly, meeting with stalling tactics, especially in the dioceses of Lebus and Havelberg. Finally, however, these dioceses came into the hands of members of Joachim's family, as did Brandenburg and the archdiocese of Magdeburg. From 1552-1555 onward, the electoral prince changed course, supporting electoral Saxony in imperial politics. He made a demonstrative profession of the Lutheran faith in the cathedral of Cölln in 1563, and this now became the dominant confession.

■ **Literature:** *ADB* 14:71–86; *RE* 9:220–27; *BBKL* 3:107–15; *TRZRK* 2:35–48.—J. Schultze, *Die Mark Brandenburg* (Berlin, vol. 3, 1963) 173–231; (vol. 4, 1964) 9–100; G. Heinrich, "Kurfürst Joachim von Hohenzollern, Markgraf von Brandenburg," in F. Reuter, ed., *Der Reichstag zu Worms von 1521* (Worms, 1971) 336–51.

PETER BAUMGART

■ **Additional Bibliography:** M. Rudersdorf, "Die Reformation in Kurbrandenburg," in *Wichmann-Jahrbuch des Diözesangeschichtsvereins Berlin* 34/35 (1994/95) 141–57.

Johann Friedrich of Saxony (electoral prince of the Ernestine line, 1532-1547). Born June 30, 1503 in Torgau, died March 3, 1554 in Weimar. He was

a close confidant of Martin Luther from 1520, and proved an important political supporter of the Reformation. He supported the Protest of Speyer in 1530, the → Confessio Augustana in 1530, and the League of → Schmalkald (1531-1547). Unyielding on religious questions—he rejected both the planned council in 1537 and the concessions made in the religious dialogue in → Regensburg in 1541—he sought a compromise in political matters (Truce of Nuremberg in 1532, Treaty of Kaaden in 1534, Truce of → Frankfurt in 1539). After the battle of Mühlberg on April 24, 1547 (War of → Schmalkald), he was the emperor's prisoner for five years, and lost the electoral dignity to his cousin → Moritz, who belonged to the Albertine line; the Ernestines retained the duchy of Saxony (Weimar). He had been a benefactor of the university of Wittenberg, but this now belonged to Albertine electoral Saxony; instead, Johann Friedrich founded the Academic College in Jena in 1548, which attained university status in 1557. Because of his steadfastness in matters of faith and his imprisonment by the emperor, he is counted among the Protestant martyrs. In political terms, his career was a failure, in that the Ernestine line lost the electoral dignity in Saxony for good.

■ **Literature:** *TRE* 17:97–103; *BBKL* 3:147–57.—G. Mentz, *J. F. der Grossmütige 1503–54*, 3 vols. (Jena, 1903–8); G. Wartenberg, "Luthers Beziehungen zu den sächsischen Fürsten," in *Leben und Werk Martin Luthers von 1526–46*, ed. H. Junghans (Göttingen, 1983) 549–71, 916–29; D. Ignasiak, *Fürst J. F. I. und die Gründung der Universität Jena* (Jena, 1996); G. Vogler, "Kurfürst J. F. und Herzog Moritz von Sachsen. Polemik in Liedern und Flugschriften während des Schmalkaldischen Krieges," *ARG* 89 (1998) 178–206.

ROLF DECOT

■ **Additional Bibliography:** G. Vogler, "Kurfürst J. F. von Sachsen und Herzog Moritz von Sachsen," *ARG* 89 (1998) 178–206; R. Kolb, "The Legal Case for Martyrdom. Basilius Monder on J. F. the Elder and the Smalcald War," in *Reformation und Recht. Festschrift G. Seebass* (Göttingen, 2002) 145–60, J. Bauer, ed., *Verlust und Gewinn. J. F. I., Kurfürst von Sachsen* (Weimar, 2003).

Johann Kasimir. Protestant Count Palatinate in Rhein, born March 7, 1543 in Simmern, died January 6, 1592 in Heidelberg. He was the younger son of the Calvinist electoral prince → Frederick

III; unlike his brother, Ludwig VI, he held fast to the Reformed confession. During his reign (1576-1583), his principality of Palatinate-Lautern (the territory around Kaiserslautern and Neustadt) became a place of refuge for Reformed Christians from the Palatinate, and the Casimirianum, a Calvinist academy founded in 1578, took the place of Heidelberg, which had become Lutheran. Contrary to the terms of the testament of Ludwig VI, Johann Kasimir alone became the regent for Frederick IV. As electoral administrator, he reintroduced Calvinism and the Reformed Church order of Frederick III in 1585. This consolidated the confessional divisions in the electoral Palatinate until 1685. Religious solidarity and political ambition led Johann Kasimir to give military aid to the → Huguenots in the French civil war (1567-1568 and 1575-1576); he also supported → William I of Orange in the Netherlands and took part in the War of Cologne in 1582-1583. In 1587 and 1591, he organized military aid to the French king → Henry IV. He attempted in vain to unite the German Protestants politically.

■ **Literature:** *NDB* 10:510ff.—F. von Bezold, *Briefe des Pfalzgrafen J. Casimir mit verwandten Schriftstücken,* 3 vols. (Munich, 1882–1903); M. Kuhn, *Pfalzgraf J. Casimir von Pfalz-Lautern* (Otterbach and Kaiserslautern, 1961); *EKO,* vol. 14; V. Press, *Calvinismus und Territoritalstaat* (Stuttgart, 1970); M. Schaab, *Geschichte der Kurpfalz,* vol. 2 (Stuttgart et al., 1992) 58ff.

EIKE WOLGAST

John of Feckenham (real name Howman). Benedictine monk in Evesham, born c. 1515 near Feckenham, died October 16, 1585 in Wisbech castle near Cambridge. He studied in Oxford and became master of novices in Evesham. Later, he taught at Oxford and was chaplain to Bishop John Bell of Worcester. From 1543, he was in the household of Bishop Edmund → Bonner in London, and Thomas → Cranmer had him imprisoned with the bishop in the Tower from 1549. He was a learned and quick-tongued controversialist in disputations with John → Jewel, John Hooper, and others. After the Catholic → Mary ascended the throne in 1553, he became her private chaplain. He became dean of St. Paul's church in London in March, 1554, and became the last abbot of the restored abbey of Westminster on November 21, 1556; in the same year, he took his doctorate in divinity at Oxford University. Queen → Elizabeth

I offered him the archbishopric of Canterbury, if he would accept the religious innovations. His refusal, and his speech in parliament against the planned ecclesiastical changes, led to the renewed dissolution of the abbey of Westminster in 1559, and to his imprisonment in the Tower in 1560. He remained imprisoned there and in other places until his death. Some of his writings survive in manuscript form.

■ **Literature:** *DNB* 18:282ff.; *DHGE* 16:803–9; *BBKL* 3:358f.—E. Taunton, *The English Black Monks of St. Benedict* (London, 1897); J. Spillmann, *Geschichte der Katholikenverfolgung in England,* vol. 4 (Freiburg, 1909) 382–87; Ph. Hughes, *The Reformation in England,* vol. 3 (London, 1954) 414f. et al.; D. M. Loades, *Maria Tudor* (Munich, 1982).

BRUNO STEIMER

■ **Additional Literature:** P. Tudor, "J. F. and Tudor Religious Controversies," in *The Cloister and the World.* Festschrift B. Harvey (Oxford, 1996) 302–22.

Jonas, *Justus* (originally Jodocus Koch). Lawyer and Lutheran theologian, born June 5, 1493 in Nordhausen, died October 9, 1555 in Eisfeld. During his studies in Erfurt (from 1506) and Wittenberg (from 1511), he joined the humanistic circle around Eobanus Hessus (1488-1540) and → Mutianus Rufus. From 1518 onward, he held lectures in law at the university of Erfurt. In 1519, he visited → Erasmus of Rotterdam; in 1521, he demonstratively accompanied Martin Luther to the imperial parliament at Worms, and in the same year he became provost, doctor of theology, and professor at the theological faculty in Wittenberg; he was also dean of this faculty from 1523 to 1533. He was Luther's collaborator and friend, and much prized as a translator of the Reformers' writings. From 1532, and later from 1539, he took part in the introduction of the Reformation into the principality of Anhalt and the duchy of Saxony; it was he who composed the relevant church orders. He was in Halle from 1541, becoming superintendent there in 1544; here too, Jonas was the author of the church order. The War of → Schmalkald led to his expulsion from Halle. After periods in Hildesheim, Coburg, and Regensburg, he became pastor in Eisfeld in 1553.

HANS-GÜNTER LEDER

■ **Sources:** *Der Briefwechsel des J. J.,* ed. G. Kawerau, 2 vols. (Halle, 1884–85; reprint, Hildesheim, 1964); W. Delius, "Drei Briefe des J. J.," *ARG* 31 (1934) 133–36;

idem, "Ergänzungen zum Briefwechsel des J. J.," *ARG* 42 (1951) 136–45.

■ **Literature:** *CEras* 2:244ff.; *TRE* 17:234–38.—M. Schellbach, *J. J.* (Essen, 1941); W. Delius, *J. J.* (Berlin, 1952); idem, *Die Reformationsgeschichte der Stadt Halle an der Saale* (Berlin, 1953); M. E. Lehmann, *J. J., Loyal Reformer* (Minneapolis, 1963); E. Koch, "Handschriftliche Überlieferung aus der Reformationszeit in der Stadtbibliothek Dessau," *ARG* 78 (1987) 321–45; *J. J. Beiträge zur 500. Wiederkehr seines Geburtstages* (Nordhausen, 1993).

Joris, *David* (pseudonym: John of Bruges). Baptist, born 1501/1502 in Ghent or Bruges, died August 23, 1556 in Basle. He trained as a painter of stained-glass windows. He was expelled from Delft in 1528 as an adherent of the Reformation. He was a member of the → Baptist movement, and subsequently an influential sectarian leader, especially because of his prophetic writings. From 1544 onward, he lived in Basle under the pseudonym "John of Bruges." After a posthumous trial for heresy, his corpse and his writings were burnt in Basle in 1559.

■ **Works:** *T'Wonderboek* (n.p., 1542, ²1551); G. K. Waite, ed., *The Anabaptist Writings of D. J. (1535–43).* (Waterloo [Ontario], 1994).

■ **Literature:** *NDB* 10:608f.; *BBKL* 3:654ff.—A. van der Linde, *D. J. Bibliographie* (The Hague, 1867); R. H. Bainton, "D. J.," *ARG* Ergänzungs-Bd. 6 (1937); P. Burckhardt, "D. J. und seine Gemeinde in Basel," *Basler Zeitschrift für Geschichte und Altertumskunde* 48 (1949) 5–106.

CHRISTOPH MAIER

■ **Additional Bibliography:** G. K. Waite, *D. J. and Dutch Anabaptism 1524–43* (Waterloo [Ontario], 1990); idem, "'Man is devil to himself.' D. J. and the Rise of a Sceptical Tradition towards the Devil in the Early Modern Netherlands," *Nederlands archief voor kerkgeschiedenis* 75 (1995) 1–29; B. Hebert, "Images et imaginaire du millenium dans le 'Wonderboeck' de D. J.," in *Formes du millénarisme en Europe à l'aube des temps modernes* (Paris, 2001) 141–55; M. G. van Veen, "Spiritualism in the Netherlands," *SCJ* 33 (2002) 129–50.

Jud (Judae, also Keller), *Leo.* Reformer in Zurich and biblical translator, born c. 1482 in Gemar (Alsace), died June 19, 1542 in Zurich. He attended the Latin school in Schlettstadt and studied in Basle and Freiburg from 1499 to 1512. He succeeded Huldrych Zwingli as priest with the cure of souls in Einsiedeln from 1519 to 1522;

here, he translated various Latin works of → Erasmus of Rotterdam and works by Martin Luther (from 1521 onward). He became pastor at St. Peter's in Zurich in February, 1523, and was Zwingli's most important collaborator and fellow combatant. After Zwingli's death in 1531, he worked together with Henrich → Bullinger, helping to overcome the crisis of the Reformation in Zurich. He wrote two catechisms, the Great (Zurich, 1534) and the Small (Zurich, 1537). He also published Zwingli's biblical commentaries, which he had copied down, and translated texts of Augustine and Jean Calvin. He became famous as a biblical translator, publishing a revised German Bible (Zurich, 1540) and a Latin translation of the Old Testament (printed posthumously in Zurich in 1543, together with a New Testament).

■ **Literature:** *CEras* 2:248ff.—L. Weisz, *L. J.* (Zurich, 1942); K.-H. Wyss, *L. J. Seine Entwicklung zum Reformator, 1519–23* (Berne, 1976); K. Deppermann, "Schwenckfeld and L. J.," in *Schwenckfeld and Early Schwenckfeldianism,* ed. P. C. Erb (Pennsburg, Pa., 1986) 211–36.

KASPAR VON GREYERZ

■ **Additional Bibliography:** *RGG*⁴ 4:596f.—F. P. van Stam, "L. J. als programmatischer Interpret Calvins," *Nederlands archief voor kerkgeschiedenis* 79 (1999) 123–41.

Julius III. Pope (February 8, 1550–March 23, 1555), formerly *Giovanni Maria del Monte,* born September 10, 1487 in Rome. After studying civil and canon law in Perugia and Siena, he became chamberlain to Julius II. He was appointed archbishop of Siponto in 1513 and held a number of offices in the curia and the papal states. He was created cardinal in 1536 and was president of the Council of Trent during the first conciliar period (1545-1547) and in Bologna (1547-1548). His election as pope was the outcome of a lengthy struggle between the imperial and the French parties, in which Julius was the compromise candidate. His electoral capitulation and pressure from the emperor forced him to summon the council to resume its activity at Trent on May 1, 1551. The suspension of the council on April 28, 1554 proved inevitable, thanks to the conspiracy of the German princes; but Julius wanted the council to promulgate the necessary dogmatic decrees and a number of general reform measures before the members departed. He became involved in a military conflict with Ottavio Farnese, whom he had appointed feudal ruler of Parma. He supported the Jesuits and entrusted to them the direction of the German college, founded in 1552. One particular success during the pontificate of Julius was the reunion of England (under → Mary I) with the Catholic Church, achieved in 1554 by Cardinal Reginald Pole; this union, however, did not last. A shadow on the pontificate was cast by his adoptive nephew Innocenzo del Monte, on whom he showered favors, creating him a cardinal in 1550. Julius, in many ways a typical Renaissance prince, can truly be called a transitional figure.

■ **Sources:** *CT,* passim.—Valuable material in the series of nuntiature reports.

■ **Literature:** *TRE* 17:445ff.—C. Erdmann, "Die Wiedereröffnung des Trienter Konzils durch Julius III.," *QFIAB* 20 (1928/29) 238–317; H. Jedin, "Analekten zur Reformtätigkeit der Päpste J. III. und Paul IV.," *RQ* 42 (1934) 305–32; 43 (1935) 87–156; idem, "Kirchenreform und Konzilsgedanke 1550–59," *HJ* 54 (1934) 401–31; Jedin vol. 1–3, passim; H. Lutz, *Christianitas afflicta. Europa, das Reich und die päpstliche Politik im Niedergang der Hegemonie Kaiser Karls V. (1552–56)* (Göttingen, 1964); *Friedenslegation des Reginald Pole zu Kaiser Karl V. und König Heinrich II. (1553–56),* ed. idem (Tübingen, 1981).

KLAUS GANZER

■ **Additional Bibliography:** *Vatikanlexikon,* ed. N. del Re (Augsburg, 1998) 365f.—A. Nova, *The Artistic Patronage of Pope J. III* (New York, 1988); Th. F. Mayer, "An Unknown Diary of J. III's Conclave by Bartolomeo Stella, a Servant of Cardinal Pole," *AHC* 24 (1992) 345–77; W. V. Hudon, "The 'Consilium de Emendanda Ecclesia' and the 1555 Reform Bull of Pope J. III," in *Reform and Renewal in the Middle Ages and the Renaissance.* Festschrift L. Pascoe (Leiden, 2000) 240–58.

Justification

1. Concept

"Justification" is a concept emphasized by Paul, an abbreviation designating the totality of God's salvific action and its acceptance by the human person. In terms of substance, this concept is identical with salvation, grace, redemption, life, salvation, the kingdom of God, rebirth, etc.; but it designates these realities under the specific aspect of the creation of the righteousness of the human person before God. This entails the uncovering of sin and its unconditional, unmerited forgiveness,

which establishes a "righteous," i.e., "right" new relationship between the human person and God, leading to an ontological and ethical renewal. In this process, God's creative will for the human person triumphs, through his grace, over human resistance. Since the meaning of the word "justification" oscillates between "declaration of righteousness" (Hebrew), "pronouncement of righteousness" (Greek), "making righteous" (Latin), and "execution" (early New High German), and since the related concept of "(God's) righteousness" must be considered in the context of the Greek philosophical concept, it is clear that the concept of "justification" already includes *in nuce* all the problems of later theological interpretations, with the controversies (and the breakdown of church unity) to which these divergent interpretations led.

If we look back at the history of theology and dogma from the perspective of the problem with which we are familiar in the West and which is central in the ecumenical process, we are surprised to note that it took a long time before Paul—and the Old Testament problem which made a deep mark on him here—came to have any influence on Christian thinking. We also discover that the doctrine of justification is mostly detached from the doctrine of grace. Sometimes the link is made, but sometimes justification completely disappears from the doctrine of grace; when it re-emerges, it never completely merges with the doctrine of grace. Systematic theology makes it a subdivision of this doctrine.

2. Martin Luther

Luther does not develop any new "doctrine of justification" in the technical sense of this term—this happened only at a later stage in Lutheran theology. However, the theology and piety of the late Middle Ages posed a personal problem to Luther, which he first tackles as a theological problem, and then must accept as an ecclesial problem. He rejects the concept of → grace as an "interior form," since this has proved to have (Semi-)Pelagian implications. Luther returns to Paul and understands justification anew as a judicial verdict of acquittal; he follows the tradition, however, in understanding this as God's action vis-à-vis the individual. Since it can no longer be thought of as something "interior," nor exclusively as something bestowed *ab extra,* but must be conceived as existing strictly outside the individual (*extra nos*), the righteousness which is bestowed on us exists only on the side of God, as his gracious disposition, his *favor* (WA 8:106, 10). Being justified is a purely *relational* reality, what Gerhard Ebeling has called a "relationship *coram*" (*nec sanctitas est in praedicamento substantiae sed relationis*, WA 40:1, 354, 3). In other words, when judgment is pronounced over sin, the attribution of justification is an acquittal; justification is "forensic," and hence can be "taken hold of" (by the *fides apprehensiva*) "only in faith" (*sola fide*). Another important factor determining Luther's elaboration of the doctrine of justification is the idea of the last judgment of God: on the last day, God will justify those who have submitted themselves to his judgment already here on earth, by accepting God's verdict on their sin in that self-condemnation which is an essential element of the faith which brings justification. An ontological "being made righteous" in the traditional sense does not disappear, but now, in keeping with the relational concept of grace, it must be thought of as a consequence of justification. In later Protestant theology—"officially" in the Reformed confessional documents since 1559, and in the Lutheran texts from 1570 onward, especially in the Formula of → Concord—this point is made by means of the distinction between "justification" and "sanctification," which are not yet distinct technical terms in Luther (cf. *BSLK* 919:24–924:17). Since justification is understood here as the synthesis of the whole gospel, the "article" of justification is the "article of faith by which the church stands or falls" (cf. WA 40:3.352.3; similarly, 39:1.205.1; 40:3.335.6-9; *BSLK* 415:21–416.6; → Articulus stantis et cadentis ecclesiae).

3. Jean Calvin

Calvin's doctrine of justification differs from Luther, not in the individual theses (*sola fides*, rejection of grace as "form," certainty of salvation, etc.), but in the relative importance attached to these. Justification is not the coordinating perspective of Calvin's doctrine as a whole, but is itself assigned a place in his "system," as a link between Christology and pneumatology, in the context of rebirth. Here it functions virtually as a counterweight, in order to prevent a moralizing misunderstanding of "rebirth" (*Inst* 3:11-16; CR 30:533-89).

4. Trent

The Council of Trent defends "effective" justification in the vocabulary of the scholastic tradition, but consciously avoids tying itself down to specific theories proposed by the various theological schools. Nevertheless, the council believes that a "forensic" understanding of justification is inappropriate even when the consequences of justification include everything that the Catholic tradition had found essential here. This is why the council—despite all the agreements it notes in its dogmatic chapters with the starting-points of Reformation teaching—finds four Protestant theses completely unacceptable, viz., the rejection of every "cooperation" in justification, the reception of justification "by faith alone," the rejection of faith and love as a reality present in the human person, and the "certainty of → salvation." The primary reason why these ideas are condemned is the fear that they might lower the level of ethical endeavor on the part of Christians (cf. especially DH 1531, 1533ff., 1538, 1539, 1563f., 1569f.).

This predominantly defensive position on the part of Trent should not make us forget two points. First, the outcome of the Pelagian and Semi-Pelagian controversies is not abandoned, but rather confirmed; this means that the *via moderna* is substantially discredited and is no longer pursued (cf. especially DH 1510-1515, 1521ff., 1551ff.). Second, justification recovers at Trent the centrality it had for Paul. The doctrine of grace is subsumed under the heading of justification—not vice versa.

■ *LThK*[3] 8:882–902 (unabridged version).

■ **Sources:** (R.=Rechtfertigung, justification) M. Luther, WA-vols. 1–2, 6–8, 18, 31 I, 39 I, 40 I–II, 56; *BSLK*: CA/ApolCA 4, 6, 18, 20; Schmalkaldische Artikel II/1; Konkordienformel, Epitome/Solida Declaratio III; J. Calvin, *Inst* 3:11–16; CR 30:533–89; DH 1520–83 (Council of Trent).

■ **Literature:** *General studies*: *RGG*[3] 5:825–46; *LThK*[2] 8:1033–50; *Neues Handbuch theologischer Grundbegriffe, Neue Auflage*, ed. P. Eicher, vol. 4 (Munich, [2]1992) 331–49; *Lexikon der katholischen Dogmatik*, ed. W. Beinert (Freiburg, [5]1997) 434ff.; *Historisches Wörterbuch der Philosophie*, ed. J. Ritter et al., vol. 8 (Basle, 1992) 251–65; *TRE* 28:282–364; *EKL*[3] 3:1455–59.—*Monographs*: W. Dantine, *Die Gerechtmachung des Gottlosen* (Munich, 1959); A. Peters, *Glaube und Werk. Luthers R.-Lehre im Lichte der Heiligen Schrift* (Berlin and Hamburg, 1962, [2]1967); G. Gloege, "Die R.-Lehre als hermeneutische Kategorie," *Theologische Literaturzeitung* 89 (1964) 161–75; E. Wolf, "Die R.-Lehre als

Mitte und Grenze reformatorischer Theologie (1950)," in *Peregrinatio*, vol. 2 (Munich, 1965) 11–21; A. Peters, "Das Ringen um die R.-Botschaft in der gegenwärtigen lutherischen Theologie," in *Theologische Strömungen der Gegenwart* (Göttingen, 1967) 24–44; K. J. Becker, *Die R.-Lehre nach Domingo de Soto* (Rome, 1969); J. Baur, *Salus christiana. Die R.-Lehre in der Geschichte des christlichen Heilsverständnisses* (Gütersloh, 1968); V. Pfnür, *Einig in der R.-Lehre? Die R.-Lehre der Confessio Augustana (1530) und die Stellungnahme der katholischen Kontroverstheologie zwischen 1530 und 1535* (Wiesbaden, 1970; *R. im neuzeitlichen Lebenszusammenhang. Studien zur Interpretation der R.-Lehre*, ed. W. Lohff and Ch. Walther (Gütersloh, 1974); G. Müller, *Die R.-Lehre. Geschichte und Probleme* (Gütersloh, 1977); W. Pannenberg, "Das Verhältnis zwischen der Akzeptationslehre des Duns Scotus und der reformatorischen R.-Lehre," in *Regnum hominis et regnum Dei,* ed. C. Bérubé, vol. 1 (Rome, 1978) 213–18; E. Jüngel, *Zur Freiheit eines Christenmenschen. Eine Erinnerung an Luthers Schrift* (Munich, 1978); W. Härle and E. Herms, *R. Das Wirklichkeitsverständnis des christlichen Glaubens* (Göttingen, 1979); Ph. Schäfer, "Hoffnungsgestalt und Gegenwart des Heils. Diskussion um die doppelte Gerechtigkeit auf dem Konzil von Trient," *Theologie und Philosophie* 55 (1980) 204–29; V. Subilia, *Die R. aus Glauben* (Göttingen, 1981); O. H. Pesch and A. Peters, *Einführung in die Lehre von Gnade und R.* (Darmstadt, 1981, ³1987/94); O. H. Pesch, *Frei sein aus Gnade. Theologische Anthropologie* (Freiburg, 1983) 190–328; O. Bayer, *Aus Glauben leben. Über R. und Heiligung* (Stuttgart, 1984); B. Hamm, "Was ist reformatorische R.-Lehre?" *Zeitschrift für Theologie und Kirche* 83 (1986) 1–38; G. Ebeling, *Lutherstudien*, vol. 2/3: *Disputatio de homine: Die theologische Definition des Menschen* (Tübingen, 1989); O. Bayer, *R.* (Neuendettelsau, 1991); K. Schwarzwäller, "Luthers R.-Lehre—heute," *Theologische Beiträge* 27 (1996) 22–43; A. Lexutt, *R. im Gespräch. Das R.-Verständnis in den Religionsgesprächen von Hagenau, Worms und Regensburg 1540/ 1541* (Göttingen, 1996); M. Beintker, *R. in der neuzeitlichen Lebenswelt* (Tübingen, 1998); E. M. Faber, *Symphonie von Gott und Mensch. Die responsorische Struktur von Vermittlung in der Theologie Johannes Calvins* (Neukirchen-Vluyn, 1999).

OTTO HERMANN PESCH

K

Karlstadt (real name: Bodenstein), *Andreas von.* Reformer, born 1486 in Karlstadt (Main), died December 24, 1451 in Basle (of the plague). He studied in Erfurt (1499-1500), Cologne (1503-1505), and Wittenberg (from 1505); he was ordained priest and took his doctorate in theology in 1510, and became professor. He became a canon of All Saints' church in 1508, and archdeacon of the same chapter in 1510/1511. In addition to theology, Karlstadt studied law, and took his doctorate in civil and canon law at the curia during a stay in Rome (1515-1516). The legal manner of thought influenced his theology, but from 1517 onward, thanks to his study of works by Augustine and the mystics (especially John Tauler), he turned from Thomistic-Scotist scholasticism to a theology more influenced by Augustine's doctrine of grace, by mystical ideas, and by an emphasis on the Bible. This led him to support Martin Luther. His 406 *Apologeticae conclusiones,* printed in 1518, provoked the → Leipzig disputation in 1519 and controversies with Johannes → Eck. The definitive breach with the Roman church came in 1520. The "events of Wittenberg" occurred during Luther's absence in 1521-1522: Karlstadt changed the Mass, collaborated in the "new order" of Wittenberg, and rejected the veneration of images in 1522 (→ Art and Reformation). In 1523-1524, he left the university and attempted to put his theology into practice as curate and pastor in Orlamünde; at the same time, his positions became more radical, especially his rejection of the real presence in the Lord's Supper and of infant baptism. He was expelled from Saxony in 1524; thereafter, he stayed in various places and had contacts with Baptist groups. During the → Peasants' War, he took a mediating position. He returned to Saxony in 1525, but fled in 1529 and came to Zurich, where he was given a deacon's prebend in the Great Minster and held the office of preacher until 1533. He became professor of Old Testament at the university of Basle in 1534 and collaborated in the project of university reform; from 1535, he was also pastor of St. Peter's church in Basle. His theology was not a completely coherent system. It was orientated to the mystical ideas of serenity, suffering, and the following of the crucified Jesus; law, Spirit, grace, and sanctification were central for Karlstadt, as was the idea of the human person as the image of God. Despite these "spiritualizing" traits, he also emphasized clearly the literal meaning of scripture. His theology influenced many individuals and groups throughout the Reformation period.

■ **Works:** E. Freys and H. Barge, *Zentralblatt für Bibliothekswesen* 21 (1904) 153–79, 209–43, 305–31 (reprint,

Nieuwkoop, 1965); E. Kähler, *K. und Augustin. Der Kommentar des A. Bodenstein von K. zu Augustins Schrift "De spiritu et litera"* (Halle, 1952); E. Hertzsch, ed., *K. Schriften aus den Jahren 1523–25* (Halle, 1956–57); *VD 16* 3:60–78; H.-P. Hasse, "K.s 'De usura,'" *ZSRG.K* 76 (1990) 310–28; idem, "K.s Predigt am 29.9.1522 in Joachimsthal," *ARG* 81 (1990) 97–119; A. Zorzin, *K. als Flugschriftenautor* (Göttingen, 1990); Köhler *BF* I/2:164–215.

■ **Literature:** *NDB* 2:356f.; *BBKL* 3:1167–71; *TRE* 17:649–57.—H. Barge, *A. Bodenstein von K.,* 2 vols. (Tübingen, 1905); reprint, Nieuwkoop, 1968); R. J. Sider, *A. Bodenstein von K. The Development of his Thought 1517–25* (Leiden, 1974); U. Bubenheimer, *Consonantia Theologiae et Iurisprudentiae. A. Bodenstein von K. als Theologe und Jurist zwischen Scholastik und Reformation* (Tübingen, 1977); C. A. Pater, "K. as the Father of the Baptist Movements," in *The Emergence of Lay Protestantism* (Toronto, 1984); H.-P. Hasse, "Zum Aufenthalt K.s in Zürich," *Zwingliana* 18 (1989–91) 366–89; U. Bubenheimer, "A. Bodenstein genannt K.," *Fränkische Lebensbilder,* vol. 14 (Würzburg, 1991) 47–64; Th. Kaufmann, *Die Abendmahlstheologie der Strassburger Reformatoren bis 1528* (Tübingen, 1992); H.-P. Hasse, *K. und Tauler* (Gütersloh, 1993); S. Looss, "M. Bucer und A. K.," in *M. Bucer and Sixteenth Century Europe,* ed. M. Lienhard (Leiden et al., 1993) 317–28; V. Gummelt, "Bugenhagens Handschrift von K.s Jeremiavorlesung aus dem Jahre 1522," *ARG* 86 (1995) 56–66; S. Looss, "K.s Bild vom Menschen in seiner Wittenberger Zeit (1520–23)," in *700 Jahre Wittenberg,* ed. S. Oehmig (Weimar, 1995) 275–78.

HERIBERT SMOLINSKY

■ **Additional Bibliography:** S. Looss, ed., *A. Bodenstein von K.* (Wittenberg, 1998); B. MacNiel, "A. von K. as a Humanist Theologian," in *Radical Reformation Studies,* ed. W. O. Packull (Aldershot, 1999) 106–19; V. Joestel, *A. Bodenstein genannt K.* (Wittenberg, 2000); U. Bubenheimer, ed., "Querdenker der Reformation," in *A. Bodenstein von K. und seine frühe Wirkung* (Würzburg, 2001); N. R. Leroux, "K.'s 'Christag predig': Prophetic Rhetoric in an 'Evangelical' Mass," *ChH* 72 (2003) 102–37; idem, "'In the Christian City of Wittenberg': K.'s Tract on Images and Begging," *SCJ* 34 (2003) 73–105.

Käser, *Leonhard.* Priest and Reformer, born c. 1480 in Raab (diocese of Passau), died August 16, 1527 in Schärding. He began his studies in Leipzig in 1500; he looked after the parish of Waitzenkirchen from c. 1516/1517. When he was accused of holding sermons in the spirit of the Reformation, he repudiated Martin Luther's doctrine with an oath (1524). He then left his parish and registered as a student at Wittenberg on June 7, 1525. He was arrested on March 10, 1527, and confessed under interrogation that he held Luther's doctrine. Despite the pleas of the princes of Saxony and Brandenburg, he was found guilty of heresy by the spiritual court (whose members included Johannes → Eck) in Passau on July 18, 1527, and was handed over to the secular arm, viz., Bavaria, and was burnt at the stake. An anonymous pamphlet which declared Käser a "martyr of Jesus Christ" went through nine editions. Some later scholars erroneously held him to be a Baptist.

■ **Sources:** *Das wahrhaftig geschicht des leydens und sterbens Lienhart Keysers seligen,* ed. Leeb-Zoepfl, 55–77 (see Literature below); J. Eck, *Warhafftige handlung, wie es mit herr Lenhart Kaeser, zu Schaerding verbrent, ergangen ist,* ed. Leeb-Zoepfl, 78–87; M. Luther, "Von Herrn L. Keisser in Baiern um des Evangelii willen verbrannt," in *WA* 23:473–76.

■ **Literature:** F. Roth, *L. Kaiser, ein evangelisches Martyrium aus dem Innviertel* (Halle, 1900); F. Leeb and F. Zoepfl, *L. K.* (Münster, 1928); A. Eckert, "L. Keysser (K.) in neuer Betrachtung," *Ostbairische Grenzmarken* 7 (1964/1965) 303–10; B. Kaff, *Volksreligion und Landeskirche* (Münster, 1977) 15–17.

GÜNTER DIPPOLD

■ **Additional Bibliography:** H. Roser, "L. K., einer der ersten evangelischen Märtyrer," in *Altbayern und Luther,* ed. H. Roser (Munich, 1996) 131ff.

Kessler, *Johannes.* Reformer of St. Gallen, born 1502/1503 in St. Gallen, where he died March 7, 1574. He began his studies in Basle, and moved to Wittenberg in 1522. He returned to the Catholic town of St. Gallen at the end of 1523; in the following year, he began expounding scripture for an ever-larger private circle. In 1525, he became a member of the commission which elaborated a new order of worship, and he supported Joachim → Vadian in the introduction of the Reformation. In 1537, he became a teacher at the municipal Latin school, and was appointed preacher in St. Laurence's church in 1542. After Vadian's death in 1551, he became the head of the Reformed Church in St. Gallen. He took a position between Martin Luther and Huldrych Zwingli on the Lord's Supper, and he opposed the violent persecution of the → Baptists. He wrote the *Sabbata,* a chronicle of the history of St. Gallen from 1519 to 1539.

■ **Works:** *Sabbata. Mit kleineren Schriften und Briefen,* ed. E. Egli and R. Schoch (St. Gallen, 1902).

■ **Literature:** *NDB* 11:546f.; *BBKL* 3:1412ff.—I. Wissmann, *Die St. Galler Reformationschronik des J. K.*

(Stuttgart, 1971); R. Feller and E. Bonjour, *Geschichts-schreibung der Schweiz*, vol. 1 (Basle and Stuttgart, ²1979) 186–89; E. Ehrenzeller, *Geschichte der Stadt St. Gallen* (St. Gallen, 1988).

BARBARA HENZE

■ **Additional Bibliography:** W. Alter, *Die Berichte von Peter Harer und J. K. vom Bauernkrieg 1525* (Speyer, 1995).

Kingdom of God. Does the kingdom of God mean "something more within history" (to use Medard Kehl's phrase)? The question of the relationship between the kingdom of God and the course of human history came to be posed in a new way from the high Middle Ages onward, as people experienced the growing autonomy of worldly realities. The more the world became autonomous, the more it appeared resistant to God's sovereign rule. This problem provides the context for the different ways in which Martin Luther and Jean Calvin understand the "kingdom of God."

Luther elaborated his doctrine of two kingdoms above all in the debate with the "→ Enthusiasts," who wanted to introduce God's rule by violent means. He accepts the increasing experience of autonomy, in that he sees God's "worldly rule" as entailing appropriate regularities and laws, which are necessary in order to ensure peaceful co-existence in human society; but since this "worldly rule" is to be enforced by human beings, it must be strictly distinguished from the "spiritual" rule, which God alone can enforce—and this happens when Christ begins to rule in individual Christians through the Word of God and the Holy Spirit. Luther understands the kingdom of God as a completely internal reality which already exists on earth. This means that he does not envisage "something more within history," in the sense of a continuous reshaping of the world in view of God's eschatological lordship. He rejects all such expectations by pointing to the cross, which tells human beings that God is totally sovereign in the enforcement of his kingdom.

Calvin too sees God's eschatological lordship as already present wherever the Spirit of God takes hold of human persons and transforms them. This brings them into an antithetical position vis-à-vis the world; they are now obliged to repel the world's influence. For Calvin, this applies not only to individuals, but to the → church as a whole,

which must employ the *legitimus ordo* ("right ordering of things") to oppose a life hostile to God. This was indeed Calvin's precise aim in his work as Reformer in Geneva—he sought to expand the sphere of God's rule in society. This is why he envisages the kingdom of God as bringing "something more within history." As the kingdom expands, there is less space for an autonomous human shaping of the world.

This view relates the presence of God's kingdom to society. In Counter-Reformation Catholicism, the perspective is reduced to the Roman church, which separates itself from the world which surrounds it.

MARKUS KNAPP

■ *LThK*³ 5:31–34 (unabridged version s.v. "Herrschaft Gottes").
■ **Literature:** *TRE* 15:221–24.—G. Forck, *Die Königsherrschaft Jesu Christi bei Luther* (Berlin, ²1988); K. R. Kim, *Das Reich Gottes in der Theologie Thomas Müntzers [und die] alternativen Anschauungen Martin Luthers* (Frankfurt/Main, 1994).

Knox, *John.* Scottish Protestant preacher and Reformer, born c. 1514 in Haddington (East Lothian), died November 24, 1572 in Edinburgh. He studied at St. Andrews and was ordained priest in 1536; thereafter, he acted as notary and domestic tutor to children of noble families. He converted to Protestantism in the early 1540s, and first became famous as the companion of the Protestant preacher George Wishart, whose execution in St. Andrews in 1546 was avenged by the murder of David Beaton, cardinal primate and archbishop of St. Andrews. Beaton's murderers were besieged in St. Andrews castle. Knox joined them there and was called to the Protestant ministry for the first time in 1547. At the end of 1547, the castle fell to the French soldiers, who compelled Knox to serve as a galley slave for the next two years.

After he was set free in 1549, he settled in England and ministered in the Protestant parishes in Berwick and Newcastle. The fiery eloquence of his sermons came to the notice of the duke of Northumberland, and led to Knox's appointment as court chaplain to → Edward VI. Knox's radical positions were based on a consistent appeal to the authority of the Bible: for example, he refused to kneel during the Mass, since this was not in accordance with scripture. This led to the introduction of the "Black rubric" in the second edition of the

Book of → Common Prayer (1552). After → Mary I became queen of England in 1553, Knox went abroad and served the English exile community in Frankfurt am Main; after his views on the liturgy split this community, he was forced to move to Geneva, where his radical positions and his political causticity found their most extreme expression in his celebrated rabble-rousing pamphlet *The First Blast of the Trumpet against the Monstrous Regiment of Women* (1558), directed against the rule of the two Maries in England and Scotland.

After → Elizabeth I became queen, Knox was refused permission to enter England, so he returned to Scotland. His iconoclastic preaching in May, 1559 unleashed a Protestant revolution against Queen Mary of Guise (died 1560), whose daughter, Queen Mary Stuart, had married the French dauphin Francis in 1558, thus aligning Scotland with the interests of Catholic France. Thanks in no small measure to Knox's activities, the Protestant rebellion of 1559 led to the acceptance of the → Confessio Scotica and the first sketch of a church order, later known as the "First Book of Discipline" (1560).

The consolidation of the Reformation was put at risk by the return of Mary Stuart in 1561, and Knox, by now preacher in St. Giles's church in Edinburgh, attacked her from the pulpit as an "idolatress." Although he had several private conversations with her, he did not succeed in winning the young queen over to Protestantism. In the meantime, Knox's political influence declined drastically; he played no part in the tumultuous events which led to Mary's abdication and her flight from Scotland in 1567-1568.

In his last years, which were marked by serious illness, he compiled his valuable *History of the Reformation of Religion in Scotland*. Knox was neither a systematic theologian nor an author of theological works. He made his mark as a powerful preacher who was completely convinced that he was God's instrument and the prophet of the divine will.

■ Literature: *The Works of J. K.,* ed. D. Laing, 6 vols. (Edinburgh, 1846–64); *J. K.'s History of the Reformation . . . in Scotland,* ed. W. C. Dickinson, 2 vols. (Edinburgh and London, 1949); *J. K.: On Rebellion,* ed. R. A. Mason (Cambridge, 1994).

ROGER A. MASON

■ Additional Bibliography: J. M. Richards, "'To promote a woman to beare rule': Talking of Queens in Mid-Tudor England," *SCJ* 28 (1997) 101–21; M. T. Courtial, "J. K. un méconnu de la réforme," *Revue réformée* 48 (1997) 55–59; R. A. Mason, ed., *J. K. and the British Reformations.* (Aldershot, 1998); D. W. Johnson, "Prophet in Scotland. The Self-image of J. K.," *Calvin Theological Journal* 33 (1998) 76–86; R. K. Marshall, *J. K.* (Edinburgh, 2000); R. G. Kyle, "J. K. Confronts the Anabaptists," *Mennonite Quarterly Review* 75 (2001) 493–515; idem, "The Thundering Scot: J. K. the Preacher," *Westminster Theological Journal* 64 (2002) 135–49; idem, "Prophet of God. J. K.'s Self awareness," *Reformed Theological Review* 61 (2002) 85–101; idem, *The Ministry of J. K.* (Lewiston, N.Y., 2002); idem, "J. K. and the Care of Souls," *Calvin Theological Journal* 38 (2003) 125–38.

Komander (Comander, a Greek form of Dorfmann; also known as Hutmacher), *Johannes.* Leader of the Reformation in Graubünden, born 1482 in Maienfeld, died February, 1557 in Chur. He attended the Latin school in Chur in 1495-1496, and studied liberal arts in Basle from 1502 to 1506. He was curate (1512-1521) and parish priest (1521-1523) in Escholzmatt (canton of Lucerne), and became parish priest of St. Martin's church in Chur in 1523. He was the author of the 18 theses that were debated in the religious dialogue at → Ilanz (January 7-9, 1526). He introduced the Reformation into Chur in 1527, and became the first president of the Graubünden synod in 1537. He collaborated in the composition of a catechism (1537; edited by E. Camenisch, "Der erste evangelische Bündner Katechismus 1537," in *Aus fünf Jahrhunderten Schweizerischer Kirchengeschichte,* Festschrift for P. Wernle [Basle, 1932] 39-79) and of the *Confessio Raetica* of 1553 (E. Camenisch, *Jahrbuch der Historisch-Antiquitarischen Gesellschaft von Graubünden* 43 [1913] 223-60, with summary in German).

■ Literature: *NDB* 3:331f.; *TRE* 19:378–84; *BBKL* 4:369ff.—W. Jenny, *J. C.,* 2 vols. (Zurich, 1969–70); H. Berger, *Bündner Kirchengeschichte,* vol. 2 (Chur, 1986) 40–78.

MARKUS RIES

■ Additional Bibliography: *RGG*[4] 2:425.

Krafft (Crato), *Adam.* Reformer in Hessen, born 1493 in Fulda, died September 9, 1558 in Marburg. He began his studies in Erfurt in 1412, taking the degrees of bachelor in 1514 and master in 1519. He was preacher in Fulda (1523) and in

Hersfeld (1525). He became court preacher to → Philip of Hessen in 1527, and professor in Marburg and visitor in 1527. He married in 1528. In 1531, he was appointed superintendent in Marburg. Krafft supported the church politics of Hessen and composed many memoranda. After his wife's death, he married again in 1548. He was a Lutheran theologian with a humanistic education, a man of "reconciliatory character" (Zeller).

■ **Literature:** *Urkundliche Quellen zur hessischen Reformationsgeschichte,* vols. 2–4 (Marburg, 1951–55); W. Schäfer, *A. K.* (Kassel, 1976); idem, "A. K. im Urteil seiner Zeitgenossen," *Jahrbuch der Hessischen Kirchengeschichtlichen Vereinigung* 27 (1976) 147–56; W. Zeller, *Theologie und Frömmigkeit,* vol. 2 (Marburg, 1978) 254–73.

GERHARD MÜLLER

Krell, *Nikolaus.* Politician in Saxony, born shortly before 1553, the son of a dynasty of Leipzig counselors, died October 9, 1601 in Dresden (by beheading). He began the study of law in Leipzig in 1571, and his travels in search of learning brought him to those strongholds of Calvinism, Valence and Geneva. In 1584, he was appointed adviser to the electoral prince of Saxony, Christian I, whom he strongly influenced throughout his life. He became privy counselor in 1586, and chancellor in 1589; this office amounted to that of a prime minister. In confessional terms, he was "neither Calvinist nor Lutheran" (→ Crypto-Calvinism). With the approval of the electoral prince, Krell pursued domestic policies which aimed at eliminating the power of the Estates. His foreign policy was aligned to the Calvinist party in the Palatinate and directed against the Habsburgs and Spain; he aimed to suppress Lutheranism by taking electoral Saxony into the Calvinist camp. He authorized the composition of the "Krell Bible," in which Luther's text was accompanied by a commentary in the style of early absolutist popular education; this project was not completed. The sudden death of electoral prince Christian I on September 25, 1591 reversed Krell's fortunes: he was imprisoned for ten years in Königstein fortress, then executed.

■ **Literature:** Th. Klein, *Der Kampf um die Zweite Reformation in Kursachsen 1586–1591* (Cologne and Graz, 1962); K. Blaschke, "Religion und Politik in Kursachsen 1586–91," in *Die reformierte Konfessionalisierung in Deutschland,* ed. H. Schilling (Gütersloh, 1986).

KARLHEINZ BLASCHKE

Kretz (Gretz, Kretzius), *Matthias.* Theologian, born c. 1480 in Haunstetten near Augsburg, died 1543 in Munich. He took his bachelor's degree in Vienna in 1502, and studied for his master's degree in Tübingen (1504-1512) and Ingolstadt (1516), where he then took his doctorate of theology in 1519. He was appointed cathedral preacher in Eichstätt in 1519, and in Augsburg in 1521. He became dean of the collegiate church in Moosburg in 1531, and dean of Our Lady's church in Munich in 1533. He corresponded with → Erasmus of Rotterdam, and drew on Erasmus's treatise on Acts 19:18 for his *Sermon on confession.* He was the representative of the Bavarian duke at the religious dialogue in → Worms in 1540. He took part in the disputation in → Baden in 1530, and was one of those involved in the drafting of the *Confutatio* (→ Confessio Augustana).

■ **Sources:** *VD* 16 11:2361–68.

■ **Literature:** *NDB* 13:16f.; *CEras* 2:274f.; *BBKL* 4:649f.

BARBARA HENZE

Kromer (Cromer), *Martin.* Important representative of the Catholic reform in Poland, born 1512/1513 in Biecz near Krakow, died March 23, 1589 in Heilsberg (East Prussia). He studied in Krakow, Padua, and Bologna, and held cathedral canonries in Krakow (1543-1544), Frauenberg (1552), and other cities. He became a royal secretary and diplomat, serving *inter alia* in Vienna. He became administrator of Ermland in 1569, coadjutor in 1570, and diocesan bishop from 1579 onward. He endeavored to raise the moral and educational standards among the clergy and laity by means of general visitations, diocesan synods, and pastoral letters. He revised the liturgical books of the diocese, supported the Jesuit institutions in Braunsberg, and confirmed in 1583 the first rule of the Congregation of Sisters of St. Catharine. He was also active in support of Catholic renewal at the Polish provincial synods. He was an excellent theological and historical writer, and contributed to the renewal of the Polish language.

■ **Works:** *Orechovius* (Cologne, 1564); *Monachus* (Cologne, 1568); *Catecheses* (Krakow, 1570); *Polonia* (Cologne, 1577).

■ **Literature:** N. Korbut, *Słownik Polskich Teologów Katolickich,* vol. 2 (Warsaw, 1982) 429–36.—A. Eichhorn, "Der ermländische Bischof M. C. als Schriftsteller, Staatsmann und Kirchenfürst," *Zeitschrift für die*

Geschichte und Altertumskunde Ermlands 4 (1867–69) 1–470; *Die deutschen Predigten und Katechesen der ermländischen Bischöfe Hosius und K.,* ed. F. Hipler (Cologne, 1885); idem, "Monumenta Cromeriana. M. K.s Gedichte, Synodalreden und Pastoralschreiben," *Zeitschrift für die Geschichte und Altertumskunde Ermlands* 10 (1894) 145–290.

BRIGITTE POSCHMANN

L

Laínez, *Diego.* Jesuit (1540), conciliar theologian and general of the Society of Jesus, born 1512 in Almazán (province of Soria), died January 19, 1565 in Rome. He took the degree of master of arts in Alcalá in 1532, and began the study of theology in Paris in 1533, where he joined → Ignatius of Loyola, accompanying him to Rome in 1537. After Ignatius's death in 1556, Laínez was vicar general, and became the second general of the Order in 1558. He took part in the Council of → Trent in 1546-1547, 1551-1552, and 1562-1563; he also participated in the religious dialogue in → Poissy in 1561.
■ **Works:** *Disputationes Tridentinae,* ed. H. Grisar, 2 vols. (Innsbruck, 1886); *Lainii Monumenta,* 8 vols. (Madrid, 1912–17).
■ **Literature:** *TRE* 20:399–404; *BBKL* 4:997–1000.—C. Sommervogel, *Bibliothèque de la Compagnie de Jésus* (Paris, vol. 4, 1893) 1596–1600; vol. 9 (1900) 579; M. Scaduto, *L'Epoca di Giacomo L.,* 2 vols. (Rome, 1964–74); L. Polgár, *Bibliographie sur l'histoire de la Compagnie de Jésus,* vol. 3/2 (Rome, 1990) 359–62; J. W. O'Malley, *Die ersten Jesuiten* (Würzburg, 1995).

GÜNTER SWITEK

■ **Additional Bibliography:** M. Scaduto, *D. L., Archivum historicum Societatis Jesu* 59 (1990) 191–225.

Lambert, *Franz* (Lambert of Avignon). Reformer in Hessen, born 1487 in Avignon, died April 18, 1530 in Frankenberg (Eder). He was a Franciscan Observant from 1501 to 1522; as *praedicator apostolicus,* he had the task of expounding biblical texts. In 1522, he preached in Berne and Zurich, where he had discussions with Huldrych Zwingli which led him to leave his Order and travel to Wittenberg, with the intention of collaborating in the work of Reformation. Although Martin Luther was skeptical, he gave him permission to hold lectures. Lambert married in 1523. He left

Saxony in the following year and attempted in vain to spread the Reformation in France; although he acquired citizen's rights in Strasbourg in 1524, he was not able to remain there. He was invited to Hessen in 1526, and this gave him a stable base for the first time. Marquis → Philip of Hessen asked him to draw up the texts which formed the basis of discussions at the synod of → Homberg (1526), and Lambert was also involved in the composition of the *Reformatio ecclesiarum Hassiae.* He became professor at the university of Marburg in 1527. The emphasis he laid on faith disturbed the humanists and interested the pietists. He wrote many academic treatises.
■ **Literature:** *TRE* 20:415–18.—*Pour retrouver F. L. Bio-bibliographie et études,* ed. P. Fraenkel (Baden-Baden, 1986).

GERHARD MÜLLER

Landeskirchentum. This concept, which has no equivalent in other European languages, designates one form of relationship between church and state. It was restricted to Germany and Switzerland, and varied throughout the course of history.

When the Reformation was introduced in the 16th century, Protestant territorial churches came into existence, replacing churches governed by bishops who were loyal to the pope. It was not the original intention that the secular authorities should take over "church government," but this system replaced the initial "community Reformation" in the aftermath of the → Peasants' War. The Protestant Estates demonstrated their ecclesiastical autonomy when they refused to carry out the Edict of Worms and made the Protestation of Speyer in 1529; this autonomy was further developed in the following period by means of → visitations, the introduction of → church orders, and the appointment and ordination of parish pastors. Despite reservations, the Reformers (Martin Luther, Philipp Melanchthon, Johannes → Bugenhagen) gave their consent to the dissolution of the episcopal church structures, so that now the princes were "emergency bishops." They saw this as necessary in order to guarantee an orderly succession in the parish ministry and a social and educational reform. The political territory and the confessional identity coalesced; this was given an interim guarantee in imperial law in the Religious

Peace of → Augsburg (1555; → *Cuius regio, eius religio*). These territorial churches became the most important type of Protestant ecclesiastical structure in those territories whose Lutheran (or, after 1648, Reformed) confession was acknowledged in imperial law, alongside the Roman Catholic diocesan constitution and the community principle of the → Baptists and other churches. The functions previously exercised by the bishop were now mostly entrusted to superintendents and consistories.

■ *LThK*³ 6:631f. (unabridged version).
■ **Literature:** *TRE* 20:427–34.—*Die territoriale Bindung der evangelischen Kirche in Geschichte und Gegenwart,* ed. K. Dumrath and H. W. Krumwiede (Neustadt [Aisch], 1972); W. Maurer, *Gesammelte Aufsätze zum evangelischen Kirchenrecht,* ed. G. Müller and G. Seebass (Munich and Tübingen, 1976).

JÖRG HAUSTEIN

Land(t)sperger, *Johannes.* Carmelite who became a Protestant theologian, born c. 1470 in Landsberg (?), died c. 1530 in the Berne region. He began his studies in Ingolstadt in 1487, moving to Leipzig in 1494. He was an early adherent of Zwingli's and Oecolampadius' Reformation. He edited the writings of Hans Huts, although he did not himself become a → Baptist. He later worked in the Berne region, and it is possible that he took part in the Berne disputation in 1528.

■ **Works:** Köhler *BF* part 1, vol. 2, nos. 1657ff., 2131–40 (microfiche); *VD 16* 11:229–38; 9; H 6217–19; P. Riedemann, *IV. Beiträge zur Geschichte der Wiedertäufer in Oberdeutschland [. . .]* 2. "J. L.," *Mittheilungen aus dem Antiquariate von S. Calvary & Co. in Berlin* 1 (1869) 111f. 130–253; *Von der Liebe zu Gott und dem Nächsten, auch wie man den Zehnten geben und [. . .] nehmen soll* (Augsburg, 1524); *Flugschriften der frühen Reformationsbewegung* (1518–24), ed. A. Laube (Berlin and Vaduz, 1983) 1210–33.
■ **Literature:** *The Mennonite Encyclopedia,* vol. 3 (Scottdale, 1957) 285.—M. Martin, *J. L.* (Augsburg, 1902); K. Schottenloher, *Philipp Ulhart* (Munich and Freising, 1921; reprint, Nieuwkoop, 1967); G. Seebass, "Hans Hut" (diss., Erlangen, 1972), vol. 1, 8–20, 78–81; vol. 2, 14–19, 77–84, 125.

DIETRICH BLAUFUSS

Lang, *Johann.* Augustinian Hermit (1506-1522), humanist, exegete, Reformer of Erfurt, born c. 1486 in Erfurt, where he died April 2, 1548. He studied in Erfurt and Wittenberg, and was ordained priest in 1507 or 1508. He taught philosophy and theology in Wittenberg from 1511 onward, and was prior in Erfurt from 1516 to 1518. He took his doctorate in theology in Erfurt in 1519. He was district vicar for Thüringen and Meissen from 1518 to 1520. He was a friend and correspondent of Martin Luther and of Konrad → Mutianus. He left the monastery in 1522, and became a Lutheran pastor in Erfurt in 1525.

■ **Works:** *Das heilig Ev. Matthei aus kriechserspach . . . yns deutsch gebracht . . .* (Erfurt, 1521); *Die Wittenberger Titusbriefvorlesung des Erfurter Augustiners J. L.,* ed. R. Weijenborg, in *Scientia Augustiniana.* Festschrift A. Zumkeller (Würzburg, 1975) 423–68; "Die Wittenberger Römerbriefvorlesung des Erfurter Augustiners J. L.," ed. R. Weijenborg, *Augustinianum* 51 (1976) 394–494.
■ **Literature:** *NDB* 13:540f.; *CEras* 2:287ff.—H. Junghans, *Der junge Luther und die Humanisten* (Weimar, 1984) 53–56.

WILLIGIS ECKERMANN

Lang, *Matthäus.* Cardinal (1512), born 1468 in Augsburg, died March 30, 1540 in Salzburg. He was one of 13 children in an impoverished patrician family, and these humble circumstances may help explain the ambition which characterized him throughout his life. He studied extensively in Ingolstadt (where he took his bachelor's degree in 1486), in Tübingen (master's degree, 1490), and in Vienna from 1493 (*licentia doctorandi* in law). He was a brilliant public speaker, a man of imposing appearance, a friend and patron of humanists. He began his career in the chancellery of Berthold von Henneberg, and entered the service of Maximilian I in 1494. The emperor ennobled him in 1507 with the title "von Wellenburg." Lang was the most influential of the imperial diplomats in the negotiations which led to the League of Cambrai (1508), Maximilian's adherence to the Fifth Council of the Lateran (1512), and the treaty of Vienna (1515). He acquired many ecclesiastical benefices, including the position of cathedral provost in both Augsburg and Constance. He became coadjutor of Gurk in 1501 and was diocesan bishop from 1505 to 1522, and coadjutor of Salzburg in 1512 and archbishop in 1519; he was ordained priest and bishop in 1519. He presided at the election of → Charles V as emperor in 1519. Charles made him viceroy in Upper and Lower Austria, and obtained the bishopric of Cartagena-

Murcia in Spain for him in 1521. Thanks to Lang's good connections at the Roman curia, he also obtained the suburbicarian bishopric of Albano in 1535.

Lang's initial reaction to Luther was a cautious attitude of "wait and see." He was present at the imperial parliament in Worms in 1521, and was a member of the imperial government imposed by Charles V on Nuremberg from 1521 to 1523, where he was a prominent opponent of the Reformation. He himself introduced the first ecclesiastical reforms at the synod of Mühldorf in 1522, and brought the Catholic party together in the Regensburg reform circle, which laid the foundations of the Counter-Reformation in southern Germany and Austria. These reforming measures, and his severe treatment of Lutheran preachers, were however overshadowed in 1523 by the rebellion ("Latin War") of the city of Salzburg and in 1525-1526 by the → Peasants' War throughout the whole territory of the archdiocese. Lang was rescued by Bavaria and the Swabian League, but he had to pay costly reparations; besides this, a secret treaty obliged him to accept the administrator of the diocese of Passau, → Ernest of Bavaria, as his coadjutor, but the Habsburgs put pressure on the pope, and he refused to sanction this appointment. The numerous laws which he promulgated made Lang a forerunner of princely absolutism. Despite all his endeavors, he failed to ward off the Reformation: the rulers in Bavaria and Austria refused to let him interfere in their government of the church in their domains. He dealt harshly with members of the → Baptist movement. Lang was a statesman rather than a bishop, a servant of the house of Habsburg, and a man who fought on behalf of the old church. He paved the way for Catholic → reform and sowed the seeds of the absolutist state with its system of civil servants.

■ **Literature:** F. Dalham, *Concilia Salisburgensia* (Augsburg, 1788); *ARCEG* 1–4; J. Obersteiner, *Bischöfe von Gurk (1072–1822)* (Klagenfurt, 1969); K. Lackenbauer, "Der Kampf der Stadt Salzburg gegen die Erzbischöfe 1481–1524" (diss., Salzburg, 1973); P. Blickle, *Landschaft und Bauernkrieg im Erzstift Salzburg 1525/26* (Salzburg, 1977); R. R. Heinisch, *Die bischöflichen Wahlkapitulationen im Erzstift Salzburg 1514–1688* (Vienna, 1977); H. Paarhammer, "Rechtsprechung und Verwaltung des Salzburger Offizialates 1300–1569" (dissertation, Salzburg, 1977); C. Bonorand, *Joachim Vadian und der Humanismus im Bereich des Erzbistum Salzburg* (St. Gallen, 1981); F. Ortner,

Reformation, Katholische Reform und Gegenreformation im Erzstift Salzburg (Salzburg, 1981); J. Sallaberger, *Bischof an der Zeitenwende. Der Salzburger Erzbischof Kardinal M. L. von Wellenburg (1519–40)* (Salzburg, 1987); *Geschichte Salzburgs—Stadt und Land,* ed. H. Dopsch and H. Spatzenegger, vol. 2 (Salzburg, 1990) 11–111; H. Bayr, "Die Personal- und Familienpolitik des Erzbischofs M. L. von Wellenburg (1519–40) im Erzstift Salzburg unter Einbeziehung des Zeitraums von 1495–1519" (dissertation, Salzburg, 1990).

FRANZ ORTNER

■ **Additional Bibliography:** J. Sallaberger, *Kardinal M. L. von Wellenburg* (Salzburg, 1997); H. Bayr, "M. L. von Wellenburg," in *Lebensbilder Salzburger Erzbischöfe aus zwölf Jahrhunderten,* ed. P. F. Kramml (Salzburg, 1999) 137–62.

Łaski, *Jan* (Joannes a Lasco), Polish Reformer, born 1499 in Łask near Łodz, died January 8, 1560. He was the nephew of Archbishop Jan Łaski of Gniezno, the royal chancellor and primate of Poland, and was educated at his uncle's court. He studied from 1514 to 1519 in Vienna, Bologna, and Padua. Thanks to his uncle, he became cathedral canon in Łęczycy, Płock, and Krakow, as well as coadjutor and cathedral dean in Gniezno itself as early as 1517. He was ordained priest in 1521 and appointed royal secretary. He was in Basle and Paris in 1524-1525, where he became a friend of → Erasmus of Rotterdam, Huldrych Zwingli, Johannes → Oecolampadius, Bonifatius → Amerbach, and later of Philipp Melanchthon. He went to Hungary, Germany, and Vienna with his brother from 1526 to 1529. After his uncle's death in 1531, he administered the archdiocese of Gniezno; he attempted unsuccessfully to become archbishop in 1535. After this date, he undertook theological studies under the guidance of important theologians, who included Stanislaus → Hosius and Andrzej Frycz-Modrzewski. He went to Frankfurt am Main in 1539, where he made closer contacts with the Protestants, then to the Netherlands (he married in Louvain in 1540) and to Emden in Frisia. He returned to Poland in 1541, and swore an oath in Krakow on February 6, 1542 that he had not left the Catholic Church. In the following year, however, he left Poland and worked to spread the Reformation; he was declared a heretic in Poland in 1544. Anna of Oldenburg invited him to organize church life in East Frisia as superintendent from 1543 to 1548, and he wrote the *Epitome doctrinae ecclesiarum Phrigiae Orientalis* in 1544 (published some time later). He was invited by Thomas → Cranmer to England in September, 1548, and he headed a → Calvinist community in London from 1550 to 1553 (*Forma ac Ratio* [Emden, 1555]). After the death of his wife, he remarried in 1553. He left England before the persecution of Protestants under → Mary I began, and returned to Emden via Denmark. At the beginning of 1553, he went to Poland via Frankfurt am Main and Wittenberg, and endeavored, as the unofficial leader of the Calvinists, to forge unity among Poland's Protestants. He was a man of ecumenical and peaceable spirit, inspired by ideas of Melanchthon (though he interpreted these in a Calvinist sense). He proposed a compromise confession in 1557 as the counterpart to the confession proposed by Hosius. Łaski supported the new translation of the Bible into Polish and published school regulations for Calvinists. He was able to spread his ideas only thanks to the support of → Albrecht the Elder of Brandenburg-Ansbach and King Sigismund II of Poland.

■ **Works:** A. Kuyper, *Joannes Lasco opera tam edita quam inedita* (Amsterdam and The Hague, 1866); *Die evangelischen Kirchenordnungen des 16.Jh.*, ed. E. Sehling, vol. 7, II/1 (Tübingen, 1963).

■ **Literature:** *Polski Słownik Biograficzny*, vol. 18 (Breslau, 1973) 237–44; *CEras* 2:297–301; *BBKL* 4:1190ff.; *TRE* 20:448–51.—U. Falkenroth, *Gestalt und Wesen der Kirche bei Joannes a Lasco* (Göttingen, 1957); B. Hall, *Joannes a Lasci* (London, 1971); O. Bartel, *J. L.* (Berlin, 1981); H. Kowalska, *Działalność reformatorska Jana Ł. w Polsce* (new edition, Warsaw, 1999).

JAN KOPIEC

■ **Additional Bibliography:** H. P. Jürgens, ed., *Johannes a Lasco* (Wuppertal, 1999); Ch. Strohm, ed., *Johannes a Lasco. Beiträge zu einem internationalen Symposium 1999 in Emden* (Tübingen, 2000); W. Kriegseisen, ed., *J. Ł.* (Warsaw, 2001); H. P. Jürgens, *Johannes a Lasco in Ostfriesland* (Tübingen, 2002).

Latimer, *Hugh,* English Reformer, born c. 1485 in Thurcaston (Leicestershire), died October 16, 1555 in Oxford. After his studies in Cambridge, Latimer converted to the Protestant faith in 1524, under the influence of Thomas → Bilney. As a respected preacher, he was involved in a number of pulpit controversies in Cambridge and other towns. He supported → Henry VIII's divorce and the king's second marriage to Anne Boleyn. As bishop of Worcester, he pursued from 1535 onward a decidedly Protestant strategy, aided by gifted priests and chaplains. He supported the Reformation church politics of Thomas → Cromwell and Thomas → Cranmer, but resigned after the publication of the Catholic "Six articles" by Henry VIII in 1539, since these confirmed traditional doctrines and practices such as transubstantiation, auricular confession, and → celibacy. He returned to public life under → Edward VI, and preached frequently at the royal court. He criticized the nobles for plundering the church. When → Mary I of England allowed the Mass to be celebrated in public again, Latimer was arrested, and was brought to trial for denying the real presence, along with Cranmer and the bishop of London, Nicholas Ridley (born c. 1500). After refusing to recant, he was declared guilty. After a second interrogation, he was burnt at the stake with Ridley.

■ **Literature:** *The Works of H. L.*, ed. G. E. Corrie, 2 vols. (Cambridge, 1844–45); D. Loades, *The Oxford Martyrs* (London, 1970); A. G. Chester, *H. L.* (New York, 1978).

RICHARD REX

■ **Additional Bibliography:** C. H. Stuart, *L., Apostle to the English* (Grand Rapids, 1986); Ph.-E. Hughes, "The Reformer's View of Inspiration," *The Churchman* 111 (1997) 337–57; C. I. Hammer, "The Oxford Martyrs in Oxford," *JEH* 50 (1999) 235–50; J. Makens, "H. L. and John Forest: Rituals of Martyrdom," *Reformation* 6 (2001–2002) 29–48.

Latomus, *Bartholomäus.* Humanist and controversial theologian, born after 1480 in Arlon (Belgian province of Luxembourg), died January 3, 1570 in Coblenz. After studying law in Freiburg and Cologne, Latomus taught rhetoric at the Collegium Trilingue in Louvain, and from 1531 onward in Paris, first at the Collège de Ste-Barbe, and from 1534 at the newly founded Collège Royal also. In these years, he published the *Oratio de studiis humanitatis* (Paris, 1534) and other works. After a study trip to Italy (1539-1540), he met his former student Johann → Sturm in Strasbourg (*Epistulae duae duorum amicorum* [Strasbourg, 1540]) and took part in the religious dialogue of → Hagenau with Martin → Bucer (1540). Bucer sought to win him over to the Reformation party, but Latomus took up the defense of the Catholic position (*Responsio B. Latomi ad epistolam M. Buceri* [Cologne, 1545]) and moved to Coblenz, where another of his former students, Ludwig von Hagen, who had become archbishop of Trier in 1541, appointed him electoral counselor. He took part in several religious dialogues; the last of these was in → Worms (1557), where he published his book *Spaltung der Augspurgischen Confession durch die newen und streitigen Theologen.*

■ **Literature:** *CEras* 2:303f.; *BBKL* 4:1217ff.—L. Keil, ed., B. L. *Zwei Streitschriften gegen Martin Bucer (1543–45)* (Münster, 1924); H. de Vocht, *History of the Foundation and the Rise of the Collegium Trilingue Lovaniense 1517–50,* vol. 2 (Louvain, 1953) 591–602; B. Caspar, *Das Erzbistum Trier im Zeitalter der Glaubensspaltung* (Münster, 1966) 204–13; Klaiber nos. 1767–89; B. von Bundschuh, *Das Wormser Religionsgespräch von 1557* (Münster, 1988) 380ff.

FERNANDO DOMÍNGUEZ

Latomus, *Jacobus* (real name: Jacques Masson). Controversial theologian, born c. 1475 in Cambron (Hennegau), died May 29, 1544 in Louvain. He studied at the Collège Montaigu in Paris and in Louvain, where he took his doctorate in theology in 1519. In 1535, he succeeded Johannes → Driedo. He was dean of the theological faculty several times (1520, 1526, 1529) and rector of the university in 1537. He provided expert advice to the Inquisition on numerous occasions, e.g., in the trials of Jacobus Praepositus (1522) and William → Tyndale (1535-1536). Latomus's own writings are polemical; his earliest works attack → Erasmus of Rotterdam in the controversy about the role of dialectics and philology in theological education (*De trium linguarum et studii theologici ratione dialogus* [Antwerp 1519]). His controversy with Martin Luther began when Louvain condemned writings by the German Reformer in 1521; Latomus defended this condemnation, and wrote in defense of the papal → primacy, as well as books on faith, works, and monastic vows, on → marriage and confession, and pamphlets attacking Johannes → Oecolampadius and Philipp Melanchthon.

■ **Works:** *Opera adversus horum temporum haereses* (Louvain, 1550); *Bibliotheca reformatoria neerlandica,* ed. S. Cramer and F. Pijper, vol. 3 (The Hague, 1905) 28–84 (*De trium linguarum*) 101–95 (*De primatu Romani Pontificis adversus Lutherum*); Klaiber nos. 1790–1804.

■ **Literature:** *CEras* 2:304ff.; *KThR* 2:6–26; *TRE* 20:491–99.—R. Guelluy, "L'évolution des méthodes théologiques à Louvain d' Érasme à Jansénius," *RHE* 37 (1941) 31–144, esp. 52–66; E. Rummel, *Erasmus and His Catholic Critics,* vol. 1 (Nieuwkoop, 1989) 63–93; R. Guelluy, "La permanence, depuis le XVIe siècle, de deux sensibilités théologiques," *Revue théologique du Louvain* 20 (1989) 308–23; D. V. N. Bagchi, *Luther's Earliest Opponents* (Minneapolis, 1991); M. Lamberigts, ed., *L'Augustinisme à l'ancienne Faculté de Théologie de Louvain* (Louvain, 1994) 7–61; M. Gielis, *Scholastiek en humanisme* (Tilburg, 1994).

FERNANDO DOMÍNGUEZ

Law and Gospel.

The *formula* "law and gospel" was coined in the Lutheran Reformation. It takes Paul's salvation-historical distinction between the law and the gospel, and elevates this to an existential dialectic which persists throughout human life: we always live under the accusation that we have not fulfilled the law, and we experience again and again, through faith in God's Word, that the gospel sets us free from the curse entailed by this accusation. The law is understood here as making known God's will for the human person—a will which is indeed valid, but which the human person is fundamentally unable to carry out. This means that the law is seen as coercion and curse (*lex accusans, reos agens, exactrix*: WA 39:I 434,3; 3:1538). The law is meant to drive one into the salvific doubt about one's own capacities, so that one may yearn for the acquittal that the gospel pronounces.

This existential dialectic between law and gospel is not present in *Martin Luther's* theology from the very outset, but it makes its appearance at an early date: the distinction in the Reformation sense is found no later than his *Short Commentary on Galatians* (1519, a revision of his 1518 lecture; cf. WA 2:466,3ff.), and the first detailed exposition of this matter dates from 1521 (WA 10:I 2,155,21-159,20: the *Postille* for Advent).

This does not mean the abandonment of central insights of the patristic and medieval tradition, which had seen Moses and Jesus as basically doing nothing more than proclaiming anew the law "written on human hearts." This tradition had also emphasized the historical significance of the law for Israel, making a distinction between the ethical commandments of the Old Testament and the casuistic law of Judaism. The law had a pedagogical and political meaning, since the so-called first use of the law (*primus usus legis*) in the hands of civil authority was intended to restrain evil, to preserve peace, to educate young people, and to proclaim the Word of God. The idea that the law brings doom is not itself new—cf. Rom 4:15; 7:9-13; Gal 3:19. What is new is that this now becomes the "function" of the law, as its "second," "theological," "convicting use" (*secundus usus legis, usus theologicus, elenchticus*). The new theological understanding takes firm root thanks to its agreement with Luther's own personal experience of the impossibility of fulfilling the law out of love alone, and also to the church praxis which shackled the gospel in legal precepts. Here, the distinction between law and gospel becomes the key to the correct understanding of human existence in the eyes of God, and of the essence and task of the church. It becomes the "basic formula of theological understanding" (*RGG* 3rd ed., 4:507). Compared with this concept, the controversy about the Calvinist understanding of the meaning of the law in the Christian life is a mere conflict about words (→ Antinomian controversy).

The *Council of Trent* does not perceive the theological-hermeneutical point of this distinction between law and gospel. This is why it does not condemn the formula itself in chs. 18-21 of the decree on justification (DH 1568-1571). All it does is to guard against ethical consequences, which the Reformers themselves had castigated as misunderstandings and abuses (CA 20:1-7: *BSLK* 75f.). The council also justifies speaking of Christ as "law giver" (*legislator*), since this term denotes that Christ is the interpreter of the will of God (a point on which Luther concurred). The function of the law as accuser, impelling us to take refuge in the gospel, is expressed by Trent (without the formula "law and gospel") when ch. 8 of the same decree (DH 1558; cf. 1526) speaks of the fear of hell as an element in penance, and ch. 16 (DH 1563; cf. 1533f.) portrays the abiding instability of the human person.

■ *LThK*[3] 4:591–94 (unabridged version).
■ **Literature:** *Neues Handbuch theologischer Grundbegriffe*, new edition, ed. P. Eicher, vol. 2 (Munich, [2]1992) 7–22; *RGG*[3] 2:1519–33; *LThK*[2] 4:831–35; *TRE* 13:126–42.—K. Barth, *Evangelium und Gesetz* (Munich, 1935; reprint, 1980); E. Kinder and K. Haendler, ed., *Gesetz und Evangelium* (Darmstadt, 1968, [2]1986); *Christlicher Glaube in moderner Gesellschaft*, vol. 13

(Freiburg, 1981) 8–77; A. Peters, *Gesetz und Evangelium* (Gütersloh, 1981); R. Oechslen, "Gesetz und Evangelium—ein lutherisches Sonderthema?" *Catholica. Vierteljahresschrift für Ökumenische Theologie* 41 (1987) 30–41; H. G. Göckeritz, "Das Gesetz in der Unterscheidung von Gesetz und Evangelium," *Neue Zeitschrift für systematische Theologie* 32 (1990) 181–94; B. Lohse, *Luthers Theologie in ihrer historischen Entwicklung und in ihrem systematischen Zusammenhang* (Göttingen, 1995) 2.10 14; 3.9; idem, "'Gesetz und Gnade'—Gesetz und Evangelium," in *Verbindliches Zeugnis*, ed. W. Pannenberg and Th. Schneider, vol. 3 (Freiburg and Göttingen, 1998).

OTTO HERMANN PESCH

■ **Additional Bibliography:** M. Horton, "Calvin and the Law—Gospel Hermeneutic," *Pro ecclesia* 6 (1997) 27–42; K. Gabris, "Luthers Auffassung vom G. und E. laut seinen Kommentaren zum Galaterbrief," in *Recent Research on Martin Luther* (Bratislava, 1999) 85–102; M. J. Suda, "Die Ethik des Gesetzes bei Luther," *Vielseitigkeit des Alten Testaments. Festschrift G. Sauer* (Frankfurt/Main, 1999) 345–56; D. J. Lose, "Martin Luther on Preaching the Law," *Word and World* 21 (2001) 253–61; C. P. Arand, "Two Kinds of Righteousness as a Framework for Law and Gospel in the Apology," *Lutheran Quarterly* 15 (2001) 417–439; J. Couenhoven, "Law and Gospel, or the Law of the Gospel?," *Journal of Religious Ethics* 30 (2002) 185–205.

Leib, *Kilian.* Augustinian canon (1486), controversial theologian and historian, born February 23, 1471 in Ochsenfurt near Würzburg, died July 16, 1553 in Rebdorf near Eichstätt. He was a canon in Rebdorf (congregation of Windesheim), and became prior in Schamhaupten in 1499. He returned to Rebdorf as prior in 1503, and was a responsible superior and a careful administrator of the monastery's economy. He corresponded with men such as Johannes → Eck, Johannes → Cochlaeus, Johannes → Reuchlin, and above all with Willibald → Pirckheimer. He was in favor of reform within the church, but he soon turned against Martin Luther, and wrote a number of highly polemical works in Latin and German, emphasizing the importance of fidelity to the church and to the fathers. He took part in the imperial parliament at Augsburg in 1530, with Bishop Gabriel von → Eyb, and at the religious dialogue in → Regensburg in 1546, with Bishop Moritz von → Hutten. As a humanist, Leib was self-taught, with a profound knowledge of the biblical languages. His chronicles offer a critical view of contemporary events from the perspective of the coteries of learned men.

■ **Works:** *Annales Maiores* (1524–48), ed. I. von Döllinger, *Beiträge zur politischen, kirchlichen und Culturgeschichte* 2 (Regensburg, 1863) 445–611; *Annales minores,* ed. K. Vollmann (Ellingen, 1999); Klaiber nos. 171f.

■ **Literature:** *NDB* 14:115; *BBKL* 4:1375–79; *KThR* 5:88–96.

PLACIDUS HEIDER

■ **Additional Bibliography:** J.-M. and K. H. Keller, "K. L. als Hebraist," *Bibliotheksforum Bayern* 22 (1994) 193–203.

Leipzig Disputation (June 27–July 16, 1519 in Pleissenburg). The origins of this disputation lie in a literary controversy between Johannes → Eck and Andreas von → Karlstadt, into which Martin Luther too was drawn; Luther's trial had come to a standstill, and Duke → George of Saxony had pleaded in his favor, against the will of the bishop of Merseburg and the theological faculty of Leipzig. Luther (who was admitted only after the disputation had begun), Eck and Karlstadt debated → indulgences, → penance, purgatory, free will, and the papal authority (to which Eck consistently appealed). Luther, who considered Eck his main opponent, denied the divine right of the papacy and relativized the councils, asserting that they were capable of error. Despite his esteem for the church fathers, he expounded the classical texts about Peter's primacy (Mt 16:18; Jn 21:17) in keeping with the principle of *sola scriptura* and denied that these scriptural texts provided any justification of the Roman → primacy. The ecclesiological dissent became clear in the statements made about the pope and councils. The → pamphlets which followed the Disputation contributed to the growth of what we might call specifically "Reformation publications."

■ **Editions:** WA 59:427–605 (Eck and Luther); O. Seitz, *Der authentische Text der LD* (Berlin, 1903); H. Emser, *De disputatione Lipsicensi* (CCath 4) (Münster, 1921); E. Iserloh and P. Fabisch, ed., *Dokumente zur Causa Lutheri,* 1/2 (Münster, 1991).

■ **Literature:** K.-V. Selge, "Der Weg zur LD zwischen Luther und Eck im Jahr 1519," in *Bleibendes im Wandel der Kirchengeschichte,* ed. B. Moeller and G. Ruhbach (Tübingen, 1973) 169–210; K.-V. Selge, "Die LD zwischen Luther und Eck," *ZKG* 86 (1975) 26–40; idem, "Kirchenväter auf der LD," in *Auctoritas Patrum,* ed. L. Grane et al. (Mainz, 1993) 197–212; L. Grane, *Martinus noster* (Mainz, 1994) 45–145; B. Lohse, *Luthers Theologie in ihrer historischen Entwicklung und in ihrem*

systematischen Zusammenhang (Göttingen, 1995) 134–43.

HERIBERT SMOLINSKY

Leisentrit(t) von Julisberg, *Johann.* Dean of the collegiate church in Bautzen, preserver and supporter of Catholicism in Upper and Lower Lausitz, born May, 1527 in Olmütz, died November 24, 1584 in Bautzen. He studied in Krakow and was ordained priest there in 1549. He became a canon in Bautzen in 1551, and dean in 1559. At the urging of Emperor → Ferdinand I, the bishop of Meissen appointed him general commissioner of both Lausitz regions in 1560, and he acted prudently to preserve the Catholic confession in his jurisdiction (the bishop of Meissen, Johannes IX von Haugwitz, had resigned his office into the hands of the Protestant cathedral chapter). He wrote a number of important pastoral-liturgical works, including German liturgical books for baptism and marriage and a pioneering hymnal; he supported reform of the Mass, with parts in the German language. With Georg → Witzel, he was the most significant advocate of Catholic liturgical reform before and during the Council of Trent.

■ **Works:** *Christianae et piae precationes in usum adolescentium* (Bautzen, 1555); *Forma germanico idiomate baptizandi infantes* (Bautzen, 1562); *Geistliche Lieder und Psalmen* (Bautzen, 1567); *Forma vernacula lingua copulandi* (Bautzen, 1568); *Ritus missam catholice auspicandi, celebrandi et peragendi* (Bautzen, 1570); *Catholisch Pfarbuch* (Cologne, 1578, often reprinted).

■ **Literature:** W. Gerblich, *J. L. und die Administration des Bistums Meissen in den Lausitzen.* (Leipzig, 1959); J. Gülden, *J. L.s pastoralliturgische Schriften* (Leipzig, 1963); W. Lipphardt, *J. L.s Gesangbuch von 1567* (Leipzig, 1963); E. Heitmeyer, *Das Gesangbuch von J. L. 1567* (St. Ottilien, 1988).

ANDREAS HEINZ

■ **Additional Bibliography:** S. Seifert, ed., *J. L.* (Leipzig, 1987).

Lemnius, *Simon* (real name: Margadant; "Lemm" was his grandmother's name). Humanist poet and opponent of Martin Luther, born 1511 in Münstertal (Graubünden), died November 24, 1550 in Chur. He studied at Wittenberg under Philipp Melanchthon from 1534 onward, but provoked Luther to anger when he praised the archbishop of Mainz, → Albrecht of Brandenburg, in his *Epi-*

179

grams (Wittenberg, 1538). This led him to engage in a literary campaign against Luther. The most important of his works in this context were the new, third book of *Epigrams* (1538), an *Apology* in prose, and the *Monachopornomachia* which appeared under a pseudonym in 1539 and became very popular, with its rude comments on the marriages of Luther, Justus → Jonas, and Georg → Spalatin. Lemnius fled in 1539 to Chur, where he taught at the Latin school until his death.

■ **Works:** *Epigrammaton libri duo* (Wittenberg, 1538); *Epigrammaton libri tres* (1538). Both works with translation in L. Mundt, *L. und Luther,* vol. 2 (Berne, 1983) 1–171; *Apologia contra decretum, quod imperio et tyrannide M. Lutheri et Iusti Ionae Viteberg. universitas coacta iniquissime et mendacissime evulgavit* (Cologne, 1539) (with translation: L. Mundt [Cologne, vol. 2, 173–253]); *Lutii Pisaei Iuvenalis Monachopornomachia* (Edition mit Übersetzung: L. Mundt [Cologne, vol. 2, 257–315]); *Amorum libri IV—Liebeselegien in vier Büchern,* ed. and trans. L. Mundt (Bern and Frankfurt/ Main, 1988); *Bucolica—Fünf Eklogen,* ed., trans., and commentary by L. Mundt (Tübingen, 1996).

■ **Literature:** L. Mundt, *L. und Luther,* 2 vols. (Berne, 1983); F. Wachinger, "L. und Melanchthon," *ARG* 77 (1986) 141–57.

FIDEL RÄDLE

Leo X, pope (March 11, 1513–December 1, 1521), formerly *Giovanni de' Medici,* born in Florence on December 11, 1475, the second son of Lorenzo the Magnificent, who decided that he should have an ecclesiastical career. He received many benefices at an early age, and his father had him created a cardinal in 1489. He was educated by leading humanists. He shared the ups and downs of his family in Florence; when they were overthrown in 1494, he fled with his cousin Giulio (later → Clement VII) through Germany, Flanders (where he became a friend of → Erasmus of Rotterdam), and France. He returned to Rome in 1500 and devoted himself to literature and the fine arts. After the death of Alexander VI, he soon acquired political influence under Julius II. He was made legate in Bologna in 1511 and was given command of the papal-Spanish army which was meant to drive the French out of Italy. After his defeat in the battle of Ravenna (April 11, 1512), he was taken prisoner and brought to Milan, but he managed to escape and returned to Rome. Here he was successful in bringing the Medici back to Florence, which he and his brother Giulio ruled until he was

elected pope; he was the de facto ruler of the city even after his election.

He was elected in a brief conclave. Since he was only a deacon, he was ordained priest on March 15, 1513, and bishop two days later; he was crowned on March 19. Supporters of church reform welcomed Leo with high expectations, but these were not fulfilled. In the political sphere, he endeavored to exclude French and Habsburg (German-Spanish) influence from Italy and to strengthen papal power—though with far less success than Julius II. He was guided principally by the desire to benefit his own family. After the French victory at Marignano in September 1515, Leo met → Francis I of France in Bologna and was obliged to cede Parma and Piacenza to him; he did, however, obtain the abrogation of the Pragmatic Sanction of Bourges. He concluded a concordat with Francis I in 1516, which gave the king extensive sovereignty over the church and remained in force until the French Revolution. Leo's intervention in Siena led to a conspiracy against his life. In the imperial election, Leo unsuccessfully supported the candidacy of Francis I of France, and also for a time the Saxon elector → Frederick the Wise. New conflicts of interest with Francis I (Ferrara) led him to form an alliance against France with Emperor → Charles V at the end of May 1521. Before his death, he experienced the conquest of Milan by imperial, Swiss, and papal troops. Leo called for a crusade against the Turks, but this came to nothing.

His entanglement in political business, often guided by nepotistic interests, and his delight in worldly luxuries led Leo to neglect his urgent spiritual tasks. This was obvious in the case of the Fifth Lateran Council, as it dragged on toward its inglorious end in 1517; although it issued good reforming decrees, those in charge of church government did nothing to make these effective. This meant that the last great possibility of self-reform before the Reformation had been squandered. Leo's pontificate shows little awareness of the responsibility that he bore. The sale of → indulgences to finance the new construction of St. Peter's prompted Martin Luther to publish his ninety-five theses toward the end of 1517; but the pope and the curia failed to recognize Luther's religious concern and the ominous consequences of his actions, just as they underestimated the widespread European hostility to Rome. In 1518,

Leo sent Cardinal Thomas → Cajetan of Vio to the imperial parliament in Augsburg to engage in a disputation with Luther, and he sent Charles of → Miltitz to Saxony in 1519, bearing the Golden Rose. It was only at the urging of Johannes → Eck that he issued the bull → Exsurge Domine against Luther on June 15, 1520, which was followed by the bull of excommunication (→ Decet Romanum Pontificem) on January 3, 1521. King → Henry VIII of England wrote a book against Luther, and Leo conferred the title "Defender of the Faith" on Henry in 1521. Charles V defended the unity of the Catholic faith and the shattered papal authority much more effectively than did the pope himself.

Leo X was a very great patron of scholars, poets, and artists (Raphael, Michelangelo, etc.). Nevertheless, his pontificate was one of the most disastrous in the history of the church. He was buried initially in St. Peter's; his tomb has been in Santa Maria sopra Minerva since 1542.

■ **Sources:** P. Bembo, *Libri XVI epistolarum Leonis X P. M. nomine scriptarum* (Venice, 1535/36; Basle, 1539); P. Jovius, *Vita Leonis X et Vita Adriani VI* (Florence, 1548, 1551); P. de Grassis, *Il Diario di Leone X,* ed. D. Delicati and M. Armellini (Rome, 1884); M. Sanudo, *I diarii XVI–LVIII* (Venice, 1886–1903); J. Hergenröther, *Leonis X P. M. Regesta,* Fasciculum 1–8 (1513–15) (Freiburg, 1884–91); *HCMA* 2:21; 3:13–18; S. Camerani, *Bibliografia Medicea* (Florence, 1964); P. Fabisch and E. Iserloh, *Dokumente zur Causa Lutheri (1517–21),* 2 vols. (Münster, 1988–1991); L. Nanni, ed., *Epistulae ad Principes,* vol. 1: *L. X. –Pius IV (1513–65). Regesten* (Rome, 1992); N. H. Minnich, *The Fifth Lateran Council (1512–17)* (London, 1993).
■ **Literature:** *EC* 7:1150–55; *TRE* 20:744–48; *BBKL* 4:1448ff.—L. von Pastor, *Geschichte der Päpste seit dem Ausgang des Mittelalters* (Freiburg, vol. 4/1, 1906; 4/2 1907) 3–6, 648–721; C. Falconi, *Leone X. Giovanni de' Medici* (Milan, 1987); R. Bäumer, "L. X. und die Kirchenreform," in *Papsttum und Kirchenreform.* Festschrift G. Schwaiger (Sankt Ottilien, 1990) 281–99; I. Ciseri, *L'ingresso trionfale di Leone X in Firenze nel 1515* (Florence, 1990); G. Bianchini, *T. Justiniani—V. Quirini. Lettera al Papa. Libellus ad L. X (1513)* (Modena, 1995).

GEORG SCHWAIGER

■ **Additional Bibliography:** *LMA* 5:1881.—F. Nitti, *Leone X e la sua politica* (Florence, 1892; reprint, Bologna, 1998); H. Feld, "Wurde Martin Luther 1521 in effgie in Rom verbrannt?," *Luther-Jahrbuch* 63 (1996) 11–18; N. Housley, "A Necessary Evil? Erasmus, the Crusades, and the War against the Turks," in *The Crusades and Their Sources.* Festschrift B. Hamilton (Aldershot, 1998) 259–79; M. Gattoni, *Leone X e la geopolitica dello Stato Pontificio* (Vatican City, 2000); R. Tewes, *Der Medici-Papst L. X. und Frankreich* (Tübingen, 2002).

Linck (Link), *Wenzeslaus.* Reformer in Nuremberg and Altenburg, born January 8, 1483 in Colditz, died March 6, 1547 in Nuremberg. He began his studies at Wittenberg as an Augustinian Hermit in 1503, and took his doctorate in theology in 1511, becoming prior in the same year. He was in Nuremberg from 1517 to 1520. He became vicar general in 1520, and left the Order in 1522. He became a preacher in Altenburg, and married in 1523. He returned to Nuremberg in 1525 as preacher at the New Hospital. His great strength was his ability to present Protestant doctrine clearly and comprehensibly in the spoken and the written word.

■ **Works:** W. Reindell, *L., Werke* (Marburg, 1894); H. van der Kolk, *L., Erbauungsschriften* (Amsterdam, 1979).—J. Lorz, *Bibliographia Linckiana* (Nieuwkoop, 1977).
■ **Literature:** J. Lorz, *Das reformatorische Wirken Dr. W. L.s* (Nuremberg, 1978); M. A. van den Broek, "Sprichwörtliche Redensart . . . in den Erbauungsschriften des . . . W. L.," *Leuvense Bijdragen* 76 (1987) 475–99; J. Lorz, "W. L.," *Fränkische Lebensbilder* 14 (Würzburg, 1991) 30–46; T. Bell, "Jesu Einzug in Jerusalem . . . als Bildrede bei Bernhard von Clairvaux, W. L. und M. Luther," *Luther* 65 (1994) 9–21.

GERHARD MÜLLER

■ **Additional Bibliography:** B. Möller, "W. L.s Hochzeit," *Zeitschrift für Theologie und Kirche* 97 (2000) 317–42.

Lindanus (van der Lindt), *Wilhelmus Damasus.* Bishop and controversial theologian, born 1525 in Dordrecht, died November 2, 1588 in Ghent. He studied in Louvain and Paris, and was professor of exegesis at the university of Dillingen from 1554 to 1557. He became vicar general in Friesland in 1557, dean in The Hague in 1560, and inquisitor in Holland, Zeeland, and Friesland in 1563. He was appointed bishop of the newly founded diocese of Roermond in 1561, but he could not take up this office until 1569. He attempted to carry out the Tridentine reform program under difficult circumstances—with diocesan synods, visitation, a seminary for the education of priests, catechesis, etc. He was appointed the second bishop of Ghent in 1588, but died less than three months later. He wrote numerous works of controversial theology and catechesis.

■ **Works:** *De optimo genere interpretandi scripturas* (Cologne, 1558); *Panoplia evangelica* (Cologne, 1560); *Dubitantius* (Cologne, 1565); *Apologeticum ad Germanos pro religionis catholicae pace* (Antwerp, 1568); *Diatriba analytica de vera Jesu Christi apud Romanos ecclesia* (Cologne, 1572); *Concordia discors* (Cologne, 1583).

■ **Literature:** *DThC* 9:772–76.—M. A. H. Willemsen, *De werken van W. L.* (Roermond, 1899); W. Schmetz, *W. van der Lindt* (Münster, 1926); P. Th. van Beuningen, *W. L. als inquisiteur en bisschop. Bijdrage tot zijn biografie (1525–76)* (Assen, 1966); Klaiber 175ff.; M. G. Spiertz, "W. L., eerste bisschop van Roermond, en zijn partijkeuze in de Nederlandse Opstand (november 1576 – juli 1578)," *Archief voor de geschiedenis van de katholieke kerk in Nederland* 31 (1989) 192–213.

PETER J. A. NISSEN

Lippomani (Lip[p]omano, Lipomanus), *Luigi.* Born 1496 in Venice, died August 15, 1559 in Rome. He studied theology at the university of Padua, and became coadjutor to the bishop of Bergamo in 1539. He was nuncio in Portugal in 1542, and was appointed bishop of Verona in 1548. He was extraordinary nuncio in Germany with Cardinal Sebastiano Piglio in 1548-1550; he was third president of the Council of Trent in 1551-1552; and he was a delegate to the imperial parliament in Augsburg in 1555. He was a politically unsuccessful nuncio to Poland in 1555-1557, and was appointed bishop of Bergamo in 1558. He was a convinced Catholic reformer and an uncompromising foe of Protestantism. He wrote numerous exegetical and apologetic works. His chef d'oeuvre, *Sanctorum priscorum patrum vitae* (vols. 1-5, Venice, 1551-1556; vols. 6-8, Rome, 1558-1560; vol. 8 published posthumously by his nephew, Girolamo Lippomani), was produced with the collaboration of Gentien → Hervet, Guglielmo → Sirleto, and others; it included the first translation of Simeon Metaphrastes (critical edition by H. Delehaye, *Analecta Bollandiana* 16 [1897] 312ff.), the first critical edition of the Martyrology of Ado of Vienne, and a translation of the *Deimōn* of John Moschus (cf. E. Mioni, *Aevum* 24 [1950] 319-31). The scholarly value of Lippomani's works is generally considered to be slight.

■ **Literature:** *HCMA* 3:132, 251, 331; *Catalogue général des livres imprimés de la Bibliothèque Nationale* 98 (Paris,

1930) 832–35; Jedin passim; *NBD* I/17 (Tübingen, 1970) XXIII–XLI; *Acta nuntiaturae Polonae* 3/1 (Rome, 1993) V–XXIX.

ALEXANDER KOLLER

■ **Additional Bibliography:** A. N. Lane, "Did Calvin Use Lippoman's 'Catena in Genesim'?" *Calvin Theological Journal* 31 (1996) 404–19.

Lipsius, *Justus* (Joost Lips). Humanist, born October 18, 1547 in Overijse near Brussels, died March 23 or 25, 1606 in Louvain. He was secretary of Cardinal Antoine Perrenot de → Granvella in Rome from 1568 to 1570. As professor of rhetoric and history at Jena, Lipsius sympathized with the Lutherans; in Leiden in 1578, he came to sympathize with the Calvinists. He was reconciled to the Catholic Church in Mainz in 1591, and became professor of ancient history and Latin in Louvain in 1592. He produced important editions of Tacitus and Seneca. His *De Constantia* (Antwerp, 1584) gave new life to certain aspects of the Roman Stoa in the early modern period. His *Politicorum . . . libri sex* (Leiden, 1589) paints the picture of a monarchical state which uses its power to promote religious unity. He is a forerunner of the idea of an autonomous morality.

■ **Works:** *Opera omnia,* 4 vols. (Antwerp, 1637ff.); *Lettres inédites,* ed. G. H. M. Delprat (Amsterdam, 1858); *Epistolae,* ed. A. Gerlo et al. (Brussels, 1978ff.).

■ **Literature:** F. van der Haeghen, *Bibliographie Lipsienne,* 3 vols. (Ghent, 1886–88); J. L. Saunders, *J. L.* (New York, 1955); G. Oestreich, *Antiker Geist und moderner Staat bei J. L.* (Göttingen, 1989); J. Lagrée, *J. L. et la restauration du stoïcisme* (Paris, 1994).

ROLAND KANY

■ **Additional Bibliography:** M. Laureys, ed., *The World of J. L.* (Turnhout, 1998); G. Tournoy, ed., *J. L., europae lumen et columen* (Louvain, 1999).

Liturgy

1. The *Reformation liturgies* belong to the "Western liturgical family" as "liturgical heirs" to the Western forms of Christian → worship; the differences among them depend on the way in which they take up this inheritance, so that we can distinguish between a Lutheran, a Reformed, and an Anglican "liturgical family." The fact of this historical continuity must not, however, obscure a very fundamental novelty in the structuring of the

communication of the Christian faith, which affects the value and the function of the liturgical action as a whole: the new role given to the Word by theological reflection means that previous modes of presenting salvation are replaced by a strictly personal relationship between the Word of God and human faith, a relationship which is mediated verbally—and this in turn affects the cultic sacramental acts, which are now interpreted as "verbal events."

2. This process is exemplified in the way in which the various Reformation churches deal with the eucharistic liturgy in its late medieval form. In *Lutheranism,* the Mass is retained as the principal act of worship on Sunday, but the inner substance of the traditional rite is removed when the offertory and the eucharistic prayer are cut out and nothing is put in their place; all that remains is in fact the external structure. The words of institution (*verba testamenti*) are detached from their previous context and now function as *summa et compendium Euangelii* (WA 6:525), a uniquely concentrated form of "God's Word" (WA 12:35). The gap which is thus created is filled by having the communion rite follow immediately after the words of institution (this too was a novelty, since the communion of the laity was not at all a regular part of the Mass in the late Middle Ages). A typical example of such a liturgy is Martin Luther's "German Mass" of 1526 (WA 19:72-113), which follows the traditional structure in the liturgy of the Word, but reduces the second part of the Mass to the rite of communion (paraphrase of the Lord's Prayer and admonition about the Lord's Supper, then the words of institution, which function as the formula of administration of the sacrament, in the following sequence: words over the bread, distribution of communion under the form of bread, then words over the chalice, distribution of communion under the form of wine).

The Reformed Church orders influenced by Johannes → Bugenhagen basically follow the "German Mass," sometimes with expansions. A characteristic of these liturgies is that the Lord's Prayer is said before the narrative of institution (a structure still found in Form A of the Lutheran altar-book of 1954). Another Reformed type preferred to follow Luther's *Formula missae* of 1523 (WA 12:205-20), retaining the traditional sequence of institution narrative, Lord's Prayer, and sign of peace (one example is the Brandenburg-Nuremberg church order of 1533).

3. It was not the Mass, but rather the late medieval form of vernacular worship with a sermon, which is the starting point of liturgical reforms in *the Reformed churches in Upper Germany and Switzerland.* This is not primarily due to the change of confession; the office of preacher existed already before the Reformation, with preachers who had good theological qualifications. At the same time, it is true that this simple liturgy, which had preserved its original catechetical function and derived originally from the "pulpit liturgy," corresponded closely to the spirituality of the Swiss Reformation; if desired, it could be easily combined with the equally simple rite of parish communion. Important examples of this form are Huldrych Zwingli's *Action oder bruch des nachtmals* (1525), the Zurich church orders of 1525 and 1535, Jean Calvin's *La Forme des Prières et Chantz ecclésiastiques* (1542), and Jan → Łaski's *Forma ac ratio tota ecclesiastici Ministri* (written for the London refugee community in 1550). Although Calvin himself desired a more frequent celebration, the custom in Zurich was to hold the Lord's Supper four times a year (at Easter and Pentecost, in the autumn, and in Christmas, each time for particular groups in the parish community), clearly in imitation of the ancient "ember days." This custom came to influence Lutheranism too, so that the initial intention to revitalize the praxis of weekly reception of communion by the parishioners was soon abandoned.

4. In the *Book of* → *Common Prayer,* the *Church of* → *England* possesses an incomparable liturgical document, both an altar-book for the church and a compilation for domestic piety. It includes orders of service and texts for morning and evening prayer, for the Mass, and for worship in church. In terms of liturgical history, one can discern here influences from the Anglo-Saxon sphere (rite of Sarum), Catholic → reform, Lutheranism, and Calvinism (especially after the revision of 1552).

■ *LThK*[3] 6:984–87 (unabridged version).

■ **Sources:** *EKO; CR; Leiturgia. Handbuch des evangelischen Gottesdienstes,* ed. K. F. Müller and W. Blankenburg, 5 vols. (Kassel, 1952–70); *Coena Domini,* ed. I. Pahl, vol. 1: *Die Abendmahlsliturgie der Reformationskirchen im 16./17.Jh.* (Fribourg, 1983).

■ **Literature:** *TRE* 1:755–84; 2:1–91; 14:54–85.—J. Smend, *Die evangelischen deutschen Messen bis zu Luthers Deutscher Messe* (Göttingen, 1896; reprint, Nieuwkoop, 1967); F. Rendtorff, *Geschichte des Gottesdienstes unter dem Gesichtspunkt der liturgischen Erbfolge* (Giessen, 1914); L. Fendt, *Der lutherische Gottesdienst des 16.Jh.* (Munich, 1923); G. Rietschel, *Lehrbuch der Liturgik,* 2., new edition prepared by P. Graff (Munich, vol. 1, 1951; vol. 2, 1952); L. Fendt, *Einführung in die Liturgiewissenschaft* (Berlin, 1958); W. Nagel, *Geschichte des christlichen Gottesdienstes* (Berlin, 1962); H. B. Meyer, *Luther und die Messe* (Paderborn, 1965); G. J. Cuming, *A History of Anglican Liturgy* (London, [2]1981); *Handbuch der Liturgik,* ed. H.-Ch. Schmidt-Lauber and K.-H. Bieritz (Leipzig and Göttingen, [2]1995).

KARL-HEINRICH BIERITZ

■ **Additional Bibliography:** B. Gordon, "Transcendence and Community in Zwinglian Worship," *Continuity and Change in Christian Worship* (Woodbridge, 1999) 128–50; G. Holderness, "'The Scripture Moveth Us in Sundry Places . . .': Strategies of Persuation in 16th Century Anglican Liturgy," *Reformation and Renaissance Review* (1999) 20–37; R. M. Kingdon, "The Genevan Revolution in Public Worship," *Princeton Seminary Bulletin* 20 (1999) 264–80; J. D. Witvliet, "Images and Themes in Calvin's Theology of Liturgy," *The Legacy of John Calvin,* ed. D. Foxgrover (Grand Rapids, 2000) 130–52; R. Kunz, *Gottesdienst evangelisch reformiert. Liturgik und L. in der Kirche Zwinglis* (Zurich, 2001).

Loher, *Dietrich.* Carthusian (1518), born before 1500 in Stratum near Eindhoven, died August 26, 1554 in Würzburg. He became prior in Hildesheim in 1539, and in Buxheim in 1543. He was one of those German Carthusians who endeavored with all their might to strengthen the old faith and its institutions in the tribulations of the Reformation period. Since Loher held that the new teachings had already been refuted by medieval authors, he had their writings printed. In particular, he edited the voluminous work of his confrère Dionysius von Rijkel (died 1471) and wrote his biography (Cologne, 1530). He also published a shortened version of John Gerson's *Monotesaron* (Cologne, 1531), the *Evangelische Peerle* (Utrecht, 1535), the *Legatus divinae pietatis* of Gertrude of Helfta (Cologne, 1536), some works by Heinrich Herp (Cologne, 1538), a lengthy collection of *Vitae patrum* (Cologne, 1547), and the *Vita* and *Dialogue* of Catharine of Siena (Cologne, 1553). With his organizational

and political gifts, he consolidated and preserved many monasteries and was able to regain possession of others (Buxheim, Erfurt, Hildesheim).

■ **Literature:** *DSp* 9:691ff.—J. Greven, *Die Kölner Kartause und die Anfänge der katholischen Reform in Deutschland* (Münster, 1935) 51–85; F. Stöhlker, *Die Kartause* (Buxheim, 1402–1803), 4 vols. (continuous pagination); (Buxheim, 1974–78) 121–49, 220–26; G. Chaix, *Réforme et Contre-Réforme catholiques* (Salzburg, 1981) (index).

HEINRICH RÜTHING

■ **Additional Bibliography:** *BBKL* 5:180f.

Lord's Supper, → Communion/Lord's Supper.

Lorichius, *Gerhard.* Humanist, born c. 1490 in Hadamar, died c. 1550. Despite initial sympathy with the Reformation, he remained in the Catholic Church and sought to renew it, taking the early church as his model. His attempts to reform the liturgy were based on the principle of the active participation in worship by all those present. Lorichius vehemently defended Catholic doctrines against Reformation attacks. He was obliged to go into exile for a short period because of his criticism of the double marriage of Marquis → Philip of Hessen. After 1547, he was parish priest in Wetzlar and Worms. He took part in the provincial synod of Mainz in 1549.

■ **Literature:** N. Paulus, "G. L.," *Der Katholik* 74 (1894) 503–29; W. Michel, "G. L. und seine Theologie," *Nassauische Annalen* 81 (1970) 160–72; M. Kunzler, "Humanistische Kirchenreform und ihre theologischen Grundlagen bei G. L., Pfarrer und Humanist aus Hadamar," *Archiv für mittelrheinische Kirchengeschichte* 31 (1979) 75–110; idem, *Die Eucharistie-Theologie des Hadamarer Pfarrers und Humanisten G. L.* (Münster, 1981).

MICHAEL KUNZLER

■ **Additional Bibliography:** B. Rücker, *Die Bearbeitung von Ovids "Metamorphosen" durch Albrecht von Halberstadt und Jörg Wickram und ihre Kommentierung durch G. L.* (Göppingen, 1997).

Lotzer, *Sebastian.* Lay theologian, born c. 1490 in Horb (Neckar). He worked as a furrier in Memmingen and was a friend of Christoph Schappeler. The five pamphlets he published between 1523 and 1525 display strong influence by Martin

Luther. In the → Peasants' War, he was the military secretary to the men of Baltring and composed the "Twelve articles of the peasantry" in February, 1525, a moderate program which included the obligation to observe biblical, divine right, the acknowledgment of the civil authority, and the renunciation of the use of violence. He later fled to St. Gallen, and nothing further is known about his life.

■ **Works:** A. Goetze, *L.s Schriften* (Leipzig, 1902).
■ **Literature:** M. Brecht, "Der theologische Hintergrund der 12 Artikel," *ZKG* 85 (1974) 30–64; M. Arnold, *Handwerker als theologische Schriftsteller* (Göttingen, 1990).

CHRISTIAN PETERS

Louise of Savoy. Regent of France, born September 11, 1476 in Pont d'Ain (department of Ain), died September 22, 1531 in Grez-sur-Loing (department of Seine-et-Marne). She was the mother of → Francis I. During her regency (1524-1526), she supported the theological faculty of Paris and the parliament in the measures they took against the circle of reformers around Bishop Guillaume → Briçonnet and Jakob → Faber Stapulensis in Meaux. Her *Journal* of events between 1508 and 1522 gives insight into her religious ideas.

■ **Literature:** *CEras* 3:201f.—G. Griffiths, "L. of Savoy and Reform of the Church," *SCJ* 10 (1979) 29–36; M. Dickman Orth, "Francis du Moulin and the Journal of L. of Savoy," *SCJ* 13 (1982) 55–66; J. K. Farge, *Orthodoxy and Reform in Early Reformation France. The Faculty of Theology of Paris* (Leiden, 1985).

BARBARA HENZE

Luke of Prague (Lukáš Pra ský). Organizer of the → Bohemian Brethren, born c. 1460 in Prague, died December 11, 1528 in Mladá Boleslav (Bohemia). He took his bachelor's degree in 1481, and was the leading theologian of the Bohemian Brethren from 1494 onward. He made contacts with the Waldensians in Italy and in France in 1498. As "counselor" (elder or bishop) from 1500, Luke governed the Brethren in practical and ecclesiastical matters, and he became their judge in 1518. He attacked Martin Luther and Huldrych Zwingli, and wrote many theological works.

■ **Literature:** A. Molnár, *Bratr Lukáš, bohoslovec Jednoty* (Prague, 1948); idem, "Luther und die Böhmischen Brüder," *Communio viatorum* 24 (1963) 47–67; E.

Peschke, *Kirche und Welt in der Theologie der Böhmischen Brüder* (Berlin, 1981) 146ff.

MILOSLAV POLÍVKA

■ **Additional Bibliography:** L. Broz, "Justification and Sanctification in the Czech Reformation," in *Justification and Sanctification in the Traditions of the Reformation* (Geneva, 1999) 38–43

Lussy, *Melchior.* Statesman in central Switzerland and supporter of Catholic reform, born 1529 in Stans, where he died November 16, 1606. He became cantonal secretary in 1551, and held the highest cantonal office several times between 1561 to 1595. He led Swiss troops in the service of the pope and of France, and he was entrusted with diplomatic missions to Rome, Venice, Milan, and Paris. In 1562, together with prince-abbot Joachim Eichhorn of Einsiedeln, Lussy represented the seven Catholic regions of Switzerland at the third period of the Council of Trent, and he collaborated with Charles → Borromeo in making possible the foundation of the Swiss seminary (Collegium Helveticum) in Milan and the permanent nunciature in Lucerne in 1579, as well as the first Capuchin monasteries in Switzerland from 1581 onward.

■ **Literature:** *NDB* 15:535f.—R. Feller, *Ritter M. L. von Unterwalden,* 2 vols. (Stans, 1906–1909); O. Vasella, *Ritter M. L.* (Olten, 1956); E. Huwyler, "Ritter M. L. (1529–1606) und das Hechhuis in Wolfenschiessen," *Schweizer Volkskunde* 82 (1992) 26–33.

MARKUS RIES

Luther, Martin, theologian and reformer
1. Life—2. Works—3. Theology: (a) Origin and Development; (b) Methodological Perspectives on the Interpretation of Luther's Texts; (c) Selected Important Themes

1. Life

He was born November 10, 1483 in Eisleben (county of Mansfeld, Thüringen), the son of a master miner in the copper mines of Mansfeld, and died there on February 18, 1546. After schooling in Magdeburg (1497-1498) and Eisenach (1498-1501), he began his studies in Erfurt in 1501, taking the degree of master of arts in 1505. At his father's wish, he began the study of law, but stopped after completing only half of his first semester. He entered the monastery of the Augustinian Hermits in Erfurt on July 17, 1505; the final impulse to this move came from a flash of lightning which nearly hit him at Stotternheim near Erfurt. He was ordained priest in autumn 1506 or spring 1507, and then studied theology, following the *via moderna*. He was moved to Wittenberg in 1508, where he continued his study of theology and attended lectures in philosophy. He took the degree of bachelor in biblical studies in March, 1509, and later the degree of bachelor in the *Sentences*. He returned to Erfurt in autumn 1509. The monastery sent him to Rome in 1510, but Luther's first contact with the religious situation in Rome did not result in any religious impulses. He was moved once again to Wittenberg in 1512, where he took his doctorate in theology and received the professorship in biblical studies which he held until his death.

After his first lectures and disputations, which were critical of scholasticism, he began to criticize the institution of → indulgences from 1516 onward. The high point was his ninety-five theses on the power of indulgences, which he sent on October 31, 1517 to → Albrecht of Brandenburg and to the bishop of his own diocese (scholars doubt whether he actually nailed his theses to the castle church in Wittenberg; this is rather unlikely). Against Luther's own intentions, these theses soon became known throughout Germany. His criticism of the way in which penance was understood and practiced, implying indirectly that the papal claims to authority contradicted scripture, led in summer 1518 to the opening of a Roman investigation of Luther on suspicion of heresy. This investigation was hampered and delayed by political considerations, but after various moves and countermoves by both sides, Luther was interrogated by Cardinal Thomas → Cajetan de Vio in Augsburg in October, 1518, after the session of the imperial parliament. A disputation with Johannes → Eck took place in → Leipzig in 1519, and the official investigation was resumed in January, 1520. At Eck's urging, the bull → *Exsurge Domine* of June 15, 1520 (which was in fact not drawn up in correct legal terms) listed "forty-one errors of Martin Luther" (DH 1451-1492) and threatened him with excommunication. After one last attempt at clarification in his *Von der Freiheit eines Christenmenschen*, Luther refused to recant, and when he burnt the books of canon law on December 12, 1520, he

threw the papal bull into the fire as well. Excommunication by → Leo X in the bull *Decet Romanum Pontificem* followed on January 3, 1521, which was given the force of imperial law by the "Edict of Worms" which the emperor promulgated at the imperial parliament in May, 1521. Luther's own electoral prince, → Frederick the Wise, protected him by having him "kidnapped" and brought to the Wartburg fortress, where he translated the New Testament.

During this period, when it was impossible for Luther to bring his influence to bear on the course of events, the various tendencies in the Reformation movement began to part company. Against the will of the electoral prince, he returned to Wittenberg in 1522, so that he could intervene in the "Wittenberg unrest" caused by the radical liturgical reforms of Andreas von → Karlstadt. The following years saw the diffusion of the Reformation in German principalities and cities; a tug of war between the emperor, the curia, and the princes about enforcing the Edict of Worms; delaying tactics on the part of → Clement VII, who rejected every idea of a council; and controversies with Thomas → Müntzer (1523), with the peasants (and the princes) in the → Peasants' War (1524-1525), with → Erasmus of Rotterdam (1525), with Huldrych Zwingli and the Upper German Protestants about the Lord's Supper (1525-1529; religious dialogue of → Marburg), with Johannes → Agricola about the law (1527, → Antinomian controversy), and with Enthusiastic, Spiritualist movements (→ Baptists; prophets of → Zwickau). Luther gave advice about the visitations which began in 1526 in electoral Saxony and other territories and cities, and about the reform of → church orders. In 1530, from the safe distance of the fortress of Coburg, he gave his theological and "strategic" support to the imperial parliament in Augsburg. He married the former nun Katharina von → Bora on June 13, 1525 (cf. WA.BR 3:482, 81ff.).

After the failure of the last attempts at reestablishing unity, and in the aftermath of the imperial parliament of Augsburg, he concentrated once more primarily on lecturing, disputations, and preaching in Wittenberg. He accompanied the reform of church structures with theological reflections and expert memoranda. The most important of these are his ecclesiological clarifications in connection with the proclamations and delays of the council from 1536 onward; the renewed debate with Agricola and those whom Luther called "antinomians," in 1538; his approval, motivated by pastoral reasons, of the double marriage of Marquis → Philip of Hessen; and his criticism of the "religious dialogues" in → Hagenau near Strasbourg, → Worms, and → Regensburg (1539-1541).

2. Works

These fall naturally into four groups, corresponding to the four phases of Luther's activity: (*a*) the period up to his conflict with Rome (1509-1517); (*b*) the controversy with the Roman curia until his excommunication (1518-1521); (*c*) clarifications within the Reformation movement itself (1522-1530); (*d*) consolidation within this movement (1531-1546). His biblical translation (→ Luther's Bible) extends across several of these phases.

Important texts in the first phase (*a*): lectures on the Psalms (*Dictata super Psalterium*, 1513-1515); on Romans (1515-1516), on Galatians (1516-1517), and on Hebrews (1517-1518); and in 1517: *Die sieben Bußpsalmen; Disputatio contra scholasticam theologiam*; 95 theses on indulgences.—In the second phase (*b*): the Heidelberg disputation; *Resolutiones* on his theses about indulgences (1518); the Leipzig disputation; short commentary on Galatians; sermons on the contemplation of the suffering of Christ, on the sacrament of penance, on baptism, on the Eucharist, *Bereitung zum Sterben* (1519); second series of lectures on the Psalms (*Operationes in Psalmos*, 1519-1521); *An den christlichen Adel deutscher Nation; De captivitate Babylonica ecclesiae praeludium; Von dem Papsttum zu Rom; Von den guten Werken; Von der Freiheit eines Christenmenschen* (1520); *Rationis Latomicae . . . confutatio* ("Antilatomus"); *Das Magnificat verdeutscht und ausgelegt; De votis monasticis iudicium* (1521); translation of the New Testament.—In the third phase (*c*): the *Invocavit* sermons; *Advents-, Weihnachts-* and *Kirchenpostille; Vom ehelichen Leben* (1522); *Daß Jesus Christus ein geborener Jude sei; Formula missae; Von weltlicher Oberkeit* (1523); *Von Kaufhandlung und Wucher* (1524); lectures on the minor prophets (1524-1527); writings on the → Peasants' War; *Fastenpostille; De servo arbitrio* (1525); *Deutsche Messe; Ob Kriegsleute auch in seligem Stande sein können* (1526); *Daß diese*

Worte Christi . . . noch feststehen; Ob man vor dem Sterben fliehen möge (1527); *Vom Abendmahl Christi. Bekenntnis; Unterricht der Visitatoren; Von der Wiedertaufe* (1528); *Kleiner* and *Großer Katechismus* (1529); *Das schöne Confitemini;* beginning of the *Tischreden* (1530).—In the fourth phase (*d*): long commentary on Galatians; lectures on Pss 2, 45, 51, 90, 101, 110, 127, 129, 130, 147 (1531-1535); on Genesis (1535-1545), series of sermons on 1 Cor 15 (1532-1533); *Von der Winkelmesse und Pfaffenweihe* (1533); *Eine einfältige Weise zu beten* (1535); disputations, especially *De homine, De iustificatione, Contra missam privatam, De sententia: Verbum caro factum est, De divinitate et humanitate Christi;* three disputations against the antinomians; *Wider die Antinomer* (1536-1540); articles of → Schmalkald (1536); *Von den Konziliis und Kirchen* (1539); *Wider Hans Worst* (1541); *Von den Juden und ihren Lügen; Vom Schem Hamphoras und vom Geschlecht Christi* (1543); *Wider das Papsttum zu Rom, vom Teufel gestiftet;* preface to the first volume of the complete edition of his Latin writings (1545, with the "great testimony to himself").—He wrote c. 2,000 sermons between 1516 and 1546.

3. Theology

(a) Origin and Development

Luther's theology begins with the personal problem of how he as a sinner can stand before God's judgment and be "righteous." This is not merely the problem of a subjectively oversensitive, scrupulous conscience, but the objective problem of his own age.

This problem oppressed Luther thanks to the confluence of four theological circumstances. *First,* the interpretation of late scholasticism experienced the commandment to love God above all things as impossible of fulfillment. *Second,* according to Ockhamist teaching (Gabriel → Biel), the absolution imparted in the sacrament of penance was valid only conditionally, since it took effect only where perfect repentance (*contrition*) existed. *Third,* Luther was confronted in his daily singing of the divine office in choir by the word and the reality of *iudicium*. *Fourth,* expectation of an imminent end of the world brought with it a general fear of judgment; in Luther's case, this was intensified by the emphasis on Christ as judge, and by the image of God as judge in Biel's *Expositio canonis missae*.

For the young professor, the personal and theological problem becomes an exegetical problem: how is one to understand the biblical concept of "God's righteousness"—and hence human righteousness? His first series of lectures on the Psalms propose an interim solution: God's righteousness is the just judgment which he pronounces on sin, and human righteousness means that one becomes "conformed" to this judgment, acknowledging it and accusing oneself. It is thus that the human person becomes true, right, "righteous." This so-called theology of *humilitas* already excludes → justification by one's own works and achievements. From 1514 onward, Luther discovers theological traditions which had been overlooked by academic theologians hitherto: works of German mystics (Johannes Tauler, → Theologia Deutsch), Augustine's anti-Pelagian writings, and "modern" exegetes who interpreted scripture on the basis of the original text. These confirmed him in his own views; at the same time, they drew a distinction between the gospel (as the promise of grace and forgiveness) and the accusatory word of judgment. This led to a consistently Augustinian anthropology of sin and justification which definitively overcame the latent semi-Pelagianism of the late medieval doctrine of justification (according to William of Ockham, the *potentia Dei ordinata* has decreed that the precondition of justification is an act of loving God above all else *ex puris naturalibus*). Luther teaches that the "righteousness of God" in Rom 1:17 is the righteousness by which God makes us righteous; this is the early dating of the "Reformation breakthrough."

The theological and exegetical problem becomes a problem for the church when Luther speaks out against the preachers of indulgences. Since he knows little about the church-political problems involved in this conflict—and nothing at all about the financial interests of his opponent, → Albrecht of Brandenburg—he cannot grasp how the whole church (in the persons of its official representatives) is suddenly arrayed against him, when all he has done is to propose a theology which lies completely within the framework of legitimate possibilities. This poses the question of the personal certainty of → salvation, which Luther answers by maintaining unconditionally the forgiveness of sins which is taken hold of in faith; the scriptural text to which he appeals here is

Mt 16:19b. This puts the coping stone on his new understanding of Rom 1:17; this is the "late" dating of the "Reformation breakthrough."

The fundamental insight which allows Luther to stand firm under the ensuing conflict works like a leaven through every aspect of his theology. Historically speaking, the sequence of individual themes which he debated may have been a matter of chance, but we can discern a remarkable "systematic" logic when we look back over these developments.

(b) *Methodological Perspectives on the Interpretation of Luther's Texts*

First, Luther is primarily an exegete, not a systematical theologian. This means that, while his scriptural commentaries may contain affirmations of a systematic-theological nature, they must not be read as the systematic exposition of Reformation thought.—*Second,* Luther is an "occasional writer," without "literary ambitions" (Lohse, 3rd ed. 1997, 114-31). When we interpret him, especially in the case of his polemical works, we must bear in mind both the situation which prompted him to write and the position of his opponents. The customary style of theological disputations in his period should make us alert to the presence of intentionally exaggerated provocations.—*Third,* Luther never presented a complete synthesis of his own theology. This means that the question about what he "really or definitively" thought cannot be answered by a chronological examination of his works; each individual case must be investigated on its own.—*Fourth,* his late works involve considerable problems of transmission, especially the lectures, disputations, and sermons which were reconstructed from notes taken by his hearers, or else written down by Luther himself after the event. This means that we cannot wholly eliminate the element of uncertainty about what Luther genuinely thought; at any rate, it is not sufficient to quote the formulations in his printed works, even when he himself authorized them in a foreword.—*Fifth,* if Luther does not write explicitly on a traditional subject, this means that he takes it for granted. This is true in particular of the trinitarian and christological profession of faith by the early church. It is unacceptable to designate as "genuinely" Lutheran only those statements in his theology which point to the future, while neglecting the traditional statements on the grounds that they are "Catholic (medieval) remnants."—*Sixth,* Luther throughout his entire life presupposed that the one Christendom in the one church did not exclude a plurality of "ceremonies." In other words, he does not simply develop an alternative ecclesiological concept from scratch. The construction of a Lutheran Church with a constitution in keeping with the principles of Luther's theology was a historical necessity; it does not signify the institutional reconstruction of an ecclesiology on his part.— *Seventh,* Luther's origins, education, and ecclesiastical socialization make him a critical, late medieval theologian. His originality, which changed world history, emerges in the context of the late Middle Ages, and continues to employ the linguistic instruments of that period. This originality consists in the theological reception— involving both positive affirmation and criticism—of the self-discovery of the subject which had begun in humanism, and hence of the consciousness and existential awareness which are typical of the early modern period.

(c) *Selected Important Themes*
(1) Scripture and Tradition

Luther intensifies the sufficiency of scripture in questions of faith (→ *sola scriptura*), which had already been taught in the late Middle Ages, since he calls into question a "harmony stabilized *a priori*" between the biblical testimony, official doctrinal teaching, and the church's tradition. This means that he subjects the church continuously—i.e., not only in cases of obvious failure on the part of the church—to a critical confrontation with the testimony of scripture and understands the working of the Spirit in the church as convincing the human conscience of the truth of the biblical word. Accordingly, he can go so far as to speak of the self-authentication of the Bible (*sacra Scriptura sui interpres*). Thus, the principle of *sola scriptura* does not at all mean the denial of binding tradition, but only that such tradition must be checked against scripture (and not *vice versa*). Luther himself sometimes argues on the basis of tradition, e.g., on the question of infant baptism.

(2) Reason and Faith/Theological Methodology

Luther is no irrationalist. All he does (in a completely traditional manner) is to insist that reason and philosophy cannot have the last word on questions of faith. This is why he criticizes scholastic theology, where this equates one particular philosophical interpretation of the truth of the faith with the truth itself (WA 39 I, 229, 6-29). In the service of faith, reason is a "very good instrument" (WA.TR 3, n. 2938b, 105, 15), and outside the realm of faith, it is reason that has been entrusted with the governance of the whole world. Accordingly, Luther both criticized and accepted Aristotle, whose writings he interpreted expertly; like the scholastics, he too employed the instruments of philosophical interpretation in the exposition of the doctrine of faith. He differed merely in his choice of instruments, e.g., in his preference of the category of "relationship" to that of *habitus,* and in his new understanding of the concept of "substance" (WA 40 II, 354, 3-5). He also employs the method of explanation by means of analogy (WA 6, 513,22-514,10).

(3) Certainty of Salvation

From the very beginning of Luther's conflict with Rome, the question at issue necessarily made this a central topic, but it first emerges in all its clarity in the documents pertaining to Luther's interrogation in Augsburg. Certainty of → salvation does not mean *securitas* in the sense of the assurance (whether empirically observable, or something to be held fast in faith) of present and future salvation. Rather, it is identical with faith itself, understood as unconditional confidence in the validity of the promise made to us in Christ of the forgiveness of sins and of righteousness before God. Such faith is incompatible with doubts about one's own salvation, since that would mean both affirming and denying that we can trust in God as the reliable source of salvation; and that in turn would mean that the words of Jesus at Mt 16:19b were a lie. Accordingly, the certainty of salvation is not based on a subjective reflection on one's own state of grace: this certainty has its formal foundations in the distinction between → law and gospel. The substantial reason for the certainty of salvation lies in the new accent in Christology, or more precisely in soteriology: the decisive point is that one not only be informed about the salvific events concerning Jesus Christ, and that one believe these to be true (the *fides historica*), but that one relate these to one's own existence (*pro me, pro nobis*). This vastly reduces the importance of the traditional problems of Christology and the doctrine of the Trinity, with which Luther was acquainted primarily in their late-scholastic version. He sometimes pokes fun at this (WA 16:217,30-218,6); he is content to affirm the dogma of the early church (WA 18:606,24-29). On occasion, he displays a sovereign neglect of the Chalcedonian terminology, emphasizing the unity of divinity and humanity in Christ in such a way that gives the impression of monophysite tendencies.

(4) Sin and Justification

His early rediscovery of Augustine led Luther to an understanding of "sin" as more than the individual sin which the human person commits, or as a quality of the human person himself: "sin" is identical with the existence of the human person as de facto in opposition to God, and is concentrated in the concept of "concupiscence," the abiding sin of pride. Sin is first of all the "basic and principal sin" which is identical with the original sin which continues to be effective in the human person; original sin in its turn is identical with the fundamental opposition of human existence to God's will, and hence is identical with unbelief. The consequence is a lifelong coexistence of righteousness and sin (→ *simul iustus et peccator*), since under these circumstances, righteousness can never be a quality which *we* ourselves possess, but is always a relationship which *God* establishes with us despite our sin. Nevertheless, Luther cannot be tied down to technical distinctions between a "forensic" and an "effective" justification, between justification and sanctification, or between a relational and a substantial understanding of grace. He makes use of various analogies in his sermons and his academic works. For example, he can speak of the "joyous exchange," the quasi-mystical experience of becoming "one cake" with Christ (WA 10 I 1,74,16ff.), of the righteousness which lies outside our own selves (*extra nos*), of acquittal for the sake of Christ, of reconciliation, of Christ's victory on our behalf over the forces of corruption, of the killing of the old Adam, or of our being saved in judgment.

(5) Basis of Ethics

Luther encountered at an early date the suspicion that his Reformation doctrine of justification undermined both theoretically and pastorally the foundations of Christian ethics. He immediately responded by drawing the consequences of his doctrine for the new ethical basis: the assurance that our sins are forgiven frees us from sin, in order that we may fight against sin. This combative freedom from sin leads the heart to react spontaneously, when it sees that which is truly good according to the will of God. Believers no longer stand under the law, but they keep the commandments of God. This allows them to hand on God's love to others, becoming "another Christ" for their neighbor (WA 7,66,25-28), and doing good to him in the manner of a sacrament. As Luther's expositions of the decalogue show, his ethics are biblically based, but do not take the form of a law.

(6) Sacraments

Luther draws consequences for the → sacraments both in terms of chronological sequence and in terms of theological substance. Baptism is the covenant in which God assures the human person the lifelong forgiveness of his sins and at the same time places him in the line of battle against sin ("drowning the old Adam": *BSLK* 516:29–517:7). The Lord's Supper (→ communion) gives us "fellowship with Christ and all the saints" (WA 2,743,11.21f., etc.), opening the will of the crucified Christ and sharing out his inheritance, viz. the promise of the forgiveness of sins (WA 6:513f.), which it makes certain (as "sign and seal," WA 7,323,5). Luther limits the number of sacraments to these two.

He does not deny the sacramental significance of → penance, but sees it as the return to baptism (which cannot be blotted out), rather than as a separate sacrament, all the more so, in that it lacks an element directly related to the senses. Luther is led to limit the number by precisely the same principle which had led scholasticism to justify the number seven. It is only Christ himself, not the church, who can bind the word and the sensuous element together to form a reliable sign of salvation; but Luther is no longer able to appeal to ecclesiastical tradition in justification of those sacraments which are not unambiguously attested in scripture. Inspired by Augustine's dictum, *accedit verbum ad elementum et fit scramentum*, he understands the external sign in the narrowest sense, viz., as a material element. Like the scholastic theologians, Luther overlooks the secondary, abbreviatory, and hence arbitrary character of the *concept* of "sacrament."

Against all the other groups in the Reformation movement, Luther held immovably in his doctrine of the Lord's Supper to the real presence of the Body and Blood of Christ, although naturally he did not explain this on the model of transubstantiation (which he held to be irrational in philosophical terms). Rather, he had recourse to the analogy of the incarnation of the Logos in the human being Jesus (WA 6:508,1-512,6). He necessarily rejects the "sacrificial character" of the Eucharist, as this was understood by his contemporaries, as "the most terrible" (yet also "the most beautiful") "papal idolatry" (*BSLK* 416:8-11). In the second half of his career, the debate with "spiritualist" devaluations of the sacraments led Luther to emphasize the importance of our obedience to what God has instituted (→ Eucharistic controversy).

(7) The Church

For Luther, the church is the "throng" of those who believe in Christ, the "Christian holy people" who listen to the voice of their Shepherd (WA 10 I 1,140,14; 50,623,223f.; *BSLK* 459:22), rather than the hierarchy (cf. WA 50:624,10f.). The true, "spiritual" church is not "invisible," but rather hidden: only in faith can it be identified as the church of Jesus Christ. The institutional form, the "external church," ought to be an "image" of the hidden church, allowing it to be recognized. Accordingly, Luther speaks of those characteristics of the church that are visible, yet can be discerned only in faith, in "lists" which never aim to be exhaustive: baptism, the Lord's Supper, the power of the keys (absolution), the office of preaching, ministries, prayer, the cross, the creed, respect for those in authority, marriage. Since these characteristics have been distorted for centuries in the church of Rome—both in theory and in practice—Luther can argue that it is not "his" church, but rather the church of the pope that is in reality the "new" church (*Wider Hans Worst*, 1541). Nevertheless, Luther does not elaborate any specific concept of the church: he limits himself to reflections on how the existing church might be corrected.

Luther adopts the traditional *understanding of* → *ministry*. The only ecclesial ministry which exists by divine right (since although the minister may be elected "democratically," the basis of his ministry is not itself democratic) is the office of preaching, which includes the administration of the sacraments; in practice, this is identical with the office of parish pastor. All other ministries, including the office of deacon, which goes back to models in scripture and the early church, depend on human law. This applies also to the bishop's office to the extent that this is distinct from the pastor's ministry; in keeping with the medieval tradition, Luther understands this distinction exclusively in terms of jurisdiction, taking it for granted that a Reformation church will have ministries higher than that of the individual pastor. In Germany, Luther also envisages the episcopal ministry as something incumbent upon the secular prince too. Under these circumstances, it is no devaluation of the episcopal office to say that bishop and pastor are equal. On the contrary, this raises the theological value of the episcopal ministry, which Luther maintained throughout his life as his own "constitutional idea" (in Bornkamm's phrase) for the church (WA 26:197,15-29). Against this background, Luther's attempts to ordain bishops must be judged "emergency ordinations"; these broke the rules of canon law, but they were not intended to affirm anything about apostolic succession, which posed such a great problem for later generations.

For Luther, the office of the pope (→ primacy) is entirely a matter of jurisdiction. Church critics in the late Middle Ages had often identified the pope with the Antichrist, and this suspicion occurs to Luther for the first time at the end of 1518, thanks to his interrogation in Augsburg, where he had the impression that the pope put himself above scripture. Nevertheless, it was only in 1536, in the articles of → Schmalkald, that Luther finally took the position (unlike Philipp Melanchthon) that even a papacy existing only *iure humano* was meaningless. His late work *Wider das Papsttum zu Rom vom Teufel gestiftet* (1545) was prompted by the active support given by the pope to the preparations for the war which the emperor was soon to unleash against the Protestant territories (→ Schmalkaldic War).

The relationship to the *Jews* is a subordinate topic which Luther takes up only as the occasion demands. In questions of detail, he is fairly open and "milder" than many at that period, but he remains within the limits of contemporary views and (church-)political options. Nevertheless, what he said was to have extremely negative effects in the long term because of Luther's authoritative position.

His understanding of the church and of ministry led him to speak only with reserve about *church reform*. There is no trace in Luther of a thoroughgoing concept of church reform, such as we find in Jean Calvin. Luther appeals only to the right and duty of Christian princes, on the basis of the priesthood of all believers, to exercise the *cura religionis* when the official church ministers fail to do so. The church must get rid of abuses and false forms of piety, but otherwise it can and should remain as it is.

(8) The Unity of Church and Society

Luther maintained this principle, but not of course in the sense of the *corpus christianum* under the pope and the emperor. The distinction between the two kingdoms (→ kingdom of God) or two "regimes" serves to free the conscience from being burdened by the worldly conditions of one's relationship to God. It also frees the "secular arm" from a situation where the hierarchy tells it what it must do, while at the same time preventing the civil authorities from intervening in things that are the preachers' responsibility. The princes too are subject to God's commandment, and must ensure that no obstacles are placed in the way of the proclamation of the gospel. Luther does not envisage any tolerance for the public celebration of false worship.

(9) Eschatology

Luther eliminates ideas that are not based in the Bible (purgatory, the mediatory role of the saints), and interprets the concrete affirmations of scripture in realistic terms, intensifying them with the vigor of his own language when he speaks of the devil, hell, the judgment and victory of Christ, and the resurrection of the dead. The true anchor of the Christian hope is God and Christ, who died and rose again—when we look to him, we see that death is the litmus test of faith, which relativizes all images and poses a critical question to any view that might seem to justify a human "right" to be raised from the dead. Luther justifies the immortality of the soul on theological grounds: it is based on the fact that God has created the human person and has spoken to him. He teaches that the soul "sleeps" after death, and sees the Last Day as the object of our yearning and our prayer ("Come, dear Last Day!": WA.BR 9, 175,17).

(10) Luther's Understanding of God

His eschatology, like all his theology, is intimately linked to his understanding of God. He does not question that God is a Trinity, but he always sees God in the light of Jesus' address as "Father"—hence as "pure grace and love" (WA 36:393,13f.). As such, God is the creator of all things, and he himself is the reason why we may trust in the goodness of all creatures. Luther seems however to neglect the good creation and to posit a disjunction between creation and redemption, when he follows the doctrine of predestination in the Augustinian tradition and sees the human person as wholly a slave under Satan and sin. The consequence is not only that the human person is completely dependent on God's mercy, but also the total lack of freedom of the will in relation to God and Satan; even our apparently free ethical endeavor serves only to deepen our corruption, so that Luther can speak of "bright shining vices." And since God—as Augustine and the Middle Ages taught—saves only a few persons (WA 18:633,15-21), we have the picture of a doubly hidden God. He is hidden in his revelation *sub contrario* or *sub contraria specie,* and he is hidden in his election of those to whom he shows mercy; we cannot ask him to justify this choice. In his controversy with → Erasmus of Rotterdam, Luther maintains this position, without paying heed to the intellectual or indeed the pastoral consequences, and reinforces it by means of a concept of the omnipotence and omniscience of God which excludes human freedom. He sees this as the ultimate anchor of the certainty of salvation, and can understand human freedom only as a gift bestowed on human persons, so that they are free to collaborate with God in the world. (Luther argues here against contemporary tendencies to emancipate the self-understanding of the human person from his relationship to God.)

■ *LThK*[3] 6:1129–40 (unabridged version).

■ **Works:** Complete critical edition: WA (with its divisions): Werke, Deutsche Bibel (DB), Briefwechsel (Br), Tischreden (TR), *Archiv zur WA* (AWA), Register-vols. (Weimar, 1883ff.)—Selected works: *L.s Werke in Auswahl,* ed. O. Clemen et al., 8 vols. (Bonn, 1912–33; reprint, Berlin, 1966); *M. L. Ausgewählte Werke,* ed. H. H. Borcherdt and G. Merz et al., 6 vols. and 7 suppl.-vols. (Munich, 1914–25; [3]1948–1965); *M. L. Studienausgabe,* ed. H.-U. Delius, 5 vols. (Berlin, 1979–92).— Survey: K. Aland, *Hilfsbuch zum L.-Studium* (Witten, [4]1996).

■ **Literature and Supplements:** General: for older literature, see the collections of sources in *RGG*[3] 4:480–520; *LThK*[2] 6:1223–30; for more recent literature: *HDThG* 2:1–69; *TRE* 21:513–94; *EKL*[3] 3:211–20.— Continuing complete bibliographies: *L.-Jahrbuch*.
■ **On 1:** Complete Biographies: M. Brecht, *M. L.,* 3 vols. (Stuttgart, 1981–87); W. von Loewenich, *M. L.* (Munich, 1981); H. A. Oberman, *L.* (Berlin, 1982); P. Manns and N. H. Loose, *M. L.* (Freiburg, 1982, 1984); G. Ebeling, *M. L.s Weg und Wort* (Frankfurt/Main, 1983); J. Rogge, *M. L.* (Gütersloh, 1983); E. W. Gritsch, *Martin— God's Court Jester* (Philadelphia, 1983); M. Lienhard, *M. L.* (Paris and Geneva, 1983); G. Brendler, *M. L. Theologie und Revolution* (Berlin and Cologne, 1983); R. Schwarz, *L.* (Göttingen, 1986); A. Beutel, *M. L.* (Munich, 1991); H. J. Genthe, *M. L.* (Göttingen, 1996).—Partial biographies and particular biographical issues: E. Iserloh, *L. zwischen Reform und Reformation. Der Thesenanschlag fand nicht statt* (Münster, [3]1968); W. Borth, *Die L.-Sache.* (Lübeck and Hamburg, 1970); D. Olivier, *Le procès de L.* (Paris, 1971; German, Stuttgart, 1972); H. Bornkamm, *M. L. in der Mitte seines Lebens* (Göttingen, 1979); *Leben und Werk M. L.s von 1526–46,* ed. H. Junghans, 2 vols. (Berlin and Göttingen, 1983); L. Grane, *Martinus noster. L. in the German Reform Movement 1518–21* (Mainz, 1994); K. Randell, *L. and the German Reformation, 1517–55* (London, [2]2000).
■ **On 3:** Introductions: G. Ebeling, *L. Einführung in sein Denken* (Tübingen, 1964, [4]1981); J. Pelikan, *Obedient Rebels* (London, 1964); D. Olivier, *La foi de L.* (Paris, 1978, German, Stuttgart, 1982); B. Lohse, *M. L. Eine Einführung in sein Leben und sein Werk* (Munich, 1981, [3]1997); O. H. Pesch, *Hinführung zu L.* (Mainz, [2]1983); E. Maurer, *L.* (Freiburg, 1999); K. Schwarzwäller, *Fülle des Lebens. L.s Kleiner Katechismus* (Münster and Hamburg, 2000).—Comprehensive studies: L. Pinomaa, *Sieg des Glaubens,* ed. H. Beintker (Berlin and Göttingen, 1964); P. Althaus, *Die Ethik M. L.s.* (Gütersloh, 1965); F. Gogarten, *L.s Theologie* (Tübingen, 1967); R. Hermann, "L.s Theologie," in idem, *Gesammelte und nachgelassene Werke,* ed. H. Beintker, vol. 1 (Göttingen, 1967); O. H. Pesch, *Theologie der Rechtfertigung bei M. L. und Thomas von Aquin* (Mainz, 1967; reprint, 1985); G. Ebeling, *L.-Studien,* 3 vols. (Tübingen, 1971–89); Th. Beer, *Der fröhliche Wechsel und Streit* (Einsiedeln, 1980); P. Althaus, *Die Theologie M. L.s.* (Gütersloh, [6]1983); U. Asendorf, *Die Theologie L.s nach seinen Predigten* (Göttingen, 1988); A. E. McGrath, *L.'s Theology of the Cross* (Oxford, 1990); A. Peters, *Kommentar zu L.s Katechismen,* ed. G. Seebass, 5 vols. (Göttingen, 1990–94); B. Lohse, *L.s Theologie in ihrer historischen Entwicklung und in ihrem systematischen Zusammenhang* (Göttingen, 1995); G. Ebeling, *L.s Seelsorge an seinen Briefen dargestellt* (Tübingen, 1997).—Important collections of articles: A. Brandenburg, *M. L. gegenwärtig* (Paderborn, 1969); W. Maurer, *L. und das evangelische Bekenntnis* (Göttingen, 1970); H. Bornkamm, *L. Gestalt und Wirkungen* (Gütersloh, 1975); G.

Scharffenorth, *Den Glauben ins Leben ziehen . . .* (Munich, 1982); G. Ebeling, *Umgang mit L.* (Tübingen, 1983); Y. Congar, *M. L.* (Paris, 1983); G. Hammer, ed., *Lutheriana* (Cologne, 1984); *M. L. Reformator und Vater im Glauben,* ed. P. Manns (Stuttgart, 1985); *L.-Jahrbuch* 52 (1985); H. A. Oberman, *Die Reformation* (Göttingen, 1986); P. Manns, *Vater im Glauben* (Stuttgart, 1988); B. Lohse, *Evangelium in der Geschichte,* vol. 1 (Göttingen, 1988); G. Müller, *Causa Reformationis* (Gütersloh, 1989); J. Wicks, *L.'s Reform* (Mainz, 1992); G. Maron, *Die ganze Christenheit auf Erden* (Göttingen, 1993); H. A. Oberman, *The Impact of the Reformation* (Grand Rapids, Mich., 1994); M. Brecht, *Reformation* (Stuttgart, 1995); K.-H. zur Mühlen, *Reformatorisches Profil* (Göttingen, 1995); R. Marius, *M. L., The Christians between God and Death* (Cambridge, Mass., 1999); T. Maschke, ed., *Ad fontes Lutheri. Toward the Recovery of the Real Luther.* Festschrift K. Hagen (Milwaukee, 2001); G. Tomlin, *L. and His World* (Oxford, 2002); D. C. McKim, ed., *The Cambridge Companion to M. L.* (Cambridge, 2003); T. J. Wengert, ed., *Harvesting M. L.'s Reflections on Theology, Ethics, and the Church* (Grand Rapids, 2003); S. W. Crompton, *M. L.* (Philadelphia, 2003).—*Monographs:* On *3.a* and *3.b:* L. Grane, *Contra Gabrielem* (Copenhagen, 1962; R. Schwarz, *Fides, spes und caritas beim jungen L.* (Berlin, 1962); K. Bornkamm, *L.s Auslegungen des Galaterbriefes von 1519 und 1531* (Berlin, 1963); M. Kroeger, *Rechtfertigung und Gesetz* (Göttingen, 1968); J. Wicks, *Man Yearning for Grace* (Wiesbaden, 1969); O. Bayer, *Promissio. Geschichte der reformatorischen Wende in L.s Theologie* (Göttingen, 1971); K.-H. zur Mühlen, *Nos extra nos. L.s Theologie zwischen Mystik und Scholastik* (Tübingen, 1972); L. Grane, *Modus loquendi theologicus* (Leiden, 1975); H. U. Delius, *Augustin als Quelle L.s* (Berlin, 1984); Th. Bell, *Divus Bernhardus. Bernhard von Clairvaux in M. L.s Schriften* (Mainz, 1993); G. Schmidt-Lauber, *L.s Vorlesung über den Römerbrief 1515/16* (Cologne, 1994); O. H. Pesch, *M. L., Thomas von Aquin und die reformatorische Kritik an der Scholastik* (Göttingen, 1994); Th. Dieter, *Der junge L. und Aristoteles. Eine historisch-systematische Untersuchung zum Verhältnis von Philosophie und Theologie* (Berlin, 2001).—On *3.c* and *3.c.1:* G. Ebeling, *Wort Gottes und Tradition* (Göttingen, 1964); F. Beisser, *Claritas scripturae bei M. L.* (Göttingen, 1966); W. Führer, *Das Wort Gottes in L.s Theologie* (Göttingen, 1984); K. Hagen, *L.'s Approach to Scripture as Seen in His "Commentaries" on Galatians 1519–1538* (Tübingen, 1993).—On *3.c.2:* B. Lohse, *Ratio und Fides* (Göttingen, 1958); B. A. Gerrish, *Grace and Reason* (Oxford, 1962); R. Malter, *Das reformatorische Denken und die Philosophie* (Bonn, 1980).—On *3.c.3:* S. Pfürtner, *L. und Thomas im Gespräch* (Heidelberg, 1961); P. Hacker, *Das Ich im Glauben bei M. L.* (Graz, 1966; I. D. K. Siggins, *M. L.'s Doctrine of Christ* (New Haven and London, 1970); U. Asendorf, *Gekreuzigt und Auferstanden* (Berlin and Hamburg, 1971); M. Lienhard, *L., Témoin de Jésus-Christ* (Paris, 1973; German, Göttingen, 1980); D.

Vorländer, *Deus Incarnatus. Die Zweinaturenchristologie L.s bis 1521* (Witten, 1974); F. Posset, *L.'s Catholic Christology According to his Johannine Lectures of 1527* (Milwaukee, 1988); M. Lienhard, *Au cœur de la foi de L.: Jésus-Christ* (Paris, 1991); S. Streiff, *"Novis Linguis Loqui." M. L.s Disputation über Joh 1, 14 "verbum caro factum est" aus dem Jahre 1539* (Göttingen, 1993); M. Kreuzer, *"Und das Wort ist Fleisch geworden." Zur Bedeutung des Menschseins Jesu bei Johannes Driedo und M. L.* (Paderborn, 1998).—*On 3.c.4–6*: A. Peters, *Glaube und Werk* (Berlin and Hamburg, 1962, [2]1967); O. Modalsli, *Das Gericht nach den Werken* (Göttingen, 1963); W. Joest, *Ontologie der Person bei L.* (Göttingen, 1967); O. H. Pesch and A. Peters, *Einführung in die Lehre von Gnade und Rechtfertigung* (Darmstadt, 1981, [3]1994); H. Blaumeister, *M. L.s Kreuzestheologie* (Paderborn, 1995).—*On sacramental regulations*: A. Peters, *Realpräsenz* (Berlin, [2]1960); C. F. Wislöff, *Abendmahl und Messe* (Berlin and Hamburg, 1969); W. Schwab, *Entwicklung und Gestalt der Sakramententheologie bei M. L.* (Frankfurt [Main] and Berne, 1977); E. Grötzinger, *L. und Zwingli* (Zurich, 1980); U. Stock, *Die Bedeutung der Sakramente in L.s Sermonen von 1519* (Leiden, 1982); J. Diestelmann, *Actio sacramentalis. Die Verwaltung des Heiligen Abendmahls nach den Prinzipien M. L.s in der Zeit bis zur Konkordienformel* (Braunschweig and Gross Oesingen, 1996); S. Dähn, *Rede als Text. Rhetorik und Stilistik in L.s Sakramentssermonen von 1519* (Bern and Frankfurt/Main, 1997).—*On 3.c.7 and 8*: W. Höhne, *L.s Anschauungen über die Kontinuität der Kirche* (Berlin and Hamburg, 1963); W. Stein, *Das kirchliche Amt bei L.* (Wiesbaden, 1974); J. Aarts, *Die Lehre L.s über das Amt in der Kirche* (Helsinki, 1982); C. A. Aurelius, *Verborgene Kirche* (Hannover, 1983); M. Lienhard, *L'Évangelie et l'Église chez L.* (Paris, 1989); *M. L. und das Bischofsamt*, ed. M. Brecht (Stuttgart, 1990); D. Wendebourg, "Das Amt und die Ämter," *Zeitschrift für evangelisches Kirchenrecht* 45 (2000) 5–37.—*Relations with Jews*: J. Brosseder, *L.s Stellung zu den Juden im Spiegel seiner Interpreten* (Munich, 1972); H. A. Oberman, *Wurzeln des Antisemitismus* (Berlin, 1981).—*On 3.c.9*: U. Asendorf, *Eschatologie bei L.* (Göttingen, 1967); F. Heidler, *L.s Lehre von der Unsterblichkeit der Seele* (Erlangen, 1983).—*On 3.c.10*: H. J. McSorley, *L.s Lehre vom unfreien Willen nach seiner Hauptschrift De servo arbitrio im Lichte der biblischen und kirchlichen Tradition* (Munich, 1967); K. Schwarzwäller, *Sibboleth. Die Interpretation von L.s Schrift de servo arbitrio seit Th. Harnack* (Munich, 1969); idem, *Theologia crucis. L.s Lehre von der Prädestination nach de servo arbitrio 1525* (Munich, 1970); R. Jansen, *Studien zu L.s Trinitätslehre* (Bern and Frankfurt/Main, 1976); W. Behnk, *Contra Liberum arbitrium pro Gratia Dei* (Bern and Frankfurt/Main, 1982); T. H. M. Akerboom, *Vrije wil en/of genade. Een theologie-historisch onderzoek naar het dispuut tussen Erasmus en Luther over de (on)vrijheid van het menselijke willen* (Nimwegen, 1995).

OTTO HERMANN PESCH

Lutheranism

1. Concept

"Lutheranism" was coined c. 1520 as a designation of the movement for ecclesiastical reform which appealed to the Wittenberg Reformer Martin Luther. It was initially employed by Luther's opponents, and was adopted within Reformation circles from c. 1560 in order to distinguish the renewal movement which appealed to Luther from other orientations, e.g., those of Huldrych Zwingli or Jean Calvin. The precise meaning of the terms "Lutheran" and "Lutheranism" long remained open within the Wittenberg Reformation, as we see in the divergences soon after Luther's death between the "true" Lutherans (→ Gnesiolutherans") and the "Philippists," adherents of Philipp Melanchthon (see below). From 1586 onward, "Lutheran Church" is used in Württemberg and electoral Saxony as the name of that church which appeals to Luther's "true doctrine of the gospel."

2. Confessional Consolidation

Lutheranism saw itself from the outset in continuity with the ancient church, referring explicitly to the intentions and affirmations of the earliest Christian period and emphasizing the importance of the three patristic professions of faith (viz., the Apostolic, Niceno-Constantinopolitan, and Athanasian creeds). This link with the tradition of the undivided church can also be seen in the rejection of "Enthusiastic" movements and of a number of theological convictions held by the Calvinist or Zwinglian Reformation. Nevertheless, the church at that period could not cope with the demand made by the Lutheran Reformation to preach freely and to live the rediscovered gospel of the unconditional grace of God which is bestowed on us in Christ; the desire to correct abuses and false theological developments had further-reaching ecclesiological consequences, because this ultimately entailed posing a question-mark against the dominant theological and ecclesiastical system under the leadership of the pope, with its mixture of spiritual authority and worldly power. Thus it was inevitable that a new ecclesial identity should develop on the basis of the → Confessio Augustana which Melanchthon drew up in 1530. This did not seek to be a new church, but to be an ancient church renewed in keeping with the gospel—and hence, a true church. After the imperial parliament of Augsburg (1530), which made it possible to promulgate new → church orders and establish new ministries of church leadership, the Lutheran Reformation, which had been in expansion since 1520, began to form autonomous Lutheran → territorial churches. These received recognition in public law through the Religious Peace of Augsburg in 1555, and a compromise solution entrusted the administration of these churches to the structures of the state.

These churches show their Lutheran identity by the appeal they make to the Confessio Augustana. They adopt the important theological orientations which Luther laid down; in keeping with his own theological approach, the church is not defined on the basis of its ministry and structures, but on the basis of its teaching and its creed.

The confessional consolidation of Lutheranism required time, and was accompanied by controversies. The variety of orientations of Luther's fellow Reformers and his pupils (Melanchthon, Johannes → Bugenhagen, Martin → Bucer, Johannes → Brenz, Andreas → Osiander, Matthias → Flacius, etc.) meant that the early history of Lutheranism was full of conflicts, concerning not only the clarification of specific doctrinal questions (viz., the → Law, good works, the freedom of the will, → original sin, → justification and sanctification), but also various influences from movements chronologically prior to the Reformation, from humanist endeavors, and from church politics. It was only after a number of attempts at mediation that the Formula of → Concord (1577) succeeded in establishing a common theological basis. The → Corpus of the Lutheran confessions of faith was brought together in the Book of Concord in 1580. It comprises the three patristic creeds, Luther's Small and Great Catechisms (1529), the Confessio Augustana (1530) with its Apology (1531), the → Schmalkaldic articles (1537), Melanchthon's treatise "On Authority" and "Primacy of the Pope" (1537), and the Formula of Concord.

ANDRÉ BIRMELÉ

■ *LThK³* 6:1143–49 (unabridged version).
■ **Literature:** *RGG⁴* 3:1043.—S. Sterhle, "Imputatio iustitiae. Its Origins in Melanchthon, Its Opposition in Osiander," *Theologische Zeitschrift* 50 (1994) 201–19; J. Diestelmann, *Actio Sacramentalis* (Gross Oesingen, 1996); M. Richter, *Gesetz und Heil* (Göttingen, 1996); F. Buzzi, "Lutero contro l'antinomismo," *Annali di scienze religiose* 2 (1997) 81–106; P. T. Ferry, "Confessionalization and Popular Preaching. Sermons against Synergism in Reformation Saxony," *SCJ* 28 (1997) 1143–66; T. J. Wengert, "Georg Major Defender of Wittenberg's Faith and Melanchthonian exegete," in *Melanchthon in seinen Schülern* (Wiesbaden, 1997) 129–55; I. Dingel, "Flacius als Schüler Luthers und Melanchthons," in *Vestigia pietatis*. Festschrift E. Koch (Leipzig, 2000) 77–92; P. F. Barton, "Heiliger Geist, Evangelium und Amt. Marginalien zum Gnesio-L.," *Wiener Jahrbuch für Theologie* 3 (2000) 51–63; G. Martens, "Die Adiaphora als theologisches Problem," *Lutherische Beiträge* 5 (2000) 117–27.

Luther's Bible. In 1521-1522, Martin Luther produced a new translation of the New Testament (published at Wittenberg, 1522) on the basis of the Greek text of → Erasmus (2nd ed., Basle, 1519). He had recourse to the language used in the chancellery of Saxony in his endeavor to write good German; at the same time, he emphasized those matters which accorded with his understanding of the faith. He drew on the help of other collaborators such as Philipp Melanchthon when he translated the Old Testament from the original text (1523-1534), and made use of already existing translations (e.g., the Worms translation of the prophets and the plenary texts). He continually improved his translation from the first complete edition (Wittenberg, 1534) until 1545. This translation spread very quickly among all classes of the people and had a long-lasting influence on the development of a unified German language.

■ **Literature:** J. J. Mezger, *Geschichte der deutschen Bibelübersetzungen in der schweizerisch-reformierten Kirche* (Basle, 1876); P. H. Vogel, "Evangelische und freikirchliche Übersetzungen im 19.Jh. in Deutschland," in *Die Bibel in der Welt* (Stuttgart, 1962) 53–69; E. Fascher, *Luthers Bibelübersetzungen im Wandel der Zeiten* (Berlin, 1968); E. Arndt, "Luthers Bibelübersetzung und ihre Bedeutung für die Entwicklung der deutschen Sprache," in *Weltwirkung der Reformation*, vol. 2 (Berlin, 1969) 416–24; W. Kolb, *Die Bibelübersetzung Luthers und ihre mittelalterlichen deutschen Vorgänger* (Saarbrücken, 1972); S. Hahn, *Luthers Übersetzungsweise im Septembertestament von 1522* (Hamburg, 1972); B. Köster, *Die L. im frühen Pietismus* (Bielefeld, 1984); S. Meurer, ed., *Die neue L.* (Stuttgart, 1985); T. Himmighöfer, *Die Neustadter Bibel von 1587/88, die erste reformierte Bibelausgabe Deutschlands* (Speyer, 1986); H. Volz, *Martin Luthers deutsche Bibel* (Hamburg, 1978); H. Gelhaus, *Der Streit um Luthers Bibelverdeutschung im 16./17.Jh.*, 2 vols. (Tübingen,

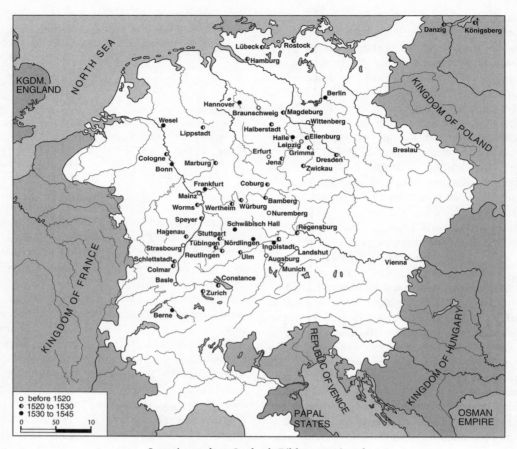

Locations where Luther's Bible was printed.

1988); D. C. Steinmetz, ed., *The Bible in the 16ᵗʰ Century* (Durham and London, 1990).

OTTO B. KNOCH/KLAUS SCHOLTISSEK

■ **Additional Bibliography:** S. Meurer, ed., *Was Christum treibet. Martin Luther und seine Bibelübersetzung* (Stuttgart, 1996); J. Schilling, "Martin Luthers Deutsche Bibel," *Luther-Bulletin* 6 (1997) 23–45; A. Beutel, "Luthers Bibelübersetzung und die Folgen," *Evangelische Theologie* 59 (1999) 13–24; C. C. Christensen, "The Reformation of Bible Illustration," *ARG* 90 (1999) 103–29; S. Füssel (Introduction), *The Book of the Books, the L.-Bible of 1534* (London 2003).

M

Madruzzo, (1) *Cristoforo.* Cardinal (1542), born July 5, 1512 on the family estate of Madruzzo near Cavedine (diocese of Trent), died July 5, 1578 in Tivoli. He studied in Padua and Bologna. He received canonries in Trent (1529), Augsburg (1534), Salzburg (1536), and Brixen (1537); he became bishop of Trent in 1539 and was administrator of Brixen from 1542 to 1578. He was ordained deacon, priest, and bishop in 1542; he attempted several times to become archbishop in Trier, Mainz, and Salzburg. Emperor → Charles V sent him to Venice in 1539 and 1542; he took the feudal oath in Ghent in 1540, and attended the religious dialogue in → Hagenau. Madruzzo employed all available diplomatic and financial means to ensure the success of the Council of Trent. He supported the translation of scripture into the vernacular and the concession of the → chalice to the laity. He opposed the transfer of the council to Bologna in 1547. He went on many political missions, attempting unsuccessfully to mediate between the emperor and the pope. He was governor of the duchy of Milan from 1555 to 1557, and moved definitively to Rome in 1560. He became a member of the Congregatio Germanica in 1573. He became sovereign of Soriano and Gallese in 1560; he was governor of Spoleto in 1566, and governor of Gualdo Tadino from 1569 to 1578. Madruzzo supported reform, but he was an ambitious man who loved splendor, and his theological education was inadequate.

■ **Literature:** Jedin 1, esp. 450–56; E. Tessadri, *Il grande cardinale* (Milan, 1953); A. Costa, *I vescovi di Trento* (Trent, 1977) 151–57; J. Gelmi, *Die Brixner Bischöfe in der Geschichte Tirols* (Bozen, 1984) 130–34; L. Dal Prà, ed., *I M. e l'Europa* (Milan, 1993) 57–62; E. Gatz, ed., *Die Bischöfe des Heiligen Römischen Reiches 1448–1648* (Berlin, 1996) 443–46.

(2) *Ludovico*, nephew of (1). Cardinal (1561), born 1532 in Trent, died April 20, 1600 in Rome. He acquired canonries in Brixen (1545) and Trent (1548), and became coadjutor in Trent in 1548. He studied in Louvain and Paris. He hosted the council in 1562-1563. He was ordained priest before May, 1565, and became bishop of Trent in 1567. He had numerous conflicts with Ferdinand II, who was ruler in Tyrol, and fled to Rome in 1568, where he rose to become a curial cardinal. He became "Protector of the German nation" in 1573, and engaged in extensive diplomatic activities as member of the Congregatio Germanica and as representative of the emperor at the papal court. In 1574, he was a member of six of the fifteen Congregations. He was reconciled with Archduke Ferdinand in 1578, and conducted a visitation in Trent from 1579 to 1581. He was appointed commissioner and general inquisitor for the empire in 1582. He held an important diocesan synod in Trent in 1593. He took part in seven conclaves, and was regarded as *papabile* in 1592. Madruzzo played an important part in Catholic renewal and the Counter-Reformation, but the large number of tasks he was given by the pope and the emperor prevented him from governing his diocese in person.

■ **Sources:** *Biblioteca Comunale di Trento.* Manuscript 2925.
■ **Literature:** *NDB* 15:423f.—B. Roberg, "Türkenkrieg und Politik," *QFIAB* 65 (1985) 192–305; 66 (1986) 192–309; S. Vareschi, *La Legazione del Card. L. M. alla dieta imperiale di Augusta 1582* (Trent, 1990); C. Nubola, *Conoscere per governare* (Bologna, 1993); B. Steinhauf, *Giovanni L. M. (1532–1600)* (Münster, 1993); see also

the review of S. Vareschi, *RHE* 90 [1995] 483–92); L. Dal Prà, ed., *L. M. e l'Europa* (Milan, 1993) 62–68; E. Gatz, ed., *Die Bischöfe des Heiligen Römischen Reiches 1448–1648* (Berlin, 1996) 446–50.

JOSEF GELMI

Magdeburg Centuriators. This name is given to the team (*collegium*) of researchers who published the "Magdeburg Centuries" (*Ecclesiastica historia . . . secundum singulas Centurias . . . per aliquot studiosos et pios viros in urbe Magdeburgica,* 8 vols., Basle [1559-1574]). Matthias → Flacius organized the work, and his fellow editors (*gubernatores*) included the theologians Johann → Wigand, who worked on Centuries 7-13 (14-16 remained in manuscript only), and Matthaeus Judex (1528-1564; he became co-rector of the Council Grammar School and deacon at St. Ulrich's church in Magdeburg in 1553, and followed Wigand to Jena and Wismar). Collaborators on the first four Centuries included also Basilius Faber (c. 1520-1576), one of the most important schoolmasters of the 16th century. New editions and summary excerpts from the Centuries were published over the next two centuries. The aim of the Centuries was to produce historical proof, based on source materials, that Martin Luther was in continuity with the true ecclesiastical tradition, and this intention gave a tremendous impetus to church-historical research. A comprehensive presentation of the opposite view, from the Roman perspective, was not published until Caesar Baronius' *Annales* in 12 volumes appeared between 1588 and 1607.

■ **Literature:** *RE* 6:90f.; *DHGE* 17:316–26; *NDB* 10:639; *TRE* 11:208f.—H. Scheible, *Die Entstehung der Magdeburger Zenturien* (Gütersloh, 1966).

ECKEHART STÖVE

Magni, *Petrus* (Peder Månsson). Born Jönköping, died May 17, 1534 in Västerås. He was rector of the school in Vadstena, where he became a Bridgetine monk in 1499. From 1508 onward, he was commissioner of his monastery in Rome and superior of St. Bridget's house there from 1511 onward. He was appointed bishop of Västerås in 1524, and consecrated in Rome. Although his own position was Catholic, he ordained three bishops in 1528 without confirmation by Rome. In 1531, although he protested secretly, he ordained the Lutheran archbishop Laurentius → Petri. He had received a humanist education and left notes on mining, agriculture, maritime law, medicine, and military strategy.

■ **Works:** *Peder Månssons skrifter,* ed. R. Geete (Stockholm, 1913–15); *Peder Månssons bref* (Stockholm, 1915).

■ **Literature:** C. Silfverstolpe, *Klosterfolket i Vadstena* (Stockholm, 1898–99) 147–51; Th. van Haag, *Die apostolische Sukzession in Schweden* (Uppsala, 1945).

JARL GALLÉN

Magnus, (1) *Johannes.* Archbishop of Uppsala, born March 19, 1488 in Linköping, died March 22, 1544 in Rome. After his studies in Louvain, Cologne, and Perugia, Magnus's patriotism led him to give active support in 1523 to King → Gustav I Vasa, who declared Archbishop Gustav Trolle (c. 1488-1535) deposed and had Magnus elected as his successor. Magnus may have taken part in the translation of the New Testament. He was sent by the king to Danzig in 1526, and did not return to Sweden. He remained in exile, and completed his history of the archbishops of Uppsala by 1536. He also made preparations to return home and fight against Lutheranism, but this came to nothing, since Rome accepted the deposition of Trolle only in 1533, when the pope officially appointed Magnus archbishop of Uppsala. Magnus was willing to accept the summons to take part in a council. While he waited, he completed his effusive history of the Goths and Sveonians in Venice in 1540. This work made a great impact in Sweden after 1560.

■ **Works:** *Historia de omnibus Gothorum Sueonumque regibus* (Venice, 1554); *Historia metropolitanae ecclesiae Upsalensis* (Rome, 1557), also in *Scriptores rerum Svecicarum medii aevi,* vol. 3/2 (Uppsala, 1876) 5–97.

■ **Literature:** *Svenskt biografiskt lexikon,* vol. 20 (Stockholm, 1973–75) 220–26.

TORE NYBERG

■ **Additional Bibliography:** K. Johannesson, "The Renaissance of the Goths in Sixteenth-Century Sweden," in *J. and Olaus M. as Politicians and Historians* (Berkeley, 1991); B. Larsson, ed., *J. M. Latin Letters* (Lund, 1992); C. Santini, ed., *I fratelli Giovanni e Olao Magno,* Atti del convegno internazionale (Rome, 1999).

(2) *Olaus.* Archbishop of Uppsala, brother of (1), born October, 1490 in Linköping, died August 1, 1559 in Rome. After studying in Rostock, he became cathedral canon in Linköping in 1518, and undertook a voyage to northern Sweden

in 1519. He was in Stockholm from 1520 to 1522, and was appointed cathedral provost in Strängnäs by King → Gustav I Vasa in 1523. He shared the exile of his brother, and published the volume of maps of Scandinavia, on which he had worked for many years, in Venice in 1539. After the death of his brother, he was appointed his successor on June 4, 1544. He took part in the opening sessions of the Council of Trent, and the pope gave him the house of St. Bridget of Sweden in Rome (the "Hospitale S. Brigide") in 1549. He made this a center of the Catholic resistance to Lutheranism, setting up a printing press and publishing his chef d'oeuvre, *Historia de gentibus septentrionalibus,* as well as posthumous works by his brother.

■ **Sources:** *Carta marina* (Venice, 1539); *Historia de gentibus septentrionalibus* (Rome, 1555); *Historia de gentibus septentrionalibus* (Rome, 1555; 3 vols. London, 1998).

■ **Literature:** *Svenskt biografiskt lexikon,* vol. 28 (Stockholm, 1992–94) 136–41.—K. Johannesson, *Gotisk renässans. Johannes och O. M. som politiker och historiker* (Stockholm, 1982).

TORE NYBERG

■ **Additional Bibliography:** K. Johannesson, "The Renaissance of the Goths in Sixteenth-Century Sweden," in *Johannes and O. M. as Politicians and Historians* (Berkeley, 1991).

Major (Meier), *Georg.* Theologian in the later Reformation period, born April 25, 1502 in Nuremberg, died November 28, 1574 in Wittenberg. He began his studies under Philipp Melanchthon and other professors in Wittenberg in 1521, taking his master's degree in 1523. He became rector of the Latin school in Magdeburg in 1539, and preacher in Wittenberg castle in 1537. After taking his theological doctorate in 1537, he became professor at Wittenberg in 1545 and retained this position, with breaks as superintendent of the diocese of Merseburg (1547-1548) and in Eisleben (1551-1552). He took part in the religious dialogue in → Regensburg in 1546. He became dean in perpetuity in the theological faculty in 1558. His marriage in 1528 to Margarete von Mochau made him brother-in-law to Andreas → Karlstadt.

His contemporaries knew Major as a schoolmaster who wrote Latin textbooks, a catechism in Latin and Low German, a Protestant version of lives of the saints, commentaries on the Psalms, and hymns. He was also an exegete who produced commentaries on the letters of Paul and homilies on both series of liturgical readings. He was renowned as a preacher, a writer of edifying literature, one of the editors of the twelve-volume edition of Luther's works (1539/1552-1559), and a controversialist who wrote polemically against the Roman understanding of the Mass, of saints, and of scripture, as well as against the Antitrinitarians.

Major is best remembered because of the *Majorist controversy* ("Majorism"). His loyalty to → Moritz of Saxony led Major to support his sovereign's church politics (Leipzig Interim, 1548; → Augsburg Interim), and loyalty to his own teacher led him to support Melanchthon's doctrine of justification, with its accentuation of the ethical dimension. These two positions provoked the opposition of the → Gnesiolutherans in Magdeburg, in Ernestine Saxony, and in northern Germany. At the end of 1551, Nikolaus von → Amsdorf accused Major of teaching that good works were necessary for salvation. Major replied in the following year: "That good works are necessary for eternal *beatitude* . . . that no one becomes blessed by means of evil works, and that no one will attain beatitude without good works" (*Auff des Ehrenwidrigen Herren Niclas von Ambsdorff schrifft* . . . [Wittenberg, 1552]); at the same time, he denied that works had any causal effect on *salvation*. He explained, with reference to Lk 17:10, that works are the obedience we owe to God, the proof of our right faith, and a means to preserve the state of grace. Amsdorf, Matthias → Flacius, and others misunderstood this position as the abandonment of the fundamental Reformation conviction, and Amsdorf went so far as to assert in 1559 that good works were actually harmful to one's salvation. On numerous occasions from 1558 onward (finally in his will, printed in 1570), Major appealed to the → Confessio Augustana and to Melanchthon's → Corpus Doctrinae, abandoning the formulation (though not the substance) of the three propositions quoted above. He dismissed every accusation that he held a "Pelagian" or "papistical" theory of meritorious works. The authors of the Formula of → Concord (1577) took Major's anti-libertinist intention seriously, and rejected Amsdorf's exaggerations, insisting that, while the link between faith and action is not meritorious, it is nevertheless "necessary" (Art. 4).

■ **Bibliographies:** *VD 16* 13:1987–2215; *TRE* 21:729 (Briefe).
■ **Literature:** *RE* 12:85–91; *NDB* 15:718f.; *HDThG* 2:113–17; *TRE* 21:725–30.—R. Kolb, "G. M. as Controversialist," *ChH* 45 (1976) 455–68; T. J. Wengert, "G. M. Defender of Wittenberg's Faith and Melanchthonian Exegete," in *Melanchthon in seinen Schülern* (Wiesbaden, 1997) 129–55.

INGE MAGER

■ **Additional Literature:** R. Keller, "Das Schriftverständnis bei G. M.," in *Humanismus und Reformation. Festschrift F. Krüger* (Münster, 2001) 123–35.

Malvenda, *Pedro de.* Spanish theologian, born c. 1505 in Burgos, died after 1561. He studied in Paris, completing the course at the faculty of arts in 1519 and taking his doctorate in theology in 1538; thereafter, he was chaplain at the imperial court, and took part in the religious dialogues in → Worms and → Regensburg (1541 and 1546), where he disputed with Martin → Bucer and with his fellow-student Juan → Díaz, who had converted to Protestantism. He collaborated with Pedro de → Soto in the → Augsburg Interim of 1548. At the Council of Trent, Malvenda was exceptional both for his knowledge and for his endeavors to achieve reconciliation. In 1561, he spoke in favor of his brother Fra Antonio in Burgos in the controversy with Cardinal Pedro González de Mendoza about the Eucharist.
■ **Literature:** Jedin vols. 2 and 3; M. Le Vassor, *Lettres et mémoirs de François de Vargas, de Pierre M.* (Amsterdam, 1699); C. Gutiérrez, *Españoles en Trento* (Valladolid, 1951) 962–65; J. I. Tellechea, *La polémica entre el card. Mendoza y el abad M.* (Madrid, 1980).

JOSÉ LUIS GONZÁLEZ-NOVALÍN

Marbach, *Johannes.* Lutheran theologian, born April 24, 1521 in Lindau, died March 17, 1581 in Strasbourg. After studies in Strasbourg and under Martin Luther in Wittenberg (1539-1541), he was in Isny from 1542 to 1545. Martin → Bucer summoned him to Strasbourg, where he was pastor in St. Nicholas's church from 1545 to 1547; additionally, he was professor of theology from 1546 and chairman of the synod of pastors from 1553. Despite opposition (e.g., by Johann → Sturm), Lutheran orthodoxy became established in Strasbourg under Marbach's leadership, and the Tetrapolitana (→ confessional documents) was replaced by the → Confessio Augustana in 1563.

■ **Literature:** *Nouveau dictionnaire de biographie alsacienne*, vol. 5 (Strasbourg, 1995) 2514.—W. Horning, *Dr. J. M.* (Strasbourg, 1896); B. Vogler, "L'affirmation de l'orthodoxie luthérienne," in *Strasbourg au cœur religieux du XVIᵉ siècle* (Strasbourg, 1977) 595–602; A. Schindling, *Humanistische Hochschule und freie Reichsstadt* (Wiesbaden, 1977).

BERNARD VOGLER

Marburg, religious dialogue (October 1-4, 1529). Since the → eucharistic controversy between Martin Luther and Huldrych Zwingli and their respective adherents made it impossible to unite the Protestant Estates in a political league, Marquis → Philip of Hessen insisted on the necessity of a dialogue in which the most important Protestant theologians could reach an agreement. Although the arguments had already been exchanged in writing, the theologians yielded to the politicians' desire and held discussions in Marburg castle, first separately (between Luther and Johannes → Oecolampadius, and Zwingli and Philipp Melanchthon), then in full assembly. The interpretation of the Lord's Supper quickly became the center of interest. While Luther emphasized the creative power of God's Word and referred to the words of institution (*hoc est*), Oecolampadius based his arguments on Jn 6:63 and maintained that the bodily act of eating was unimportant, and Zwingli demanded that those who received communion must have faith. It proved impossible to reach a consensus. On October 4, at Philip's request, Luther drew up fifteen "Marburg articles," noting that consensus existed on fourteen of these; disagreement existed on the last point, viz., whether "the Body and Blood of Christ are bodily present in the bread and wine" in the Lord's Supper. This divergence led to fresh controversies in the ensuing period (→ eucharistic controversy).

■ **Sources:** *Das MR 1529*, ed. G. May (Gütersloh, ²1979).
■ **Literature:** *TRE* 22:75–79.—W. Köhler, *Das MR 1529* (Leipzig, 1929).

GERHARD MÜLLER

■ **Additional Bibliography:** I. L. Snavely, "'The Evidence of things unseen.' Zwingli's 'Sermon on Providence' and the Colloquy of Marburg," *Westminster Theological Journal* 56 (1994) 399–407; W. H. Neuser, "Die abschliessenden Einigungsversuche auf dem MR 1529. Zwei unerkannte Unionsformeln," in *Ordenlich und fruchtbar*. Festschrift W. van't Spijker (Leiden, 1997) 43–52.

Marcello, *Cristoforo*. Theologian and humanist, born in a noble Venetian family, died 1527 in Gaeta (?). He worked initially in Padua, and became apostolic protonotary in the Roman curia in 1500. He was appointed archbishop of Corfu in 1514. He published under his own name the book of papal ceremonies which had been compiled by Agostino Patrizi Piccolomini, adjusting the vocabulary to suit humanist taste: *Rituum ecclesiasticorum sive sacrarum caerimoniarum SS. Romanae Ecclesiae libri tres non ante impressi* (Venice, 1516; reprint Ridgewood, 1965). Marcello was one of the first to write against Martin Luther. He died as a result of injuries received during the → Sack of Rome.

■ **Works:** *Universalis de anima traditionis opus* (Venice, 1508; reprint, Farnborough, 1969); *In quarta Lateranensis concilii sessione habita oratio* (Rome, 1513); *De authoritate summi pontificis et his quae ad illam pertinent adversus impia Martini Lutheri dogmata* (Florence, 1521; reprint, Farnborough, ²1969).
■ **Literature:** F. Lauchert, *Die italienischen literarischen Gegner Luthers* (Freiburg, 1912) 231–38; F. Tamburini and J. Nabuco, *Le Cérémonial Apostolique avant Innocent VIII* (Rome, 1966) 34*–38*; N. H. Minnich, "Concepts of Reform Proposed to the Fifth Lateran Council," *AHP* 7 (1969) 163–251, esp. 181ff.; J. W. O'Malley, *Praise and Blame in Renaissance Rome* (Durham, N.C., 1979); M. Dykmans, *L'œuvre de Patrizi Piccolomini*, vol. 1 (Vatican City, 1980) 33*–42*.

PETER WALTER

Marcellus II. Pope (April 9-May 1, 1555), formerly *Marcello Cervini*, born May 6, 1501 in Montefano near Macerato, son of a noble family from the city of Montepulciano. He was a friend of those who wished to reform the Catholic Church. He was tutor to Cardinal Alessandro Farnese, the influential nephew of → Paul III, and became his secretary. He was made bishop of Nicastora and cardinal in 1539, bishop of Reggio-Emilia in 1540, and bishop of Gubbio in 1544. He was sent on diplomatic missions to Germany (Emperor → Charles V) and France (King → Francis I). He was one of the presidents of the Council of Trent from 1545 onward. He was made cardinal librarian in 1548. Under Julius II, he worked in favor of reform in the second period of the council (1551-1552) and in Rome. He retained his baptismal name when he became pope. He resolved to carry out reforms, but died after only three weeks in office. The *Missa papae Marcelli* of Giovanni Pier-luigi da Palestrina bears his name. He was buried in St. Peter's.

- **Sources:** *NDB* Abteilung I; *CT*.
- **Literature:** *HKG* 4:476–505; *DBI* 24:111ff.; *BBKL* 5:771–75.—P. Polidori, *De vita, gestis et moribus Marcelli II* (Rome, 1744); L. von Pastor, *Geschichte der Päpste seit dem Ausgang des Mittelalters.* (Freiburg, vol. 5, 1909) 874f. (index); (vol. 6, 1913) 317–56, 708, 715; *HCMA* 3:26, 33, 193, 256, 284; Jedin vols. 1–3; M. Dykmans, "Quatre lettres de Marcel Cervini, cardinal-légat auprès de Charles Quint en 1540," *AHP* 29 (1991) 113–71; W. V. Hudon, *Marcello Cervini and Ecclesiastical Government in Tridentine Italy* (De Kalb, Ill., 1992).

GEORG SCHWAIGER

- **Additional Bibliography:** R. Spataro, "Il cardinale Cervini e l'argomentazione patristica durante la quarta sessione del Concilio di Trento," *Salesianum* 59 (1997) 33–49; J. I. Tellechea Idigoras, "Marcelo II y su breve pontificado, según documentos de Simancas," *Salmanticensis* 46 (1999) 411–29; P. Piacentini, *La biblioteca di Marcello II Cervini* (Vatican, 2001).

Margaret of Parma. Duchess, vicereine of the Netherlands (1559-1567 and 1580-1583), born December 28, 1522 in Oudenaarde, illegitimate daughter of Emperor → Charles V and Jeanne van den Gheynst, died January 18, 1586 in Ortona. The De Douvin family brought her up in Brussels. She married Alessandro de' Medici, duke of Florence, in 1536, and took over the reins of government when he was murdered in 1537. She followed her father's wishes and married Ottavio Farnese, later duke of Parma, in 1538. This embroiled her in the conflicts between the great Italian families and the Vatican. She was appointed vicereine of the Netherlands by → Philip II in 1559, but after lengthy political and religious clashes, she was forced to bow to pressure from the aristocratic opposition under → William I of Orange and dismiss her counselor, Antoine Perrenot de → Granvella, in 1564. After making further concessions, she was left only with the role of transmitting information between the Dutch opposition and the Spanish crown. When Philip II bestowed far-reaching authority on the duke of → Alba, who arrived in the Netherlands at the head of a strong military force, Margaret realized that this amounted to an even greater reduction of her own authority, and she returned to Italy in December, 1567. She became vicereine again in 1580. Her second period of office was

marked by power struggles with her son, Alessandro Farnese, which Margaret ultimately lost. She retired to Ortona in Italy in 1583.

- **Literature:** B. Hamann, ed., *Die Habsburger. Ein biographisches Lexikon* (Vienna, 1988) 275ff.—J. de Jonghe, *Madama M. van Oostenrijk, Hertogin van Parma en Piacenza 1522–86* (Amsterdam, [3]1981); A. Puaux, *Madama, Fille de Charles V, Regente de Pays-Bas* (Paris, 1987).

JENS GRÜHN

- **Additional Literature:** G.-H. Dumont, *Marguerite de Parme* (Brussels, 1999).

Marius (real name Mair, Mayr), *Wolfgang.* Cistercian (1490), humanist, born October 18, 1469 in Dorfbach, died October 11, 1544 in Aldersbach. He studied in Heidelberg from 1493 to 1497, and became abbot of Aldersbach in 1514. Marius wrote poetry and a history of his own monastery, as well as controversial writings against Martin Luther, some of which have been published by Wiest (vol. 4).

- **Works:** *Christi fasciculus florido heroici poematis charactere digestus* (Landshut, 1515; German, Tegernsee, 1580); S. Wiest, ed., *De W. M. . . . scriptore,* 4 vols. (Ingolstadt, 1788–92); M. Hartig, ed., "Die Annales ecclesiae Alderspacensis des W. M.," *Verhandlungen des historischen Vereins von Niederbayern* 42 (1906) 1–112; 43 (1907) 1–113; M. Gloning, ed., "Aus der Gedichtesammlung des Abtes M. von Aldersbach," *Studien und Mitteilungen zur Geschichte des Benedictinerordens und seiner Zweige* 32 (1911) 699–702, 33 (1912) 76–89.
- **Literature:** *NDB* 16:218f.—J. Oswald, "Der Humanistenabt W. M.," L. Schrott, ed., *Bayerische Kirchenfürsten* (Munich, 1964) 149–59; J. Oswald, "Die Gedichte des Abtes W. M.," *Ostbairische Grenzmarken* 7 (1964/65) 310–19; idem, "Abt W. M.," in *Speculum historiale.* Festschrift J. Spörl (Munich, 1965) 354–74; idem, "Bayerische Humanistenfreundschaft," in D. Albrecht et al., eds., Festschrift M. Spindler (Munich, 1969) 401–20; F. Lenhardt, "Der Altar des Abtes W. M. . . . im Ingolstädter Münster," *Sammelblätter des historischen Vereins Ingolstadt* 92 (1983) 145–69; W. Hauer, *1250 Jahre Aldersbach* (Aldersbach, 1985) 93f.

CLAUDIA SCHWAAB

Marpeck (Marbeck), *Pilgram.* Leader in the → Baptist movement, born c. 1495, died 1556 in Augsburg. He worked in the municipal administration of Rattenberg am Inn, becoming mayor in 1522 and supervisor of the mines from 1525-1528, and then in the administration of Strasbourg

(1528-1532). He was expelled from both cities because of his membership in the Baptist movement. After a long period as an itinerant, he was entrusted with public office in Augsburg from 1544 onward. He regarded his political activities as a Christian task, and he influenced both the Mennonites (→ Menno Simons) and the → Hutterite Brethren.

■ **Literature:** *BiDi* 17:33–73.—J. Kiwiet, *P. M.* (Kassel, 1958); W. Klassen, *Covenant and Community* (Grand Rapids, Mich., 1968); N. Blough, *Christologie anabaptiste* (Geneva, 1984); S. B. Boyd, *P. M.* (Mainz, 1992); J. D. Rempel, *The Lord's Supper in Anabaptism* (Waterloo [Ontario], 1993).

STEPHEN B. BOYD

■ **Additional Bibliography:** G. L. Dipple, "Sebastian Franck in Strasbourg," *Mennonite Quarterly Review* 73 (1999) 783–802; W. O. Packull, "Preliminary Report on P. M.'s Sponsorship of Anabaptist 'Flugschriften,'" *Mennonite Quarterly Review* 75 (2001) 75–88; N. Blough, "'The Uncovering of the Babylonian Whore': Confessionalization and Politics Seen from the Underside," *Mennonite Quarterly Review* 75 (2001) 35–55.

Marriage

1. The Middle Ages considered marriage as a second-class ethical conduct, but the *Reformation* sought to give marriage a higher rank, on the basis of the earliest biblical testimony, teaching that marriage and the unmarried state are equally valuable ways of serving God. According to the Reformation confessions of faith, celibacy is a "special gift" of God which only "a few possess." This means that it is inadmissible to compel an entire professional body, such as priests, to live in → celibacy (→ Confessio Augustana 23). Marriage is not impure; on the contrary, it is God's good ordering for his creation and a "natural right" that no one may be forbidden to exercise (Confessio Augustana and Apology CA 23). It is not a → sacrament in the strict sense of communicating grace like baptism, the Lord's Supper (→ communion), and penance, but it is a "sacrament" in a wider sense (Apology CA 13), since it is not a merely human reality, but a "divine covenant" (Apology CA 23). It belongs not to the human order, but to the divine—though to the order of creation rather than to the order of redemption and salvation. This is why Luther can call it "a worldly matter." Marriage is not itself

grace, but lives on the basis of grace. The shadows of human inadequacy fall on marriage, just as they fall on every ordering in creation. Marriage lives on the basis of forgiveness. The fragile pledge, which the marriage partners give each other, can persist only because it is supported and rooted in God's utterly faithful pledge, which is eternally antecedent to ours. Although marriage is in principle indissoluble, the Reformation holds that divorce is possible in borderline cases. Precisely the fragility and the de facto failure of marriage show that it is not an end in itself: it has a transcendental reference point, viz., the *sola gratia*.

HORST G. PÖHLMANN

2. The *Council of Trent* resolutely maintained the sacramental character of marriage and insisted that only the church has legal responsibility for marriage. It did not however offer any dogmatic definition of the essence of this sacrament, nor did it answer the question (already a matter of dispute in scholasticism) whether Christ himself had instituted marriage (DH 1797-1816). The council was more concerned with the introduction (reached only after difficult debates) of the obligation to observe the ecclesiastical forms, as a condition of the validity of a marriage. The central passage of the reform decree *Tametsi* specifies that the parish priest shall speak the following confirmatory sacramental formula: "I join you in marriage in the name of the Father and of the Son and of the Holy Spirit …" (DH 1814).

URS BAUMANN

■ *LThK*[3] 3:489ff. (1.) 471–74 (2.) (unabridged version).
■ **Literature:** (E.=Ehe, marriage) U. Baumann, *Die E.— ein Sakrament?* (Zurich, 1988); N. Schöch, "La solennizzazione giuridica della 'forma canonica' nel decreto 'Tametsi' del Concilio di Trento," *Antonianum* 72 (1997) 637–72; J. Witte, "Between Sacrament und Contract. Marriage as Covenant in John Calvin's Geneva," *Calvin Theological Journal* 33 (1998) 9–75; S. H. Hendrix, "Luther on Marriage," *Lutheran Quarterly* 14 (2000) 335–50; B. Möller, "Wenzel Lincks Hochzeit. Über Sexualität, Keuschheit und E. in der frühen Reformation," *Zeitschrift für Theologie und Kirche* 97 (2000) 317–42.

■ **Additional Literature:** M. Arnold, "Formation et dissolution du lien conjugal chez Bucer et Luther," *Revue d'histoire et de philosophie religieuse* 81 (2001) 259–76; C. Euler, "Heinrich Bullinger, Marriage, and the English Reformation," *SCJ* 34 (2003) 367–93.

Marschalk, *Nikolaus* (Nicolaus Marescalcus Thurius). Humanist, born c. 1470 in Rossla (Thüringen), died July 12, 1525 in Rostock. He began his studies in Erfurt in 1492, taking the degree of master of arts in 1496. He was the central figure in a group of humanist scholars. As a supporter of the study of Greek and Hebrew, he influenced Martin Luther. He taught at the university of Wittenberg from 1502; after a period as ducal counselor in Schwerin (1505-1510), he taught at the university of Rostock. He edited and wrote many works, including philological textbooks and historical works.

■ **Literature:** *Literaturlexikon. Autoren und Werke deutscher Sprache,* ed. W. Killy, vol. 7 (Gütersloh and Munich, 1990) 495; *NDB* 16:252f.—H. Junghans, *Der junge Luther und die Humanisten* (Göttingen, 1985); Th. Haye, "Notizen zu N. M.," *Daphnis* 23 (1994) 205–36.

THOMAS HAYE

Mary I of England (also known as Bloody Mary). Queen (1553-1558), born February 18, 1516 in Greenwich, daughter and sole surviving child of → Henry VIII and Catharine of Aragon, died November 17, 1558 in London. In 1523, Juan Luis → Vives wrote his *De institutione foeminae christianae,* providing guidelines for a suitable education for Mary. In the late 1520s, Henry began to call into question the legality of his marriage to Catharine, and hence the legitimacy of Mary's birth. Mary refused to acknowledge Henry's divorce from Catharine in 1533. After Henry's second wife, Anne Boleyn, gave birth to the future → Elizabeth I in 1534, the Act of Succession in the same year excluded Mary from succession to the throne. She made a formal protest against the loss of her status as heir, but yielded after the death of her mother in January, 1536. This caused her father to look on her with greater favor, and she received extensive properties in East Anglia, where she remained during the reign of her Protestant half-brother, → Edward VI. She opposed his religious views, and retained the celebration of the Mass in her domestic chapel; she was protected by her cousin, Emperor → Charles V. Finally, after Edward died in 1553, her territorial power base enabled her to thwart the attempt of the duke of Northumberland to crown Jane Grey (his son's wife) as queen.

As soon as Mary ascended the throne, she began the restoration of Roman Catholicism in England. The Mass was immediately permitted, and Edward's laws about religion were declared void in December, 1553. In 1554, she made an extremely unpopular marriage with → Philip of Spain; thanks both to her age and to her weak health, no children were born of this union. On November 30, 1554, Cardinal Reginald → Pole imparted in parliament the formal absolution of the kingdom of England from schism; however, those who had acquired church property were allowed to keep it. Mary did not shrink from harsh methods in her work of restoration, and c. 300 Protestants were burnt as heretics, including Thomas → Cranmer and Hugh → Latimer. She had some monasteries reopened, and the English church witnessed a notable restoration of Catholic liturgy and praxis under Pole, whose disciplinary laws anticipated the decrees of the Council of Trent. In domestic politics, Mary faced opposition (e.g., the revolt of Thomas Wyat in 1554); in external politics, she had to accept the loss of Calais in 1558. Her popularity sank, thanks to inflation, epidemics, and a high war tax. Since there was no reliable Catholic heir, Mary's lifework was highly vulnerable, and it collapsed within a few months thanks to the rapid swing of the religious pendulum under her half-sister → Elizabeth.

■ **Literature:** D. Loades, *The Reign of Mary Tudor* (London, 1979); R. Wingfield, *Vitae Mariae Reginae,* ed. D. MacCulloch (London, 1984); D. Loades, *Mary Tudor* (Oxford, 1992); E. Duffy, *The Stripping of the Altars* (New Haven, 1992) chap. 16.

RICHARD REX

■ **Additional Bibliography:** C. Erickson, *Bloody Mary* (London, 1995); J. M. Richards, "'To promote a woman to beare rule.' Talking of Queens in Mid-Tudor England," *SCJ* 28 (1997) 101–21; J. White, "The Funeral Sermon for Queen Mary I Tudor," *Ephemerides liturgicae* 111 (1997) 164–93; Th. Betteridge, "'Making New Novelties Old.' Marian Histories of the Henrician Reformation," *Reformation* 2 (1998) 149–73; J. Edwards, "A Spanish Inquisition? The Repression of Protestantism under Mary Tudor," *Reformation and Renaissance Review* 2 (2000) 62–74; M. A. Panzer, "M. I.," in *Englands Königinnen,* ed. M. A. Panzer (Regensburg, 2001) 72–92; J. R. Wright, "Marian Exiles and the Legitimacy of Flight from Persecution," *JEH* 52 (2001) 220–43.

Mary Queen of Scots (1542–1587). Born December 8, 1542 in Linlithgow, daughter of James V (died 1542) and Mary of Guise (died 1560), died February 8, 1587 in Fotheringhay. When → Henry VIII attempted after the death of Mary's father to enforce her engagement to his son → Edward (VI), in order to unite the independent kingdoms of England and Scotland in the struggle against the superior Catholic might of France, Spain, and Rome, her mother had her brought to France in 1548, and she grew up in the Catholic faith at the French royal court. She was engaged to the later king Francis II of France in 1558.

He died in 1560, and Mary returned in the following year to Scotland, where the Reformers had deposed her mother as regent in October, 1559, and the Protestant faith had been declared the religion of state by parliament in July, 1560. Mary acknowledged the Reformed faith in public, but she refused throughout her life to ratify this law, and regularly attended Mass in her chapel at Holyrood. In 1565, she married her cousin, Lord Henry Darnley, and bore him a son, later James VI of Scotland and I of England. In 1566, her secretary and confidant David Rizzio was murdered by her husband and by Protestant lords whom Mary had threatened with legal proceedings. Mary turned from Darnley, and was accused of involvement in his murder in 1567, initially because she so quickly married James Bothwell, one of the main suspects, and subsequently because of the so-called casket letters, whose authenticity is doubted today. Mary was imprisoned and forced to abdicate in favor of her son, who was crowned king in a Protestant ceremony celebrated by John → Knox.

In May, 1568, Mary succeeded in escaping from Loch Leven, where she was held prisoner. After her followers were defeated at Langside that same year, she sought refuge with → Elizabeth I, whose demand that Mary be reinstated as queen of Scotland was rejected by the Scots. Elizabeth reacted by having Mary imprisoned, under suspicion of involvement in Darnley's murder. During the eighteen years of her imprisonment, Mary was suspected of complicity in a number of plots to overthrow Elizabeth, including the conspiracy by Anthony Babington (1586) which led to her execution.

Mary's contradictory policies have been interpreted in a great variety of ways up to the present day: she is portrayed as tolerant in religious manners, as indecisive, or as an opportunist. We are at any rate entitled to assume that Mary's conduct in a period of religious upheaval was determined, not so much by her own personal faith, as by her desire to become queen of England—as great-grandchild of Henry VII, she was in fact the legitimate heir to Elizabeth's throne.

■ **Literature:** T. F. Henderson, *Mary, Queen of Scots*, 2 vols. (London, 1905); I. B. Cowan, *The Enigma of Mary Stewart* (London, 1971); G. Donaldson, *Mary, Queen of Scots* (London, 1974); idem, "All the Queen's Men," in *Power and Politics in Mary Stewart's Scotland* (London, 1983); A. Plowden, *Two Queens in One Isle* (Brighton, 1984); J. Wormald, *Mary, Queen of Scots* (London, 1987); D. und J. Steele, *Mary Stuart's Scotland* (London, 1987); M. Lynch, ed., *Mary Stewart. Queen in Three Kingdoms* (Oxford, 1988); M. Lee, "The Daughter of Debate: Mary, Queen of Scots after 400 Years," *Scottish Historical Review* 68 (1989) 70–79; R. M. Kingdon, "Knox and the Anti-Marian Resistance," in *The Cambridge History of Political Thought, 1450–1700*, ed. J. J. Burns and M. Goldie (Cambridge, 1991) 194–200; A. A. Macdonald, "Mary Stewart's Entry to England: An Ambiguous Triumph," *Innes Review* 42 (1991) 101–10; M. Duchein, *M. Stuart* (Zurich, 1992); R. Guerdon, *Marie Stuart: reine de France et d'Ecosse* (Paris, 1995).

SABINE SCHARBERTH

■ **Additional Literature:** J. E. A. Dawson, *The Politics of Religion in the Age of Mary, Queen of Scots* (Cambridge, 2002); A. E. MacRobert, *Mary Queen of Scots and the Casket Letters* (London, 2002); A. Weir, *Mary, Queen of Scots, and the Murder of Lord Darnley* (New York, 2003).

Massarelli, *Angelo.* Bishop of Telese (1557), born 1510 in Sanseverino (Marches of Ancona), died July 16, 1566 in Rome. He studied civil and canon law in Siena, and became secretary to Cardinal Hieronymus → Aleander the Elder in 1538, then secretary to Marcello Cervini (later Pope → Marcellus II) in 1545; he accompanied Cervini to the Council of Trent in 1545 and was appointed secretary of the council on April 1, 1546. He held this office in all three periods of the council and carried out his duties conscientiously, although the sheer amount of work was sometimes too great for him. He wrote the minutes of the council and kept a journal.

■ **Works:** Protocols of the congregations and sessions: *CT* 4–9; 7; diaries: *CT* 1–2; *Decreta septem priorum sessionum Concilii Tridentini sub Paulo III Pontifice Maximo ex autografo A. M.*, ed. S. Kuttner (Washington, 1945).

■ **Literature:** S. Merkle, "De A. M. Concilii secretario et Diariorum Actorumque scriptore," *CT* 1:LXVIII–CXX;

idem, "Lücken in den Protokollen des Tridentinums ihre Ergänzung," *ZSRG.K* 27 (1938) 154–79; Jedin vol. 2–4/2.

KLAUS GANZER

Mathesius, *Johannes.* Lutheran theologian, born June 24, 1504 in Rochitz (Saxony), died October 7, 1565 in St. Joachimsthal (Bohemia). After studying at Ingolstadt and other universities, he came to Wittenberg in 1529, where he studied under Philipp Melanchthon. He became rector of the Latin school in Joachimsthal in 1532 and helped shape its humanistic orientation. He returned to Wittenberg for further studies, and was one of those who noted down Martin Luther's table talk (1540-1542). Luther ordained him in 1542, and he became pastor of the parish of Joachimsthal in 1545. About 1,500 sermons survive; especially noteworthy are the sermons in which Mathesius created the first Protestant biography of Luther, portraying him as prophet, teacher, and pastor. His homilies on the Sermon on the Mount are significant source material both for historians and for scholars of the development of the German language.

■ **Literature:** *NDB* 16:369f.; *BBKL* 5:1000–11.—G. Loesche, *J. M.*, 2 vols. (Gotha, 1895), includes a list of writings; H. Volz, *Die Lutherpredigten des J. M.* (Leipzig, 1930); H. Wolf, *Die Sprache des J. M.* (Cologne and Vienna, 1969); R. Kolb, *For All the Saints: Changing Perceptions of Martyrdom and Sainthood in the Lutheran Reformation* (Macon, 1987) 109–37.

HERIBERT SMOLINSKY

■ **Additional Bibliography:** A. Eckert, "Analytischer Vergleich der Abendmahlslehre . . . [von] J. M. . . . ," *Communio viatorum* 41 (1999) 5–29.

Maximilian II (emperor 1564-1576). Born July 31, 1527 in Vienna, son of Emperor → Ferdinand I, died October 12, 1576 in Regensburg. Through his tutor, Wolfgang Schüber, a pupil of Luther who was dismissed from office in 1538, Maximilian came into contact at an early age with the Protestant movement. He accompanied his uncle, → Charles V, in the Schmalkaldic War, and married Maria, a daughter of Charles, in 1548. He was viceroy in Spain from 1548 to 1550. Protestant innovations demanded by his court chaplain, Sebastian Pfauser, and by Lutheran nobles set him at odds with the emperor; Maximilian acquired a "Lutheran library" and exchanged letters with Protestant princes. However, political reasons induced him to remain a Catholic: Charles and → Paul IV put pressure on him; little help was to be expected from the Protestant princes; and Maximilian himself hoped to succeed to the empire and perhaps also to the Spanish throne. He became king of Bohemia and Roman-German king in 1562, king of Hungary in 1563, and emperor in 1564. In keeping with Ferdinand I's division of his domains into three parts, Maximilian received Bohemia, Hungary, Upper and Lower Austria.

As emperor, he sought to unite the confessions, and as sovereign in Austria, under pressure from the wars against the Turks, he granted the Protestant nobles freedom of confession and of worship in the Religious Concession of 1568. He approved the church order drawn up by David → Chytraeus and promulgated the Religious Assurance in 1571. In 1567, he published regulations for monastic reform, and set up the so-called Monastery Council in 1568. He granted the Lutherans and → Utraquists in Bohemia religious freedom in 1575. His religious policies were motivated by the hope that reforms such as priestly marriage (→ celibacy) and the → chalice for the laity, as well as the observance of the Religious Peace of → Augsburg, would promote a convergence among the various confessions. He had problems with Rome, not only because of what was perceived as unreliability on the confessional question, but also because → Pius V raised Cosimo de' Medici to the rank of archduke in 1569. Maximilian attempted in vain to secure the Polish crown in 1572-1573 and 1575. He died during the imperial parliament in Regensburg in 1576, and was buried in St. Vitus' cathedral in Prague.

■ **Sources:** M. Koch, ed., *Quellen zur Geschichte des Kaisers M. II.*, 2 vols. (Leipzig, 1857–61); W. E. Schwarz, ed., *Briefe und Akten zur Geschichte M.s II.*, 2 vols. (Paderborn, 1889–91); V. Bibl, ed., *Die Korrespondenz M.s II. 1564–67*, 2 vols. (Vienna, 1916–21); R. Rodriguez Raso, ed., *Maximiliano de Austria, gobernador de Carlos V en España. Cartas al emperador* (Madrid, 1963).

■ **Literature:** *NDB* 16:471–75.—O. H. Hopfen, *Kaiser M. II. und der Kompromisskatholizismus* (Munich, 1895); V. Bibl, *M. II. Der rätselhafte Kaiser* (Hellerau-Dresden, 1929); R. Vocelka, "Die Begräbnisfeierlichkeiten für M. II.," *Mitteilungen des Instituts für Österreichische Geschichtsforschung* 84 (1976) 105–36; M. Altfahrt, "Die politische Propaganda für M. II.,"

205

Mitteilungen des Instituts für Österreichische Geschichtsforschung 88 (1980) 283–312; 89 (1981) 53–92; A. Bues, *Die habsburgische Kandidatur für den polnischen Thron während des Ersten Interregnums in Polen 1572/73* (Vienna, 1984); F. Edelmayer, *M. II., Philipp II. und Reichsitalien* (Stuttgart, 1988); F. Edelmayer and A. Kohler, ed., *Kaiser M. II., Kultur und Politik im 16.Jh.* (Vienna and Munich, 1992).

JOHANN RAINER

■ **Additional Bibliography:** M. Lanzinner, *Friedenssicherung und politische Einheit des Reiches unter Kaiser M. II. 1564–76* (Göttingen, 1993); P. Luttenberger, *Kurfürsten, Kaiser und Reich. Politische Führung und Friedenssicherung unter Ferdinand I. und M. II.* (Mainz, 1994); A. Edel, *Der Kaiser und Kurpfalz. Eine Studie zu den Grundelementen politischen Handelns bei M. II* (Göttingen, 1997); H. Louthan, *The Quest for Compromise. Peacemakers in Counter-Reformation Vienna* (Cambridge, 1997); P. Sutter Fichtner, *Emperor M. II* (New Haven, 2001).

Mediating theology. This concept (*Vermittlungstheologie*) has been coined by historians to designate a theology which endeavored in the period of → confessionalization to mediate between the extreme positions in the conflict between the religious parties. The goal was unity or *concordia,* but without denying any aspect of the truth. In order to avoid confessionalistic positions, these theologians mostly took their stance on the Bible and on the teaching and praxis of the early church; they spoke of a *via media* and pleaded for a comprehensive reform of the church as the necessary precondition of religious unification. Their methodology sought the path of moderation, urging that various methods be adopted: literary publications, → religious dialogues, conferences of scholars, and a council which would achieve unity. *De sarcienda ecclesiae concordia,* a work by → Erasmus of Rotterdam (Basle, 1535), had a great influence on mediating theology. Its representatives include Georg → Witzel, Georg → Cassander, Claude d'Espérance, and François → Bauduin; Hugo Grotius counted Philipp Melanchthon too among the mediatory theologians. It is a matter of scholarly dispute whether those who taught a double righteousness (e.g., Johann → Gropper, Albert → Pigge, Girolamo → Seripando) can be considered mediatory theologians.

Since this concept is very broad and can be expanded by means of additional descriptions (irenicists, *moyenneurs,* center party), it is necessary to specify precisely what is meant in each case, and to see these theologians in the context of the confessional history of the 16th and 17th centuries. We must also bear in mind that this concept involves not only mediation between Roman Catholic and Protestant positions, but also mediation within Protestantism itself.

■ **Literature:** *TRE* 16:268–73.—F. W. Kantzenbach, *Das Ringen um die Einheit der Kirche im Jahrhundert der Reformation* (Stuttgart, 1957); M. Turchetti, *Concordia o tolleranza? François Bauduin i "moyenneurs"* (Geneva, 1984); B. Henze, *Aus Liebe zur Kirche Reform. Die Bemühungen Georg Witzels um die Kircheneinheit* (Münster, 1995); M. E. H. N. Mout, H. Smolinsky, and J. Trapman, eds., *Erasmianism, Idea and Reality* (Amsterdam, 1997); T. Wanegffelen, *Ni Rome ni Genève* (Paris, 1997).

HERIBERT SMOLINSKY

Medici, *Catharine de'.* Queen of France, born April 13, 1519 in Florence, died January 1, 1589 in Blois. She was the daughter of Lorenzo de' Medici, duke of Urbino, and Madeleine de la Tour d'Auvergne. She married the future king → Henry II of France in 1533, a marriage arranged by → Clement VII to further his own political goals. After Henry's death in 1559, Catharine was regent for her sons Francis II (died 1560) and → Charles IX, while they were minors. She preserved peace within France and maintained the power of the crown. Initially, she favored the → Huguenots, but she later bore responsibility for St. → Bartholomew's Eve (August 24, 1572) together with her son, Henry of Anjou (→ Henry III), and the duke of → Guise. She fled from the Guise faction to Blois in 1588.

■ **Sources:** *Lettres,* ed. H. de la Ferrière et al., 10 vols. (Paris, 1880–1909).

■ **Literature:** L. Romier, *Catholiques et Huguenots à la Cour de Charles IX* (Paris, 1924); idem, *Le royaume de Cathérine de Médicis,* 2 vols. (Paris, ²1925); J. Héritier, *K. von M.* (Stuttgart, 1964); H. R. Williamson, *Catherine de'M.* (London, 1973); I. Mahoney, *K. von M.* (Munich, ⁵1997).

KLAUS JAITNER

■ **Additional Bibliography:** J. Orieux, *K. von M.* (Augsburg, 1998); R. J. Knecht, *Catherine de'M.* (London, 1998); idem, *The French Civil Wars* (Harlow, 2000); K. Crawford, "Catherine de M. and the Performance of Political Motherhood," *SCJ* 31 (2000)

643–73; M. G. Paulson, *Catherine de M.: Five Portraits* (New York, 2002).

Medina, *Miguel de.* Franciscan (1509), theologian, born after 1500 in Belalcázar (Córdoba), died May 1, 1578 in Toledo. He studied in Córdoba and Alcalá, and applied unsuccessfully for the professorship of biblical studies in Alcalá in 1560. He attended the Council of Trent in 1562. → Pius V commissioned him in 1567 to write against the → Magdeburg Centuriators; however, his writings were never published. He was obliged to give an account of himself before the Inquisition after he published the scriptural commentaries of Johannes → Wild, which the Sorbonne had placed on the Index, in a revised form in Spain, and he defended these works against the accusations by Domingo de → Soto that they contained Lutheran tendencies. The investigation ended in 1578, after Medina's death, with his acquittal.

■ **Works:** *Apologeticum pro lectione apostolica* (Alcalá, 1558); *De recta in Deum fide* (Venice, 1563); *Disputationes de indulgentiis* (Venice, 1564, 1569); *Tratado de la cristiana y verdadera humildad* (Toledo, 1570).
■ **Literature:** DThC 10:486f.—J. L. Orella y Unzue, *Respuestas católicas a las Centurias de Magdeburgo (1559–88)* (Madrid, 1976); I. Vázquez Janeiro, "Un erasmista olvidado: Fray M. de M. OFM († 1578)," *Miscellanea Historiae Pontificiae* 50 (1983) 261–81; idem, "Cultura y censura en el siglo XVI," *Anton* 63 (1988) 26–73.

FERNANDO DOMÍNGUEZ

Megander (real name: Grossmann), *Kaspar.* Swiss Reformer, born 1495 in Zurich, where he died August 17, 1545. He was an early follower and collaborator of Huldrych Zwingli. He was invited to become professor of theology and preacher in Berne in 1528, but he was dismissed from office by the city council in 1537, since he opposed the attempts at union which were promoted by Martin → Bucer, and held fast to Zwingli's doctrine of the Lord's Supper. Megander then became cathedral canon and archdeacon in Zurich. His writings include biblical commentaries. It was he who elaborated the church constitution for Waadtland in 1537.

■ **Literature:** RE³ 12, 501ff.; RGG³ 4:828.—K. Guggisberg, *Bernische Kirchengeschichte* (Berne, 1958) index.

BURKHARD NEUMANN

■ **Additional Bibliography:** "Ein Berner 'Kunzechismus' von 1541. Bucers verloren geglaubte Bearbeitung des Meganderschen Katechismus," *Zwingliana* 24 (1997) 81–94.

Melanchthon (real name: Schwartzerdt), *Philipp.* Humanist and reformer, born February 16, 1497 in Bretten, died April 19, 1560 in Wittenberg. His studies at the universities of Heidelberg (1509-1512) and Tübingen (1512-1518) were wholly within the parameters of scholasticism, and made no lasting impression on him; he was more deeply influenced by the humanist reforming theology (→ humanism) which developed in the second decade of the 16th century and was inspired above all by → Erasmus of Rotterdam. On the recommendation of Johannes → Reuchlin, a distant relative, he was made professor of Greek at the university of Wittenberg in 1518, and took the degree of bachelor in biblical studies in 1519. His first theological utterances in Wittenberg were themselves an important contribution to the humanist reforming theology; however, the sheer dominance of the doctrinal conflicts in the Reformation period prevented the development of an autonomous theology along these lines.

In Wittenberg, Melanchthon met Martin Luther, and this encounter had tremendous consequences for his subsequent life; in his will, he acknowledges that it was from Luther that he learned the gospel. Beginning with the → Leipzig disputation in 1519, Melanchthon was an open supporter of Luther, and he himself became one of the spokesmen of the developing Reformation theology from 1521 onward. His first theological work, the *Loci communes rerum theologicarum seu hypotyposes theologicae* (Wittenberg, 1521), often called the first Protestant dogmatics, contains a number of one-sided affirmations which he corrected in the course of the 1520s by means of a new definition of the relationship between faith and reason, and between grace and freedom (commentary on Colossians [Hagenau, 1527]). This one-sidedness was definitively overcome in the early 1530s (commentary on Romans [Wittenberg, 1532], and *Loci communes theologici* [Wittenberg, 1535]; revised version: *Loci theologici* [Wittenberg, 1543-1544]; last edition published during Melanchthon's own lifetime: *Loci praecipui theologici* [Wittenberg and Leipzig, 1559]).

Apart from extensive activity in church politics and the educational sphere (→ church orders, school regulations, etc.) and his academic teaching with its literary spin-offs in the form of commentaries on biblical and classical texts, a commentary on Aristotle, and textbooks, Melanchthon was a prominent participant in endeavors to achieve unity, and in → religious dialogues. This work corresponded to his deepest personal convictions, and it was he who gave the standard account of the Protestant side when he composed the → Confessio Augustana (1530), the Apologia for the Augsburg Confession (1531), the *Tractatus de potestate et primatu papae* (written 1537, published Strasbourg, 1540), and the *Confessio Saxonica* (1551).

Although he was the leading representative of the German Reformation alongside Luther, and there was never any breach between the two men, he was accused by younger students of Luther (the → Gnesiolutherans) of → Crypto-Calvinist and Crypto-Catholic tendencies, and he was harshly attacked. In the history of education, Melanchthon is regarded both as the creator of the German school, with its emphasis on scholarly learning, and as the organizer who laid down the guidelines for the Protestant universities. He was a polymath who wrote widely used textbooks in virtually every subject, and even in his lifetime he was given the honorific title *Praeceptor Germaniae* ("Germany's teacher"). In the history of philosophy, Melanchthon's humanistic reception of Aristotle makes him the father of German scholastic philosophy. Earlier scholars often saw his understanding of philosophy, relating it to language, history, and praxis, and linking Aristotle, linguistic humanism, dialectics and rhetoric, as a superficial eclecticism; today, it is seen rather as an important example of the transformation process undergone by philosophy in the early modern period.

Melanchthon's significance in the history of the church and of theology has been a matter of dispute among both Protestants and Catholics. It is probably true to say that he exercised a stronger influence than Luther on the process whereby the Reformation movement took the form of a *church*. At any rate, unlike Luther, Melanchthon was a highly important mediator between the Reformation and humanism (Luther and Erasmus), between Lutheran and Reformed Protestants, and between Lutheranism and Catholicism, and today's ecumenical climate suggests a new assessment of Melanchthon.

■ **Works:** CR 1–28; *Supplementa Melanchthoniana. Werke Ph. M.s, die im CR vermisst werden,* 5 vols. (Leipzig, 1910–29; new printing, Frankfurt/Main, 1968); *M.s Werke in Auswahl,* 7 vols., ed. R. Stupperich (Gütersloh, 1951–75); *M.s Briefwechsel. Kritische und kommentierte Gesamtausgabe,* ed. H. Scheible (Stuttgart, 1977ff.); *Loci communes 1521* (Latin-German), trans. H. G. Pöhlmann (Gütersloh, 1993); *M.* (German), 2 vols., ed. M. Beyer et al. (Leipzig, 1997).

■ **Literature:** TRE 22:371–410.—W. Hammer, *Die M.-Forschung im Wandel der Jahrhunderte,* 4 vols. (Gütersloh, 1967–96); V. Pfnür, *Einig in der Rechtfertigungslehre?* (Wiesbaden, 1970); S. Wiedenhofer: *Formalstrukturen humanistischer und reformatorischer Theologie bei Ph. M.,* 2 vols. (Berne, 1976); idem, "Zum katholischen M.-Bild im 19. und 20.Jh.," *Zeitschrift für Katholische Theologie* 102 (1980) 425–54; E. P. Meijering, *M. and Patristic Thought* (Leiden, 1983); S. Rhein, "Philosophie und Dichtung" (diss., Heidelberg, 1987; J. R. Schneider, *Ph. M.'s Rhetorical Construct of Biblical Authority* (Lewiston, N.Y., 1990); J. Knape, *Ph. M.s "Rhetorik"* (Tübingen, 1993); O. Berwald, *Ph. M.s Sicht der Rhetorik* (Wiesbaden, 1994); G. Frank, *Die theologische Philosophie Ph. M.s* (Leipzig, 1995); H. Scheible, *M. und die Reformation,* ed. R. Decot and G. May (Mainz, 1996); H. Scheible, *M.* (Munich, 1997); idem, ed., *M. in seinen Schülern* (Wiesbaden, 1997); *Ph. M.,* ed. J. Haustein (Göttingen, ²1997).—Series: *M.-Schriften der Stadt Bretten,* vol. 1ff. (Sigmaringen, 1988ff.).

SIEGFRIED WIEDENHOFER

■ **Additional Bibliography:** *Humanismus und Wittenberger Reformation. Festschrift anlässlich des 500. Geburtstages des Praeceptor Germaniae Ph. M. am 16.2.1997* (Leipzig, 1996); G. Binder, ed., *Ph. M. Exemplarische Aspekte seines Humanismus* (Trier, 1998); M. H. Jung, *Frömmigkeit und Theologie bei Ph. M. Das Gebet im Leben und in der Lehre des Reformators* (Tübingen, 1998); G. Wartenberg, ed., *Ph. M. als Politiker zwischen Reich, Reichsständen und Konfessionsparteien* (Wittenberg, 1998); R. Friedrich, ed., *500 Jahre Ph. M.* (Wiesbaden, 1998); K. Maag, ed., *M. in Europe* (Grand Rapids, Mich., 1999); *Werk und Rezeption Ph. M. in Universität und Schule bis ins 18.Jh.* (Leipzig, 1999); G. Frank, ed., *Der Theologe M.* (Stuttgart, 2000); M. Becht, *Pium consensum tueri* (Münster, 2000); W. Matz, *Der befreite Mensch* (Göttingen, 2001); T. J. Wengert, "Bearing Christ as M.'s Contribution to 'The Book of Concord,'" *Lutheran Quarterly* 15 (2001) 396–416; J. Löhr, *Dona Melanchthonia.* Festschrift H. Scheible (Stuttgart, 2001); G. B. Graybill, *The Evolution of P. M.'s Thought on Free Will* (Oxford, 2002); H. Scheible, "P. M.," in *The Reformation Theologians,* ed. C. Lindberg (Boston, 2002) 67–82.

Melander, *Dionysius* the Elder. Dominican (1505/1506), Protestant theologian, born c. 1486 in Ulm, died July 10, 1561 in Kassel. Melander embraced the Reformation in 1522 and was preacher in Frankfurt am Main from 1525 to 1535, then court preacher to → Philip of Hessen in Kassel from 1536 to 1561. He was in contact with Martin → Bucer, Wolfgang → Capito, Huldrych Zwingli, Johannes → Oecolampadius, and Heinrich → Bullinger. He was receptive to the Reformed doctrine of the Upper German and Swiss Protestants, and sought to spread this teaching in Frankfurt. He celebrated the marriage of Philip and Margarete von der Saale in 1540, which meant that the marquis lived in bigamy. Melander defended Philip's double marriage, and the marquis entrusted his court preacher with various church-political tasks in Hessen, including the → church order, synods, visitations, and religious negotiations.
■ **Literature:** *NDB* 17:1.—K. M. Sauer, "D. M. der Ältere. Leben und Briefe," *Jahrbuch der Hessischen Kirchengeschichtlichen Vereinigung* 29 (1978) 1–36; J. Telschow and E. Reiter, *Die evangelischen Pfarrer von Frankfurt am Main* (Gelnhausen, 1980); K. M. Sauer, "Kirchliche Einheit bei unterschiedlichen Lehrmeinungen," *Jahrbuch der Hessischen Kirchengeschichtlichen Vereinigung* 44 (1993) 5–24.

HERIBERT SMOLINSKY

Melius (real name: Juhász), *Peter.* Hungarian Reformer, born c. 1536 in Horhi (county of Somogy), died December 15, 1572 in Debrecen. He studied from 1556-1558 in Wittenberg under Philipp Melanchthon and others. From 1558 onward, he worked in Debrecen, where he embraced → Calvinism and was elected bishop in 1561. It was thanks to him that Debrecen became the center of Hungarian Calvinism. In 1562, together with Gregor Szegedi and Georg Czeglédi, he drew up the so-called *Confessio Debrecinensis.* Melius played a decisive role in the organization of the Reformed Church in Hungary and in the struggle against the Unitarians in Transylvania.
■ **Literature:** *HDThG* 2:291f.; *BBKL* 5:1223ff.; *OER* 3:47ff.—I. Botta, *M. P. ifjúsága (Die Jugend von P. M.)* (Budapest, 1978; with German summary).

MICHAEL BECHT

Menius, *Justus* (real name: Jodocus Menig). Reformer, born December 13, 1499 in Fulda, died

August 1, 1558 in Leipzig. He began his studies in Erfurt in 1514 and studied under Martin Luther and Philipp Melanchthon from 1519 onward. He was curate in Mühlberg from 1523 to 1525, then pastor in Erfurt (1525) and superintendent first in Eisenach (1529), then in Gotha (1546). From 1528 onward, he was frequently involved in visitations in Thüringen. He took part in the religious dialogue in → Marburg, in the negotiations for the concord of → Wittenberg, the assembly of Schmalkalden, and the religious dialogues in → Hagenau and → Worms. In addition to translations of works by Luther and polemical pamphlets of his own, he wrote the *Oeconomia christiana* (Wittenberg, 1529), in which he took up the economic literature of classical antiquity and developed this theme in biblical terms.
■ **Literature:** *TRE* 22:439–42; *BBKL* 5:1263–66.—H. Gottwald, *Vergleichende Studie zur Ökonomik des Aegidius Romanus und des J. M.* (Frankfurt/Main, 1988).

MICHAEL BECHT

■ **Additional Bibliography:** L. D. Peterson, "J. M., Philipp Melanchthon, and the 1547 Treatise 'Von der Notwehr Unterricht,'" *ARG* 81 (1990) 138–57.

Menno Simons. Dutch Catholic priest, born 1498 in Witmarsum, died 1561 in Wüstenfelde near Oldesloe. After reading books by Martin Luther, he joined the → Baptists in 1536. When the moderate wing of this movement separated from the revolutionaries (Münster, Amsterdam), Menno Simons had himself rebaptized and became their Elder in 1537. He worked primarily in the Netherlands and northern Germany. As teacher, pastor, and organizer of the Baptists who were willing to suffer for their beliefs, he wrote both edifying and polemical works, including his chef d'oeuvre, *Das Fundament der christlichen Lehre.* The Mennonites bear his name today.
■ **Works:** *Die vollständigen Werke M.'* (Aylmer, Ont., and La Grange, Ind., 1971).
■ **Literature:** J. A. Brandsma, *M. von Witmarsum. Vorkämpfer der Täuferbewegung in den Niederlanden.* (Maxdorf, ²1983); H. J. Goertz, "M. Ein antiklerikaler Pazifist," in idem, *Die Täufer. Geschichte und Deutung* (Munich, ²1988) 60–68.

HANS JÖRG URBAN

■ **Additional Bibliography:** J. Reimer, *M. S.* (Lage, 1996); S. Voolstra, *M. S.* (North Newton, 1996); A. Friesen, *Erasmus, the Anabaptists, and the Great Commission* (Grad Rapids, 1998).

Mensing, *Johannes.* Dominican (1495), Catholic controversial theologian, born 1475 in Zutphen or Zwolle, died August 8, 1547. He began his studies in Wittenberg in 1515-1516, taking his licentiate in theology in 1517. He matriculated in Frankfurt on the Oder in 1518-1519, where he took his doctorate. From 1519 onward, he was regent of the Dominican house of studies in Magdeburg and prior of the monastery there, and became court preacher in Dessau c. 1527. He became professor of theology in Frankfurt on the Oder in 1529, and was provincial of the Saxon province from 1534 to 1539. He was appointed auxiliary bishop of Halberstadt in 1539. At the imperial parliament in Augsburg in 1530, he collaborated in the *Confutatio* of the → Confessio Augustana, and took part in the religious dialogues in → Worms and → Regensburg in 1540-1541. His works of controversial theology dealt primarily with the sacrifice of the Mass, the doctrine of justification, and the priesthood.

■ **Catalogue of Works:** *VD 16* 13:570–73; Klaiber nos. 2103–17; Köhler *BF* 3:80–85.
■ **Literature:** *NDB* 17:88f.; *KThR* 3:48–64.—V. Pfnür, *Einig in der Rechtfertigungslehre?* (Wiesbaden, 1970) 324–68; D. Fabricius, *Die theologischen Kontroversen in Lüneburg im Zusammenhang mit der Einführung der Reformation in Lüneburg* (Lüneburg, 1988).

HERIBERT SMOLINSKY

Mercier (Mercerus), *Jean.* Biblical philologist, born at Uzès, where he died in 1570. He was a student of Franciscus → Vatablus, and succeeded him at the Collège Royal. After his conversion to Protestantism, he was obliged to leave France, and lived for a time in Venice. His fame rests primarily on his edition of the Targums.

■ **Works:** *Tabula in grammaticam linguae Chaldeae* (Paris, 1560); *Libellus de abbreviaturis Hebraeorum tam Talmudicorum quam masoritarum et aliorum rabbinorum* (Paris, 1561); *In Genesim commentarium,* ed. Th. Beza (Geneva, 1598); *Annotationes in Pagnini Thesaurum* (Lyons, 1575, often reprinted); *Commentaria in Jobum et Salomonis Proverbia, Eclesiasten, Canticum Canticorum* (Amsterdam, 1651).
■ **Literature:** *Encyclopaedia Judaica,* ed. C. Roth et al., vol. 11 (Jerusalem, 1971) 1381f.—*La France protestante* 7 (1958) 239ff.; F. Domínguez, *Gaspar de Grajal* (Münster, 1998) 373f.

FERNANDO DOMÍNGUEZ

Miltiz, *Karl von.* Curial diplomat, born 1490 in Rabenau near Dresden, died November 20, 1529.

He was appointed notary and private chamberlain in Rome in 1514, and was sent in the summer of 1518 to → Frederick the Wise in Saxony with the Golden Rose and the demand that Martin Luther be handed over. He was a loquacious man with a high sense of his own importance, and he conducted negotiations with Luther and made him promises on his own account. His role was finished by summer of 1519. He lived in Germany from 1523 onward, as cathedral canon of Mainz and Meissen.

■ **Literature:** *DThC* 10:1765ff.; *BDG* 2:57; *LThK²* 7:422; *BBKL* 5:1538f.; *NDB* 17:532ff.—H. A. Creutzberg, *K. von M.* (Freiburg, 1907); P. Kalkoff, *Die Miltitziade* (Leipzig, 1911).

KLAUS GANZER

■ **Additional Bibliography:** H.-G. Leder, *Ausgleich mit dem Papst. Luthers Haltung in den Verhandlungen mit M. 1520* (Stuttgart, 1969).

Ministry, church. The interpretation and shaping of ecclesiastical ministry by the Reformers developed in response to specific situations.

The controversy about indulgences led Martin Luther to question the theory of authority as *potestas iurisdictionis.* Jesus did not give the "keys" to Peter alone (Mt 16:18f.), nor did he entrust the authority to bind and loose to the apostles alone (Mt 18:18); on the contrary, "all Christians" enjoy this authority (WA 12:184). The "universal priesthood" (WA 12:317; 15:720) is the decisive reality, and this is why baptism must replace the sacrament of ordination (cf. WA 6:560-567), and everyone must be permitted to administer the → sacraments (WA 6:566). Nevertheless, the individual may not make use of this *potestas* without the approval of the community or a call received from a superior (ibid.; → ordination). Ministry is essentially "service of the Word" (*ministerium Verbi*) and includes both preaching and the administration of the sacraments (cf. → Confessio Augustana [CA] 5:1).

Luther emphasized other aspects in his debate with the → Baptists: election by the community or a calling by the secular ruler is a precondition of the public exercise of the ministry of the Word (WA 8:495; 17/1:360-367), and there is a "difference between the preacher and the laity" (WA 30/3:525). The ministry was instituted by Christ (WA 28:470; 50:633).

According to CA 5:1-2, God himself "instituted" the ministry of preaching. Philipp Melanchthon states explicitly that God is "present" in the ministry (Apologia for CA 13:12). All that matters is that the Word be genuinely audible in this "function": where this is the case, the office-bearer represents the person of Christ (ibid., 7:28) and acts in his stead (ibid., 48).

Martin → Bucer and Jean Calvin attach importance to the structuring of the ministry. Appealing to Rom 12:6ff., 1 Cor 12:7f., and Eph 4:11, Calvin legitimated four articulations of the ministry: pastors, teachers, elders, and deacons (*Inst* 4:3,1 and 8f.). The elders are charged with church discipline, and the deacons are responsible for social work. Calvin sees the ministry as the instrument of the lordship of Christ, who wishes to establish, gather, and lead his church, preserving it in the pure doctrine of the gospel, through the activity of human persons (ibid., 1:4f.; *Confessio Helvetica posterior* 18). Calvin affirms the sacramental quality of ordination by the laying-on of hands (in keeping with 1 Tim 4:14 and 2 Tim 1:6), provided that the purity found in the early church is present also today (*Inst* 4:19,28 and 31). The ministerial charism and a "spiritual character" are imparted by the Holy Spirit to those ordained (*consecrati*, ibid.). With the same reservation about purity, Calvin accepts the special preeminence of the local community and of the bishop of Rome: a genuine Petrine ministry promotes unity (cf. CR 35:611; 75:453; *Inst* 4:7,5 and 8f.). The ministry is in accord with Christ as long as the minister is elected by the community (*Inst* 4:3,10 and 15; *Confessio Gallicana* 27) and the spirit of collegiality prevails (CR 79:196-200), in keeping with the church (*Inst* 4:4,1) and the councils (*Inst* 9,8) of the first four centuries.

■ Literature: (A.=Amt, ministry) *TRE* 2:522–74.—G. Dix, *The Ministry in the Early Church* (London, 1946); P. Fraenkel, *Testimonia Patrum. The Function of the Patristic Argument in the Theology of Philipp Melanchthon* (Geneva, 1961); J. Aarts, *Die Lehre Martin Luthers über das A. in der Kirche* (Helsinki, 1972); A. Ganoczy, *Ecclesia ministrans. Dienende Kirche und kirchlicher Dienst bei Calvin* (Freiburg, 1968); W. Stein, *Das kirchliche A. bei Luther* (Wiesbaden, 1974).

ALEXANDRE GANOCZY

■ Additional Bibliography: M. Hauser, *Prophet und Bischof. Huldrych Zwinglis Amtsverständnis im Rahmen der Zürcher Reformation* (Fribourg, 1994); G. L. Dipple, "Luther, Emser and the Development of Reformation Anticlericalism," *ARG* 87 (1996) 38–56; W. van't Spijker, *The Ecclesiastical Offices in the Thought of Martin Bucer* (Leiden, 1996); H. Goertz, *Allgemeines Priestertum und ordiniertes A. bei Luther* (Marburg, 1997); B. Peter, *Der Streit um das kirchliche A. Die theologischen Positionen der Gegner Martin Luthers* (Mainz, 1997); F. Soto-Hay y García, "Sacerdocio ministerial y sacerdocio real," *Anámnesis* 10 (2000) 109–32; D. Wendebourg, "The Ministry and Ministries," *Lutheran Quarterly* 15 (2001) 159–94.

Monheim, *Johannes.* Humanist and schoolmaster in the Lower Rhine area, born c. 1509 in Klausen near Elberfeld, died September 8/9, 1564 in Düsseldorf. He took the degree of master of arts in Cologne in 1529 and headed the church school in Essen from 1532 to 1536. Thereafter, he was head of the cathedral school in Cologne, and became rector of the newly founded humanistic grammar school in Düsseldorf in 1545. Monheim wrote several textbooks. Under his leadership, the school flourished greatly, but he became involved in the confessional controversy. His *Catechismus* (Düsseldorf, 1560) led the Jesuits in Cologne and others to suspect him of holding Calvinist views.

■ Works: *Katechismus,* facsimile edition with German translation (Cologne, 1987); *VD 16* 14:147f., with list of works.

■ Literature: *NDB* 18:36f.—H. Jedin, "Der Plan einer Universitätsgründung in Duisburg," in *Die Universität Duisburg,* ed. G. von Roden (Duisburg, 1968) 1–32; *Ausstellungskatalog "Humanismus und Reform am Niederrhein. Konrad Heresbach 1496–1576"* (Bielefeld, 1996)

HERIBERT SMOLINSKY

More (Morus), Sir *Thomas.* Saint (1935; feast June 22), English humanist, judge, statesman, martyr, born 1477/1478 in London, where he died July 6, 1535. He was brought up in the household of Archbishop John Morton, who made it possible for him to study at Oxford. He studied civil and canon law at Lincoln's Inn in London. He lived for a period in the Charterhouse, desiring to discover whether he had a vocation to the priesthood, but he decided in favor of a life in the world. He made a thorough study of classical antiquity; he was a close friend of → Erasmus of Rotterdam and was the center of a circle of European humanists (Thomas Linacre, William Grocyn, John Colet; Juan Luis → Vives, Frans Cranevelt, etc.). He took good care of his family. He was a deputy sheriff and a much sought-after legal advocate, serving as legal attaché on diplomatic missions. He had a successful career at the court of King → Henry VIII, rising to the office of lord chancellor (in succession to Cardinal Thomas → Wolsey). He resigned from this post after the "submission of the clergy," and refused (like Bishop John → Fisher) to accept the royal supremacy over the church (Act of → Supremacy). He was thrown into the Tower of London and found guilty of "high treason" on the basis of blatant perjury. He was beheaded; his daughter Margaret kept his head, which is preserved in St. Dunstan's church in Canterbury today.

More's religious and theological significance lies first in the testimony of his life. He unwaveringly followed his conscience and carried out his obligations to his family and in service of the state. He was loyal to his faith, even when his friends— and the entire English episcopate, with the exception of Fisher—yielded to the king. He patiently suffered martyrdom; indeed, as his letters from the Tower show, he went to his death joyfully. Second, his numerous meditative and controversial theological writings show that he—as a layman— was the leading English apologist in the Reformation period. He wrote against Martin Luther (*Responsio ad Lutherum,* 1523), Johannes → Bugenhagen (*Epistolae,* 1526), William → Tyndale (*Dialogue concerning Heresies,* 1529; *Confutation of Tyndale's Answer,* 1532-1533), Simon Fish (*Supplication of Souls,* 1529), John → Frith (*Letter to Frith,* 1533), Christopher St. German (*Apology,* 1533; *Debellation of Salem and Bysanze,* 1533), and George Joye (*Answer to the Supper of the Lord,* 1534). His letters from the Tower and his meditative writings allow us to see something of the deep spirituality on which his courage was based: *Four Last Things* (c. 1520-1525), *Dialogue of Comfort* (1534), *Treatise of the Passion* (1534), *Treatise of the Blessed Body* (1534), *De Tristitia Christi* (1534-1535). He became world-famous through *Utopia* (1516), a humanist work which can be interpreted on several levels; it responds to the social criticism of his age by painting the picture of a "communist" island state, Utopia (literally, the land of "nowhere"), where life is based on the cardinal virtues. His *Historia Richardi Tertii* (c. 1515) portrays a Machiavellian usurper on the English throne. His epigrams are partly his own, partly

translations from the anthology by Maximus Planudes.

■ **Works:** *The Yale Edition of the Complete Works of St. Th. M.,* vols. 1ff. (New Haven and London, 1963ff.); *Th. M. Werke,* ed. H. Schulte Herbrüggen, 6 vols. (Munich, 1983–85; Düsseldorf, 1988); *The Correspondence of Sir Th. M.,* ed. E. F. Rogers (Princeton, N.J., 1947); *Th. M. Neue Briefe,* ed. H. Schulte Herbrüggen (Münster, 1966).—Bibliographies: R. W. Gibson, *Sir Th. M., A Preliminary Bibliography* (New Haven, 1961); C. Smith, *An Updating of Gibson's Bibliography* (St. Louis, 1981).

■ **Sources:** Biographies from the age of the Tudors: of his son-in-law W. Roper, of N. Harpsfield, and of "Ro. Ba." (a pseudonym of an unknown author) and of Th. Stapleton, critical edition: Early English Text Society (London, vol. 186, 1932; vol. 197, 1935; vol. 222, 1950); *Letters and Papers (Henry VIII),* ed. J. S. Brewer and J. Gairdner, 23 vols. (London, 1862–1932).

■ **Literature:** *DSp* 15:849–65.—H. Holeczek, *Humanistische Bibel-Philologie als Reformproblem bei Erasmus von Rotterdam, Th. M. und William Tyndale* (Leiden, 1975); R. S. Sylvester and G. Marc'hadour, *Essential Articles for the Study of Th. M.* (Hamden, Conn., 1977); J. B. Trapp and H. Schulte Herbrüggen, "The King's Good Servant," in *Sir Th. M.* (London, 1977); A. Fox, "Th. M.," in *History and Providence* (Oxford, 1982); R. C. Marius, *Th. M.* (New York, 1984); E. Baumann, *Th. M. und der Konsens (theologisch-geschichtliche Analyse der "Responsio ad Lutherum")* (Paderborn, 1993); J. Timmermann, *Sterbehilfe in Utopia* (Bochum, 1993).— Journal: *Moreana,* ed. G. Marc'hadour, 1 (Angers, 1963) and subsequent issues.

                                        HUBERTUS SCHULTE HERBRÜGGEN

■ **Additional Bibliography:** G. B. Wegemer, *Th. M.* (Princeton, N.J., 1995); P. Ackroyd, *The Life of Th. M.* (New York, 1998); D. Herz, *Th. M. zur Einführung* (Hamburg, 1999); J. Guy, *Th. M.* (London, 2000); D. Trevor, "T. M.'s 'Responsio ad Lutherum' and the Fictions of Humanist Polemic," *SCJ* 32 (2001) 743–64; E.-M. Ganne, *T. M., L'homme complet de la Renaissance* (Montrouge, 2002); A. De Silva, *T. M.* (London, 2003).

Moritz of Saxony. Duke (1541), electoral prince from 1547, born March 21, 1521 in Freiberg, died July 11, 1553 near Sievershausen (near Lehrte). He was educated in Halle, Dresden, Wittenberg, and Torgau. He succeeded his father, Henry the Pious, as ruler of Albertine Saxony in 1541, and supported the development of the Lutheran territorial church within his domains, as well as the reform of the university of Leipzig and of government administration. He founded schools. The Truce of Wurzen (1542) consolidated his influence over this small territory, at the expense of electoral prince → Johann Friedrich. Under the influence of Duke → George of Saxony, Marquis → Philip of Hessen, and important counselors such as Georg von Karlowitz, he kept his distance from the → Schmalkaldic League and pursued a policy of support for the emperor until 1548; thanks to this policy, and to the Treaty of Regensburg (June 19, 1546), Moritz received both the electoral dignity and parts of the Ernestine territories in 1547, after the Schmalkaldic War was over. Moritz himself always remained a Protestant; with the Leipzig Interim (→ Augsburg Interim), which was negotiated in 1548-1549 and envisaged the Adiaphora as offering a potential for mediation and reconciliation, he attempted to take a middle course in the religious question (→ Adiaphora controversy). This course was politically motivated and was the object of a furious controversy; it ended in 1551 with the *Confessio Saxonica* (→ Mediating theology). Moritz initiated a different policy vis-à-vis → Charles V, designed to weaken the emperor's power, when he joined the princely opposition, putting himself at its head in the Treaty of Torgau (1551). He concluded the Treaty of Chambord with King → Henry II of France on January 15, 1552. After the defeat of the emperor, the war, in which Moritz was the driving force, led to the suspension of the Council of → Trent in 1552. Another fruit of this defeat was the Treaty of → Passau, which guaranteed the Protestants the right to retain their possessions; this came about through the agency of King → Ferdinand I, and pointed the way to the Religious Peace of → Augsburg. Moritz died of wounds received in the battle of Sievershausen against Marquis Albrecht Alkibiades of Brandenburg-Kulmbach. His primary political concern was always his own power, and he was a lifelong Protestant. He laid the foundations of the electoral principality of Albertine Saxony, which was consolidated and expanded by his brother August, who succeeded him.

■ **Works:** *Politische Korrespondenz des Herzogs und Kurfürsten M. von Sachsen,* vols. 1–2, ed. E. Brandenburg (Leipzig, 1900–1904; reprint, Berlin, 1982–83); vols. 3–4, ed. J. Herrmann and G. Wartenberg (Berlin, 1978–92); *TRE* 23:308f.
■ **Literature:** *TRE* 23:302–11; *BBKL* 6:137–42; *NDB* 18:141ff.; *TRZRK* 2³:8–32.—K. Blaschke, *M. von Sachsen* (Göttingen, 1983); G. Wartenberg, *Landesherrschaft und Reformation. M. von Sachsen und die albertinische Kirchenpolitik bis 1546* (Weimar, 1988); idem, "M. von Sachsen," in *Kaiser—König—Kardinal: deutsche Fürsten*

1500–1800, ed. R. Straubel and U. Weiss (Leipzig, 1991) 106–14; G. Wartenberg, "M. von Sachsen," in G. Vogler, ed., *Europäische Herrscher* (Weimar, 1988) 106–22.

HERIBERT SMOLINSKY

■ **Additional Bibliography:** J.-P. Bois, *Maurice de Saxe* (Paris, 1992); G. Vogler, "Kurfürst Johann Friedrich und Herzog M. von Sachsen," *ARG* 89 (1998) 178–206; J. Herrmann, "M. von Sachsen, evangelischer Christ und Judas zugleich," *ARG* 92 (2001) 87–118.

Mörlin, *Joachim.* Lutheran theologian, born April 6, 1514 in Wittenberg, died May 23, 1571 in Königsberg. He began his studies in Wittenberg in 1532, taking the decree of master of arts in 1535 and his doctorate in 1540. In the latter year, he became superintendent in Arnstadt, but was dismissed from this post in 1543. From 1544 to 1550, he was superintendent in Göttingen, but he was dismissed once again, thanks to his uncompromising position in the discussions within Protestantism and to his strict rejection of the → Augsburg Interim. He was cathedral canon and theological adviser to Duke → Albrecht of Brandenburg-Ansbach in Königsberg from 1550 to 1553, but he had to give up this post too, after he became involved in violent controversies with Andreas → Osiander about the doctrine of → justification. He was superintendent in Braunschweig from 1553 to 1567, and wrote extensively. Here, along with Martin → Chemnitz, Mörlin participated as a strictly Lutheran theologian in various stages of the formation of the Lutheran confession (*Corpus Doctrinae,* 1563). From 1567 until his death, he was once again in Prussia as bishop of Samland.
■ **Works:** *VD* 16 14:102–6.
■ **Literature:** *BBKL* 6:8–11; *NDB* 17:679f.; *TRE* 23:193–96.—J. Diestelmann, "J. M. und Philipp Melanchthon," in *Einträchtig lehren.* Festschrift J. Schöne (Gross Ösingen, 1997) 95–107; I. Gundermann, "Die Kirchenvisitationen des Bischofs J. M. im Jahre 1569," in *"Alles ist euer, ihr aber seid Christi."* Festschrift D. Meyer (Cologne, 2000) 245–67.

BRUNO STEIMER

■ **Additional Literature:** J. Diestelmann, "Das bischöfliche Lehramt des Superintendenten am Beispiel J. M.s," *Lutherische Beiträge* 7 (2002) 87–96.

Morone, *Giovanni.* Cardinal (1542), born January 25, 1509 in Milan, died December 1, 1580 in

Rome. He studied in Padua, and became bishop of Modena in 1529. He was appointed nuncio in Germany in 1536, and took part in the religious dialogues in → Hagenau (1540), → Worms (1541), and Speyer (1542). He was appointed papal legate to the Council of Trent in 1542, and was legate in Bologna in 1544. He was also bishop of Novara from 1553 to 1560. He was papal legate at the imperial parliament in Augsburg in 1555. He was imprisoned by → Paul IV in Castel Sant'Angelo from 1557 to 1559 on suspicion of heresy, but was fully rehabilitated by → Pius IV in 1560. He was president of the Council of Trent in 1563, and became cardinal bishop and dean of the college of cardinals in 1570. He was papal legate at the imperial parliament in Regensburg in 1576.

Morone was not only a complete master of Renaissance diplomacy; under the influence of the Italian reform circles in the 1530s and 1540s, and especially thanks to Gasparo → Contarini, he became a man of deep personal piety. He was a friend of Contarini, Reginald → Pole, and other proponents of Catholic → reform. The formula about justification proposed at the religious dialogue in → Regensburg (1541) led Paul IV to see him as a Crypto-Lutheran; the extensive acts of the Inquisition's investigation of Morone have recently been published in a critical edition. After his rehabilitation, Pius IV offered him the post of head of the Secretariat of State, but Morone refused this. His great achievement was the resolution of the great crisis of the Council of Trent; as its president, he brought the council safely to a conclusion. He was considered *papabile* in two conclaves. Morone was one of the most important representatives of Italian → Evangelism, and his biography shows "how slow and full of bitter experiences was the process whereby a genuine *Riformatore* grew to human and religious maturity" (Lutz, 380).

■ **Sources:** H. Laemmer, *Monumenta Vaticana* (Freiburg, 1861); F. Dittrich, *HJ* 4 (1883) 395–472, 618–73; *Nuntiaturberichte G. M.s vom deutschen Königshofe 1539–40*, ed. idem (Paderborn, 1893); *NBD*, I. Abteilung, vols. 2, 5, 6, and 17; *CT* vols. 1–13; J. Šusta, *Die römische Kurie und das Konzil von Trient*, 4 vols. (Vienna, 1904–14); *ARCEG* 2–4; *Il processo inquisitoriale del cardinal G. M.*, ed. M. Firpo and M. Dario, 6 vols. (Rome, 1981–95).

■ **Literature:** L. von Pastor, *Geschichte der Päpste seit dem Ausgang des Mittelalters*, vols. 5–9 (Freiburg, 1909–23); G. Constant, *La légation du Cardinal M. près l'Empereur et le Concile de Trente* (Paris, 1922); H. Jedin,

Krisis und Wendepunkt des Trienter Konzils (Würzburg, 1941); J. Grisar, "Die Sendung des Kardinals M. als Legat zum Reichstag von Augsburg 1555," *Zeitschrift des Historischen Vereins für Schwaben* 61 (1955) 341–87; P. Prodi, *Il cardinale Gabriele Paleotti*, 2 vols. (Rome, 1959–67); H. Lutz, "Kardinal M.," in *Reform, Konzil und europäische Staatenwelt: Il Concilio di Trento e la Riforma Tridentina*, vol. 1 (Rome, 1965) 363–81; Jedin, vols. 1–4; P. Simoncelli, *Il caso Reginald Pole* (Rome, 1977); idem, *Evangelismo italiano del Cinquecento* (Rome, 1979); M. Firpo and D. Marcatto, "G. M. e Lorenzo Davidico," *Bolletino storico per la provincia di Novara* 82 (1991) 1–139; K. Ganzer, "Aspekte der katholischen Reformbewegungen im 16.Jh.," *Abhandlungen der geistes- und sozialwissenschaftlichen Klasse der Akademie der Wissenschaften und der Literatur in Mainz* (1991) n. 13; M. Firpo, *Inquisizione Romana e Controriforma* (Bologna, 1992); E. G. Gleason, *Gasparo Contarini* (Berkeley, 1993).

KLAUS GANZER

Mosellanus (real name: Schade), *Petrus.* Humanist, born c. 1493 in Bruttig (Latin name: Protegensis) near Cochem, died April 19, 1524 in Leipzig. He studied in Cologne and moved to the university of Leipzig in 1515, where he became professor of Greek in 1517. He was attacked by Jacobus → Latomus for emphasizing the importance of the ancient languages for theology in his *Oratio de variarum linguarum cognitione paranda* (Leipzig, 1518). It was he who opened the proceedings at the → Leipzig Disputation (*De ratione disputandi praesertim in re theologica* [Leipzig, 1519]). He took the degree of master of arts in 1520. He composed the rhetorical handbook *Tabulae de schematibus et tropis* (Frankfurt am Main, 1516; often reprinted) and the school textbook *Paedologia* (Leipzig, 1518; often reprinted; ed. by H. Michael [Berlin, 1906]). He produced editions, commentaries, and translations of Gregory Nazianzen and many other ancient authors.

■ **Catalogue of Works:** *VD 16* 18:169–79.

■ **Literature:** *BBKL* 6:169ff.; *NDB* 18:170f.; *CEras* 2:466f.—O. G. Schmidt, *P. M.* (Leipzig, 1867); R. Weier, "Die Rede des P. M. 'Über die rechte Weise, theologisch zu disputieren,'" *Trierer Theologische Zeitschrift* 83 (1974) 232–45; R. Schober, *P. M.* (Koblenz, 1979); U. M. Kremer, "M. Humanist zwischen Kirche und Reformation," *ARG* 73 (1982) 20–34; U. M. Kremer, "P. M. und J. Pflug," in *Pflugiana*, ed. E. Neuss and J. V. Pollet (Münster, 1990) 3–22.

PETER WALTER

Mosham, *Ruprecht von.* Imperial counselor and dean of the cathedral in Passau (from 1522), born September 24, 1493 in Thaneck (Styria), committed suicide April/May, 1543 in Passau. He took his doctorate in civil and canon law in 1514, and was ordained priest in 1534. His fanatical speeches and writings urged the reestablishment of religious unity through the destruction of the four "Antichrists," viz., the papacy, Lutheranism, Zwinglianism, and the Baptist movement; this would allow Europe to resist the danger which threatened from the Turks. He fled from Passau in 1539, and was deposed from office because of heresy. After a propaganda journey through Germany, he was arrested in 1542 and imprisoned in the Oberhaus fortress in Passau.

■ **Literature:** M. Heuwieser, "R. von M.," in *Beiträge zur bayerischen Geschichte.* Festschrift S. Riezler (Gotha, 1913) 115–92; R. Bauerreiss, *Kirchengeschichte Bayerns,* vol. 6 (Augsburg, 1965) 55–59; F. Mader, *Tausend Passauer* (Passau, 1995) 197.

MANFRED EDER

Müller, *Gallus.* Theologian, born c. 1490 in Fürstenberg near Donaueschingen, died July 16, 1546 in Meran. He studied in Freiburg and Cologne; he was in Tübingen from 1509 onward, where he took his doctorate in theology and became professor of theology in 1519; he was appointed parish priest at the same time. He took part in the → Baden disputation in 1526. After the introduction of the Reformation, he lived in Rottenburg (1534-1535), then in Freiburg; he became court preacher in Innsbruck in 1535, and was counselor to the archduke and to the bishop of Brixen. The task of fighting the Baptist movement in Tyrol was entrusted to Müller. He took part in the religious dialogue of → Hagenau in 1540. He became parish priest in Meran in 1543.

■ **Literature:** *Mennonitisches Lexikon,* ed. Ch. Hege and Ch. Neff, vol. 3 (Karlsruhe, 1958) 176ff.—H. Hermelink, *Die theologische Fakultät in Tübingen vor der Reformation* (Tübingen, 1906) 203f.; A. Nägele, "Dr. G. M. von Fürstenberg," *Freiburger Diözesan-Archiv* 66 (1938) 97–164; G. Mecenseffy, *Quellen zur Geschichte der Täufer,* vol. 14: *Österreich,* 3. Teil (Gütersloh, 1983) 312, 316, 361, 373f., 377, 379, 383–86, 389f., 414, 430, 469, 491, 504, 527.

JOSEF GELMI

Münster, *Sebastian.* Hebraist, born January 20, 1488 in Ingelheim, died May 16, 1552 in Basle. He was a Franciscan from 1505 to 1529. After studies at various institutes of his Order, he became lector in Tübingen (1514) and in Basle (1518), where he edited writings by Martin Luther. He became lector in Heidelberg in 1521, and professor of Hebrew in Basle in 1529. He was also professor for Old Testament exegesis in 1542-1544. He wrote numerous works on Hebrew grammar and lexicography. He edited the Old Testament with a new Latin translation and a commentary which drew on the insights of Jewish authors (Basle, 1534-1536, 2nd ed. 1546). He became famous above all through his illustrated work of geography and history, the *Cosmographia* (Basle, 1544; often reprinted and translated).

■ **Works:** *Briefe S. M.* (Latin and German), ed. K. H. Burmeister (Frankfurt/Main, 1964).

■ **Literature:** *BBKL* 6:316–26; *TRE* 23:407ff.—K. H. Burmeister, *S. M.* (Wiesbaden, 1964); idem, *S. M.* (Basle, ²1969); I. Zinguer, ed., *L'Hebreu au temps de la renaissance* (Leiden, 1992).

KARL HEINZ BURMEISTER

■ **Additional Bibliography:** S. G. Burnett, "A Dialogue of the Deaf. Hebrew Pedagogy and Anti-Jewish Polemic in S. M.'s 'Messiahs of the Christians and the Jews,'" *ARG* 91 (2000) 168–90.

Müntzer, *Thomas.* Born December 20/21, 1490 in Stolberg (Harz), executed May 27, 1525 in Görmar. He came from an upwardly mobile family, and matriculated in Leipzig in 1506. In 1512, he moved to Frankfurt on the Oder, where he took the degree of master of arts. He was ordained priest and received a benefice in Brandenburg in 1514; later, he became provost of the canonesses' church in Frose. He came under the influence of Andreas von → Karlstadt and Martin Luther in Wittenberg c. 1517, and his criticism of scholasticism and the church hierarchy led to conflicts in Jüterbog as early as 1519. He was father confessor in the convent of Cistercian nuns in Weissenfels, and studied church history and mystical texts by authors such as Johannes Tauler. On Luther's recommendation, he came to Zwickau as preacher in 1520. Here, his theology, with its "spiritualist" and apocalyptic character, brought him into contact with the "prophets of → Zwickau," and controversies with both Catholics and followers of Luther led the municipal council to dismiss him in 1521. He made contact with the Hussite reform movement and went to Prague, where his "Prague Manifesto" proclaimed an anticlerical Reformation that would encompass the whole world. At that period, he hoped that this would be brought about by the Bohemians; later, he pinned his hopes on the princes of Saxony, and later still, on the rebellious peasants. He was expelled from Prague, and during the time of his "exile" (from the end of 1521 to March, 1523), he came to identify his own person very closely with his theological ideas.

As pastor of St. John's church in the electoral Saxon enclave of Allstedt, he consistently used the German language and introduced a reform of the Mass, the divine office, baptism, and burial services in keeping with his own theology in Eastertide of 1523. He was convinced that the human person can come to true faith in God only by following Christ in suffering and in despair over all earthly things, and this led him to criticize the Lutheran doctrine of → justification. His sermons, with their vigorous polemic, attracted many people, provoking conflicts with local Catholic rulers, and after violence broke out in Allstedt, Duke Johann of Saxony intervened (as Luther had wished). Müntzer tried unsuccessfully to win Johann over to his side in a sermon on Daniel 2 in July, 1524. When the people of Allstedt could no longer guarantee his safety, Müntzer went to Mühlhausen in Thüringen. Together with Heinrich Pfeiffer, a former Cistercian monk, he aggravated the already-existing tensions between the municipal council and the parish, and was therefore expelled. He went via Bibra (where he won over Hans Hut, later a Baptist leader) to Nuremberg, where he made a profound impression on Johann→ Denck and published his anti-Lutheran pamphlets. He then went to the southwest, meeting Johannes → Oecolampadius in Basle, and probably also encountering Balthasar → Hubmaier in Waldshut. He preached to the rebellious peasants (→ Peasants' War). In the meantime, the Reformation had been introduced into Mühlhausen, and Müntzer returned there in February, 1525. Since he looked on the rebellious peasants as warriors for the great Reformation and for the kingdom of Christ, he followed the biblical example of Gideon and took 300 men with him to Frankenhausen, intending to come to the peasants' aid. In his fiery sermons, he interpreted the struggle against the princes as the eschatological battle against the godless: God himself would fight on behalf of the peasants. Their defeat did not cause him to alter his theology: he understood this as a consequence of their "selfishness," and his own execution as a vicarious dying in their stead. He continued after his death to influence the traditions associated with Hut and the Hutterite Baptist movement. Socialist authors (including Friedrich Engels and Ernst Bloch) and historians in communist East Germany appealed to Müntzer as a pioneer and forerunner.

■ **Works:** *Schriften und Briefe,* ed. G. Franz (Gütersloh, 1968).

■ **Literature:** *OER* 3:99–102; *TRE* 23:414–36.—H.-J. Goertz, *Th. M.* (Munich, 1989); G. Vogler, *Th. M.* (Berlin, 1989); S. Bräuer and H. Junghans, eds., *Der Theologe Th. M.* (Munich, 1989).

GOTTFRIED SEEBASS

■ **Additional Bibliography:** B. Lohse, *Th. M. in neuer Sicht. M. im Licht der neueren Forschung und die Frage nach dem Ansatz seiner Theologie* (Göttingen, 1991); P. Matheson, "The Cornflower in the Wheatfield: Freedom and Liberation in T. M.," *ARG* 89 (1998) 41–54; T. Quilisch, *Das Widerstandsrecht und die Idee des religiösen Bundes bei Th. M.* (Berlin, 1999); A. Bradstock, "T. M.: Mystic and Apocalyptic Revolutionary?," *Reformation* (2000) 27–53.

Murner, *Thomas.* Franciscan Conventual (1490), preacher, writer, lawyer, Catholic controversial theologian, born December 24, 1475 (?) in Oberehnheim (Obernai, Alsace), where he died 1537. He was ordained priest in 1494 and studied thereafter in Freiburg (where he took his doctorate in theology in 1506), Cologne, Paris, Rostock, Krakow, Prague, Vienna, Trier (where he held lectures on Roman law in 1515), and Basle (where he took his doctorate in civil and canon law in 1519). He was lector and guardian in a number of monasteries (Freiburg, Berne, Frankfurt, Strasbourg, Speyer). He fled from Strasbourg to Oberehnheim in 1524 because of the Reformation, and from that town to Lucerne in the following year because of the → Peasants' War. He took part in the disputation of → Baden in 1526. He became parish priest in Lucerne in 1527, and in Oberehnheim in 1533.

He was a gifted writer, becoming *poeta laureatus* in 1505, a good observer with a critical eye, a man who favored reform and was interested in education. His writings cover several fields. The pedagogical writings, such as the *Logica memorativa* (a game designed to improve memory techniques: Krakow, 1507; often reprinted), were the fruit of his work as university teacher. He was the first to translate Vergil's *Æneid* and the *Institutions* of Justinian I into German. A dispute with Jakob → Wimpfeling led him to state his position on questions of the history of Alsace in the *Germania nova* (Strasbourg, 1502). The *Tractatus perutilis de phitonico contractu* (1499, no place of publication mentioned) takes its starting point in a lameness which Murner contracted as a child, and deals with the problems connected with witches. His book about the trial of Johannes Jetzer (1509) was a contribution to the controversy between Franciscans and Dominicans about the immaculate conception of Mary. His satires and poems are partly based on his sermons; under the influence of Sebastian → Brant and Johannes → Geiler von Kaysersberg, these take up the motif of the fool and engage in moral criticism (*Narrenbeschwörung* [Strasbourg, 1512]; *Schelmenzunft* [Frankfurt am Main, 1512]; the allegorical poem *Badenfahrt* [Strasbourg, 1514]; *Die Mühle von Schwindelsheim* [Strasbourg, 1515]; *Die Geuchmat* [Basle, 1519]).

From 1520 onward, Murner was involved in controversies with Reformers, in particular with Martin Luther, Martin → Bucer, and Huldrych Zwingli. His best-known work, *Von dem großen Lutherischen Narren,* an illustrated satirical poem, appeared in Strasbourg in 1522. He held a debate with Bucer on the Lord's Supper in Strasbourg in the following year. He stated his position on the Swiss Reformation in 1522, e.g., in the "Bear" satires about Berne and in controversial writings against Zwingli; he was the editor of the Proceedings of the Baden disputation. His last work, written between 1532 and 1535 and preserved in manuscript, is a German translation of the world chronicle of the Venetian humanist Marcus Antonius Sabellicus (facsimile ed., Karlsruhe, 1987). His polemical theological works centered on the Mass, the papacy, the defense of the Roman Catholic priesthood, and the veneration of the saints. Despite all his modernity and his criticism of his own age, Murner, in whose life and works we find a mixture of humanism and the endeavor to reform the church, remained ultimately the representative of a conservative, moralizing worldview which accepted the traditional authori-

ties. Thanks to his skillful use of the various literary styles and means of communication, he became one of the most important popular writers and satirists of the 16th century.

■ **Works:** *Th. M.s Deutsche Schriften,* ed. F. Schultz, 9 vols. (Strasbourg and Berlin, 1918–1931).—List of works: Klaiber nos. 2185–2241; Köhler *BF* 3:102–17; *VD 16* 14:287–97.

■ **Literature:** *NDB* 18:616ff.; *BBKL* 6:366–69; *TRE* 23:436ff.; *Encyclopédie de l'Alsace,* vol. 9 (Strasbourg, 1984) 5393ff.; *KThR* 3:19–32.—Th. von Liebenau, *Der Franziskaner Th. M.* (Freiburg, 1913); *Ausstellungskatalog, Th. M. Elsässischer Theologe und Humanist,* ed. der Badischen Landesbibliothek Karlsruhe—Bibliothèque Nationale et Universitaire Strasbourg (Karlsruhe, 1987); D. V. N. Bagchi, *Luther's Earliest Opponents* (Minneapolis, 1989); H. Heger, "Th. M.," in S. Füssel, ed., *Deutsche Dichter der frühen Neuzeit (1450–1600)* (Berlin, 1993) 296–310; M. Lienhard, "La controverse entre M. et Bucer au sujet de la Sainte Cène," *Revue d'Alsace* 122 (1996) 223–37.

HERIBERT SMOLINSKY

Musculus (Meusel), *Andreas.* Lutheran theologian, born November 29, 1514 in Schneeberg (Saxony), died September 29, 1581 in Frankfurt on the Oder. He began his studies in Leipzig in 1531, completing them in Wittenberg and Frankfurt on the Oder. He took his doctorate in theology in Frankfurt in 1546, and became rector of the university and professor of theology. He was an adviser to the electoral prince of Brandenburg, and became general superintendent of the marquisate of Brandenburg in 1566. As a → Gnesiolutheran, he attacked the → Augsburg Interim and Philippism. He played a central role in church politics in Brandenburg: he was the main author of the church order (1572), carried out visitations, and compiled a hymnal and a catechism. He was the first in Germany to draw up regulations for a girls' school.

■ **Works:** *VD 16* 14:7117–7266; Partial collection: *Teufelbücher in Auswahl,* ed. R. Stambaugh, vol. 4 (Berlin and New York, 1978).

■ **Literature:** *BBKL* 6:380f.; *NDB* 18:626f.—R. Mau, "Bekenntnis und Machtwort . . . ," in *450 Jahre Evangelische Theologie in Berlin,* ed. G. Besier and Ch. Gestrich (Göttingen, 1989) 39–64; F. Weichert, "A. M.," in *Berlinische Lebensbilder. Theologen,* ed. G. Heinrich (Berlin, 1990) 17–28; E. Koch, "'Das Geheimnis unserer Erlösung.' Die Christologie des A. M. . . . ," in *Veritas et Communicatio.* Festschrift U. Kühn (Göttingen, 1992) 143–56; idem, "A. M. und die Konfessionalisierung im Luthertum," in *Die lutherische Konfessionalisierung in*

Deutschland, ed. H.-Ch. Rublack (Gütersloh, 1992) 250–70.

BARBARA HENZE

■ **Additional Bibliography:** R. Kolb, "A. M. Katechismus aus den Vätern," *Lutherische Theologie und Kirche* 24 (2000) 114–34; A. Baumann-Koch, *Frühe lutherische Gebetsliteratur bei A. M. und Daniel Cramer* (Frankfurt/Main, 2001).

Musculus (Müslin), *Wolfgang.* Reformer, born September 8, 1497 in Dieuze (Lorraine), died August 30, 1563 in Berne. He entered the Benedictine monastery of Lixheim in 1512, but became an adherent of Martin Luther in 1518 and refused to accept election as prior. He went to Strasbourg in 1527 as student and fellow worker of Wolfgang → Capito, Martin → Bucer, and Matthäus → Zell. As preacher in Augsburg from 1531 to 1548, he played an outstanding role in the spread of the Reformation in that city. He became professor in Berne in 1549. He was a signatory to the → Wittenberg Concord in 1536 and took part in the religious dialogues of → Worms and → Regensburg in 1540-1541. He sought to promote the use of arguments (rather than mere polemic) in the controversies which raged among Protestants, and between Protestants and Catholics. He was an important patristic scholar, exegete, and systematic theologian, and is considered a representative of the path taken by the Reformation in "Upper Germany."
■ **Literature:** *TRE* 23:439ff.—R. Dellsperger et al., *W. M. (1497–1563) und die oberdeutsche Reformation* (Berlin, 1997).

RUDOLF DELLSPERGER

■ **Additional Bibliography:** H. J. Selderhuis, "Die Loci communes des W. M.," in *Ordenlich und fruchtbar.* Festschrift W. van't Spijker (Leiden, 1997) 171–90; R. Bodenmann, *W. M.* (Geneva, 2000); J. Th. Ford, "W. M. on the Office of the Christian Magistrate," *ARG* 91 (2000) 149–67.

Music and the Reformation
1. Martin Luther

No other event in church history is so intimately linked to music as the Reformation of Martin Luther—for music was an essential element of his personality. The Latin school had instructed him in *musica* as one of the "seven liberal arts," and he himself was a musician who sang in choirs and played the lute. This made it possible for him, in the course of his intellectual and religious development, to give music a place in his theology and to integrate music into the conception and praxis of Reformed worship (→ liturgy). Luther's understanding of music, with its cosmological and ethical orientation, and especially in the view (which goes back to Augustine) that music is a "gift of God," is fundamentally medieval, but it is also clear that Luther was familiar with some later theoretical writings about music, e.g., by Johannes Tinctoris (c. 1435-1511). In terms of the history of music, the fact that Luther attributed to music the "second place" after theology was tremendously important; and characteristically, he understood this ranking of music on the basis of his doctrine of → justification: "Since the free gift of the grace of God demands a joyful faith, music—as a *nobilis, salutaris, laeta creatura* [noble, salutary, joyful creature]—belongs to the Christian life, and is a *donum divinum et excellentissimum* [divine and most excellent gift] against Satan, the *spiritus tristitiae* [spirit of sadness]" (*Economion musices,* 1538). Here, Luther has in mind singing both in unison and in harmony, and the musical proclamation of the Word of God, and he appeals to the Dutch composer Josquin Desprez (c. 1440-1521) as his chief witness: *Sic praedicavit Deus evangelium etiam per musicam, ut videt in Josquin* ["Thus God preached the gospel through music too, as Josquin shows"] (WA 3:153)—an observation which has been analytically confirmed in recent musicological research. Two aspects are important in the Reformer's views about musical praxis: first, his position on unison music in worship ("chant"), and second, his position on part-song ("figural song"); in this context, music for the organ and other instruments is a peripheral concern.

(a) Unison Music in Worship

Here, the situation was made clear once and for all by Luther's important writings on the liturgy in the period from 1523 to 1525. His order of service, especially the Mass with the abolition of the consecration and the denial of any sacrificial character (→ Communion), demanded "the active participation of the community, which listened to the Word and responded in praise and confession. He considered the ideal form of active participation to be . . . the strophic vernacular hymn with rhymes" (Blankenburg, 1341). This later came to be known as the Protestant chorale (a concept which translates into German the term *cantus choralis* of the ancient church and transfers its liturgical importance to the new genre). Luther himself played a key role in the creation of such chorales. As a poet, he took up the ancient tradition and translated Latin hymns (e.g., *Nun komm, der Heiden Heiland*) and other liturgical texts (*Verleih uns Frieden gnädiglich*); he also added extra strophes to medieval German hymns (e.g., *Gelobet seist, du, Jesu Christ,* and *Mitten wir im Leben sind*). He also wrote poetic versions of biblical texts (e.g., *Vom Himmel hoch, da komm ich her*) and introduced metrical psalms into community worship as a new type of chorale (e.g., *Ein feste Burg ist unser Gott,* or *Aus tiefer Not schrei ich zu dir*). He himself composed the melodies to the three last-mentioned hymns and to several others; his musical secretary, Johann → Walter, composed the melodies for other hymns from Luther's pen (e.g., *Ach Gott vom Himmel sieh darein,* and *Mit Fried und Freud ich fahr dahin*). These provided models for the creation of numerous Reformation chorales in the course of the 16th century, some of which are still in use today; they have long found a place in Catholic worship too.

Luther did not simply replace the Latin chant with German chorales. Initially, he preserved alongside the community singing (in German) the traditional musical ordinary and proper of the Mass for the pastor and the choir, while some texts continued to be sung in Latin. It was only gradually that he introduced German texts, e.g., the "German Kyrie" and "German Gloria," and created the German form of the introit psalmody and musical cantillation tones for the readings and prayers. The starting-point of Luther's liturgical reform meant that he had an ambivalent relationship to the musical tradition. On the one hand, here as elsewhere, he was concerned about "continuity with the true apostolic church," from which he held that "the pope in Rome has fallen away" (Söhngen, 98); on the other hand, however, he recognized that in the ordinary of the Mass one "finds nothing about sacrifice, but simply praise and thanksgiving," and that therefore such texts could be retained.

(b) *Part-singing in Worship*

Luther did not make any equally specific observations on "figural music." Nor was this necessary, since the situation here was clear: the governing principle was the continuity displayed in the fact that Protestant and Catholic church music shared the same repertoire. Both churches sang the same polyphonic liturgical music in Latin—Masses, motets, canticles, and psalms—throughout the 16th century and beyond. Luther himself composed a short motet, *Non moriar, sed vivam* ("I shall not die, but live"). Here we should mention the fact that Ludwig Senfl (1486-1542/1543), the solidly Catholic kapellmeister at the court of Duke → William IV of Bavaria (who also employed Johannes → Eck), set Psalm 132/133 to music for the imperial parliament in Augsburg in 1530. The significant opening verse—*Ecce quam bonum, et quam jucundum habitare fratres in unum* ("Behold, how good and delightful it is when brethren dwell together in unity")—reminds us that Luther's age did not conceive of a specifically Catholic and a specifically Protestant church music, and this conviction remained throughout the 16th century, long after the confessional division had become an established fact.

Nevertheless, a large number of specifically Protestant pieces of figural music were composed in this period, especially polyphonic settings of chorale melodies. A key role here was played by Johann Walter and his *Geystlichen gesang Buchleyn* (Wittenberg, 1524, with a preface by Luther; often reprinted and revised). Walter conducted a (non-church) choir in Torgau, which provided the model for the Protestant church choirs which have made an important contribution to church life ever since. He was also the creator of the German Passion, which consisted of purely vocal music. For the words of the individual persons in the narrative, he followed the model of the unison Latin Passions, adapting the tone used for the scriptural text with masterly flexibility to the language of Luther's translation; for the words of the crowd, he composed simple four-part settings. Georg Rhau (1488-1548), who had published Luther's *Great Catechism* and other works in Wittenberg, also supported Luther's commitment to figural music in early Protestant worship; he published music for use in the Latin schools which provided the basic general preparation for liturgical music.

The German Reformation was an exceedingly important event in the history of music. It laid the foundations on which an independent Protestant church music could develop; with the "decline" of the Lutheran liturgy (to use Graff's term), this in its turn became one of the essential foundations of German music as a whole. This confessionalization was not an isolated process; there was continuous and varied contact with Catholic church music and Catholic spiritual music.

2. Jean Calvin and Huldrych Zwingli

A particularly clear light is shed on the role played by the Lutheran Reformation in the history of German music when we compare this with the effects of Jean Calvin's Reformation in the French-speaking regions. Calvin affirmed that since the link between music and the biblical word was indissoluble, only biblical psalms and canticles were to be sung in worship—his liturgy had no place for the preservation of the ecclesiastical musical tradition (or for the use of musical instruments). A key work here was Calvin's publication of 22 versified Psalms, *Aulcuns pseaulmes et cantiques mys en chant* (Strasbourg, 1539; the book also includes versifications by Clément Marot), which formed the basic stock for the so-called → Huguenot Psalter and for many settings of the Psalms for part-singing. The one-sidedness and purism of Calvin's understanding of music explains why his Reformation as a whole had only a slight significance in musical history—especially when compared to the impact made by Luther.

The Reformation of Huldrych Zwingli was wholly without significance in this context; indeed, it had a negative impact, since his liturgical reform went hand in hand with a rigorous rejection of singing and music. This went as far as the destruction of church organs. The reasons for this have not yet been completely clarified; Zwingli himself had had a good training in musical theory and praxis.

3. Post-Reformation Catholic Church Music

What influence did the Reformation have on Catholic church music? The situation is not simple; when we think of the Counter-Reformation, we may be inclined to think that the Jesuits played a central role here, but in fact they tended in the 16th century to be cautious about the use of church music. It was only in 17th-century Ger-

many that Jesuits in the Rhineland reacted to the central importance of the Protestant chorale singing by a new emphasis on hymns in the German language; the outstanding figure here is Friedrich Spee von Langenfeld (1591-1635). About the same time, the Jesuit Collegium Germanicum et Hungaricum in Rome, under its kapellmeister, Giacomo Carissimi (1605-1674), cultivated the Latin oratorio as an eloquent instrument of religious renewal.

In the context of the Catholic reform, we must mention the Congregation of the Oratory, founded by Philip Neri in Rome in 1575. Music played an essential role in their worship, which was the birthplace of the "oratorio" genre. The music in St. Philip's services was exclusively in Italian. The link with Luther's high esteem for the vernacular was not made explicitly at that period, but the Oratorians may have been aware of it; at any rate, however, this referred only to the polyphonic music sung by the choir, not to the participation by the community.

■ **Literature:** W. Blankenburg, "Martin Luther," in *Die Musik in Geschichte und Gegenwart*, ed. F. Blume, vol. 8 (Kassel, 1960) 1334–46 ; *RGG*[4] 4:1238–41.—P. Graff, *Geschichte der Auflösung der gottesdienstlichen Formen* (Göttingen, 1921), 2nd enlarged edition, 1937-1939; F. Blume, *Die evangelische Kirchenmusik* (Potsdam, 1931), 2nd (enlarged) edition published as *Geschichte der evangelischen Kirchenmusik* (Kassel, 1965); M. Jenny, *Zwinglis Stellung zur Musik im Gottesdienst* (Zurich, 1966); O. Söhngen, *Theologie der Musik* (Kassel, 1967); Ch. Garside, *The Origins of Calvin's Theology of Music* (Philadelphia, 1979); M. Jenny, *Luther, Zwingli, Calvin in ihren Liedern* (Zurich, 1983); C. Schalk, *Luther on Music* (St. Louis, 1988); H. Guicharrousse, *Les musiques de Luther* (Geneva, 1995); A. Schneiderheinze, *Johann Walter und die Musik der Reformation* (Torgau, 1996); J. C. Mahrenholz, "Luthers Lieder," *Luther* 68 (1997) 67–82; R. Wagner Öttinger, *Music as Propaganda in the German Reformation* (Aldershot, 2001).

GÜNTHER MASSENKEIL

Mutianus Rufus, *Conradus* (real name: Konrad Muth). Humanist, born October 15, 1470/1471 in Homberg, died March 30, 1526 in Gotha. He began his studies in Erfurt in 1486, taking the degree of master of arts in 1492. From 1494 onward, he studied in Bologna, Rome, and Ferrara (where he took his doctorate in canon law in 1501). He became a canon in St. Mary's collegiate church in Gotha in 1503; he was active as scholar (without any professional position) and as head of a humanist circle to which men such as Georg → Spalatin, → Crotus Rubeanus, Ulrich von → Hutten, Johann → Lang, and Eobanus Hessus (1488-1540) belonged. He initially supported Martin Luther, but later parted company with him.

■ **Sources:** *Der Briefwechsel des M. R.,* ed. C. Krause (Kassel, 1885); *Der Briefwechsel des C. M.,* ed. K. Gillert, 2 vols. (Halle, 1890).

■ **Literature:** *CEras* 2:473f.; *NDB* 18:656f.—F. Halbauer, *M. R. und seine geistesgeschichtliche Stellung* (Leipzig and Berlin, 1929; reprint, Hildesheim, 1972); L. W. Spitz, *The Religious Renaissance of the German Humanists* (Cambridge, Mass., 1963) 130–54; R. W. Scribner, "The Erasmians and the Beginning of the Reformation in Erfurt," *Journal of Religious History* 9 (1976/ 1977) 3–31; J.-C. Margolin, "M. R. et son modèle érasmien," in *L'Humanisme allemand* (Munich and Paris, 1979) 169–202; H. Junghans, *Der junge Luther und die Humanisten* (Göttingen, 1985); E. Kleineidam, *Universitas studii Erffordensis,* vol. 2 (Leipzig, ²1992).

PETER WALTER

Myconius (Mecum), *Friedrich.* Reformer, born December 26, 1490 in Lichtenfels, died April 7, 1546 in Gotha. He became a Franciscan in 1510 and was ordained priest in 1516. He came via Leipzig to Weimar, but was transferred back to Leipzig because of his Protestant preaching; he was then transferred to Annaberg, but fled to Zwickau in 1524. After a brief activity as preacher in electoral Buchholz, he became preacher (1524) and pastor (1525) in Gotha. He carried out a visitation of the district of Tenneburg in 1526. He became superintendent in Gotha in 1527. He played a central role in the visitations of Thüringen in 1527-1528 and 1533, and in the duchy of Saxony in 1539. Together with Justus → Menius, he was appointed general visitor of Thüringen in 1537. He was a central figure in the introduction of the Reformation in Leipzig and Annaberg. He took part in a disputation in Düsseldorf and in the religious dialogue in → Marburg (1529), the → Wittenberg Concord (1536), and the negotiations in Schmalkalden (1537), Frankfurt, Nuremberg (1539), and Hagenau (1540). His negotiations with King → Henry VIII in England in 1538 did not lead to any concrete results.

■ **Works:** *Geschichte der Reformation,* ed. O. Clemen (Leipzig, 1914; reprint, Gotha 1990); *Handlung und Disputation* (1527), ed. C. Schmitz, *Der Observant J. Heller von Korbach* (Münster, 1913).

■ **Literature:** P. Scherffig, *F. Mekum von Lichtenfels* (Leipzig, 1909); H.-U. Delius, "F. M., das Leben und Werk eines thüringischen Reformators" (dissertation, Münster, 1956); idem, *Der Briefwechsel des F. M.* (Tübingen, 1960); H. Ulbrich, *F. M. Lebensbild und neue Funde zum Briefwechsel des Reformators* (Tübingen, 1962); H.-U. Delius, "Königlicher Supremat oder evangelische Reformation der Kirche. Heinrich VIII. von England und die Wittenberger 1531–40," *Wissenschaftliche Zeitschrift der Universität Greifswald* 20 (1971) 283–91.

HANS-ULRICH DELIUS

Myconius (real name: Geisshüsler), *Oswald.* Swiss Reformer, born 1488 in Lucerne, died October 14, 1552 in Basle. After a humanist education in Rottweil and at the university of Basle (1510-1514), he became a schoolmaster in Basle and Zurich, and then from 1519 in Lucerne, whence he was expelled as a "Lutheran" in 1522. He taught in Einsiedeln, then again in Zurich from 1524 until the death of his friend Huldrych Zwingli, whose first biography he wrote. He then moved to Basle and became a preacher; he succeeded Johannes → Oecolampadius as professor and Antistes in 1532. The Basle Confession of 1534 is basically his work. Although his reconciliatory attitude on theological questions awakened suspicions for a time in Zurich and Berne, he proved an obstinate defender of ecclesiastical autonomy vis-à-vis the university and the city council. His few books are less important than his voluminous correspondence.

■ **Works:** *Vom Leben und Sterben H. Zwinglis* (Latin and German), ed. E. G. Rüsch (St. Gallen, 1979).

■ **Literature:** *CEras* 2:475; *BBKL* 6:412ff.; *NDB* 18:662f.—M. Kirchhofer, *O. M., Antistes der Baslerischen Kirche* (Zurich, 1813); K. R. Hagenbach, *J. Oekolampad und O. M., die Reformatoren Basels* (Elberfeld, 1859); W. Brändly, *Geschichte des Protestantismus in Stadt und Land Luzern* (Lucerne, 1956); J. V. Pollet, *Martin Bucer,* vol. 2 (Paris, 1962) 335–69; E. Fabian, "Zur Biographie und zur geplanten Erstausgabe der Briefe und Akten von O. M. und seiner Basler Mitarbeiter," *Zwingliana* 19 (1991/92) 115–30.

RAINER HENRICH

N

Nacchianti (Naclante, Naclantus), *Giacomo* (Jacopo). Dominican (1518), bishop of Chioggia (1544), born in Florence, died April 25, 1569 in

Chioggia. He studied in Bologna and was lector in Perugia from 1539 to 1541, then in Rome. He was present at all three periods of the Council of Trent. For a time, he was suspected of heresy, since he initially opposed the attribution of an equal rank to scripture and tradition as sources of the faith.

■ **Works:** *Opera,* 2 vols. (Venice, 1567).

■ **Literature:** *DThC* 11:1–3; *BBKL* 6:426ff.—F. Lauchert, *Die italienischen literarischen Gegner Luthers* (Freiburg, 1912) 584–612; A. Walz, *I domenicani al concilio di Trento* (Rome, 1961) passim.

VIOLA TENGE-WOLF

Nadal, *Jerónimo* (Hieronymus Natalis). Jesuit (1545), visitor and author, born August 11, 1507 in Palma de Mallorca, died April 3, 1580 in Rome. He studied in Alcalá and Paris, where he met → Ignatius of Loyola. He was ordained priest in Avignon in 1538. He was one of the founders of the college in Messina, where he was rector and professor from 1548 to 1552. His Order charged him with commissions in Spain and Portugal from 1552 to 1556. In 1558, he was appointed Assistant for the northern provinces; he was visitor in Spain, Portugal, the Netherlands, and Germany from 1560 to 1562. In 1562-1563, he was a member of the theological commission which met in Innsbruck with the aim of achieving an agreement between → Ferdinand I and Giovanni → Morone about the council. He attended the imperial parliament in Augsburg with Peter Canisius, as adviser to the papal legate, Giovanni Francesco Commendone, and was visitor in Germany until 1568. From 1565 to 1573, he was assistant for the Spanish province, and was vicar general of his Order in 1571-1572. His great achievement was the introduction of the *Constitutiones.* He lived in Hall in Tyrol as a writer from 1573 to 1579.

■ **Works:** *Evangelicae Historiae Imagines ex ordine Evangeliorum . . .* (Antwerp, 1593); *Adnotationes et Meditationes in Evangelia . . .* (Antwerp, 1595); *Epistolae . . .,* ed. F. Cervós, 4 vols. (Madrid, 1898–1905); *Pláticas espirituales . . . en Coimbra* (1561), ed. M. Nicolau (Granada, 1945); *Epistolae et Monumenta 5. Commentarii de Instituto SJ* (Rome, 1962); *Orationis observationes,* ed. M. Nicolau (Rome, 1964); *Scholia in Constitutiones SJ,* ed. M. Ruiz Jurado (Granada, 1976); *J. N. Der geistliche Weg. Erfahrungen und Lehre nach . . . "Orationes observationes,"* trans. J. Stierli (Einsiedeln, 1991); *Contemplation dans l'action. Écrits spirituels,* ed. F. Èvais and A. Lauras (Paris, 1994).

■ **Literature:** *DSp* 11:3–15.—C. Sommervogel, *Bibliothèque de la Compagnie de Jésus,* vol. 5 (Brussels and Paris 1894) 1517–20; A. Astraín, *Historia de la Compañia de Jesús en la Asistencia de España,* vols. 1–3 (Madrid, 1902–9); M. Nicolau, *J. N. Sus obras y doctrinas espirituales* (Madrid, 1949); L. Polgár, *Bibliographie sur l'histoire de la Compagnie de Jésus,* vol. 3 (Rome, 1990) 14532–570; J. W. O'Malley, "Unterwegs in alle Länder der Welt. Die Berufung des Jesuiten nach J. N.," *Geist und Leben* 59 (1986) 247–60; W. Bangert, "J. N.," in *Tracking the First Generation of Jesuits,* ed. Th. M. McCoog (Chicago, 1991).

JOHANNES WRBA

■ **Additional Bibliography:** J. E. Vercruysse, "N. et la Contre-Réforme," *Gregorianum* 72 (1991) 289–315; G. Palumbo, "I miracoli promessi e negati. Le 'Meditationes' di N. . . . ," in *Il pubblico dei santi,* ed. P. Golinelli (Rome, 2000) 285–319.

Nantes, Edict of. This edict, an expression of the royal power promulgated on April 13, 1598, guaranteed religious peace and thereby put an end to more than thirty years of military clashes between Catholics and → Huguenots in France. It consists of four documents; the *édit solennel et public* with 92 general articles; 56 secret articles; a document laying down the income of the pastors; and a document (April 30) which gives the Reformed party military guarantees, including 51 places of refuge. Although the edict granted a number of guarantees to the Protestants—freedom of conscience and of worship (restricted to certain places), recognition of their ecclesiastical structures, the possibility of founding schools, colleges, and academies, access to offices of state, and the establishment of four confessionally mixed courts of justice—it also gave the Catholic party a basis for reconquest. To begin with, the edict was applied conscientiously (1600-1620), but then it clashed with the continuation of the wars (1620-1629). It was observed as well as circumstances allowed between 1629 and 1661, but then it was applied "rigorously," which made persecutions possible. It was abolished by the Edict of Fontainebleau on October 10, 1685.

■ **Literature:** *Dictionnaire de l'Ancien Régime,* ed. L. Bely (Paris, 1996).—F. J. Baumgartner, *Change and Continuity in the French Episcopate. The Bishops and the Wars of Religion* (Durham, 1986); M. Pernot, *Les guerres de religion en France* (Paris, 1987); G. Deregnaucourt, *La vie religieuse en France aux XVIᵉ, XVIIᵉ, XVIIIᵉ siècles* (Gap, 1994); G. de Groër, *Réforme et Contre-Réforme en*

France (Paris, 1995); O. Christin, *La paix de religion. L'Autonomisation de la raison politique au XVIᵉ siècle* (Paris, 1997); B. Cottret, *1598. L'Édit de N.* (Paris, 1997); G. Saupin, *L'Édit de N. en 30 questions* (Mougon, 1997); B. Roussel, ed., *Coexister dans l'intolérance. L'Édit de N. (1598)* (Paris and Geneva, 1998); M. Venard, "La France avant l'édit de N.," in *L'acceptation de l'autre. De l'édit de N. à nos jours,* ed. J. Delumeau (Paris, 2000) 21–34; L. Theis, "La France de L'édit de N.," in *L'acceptation de l'autre. De l'édit de N. à nos jours,* 35–44.

GERALD CHAIX

■ **Additional Literature:** K. Cameron, ed., *The Adventure of Religious Pluralism in Early Modern France* (Oxford, 2000); R. Whelan, *Toleration and Religious Identity: The Edict of Nantes and Its Implications in France, Britain and Ireland* (Dublin 2003).

Naumburg, assembly of princes. The Protestant imperial Estates assembled in Naumburg from January 20 to February 8, 1561 with the aim of securing a theological unification of the Protestant party on the basis of the → Confessio Augustana, and a common position with regard to the Council of Trent, which → Pius IV had convoked anew. Neither aim was achieved, since the Flacians (supporters of Matthias → Flacius; → Gnesio-lutherans) and the Philippists (supporters of Philipp Melanchthon) could not agree on the binding text of the Confessio Augustana: electoral prince → Frederick III of the Palatinate pleaded for the *Confessio Augustana Variata* of 1540, since this did not completely exclude the Reformed understanding of the Lord's Supper, but Duke → Johann Friedrich of Saxony insisted, in keeping with orthodox Lutheranism, on the *Invariata* of 1530. Johann Friedrich caused the breakdown of the negotiations by leaving Naumburg early. The invitation to the council, which Emperor → Ferdinand I had sent to the assembled princes, was harshly refused.

■ **Literature:** R. Calinich, *Der Naumburger Fürstentag 1561* (Gotha, 1870); K. Schornbaum, "Zum Tage von Naumburg 1561," *ARG* 8 (1910/11) 181–214; Jedin vol. 4/1; H. Rabe, *Deutsche Geschichte 1500–1600* (Munich, 1991).

ANTON SCHINDLING

Nausea, *Friedrich.* Catholic controversial theologian, born 1491/1496 in Waischenfeld (Upper Franconia), died February 6, 1552 in Trent. He took his bachelor's and master's degrees at the university of Leipzig in 1514, and became a teacher in Bamberg in 1517. He was in Pavia and Padua from 1518-1519 onward, and took his doctorate in civil and canon law in Pavia in 1523. He wrote extensively, and corresponded with → Erasmus of Rotterdam, whom he praised lavishly in his book *Monodia* (1536). In 1524, he was appointed Count of the Latin Palace and notary of the Apostolic See, and he took part in the imperial parliament and Convent in → Regensburg as secretary to Cardinal Lorenzo → Campeggi. Thereafter, he was cathedral preacher in Mainz, an activity to which 25 volumes of sermons bear witness. Despite his eloquence, he had no lasting success as a public speaker. He became doctor of theology in Siena in 1534, and King Frederick I appointed him in the same year court preacher and counselor. He became coadjutor to Bishop Johannes → Fabri of Vienna in 1538. Nausea was instructed by the emperor to take part in the religious dialogues in → Hagenau (1540) and → Worms (1540-1541), and he accepted at the urging of the pope, although he himself completely rejected such dialogues, since he believed that only a universal council could decide on the many controversial doctrines involved. He became bishop of Vienna in 1541; his only success was as preacher and as author of a *Catechismus catholicus,* since he was basically unable to redress the problems of his small diocese, which was hopelessly impoverished and under constant threat from the Turks. He attended the Council of Trent as orator of King Ferdinand from September, 1551 to January, 1552, taking part in the debates on the Eucharist, on the → chalice for the laity, penance, the Mass, priestly ordination and the anointing of the sick. Although Nausea was a humanist, diplomat, preacher, and bishop who did exemplary work in his own period, he was forgotten soon after his death.

■ **Principal Works:** *De reformanda ecclesia* (Mainz, 1527); *Evangelicae veritatis homiliarum centuriae quatuor* (Cologne, 1532) 51540; *Libri mirabilium septem* (Cologne, 1532); *Predigt evangelischer Wahrheit über alle Evangelien* (Cologne, 1535, often reprinted); *Catechismus catholicus* (Cologne, 1543, ²1552/53); *Epistolarum miscellanearum ad Fridericum Nauseam Blancicampianum episcopum Viennensem libri X* (Basle, 1550).—List of works: H. Gollob, *Bischof F. N. Probleme der Gegenreformation* (Vienna, 1952; Niewkoop, ²1967) 136–53; Klaiber nos. 213–19.

■ **Sources:** *ARCEG* 1 (1959) 334–44; 2 (1960) 547–53; 4 (1969) 353ff.; *ZKG* 20 (1900) 500–545; 21 (1901) 537–94; *CT* vols. 4–6, 7/2–3, 8–10, 12²–13.

■ **Literature:** *KThR* 2:92–103; *BBKL* 6:506–13; *TRE* 24:230–35; *NDB* 18:75f.—J. Metzner, *F. N. aus Waischenfeld, Bischof von Wien* (Bamberg, 1884); E. Wenzel, *F. N., Bischof von Wien, ein Kirchenfürst als Pädagoge* (Leitmeritz, 1890); H. Jedin, "Das konziliare Reformprogramm F. N.s," *HJ* 77 (1958) 229–53; J. Beumer, "F. N. und seine Wirksamkeit zu Frankfurt, auf den Colloquien zu Hagenau und Worms und auf dem Trienter Konzil," *Zeitschrift für Katholische Theologie* 94 (1972) 29–45; H. Immenkötter, "F. N. und die Augsburger Religionsverhandlungen," in *Reformatio Ecclesiae. Festschrift E. Iserloh* (Paderborn, 1980) 467–86; K. Fischer, "Verwaltung und Hofleitung unter dem Wiener Bischof N. (1541–52)" (diss., Vienna, 1981); E. Honee, "Über das Vorhaben und Scheitern eines Religionsgesprächs. Ein Verfahrensstreit auf dem Konvent von Hagenau (1540)," *ARG* 76 (1985) 195–215; I. Bezzel, "Das humanistische Frühwerk F. N.s (1496– 1552)," *Archiv für die Geschichte des Buchwesens* 26 (1986) 217–37; G. Ph. Wolf, "F. N.," *ZBKG* 61 (1992) 59–101.

HERBERT IMMENKÖTTER

Neander, *Michael* (real name: Michael Neumann). Pedagogue and philologist, born 1525 in Sorau/Zary (Lower Lausitz), died April 26, 1495 in Ilfeld (Harz). He began his studies under Martin Luther and Philipp Melanchthon in Wittenberg in 1543, and became a teacher in Nordhausen in 1547. Three years later, he moved to the monastery school in Ilfeld, becoming its rector and administrator in 1559. He was a learned humanist in many disciplines, especially well acquainted with the classical languages. He united Protestant piety with a classical education and practical knowledge, and was one of the most important Protestant schoolmasters in the 16th century. He became famous above all thanks to his textbooks (particularly his Greek and Hebrew grammars, and his compendia of history, geography, and physics). He also published editions of more than forty classical texts. His preface (340 pages) to the *Graecae linguae erotemata* (Basle, 1565; often reprinted) amounts to an attempt at writing the history of literature. His theology was based on that of Luther, and he was also greatly influenced by Johannes Tauler.

■ **Works:** *Bedenken [...], wie ein Knabe zu leiten und zu unterweisen* (Eisleben, 1580, often reprinted; also printed in R. Vormbaum, *Die evangelischen Schulordnungen des 16.Jh.* (Gütersloh, 1860) 746–65); *Theologia Christiana* (Leipzig, 1595); F. Latendorf, ed., *M. N.s*

deutsche Sprichwörter (Schwerin, 1864); *VD 16* 14:342–428 (bibliography).

■ **Literature:** M. Klemm, *M. N. und seine Stellung im Unterrichtswesen des 16.Jh.* (Grossenhain, 1884); H. Heineck, *Aus dem Leben M. N.s.* (Nordhausen, 1925); E. Koch, "M. N. als Theologe," in *Bekenntnis zur Kirche. Festschrift E. Sommerlath* (Berlin, 1960) 112–25; M. Büttner, "M. N. und das erste Geographielehrbuch in Deutschland," in idem, ed., *Zur Entwicklung der Geographie* (Paderborn and Munich, 1982) 97–112.

WERNER RAUPP

O

Obscure Men, Letters of (*Epistolae obscurorum virorum*). This was the high point of humanistic satire in Germany, originating in the controversy which broke out in 1511 between the Hebraist Johannes → Reuchlin and Johannes → Pfefferkorn, a convert from Judaism, about the confiscation of the religious books of the Jews. The immediate occasion for the composition of this satire was the *Clarorum virorum epistolae,* letters sent by "prominent" scholars to Reuchlin, which he published in 1514 as testimonies to solidarity among the humanists. In autumn of 1515, under a fictional printer's name and location, appeared a collection of 41 letters, written with malicious skill in a rudimentary Latin. Their authors, allegedly pupils of Master Ortwinus → Gratius in Cologne, revealed themselves to be the depraved products of a perverted scholasticism; the real author of most of these texts is held to be the Erfurt humanist → Crotus Rubeanus. A second edition appeared in 1516, with an appendix of seven letters from the pen of Ulrich von → Hutten, who was chiefly responsible for Part II of the *Epistolae,* a collection of 62 anonymous texts which appeared in 1517 and made a direct contribution, with polemic and propaganda, to the Reuchlin controversy. The *Epistolae* have their place in a tradition of facetious university, monastic, and jesting satires and comical tales. The polarizing power of their vigorous caricatures is due to their turning the conventions of humanistic epistolary literature upside-down by the conscious use of a barbarous style.

■ **Editions:** E. Böcking, *U. Hutteni Operum supplementum,* 2 vols. (Leipzig, 1864–70); A. Bömer, *Epistolae obscurorum virorum,* 2 vols. (Heidelberg, 1924; reprint, Aalen, 1978).—Translation: P. Amelung, *Briefe der*

Dunkelmänner (Munich, 1964); *Dunkelmännerbriefe* (Frankfurt/Main, 1991).

■ **Literature:** G. Hess, *Deutsch-lateinische Narrenzunft* (Munich, 1971); H. J. Overfield, *Humanism and Scholasticism in Late Medieval Germany* (New Jersey, 1984); R. Hahn, "Huttens Anteil an den Epistolae obscurorum virorum," *Pirckheimer-Jahrbuch* 4 (1988) 79–111; E. Meuthen, "Die Epistolae obscurorum virorum," in *Ecclesia militans.* Festschrift R. Bäumer, vol. 2 (Paderborn, 1988) 53–80.

FRANZ JOSEF WORSTBROCK

■ **Additional Bibliography:** J. V. Mehl, "Printing the Metaphor of Light and Dark. From Renaissance Satire to Reformation Polemic," in *Books Have Their Own Destiny.* Festschrift R. V. Schnucker (Kirksville, 1998) 83–92; S. Kivistö, *Creating Anti-eloquence: 'Epistolae obscurum virorum' and the Humanist Polemics on Style* (Helsinki, 2002).

Ochino, *Bernardino.* Preacher, born c. 1487 in Siena, died 1564/1565 in Slavkov (Austerlitz). He became a Franciscan Observant in 1503/1504, and became provincial minister of the Sienese province in 1523, and vicar general of the north Italian province in 1533. He joined the Capuchins, because their way of life was stricter, in 1534, becoming vicar general in 1538; he was reelected to this position in 1541. He preached in all the major cities in Italy, attracting huge crowds. He was summoned to Rome on suspicion of heresy in 1542, but after meeting Pietro Martire → Vermigli in Florence, he fled via Graubünden to Geneva, where Jean Calvin permitted him to preach. He journeyed in 1545 via Basle and Strasbourg to Augsburg, and went to England in 1547, remaining there until → Mary I became queen in 1553. He then returned to Switzerland, and became pastor in Zurich in 1555, but was expelled from the city in 1563 because of his antitrinitarianism. He spent his last years in Poland and Moravia.

■ **Literature:** *DSp* 11:575–91; *BBKL* 6:1085–89; *TRE* 25:1–6.—K. Benrath, *B. O. von Siena* (Leipzig, 1875; reprint, Nieuwkoop, 1968); Ph. McNair and J. Tedeschi, "New Light on B. O.," *Bibliothèque d'humanisme et renaissance* 35 (1973) 289–301; V. Marchetti, *Gruppi ereticali senesi del cinquecento* (Florence, 1975); M. Firpo, *Inquisizione romana e controriforma* (Bologna, 1992).

GIUSEPPE ALBERIGO

■ **Additional Bibliography:** E. Campi, *Michelangelo e Vittoria Colonna. Un dialogo artistico-teologico ispirato da B. O.* (Turin, 1994); E. Campi, "B. O.'s Christology and 'Mariology' in His Writings of the Italian Period (1538–42)," in *Protestant History and Identity in 16th Century Europe* (Aldershot, 2002) 108–22.

Oecolampad(ius) (real name: Huschin, Huszschyn), *Johannes.* Humanist and reformer of Basle, born 1482 in Weinsberg (Württemberg), died November 23, 1531 in Basle. He studied under Jakob → Wimpfeling in Heidelberg from 1499 to 1506, taking the degree of master of arts in 1503; he also spent a short period in Bologna, where he may have studied law. He served the Palatinate as tutor to the princes in Mainz from 1506 to 1508, and then continued his study of theology and of the classical languages, probably returning to Heidelberg; the year of his ordination to the priesthood is unknown. He received the preacher's prebend at St. Johannes in Weinsberg in 1510; he was in Tübingen in 1513, where he had contact with Philipp Melanchthon and Johannes → Reuchlin. He returned to Heidelberg, and was in Basle in 1515-1516 as a collaborator of → Erasmus. In 1518, he was appointed penitentiary at the Minster in Basle, took his doctorate in theology, and became cathedral preacher in Augsburg. He began to speak out in support of Martin Luther, but withdrew to the monastery of Altomünster in 1520 in order to clarify his own position. In this period, he studied the church fathers and wrote sermons and his *Iudicium de Luthero.* He left Altomünster in 1522; after a brief period as chaplain in the castle of Franz von → Sickingen, he settled in Basle for good in November, 1522. He worked as corrector in the printing press of Andreas Cratander, published translations of the church fathers, and began to hold lectures at the university, which were also open to the public. Oecolampadius became the leader of the Reformation movement in Basle, and soon became a close friend of Huldrych Zwingli. He was constantly in contact with the Reformers in Strasbourg and Constance. He became professor in 1523 and pastor first in St. Martin's (1525), then in the Minster (1529). In the controversy about the → Eucharist in Upper Germany (1524-1529), Oecolampadius maintained a symbolic understanding of the Lord's Supper (*De genuine verborum . . . expositione* [Strasbourg, 1525]; *Antisyngrammata* [Zurich, 1526], written against

225

Johannes → Brenz and others). On November 1, 1525, he held the first celebration of the Protestant Lord's Supper in Basle; the Protestant order of service for the city was published in 1526. Oecolampadius took part in the disputations in → Baden and Berne (1528), and in the religious dialogue in → Marburg. The council in Basle finally enforced the Reformation in 1529, after much hesitation and after conflicts which culminated in the destruction of church images (→ Art and Reformation). Oecolampadius created the special ministry of "presbyter" in 1520 to carry out the controversial function of church discipline, but he succeeded only in part in making his ideas a reality. In addition to this question, his last years were occupied by the struggle against the → Baptist movement, by church visitations, and by the reorganization of the school sector. His last journey, with Martin → Bucer and Ambrosius → Blarer, was at the service of the Reformation in the cities of Ulm, Memmingen, and Biberach. He died only six weeks after Zwingli. His widow, Wibrandis Rosenblatt (1504-1564), whom he had married in 1528, married Wolfgang → Capito in 1532, and Bucer in 1542.

■ **Catalogue of Works:** E. Staehelin, *O.-Bibliographie* (1918/28) (Nieuwkoop, ²1963); *VD 16* 15:110–28.

■ **Sources:** E. Staehelin (compiler), *Briefe und Akten zum Leben O.s,* 2 vols. (Leipzig, 1927–34; reprint, New York and London, 1971) (supplementary material in *Basler Zeitschrift für Geschichte und Altertumskunde* 65 [1965] 165–94); E. Dürr and P. Roth, eds., *Aktensammlung zur Geschichte der Basler Reformation,* 6 vols. (Basle, 1921–50).

■ **Literature:** *BBKL* 6:1133–50; *TRE* 25:29–36.—K. R. Hagenbach, *J. O. und Oswald Mykonius, die Reformatoren Basels, Leben und ausgewählte Schriften* (Elberfeld, 1859); E. Staehelin, ed., *Das Buch der Basler Reformation* (Basle, 1929); idem, *Das theologische Lebenswerk J. O.s.* (Leipzig, 1939; reprint, New York and London, 1971); P. Roth, *Durchbruch und Festsetzung der Reformation in Basel* (Basle, 1942); G. Lenckner, "Wie hiess J. Ökolampad von Haus aus?," *Württembergisches Franken* 46 (1962) 52f.; A. Demura, "Church Discipline according to J. O. in the Setting of His Life and Thought" (dissertation, Princeton, 1964); *Gestalten der Kirchengeschichte,* ed. M. Greschat, vol. 5 (Stuttgart, 1981) 117–28.

CHRISTOPH WEISMANN

■ **Additional Bibliography:** K. Hammer, "Der Reformator O.," *Zwingliana* 19 (1991/92) 157–70; Th. A. Fudge, "Icarus of Basel? O. and the Early Swiss Reformation," *Journal of Religious History* 21 (1997) 268–84; O. Kuhr, *Die Macht des Bannes und der Busse.*

Kirchenzucht und Erneuerung der Kirche bei J. O. (Berne, 1999).

Oldendorp, *Johannes.* Lawyer, born 1480/1490 in Hamburg, died June 3, 1567 in Marburg. After studies in Bologna and other towns, he alternated all his life between university teaching and political activity in Rostock, Frankfurt on the Oder, Greifswald, Lübeck, Cologne, and Marburg, where he became professor in 1543. He was the first to propose a Protestant doctrine of natural law, laying the foundations in his book *Wat byllick unn recht ys* (Rostock, 1529), which makes fairness a comprehensive legal principle, and in his *Iuris naturalis gentium et civilis eisagoge* (Cologne, 1539). His book *Van Ratslagende* (Rostock, 1530) is a classic presentation of the structure and spirit of a Christian society.

■ **Works:** *Opera,* 2 vols. (Basle, 1559; reprint, Aalen, 1966).—Selected works: E. Wolf, ed., *Quellenbuch zur Geschichte der deutschen Rechtswissenschaft* (Frankfurt/Main, 1949) 49–101.—Catalogue: *VD 16* 15:151–63.

■ **Literature:** *TRE* 25:235.—E. Wolf, *Grosse Rechtsdenker der deutschen Geistesgeschichte* (Tübingen, ⁴1963) 138–76; H. Maier, *Die ältere deutsche Staats- und Verwaltungslehre (Polizeiwissenschaft).* (Munich, ²1980); M. Stolleis, *Geschichte des öffentlichen Rechts in Deutschland,* vol. 1 (Munich, 1988); B. Pahlmann, "J. O.," in G. Kleinheyer and J. Schröder, eds., *Deutsche und europäische Juristen aus neun Jahrhunderten* (Heidelberg, ⁴1996) 313–16.

ALEXANDER HOLLERBACH

Olevian, *Caspar.* Reformed theologian, born August 8, 1536 in Trier, died March 15, 1587 in Herborn. He studied civil and canon law in Orleans and Bourges, taking his doctorate in law in 1557. He then studied theology in Geneva and Zurich. He took part in the attempt to introduce the Reformation into Trier in 1559. In 1560, he became head of the Collegium Sapientiae in Heidelberg, and was appointed professor of theology in 1561 and pastor in St. Peter's and in the Holy Spirit church in 1562. Under electoral Prince → Frederick III, he was a member of the Heidelberg ecclesiastical council. He was one of those who played a decisive role in the conversion of the Palatinate to the Reformed confession in 1563, through the introduction of the → Heidelberg catechism and a corresponding church order. In 1564, he took part with Lutheran theologians from Württemberg in the Colloquium of Maulbronn on the Lord's Supper and Christology; in 1566, he took part with the Lutheran pastors of the Upper Palatinate in the religious dialogue of Amberg. The reintroduction of the Lutheran confession in the electoral Palatinate in 1576-1577 led to his dismissal from all his offices. He became court preacher and tutor to the princes in Berleburg in 1577, and influenced the establishment of the Reformed Church structures there. He became pastor in Herborn and professor at the newly founded college there in 1584. In philosophy, he followed Petrus Ramus; along with Johannes Piscator and Zacharias → Ursinus, he brought the teachings of Jean Calvin and Heinrich → Bullinger to Germany, presenting this doctrine in a covenantal theology centered on Christ, which had a strong influence on Johannes Coccejus.

■ **Principal Works:** *De substantia foederis gratuiti inter Deum et electos* (Geneva, 1585); *Der Gnadenbund Gottes* (Herborn, 1590), facsimile edition, ed. G. Franz et al. (Cologne, 1994).

■ **Literature:** *TRE* 25:237ff.

HEINER FAULENBACH

■ **Additional Bibliography:** L. D. Bierma, *German Calvinism in the Confessional Age. The Covenant Theology of C. O.* (Grand Rapids, Mich., 1997); R. S. Clark, "The Catholic-Calvinist Trinitarianism of C. O.," *Westminster Theological Journal* 61 (1999) 15–39.

Ordination. The Reformers took it for granted that a public ministry in the church required ordination (*rite vocatus:* Confessio Augustana 14; Calvin, *Inst* 4:3 and 10). Lutheran theologians thought here of the one *ministerium* of the public proclamation of the gospel and administration of the sacraments; Reformed theologians thought of the → ministries of pastor, teacher, elder, and deacon. Ordination took the form of a laying-on of hands, understood as an effective invocation of the Holy Spirit. In the Reformed understanding, it presupposed that those ordained had been elected by the community; the ordination itself was carried out by the parish pastors (*Inst* 4:3 and 16). Ordination is valid *iure divino,* whereas the distinction between bishops and priests is only *iure humano* (Melanchthon, *Tractatus de potestate* 63-66, appealing to Jerome); the bishops at that time refused to ordain Protestant pastors for the

parishes. Ordination is not counted by the Reformation among the sacraments in the strict sense, although neither Philipp Melanchthon nor Jean Calvin had reservations about using this term (Apologia for Confessio Augustana 13:11; *Inst* 4:19 and 28).

■ *LThK*[3] 7:1111f. (unabridged version).

■ **Literature:** *Gemeinde—Amt—O.,* ed. F. Viering (Gütersloh, 1970); J. Heubach, *Die O. zum Amt der Kirche* (Berlin, 1956); H. Lieberg, *Amt und O. bei Luther und Melanchthon* (Berlin, 1962); F. Schulz, "Evangelische O.," *Jahrbuch für Liturgik und Hymnologie* 17 (1972) 1–54; idem, "O. im Gemeindegottesdienst," *Jahrbuch für Liturgik und Hymnologie* 23 (1979) 1–31; *Handbuch der Liturgik,* ed. H.-Ch. Schmidt-Lauber and K.-H. Bieritz (Leipzig, 1995) 371–91.

ULRICH KÜHN

■ **Additional Bibliography:** G. D. Gallaro, "Martin Lutero sull' ordinazione ministeriale," *Kanon* 13 (1996) 185–96; A. R. Sander, "'. . . haben wir im durch die Christliche offentliche O. . . . das predigambt . . . befholen.' Theologische Anmerkungen zu einem O.-Zeugnis des 16.Jh.," in *Festhalten am Bekenntnis der Hoffnung.* Festschrift R. Slenczka (Erlangen, 2001) 99–118; J. M. Kittelson, "Historical and Systematic Theology in the Mirror of Church History: The Lessons of 'Ordination' in 16th Century Saxony," *ChH* 71 (2002) 743–73.

Original sin

1. The *Reformers* emphasized above all three determinants of original sin: the loss of the fear of God, the inability to believe confidently in God, and concupiscence, which they also formally identified with original sin (Confessio Augustana 2: *vere sit peccatum*). Here the Augustinian link between original and sin and concupiscence, which Martin Luther had repristinated, became a question of controversial theology which linked fundamental definitions of theological anthropology with a specific understanding of the doctrine of → justification and of grace.

EBERHARD SCHOCKENHOFF

2. The *Council of Trent* refused to accept an indissoluble link between original sin and concupiscence, declaring in its decree on original sin (DH 1510-1516) that Adam by his sin lost both for himself and for us the holiness (*sanctitas*) and righteousness (*iustitia*) which God had bestowed on him. In terms of its origin, original sin is one single reality (*origine unum est*), but at the same

time, it is in all persons and belongs to each of them (*omnibus inest unicuique proprium*)— against the doctrine of imputation proposed by Albert → Pigge and → Ambrosius Catharinus. Original sin is transmitted by procreation, not by imitation (*propagatione, non imitatione*), so that even small children have original sin. Through baptism, the guilt of original sin is removed, but concupiscence remains. This comes from sin, and inclines us to sin, but it is not itself a genuine sin.

HELMUT HOPING

■ *LThK*³ 3:744–45 (s.v. Erbsünde); 6:271–74 (s.v. Konkupiszenz) (unabridged version).
■ **Literature:** *RGG*⁴ 3:1394–97.—T. Kleffmann, *Die Erbsünde-Lehre in sprachtheologischem Horizont* (Tübingen, 1994); S. Greiner, "Konkupiszenz und Busse," *Catholica* (Münster) 51 (1997) 53–83; B. Pitkin, "Nothing but Concupiscence. Calvin's Understanding of Sin and the 'Via Augustini,'" *Calvin Theological Journal* 34 (1999) 347–69.

■ **Additional Literature:** A. N. Lane, "Albert Pighius's Controversial Work on Original Sin," *Reformation and Renaissance Review* 2 (2000) 29–61.

Orozco, *Alonso de.* Blessed (1882), Augustinian Hermit (1522), theologian and spiritual writer, born October 17, 1500 in Oropesa near Toledo, died September 19, 1591 in Madrid. He was prior in several monasteries and held other offices in his Order. He was preacher and adviser to → Charles V and → Philip II, and wrote voluminous exegetical, ascetical, and homiletic works.

■ **Works:** *Recopilación de todas las obras* (Valladolid, 1554, often reprinted); *Obras,* 7 vols. (Madrid, 1736, often reprinted); *Antología de sus obras,* ed. J. Díez (Madrid, 1991).
■ **Literature:** *DSp* 1:392–95; *DHEE* 3:1842.—A. J. Bulovas, *El amor divino en la obra del Beato A. de O.* (Madrid, 1973); G. Díaz Díaz, *Hombres y Documentos de la Filosofía Española,* vol. 1. (Madrid, 1980) 189–95; T. Aparicio López, *Fray A. de O.* (Valladolid, 1991); R. Lazcano, "Bibliografia fundamental del Beato A. de O.," *La Ciudad de Dios* 204 (1991) 205–54; idem, ed., *Figura y obra de A. de O.* (Madrid, 1992); K. Reinhardt, *Bibelkommentare spanischer Autoren,* vol. 2 (Madrid, 1999) 139–47.

FERNANDO DOMÍNGUEZ

Orzechowski (Orichovius), *Stanisław,* polemical Polish author, born November 11, 1513 in Orze-

chowice near Przemyśl, died end of 1566. He studied in Krakow (1526-1528), Vienna, Wittenberg, and Leipzig (where he met Philipp Melanchthon in 1531). He was in Italy from 1531 to 1537, and again from 1538 to 1541 (Padua, Bologna, Venice, Rome). In 1541, he returned to Przemyśl and was ordained priest, becoming parish priest in Zórawica. In the following years, he wrote polemic works (*Fidelis subditus* [Krakow, 1543]) against the papacy (→ primacy) and → celibacy (*De lege coelibatus contra Siricium* [Krakow, 1548]) and on other themes, worked actively for Christian reunification, and defended the Orthodox church (*Baptismus Ruthenorum* [Krakow, 1544]). When he married in 1551, he was excommunicated and stripped of all his ecclesiastical benefices and prebends. Orzechowski appealed in 1552 to the Polish parliament, to the university of Krakow, and even to → Julius III, and he was dispensed from celibacy in 1561. Despite these conflicts with his bishop, Orzechowski also wrote polemically against Protestantism (*Fidei Catholicae Confessio* [Krakow, 1561]). His political theories followed the understanding of the state in classical antiquity.

■ **Works:** *Orichoviana,* ed. J. Korzeniowski, vol. 1 (Krakow, 1891); *Wybór pism,* ed. J. Starnawski (Breslau, 1972).
■ **Literature:** *Polski Słownik Biograficzny,* vol. 24 (Breslau, 1979) 287–92; *Słownik polskich teologów katolickich,* vol. 3 (Warsaw, 1982) 265–71; *BBKL* 6:1294ff.

JAN KOPIEC

Osiander, (1) *Andreas.* Reformer, born December 19, 1496/1498 in Gunzenhausen, died October 17, 1552 in Königsberg. He matriculated in Ingolstadt in 1515, and his humanistic studies gave him a mastery of Hebrew and Greek. After his ordination to the priesthood in 1520, he was appointed teacher of Hebrew in the Augustinian monastery in Nuremberg, where he became acquainted with the writings of Martin Luther. He was appointed preacher at St. Laurence's in 1522, and did his utmost to spread the Reformation movement. In the religious dialogue of March, 1525, at which Osiander spoke on behalf of the Protestant party, the city accepted the Reformation, and Osiander's expert memoranda in the following years translated the theology of the Reformation into new social and ecclesiastical structures; he helped repel both Zwinglians and → Baptists, and defended the Reformation of the city vis-à-vis the emperor and the empire. The church order which he elaborated between 1530 and 1533 led to serious tensions with his colleagues in office and with the council secretary, Lazarus → Spengler. He irritated the city council by the controversy about general absolution and by his rigid position in religious negotiations both within the → Schmalkaldic League and with the emperor. Since he now had fewer public duties, he found the time to compose a harmony of the Gospels, to engage in apocalyptic speculations, to edit Nikolaus Copernicus's *De revolutionibus,* and to defend the Jews against accusations of ritual murder. In the Interim period (→ Augsburg Interim), he was once again a much-sought-after counselor, but when the Council of Nuremberg disregarded his advice and accepted an order of worship in keeping with the Interim, he went in 1548 to Königsberg, to Duke → Albrecht the Elder of Brandenburg-Ansbach, who had looked on Osiander as his spiritual father since 1522. Tensions with his colleagues in church and university arose when the duke created a vacancy for Osiander as pastor of the parish of Altstadt and appointed him professor at the university, in breach of the statutes. A violent controversy arose over the highly individual character of his theology, which employed a strongly scholastic concept of God and united Christology and justification in a manner that excluded a theory of pure imputation. The duke supported Osiander in this "Osiandric" conflict, even after his death, but his contemporaries and later generations of Lutherans (Formula of → Concord) agreed in condemning him.

■ **Works:** *Gesamtausgabe,* vols. 1–6, ed. G. Müller, vols. 7–10, ed. G. Seebass (Gütersloh, 1975–97); *Bibliographia Osiandrica,* prepared by G. Seebass (Nieuwkoop, 1971).
■ **Literature:** *TRE* 25:507–15.—E. Hirsch, *Die Theologie des A. O.* (Göttingen, 1919); G. Seebass, *Das reformatorische Werk des A. O.* (Neustadt [Aisch], 1967); M. Stupperich, *O. in Preussen (1549–52)* (Berlin, 1973).

GOTTFRIED SEEBASS

■ **Additional Bibliography:** R. Hauke, *Gott-Haben—um Gottes Willen. A. O.s Theosisgedanke* . . . (Frankfurt/Main, 1999); G. Zimmermann, *Prediger der Freiheit. A. O. und der Nürnberger Rat 1522–48* (Mannheim, 1999); J. Kammerling, "A. O.'s Sermons on the Jews," *Lutheran Quarterly* 15 (2001) 59–84; G. Martens, "'Ein uberaus grosser unterschiedt.' Der Kampf des A. O.

gegen die Praxis der allgemeinen Absolution in Nürnberg," *Festhalten am Bekenntnis der Hoffnung.* Festschrift R. Slenczka (Erlangen, 2001) 144–64.

(2) *Lukas* the Elder. Lutheran theologian, son of (1), born December 15, 1534 in Nuremberg, died September 17, 1604 in Stuttgart. After studies in Königsberg and Tübingen, he worked from 1555 onward as pastor in Göppingen, Blaubeuren, and Stuttgart. He took his doctorate in theology at Tübingen in 1567. He was appointed court preacher in Stuttgart in 1567, and preacher in the collegiate church in the same city in 1593. He became prelate of Adelberg in 1596. He was expelled from this state in 1598 after he had criticized the tolerant policy of Duke Frederick vis-à-vis the Jews. He worked in Esslingen until he was invited to return to Stuttgart. Osiander collaborated in the elaboration of the Formula of → Concord and its translation into Latin, and was a participant in religious dialogues, e.g., in Montbéliard (1586) and Regensburg (1594). He exchanged letters with Patriarch Jeremiah II of Constantinople, and was an adviser to Gebhard Truchsess von → Waldburg, archbishop of Cologne when the latter unsuccessfully attempted to introduce the Reformation.

■ **Works:** *Biblia sacra latina,* 7 vols. (Tübingen, 1573–86) (text of the Vulgate with commentary); *Institutio christianae religionis* (Tübingen, 1582); *Epitome historiae ecclesiasticae,* 6 vols. (Tübingen, 1592–1603) (continuation of the Magdeburg Centuriators); *Bawren Postilla,* 5 vols. (Tübingen, 1597–1600) (popular sermons).—Catalogue: *VD 16* 15:259–75.
■ **Literature:** *BBKL* 6:1299–1304.—H. Wolter, "Die Kirche im Religionsgespräch zwischen Gregor von Valencia und L. O.," in *Sentire Ecclesiam.* Festschrift H. Rahner (Freiburg, 1961) 350–70; J. A. Steiger, *Melancholie, Diätetik und Trost. Die Konzepte der Melancholie-Therapie im 16. und 17.Jh.* (Heidelberg, 1996) 51–58.

JOHANN ANSELM STEIGER

■ **Additional Bibliography:** U. Bubenheimer, "Streittheologie in Tübingen am Anfang des 17.Jh.," *Kirchliche Zeitgeschichte* 7 (1994) 26–43.

Oswald, *Wendelin.* Dominican preacher, born in Sommeri (canton of Thurgau), died July 14, 1541 in Einsiedeln. He studied in Cologne, Paris, and Freiburg. He was prior in Constance from 1518 to 1520, and was father confessor to the Dominican nuns of St. Catharine's convent in the town of St.

Gallen from 1520 onward. He was appointed preacher at the Minster in St. Gallen in 1522. Since he resolutely opposed Huldrych Zwingli and the Reformation, restrictions were placed on his activity from 1524 onward. He took part in the → Baden Disputation in 1526, and was preacher in Einsiedeln in 1527, where a source from 1530 speaks of him as a Benedictine monk.

■ **Literature:** *BBKL* 6:1330f.—N. Paulus, *Die deutschen Dominikaner im Kampf gegen Luther* (Freiburg, 1903) 323ff.

VIOLA TENGE-WOLF

Otter (Ot[h]er), *Jakob.* Protestant theologian, Reformer of Esslingen, born c. 1485 in Lauterburg (Lower Alsace), died March 15, 1547 in Esslingen. He studied in Heidelberg from 1505 to 1507. After a period as secretary to → Geiler von Kaysersberg and editor of his writings in Strasbourg, he continued his studies in Freiburg from 1510 onward. Here, he became an adherent of the theological professor Johannes Brisgoicus (died 1539), and took his licentiate in theology in 1517. He became parish priest in Wolfenweiler in 1518, and preacher in Kenzingen in 1522; when he embraced Protestantism, the Austrian government applied pressure, and Otter was obliged to leave Kenzingen. He went via Strasbourg (with whose theologians he remained in contact throughout his life), Neckarsteinach, Berne, Solothurn, and Aarau to Esslingen, where he arrived in 1532. Here he succeeded Ambrosius → Blarer. In 1534, he drew up regulations for the Latin and German schools, and he signed the Concord of → Wittenberg on behalf of the Upper Germans in 1536.

■ **Sources:** *VD* 16 15:1463–71; *Quellen zur Geschichte der Täufer,* vol. 8 (Gütersloh, 1960); *Correspondance de Martin Bucer,* vol. 2 (Leiden, 1989); Jakob Wimpfeling, *Briefwechsel,* vol. 2 (Munich, 1990).

■ **Literature:** *BBKL* 6:1344f.—M. Brecht, "Esslingen im geistigen Ringen der Reformationszeit," *Esslinger Studien* 20 (1981) 59–71; T. M. Schröder, *Das Kirchenregiment der Reichsstadt Esslingen* (Esslingen, 1987) esp. 115–31; R. Lusiardi, *Ackerbürgerstadt und Evangelium . . . Kenzingen: Zeitschrift für die Geschichte des Oberrheins* 141 (1993) 185–211.

BARBARA HENZE

Ottheinrich of the Palatinate. Palatinate count of Neuburg ("Young Palatinate") from 1505 to 1559,

electoral prince of the Palatinate from 1556 to 1559, born April 10, 1502 in Amberg, died February 12, 1559 in Heidelberg. In 1542, Ottheinrich introduced the Reformation into the principality of Neuburg (which had been created for him and his brother Philipp in 1505). He promulgated a church order composed by Andreas → Osiander in 1543. When he became bankrupt in the following year, thanks to the luxurious lifestyle of his court and extensive building projects, the parliamentary Estates assumed the reins of government. He fled during the turbulence of the → Schmalkaldic War in 1546, and spent the next years in Heidelberg and Weinheim, until his principality was restored to him in the Treaty of → Passau (1552)—although he rejected the other points of this treaty, and later rejected the Religious Peace of → Augsburg (1555). As soon as he received the electoral dignity of the Palatinate in 1556, he introduced the Reformation in the electoral Palatinate and promulgated a strictly Lutheran church order (April, 1556). With the help of Philipp Melanchthon, Ottheinrich reformed the university in Heidelberg, where he resided, and founded the world-renowned "Bibliotheca Palatina," to which he presented in 1557 the extensive library of the secularized Benedictine abbey of Lorsch.

■ **Literature:** *Handbuch der bayerischen Geschichte,* founding editor, M. Spindler; ed. A. Kraus, vol. 3/3 (Munich, ³1995) 89f., 126f., and passim; *BBKL* 6:1348–52.

MANFRED EDER

■ **Additional Bibliography:** W. von Moers-Messmer, *Heidelberg und seine Kurfürsten* (Ubstadt-Weiher, 2001); B. Zeitelhack, ed., *Pfalzgraf O.: Politik, Kunst und Wissenschaft im 16. Jahrhundert* (Regensburg, 2002).

P

Pack, *Otto von.* Vice-chancellor of Duke → George of Saxony, born c. 1480, died February 8, 1537; the "Packian Quarrels" are named after him. In January, 1528, Pack handed Marquis → Philip of Hessen faked documents about an alleged military league of Catholic princes (→ Ferdinand I, the electoral princes of Mainz and Brandenburg, the dukes of Saxony and Bavaria, the archbishop of Salzburg, the bishops of Bamberg and Würzburg). Philip took up arms and invaded the ecclesiastical territories in Franconia. When the forgery came to light, Philip halted his campaign, but he compelled the electoral prince of Mainz to give him the right to try the clergy in Hessen in his own courts (Treaty of Hitzkirchen, June, 1528); the Franconian bishops were also obliged to pay him reparations to cover the cost of his weaponry. The Catholic Estates in the empire reacted by defending their cause more decisively at the imperial parliament in Speyer in 1529. Pack was on the run for many years, until Duke George had him condemned and executed.

■ **Literature:** K. Dülfer, *Die Packschen Händel* (Marburg, 1958); A. Kohler, *Antihabsburgische Politik in der Epoche Karls V.* (Göttingen, 1982); W. Heinemeyer, "Das Zeitalter der Reformation," in idem, ed., *Das Werden Hessens* (Marburg, 1986) 225–66.

ANTON SCHINDLING

Paleario, *Aonio* (real name: Antonio della Paliga[ra]). Humanist, born 1503 in Veroli (Latium), died July 3, 1570 in Rome. After studies in Rome, he taught in schools in Perugia and Siena. He continued his studies in 1531-1532 and 1534-1536 in Padua, where he met Pietro → Bembo and turned to philosophy, under the influence of Pietro Pomponazzi. Paleario, who was also influenced by Bernardino → Ochino, was accused of heresy in 1542 because of his teaching about purgatory, but Jacopo → Sadoleto defended him successfully. He was in Lucca from 1546 to 1555 and thereafter in Milan, where he was once again tried for heresy in 1559-1560, but again acquitted. After the publication of his books, Paleario's doctrine of justification and his criticism of the pope and the church led to new accusations, and he was imprisoned. He was transferred to Rome, condemned as a recidivist heretic, and executed in Castel Sant'Angelo.

■ **Works:** *Opera* (Basle, n.d. [1567]); *Actio in pontifices Romanos*, ed. G. Paladina, *Opuscoli e lettere di riformatori italiani del cinquecento*, vol. 2 (Bari, 1927) 19–170; *Dell'economia o vero del governo della casa*, ed. S. Caponetto (Florence, 1983).

■ **Literature:** *CEras* 3:45f.; *BBKL* 6:1451ff.—G. Morpurgo, *Un umanista martire, A. P., e la riforma teorica italiana* (Città di Castello, 1912); V. Marchetti, *Gruppi ereticali senesi del cinquecento* (Florence, 1975); S. Caponetto, *A. P. e la Riforma protestante in Toscana*

(Turin, 1979); E. Gallina, *A. P.,* 3 vols. (Sora, 1989); S. Seidel Menchi, *Erasmus als Ketzer* (Leiden, 1993).

GIUSEPPE ALBERIGO

Paleotti, *Gabriele.* Cardinal (1565), canon lawyer, born October 4, 1522 in Bologna, died July 22, 1597 in Rome as cardinal bishop of Sabina. He was a much-appreciated professor of law in Bologna from 1546 to 1556, then auditor at the Rota from 1556 to 1566. He was adviser to the papal legates at the Council of Trent, especially to Cardinal Giovanni → Morone, in 1562-1563, and his diary is an important source of historical information about the council (ed. S. Merkle, *CT* 3/1:231-762). He became bishop of Bologna in 1566 and was made the first archbishop of this see in 1582. Here he worked closely with Charles → Borromeo to carry out the Tridentine reform. He spent his last years in Rome.

■ **Principal Works:** *De nothis spuriisque filiis* (Venice, 1550, often reprinted); *Discorso sulle imagini sacre e profane* (Bologna, 1582; Latin, Ingolstadt, 1594); *De s. consistorii consultationibus* (Rome, 1592, often reprinted); *Episcopale Bononiense* (Bologna, 1580); *Archiepiscopale Bonon* (Rome, 1594); *De bono senectutis* (Rome, 1595).—"P.s Rota-Entscheidungen," in *Decisionum novissimarum SRR* (Venice, 1618) 202–330.

■ **Literature:** *DThC* 11:1821ff.—S. Merkle, "Kardinal G. P.'s Litterarischer Nachlass," *RQ* 11 (1897) 333–429; P. Prodi, *Il Cardinale G. P.,* 2 vols. (Rome, 1959–67); C. Hecht, "Katholische Bildertheologie im Zeitalter von Gegenreformation und Barock: Studien zu Traktaten von Johannes Molanus, G. P. und anderen Autoren" (diss., Berlin, 1997).

PAOLO PRODI

■ **Additional Literature:** G. Dossetti, "La chiesa di Bologna e il Concilio," *CrS* 23 (2002) 705–46.

Pamphlets. This early form of mass publicity became popular in the late Middle Ages. Most pamphlets dealt polemically with issues of the day, and their aim was to influence public opinion. They were particularly numerous in periods of general turmoil (e.g., the Reformation and the Thirty Years' War). Since they were written for a poorly educated public, their criticism tends to be crude and populist, sometimes even obscene; they are full of heavy-handed mockery, and the written word is supported by woodcuts, often on the title page. They deal with topics of morals and propriety, often in combination with urgent issues in religion and politics (Martin Luther, the clash between the confessions, or war). In the 16th century, particularly large numbers of pamphlets were published in the early years of the Reformation up to the Peasants' War of 1525, and later in the controversy about the → Augsburg Interim and the Council of Trent. They make use of various literary forms: the treatise, the sermon in verse and prose, dialogue, theatrical conversations. Luther published masterly pamphlets from 1517 onward, some running to 100 pages (e.g., *An den christlichen Adel,* probably the most influential pamphlet produced in this period); he used these above all to address circles of laypersons who had no other means of access to his theological reflections. Many prominent publicists wrote pamphlets (on the Protestant side, in addition to Luther, we find Ulrich von → Hutten, Johann → Eberlin von Günzberg, and Heinrich von Kettenbach; on the Catholic side we find Thomas Murner and Daniel von Soest).

The pamphlets helped turn the Reformation into a popular movement. They criticized the notorious abuses and wrote polemically against the pope and the hierarchy, the clergy, the monks, → celibacy, and → indulgences; they lauded the Protestant path to salvation, pouring scorn on prominent representatives of the Catholic Church and praising Luther. The opponents of the Reformation employed the same weapons, but the Catholic pamphlets were fewer and (with some exceptions) inferior in quality to the Protestant publications. The religious aspect was frequently combined with economic and social considerations (e.g., on the knights' movement and on the Peasants' War). As documents aimed at a wide public, the pamphlets are an excellent source of historical information, but a cautious and critical methodology is required, if they are to be interpreted correctly.

■ **Sources:** *Satiren und Pasquillen aus der Reformationszeit,* ed. O. Schade, 3 vols. (Hannover, ²1863); *Flugschriften aus den ersten Jahren der Reformation,* ed. O. Clemen, 4 vols. (Leipzig, 1904–11); *Flugschriften zur Ritterschaftsbewegung 1523,* ed. K. Schottenloher (Münster, 1929); *Flugschriften und Streitschriften der Reformation in Westfalen 1523–83,* ed. Th. Legge (Münster, 1933); *Die Sturmtruppen der Reformationszeit,* ed. A. E. Berger (Leipzig, 1931); Köhler *BF.*
■ **Literature:** *TRE* 11:240–46.—K. Schottenloher, *Flugblatt und Zeitung* (Berlin, 1922); *BDG* n. 36879–996;

H.-J. Köhler, ed., *Flugschriften als Massenmedium der Reformationszeit* (Stuttgart, 1981).

ERNST WALTER ZEEDEN

■ **Additional Bibliography:** M. Arnold, *Handwerker als theologische Schriftsteller. Studien zu Flugschriften der frühen Reformation (1523–25)* (Göttingen, 1990); B. Möller, *Städtische Predigt in der Frühzeit der Reformation. Eine Untersuchung deutscher Flugschriften der Jahre 1522–29* (Göttingen, 1996); I. B. Vogelstein, "Reformation Pamphlets," *Philosophy and Theology* 10 (1997) 501–24; R. Walinski-Kiehl, "Pamphlets, Propaganda and Witch-hunting in Germany c. 1560—c. 1630," *Reformation* 6 (2001/02) 49–74; B.-M. Schuster, *Die Verständlichkeit von frühreformatorischen Flugschriften* (Hildesheim, 2001).

Panvini(o), *Onofrio.* Augustinian Hermit (1541), church historian, born February 24, 1530 in Verona, died April 7, 1568 in Palermo. He wrote a history of his Order. He entered the service of Alessandro Farnese the Elder in 1554, and accompanied him to the conclave of 1559, where he wrote a *Diarium* about the election of → Pius IV (*CT* 2:575-601). Panvinio made extensive studies of the classical Roman period and of the history of the church and the popes. He dedicated his monograph *De comitiis imperatoriis* (Barcelona, 1558) to → Philip II. This book deals with the origins of the college of electoral princes, and its conclusions are astonishingly akin to those of modern scholarship. His printed works draw on only a small part of the enormous wealth of material which he collected for his history of the Roman churches and catacombs and of the popes and cardinals. Excerpts from his iconography of the popes (a work undertaken at the request of Johann Jakob → Fugger and surviving in Codex latinus Monacensis 155-160) were published after his death. He did not realize his aim of publishing a scholarly refutation of the → Magdeburg Centuriators.
■ **Principal Works:** *Epitome vitarum Romanorum Pontificum* (Venice, 1557); *De episcopatibus, titulis et diaconiis cardinalium* (Venice, 1557); *De antiquis Romanorum nominibus* (Venice, 1558); *In quinque Fastorum libros commentarii* (Venice, 1558); *De varia Romanorum Pontificum creatione,* Codex latinus monacensis 147–52; introduction by A. Mai in *Spicilegium Romanum,* vol. 9 (Rome, 1843) 530f.; *De cardinalium origine,* in *Spicilegium Romanum,* vol. 9, 430ff.; *De ecclesiis Urbis Romae,* in *Spicilegium Romanum,* vol. 9, 441ff.; *De ritu sepeliendi mortuos apud veteres christianos et eorum coemeteriis* (Cologne, 1568);

Chronicon ecclesiasticum usque ad Maximilianum II (Venice, 1568).
■ **Literature:** J. F. Ossinger, *Bibliotheca Augustiniana historica, critica et chronologica* (Ingolstadt and Augsburg, 1768) 656–62; D. A. Perini, *O. P. e le sue opere* (Rome, 1899); O. Hartig, "Des Onuphrius Panvinius Sammlung von Papstbildnissen in der Bibliothek J. J. Fuggers," *HJ* 38 (1917) 284–314; *Bibliographia augustiniana*, vol. 3 (Florence, 1935) 53–65; J.-L. Ferrary, *O. P. et les antiquités romaines* (Rome, 1996).

KLAUS GANZER

Pappus, *Johannes.* Lutheran theologian, born January 16, 1549 in Lindau, died July 13, 1610 in Strasbourg. After studies in Strasbourg, Tübingen (doctor of theology, 1573), and Basle, he became first professor of Hebrew at the academy in Strasbourg (1570), then professor of theology (1578). In the latter year, he also became pastor at the Minster, and was appointed preacher in the collegiate church in 1593. As president of the imperial-municipal synod, Pappus headed the church in Strasbourg after the death of Johannes → Marbach, and ensured the victory of Lutheranism in Strasbourg against the opposition of Johann → Sturm (church order of 1598). Pappus was embroiled in the controversies about the Formula of → Concord and in debates with the Catholic Church (religious dialogue of Emdingen, 1590). He wrote c. 30 works of controversial theology, exegesis, and church history.
■ **Works:** F. Ritter, *Répertoire bibliographique*, vol. 2/3 (Strasbourg, 1945) nos. 1755–66; vol. 4 (Strasbourg, 1960) nos. 2814–18; *VD 16* 15:319–42.
■ **Literature:** *BBKL* 6:1497–1502; *Nouveau Dictionnaire de Biographie Alsacienne* 29 (Strasbourg, 1997) 2942.— W. Horning, *Dr. J. P.* (Strasbourg, 1891); M.-J. Bopp, *Die evangelischen Geistlichen und Theologen im Elsass* (Neustadt [Aisch], 1959) n. 3908.

CHRISTOPH WEISMANN

Paracelsus (real name: Theophrastus Bombast von Hohenheim). Doctor, natural philosopher, and lay theologian, born 1493 or 1494 in Einsiedeln, died September 24, 1541 in Salzburg. After his studies (which, according to his own account, were concluded with a doctorate in medicine in Ferrara) and years of extensive wanderings through Europe, he was in Salzburg in 1524-1525; his relations with the rebels remain unclear. It was here that he wrote his earliest theological works, mostly of a speculative nature, on the doctrine of God and of Mary, whom he included in the Trinity as "wife of God" and "goddess." These were followed by an extremely polemical treatise against the "Christian idolatry" of the "church with walls," employing "spiritualistic" arguments. At this period, he also began exegetical work on Matthew 1-5. He sympathized with the Reformation for a time: he probably wrote a letter to Martin Luther and others in Wittenberg in 1525, and he was influenced by Huldrych Zwingli, and possibly also by Thomas → Müntzer. He worked briefly in Basle in 1527 as city doctor and university teacher, then wandered through Upper Germany and the Alpine region: he was in Nuremberg in 1529 (where he met Sebastian → Frank) and in St. Gallen in 1531 (where he sought in vain the approval of Joachim → Vadian). He had by now distanced himself from all the churches, but he had contacts with the monastery of St. Gallen in 1533, and with the abbot of Pfäffers in 1535. He wandered through Carinthia in 1537-1538, and was again in Salzburg in 1540. He was buried according to the Catholic rite.

His first writings, on medicine and natural philosophy, already display a close connection (on which Paracelsus himself commented) with theological ideas. This is reminiscent of the anthropocentric image of the world and of the human person in Renaissance Neo-Platonism, whose soteriology envisaged the goals of deification and immortality (Marsilio Ficino, Giovanni Pico della Mirandola, Heinrich C. Agrippa von Nettesheim).

In keeping with the symbolism of two lights in Paracelsus's epistemology—viz., the light of nature and the light of the spirit—his theology is permeated by a speculation which is a variation on Paul's argumentation in 1 Cor 15: the Christian who is born in baptism from the limbo of Abraham or of Christ is transformed by the heavenly nourishment of the Eucharist (while preserving his personal identity) from the Adamic-mortal identity into the divine-immortal identity, and this allows him here on earth to have a share in the divine power to perform miracles and to heal, just like Christ and the apostles. Paracelsus holds that the individual Christian matures towards perfection (the *vita beata*), and this makes him reject both war and the death penalty; he is also skeptical vis-à-vis martyrdom. This basic attitude is combined with an ethos which follows the principle of poverty maintained by the Franciscan "Spirituals"—with harsh criticism of the church and the pope, an apocalyptic translated from the future tense into the present, the expectation of a *papa angelicus,* and idealized communist utopias. All this provides the criterion (Mt 7:20) for distinguishing true Christians from the seducers who will appear at the end of the age (Mt 24:5f.).

His voluminous exegetical, dogmatic-polemical, and ethical writings are just as ample as his medicinal and natural-philosophical writings (which themselves contain many theological passages) and his speculative political "prognostications." During Paracelsus's lifetime, only a small portion of his works were printed, exclusively medicinal writings and prognostications. Editions of his surgical writings were placed on the Index in Parma in 1580, and he himself as an author was placed on the Roman Index in 1596. In the following centuries, his theological writings (with the exception of a few treatises) were transmitted only in manuscript. He was influential in "Spiritualistic" and radical reforming Protestantism, as well as in the Catholic sphere (→ Ernest of Bavaria, Johann → Leisentritt) and the transconfessional milieu in the 16th and 17th centuries.

■ **Works:** *Erste Gesamtausgabe von J. Huser,* 10 vols. (Basle, 1589–90), supplementary vols. 1603–5; *Sämtliche Werke,* 1. Abteilung (medicine, natural science, and philosophical writings), ed. K. Sudhoff, 14 vols. (Munich and Berlin, 1922–1933); 2. Abteilung (theological and religio-philosophical writings), vol. 1, ed. W. Matthiessen (Munich, 1923); vol. 2ff., ed. K. Goldammer (Wiesbaden and Stuttgart, 1955ff.).
■ **Bibliographies:** K.-H. Weimann, *P. Bibliographie 1932–60* (Wiesbaden, 1963); R. Dilg-Frank, "Bibliographie 1960–80," in *Paracelse,* ed. A. Faivre and F. Tristan (Paris, 1980) 269–80; J. Telle, "Bibliographie zum frühneuzeitlichen Paracelsismus," *Analecta Paracelsica,* ed. idem (Stuttgart, 1994) 556–64; J. Paulus, *P. Bibliographie 1961–1986* (Heidelberg, 1997).
■ **Literature:** TRE 25:699–705.—K. Biegger, *De invocatione BMV. P. und die Marienverehrung* (Stuttgart, 1990); U. Gause, *P. Genese und Entfaltung seiner frühen Theologie* (Tübingen, 1993); U. Benzenhöfer, *P.* (Reinbek, 1997); A. Weeks, *P. Speculative Theory and the Crisis of Early Reformation* (Albany, N.Y., 1997); *P. The Man and His Reputation,* ed. O. P. Grell (Leiden, 1998).

HARTMUT RUDOLPH

■ **Additional Bibliography:** P. Letter, *P.* (Krummwisch, 2000).

Parker, *Matthew.* Protestant reformer and first archbishop of Canterbury under → Elizabeth I (1559), born August 6, 1504 in Norwich, died May 17, 1575 in Lambeth. He was educated in Cambridge, where he first became acquainted with Protestant ideas, and became chaplain to Elizabeth's mother, Anne Boleyn, in 1535. He became Master of Corpus Christi College in Cambridge in 1544 and married in 1547. This subsequently displeased Elizabeth, and she never appointed another married clergyman to the office of archbishop. During the period of the Catholic reaction under → Mary I, Parker remained in England, but led a secluded life, without getting involved in the liturgical controversies of the English exiles; this recommended him to Elizabeth in 1559. Other factors in his favor were his loyalty to her mother and the support Parker received from Elizabeth's minister William Cecil, another Cambridge scholar. As archbishop, Parker played a leading role in making the "Elizabethan Settlement" a reality, by commissioning the 1563 version of the *Thirty-Nine* → *Anglican Articles* and the "Bishops' Bible" of 1568. This Bible was intended to counteract the growing popularity of the "Genevan Bible." Parker devoted a great deal of time to the attempt to impose uniformity on the extreme Protestants (or → "Puritans"), e.g., with regard to the wearing of the surplice in church services.
■ **Literature:** V. J. K. Brook, *Archbishop P.* (Oxford, 1962); P. Collinson, *The Elizabethan Puritan Movement* (London, 1967); W. P. Haugaard, *Elizabeth and the English Reformation* (Cambridge, 1968).

PETER MARSHAL

■ **Additional Bibliography:** N. C. Bjorklund, *M. P. and the Reform of the English Church during the Reigns of Henry VIII and Edward VI* (Irvine, Calif., 1987); B. S. Robinson, "'Darke speech.' M. P. and the Reforming of History," *SCJ* 29 (1998) 1961–83; B. Usher, "The Deanery of Bocking and the Demise of Vestiarian Controversy," *JEH* 52 (2001) 434–55; N. B. Bjorklund, "'A Godly Wyfe is an Helper': M. P. and the Defense of Clerical Marriage," *SCJ* 34 (2003) 347–65.

Passau, Treaty of. In the course of the negotiations of the assembly of the Estates in Passau (May 31–August 8, 1552), a confessionally neutral group of imperial princes, under the leadership of the electoral Palatinate, Jülich, and Württemberg, persuaded King → Ferdinand to end the state of war between electoral prince → Moritz of Saxony and Emperor → Charles V. After an initial refusal, the emperor ratified the treaty of Passau (August 2, 1552) on August 15. It envisaged the liberation of Marquis → Philip of Hessen, a restitution of property, and a general amnesty in regard to the religious war. The "Christian settlement" of the confessional division was postponed to an imperial parliament which was to be prepared by a commission with equal Catholic and Protestant membership, and to be held within six months. A provisional "state of peace" between Lutherans and Catholics was proclaimed; this was to be governed by the regulations of imperial law and by the "king's peace." The treaty anticipated the Religious Peace of → Augsburg (1555) by formulating a "principle of toleration" (in Luttenberger's phrase) which no longer insisted upon religious unity as a precondition before political stability could be reestablished. The electoral princes and the most important of the imperial princes (including the bishops) began to dismantle the confessional confrontation by means of the political compromise they had reached in the imperial assemblies, "so that a situation where the emperor had decided constitutional issues was replaced by a constitutional agreement among the Estates" (Angermeier).

■ **Literature:** *Neue und vollständigere Sammlung der Reichs-Abschiede,* vol. 3 (Frankfurt/Main, 1747) 1–10; H. Barge, *Die Verhandlungen zu Linz und Passau und der Vertrag von Passau vom Jahre 1552* (Stralsund, 1893); W. Kühns, *Geschichte des Passauischen Vertrages 1552* (Göttingen, 1906); G. Bonwetsch, *Geschichte des Passauischen Vertrages von 1552* (Göttingen, 1907); H. Lutz, *Christianitas afflicta. Europa, das Reich und die päpstliche Politik im Niedergang der Hegemonie Kaiser Karls V. (1552–1556)* (Göttingen, 1964); A. P. Luttenberger, *Glaubenseinheit und Reichsfriede. Konzeptionen und Wege konfessionsneutraler Reichspolitik (1530–52)* (Göttingen, 1982) 651–713; *Säkulare Aspekte der Reformationszeit,* ed. H. Angermeier and R. Seyboth (Munich and Vienna, 1983).

WINFRIED BECKER

■ **Additional Bibliography:** V. H. Drecoll, *Der Passauervertrag* (Berlin, 2000); H. Neuhaus, "Der P. V. und die Entwicklung des Reichsreligionsrechts," in: *Bürgerliche Freiheit und chriastliche Verantwortung. Festschrift C. Link* (Tübingen, 2003) 751–65.

Paul III. Pope (October 13, 1534–November 10, 1549), formerly *Alessandro Farnese,* born in Feb-

ruary, 1468 in Canino near Viterbo or in Rome. He received a humanist education in Rome. He owed his successful curial career to Pope Alexander VI, who had been the lover of Alessandro's sister, Giulia Farnese. He was created cardinal deacon in 1493 and became dean of the college of cardinals in 1524. His lifestyle was no different from that of the other Renaissance popes. He had several children while a cardinal; his favorite was Pier Luigi. As pope, he practiced an excessive nepotism: two grandsons became cardinals, while his third grandson became duke of Urbino, and his son Pier Luigi received Parma and Piacenza. Paul realized that the vacillating policies of his predecessor, → Clement VII, could not be continued. Accordingly, he attempted to maintain neutrality vis-à-vis Emperor → Charles V and France. Although he was personally disinclined to reform, he saw its inevitability and made men of the reforming party cardinals (e.g., John → Fisher, Gasparo → Contarini, Giampietro Carafa [later → Paul IV], Jacopo → Sadoleto, Reginald → Pole, Giovanni → Morone, Gregorio → Cortese). He supported movements of religious renewal, both the reform of the older Orders and the foundation of new Orders (Theatines, Barnabites, Ursulines, Capuchins). He confirmed the Jesuit Order in 1540. He set up a commission for reform in 1536, which produced the *Consilium delectorum cardinalium et aliorum praelatorum de emendenda ecclesia* in 1537. Paul was suspicious of the discussions with Protestants (→ Hagenau, → Worms, → Regensburg, 1540-1541) by means of which Charles V sought to achieve unity among the confessional parties in the empire. The spread of the ideas of the Protestant Reformation in northern Italy and the growing influence of the adherents of Juan de → Valdés in Naples led to the foundation of the Inquisition in the Roman curia in 1542 (bull *Licet ab initio*) with Carafa as its leading proponent.

From the beginning of his pontificate, Paul planned to hold a council, but the first convocations (Mantua and Vicenza in 1537, Trent in 1542) led to nothing. After Charles V had won the commitment of the French king to a council in the Peace of Crépy (1544), it was finally possible to open the council at Trent on December 13, 1545. The sessions of the first period (1545-1548) produced a number of important dogmatic degrees. The legates transferred the council to Bologna when it was alleged that typhus fever had broken out; when the emperor protested, Paul ruled that no new decrees should be promulgated in Bologna. The council was suspended on September 14, 1549.

Paul had made money and an auxiliary troop of soldiers available to the emperor for the → Schmalkaldic War in a treaty of 1546. In the following years, grave dissensions arose between Paul and Charles V because of the way the emperor handled the religious question, and because of the pope's family politics. The proclamation of the → Augsburg Interim by the emperor in 1548 enraged the pope. The murder of his son Pier Luigi in 1548 brought these tensions to their high point, since Ferrante Gonzaga, the imperial viceregent in Milan, was privy to the conspiracy.

Paul failed to persuade Charles V and the French king to end the English schism by taking military action against → Henry VIII. Nevertheless, Paul gave the emperor vigorous support in his attempts to ward off the Turkish threat.

Paul was a patron of the arts and sciences. Michelangelo was appointed chief architect, sculptor, and painter in the Vatican Palace, and the *Last Judgment* in the Sixtine Chapel was painted in this period.

Paul's pontificate tends to be portrayed as a period of transition, and his character is often judged to be ambivalent. Elisabeth G. Gleason is surely not wrong to see him in her recent essay as the first pope of the → Counter-Reformation. Through the changes which his appointments made to the college of cardinals, his introduction of reforms (*Consilium de emendanda ecclesia*), his support of the reforming Orders of Jesuits and Capuchins, the foundation of the Inquisition, and the convocation of the Council of Trent, he showed that he was serious in his leadership and defense of the Catholic Church.

■ **Sources:** Valuable material can be found in the various series of nunciature reports.—*CT.*
■ **Literature:** *DThC* 12:9–20; *EC* 9:734ff.; *TRE* 26:118–21.—L. von Pastor, *Geschichte der Päpste seit dem Ausgang des Mittelalters*, vol. 5 (Freiburg, 1909); C. Capasso, *Paolo III*, 2 vols. (Messina and Rome, 1925); L. Dores, *La cour de pape P. III*, 2 vols. (Paris, 1932); W. Friedensburg, *Kaiser Karl V. und Papst P. III.* (Leipzig, 1932); G. Drei, *I Farnese* (Rome, 1954); G. Müller, "Die drei Nuntiaturen Aleanders in Deutschland," *QFIAB* 39 (1959) 222–76, 328–42; H. Jedin, "Die Päpste und das

Konzil in der Politik Karls V.," in *Karl V.*, ed. P. Rassow and F. Schalk (Cologne and Graz, 1960) 104–17; K. Repgen, *Die Römische Kurie und der Westfälische Friede*, vol. 1/1: *Papst, Kaiser und Reich 1521–1644* (Tübingen, 1962); H. Lutz, *Christianitas afflicta* (Göttingen, 1964); Jedin vols. 1–3; E. G. Gleason, "Who Was the First Counter-Reformation Pope?," *CHR* 81 (1995) 173–84; J. S. Panzer, "The Popes and Slavery," *Homiletic and Pastoral Review* 97 (1996) 22–29 (on "Sublimis Deus"); R. Zapperi, "Die vier Frauen des Papstes," in *Das Leben P.s III. zwischen Legende und Zensur* (Munich, 1997).

KLAUS GANZER

■ **Additional Bibliography:** R. Zapperi, *La leggenda del Papa Paolo III. Arte e censura nella Roma pontificia* (Turin, 1998); C. Robertson, "Two Farnese Cardinals and the Question of Jesuit Taste," *The Jesuits*, ed. J. W. O'Malley (Toronto, 1999) 134–47; M. Schmidt, "'Papst P. wünschte, dass er die von Clemens angeordnete Arbeit fortsetzen möge.' Neues zur Genese von Michelangelos 'Jüngstem Gericht' in der Sixtinischen Kapelle unter P. III.," *Das Münster* 53 (2000) 16–29.

KLAUS GANZER

Paul IV. Pope (May 23, 1555–August 18, 1559), formerly *Giampietro Carafa*, born June 28, 1476 in Capriglio, into a noble Neapolitan family. He was a nephew of Cardinal Oliviero Carafa, to whom he owed his successful career in the curia. He became bishop of Chieti in 1505. He was nuncio in Naples in 1505-1506, in England in 1513, and in Spain in 1515, where tensions arose between Carafa and the Spanish court. He was appointed archbishop of Brindisi in 1518. He was closely connected to the "Oratory of divine love" in Rome, and he founded the Order of Theatines in 1524 with → Cajetan of Thiene. He was created cardinal in 1536 and became dean of the college of cardinals in 1553. He was appointed archbishop of Naples in 1549. He was a member of the commission for the *Consilium de emendanda ecclesia*. Cardinal Alessandro Farnese the Younger played a decisive role in his election as pope. The negative experiences during his legation in Spain and insults on the part of → Charles V generated in him a deep antipathy to the Habsburgs, and he suspected the emperor of not being genuinely Catholic. He considered the Religious Peace of → Augsburg (1555) to be invalid; the same applied to Charles's abdication and the election of → Ferdinand I as emperor. Paul joined a military alliance with France against Spain in 1555, in the hope that he could destroy the Habsburg world empire. This, however, led to political disaster: Duke Fernando → Alba invaded the papal states, and Paul was obliged to make a peace treaty with Spain in 1557.

After the collapse of his political ambitions, Paul turned his attention to activity within the church. His goal was to use the fullness of papal authority to introduce decisive reforms in the church; he sought to prevent a continuation of the Council of Trent. He extended the work of the Roman Inquisition, which was given a position above all other curial offices and did not shrink from confrontation with even the highest-placed officials in the church. On Paul's orders, Cardinal Giovanni → Morone was imprisoned in Castel Sant'Angelo, and the Inquisition began proceedings against him; it was also intended that proceedings be taken against Cardinal Reginald → Pole. Paul published the Index of Prohibited Books in 1559, which subsequently had to be withdrawn and revised. He also took strong measures against the Jews. Nepotism in the old style flourished under Paul IV, who made his nephew Carlo Carafa a cardinal and entrusted all political business to him in 1555. Carlo was a man without spiritual interests or conscience, and all that he did was intended to increase the power of his family. Another nephew, Giovanni Carafa, was made Captain General of the church in the same year, and the two brothers exploited their supreme authority to the full. When Paul came to realize the extent of their crimes, he removed them from their offices and banished them from Rome in 1559; both were executed under → Pius IV.

Paul IV himself was a man of integrity, but his lack of intellectual sensibilities and his erratic character meant that his pontificate did not help the cause of reform.

■ **Sources:** Valuable material can be found in the various series of nunciature reports.
■ **Literature:** *DBI* 19:497–509; *DThC* 12:20–23; *EC* 9:736ff.; *TRE* 26:121–24.—L. von Pastor, *Geschichte der Päpste seit dem Ausgang des Mittelalters*, vol. 4/2, 5 and 6 (Freiburg, 1907–1913); L. Riess, *Die Politik P.s IV. und seiner Nepoten* (Berlin, 1909); P. Paschini, *S. Gaetano Thiene, Gian Pietro Carafa e le origini dei Chierici Regolari Teatini* (Rome, 1926); M. S. de Otto, *Paulo IV y la Corona de España* (Saragossa, 1943); L. Serrano, "El papa Paulo IV y España," *Hispania* 3 (1943) 293-325; T. Torriani, *Una tragedia nel Cinquecento romano. Paolo IV e i suoi nepoti* (Rome, 1951); H. Lutz, "Reformatio Germaniae," *QFIAB* 37 (1957) 222–310; R. De Maio, *Alfonso Carafa, cardinale di Napoli* (Vatican City, 1961; reprint, 1981); K. Repgen, *Die Römische Kurie und der Westfälische Friede*, vol. 1/1 (Tübingen, 1962); H. Lutz, *Christianitas afflicta* (Göttingen, 1964); idem, "Kardinal Morone," in *Il Concilio di Trento e la Riforma Cattolica*, vol. 1 (Rome, 1965) 363–81; H. Jedin, "Kirchenreform und Konzilsgedanke 1550–55," in *Kirche des Glaubens, Kirche der Geschichte*, vol. 2 (Freiburg, 1966) 237–63; Jedin vol. 1–3; P. Simoncelli, *Il caso Reginald Pole* (Rome, 1977); idem, *Evangelismo italiano del Cinquecento* (Rome, 1979); M. Firpo and D. Marcatto, *Il processo inquisitoriale del cardinal Giovanni Morone*, 6 vols. (Rome, 1981–95); D. Chiomenti Vassalli, *Paolo IV e il processo Carafa* (Milan, 1993).

KLAUS GANZER

■ **Additional Bibliography:** A. Aubert, *Paolo IV. Politica, inquisizione e storiografia* (Florence, 1999).

Peasants' War. The name "German Peasants' War" is given to the rebel movements in Swabia, Upper and Lower Rhineland, Franconia, the Rhine-Main region, Fulda, Salzburg, Graubünden, Tyrol, and the neighboring Alpine regions of Austria in the period between 1524 and 1526. The high point of these conflicts was from March to June, 1525. Many of the rebels were prosperous farmers from the countryside, but they also included members of the lower classes in towns where the citizens had smallholdings, as well as workers in the mines. Their leaders were farmers, a few aristocrats (Florian Geyer, Götz von Berlichingen), officials in the service of the local rulers (Wendel Hipler, Friedrich Weigandt, Michael Gaismair), and Protestant preachers (Balthasar → Hubmaier, Christoph Schappeler, Thomas → Müntzer).

Local and regional circumstances meant that the individual uprisings had different causes, took different courses, and employed varying measures of violence; their impact was not uniform, and they were put down in different ways. Nevertheless, the repressive policies of the local princes regarded all these rebellions as one and the same phenomenon, which contemporaries called "the Peasants' War" (in the singular). A general overview is problematic, in view of the variety of factors which led to the uprisings; this verdict applies to the Marxist thesis of an "early citizens' revolution," to Blickle's thesis about the "revolution of the common man," and *a fortiori* to Oberman's interpretation of the Peasants' War as a Protestant "revolt of faith." Local historians have taken another path, uncovering the variety of causes which led to the local uprisings: the social and economic oppression took the form of serfdom, tithes, taxes, restrictions by the local rulers on the use of woods and common land, and the reduction of the autonomy of village communities.

In the political sphere, one cause of the uprisings was pressure from the emergent early-modern territorial state. Since this differed from one region to another, the proposed models of a new societal organization likewise varied—in regions with many small territories, a fellowship of groups of peasants was proposed as a "Christian union" which would embrace all these territories; where stable territorial states existed, a corresponding constitution was envisaged. The → Reformation provided the occasion for the rebel movement, rather than its cause. At the same time, it is true that the "conflagration" of the Peasants' War (to use Moeller's phrase) would never have happened without the spread of Reformation preaching. The Reformation also suggested the idea of a "divine right" based on the Bible, to which the Upper Swabians appealed in support of the demands they made in the twelve Articles of Memmingen (written by Schappeler and the furrier Sebastian → Lotzer). These articles found a wide diffusion throughout the area of the revolt; their mixture of radical and moderate demands, some appealing to divine right and others to ancient laws, makes them a kind of overarching "manifesto of the Peasants' War" (Blickle).

In Thüringen, the Peasants' War took on a special character thanks to Müntzer's apocalyptic, chiliastic theology. Martin Luther's initial reaction to the twelve articles was an *Exhortation to Peace,* but he subsequently wrote his pamphlet *Wider die räuberischen und mörderischen Rotten der Bauern,* aimed especially at Müntzer. The rebellion produced its own program in Tyrol too, where Gaismair proposed a Christian egalitarian utopian vision of the state.

The princes took a terrible vengeance on the rebels: as many as 100,000 fell in the battles of the Peasants' War, or were executed. The Peasants' War did not, however, only lead to a loss of rights on the part of the peasants; in the long term, their legal position improved and they were given guarantees, e.g., by territorial constitutions in southwest Germany. Conflicts between the rulers and their subjects ceased to be a cause of violent uprisings in these regions from 1525 onward; instead, they became a matter to be settled before the imperial courts.

■ **Literature:** G. Franz, *Der Deutsche Bauernkrieg* (Darmstadt, [11]1977); P. Blickle, ed., *Der Deutsche Bauernkrieg von 1525* (Darmstadt, 1985); idem, *Unruhen in der ständischen Gesellschaft* (Munich, 1988); *TRZRK*; P. Blickle, *Die Revolution von 1525* (Munich and Vienna, [3]1993); H. Buszello, P. Blickle, and R. Endres, eds., *Der deutsche Bauernkrieg* (Paderborn, [3]1995).

ANTON SCHINDLING

■ **Additional Bibliography:** T. A. Brady, "German Civic Humanism? Critique of Monarchy and Refashioning of History in the Shadow of the German Peasants' War," in *Querdenken.* Festschrift H. R. Guggisberg (Mannheim, 1996) 41–55; C. S. Shim, "A Theological Exposition of Luther's Attitude toward Peasants' War," *Chongshin Theological Journal* 1 (1996) 49–69; H. Buszello et al., *Studien zum deutschen Bauernkrieg* (Mühlhausen, 1997); P. Blickle, *Der Bauernkrieg* (Munich, 1998); idem, *From the Communal Reformation to the Revolution of the Common Man* (Leiden, 1998); G. P. Sreenivasan, "The Social Origins of the Peasants' War of 1525 in Upper Swabia," *Past and Present* 171 (2001) 30–65.

Pelargus (real name: Storch), *Ambrosius.* Dominican, born c. 1493 in Nidda (Hessen), died July 5, 1561 in Trier. He studied in Frankfurt am Main and Heidelberg, and worked as preacher in Basle from 1525 to 1529, where he defended the Catholic doctrine of the Mass against Johannes → Oecolampadius. He worked in Freiburg from 1529 to 1533, writing five short works against the contemporary iconoclasts (→ Art and Reformation) and the → Baptists. He took his doctorate in theology in Freiburg in 1534, and maintained contact with → Erasmus of Rotterdam. He was professor of theology at the university of Trier from 1533 until 1561, and was the first priest to be appointed preacher in the cathedral there in 1545. He took part in the religious dialogues in → Hagenau and → Worms in 1540. He participated in the Council of Trent as procurator of the archbishop in 1546-1547, and accompanied his archbishop to Trent as conciliar theologian in 1551-1552, where he took part above all in the debates on the Eucharist, penance, and the sacrifice of the Mass. In 1561, after the Jesuits had been invited to Trier, he was the only professor in the theological faculty who accepted the archbishop's order to authorize them to teach theology, philosophy, and classical languages at the university of Trier.

■ **Literature:** *BBKL* 10:1561–65.—N. Paulus, *Die deutschen Dominikaner im Kampf gegen Luther* (Freiburg, 1903) 190–212; A. Walz, *I domenicani al concilio di Trento* (Rome, 1961); B. Caspar, *Das Erzbistum Trier im Zeitalter der Glaubensspaltung* (Münster, 1966) esp. 213–22; Jedin vols. 2 and 3 (index); Klaiber nos. 2443–46.

JOSEF STEINRUCK

Pellikan (real name: Kürsner), *Konrad.* Hebraist, born January 8, 1478 in Ruffach (Alsace), died April 6, 1556 in Zurich. He was a Franciscan from 1493 to 1526, and was the first Christian to write a textbook of the Hebrew language (printed Strasbourg, 1504). He was an adherent of Martin Luther in Basle from 1519 onward, and was professor of Old Testament from 1523 to 1526. He was "reader" (i.e., professor) of the Hebrew Old Testament in Zurich from 1526 to 1556, and also researched into Jewish literature. Members of other confessions appreciated his *Commentaria Bibliorum*, the only complete commentary on scripture published in the 16th century, too, thanks to its philological thoroughness and its brief explanations of the texts (7 vols., Zurich, 1532-1539, 2nd ed. 1536-1546, 3rd ed. 1582).
■ **Literature:** *CEras* 3:65f.—C. Zürcher, *K. P.s Wirken in Zürich 1526–56* (Zurich, 1975); M. Rose, "K. P.s Wirken in Zürich 1526–56," *Zwingliana* 14 (1977) 380–86; R. G. Hobbs, "Monitio amica: Pellican à Capiton sur le danger des lectures rabbiniques," in *Horizons européens de la réforme en Alsace.* FG J. Rott (Strasbourg, 1980) 81–94.

SIEGFRIED RAEDER

■ **Additional Literature:** R. G. Hobbs, "Conrad P. and the Psalms," *Reformation and Renaissance Review* 1 (1999) 72–99.

Penance, sacrament. The roots of the Reformation lay in a protest against the medieval doctrine of penance and of penitential praxis, which had concentrated on the sacrament of confession and on works of satisfaction. Martin Luther's first Wittenberg thesis (WA 1:233) affirmed that Christ had ordained that the Christian life as a whole should be determined by penitence. A Christian must "clothe himself in his baptism every day" (WA 15:418ff.); the old Adam in us should "be drowned . . . by daily penance and repentance, and die with all our sins and evil desires." Every day, "a new human being should

emerge and arise, to live eternally for God in righteousness and purity" (WA 30/1:312). In the *mortificatio* and the *regeneratio nostri,* it is God himself who is at work in the human person (Philipp Melanchthon, *Loci communes* 8:63f.). This means that repentance and satisfaction are not something that the penitent himself performs, something that could win him the forgiveness of sins: we are made righteous only by faith in God's action, which reconciles the sinner (→ justification; → sola fide). Jean Calvin understands penance as the continuous practice of self-denial and "putting the flesh to death": it is in this process that God's Spirit raises us to new life. The one who is raised to a life by the power of the Spirit bears visible fruits of repentance (*Inst* 3:4, 8; 3:16).
■ **Literature:** R. Schwarz, *Vorgeschichte der reformatorischen Busstheologie* (Berlin, 1968); S. Hausamann, *Busse als Umkehr und Erneuerung von Mensch und Gesellschaft* (Zurich, 1975); B. Lohse, "Beichte und Busse in der lutherischen Reformation," in *Lehrverurteilungen—kirchentrennend?,* vol. 2, ed. K. Lehmann (Freiburg and Göttingen, 1989) 283–95.

JÜRGEN WERBICK

■ **Additional Bibliography:** D. Myers, "Ritual, Confession, and Religion in Sixteenth-century Germany," *ARG* 89 (1998) 125–43.

Pérez de Ayala, *Martín.* Spanish theologian and bishop, born November 11, 1503/1504 in Segura de la Sierra (Jaén), died August 5, 1566 in Valencia. He entered the Order of St. James in 1525 and studied in Alcalá and Salamanca. From 1525 to 1540, he taught philosophy and theology, first in Granada and then in Jaén. He was appointed bishop of Cadiz in 1548 and bishop of Segovia in 1560; he became archbishop of Valencia in 1564. He held numerous visitations, three diocesan synods, and a provincial council (1565). He attended several sessions of the Council of Trent (1546, as theologian of → Charles V; 1551-1552; and 1562) and upheld the views of the strict reforming party. He emphasized the divine origin of episcopal authority, tradition as a comprehensive source of faith, and the *sensus ecclesiae* as the abiding doctrine of faith held by the whole church. His *De traditionibus* is the first complete and systematic treatise on this subject. As Josef Rupert Geiselmann has noted, he was the first to make a clear distinction between divine, apostolic, and ecclesiastical traditions and to set out in detail their varying relationships to scripture (which was not self-explanatory) and to the church's magisterium, as well as the origin and authority of the various individual traditions. He was one of the outstanding theologians of his age.

■ **Principal Works:** *Dilucidarium quaestionum super 5 universalia Porphyrii* (Granada, 1537); *De divinis, apostolicis atque ecclesiasticis traditionibus* (Paris, 1549; Venice, 1551; Cologne, 1549, 1560, often reprinted); *Catecismo* (Pavia, 1552); *Aviso de buen morir* (Pavia, 1552); *Compendio . . . de la Orden de Santiago* (Pavia, 1552); *Doctrina Cristiana per modo de diálogo* (Milan, 1554); *Concilium Valentiae cel. 1565* (Valencia, 1566); *Doctrina Cristiana en lengua Arabiga y Castellana . . .* (Valencia, 1566); *Confesionario* (Valencia, 1582, often reprinted); *Catecismo en forma de diálogos* (Valencia, 1599).—Council votes: *CT* 8:640ff.; 9:73–77, 137–41, 928ff.; 11:613f. (letter to Charles V).—Autobiography: M. Serrano y Saenz, *Nueva Biblioteca de Autores Españoles,* vol. 2 (Madrid, 1927) 211–38.

■ **Literature:** *DThC* 1:2652.—M. Solana, *Estudios sobre el Concilio de Trento . . .* (Santander, 1946); C. Gutiérrez, *Españoles en Trento* (Valladolid, 1951) 774–92; H. Jedin, "Die Autobiographie des Don M. P.," *Gesammelte Aufsätze zur Kulturgeschichte Spaniens* 11 (1955) 122–64; G. Navarro, "El arzobispo don M. P. (Apuntes de su vida y obra)," *Boletín del Instituto de Estudios Giennenses* (Jaén) 4/13 (1957) 175–80; A. Palau y Dulcet, *Manual del librero hispanoamericano,* vol. 13 (Barcelona, ²1961) 29f.; A. Marím Ocete, "M. Pérez de Ayala: Edición de una respuesta suya inédita a la consultación sobre la celebración de los Concilios provinciales," *Archivo teológico Granadino* 25 (1962) 96–104; J. R. de Diego, "La sentencia de M. P. sobre la relación entre la escritura y la tradición," *Archivo teológico Granadino* 30 (1967) 5–211; A. Miralles, *El concepto de tradición en M. P.* (Pamplona, 1980); A. García y García-Estévez, "El carácter episcopal según Don M. P.," *Salmanticensis* 41 (1994) 273–90.

JOHANNES STÖHR

■ **Additional Bibliography:** A. Galino Garcia, "La justificación por la fe. Los votos de los segovianos en Trento," in *Ecclesia una.* Festschrift A. Gonzalez Montes (Salamanca, 2000) 379–98.

Pérez de Pineda, *Juan.* Spanish Protestant, born after 1500 in Montilla, died 1566 in Paris. He became secretary to the Spanish ambassador in Rome c. 1520. He was in Seville from 1540 onward, and had contacts with Juan → Gil and Constantino → Ponce. When these men were persecuted by the Inquisition, he left Spain and arrived in Geneva in 1556, after a short stay in Paris. He won the esteem of Jean Calvin and Theodor → Beza, and founded the community of Spanish exiles in Geneva. After many travels, he became chaplain to Queen Renée of France. He published a free translation of Calvin's catechism (*Sumario breve de la doctrina christiana,* Geneva, 1556; often reprinted) as well as translations of books of the Bible with his own commentaries. He also published biblical commentaries by Juan de → Valdés.

■ **Literature:** E. Boehmer, *Bibliotheca Wiffeniana,* vol. 2 (Strasbourg and London, 1883) 57–100; A. G. Kinder, *Spanish Protestants and Reformers in the Sixteenth Century* (London, 1983) n. 372–82; C. Gilly, *Spanien und der Basler Buchdruck bis 1600* (Basle and Frankfurt/Main, 1985); A. G. Kinder, "J. P. (Pierius)," *Diálogo ecuménico* 21 (1986) 31–64; K. Reinhardt, *Bibelkommentare spanischer Autoren,* vol. 2 (Madrid, 1999) 188f.

FERNANDO DOMÍNGUEZ

Petri, (1) *Olaus.* Leading Reformer of Sweden, born January 6, 1493 in Örebro (Sweden), died April 9, 1552 in Stockholm. He studied in Uppsala, Leipzig, and Wittenberg, taking his bachelor's degree in March, 1517. He was promoted to the degree of master in February, 1518 and returned in the same year to Sweden, where he became secretary to Bishop Matthias of Strängnäs. He was ordained deacon in 1520. Petri began to preach in support of the Reformation, and moved to Stockholm, where he worked as a municipal secretary and began his career as a writer, publishing a catechism (1527), a hymnal (1528), a liturgical order of service (1529, revised 1541), a book for domestic worship (1530), a missal (1531), and his chronicle of Swedish history (1530).

Petri was chancellor to → Gustav I Vasa for three years. He was ordained priest in 1539 and became a curate in Stockholm. He was accused of high treason in 1530 and condemned to death, but he was reprieved and succeeded in regaining the king's confidence. He was a true pupil of Luther, and was also influenced by → humanism.

■ **Editions:** *O.-P. Samlade Skrifter,* ed. B. Hesselman, 4 vols. (Uppsala, 1914–18).

■ **Literature:** *TRE* 26:260–63.—G. T. Westin, *Historieskrivaren Olavus P.* (Lund, 1946); R. Murray, *Olavus P.* (Stockholm, 1952); S. Kjöllerström, *Guds och Sveriges lag under reformationstiden* (Lund, 1957); S. Ingebrand, *Olavus P. reformatoriska åskådning* (Uppsala, 1964); C. Gardemeister, *Den suveräne Guden. En studie i Olavus P.s teologi* (Lund, 1989).

INGMAR BROHED

■ **Additional Bibliography:** F. Hallencreutz, *O. P.* (Uppsala, 1994); T. Jäger, *Olavus Petri, Reformator in Schweden . . .* (Bonn, 1995); H. U. Bächtold, ed., *Olavus P. und die Reformation in Schweden* (Zug, 2002).

(2) *Laurentius.* First archbishop of the Evangelical Lutheran Church of Sweden, brother of (1), born 1499 in Örebro, died October 26, 1573 in Uppsala. He studied in Wittenberg in the 1520s, and was elected archbishop by a national church council in 1531. He was consecrated by Petrus → Magni, bishop of Västerås, who had been consecrated bishop according to the Catholic rite in Rome in 1524. This is the reason for the affirmation that a Roman Catholic apostolic succession was maintained in the Swedish Lutheran Church. King → Gustav I Vasa had reduced the extent of church property, and Petri defended this action; at the same time, however, he emphasized the church's independence in religious matters.

Petri acted with moderation in the introduction of the Reformation. His theological writings had a tremendous influence on the Swedish Reformation, and he was one of the scholars who translated the Bible into Swedish ("Gustav Vasa Bible" [Uppsala, 1541]). He published a church hymnal (1553, revised editions 1562, 1567), the Swedish edition of Martin Luther's *Catechism* (1562), and the first Swedish church order (Uppsala, 1571). This confirmed the episcopal structure of the Swedish church and preserved many older liturgical traditions. Petri's theology was influenced by Luther, Johannes → Brenz, and (to a lesser extent) Philipp Melanchthon.

■ **Catalogue of Works:** R. Kick, *Tel un navire sur la mer déchaînée. La communauté chrétienne dans l'œuvre de L. P., archevêque d'Uppsala (1531–73)* (Lund, 1997).
■ **Literature:** Å. Andrén, *Högmässa och nattvardsgång i reformations-tidens svenska kyrkoliv* (Stockholm, 1954); B. Ahlberg, *L. P. nattvardsuppfattning* (Lund, 1964); S. Kjöllerström, *Kräkla och Mitra. En undersökning av biskopsvigningen i Sverige under reformationstidevarvet* (Lund, 1965); I. Brohed, ed., *Reformationens konsolidering i de nordiska länderna 1540–1610* (Oslo, 1990); C. Palmblad, *Mässa på svenska. Den reformatoriska mässan i Sverige mot den senmedeltida bakgrunden* (Lund, 1998).

INGMAR BROHED

Peucer, *Caspar.* Doctor and historian, born January 6, 1525 in Bautzen, died September 25, 1602 in Dessau. He began his studies in Wittenberg in 1540, and had close scholarly and personal contacts in this period with Philipp Melanchthon, whose youngest daughter, Magdalena, he married in 1550. After studies in mathematics and medicine, he became professor of higher mathematics in Wittenberg in 1553. He took his doctorate in medicine in 1560, and became personal physician to electoral prince August of Saxony in 1570. He wrote the continuation of Melanchthon's universal history (the *Chronicon Carionis*). As the theological and literary executor of his father-in-law, he was accused of → Crypto-Calvinism and was imprisoned under harsh conditions from 1574 to 1586.

■ **Works:** *Commentarius de praecipuis divinationum generibus* (Wittenberg, 1553); *Kurtze historische Erzelung von dem fürstlichem Hause zu Anhalt* (Wittenberg, 1572); *Historia carcerum et liberationis divinae* (Zurich, 1605).
■ **Literature:** R. Kolb, *C. P.'s Library* (St. Louis, 1976); U. Neddermeyer, "K. P. Melanchthons Universalgeschichtsschreibung," in *Melanchthon in seinen Schülern,* ed. H. Scheible (Wiesbaden, 1997) 69–101.

STEFAN RHEIN

■ **Additional Bibliography:** W. Janse, "Wittenberg 'Calvinizans.' The Involvement of Melanchthon, P., and Elber in the Bremen Sacramentian Controversy, 1560," in *Ordenlich und fruchtbar.* Festschrift W. van't Spijker (Leiden, 1997) 53–67; R. Bröer, "Gesundheitspädagogik statt Tröstung. Die theologische Bewältigung von Krankheit bei Philipp Melanchthon und C. P.," *Sudhoffs Archiv* 85 (2001) 18–44; U. Koch, ed., *Zwischen Katheder, Thron und Kerker: Leben und Werk des Humanisten C. P.* (Bautzen, 2002).

Peutinger, *Conrad.* Humanist and politician, born October 15, 1465 in Augsburg, where he died December 28, 1547. He studied law in Padua and Bologna from 1482 to 1488, and had contacts with Italian humanists (Giovanni Pico della Mirandola, Ermolao Barbaro the Younger, Marsilio Ficino, Pomponius Laetus). He took his doctorate in law in Padua in 1491. His marriage to Margarete Welser and his post as municipal secretary of Augsburg (1497-1534) made Peutinger one of the leading men in the city, and an influential politician. He was a close associate of Emperor Maximilian I, whom he advised on both political and personal matters (*Geschichte Habsburgs* and other books). On the imperial level, he represented the interests of the Upper German cities and of the great merchants of Augsburg, writing memoranda on monopolies and on foreign trade. Peutinger corresponded with numerous humanists and princes and was an important historian and expert in classical inscriptions; he researched into numismatics, had a collection of antiquities, and published the Tabula Peutingeriana, a copy of a Roman road map. He also edited Latin inscriptions and texts relating to German and imperial history. He favored reform in the church, and was initially sympathetic to Martin Luther. He took part in an attempt at mediation between the religious parties in Worms in 1521, under the auspices of → Erasmus of Rotterdam and Johannes → Faber. However, he remained in the Roman Catholic Church, since he was convinced that reform must take place under the aegis of the imperial authorities. After the Reformation was introduced into Augsburg, Peutinger withdrew from public life in 1534.

■ **Sources:** *K. P.s Briefwechsel,* ed. E. König (Munich, 1923); *Historische Kataloge der Bayerischen Staatsbibliothek München,* vol. 11 (Wiesbaden, 1996) 552–55; *VD 16* 15:678f.

■ **Literature:** *BBKL* 7:392–97; *Deutsche biographische Enzyklopädie,* vol. 7 (Munich, 1998) 630; *CEras* 3:74ff.—H. Lutz, *C. P. Beiträge zu einer politischen Biographie* (Augsburg, 1958); B. Trautner, "Willibald Pirckheimer und C. P.," *Pirckheimer Jahrbuch* 5 (1989/90) 109–39.

HERIBERT SMOLINSKY

■ **Additional Bibliography:** A. Gössner, "K. P.s 'mittlerer Weg,'" *ZBKG* 67 (1998) 1–11; H. Lutz, *Conrad P.* (Augsburg, 2001); H. Lutz, *C. P.: Beiträge zu einer politischen Biographie* (Augsburg, 2001).

Pezel, *Christoph.* Theologian, born March 5, 1539 in Plauen (Vogtland), died February 2, 1604 in Bremen. After studies in Jena and Wittenberg, where Philipp Melanchthon directed his work in 1557, he became schoolmaster in Plauen and Annaberg. From 1567 onward, he taught philosophy in Wittenberg, and then theology from 1569. He took his doctorate in theology there in 1570. He was accused of holding → Crypto-Calvinist views and dismissed from office in 1574. He was expelled from Saxony in 1576, but was invited to Dillenburg by Count Johann VI of Nassau-Dillenburg in 1577 and commissioned to set up a school of higher studies in Siegen. He became Reformed pastor in Herborn in 1578, and was sent in 1581 to Bremen, where he became pastor in St. Mary's

church and superintendent in 1584. Pezel wrote extensively, and attacked the elaboration of a Lutheran → Concord.

■ **Catalogue of Works:** *VD 16* 15:680–86.

■ **Literature:** J. Moltmann, *Ch. P. und der Calvinismus in Bremen* (Bremen, 1958); R. Wetzel, "Ch. P.," in H. Scheible, ed., *Melanchthon in seinen Schülern* (Wiesbaden, 1997) 465–566.

CHRISTIAN PETERS

■ **Additional Bibliography:** H. Klüting, "'Wittenberger Katechismus' und 'Wittenberger Fragstücke.' Ch. P. und die Wittenberger Theologie," *ZKG* 112 (2001) 1–43.

Pfefferkorn, *Johannes* (initially: Josef). Convert from Judaism, born 1469 in Nuremberg, died 1522/1523 in Cologne. He became a Christian in 1504, and worked until 1513 as an unsuccessful itinerant preacher and missionary among the Jews; from 1514 onward, he was master of a hospital in Cologne. As a convert from Judaism, Pfefferkorn faced both high expectations and the demand that he justify himself. This led him to write religious and political pamphlets against the Jews between 1507 and 1521. In his *Judenspiegel* (1507), he demanded that all Jewish writings other than the Bible be confiscated; later, he went so far as to demand that all Jews be expelled. After Pfefferkorn received imperial authorization to confiscate writings, the archbishop of Mainz commissioned a number of expert memoranda in 1510 on the question how one should deal with Jewish books, and the Hebraist Johannes → Reuchlin protested against an indiscriminate destruction of all the rabbinic writings. Pfefferkorn defended himself against Reuchlin's criticism in his pamphlet *Handt Spiegel* (1511), to which Reuchlin at once replied in his *Augenspiegel.* The controversy between Pfefferkorn and Reuchlin developed into a merciless public fight, with polemical pamphlets by the Cologne theologians on the one side and Reuchlin's humanist friends on the other (Letters of → Obscure Men, 1515 and 1517).

■ **Literature:** H. A. Oberman, *Wurzeln des Antisemitismus. Christenangst und Judenplage im Zeitalter von Humanismus und Reformation* (Berlin, [2]1983); H.-M. Kirn, *Das Bild vom Juden im Deutschland des frühen 16.Jh., dargestellt an den Schriften J. P.s* (Tübingen, 1989); E. Martin, *Die deutschen Schriften des J. P.* (Göppingen, 1994).

ANDREAS METZ

Pfeffinger, *Johannes.* Lutheran theologian, born December 27, 1493 in Wasserburg (Inn), died January 1, 1573 in Leipzig. He was ordained priest in 1518 and became preacher at the collegiate church in Passau in 1521. He embraced the Reformation in 1523 and fled to Wittenberg, where he continued his studies. He became superintendent in Leipzig in 1540. He took his doctorate in theology in 1543 and became professor at the university of Leipzig. He was vehemently attacked by the → Gnesiolutherans as a Philippist and one of the authors of the Leipzig Interim (→ Augsburg Interim). He unleashed the synergistic controversy at the Disputation of → Leipzig in 1550.

■ **Works:** *VD 16* 16:2322–57.
■ **Literature:** *TRE* 20:721–29; *BBKL* 7:413–16.—G. Wartenberg, "Philipp Melanchthon und J. P.," in *Philipp Melanchthon und Leipzig* (Leipzig, 1997) 40–50.
                                                              BRUNO STEIMER

■ **Additional Literature:** E. Rummel, *The Case against Johann Reuchlin: Religious and Social Controversy in 16th Century Germany* (Toronto, 2002).

Pflug, *Julius.* Bishop of Naumburg, born 1499 in Eythra near Leipzig, died September 3, 1564 in Zeitz. He became cathedral canon in Meissen in 1514. He received minor orders in 1516; in 1519, he was ordained subdeacon and became archdeacon of Lower Lausitz. He was at the court in Dresden in 1522, and was appointed assessor at the supreme court in Leipzig in 1522. He was appointed cathedral canon in Zeitz in 1522, and provost of the cathedral in 1523; subsequently, he acquired canonries in the cathedrals of Merseburg (1528), Mainz (1530), and Naumberg (1532), and became dean of the cathedral of Meissen in 1537. He fled to Mainz in 1539, after the Revolution was introduced forcibly into Meissen and St. Benno's tomb was destroyed; it was at this time that he became cathedral canon in Magdeburg. He was elected bishop of Naumburg on January 20, 1541, but was unable to exercise this office until 1547 (Nikolaus von → Amsdorf; *Supplication und Replica widder des Durchleuchtigsten und Hochgebornen Churfürsten zu Sachsen tätliche handlungen,* published without indication of place, 1542).

Pflug's writings reveal the thorough education he had acquired in his studies of law, ancient languages, and philosophy in Leipzig from 1510 to 1517 and again from 1522 to 1524, where his pro-

fessors included Richard Crocus and Petrus → Mosellanus (at whose funeral Pflug preached: *Oratio funebris in mortem Petri Moselani* [Wittenberg, 1524]). He also studied in Bologna and Padua (under Romolo Amaseo) from 1517 to 1520, and in Rome from 1525 to 1527 under Gregorius Haloander and Lazzaro Bonamico, and under Cardinal Nikolaus von → Schönberg, who was his uncle. He studied in Venice in 1528-1529. His writings included commentaries on Romans, Galatians, and other books of scripture, theological monographs (especially on → justification, the → church, and the → sacraments), memoranda on church reform and on the confessional question, and pastoral letters. Most of his library has been preserved in Zeitz. It contains c. 1,500 books in the fields of theology (especially biblical works in Hebrew, Aramaic, and Syriac, and works of the Greek fathers), law, medicine, history, poetry, and philosophy. Pflug exchanged humanistic letters with men such as Caspar Borner, Joachim → Camerarius, Johannes → Cochlaeus, → Crotus Rubeanus, Caspar → Cruciger, Johann → Hess, Johannes von Maltitz, Philipp Melanchthon, Johannes Metzler, and Willibald → Pirckheimer. His endeavors on behalf of church reform and the restoration of Christian unity were influenced especially by → Erasmus of Rotterdam, whose book *De sarcienda Ecclesiae concordia* (1533) was dedicated to Pflug, and by Georg → Witzel. Pflug took part in the regional religious dialogues in Leipzig in 1534 and 1539 as adviser to Duke → George of Saxony and confidant of Bishop Maltitz of Meissen (*Christliche Lehre zu gründlichem Unterricht des rechten Glaubens und gottseligen Wandels* [Mainz, 1541]; Pflug was one of the authors of this work in his capacity as dean of the cathedral of Meissen in 1539). He argued in favor of granting the → chalice to the laity and priestly marriage (→ celibacy). Pflug took part in all the religious dialogues on the level of the empire from 1530 onward (as joint spokesman in 1541, joint president in 1546, and president in 1547). The conception of the → Augsburg Interim—fellowship in the common faith, while accepting a variety of ecclesiastical customs—is basically his idea. He attended the Council of Trent from November 20, 1551 to March 25, 1552. He held a speech about church reform, and translated his ideas into action in the catechism he published: *Institutio christiani hominis* (Cologne, 1562, 1564). In his admonitions (cf. list of his writings), he addressed the people, the pastors (almost all of whom were married), the subjects of the ecclesiastical rulers, and all Germans.

■[Works (in addition to those named above): *Christliche Ermanung zur Busse* (Erfurt, 1550); *Christliche Erinnerung und Ermanung* (n.p., 1553, 1555); *Christliche Ermanungen, Welche die Seelsorgere . . . Bey dem Sacrament der Tauffe . . . des Altars: Bey der Verehlichung: Bey den Krancken: gebrauchen sollen vnd mögen* (Erfurt, 1550); *Von christlicher Busse und dem gesetze Gotts* (n.p., 1556; Cologne, 1562); *Policey Ordennung* (n.p., 1556); *Christliche Ermanung an des Naumburgischen Stieffts vnderthanen vnd vorwandten, wes sie sich bey dem vorgefallenem hochbeschwerlichem missvorstand in Religions sachen halten sollen . . .* (Cologne, 1562); *Oratio funebris de morte Caroli V. Imperatoris . . .* (Dillingen, 1559); *De Republica Germaniae seu Imperio constituendo* (Cologne, 1562; Antwerp 1562, 1563); *Gründtlicher vnd Christlicher Bericht, Ob einer mit gutem gewissen die alte Catholische Religion verlassen, vnd sich der Augspurgischen Confession anhangen möge* (Cologne, 1571); E. Hoche, ed., *De ecclesiae concordia et salute ad Germanos Pars I: Programm des königlichen Stiftsgymnasiums in Zeitz* (Zeitz, 1865) 1–24; *CT* 12:290–95; *RQ* 50 (1955) 29–43; *ARCEG* 3–6, passim.—Letters: J. V. Pollet, ed., *J. P., Correspondance,* 5 vols. (Leiden, 1969–82).—For the handwritten literary remains, see V. Marcolino and V. Pfnür, *Bibliographia Pflugiana* (Münster, 1999).
■ Literature: *DSp* 12:1253–58; *CEras* 3:77f.; *TRE* 26:449–53; *OER* 3:252f. – E. Neuss and J. V. Pollet, ed., *Pflugiana* (Münster, 1880); *Gestalten der Kirchengeschichte,* ed. M. Greschat, vol. 6 (Stuttgart, 1981) 129–46; Th. Freudenberger, "J. P. über den Laienkelch," *AHC* 21 (1989) 418–27; J. V. Pollet, *J. P. (1499–1564) et la crise religieuse dans l'Allemagne du XVIᵉ siècle* (Leiden, 1990); F. Prause, *J. P. (1499–1564). Versuch einer Standortbestimmung eines Vermittlungstheologen in den dreissiger Jahren des 16.Jh.* (Münster, 1992).

VINZENZ PFNÜR

■ Additional Bibliography: S. Kröner, ed., *J. P.* (Naumburg [Saale], 2001).

Pfyffer, *Ludwig.* Prominent Swiss politician of the Catholic → reform, born 1524 in Lucerne, where he died March 17, 1594. He made his career in the pay of the French from 1553 onward, and was a leader (the "Swiss king") in Catholic Switzerland from 1569. He negotiated an alliance of the Catholic towns in 1586, and an alliance with Spain in 1587. As mayor, he energetically promoted the foundation of Jesuit houses from 1571 onward. Although he had contacts with papal Visitors (Giovanni Antonio → Volpe; Giovanni Francesco

Bonomi), he rejected the idea of a permanent nunciature.
■ Literature: *Handbuch der Schweizer Geschichte,* vol. 1 (Zurich, 1972) 590ff.; *Helvetia Sacra,* vol. 7 (Berne, 1976) 115–18.—J. Studhalter, *Die Jesuiten in Luzern 1574–1652* (Stans, 1973) 57–113, 222.

JOSEF SIEGWART

Philip I of Hessen, "the Magnanimous." Marquis (from 1518), born November 13, 1504 in Marburg, died March 31, 1567 in Kassel. He was the most prominent of the first generation of typical Protestant princes in Germany. His mother ruled as regent until 1518, and he experienced in these years the threat posed to his state by a corporate government (1509-1514); accordingly, his central political aim was to extend and consolidate his own personal rule. Philip played a decisive role in military actions against Franz von → Sickingen (1522-1523), the peasants in central Germany (1525), and the → Baptists in Münster (1534-1535). He was sympathetic to the Reformation from the imperial parliament of Worms (1521) onward; he had studied theology, and Philipp Melanchthon made such an impression on him that he professed the Protestant faith openly in 1524 and became one of the political leaders of the Reformation. He reorganized the church structure and ecclesiastical property in Hessen in 1526-1527; initially, he followed the conception of a territorial church based on the parishes, as developed by Franz → Lambert of Avignon, but he abandoned these ideas when Martin Luther objected. Philip founded the first Protestant university at Marburg in 1527. He sought to bring about unity among the Protestants by means of the religious dialogue in → Marburg in 1529. His sense of his own duty as an imperial prince and his keen political awareness of risks to the Reformation made Philip a resolute champion of the opposition to the imperial and religious policies of Emperor → Charles V on the part of the Protestant imperial princes. He succeeded in building a bridge to the Protestant imperial cities in Upper Germany in the → Schmalkaldic League (1531), despite all the disagreements; he also saw the need for solidarity and for the consolidation of the Reformation as overriding the traditional differences between the princes and the Estates. He played a central role in the restoration to power of

Duke → Ulrich of Württemberg in 1534. His bigamous marriage to Margarethe von der Saale gravely damaged his own prestige and the Protestant cause. After 1540, he was helpless against the pressure applied by the emperor. He was commander-in-chief in the → Schmalkaldic War, together with electoral prince → Johann Friedrich of Saxony. After the defeat at Mühlberg (Elbe), Philipp submitted in 1547 to Charles V, who kept him in prison until he was freed in 1552 under the terms of the Treaty of → Passau, thanks in no small measure to the help of electoral prince → Moritz of Saxony. The old vigor was now gone from the policy of consolidating and extending his own power, which Philip had conducted as a territorial prince; nevertheless, he continued even after 1555 to pursue a policy of uniting all the Protestants in the empire. He was a force for integration on the imperial level, providing a rallying-point which was not limited to the Protestant confession. He dedicated himself with great zeal to the consolidation of his territory, which he divided among his four sons before his death. This regulation of the succession was the first step in a process which led later to the definitive partition of Hessen into a Reformed territory centered on Kassel and a Lutheran territory centered on Darmstadt.

■ **Sources:** *Politisches Archiv des Landgrafen Ph., Inventar der Bestände,* vols. 1–2, ed. F. Küch (Leipzig, 1904–10); vols. 3–4, ed. W. Heinemeyer (Marburg, 1954–59); *Briefwechsel Landgraf Ph.s des Grossmüthigen von Hessen mit Bucer,* ed. M. Lenz, 3 Teile (Leipzig, 1880–91).

■ **Literature:** *TRZRK* 4:254–88.—Ch. von Rommel, *Ph. der Grossmütige,* 3 vols. (Giessen, 1830); W. Sohm, *Territorium und Reformation in der hessischen Geschichte 1526–1555* (Marburg, 1915, ²1957); G. Müller, *Franz Lambert von Avignon und die Reformation in Hessen* (Marburg, 1958); R. Hauswirth, *Landgraf Ph. von Hessen und Zwingli* (Tübingen, 1968); V. Press, "Landgraf Ph. der Grossmütige von Hessen," in K. Scholder, ed., *Protestantische Profile* (Königstein [Taunus], 1983) 60–77; W. Heinemeyer, *Das Zeitalter der Reformation, Das Werden Hessens,* ed. idem (Marburg, 1986) 225–66; M. Rudersdorf, *Ludwig IV. Landgraf von Hessen-Marburg 1537–1604. Landesteilung und Luthertum in Hessen.* (Mainz, 1991).

MANFRED RUDERSDORF

■ **Additional Bibliography:** W. Heinemeyer, *Ph. der Grossmütige und die Reformation in Hessen* (Marburg, 1997); F. Krapf, *Landgraf Ph. der Grossmütige von Hessen und die Religionskämpfe im Bistum Münster, 1532–36*

(Marburg, 1997); R. A. Cahill, *P. of Hesse and the Reformation* (Mainz, 2001).

Philip II of Spain. King (from 1556), born May 21, 1527 in Valladolid, son of → Charles V and Isabella of Portugal, died September 13, 1598 in the Escorial. Philip received a thorough humanistic education and was entrusted with tasks of government at an early age, thanks to his father's lengthy absence from Spain. In 1543, he married Maria Manuela of Portugal, who died two years later while giving birth to their son, Don Carlos. Philip married three more times: the English queen → Mary Tudor (1554), Isabella of Valois (1559), and Anna von Habsburg (1570); this last marriage produced the only male heir who survived him, viz., King Philip III.

After Charles V abdicated in 1556, Philip became ruler over the western part of his father's domains, which included the Spanish kingdoms, the Italian territories of Milan, Naples, Sicily, and Sardinia, Franche-Comté, the Netherlands, and the West Indies. In 1565, his sovereignty was extended to include the Philippines (which were named after him). Philip renewed the structures of administration and established the so-called polysynodal government system, which characterized Spanish institutions throughout the Ancien Régime. The two great goals of his domestic and foreign policy were the extension of Spanish hegemony and the defense of Catholicism. Not a few of his contemporaries held that he sought to throw a religious cloak over his real political goals, but both goals were in fact one single aim in Philip's thinking: in order to guarantee the success of the Catholic cause, it was necessary for the Spanish monarchy to strengthen its position.

Philip's reign consists of two phases, the "Mediterranean" and the "Atlantic." The briefer Mediterranean phase was dominated by the political and religious problems in the Iberian peninsula and in his Italian domains, as well as by the struggle against the Turkish threat in the Mediterranean. The first set of problems can be seen in the war fought by the kingdom of Naples against the anti-Habsburg Pope → Paul IV in 1556; in the destruction of the Lutheran centers in Valladolid and Seville in 1559 at the behest of the Spanish Inquisition (which must be seen in the context of the tensions with → Pius IV caused by the resumption of the Council of Trent and the conclusion of its last session in 1562-1563); in the jurisdictional conflicts between the ecclesiastical and the secular powers in the Spanish domains in Italy during the pontificate of → Pius V; and in the crushing of the rebellion of the Moriscos in the kingdom of Granada (1568-1571). In the aftermath of the Peace of Cateau-Cambrésis with France (1559), Philip was able to devote his energies to the struggle against Islam. The first consequence was his support of the Maltese knights, who were hard pressed by the Berbers (1565). This policy culminated in the league he formed with the Holy See and Venice, which made possible the victory over the Turks at Lepanto in 1571.

In the second phase of his reign, Philip concentrated on the Atlantic side of his domains. The uprising in the Netherlands in 1566 was a fruit of the spread of → Calvinism and of the disaffection caused by the Spanish policy of centralization. The harsh repressive methods employed by the duke of → Alba proved ineffective, but Duke Alessandro Farnese succeeded in winning the southern, Catholic provinces back to submission to Spain from 1578 onward. After the death of the last king of the Avis dynasty in 1580, Philip was able to make good his claims to the Portuguese throne. For the first time in history, the entire Iberian peninsula was subject to one single ruler, and Philip extended his domains in South America to include the rich Brazilian colonies. His struggle against the Protestant powers in Europe did not meet with a positive outcome: his attempt at an invasion of England led to the destruction of Spanish maritime power (the so-called invincible Armada) in 1588, and the military support he gave the French Catholics did not prevent the Calvinist → Henry (IV) of Navarre from becoming king of France. On May 2, 1598, France and Spain signed the Peace Treaty of Vervins. Philip died in the Escorial, a monastery and seat of government which he had built for himself. Its buildings are a monument to the golden age of the Spanish monarchy.

Recent historical scholarship sees Philip's person and politics in a different light than earlier scholars. The "Black legend" (leyenda negra) painted the picture of a bigoted and intolerant despot, a cruel father who was guilty of the death of his son, Don Carlos, and a mediocre and pedantic man. Researches in the last two decades

have brought about a profound revision of this gloomy portrait. Philip was a loving father who bore no responsibility for the death of his son in 1568. He was a man who appreciated art and music and had expert knowledge of both these fields, a patron of artists, a benefactor and collector of art. Despite his excessive pedantry and his instinctive distrust of his collaborators, he frequently displayed the ability to discern the true extent of important political problems. However, his working methods, his tendencies toward centralization, and the recurring financial difficulties of the monarchy—the crown had to postpone the payment of its debts three times (in 1557, 1575, and 1596)—meant that he was not always able to achieve his goals.

There has been a similarly profound change in the evaluation of Philip's religious politics. In the past, his attitude towards the church was often called "caesaropapist," but today it seems clear that his policies were inspired by the principles of "regalism": in other words, he attempted to impose forms of state control on the various spheres of church life in his domains. He even attempted to influence the actions of the pope, when it was a case of defending the interests of the Catholic cause, and all the popes in the second half of the 16th century were forced to acknowledge that Spain was the only power on which the Apostolic See could count for support in its struggle against Protestantism and Islam. Besides this, Philip's use of his authority to control the church served to promote the enforcement of the conciliar decrees of Trent in his realm. These decrees were accepted in their entirety and published in Spain in July, 1564.

■ **Sources:** *Colección de documentos inéditos para la historia de España,* 113 vols. (Madrid, 1842–95, index); *Correspondance de Philippe II sur les affaires des Pays-Bas (1558–77),* 5 vols., ed. L. P. Gachard (Brussels, 1848–79); *Correspondance de Marguerite d'Autriche avec Philippe II,* 3 vols., ed. idem (Brussels, 1867–81); *Correspondencia diplomática entre España y la Santa Sede durante el pontificado de S. Pío V,* 4 vols., ed. L. Serrano (Madrid, 1914); *Correspondencia privada de Felipe II con su secretario Mateo Vázquez,* ed. C. Riba García (Madrid, 1959); *Cartas de Felipe II a sus hijas,* ed. F. J. Bouza Álvarez (Madrid, 1988).

■ **Literature:** *BBKL* 7:454–71.—F. Braudel, *La Méditerranée et le monde méditerranéen à l'époque de Philippe II,* 2 vols. (Paris, 1966); P. Pierson, *Philip II of Spain* (London, 1975); G. Parker, *Philip II.* (London, 1979); F. Edelmayer, *Maximilian II., Ph. II. und Reichsitalien. Die*

Auseinandersetzungen um das Reichslehen Finale in Ligurien (Stuttgart, 1988); J. Buckler, *Philip II and the Sacred War* (Leiden and New York, 1989); F. Checa, *Felipe II, mecenas de las artes* (Madrid, 1992); *La corte de Felipe II*, ed. J. Martínez Millán (Madrid, 1994); H. Kamen, *Felipe de España* (Madrid, ⁹1998); M. Fernández Álvarez, *Felipe II y su tiempo* (Madrid, 1998); *Felipe II y el arte de su tiempo* (Madrid, 1998); A. Borromeo, "Felipe II y el absolutismo confesional: Felipe II, un monarca y su época," in *La Monarquía Hispánica* (Madrid, 1998) 185–95.

AGOSTINO BORROMEO

■ **Additional Bibliography:** H. Kamen, "La politica religiosa de Felipe II," *Anuario de historia de la iglesia* 7 (1998) 21–33; A. Molinié, ed., *Philippe II et l'Espagne* (Paris, 1999); C. Slade, "The Relationship between Teresa of Avila and P.," *Reformation and Renaissance Review* 1 (1999) 72–99; P. Williams, *Philip II* (Basingstoke, 2001); M. Vasold, *Ph. II.* (Hamburg, 2001).

Pigge (Pighius), *Albert*. Catholic controversial theologian, born c. 1490 in Campen (province of Overijssel), died December 28, 1542 in Utrecht. He took the degree of master of arts in Louvain in 1509, and then began the study of theology. He studied in Paris from 1518 to 1522, and then entered the service of Pope → Hadrian VI in Rome. He was appointed private chamberlain to the pope in 1525. He was in the Netherlands from 1531, becoming provost of St. John's church in Utrecht in 1535. Pigge was an adviser to the nuncios, and took part (though not as a full participant) in the religious dialogues of → Worms and → Regensburg in 1540-1542; this led to a literary controversy with Martin → Bucer. In addition to astrological writings and works on calendar reform, and a theological debate with the Greeks, Pigge is important above all as an anti-Reformation controversial theologian. Pigge's doctrine of free will and predestination was directed against Calvin, who replied with a treatise of his own (CR 6:225-404). Pigge maintained the doctrine of double righteousness, which was discussed at Trent, but remained a matter of dispute even after the council; his writings on this subject were placed on the Index in Lisbon in 1624. His chef d'oeuvre, *Hierarchiae Ecclesiasticae Assertio* (Cologne, 1538; often reprinted), played down the importance of councils and proposed an exaggerated papalist doctrine, according to which the infallible pope could never become a heretic.

■ **Sources:** W. Friedensburg, "Beiträge zum Briefwechsel der katholischen Gelehrten Deutschlands im Reformationszeitalter," *ZKG* 23 (1902) 110–55; *CT* passim.
■ **Catalogue of Works:** H. Jedin *Studien über die Schriftstellertätigkeit P.s.* (Münster, 1931) 7–47; Klaiber nos. 2510–22; *VD 16* 16:98ff.
■ **Literature:** *TRE* 26:632ff.; *CEras* 3:84f.; *KThR* 1:98–106; *BBKL* 7:610ff.—G. Melles, *Albertus Pighius en zijn strijd met Calvin over het Liberum arbitrium* (Kampen, 1973); H. J. Sieben, *Die katholische Konzilsidee von der Reformation bis zur Aufklärung* (Paderborn, 1988) passim; H. Rimbach, *Gnade und Erkenntnis in Calvins Prädestinationslehre. Calvin im Vergleich mit Pighius, Beza und Melanchthon* (Frankfurt/Main, 1996) 123–51.

HERIBERT SMOLINSKY

■ **Additional Bibliography:** A. N. Lane, "When Did A. Pighius Die?," *Nederlands archief voor kerkgeschiedenis* 80 (2000) 327–42; A. N. Lane, "A. P.'s Controversial Work on Original Sin," *Reformation and Renaissance Review* 2 (2000) 29–61.

Pirckheimer. A family that emigrated from the Donauried area to Nuremberg and rose to the dignity of city councilors:

(1) *C(h)aritas*. Poor Clare (1479), born March 21, 1467 in Eichstätt, died August 19, 1532 in Nuremberg. She was the oldest daughter of Dr. Johann Pirckheimer, a lawyer at the court of the bishop of Eichstätt. She entered the Poor Clare convent in Nuremberg at the age of twelve, and became abbess on December 20, 1503. She was outstanding both for her piety and for her humanistic education, and she maintained contact with her brother Willibald [see (2), below] and numerous theologians and intellectuals (Sixtus Tucher, Kaspar Nützel, Christoph → Scheurl, Conradus Celtis, → Erasmus of Rotterdam, Stephan Fridolin, Konrad → Pellikan, and others). C(h)aritas and her nuns read the Bible and the church fathers in Latin. After the Reformation was introduced into Nuremberg and the city council endeavored to persuade the nuns to abandon the religious life, they appealed to their freedom of conscience. C(h)aritas got Philipp Melanchthon involved, and initially succeeded in preventing the closure of her convent, but it was condemned to extinction in the long term. Her sister Klara was also a nun in this convent. She succeeded C(h)aritas as abbess in 1532-1533.

■ **Sources:** *C.-P.-Quellensammlung,* 4 Hefte (Landshut, 1961–66) Heft 2: Denkwürdigkeiten; Heft 3: Briefe, both ed. J. Pfanner.

■ **Literature:** *LMA* 6:2173f.—L. Kurras and F. Machilek, eds., *Ausstellungskatalog "C. P."* (Munich, 1982); M. H. Jung, "Die Begegnung Melanchthons mit C. P.," *Jahrbuch für fränkische Landesforschung* 56 (1996) 235–57; F. Machilek, "Menschenwürde und Gewissensfreiheit," in *In Würde leben.* Festschrift E. L. Grasmück (Bonn, 1998) 49–71.

■ **Additional Literature:** S. B. Knackmuss, "Die Äbtissin und das schwarze Schaf oder zur 'vox ipsissima' einer 'inutilis abatissa'," *Collectanea Franciscana* 73 (2003) 93–159.

(2) **Willibald.** Humanist, brother of (1), born December 5, 1470 in Eichstätt, died December 22, 1530 in Nuremberg. He studied in Padua and Pavia from 1488 to 1495, and was a member of the municipal council from 1496 to 1523 (with a break between 1502 and 1505), serving as legal adviser, envoy, and military commander. He became an imperial counselor in 1500. He was a personal friend or a correspondent of Albrecht Dürer and leading humanists such as Giovanni Pico della Mirandola, → Erasmus of Rotterdam, → Beatus Rhenanus, Johann Trithemius, and other intellectuals. He read Greek, and was a prominent author of both prose and verse, as well as translator and reviser of classical works (especially satires) and patristic texts. Initially, he took an unambiguously positive view of the Reformation, but he distanced himself from this movement as time went on, thanks to the violent conflicts and to his own personal experiences— especially in connection with St. Klara's convent [see (1), above]. In this period, he developed his own independent humanistic-Christian theology: "I am neither a Lutheran nor an Eckian, but a Christian."

■ **Works:** *Opera,* ed. M. Goldast (Frankfurt/Main, 1610); *W.-P.-Briefwechsel,* vols. 1–2, ed. E. Reicke (Munich, 1940–56), vol. 3, ed. D. Wuttke (Munich, 1989); *Eckius dedolatus* (Latin and German), ed. N. Holzberg (Stuttgart, 1983).

■ **Literature:** *BBKL* 7:628–33.—N. Holzberg, *W. P. Griechischer Humanismus in Deutschland* (Munich, 1981); D. Wuttke, *Der Humanist W. P.* (Nuremberg, 1994).—*P.-Jahrbuch* 1 (Nuremberg, 1985) ff. 12 (Wiesbaden, 1997) ff.

FRANZ MACHILEK

Pithou, *Pierre.* Lawyer and historian, born November 1, 1539 in Troyes, died November 1, 1596 in Nogent-sur-Seine. He studied law in Bourges and Valence, where he was the pupil and friend of Jacques Cujas (1522-1590). Initially, he was attracted by the Reformation, but he rejoined the Catholic Church after he barely escaped with his life in the massacre of St. → Bartholomew's Eve. His writings, which are mostly concerned with the early history of France and of Europe, gave French humanism a Gallican-national orientation which was to have important consequences. In his writings and his political activities, he supported the path of → Henry IV to power.

■ **Works:** *Opera sacra, iuridica, historica, miscellanea,* ed. Ch. Labbé (Paris, 1609).

■ **Literature:** *DThC* 12:2235–38; *BBKL* 7:651–56.—R. Zuber, "Tombeaux pour les P.," in *Mélanges sur la littérature de la Renaissance.* Festschrift V.-L. Saulnier (Geneva, 1984) 331–42; F. Lestringant and D. Ménager, eds., *Études sur la Satyre Ménippée* (Geneva, 1987) passim; *Les Pithous, les Lettres et la Paix du Royaume. Actes du colloque de Troyes, avril 1998* (Paris, 1999).

PIERRE E. LEROY

Pius IV. Pope (December 25, 1559–December 9, 1565), formerly *Gian Angelo de'Medici* (not related to the Medici of Florence), born March 31, 1499 in Milan. After studies in medicine and jurisprudence, he came to Rome in 1526 and held various offices in the church state. In 1542-1543, he was apostolic commissioner to the troops whom → Paul III sent against the Turks, and his career began to prosper under this pope. He received major orders when he was appointed archbishop of Ragusa in 1545. He was general commissioner to the papal auxiliary troops in the → Schmalkaldic War in Germany. He was created cardinal in 1549, but held no important offices during this period, since he did not sympathize with → Paul IV's desire for reform. He was elected in the difficult conclave in 1559 as a candidate of last resort, and he immediately changed the political course, endeavoring to establish good relations with Emperor → Ferdinand I and King → Philip II of Spain. Within the church, he toned down the harsh measures taken by Paul IV; for example, he rehabilitated Cardinal Giovanni → Morone. He pronounced sentence on the two nephews of Paul IV, who were executed; he himself, however, showered favors on a large number of his relatives. His favorite nephew, Charles → Borromeo, was created cardinal and administrator of the archdiocese of Milan in 1560, receiving the post of secretary of state. He honored the obligation he had accepted in his electoral capitulation, and after overcoming numerous political difficulties, summoned the council to meet at Trent again. It opened on January 18, 1562. When the controversies about the residential obligation of bishops, the papal → primacy, and the character of the episcopal office almost led to the collapse of the council, he appointed Morone its president. Thanks to Morone's skill, it proved possible to bring the council to a positive conclusion on December 3/4, 1563. Pius confirmed the decrees of the council as a whole by word of mouth on January 26, 1564, and in a solemn manner by the decree *Benedictus Deus* of June 30, 1564. He published the Index of Forbidden Books in March, 1564 and the Tridentine Profession of Faith in November, 1564, after he had reorganized the Rota, the Apostolic Penitentiary, and the Apostolic Chamber. Under pressure from Emperor → Maximilian II and the Bavarian dukes, Pius gave permission in 1564 for communion to be administered under both kinds in Germany, Austria, Bohemia, and Hungary (→ chalice for the laity). He promoted the arts and sciences. Discontent among the populace in the church state led to an unsuccessful conspiracy.

Pius was a transitional figure. Although he was personally marked by the Renaissance mentality—he had several illegitimate children before becoming pope—he could not close his eyes to the necessity of reforming the church. At the same time, he sought to save as much as possible of the old structures of the Roman curia.

■ **Sources:** *CT*; *NDB(G)* II:1–4.
■ **Literature:** *DThC* 12/2:1633–47; *EC* 9:1496; *Cath* 11:253f.; *BBKL* 7:665; *TRE* 26:652–55.—Th. von Sickel, *Zur Geschichte des Konzils von Trient* (Vienna, 1872); J. Šusta, *Die römische Curie und das Concil von Trient unter P. IV.*, 4 vols. (Vienna, 1904–14); L. von Pastor, *Geschichte der Päpste seit dem Ausgang des Mittelalters*, vol. 7 (Freiburg, 1920); F. Häfele, "Papst P. IV. und seine Nepoten," *Vierteljahresschrift für Geschichte und Landeskunde Vorarlbergs* 5 (1921) Heft 1; M. Constant, *Concession à l'Allemagne de la Communion sous les deux espèces*, 2 vols. (Paris, 1923); P. Paschini, *Il primo soggiorno di S. Carlo Borromeo a Roma* (Rome, 1935); H. Jedin, *Krisis und Wendepunkt des Trienter Konzils (1562/63)* (Würzburg, 1941); Jedin vol. 4/1–2; K. Ganzer, "Das Konzil von Trient—Angelpunkt für eine Reform der Kirche?," *RQ* 84 (1989) 31–50; idem, "Aspekte der katholischen Reformbewegungen im

16.Jh.," in *Abhandlungen der geistes- und sozialwissenschaftlichen Klasse der Akademie der Wissenschaften und der Literatur in Mainz* (Wiesbaden, 1991), n. 13.

KLAUS GANZER

■ **Additional Bibliography:** *Vatikanlexikon,* ed. N. Del Re (Augsburg, 1998) 586–89.—R. Rezzaghi, "Cronoca di un conclave. L'elevazione di Pio IV," *Salesianum* 48 (1986) 539–81.

Pius V. Pope (January 7, 1566–May 1, 1572), saint (feast, April 30), Dominican (1518), formerly *Michele Ghislieri*, born January 17, 1504 in Bosco near Alessandria. After studies in Genoa, he was ordained priest in 1528 and taught philosophy and theology in Pavia. As inquisitor of the diocese of Como, he came to the appreciative notice of Giampietro Carafa (later → Paul IV); under → Julius III, he became general commissioner of the Inquisition in Rome. He was appointed bishop of Sutri and Nepi in 1556 and created cardinal in 1557. He was appointed grand inquisitor of the Roman church in 1558, and bishop of Mondovì in 1560. Charles → Borromeo played the decisive role in his election as Pope. Pius entrusted the most important curial offices to men of the school of Paul IV. His twenty-five-year-old great-nephew, the Dominican Michele Bonelli, became "cardinal nephew."

The Council of Trent had left a number of tasks to be completed by the pope: the → Catechismus Romanus was published in 1566, the Roman Breviary in 1568, and the Roman Missal in 1570. The Apostolic Penitentiary was reorganized and its authority limited to the *forum internum*. Pius insisted on the clergy's residential obligation and promoted the foundation of seminaries. He was especially zealous for the Inquisition—every tendency to deviate from the faith was to be pursued with the strictest measures, and numerous persons were condemned to death. Pius proposed to take up afresh the inquisitional investigation of Cardinal Giovanni → Morone, whom Pius IV had rehabilitated. In the so-called controversy about grace, Pius condemned seventy-six propositions of Michael → Bajus and his adherents. In France, where → Calvinism was spreading, Pius aimed to destroy the → Huguenots completely, and he objected to the Peace of Saint Germain (1570). In the case of England, he resolved to act resolutely against → Elizabeth I, and he declared her guilty of heresy in the bull *Regnans in excelsis* (February 2, 1570). This meant that she was excommunicated and lost her right to the English throne; her subjects were freed from their oath of loyalty to her. This, the very last sentence of deposition pronounced by a pope against a ruler, was a grave mistake, which made the situation of the English Catholics worse. Pius was dissuaded from making a formal protest against the Religious Peace of → Augsburg (1555). The development of much stronger royal control of the church in Spain put a strain on relations between Pius and → Philip II, but the pope succeeded in realizing the Holy League between Spain and Venice against the Turks. After the victory of the armada under Don John of Austria in the Gulf of Lepanto on October 7, 1571, Pius established the feast of Our Lady of Victories (later renamed the feast of the rosary).

Pius was completely uninterested in classical art, and the cardinals had great difficulty in dissuading him from getting rid of the precious antiquities ("pagan images of the gods") which belonged to the papacy. He supported new editions of the works of Bonaventure and Thomas Aquinas. Pius was a man of great religious zeal and ascetic strictness, whose overriding priority was always the reform of the church. His narrowness of spirit made him the embodiment of the intransigent Catholic reformer of the 16th century, a man with no understanding of the kind of religious intellectual attitude, inspired by → humanism, that one finds in such figures as Gasparo → Contarini and Reginald → Pole.

■ **Sources:** *Lives:* G. Catena, *Vita del gloriosissimo papa Pio V.* (Rome, 1582, often reprinted); J. A. Gabuzzi, *De vita et rebus gestis Pii V P. M. libri VI.* (Rome, 1605).— *Epistulae apostolicae,* ed. F. Goubeau (Antwerp, 1640); W. E. Schwarz, *Der Briefwechsel Maximilians II. mit P. V.* (Paderborn, 1889); L. Serrano, *Correspondencia diplomatica entre España, Venecia y la Santa Sede durante el pontificado de S. Pio V,* 4 vols. (Madrid, 1914); *NDB(G)* II:5–7.
■ **Literature:** *DThC* 12:1647–53; *EC* 9:1498ff.; *Cath* 11:255–58; *BBKL* 7:665ff.; *TRE* 26:655–59.—B. Hilliger, *Die Wahl P.' V. zum Papste* (Leipzig, 1891); L. Serrano, *La Liga de Lepanto entre España, Venecia y la Santa Sede (1570–73),* 2 vols. (Madrid, 1918–1920); Ch. Hirschauer, *La politique de S. Pie V en France (1566–1572)* (Paris, 1926); B. de Meester, *Le Saint-Siège et les troubles des Pays-Bas 1566–1570* (Louvain, 1934); L. Browne-Oll, *The Sword of St. Michael. S. P. V.* (Milwaukee, 1943); E. van Eijl, "Les censures des universités d'Alcalà et de Salamanque et la censure du Pape Pie V contre Michel Baius (1565–67)," *Revue d'histoire*

ecclésiastique 48 (1953) 719–76; idem, "L'interprétation de la bulle de Pie V portant condamnation de Baius," *Revue d'histoire ecclésiastique* 50 (1955) 499–542; G. Grente, *Le pape des grands combats, S. Pie V.* (Paris, ²1956;) K. M. Setton, *The Papacy and the Levant,* vol. 4 (Philadelphia, 1984); N. Lemaitre, *Saint Pie V.* (Paris, 1994).

KLAUS GANZER

■ **Additional Bibliography:** *Vatikanlexikon,* ed. N. Del Re (Augsburg, 1998) 589ff.—A. d'Andigne, "Saint Pie V et la victoire de Lépante," *Pensée catholique* 248 (1990) 74–86; E. García Hernan, "Pio V y el Mesianismo profetico," *Hispania sacra* 45 (1993) 83–102.

Plettenberg, *Wolter von.* Knight of the Teutonic Order, Master of his Order in Livonia from 1494 to 1535; born c. 1450 near Soest, died February 28, 1535 in Wenden/Cesis. His period in office was a time of economic and cultural prosperity for the medieval territory of Livonia. Plettenberg ensured external peace by two successful preventive strikes against the numerically far superior forces of the grand-principality of Moscow, the second time at Lake Smolina in 1502. He was himself a convinced adherent of the Catholic faith, but he tolerated the diffusion of the Reformation in Livonia, without however secularizing the state, which was governed by his Order (as happened in Prussia).
■ **Literature:** L. Arbusow, *W. von P. und der Untergang des Deutschen Ordens in Preussen* (Leipzig, 1919); *W. von P. Der grösste Ordensmeister Livlands,* ed. N. Angermann (Lüneburg, 1985); *Baltische Länder,* ed. G. von Pistohlkors (Berlin, 1994).

ROLAND GEHRKE

■ **Additional Bibliography:** N. Angermann, ed., *W. von P.* (Lüneburg, 2001).

Poissy, religious dialogue. During a national synod of the French bishops in this city on the Seine in September-October, 1561, a religious dialogue between Catholic and Calvinists took place. Catharine de → Medici hoped that this assembly would achieve a theological reconciliation between the religious parties, but the dialogue brought no lasting results. The Catholic participants included Cardinal Charles → Guise and the Jesuit Diego → Laínez; the Calvinists included Theodor → Beza and Pietro Martire → Vermigli.
■ **Sources and Literature:** *Diario dell'Assemblea de' Vescovi à P.,* ed. J. Roserot de Melin, *Mélanges*

d'archéologie et d'histoire 39 (1921–22) 47–151; H. O. Evennett, *The Cardinal of Lorraine and the Council of Trent* (Cambridge, 1930) 283–394; idem, "Claude d'Espence et son 'Discours du Colloque de P.,'" *Revue historique* 164 (1930) 40–78; W. P. Fischer, *Frankreich und die Wiedereröffnung des Konzils von Trient 1559–62* (Münster, 1972) 214–39; D. Nugent, *Ecumenism in the Age of the Reformation. The Colloquy of P.* (Cambridge, Mass., 1974); Jedin 4/1:51–55.

KLAUS GANZER

■ **Additional Bibliography:** M. Turchetti, "Une question mal posée. La Confession d'Augsbourg, le cardinal de Lorraine er les moyenneurs au Colloque de P. en 1561," *Zwingliana* 20 (1993) 53–102.

Pole, *Reginald.* Cardinal, archbishop of Canterbury, born March 3, 1500 in Stourton Castle (Staffordshire), died November 17, 1558 in Lambeth; he was a relative of King → Henry VIII. During his studies in Oxford, he came in contact with Thomas → More and other English humanists. He received ecclesiastical benefices at an early age. A pension from the king allowed him to study at the universities of Padua and Venice between 1519 and 1526; in this period, he became a friend of Italian humanists such as Marc Antonio Flaminio and Pietro → Bembo, and corresponded with → Erasmus of Rotterdam. He visited the university of Paris in 1529-1530, hoping to obtain a memorandum favorable to the divorce of King Henry VIII. He refused the king's offers of the bishoprics of York and Winchester, and returned to Padua and Venice in 1532, where he came under the influence of representatives of the humanistic reform movement (Giampietro Carafa [later Pope → Paul IV], Gian Matteo → Giberti, Gregorio → Cortese, Gasparo → Contarini). He now devoted himself to the study of scripture and the fathers.

After the outbreak of the English schism, he refused to return to England, and composed the book *Pro ecclesiae unitatis defensione* (1535-1536), in which he defended the primatial rights of Rome. → Paul III summoned him to Rome and made him a member of the reform commission which produced the *Consilium de emendanda ecclesia.* He was created cardinal on December 22, 1536 and was ordained a deacon. Paul III employed him frequently as a legate; he attempted in vain to negotiate a peace between → Francis I and → Charles V in 1537 and 1539. He was appointed legate of the papal patrimony in Viterbo in 1541, and here he became the intellectual and religious center of a circle of like-minded sympathizers with religious reform (Vittoria Colonna, Flaminio, Ludovico → Beccadelli, Luigi Priuli, Vettore Soranzo, and others). He was appointed papal legate to the Council of Trent in 1542 and in 1545. He was profoundly disappointed at the course taken by the debate on → justification at the council, since he held that legitimate theological views were excluded from the discussion. This led him to lay down his function as conciliar legate on October 16, 1545. He was *papabile* in the conclave of 1549, as the candidate of the emperor's party and of the supporters of reform, but his candidature was destroyed by the accusation by Carafa (Paul IV) that he held heretical views.

After → Mary I ascended the English throne, she requested that he be sent as papal legate for England and furnished with extensive faculties. He was appointed archbishop of Canterbury on December 11, 1555; he was ordained priest and bishop in 1557. He declared the reunion of the English church with Rome in November, 1554, and he reorganized church life at a provincial synod. His decree on seminaries was a forerunner of the seminary decree of the Council of Trent. He attempted to prevent the marriage of the queen with → Philip II of Spain. Paul IV dismissed him from the office of legate in 1557 and summoned him to Rome, intending to open proceedings against him on the grounds of heresy; but Pole died (only a few hours after the queen herself) before the Inquisition could begin this investigation.

Pole was a man of outstanding learning, with a piety deeply marked by the humanistic reform movement. He was one of the best representatives of Italian → Evangelism, a friend of Contarini, Giovanni → Morone, and others. His piety was united to a noble character and wide political experience.

■ **Principal Works:** *Epistolae R. P. et aliorum ad ipsum,* ed. A. M. Quirini, 5 vols. (Brescia, 1744–57); *Pro ecclesiasticae unitatis defensione* (Rome, n.d. [1553/54]); *Reformatio Angliae* (Rome, 1562); *De concilio* (Rome, 1562); *Epistula de sacramento Eucharistiae* (Cremona, 1583); *NBD* I, 15, ed. H. Lutz (Tübingen, 1981); S. M. Pagano and C. Ranieri, *Nuovi documenti su Vittoria Colonna e R. P.* (Vatican City, 1989); *The Correspon-*

251

dence of R. P., ed. T. F. Mayer, vol. 1ff. (Aldershot, 2002–).

■ **Literature:** *BBKL* 7:789–93.—F. Gasquet, *Cardinal P. and His Early Friends* (London, 1927); W. Schenk, *R. P., Cardinal of England* (London, 1950); G. B. Parks, "The Parma Letters and the Dangers to Cardinal P.," *CHR* 46 (1960/61) 299–317; H. Lutz, *Ragione di Stato und christliche Staatsethik im 16.Jh.* (Münster, 1961); idem, *Christianitas afflicta* (Göttingen, 1962); H. Jedin, "Kardinal P. und Vittoria Colonna," in *Kirche des Glaubens, Kirche der Geschichte*, vol. 1 (Freiburg, 1966) 181–94; T. Bozza, *Nuovi studi sulla Riforma in Italia. Il Beneficio di Cristo* (Rome, 1976); P. Simoncelli, *Il caso R. P.* (Rome, 1977); idem, *Evangelismo italiano del Cinquecento* (Rome, 1979) passim; M. T. Dainotti, *La via media. R. P.* (Bologna, 1987).

KLAUS GANZER

■ **Additional Bibliography:** Th. M. MacCoog, "Ignatius Loyola and R. P.," *JEH* 47 (1996) 257–73; J. I. Tellechea Idigoras, "El retorno de Inglaterra al Catolicismo. Tres cartas del Cardenal R. P. a Carlos V (1553)," *Dialogo ecumenico* 32 (1997) 183–93; K. Diez, "Das Verhältnis von Rechtfertigungslehre und Ekklesiologie im Denken R. P.s," in *Ecclesia tertii millennii advenientis. Festschrift A. Anton* (Casale Monferrato, 1997) 372–90; T. F. Mayer, *R. P.: Prince and Prophet* (Cambridge, 2000); idem, *Cardinal P. in European Context* (Aldershot, 2000); D. M. Loades, "Cardinal P.," *Reformation* 7 (2002) 197–205.

Polentz, *Georg von.* Bishop of Samland, born 1478 in a noble family in Meissen, died April 28, 1550 in Balga. He studied civil and canon law in Leipzig and in Italy, where he took his licentiate. He met → Albrecht the Elder of Brandenburg-Ansbach in the camp of Maximilian I outside Padua, and he entered the Teutonic Order with him in 1511; he was domestic commander in Königsberg in 1516, and became bishop of Samland in 1519. He was regent in Eastern Prussia from 1522 to 1525, while Albrecht was in the empire, and was the first bishop to introduce the Reformation into the territory which was governed by the Order, with Lutheran preaching in the cathedral in Königsberg in 1523. His theological adviser was Johannes → Briesmann. In 1525, Polentz ceded to Albrecht the territories which had hitherto been subject to the bishopric of Samland, receiving in return the district of Balga with its revenues. Polentz was a lawyer who had not studied theology in any depth, and he held aloof from the controversies about theological doctrines which raged in the duchy of Prussia. Nevertheless, he worked hard to build up the Evangelical Lutheran territorial church in the duchy, carrying out visitations and promulgating church orders for the region.

■ **Literature:** *TRZRK* 2:220–33.—W. Hubatsch, *Albrecht von Brandenburg-Ansbach* (Heidelberg, 1960); A. Zieger, *Das religiöse und kirchliche Leben in Preussen und Kurland im Spiegel der evangelischen Kirchenordnungen* (Cologne and Graz, 1967); E. Wolgast, *Hochstift und Reformation* (Stuttgart, 1995).

ERNST MANFRED WERMTER

Poliander (real name: Gramann or Graumann), *Johann.* Theologian, reformer in Eastern Prussia, born December 26, 1486 in Neustadt (Aisch), died April 29, 1541 in Königsberg. He studied in Leipzig, taking the degree of master of arts in 1516. In the same year, he became a schoolmaster at St. Thomas' School in Leipzig; he was appointed its rector in 1520. He was Johannes → Eck's secretary at the → Leipzig disputation. He came under the influence of Martin Luther and Philipp Melanchthon, and studied at Wittenberg for a short period in 1519. From 1522 to 1525, he preached Reformation doctrine in the cathedral of Würzburg, then in Nuremberg and Mansfeld. On Luther's recommendation, Poliander was appointed pastor in Königsberg in 1525; here he was adviser to the duke and carried out visitations and a school reform. He wrote texts for hymns, and was involved in the struggle against the influence of the "Spiritualists" and Baptists in Prussia. He left a collection of sermons and expositions of scripture by Luther from the years 1519-1521 (WA 9:314-676).

■ **Sources:** *VD 16* 16:297.

■ **Literature:** *RGG³* 2:1823f.; *BBKL* 2:285.—W. Hubatsch, *Albrecht von Brandenburg-Ansbach* (Heidelberg, 1960); H.-Ch. Rublack, *Gescheiterte Reformation. Frühreformatorische und protestantische Bewegungen in süd- und westdeutschen geistlichen Residenzen* (Stuttgart, 1978) 14–18.

HERIBERT SMOLINSKY

Ponce de la Fuente, *Constantino.* Preacher and catechist, born c. 1502 in San Clemente (Cuenca), died 1560 in Seville. He studied in Alcalá and Seville from 1524 to 1534, becoming preacher in the cathedral of Seville in the latter year. He was at the court of → Charles V from 1548 onward, and accompanied the emperor to Flanders and Germany. He returned to Seville in 1550 and was appointed cathedral canon in 1556. He was imprisoned by the Inquisition in 1558. He was burnt as a Lutheran in a posthumous auto-da-fé.

■ **Works:** L. Usoz, ed., *Reformistas antiguos españoles*, vol. 9 (Madrid, 1863); *Obras*, 2 vols. (Nashville, Tenn., 1902).

■ **Literature:** *DHEE* 3:1991; *OER* 3:294f.—J. R. Guerrero, *Catecismos españoles del siglo XVI. La obra catequética del Dr. C. P.* (Madrid, 1969); A. Huerga, *Predicadores, alumbrados e inquisición en el siglo XVI.* (Madrid, 1973); M. P. Aspe Ansa, *C. P.* (Madrid, 1975); K. Wagner, *El doctor C. P.* (Seville, 1979); J. C. Nieto, *El Renacimiento y la otra España* (Geneva, 1997) 217–70, 309–62, and passim; K. Reinhardt, *Bibelkommentare spanischer Autoren*, vol. 2 (Madrid, 1999) 200ff.

FERNANDO DOMÍNGUEZ

Porcia, Count *Bartolomeo*. Born c. 1540 in an ancient aristocratic family in Friuli, died August 12, 1578 in Prague. He studied theology in Prague, and joined the reforming circle around Charles → Borromeo in 1562; Borromeo ordained him in 1566, and he became commendatory abbot of the monastery of Moggio in 1567. He was appointed apostolic visitor of the diocese of Aquileia in 1569, and helped as nuncio in the introduction of the Tridentine reforms in southern Germany, above all in his dealings with Johann Jakob von Kuen-Belasy (archdiocese of Salzburg), Duke → Albrecht V of Bavaria, Archduke Ferdinand (south-west Austria), and Archduke Karl (central Austria). He transferred the center of his activities to Upper Rhineland in 1575-1576. He accompanied Cardinal Giovanni → Morone to the imperial parliament in Regensburg in 1576. He was appointed extraordinary nuncio to give support to → Ernest of Bavaria against Gebhard von → Waldburg in the election of the archbishop of Cologne (1577-1578), and became nuncio at the imperial court in 1578. He was the most important of the reforming nuncios whom → Gregory XIII sent to the empire. Torquato Tasso praised his learning and his diplomatic skill.

■ **Sources:** J. Hansen, *NBD* III/1 (Berlin, 1892) (Cologne); K. Schellhass, *NBD* III/3–5 (Berlin, 1896–1909) (southern Germany).

■ **Literature:** L. von Pastor, *Geschichte der Päpste seit dem Ausgang des Mittelalters*, vol. 9 (Freiburg, 1923) 453–66, 490–510; P. Paschini, "Un diplomatico friulano della Controriforma B. P.," *Memorie storiche forogiuliesi* 12 (1934) 17–51; J. Rainer, "B. P. als Nuntius bei Erzherzog Ferdinand II. von Tirol 1573/74," *Tiroler Wirtschaftsstudien* 26 (1969) 347–60; G. Paolin, "La

visita apostolica di B. da P. nel Goriziano nel 1570," in *Katholische Reform und Gegenreformation in Innerösterreich 1564–1628*, ed. F. M. Dolinar (Graz, 1994) 133–42.

ALEXANDER KOLLER

Predestination. The consistent application of the Reformation principle of *sola gratia* leads Martin Luther and Jean Calvin to propose (each in his own way) an absolute, double predestination; Philipp Melanchthon attempted to find a mediating position between these two.

Luther's understanding of predestination takes definitive form in his lectures on Romans and in *De servo arbitrio*. The starting point is → justification by grace alone: this presupposes an absolute predestination on God's part, both because the human being is totally corrupt as a result of → original sin, and because God alone accomplishes all things. Both these principles exclude any cooperation by human free will in salvation. The "hidden God" (*Deus absconditus,* WA 18:684f.) accomplishes eternal salvation and eternal damnation, and neither of these depends on any preconditions in the human person (WA 18:730f.); God is the absolute cause both of election and rejection (WA 56:428). When one is troubled by the question of the fate to which one is predestined, one will find the ultimate certainty of salvation by looking to Jesus Christ, the *Deus revelatus* who is the concrete form taken by the God of grace (WA.BR 6, n. 1811).

Calvin's teaching is found in definitive form in the *Institutio* of 1559. His strict systematic theology proposes a rigorous double predestination: "'Predestination' is the name we give to God's eternal decree, whereby he alone has resolved what is to become of each individual human being in accordance with the divine will. For all are not created with the same destiny: eternal life is appointed beforehand for some, and eternal damnation for others" (*Opera Selecta* [OS] 4:374). The fundamental motif in Calvin's systematic presentation of predestination is a radical Reformation theocentrism: he emphasizes the honor which belongs to God alone, his unlimited sovereignty, God as exclusive and unconditioned cause of all things, the unimpeachable divine righteousness, and the impenetrable mystery. Above all, Calvin wants to refute the accusation that absolute reprobation makes God the cause of evil (CR 37:257-61; 36:353-66). In order to tone down the harshness of the *decretum horribile* (OS 4:401) and the terrible doubts about one's own election which the Christian may experience, Calvin points to the certainty of salvation in Jesus Christ, who reveals to us the gospel of the Father's love.

GEORG KRAUS

■ *LThK*[3] 8:468–73 (unabridged version).
■ **Literature:** G. Rost, *Der P.-Gedanke in der Theologie Martin Luthers* (Berlin, 1966); F. Brosché, *Luther on Predestination* (Uppsala, 1978); J. H. Rainbow, *The Will of God and the Cross* (Allison Park, 1990); M. Wriedt, *Gnade und Erwählung* (Mainz, 1991); H. Rimbach, *Gnade und Erkenntnis in Calvins P.-Lehre* (Frankfurt/ Main, 1996); W. H. Neuser, "Calvin the Preacher," *Hervormde Teologiese Studies* 54 (1998) 60–78; Th. Buske, "Praedestinatio in praedicatione," *Theologische Zeitschrift* 55 (1999) 303–25; E. M. Faber, "Immer schon überholt? Zur Frage der P. in der Theologie J. C.s," *Theologische Zeitschrift* 56 (2000) 50–68.
■ **Additional Literature:** J. A. Mahn, "Beyond Synergism: The Dialectic of Grace and Freedom in Luther's 'De servo arbitrio,'" *Augustinian Studies* 33 (2002) 239–58; M. B. Pranger, "Calvin's Concept of Predestination and the Language of Dispossession," *Augustiniana* 52 (2002) 291–309.

Prée (Pratanus), *Laurent de la*. Born 1519, died April 1, 1577 in Tournai. As a cleric of the diocese of Cambrai, he accompanied his bishop, Robert de Croy, to the Council of Trent in June, 1546. Thereafter, he entered the service of Cardinal Cristoforo → Madruzzo, who gave him the task of composing the *Epilogus*, a diary of events at the council from March of 1545 to March of 1547 which is written from the emperor's point of view. He is attested as vicar of Cardinal Antoine Perrenot de → Granvella in the abbey of St-Amand-des-Eaux in 1565. He was appointed archdeacon of Tournai in 1573.
■ **Works:** *Epilogus: CT* 2:363–95.
■ **Literature:** *CT* 2:XLIX–LXI; Jedin 2:436ff.

KLAUS GANZER

Prierias (real name: Mazzolini), *Sylvester*. Dominican (1471), born 1456 in Prierio, died 1527 in Rome. In the period from 1495 to 1508, he was professor in Bologna and Padua, and prior in Milan, Verona, and Genoa. He was vicar general of his Order's province in Lombardy from 1508 to

1510; from 1510 to 1515, he was prior in Bologna, Cremona, and Venice. In 1515, he became professor at the Sapienza university in Rome and master of the Sacred Palace. His debate with Martin Luther begins with a dialogue in the style of academic disputations (*In praesumptuosas Martini Luther conclusiones de potestate papae dialogus* [Rome, 1518; CCath 41:52-107]), then takes the form of a friendly exhortation (*Replica ad F. Martinum Luther Ordinis Eremitarum* [Rome, 1518; CCath 41:116–28]), culminating in total rejection (*Errata et argumenta Martini Lutheri recitata, detecta, repulsa et copiosissime trita* [Rome, 1520; cf. CCath 41:138–89]). For Prierias, only Peter was personally appointed by Christ as bishop, and the pope is *virtualiter* the church. His dictionary of pastoral theology (*Summa summarum, quae Silvestrina dicitur* [Bologna, 1514]) went through forty editions, and his collection of sermons (*Aurea Rosa* [Bologna, 1503]) was published in twenty editions.
■ **Works:** F. Michalski, *De Sylvestri Prieratis . . . vita et scriptis* (Münster, 1892); Klaiber nos. 2596–2622.
■ **Literature:** *DSp* 12:2347ff.; *TRE* 3:376–79; *CEras* 3:120f.; *BBKL* 7:948ff.; *OER* 3:341f.; *KThR* 1:26–36.—U. Bubenheimer, *Consonantia Theologiae et Iurisprudentiae* (Tübingen, 1977); U. Horst, *Zwischen Konziliarismus und Reformation* (Rome, 1985); M. Tavuzzi, *P.* (Durham, N.C., 1997).

VINZENZ PFNÜR

■ **Additional Bibliography:** R. Saarinen, "Liberty and Dominion: Luther, P. and Ringleben," *Neue Zeitschrift für systematische Theologie und Religionsphilosophie* 40 (1998) 171–81.

Primacy. The Reformation does not begin with an attack on the papal primacy as such, although this was how its opponents understood the situation. Martin Luther declared his willingness to obey the pope, and this attitude gave way to a more radical criticism only when it became clear that Rome rejected the concerns which were dear to the Reformation. It soon occurred to him—initially only as a worried thought (from December, 1518 onward), but then as a solid conviction (from October, 1520)—that the pope was "Antichrist" (2 Thess 2:4). From then on, this verdict was a constant element in Protestant polemics; it is also affirmed in the Lutheran → confessional writings. The theological kernel of this apocalyptic-eschatological verdict consists of three accusations:

(*a*) the pope makes himself "judge over scripture"; (*b*) he lays down "new articles of the faith"; and (*c*) the Catholic Church affirms that obedience to the pope is "necessary for salvation." Nevertheless, we often find in Luther's writings (and more clearly still in Philipp Melanchthon) a measure of openness vis-à-vis a papacy that "opens the door to the gospel" (in Melanchthon's words); the accusations would no longer apply to such a papacy.

HARDING MEYER

■ *LThK*³ 8:593 (unabridged version).
■ **Literature:** E. Bizer, *Luther und der Papst* (Munich, 1958); R. Bäumer, *Martin Luther und der Papst* (Münster, ⁵1987); M. Lienhard, "Les réformateurs protestants du XVIᵉ siècle et la papauté," *Positions luthériennes* 46 (1998) 157–73; H. Meyer, "Suprema auctoritas ideo ab omni errore immunis," in *Il ministero petrino e l'unità della Chiesa* (Venice, 1999) 25–46; V. Leppin, "Luthers Antichristverständnis vor dem Hintergrund der mittelalterlichen Konzeptionen," *Kerygma und Dogma* 45 (1999) 48–63.

■ **Additional Literature:** W. V. Hudon, "The Papacy in the Age of Reform, 1513–1644," in *Early Modern Catholicism*. Festschrift J. W. O'Malley (Toronto, 2001) 46–66; J. Haustein, "Das Papsttum aus der Sicht der Reformatoren," *Amt und Gemeinde* 52 (2001) 170–82.

Protestantism

1. Concept

In the broadest sense, this concept is the indispensable name for that part of Western Christianity which separated from the Roman church in the course of the → Reformation. A central aspect of the history of Protestantism is the continuous reinterpretation of this term, as different aspects are emphasized in relation to Catholicism. Initially, it was applied only to the large Lutheran (→ Lutheranism) and Reformed (→ Calvinism) Churches.

2. Origin of the Name

At the imperial parliament in Speyer in 1529, electoral Prince → Johann of Saxony, Marquis → George of Brandenburg-Ansbach, Duke Ernest of Braunschweig-Lüneburg, Marquis → Philip of Hessen, and Prince Wolfgang of Anhalt protested against the abrogation of the decision of the imperial parliament in 1526, which had in effect given a free license to the Reformation, by leaving it up to the individual imperial cities to decide whether they would put into practice the Edict of Worms (1521), which had proscribed the Reformation. The princes were subsequently joined in their protest by fourteen imperial cities. The protesters refused to accept the majority decision of 1526, because "In matters pertaining to the honor due to God and to our soul's salvation and eternal bliss, each one must stand before God and give an account of himself" (*Deutsche Reichstagsakten,* new series 7:1277).

Protests were not illegal. They were a common means of disputing the validity of unacceptable decisions; for example, the imperial cities had protested in 1524 when the Edict of Worms was promulgated anew. Despite the appeal to the individual conscience and to the legal responsibility of the imperial Estates, this protest did not amount to a schism in the church, although it certainly took the first step in this direction.

The word "Protestantism" has an undeniably negative coloring, which made it easy for opponents to accuse "Protestants" of sedition and of falling away from the one truth. On the positive side, however, the claim to freedom of conscience had the potential to transform the whole of society.

To begin with, the concept of "Protestantism" did not make any further affirmations about Reformation doctrine—this too was one of its weaknesses. In the ensuing period, when a name was needed for those in the empire who did not submit to imperial religious legislation, they were called "Evangelical" or "Christian protesting" Estates. This designation was not limited to those who belonged to the defensive alliance of the → Schmalkaldic League; at times, it was a more important "identifying label" than declared adherence to the → Confessio Augustana.

3. The Term Is Used More Widely

This name was first applied to Reformation Christians as a whole in the historical work of the Strasbourg politician and historian Johannes → Sleidanus, *De statu religionis et reipublicae Carolo V Caesare Commentarii* (Strasbourg, 1555). Sleidanus was acquainted with the religious situation in England and France, and had been a member of the Strasbourg delegation to the Council of Trent in 1551-1552. He derived the term "Protestants" from the behavior of these persons at the imperial parliaments in Speyer and Augsburg (1530), in the Schmalkaldic League, and at Trent; he applied it not only to Germans, but also to other peoples. The concept spread thanks to those who read Sleidanus' book in Latin and in translations; in western Europe, "Protestants" was preferred to "Protesters." In 1564, the Catholic theologian Georg → Cassander published a comparison of *Articuli inter catholicos et protestantes controversi* (printed at Cologne, 1577).

MICHAEL BRECHT

■ *LThK*[3] 8:656–61 (unabridged version).
■ **Literature:** R. Wohlfeil, *Gewissensfreiheit als Bedingung der Neuzeit. Fragen an die Speyerer Protestation von 1529* (Göttingen, 1980).

■ **Additional Literature:** G. Bray, "Was the Reformation a Tragedy?," *The Churchman* 114 (2000) 137–52; M. Ohst, "'Reformation' versus 'P.'?: Theologiegeschichtliche Fallstudien," *Zeitschrift für Theologie und Kirche* 99 (2002) 441–79.

Puritans. This term is applied to the adherents of a religious and theological trend in the English Reformation, which began under → Elizabeth I as a movement for reform within the church. In the context of the struggle between king and parliament in the early 17th century, Puritanism became a power which transformed both church and state. After the restoration of the Church of → England in 1660, it became a spiritual and theological movement whose heirs today are the Anglo-Saxon Evangelicals.

Puritanism is strongly influenced by → Calvinism. Its piety is characterized by an explicit consciousness of being redeemed and chosen by God, and by a serious striving after holiness. This takes the form of strict self-discipline, with Sunday observance in the manner of the Old Testament Sabbath and the rejection of dancing, theater, and similar things. The Puritans' high esteem for the Bible led them to reject cultic-sacramental piety; their consciousness of standing in a direct relationship to God led them to do without any priestly mediation; and their conviction of the equality of all believers led them to reject hierarchical structures.

The name was first applied by their opponents in the 1560s to those who refused to accept the "compromise" of the Elizabethan church order and demanded that the church be "purified" from all the remnants of Catholicism in its worship and its constitution. Their rejection of the traditional liturgical vestments led to the first conflict with the state church (the Vestiarian controversy). From the 1570s onward, their criticism was increasingly directed at the episcopal office. While moderate Puritans demanded the reform of this ministry as an office of preaching and pastoral care, with greater rights for the parochial clergy, the more radical voices followed Thomas Cartwright (1535-1603) in seeking to establish a Presbyterian church structure. From the 1580s on, the Puritans were persecuted as "dissenters," and when James I proved unwilling to make any substantial concessions, all they could do was offer a passive resistance. From 1620 onward, many Puritans escaped the pressure of persecution from church and state by emigrating to America (Pilgrim fathers).

■ *LThK*[3] 8:745f. (unabridged version).
■ **Literature:** W. Haller, *The Rise of Puritanism* (London, [3]1957); P. Miller, *Errand into the Wilderness* (New York, [2]1964); B. White, *The English Separatist Tradition* (Oxford, 1971); P. Lake, *Moderate Puritans and the Elizabethan Church* (Cambridge, 1982); P. Collinson, *English Puritanism* (London, 1987); idem, *The Elizabethan Puritan Movement* (London, [2]1990); S. Foster, *The Long Argument* (Chapel Hill, N.C., 1991).

GEORG HINTZEN

■ **Additional Bibliography:** F. J. Bremer, ed., *Puritanism* (Boston, 1993); W. Lamont, *Puritanism and Historical Controversy* (Montreal, 1996); D. Oldridge, *Religion and Society in Early Stuart England* (Aldershot, 1998); C. Gribben, *The Puritan Millennium. Literature and Theology 1550–1682* (Dublin, 2000); F. Luttmer, "Persecutors, Tempters and Vassals of the Devil: The Unregenerate in Puritan Practical Divinity," *JEH* 51 (2000) 37–68.

R

Rab, *Hermann.* Dominican (1487), provincial (1514-1534), born Bamberg, died January 5, 1534 in Leipzig. He began his studies in Leipzig in 1486, and took his doctorate in theology in 1512. He became professor in 1514. He worked hard to ensure the strict observance of his Order's rule, and succeeded in uniting both the observant and the non-reformed monasteries in the province of Saxony in 1517. Rab was an opponent of the Reformation. He gave Johannes → Tetzel his protection, and supported the theological faculty in Leipzig by sending students from the Dominican Order to study there. During his period in office, the monastery in Leipzig became a center of his province's opposition to the Reformation and a place of refuge for those forced to leave their own monasteries from 1525 onward. It is highly unlikely (as has been alleged) that the Roman proceedings against Martin Luther were prompted by an accusation on the part of Rab.

■ **Literature:** *BBKL* 7:1145f.—G. Löhr, *Die Kapitel der Provinz Saxonia* (Vechta and Leipzig, 1930); K.-B. Springer, *Widerstand und Anpassung* (Berlin, 1999).

KLAUS-BERNWARD SPRINGER

Rauch (von Ansbach), (1) *Bartholomäus*. Dominican, born in Ansbach, died after 1533. He studied in Heidelberg and Cologne from 1513 onward, was lecturer in Leipzig in 1520, and was appointed one of the regents of studies in his Order in 1523, an office he shared with his brother Petrus [see (2), below] in 1528-1529. He was prior in Leipzig and an influential preacher.

(2) *Petrus* (also known as Peter Anspach). Dominican (1514), born 1495 in Ansbach, died November 1, 1558 in Bamberg. He studied in Vienna, Heidelberg, Cologne, and Leipzig from 1514 onward. He was commentator on the *Sentences* and regent of studies in Leipzig in 1528-1529. Between 1529 and 1532, he continued his studies in Leipzig and Frankfurt on the Oder, and was at the same time court preacher and tutor to the princes in Dessau, then municipal preacher in Frankfurt on the Oder. He was appointed court preacher to the electoral princes → Joachim I and → Joachim II of Brandenburg in 1533. He entered the service of → Albrecht of Brandenburg in 1539, and matriculated at the university of Erfurt in the same year, becoming lecturer in theology and preacher at the church of Sts Mary and Laurence. He took his doctorate in theology in Mainz in 1543 and taught in the theological faculty there. He became auxiliary bishop in Bamberg in 1546, and cathedral preacher in 1548; he was kept a hostage in place of the bishop in 1553. He wrote works of controversial theology and history.— Both brothers persisted in their conservative opposition to the Reformation and in their commitment to the numerically weaker Catholic party.

■ **Works:** *On 2: Antithesis der Lutherischen Bekenntniss* (Frankfurt [Oder], 1531); O. Clemen, ed., *Briefe von H. Emser . . .* (Münster, 1907).

■ **Literature:** *On 1 and 2: BBKL* 7:1398–1401.—G. Löhr, *Die Kapitel der Provinz Saxonia . . .1513–40* (Vechta, 1930); idem, *Die Dominikaner an der Leipziger Universität* (Vechta and Leipzig, 1934).

KLAUS-BERNWARD SPRINGER

Ravesteyn, *Josse* (Jodocus; also known as Tiletanus, because of his birthplace). Theologian, born c. 1506 in Tielt (West Flanders), died February 7, 1570 in Louvain. He studied in Louvain, taking the degrees of master of arts in 1525 and doctor of theology in 1546. He became professor of theology there in the latter year. He was president of Houterlee college from 1540 to 1553, and rector of the university in 1551. He took part in the Council of Trent in 1551, and was present at the religious dialogue of → Worms in 1557. In Louvain, Ravesteyn opposed those of his colleagues (e.g., Jan → Hessels and especially Michael → Bajus) who criticized the scholastic methodology and demanded a reform of theology based on scripture and the church fathers. Ravesteyn had a number of Bajus's teachings censured by the universities of Alcalá and Salamanca, and compelled him to submit to this verdict in 1567. In the same year, he succeeded in having the Protestants expelled from Louvain; his theology replied to their principle of → *sola scriptura* by emphasizing the legitimacy of the appeal to tradition.

■ **Works:** *Confessionis sive doctrinae quae nuper edita est . . . succinta confutatio* (Louvain, 1567); *Catholicae confutationis . . . contra varias et inanes cavillationes Mat. Flacci Illyrici, apologia seu defensio* (Louvain, 1568); *Apologia seu defensio decretorum ss. Concilii Tridentini . . . adversus censuras et examen Martini Kemnitii*, 2 vols. (Louvain, 1568–70).

■ **Literature:** *Biographie nationale*, ed. die Belgische Akademie der Wissenschaften, vol. 18 (Brussels, 1905) 802–6; *DThC* 13:1793; *BBKL* 7:1422ff.—P. Polman, *L'élément historique dans la controverse religieuse du XVIe siècle* (Gembloux, 1932); M. Lamberigts, ed., *L'augustinisme à l'ancienne faculté de théologie de Louvain* (Louvain, 1994).

MATHIJS LAMBERIGTS

257

Reform, Catholic

1. Concept

Hubert Jedin took up a suggestion by Wilhelm Maurenbrecher and elaborated the concept of "Catholic reform" to designate the self-reflection of the Catholic Church in the 15th and 16th centuries on the ideal of Catholic life, which was to be realized through internal renewal. Jedin distinguished this from the "Counter-Reformation," in which the Catholic Church asserted its identity in the struggle against Protestantism (*Katholische Reformation . . .* , 38). This distinction has found broad acceptance, although recent researches into → confessionalization have modified it somewhat.

2. Plurality of Reform Movements

Church reform was one of the most central themes in the late Middle Ages. "Without a council there can be no reform"—this conviction found expression in the decree *Frequens* (Council of Constance, October 9, 1417), which obligated the popes to hold reforming councils at regular intervals. The attempt to reform the church by means of conciliarism was unsuccessful, but the 15th and 16th centuries saw many outbreaks of reform, some spontaneous, others less so. There were reform movements in religious life: Benedictine monastic congregations such as Santa Giustina in Italy and Bursfeld in Germany; the movements in the mendicant Orders for a strict observance of their rules; and the congregation of Windesheim in the Order of canons regular. Bishops in many countries were zealous for reform, and the Catholic sovereigns Ferdinand of Aragon and Isabella of Castile undertook the task of renewal in the Spanish church in the 15th century. Girolamo Savonarola was a prophetic figure with a lasting influence. The humanist movement also generated many reforming impulses, e.g., a greater concentration on the study of scripture (so-called biblical humanism) and the church fathers, especially Augustine; here, we may mention names such as → Erasmus of Rotterdam, Johannes → Reuchlin, Jakob → Faber Stapulensis, and Thomas → More. The aim was to make the Christian life more spiritual—Erasmus's *philosophia Christi*—and this was also the aim of the *devotio moderna*. Erasmus had great influence on intellectual life and piety in Spain and Italy. The names → "Evangelism" and "Spirituali" are

given to the circles which met in Italy to promote renewal, though these never in fact formed one uniform movement; here, we may mention names such as Gasparo → Contarini, Paolo Giustiniani, Vincenzo Quirini, Gian-Matteo → Giberti, Giampietro Carafa (later Pope → Paul IV), Reginald → Pole, Vittoria Colonna, Bernardino → Ochino, and Juan Valdés. They had much in common; for most of them, the question of the path to salvation (i.e., the question of → justification) played a central role; cf. Contarini's experiential recognition that justification was by grace, not by works. The book *Trattato utilissimo del beneficio di Giesu Cristo crocifisso verso i cristiani* (first published 1543) was very influential.

The spontaneous movement which arose around Martin Luther must be seen initially against the background of these great waves of religious reform movements in the late Middle Ages—although it soon took a very different path. Both the Catholic reform movements and the Protestant movements generated by the Reformers ended with the confessionalization process in the mid-16th century.

3. Catholic Reform and Confessionalization

Catholic reform took on a new quality from the middle of the 16th century onward. Increasingly, it tended to draw boundary lines vis-à-vis the Protestant confessions, while it also resembled the "princes' Reformation" in the Protestant sphere, in that it increasingly obeyed the directives of the local rulers, who governed the church in a more direct manner than had been the case in the late Middle Ages. All this gave the Catholic reform a "Counter-Reformation" orientation. Under → Paul III, it gained a foothold in Rome itself: new cardinals were created (Contarini, Carafa, Marcello Cervini [later Pope → Marcellus II], Pole, etc.), and a reform commission was set up (*Consilium de emendanda ecclesia*). However, the Catholic reformers in Italy took a variety of paths. Contarini, and later Giovanni → Morone, were disavowed by Rome after they had given their consent at the religious dialogue of → Regensburg (1541) to a formulation of the doctrine of justification which was intended to reestablish Christian unity. The Roman Inquisition was reorganized on July 21, 1542 with Carafa as its main initiator. The "Spirituali" and the adherents of Italian Catholic "Evangelism" were now systematically suspected of heretical leanings, especially on the question of justification. This led to repressive actions, which increased dramatically after Carafa became pope. Cardinal Morone was imprisoned, and proceedings began against him on the grounds of heresy; the pope planned to take the same steps against Cardinal Pole. The Index of Forbidden Books was another repressive measure. Rome tended increasingly to follow the policy of a strict confessionalistic demarcation, and this had an effect on the Council of Trent, e.g., in the discussion and final redaction of the decree on justification, which rejected the Augustinian theology of Girolamo → Seripando. Most Italian historians apply the term *controriforma* to the process whereby the intransigent reforming orientation won the day in Rome. Theologically speaking, the confessionalistic orientation of the Catholic reform entailed a narrower and impoverished approach, since valuable impulses from humanist intellectual circles were excluded, and scholasticism was restored to its dominant position.

4. The Significance of Trent

The Council of Trent formulated far-reaching reform decrees, especially in its third period (1562-1563), e.g., on improved qualifications for bishops and parish priests, the creation of seminaries for the education of the clergy, raising the level of pastoral care, regular visitations and local synods, and on religious life. This body of reforming law was however a compromise—with all the weaknesses inherent in compromises. The late-medieval curial system was left basically untouched; and although the bishops received considerable authority to carry out reform as "delegates of the Apostolic See," the regulations they issued could still be rendered void by means of exemptions, papal dispensations, privileges, etc.—as often happened in practice.

5. Post-Tridentine Reforms

The Tridentine decrees offered an important instrument for carrying out Catholic reform, and these measures were supported by bishops such as Charles → Borromeo, Bartholomaeus a Martyribus, and Julius Echter von Mespelbrunn, by zealous pastors such as Philip Neri, and to a significant degree also by Orders such as the Jesuits and Capuchins. Post-Tridentine popes likewise supported reform, but their role should not be over-

estimated, since their insistence on retaining Roman centralism often hampered this reform. The history of the implementation of the Tridentine decrees is extremely complex, varying from country to country and from Order to Order.

■ **Sources:** General: *CT*—also *ARCEG*.

■ **Literature:** (KR=Katholische Reform) *TRZRK.*—W. Maurenbrecher, *Geschichte der katholischen Reformation,* vol. 1 (Nördlingen, 1880); J. Greven, *Die Kölner Kartause und die Anfänge der KR in Deutschland* (Münster, 1935); V. Beltrán de Heredia, *Historia de la Reforma de la Provincia de España 1450–1550* (Rome, 1939); V. Martin, *Le gallicanisme et la réforme catholique* (Paris, 1939); G. M. Monti, *Studi sulla Riforma Cattolica e sul Papato nei secoli XVI–XVII* (Trani, 1941); P. Paschini, *Tre ricerche sulla storia della Chiesa nel Cinquecento* (Rome, 1945); H. Jedin, *Katholische Reformation oder Gegenreformation?* (Lucerne, 1946); idem, "Concilio e Riforma nel pensiero del card. B. Guidiccioni," *RSCI* 2 (1948) 33–60; P. Janelle, *The Catholic Reformation* (Milwaukee, 1949); G. Schreiber, "Tridentinische Reformdekrete in deutschen Bistümern," *ZSRG.K* 38 (1952) 395–452; H. Jedin, *Contarini und Camaldoli* (Rome, 1953); J. I. Tellechea, "F. de Vitoria y la Reforma Católica," *Revista Española de Derecho canónico* 11 (1957) 3–48; G. Alberigo, "Studi e problemi relativi all'applicazione del Concilio di Trento in Italia," *Rivista storica italiana* 70 (1958) 239–98; H. Jedin, "Das Bischofsideal der KR," in *Kirche des Glaubens, Kirche der Geschichte,* vol. 2 (Freiburg, 1966) 75–117; W. Reinhard, "KR und Gegenreformation in der Kölner Nuntiatur: 1584–1621," *RQ* 66 (1971) 8–65; K. D. Schmidt, *Die KR und die Gegenreformation* (Göttingen, 1975); A. Cistellini, *Figure della riforma pretridentina* (Brescia, ²1979); M. Heckel, *Deutschland im konfessionellen Zeitalter* (Göttingen, 1983); E. W. Zeeden, *Konfessionsbildung. Studien zur Reformation, Gegenreformation und KR* (Göttingen, 1985); K. Ganzer, "Das Tridentinum—Angelpunkt für eine Reform der Kirche?," *RQ* 84 (1989) 31–50; idem, *Aspekte der katholischen Reformbewegungen im 16.Jh.* (Stuttgart, 1991); idem, "Die Trienter Konzilsbeschlüsse und die päpstlichen Bemühungen um ihre Durchführung während des Pontifikats Clemens' VIII. (1592–1605)," in *Das Papsttum, die Christenheit und die Staaten Europas 1592–1605,* ed. G. Lutz (Tübingen, 1994) 15–23.

KLAUS GANZER

■ **Additional Bibliography:** J. C. Olin, *The Catholic Reformation* (New York, 1992); N. H. Minnich, *The Catholic Reformation* (Aldershot, 1993); R. P. Hsia, *Gegenreformation: Die Welt der katholischen Erneuerung.* (Frankfurt/Main, 1998); M. A. Mullett, *The Catholic Reformation* (London, 1999); R. Bireley, *The Refashioning of Catholicism* (Washington, 1999); M. Peters, "One, Holy, Catholic, and Apostolic? Themes and Issues in Reformation Era Catholic Preaching," in *Caritas et* *reformatio.* Festschrift C. Lindberg (St. Louis, 2002) 167–78.

Reformation.

1. Concept—2. Martin Luther's Reformation—3. The Conflict with the Church—4. The Development of Reformation Theology—5. Reformation Movements—6. Various Solutions—7. The Political Consolidation of the Reformation—8. Evaluation

1. Concept

Leopold von Ranke was the first scholar to apply the term "Reformation" to one particular epoch of German and European history, in which—thanks to the new theological approach taken by Martin Luther (1485-1546)—a far-reaching transformation of the ecclesiastical, political, and societal situation took place from the first half of the 16th century onward. The term *reformatio* was already current in classical antiquity, where it denoted the endeavor to improve decadence and abuses by a return to the good old ways. In the Christian Middle Ages, people were convinced that God had created the world perfect, and that every change therefore represented a rebellion against the ordering which God had intended. Accordingly, when—in view of incontestable empirical evidence that the church, the empire, and society were in need of renewal—the demand for a reform of the head and the members began to be voiced from the early 15th century onward, this "reform" was understood as a restoration. The concept of *reformatio* became shorthand for far-reaching expectations and hopes. "It signified the idea of a renewal of the various spheres of life, based on the indissoluble unity and the mutual compenetration of spiritual and secular life, and on a belief in the divine righteousness" (Wohlfeil, 46). While some endeavored to restore the original situation where ancient law prevailed, hoping thereby to realize the norms laid down for the church by the law of Christ (or the norms established for the world in the natural law), there were others who sought to adapt the ancient tradition to changed contemporary demands.

In the aftermath of the historical event of the "Reformation" in the 16th century, we can discern an increasing tendency among scholars to apply this concept to one clearly delineated complex of events in the period between 1517 and 1555.

2. Martin Luther's Reformation

The Reformation is generally held to begin with the ninety-five theses on → indulgences which Luther sent on October 31, 1517 to his metropolitan, the archbishop of Magdeburg, → Albrecht von Brandenburg, and to his local bishop, Hieronymus Schulze of Brandenburg; but this is a retrospective evaluation, made possible only by our knowledge of the history of the Reformation as a whole. At that time, Luther's actions were pastorally motivated: his intention was not in the least to perform a revolutionary action or to make a public protest; and this is why scholars are right to question the historicity of the story (first told after his death) that he nailed the theses to the door of the castle church in Wittenberg (Iserloh). The theses made a tremendous impact even without such dramatic actions on Luther's part, for although → indulgences were a peripheral question as far as theology was concerned, they were central to church practice at that period. By c. 1500, indulgences had developed in people's consciousness into a special offer of salvation made by the church. Their efficacy was linked to the legal institution of the church, and in particular to the *plenitudo potestatis* of the pope—and this meant that criticism of indulgences could be interpreted as an attack on the papacy.

There were many indulgences; Luther's critique was directed specifically against the indulgence connected with the building of new St. Peter's in Rome, which was promoted by Albrecht of Brandenburg and preached by the Dominican Johannes → Tetzel. The Roman curia had suggested to Albrecht that he might recoup in this way the immense expenses involved in his election as archbishop of Mainz and the fee he had paid for the Roman dispensation which allowed him (against the letter of canon law) to retain the archbishopric of Magdeburg and the bishopric of Halberstadt in addition to Mainz; this outlay had been financed in advance by a loan from the banking house of → Fugger. After long internal struggles and a thorough study of scripture had convinced Luther that the certainty of → salvation was not to be won through the use of external means of salvation, but only by faith in the assurance of salvation which God makes in his Word, he was compelled to see indulgences as a deviation from the heart of Christianity.

The background to this new experience and insight was first of all Luther's personal search for salvation, i.e., for the certainty that he himself was saved; this was what led him to enter the Augustinian monastery in Erfurt in 1505. Despite his intense efforts, he was forced to recognize that the endeavors recommended by late-medieval theology in order that one might merit the grace of God—indulgences, fasting, frequent prayer, veneration of the saints and of relics, monastic life, endowments for the celebration of Masses, pilgrimages, and the blessing of objects—ultimately remained insufficient, since certainty in questions of salvation could be attained only by faith in the gospel of God's assurance of salvation (*solus Christus = sola gratia*, → *sola fide*).

This is the heart of the Lutheran doctrine of → justification, and it was a genuinely new interpretation by Luther of the gospel, taking his starting point in its christological center. He found confirmation of these insights in his study of the church fathers, especially Augustine. In the debate with the scholastic theology of the Middle Ages, the humanists' demand that one must return to the ancient sources provided an important inspiration for the theologians to study the biblical and patristic texts with greater thoroughness. The humanists gave priority to philology, rhetoric, and history, rather than to logic and metaphysics. In the sphere of piety, the mystics and the *devotio moderna* (a movement which began in the Netherlands in the late 14th century) sought a direct encounter with God on the basis of personal experience, taking the biblical text as their guide.

Most of the professors at the new university of Wittenberg (founded 1502) shared this background in biblical studies and humanism and worked together to realize a thoroughgoing reform of theological studies. This meant that Luther's theology was readily understood by his colleagues, many of whom agreed with him. While he was in the Wartburg fortress (1521-1522), some of his university colleagues—Andreas von Bodenstein (known as → Karlstadt), Justus → Jonas, Johann Dölsch, Hieronymus Schurf, Christian Beyer, and Philipp Melanchthon—drew practical consequences from his theoretical considerations, and changed the forms of worship and the ecclesiastical structures in Wittenberg. They were also influenced by the prophets of → Zwickau, who claimed that they were directly guided by the Holy Spirit. Priests married, and monks left their monasteries. Luther responded to these events by rejecting the claim that vows which were impossible to keep had no validity; rather, he appealed to Christian freedom, arguing that the gospel alone suffices for salvation. We are not permitted to posit any additional conditions for its attainment, nor do religious vows guarantee salvation (*De votis monasticis iudicium*, 1521). The Mass was altered, with communion under both kinds and the abolition of vestments; its sacrificial character was denied (→ Communion). Altars and images of the saints were removed. Despite the opposition of the electoral prince, the city council in Wittenberg sanctioned a → church order, confirming the changes which had already been made and setting up a common fund to which all ecclesiastical revenues (stipends, endowments, benefices, money belonging to fraternities, etc.) were to be paid. In his *Invocavit* Lenten sermons (1522), Luther revoked most of these changes, since they had been made without due consideration for the laity, whose consciences were oppressed by them; but they were gradually put into practice in the following years (Luther's *Deutsche Messe*, 1526; → Liturgy).

The new Reformation ideas, which developed in quick succession from 1517 onward, were spread not only by Luther himself, but also by his colleagues, especially Karlstadt (with whom he parted company on theological grounds in 1524, because of the → eucharistic controversy) and Melanchthon. The latter was a vocal supporter of Luther from 1518 onward, and offered a summary of Reformation theology in his *Loci communes* (1521). This book was ideal for teaching purposes, and helped the Reformation to win wide acceptance, especially among preachers who had had a humanist education, among the monks, and at the universities. These in turn spread the new ideas among wide sections of the people, first in the cities, but then also in the countryside. The fact that this movement soon came into conflict with the curia tended to be seen as a positive element, in view of the animosity towards Rome which had built up in Germany over the decades; and this conflict led Luther and others to take the biblical texts as their criterion when they evaluated the traditional ecclesiastical structure, the power relationships, and the competence of the church to make doctrinal decisions.

3. The Conflict with the Church

Luther's theses and his ensuing writings soon provoked a clash with the Roman church. Albrecht of Brandenburg had sent the relevant documents to Rome, but without making a formal accusation. The Dominican Order—to which Johannes Tetzel, who had held the sermons on indulgences for Albrecht, belonged—reacted differently. In Rome, the whole problem of grace, justification, and penance, which Luther had raised, was ignored: the case was treated as a conflict about authority (cf. Sylvester → Prierias, *In praesumptuosas Martini Luther conclusiones de potestate papae dialogus,* 1518; and the interrogation of Luther by Cardinal Thomas → Cajetan at the imperial parliament in Augsburg in October, 1518). When it became obvious that the curia was incapable of reacting appropriately to the specifically theological questions, Luther became firmly convinced that the pope and his collaborators were defending not the gospel but their own canon law—and this meant that the Antichrist reigned in Rome (although this did not entail that the → church as a whole belonged to the Antichrist). Luther saw the conflict with the Roman curia as a struggle to specify which norms were to be binding on Christians. Is the highest authority to be found in the ecclesiastical (and in the last resort, the papal) ministry, or in the Bible (→ *sola scriptura*)? He saw himself as engaged in an apocalyptic battle between the word of human beings and the Word of God. This is why he refused at the disputation in → Leipzig (June 27–July 16, 1519) to accept conciliar decisions merely because of the formal authority these possessed: they were to be accepted only insofar as they represented the contents of sacred scripture.

The proceedings against Luther stagnated in the interval between the death of Emperor Maximilian and the election of → Charles V on June 28, 1519, since the vote of the electoral prince of Saxony, Luther's own sovereign, was important in the election of the emperor. Although the bull → *Exsurge Domine* (June 15, 1520), which threatened Luther with excommunication, also incriminated forty-one propositions extracted from his writings, the proceedings were conducted primarily on formal grounds: Luther was accused of disobedience to the church and the papacy. The definitive condemnation and sentence of excommunication were pronounced in the bull → *Decet Romanum Pontificem* (January 3, 1521).

In the Middle Ages, condemnation by the church led automatically to proscription by the state. Since most of the territorial princes were no longer willing to accept this link, Charles V was unable to proceed at once to the declaration that Luther was now an outlaw. Ultimately, he was forced to promulgate the Edict of Worms (May 8) in his own name; but the refusal by the overwhelming majority of the territorial rulers to implement this edict gave the Reformation movement the space it needed to develop.

4. The Development of Reformation Theology

Growing opposition and public debates led Luther to attempt a clarification of his basic convictions in a series of books. He sought to formulate precise theological affirmations on the basis of scripture. His work *Von der Freiheit eines Christenmenschen* is a tranquil presentation of the doctrine of justification, which was the basis of his entire theology, but earlier writings in 1520 had also argued on the basis of the Bible against fundamental convictions of the medieval church. His work *An den christlichen Adel deutscher Nation* rejects the division of Christendom into "Estates," and rediscovers the common priesthood of all believers, though retaining a functional ministry in the church. Here, he skillfully takes up various demands for reform which had been made repeatedly in the last hundred years in the → *Gravamina* of the German Nation, and he develops a concrete program for reform. *De captivitate Babylonica* calls into question the very center of the medieval church, which understood itself as the sacramental mediator of salvation. Appealing to the biblical evidence, and employing the scholastic concept of "sacrament," Luther accepts only baptism and the Eucharist as genuine sacraments, while respecting the other five "signs" as pious customs. Above all, however, he strips the sacraments of their function as means of salvation to be used by the church: as *verba visibilia,* they are a dimension of God's gracious dealings with the human person, and all that is needed in the one who receives them is faith.

Vom Papsttum zu Rom wider den hochberühmten Romanisten zu Leipzig is an occasional work, like most of Luther's writings in this period. Here, he elaborates the basic outlines of his ecclesiology: the church is not primarily an external institution, but an object of faith. It is indeed always visible and can be experienced in the course of history; nevertheless, the church is primarily the assembly of those who are united in faith in that Word by which God gives them guidance.

It is astonishing to see how rapidly Luther succeeded—on the basis of scripture—in developing his position with regard to so many themes of theology, pastoral care, and the concrete form of the church. Church reform had indeed been demanded for the past two hundred years, though without effect; but *this* approach fell on fertile soil, because Luther was not treating symptoms, but tackling the problems on the basis of the very heart of Christian theology.

5. Reformation Movements

This new theology, prepared by → humanism, supported by the printing presses (→ pamphlets), and spread by learned theologians in the monasteries and the big towns, quickly found adherents and led to a Reformation movement, so that changes in keeping with the gospel were demanded not only in the cities, but also in the countryside. One explanatory factor for this impact was the extraordinary openness to religious questions at the beginning of the 16th century. The legacy of the rigid church life of the Middle Ages was a yearning for spiritual renewal. Once the movement had begun, other Reformers appeared in many places. The substance of their preaching was largely based on Luther, but they had emphases of their own. In Switzerland and southern Germany, the theology and writings of Huldrych Zwingli were particularly important. Some years later, Jean Calvin reformed and organized an independent church structure in Geneva. Almost every imperial city and territory which came to embrace the Reformation had its own Reformer. There were also groups which accentuated particular aspects, such as the → Baptists or the "Spiritualists."

The Reformation might perhaps have remained within the boundaries of the church structures which already existed, leading to a broader spectrum within theology and to a gradual restructuring, had not the new theological ideas been linked to political interests.

In the first phase, there is a discernible differentiation among the social classes in terms of their openness to the Reformation. It found quick acceptance among many of the lower aristocracy, whose social and economic situation in the early 16th century was critical. As early as 1521, Lutheran doctrines were widely held in the Austrian crown lands, especially Styria. One spectacular aristocratic action, the so-called Feud of Sickingen, caused a tremendous sensation in 1522-1523. After reading Luther's writings and consulting his humanist advisers in his main residence, Ebernburg near Kreuznach, Franz von → Sickingen became convinced that he was called by God to take up weapons on behalf of the new doctrine. However, his campaign against the archdiocesan territory of Trier was a failure, and although many of the knights joined the Reformation, they lost all their political significance after Sickingen's defeat.

Historians such as Dickens have drawn attention to the leading role played by the cities in the implementation of the Reformation. It appears that the Reformation gave new impetus to a longstanding development in the direction of communal self-administration; this had long-term effects only in Switzerland and in some southern German territories (Blickle). From 1522-1523, the municipal authorities in a number of southern German imperial cities began to introduce the Reformation officially, often at the urging of the populace. This was a legal act: the episcopal jurisdiction was suspended, and the traditional church order was replaced by new regulations approved by the council. This meant in concrete terms that from now on, the municipal authorities considered priests, monks, and nuns as citizens under their oversight. The cities claimed the right to have charge (or at least the inspection) of ecclesiastical goods (buildings, churches, monasteries, revenues, and real estate). The right of external persons such as bishops or abbots to appoint the clergy was abolished and replaced by the election of pastors. Behind such changes lies the idea that the city is a miniature *corpus christianum* in which the council has the responsibility for the citizens' well-being both on earth and in eternity (Moeller).

To some extent, the reception of the Reformation in the countryside supplied justification for implementing reforms which had been demanded—sometimes with violence—for over a hundred years. The → Peasants' War of 1525 linked the Reformation movement to societal reform: this war was occasioned by social demands which it sought to realize, but at the same time, the Reformation provided a new justification and legitimation. The peasants demanded the preaching of the pure gospel and the election of the pastor by his parish, appealing to the "divine right" found in scripture—and they affirmed that scripture was the tribunal before which every traditional secular and ecclesiastical structure must give an account of itself.

Luther castigated this appeal to the gospel in support of societal demands as an abuse. He issued an exhortation to restraint, once the peasants' rebellion had been put down. This was the end of the first phase of the Reformation as a spontaneous movement supported by wide sectors of the people. Those who had hitherto been leaders—the lower aristocracy, the cities, the peasants, and the "man in the street" (Blickle)—ceased to be important; increasingly, the center stage came to be occupied by the territories and the local rulers.

Until his death on February 18, 1546, Luther remained the leading theologian of the Reformation. The public confrontation with the Catholic party was led by the imperial Estates and their legal counselors, especially at the imperial parliaments.

6. Various Solutions

Since the Edict of Worms (1521) did not succeed in halting the onward march of the Reformation, this movement gradually became a major political issue. Most people at that time saw the biblically based insights and initiatives of the Reformation as justified, but it was unclear how these could be implemented in a manner consistent with the law. While the imperial parliament of Augsburg was under preparation in 1553, the imperial counselor Sigismund Seld summarized four conceivable paths to a solution of the religious question within the church in the empire: a general council, a national council, an imperial assembly, or a religious dialogue. All these were attempted in the first half of the 16th century. A general council would have been the safest way to clear up the theological divergences, and those imperial Estates which were sympathetic to Luther had demanded such a council since 1523;

but various reasons induced the popes to prevent the convocation of such a council. When it did finally meet in Trent at the end of 1545, the Reformation churches were already established bodies. The second imperial parliament, which met in Nuremberg in the spring of 1524, summoned a German national council to meet in Speyer at the end of that year, but this was forbidden by Pope → Clement VII and by the emperor, on the grounds that it was not permissible for one individual nation on its own to change church ordinances.

The only remaining path was the attempt to employ imperial assemblies or parliaments to find a *modus vivendi* between those imperial Estates which supported the implementation of the Edict of Worms and those which opposed this decree. For the Catholic Estates in the empire, all that this path could achieve was an interim solution "until a council meets." The adherents of the Reformation held that once a renewal based on the Bible had been achieved, the matter was non-negotiable.

7. The Political Consolidation of the Reformation

When foreign wars compelled Emperor → Charles V to absent himself from the empire for nearly ten years in the aftermath of the imperial parliament of Worms (1521), he entrusted the government to an imperial regency. Since neither this body nor the imperial parliaments proved capable of enforcing the Edict of Worms, another solution had to be sought. The imperial Mandate of Nuremberg in 1523 coined an initial compromise formula: from now on, nothing other than the gospel was to be preached. Obviously, however, this formula could be interpreted in keeping with either Catholicism or the Reformation.

The territorial rulers saw the peasants' revolution as a threat to their sovereignty; and the reforms which had already been put into practice gave them a greater measure of influence on church life in their territories. These two factors made compromises necessary, in order to help avoid future unrest and to maintain what had been achieved. This is why those imperial Estates which sympathized with Luther and did not desire any return to the old church could no longer accept the position of the emperor, who wanted the Edict of Worms implemented and all changes in liturgy and theology to be avoided. The imperial parliament of Speyer (1526) proposed a compromise: the implementation of the Edict of Worms and the resolution of the religious question would be left to the conscience of each individual imperial Estate, until a council met.

From the late Middle Ages onward, the princes sought the supreme authority over church life in their territories, since this would give them control over vast tracts of land and financial resources, as well as over the educational sector and the care for the poor and the sick. Ultimately, this was indispensable if they were to build up and consolidate their territorial lordship. This was why the princes could not allow the Reformation movement to go on developing freely: they found it necessary to take control of this movement, either by deciding that the old religion would be preserved, or by personally introducing the Reformation into their territories. Large territories such as Hessen (synod of → Homberg, 1526) and Saxony (Instruction for electoral Saxony, 1527) now began to remove church life as a whole in their territories from episcopal jurisdiction, and to restructure it by means of a new → church order. It was only this process that led to the birth of legally independent churches, and consequently to the break-up of the medieval church. In order to translate these goals into practice, the princes had visitations carried out in close collaboration between their counselors and the theologians. The desire to halt this development led the Catholic majority at the imperial parliament in Speyer to annul the decision of 1526. A response by five princes (electoral Saxony, Brandenburg-Ansbach, Lüneburg, Hessen, and Anhalt) and fourteen cities (including Strasbourg, Nuremberg, Ulm, and Constance) appealed above all to the protesters' conscience (→ Protestantism).

The priority of the imperial parliament which met at Augsburg in 1530, and was attended once again by Charles V, was to resolve political questions; but it also sought a provisional settlement of the religious question on the imperial level. The Protestant imperial Estates presented a statement of their own faith and a justification of the changes that had been made, in the → Confessio Augustana, a text composed under the theological guidance of Philipp Melanchthon, but the Catholics rejected this document in their *Confutatio*. The emperor ordered negotiations to be held; both sides agreed that they had found a large measure of rapprochement in theology, but not in questions of (church) politics, where the two positions were irreconcilable. On the one hand, the emperor, as protector of the church, and the Catholic imperial Estates maintained the traditional external, ritual, and legal ordering of the church, which was crystallized in their eyes above all in the celebration of the Mass; but they were willing to tolerate divergent theological views until a council should take a decision on these matters. On the other hand, the Protestant imperial Estates, and in particular their theologians, were unwilling to accept any compromises on fundamental theological questions, which were crystallized in their eyes above all in the renewed Reformation liturgy. Thus the attempt to find a compromise collapsed ultimately because of the question of Mass *vs.* Lord's Supper.

The first confessional leagues had formed in the 1520s (→ Dessau League of Catholic princes in 1525, as a reaction to the Peasants' War; Torgau League in 1526, to safeguard the Reformation). The Protestant rulers united in the → Schmalkaldic League under the leadership of Philip of Hessen (1531), but it proved impossible to gather all the Protestant forces in one body, after the religious dialogue of → Marburg between → Zwinglians and → Lutherans (1529) had broken down over the question of the Lord's Supper. This alliance of Protestant imperial Estates represented a political and military power which even the emperor had to respect, and since he faced external threats from the Turks and from France, he was continually obliged in the ensuing period to make new compromises (Truce of Nuremberg, 1532; Truce of → Frankfurt, 1539). Religious dialogues (→ Worms and → Hagenau, 1540, → Regensburg, 1540-1541) made one final unsuccessful attempt to find a provisional compromise which would hold until the council met.

Although both sides asserted that a future council would be able to find a workable solution, they had very different ideas about such a council. While the Catholics envisaged a traditional medieval council held under the pope's authority, the Protestants demanded a "free [i.e., free from the pope] Christian [i.e, with equal rights for all parties] council on German territory." After various false starts, the council finally assembled in Trent in December, 1545, but the Protestants refused to participate, since it was under the pope's supreme authority and therefore not

265

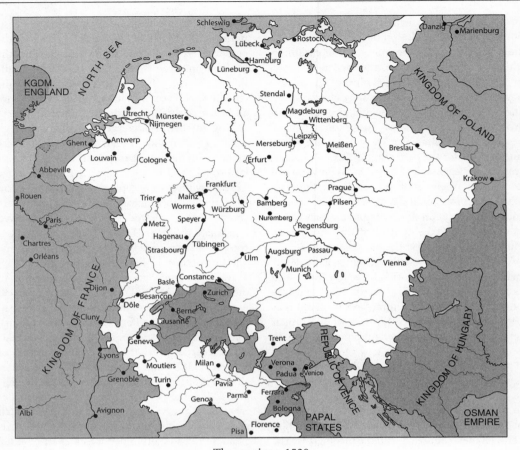

The empire c. 1520

"free." The emperor, then at the zenith of his power, resolved to use military force to compel the Protestants to take part in the council. In the course of the → Schmalkaldic War (1546-1547), Charles won total victory over the Protestants at the battle of Mühlberg (April 24, 1547) and captured their leaders, Philip of Hessen and electoral Prince → Johann Friedrich of Saxony (whose electoral dignity was given to his cousin → Moritz of Saxony, and remained thereafter in the Albertine line of the Wettin dynasty). However, Pope → Paul III transferred the council temporarily from Trent to Bologna—a city in the papal state— and this move prevented the emperor's military victory from achieving its church-political goal.

Instead of the hoped-for council, the imperial parliament in Augsburg (1547-1548) proclaimed the → Augsburg Interim, a provisional resolution of the religious and ecclesiastical question which

had the force of imperial law and was originally meant to apply to both religious parties. The refusal of the Catholic imperial estates to implement this compromise in their territories, and the opposition by the Roman curia to a number of the concessions it made to the Protestants (marriage for priests [→ celibacy], → chalice for the laity, abandonment of claims to secularized church properties), watered down the Interim, so that it became a special law applicable to the Protestant imperial Estates alone. The result was that they too refused to accept it.

The rebellion of the princes destroyed the last possibility for Protestant theologians to take part in the newly convoked Council of Trent in 1551-1552. For a short period, both religious parties made common cause, since both had come to feel the need to safeguard the gains they had achieved and to avoid further losses. In these circumstances, the emperor's brother, King → Ferdinand, succeeded in negotiating a political compromise between the religious parties, first in the Treaty of → Passau (1552), and finally in the Religious Peace of → Augsburg (1555). Imperial law now recognized both the Catholic Church and the adherents of the Confessio Augustana. The local ruler was allowed to determine freely the confession in his territories (→ *Cuius regio, eius religio*), with the exception of those states with clerical rulers (→ ecclesiastical reservation). This echoed the agreement made at Speyer in 1526, though replacing the time-limit ("until a council meets") with an unlimited validity. A compromise on the substantial issues which divided the parties was postponed; but in fact, with the exception of the religious dialogue held in Worms in 1557, there was no further attempt at such a compromise. The Religious Peace became possible because, despite the differences between the confessions, both religious parties wanted the empire to remain capable of functioning. This Peace helped avoid bloody religious wars in the empire, but the tensions caused by the question of who should possess church property finally exploded in the Thirty Years' War.

8. Evaluation

On the one hand, the Reformation can be seen as the conclusion of more than two hundred years' endeavor to reform the state and the church. In this context, Martin Luther himself is seen as belonging theologically and in terms of his mentality to the Middle Ages (Oberman). On the other hand, the Reformation generated a modernizing impulse in theology, church, and society. Reforms and renewals took place in every sector.

The Catholic Church confronted the theological questions posed by the Reformation in the Council of Trent. The problems connected with scripture and tradition, justification, and the sacraments, as well as many abuses in ecclesiastical praxis, were dealt with, at least in the sense that theological thinking and forms of piety now differed from the status quo before the Reformation. Accordingly, the Reformation did produce a reform of the church as a whole. It did not, however, succeed in renewing the church as a whole: rather, the effect was a break-up, or a pluralistic articulation, of the Western church—a pattern that can be observed in state and society also from

the late Middle Ages onward. This pluralistic articulation was linked in the following centuries to developments in the individual states, each of which gave a privileged position to its official church. It was only the separation between state and church in the modern period which made it possible for the Western Christian churches to hold an ecumenical dialogue which no longer needed to take into account the interests of the state.

It is impossible to overlook the impulses generated by the Reformation in the educational sector. It is above all thanks to Philipp Melanchthon that a coherent educational system from primary schools via grammar schools to universities was developed, with textbooks for each phase. One generation later, the same system was developed in the Catholic Church, especially by the Jesuits, in the process of implementation of the Tridentine reforms. We could say that this realized the ideas of → Erasmus of Rotterdam, who had insisted that the reform of church and society would come about by means of education.

■ Sources: *CT*; H. A. Oberman, A. M. Ritter, and H.-W. Krumwiede, *Kirchen- und Theologiegeschichte in Quellen*, 4 vols. (Neukirchen-Vluyn, 1977ff.); M. Luther, *Studienausgabe* (Berlin, 1979ff.); E. W. Zeeden, ed., *Repertorium der Kirchenvisitationsakten aus dem 16. und 17.Jh.* (Stuttgart, 1982ff.); *WA*; P. Fabisch and E. Iserloh, eds., *Dokumente zur Causa Lutheri (1517–21)*, 2 Teile (Münster, 1988–91).

■ Literature: Jedin; *OER*; *HKG* vol. 4; *HDThG*; *TRZRK*; *KThR*; *GCh* vols. 7 and 8; H. J. Hillerbrand, *Historical Dictionary of the Reformation and Counter-reformation* (Lanham, Md., 2000).—K. Brandi, *Der Augsburger Religionsfriede vom 25. September 1555* (Göttingen, [2]1927); A. Herte, *Das katholische Lutherbild im Banne der Lutherkommentare des Cochlaeus*, 3 vols. (Munich, 1943); J. Lortz, *Die R. in Deutschland* (1939) (Munich, [4]1962, 1982); H. Lutz, *Christianitas afflicta. Europa, das Reich und die päpstliche Politik im Niedergang der Hegemonie Karls V.* (Göttingen, 1964); B. Moeller, "Frömmigkeit in Deutschland um 1500," *ARG* 56 (1965) 5–31; H. A. Oberman, *Spätscholastik und R.*, 2 vols. (Tübingen, 1965–77, [2]1979); M. Heckel, *Staat und Kirche nach den Lehren der evangelischen Juristen Deutschlands in der ersten Hälfte des 17.Jh.* (Munich, 1968); E. Iserloh, *Luther zwischen Reform und R. Der Thesenanschlag fand nicht statt* (Münster, [3]1968); W. Borth, *Die Luthersache (Causa Lutheri) 1517–24* (Lübeck and Hamburg, 1970); J. Engel, *Die Entstehung des neuzeitlichen Europa* (Stuttgart, 1971); H. Rabe, *Reichsbund und Interim. Die Verfassungs- und Religionspolitik Karls V. und der Reichstag von Augsburg 1547/48* (Cologne and Vienna, 1971); R. Bäumer, ed., *Luther-*

prozess und Lutherbann (Münster, 1972); F. Reuter, ed., *Der Reichstag zu Worms von 1521* (Worms, 1971), supplementary volume: *Luther in Worms* (Worms, 1973); G. Dickens, *The German Nation and Martin Luther* (London, 1974); H. Immenkötter, *Um die Einheit im Glauben. Die Unionsverhandlungen des Augsburger Reichstages im August und September 1530* (Münster, ²1974); R. van Dülmen, ed., *Das Täuferreich zu Münster 1534/35* (Munich, 1974); E. Walder, ed., *Religionsvergleiche des 16.Jh.* (Berne, 1974); S. E. Ozment, *The R. in the Cities* (London, 1975); W. Reinhard, "Gegenreformation als Modernisierung," *ARG* 68 (1977) 226–52; O. Brosse et al., *Lateran V und Trient* (Mainz, 1978); I. W. Frank, "Kirchengewalt und Kirchenregiment in Spätmittelalter und früher Neuzeit," *Innsbrucker historische Studien* 1 (1978) 33–60; B. Moeller, ed., *Stadt und Kirche im 16.Jh.* (Gütersloh, 1978); H. Bornkamm, *Martin Luther in der Mitte seines Lebens* (Göttingen, 1979); W. Mommsen, ed., *Stadtbürgertum und Adel in der R.* (Stuttgart, 1979); R. Decot, *Religionsfriede und Reichsreform. Der Mainzer Kurfürst und Erzbischof Sebastian von Heusenstamm* (Wiesbaden, 1980); E. Iserloh, ed., *Confessio Augustana und Confutatio. Der Augsburger Reichstag 1530 und die Einheit der Kirche* (Münster, 1980); G. Östreich, *Strukturprobleme der frühen Neuzeit* (Berlin, 1980); M. Brecht, *Martin Luther*. 3 vols. (Stuttgart, 1981–87); G. Ebeling, *Luther. Einführung in sein Denken* (Tübingen, 1981); H. A. Oberman, *Luther* (Berlin, 1982); A. Ravier, *Ignatius von Loyola gründet die Gesellschaft Jesu* (Würzburg, 1982); R. Wohlfeil, *Einführung in die Geschichte der deutschen R.* (Munich, 1982); M. Heckel, *Deutschland im konfessionellen Zeitalter* (Göttingen, 1983); H. Junghans, ed., *Leben und Werk Martin Luthers von 1526 bis 1546*, 2 vols. (Berlin, 1983); O. H. Pesch, *Hinführung zu Luther* (Mainz, ³1983); W. Reinhard, "Zwang zur Konfessionalisierung," *ZHF* 10 (1983) 257–77; P. Warmbrunn, *Zwei Konfessionen in einer Stadt. Das Zusammenleben von Katholiken und Protestanten in den paritätischen Reichsständen Augsburg, Biberach, Regensburg und Dinkelsbühl von 1548 bis 1648* (Wiesbaden, 1983); P. Blickle, *Gemeinde-R.* (Munich, 1985); U. Horst, *Zwischen Konziliarismus und R. Studien zur Ekklesiologie im Dominikanerorden* (Rome, 1985); H. Angermeier, *Die Reichsreform 1410–1555* (Munich, 1985); P. Blickle, ed., *Der deutsche Bauernkrieg* (Darmstadt, 1985); E. W. Zeeden, *Konfessionsbildung* (Stuttgart, 1985); C. Augustin, *Erasmus von Rotterdam* (Munich, 1986); J. Lecler et al., eds., *Trient* (Mainz, 1987); B. Moeller, *Reichsstadt und R.* (Berlin, 1987); O. H. Pesch, *Theologie der Rechtfertigung bei Martin Luther und Thomas von Aquin* (Mainz, ²1987); A. Schindling, "Reichskirche und R. Zu Glaubensspaltung und Konfessionalisierung in den geistlichen Fürstentümern des Reiches," in *Neue Studien zu frühneuzeitlichen Reichsgeschichte*, ed. J. Kunisch (Berlin, 1987) 81–112; B. Lohse, ed., *Der Durchbruch der reformatorischen Erkenntnis bei Luther* (Stuttgart, 1988); R. Decot, ed., *Vater im Glauben.*

Studien zur Theologie Martin Luthers. Festschrift P. Manns (Stuttgart, 1988); H. Schilling, *Aufbruch und Krise. Deutschland 1517–1648* (Berlin, 1988); idem, "Die Konfessionalisierung im Reich," *Historische Zeitschrift* 246 (1988) 1–45; R. Decot and R. Vinke, ed., *Zum Gedenken an Joseph Lortz (1887–1975). Zur Reformationsgeschichte und Ökumene* (Stuttgart, 1989); P. Blickle and J. Kunisch, *Kommunalisierung und Christianisierung. Voraussetzungen und Folgen der R. 1400–1600* (Berlin, 1989); R. P. Hsia, *Social Discipline in the R.: Central Europe 1550–1750* (London and New York, 1989); H. Rabe, *Reich und Glaubensspaltung. Deutschland 1500–1600* (Munich, 1989); A. Kohler, *Das Reich im Kampf um die Hegemonie in Europa 1521–1648* (Munich, 1990); F. Seibt, *Karl V. Der Kaiser und die R.* (Berlin, 1990); A. Beutel, *Martin Luther* (Munich, 1991); F. Jürgensmeier, ed., *Albrecht von Brandenburg* (Mainz, 1991); H. Lutz, *R. und Gegenreformation* (Munich, ³1991); H. R. Schmidt, *Konfessionalisierung im 16.Jh.* (Munich, 1992); H.-J. Goertz, *Religiöse Bewegungen in der frühen Neuzeit* (Munich, 1993); H.-Ch. Rublack, ed., *Die lutherische Konfessionalisierung in Deutschland* (Gütersloh, 1993); B. Lohse, *Luthers Theologie in ihrer historischen Entwicklung und in ihrem systematischen Zusammenhang* (Göttingen, 1995); W. Reinhard and H. Schilling, *Die katholische Konfessionalisierung* (Gütersloh, 1995); B. Lohse, *Martin Luther. Eine Einführung in sein Leben und Werk* (Munich, ³1997); B. Moeller and E. Buckwalter, ed., *Die frühe R. in Deutschland als Umbruch* (Gütersloh, 1998); P. Blickle, *Die R. im Reich* (Stuttgart, 2000); R. Mau, *Evangelische Bewegung und frühe Reformation 1521–32* (Leipzig, 2000); E. Rummel, *The Confessionalization of Humanism in Reformation Germany* (Oxford, 2000); A. Lexutt, ed., *Relationen—Studien zum Übergang vom Spätmittelalter zur Reformation.* Festschrift K.-H. zur Mühlen (Münster, 2000).—Bibliographies: *ARG* Literaturbericht 1 (1972) ff.; W. Dotzauer (compiler), "Quellenkunde zur deutschen Geschichte der Neuzeit," in *Das Zeitalter der Glaubensspaltung 1500–1618* (Darmstadt, 1987).

ROLF DECOT

■ **Additional Literature:** J. E. Carney, *Renaissance and R.: A Biographical Dictionary* (Westport, 2001); D. C. Steinmetz, *Reformers in the Wings: From Geiler von Kaysersberg to Theodore Beza* (Oxford, ²2001)C. Scott Dixon, *The R. in Germany* (Oxford, 2002); A. Levi, *Renaissance and R.: The Intellectual Genesis* (New Haven, 2002); C. Lindberg, *The R. Theologians* (Oxford, 2002); J. Witte, *Law and Protestantism: The Legal Teachings of the Lutheran R.* (New York, 2002); P. Collinson, *The R.* (London, 2003); H. A. Oberman, *The Two Reformations* (New Haven, 2003); D. MacCulloch, *R. Europe's House Divided, 1490–1700* (London, 2003); A. E. McGrath, *The Intellectual Origins of the European R.* (Oxford, ²2004); P. G. Wallace, *The Long European R.* (Basingstoke, 2004).

Reformed churches

1. Concept

This name refers to the Reformation preached by Jean Calvin, and is given to those Protestant communities which stand in the tradition of → Calvinism. It was coined in the 16th century as a polemical Lutheran name for that Protestant community which understood itself as "reformed in accordance with God's Word" (see below). This means that the terms "Calvinism/Calvinist" and "Reformed churches/Reformed" are often used interchangeably today.

BRUNO STEIMER

2. Origin and Characteristics

The original home of the Reformed churches is Switzerland, where they came into existence as the fruit of the activity of Reformers such as Huldrych Zwingli, Martin → Bucer, Calvin, and John → Knox. Their intention was not to found a new → church, but to renew the entire Christian church; the creation of a new ecclesiastical organization was understood as at best a temporary solution. The most important characteristic of a Reformed Church is the conviction that the church is "reformed in accordance with God's Word and is in constant need of reform" (*ecclesia reformata et semper reformanda*). The Reformed → confessional documents played an important role in the spread of this type of church. The decisions of the synod of Chanforan in 1532 meant that the Waldensians were close to the Reformed position. The Reformation entailed the return to scripture and to zealous preaching, which often meant the exposition of all the books of the Bible (*lectio continua*). Indulgences, the veneration of images and of the saints (→ Art and Reformation), and a piety which attached value to human achievements were all called into question; the Mass was replaced by an act of worship centered on the sermon, which spoke of God's grace and the claim he made on the whole of human life. Following the practice in the Hussite movement since 1414, the Lord's Supper (→ Communion) was administered to the entire community under both kinds (bread and wine). In addition to the principles of *solus Christus*, → *sola scriptura, sola gratia,* and → *sola fide*, great weight was attached to the principle of the common priesthood of all believers. In Geneva, church discipline was seen as the third characteristic of the true church, alongside the proclamation of the Word and the administration of the sacraments.

MILAN OPOČENSKÝ

■ **Literature:** *Historical Dictionary of Reformed Churches* (Lanham, 1999); *Dictionary of the Presbyterian and Reformed Tradition in America* (Downers Grove, Ill., 1999)—W. Hollweg, *Der Augsburger Reichstag von 1566 und seine Bedeutung für die Entstehung der Reformierten Kirche und ihres Bekenntnisses* (Neukirchen-Vluyn, 1964); K. Halaski, ed., *Die Reformierte Kirchen* (Stuttgart, 1977); E. A. Pettegree, *Calvinism in Europe 1540–1620* (Cambridge, 1994); E. Wolgast, *Reformierte Konfession und Politik im 16.Jh.* (Heidelberg, 1998); B. Nischan, *Lutherans and Calvinists in the Age of Confessionalism* (Aldershot, 1999).

Regensburg Book. At a secret meeting in Worms from December 15-31, 1540, Johann → Gropper, Gerhard Veltwyk, Martin → Bucer, and Wolfgang → Capito negotiated the "Book of Worms," which was debated and reformulated in the religious dialogue of → Regensburg between April 27 and May 22, 1541 under the auspices of the imperial parliament which met in that city. This work was undertaken by Julius von → Pflug, Johannes → Eck, and Gropper from the Catholic party, and Philipp Melanchthon, Bucer, and Johannes Pistorius the Elder from the Protestant party (M. Bucer, *Deutsche Schriften*, 9/1:328-483). It contains twenty marginal notes made by Gropper at the request of the papal legates, Gasparo → Contarini and Giovanni → Morone. The first part of the text compares the articles professed by the religious parties on the state of Adam and Eve in paradise (art. 1), free will (2), sin (3-4), and → justification (5); the second part (6-9 and 19) deals with ecclesiology. The authority of the → church to expound sacred scripture (6-9) and the ecclesiastical hierarchy (19) were topics of dispute; there was a greater rapprochement in the third part, dealing with sacramental doctrine in general (10), ordination (11), baptism (12), confirmation (13), → marriage (16), and extreme unction (17). The doctrine of transubstantiation prevented agreement on the Eucharist (14), and the doctrine of satisfaction prevented agreement on sacramental confession (15). A fourth part (18 and 20-23) on unity and ceremonies, and on the external form of the church, did not make comparisons between the two sides. The Regensburg Book was presented to Emperor → Charles V on

May 31, 1541, accompanied by nine articles in which the Protestants expressed their criticism (CR 4:348-76). It was approved by the imperial parliament on July 29, 1541 (CR 4:626ff.), which directed that further reforms should be carried out in the church on the basis of the sixteen articles where some consensus had been reached; the seven articles where no comparable consensus existed were to be compared in a definitive manner at the imminent council; if however this council were to be delayed, a national council or imperial parliament would see to this matter.

■ **Literature:** *TRE* 28:432–37, 654–81.—J. Mehlhausen, "Die Abendmahlsformel des RB," in *Studien zur Geschichte und Theologie der Reformation. Festschrift E. Bizer* (Neukirchen-Vluyn, 1969) 189–211; R. Braunisch, "Die 'Artikell' der 'Wahrhafftigen Antwort' (1545) des Johannes Gropper. Zur Verfasserfrage des Worms-Regensburger Buches (1540/ 1541)," in *Von Konstanz nach Trient. Festgabe A. Franzen* (Paderborn, 1972) 519–45; K.-H. zur Mühlen, "Die Einigung über den Rechtfertigungsartikel auf dem Regensburger Religionsgespräch von 1541—eine verpasste Chance?," *Zeitschrift für Theologie und Kirche* 76 (1979) 331–59; V. Pfnür, "Die Einigung bei den Religionsgesprächen von Worms und Regensburg 1540/41 eine Täuschung?," in G. Müller, ed., *Die Religionsgespräche der Reformationszeit* (Gütersloh, 1980) 55–88; A. Lexutt, *Rechtfertigung im Gespräch. Das Rechtfertigungsverständnis in den Religionsgesprächen von Hagenau, Worms und Regensburg 1540/41* (Göttingen, 1996); V. Ortmann, "Die Tätigkeit M. Bucers bei den Religionsgeprächen in Leipzig, Hagenau, Worms und Regensburg 1539–41" (diss., Bonn, 1997). → Regensburg, religious dialogues; → Worms, religious dialogues.

KARL-HEINZ ZUR MÜHLEN

Regensburg Convent and League (July 6, 1524). The imperial parliament of Nuremberg (1524) demanded the convocation of a national council. In order to render this superfluous and to protect southern and western Germany from the Reformation, the papal legate, Lorenzo → Campeggi, with the support of Bavaria, decided on a reform program and the creation of an anti-Lutheran league. On May 8, he and Archduke → Ferdinand sent invitations to the Regensburg Convent, which began on June 27. Agreement was reached on July 6 that the Edict of Worms should be enforced more strictly; if this met with opposition, the members of the league would help each other. Clergy reform was another subject of agreement.

The secular princes insisted on church reform, but the clerical princes were not willing to implement this. Campeggi promulgated reforming ordinances for the entire German church on July 7, but he was not able to put these into practice. The Regensburg League was the first official step towards the realization of Catholic → reform, and the first of the confessional leagues.

■ **Literature:** *LThK²* 8:1095.—*ARCEG* 1:294–393; W. Friedensburg, "Der Regensburger Convent 1524," in *Historische Aufsätze* (Hannover, 1886) 502–39; W. Borth, *Die Luthersache 1517–24* (Lübeck, 1970) 161–68; G. B. Winkler, "Der Regensburger Konvent," in *Reformatio Ecclesiae. Festschrift E. Iserloh* (Paderborn, 1980) 413–25; E. Wolgast, "Die deutschen Territorialfürsten," *Schriften des Vereins für Reformationsgeschichte* 199 (1998) 422f.

ROSEMARIE AULINGER

Regensburg, religious dialogues

(1) *April 27–May 22, 1541.* After preliminary dialogues in → Hagenau and → Worms in 1540-1541, a religious dialogue was held on the occasion of the imperial parliament in Regensburg. Its subject was the Book of Worms, which had been negotiated by Johann → Gropper and Gerhard Veltwyk for the Catholic party, and Martin → Bucer and Wolfgang → Capito for the Protestant party (M. Bucer, *Deutsche Schriften*, 9/1:328-483). After the papal legates, Gasparo → Contarini and Giovanni → Morone, succeeded in having twenty textual changes inserted, it was presented by Emperor → Charles V to the dialogue partners whom he had selected: Johannes → Eck, Gropper, and Julius von → Pflug on the Catholic side, and Philipp Melanchthon, Bucer, and Johannes Pistorius on the Protestant side. Nicolas Perrenot de → Granvella and the Palatine count Friedrich II presided at the dialogue, which succeeded in reaching agreement on the doctrine of sin and of grace, including → justification (art. 1-5) under the double aspect of a *iustitia imputata* and *inhaerens* (which was rejected both by Martin Luther [WA.BR 9:406-409 n. 3616] and by the Roman curia). A varying measure of consensus was achieved on some elements of sacramental doctrine (art. 10-13, 16, 17) and aspects of the external form of the → church (18, 20-23), but the religious dialogue in Regensburg broke down on the questions of the authority and structure of the church (6-9, 19), transubstantiation (14), and sacramental confession (15). Sixteen articles

where agreement existed and seven articles without consensus, in addition to nine contradictory articles by the Protestants, were presented to Charles V in the → Regensburg Book on May 31, 1541. In the resolution approved by the imperial parliament on July 29, 1541, the emperor recommended further reforms in the church in keeping with the articles where consensus existed, until a council should be held.

(2) *January 27–March 20, 1546.* In order to conceal the preparations he was making for the → Schmalkaldic War (1546-1547), Charles V had the imperial parliament of Worms (1545) resolve that a new religious dialogue should be held. The Catholic participants were Eberhard → Billick, Johannes Hoffmeister, and Pedro de → Malvenda; the Protestant participants were Johannes → Brenz, Bucer, Erhard → Schnepff, and Georg → Major. Malvenda's critique of the doctrine of justification took the discussion back to the stage before the religious dialogue which had taken place in Regensburg four years earlier; and when the participants were informed that the dialogue was to be kept a secret, the delegation from electoral Saxony took its leave. This meant that the dialogue in March, 1546 ended without any results.

■ Literature: *RE* 23:637ff.—*BDG* nn. 41390–98; Th. Brieger, *Casparo Contarini und das Regensburger Concordienwerk des Jahres 1541* (Gotha, 1870); W. Herbst, *Das Regensburger Religionsgespräch von 1601* (Gütersloh, 1928); P. Simoncelli, *Evangelismo italiano del Cinquecento* (Rome, 1979) passim; B. Bauer, "Das Regensburger Kolloquium 1601: Um Glauben und Reich. Kurfürst Maximilian I," in *Beiträge zur Bayrischen Geschichte und Kunst 1573–1657* vol. 1/1 (Munich, 1980) 90–99; C. Augustijn, "The Quest of Regensburg 1541 as a Turning Point," *ARG* special volume "Die Reformation in Deutschland und Europa. Interpretationen und Debatten" (Gütersloh, 1993) 64–80; E. G. Gleason, *Gasparo Contarini* (Berkeley, 1993) 186–256.

KARL-HEINZ ZUR MÜHLEN

Reina, *Casiodoro de.* Spanish Protestant, born c. 1520 in Seville, died March 20, 1594 in Frankfurt am Main. He was the intellectual leader of those monks of the Hieronymite monastery of San Isidoro who fled to Geneva in 1557. He was in Frankfurt in 1558, and then in London, where he was pastor of a Reformed Spanish community. He produced the first Spanish translation of the Bible from the original languages (Basle, 1569; often reprinted; *La Biblia del Oso,* 4 vols., Madrid, 1986-1987); this remained the only Spanish translation until the mid-20th century.

■ Literature: *DHEE* supplement vol., 642–45.—A. G. Kinder, *C. de R.* (London, 1975); *BiDi* 4:99–153; C. Gilly, *Spanien und der Basler Buchdruck bis 1600* (Basle and Frankfurt/Main, 1985) 353–436; K. Reinhardt, *Bibelkommentare spanischer Autoren,* vol. 2 (Madrid, 1999) 233f.

FERNANDO DOMÍNGUEZ

Religious dialogues. These were held in the early church and in the Middle Ages, but it was only in the 16th century that they took on central importance as a political and religious instrument for comparing and reconciling religious positions. This significance was a fruit of the disputations which were held by scholars and city councils in the first half of the century with the purpose of introducing, legitimating, or criticizing the → Reformation, e.g., in Zurich (1523), → Ilanz (1526), Baden (1526; → Baden disputation), Berne (1528), and Leipzig (1534 and 1539). An unofficial religious dialogue was held in Augsburg in 1530. After the Truce of → Frankfurt in 1539, the era of religious dialogues on the imperial level began, with gatherings in → Hagenau, → Worms, and → Regensburg (1540-1541), then again in Regensburg (1546) and Worms (1557). These were a national substitute for the council which had been convoked in 1536, but which assembled, after repeated delays, only in 1545. The religious dialogues in Regensburg (1546) and Worms (1557) were not significant, since they were an instrument of religious politics rather than a serious attempt to compare and reconcile divergent religious positions; the same applies to the religious dialogues of → Poissy (1561) and Thorn (1545), which likewise covered more than one local region.

Religious dialogues on the local level came back into vogue in the second half of the 16th century, especially after the Council of Trent (1545-1563). Some of these helped promote understanding among the Protestants themselves: e.g., Maulbronn (1564), → Altenburg (1568-1569), Sandomierz (1570), Mömpelgard (1586), Meissen (1568-1569), Zerbst (1570), and Quedlinburg (1583). Others promoted the goals of the → Counter-Reformation: e.g., Baden-

Baden (1589), Emmendingen (1590), and Regensburg (1601 and 1615).

■ **Literature:** G. Müller, *Die Religionsgespräche der Reformationszeit* (Gütersloh, 1980); M. Hollerbach, *Das Religionsgespräch als Mittel der konfessionellen und politischen Auseinandersetzung im Deutschland des 16.Jh.* (Frankfurt/Main, 1982); Th. Fuchs, *Konfession und Gespräch* (Cologne, 1995); G. Kuhaupt, *Veröffentlichte Religionspolitik* (Göttingen, 1997); C. Augustijn, "Melanchthon und die Religionsgespräche," in *Der Theologe Melanchthon* (Stuttgart, 2000) 213–26.—Cf. the literature cited in the individual contributions above.

KARL-HEINZ ZUR MÜHLEN

Reublin, *Wilhelm.* Born c. 1484 in Rottenburg, date and place of death unknown. He studied in Freiburg and Tübingen, and became parish priest in Griessen before 1510. He was given the cure of souls at St. Alban's church in Basle in 1521, but was expelled from the city in the following year because he had preached against the Mass and the precepts about fasting. He married in Witikon in 1522, and became the leader of the → Baptists there, until he was compelled to leave the city in 1525. He spread the Baptist movement in Schaffhausen, Waldshut, Strasbourg, Reutlingen, and Esslingen. After a period of imprisonment in Strasbourg (1528-1529), he went to Moravia. He split the Baptist community in Austerlitz in 1530 and founded a community of his own in Auspitz, but this community in turn rejected him. He returned to Rottenburg, and parted company with the Baptists in 1531. He was a frequent visitor to Zurich, Basle, Augsburg, and Znaim; the last record of him is from 1559.

■ **Literature:** *Mennonitisches Lexikon,* vol. 3 (Karlsruhe, 1958) 477; *RGG*[3] 5:1074; *BBKL* 8:76f.—M. Krebs and H.-G. Rott, eds., *Quellen zur Geschichte der Täufer,* vol. 7: *Elsass* 1 (Stuttgart, 1959).

JOHANNES MADEY

Reuchlin, *Johannes.* Humanist, born January 29, 1455 in Pforzheim, died June 30, 1522 in Stuttgart. After schooling in Pforzheim, Reuchlin studied the basic *artes* and jurisprudence in Freiburg, Basle, Orleans, and Poitiers. As a student, he published a Latin dictionary (*Vocabularius breviloquus,* Basle, 1478); as a young man, he was particularly interested in the Greek language, which he learned from the Greek exiles Konto-

blakes and Hermonymos. He began his legal career in 1482, as doctor of imperial laws, at the court of Count Eberhard V of Württemberg, and rose to become a judge of the Swabian League.

His academic reputation in later centuries as "founder of Christian humanism" and "leader of academic cabbalistic studies in the West" is based on his grammar (with dictionary) *De rudimentis hebraicis* (Pforzheim, 1506) and his studies of the cabbala, *De verbo mirifico* (Basle, 1494) and *De arte cabalistica* (Hagenau, 1517). It was above all his studies of the Hebrew language under Jewish scholars such as Jakob ben Jechiel, the emperor's personal physician, that made Protestant historians of the Reformation look on Reuchlin—a humanist who himself always remained faithful to the Catholic Church—as a pioneer in the discovery of the *veritas hebraica.*

Another reason why Reuchlin was included among the pre-Reformation witnesses to the faith was his involvement in the controversy about the preservation of Jewish literature. Johannes → Pfefferkorn, a convert from Judaism, started moves to have all Jewish writings confiscated, and a number of scholars were asked for their opinion on this question. Reuchlin was the only one to protest against Pfefferkorn's actions, in a memorandum drawn up in 1510. He argued on legal grounds (the Jews enjoyed the legal protection of the emperor, which included a guarantee of their right to property), on theological and philosophical grounds (the Jewish tradition is in harmony with the Christian tradition, and is evidence of the existence of the Christian God), and on academic and philological grounds (the Jewish writings are useful for the work of Christian exegesis). Proceedings against Reuchlin on the suspicion of heresy began, and the Dominican Order took this as far as the papal courts in Rome. He was condemned in 1520 to bear the costs of the trial and condemned to silence. Thanks to the public support given to Reuchlin in the "Letters of → Obscure Men," a clever verbal satire which poked fun at the abysmal lack of culture on the part of Reuchlin's opponents, this debate has come to be seen as a milestone in the history of tolerance and of censorship in the early modern period. The humanistic "Reuchlinists" do not take up the issue of the Jewish writings, but turn the whole controversy into a matter of principle, a conflict between backwoods scholasticism and enlightened humanism. The "Letters" also display an antipathy toward theology, since the lay humanists rebel against the monopoly claimed by academic (scholastic) theologians on both knowledge and interpretation.

The theological topics which interested Reuchlin are found scattered throughout his writings. His comedy *Sergius* (written in Erfurt c. 1504) is a polemic against the excesses of popular piety (relics and the pilgrimage "business"). He devoted considerable time to the edition and translation of Greek and Latin church fathers such as Athanasius and Proclus. His studies of the cabbala are clearly written from a Christian perspective. In his theoretical writings on preaching, he combines Cicero's ideas about rhetoric and biblical affirmations with pastoral interests, aiming principally at the moral education of the hearers. He frequently dealt with Marian themes, translating the sermon about Mary by Proclus and writing a detailed commentary (never printed) on the Marian sequence *Ave virginalis forma.* He was a member of the Salve-Regina fraternity.

■ **Works:** *De arte praedicandi* (Pforzheim, 1504); *Augenspiegel* (Tübingen, 1511); *Defensio contra calumniatores suos Colonienses* (Tübingen, 1514); *De accentibus et orthographia linguae hebraicae* (Hagenau, 1518); *Sämtliche Werke,* vol. 1/1, ed. W.-W. Ehlers (Stuttgart, 1996) (*De verbo mirifico*).

■ **Literature:** *BBKL* 8:77–80.—L. Geiger, *J. R.* (Leipzig, 1871; reprint, 1964); S. Rhein, "Reuchliniana I–III," in *J. R. (1455–1522)* ed. H. Kling (Sigmaringen, ²1994) 277–325; C. Zika, *R. und die okkulte Tradition der Renaissance* (Sigmaringen, 1998); *R. und die politischen Kräfte seiner Zeit,* ed. S. Rhein (Sigmaringen, 1998).

STEFAN RHEIN

■ **Additional Bibliography:** M. R. Ackermann, *Der Jurist J. R.* (Berlin, 1999); G. Dörner, ed., *R. und Italien* (Stuttgart, 1999).

R(h)adinus (Radini, Rodaginus, also known as Tedescus, Tedeschi, Todisc[h]us, -ius), *Thomas* (Tommaso). Dominican theologian, born March 15, 1488 in Piacenza, died May, 1527 in Rome (during the → Sack of Rome). He was professor of theology in Rome, and became the deputy of Sylvester → Prierias, master of the Sacred Palace, c. 1520. He became known in Germany through his *Oratio ad principes et populos Germaniae* (Cologne, 1520), a response to Martin Luther's pamphlet *An den christlichen Adel.* This provoked

Philipp Melanchthon's *Didymi Faventini adversus Thomam Placentinum oratio,* to which Rhadinus in turn replied in his *Oratio in Philippum Melanchthonem* (Leipzig, 1522).

■ **Catalogue of Works:** *VD 16* R:84–87.

■ **Literature:** *CEras* 3:131.—R. Stupperich, "Melanchthon und R.," *ZKG* 100 (1989) 340–52; D. V. N. Bagchi, *Luther's Earliest Opponents* (Minneapolis, 1991); M. Tavuzzi, "An Unedited Oratio by Tommaso R. Tedeschi O.P.," *AHP* 32 (1994) 43–63.

BARBARA HENZE

Rhegius, *Urbanus* (real name: Urban Rieger). Humanist and Reformation theologian, born May, 1489 in Langenargen (Bodensee), died May 27, 1541 in Celle. He studied in Freiburg and Ingolstadt, and was a pupil of Johannes → Eck. He was crowned poet laureate in 1517. He was ordained priest in 1519 and took his doctorate of theology in Basle in 1520; he succeeded Johannes → Oecolampadius as cathedral preacher in Augsburg in 1520, where it was his task to publish the bull *Exsurge Domine* in the cathedral on December 30, 1520. He was dismissed from office in 1521, and became preacher at St. Anne's church in Augsburg in 1524. He married in 1525. He performed the services of a go-between during the composition of the → Confessio Augustana. After the imperial parliament of 1530, he was invited by Duke Ernest the Confessor to come to Braunschweig-Lüneburg as superintendent. Rhegius took part in important events and decisions of the Reformation period (Concord of → Wittenberg, 1536; Assembly of Schmalkalden, 1537; religious dialogue in → Hagenau, 1539).

■ **Works:** *Opera . . . latine edita,* ed. E. Regius, 3 Teile (Nuremberg, 1562); *Deutsche Bücher und Schriften,* ed. idem, 4 Teile (Nuremberg, 1562); *Poemata iuvenilia,* ed. G. Wagner (Wittenberg, 1711).

■ **Literature:** *BBKL* 8:122–34.—G. Uhlhorn, *U.Rh. Leben und ausgewählte Schriften* (Elberfeld, 1861; reprint, Nieuwkoop, 1968); M. Liebmann, *U. Rh. und die Anfänge der Reformation* (Münster, 1980); H. Zschoch, *Reformatorische Existenz und konfessionelle Identität. U.Rh. als evangelischer Theologe in den Jahren 1520–30* (Tübingen, 1995).

MAXIMILIAN LIEBMANN

■ **Additional Bibliography:** S. H. Hendrix, *Die Bedeutung des U. Rh. für die Ausbreitung der Reformation: Humanismus und Wittenberger Reformation* (Leipzig, 1996) 53–72; R. Cole, "Interpreting an Early Reformation Pamphlet by U.Rh.," in *Books Have Their*

Own Destiny. Festschrift R. V. Schnucker (Kirksville, 1998) 39–46.

Rink (Rinck), *Melchior.* Leader of the Baptists in eastern Hessen, born c. 1493, date of death unknown. He was Catholic curate in Hersfeld in 1523, where he endeavored to introduce Reformation thinking, but he was expelled from the city. While pastor near Eisenach, he came under the influence of Thomas → Müntzer. He was in Worms and Landau from 1525 to 1528. After embracing the Baptist movement, he founded a Baptist community in Hersfeld (1528) and in Sorga. He was expelled after the civic and ecclesiastical authorities had raised accusations against him. On his return in 1529, he was arrested, and sentenced to lifelong imprisonment in 1531.
■ Literature: *BBKL* 8:369ff.—E. Geldbach, *Leben und Lehre des hessischen Täuferführers M. R.* (Marburg, 1969) (manuscript); H. Beulshausen, *Die Geschichte der osthessischen Täufergemeinden* (Giessen, 1981).

ALOYS KLEIN

Rorer (Rohrer), *Thomas.* Lutheran theologian, born 1521 in Ingolstadt, died after 1582 in Gutenbrunn (Austria). After studies in his hometown, he became a Premonstratensian in Windberg. He was ordained priest in 1542 and became curate in Viechtach. He converted to Lutheranism in 1545, and was appointed preacher in Cham in the Upper Palatinate, where he married. He was curate in Weiden in 1550, and became pastor in Bruck in 1555. He was in Rennertshofen near Neuburg in 1562, and helped consolidate the Reformation in the county of Ortenburg in 1564. He became pastor in Giengen (Brenz) in 1570. In 1572, he became pastor in Pottenbrunn (Austria), and in Gutenbrunn in 1579. He can be considered the successor of Matthias → Flacius, as one of the most important Protestant writers in Bavaria.
■ Literature: F. W. Kantzenbach, "Der Prädikant Th. R.," *ZBKG* 25 (1956) 152–65; N. Backmund, *Kloster Windberg* (Windberg, 1977) 82f., 158.

MANFRED EDER

Rothmann, *Bernhard.* Protestant preacher and Baptist theologian, born c. 1495 in Stadtlohn (Westphalia), date of death unknown. He attended schools in Deventer and Münster, and became a teacher in Warendorf. From 1529 onward, he was curate in the collegiate church of St. Maurice outside Münster. He traveled to Wittenberg, Marburg, and Strasbourg. Prince Bishop Friedrich von Wied expelled him from the territory which was subject to the diocese of Münster because of his Protestant sermons, but he found refuge in the city of Münster itself, where he became pastor in St. Lambert's church (February 23, 1532). After other Protestant preachers were appointed in Münster, Rothmann and several of his colleagues turned against infant baptism in 1533. Dutch Melchiorites (Melchior → Hoffman) baptized Rothmann on January 5, 1534. During the rule of the → Baptists (from February 24, 1534), Rothmann was eclipsed by the prophets Jan van Leiden and Jan Matthijs, but he worked to the last to help the besieged Baptist city. When Münster was captured on June 25, 1535, he escaped, and probably made his way to Oldenburg. Theologically, he was influenced by Philipp Melanchthon, Huldrych Zwingli, Wolfgang → Capito, Johannes → Campanus, and Hoffman. His writings from 1534-1535 were intended to prepare the way for the return of Christ, and won acceptance in the Baptist movement.
■ Works: *Die Schriften B. R.s,* ed. R. Stupperich (Münster, 1970).
■ Literature: *BBKL* 8:825ff.—M. Brecht, "Die Theologie B. R.s," *Jahrbuch für westfälische Kirchengeschichte* 78 (1985) 49–82; W. de Bakker, "B. R.," in *The Dutch Dissenters*, ed. I. Horst (Leiden, 1986) 105–16; R. Klötzer, *Die Täuferherrschaft von Münster* (Münster, 1992).

RALF KLÖTZER

Rythovius, *Balduinus Martinus* (Maarten van Riethoven). First bishop of Ypres (Belgium), born 1511 in Riethoven (Netherlands), died October 9, 1583 in St. Omer (department of Pas-de-Calais). He was professor in Dillingen and Louvain, and took part in the religious dialogue in → Worms in 1557. In 1561, he was appointed bishop of Ypres, a diocese erected in 1559. He took part in the last session of the Council of Trent in 1563, and implemented the decisions of the council in his diocese, opening the first Tridentine seminary in the Netherlands in 1565. He appealed to the duke of → Alba to exercise moderation in his dealings in the Netherlands. When the Calvinists seized power in the city of Ghent on October 28, 1577,

Rythovius and the bishop of Bruges were taken captive, and remained in prison until 1581.

■ **Literature:** *Biographie nationale,* ed. die Belgische Akademie der Wissenschaften, vol. 20 (Brussels, 1908–10) 725–64.—A. Iweins, *Esquisse historique et biographique sur R., premier évêque d'Ypres* (Brügge, 1859); M. Dierickx, *De oprichting der nieuwe bisdommen in de Nederlanden onder Filips II 1559–70* (Antwerp and Utrecht, 1950); P. H. Verhoeven, *Maarten van Riethoven, eerste bisschop van Ieper* (Wetteren, 1961).

PETER J. A. NISSEN

S

Sachs, *Hans.* Poet and cobbler, born November 5, 1494 in Nuremberg, where he died January 19, 1576. He embraced the Reformation at an early date. In his lyric poem *Die Wittembergisch Nachtigall* (1523), which made him famous, he offered a popular summary of Martin Luther's teachings. Much of his other work—more than 6,000 *Meisterlieder,* lyric poems, prose dialogues, plays for the carnival season, comedies, and tragedies—is intended to serve the cause of the Reformation.

■ **Works:** *Werke,* ed. A. von Keller and E. Goetze, 26 vols. (Stuttgart, 1870–1908); *Repertorium der Sangsprüche und Meisterlieder,* ed. H. Brunner and B. Wachinger (Tübingen, 1986ff.).

■ **Literature:** N. Holzberg, *H. S. Bibliographie* (Nuremberg, 1976); E. Bernstein, *H. S.* (Reinbek, 1993).

HORST BRUNNER

■ **Additional Bibliography:** B. Hamm, "'Ist das gut evangelisch?' H. S. als Wortführer und Kritiker der Reformation," *Luther* 66 (1995) 125–40; idem, *Bürgertum und Glaube* (Göttingen, 1998).

Sack of Rome. This name is given to the plundering (*sacco* in Italian) of Rome by the troops of → Charles V in 1527. The emperor sought to enforce his claims to sovereignty in Italy against the League of Cognac, to which Pope → Clement VII belonged. His soldiers were initially under the command of Duke Charles de Bourbon, who died during the assault on Rome on May 5; deprived of their leader, they plundered and murdered without restraint. Clement fled to Castel Sant'Angelo, but was forced to surrender on June 5 and was taken captive, until he was able to ransom himself

on December 6. The Sack of Rome, a catastrophe generally perceived as a punishment of Renaissance Rome, opened the path to repentance and renewal.

■ **Literature:** L. von Pastor, *Geschichte der Päpste seit dem Ausgang des Mittelalters,* vol. 4/2 (Freiburg, 1956) 228–322; M. Lenzi, *Il S. del 1527.* (Rome, 1978); E. A. Chamberlain, *The Sack of Rome* (London, 1979); C. Chaffin, *Olympiodoros of Thebes and the Sack of Rome* (New York, 1993); V. J. Pitts, *The Man Who Sacked Rome* (New York, 1994); L. Guicciardini, "The Sack of Rome, "*CHR* 80 (1994) 353–57.

JOSEF GELMI

■ **Additional Bibliography:** K. Gouwens, *Remembering the Renaissance. Humanist Narratives of the Sack of Rome* (Leiden, 1998).

Sacraments

1. An essential aspect in the *Reformation understanding of sacraments* is their "positive character," i.e., the fact that they were instituted by God himself. Since only God can link his grace to visible signs, it follows that only those signs or actions which the Bible explicitly attests as instituted by God (*mandatum Dei*) can count as "sacraments." This means that the natural symbolic character of sacramental signs and rites is seldom a topic of theological reflection; indeed, this is sometimes explicitly denied. All the emphasis lies on God's action, which is the only decisive factor, and on the character of the sacraments as his gifts. At the same time, the significance of the Word is underlined, both in relation to the sacrament itself and in the concrete form of the sacrament. The Lutheran tradition tends to give Word and sacrament an equal rank, while the Reformed tradition explicitly considers the Word the higher and primary means of grace.

For *Martin Luther,* the sacraments are signs instituted by God as contexts in which the human person is assured of God's salvation by means of a sign. Faith (*fides*), the pure act of entrusting oneself to God's promise (*promissio*), is the necessary condition of the salvific efficacy of the sacraments. Nevertheless, Luther explicitly safeguards their objective character: faith does not create the sacraments, but receives them (*BSLK* 701:41f.). Philipp Melanchthon emphasizes more clearly the character of the sacraments as *ritus,* symbolic actions by the church (cf. the definition in the Apologia for the → Confessio Augustana 13:3). They are signs which bear witness to God's will in regard to the human person (CA 13). In general, Melanchthon underlines the ecclesiological aspect of the sacraments more strongly than Luther, and CA 7 makes clear the significance of the sacraments for the constitution of the → church. The Lutheran concept of "sacrament" leaves the number of sacraments somewhat open; cf. the different evaluations of → penance and the statements in CA and ApolCA 13. At the same time, there is little interest in formulating an explicit concept of "sacrament," which tends to be accepted only at a secondary stage of reflection, in order not to obscure the specific character of what God himself has instituted. On the basis of the biblical concept of *mystērion,* Luther can call Jesus Christ the true *sacramentum* from whom the sacramental signs are derived (WA 6:86,7; 501,37f.).

The *Reformed tradition* developed a clearer concept of "sacrament," covering the sacraments of both the Old and the New Testaments which seal the covenant of grace. The Bible attests the institution of two sacraments of the new covenant, viz., baptism and the Lord's Supper. Huldrych Zwingli interprets the sacrament as a purely human sign whereby we profess our faith, since the Spirit who bestows grace is not in need of any visible element. Jean Calvin, whose position came to be more influential within the Reformed tradition, understands the sacrament as a seal on God's promise, which God gives us as an external sign in order to strengthen our weak human faith. Calvin emphasizes the pneumatological dimension: the power of the sacrament is derived, not from its character as sign, but from the Spirit of God. Nevertheless, the sacrament is rightly called an efficacious sign of grace. Calvin does not simply posit a parallel between the external sign and the internal effect. The centrality of the Word as the means of salvation in Reformed thinking, and its understanding of grace in personal terms, leads this tradition to see the specific quality of the sacrament not in its substance (i.e., the sacrament as a gift which bestows salvation), but rather in its form: the sacraments complement the Word of God by emphasizing the bodiliness and the individuality of the human person, as well as the ecclesiological significance of faith.

Articles 25-31 of the *Thirty-Nine* → *Anglican Articles* of the *Church of* → *England* and the catechism in the Anglican *Book of* → *Common Prayer*

understand the sacraments not primarily as human signs of the profession of faith, but as efficacious signs of grace and of God's goodwill toward the human person. The sacraments strengthen and confirm our faith. The New Testament testimony makes baptism and the Lord's Supper the sacraments of the gospel, whereas the other signs called "sacraments" were not explicitly instituted by God. If the sacrament is to be efficacious for salvation, the one who receives it must be worthy. However, the unworthiness of a church minister does not make the sacraments invalid, since they are inseparably linked to institution by Christ and to his promise.

BURKHARD NEUMANN

■ *LThK*[3] 8:1447ff. (unabridged version).
■ **Literature:** J. Rohls, *Theologie reformierter Bekenntnisschriften* (Göttingen, 1987); U. Stock, *Die Bedeutung der S. in Luthers Sermonen von 1519* (Leiden, 1992); I. Green, *The Christian's ABC. Catechism and Catechizing in England c. 1530–1740.* (Oxford, 1996); M. Lienhard, "Luther est-il 'protestant'? Le sacrement chez Luther et dans la tradition luthérienne," *Revue d'histoire et de philosophie religieuses* 77 (1997) 141–64; Y. H. Lee, "Calvin's Doctrine of the Sacraments," *Yonsei Journal of Theology* 2 (1997) 119–47.

2. The *Council of Trent* approved its decree on the sacraments (DH 1600-1613) in 1547, taking the texts of the Council of Florence as guidelines. Technical terms of scholastic theology were avoided. No definition of the essence of the sacraments was made, since the intention was to state the bare minimum required in order to reject the Reformation doctrines about the number of the sacraments and about their efficacy through faith alone; the Reformers were not mentioned by name. Those propositions which rejected the Reformers' teachings were protected by the anathema. These concerned the institution of the seven sacraments by Jesus Christ (the council spoke in greater detail about this in its treatment of the individual sacraments); their relationship to faith; the *opus operatum*; the existence of the indelible sacramental character; the authority required for the administration of the sacraments; the intention of the minister; the lack of an *obex* (impediment) in the recipient. It is clear that Trent regarded the praxis of infant baptism as the norm when drawing up its text on the sacraments as a whole, and this means that the personal and liturgical perspective of the sacraments is not brought

out. The text posits a relationship between the sacraments and justification, but it does not teach that all seven are equal in rank or necessary for salvation.

HERBERT VORGRIMLER

■ *LThK³* 8:1440ff. (unabridged version).
■ **Literature:** J. Lligadas Vendrell, *La eficacia de los sacramentos. "Ex opere operato" en la doctrina del Concilio de Trento* (Barcelona, 1983); A. Duval, *Des sacrements au Concile de Trente* (Paris, 1985).

■ **Additional Literature:** N. H. Gregersen, "The Chalcedonian Structure of Martin Luther's Sacramental Realism," in *Kirche zwischen Heilsbotschaft und Lebenswirklichkeit.* Festschrift T. Jorgensen (New York, 1996) 177–96; M. D. Tranvik, "Luther on Baptism," *Luther Quarterly* 13 (1999) 75–90; G. Müller, "Die Kritik des Martin Chemnitz an der Sakramentenlehre des Konzils von Trient," in *Reformation und Katholizismus.* Festschrift G. Maron (Hannover, 2003) 178–99.

Sadoleto, *Jacopo.* Humanist reform theologian, born July 12, 1477 in Modena, died October 18, 1547. He became secretary to → Leo X in 1511, and was appointed bishop of Carpentras near Avignon in 1517; Pope → Hadrian VI dismissed him from office in 1523. Giles of Viterbo kindled his interest in theological matters, and he began to take a new interest in his diocese. Although his intention was to devote his energies to writing, he was secretary to → Clement VII from 1524 to 1527. He was created cardinal in 1536, and was in Rome from 1536 to 1538 as a member of the reform commission set up by → Paul III, where he submitted a memorandum of his own. He endeavored to achieve reconciliation in a humanist spirit between 1537 and 1539 (Philipp Melanchthon; Johann → Sturm; Geneva). He was mild in his dealings with the Waldensians in Provence; although he later adopted a policy of severity, he was not responsible for the massacre in 1545. He was sent as papal legate to → Francis I in 1542-1543 and was present at the meeting in Busseto. He raised his voice in Rome in support of a council (1545-1547) and was a critic of the pope's policies. He perceived reform as a problem of morality and education, and unity was more important in his eyes than truth; he was a foe of the Jews. Sadoleto composed humanistic poetry, Aristotelian-Neoplatonic philosophical writings, and exegetical works (on Psalms 50 and 93, and on the Letter to the Romans, a semi-Pelagian text written in 1535), as well as systematic theological monographs which remain unpublished. He was a student of the church fathers, especially John Chrysostom, and he wrote dialogues in which the voice of rhetoric and morality argues against the voice of scholasticism.

■ **Works:** *Gesamtausgabe* (Mainz, 1607); *Gesamtausgabe,* 4 vols. (Verona, 1737–38); A. Mai, *Spicilegium Romanum,* vol. 2 (Rome, 1839) 101–78.
■ **Sources:** *Epistolae,* 5 vols. (Rome, 1759–67); A. Ronchini, ed., *Lettere* (Modena, 1872); *Acta Nuntiaturae Gallicae,* vol. 3 (Paris, 1963).
■ **Literature:** *BBKL* 8:1164–69.—R. M. Douglas, *J. S.* (Cambridge, Mass., 1959); W. Reinhard, *Die Reform in der Diözese Carpentras* (Münster, 1966); M. Venard, *Réforme protestante, Réforme catholique dans la province d'Avignon* (Paris, 1993); G. Gesigora, *Ein humanistischer Psalmenexeget des 16.Jh. J. S.* (Frankfurt/Main, 1997).

WOLFGANG REINHARD

Saints, veneration

1. The Reformers

Not only individual abuses of popular piety were considered to be diametrically contradictory of the fundamental religious principles of the Reformation; the same applied in a particular manner to the teaching of the Catholic magisterium that it was possible to ask the saints in heaven for their intercession and for the mediation of grace which aided the Christian here on earth (though not a grace which justified or sanctified). For the Reformers, God alone can be adored (i.e., venerated), and Christ is the only mediator between God and human beings; the believer must place his hope on Christ alone for the forgiveness of sins and → justification. Besides this, since there is no example in scripture of prayer to deceased saints, veneration of the saints also infringes the principle of *sola scriptura.* The veneration of the saints was linked to other Catholic doctrines which were criticized, viz., the treasury of merits of the saints, → indulgences, prayer for the dead, and the celebration of the Mass in honor of the saints. This is why Martin Luther calls the invocation of the saints one of the "dechristianized abuses" (→ Schmalkaldic articles II/2): people think that Christ is a severe judge, so they flee from him and turn to the saints in the hope that they will appease him (WA 30/III:312; → Confessio Augustana 21). Accordingly, the cult of the saints is an "appalling idolatry"

(Philipp Melanchthon, *Confessio Saxonica*, CR 23: LXXXIX); for Calvin, it contradicts the honor which is due to God alone (*Inst* I 12:1; III 20:24-27).

This does not, however, entail the total abolition of the veneration of the saints. This has its place in the ecclesial fellowship which embraces all who believe in Christ (Luther, WA 2:745 and 748). The Confessio Augustana and its Apologia (21) speak of a threefold honor which is owed to the saints: first, they are remembered, and God is thanked for giving them to Christendom as examples of the gifts he bestows and as teachers. Second, they themselves are to be praised, because Christ too praised and rewarded his true stewards. Third, the saints are honored when one follows their example, thereby experiencing consolation, the certainty that one's sins are forgiven, and a strengthening in faith. Nevertheless, one may not ask the saints for their intercession, in the sense that one would put one's trust in the saints to win salvation for the Christian.

2. *The Council of Trent*

Trent takes up the affirmations of the second Council of Nicaea (DH 600; cf. also the Council of Florence, DH 1304) and teaches, in view of the objections by the Reformers, that it is "good and profitable" to invoke the intercession of the saints who reign with Christ in heaven, "in order to obtain benefits from God [!] through [!] his Son Jesus Christ, who alone is our redeemer and savior" (DH 1821). It is in this sense that one should venerate the saints, their relics, and their images (→ Art and Reformation). The cult of the saints has nothing to do with idolatry (DH 1821-1825).

■ *LThK*[3] 4:1298, 1301 (unabridged version).

■ **Literature:** *EKL*[3] 2:445; *RGG*[3] 4:664ff.

GERHARD LUDWIG MÜLLER

■ **Additional Bibliography:** M. Lienhard, "La sainteté et les saints," *Etudes théologiques et religieuses* 72 (1997) 375–87; A. Dörfler-Dierken, "Luther und die heilige Anna," *Luther-Jahrbuch* 64 (1997) 19–46; T. Fuchs, "Protestantische Heiligen-memoria im 16. Jahrhundert," *Historische Zeitschrift* 267 (1998) 587–614; O. H. Pesch, "Von der wahren und falschen Ehrung der Heiligen. Eine Predigt in Hamburg—in der Person Johannes Bugenhagens," *Wort und Antwort* 41 (2000) 124–29; S. Cavallotto, "'Heiligentexte,' 'devozione' ai santi e riforma liturgica nelle Chiese protestanti (1522–1552)," *Hagiographica* 8 (2001) 233–56.

Salvation, certainty of

1. *The Reformation*

Martin Luther emphasizes that, thanks to the assurances God has made, faith brings about the certainty of salvation, of grace, and of the forgiveness of sins; the word of forgiveness spoken in absolution is the paradigm he follows here. Accordingly, the → Confessio Augustana affirms: "Only faith overcomes the terrors of sin and death, since it looks to the promise and knows that God forgives, because Christ did not die in vain" (*BSLK* 189:32-36). In other words, the basis of the certainty of salvation is not human existence or human action. It is identical with faith in the sense of a stable confidence ("fiducial" faith), and is therefore something other than a merely theoretical or psychological certainty.

2. *The Council of Trent*

The council replied to this position by citing Phil 2:12 and insisting that Christians must "work out their salvation in fear and trembling." Recent research has shown that the Tridentine decree on → justification (especially DH 1533f., 1540f., 1562-1566, 1572f.) agrees with Luther in rejecting a false understanding of the certainty of salvation, and underscores what he and the Reformers saw as the central issue (cf. LK 1:62,10-20). The council does however concede that talk of "certainty of salvation" remains open to the misunderstanding that our absolute confidence in God's Word would be based on our own certainty; Trent correctly rejects such a certainty as "vain" (cf. ibid., and DH 1533).

■ *LThK*[3] 4:1344ff. (unabridged version).

■ **Literature:** (H.=Heilsgewissheit) *LThK*[2] 5:157–60; *TRE* 14:759–63.—A. Stakemeier, *Das Konzil von Trient über die H.* (Heidelberg, 1947); S. Pfürtner, *Luther und Thomas im Gespräch* (Heidelberg, 1961); L. Ullrich, "H.," in *Theologisches Jahrbuch* (Leipzig, 1985) 381–401; "Ökumenischer Arbeitskreis evangelischer und katholischer Theologen," in *Lehrverurteilungen—kirchentrennend?*, vols. 1–3 (Freiburg and Göttingen, 1986–94) (LK); O. H. Pesch and A. Peters, *Einführung in die Lehre von Gnade und Rechtfertigung* (Darmstadt, [3]1994).

JOSEF WOHLMUTH

Sattler, *Michael.* Baptist theologian, born c. 1490 in Staufen (Breisgau), died May 20, 1527 near Rottenburg (Neckar). He was a Benedictine monk in the monastery of St. Peter's in the Black Forest, and documents attest him as prior. He joined the → Baptist movement in Zurich in 1525 and headed the Baptist synod in Schleitheim (Schaffhausen) in 1527. As the author of the "Confession of Schleitheim," he played a determinative role in the Baptist movement in Switzerland and southern Germany. This text rejected infant baptism, the taking of oaths, and military service; it urged the creation of voluntary communities which lived separate from the world. He influenced the development of a pacifist Free Church ecclesiological model. He was tried, tortured, and executed in 1527.

■ **Literature:** *BBKL* 8:1403–8.—M. Haas, "M. S.," in *Radikale Reformatoren,* ed. H.-J. Goertz (Munich, 1978) 195–242; K. Deppermann, *Protestantische Profile von Luther bis Francke* (Göttingen, 1992) 48–64; H. O. Mühleisen, "M. S.," in *Edith-Stein-Jahrbuch,* vol. 4 (Würzburg, 1998) 225–42.

G. MICHAEL SCHMITT

Scaliger, *Joseph Justus.* French Reformed philologist, born August 5, 1540 in Agen (department of Garonne), died January 21, 1609 in Leiden. After humanistic studies under his father, Julius Caesar Scaliger, and in Paris, he converted to Calvinism in 1562, and took part several times in the Wars of Religion on the Huguenot side. He was professor in Geneva from 1572 to 1574, and then worked as a private scholar in France. From 1593 to 1609, he was the successor to Justus → Lipsius as professor in Leiden, and it was thanks to him that Holland became the center of all philological research in Europe. He is considered the greatest editor of texts and philological commentator in his period. He also carried out epigraphical research, and is the founder of the academic study of chronology (e.g., *De emendatione temporum,* Paris, 1588, 2nd edition with critical excursus, 1598; *Thesaurus temporum,* Leiden, 1606, 2nd edition 1608). His polemical discussion of contemporary confessional issues (in the context of his philological writings) provoked numerous literary controversies, especially with Jesuit scholars. One of his opponents, Dionysius Petavius, deserves mention because of his improvements to Scaliger's chronology (*De doctrina temporum* [Paris, 1627]).

■ **Literature:** *LThK*¹ 9:357; *RGG*³ 5:1380f.; *BBKL* 8:1489–92.—*Autobiography of J. J. S.,* ed. G. W. Robinson (Cambridge, Mass., 1927); C. M. Bruehl, "J. J. S.: ein Beitrag zur geistesgeschichtlichen Bedeutung

der Altertumswissenschaft," *Zeitschrift für Religions- und Geistesgeschichte* 12 (1960) 201–18; 13 (1961) 45–65; R. Smitskamp, ed., *The S. Collection* (Leiden, 1993).

ERNST WALTER ZEEDEN

■ **Additional Bibliography:** A. Grafton, *J. S.* vols. 1ff. (Oxford, 1983ff.); H. J. de Jonge, "J. S.'s Historical Criticism of the New Testament," *Novum Testamentum* 38 (1996) 176–93.

Schatzgeyer (Sasger, Schatzger), *Kaspar.* Franciscan Observant, controversial theologian, born 1463/1464 in Landshut, died September 18, 1527 in Munich. After studies in Ingolstadt and other towns, he was appointed lector in Landshut in 1487. He was lector in Ingolstadt from 1489 to 1496, and then in Munich (1498), where he became guardian in 1499. He was appointed preacher and lector in Ingolstadt in 1508. He was provincial of the Upper German province of the Franciscan Observants from 1514 to 1517, and again from 1520 to 1523; he was guardian in Nuremberg from 1517 to 1520, and in Munich from 1523 to 1527. He engaged in debates with the Franciscan Conventuals in 1516, and with the Reformers from 1522 onward; here he argued on the basis of scripture, discussing the doctrine of the Eucharist and the sacraments, monastic vows, and Christian freedom. Initially, he sought to maintain a mediating position which did not dismiss the concerns of the Reformation, but he adopted a harsher tone as the controversies developed.

■ **Works:** *Apologia status fratrum ordinis minorum de observantia* (Basle, 1516); *Scrutinium divinae scripturae pro conciliatione dissidentium dogmatum* (Basle, 1522, often reprinted), ed. U. Schmidt (Münster, 1922); *Omnia opera* (Ingolstadt, 1543); *Schriften zur Verteidigung der Messe,* ed. E. Iserloh and P. Fabisch (Münster, 1984); *Von der waren Christlichen und Evangelischen freyheit* (Munich, 1524); *De vera libertate evangelica* (Tübingen, 1525, often reprinted), ed. Ph. Schäfer (Münster, 1987).—*Catalogue of Works: VD 16* 18:198–203; Klaiber nos. 2761–96.

■ **Literature:** *KThR*² 1:56–63; *DSp* 14:403f.; *OER* 4:1f.— H. Klomps, *Kirche, Freiheit und Gesetz bei dem Franziskaner-Theologen K. Sch.* (Münster, 1959); E. Komposch, *Die Messe als Opfer der Kirche. Die Lehre K. Sch.s über das eucharistische Opfer* (Munich, 1965); P. L. Nyhus, "Caspar Sch. and Conrad Pellican," *ARG* 61 (1970) 179–204; D. V. N. Bagchi, *Luther's Earliest Opponents* (Minneapolis, 1991); K. Diez, "*Ecclesia—non est civitas platonica*" (Frankfurt/Main, 1997) 184–203.

HERIBERT SMOLINSKY

Schauenburg, *Count Adolf III von.* Electoral prince and archbishop of Cologne (1546-1556), born 1511, died 1556 in Brühl castle. He studied in Louvain, and became cathedral canon in Liège in 1528 and provost of the chapter in 1533. He became cathedral canon in Cologne and in Mainz in 1529, dean of the collegiate church of St. Gereon in Cologne in 1529, and provost of the same church in 1533; in the latter year, he also became provost of the collegiate church of the Holy Spirit in Liège. The cathedral chapter of Cologne elected him as coadjutor to Archbishop Hermann V von → Wied in 1533. After Wied was deposed from office, Schauenburg became archbishop on December 11, 1546; the formal election by the cathedral chapter took place on January 24, 1547. He was ordained priest on May 3, 1547, and bishop on April 18, 1548. He attempted to implement in his archdiocese the decisions of the imperial parliament of Augsburg concerning confessional politics and church reform (→ Augsburg Interim). Johannes → Gropper, canon of the cathedral in Cologne, was the driving force behind church reform. Schauenburg held regular diocesan synods from 1548 to 1551. The statutes of the provincial synod held in 1549 were a new high point of the pre-Tridentine reform, after the provincial council of 1536. Schauenburg's personal attendance at the Council of Trent underscored his seriousness about reform.

■ **Literature:** J. Hartzheim, *Concilia Germaniae,* vol. 6 (Cologne, 1765); O. R. Redlich, *Jülich-bergische Kirchenpolitik am Ausgange des Mittelalters und in der Reformationszeit,* vol. 1 (Bonn, 1907; reprint, 1986); R. Schwarz, *Personal- und Amtsdaten der Bischöfe der Kölner Kirchenprovinz von 1500 bis 1800* (Cologne, 1914); H. Foerster, *Reformbestrebungen A.s III. von Schaumburg (1547–56) in der Kölner Kirchenprovinz* (Münster, 1925); A. Franzen, *Die Kelchbewegung am Niederrhein* (Münster, 1955); K. Repgen, "Der Bischof zwischen Reformation, katholischer Reform und Konfessionsbildung," in *Der Bischof in seiner Zeit,* ed. P. Berglar et al. (Cologne, 1986) 245–314.

HANSGEORG MOLITOR

Scheurl, *Christoph.* Humanist and legal scholar, born November 11, 1481 in Nuremberg, where he died June 14, 1542. His father came from Breslau, and his mother belonged to the patrician Tucher family. He studied in Heidelberg (1497) and Bologna (1498, where his professors included Lorenzo → Campeggi). He took his doctorate in civil and canon law in Bologna in 1506. He was professor of jurisprudence in Wittenberg from 1507 to 1512, and became rector of the university. He was appointed consultant to the Council of Nuremberg in 1512, and carried out many diplomatic missions for his hometown. He was initially an adherent of Martin Luther, whom he supported at the religious dialogue in Nuremberg in 1525; however, he disliked the separatist development of the Reformation, and opposed it from 1530 onward. He was active as an author and exchanged many letters with such figures as Johannes → Eck and Charitas → Pirckheimer.

■ **Literature:** *BBKL* 9:178–85.—M. Gossmann, "Bibliographie der Werke Ch.Sch.s," *Archiv für die Geschichte des Buchwesens* 10 (1969) 373–95.

ROLF DECOT

■ **Additional Bibliography:** I. Backus, "Ch.Sch. and His Anthology of 'New Testament Apocrypha,'" *Apocrypha* 9 (1998) 133–56.

Schiner, *Matthäus.* Cardinal, prince bishop of Sion, born c. 1465 in Mühlebach near Ernen (canton of Valais), died October 1, 1522 in Rome. He studied in Sion and Como, and was ordained priest in 1489. He was curate in Obergesteln in 1493, and was involved in the overthrow of Prince Bishop Jost von Silenen in 1496. Subsequently, he was parish priest of Ernen and non-residentiary cathedral canon. He became dean of the cathedral in 1497. The pope nominated him prince bishop of Sion, and hence territorial ruler of Valais, on September 20, 1499. He was consecrated in Rome on October 13 of the same year. He was created cardinal priest of Santa Pudenziana in 1511. He was bishop of Novara and papal legate from 1512 to 1515. The emperor nominated him bishop of Catania in 1519.

Schiner was a reforming bishop who carried out visitations, built churches, and promoted clerical discipline. An opponent of France, he negotiated an alliance between Julius II and the Swiss confederation in 1510. He acquired papal soldiers for the battles of Pavia (1512) and Novara (1513), and won Bellinzona and the Blenio valley for Switzerland. He was expelled from his diocese in 1517, in the course of the reconciliation between → Leo X and France, but he became an influential counselor of → Charles V. He had contacts with humanists, and was an important opponent of

Martin Luther at the imperial parliament of Worms in 1521. He had good prospects as a candidate at the papal election in 1521. He supported → Hadrian VI in Rome. He died of the plague and was buried in Santa Maria dell'Anima.

■ **Literature:** E. Gatz, ed., *Die Bischöfe des Heiligen Römischen Reiches 1448–1648* (Berlin, 1996) 635ff.; *BBKL* 9:213ff.; *LMA* 7:1467.—A. Büchi, *Korrespondenzen und Akten zur Geschichte des Kardinals M.Sch.*, 2 vols. (Basle, 1920–25); E. F. Müller, *Kardinal M.Sch. als Staatsmann und Kirchenfürst*, 2 vols. (Zurich and Fribourg, 1923–37); *Kardinal M.Sch. und seine Zeit. Festschrift zum 500. Geburtstag* (Brig, 1967–68); L. Carlen, "Kaiser Maximilian I. und Kardinal M.Sch.," *Anzeiger der philosophisch-historischen Klasse der Österreichischen Akademie der Wissenschaften* 117 (1980) 230–48; idem, *Kultur des Wallis 1500–1800* (Brig, 1984) 6–13; idem, "Kardinal Sch. in Rom," *Walliser Jahrbuch* 56 (1987) 19–26.

MARKUS RIES

Schlegel, *Theodul.* Premonstratensian, leader of the Catholic party in the Reformation controversies in Switzerland, born c. 1485 in Chur, where he died January 23, 1529. After studies in Tübingen and Heidelberg, he entered the monastery of St. Lucius in Chur, where he became abbot in 1515. He served Graubünden as a diplomat. He was initially open to church reforms, but headed the Catholic party from 1522-1523 onward. He fought against the Reformer Johannes → Komander and represented the Catholic party at the religious dialogue in → Ilanz (January 7-9, 1526). He was implicated in the plans of Paul Ziegler, bishop of Chur, who wanted to resign his see in favor of Gian Angelo de'Medici (later Pope → Pius IV); this would have given support to foreign claims on the territory of Graubünden, and Schlegel was executed for high treason.

■ **Literature:** *BBKL* 9:250–53.—O. Vasella, *Abt Th.Sch. von Chur und seine Zeit 1515–1529* (Fribourg, 1954); H. Berger, *Bündner Kirchengeschichte,* vol. 2 (Chur, 1986); G. Jäger, "Die Reformation in der Stadt Chur," in *Churer Stadtgeschichte,* vol. 1 (Chur, 1993) 434ff.

MARKUS RIES

Schmalkaldic Articles. This confessional document was drawn up by Martin Luther in 1536, at the request of the electoral prince of Saxony, → Johann Friedrich, in order to clarify his own position in view of the council which → Paul III had summoned to meet at Mantua in 1537. He makes a distinction between those articles about which there is no controversy (the Trinity and the incarnation); those articles on which no concession is permissible (→ justification by faith, the Mass, the invocation of the saints, collegiate churches and monasteries, the papacy [→ primacy]); and those articles where agreement seems possible with scholars and reasonable Catholics (sin, → law, the gospel, the → sacraments, ecclesiology [→ church], → justification and works, human institutions). The articles were approved by the electoral prince and by the Wittenberg theologians, although Philipp Melanchthon had his reservations about the harsh formulations in the antipapal article. However, they were not accepted by the assembly of the → Schmalkaldic League in February, 1537, since Luther was ill, Melanchthon intervened, and it was clear *a priori* that the council would be rejected. The articles acquired the status of a basic doctrinal formulation in some cities and territories, and strictly Lutheran theologians (Matthias → Flacius, the → Gnesiolutherans) set great store by them. They became an official confessional document through their inclusion in the Book of Concord in 1580 (Formula of → Concord).

■ **Editions:** *BSLK*[10] 405–68; H. Volz and H. Ulbrich, eds., *Urkunden und Aktenstücke zur Geschichte von Martin Luthers Schwabacher Artikeln (1536–74)* (Berlin, 1957).

■ **Literature:** H. Volz, "Zur Entstehungsgeschichte von Luthers Schwabacher Artikeln," *ZKG* 74 (1963) 316–20.

ROLF DECOT

■ **Additional Bibliography:** K. Hagen, "The Historical Context of the Smalcald Articles," *Concordia Theological Quarterly* 51 (1987) 245–53; H. P. Hamann, "The Smalcald Articles as a Systematic Theology," *Concordia Theological Quarterly* 52 (1988) 29–40; W. R. Russell, "A Neglected Key to the Theology of Martin Luther: The Schmalkald Articles," *Word and World* 16 (1996) 84–90.

Schmalkaldic League. This political and military defensive alliance (1531-1547) was set up by the Protestants under the leadership of Hessen and electoral Saxony, after religious negotiations had broken down and a resolution approved by the imperial parliament in Augsburg on November 19, 1530 had threatened to impound the goods of the Protestants (→ Charles V). → Philip of Hessen had endeavored since the imperial parliament of 1529 in Speyer to strengthen the Protestant

281

imperial Estates by means of an alliance (cf. the religious dialogue at → Marburg in 1529); this led to an initial agreement in the Conclusion of Schmalkalden, signed on December 31, 1530 by electoral Saxony, Hessen, Braunschweig-Lüneburg, Wolfgang of Anhalt, Gebhard and Albrecht of Mansfeld, Magdeburg, and Bremen, after Martin Luther had affirmed, during the negotiations in Torgau in October, 1530, that there could exist (under certain conditions) a right to armed resistance to the emperor. After further members joined the League—Strasbourg, Constance, Ulm, Reutlingen, Memmingen, Lindau, Biberach, Isny, and Lübeck—the deeds of foundation were dated February 27, 1531. The League sought the support of foreign powers (France, England, Denmark), but without positive results. Although it was not restricted to one region like the Swabian League, it did not succeed in uniting all the signatories to the → Confessio Augustana, since Brandenburg-Ansbach and Nuremberg refused to join it.

It was initially decided that the league would last for six years; during this period, other principalities and Estates joined it, and it proved so powerful that the emperor (who was under threat both from the Turks and from France) had to make the Truce of Nuremberg in 1532 and conclude other agreements which bought him time. Assemblies of the league were held in 1533 and 1535 to draw up a constitution, which envisaged Philip of Hessen as leader of the southern region, and the electoral prince of Saxony as leader of the northern region. The league was extended for a further ten years at the assembly in Schmalkalden in 1537. When his double marriage (1540) became known, Philip was compelled to make a secret agreement with the emperor; this weakened the league. When the Protestants refused to attend the council which opened in Trent in 1545, the emperor waged the *Schmalkaldic War* against them (1546-1547), and won the decisive victory at the battle of Mühlberg on April 24, 1547. With the capture of its leaders, Philip of Hessen and electoral prince Johann Friedrich, the Schmalkaldic League collapsed.

The confessional basis of the league was the Confessio Augustana. This excluded the Zwinglian cities in Upper Germany and Switzerland, but welded the Lutherans together. Its significance consisted in the fact that it ensured the political and military consolidation of Protestantism for

seventeen years, so that the Reformation movement could no longer be defeated—neither by the emperor at the "armor-clad" imperial parliament in Augsburg (1547-1548) nor by the Council of Trent (second period, 1551-1552). Ultimately, the adherents of the Confessio Augustana won the day in the imperial parliament of 1555, with the Religious Peace of → Augsburg.

■ **Editions:** *Die Schmalkaldischen Bundesabschiede 1530–32, 1533–36*, ed. E. Fabian (Tübingen, 1958).
■ **Literature:** (SChB=Schmalkaldischer Bund) E. Fabian, *Die Entstehung des SchB und seiner Verfassung 1529–31/33* (Tübingen, ²1962); S. Jahns, *Frankfurt, Reformation und SchB.* (Frankfurt/Main, 1976); G. Schlütter-Schindler, *Der SchB und das Problem der causa religionis* (Frankfurt/Main, 1986); Th. Brady, *Zwischen Gott und Mammon. Protestantische Politik und deutsche Reformation* (Berlin, 1996).

ROLF DECOT

■ **Additional Bibliography:** G. Wartenberg, "Die Schlacht bei Mühlberg in der Reichsgeschichte als Auseinandersetzung zwischen protestantischen Fürsten und Kaiser Karl V.," *ARG* 89 (1998) 167–77; G. Vogel, "Kurfürst Johann Friedrich und Herzog Moritz von Sachsen," *ARG* 89 (1998) 178–206; R, Kolb, "The Legal Case for Martyrdom: Basilius Monner on Johann Friedrich the Elder and the Smalcald War," in *Reformation und Recht*. Festschrift G. Seebass (Tübingen, 2002) 145–60; G. Haug-Moritz, *Der Sch.* (Leinfelden-Echterdingen, 2002).

Schnepf(f), *Erhard.* Reformer in Württemberg, born November 1, 1495 in Heilbronn, died November 1, 1558 in Jena. He studied in Erfurt and Heidelberg, and was present at Martin Luther's disputation in Heidelberg in 1518. He became a Protestant preacher in Weinsberg in 1520, and in Wimpfen in 1524. He was one of the fourteen signatories to the *Syngramma Suevicum* (the others included Johannes → Brenz), which supported the Lutheran doctrine of the Lord's Supper. He helped implement the Reformation in Weilburg in 1526, and became professor in Marburg in 1528. He accompanied the marquis of Hessen to the imperial parliaments in Speyer (1529) and Augsburg (1530). In 1534, Duke → Ulrich summoned him to Stuttgart, in order that he might introduce the Reformation in northern Württemberg. He came to an agreement in 1534 with Ambrosius → Blarer on the mediatory Concord of Stuttgart, and he took part in the religious dialogues of → Hagenau, → Worms, and →

Regensburg (1541, 1546). He was appointed professor in Tübingen in 1544, but was expelled from this post because of the → Augsburg Interim. He was appointed visitor in the Ernestine territories in 1554. He parted company with Brenz in the controversy about Andreas → Osiander, and came under the influence of Nikolaus von → Amsdorf and Matthias → Flacius. In the Majorist controversy (Georg → Major), he wrote against the Wittenberg theologians. He attended the religious dialogue of Worms in 1557. At the close of his life, he was theologically isolated.

■ **Sources:** *VD 16*; K. H. May, "Veröffentlichungen des D. E.Sch. 1952" (typescript in the university library, Marburg); T. Schiess, *Briefwechsel der Brüder A. und Th. Blarer*, 3 vols. (Freiburg, 1908–12); *Beiträge zur Bayerischen Kirchengeschichte* 25 (1919); WA.BR; *Blätter für württembergische Kirchengeschichte* 35 (1931) and 38 (1934); *Melanchthons Briefwechsel. Gesamtausgabe*, ed. H. Scheible, vols. 1ff. (Stuttgart, 1977ff.).

■ **Literature:** RE[3] 17, 670–74; *BBKL* 9:574ff.; *OER* 4:16f.; *TRE* 30:233ff.—J. Hartmann, *E.Sch.* (Tübingen, 1870); K.-D. Zippel, "E. Sch.," in K. Brinkel and H. von Hintzenstern, *Ach, Herr Gott, wie reich tröstest du*, vol. 2 (Berlin, 1963) 151–60; M. Brecht and H. Ehmer, *Südwestdeutsche Reformationsgeschichte* (Stuttgart, 1984); H. Ehmer, "E.Sch.," *Blätter für württembergische Kirchengeschichte* 87 (1987) 72–126.

CHRISTIAN PETERS

■ **Additional Bibliography:** W. Schmidt, "Der Weilburger Reformator E.Sch.," *Jahrbuch der Hessischen Kirchengeschichtlichen Vereinigung* 47 (1996) 31–39; V. Leppin, "Theologischer Streit und politische Symbolik. Zu den Anfängen der württembergischen Reformation 1534–38," *ARG* 90 (1999) 159–87.

Schoepper, *Jacob.* Theologian, preacher, and poet, born 1512/1516, died June 11, 1554 in Dortmund. He was priest at St. Mary's church and teacher at the grammar school in Dortmund, where he promoted church reform in keeping with the regulations of Jülich-Kleve-Berg and the provincial synod of Cologne. The third volume of his posthumously published sermons was placed on the Index because it maintained the doctrine of double righteousness; some of the dramas he composed for performance in his school contain sarcastic criticism of the church.

■ **Works:** *Catechismus* (Dortmund, 1549, often reprinted); *Comoediae et tragoediae sacrae et novae* (Dortmund, 1552, often reprinted); *Institutio christiana* (Cologne, 1555, often reprinted); *Conciones*, ed. J.

Lambach, 3 vols. (Dortmund, 1557–1558, often reprinted; German by C. Hipparius, 3 vols. (Cologne, 1561–62).

■ **Literature:** A. Döring, *Johann Lambach und das Gymnasium zu Dortmund* (Berlin, 1875) 80–111; U. Olschewski, *Erneuerung der Kirche durch Bildung und Belehrung des Volkes* (Münster, 1999).

URSULA OLSCHEWSKI

Schönberg, *Nikolaus von.* Dominican (1497), born August 11, 1472 in Meissen, died September 11, 1537 in Rome. He studied civil and canon law in Pisa. After hearing a sermon by Girolamo Savonarola, he entered the monastery of San Marco. He was *definitor* of the Reform congregation from 1504 to 1506. He was prior in Lucca (1503-1505), Siena (1506), and Florence (1506-1508); at the same time, he was *socius* of Jean Clerée, Master of the Order. He was procurator of the Order under Thomas → Cajetan from 1508 to 1515, and became professor at the Sapienza university in Rome in 1510. He was appointed visitor of the German province of his Order in 1512. From 1513 onward, he was procurator of Duke → George of Saxony at the Fifth Council of the Lateran and at the curia. From 1517, he and Gian Matteo → Giberti were the most important advisers to the "cardinal nephew," who subsequently became Pope → Clement VII. He carried out business for the emperor under → Paul III. He was frequently sent as legate to various European countries. He was archbishop of Capua from 1520 to 1536, and was created cardinal of San Sisto in 1535. He was involved in the negotiation of the Peace of Cambrai (1529); he was governor of Florence from 1530 to 1532.

He influenced the course of events surrounding Martin Luther. He supported his great-nephews, Karl von → Miltiz and Johannes von → Pflug, and later adopted a mediatory position vis-à-vis the new doctrines. He supported the cause of church reform. In 1536, he advised Nicholas Copernicus to publish his studies.

■ **Works:** *Orationes vel potius divinorum eloquiorum enodationes* (Leipzig, 1512).

■ **Literature:** *BBKL* 9:619f.—J. V. Pollet, *Julius Pflug* (Leiden, 1990); A. Morisi Guerra, "La paraphrasis in beati Johannis Apostoli canonicam epistolam di N.Sch.," in *Frate Girolamo Savonarola e il suo movimento* (Pistoia, 1998) 425–40.

KLAUS-BERNWARD SPRINGER

Schwabach Articles. This profession of faith in seventeen articles was drawn up by Martin Luther and his collaborators, and was presented in Schwabach (Franconia) by electoral Saxony and Brandenburg-Ansbach to the delegates of the Upper German cities on October 16, 1529. These articles are a part of the crystallization process of the Protestant confession of faith. They were born of a threefold necessity: central affirmations by Luther must be summarized in a form easy to teach and to learn; the Protestant party had to make preparations for the council which was envisaged by the imperial parliament at Nuremberg in 1524; and boundary lines had to be drawn vis-à-vis → Enthusiasts and other groups (cf. Luther's *Vom Abendmahl Christi Bekenntnis,* 1528 [WA 26:499-509], which the contents—though not the form—of the Schwabach Articles follow). The resolution of the imperial parliament at Speyer on April 22, 1529 gave new impetus to endeavors to unite the Protestant imperial Estates, but the Schwabach assembly, held two weeks after the religious dialogue in → Marburg (October 1–3, 1529), had produced a document with fifteen articles and did not lead to unity among the Upper German Protestants. In Saxony, the Schwabach Articles enjoyed the status of a summary of the Protestant confession. Their subject matter and their structure served as a model for the doctrinal articles of the → Confessio Augustana (1530).
■ **Text:** *BSLK*[10] 50–137.
■ **Literature:** W. Maurer, "Zur Entstehung und Textgeschichte der SchA," in S. Hermann and O. Söhngen, eds., *Theologie in Geschichte und Kunst* (Witten, 1968) 134–51; G. Seebass, "Die reformatorischen Bekenntnisse vor der Confessio Augustana," in P. Meinhold, ed., *Kirche und Bekenntnis* (Wiesbaden, 1980) 26–55.

ROLF DECOT

Schwenckfeld, *Kaspar von.* Mystical "Spiritualist," born 1489 in a family of the lower aristocracy in Ossig (Lower Silesia), died December 10, 1561 in Ulm. After studies in Cologne and Frankfurt on the Oder, he was at the court of Liegnitz from 1518 onward. He was a self-taught theologian who became a key figure in the Reformation among the Silesian aristocracy. After 1521, he won Duke Friedrich II over to the Reformation in Liegnitz; from this city, it spread through the whole of Silesia from 1524. In the → eucharistic controversy, Schwenckfeld took the side of Andreas von → Karlstadt and Huldrych Zwingli against Martin Luther. The spiritualizing tendency in his theology, which rejected the external form of the → church, aroused suspicions that he belonged to the → Baptist movement. He was compelled to leave Liegnitz, and went to Upper Germany (Strasbourg, Augsburg, Ulm), where he subsequently parted company with the Swiss/Upper German Reformation. After his teachings were condemned by the → Schmalkaldic League, he confined his literary activities and his correspondence (above all with Pilgram → Marpeck) to the underground.

His doctrine was fully elaborated by c. 1540. Pneumatological and soteriological insights give it its specific character. Sin is the very nature of the human person; even before Adam's fall, human beings needed the knowledge of Christ in order to become the image of God. Christ's human nature was deified after his ascension (subsequently, Schwenckfeld taught that this deification happened before the ascension), and his transfigured flesh is the food of believers (doctrine of the heavenly flesh of Christ). Since material things cannot mediate the Spirit, Schwenckfeld links God only to the interior dimension of the human person, not to external rites such as sacraments.

The recognition that his piety could be lived only in small circles led to the formation of conventicles, which became influential for a time among the patrician families of Ulm and Augsburg and among the imperial knights. Schwenckfeldian circles existed in East Prussia, Silesia (until 1826), and Lausitz. Thanks to emigrants from Silesia, his teaching took on a specific ecclesiological form in Pennsylvania, where the Schwenckfeld church was founded in 1734. This church published his writings and promoted valuable research in theology and church history.
■ **Works:** *Corpus Schwenckfeldianorum,* 19 vols. (Pennsburg, Pa., 1907–61).
■ **Literature:** *BBKL* 9:1215–35.—E. Hirsch, "Sch. und Luther," in *Lutherstudien,* ed. idem, vol. 2 (Gütersloh, 1954) 35–67; H. Weigelt, *Spiritualistische Traditionen im Protestantismus. Die Geschichte des Schwenckfeldertums in Schlesien* (Berlin, 1973); A. Sciegienny, *Homme carnel, homme spirituel. Études sur la christologie de C.Sch.* (Wiesbaden, 1975); R. E. McLaughlin, *C.Sch. Reluctant Radical* (New Haven and London, 1986); *Sch. and Early Schwenckfeldianism,* ed. P. C. Erb (Pennsburg, Pa., 1986); G. Mühlpfort, *Sch. und die Schwenckfelder, Wegscheiden der Reformation,* ed. G. Vogler (Weimar, 1994) 115–50.

MATTHIAS ASCHE

■ **Additional Bibliography:** R. E. McLaughlin, *The Freedom of Spirit, Social Privilege, and Religious Dissent. C.Sch. and the Schwenkfelders* (Baden-Baden et al., 1996); P. G. Eberlein, *C. von Sch., der schlesische Reformator und seine Botschaft* (Metzingen, 1999); H. Weigelt, "Sebastian Franck und C.Sch. in ihren Beziehungen zueinander," *Von Sch. bis Löhe. Festschrift H. Weigelt* (Neustadt [Aisch], 1999) 21–38.

Selnecker, *Nikolaus.* Protestant theologian, born December 5, 1530 in Hersbruck, died May 24, 1592 in Leipzig. He became court preacher in Dresden in 1558. He was appointed professor of theology in Jena in 1565, and in Leipzig in 1568, but was frequently dismissed from office in the latter city. He was a quarrelsome man, and his theology and his poetry aroused controversy because he was seen as too close to Martin Luther (doctrine of the Lord's Supper) and Philipp Melanchthon (justification). The Psalms played a central role for him: he wrote a commentary which was often reprinted, and recast many Psalms in a variety of metrical forms. Some of his hymns are still found in Protestant hymnals today. He is one of the intellectual fathers of the Formula of → Concord (1580).

■ **Literature:** *BBKL* 9:1376–79. – A. Eckert, "Aus dem Leben und Werk N. S.s," *ZBKG* 48 (1979) 19–27; idem, "Die Abendmahlslehre von N. S.," *ZBKG* 54 (1985) 44–65; G. Fuchs, *Psalmdeutung im Lied. Die Interpretation der "Feinde" bei N. S.* (Göttingen, 1992); I. Dingel, *Concordia controversa* (Gütersloh, 1996) passim.

GUIDO FUCHS

■ **Additional Bibliography:** H. P. Hasse, "Die Lutherbiographie von N. S.," *ARG* 86 (1995) 91–123; R. Kolb, "The Doctrine of Christ in N. S.'s Interpretation of Psalms 8, 22 and 110," in *Biblical Interpretation in the Era of the Reformation.* Festschrift D. C. Steinmetz (Grand Rapids, 1996) 313–32; R. Kolb, "Seelsorge und Lehre in der Spätreformation am Beispiel von N. S.s Abhandlung zur Prädestinationslehre (1565)," *Lutherische Theologie und Kirche* 25 (2001) 14–34.

Seripando, *Girolamo.* Augustinian Hermit (1507), theologian, cardinal, and legate at the Council of Trent, born probably October 6, 1492 in Naples, died March 17, 1563 in Trent. He became the general secretary of the Augustinian Hermits in 1514, and was rector of the *studium generale* in Bologna from 1517 onward. He became vicar of the Observant congregation of San Giovanni a Carbonara in Naples in 1524. At the wishes of → Paul III, he became general of his Order in 1538. He promoted reforms in his Order through visitations in Italy, France, and Spain, and fought against the influence of the Reformation. Seripando was deeply marked by Christian Platonism, and owed much to humanism and to Italian → "Evangelism," with its central orientation to scripture and to the theology of St. Augustine. As general of his Order, he took part in the first period of the Council of Trent, and played a key role in the preparation of its dogmatic decrees. In the discussion of → original sin and → justification, he did not succeed in introducing his own views of concupiscence and of the event of justification (with regard to the role of faith and the significance of the righteousness of Christ) into the formulations of the conciliar decrees. He was accused of making too many concessions to the Lutheran doctrine of justification. He laid down the office of general in 1551, because of illness. He was sent as ambassador of Naples to the emperor in Brussels in 1553. He was appointed archbishop of Salerno in 1554 and was a zealous pastor. He was created cardinal in 1561 and was conciliar legate at the third period of the Council of Trent, where he guided above all the work on dogmatic questions. In the great controversies about the decree on ordination and the duty of residence, he attempted to mediate between the endeavors of the Roman curia and the intentions of the episcopal opposition, but without success; he fell out of favor in Rome. He died during the great crisis of the council, shortly after Cardinal Ercole → Gonzaga. Seripando was one of the great figures of the movement for religious reform in 16th-century Italy. Despite the setbacks he suffered, he had a great influence on the Council of Trent.

■ **Works:** *Commentarius in ep. Pauli ad Galatas* (Antwerp, 1567; Venice, 1569; with *Commentarius in ep. ad Romanos,* Naples, 1601); *Doctrina orandi sive expositio orationis Dominicae* (Louvain, 1661); *Prediche sopra il simbolo degli Apostoli* (Venice, 1567; Rome, 1585; Salerno, 1856); *Diarium de vita sua 1513–62,* ed. D. Gutiérrez, *Analecta Augustiniana* 26 (1963) 5–193.—Commentary on the Council of Trent, *CT* 2:397–488; numerous tractates in *CT* 12:483–96, 517–21, 549–53, 613–37, 824–49; *De iustitia et libertate christiana,* ed. A. Forster (Münster, 1965).—Literary remains in Biblioteca Nazionale Neapel; selection with source investigations in H. Jedin, *G. S.,* vol. 2 (Würzburg, 1937) 335–656.

■ **Literature:** *BBKL* 9:1456ff.—H. Jedin, *G. S.,* 2 vols. (Würzburg, 1937); E. Stakemeier, *Der Kampf um*

Augustin auf dem Tridentinum (Paderborn, 1937); A. Balducci, *G. S. Arcivescovo di Salerno* (Cava, 1963); A. Forster, *Gesetz und Evangelium bei S.* (Paderborn, 1963); Jedin vol. 2; A. Marranzini, *Il Cardinale G. S., arcivescovo di Salerno, legato pontificio al Concilio di Trento* (Salerno, 1994); A. Cestaro, ed., "G. S. e la chiesa del suo tempo nel V. centenario della nascita," in *Thesaurus Ecclesiarum Italiae recentioris aevi,* vol. 7/8 (Rome, 1997) (with numerous individual contributions).

KLAUS GANZER

■ **Additional Bibliography:** F.C. Cesareo, *A Shepherd in Their Midst: The Episcopacy of G. S. (1554–63)* (Villanova, Pa., 1999).

Servet (Servetus, Serveto), *Michael.* Theologian, natural philosopher, and doctor, born 1511 in Villanueva de Sijena (province of Huesca in Spain), died October 27, 1553 in Geneva. He was a servant of the Franciscan Juan de Quintana, who made it possible for him to study law in Toulouse (1528-1529); after Quintana became father confessor to → Charles V, he took Servet with him to the imperial coronation in Bologna in 1530. Thereafter, Servet stayed with Johannes → Oecolampadius in Basle, and became acquainted with Martin → Bucer and Wolfgang → Capito in Strasbourg. His book *De Trinitatis erroribus libri septem* was published in Hagenau in 1531. Here he maintained modalistic views, which he repeated, despite vehement protests, in his *Dialogorum de Trinitate libri duo,* published in Hagenau in 1532. The second book presents Servet's own doctrine of the Lord's Supper: the divine matter of the body of Christ is present in the bread, and the one who eats it becomes more divine. Servet fled from the Inquisition to Paris, where he adopted the name Michel de Villeneuve and studied medicine. In Lyons, he edited the *Geography* of Ptolemy, and then published biblical translations and glosses. He continued his medical studies in Paris, where he held lectures in geography and astrology. Here, he published treatises on natural science from 1537 onward. Bishop Pierre Palmier invited him to Vienne in 1540, and he worked undisturbed as a doctor in that city until his true identity was revealed in 1553, thanks to letters sent from Geneva. His chef d'oeuvre had already been published in Vienne that year, viz., the *Christianismi restitutio,* a summary of his theological views and his *Weltanschauung.* This book also contains a description of the lesser circulation of the blood, which he had probably discovered during his medical studies in Paris. He was arrested by the Inquisition, but managed to escape. He was condemned to death *in absentia* and burned *in effigie* (i.e., a picture of him was thrown into the flames). While he was making his way to Italy, he was recognized during a service in Geneva on August 13, and Jean Calvin had him arrested. After memoranda from Zurich, Schaffhausen, Berne, and Basle had all reached the same conclusions, his trial ended with the sentence of death on October 27, 1553, and he was burned at the stake on the same day.

Both Catholic and Protestant contemporaries saw Servet's antitrinitarianism (→ Antitrinitarians) as an attack on the very heart of Christianity, and hence as a crime deserving death; however, Sebastian → Castellio reacted to the verdict with a plea for freedom of conscience and tolerance. Servet's aim, inspired by humanism, was to revitalize the theology of the early church, which had been corrupt since the time of Constantine and the Council of Nicaea. He had an excellent knowledge of scripture and the fathers, and sought to harmonize Neoplatonic dualism and Jewish monotheism from a Christian standpoint. He saw history as a continuous revelation both of God (beginning with Mount Sinai, then in the prophets, and reaching fulfillment in Jesus) and of Satan (in the powers that fought against God, and in the church of the pope). Servet elaborated an alternative understanding of religion, of Jesus, and of the church.

■ **Literature:** *BBKL* 9:1470–79.—R. H. Bainton, *M. S.* (Gütersloh, 1960); J. B. Fernández, *M. S., su vida y su obra* (Madrid, 1970); C. Manzoni, *Umanesimo ed eresia. M. S.* (Naples, 1974); J. Friedman, *M. S. A Case Study in Total Heresy* (Geneva, 1978); H. R. Guggisberg, *Sebastian Castellio 1616–63* (Göttingen, 1997).

ROLF DECOT

■ **Additional Bibliography:** G. T. Park, "Le problème de la liberté de conscience chez Calvin et Castellion," *Chongshin Theological Journal* 5 (2000) 202–32; M. Hillar, *M. S.: Intellectual Giant, Humanist, and Martyr* (Lanham, 2002).

Severoli, *Ercole.* Born after 1510, died 1571 in Rome. He was *promotor* of the Council of Trent, with the duty of proffering legal assistance and maintaining the rights of the synod; he ended his life as general procurator of the Apostolic Treasury. Reports which he sent to Cardinal Alessandro Farnese the Younger about the conciliar negotiations were given the literary form of a diary of the council; Sebastian Merkle was the first to identify Severoli as its author. He is a reliable and well-informed source of information about the events at the council.

■ **Works:** *De remissionibus litigatorum* (Venice, 1548); council diary in *CT* 1:1–147.

■ **Literature:** *BBKL* 9:1513ff.—*CT* 1:XXXVI–LXVIII; S. Merkle, "Hercules S. und sein Tagebuch über das Trienter Konzil," *HJ* 16 (1895) 749–76; Jedin vol. 1–3, passim (index).

KLAUS GANZER

Seydel (Seidel, Sedelius), *Wolfgang*. Benedictine (1517), humanist, and court preacher, born 1491/1492 in Mauerkirchen near Braunau (Upper Austria), died June 11, 1562 in Tegernsee. He was ordained priest in 1521 or 1522, and was ducal preacher at the Augustinian church in Munich from 1532 to 1560. He composed the *Mirror of Princes* for Duke William IV in 1547, attended the Council of Trent in 1552, and taught in Salzburg from 1552 to 1555. His sermons were wholly consecrated to the aims of the Counter-Reformation. Seydel was a man of universal learning, in whom the Tegernsee humanist tradition reached its zenith.

■ **Literature:** *BBKL* 14:1474f.—H. Pöhlein, *W. S.* (Munich, 1951); W. Müller, "Die Anfänge der Humanismusrezeption im Kloster Tegernsee," *Studien und Mitteilungen zur Geschichte des Benedictinerordens und seiner Zweige* 92 (1981) 28–90, esp. 72ff.; B. Singer, *Die Fürstenspiegel in Deutschland im Zeitalter des Humanismus und der Reformation* (Munich, 1981) 250–70.

MANFRED EDER

■ **Additional Bibliography:** S. Pfaff, "Der Codex Vadiana 404 von W. S. (1492–1562)" (first part of a 3-vol. work; dissertation, Munich, 1994).

Sickingen, *Franz von.* Imperial knight, born March 2, 1481 in Ebernburg near Kreuznach, died May 7, 1523 in Nanstein castle near Landstuhl. After taking over his family property in 1505, Sickingen consolidated his position in central Rhineland by building a fortress and hiring mercenaries, but above all by the armed feuds he initiated against Worms, Metz, the marquis of Hessen, and the city of Frankfurt. After a brief period in the service of → Francis I of France, he changed to the side of Emperor Maximilian I in 1518, after his outlawry within the imperial territory had been revoked. In 1519, he took part in the actions carried out by the Swabian League against Duke → Ulrich of Württemberg; as a military commander, he guaranteed the election of → Charles V to the imperial throne. Ulrich von → Hutten introduced him to the teachings of Martin Luther. He supported Johannes → Reuchlin and offered other Reformers (including Martin → Bucer, Johannes → Oecolampadius, Johannes Schwebel, and Kaspar Aquila) refuge in his fortresses. After his relations with the emperor had cooled, Sickingen let himself be elected commanding officer of the Landauer League by the knights of Rhineland and Franconia in 1522, and he began the fatal feud against Richard von Greiffenclau, electoral prince of Trier. Sickingen was compelled to retreat before Trier and was once again declared an outlaw. He was mortally wounded in an attack on his fortress of Nanstein by the troops of the electoral princes of Trier and the Palatinate, and the marquis of Hessen, who were charged with enforcing the sentence of outlawry.—Sickingen's life displays a striking contrast between his actions (committed support of the Reformation and intervention on behalf of the lower aristocracy, with the aim of strengthening his own position of power) and his political ideals (raising the prestige of the empire, and uniting with the emperor to preserve the rights and freedoms of the knights against the increasing power of the princes and cities).

■ **Literature:** *BDG* 2:20010–67; 5:49329–339; 7:58243–54; *ADB* 34:151–58; *BBKL* 10:24ff.—K. Baumann, *F. von S. Pfälzer Lebensbilder,* vol. 1 (Speyer, 1964) 23–42; V. Press, "Ein Ritter zwischen Rebellion und Reformation," *Blätter für pfälzische Kirchengeschichte und religiöse Volkskunde* 50 (1983) 151–77; G. Birtsch, "F. von S.," *Vor-Zeiten, Geschichte in Rheinland-Pfalz,* vol. 4, ed. D. Lau and F.-J. Heyen (Mainz, 1988) 87–108; V. Press, "F. von S.," *"Ulrich von Hutten." Ausstellungskatalog,* compiled by P. Laub (Kassel, 1988) 293–306; R. Scholzen, *F. von S.* (Kaiserslautern, 1996).

ALEXANDER KOLLER

■ **Additional Bibliography:** O. Böcher, "Die Theologen der Ebernburg," *Blätter für pfälzische Kirchengeschichte und religiöse Volkskunde* 66/67 (1999/2000) 403–23.

Sim(m)ler, *Josias.* Reformed Protestant theologian and historian, born November 6, 1530 in

Kappel (Albis), died July 2, 1576 in Zurich. After studying theology and the natural sciences in Zurich, Basle, and Strasbourg, he entered the service of church and school in Zurich in 1549. He was appointed professor of Old Testament in Zurich in 1563. He became famous as translator, author of obituary notices (Pietro Martire → Vermigli, Konrad Gessner, Heinrich → Bullinger), and writer of theological and apologetic works. His book *Vallesiae descriptio* (Zurich, 1574; often reprinted) had a lasting influence on the academic study of the Alpine region; his *De republica Helvetiorum* (Zurich, 1576; often reprinted) was a similarly important presentation of Swiss civil law.

■ Literature: *Literaturlexikon. Autoren und Werke deutscher Sprache,* ed. W. Killy, vol. 11 (Munich, 1991) 45; *BBKL* 14:1298–1303.—R. Feller and E. Bonjour, *Geschichtsschreibung der Schweiz,* vol. 2 (Basle and Stuttgart, ²1979) 160–63.

HANS ULRICH BÄCHTOLD

■ **Additional Bibliography:** E. Campi, "Le 'preces sacrae' di Pietro Martire Vermigli," in *Oratio* (Göttingen, 1999) 197–210.

Simonetta, (1) *Giacomo.* Celebrated canon lawyer, born 1475 in Milan, died November 1, 1539 in Rome. He was secretary to the Signatura from 1512 to 1535, and dean of the Rota from 1523 to 1528. He was appointed bishop of Pesaro in 1528, and subsequently held the sees of Perugia, Lodi, and Sutri. He was created cardinal in 1535, and appointed legate for the council which the pope planned to hold in Vicenza. The advice which Simonetta gave played an important role in the Roman decision about the marriage of King → Henry VIII of England.

■ Works: *De reservatione beneficiorum* (Cologne, 1583; Rome, 1589); *De Signatura gratiae et iustitiae* (manuscript).
■ Literature: J. von Schulte, *Geschichte der Quellen und der Literatur des kanonischen Rechts,* vol. 3 (Stuttgart, 1880) 442; E. Sol, *L'œuvre canonique du Card. G. S.* (Rome, 1902); L. von Pastor, *Geschichte der Päpste seit dem Ausgang des Mittelalters,* vol. 5 (Freiburg, 1909) index; Jedin, vol. 1.

(2) *Ludovico.* Nephew of (1), died April 30, 1568 in Rome. He worked as a lawyer in Milan and Pavia, and became bishop of Pesaro in 1537. He was secretary to the Signatura from 1540 to 1549, and attended the Council of Trent from 1545 to 1548. He became datary to → Pius IV in 1560. He was created cardinal in 1561, and was the leader of the curial party in Trent, who wanted to eliminate the obligation of bishops to reside in their sees. He was removed from power by Giovanni → Morone.

■ Literature: J. Šusta, *Die Römische Curie und das Conzil von Trient unter Pius IV.,* vols. 1–4 (Vienna, 1904–14) index; E. Sol, "Il card. L. S., datario di Pio IV e legato al Concilio di Trento," *Archivio della reale societa Romana* 26 (1903) 185–247; G. Alberigo, *I vescovi italiani al Concilio di Trento* (Florence, 1959) 106ff.; Jedin.

UWE NEDDERMEYER

Simul iustus et peccator. This formula was coined by Martin Luther, and has become a specifically Lutheran summary of his understanding of the → justification of the sinner by faith alone, although it is neither the starting point nor the only synthesis of Luther's doctrine of justification. It affirms that even those who are baptized are truly sinners, thanks to their abiding concupiscence which is in opposition to God. However, this basic sin no longer separates them from God, since he does not reckon it to their account for the sake of Christ. This means that believers are truly righteous in Christ before God. Variations of the formula are *partim iustus, partim peccator* ["partly just, partly sinner"] or *peccator in re, iustus in spe* ["sinner in present reality, just in hope"].

This formula goes back to Augustine's theology. It is generated by four factors: *first,* Ps 31(32):2, which says that God "does not count" (*non imputavit*) sins; *second,* the understanding of grace as the love which literally turns the sinner around from his love of self (→ original sin) and points him in the direction of God; *third,* the experience that self-seeking (concupiscence) remains as an ineradicable tendency; and *fourth,* the consequent thesis that original sin *transit reatu, manet actu* ["passes away in terms of guilt, but remains in terms of what we do"]. Thus, although sin no longer separates us from God, it remains as an empirical fact. This means that the new relationship to God is not based on a fundamental change in the human person, but on the fact that God does not reckon sin to our charge, and consequently on a change in our relationship to him which generates the beginning of love for God (Augustine, *Enarrationes in Psalmos* 31:1; *De nuptiis et concupiscentia ad Valerium* 1:25).

Augustine does not maintain the concept of *simul iustus et peccator* in its entirety, but he teaches a dynamic simultaneity of abiding concupiscence and growing love for God. One constant aim of Luther's formula is to preserve this simultaneity, which is also expressed in the variants quoted above.

As early as his first lectures on the Psalms (1513-1515), Luther encountered the problematic verse 31(32):2, which he interpreted as follows: when God is said not to reckon sin, this means that he reckons righteousness (WA 3:175,9f.). In his preparation for his lectures on Romans (1515-1516), he read Augustine's anti-Pelagian writings, and Luther already employs the formula in keeping with Augustine's position, when he debates with Gabriel → Biel's position in his lectures (WA 56:269,21f.; 272,7ff.; and often). At the same time, he sees no problem in retaining and frequently employing the concept of the "infusion" of grace, although he is aware of the deformation of this notion in late scholasticism, and of the effects which this had on pastoral care. It is only when the further development of his theology leads him to abandon and indeed to attack the scholastic idea of grace as a form or quality, that the *simul iustus et peccator* acquires full definition in the sense of an ontic, abiding sin which God in his grace (or "favor") does not reckon to the human person's charge, thereby allowing the sinner to appear at the same time just in God's eyes. This development runs parallel to the distinction between → law and gospel, since the law convicts the human person of his sin and makes it possible for him to understand his own self-seeking as what it truly is, viz., the abiding basic sin of unbelief. In other words, Luther develops his formula on the basis of his reception of, and continuing reflection on, Augustine's anti-Pelagian theology. It might be suspected that the idea of God's refusal to reckon sin to our charge, and hence the *simul iustus et peccator*, was derived from the late medieval Scotist-Ockhamist theory of *acceptatio*, but this has not yet been proved; it is at any rate clear that Luther's Ockhamist education would not have prevented him from thinking in these terms (against McGrath, 82, and Dettloff: *TRE* 28:309f., 314f.; agreeing with Kroeger, 74-85, Wicks, 92, 95f., *et al.*). Rather, as Faber (437ff.) suggests, the trajectory goes from the Ockhamists to Jean Calvin.

The *Council of Trent* argues in recognizably scholastic categories, but it does not tie itself down to one particular academic theological theory about grace as form. This is why it does not explicitly reject the *simul iustus et peccator*. Substantially, however, the rejection is clear: *non modo reputamur, sed vere iusti nominamur et sumus . . .* ["we are not merely reputed just, but are truly said to be just, and we are just"] (DH 1529; cf. 1560f.).

■ *LThK*[3] 9:612–15 (unabridged version).

■ **Source Texts:** Augustine, *Enarrationes in Psalmos* 31, 2; *De nuptiis et concupiscentia* I, 25 and 28–29; M. Luther, WA 3, 171, 25 and 172, 26 = WA 55 I, 290, 1 – 291, 8; 3, 174, 1 – 175, 17; 287, 32 – 288, 7 (*Erste Psalmenvorlesung*, 1513/15); 56, 268, 26 – 291, 14; 339– 54 (*Römerbriefvorlesung*, 1515/16); 8, 82, 19 – 126, 14 (*Antilatomus*, 1521); J. Calvin, *Inst* II, 1; III, 11–18 (1559).

■ **Literature and Supplements:** R. Hermann, *Luthers These "Gerecht und Sünder zugleich"* (Gütersloh, 1930; Darmstadt, [2]1960); W. Link, *Das Ringen Luthers um die Freiheit der Theologie von der Philosophie* (Munich, 1940; [2]1955) 77–165; W. Joest, *Gesetz und Freiheit* (Göttingen, 1951; [4]1968) 55–82; idem, "Paulus und das Luthersche S.," *Kerygma und Dogma* 1 (1955) 269–320; A. Peters, *Glaube und Werk* (Berlin and Hamburg, 1962; [2]1967) 137–83; R. Kösters, "Luthers These 'Gerecht und Sünder zugleich,'" *Catholica* 18 (1964) 48–77, 193–217; 19 (1965) 138–62; 171–85; K. O. Nilsson, *Simul* (Göttingen, 1966) 192–208, 309–57; E. Schott, "Zugleich," in *Vierhundertfünfzig Jahre Lutherische Reformation 1517–1967. Festschrift F. Lau* (Göttingen, 1967) 333–51; O. H. Pesch, *Theologie der Rechtfertigung bei Martin Luther und Thomas von Aquin* (Mainz, 1967; [2]1985) 109–22, 526–37, 548ff.; M. Kroeger, *Rechtfertigung und Gesetz* (Göttingen, 1968) 72–85; J. Wicks, *Man Yearning for Grace. Martin Luther's Early Spiritual Teaching* (Wiesbaden, 1969); O. Bayer, *Promissio* (Göttingen, 1971) 139, 153–57, 301, 342f.; G. Ebeling, *Wort und Glaube*, vol. 3 (Tübingen, 1975) 187–90; J. F. McCue, "S. in Augustine, Aquinas, and Luther," *Journal of the American Academy of Religion* 48 (1980) 81–96; N. Nicol, *Meditation bei Luther* (Göttingen, 1984) 91–101, 117–50; E. Iserloh, "Gratia und Donum," in *Kirche— Ereignis und Institution*, vol. 2 (Münster, 1985) 70–87; G. Ebeling, *Lutherstudien*, vol. 3 (Tübingen, 1985) 74– 107, 223, 310; A. McGrath, *The Intellectual Origin of the European Reformation* (Oxford, 1987) 77–82; P. Manns, "Fides absoluta—fides incarnata (1965)," in *Vater im Glauben. Studien zur Theologie M. Luthers* (Stuttgart, 1988) 1–48, esp. 24–48; idem, "Zum Gespräch zwischen Martin Luther und der katholischen Theologie (1987)," in *Vater im Glauben. Studien zur Theologie M. Luthers*, 441–532, esp. 151f.; B. Lohse, "Die Bedeutung Augustins für den jungen Luther (1965)," in *Evangelium in der Geschichte*, vol. 1 (Göttingen, 1988) 11–30; G. Ebeling, *Lutherstudien*, vol. 2/3 (Göttingen, 1989) 425–30, 458

536, 563,; T. Mannermaa, *Der im Glauben gegenwärtige Christus* (Hannover, 1989) 62–79; W. Pannenberg, *Systematische Theologie* (Göttingen, vol. 2, 1991) 266–90; (vol. 3, 1993) 274–87; J. Wicks, *Luther's Reform* (Mainz, 1992) 59–83 (commentary on all the texts of Luther); S. Peura, *Mehr als ein Mensch? Die Vergöttlichung als Thema der Theologie M. Luthers von 1513–19* (Mainz, 1994) 144–74, 244–94; B. Lohse, *Luthers Theologie in ihrer historischen Entwicklung und in ihrem systematischen Zusammenhang* (Göttingen, 1995) 64ff., 82ff., 263–73; idem, "Luther und Bernhard von Clairvaux (1994)," in *Evangelium in der Geschichte* [vol. 2] (Göttingen, 1998) 255–84, esp. 273f.; E.-M. Faber, *Symphonie von Gott und Mensch. Die responsorische Struktur von Vermittlung in der Theologie J. Calvins* (Neukirchen-Vluyn, 1998) 168–84, 437–61; Th. Schneider and G. Wenz, eds., *Gerecht und Sünder zugleich? Ökumenische Klärungen.* (Freiburg and Göttingen, 2001).

OTTO HERMANN PESCH

Sirleto, *Guglielmo.* Cardinal, born 1514 in Guardavalle near Stilo (Calabria), died October 6, 1585 in Rome. He studied in Naples. From c. 1540 onward, he lived in Rome, where he joined the household of Cardinal Marcello Cervini (later Pope → Marcellus II). He was tutor to Cervini's nephews, and became custodian of the Vatican Library in 1554. During the Council of Trent, he conducted an intensive correspondence with the legates Cervini (during the first period) and Girolamo → Seripando (third period), supplying them from the Vatican Library with texts from church fathers, theologians, councils, etc., which were relevant to the questions discussed at Trent. It is not possible to estimate exactly the extent to which the conciliar texts are the fruit of his work. → Paul IV made him a member of a commission for church reform in 1556, and appointed him apostolic protonotary. At the request of Charles → Borromeo, → Pius IV created him cardinal in 1565. He was bishop of San Marco from 1566 to 1568, and of Squillace from 1568 to 1573. → Pius V summoned him to Rome, where he then worked on the revision of the Index, guided the final redaction of the → *Catechismus Romanus,* and played a key role in the new editions of the missal and the breviary, and in the reform of the calendar under → Gregory XIII. Sirleto had been involved in improvements to the text of the Bible since his time with Cervini, and now he became a member (and later chairman) of the commission for the revision of the Vulgate text; he also worked for the commission on the Septuagint. He was a member of the Congregation of the Index and the Congregation for the Greeks. He became cardinal librarian of the Vatican in 1572. Sirleto was an outstanding scholar, and his tireless study and organizational work made a great contribution to the Vatican Library.

■ **Works** (mostly unpublished): *Textkritischer Kommentar zum Neuen Testament* (Vaticanus latinus 6132–43; 6151); "Adnotationes variarum lectionum in psalmos," in *Biblia regia,* vol. 3 (Antwerp, 1569); *Konzilsbriefe an Cervini* (Vaticanus latinus 6177); *CT* 10:929–55; *Konzilsbriefe an Seripando* (Vaticanus latinus 6179).

■ **Literature:** *BBKL* 10:532f.—L. von Pastor, *Geschichte der Päpste seit dem Ausgang des Mittelalters,* vols. 5–10 (Freiburg, 1909–1926); H. Höpfl, *Kardinal W. Sirlets Annotationen zum Neuen Testament* (Freiburg, 1908); S. Merkle, "Ein patristischer Gewährsmann des Tridentinums," in *Beiträge zur Geschichte des christlichen Altertums und der byzantinischen Literatur.* Festgabe A. Ehrhard (Bonn, 1922) 342–58; P. Paschini, "G. S. prima del cardinalato," in *Tre ricerche sulla storia della chiesa nel Cinquecento* (Rome, 1945) 155–281; A. P. Frutaz, "La riforma del Messale," in *Problemi di vita religiosa in Italia nel Cinquecento* (Padua, 1960) 187–214; R. de Maio, *La Bibliotheca Apostolica Vaticana sotto Paolo IV e Pio IV* (Vatican City, 1962) 265–313; G. Denzler, *Kardinal G. S.* (Munich, 1964); J. Bignami-Odier, *La Bibliothèque Vaticane de Sixte IV à Pie XI* (Vatican City, 1973); L. Calabretta et al., eds., *Il card. G. S. Atti del convegno di studio nel IV centenario della morte, 5–7 ottobre 1986* (Catanzaro, 1989).

KLAUS GANZER

■ **Additional Bibliography:** C. Alonso, "Cartas de Agustinos y sobre Agustinos al Card. S.," *Analecta Augustiniana* 63 (2000) 97–139.

Sittard (family name: Esche), *Matthias.* Dominican (c. 1538), celebrated preacher in the Reformation period, born February 2, 1522 in Sittard (Netherlands), died October 31, 1566 in Vienna. He preached in Aachen and Cologne. He took part in the religious dialogue of → Worms in 1557, and was preacher at the imperial court and father confessor to → Ferdinand I and → Maximilian II from 1559 onward. He was a theological counselor in Innsbruck in 1563. In 1566, he preached against the Reformers at the imperial parliament in Augsburg, emphasizing that love was the best means to achieve reunification.

■ **Works:** *VD 16* 19:6604–07.

■ **Literature:** *BBKL* 10:573ff.—J. Quétif and J. Echard, *Scriptores Ordinis Praedicatorum*, vol. 2 (Paris, 1721) 215f.; N. Paulus, *Die deutschen Dominikaner im Kampfe gegen Luther* (Freiburg, 1903) 163–81; A. Walz, *Compendium historiae Ordinis Praedicatorum* (Rome, ²1948) 472, 476.

MEINOLF LOHRUM

Sixtus V. Pope (April 24, 1585–August 27, 1590), Franciscan Conventual (1534), formerly *Felice Peretti* (as cardinal, *Montalto*), born December 13, 1521 in Grottamare (Marches of Ancona) into a poor family. He studied in Ferrara and Bologna. He became vicar general of the Order of Friars Minor and was appointed bishop of Sant'Agata dei Goti in 1566. He was created cardinal in 1570 and was bishop of Fermo from 1571 to 1577. Thanks to earlier tensions, he was excluded from church politics under → Gregory XIII. When he became pope, Sixtus acted with severity against the banditry in the church state. He endeavored to improve living conditions in the church state in general and established a healthy financial situation by making rigorous savings in the budget of the papal court and by greatly increasing the number of curial offices for sale. He was also active as patron of the arts and sciences, and he put up many buildings in Rome (Acqua Felice, Via Sistina; he erected the obelisk and completed the dome of St. Peter's). His reorganization of the curia included the limitation of the number of cardinals to seventy and the setting up of fifteen congregations of cardinals which were directly responsible to the pope (Constitution *Immensa aeterni*, 1588). His headstrong conduct with regard to the new edition of the Vulgate caused great embarrassment, and the text had to be re-issued under Clement VIII. Sixtus's policies were born of the conviction that secular rulers were subordinate to the pope both in spiritual and in temporal matters. In France, the course of events indicated that Henry of Navarre, who had Calvinist sympathies, would gain the throne (→ Henry IV), and → Philip II of Spain put pressure on Sixtus to join an alliance against Henry. The pope did indeed declare in 1585 that, since he was a heretic, Henry had forfeited all claims to the throne, but he attempted to avoid a total dependence on Spain. The collapse of his attempts to regain England for the Catholic Church (execution of → Mary Queen of Scots in 1587, defeat of the Spanish Armada in 1588) disappointed Sixtus.

Sixtus possessed exceptional talents and was highly skilled in administration and in financial matters. He had an exaggerated idea of his own papal dignity, and he had no hesitations in showering favors on his own family. Nevertheless, he is one of the most important popes of the 16th century.

■ **Literature:** *DThC* 14/2:2217–38; *EC* 11:782–87; *BBKL* 10:599–609.—M. de Bonard, "S. V., Heinrich IV. und die Liga," *Revue des questions historiques* 60 (1932) 59–140; A. von Hübner, *Der eiserne Papst* (Berlin, 1932); J. Grisar, "Päpstliche Finanzen . . . ," in *Miscellanea Historiae Pontificiae*, vol. 7 (Rome, 1943) 205–366; F. Sarazani, *La Roma di Sisto V, "er papa tosto." Potere assoluto e grandezza irrazionale di un personaggio entrato nella fantasia popolare* (Rome, 1979); N. Del Re, "Sisto V e la sua opera di organizzazione del governo centrale della Chiesa e dello Stato," *Idea* 36 (1980) 41–53; R. Schiffmann, *Roma felix. Aspekte der städtebaulichen Gestaltung Roms unter Papst S. V.* (Frankfurt/Main, 1985); I. De Feo, *Sisto V* (Milan, 1987); *Studia Sixtina nel IV centenario del pontificato di Sisto V* (Rome, 1987); *Roma e Sisto V. Le arti e la cultura*, ed. M. L. Madonna (Rome, 1993).

KLAUS GANZER

■ **Additional Bibliography:** I. Polverini Fosi, "Justice and Its Image. Political Propaganda and Judicial Reality in the Pontificate of S. V," *SCJ* 24 (1993) 75–96; "Celebrazioni del IV centenario del pontificato di Sisto V," in *Atti del Convegno di studi "Montalto e il Piceno in età sistina"* (Ascoli-Piceno, 1994); E. García Hernán, "La curia romana, Felipe II y Sixto V," *Hispania sacra* 46 (1994) 631–60; L. J. Villalon, "San Diego de Alcalá and the Politics of Saint-Making in Counter-Reformation Europe," *CHR* 83 (1997) 691–715; R. B. Trabold, "Soziales Mäzenatentum im Frühbarock. Betrachtungen zur päpstlichen Kunstförderung unter S. V. . . . ," in *Im Gedächtnis der Kirche neu erwachen*. Festschrift G. Adriányi (Cologne, 2000) 621–28.

Sleidan(us) (real name: Philippi), *Johannes*. Protestant historian of the Reformation period, born c. 1506 in Schleiden, died October 31, 1556 in Strasbourg. After studying law in Liège, Cologne, and Louvain, he lived in France from 1533 onward, where he was secretary to the brothers → Du Bellay from 1537 to 1544. He was an observer for France at the religious dialogues in → Hagenau and → Regensburg. From 1544, he worked in Strasbourg, and was sent on diplomatic missions to England (1545), the Council of Trent (1551-1552), and France (1552). Jean Calvin won him over to the Reformation, and he wrote the antipapal work *Zwei Reden an Kaiser und Reich* (1540). He translated Martin → Bucer's catechism into Latin in 1544. His chef d'oeuvre, the *Kommentarien* (1555), is a chronicle of the → Schmalkaldic League, commissioned at the insistence of Bucer and Jakob → Sturm in 1545. This is a strictly chronological presentation of events between 1517 and 1555, relying on the archives of Hessen, Strasbourg, the electoral Palatinate, and electoral Saxony. It remained the basic history of the Reformation until the 19th century. His *Weltchronik* (1556) follows the structure of four kingdoms which rule the world.

■ **Principal Works:** *Ioan. Sleidani De Statu Religionis et Reipublicae, Carolo quinto, Caesare, Commentarii* (Strasbourg, 1555).
■ **Literature:** W. Friedensburg, *J. S. Der Geschichtsschreiber und die Schicksalsmächte der Reformation* (Leipzig, 1935); T. Brady, *Zwischen Gott und Mammon. Protestantische Politik und deutsche Reformation* (Berlin, 1996).

ROLF DECOT

Slotanus (van der Slooten), *Johannes* (also known as J. S. Geffensis). Dominican controversial theologian, born in Geffen near 's-Hertogenbosch, died July 9, 1560 in Cologne. He took his doctorate in theology in 1554 and became professor of theology in Cologne and inquisitor for the archdioceses of Cologne, Mainz, and Trier (following Tilmanus → Smeling in both positions). He wrote *inter alia* against Justus Velsius (born 1510 or 1515; died after 1581), the humanist and nonconformist who taught in Cologne from 1550 to 1556.

■ **Works:** *Apologiae Iusti Velsii Hagani Confutatio* (Cologne, 1557); *Disputationum adversus haereticos liber unus* (Cologne, 1558).—Catalogue of works: *VD 16* 19:246ff.
■ **Literature:** *BBKL* 10:638f.—E. Meuthen, "Die alte Universität," in *Kölner Universitätsgeschichte*, vol. 1 (Cologne and Vienna, 1988) 427f.

BARBARA HENZE

Smeling(us), *Tilman(us)*. Dominican controversial theologian, born before 1500 in Siegburg, died 1557 in Cologne. He began his studies in Cologne in 1504, taking his licentiate in theology in 1525. He taught theology in Cologne from 1535 to 1553/1554. He served from 1529 to 1554 (and at other periods) as prior of the Dominican monastery in that city. He was inquisitor for the

archdioceses of Cologne, Mainz, and Trier from 1538/1539 to 1553/1554. He revised Johannes → Eck's *Enchiridion* (ed. P. Fraenkel [Münster, 1979] 35*-37*).

■ **Principal Works:** *De septem sacramentis* (Cologne, 1538, often reprinted).
■ **Literature:** *BBKL* 10:648f.—E. Meuthen, *Die alte Universität: Kölner Universitätsgeschichte*, vol. 1 (Cologne and Vienna, 1988) 427.

BARBARA HENZE

Socinians. When we bear in mind the exceptional importance of the role played by Socinianism in the genesis of the modern understanding of the human person and of the world, it is strange that historians of dogma and of philosophy in western Europe have paid little attention to this phenomenon. Socinianism, which was inspired by late-medieval nominalism and humanistic philological studies of the Bible, was a conduit which transported this kind of thought into Enlightenment philosophy. This means that the investigation of Socinianism in the context of the history of ideas would shed valuable light on Enlightenment philosophy itself.

The priority which William of Ockham accorded to the logical (rather than to the ontological) had already entangled him in difficulties, when he attempted to explain the dogma of the Trinity: the comprehensible argument that "one" could not simultaneously be "three" led him to see the Trinity as *sola fide tenendum,* in order to protect this dogma from possible attack by the logicians. This means that nominalism had already cordoned the trinitarian dogma off from the intellectual sphere; moderate Reformers had continued to teach it out of a sheer "obedience of faith," handing it on rather in the manner of a precious but obsolete heirloom. The disquiet this caused finally exploded in Socinianism.

In 1546, forty disputants "who have called into question the traditional doctrine of the triune God" (Andreas Wissowatius, in *Biblioteca Anti-Trinitariorum,* 210) met near Venice. Persecution compelled most of them to flee to Switzerland. This group included the highly educated patrician *Lelio Sozzini* (Latinized as Laelius Socinus, born 1525 in Siena, died 1562 in Zurich) and his nephew *Fausto Sozzini* (Latinized as Faustus Socinus, born 1539 in Siena, died 1604 in Lucławice in Poland), whose name was applied to this movement of critics of the Trinity. When Jean Calvin had the Spanish physician Michael → Servet (who had published his *De Trinitatis erroribus libri septem* in 1531) burned at the stake in Geneva in 1553, this was a signal to the Antitrinitarian refugees in Switzerland that they must flee once again. Like other Protestant groups, they emigrated to Poland. When the synod of Piotrków attempted to unite the religious exiles in 1565, the Socinians became a separate *ecclesia minor* which rejected the doctrine of the divine *trinitas* and the divinity of Christ and of the Holy Spirit. Their decisive arguments in favor of the divine *unitas* led them to be described as Neo-Arians or Unitarians, as *Trinitatis oppugnatores,* or as → Antitrinitarians. The small town of Raków near Sandomierz quickly became an influential educational Socinian center, publishing criticisms of dogma, and especially of the Trinity, which were read throughout the whole of Europe.

■ *LThK*[3] 9:796ff. (unabridged version).

■ **Works:** M. Servet, *De Trinitatis erroribus libri septem* (n.p. [Hagenau], 1531; reprint Frankfurt/Main, 1965); idem, *Christianismi Restitutio* (n.p., 1553; reprint, Frankfurt, 1966); *Per la storia del secolo XVI in Europa. Testi raccolti da C. Cantimori e E. Feist* (Rome, 1937); *Bibliotheca Fratrum Polonorum, qui Unitarii appellantur,* vols. 1–9 (Amsterdam, 1668–69; vol. 1: "Irenopoli 1656" and vol. 9: "Eleutheropoli 1692" are fictitious assertions); *Bibliotheca Anti-Trinitariorum . . . Opus posthumum Christophori Chr. Sandii. Accedunt . . . Compendium Historiae Ecclesiasticae Unitariorum, qui Sociniani vulgo audiunt, . . . Freistadii* (= Amsterdam, 1684; reprint, with a foreword by L. Szczucki, Warsaw, 1967); A. Wissowatius, *Religio rationalis (1685). Editio trilinguis* (Latin, French, German), ed. Z. Ogonowski (Wolfenbüttel, 1982).—Rejoinders: J. A. Comenius, *Antisozinianische Schriften,* reprint, ed. E. Schadel (Hildesheim, 1983) (8 individual writings, Amsterdam, 1659–62, 7*–72*: Introduction and Bibliography); G. W. Leibniz, "Defensio Trinitatis (1669)," *Philosophische Schriften,* vol. 1, ed. P. Ritter and W. Kabitz (Berlin, 1971) 515–30.

■ **Literature:** *HDThG* 3:1–70; *Dicionário Teológico* (Salamanca, 1992) 1408–23.—O. Fock, *Der Sozinianismus* (Kiel, 1847; reprint, Aalen, 1970); H.-W. Gensichen, "Die Wittenberger antisozinianische Polemik" (dissertation typescript, Göttingen, 1942); E. M. Wilbur, *A History of Unitarianism,* 2 vols. (Cambridge, Mass., 1947–1952); D. Cantimori, *Italienische Häretiker der Spätrenaissance* (Basle, 1949); G. Mühlpfordt, "Arianische Exulanten als Vorboten der Aufklärung," *Renaissance und Humanismus in Mittel- und Osteuropa,* vol. 2 (Berlin, 1962) 220–46; P. Wrzecionko, "Die Theologie des Rakower Katechismus," *Kirche im Osten* 6 (1963) 73–110; F. Sánchez-Blanco, *M. Servets Kritik an der*

Trinitätslehre (Frankfurt/Main, 1977); R. Dán and A. Pirnát, eds., *Antitrinitarianism in the Second Half of 16th Century* (Budapest and Leiden, 1982); L. Szczucki, ed., *Socinianism and Its Role in the Culture of XVIth to XVIIth Centuries* (Warsaw, 1983); S. Wollgast, "Der Sozinianismus in Deutschland," in idem, *Philosophie in Deutschland zwischen Reformation und Aufklärung, 1550–1660* (Berlin, 1988) 346–422; E. Schadel, "Zu Leibniz' 'Defensio Trinitatis,'" in *Actualitas omnium actuum. Festschrift H. Beck* (Frankfurt/Main, 1989) 235–305; W. Deppert, W. Erdt, and A. de Groot, eds., *Der Einfluss der Unitarier auf die europäisch-amerikanische Geistesgeschichte* (Frankfurt/Main, 1990); E. Schadel, "Antitrinitarischer Sozinianismus als Motiv der Aufklärungsphilosophie," in idem, *Kants "Tantalischer Schmertz"* (Frankfurt/Main, 1998) 31–108.

ERWIN SCHADEL

Sola fide

1. This expression, like the other so-called exclusive particles (*sola gratia,* → *sola scriptura*), is one of the precisions in the doctrine of → justification which the *Reformers* and their successors considered necessary in their debate with scholastic doctrine. This particular precision was intended to make it completely clear that God's justifying grace is imparted to the human person in no other way, and under no other conditions, than through the reception of this grace in trusting faith. For Martin Luther, it is "clear and certain that alone such a faith makes us righteous" (→ Schmalkaldic Articles 2:1). According to the → Confessio Augustana (IV), we do not attain righteousness before God "by merit, work, and satisfaction," but "out of grace for the sake of Christ through faith," i.e., through that faith whose referent is the satisfaction carried out by Christ in his death; only in this way is the troubled conscience assured of the consolation of justification. Luther calls faith "something alive, active, and powerful . . . which must of necessity always be doing good" (Preface to Lectures on Romans, 1522). Later Lutheran doctrine denied that this activity on the part of faith had any causal connection to justification itself; the spiritual reasoning here was the desire not to water down the consolation provided by the message that we are justified.

ULRICH KÜHN

2. Rejecting the Reformation doctrine of justification and the emphatic Protestant formulation that salvation is given by faith alone, the *Council of*

Trent declared: "If anyone shall affirm that a godless person is justified by faith alone, in the sense that nothing else is required in the way of human collaboration with the grace that makes us righteous; and if anyone shall affirm that it is not in the least necessary that such a person make himself ready and prepared by the endeavor of his own will—let him be anathema" (DH 1559). Since the council regarded the principle of *sola fide* as abandoning both ethics and the ecclesial mediation of salvation, it emphasized that the human person, touched by God's grace, must personally collaborate in the event of justification by giving his assent and accepting justification: "If faith is not accompanied by hope and love, it does not bring about perfect union with Christ, nor does it make one a living member of Christ's body" (DH 1531). The believer is not wholly passive in the event of justification, where it is not God alone who is active—for that would be an event external to the human person (the so-called *iustitia aliena*) where the one who is justified would remain a sinner (→ *simul iustus et peccator*).

Ecumenical discussions have made it clear that these mutual doctrinal condemnations do not affect the ecumenical partner, but rather—to the extent that they genuinely affect anyone—exclude extreme positions which no one upholds today. In the terminology of the Reformation, "faith" already includes hope and love, since it is the comprehensive act of confidence and of the gift of self which is made concrete in works of love. Consequently, the formulation *sola fide* does not make Christian conduct irrelevant to our relationship to God. Rather, works of love of our neighbor are necessary fruits of faith, and cannot be detached from faith. Accordingly, the Reformation concept of faith implies the same requirement of good deeds which is made explicit in the words of the Council of Trent.

PETER NEUNER

■ *LThK*[3] 9:701ff. (unabridged version).
■ **Literature:** O. H. Pesch, *Theologie der Rechtfertigung bei Martin Luther und Thomas von Aquin* (Mainz, 1967; [2]1985); *Lehrverurteilungen—kirchentrennend?*, vol. 1 (Freiburg and Göttingen, 1986); H. G. Anderson et al., *Justification by Faith* (Minneapolis, 1985) esp. 13–74; G. Schramm, "Selig werden allein durch den Glauben," in *Zugänge zu Martin Luther*. Festschrift D. von Heymann (Frankfurt/Main, 1997) 145–62; V. Grossi, "La dottrina tridentina della giustificazione," *Lateranum* 66 (2000) 481–507; O. H. Pesch, "La reponse du Concile de Trente. Les décisions doctrinales anti-réformatrices et leurs conséquences," *Positions luthériennes* 48 (2000) 331–57; M. S. Fernandez-García, "Gabriel Biel, Lutero y la justificación por la sola fe," *Scripta theologica* 30 (1998) 891–96.
■ **Additional Literature:** C. P. Arand, "Melanchthon's Rhetorical Argument for 'Sola Fide' in the Apology," *Lutheran Quarterly* 14 (2000) 281–308.

Sola scriptura

1. The *Reformation* formula *sola scriptura* was reformulated in the 19th century as the "scriptural principle"; the history of this concept shows considerable variations in emphasis, and indeed breaks in continuity. The Reformation agreed with the critique of church institutions implied by the late-medieval concept of *sola scriptura*, but introduced a fundamentally new soteriological dimension by linking this to the other "exclusive particles" (*solo Christo, sola gratia*, and → *sola fide*). Sacred scripture has a unique status as the Word of God which is preached and the gospel which is believed, since it *Christum treibet* (in Martin Luther's words): by the power of the Holy Spirit, scripture expounds its own self and awakens faith. Only this gives scripture authority as divine law, as rational natural law, as human tradition, and as a "letter" which can be applied to praxis; in other words, only this makes scripture the church's book. All the Reformers agreed in seeing scripture in its (christological) *sensus historicus* as the sole epistemological principle of theology. The Formula of → Concord (1577: *BSLK* 837) calls scripture the *unica regula et norma*.

WALTER SPARN

2. The basic principles of the doctrine of justification led Luther to criticize particular traditions, and this in turn led to the Reformation scriptural principle. Scripture and tradition are related in the same way as gospel and church, or God's Word and human words, although the Reformers too acknowledged the value of those traditions which were in accordance with scripture. The definitions of what was genuinely in accordance with scripture called into question the role of the church's magisterium as authoritative interpreter of the Bible. The *Council of Trent* declares that the one gospel is present both in scripture *and* in tradition, and it makes apostolicity, linked with con-

tinuity and catholicity, the criterion for the distinction between apostolic tradition and human traditions (DH 1501, 1504). The new element in the Tridentine response to the Reformation is the council's emphasis on the active role of the church's magisterium as authoritative interpreter of scripture (DH 1507).

JOACHIM DRUMM

■ *LThK*[3] 9:266ff. (unabridged version s.v. Schriftprinzip); 10, 153ff. (unabridged version s.v. Tradition).
■ **Literature:** F. Kropatschek, *Das Schriftprinzip der lutherischen Kirche. Geschichtliche und dogmatische Untersuchungen*, vol. 1: *Die Vorgeschichte. Das Erbe des Mittelalters* (Leipzig, 1904); I. Backus, *Das Prinzip ,S.' und die Kirchenväter in den Disputationen von Baden (1526) und Bern (1528)* (Zurich, 1997); J. Ringleben, "Claritas scripturae," *Theologische Rundschau* 62 (1997) 103–10; E. Mühlenberg, "Scriptura non est autentica sine authoritate ecclesiae (Johannes Eck). Vorstellung von der Entstehung des Kanons in der Kontroverse um das reformatorische Schriftprinzip," *Zeitschrift für Theologie und Kirche* 97 (2000) 183–209.
■ **Additional Literature:** M. D. Thompson, "'Claritas scripturae' in the Eucharistic Writings of Martin Luther," *Westminster Theological Journal* 60 (1998) 23–41; W. G. Crampton, *By Scripture Alone* (Unicoi, 2002).

Sonnius (also: van de Velde, de Campo), *Franciscus*. Controversial theologian, born August 12, 1506 (or 1507) in Son near Eindhoven, died June 29, 1576 in Antwerp. He studied in Louvain, where he took his doctorate in theology in 1539. He was professor of theology in Louvain and cathedral canon in Utrecht from 1544 onward; he was inquisitor from 1549 to 1560; he was theologian of the bishop of Cambrai (or Tournai?) in 1546-1547, and attended the Council of Trent in 1551 both as representative of his university and as an imperial theologian. He took part in the religious dialogue of → Worms in 1557. → Philip II sent him to Rome in 1558-1559 in connection with the erection of new dioceses. He was appointed the first bishop of the new diocese of 's-Hertogenbosch in 1561, and first bishop of the new diocese of Antwerp in 1570.
■ **Works:** *Examen tyronum militiae christianae* (Utrecht, 1554; 's-Hertogenbosch, [2]1570); *Ondersoeckinghe der jonghers oft si kerstelijck onderwezen zijn* (Utrecht, 1554; Antwerp, [2]1574); *Claer bewys uyten woorde Godts van tghene dat men kerstelyk behoort te ghelooven ende te beleven* (Louvain, 1555; Antwerp, [3]1568); *Demonstrationum religionis christianae ex verbo Dei libri III.*

(Louvain and Antwerp, 1555–57, often reprinted); *Succincta demonstratio . . . errorum cuiusdam confessionis Calvinisticae* (Louvain, 1567, often reprinted).
■ **Sources:** *Francisci Sonii ad Viglium Zuichemum Epistolae,* ed. P. F. X. de Ram (Brussels, 1850); *CT* 7:1ff.
■ **Literature:** *Biographie nationale,* ed. die Belgische Akademie der Wissenschaften, vol. 23 (Brussels, 1921–24) 179–224.—Th. Goossens, *F. S. in de pamfletten* ('s-Hertogenbosch, 1917); A. Erens, *Tongerloo en 's-Hertogenbosch* (Tongerloo, 1925); M. Dierickx, *De oprichting der nieuwe bisdommen in de Nederlanden onder Filips II.* (Antwerp and Utrecht, 1950); idem, *Documents inédits sur l'érection des nouveaux diocèses aux Pays-Bas,* 3 vols. (Brussels, 1960–62); *Bossche bijdragen* 25 (1969) Heft 1; P. J. Begheyn, "F. S. als inkwisiteur," *Bossche bijdragen* 30 (1970/71) 85–154; C. de Clercq, "F. S. controversiste et apologiste," in *De Gulden Passer* 56 (1978) 137–53; Jedin vol. 3 (index); W. van der Meeren, "Een dorpsgenoot: F. S.," in *Heem Son en Breughel* (1995) 50–73.

KLAUS GANZER

Soto, *Domingo de.* Dominican (1524), philosopher and theologian, born 1495 in Segovia, died November 15, 1560 in Salamanca. He studied philosophy in Alcalá from c. 1512 to 1516, and in Paris from 1516 onward. He taught philosophy and studied theology in Alcalá from 1520 to 1524. He lectured in the Dominican monastery in Salamanca from 1525 to 1532, occasionally deputizing for Francisco de → Vitoria at the university in that town, where he was second professor of theology from 1532 to 1549, and first professor from 1552 to 1560. He was four times prior of St. Stephen's (1540-1542; 1544-1545; 1550-1552; 1556-1560). He attended the Council of Trent from 1545 to 1547 as theologian to → Charles V, and was in Germany as the emperor's father confessor from 1548 to 1550. He presided at the disputation in Valladolid between Bartolomé de Las Casas and Juan Ginés de Sepúlveda (1550-1551). In marked contrast to other professors at the Dominican faculty in Salamanca, who had little use for philosophy, Soto's writings display an independent philosophical knowledge which he had acquired outside his Order. He had a lasting influence through his reforms of the study of arts and through the textbooks which he wrote in order to translate his ideas into praxis. Like many other theologians in Salamanca, Soto—who had to carry out a great number of tasks in public life—accommodated the material of his lectures to the needs of the jurists who dominated university life

(*De iustitia et iure*). His writings connected with the Council of Trent (*De natura et gratia*, commentary on Romans) were generated by the discussions about the decree on justification, in which Soto played a key role. Unlike his predecessors Vitoria and Melchior Cano, Soto rejected humanistic philological study of the Bible; on this point, he influenced both Bartolomé de Medina and Domingo Bañez. His contemporaries agreed that Soto's achievements as a theologian were far inferior to his philosophical writings, especially in his analysis of economic structures and of Spanish colonial policies, and in the philosophy of law.

■ **Works:** *Summulae* (Burgos, 1529, often reprinted); *De ratione tegendi et detegendi secretum relectio* (Salamanca, 1541); *In dialecticam Aristotelis commentarii* (Salamanca, 1543, often reprinted); *Super VIII libros Physicorum commentaria* (Salamanca, 1545, often reprinted); *Super octo libros physicorum quaestiones* (Salamanca, 1545, often reprinted); *Deliberatio de causa pauperum* (Salamanca, 1545); *De natura et gratia* (Venice, 1547, often reprinted); *Apologia qua R. P. Ambrosio Catharino de certitudine gratiae respondet* (Venice, 1547); *In epistolam ad Romanos* (Antwerp, 1550); *De cavendo iuramentorum abusu* (Salamanca, 1551); *Summa de la doctrina christiana* (Salamanca, 1552); *De iustitia et iure* (Salamanca, 1553, often reprinted); *Annotationes in commentarium Ioannis Feri super Ev. Ioannis* (Salamanca, 1554); *In quartum Sententiarum* (Salamanca, 1557); *De extremo iudicio* (Louvain, 1567); *De sacra doctrina*, ed. C. Pozo, *Fuentes para la historia del método teológico en la Escuela de Salamanca* (Granada, 1962) 121–217; *Relectio de haeresi*, ed. idem, *Archivo teológico Granadino* 26 (1963) 223–61; *Relectio de sacro canone et eius sensibus*, ed. J. C. Martín de la Hoz, *Scripta Theologica* 14 (1982) 757–806; "Relectio de catalogo librorum sacrae scripturae," ed. J. Belda Plans and J.C. Martín de la Hoz, *Burgense* 24 (1983) 263–315; *Relecciones y opúsculos* I, ed. J. Brufau Prats (Salamanca, 1995).

■ **Literature:** DThC 14:2423–31; DHEE 4:2507; BBKL 10:831–36.—M. Solana, *Historia de la filosofía española. Época del Renacimiento*, vol. 3 (Madrid, 1940) 91–130; V. Muñoz Delgado, "D. de S. y la ordenación de la enseñanza de la lógica," *Ciencia Tomista* 87 (1960) 467–528; idem, "Reflexiones acerca de la naturaleza de la lógica en la obra de D. de S.," *Estudios* 20 (1964) 3–45; V. Beltrán de Heredia, "D. de S.," *Estudio biográfico documentado* (Madrid, 1961); J. Quétif and J. Echard, *Scriptores Ordinis Praedicatorum*, vol. 2 (reprint, Turin, 1961) 171ff.; K. J. Becker, *Die Rechtfertigungslehre nach D. de S.* (Rome, 1967); D. Ramos-Lissón, *La ley según D. de S.* (Pamplona, 1976); Klaiber nos. 2908–21; I. Jericó Bermejo, "'Condere articulum fidei et condere Sacram Scripturam': El poder eclesial según D. de S.," *Archivo teológico Granadino* 56 (1993) 63–130; L. Jiménez Patón, "'De Natura et Gratia' de D. de S. en la controversia

Luterana," *Communio* 27 (Seville, 1994) 187–270; 28 (1995) 261–304; 29 (1996) 273–336; 30 (1997) 275–309; J. Belda Plans, "D. de S. y la reforma de la Teología en el siglo XVI," *Anales Valentinos* 21 (1995) 193–221; idem, "D. de S. y la defensa de la Teología Escolástica en Trento," *Scripta Theologica* 27 (1995) 423–58; F. Domínguez, *Gaspar de Grajal* (Münster, 1998) 221–27 249–56, and passim; K. Reinhardt, *Bibelkommentare spanischer Autoren*, vol. 2 (Madrid, 1999) 320–23.

FERNANDO DOMÍNGUEZ

■ **Additional Bibliography:** S. DiLiso, *D. de S.* (Bari, 2000); W. A. Wallace, *D. de S. and the Early Galileo: Essays on Intellectual History* (Aldershot, 2003).

Soto, *Pedro de.* Dominican (1518), controversial theologian, born c. 1500 in Alcalá, died April 20, 1563 in Trent. After studies in Salamanca and various activities within his Order, he was father confessor to → Charles V from 1542 to 1548. He was one of the founders of the university of Dillingen in 1549, and was professor there until 1555. As vicar general of the Dominican province of Lower Germany, Soto devoted particular care to the restoration of studies in his Order. He was professor of theology at Oxford in 1555-1556. He was papal theologian during the last session of the Council of Trent. He wrote catechetical and pastoral works (*Compendium doctrinae catholicae* [Ingolstadt, 1549]; *Tractatus de institutione sacerdotum* [Dillingen, 1558]). His letters to Ruard → Tapper on the methodology to be employed in the controversial theological discussion of the doctrine of grace (printed in the appendix to A. Réginald, *De mente Sacri Concilii Tridentini circa gratiam se ipsa efficacem* [Antwerp, 1706]) played an important role in the controversies around Michael → Bajus. He replied to the → Confessio Virtembergica (1551) in an *Assertio catholicae fidei* (Cologne, 1555), which provoked the author of the Confessio to compose a detailed apologia for his work; Soto replied to this with a *Defensio catholicae confessionis* (Antwerp, 1557). After Soto's death, this debate was continued by Wilhelmus → Lindanus.

■ **Literature:** BBKL 10:836–39; DSp 10:1084f.—V. D. Carro, *El Maestro Fray P. de S. OP (Confesor de Carlos V) y las controversias político-teológicas en el siglo XVI*, 2 vols. (Salamanca, 1931–50); C. Gutiérrez, *Españoles en Trento* (Valladolid, 1951); V. Proaño Gil, "El concepto de tradición en P. de S.," *Burgense* 3 (1962) 215–37; Klaiber nos. 2922–31; F. Domínguez Reboiras, *Gaspar de Grajal* (Munich, 1998, 333–46.

FERNANDO DOMÍNGUEZ

Sotomaior, *Luiz de.* Dominican (1543), exegete and theologian, born 1526 in Lisbon, died May 20, 1610 in Coimbra. He studied at the college of his Order in Lisbon from 1543 to 1548, then at the Dominican college and the university of Louvain from 1549 to 1554. He accompanied Pedro de → Soto to England in 1554, and was father confessor to → Mary I and teacher of theology at Oxford until 1558. He taught in Louvain from 1558 to 1561; he was a conciliar theologian at Trent in 1561-1562; he subsequently taught at Louvain and Dillingen from 1562 to 1565. He was in the monastery in Lisbon from 1565 to 1567. He was professor of biblical studies at Coimbra from 1567 to 1598. He was an important representative of the humanistic philological study of the Bible.

■ **Works:** *Cantici canticorum interpretatio* (Lisbon, 1599); *Ad canticum canticorum notae posteriores et breviores* (Paris, 1611); *In I–II Tim. et Tit.* (Paris, 1610); *Kommentare zu Ijob, Lk und Joh* (manuscript).
■ **Literature:** J. Quétif and J. Echard, *Scriptores Ordinis Praedicatorum,* vol. 2 (reprint, Turin, 1961) 374; M. A. Rodrigues, *A Cátedra de Sagrada Escritura na Universidade de Coimbra. Primeiro século (1537–1640)* (Coimbra, 1974) 157–260.

FERNANDO DOMÍNGUEZ

Spalatin (real name: Burckhardt), *Georg.* Protestant theologian, humanist, lawyer, counselor of princes, born January 17, 1484 in Spalt near Nuremberg, died January 16, 1545 in Altenburg. He studied in Erfurt (where he joined the humanist circle around → Mutianus Rufus) and Wittenberg. He was appointed teacher of the novices in the monastery of Georgenthal near Gotha in 1505, and was ordained priest in 1508. He was summoned to Torgau as tutor to the princes, and → Frederick III (the "Wise") also employed him as librarian and historian. In 1511, he moved to Wittenberg, where he became private secretary, spiritual adviser, and court preacher to the electoral prince. He first met Martin Luther in 1514, and it was he, as Luther's patron and contact at court, who ensured that the prince would protect the Reformer in the decisive years 1517-1522. Spalatin attempted in vain to mediate between Luther and → Erasmus of Rotterdam. After the death of the electoral prince, he married in 1525 and took over the parish of Altenburg, becoming superintendent in 1528. He was a member of the visitation commission from 1527 onward, and helped establish the system of church government under the authority of the prince. He served the electoral princes Johann and → Johann Friedrich as counselor (e.g., at Augsburg in 1530, and at Schweinfurt and Nuremberg in 1532). His edifying treatises helped the spread of the Reformation, as did his translations of works by Luther, Philipp Melanchthon, and Erasmus. In his last years, he concentrated on historical studies: *Annales reformationis* (Leipzig, 1718); *Chronica . . . der Churfürsten . . . zu Sachsen* (Wittenberg, 1541).

■ **Works:** H. Volz, "Bibliographie der im 16.Jh. erschienenen Schriften G. S.s," *Zeitschrift für Bibliothekswesen und Bibliographie* 5 (1958) 83–119.
■ **Literature:** *BBKL* 10:865–68.—I. Höss, *G. S.* (Weimar, 1956; ²1989); G. Wartenberg, *Landesherrschaft und Reformation* (Gütersloh, 1988); I. Ludolphy, *Friedrich der Weise* (Göttingen, 1989).

ROLF DECOT

■ **Additional Bibliography:** W. Petke, "Das Breve Leos X. an G. P. von 1518 über die Verleihung der Goldenen Rose an Friedrich den Weisen," *Archiv für Kulturgeschichte* 80 (1998) 67–104; Ch. Meckenborg and A.-B. Riecke, "Die 'Chronik der Sachsen und Thüringer' von G. S.," in *Fata Libellorum,* ed. R. Bentzinger et al. (Göppingen, 1999) 131–62.

Spengler, *Lazarus.* Secretary to the Nuremberg city council and theologian, born March 13, 1479 in Nuremberg, where he died September 7, 1534. After studies in Leipzig, he entered the service of his home town in 1496, becoming secretary to the council in 1507. He was a friend of Albrecht Dürer, Willibald → Pirckheimer, and Johannes von → Staupitz, and embraced Martin Luther's teachings at an early date: he composed a speech in defense of Luther in 1519. He played a central role in the introduction of the Reformation into Nuremberg and strongly influenced the religious policies of the imperial cities. He is a typical example of those municipal councilors who combined religious politics, concern for the common good, and personal piety.

■ **Works:** *L. S. Schriften,* vol. 1 (Gütersloh, 1995) (additional vols. in preparation).
■ **Literature:** *BBKL* 10:939ff.—H. von Schubert, *L. S. und die Reformation in Nürnberg* (Leipzig, 1934; reprint, New York and London, 1971); B. Hamm, *Bürgertum und Glaube* (Göttingen, 1996).

ROLF DECOT

■ **Additional Bibliography:** H. Roser, *Franken und Luther* (Munich, 1996) 20–27; W. Huber, "Der

Nürnberger Ratsschreiber L. S. als Apologet der Reformation," *ZBKG* 66 (1997) 1–11; B. Hamm, "Der Nürnberger Ratsschreiber L. S. als Rechtsdenker und Advokat der Reformation," in *Recht und Verfassung im Übergang vom Mittelalter zur Neuzeit*, vol. 1 (Göttingen, 1998) 230–57; idem, "Das erste persönliche Glaubensbekenntnis der reformation: L. S. un die Anfänge der evangelischen Bekenntnisbildung," in R. Suntrup et al., eds., *Self-fashioning* (Frankfurt am Main, 2003) 251–84.

Speratus (real name: Hoffer), *Paul*. Born December 13, 1484 in Rötlen near Ellwangen, died August 12, 1551 in Marienwerder. In 1503, he began the study of philosophy, theology, and canon law in Freiburg, Paris, and Italy. He was ordained priest in 1506. He was appointed notary in Salzburg in 1512, and worked for a time there as a preacher, until 1517-1518. He was cathedral preacher in Würzburg (possibly already as a Lutheran) in 1520-1521. He preached a sermon on the married state and against monastic vows in St. Stephen's cathedral in Vienna on January 12, 1522. He was pastor in Iglau in 1522-1523; after his arrest in Olmutz in the summer of 1523, he was expelled from Bohemia by the king. He was in Wittenberg in 1523-1524, where he translated three of Martin Luther's Latin works into German and published the *Book of Eight Hymns* with him: he and Luther are the two earliest authors of Protestant hymns. He was invited to come to Königsberg by → Albrecht the Elder of Brandenburg-Ansbach in 1523, and he collaborated in the composition of the Lutheran Prussian church order in 1526. As ducal counselor, he took part in the first church visitations in Prussia in 1526 and 1528. He was appointed Lutheran bishop of Pomesania in 1530, and it is probable that he was the main author of the *Constitutiones synodales evangelicae* (1530), a manual of distinctively Protestant doctrine. He was a bitter enemy of → Schwenckfeldian and → Enthusiastic tendencies in the duchy of Prussia (1531-1535).—The Lutheran character of the local church in Prussia is primarily the work of Speratus. As bishop, he was a conscientious and zealous pastor of a difficult diocese.

■ **Literature:** *BBKL* 10:973ff.

ERNST MANFRED WERMTER

■ **Additional Bibliography:** W. von Meding, "Luther und S.," *Musik und Kirche* 64 (1994) 188–99; K. Burba, "'Es ist das Heil uns kommen her.' Von S. selbst der Gemeinde erläutert," *Blätter für württembergische Kirchengeschichte* 95 (1995) 27–48; H. Roser, *Franken und Luther* (Munich, 1996) 43f.; M. Brecht, "Erinnerung an P. S., ein enger Anhänger Luthers in den Anfängen der Reformation," *ARG* 94 (2003) 105–33.

Stadion, *Christoph von*. Bishop of Augsburg (1517), born March 1478 in Schelklingen (Württemberg), died April 15, 1543 in Nuremberg (tomb in the parish church in Dillingen). He studied from 1490 to 1506 in Tübingen, Ferrara, Bologna, and Ferrara. In the latter year, he took his doctorate in canon law and was appointed canon in Augsburg. He was appointed legal officer to the bishop in 1512, and defended the refusal to admit Augsburg patricians as members of the cathedral chapter. In March, 1517, at the wish of Bishop Heinrich von Lichtenau (and possibly also of Jakob → Fugger), he was appointed coadjutor with the right of succession; he was consecrated on July 5 in Dillingen. He convoked a diocesan synod on October 20, 1517, but this was a largely unsuccessful enterprise. The Reformation soon took hold of wide areas of the diocese, and Johannes → Eck managed only with difficulty to promulgate in Augsburg the bull → *Exsurge Domine* which threatened Martin Luther with excommunication. Augsburg itself became a center of the new teaching: a major role was played by St. Anne's, the monastery of the Carmelites of the Immaculate Conception of Mary, and the → Baptists too found many adherents in the city, which was predominantly Zwinglian around the year 1527. Stadion, a humanist indebted to the influence of his friend → Erasmus of Rotterdam, sought a middle path between the confessions. At the imperial parliament in Augsburg in 1530, he maintained that the church could make concessions on the question of communion under both kinds (→ chalice for the laity), the vernacular in the liturgy, and clerical marriage (→ celibacy), without thereby abandoning its doctrine and its legal system. This won the approval of Emperor → Charles V and the Protestant imperial princes, but the Roman curia looked on such utterances with deep misgivings. Stadion also displayed a fundamentally irenical attitude in the conduct of the imperial business which was entrusted to him; at the religious dialogue in → Hagenau (1540), he was accused of seeming more a Lutheran than a

Catholic. Stadion suffered profoundly under such suspicions, since he was a man of personal integrity and completely faithful to the Catholic Church.

The confessional development in his diocese after 1530 affected him even more deeply. In 1534, Duke → Ulrich of Württemberg accepted the → Confessio Augustana, which meant that many parishes in his territories were lost to the Catholic Church. In 1537, the Catholic clergy were expelled from Augsburg, and the cathedral chapter took up provisional residence in Dillingen. In 1539, the counts of Oettingen introduced the Reformation in the Ries region. In 1542, → Ottheinrich of Palatinate-Neuberg converted to the Lutheran teachings. Besides this, most of the imperial cities in the diocese became Protestant. When Stadion died after suffering a stroke at the imperial parliament in Nuremberg, he left behind him a basically well-ordered ecclesiastical territory, but the religious situation in his diocese was disastrous.

■ **Literature:** *Handbuch der Bayerischen Kirchengeschichte,* ed. W. Brandmüller et al., vol. 2 (St. Ottilien, 1993) passim; *BBKL* 10:1087–90.—F. Zoepfl, *Das Bistum Augsburg und seine Bischöfe im Reformationsjahrhundert* (Munich and Augsburg, 1969) 1–172; A. Schmid, "Humanistenbischöfe. Untersuchungen zum vortridentinischen Episkopat in Deutschland," *RQ* 87 (1992) 159–92; E. Gatz, ed., *Die Bischöfe des Heiligen Römischen Reiches 1448–1648* (Berlin, 1996) 678f.

PETER RUMMEL

Stancaro, *Francesco.* Italian Protestant theologian and humanist, born c. 1501 in Mantua, died November 12, 1574 in Stopnica (Poland). He was initially a monk and priest, and published a Hebrew grammar in 1530. After he professed the Protestant faith, he was persecuted by the Inquisition and was compelled to leave Italy. He was professor of Hebrew in Vienna from 1544 to 1546. He took his doctorate in theology at Basle in 1546. He became professor of Old Testament in Krakow in 1549, but he came under suspicion of heresy, and had to leave this city the following year. Thereafter, he worked as a reformer in Galicia, where he composed the *Canones reformationis ecclesiarum Polonicarum* (Frankfurt on the Oder, 1552). In 1551, he was appointed professor of Hebrew in Königsberg, where he challenged Andreas → Osiander's doctrine of justification. Stancaro maintained that Christ is mediator only in terms

of his human nature, and this threatened to dissolve the doctrine of the two natures of Christ. After periods spent in Frankfurt on the Oder, Hungary, and Transylvania, where his teachings met with opposition, he returned definitively to Poland in 1559. After he had accused Philipp Melanchthon of Arianism, Stancaro was condemned by a number of synods. This general rejection of his teachings led him to found a church of his own, but this did not last long (1561-1571), and he was finally reconciled with the Reformed Church at the synod of Oleśnica. His criticism of leading theologians of the Reformation was a contributory factor to divisions in the Protestant movement and to the spread of Antitrinitarianism (→ Antitrinitarians) in Poland.

■ **Literature:** *BBKL* 10:1148–52.—L. Hein, *Italienische Antitrinitarier und ihr Einfluss auf die Reformation in Polen während der beiden Jahrzehnte vor dem Sandomirer Konsens (1570)* (Leiden, 1974) 66–118; W. Urban, "Die grossen Jahre der stancarianischen 'Häresie' (1559–63)," *ARG* 81 (1990) 309–19.

MICHAEL BECHT

Stapleton, *Thomas.* Catholic controversial theologian, born July, 1535 in Henfield (England), died October 12 (or 3), 1598 in Louvain. He refused to take the oath of Supremacy (Act of → Supremacy) and left England in 1563. He took his doctorate in theology at → Douai in 1571, and was professor of exegesis there until he became professor in Louvain in 1590, as the successor to Michael → Bajus. Stapleton's writings were primarily concerned with authority in the church and with justification.

■ **Principal Works:** *Principiorum fidei doctrinalium demonstratio methodica* (Paris, 1578); *Relectio* (Antwerp, 1596); *Universa iustificationis doctrina* (Paris, 1581); *Tres Thomae* (Douai, 1588) (apostle Thomas, Th. Becket, Th. Morus), partial Eng. trans. by Ph.E. Hallet, *The Life and Illustrious Martyrdom of Sir Thomas More* (London, 1928; reprint, ed. E. E. Reynolds, New York, 1960).—Complete edition: *Opera omnia,* 4 vols. (Paris, 1620).—Catalogue of works: A. F. Allison and D. M. Rogers, *The Contemporary Printed Literature of the English Counter-Reformation,* vol. 1 (Aldershot, 1989) 154–64.

■ **Literature:** *NCE* 13:643f.; *Encyclopedic Dictionary of Religion,* vol. 3 (Washington, 1979) 3379.—M. J. Scheeben, *Gesammelte Schriften,* ed. J. Höfer et al., vol. 1 (Freiburg, 1941) nn. 1087f.; M. R. O'Connell, *Th. S. and the Counter-Reformation* (New Haven and London,

1964); H. Schützeichel, "Das Wesen der kirchlichen Lehrautorität nach Th. S.," *Catholica* 19 (1965) 303–10; idem, *Wesen und Gegenstand der kirchlichen Lehrautorität nach Th. S.* (Trier, 1966); M. Seybold, *Glaube und Rechtfertigung bei Th. S.* (Paderborn, 1967); idem, "Zur theologischen Anthropologie bei Michael Baius (1513–89) und Th. S. (1535–98)," in *Wahrheit und Verkündigung*. Festschrift M. Schmaus, vol. 1 (Munich et al., 1967) 799–818; J. de Landtsheer, "The Correspondence of Th. S. and Johannes Moretus," *Humanistica Lovaniensia* 45 (1996) 430–503.

HERIBERT SCHÜTZEICHEL

Staupitz, *Johann(es) von.* Augustinian Hermit (before 1490), then Benedictine (1522), born c. 1465 in a noble family in Motterwitz (Saxony), died December 28, 1524 near Salzburg. After studies in Cologne and Leipzig, he entered the monastery of the Augustinian Hermits in Munich, where he became prior in 1490. From 1497 onward, he was in Tübingen from 1497, becoming prior in 1498 and taking his doctorate in theology in 1500. Electoral Prince Frederick III invited him to become one of the founding members of the university which he erected in 1502. Staupitz was the first dean of the theological faculty, and was professor of biblical studies in Wittenberg until 1512; he was also vicar general of the Observants in his Order in Germany from 1503 to 1520. After attempts to unite with other Observant congregations came to nothing, he intensified his preaching activity in southern Germany (Nuremberg, Munich, Salzburg). Initially, he supported Martin Luther, but he withdrew to Salzburg in 1520, where he became abbot of the Benedictine monastery of St. Peter's in 1522.

His sermons show an eclectic theology with a pastoral emphasis, formulated in a language which remains close to the biblical texts; he was receptive to the late-medieval appeals for church reform. At the center of his theology is the revelation of God's mercy in the suffering and death of Christ, and the personal appropriation of the gift of salvation. His emphasis on the unique efficacy of Christ for human salvation, and his clear reservations about the sacramental mediation of salvation by the church, show Staupitz's recourse to the anti-Pelagian theology of Augustine. We also find numerous borrowings from mystical literature, especially in ethical directives about how to live in conformity with Christ.

■ **Works:** *Deutsche Schriften,* ed. J. F. K. Knaake (Potsdam, 1867); *Tübinger Predigten,* ed. G. Buchwald and E. Wolf (Leipzig, 1927); *Sämtliche Schriften,* ed. L. Graf zu Dohna and R. Wetzel, vols. 1ff. (Berlin, 1979ff.).
■ **Literature:** *BBKL* 10:1250–53.—Th. Kolde, *Die deutsche Augustiner-Congregation und S.* (Gotha, 1879); N. Paulus, "J. von S.," *HJ* 12 (1891) 309–46; E. Wolf, *S. und Luther* (Leipzig, 1927); D. C. Steinmetz, *Misericordia Dei* (Leiden, 1969); H. A. Oberman, "Tuus sum, salvum me fac," in *Scientia Augustiniana,* ed. C. P. Mayer et al. (Würzburg, 1975); W. Eckermann, "Neue Dokumente zur Auseinandersetzung zwischen J. von S. und der sächsischen Reformkongregation," *Analecta Augusti* 40 (1977) 279–96; J. Sallaberger, "J. von S.," *Augustinianum* 28 (1978) 108–54; D. C. Steinmetz, *Luther and S.* (Durham, 1980); R. Wetzel, "S. und Luther," in *Martin Luther,* ed. V. Press et al. (Stuttgart, 1986) 75–87; B. Lohse, "Zum Wittenberger Augustinismus," in *Augustine, the Harvest, and Theology (1300–1650)*. Festschrift H. A. Oberman (Leiden, 1990) 89–109; R. Wetzel, "S. Augustinianus," in *Via Augustini,* ed. H. A. Oberman et al. (Leiden, 1991) 72–115; M. Wriedt, *Gnade und Erwählung* (Mainz, 1991); idem, "S. und Augustin," in *Auctoritas Patrum,* ed. L. Grane et al. (Mainz, 1993) 227–57; A. Zumkeller, *S. und seine christliche Heilslehre* (Würzburg, 1994); M. Wriedt, "S. als Gründungsmitglied der Wittenberger Universität," in *700 Jahre Wittenberg,* ed. S. Oehmig (Weimar, 1995) 173–86.

MARKUS WRIEDT

■ **Additional Bibliography:** B. Hamm, "Between Severity and Mercy: Three Models of pre-Reformation Urban Preaching: Savonarola—S.—Geiler," in *Continuity and Change*. Festschrift H. A. Oberman (Leiden, 2000) 321–58; B. Hamm, "J. von S.," *ARG* 92 (2001) 6–42; F. Posset, *The Front-runner of the Catholic Reformation: The Life and Works of J. von S.* (Aldershot, 2003).

Stifel, *Michael.* Protestant theologian and mathematician, born c. 1487 in Esslingen, died April 19, 1567 in Jena. As a member of the Augustinian monastery in his hometown, Stifel published an apocalyptic interpretation of Martin Luther's activities in terms of the history of salvation, which led to a literary controversy with Thomas → Murner. Thanks to Luther's intervention, he became court preacher in Mansfeld in 1523, and in Tollet (Tyrol) in 1525. He was appointed pastor in Lochau in 1528. Stifel employed numerical calculations (*gematria*) to show that Christ would return in judgment on October 19, 1533; when this failed to happen, he was placed under house arrest for a period. He became pastor in Holzdorf in 1534. From 1547 to 1554, he worked in various towns in Prussia, and thereafter in Brück. He was in Jena from 1559 onward, where he taught mathematics at the university and supported Matthias → Flacius against Andreas → Osiander.

■ **Works:** *Von der christförmigen Lehre Luthers* (Strasbourg, 1522), ed. W. Lucke, in *Flugschriften aus den ersten Jahren der Reformation*, O. Clemen, ed., vol. 3 (Leipzig, 1909) 261–352; *Rechenbüchlein vom Endchrist* (Wittenberg, 1532); *Arithmetica integra* (Nuremberg, 1544; partial German trans. by S. Bauer et al., in *Esslinger Studienzeitschrift* 28 (1989) 75–129.—List of works: *VD 16*, 19:585ff.

■ **Literature:** J. E. Hofmann, *M. S.* (Wiesbaden, 1968); *Esslinger Studienzeitschrift* 28 (1989) 25–142 (additional contributions); K. Reich, "Die Beziehung M. Luthers zu M. S.," *Esslinger Studienzeitschrift* 29 (1990) 17–36; idem, "Melanchthon und die Mathematik seiner Zeit," in G. Frank and S. Rhein, eds., *Melanchthon und die Naturwissenschaften seiner Zeit* (Sigmaringen, 1998) 105–21, esp. 119f.

CHRISTIAN PETERS

■ **Additional Bibliography:** W. Meretz, *Der Mathematiker M. S. zu Esslingen (1487? and 1567) als Dichter von Reformationsliedern* (Berlin, 1998).

Stigel, *Johann.* Protestant neo-Latinist poet, born May 13, 1515 in Gotha, died February 11, 1562 in Jena. After his studies of the classical languages, he was appointed *professor poesis* at Wittenberg in 1543; from 1547, he taught at the newly founded university of Jena. He exchanged many letters with Philipp Melanchthon. His poetical gifts found expression in his many-sided Latin compositions (including translations, epigrams, and epitaphs, especially in distiches) which dealt both with Christian subjects (the catechism and Psalms) and with contemporary topics (the Reformation, Luther, the emperor or the empire).

■ **Works:** J. Gruter, *Delitiae Poetarum Germanorum*, vol. 6 (Frankfurt/Main, 1612) 318–574.

■ **Literature:** *ADB* 36:228ff.; *Literaturlexikon. Autoren und Werke deutscher Sprache*, ed. W. Killy, vol. 11 (Gütersloh and Munich, 1991) 205f.—S. Rhein, "J. S. Dichtung im Umkreis Melanchthons," in *Melanchthon in seinen Schülern*, ed. H. Scheible (Wiesbaden, 1997) 31–49.

OTTO NEUDECK

■ **Additional Bibliography:** B. Schäfer, "Mit den Waffen der Dichtkunst für die Reformation. Melanchthons Schüler J. S.," in *Humanismus und Wittenberger Reformation* (Leipzig, 1996) 389–407.

Strauss, *Jakob.* Protestant theologian, born c. 1480 in Basel, died after 1527. He studied in Basle and took his doctorate in theology. He entered the Dominican Order, and worked from 1521 as preacher in Tyrol (Schwaz and Hall). Under pressure from the bishop of Brixen, he moved to Wittenberg in 1522. Martin Luther recommended him to count Georg of Wertheim, but his impetuous temperament led to his dismissal. He worked in Eisenach, Nuremberg, Schwäbisch-Hall, and Baden-Baden (1525-1526). In 1525-1527, he intervened in the → eucharistic controversy against Huldrych Zwingli and Johannes → Oecolampadius, but nothing is known of his subsequent activities. His polemic was directly against ecclesiastical abuses (the Mass, images, purgatory, usury, priestly celibacy), and he urged the establishment of a communal life of love like that of the earliest Christian community.

■ **Literature:** *BBKL* 9:34–37.—H. Barge, "Die gedruckten Schriften des evangelischen Predigers J. S.," *ARG* 32 (1935) 100–121, 248–52; idem, *J. S.* (Leipzig, 1937); J. Rogge, *Der Beitrag des Predigers J. S. zur frühen Reformationsgeschichte* (Berlin, 1957); S. E. Buckwalter, *Die Priesterehe in Flugschriften der frühen Reformation* (Gütersloh, 1998).

ROLF DECOT

Strigel, *Victorinus.* Lutheran theologian, born December 26, 1524 in Kaufbeuren, died June 26, 1569 in Heidelberg. He began his studies at Wittenberg in 1542, where he was a pupil of Philipp Melanchthon; he took the degree of master of arts in 1544. After working as a schoolmaster in Wittenberg and Erfurt, he was called to the university of Jena in 1548. Here he also became involved in the religious politics of the Ernestine dukes. From 1557 onward, Strigel came into conflict with the Gnesiolutheran Matthias → Flacius over the freedom of the human will. Strigel appealed to Melanchthon's teaching and rejected the decision to publish the Weimar *Book of Confutation;* this led to his imprisonment. He was rehabilitated in 1562, and taught in Leipzig from 1563, until he was forced to leave the city in 1567 because of his doctrine of the Lord's Supper. Finally, he taught ethics in Heidelberg.

■ **Literature:** *VD 16* nos. 9580–9648; H. Kropatschek, "Das Problem theologischer Anthropologie auf dem Weimarer Gespräch von 1560 zwischen Matthias Flacius Illyricus und V. S." (theological dissertation, Göttingen, 1943); R. C. Schultz, "Original Sin: Accident or Substance. The Paradoxical Significance of FC I, 53–62 in Historical Context," in L. W. Spitz and W. Lohff, eds., *Discord, Dialogue, and Concord* (Philadelphia, 1977) 38–57; E. Koch, "V. S.," in H. Scheible, ed., *Melanchthon in seinen Schülern* (Wiesbaden, 1997) 391–404.

MICHAEL BECHT

■ **Additional Literature:** V. Stolle, "Der Gnadenstuhl als Brennpinkt einer biblischen Theologie: Ausgestaltung und Weiterführung reformatorischer Ansätze bei V. S.," in *Wortlaute*. Festschrift H. Günther (Gross Ösingen, 2002) 167–94.

Stumpf, *Johannes*. Swiss Reformed historian, born April 23, 1500 in Bruchsal, died c. 1576 in Zurich. He was the son of the town mayor; after studies in Strasbourg and Heidelberg, he was appointed notary to the bishop of Speyer in 1520. He entered the Military Order of St. John in 1521; the following year, he became prior in Bubikon, where he introduced the Zwinglian Reformation. In 1532, he took on the additional office of dean of the chapter of Ober-Wetzikon. He was Reformed pastor in Stammheim from 1543 to 1562; from 1547 onward, he was also dean of the chapter of Stein. In addition to numerous short historical, geographical, and theological monographs, which were commissioned and sponsored by his father-in-law, Heinrich Brennwald, by Gilg → Tschudi, and Joachim → Vadian, his most important work is the thirteen-volume *Schweizerchronik,* which remained the standard presentation of Swiss history until the 18th century, thanks to its comparative topographical and historical methodology and its coverage of Switzerland as a whole. His chronicle of the Reformation includes the earliest biography of Huldrych Zwingli, whom Stumpf defends in his narrative of the → eucharistic controversy.
■ **Works:** *Schweizer und Reformationschronik,* ed. E. Gagliardi et al., 2 vols. (Basle, 1952–55).
■ **Literature:** *BBKL* 11:133–36.—L. Weisz, *Landtafeln des J. S. 1538–1547* (Berne, 1942); E. Bonjour and R. Feller, *Geschichtsschreibung der Schweiz*, vol. 1 (Basle, 1962) 100–187; R. Henrich, "Zu den Anfängen der Geschichtsschreibung über den Abendmahlsstreit bei Heinrich Bullinger und J. S.," *Zwingliana* 20 (1993) 11–51.

MATTHIAS ASCHE

Sturm, *Jakob*. President of the free imperial city of Strasbourg, born August 10, 1489 in an old patrician family in Strasbourg, where he died October 30, 1553. He was a protégé of Jakob → Wimpfeling, and studied theology in Freiburg and jurisprudence in Liège and Paris. While secretary to the cathedral provost in Strasbourg (1517-1523), he converted to Protestantism, and was entrusted with various administrative tasks in Strasbourg from 1524 onward. As president of the city, he ensured that the Reformation took an orderly course in the imperial city, and he soon became the leading political representative of the Reformation in Upper Germany. After the imperial parliament in Augsburg in 1530, at which he presented the Confessio Tetrapolitana, he worked with Marquis → Philip of Hessen to consolidate the Protestant party. He organized the support of Strasbourg for the restoration of Duke → Ulrich of Württemberg, in order that the latter could consolidate the Reformation in the southern regions of the empire. He played a key role in the → Schmalkaldic League, where he was the spokesman of the southern German cities. He consulted closely with the Strasbourg theologian Martin → Bucer and did all he could on the political level to achieve a rapprochement between the Reformation in Upper Germany and Wittenberg. Thanks to his politics, Strasbourg played a leading role in the development of the Reformation in Germany.
■ **Literature:** *BBKL* 11:141–45.—H. Virck et al., eds., *Politische Korrespondenz der Stadt Strassburg im Zeitalter der Reformation (1517–55)*, 5 vols. (Strasbourg and Heidelberg, 1882–1933); E. Fabian, *Die Entstehung des Schmalkaldischen Bundes* (Tübingen, 1962); Th. A. Brady, *Ruling Class, Regime and Reformation at Strasbourg (1520–55)* (Leiden, 1978); M. Lienhard and J. Willer, *Strassburg und die Reformation* (Kehl, 1982); Th. A. Brady, "Protestant Politics," in *J. S. (1489–1553) and the German Reformation* (Atlantic Highlands, N.J., 1995).

FRANZ BRENDLE

■ **Additional Bibliography:** Th. A. Brady, "'There Are Two Sturms at Strasbourg.' The History of a Very Long Confusion," in *Gemeinde, Reformation und Widerstand*. Festschrift P. Blickle (Tübingen, 1998) 233–42.

Sturm, *Johannes*. Protestant reformer of studies, born October 1, 1507 in Schleiden (Eifel), died March 3, 1589 in Strasbourg. He attended the school of the Brethren of the Common Life in Liège from 1521 to 1524, and studied thereafter at the university of Louvain. During his stay in Paris

(1529-1537), he encountered the humanistic system of studies and embraced the Reformation. He came to Strasbourg in 1537, and was appointed in the following year rector for life at the newly founded grammar school (*gymnasium illustre*) in the imperial city. He was a proponent of a rhetorical humanism influenced by Cicero, and wrote both theoretical introductions to study and textbooks on dialectics and oratory. He also founded grammar schools in Hornbach and Lauingen on the Danube. The academy of higher studies in the imperial city of Nuremberg in Altdorf and many Protestant *gymnasia illustria* were set up in accordance with Sturm's plan of studies. He was particularly interested in helping the aristocracy to study. In theological terms, he maintained the traditions of the Upper German Reformation and sympathized with the Reformed party; this led to conflicts with the representatives of Lutheran Orthodoxy in Strasbourg, and the council of the imperial city dismissed him from the post of rector in 1581. Alongside Philipp Melanchthon, Sturm was the most important Protestant reformer of studies in the Reformation period. His synthesis of humanism and Reformation found expression in the goal of a *sapiens atque eloquens pietas*. In the process of confessionalization, boundary lines began to be drawn more and more clearly; in this context, Sturm proposed the alternative of an irenical Christianity in the spirit of → Erasmus. This basic attitude allowed him to appreciate the pedagogical endeavors of the Jesuits.

■ Literature: *BBKL* 11:145–49.—J. Rott, ed., *J. S., Classicae epistolae sive scholae Argentinenses restitutae* (Paris and Strasbourg, 1938); A. Schindling, *Humanistische Hochschule und freie Reichsstadt. Gymnasium und Akademie in Strassburg 1538–1621* (Wiesbaden, 1977); idem, "Humanistische Reform und fürstliche Schulpolitik in Hornbach und Lauingen," *Neuburger Kollektaneen* 33 (1980) 141–86; J. F. Collange, "Philipp Melanchthon et Jean S., humanistes et pedagogues de la réforme," *Revue d'histoire et de philosophie religieuses* 68 (1988) 5–18.

ANTON SCHINDLING

■ **Additional Bibliography:** U. Asendorf, "'Diversa, non contraria.' J. S. und der christliche Humanismus," *Lutherische Monatshefte* 36 (1997) 9f.; Th. A. Brady, "'There Are Two Sturms at Strasbourg.' The History of a Very Long Confusion," in *Gemeinde, Reformation und Widerstand.* Festschrift P. Blickle (Tübingen, 1998) 233–42.

Supper, Lord's. → Communion/Lord's Supper.

Supremacy, Act of. In this law, passed on November 3, 1534, King → Henry VIII was declared "Supreme Head on Earth of the Church of → England." This gave binding legal force to a title which Henry had first extorted from the Convocation of Clergy at the synod of Canterbury in 1531, but without the limitation expressed in that earlier version, viz., "as far as the law of Christ allows." That 1531 version was itself a watershed, revealing the increased pressure applied to the clergy by the king in order to get their approval of his divorce from Catharine of Aragon. The law of 1534 set the seal on Henry's victory over the clergy, which had already been won in the spring of the same year when the Act of Succession was accepted virtually without opposition: this was an oath of allegiance to Anne Boleyn's daughter Elizabeth, and those who took this oath acknowledged Henry's second marriage.

The law of 1533 which limited the right of appeal to Rome had already spoken of "the king's plenary . . . power," and the Act of Supremacy meant that he now possessed that *plenitudo potestatis* which canon law attributed to the pope. Henry himself boasted that he was now both king and pope. A first "Treason Act" passed at the end of 1534 declared the denial of this royal title by word of mouth or in writing to be high treason. This supplied the legal basis for the condemnation to death of Thomas → More, John → Fisher, and a number of Carthusians, who had called the royal supremacy into question.

During the turbulent (and ultimately frustrating) diocesan visitation carried out by Archbishop Thomas → Cranmer, some had demanded the introduction of an oath, and from 1535 onward, many clergy, especially those belonging to religious orders and collegiate churches, were required to take an oath which confirmed the royal supremacy and repudiated the papacy. This oath must not be confused with the oath that had already been demanded from all male adults in an appendix to the Act of Supremacy in the previous year (it was because of their refusal to take this earlier oath that Fisher and More had been arrested in April, 1534). This second oath of supremacy did not enjoy legal force until 1536, when a further law declared the papal authority to be null and void, and imposed this oath under threat of penalties on all who held royal or ecclesiastical office, on all academics, and on all the clergy. The Protestant martyr John Bradford recalled at a later date that he had been obliged to take this oath no less than six times.

When → Mary I became queen in 1553, she abolished the title "supreme head," and the Act of Supremacy and the relevant legislation were abrogated in 1554. The very first statute of her half-sister → Elizabeth I in 1559 reintroduced the supremacy, although—primarily out of consideration for Calvinist sensibilities—the exalted title which Henry had employed in the act and the oaths was replaced by the more modest designation "supreme governor of this realm . . . as well in all spiritual or ecclesiastical things or causes as temporal."

■ Sources: *The Tudor Constitution, Documents and Commentary*, ed. G. R. Elton (Cambridge et al., ²1982).
■ Literature: C. Cross, *The Royal Supremacy in the Elizabethan Church* (London, 1969); G. R. Elton, *Policy and Police* (Cambridge, 1972); D. MacCulloch, *Thomas Cranmer* (New Haven and London, 1996); *GCh* 8:524–34.

RICHARD REX

■ Additional Literature: C. Cross, *The Elizabethan Religious Settlement* (Bangor, 1992); A. Ryrie, "Divine Kingship and Royal Theology in Henry VIII's Reformation," *Reformation* 7 (2002) 49–77.

Surius, Laurentius. Carthusian (1540), Catholic historian of the Reformation and hagiographer, born 1523 in Lübeck, died May 28, 1578 in Cologne. It was probably during his studies in Frankfurt on the Oder that he embraced Protestantism. He lived in Cologne from 1537 onward; through his friendship with Peter → Canisius, he returned to the Catholic faith. Contact with Canisius led to contact with the reform circle around Johann → Gropper and with the Charterhouse in Cologne, which made a deep impression on him. The influence of Johannes Justus Landsberg led him to enter the monastery. In the period between 1545 and 1563, Surius, a humanist with great linguistic gifts, produced Latin translations both of German and Dutch mystics from the late Middle Ages (John Tauler, Jan van Ruusbroec, Henry Suso, etc.) and of writings by the Catholic controversialists Michael → Helding, Johannes → Fabri,

Gropper, Friedrich Staphylus, and Martin → Eisengrein. He published a collection of patristic homilies (Cologne, 1567) and the works of Leo the Great (Cologne, 1568). He published a history of the years 1500 to 1564 as a continuation of the world chronicle of Johann Nauclerus (Cologne, 1564). This was greatly expanded in a separate publication under the title *Commentarius brevis rerum in orbe gestarum* (Cologne, 1566; this went through many editions and continuations, by Surius himself or by later scholars); the work is an uncritical compilation from the writings of Johannes → Cochlaeus, Johannes → Sleidanus, and others, with the aim of refuting Sleidanus and destroying his scholarly influence. Surius also produced a continuation of Petrus Crabbe's collection of conciliar texts: *Conciliorum omnium tum generalium tum provincialium* (4 vols., Cologne, 1567; 2nd ed., Venice, 1585). This was a valuable work in its own period, but it has been criticized for the arbitrary use Surius makes of his material.

His chef d'oeuvre is the *De probatis Sanctorum historiis* (6 vols., Cologne, 1570-1575; expanded 2nd ed., Cologne 1576-1581 [from vol. 3 onward, the revision is by J. Mosander]; many later Latin and German editions). Alongside the work of Boninus Mombritius, this is the most important hagiographical collection before the Bollandist enterprise began. Surius gathered his material from Luigi → Lippomani and other printed and manuscript sources, which were supplied by the publisher Gerwin Calenius, by Canisius and other Jesuits, and by friends of the Cologne Charterhouse in Rhineland, Flanders, and Italy. Surius was criticized for his selection of material and for his omissions, as well as for the uniform style he imposed on the texts, but he appealed in justification to the aim of his work, viz., to edify Catholics and strengthen them in the fight for their faith.

■ Literature: *DThC* 14:2842–49; *BBKL* 11:276ff.—K. Etzrodt, "L. S. . . ." (dissertation, Halle, 1889); H. Quentin, *J.-D. Mansi et les grandes collections conciliaires* (Paris, 1900) 17ff.; P. Holt, "Die Sammlung von Heiligenleben des L. S.," *Neues Archiv der Gesellschaft für Ältere Deutsche Geschichtskunde zur Beförderung einer Gesamtausgabe der Quellenschriften deutscher Geschichten des Mittelalters* 44 (1922) 341–64; idem, "L. S. und die kirchliche Erneuerung im 16.Jh.," *Jahrbuch des Kölnischen Geschichtsvereins* 6/7 (1925) 51–84; A. de Wilt, "Heeft L. S. OCarth de 'Evangelische Peerle' in het Latijn vertaald," *Ons Geestelijk Erf* 27 (1953) 62–88; A. Winklhofer, "Johannes vom Kreuz und die S.-Übersetzung der Werke Taulers," in J. Auer and H.

Volk, eds., *Theologie in Geschichte und Gegenwart* (Munich, 1957) 317–48; N. Trippen, "Der Kölner Kartäuser L. S. (1523–78)" (typescript, Bonn, 1960); G. Chaix, *Réform et Contre-réform catholiques. Recherches sur la chartreuse de Cologne au XVIe siècle,* 3 vols. (Salzburg 1982); A. Wienand, "L. S.," in M. Zadnikar and A. Wienand, eds., *Die Kartäuser . . .* (Cologne, 1983) 276–87; G. Chaix, "L. S. (1523–78)," in *Rheinische Lebensbilder,* vol. 11 (Cologne, 1988) 77–100.

NORBERT TRIPPEN

Sutor (real name: Cousturier), *Petrus.* Carthusian (1511), theologian, born c. 1475 in Chêmeré-le-Roy (department of Mayenne), died June 18, 1537 in Le Parc. He completed his studies in Paris with the doctorate in theology in 1510, and entered the Parisian Charterhouse of Vauvert in the following year. He served as prior in this monastery (1517-1519) and in other Charterhouses: Val-Dieu (1514-1517), Troyes (1523-1525), and Le Parc (from 1531). He engaged in controversy with Jakob → Faber Stapulensis about the three marriages of St. Anne, with → Erasmus of Rotterdam about the translation of the Bible, and with Martin Luther about religious vows.

■ **Works:** *De vita cartusiana* (Paris, 1522, often reprinted); *De triplici connubio divae Annae* (Paris, 1523); *De tralatione Bibliae et novarum reprobatione interpretationum* (Paris, 1525); *Antapologia . . . in quandam Erasmi apologiam* (Paris, 1526); *Apologeticum in novas Anticomaritas praeclaris Beatissimae Virginis Mariae laudibus detrahentes* (Paris, 1526); *Apologia . . . adversus damnatam Lutheri haeresim de votis monasticis* (Paris, 1531); *De potestate ecclesiae in occultis* (Paris, 1534).

■ **Literature:** *DThC* 3:1987f.; A. Gruys, *Cartusiana. Un instrument heuristique,* vol. 1 (Paris, 1977) 66; J. K. Farge, *Biographical Register of Paris Doctors of Theology, 1500–1536* (Toronto, 1980) 119ff.; *CEras* 1:352f.; *BBKL* 11:279–83.—H. Bernard-Maître, "Un théoricien de la contemplation à la chartreuse parisienne de Vauvert, Pierre Cousturier dit 'Sutor,'" *Revue d'ascétique et de mystique* 32 (1956) 174–95; E. Rummel, *Erasmus and His Catholic Critics,* vol. 2 (Nieuwkoop, 1989) 61–73.

PETER WALTER

T

Tapper, *Ruard.* Controversial theologian, born February 14, 1487 in Enkhuizen (Netherlands), died March 2, 1559 in Brussels. He began his stud-ies in Louvain in 1503, and became professor of theology at that university in 1519. He became rector of the university in 1530. In 1535, he became dean of the chapter of St. Peter's, and thereby also dean of the theological faculty; in 1531, he was appointed inquisitor general of the Netherlands. He was a conciliar theologian at Trent in 1551-1552. He drew up reform plans for the church in the Netherlands. In the name of his faculty, he compiled a catalog of thirty-two articles of faith which summarized the pre-Tridentine Catholic doctrine; he used this text as the basis of his lectures from 1545 onward. His chef d'oeuvre, the unfinished *Explicatio articulorum . . .* (2 vols., Louvain, 1555-1557), contains explanations of twenty of the articles. During his final years, he joined Josse → Ravesteyn in combating the doctrine of grace proposed by Michael → Bajus and Jan → Hessels.

■ **Works:** *Omnia, quae haberi potuerunt, opera,* ed. W. Lindanus (Cologne, 1582; new edition, Ridgewood, N.J., 1964); Klaiber nos. 3061–70.

■ **Literature:** *Biographie nationale,* ed. die Belgische Akademie der Wissenschaften, vol. 24 (Brussels, 1926–29) 555–77; *DThC* 15:52ff.; *KThR* 4:58–74.—J. Étienne, "Un théologien louvaniste, R. T.," in *Scrinium Lovaniense.* Festschrift É. van Cauwenbergh (Louvain, 1961) 381–92; M. Schrama, "R. T. über die Möglichkeit, gute Werke zu verrichten," in M. Lamberigts, ed., *L'Augustinisme à l'ancienne Faculté de Théologie de Louvain* (Louvain, 1994) 63–98; F. Domínguez Reboiras, *Gaspar de Grajal* (Münster, 1998) 292f. and passim.

FERNANDO DOMÍNGUEZ

Tausen, *Hans Andreas* (Johannes Tausanus). Member of the Military Order of St. John (1516-1526), Danish Reformer and bishop, born 1494 in Birkende (Fünen), died November 11, 1561 in Ripen. He went to school in the monastery of Antvordskov and then studied philosophy and theology in Rostock (1516-1521); he studied in Copenhagen under the biblical humanist Poul → Helgesen in 1521, in Louvain in 1522, and in Wittenberg in 1523-1524. On his return to Denmark, he became a monk in Wiberg, but left his Order in 1526 and received a royal letter of protection as Protestant preacher. After the reorganization of the church in Wiberg, he was appointed to Copenhagen in 1529 in order to reform church life there too. He was an outstanding Lutheran theologian, and was appointed lector in Hebrew at the university of Copenhagen in 1537. He became lector and cathedral preacher in Roskilde in 1538, and was appointed bishop of Ripen in 1541; he was ordained bishop by Johannes → Bugenhagen in 1542. In addition to numerous polemical writings—directed especially against his old teacher Helgesen—he published a translation of the Pentateuch in 1535, a book for domestic worship and sermons on the passion in 1539, and a Danish hymnal in 1544.

■ **Publications:** *Smaaskrifter,* ed. H. F. Rørdam (Copenhagen, 1870); *H. T.'s Oversættelse af de fem Mosebøger,* ed. B. Kornerup (Copenhagen, 1931); *Postil,* 2 vols., ed. idem (Copenhagen, 1934); *Psalmebogen,* ed. P. Gamrath (Copenhagen, 1944); *Skrifter fra Reformationstiden,* vol. 1, ed. M. S. Lausten and I. Bom (Copenhagen, 1970).
■ **Literature:** *Dansk Biografisk Leksikon,* compiled by C. F. Bricka, ed. P. Engelstoft et al., vol. 14 (Copenhagen, 1944) 378–85; *BBKL* 11:580ff.—M. Schwarz Lausten, *Reformationen i Danmark* (Copenhagen, 1987); idem, *Christian den 3. og kirken 1537–59* (Copenhagen, 1987) 110–14; T. Svendrup, *H. T. Den danske Luther* (Copenhagen, 1994).

KAARE RÜBNER JØRGENSEN

Tetzel, *Johann.* Dominican, preacher of indulgences, born c. 1465 in Prina, died August 11, 1519 in Leipzig. He studied in Leipzig, possibly taking his bachelor's degree in 1487, and entered the Order in that city. He was for a time prior in Glogau, and was appointed inquisitor for Poland in 1509, and subsequently for his Order's province in Saxony. He took part in numerous campaigns connected with indulgences from 1504 onward; from 1516, he was Giovannangelo → Arcimboldi's subcommissioner for the proclamation of the indulgence of St. Peter's, and he was appointed general subcommissioner of → Albrecht of Brandenburg for the indulgence of St. Peter's in the ecclesiastical territories of Magdeburg and Halberstadt in 1517. His preaching of indulgences—which was blatant and vulgar, but not completely at variance with the official church line—attracted criticism from all sides (Hieronymus → Emser, Johannes → Cochlaeus, Johannes → Eck, Johannes Lindner, Karl von → Miltiz), and was a contributory factor to Luther's 95 theses of 1517. Tetzel himself wrote copiously on the subject of → indulgences; at the university of Frankfurt on the Oder in 1518, he defended theses which Konrad → Wimpina had drawn up against the Wittenberg Reformer.

■ **Works:** Klaiber nos. 3071–75; *VD 16* 20:283.
■ **Literature:** *BBKL* 11:725f.—P. Fabisch and E. Iserloh, eds., *Dokumente zur Causa Lutheri (1517–21),* Teil 1 (Münster, 1988) 246–53; C. V. N. Bagchi, *Luther's Earliest Opponents* (Minneapolis, 1991); L. Grane, *Martinus Noster* (Mainz, 1994); W. E. Winterhager, "Kurbrandenburg als Zentrum des frühen Kampfes gegen Luther," *Wichmann-Jahrbuch des Diözesangeschichtsvereins Berlin* 34–35 (1994–95) 113–40; idem, "Die Disputation gegen Luthers Ablassthesen an der Universität Frankfurt/Oder im Winter 1518," *Wichmann-Jahrbuch des Diözesangeschichtsvereins Berlin* 36–37 (1996–97) 129–67.

HERIBERT SMOLINSKY

■ **Additional Bibliography:** R. Decot, "J. T.," *Wort und Antwort* 40 (1999) 183f.

Thamer, *Theobald.* Born 1502 in Oberehnheim (Alsace), died May 23, 1569 in Freiburg. He began his studies in Wittenberg in 1535, and was appointed professor of Greek in Frankfurt on the Oder in 1540. He became professor of theology and preacher at St. Elizabeth's church in Marburg in 1543, but he was suspended from this post on August 8, 1549, after he ceased to maintain the principle of → *sola fide* in the doctrine of → justification. He was preacher at St. Bartholomew's church in Frankfurt am Main from December 10, 1549 onward, but was dismissed at the end of 1552 or in 1553. He traveled to Rome and converted to the Catholic Church. He took his doctorate in theology at Siena in 1556, and was appointed court preacher to the bishop of Minden in the same year. He became a canon of Mainz in 1558, and was appointed professor in Freiburg in 1566. His Christology and his doctrine of justification (which was influenced by Aristotle) differed both from Lutheran and from Catholic positions.

■ **Sources:** *VD 16* 20:679–88.
■ **Literature:** *BBKL* 11:769–75; *OER* 4:149f.—*BiDi* 3:71–152, esp. 71–74; I. Backus, "La doctrine des bonnes œuvres de Th.Th.," in *Les Dissidents du XVIe s. entre l'Humanisme et le Catholicisme,* ed. M. Lienhard (Baden-Baden, 1983) 205–17.

BARBARA HENZE

Theologia crucis. Despite its connection with monastic theology, mysticism, and the late-medieval piety which was centered on the cross, Luther's "theology of the cross" is something genuinely new. Although the expression *theologia cru-*

cis is found only in a few of his writings, from the period between 1518 and 1520 (cf. especially the "Heidelberg Disputation" 19-24: WA 1:361ff.; *Resolutiones* on the theses about indulgences: WA 1:613f.), the reality itself permeates everything the Reformer wrote.

For Luther, the *theologia crucis* means that theological knowledge takes its starting point in a sharp antithesis between God and the world, or between reason and faith (cf. von Loewenich), thanks to the principle that God is hidden under that which is his opposite (*sub contrario absconditum*, WA 56:392). This methodological approach is generated at a deeper level by the anthropological problems connected with sin: when the human being perverted everything through a self-centered misuse of God's gifts, God reacted by reversing everything, so that the cross now became the path of salvation (cf. WA 1:362f.; 5:70). God must confront the human person with his own nothingness, letting him be assailed by the law and by other sufferings (the *opus alienum*), so that he can bring him through the word of the gospel (or through grace) into a mode of existence characterized by the strictly relational realities of faith, hope and love—for only such an existence is in accord with the calling to which the human person is summoned as a created being, only such an existence is a participation in the Being and virtues of God (the *opus proprium*). Hence, the *theologia crucis* is at the heart of anthropology. At the same time, it provides a critical guarantee that the doctrine of → justification will not succumb to what Luther saw as the Pelagian tendencies of late scholasticism, which linked the reception of grace and growth in grace to human achievements (in the form of merits, or of *facere quod est in se*, "doing what one can"). Luther fears that God may be perverted into an instrument of the human person's self-glorification (*theologia gloriae*), and this leads him at this point in his argumentation to relativize drastically every "achievement" of which the human person might boast before God (not only indulgences and merits, but also, for example, the Mass as a sacrifice).

Finally, the christological dimension is a decisive element in Luther's *theologia crucis*. In the light of Jesus' abandonment by the Father on the cross, Luther radicalizes the concept of the "wonderful exchange" which the church fathers had applied to the incarnation: Christ became "sin"

and a "curse" on the cross for us (cf. Isa 53; Gal 3:13; 2 Cor 5:21), taking upon himself all our guilt and bestowing on us in exchange his own righteousness and his divine Being. This makes him the origin (*sacramentum*) of all salvation for us. In the utter humiliation which he accepted for the sake of human beings, he remains still the archetype (*exemplum*) of Christian existence, and indeed the normative form of the → church; it is at this point that Luther presents his critique of the church.

This approach is somewhat one-sided, precisely because of its novelty and its theological greatness. From a Catholic perspective, a dialectical definition of the relationship between God and the human person or the world—and consequently of the relationship between reason and faith—in the form of a radical "either/or" is not acceptable. Nor can the extreme relativization of human activity (including the sacramental signs) be accepted as it stands. However, recent research has shown that Luther's thinking is capable of further development. This means that his *theologia crucis* has an extraordinary potential for the ecumenical dialogue and for the presence of the church in today's world; but this theme awaits exploration.

Although the *theologia crucis* is important in general terms in the Reformed Church, it was not dealt with in such a broad perspective either by Huldrych Zwingli and Jean Calvin, or in the following period. Here, the emphasis lies on the cross as the basis of all salvation; in the Christian life, this salvation comes to take the form of configuration to Christ.

■ *LThK*[3] 6:454ff. (unabridged version s.v. Kreuzestheologie).

■ **Literature:** *TRE* 19:762–68, 774–79.—W. von Loewenich, *Luthers ThC.* (Munich, 1929); J. E. Vercruysse, "Luther's Theology of the Cross," *Gregorianum* 57 (1976) 523–48; P. Bühler, *Kreuz und Eschatologie* (Tübingen, 1981); J. E. Vercruysse, "Gesetz und Liebe. Die Struktur der Heidelberger Disputation Luthers," *Luther-Jahrbuch* 48 (1981) 7–43; E. Thaidigsmann, *Identitätsverlangen und Widerspruch. Kreuzestheologie bei Luther, Hegel und Barth* (Munich and Mainz, 1983); E. van der Veer, *Cruciale verborgenheid* (Kampen, 1992); H. Blaumeiser, *Martin Luthers Kreuzestheologie* (Paderborn, 1995).

HUBERTUS BLAUMEISER

■ **Additional Bibliography:** K. Schwarzwäller, *ThC.* (Munich, 1970); G. Tomlin, "The Medieval Origins of

Luther's Theology of the Cross," *ARG* 89 (1998) 22–40; H. O. Kadai, "Luther's Theology of the Cross," *Concordia Theological Quarterly* 63 (1999) 169–204; R. Kolb, "Luther on the Theology of the Cross," *Lutheran Quarterly* 16 (2002) 443–66; J. A. Nestingen, "Luther on Marriage, Vocation, and the Cross," *Word and World* 23 (2003) 31–39.

Theologia Deutsch

Theologia Deutsch (also known as "Der Franck-forter"). This text was discovered by Martin Luther, who gave it its title and published it in a shorter edition in 1516 and in a more detailed edition in 1518 as *Eyn deutsch Theologia*. It was reprinted eight times in the 16th century, and appeared in 14 editions in contemporary High German. Johann Arndt reedited it in 1597 and understood his own *Wahres Christentum* as a commentary on the *Theologia Deutsch*. Philipp Jakob Spener published it in 1681 as an appendix to the sermons of Johannes Tauler. Since then, the work has appeared in numerous new editions and has been translated into many European languages.

Following the Bronnbach manuscript, the work is dated to 1497. Scholars do not agree on the question of authorship (candidates include Johannes von → Staupitz and Johannes de Franc-fordia). The treatise is in the tradition of late-medieval works of pious edification and of treatises on the imitation of Christ. It had a great influence on early German pietism. It eschews speculation and speaks of a life that follows Jesus, the love that comes from the heart, a faith that is alive and active, and the transformation of one's life through frequent reading and continuous spiritual exercises into the "sacred life of Christ" (Arndt). The author, a representative of mystical popular piety, combats the "Brethren of the Free Spirit," whose views were close to those of the heretical Begards.

The *Theologia Deutsch* begins with an introduction (chs. 1-2), followed by part I (on the essence of the union between the believer and God, chs. 3-13), part II (on the path to this union, chs. 14-43), and the conclusion (chs. 43-44). Its description of the yearning for God and of eternal fellowship with God has attracted Christians of all confessions up to the present day.
- **Editions:** F. Pfeiffer, *ThD.* (Gütersloh, ³1875); A. M. Haas, *ThD.* (Einsiedeln, ²1993).
- **Literature:** *RE* 19:626–31; *DSp* 15:459–63.—R. Haubst, "Johannes von Frankfurt als der mutmasslicher Verfasser von 'Eyn deutsch Theologia,'" *Scholastik* 33 (1958) 375–93; E. Zambruno, *La "ThD" o la via per giungere a Deo* (Milan, ²1991).

GERHARD RUHBACH

- **Additional Literature:** D. Blamires, *The Book of the Perfect Life. ThD—Theologia Germanica* (Oxford, 2003).

Thomas Illyricus

Thomas Illyricus. Franciscan (c. 1486), controversial theologian and preacher, born c. 1465/1470 in Vrana near Biograd (Croatia), died 1528 in Carnolès near Menton (department of Alpes-Maritimes). He went on pilgrimages to Santiago de Compostela and the Holy Land, and undertook preaching journeys through Croatia, Italy, and France. He was appointed inquisitor general for Piedmont, Savoy, and the Dauphiné in 1527. He was one of the earliest literary opponents of Martin Luther. He is venerated in the Franciscan Order as Blessed (feast: May 13).
- **Works:** *Sermones aurei* (Toulouse, 1521); *Libellus de potestate summi pontificis ... qui intitulatur clipeus status papalis* (Turin, 1523); *In Lutherianas haereses clipeus Catholicae ecclesiae* (Turin, 1524).
- **Literature:** *DSp* 15:827–30; *BBKL* 11:1388ff.—F. Lauchert, *Die italienischen literarischen Gegner Luthers* (Freiburg, 1912) 240–69; R. M.-J. Mauriac, "Nomenclature et description sommaire des œuvres de Fr. Th.," *Archivum Franciscanum historicum* 18 (1925) 374–85; A. Bacotich, "Degli scritti a stampa e della vita di fra Tommaso Illirico," *Archivio storico per la Dalmazia* 6 (1931) 574–87; R. M.-J. Mauriac, "Un réformateur catholique: Th.," *Études franciscaines* 46 (1934) 329–47, 434–56, 584–606; 47 (1935) 58–71; S. J. Skunca, "Toma Ilirik iz Vrane," *Zadarska revija* 6 (1991) 75–94.

FRANJO ŠANJEK

Timann

Timann (Tiemann, Tiedemann), *Johannes* (also Johannes Amsterdamus). Lutheran theologian, born before 1500 in Amsterdam, died February 17, 1557 in Nienburg on the Weser. He was prior of the Augustinian monastery in Antwerp, and fled to Wittenberg in 1522. In 1524, he became pastor in St. Martin's church in Bremen, where he worked with Jakob Propst to introduce the Reformation. Timann drew up church orders for East Frisia (1529, with Johann Pelt), Bremen (1534), and Lippe (1538, with Adrian Buxschoten), and represented Bremen at the Hamburg Assembly (1535), the assemblies of the → Schmalkaldic League, and the religious dialogues in → Worms and → Regensburg (1540-1541). He wrote against the → Augsburg Interim and compiled quotations from patristic and Lutheran authors in support of a new consensus in the church. He gave considerable impetus to the formation of the Lutheran confession in northern Germany during the → eucharistic controversy, when he and Albert → Hardenberg (cathedral preacher in Bremen and a pupil of Martin → Bucer) appealed to the new Christology of Johannes → Brenz in support of the real presence in the sacrament.

■ **Works:** *Hospitium Ecclesiae*, vol. 18 (Bremen, 1991) 143–54.

■ **Literature:** *RE* 19:778–81; *RGG*[3] 6:902; *BDG* 2:21296–302; *TRE* 7:156ff.; 18, 679f.; *EKO* vols. 6 and 7, index; *Deutscher Biographischer Index*, vol. 8 (Munich, [2]1998) 3570.—Th. Mahlmann, *Das neue Dogma* (Gütersloh, 1969) index; *Die Nachlässe in den Bibliotheken der BRD*, compiled by T. Brandis (Boppard, [2]1981) 380; W. Janse, *A. Hardenberg* (Leiden, 1994) index.

WIM JANSE

■ **Additional Literature:** A. Sprengler-Ruppenthal, "Joannes Amsterdamus Bremensis als Kirchenrechtler," *ZSRG.K* 120 (2003) 463–531.

Titelmans, *Frans* (also Franciscus Hasseltensis). Franciscan Observant (1523) and later Capuchin (1536), theologian, born 1502 in Hasselt (Belgium), died September 12, 1537 in Anticoli (Latium). He studied philosophy at the university of Louvain, taking the degree of master of arts in 1521; he then studied theology in the Observant Order. He first taught philosophy at Louvain; from 1527 onward, he also taught theology, especially exegesis. Under the influence of Jacobus → Latomus, Titelmans gave preference to the Vulgate and criticized humanists such as Lorenzo Valla, Jakob → Faber Stapulensis, and → Erasmus of Rotterdam, with whom a controversial debate ensued. In 1536, Titelmans went to Italy and joined the Capuchin Order, devoting himself to the care of the sick. His books were reprinted more than 200 times in the 16th century.

■ **Works:** *Elucidatio in omnes epistolas apostolicas* (Antwerp, 1528); *Tractatus de expositione mysteriorum missae* (Antwerp, 1528); *Collationes V super epistolam ad Romanos* (Antwerp, 1529); *Libri XII de consideratione rerum naturalium* (Antwerp, 1530); *Elucidatio in omnes psalmos* (Antwerp, 1531); *Libri II de authoritate libri Apocalypsis* (Antwerp, 1531); *Summa mysteriorum christianae fidei* (Antwerp, 1532); *Libri VI de consideratione dialectica* (Antwerp, 1533); *Commentarii in Ecclesiasten* (Antwerp, 1536); *Elucidatio paraphrastica in . . . Euangelium secundum Ioannem* (Antwerp, 1545); *Paraphrastica elucidatio in . . . Euangelium secundum Matthaeum* (Antwerp, 1545); *Paraphrastica elucidatio in librum D. Job* (Antwerp, 1547); *Doctissimi commentarii in Cantica Canticorum* (Antwerp, 1547).

■ **Literature:** *CEras* 3:326f.; *Cath* 15:12f.; *BBKL* 12:190ff.—B. de Troeyer, *Bio-Bibliographia Franciscana Neerlandica saeculi XVI* (Nieuwkoop, vol. 1, 1969) 87–100; vol. 2, 1970) 278–365; J. H. Bentley, "New Testament Scholarship at Louvain in the Early Sixteenth Century," *Studies in Medieval and Renaissance History* n.s. 2 (1979) 53–79; idem, *Humanists and Holy Writ* (Princeton, N.J., 1983) 199–211; E. Rummel, *Erasmus and His Catholic Critics*, vol. 2 (Nieuwkoop, 1989) 14–22.

MATHIJS LAMBERIGTS

■ **Additional Bibliography:** I. Backus, "The Church Fathers and the Canonicity of the Apocalypse in the 16th Century," *SCJ* 29 (1998) 651–65.

Toledo, *Francisco de,* Jesuit (1558). Cardinal (1593), theologian, philosopher, exegete, and church diplomat, born 1532/1533 in Cordoba, died September 14, 1596 in Rome. After studies in Valencia and Salamanca, he taught philosophy at the latter university and was ordained priest in 1558. He was summoned to the Collegium Romanum in the following year, and while still a novice in the Jesuit Order he taught philosophy (1559-1562), then theology (1562-1568). He was appointed preacher in the Apostolic Palace in 1569, and subsequently also theologian in the Penitentiary. The popes entrusted him with many church-political missions (e.g., to Poland and Austria in order to persuade the princes to take part in the war against the Turks; to Louvain on the occasion of the verdict pronounced on Michael → Bajus). He played a central role in the conversion of → Henry IV of France. He wrote commentaries on Aristotle, a casuistic *summa*, and exegetical works; his theological writings (including a commentary on the *Summa theologiae*) were first printed in 1869/1870. Toledo brought the reforms of Salamanca to Rome. He was a gifted teacher and a proponent of an open Thomism (against Thomas → Cajetan). He was the first Jesuit to teach the *praedestinatio post praevisa merita* (→ Predestination), which later became the general doctrine in his Order. He was the first Jesuit to be created a cardinal.

■ **Works:** *Omnia . . . opera*, 2 vols. (Lyons, 1587–1588); *Instructio sacerdotum* (Lyons, 1599); exegetical works (Rome, 1588f. [John]; Venice, 1600 [Luke]; Rome, 1602 [Romans]).

■ **Literature:** C. Sommervogel, *Bibliothèque de la Compagnie de Jésus*, vol. 8 (Brussels and Paris, 1898) 64–82; *DHEE* 4:2572f.; *DSp* 15:1013–17; *BBKL* 12:288–91.—R. Villoslada, *Storia del Collegio Romano* (Rome, 1954) 75f.; J. Leal, "El simbolismo del 'agua' en el cuarto Evangelio según el Cardenal T.," *Archivo teológico Granadino* 25 (1962) 239–55; I. Tellechea, "Censura inédita de T. sobre el Catecismo de Carranza, cotejo con la de Melchor Cano," *Revista española de teología* 29 (1969) 3–35; J. Theiner, *Die Entwicklung der Moraltheologie zur eigenständigen Disziplin* (Regensburg, 1969) 89–92; K.-H. Kleber, *De parvitate materiae in sexto* (Regensburg, 1971) 165f., 195f.; Ch. H. Lohr, *Latin Aristotle Commentaries*, vol. 2 (Florence, 1988) 458–64; K. Reinhardt, *Bibelkommentare spanischer Autoren*, vol. 2 (Madrid, 1999).

HELMUT WEBER

■ **Additional Literature:** G. J. MacAleer, "Jesuit Sensuality and Feminist Bodies," *Modern Theology* 18 (2002) 295–405.

Toledo, *Francisco Álvarez de.* Spanish diplomat, year of birth unknown (Buschbell dates it between 1510 and 1520), died October 4, 1555 in Siena. He became prior of Roncesvalles in 1545, but probably was not himself a member of the Order of Augustinian canons. On December 31, 1545, he was appointed the second ambassador of Emperor → Charles V to the Council of Trent (*CT* 10:301), and he delivered his credentials in Trent on April 5, 1546. In addition to his activity at the council, he carried out diplomatic missions in Florence and Rome. After the council was transferred to Bologna, he returned to the imperial court. From April 29, 1551 onward, he was the emperor's orator in the second session of Trent. He was in Florence on imperial business in 1553-1554, and was appointed governor of Siena early in 1555.

■ **Sources:** *CT* 5–7; 10; 11.
■ **Literature:** G. Buschbell, "F. de T. und seine Tätigkeit in kaiserlichen Diensten während des ersten Abschnittes des Konzils von Trient," *HJ* 52 (1932) 356–88; C. Gutierrez, *Españoles en Trento* (Valladolid, 1951) 440–45; Jedin vols. 2 and 3; *NBD* I/13.

KLAUS GANZER

■ **Additional Bibliography:** J. Baumgartner, "F. de T. im Widerstreit der Meinungen," *Neue Zeitschrift für Missionswissenschaft* 53 (1997) 113f.

Torgau, Articles of. These were a preliminary stage in the composition of the → Confessio Augustana. In order to help prepare for the impe-rial parliament which met in Augsburg in 1530, electoral Prince → Johann of Saxony asked the Wittenberg theologians to compose a memorandum justifying the alterations in ecclesiastical customs (the Mass, church holidays, monastic institutions, → celibacy, episcopal jurisdiction) which had been carried out in the course of visitations from 1525-1526 onward. Philipp Melanchthon produced the final version of the articles at the end of March, 1530. During the imperial parliament, he expanded them by drawing on the → Schwabach Articles, thus forming the Confessio Augustana. The Articles of Torgau are the basis of CA 22-28.

■ **Literature:** *BSLK* 85–124; G. Wenz, *Theologie der Bekenntnisschriften der evangelisch-lutherischen Kirche*, vol. 1 (Berlin and New York, 1996).

ROLF DECOT

Torres (Turianus), *Francisco.* Jesuit (1567), Greek scholar and controversial theologian, born c. 1509 in Herrera (diocese of Palencia), died November 21, 1584 in Rome. He studied in Alcalá, and came to Rome c. 1540. He was a member of the household of Cardinal Giovanni Salviati until 1553. He was appointed a member of → Paul IV's reform commission in 1556 and was a papal theologian at the Council of Trent in 1561-1563. He argued that bishops were required *iure divino* to reside in their dioceses. He devoted himself to studying the Greek fathers and Byzantine theologians, editing and translating Greek and Byzantine texts. He published the first edition of the Apostolic Constitutions (Venice, 1563). He wrote a number of controversial theological works. Although his writings display considerable learning, they are occasionally somewhat uncritical.

■ **Principal Works:** *De residentia pastorum iure divino . . . sancita* (Florence, 1551); *De iustificatione* (Rome, 1557); *Dogmatici characteres verbi Dei* (Florence, 1561); *De votis monasticis* (Rome, 1566); *De hierarchicis ordinationibus* (Dillingen, 1569); *De redditibus ecclesiasticis* (Rome, 1576; Paris 1577); *De SS. eucharistia* (Rome, 1576; Paris, 1577).
■ **Literature:** C. Sommervogel, *Bibliothèque de la Compagnie de Jésus*, vol. 8 (Brussels and Paris, 1898) 113–26; *BBKL* 12:432f.—H. Jedin, *Seripando*, vol. 2 (Würzburg, 1937) passim; C. Gutierrez, *Españoles en Trento* (Valladolid, 1951) 446–73; O. Kresten, "Zu griechischen Handschriften des F. T.," *Römische Historische Mitteilungen* 12 (1970) 179–96; P. Petitmangin, "Deux 'bibliothèques' de la Contre-Réforme: la 'Panoplie' du Père T. et la 'Bibliotheca

Sanctorum Patrum,'" in *The Uses of Greek and Latin*, ed. A. C. Dionisotti (London, 1988) 127–53.

KLAUS GANZER

Tournon, *François de*. French statesman, born 1489 in Tournon-sur-Rhône (department of Ardèche), died April 21, 1562 in St-Germain-en-Laye. He amassed a great number of benefices in the course of his life, becoming abbot of Chaise-Dieu (1519), archbishop of Embrun (1518-1526), archbishop of Bourges (1526-1537), abbot of Saint-Germain-des-Prés (1533), archbishop of Auch (1538), and archbishop of Lyons (1551-1562). He served the French crown as counselor from 1525 onward, and carried out many diplomatic missions. He was created cardinal in 1530, and was in Rome in 1532, where → Clement VII charged him with the investigation of the question of the marriage of King → Henry VIII of England. He was the leading minister in France from 1537 to 1547, and played a key role in negotiating the Peace of Nice (1538) between → Charles V and → Francis I in the presence of → Paul III. He fell from favor under King → Henry II in 1547 and withdrew to Rome for several years, where he mediated between → Julius III and the Farnese family (War of Parma, 1551-1552) and between the Carafa and Colonna families (1555). In the latter year, he led the negotiations for a secret alliance between Henry II and → Paul IV against Spain. He returned to France in 1559, where he served as counselor to Catharine de → Medici, Francis II, and → Charles IX. He was a patron of poets and humanists, and an energetic defender of Catholicism against Lutheranism, the Waldensians, and Calvinism. He founded several colleges.

■ **Sources:** R. Ancel, *Nonciature de Paul IV*, vol. 1, 2 parts (Paris, 1909–11) index; M. François, *Correspondance du cardinal F. de T. 1521–1562* (Paris, 1946); J. Lestocquoy, *Acta nuntiaturae Gallicae*, vols. 1, 3, 6, 9, 14 (Rome, 1961–77) index.
■ **Literature:** G. Moroni, *Dizionario di erudizione storico-ecclesiastica*, vol. 79 (Venice, 1856) 14ff.; C. Sommervogel, *Bibliothèque de la Compagnie de Jésus*, vol. 8 (Brussels and Paris, 1898) 194; L. von Pastor, *Geschichte der Päpste seit dem Ausgang des Mittelalters*, vol. 4 (Freiburg, 1907) 2–7, index; H. Fouqueray, *Histoire de la Compagnie de Jésus en France*, vol. 1 (Paris, 1910) index; *HCMA* 3:20f., 125, 135, 190; *OER* 4:164.— Ch. Fleury, *Vie de F. de T.* (Paris, ²1729); M. François, *Le Cardinal F. de T.* (Paris, 1951).

ALEXANDER KOLLER

■ **Additional Literature:** A. Saunier-Seïté, *Le cardinal de T.* (Paris 1997).

Toussain (Tossanus), (1) *Peter.* Reformer in Montbéliard, born 1499 in St-Laurent (Lorraine), died October 5, 1573 in Montbéliard. After contacts with Jakob → Faber Stapulensis, he became a canon in Metz (1515), where he became acquainted with Martin Luther's teaching. From 1535 onward, he worked at the request of Duke → Ulrich in the county of Montbéliard, which belonged to Württemberg, in order to continue the work of Reformation which Guillaume → Farel had begun. Initially, the confession of the Protestant church was left an open question; the introduction of the church order of Württemberg (translated into French) in 1560 signaled a change of direction, towards Lutheranism. Toussain composed a compromise liturgy, which was accepted. He was dismissed from office in 1571, during the visitation by Jakob → Andreae.

IRENE DINGEL

■ **Literature:** *BBKL* 12:360ff.—J. Viénot, *Histoire de la Réforme dans le pays de Montbéliard*, 2 vols. (Montbéliard, 1900); idem, "Le Réformateur de Montbéliard," *Revue Chrétienne* 47 (1900) 371–84; J.-M. Debard, "P. T. et la réforme dans le Comté de Montbéliard," *Positions luthériennes* 40 (1992) 3–31.
■ **Additional Bibliography:** F. Pichard, "Pierre T., réformateur du pays de Montbéliard," *Positions luthériennes* 47 (1999) 329–50.

(2) *Daniel.* Reformed theologian and apologist for the Reformed confession of faith, son of (1), born July 15, 1541 in Montbéliard, died January 16, 1602 in Heidelberg. He was pastor in Orleans from 1562, in Montbéliard in 1570-1571, then again in Orleans from 1571 on. After St. → Bartholomew's Eve, he came via Basle to Heidelberg in 1573, and was appointed court preacher to electoral Prince → Frederick III. He was dismissed from this office in 1576, in the course of the change of confession under Ludwig II, and entered the service of the Palatinate count Johann Casimir, becoming professor at the Casimirianum college in Neustadt (Haardt) in 1578. When the Reformed confession was reintroduced under Friedrich IV in 1583, Toussain returned to Heidelberg, where he worked as professor, superintendent (1586), and rector of the university (1594).

311

■ **Literature:** *BBKL* 12:353–58.—F. W. Cuno, *Daniel Tossanus der Ältere*, 2 vols. (Amsterdam, 1898); I. Dingel, *Concordia controversa* (Gütersloh, 1996) 129ff.; R. Bodenmann, "D. T. (1541–1602): Auteur inconnu d'un traité contre les luthériens (1576) et éditeur inattendu d'un texte de Martin Bucer," *ARG* 88 (1997) 279–321.

IRENE DINGEL

Treger (Träyer, Dreiger), *Konrad.* Augustinian Hermit (before 1503), controversial theologian, born c. 1480 in Fribourg, where he died November 25, 1542. After studies in Paris and Freiburg, where he took his doctorate in theology in 1516, he became prior in Fribourg (1513-1514) and in Strasbourg (from 1517 onward). He became provincial and head of the *studium generale* in Strasbourg in 1518. In 1521, he presented for disputation theses on the doctrines of justification and predestination which were influenced by St. Augustine's theology. He attacked the Reformers in Strasbourg in his *Paradoxa centum . . . de ecclesiae conciliorumque auctoritate* (Strasbourg, 1524) and *Vermanung . . . an ein lobliche gemeyne Eydgnoßschaft* (Freiburg, 1524); the latter text claimed that Reformation theology was close to that of the Hussites. After a brief imprisonment, Treger returned to Fribourg in 1524. He took part in the disputation of → Baden (1526) and the religious dialogues in Berne (1528) and Lausanne (1530).

■ **Catalogue of Works:** *VD 16* 20:503f.
■ **Sources:** *Martin Bucers Deutsche Schriften* (Gütersloh, vol. 2, 1962) 15–173; (vol. 4, 1975) 15–164.
■ **Literature:** *KThR* 5:74–87; *BBKL* 12:438–42.—M. Schulze, "'Via Gregorii' in Forschung und Quellen," in H. A. Oberman, ed., *Gregor von Rimini* (Berlin and New York, 1981) 1–126, esp. 54–57; Th. Kaufmann, *Die Abendmahlstheologie der Strassburger Reformatoren bis 1528* (Tübingen, 1992).

HERIBERT SMOLINSKY

Trent, Council

1. Events Leading to the Council (1521-1545)—2. The Council (1545-1563)—3. Significance—4. Subsequent Influence

1. Events Leading to the Council (1521-1545)

In the aftermath of the imperial parliament at Worms (1521), which condemned Martin Luther, many voices were raised to demand that a council be held. At the imperial parliament in Nuremberg in 1522-1523, all the estates called for "a free Christian council on German territory," but this request was refused by Rome. → Clement VII (1523-1534) pursued evasive tactics, since he feared that a council would promulgate far-reaching reforms and also contest his election as pope (on the grounds of his illegitimate birth). An additional complication was the clash between Emperor → Charles V and King → Francis I of France. When he crowned Charles as emperor in Bologna in 1530, Clement gave his assent to the convocation of a council, but he linked this to the fulfillment of conditions which in effect made a council impossible.

→ Paul III (1534-1549) recognized that a council was inevitable. While Charles was in Rome in 1536, it was agreed to hold a council, and a bull dated June 2, 1536 convoked it for Mantua on May 23, 1537. However, this came to nothing. France refused to attend, because of its opposition to Charles; → Henry VIII of England sought to prevent the council; and the → Schmalkaldic League refused the invitation. Restrictive conditions imposed by the duke of Mantua led to the transfer of the council to Vicenza on October 8, 1537, but the papal legates waited in vain for orders from Rome, and the council was suspended *ad beneplacitum* on May 21, 1539.

In the ensuing period, Charles V attempted to reunite the Catholic and Protestant parties by means of religious dialogues (→ Hagenau, → Worms, and → Regensburg). When the imperial parliament at Regensburg in 1541 failed to achieve an agreement with the Protestants, Paul III revived the plan to hold a council and decreed on May 22, 1542 that it would begin on All Saints Day of that year in Trent; the imperial estates had accepted this location, and Pietro Paolo Parisio (1473-1545), Giovanni → Morone, and Reginald → Pole were sent as papal legates. Only a few prelates appeared in Trent, however, and the tensions between the emperor and the pope proved irresoluble (thanks in part to Paul's neutrality in the conflicts between Charles and France). On July 6, 1543, Paul suspended the council, without indicating a date for its resumption.

After he defeated Francis I, Charles obligated him in the Peace of Crépy (September 18, 1544) to send representatives to a council which was to be held in Trent, Cambrai, or Metz. Paul III then summoned the council to meet in Trent on March

15, 1545, with the task of overcoming the religious division, reforming the church, and liberating those Christians who were under the rule of unbelievers. The emperor's plan was first to subjugate the Protestants by military force and then compel them to attend the council. He intended to implement the conciliar decisions in the name of the empire and of imperial law, thus reestablishing religious unity.

2. The Council (1545-1563)
First Period (1545-1548)

After considerable delays, the council opened in the cathedral in Trent on December 13, 1545. The papal legates were Giovanni Maria del Monte (later Pope → Julius III), Marcello Cervini (later Pope → Marcellus II), and Pole. The bishops (including titular bishops) and religious superiors (in the case of the abbots, the representatives of their congregations) had the right to vote on conciliar decisions; this right was not extended to the procurators of those who were absent. The question whether dogmatic issues or church reform should be discussed first was decided on January 22, 1546 when it was resolved to deal with both areas simultaneously; this decision was not accepted by Paul III, but it guided de facto the work of the council until its conclusion.

Conciliar procedure involved three steps. First, the conciliar theologians (who had no voting rights) prepared the dogmatic texts in the "congregations of the theologians." In most cases, they took their starting point in theses put forward by the Reformers (sometimes taken out of context). Second, these provisional texts were presented by the legates to the council fathers (who had voting rights) in the "general congregation" where they were discussed and voted upon. Deputations were convened ad hoc to consider the proposed alterations and reformulate the texts, which were then put to the vote as often as was necessary, until a consensus emerged. Third, the canons and the doctrinal and reform decrees were published in the solemn "sessions" of the council.

The dogmatic texts are wholly orientated to the debate with the Reformers. A number of important decrees were published during the first period. The council declared that the revealed truth is contained in libris scriptis et sine scripto traditionibus ("in the written books and unwritten traditions"); accordingly, the biblical books—i.e.,

the entire canon of the Old and New Testaments—and those traditions handed on by the apostles which are relevant tum ad fidem, tum ad mores ("to faith and to morals") must be accepted pari pietatis affectu ("with the same sentiment of religious devotion"). The Vulgate is recognized as "authentic," i.e., probative in the realm of theological questions; but this does not mean that the biblical languages are to be excluded from study (Session IV, April 8, 1546).

The decree on → original sin rejects the Lutheran doctrine of concupiscence (Session V, June 17, 1546). Influenced by St. Augustine, Girolamo → Seripando had argued that concupiscence could be termed "sin" in a certain sense, since it is the consequence of original sin and its penalty, and the root and cause of many actual sins; and the very existence of concupiscence prevents the human person from completely fulfilling the law of God. This view was not accepted, since it was considered too close to the position of the Reformers. In the same session, the council fathers published a decree on the establishment of the office of lector in cathedrals and collegiate churches, with the aim of improving the education of priests. Session VI (January 13, 1547) gave its approval to the decree on justification, which had gone through many drafts in lengthy discussions. Cardinal Pole resigned his office in October of 1546, primarily because of his dissatisfaction at the work on this decree: he considered that it paid too little attention to the imputation of Christ's own righteousness in the forgiveness of sins.

Most of the concerns put forward by Seripando (who had played a key role in the composition of several drafts of the decree) were rejected. For Seripando, → justification primarily means that the sinner is linked to Christ: through faith, his sins are forgiven, and the righteousness of Christ is imparted and applied to him. Caritas, which is God's gift, empowers the human person for good conduct, but since he never succeeds in achieving a perfect righteousness, the infused righteousness is complemented by the application to him of the righteousness of Christ; this is the so-called double righteousness.

The final text of the decree declares in 16 doctrinal chapters and 33 canons that the human person cannot merit the grace of justification through his own achievements. However, he must collaborate by assenting to what God does. Justification consists in the sanctification and renewal of the inner person. In justification, where baptism is the instrumental cause, faith, hope, and love are infused into the human person. Faith is the beginning of human salvation, and the basis and root of justification. The grace of justification can grow through faith and good works; when this grace is lost, it can be regained by → penance. This decree, for all its good points, is somewhat one-sided.

The same session published a decree on the obligation of bishops and parish priests to reside in their dioceses or parishes. This met with considerable objections, since it did not envisage the possibility of exemptions and papal dispensations.

Session VII (March 3, 1547) published a decree on the → sacraments in general, i.e., on the concept of "sacrament" (as efficacious sign), the number of sacraments (seven), and the sacraments of baptism and confirmation. A reform decree also forbade the accumulation of benefices and abolished some exemptions.

A number of alleged cases of typhus fever in Trent led the legates to decide on the transfer of the council to Bologna, which lay in the papal states. This decision was made known in Session VIII (March 11, 1547), but the fourteen imperial bishops refused to move from Trent. In Bologna, the discussion of the sacraments, the Mass, and necessary measures of reform continued, but the pope bowed to the emperor's opposition, and no decrees were published there. Charles V made a formal protest both in Bologna and in Rome against the transfer of the council. Paul III informally ordered the suspension of the work of the council on February 3, 1548; he suspended it formally on September 14, 1549.

Second Period (1551-1552)

Paul's successor, Julius III (1550-1555), yielded to the demand of the emperor and convoked the council to meet again in Trent on May 1, 1551. France declined to participate, out of opposition to Charles V. The council presidents were Cardinal Marcello Crescenzio, Archbishop Sebastiano Pighino of Siponto, and Bishop Luigi → Lippomani of Verona. The Protestants declared that they would participate only if the council was not held under the authority of the pope, and provided that the decrees published during the first period were reopened for discussion on the basis of the principle of *sola scriptura*.

Württemberg, Strasbourg, electoral Saxony, and electoral Brandenburg sent envoys to Trent, but they did not enter into negotiations with the participants in the council. Germany was relatively strongly represented in this period, which was attended by the three archbishops from Rhineland, eleven bishops, and the theologians Johann → Gropper and Eberhard → Billick; theologians from the university of Louvain in the Netherlands were also present. Thanks to the preliminary work done at Bologna, Session XIII (October 11, 1551) was able to publish a decree on eucharistic doctrine which included the definition of the real presence and transubstantiation; articles on communion under both kinds were postponed until the arrival of the Protestants. Session XIV (November 25, 1551) published a decree on the sacrament of penance, emphasizing the necessity of individual confession, the judicial character of absolution, and satisfaction. Another decree concerned the sacramental character of the anointing of the sick. A reform decree laid down the requirements for ordination, the obligation on the part of bishops to oversee the lifestyle of the clergy, and questions about the appointment to benefices. The revolt of the German princes (→ Moritz of Saxony) against the emperor and the war in which this resulted brought about a suspension of the council (Session XVI, April 28, 1552).—Nothing came of Julius' intention to publish a reform bull containing several reform decrees of the council which still awaited their confirmation, since Spain and Portugal attempted to impose such decrees on their own.

→ Paul IV (1555-1559) endeavored in vain to carry out church reform with the aid of a papal reform commission. His plans to hold a council in Rome itself under the eyes of the pope did not materialize.

Third Period (1562-1563)

→ Pius IV (1559-1565) reconvened the council in Trent. → Calvinism had had great success in France, and there was a risk that a French national council might be held; an assembly of the clergy in → Poissy (religious dialogue, September 9–October 9, 1561) came very close to such a synod. Both France and Emperor → Ferdinand I demanded the convocation of a new council, while → Philip II of Spain insisted on a continuation of the previous council. In his bull of convocation (November 29,

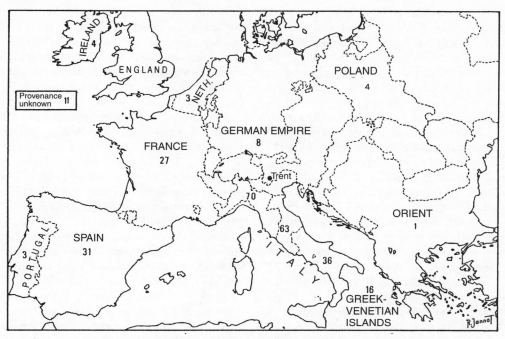

Council of Trent: Provenance of participants in the last session (1562)

1560), Pius IV avoided this contested question. At the assembly of princes in → Naumburg on February 5, 1561, the Protestant Estates in Germany once again refused to send delegates to the council.

The council opened on January 18, 1562; the papal legates in the first phase were Ercole → Gonzaga, Seripando, Stanislaus → Hosius, and Ludovico → Simonetta. Since the imperial party had issued a veto against the continuity of the council, discussions were limited initially to questions of church reform. The problem of bishops' and priests' obligation of residence was taken up again. The Spaniards, the bishops from the imperial domains, and some Italians demanded a declaration that this obligation was *de iure divino,* so that it would no longer be possible to give a simple dispensation. This demand just failed to secure a majority in the voting, and the pope forbade the continuation of the discussion of this issue; it was postponed until the discussion of the decree on the sacrament of orders.

After the opposition of the French and of the emperor to a continuation of the council had been overcome, the issues which had been postponed were taken up. Session XXI (July 16, 1562) pub-

lished a decree on communion under both kinds, which affirmed that the laity (unlike the priestly celebrant of the Mass) were not obligated by divine right to receive communion from the → chalice; Christ is fully present under each of the sacramental species. After vigorous controversies, the decree on the sacrifice of the Mass was accepted in Session XXII (September 17, 1562). The Mass is defined here as a true and genuine sacrifice, a veritable expiatory sacrifice for the living and the dead. It is, however, no new sacrifice, but rather the *repraesentatio, memoria,* and *applicatio* of the sacrifice of the cross. The sacrifice of the cross and the sacrifice of the Mass are identical; it is only the mode of sacrificing (*ratio offerendi*) that differs. The council did not succeed in formulating a theologically convincing reason for postulating this unity between the sacrifice of the cross and the sacrifice of the Mass. The council passed on to the pope the request by the emperor and the duke of Bavaria to grant the chalice to the laity in their domains; after the council, on April 16, 1564, Pius granted an indult for the chalice in Germany, Austria, Bohemia (Prague), and Hungary (Esztergom).

Thirteen French bishops under Cardinal

315

Charles → Guise arrived in Trent in November, 1562. This intensified the ecclesiological debates. There were vigorous discussions of the decree on the sacrament of orders and the problem of the obligation of residence. The debates centered on the essence of the episcopal office, its position within the hierarchy, and the extent and definition of the papal → primacy. Since the French rejected a formulation of the primacy which called the pope *universalis ecclesiae episcopus,* held fast to the superiority of a council vis-à-vis the pope (cf. the councils of Constance and Basle), and agreed with most of the Spaniards in maintaining that the obligation of residence was based both in divine and in human law, the council as a whole entered a situation of stalemate in January, 1563. Things were made worse by the deaths of the legates Gonzaga and Seripando in March.

In February, Guise held discussions with the emperor in Innsbruck, as a result of which Ferdinand I sent two letters to the pope on March 3, demanding that he resolve the situation. Cardinal Morone, who was appointed first legate to the council, was in Innsbruck in April and May, and persuaded the emperor and then Guise to accept a compromise which would exclude any definition of the episcopal office and of the relationship between the papal primacy and the episcopate, but would aim at putting wide-reaching church reforms into practice. This why the decree on the sacrament of orders, published in Session XXIII (July 15, 1563), has something of the character of a theological stopgap. It defines the sacramentality of priestly ordination and the divine institution of an ecclesiastical hierarchy. The council failed in its attempt to derive the church's ministry entirely from sacrifice, for otherwise the bishop's office would mean nothing more vis-à-vis the priest than a greater jurisdictional authority. For the council, it is the bishop, not the priest, who is the real starting-point for the discussion of ministry; and the bishop is the pastor of the local church which is entrusted to his care (cf. Freitag, 368-85). The exclusion of any definition of the essence of the episcopal office meant that this endeavor by the council to overcome an understanding of ministry purely in terms of the priesthood had no lasting effect.

In Session XXIV (November 11, 1563), the sacramentality of → marriage was defined, but no precise dogmatic definition of the nature of this sacrament was offered, nor was it specified whether it was instituted by Christ. After lively discussions, the decree *Tametsi* made the validity of marriage dependent on the observation of the obligatory form (i.e., the exchange of consent in the presence of the parish priest and two witnesses).

The furthest-reaching reform decrees of the council were published in its final six months. These included the decree on seminaries in Session XXIII (July 15, 1563), which obligated the bishops to erect seminaries (though not in opposition to the university faculties of theology), and the two reform decrees of Sessions XXIV and XXV (November 11 and December 3-4). It was the great merit of Morone to have initiated the reform proposals and steered them through the turbulent waters of church politics to a happy conclusion. His diplomatic skills succeeded in winning over the various players (the pope, the curia, the emperor, Spain, France, etc.) and neutralizing them, so that the compromise of a reform program could be achieved. The most important regulations concern the appointment of suitable men as bishops and the endeavor to improve the quality of those who exercised church ministry. The preaching of the faith must once again become a priority (*praedicationis munus, quod episcoporum praecipuum est:* Session XXIV, *De Reformatione* 4). Regular visitations and more frequent diocesan and provincial synods were intended to guarantee the stability of the reforms. The decree on religious life aimed to remove abuses in monasteries. Regulations about indulgences and the veneration of saints, relics, and images (→ Art and Reformation) sought to direct the exercise of piety in an orderly manner. The desire to improve pastoral care runs through many of the reform decrees.

At the concluding Session (XXIV), the decrees which had been published earlier were read aloud and then signed by the council fathers. The council asked the pope to complete work on the Index of Forbidden Books, the catechism, the missal, and the breviary. On January 26, 1564, Pius IV confirmed the conciliar decrees by word of mouth. Written confirmation followed in the bull *Benedictus Deus* on June 30 of that year.

3. Significance

The Council of Trent saw its task as presenting the doctrine of the Catholic faith in a clear demarcation vis-à-vis the teachings of the Reformers. This confrontation with the Protestants frequently entailed a thorough reflection on the Catholic theological positions, and this process meant that some doctrines (e.g., the teaching on justification) were formulated in detail for the first time. The challenges of the Reformation made it necessary to define the Catholic theological identity. However, the theological work was carried out to a large extent from the perspective of confessionalism—in other words, the attempt was made to draw clear boundary lines vis-à-vis the other party—and this meant that the fear of making too many concessions to the foe led the council to reject valuable impulses from a humanistic theology orientated more strongly to the Bible and the fathers (cf. Contarini, Seripando, Pole). Disagreements within Catholicism meant that central questions of ecclesiology (the episcopal office, papal → primacy) were not dealt with by the Tridentine decrees.

Although the council agreed on far-reaching reform decrees, its work of reform was a compromise. For example, although it did intervene in some specific competences and practices of the Roman curia, it did not affect in any direct way the organization of the curia or of its organs and tribunals. This frequently impeded the implementation of the council, since it was possible to employ papal dispensations and exemptions to circumvent the ordinances of the local bishops. The work of reform "was far from achieving the goals . . . of the leaders of the Catholic reform movement in that century" (Jedin 4/2:85). Of all the Tridentine reform decrees, it was those aimed at raising the intellectual and spiritual level of the clergy which were most put into practice, and this led to improved pastoral care.

4. Subsequent Influence

In the ensuing period, the dogmatic decrees formed the basis on which a Catholic identity could develop in the age of confessionalism. The implementation of the reform decrees was a very complex matter; their impact differed from one country, diocese, or religious Order to another. The council offered instruments for the reform of the church, but the transformation came from the atmosphere generated by a reform mentality—and this was the fruit, not of the council alone, but of all those engaged in the renewal of the Catholic Church. Many individuals and renewed or new Orders (Jesuits, Capuchins) played an important role in bring about these reforms.

While the council made a fundamental contribution to the development of Catholic identity in the early modern period, its limitations must not be overlooked.

■ **Sources:** Jedin; G. Alberigo, *Conciliorum oecumenicorum decreta* (Bologna, ³1973) 657–799; J. Le Plat, *Monumentorum ad historiam concilii Tridentini potissimum illustrandam spectantium amplissima collectio*, 7 vols. (Louvain, 1781–87); *Jacobi Lainez Disputationes Tridentinae*, ed. H. Grisar, 2 vols. (Innsbruck, 1886); *CT*; J. Šusta, *Die Römische Kurie und das Konzil von T. unter Pius IV.*, 4 vols. (Vienna, 1904–14); J. Tellechea Idigoras, "Cartas y documentos tridentinos inéditos," *Hispania Sacra* 16 (1963) 191–248; M. Calini, *Lettere conciliari 1561–63*, ed. A. Marani (Brescia, 1963); N. Rodolico and A. d'Addario, *Osservatori toscani al Concilio di Trento* (Florence, 1965).

■ **Literature:** P. Sarpi, *Istoria del Concilio Tridentino* (London, 1619), critical edition by G. Gambarin, 3 vols. (Bari, 1935); P. Sforza Pallavicino, *Istoria del Concilio di Trento* (Rome, 1655), in particular the edition of F. A. Zaccaria, 5 vols. (Faenza, 1792–96) (on this, see H. Jedin, *Der Quellenapparat der Konzilsgeschichte Pallavicinos* [Rome, 1940]); H. Jedin, *Girolamo Seripando*, 2 vols. (Würzburg, 1937); idem, *Krisis und Wendepunkt des Trienter Konzils 1562–63* (Würzburg, 1941); G. Schreiber, ed., *Das Weltkonzil von T., sein Werden und Wirken*, 2 vols. (Freiburg, 1951); C. Gutiérrez, *Españoles en Trento* (Valladolid, 1951); I. Rogger, *Le nazioni al Concilio di Trento* (Rome, 1952); G. Alberigo, *I vescovi italiani al Concilio di Trento 1545–1547* (Florence, 1959); P. Prodi, *Il Cardinale Gabriele Paleotti (1522–97)*, 2 vols. (Rome, 1959–67); H. O. Evennett, "Three Benedictine Abbots at the Council of Trent 1545–47," *Studia monastica* 1 (1959) 343–77; A. Walz, *I Domenicani al Concilio di Trento* (Rome, 1961); G. Alberigo, *Lo sviluppo della dottrina sui poteri nella Chiesa Universale* (Rome, 1964); P. Meinhold, "Die Protestanten am Konzil zu T.," in *Il Concilio di Trento e la riforma tridentina*, vol. 1 (Freiburg, 1965) 277–315; J. Steinruck, *J. B. Fickler* (Münster, 1965); H. D. Wojtyska, *Cardinal Hosius Legate to the Council of Trent* (Rome, 1967); W. P. Fischer, *Frankreich und die Wiedereröffnung des Konzils von T. 1559–1562* (Münster, 1972); R. Bäumer, ed., *Concilium Tridentinum* (Darmstadt, 1979); Jedin; K. Ganzer, "Benediktineräbte auf dem Konzil von T.," in *Studien und Mitteilungen zur Geschichte des Benediktinerordens und seiner Zweige* 90 (1979) 151–213; idem, "Das Konzil von T. und die Annaten," in *Römische Kurie, kirchliche Finanzen, Vatikanisches Archiv. Festschrift H. Hoberg*, vol. 1 (Rome, 1979) 215–47; H. Jedin and P. Prodi, eds., *Il Concilio di Trento come crocevia della politica europea* (Bologna, 1979); K. Ganzer, "Vertretung der Gesamtkirche auf dem Konzil von T.? Zur Stellung der Prokuratoren abwesender Bischöfe auf der dritten Tagungsperiode des Konzils (1562–63)," in *Ecclesia militans. Festschrift R. Bäumer*, vol. 1 (Paderborn, 1988) 253–77; Th. Freudenberger, "Vertretung der Gesamtkirche auf dem Konzil von T. Die Vertretung der deutschen Bischöfe 1545–52," in *Ecclesia militans. FS R. Bäumer*, 1:233–52; K. Ganzer, "Das Konzil von T.—Angelpunkt für eine Reform der Kirche?," *RQ* 84 (1989) 31–50; idem, "Gallikanische und römische Primatsauffassung im Widerstreit," *HJ* 109 (1989) 109–63; J. Freitag, *Sacramentum ordinis auf dem Konzil von T.* (Innsbruck and Vienna, 1991); K. Ganzer, "Das Konzil von T. und die theologische Dimension der katholischen Konfessionalisierung," in *Die katholische Konfessionalisierung*, ed. W. Reinhard and H. Schilling (Münster, 1995) 50–69; C. Gutiérrez, *Trento, un problema: la última convocación del Concilio (1552–62)* (Madrid, 1995); G. Alberigo and I. Rogger, eds., *Il concilio di Trento nella prospettiva del terzo millennio* (Brescia, 1997; numerous essays); C. Mozzarelli and D. Zardin, eds., *I tempi del concilio. Religione, cultura e società nell'Europa tridentina* (Rome, 1997); A. Tallon, *La France et le Concile de Trente (1518–63)* (Rome, 1997); P. Prodi and W. Reinhard, eds., *Il concilio di Trento e il moderno* (Bologna, 1996; numerous contributions; German trans.: *Das Konzil von T. und die Moderne* [Berlin, 2001]).

KLAUS GANZER

■ **Additional Bibliography:** V. Peri, "Trento. Un concile tutto occidentale," in *Cristianesimo nella storia. Festschrift G. Alberigo* (Bologna, 1996) 213–77; M. Mullett, *The Catholic Reformation* (London, 1999); A. Tallon, *Le concile de Trente* (Paris, 2000); K. Ganzee, "Gesamtkirche und Ortskirche auf dem Konzil von T.," *RQ* 95 (2000) 167–78.

Tridentine liturgy. This name is given to the forms of worship laid down for the entire church (to the extent that it followed the Roman rite) in the liturgical books published by the popes at the request of the Council of Trent. → Pius V published the reformed *Breviarium Romanum* in 1568 and the *Missale Romanum* in 1570, although dioceses and Orders with a tradition of their own which was more than two hundred years old were permitted to retain this. This meant that the reception of the Roman liturgy in France and Germany (e.g., Münster, Cologne, Trier) was not completed until the end of the 19th century. The *Pontificale Romanum* appeared in 1556 and the *Caeremoniale Episcoporum* in 1600. Finally, the *Rituale Romanum* appeared in 1614, although Paul V did not impose its use, but limited himself

to a recommendation. This meant that diocesan rituals approved by the local bishop remained in use in many parts of the Western church after Trent, preserving local variations in the celebration of the sacraments, blessings, and processions. The Congregation of Rites was set up in 1588 to oversee the observation of the unified Roman liturgy and to ensure its authentic interpretation.

■ **Literature:** H. Jedin, "Das Konzil von Trient und die Reform der liturgischen Bücher," *Ephemerides Liturgicae* 59 (1945) 5–38; *Das Weltkonzil von Trient, sein Werden und Wirken*, ed. G. Schreiber, vol. 1 (Freiburg, 1951) 325–36; A. Heinz, "Im Banne der römischen Einheitsliturgie," *RQ* 79 (1984) 37–92; J. Lenssen, *Der Tradition und der Erneuerung der Messfeier verpflichtet* (Würzburg, 1988); B. Kranemann and K. Richter, eds., *Zwischen römischer Einheitsliturgie und diözesaner Eigenverantwortung* (Altenberge, 1997); J. M. Pomarès, *Trente et le Missel* (Rome, 1997).

ANDREAS HEINZ

■ **Additional Literature:** S. Ditchfield, "Giving Tridentine Worship Back Its History," in *Continuity and Change in Christian Worship* (Woodbridge, 1999) 199–226;

Truber, *Primus* (Primo Trubar). Slovenian Reformer, born 1508 in Rašica (Dolenjska), died June 28, 1586 in Derendingen near Tübingen. After studies in Rijeka, Salzburg, and Vienna, he was ordained priest in 1530. In 1541, he became acquainted with the Reformation in Switzerland, thanks to Heinrich → Bullinger. He was appointed canon of the cathedral of Ljubljana in 1541. After he came under suspicion of holding Protestant views, he fled to Veit → Dietrich in Nuremberg in 1548. Dietrich obtained for him the post of preacher in Rothenburg (Tauber), where he wrote his *Catechismus* and *Abecedarium* (both published in Tübingen, 1550), the first books in the Slovenian language to be printed. He became pastor in Kempten in 1551. The Slovenian translation of the New Testament appeared between 1555 and 1560; he was in Urach in 1561 to see to the printing of Protestant writings in Slovenian and Croatian. He became superintendent in Ljubljana in the same year, and he composed the first Lutheran Church order in the Austrian crown lands, the *Cerkovna ordninga* (Tübingen, 1564; reprinted Munich, 1973). He was obliged to leave his native land for good in 1565, and became pastor first in Lauffen (Neckar), then in 1566 in Derendingen.

■ **Works:** *Briefe,* ed. T. Elze (Tübingen, 1897); *Pisma* (letters), ed. J. Rajhman (Ljubljana, 1986); *Deutsche Vorreden zum slowenischen und kroatischen Reformationswerk,* ed. O. Sakrausky (Vienna, 1989).
■ **Literature:** *Slovenski biografski leksikon,* vol. 4 (Ljubljana, 1991) 206–25.—M. Rupelj, *P. T.* (Ljubljana, 1962); B. Berčič, ed., *Abhandlungen über die slowenische Reformation* (Munich, 1968); A. Bernard, "La Réforme et le livre slovène," *Bulletin de la Société de l'Histoire du Protestantisme Français* 141 (1995) 5–26.

FRANCE MARTIN DOLINAR

Truchsess von Pommersfelden, *Lorenz.* Born August 8, 1473, died December 20, 1543 in Würzburg. After studies in Heidelberg and Paris, he became a cathedral canon in Würzburg and in Mainz (where he rose to become dean of the cathedral); he also held benefices in other churches of secular canons. As the intellectual leader in the assembly of the cathedral chapters in the ecclesiastical province of Mainz in 1525, he opposed the Reformation ("Counsel of Mainz") and attempted to reform the cathedral chapter. The question of the autonomy of the chapter vis-à-vis the archbishop of Mainz (Cardinal → Albrecht von Brandenburg) caused a conflict between Truchsess and Albrecht. He was imprisoned when he refused to give his consent to the Treaty of Hitzkirchen (June 11, 1528), which had been concluded between Albrecht and Marquis → Philip of Hessen on the occasion of the "Packian quarrels" (Otto von → Pack); this treaty imposed a payment of 40,000 guilders on the archiepiscopal territory, and required the archbishop to renounce for a time the spiritual jurisdiction in Hessen and electoral Saxony. Truchsess was released after a short time; in return, he renounced the office of dean and withdrew to Würzburg, where he worked energetically for the cause of the Counter-Reformation.
■ **Literature:** J. B. Kissling, *L. T.* (Mainz, 1906); A. Amrhein, *Reformationsgeschichte: Mitteilungen aus dem Bistum Würzburg* (Münster, 1923) 183 (index); *Auctarium Chartularii Universitatis Parisiensis,* vol. 6 (Paris, 1964) 687, 704f.; G. Fouquet, *Das Speyerer Domkapitel im späten Mittelalter,* vol. 2 (Mainz, 1987) 835ff.

ALFRED WENDEHORST

Trutfetter, *Jodocus.* Philosopher and theologian, born in Eisenach, died May 9, 1519 in Erfurt. He began his studies in Erfurt in 1476, taking the degree of master of arts in 1484. He taught philosophy at that university and was one of the main representatives of the nominalist *via moderna,* which was receptive to humanism. He took his doctorate in theology in 1504, and taught theology from 1506-1507 in Wittenberg, then in Erfurt from 1510 on. He upheld the importance of natural reason for theology. He parted company at an early date with Martin Luther (who had studied under him from 1501 to 1505), and broke off relations with him in 1518.
■ **Works:** *Breviarium dialecticum* (Erfurt, 1500); *Summule totius logice* (Erfurt, 1501); *Summa in totam physicam* (Erfurt, 1514).
■ **Literature:** W. Urban, "Die 'via moderna' an der Universität Erfurt am Vorabend der Reformation," in H. A. Oberman, ed., *Gregor von Rimini* (Berlin and New York, 1981) 311–30; E. Kleineidam, *Universitas Studii Erffordensis,* vol. 2 (Leipzig, ²1992) 290ff., and passim; G.-R. Tewes, "Die Erfurter Nominalisten und ihre thomistischen Widersacher in Köln, Leipzig und Wittenberg," in A. Speer, ed., *Die Bibliotheca Amploniana* (Berlin and New York, 1995) 447–88.

ULRICH G. LEINSLE

Tschudi, *Aegidius* (Gilg). Catholic politician and polymath historian, born February 5, 1505 in Glarus, where he died February 28, 1572. He attended school while Huldrych Zwingli was parish priest in Glarus, and received a humanist education under Heinrich Glareanus in Basle. He traveled through Switzerland, Italy, and France between 1517 and 1529, copying inscriptions and studying in libraries. He was several times governor in the Common Estates. He held various offices in Glarus from 1536 onward, and was the highest official in the canton from 1558 to 1560. He was highly respected in the Swiss towns and monasteries as a mediator and legal adviser. He belonged to the Catholic party, and attempted to work as a peacemaker after the introduction of the Reformation. He wrote a treatise on purgatory (printed Heidelberg, 1925). His attempt to recatholicize his valley by force, against the wishes of the Protestant majority, led to the "Deal of Glarus" in 1560: when → Pius IV, Spain, and France refused to take part in an armed combat, Tschudi was obliged to yield, and the Swiss confederation laid down the principle of confessional parity for Glarus in 1564. From that time onward, Tschudi restricted himself to academic work. He wrote an important chronicle of Swiss history from 1000 to 1470 (printed Basle, 1734-1736) and published several Swiss maps.

■ **Works:** *Die uralt wahrhafftig Alpisch Rhetia* (Basle, 1538; Latin, Basle, 1538); *Chronicon Helveticum,* ed. J. R. Iselin (Basle, 1734–36; new ed., ed. P. Stadler and B. Stettler, vols. 1ff. (Berne, 1968ff.).

■ **Literature:** *Historisch-Biographisches Lexikon der Schweiz,* vol. 7 (Neuenburg, 1937) 79f.; *BBKL* 12:665–70.—M. Wick, "Der 'Glarnerhandel,'" *Jahrbuch des Historischen Vereins des Kantons Glarus* 69 (1982) 47–240; P. Ochsenbein and K. Schmucki, *Bibliophiles Sammeln und historisches Forschen. Der Schweizer Polyhistor Ae. T. (1505–72) und sein Nachlass in der Stiftsbibliothek St. Gallen* (St. Gallen, 1991).

MARKUS RIES

■ **Additional Literature:** K. Koller-Weiss et al., eds., *A. T. und seine Zeit* (Basle, 2002).

Tyndale, *William.* English translator of the Bible and Reformer, born 1494 (?) in Gloucestershire, died October 6, 1536 in Vivorde near Brussels. He produced the first English translation of the New Testament (1525) and the Old (from 1530 onward) from the original languages.

■ **Works:** H. Walter, ed., *W. T.* (Cambridge, 1848–50); S. L. Greenslade, ed., *The Work of W. T.* (London and Glasgow, 1938); G. E. Duffield, ed., *The Work of W. T.* (Appleford, 1964); D. Daniell, ed., *T.'s New Testament* (New Haven and London, 1989); idem, ed., *T.'s Old Testament* (New Haven and London, 1992); A. M. O'Donnell, ed., *The Independent Works of W. T.,* vol. 1ff. (Washington, 2000ff.).

■ **Literature:** D. Daniell, *W. T.* (New Haven and London, 1994); J. T. Day et al., eds., *Word, Church, and State* (Washington, 1998).

CHRISTOPH HEIL

■ **Additional Bibliography:** P. Collinson, "W. T. and the Course of the English Reformation," *Reformation* 1 (1996) 72–97; C. P. Thiede, "T. and the European Reformation," *Reformation* 2 (1997) 283–300; B. Moynahan, *W. T.—If God Spare My Life* (London, 2002); idem, *God's Bestseller: W. T., Thomas More, and the Writing of the English Bible* (New York, 2003).

U

Ubiquity, doctrine. Martin Luther employed this doctrine against Huldrych Zwingli in the → eucharistic controversy, as the christological foundation of his assertion of the genuine and bodily presence of Christ in the Lord's Supper: since the human nature of Christ shares in the divine characteristics of the Logos, it follows that he can be bodily present in his human nature in every place (Latin: *ubique*) where the Lord's Supper is received (cf. *Vom Abendmahl Christi, Bekenntnis,* WA 26:326,29-343,34). The Formula of → Concord proclaimed this bodily presence of Christ as binding doctrine, and condemned contrary doctrinal positions (*Solida Declaratio* 7:55, *BSLK* 989:41ff.; 7:117f., *BSLK* 1113:1-13). The doctrine of ubiquity is however more than just a "theory about the Lord's Supper." It must be seen in the context of Luther's Christology as a whole: "I need to know a place where I find God and all things." This "place" is the Son of God, who has become a human person: in his humanity, God is found (Martensen).

■ *LThK*³ 10:340 (unabridged version).

■ **Literature:** *LThK*² 10:442ff. (H. L. Martensen); *EKL*³ 4:999ff.—*Lehrverurteilungen—kirchentrennend?,* vol. 1 (Freiburg and Göttingen, 1986) 98–124, 192f.

LOTHAR ULLRICH

Ulrich of Württemberg (duke 1498-1550). Born February 8, 1487 in Reichenweier (Alsace), died November 6, 1550 in Tübingen. He grew up under difficult family circumstances and assumed the reins of government in 1503. In order to crush the peasant revolt of "Poor Konrad" (which was the result of an increasing burden of taxation), Ulrich joined forces with the Estates in his domains, and was compelled in the Treaty of Tübingen (1514) to concede them a considerable say in political business in the duchy. The murder of his aristocratic servant Hans von Hutten and the breakdown of his marriage to Sabina of Bayern in 1511 isolated the duke politically, and he was declared an outlaw. After he attacked the imperial city of Reutlingen, the Swabian League expelled him from his duchy in 1519, and ceded it to → Charles V in compensation for the costs of the war. During his exile in Switzerland, Ulrich embraced the Reformation. In 1534, with the help of Marquis → Philip of Hessen, he succeeded in reconquering Württemberg, and his lands were restored to him as an Austrian fief in the Treaty of Kaaden. Here he introduced the Reformation, with the support of Erhard → Schnepff and

Ambrosius → Blarer, guaranteeing its stability by means of the territorial ordinance of 1536 which established the order of worship and secularized all church property. After the defeat of the → Schmalkaldic League, of which he had been a member, he had to submit to Charles V in 1547; he was obliged to tolerate the Spanish occupation of his domains, and pressure from the emperor forced him to introduce the → Augsburg Interim. When he failed to observe the obligations incumbent upon his fief, King → Ferdinand initiated proceedings against him for felony. This meant that when Ulrich died, the situation of his duchy was unclear and dangerous.

■ **Literature:** L. F. Heyd, *U., Herzog von Württemberg,* 3 vols. (Tübingen, 1841–44); V. Press, "Herzog U. (1498–1550)," in R. Uhland, ed., *900 Jahre Haus Württemberg* (Stuttgart, ³1985) 110–35; F. Brendle, *Dynastie, Reich und Reformation. Die württembergischen Herzöge U. und Christoph, die Habsburger und Frankreich* (Stuttgart, 1998); idem, "Herzog U.—ein verkannter Reformationsfürst?," in S. Hermle, ed., *Reformationsgeschichte Württembergs in Porträts* (Holzgerlingen, 1999) 199–225; V. Leppin, "Theologischer Streit und politische Symbolik. Zu den Anfängen der württembergischen Reformation 1534–38," *ARG* 90 (1999) 159–87.

FRANZ BRENDLE

■ **Additional Literature:** C. Methuen, "Securing the Reformation through Education: The Duke's Scholarship System of Sixteenth-Century Württemberg," *SCJ* 25 (1994) 841–52.

Uniformity, Acts of. This term is applied to four parliamentary laws of 1549, 1552, 1558, and 1662 which ordered the worship of the Anglican Church (→ liturgy). They are based on the supposition that all English subjects were members of the Church of → England which parliament had established. This is why they do not envisage the worship of non-Anglican churches; indeed, these are regarded as infringements of the law.

The Acts of Uniformity provide the basis for the various versions of the *Book of* → *Common Prayer.* They give a brief outline of the changes made in relation to that liturgy which had previously been celebrated in England, then set out the penalties for those who deviate from the worship regulated by law; these extend to lifelong imprisonment. The 1662 Act is still in force, as the legal basis of today's *Book of Common Prayer.*

■ *LThK*³ 10:409 (unabridged version).

■ **Sources:** H. Gee and W. J. Hardy, eds., *Documents Illustrative of English Church History* (London, 1896).
■ **Literature:** G. J. Cuming, *A History of Anglican Liturgy* (London, ²1982); Th. A. Schnitker, *The Church's Worship* (Frankfurt/Main, 1989).

THADDÄUS A. SCHNITKER

■ **Additional Literature:** C. Cross, *The Elizabethan Religious Settlement* (Bangor, 1992).

Urban VII, pope (September 15–27, 1590), formerly *Gianbattista Castagna,* born August 4, 152, in Rome, a member of a noble Genoese family. He studied civil and canon law in Perugia, Padua, and Bologna, where he became doctor in both laws. He was archbishop of Rossano from 1553 to 1573 and took part in the last period of the Council of Trent. He was nuncio in Spain from 1565 to 1572, and patriarch of Venice from 1573 to 1576. He attended the Diet of Pacification at Cologne in 1578-1579, which met to resolve the conflict about Flanders, and he was created cardinal in 1583. Although he was already *papabile* in 1585, he led an existence out of the limelight under → Sixtus V. He was elected in 1590 as the candidate of the Spanish-Tuscan party, but died of malaria only twelve days later.

■ **Sources:** *NBD* III, 2:197–202, 223–370; A. Buffardi, *Nunziature di Venezia 11* (Rome, 1972).
■ **Literature:** *BBKL* 12:928f.; N. Del Re, ed., *Vatikanlexikon* (Augsburg, 1998) 798.—L. Arrighi, *Vita Urbani VII* (Bologna, 1614); L. von Pastor, *Geschichte der Päpste seit dem Ausgang des Mittelalters,* vol. 10 (Freiburg, 1926) 503–18; E. Gracía Hernán, "Urbano VII. Un papa de trece dias," *Hispania sacra* 47 (1995) 561–86.

ALEXANDER KOLLER

Ursinus, *Zacharias.* Reformed theologian, born July 18, 1534 in Breslau, died March 6, 1583 or 1584 in Neustadt (Haardt). After studies under Philipp Melanchthon in Wittenberg (1550-1557) and a journey to Heidelberg, Strasbourg, Basle, Zurich, Geneva, Lyons, and Paris, Ursinus taught in Breslau, where he came under suspicion of → Crypto-Calvinism. He went to Zurich in 1561. He was appointed as head of the Sapientia college in Heidelberg in 1561, and succeeded Caspar → Olevian as professor of theology there in 1562. Poor health forced him to resign from this office in 1568. He is considered the main author of the → Heidelberg catechism, which presents a synthesis of Calvinism and Philippism, and the main writings from his own pen have the same aim. The restoration of Lutheranism in Heidelberg in 1576 led him to move to Neustadt, where he worked as professor of theology and head of the Casimirianum college. His systematic theology belongs in the category of → covenant theology.

■ **Works:** *Augspurgischer Confession, derselben Apologia und Repetition* (Heidelberg, 1566); *Explicationes catecheticae* (Heidelberg, 1598); *Opera theologica*, 3 vols. (Heidelberg, 1612); *Der Heidelberger Katechismus und vier verwandte Katechismen*, ed. A. Lang (Leipzig, 1907).—Letters: "Briefe des Heidelberger Theologen Z. U. aus Heidelberg und Neustadt a.H.," ed. H. Rott, *Neue Heidelberger Jahrbücher* 14 (1906) 39–172.

■ **Literature:** *BBKL* 12:953–60.—K. Sudhoff, *C. Olevianus und Z. U.* (Elberfeld, 1857); E. K. Sturm, *Der junge Z. U.* (Neukirchen-Vluyn, 1972); D. Visser, *Z. U.* (New York, 1983; Kampen, 1991).

WILLEM VAN'T SPIJKER

■ **Additional Literature:** D. Visser, "The Covenant in Z. U.," *SCJ* 18 (1987) 531–44; L. D. Bierma, "Remembering the Sabbath Day: U.'s Exposition of Exodus 20:8–11," in *Biblical Interpretation in the Era of the Reformation*. Festschrift D. C. Steinmetz (Grand Rapids, 1996) 272–91.

Utraquists. This collective term is applied to various tendencies among the Bohemian Reformers in the 16th and 17th centuries who demanded and practiced the reception of the Eucharist under both kinds (Latin: *sub utraque specie*), viz., the Hussites and Calixtines. The noun "utraquism" refers to this demand that the → chalice be administered to the laity.

LOTHAR ULLRICH

V

Vadian (von Watt), *Joachim*. Humanist, mayor of St. Gallen, Reformer, born November 29, 1484 in St. Gallen, where he died April 6, 1551. He began his studies at the university of Vienna in 1501, taking the degree of master of arts in 1509. He became professor of poetics in 1512, and was rector of the university of Vienna in the winter semester of 1516-1517. He took his doctorate in

medicine in 1517 and returned to St. Gallen as municipal doctor in 1518. He became a member of the city council in 1521, and was mayor for several periods between 1526 and 1551. While in Vienna, he edited and wrote commentaries on classical and medieval texts; in St. Gallen, he also wrote biblical commentaries and works of theology, history, and natural history, including the *Große Chronik der Äbte des Klosters St. Gallen* (1529). He was a friend of Huldrych Zwingli, with whom he exchanged correspondence. He supported the diffusion of Reformation treatises and the reading of scripture. Although Konrad → Grebel was his brother-in-law, Vadian was an opponent of the → Baptists. He introduced the Reformation into St. Gallen from 1526 onward, despite the opposition of the abbey in the city, and it was thanks to his moderate policies that the Reformation survived even after the second Peace of Kappel (1531) and the restitution of the monastery to the Catholic party. He was highly respected as a diplomat and humanist, and was president at the second Zurich disputation (1523) and at the religious dialogue in Berne (1528).

■ **Literature:** *RGG*³ 6:1223; *BBKL* 12:1003–13; *Schweizer Lexikon*, vol. 11 (Visp, 1999) 402.—W. Näf, *V. und seine Stadt St. Gallen*, 2 vols. (St. Gallen, 1944–57); D. Demandt, "Die Auseinandersetzungen des Schmalkaldischen Bundes mit Herzog Heinrich dem Jüngeren von Braunschweig im Briefwechsel des St. Galler Reformators V.," *Zwingliana* 22 (1995) 45–66; F. Graf-Stuhlhofer, "V. als Lehrer am Wiener Poetenkolleg," *Zwingliana* 26 (1999) 93–98.—Series: *V.-Studien* 1–16 (St. Gallen, 1945–98).

MARKUS RIES

Valdés, (1) *Alfonso de*. Spanish politician, born c. 1500 in Cuenca, died October 6, 1532 in Vienna. He was a constant companion of → Charles V, and it was he who composed the Latin letters which the emperor sent to Italy and Rome from 1526 onward. His *Diálogo de las cosas ocurridas en Roma* (1529) is a defense of the imperial politics with regard to the → Sack of Rome. He was a friend of → Erasmus of Rotterdam, and supported church reforms. He is the probable author of the *Diálogo de Mercurio y Carón* (1528).

■ **Works:** *Obra completa*, ed. A. Alcalá (Madrid, 1996).
■ **Literature:** *BBKL* 12:1035ff.—G. Bagnatori, *Bulletin Hispanique* 57 (Bordeaux, 1955) 353–74; D. Donald, *A. de V. y su epoca* (Cuenca, 1983).

KLAUS GANZER

■ **Additional Bibliography:** M. Sievernich, "Sünde als Kriegsgrund in der frühen Neuzeit," *Theologie und Philosophie* 71 (1996) 547–65; J. Corbet, "Lutheranism and the Limits of Humanist Dialogue: Erasmus, A. de V. and Thomas More," *Literature and Theology* 17 (2003) 265–80.

(2) *Juan de.* Spanish reformer, twin brother of (1), born c. 1500 in Cuenca, died July 12/20, 1541 in Naples. As a young man in Escalona, he was profoundly influenced by Pedro Ruiz de Alcarez and by Alumbradism. He began his studies in Alcalá in 1526, and the writings of → Erasmus of Rotterdam made a deep impression upon him. In 1529, Valdés composed the *Diálogo de doctrina cristiana,* which moved the Inquisition to begin investigating him; he left for Italy and was chamberlain to → Clement VII in Rome from 1530 to 1534. In the latter year, he moved to Naples, where he became the initiator and center of a circle of well-educated, upper-class clergy and laity who were interested in religion, including Giulia → Gonzaga, Vittoria Colonna, Pietro Martire → Vermigli, Bernardino → Ochino, and Pietro → Carnesecchi. His theology was extremely influential in 16th-century Italy. It drew its inspiration from the Alumbrados and Erasmus, and aimed at church reforms and a deepening of the inner spirituality of the individual. It does not fit into the categories of Protestant theology or of post-Tridentine Catholic theology; rather, it belongs to the sphere of a pre-Tridentine theology which remained open at many points—the kind of theology which we find in many representatives of Italian → "Evangelism."

■ **Collected Works:** *Obras completas,* ed. A. Allcalá, vol. 1ff. (Madrid, 1997ff.).

■ **Principal Works:** *Diálogo de doctrina cristiana* (Alcalá, 1529; new ed., ed. M. Bataillon, Coimbra, 1925; Catalan ed., ed. J. Pérez de Pineda, Barcelona 1994; Italian ed., ed. T. Fanlo y Cortés, Turin, 1991; French ed., ed. Ch. Wagner, Paris, 1995); *Diálogo de la lengua,* ed. C. Barbolani (Madrid, ⁴1990); *Alfabeto cristiano,* ed. M. Firpo (Turin, 1994); *Le cento e dieci divine considerazioni* (Basle, 1550; ed. E. Böhmer, Halle, 1860; Spanish ed., Salamanca, 1975); *Modo che si dee tenere nel'insegnare e predicare il principio della religione christiana* (Rome, 1545).

■ **Literature:** *DSp* 16:122–30; *BBKL* 12:1040–51.—E. Böhmer, *Lives of the Twin Brothers J. and A. V.* (London, 1883); E. Cione, *J. de V. La sua vita e il suo pensiero religioso* (Naples, ²1963); C. Gilly, "J. de V. Übersetzer und Bearbeiter von Luthers Schriften in seinem Dialog de doctrina," *ARG* 74 (1983) 257–305; D. A. Crews, *J. de*

V. and the Imperial Ideology of Charles V (Ann Arbor, Mich., 1984); W. Otto, *J. de V. und die Reformation in Spanien im 16.Jh.* (Frankfurt/Main, 1989); M. Firpo, *Tra Alumbrados e "Spirituali." Studi su J. de V. e il Valdesianesimo nella crisi religiosa del 500 italiano* (Florence, 1990); idem, *Riforma protestante ed eresie nell'Italia del Cinquecento* (Rome and Bari, 1993); F. A. James III, "J. de V. before and after Peter Martyr Vermigli," *ARG* 83 (1992) 180–208; M. Firpo, *Dal sacco di Roma all'Inquisizione. Studi su J. de V. e la Riforma italiana* (Alessandria, 1998).—Bibliography: *BiDi* 9:111–95.

KLAUS GANZER

Valera, *Cipriano de.* Spanish Protestant, born 1532, died 1602 (?). He fled to Geneva in 1557 along with Antonio del → Corro, Casiodoro de → Reina, and others. Subsequently, he studied theology in Cambridge and Oxford, and was pastor in a number of Reformed Spanish parishes in the Netherlands. He became famous above all thanks to his revision of de Reina's translation of the Bible, published in 1602.

■ **Literature:** P. J. Hauben, *Three Spanish Heretics and the Reformation* (Geneva, 1967); A. G. Kinder, "C. de V.," *Diálogo ecuménico* 20 (1985) 165–79; K. Reinhardt, *Bibelkommentare spanischer Autoren,* vol. 2 (Madrid, 1999) 374f.

FERNANDO DOMÍNGUEZ

Vargas y Mexía (Messia, Mejía), *Francisco de.* Lawyer and diplomat, born 1500, died before April 20, 1566 in Sisla near Toledo. Virtually nothing is known of his legal studies and career. → Charles V appointed him legal adviser at the Council of Trent (1542-1545); when he protested in Bologna on January 16, 1548 against the transfer of the council, he was described as *procurator generalis fisci* of the kingdom of Castile (*CT* 6:687). He was Spanish ambassador in Venice from 1552 to 1558. He was offered the post of ambassador to the imperial court in 1559, but did not accept this position; instead, he went as ambassador to Rome, where he exercised considerable influence on the conclave and on the policies of → Pius IV with regard to the council until 1563. However, he fell from the pope's favor because of his abrupt manners, and had to be recalled. His concern for the church sometimes led him to very harsh criticism of the pope's policies with regard to the council; but there was never any doubt about his wide knowledge, which also embraced theological matters, or about his personal integrity.

■ **Works:** *De episcoporum iurisdictione et Pontificis Maximi auctoritate responsum* (Rome, 1563); J. T. de Rocaberti, *Bibliotheca maxima Pontificia*, vol. 11 (Rome, 1698) 519–66; *CT* 13/1:178–82: C. Gutiérrez (1951; see below) 490ff.; Council letters: H. O. Evennett, "The Manuscripts of the Vargas-Granvelle-Correspondence," *JEH* 11 (1960) 219–24; G. Buschbell, *CT* 11; "Berichte aus Rom, 1559–63," *Colección de documentos inéditos para historia de España,* vol. 9 (Madrid, 1846) 81–406; J. I. Döllinger, *Beiträge . . . ,* vol. 1 (Regensburg, 1862) 263–543.

■ **Literature:** *DHEE* 4:2713f. – G. Constant, *Rapport sur une mission scientifique aux archives d'Autriche et d'Espagne* (Paris, 1910) 360–85; L. von Pastor, *Geschichte der Päpste seit dem Ausgang des Mittelalters,* vol. 7 (Freiburg, 1920) 28ff., 241ff., 548ff.; C. Gutiérrez, *Españoles en Trento* (Valladolid, 1951) 478–93; idem, "Nueva documentación tridentina, 1551–52," *AHP* 1 (1963) 179–240; idem, "Memorial de F. de V. sobre reforma (año 1545)," in *Reformata Reformanda.* Festschrift H. Jedin, vol. 1 (Münster, 1965) 531–76; Jedin 1–4, passim.

HUBERT JEDIN

Vatablus (Vatable), *Franciscus.* Greek and Hebrew scholar, born before 1500 in Gamaches (Picardy), died March 16, 1547 in Paris. After studying Greek and Hebrew in Paris and Avignon, he was a collaborator of Jakob → Faber Stapulensis in Paris and Meaux from 1516 onward. He edited texts of classical philosophers, including Aristotle's writings on natural philosophy (Paris, 1518). He became the first Hebrew teacher at the Collège Royal in 1530. An edition of the Bible published under his name in 1545 (and often reprinted) offers the Latin translation of the Old Testament by Leo → Jud, with text-critical notes by Vatablus and other authors inserted by the publisher, Robert Estienne. Vatablus's name was employed in order to obtain permission from the Sorbonne to print the book; nevertheless, it was placed on the Index in 1547. After a revision ordered by the Inquisition, the work was allowed to be published in Spain (Salamanca, 1584).

■ **Literature:** *CEras* 3:379.—D. Barthélemy, *Critique textuelle de l'ancien testament,* vol. 2 (Fribourg, 1986) *34 and *43; G. Bedouelle, *Le temps des réformes et la Bible* (Paris, 1989) 168ff., and passim; F. Domínguez Reboiras, *Gaspar de Grajal* (Münster, 1998) 497–510.

FERNANDO DOMÍNGUEZ

Vega, *Andrés de.* Franciscan (1538), Scotist theologian, born 1498 in Segovia, died September 13/21, 1549 in Salamanca. He studied theology under Francisco de → Vitoria in Salamanca, taking his doctorate in 1537. He was professor of studies of Thomas from 1532 to 1538, and possibly also professor of studies of Scotus; he deputized for Vitoria in 1536-1537. He attended the Council of Trent as the theologian of Cardinal Pedro Pacheco, and took part in the discussions about the Vulgate and above all about justification. When the council was transferred to Bologna, he withdrew to Venice to write his explanation of the Tridentine decree on justification, returning to Spain at the beginning of 1549.

■ **Works:** *Opusculum de iustificatione, gratia et meritis* (Venice, 1546, often reprinted); *Tridentini decreti de iustificatione expositio et defensio libris XV distincta* (Venice, 1548); both works were published together as *De iustificatione doctrina universa,* ed. P. Canisius (Cologne, 1572).

■ **Literature:** *DHEE* 4:2720; *BBKL* 12:1181–84.—S. Horn, *Glaube und Rechtfertigung nach dem Konzilstheologen A. de V.* (Paderborn, 1972).

KLAUS REINHARDT

■ **Additional Bibliography:** A. Galindo García, "La justificación por la fe," in *Ecclesia una.* Festschrift A. Gonzalez Montes (Salamanca, 2000) 379–98.

Vehe, *Michael.* Dominican, born at the close of the 15th century in Biberach (Riss), died April, 1539 in Halle (tomb in the collegiate church). He entered the Dominican monastery in Wimpfen at a young age. He studied theology in Heidelberg, where he taught from 1508 and took his doctorate in theology in 1513. He became prior of the monastery in Heidelberg in 1515. At the provincial chapter in Frankfurt in 1520, he was a member of the commission which attempted to resolve the controversy about Johannes → Reuchlin. He collaborated in the *Refutatio* of the → Confessio Augustana. In 1532, Cardinal → Albrecht of Brandenburg appointed him provost of the "new collegiate church" in Halle. Vehe wrote a number of works against the Reformation teachings. His theological chef d'oeuvre is the *Assertio sacrorum quorundam axiomatum* (Leipzig, 1535), in which he deals with all the controversial subjects relevant to the debates between Catholics and Protestants. His most significant work was the publication of the first German Catholic hymnal with musical notation (*Ein New Gesangsbüchlin Geystlicher Lieder* . . . [Leipzig, 1537; 2nd ed. Mainz, 1567]). Its 52 hymns were an important source on which all later Catholic hymnals drew.

■ **Sources:** *Ein New Gesangbüchlin Geistlicher Lieder. Faksimile der ersten Ausgabe Leipzig 1537, mit einem Geleitwort*, ed. W. Lipphardt (Mainz, 1970).

■ **Literature:** *BBKL* 12:1188f.—W. Bäumker, *Das katholische deutsche Kirchenlied*, vol. 1 (Freiburg, 1886) 124–29; N. Paulus, *Die deutschen Dominikaner im Kampf gegen Luther (1518–36)* (Freiburg, 1903) 215–31; G. Marx, "Das Verständnis vom Messopfer bei M. V.," W. Ernst et al., eds., *Dienst der Vermittlung* (Leipzig, 1977) 249–73; E. Heitmeyer, *Das Gesangbuch von Johann Leisentrit 1567* (St. Ottilien, 1988) 50–57.

PETER EBENBAUER

Vergara, *Juan de.* Humanist and biblical philologist, born September 4, 1492 in Toledo, where he died February 22, 1557. He began his studies in Alcalá in 1509, and began collaboration on the Complutensian Polyglot Bible in 1514. He was appointed cathedral canon in Toledo in 1516, and was secretary to Francisco Ximénez de Cisneros and his successors. He traveled to Flanders in 1520, where he met → Erasmus of Rotterdam; Vergara attempted to mediate between Erasmus and his Spanish opponents, who included Diego López de → Zúñiga. In the course of the Inquisition proceedings against Juan de → Valdés and Bernardino Tovar, Vergara too came under suspicion of heresy, but escaped with only a mild penalty.

■ **Literature:** *DHEE* 4:2737–42; *CEras* 3:384–87; *OER* 4:227f.—C. Gilly, *Spanien und der Basler Buchdruck bis 1600* (Basle, 1985) passim; A. Sáenz-Badillos, *La filología bíblica en los primeros helenistas de Alcalá* (Estella, 1992) 321–65; K. Reinhardt, *Bibelkommentare spanischer Autoren*, vol. 2 (Madrid, 1999) 397f.; L. A. Homza, *Religious Authority in the Spanish Renaissance* (Baltimore and London, 2000) 1–48.

FERNANDO DOMÍNGUEZ

Vergerio, *Pietro Paolo* the Younger. Born 1497/ 1498 in Capodistria (Koper), died October 4, 1565 in Tübingen. After legal studies in Padua, he worked as a lawyer in Verona, Padua, and Venice. He married in 1526; after the death of his wife, he entered church service in 1532. He traveled to Germany in 1535-1536, seeking the approval of the imperial princes for the council which → Paul III planned to hold; in November, 1535, he met Martin Luther in Wittenberg, who made a nega-

tive impression on him. Vergerio was disappointed in Paul III, who appointed him bishop of dioceses with only modest revenues (first Modrus, then Capodistria), and he began to look for new patrons, especially Cardinals Ercole → Gonzaga and Ippolito d'Este; he accompanied the latter to the court of → Francis I of France in 1540. Here he made the acquaintance of Margaret of Navarre, who sympathized with the Reformation doctrine of grace.

After taking part in the religious dialogues of → Worms and → Regensburg, he returned to his diocese, which he now endeavored to reform in keeping with his new convictions. In 1545, the Inquisition began the investigation of charges that he was spreading erroneous teachings, and this led to his condemnation on July 3, 1549. He was deposed from his office as bishop and excommunicated. Immediately before this, however, after appealing in vain to the Council of Trent, Vergerio had fled to Switzerland, where he converted to Protestantism. He was pastor in Vicosoprano (Bergell) from 1550 to 1553; after tensions with the Swiss pastors, he became counselor to Duke → Christoph of Württemberg in Tübingen in the latter year. Until his death, he traveled extensively in support of the Reformation.

He was the first Catholic bishop (and former nuncio) to become a Protestant, and this caused a tremendous sensation. His writings display strong anti-Catholic polemic against the pope and the council. He did not fit unambiguously into any one of the various Reformation movements. Although he was tirelessly active in central Europe, his Protestant propaganda was directed primarily to his own homeland, which was the meeting point of the Italian and the Slavic cultures; he supported the translation of the New Testament into Slovenian by Primus → Truber.

■ **Works:** Inventory of writings in F. Hubert (see below) 261–319; a portion of his work in *Opera*, vol. 1 (Tübingen, 1563); *Iuris civilis scholastici praelectio* (Venice, 1523); *De republica Veneta* (Venice, 1526); *Oratio habenda in funere Altobello Averoldi* (Venice, 1531) in F. Gaeta, ed., *RSCI* 13 (1959) 397–406; *De pace et unitate ecclesiae* (Venice, 1542) in H. Laemmer, ed., *Monumenta Vaticana historiam ecclesiasticam saeculi XVI illustrantia* (Freiburg, 1861) 312–17; "Articoli che sono in controversia da disputarsi in Concilio," *CT* 12 (1930) 431–39; *Lettera al doge Francesco Donà* (Venice, 1545) in A. Stella, ed., *Atti del Istituto Veneto di scienze, lettere ed arti* 128 (1969–70) 1–39; *Storia di Francesco Spiera* (Padua, 1548); *Instruttion christiana* (Poschiavo,

325

1549); *Dodici trattatelli di M. P. P. V.* (Basle, 1550) in E. Comba, ed., *Biblioteca della Riforma,* 2 vols. (Rome, 1883–84); *Ai fratelli d'Italia* (n.p., 1562).

■ **Sources:** E. von Kausler and Th. Schott, *Briefwechsel zwischen Christoph Herzog von Württemberg und P. P. V.* (Tübingen, 1875); G. Capasso, "Nuovi documenti Vergeriani," *Archivio Storico per Trieste, l'Istria e il Trentino* 4 (1889) 207–21; W. Friedensburg, "Eine Streitschrift gegen das Trienter Konzil," *ARG* 8 (1910/11) 323–33; idem, "Vergeriana 1534–50," *ARG* 10 (1912/13) 70–100; *NBD* I/1 (1892); I/2–7 (index); *Bullingers Korrespondenz mit den Graubündnern,* ed. T. Schiess, 3 vols. (Basle, 1904–1906; reprint, Nieuwkoop, 1968); F. Gaeta, *Nunziature di Venezia,* vol. 1 (Rome, 1958) (index); vol. 2 (Rome, 1960) (index); J. Sydow, "Unbekannte Briefe des P.P.V. des Jüngeren im Regensburger Stadtarchiv," *Verhandlungen des Historischen Vereins für Oberpfalz und Regensburg* 99 (1958) 221–29; J. Lestocquoy, *Acta nuntiaturae Gallicae,* vol. 1 (Rome, 1961) (index); *NBD* I/1, suppl. vol. with index (1963); H. D. Wojtyska, *Acta nuntiaturae Polonae,* vol. 3/1 (Rome, 1993) (index).

■ **Literature:** *EC* 12:1263; *DSp* 16:409ff.; *OER* 4:228f.— C. H. Sixt, *P. P. V.* (Braunschweig, 1855; new ed., 1872); F. Hubert, *V.s publizistische Tätigkeit nebst einer bibliographischen Übersicht* (Göttingen, 1893); *HCMA* 3:216, 247; P. Paschini, *P. P. V. il giovane e la sua apostasia* (Rome, 1925); D. Cantimori, *Italienische Häretiker der Spätrenaissance* (Basle, 1949, expanded Italian ed., ed. A. Prosperi, Turin, 1992); *BDG* nn. 21719–741; G. Müller, "P. P. V. in päpstlichen Diensten," *ZKG* 77 (1966) 341–48; A. Jacobson Schutte, *Pier. P. V.* (Geneva, 1977; suppl. Italian ed., Rome, 1988); Jedin vol. 1 s.v.; F. Tomizza, *Il male viene dal Nord* (Milan, 1984); A. Niero, "P. P. V.," in *Istria e Dalmazia,* ed. F. Semi, vol. 1 (Udine, 1991) 173–80; R. A. Pierce, "A. Mainardo, P.P.V., and the Anatomia Missae," *Bibliothèque d'Humanisme et Renaissance* 55 (1993) 25–42; *P. P. V. il Giovane,* ed. U. Rozzo (Udine, 2000); M. A. Overell, "V.'s Anti-Nicodemite Propaganda and England, 1547–58," *JEH* 51 (2000) 296–318.

ALEXANDER KOLLER

■ **Additional Bibliography:** E. Rummel, "V.'s Invective against Erasmus and the Lutherans," *Nederlands archief voor kerkgeschiedenis* 80 (2000) 1–19.

Vermigli, *Pietro Martire* (Petrus Martyr). Augustinian canon (1514-1542), theologian and Reformer, born September 8, 1499 in Florence, died December 12, 1562 in Zurich. He studied in Padua from 1518 to 1526, and held various positions as teacher and in the government in his Order in Vercelli, Bologna, Spoleto, and Naples between 1526 and 1540. Together with Bernardino → Ochino and Juan de → Valdés,

Vermigli studied the writings of the Reformers. Cardinals Gasparo → Contarini and Reginald → Pole helped him avoid a formal accusation on the grounds of the doctrine of purgatory which he preached. He promoted reforms as visitor of his Order and prior in Lucca (1541-1542), *inter alia* through the foundation of an academy; but when he received a summons from the Roman Inquisition, he fled along with Ochino. Vermigli taught Old Testament in Strasbourg from 1542 to 1547; from 1548 until the death of → Edward VI in 1553, he was canon of Christ Church and Regius professor of theology in Oxford. In 1553, he resumed his professorship in Strasbourg. He moved to Zurich in 1556 and remained there until his death. In 1561, he and Theodor → Beza defended the Huguenot position at the religious dialogue of → Poissy. Although Vermigli is best known for his role in controversies about sacramental theology (e.g., against Johannes → Marbach and Stephen → Gardiner), Christology (against Johannes → Brenz), and the doctrine of predestination (e.g., against Theodor → Bibiliander), his primary importance is as an exegete who also drew on rabbinic interpretations of the Bible. His main works include commentaries on Genesis, Judges, the books of Samuel and Kings, Lamentations, Romans, and 1 Corinthians, as well as on the *Nicomachaean Ethics* of Aristotle. The *Loci communes,* compiled from his works by his students after his death (Zurich, 1576; often reprinted), became an influential textbook of Reformed dogmatics.

■ **Collected Works:** *The Political Thought of P. M. V. Selected Texts and Commentary,* ed. R. M. Kingdon (Geneva, 1980); *The P. M. Library,* vols. 1ff. (Kirksville, Mo., 1994ff.)—Catalogue of works: R. M. Kingdon, J. P. Donnelly, and M. W. Anderson, *A Bibliography of the Works of P. M. V.* (Kirksville, Mo., 1990).

■ **Literature:** J. C. McLelland, *The Visible Words of God* (Edinburgh, 1957); P. McNair, *P. M. in Italy* (Oxford, 1967); M. W. Anderson, "P. M.," *A Reformer in Exile (1542–62)* (Nieuwkoop, 1975); S. Corda, "Veritas sacramenti," in *A Study in V.'s Doctrine of the Lord's Supper.* (Zurich, 1975); J. P. Donnelly, *Calvinism and Scholasticism in V.'s Doctrine of Man and Grace* (Leiden, 1976); J. C. McLelland, ed., *P. M. V. and Italian Reform* (Waterloo, Ont., 1980); F. A. James, *P. M. V. and Predestination* (Oxford, 1998).

JOSEPH C. MCLELLAND

■ **Additional Bibliography:** E. Campi, "P. M. V. Europäische Wirkungsfelder eines italienischen Reformators," *Zwingliana* 27 (2000) 29–46; J. A. Löwe, "'The

Bodie and Bloud of Christ Is Not Carnallie and Corporallie in the Bread and Wine': Zwinglian Traits in the Eucharist Theology of P. M. V.," in A. Schindler, ed., *Die Zürcher Reformation* (Bern, 2001) 317–26; E. Campi, ed., *P. M. V.: Humanism, Republiccanism, Reformation* (Geneva, 2002); T. Kirby, "'The Charge of Religion Belongeth unto Princes': P. M. V. on the Unity of Civil and Ecclesiastical Jurisdiction," *ARG* 94 (2003) 161–75.

Villavicencio, *Lorenzo de.* Augustinian hermit (1539), preacher, and theologian, born c. 1520 in Jerez de la Frontera, died February, 1583 or November, 1585 in Madrid. He studied in Louvain from 1552-1558. He became prior in that town and provincial in the Netherlands; he was an agent of the Inquisition in the Netherlands and at the Frankfurt assembly. As a secret agent of → Philip II in Flanders, he exchanged many letters with the king and with the royal secretaries. He was a friend of Josse → Ravesteyn and was involved in the controversy about Michael → Bajus. He made slight corrections to various works of Protestant authors (e.g., Andreas → Hyperius), which he considered important, and published these under his own name, in order that they might not be placed on the Index, but would be available to Catholic readers.

■ **Literature:** *DHEE* 4:2765f.—F. Domínguez Reboiras, *Gaspar de Grajal* (Münster, 1998) 346–51; L. Hell, *Entstehung und Entfaltung der theologischen Enzyklopädie* (Mainz, 1999) 45ff.; K. Reinhardt, *Bibelkommentare spanischer Autoren*, vol. 2 (Madrid, 1999) 407ff.

FERNANDO DOMÍNGUEZ

Viret, *Pierre.* Reformer in the Waadt region, born 1511 in Orbe, died March, 1571 in Orthez. He began his studies at the Collège Montaigu in Paris in 1527, where he became acquainted with Guillaume → Farel. From 1531 onward, he preached in Orbe, Grandson, Payerne, and Geneva against the Catholic confession. He married Elisabeth Turtaz in 1538; she died in 1546, and in the same year he married Sébastienne de la Harpe. He was in contact with Jean Calvin. He was pastor in Lausanne from 1535 to 1539, and taught at the academy in that city from 1537 to 1559. His attempt to introduce a rigid church order met with opposition from Berne, and he was expelled from the Waadt region in 1559; he then worked as a preacher in Geneva from 1559 to 1561. He was

elected as Reformed pastor in Lyons, but he was obliged to flee after becoming involved in conflicts in Vienna and in Orange (1565). Queen Jeanne d'Albret of Navarre appointed him professor of theology at the college of Orthez, which she had founded.

■ **Works:** (selected): *Disputations chrestiennes* (Geneva, 1544); *Instruction chrestienne* (Geneva, 1556); *De la Providence Divine* (Lyons, 1564).

■ **Literature:** *BBKL* 17:1492; *Schweizer Lexikon*, vol. 12 (Visp, 1999) 68f.—G. Bavaud, *Le réformateur P. V.* (Geneva, 1986); M. Campiche, *Le réforme en Pays de Vaud 1528–1619.* (Lausanne, 1985); D. Nauta, *P. V.* (Kampen, 1988); D. Troilo, *P. V. et l'anabaptisme* (Strasbourg, 1993); idem, "L'œuvre de P. V.," *Bulletin de la Société de l'Histoire du Protestantisme Français* 144 (1998) 759–90; B. Roussel, "P. V. en France," *Bulletin de la Société de l'Histoire du Protestantisme Français* 144:803–39; O. Favre, "P. V. et la discipline ecclésiastique," *La Revue reformée* 49 (1998) 55–75.

MARKUS RIES

■ **Additional Literature:** J. M. Berthoud, "P. V. and the Sovereignty of the Word of God over Every Aspect of Reality," in *A Comprehensive Faith.* Festschrift R. J. Rushdoony (San Jose, 1996) 93–106.

Visitation. The earliest recorded visitations were carried out in the 4th century. The few visitations which were carried out in Germany in the late Middle Ages involved the inspection of church finances. Their rarity was due to the secular activities of the German bishops (a result of Ottonian and Salic church politics), to the large number of privileges and exemptions, and to the weak position of the bishops in the empire. It was only as a result of the Reformation that visitations acquired a new importance. The introduction of a new system of church government mostly began with a visitation, which followed the model of the first great visitation in Saxony in 1528, for which Martin Luther wrote the preface and Philipp Melanchthon the guidelines.

The Catholic Church created a new framework for visitations in the Council of Trent, which strengthened the position of the bishops by obligating them to visit their entire diocese annually or biannually, and by removing exemptions: the bishops were now allowed to carry out visitations of exempt persons or regions as "delegates of the Apostolic See" (Session XXIV chs. 3 and 9 *de reformatione*, Session XXI ch. 8 *de reformatione*).

Visitations began in Italy, where Charles → Borromeo, archbishop of Milan, provided the classic example. As they spread beyond Italy, they became one of the most important instruments of the Tridentine reform. In Catholic Germany, visitations began in a cautious manner at the end of the 16th century; in the early 17th century, they were intensified and registered their first successes in correcting abuses in the ministry and lifestyle of the clergy.

■ *LThK*[3] 10:816f. (unabridged version).

■ **Literature:** E. W. Zeeden and H. Molitor, eds., *Die V. im Dienst der kirchlichen Reform* (Münster, [2]1977); P. Th. Lang, "Die Erforschung der frühneuzeitlichen Kirchen-V.," *Rottenburger Jahrbuch für Kirchengeschichte* 16 (1997) 185–94; C. Nubola and A. Turchini, eds., *Le visite pastorali fra storia sociale e storia religiosa d'Europa* (Bologna, 1999); P. Th. Lang, "V.-Protokolle und andere Quellen zur Frömmigkeitsgeschichte," in M. Maurer, ed., *Geschichte und Überlieferung*.

PETER THADDÄUS LANG

Vitoria, *Francisco de.* Dominican (1506), theologian, born 1483 in Burgos (probably of Jewish ancestry), died August 12, 1546 in Salamanca. He studied philosophy and theology in Paris from 1507 to 1512; his most important teachers were Juan de Celaya and Petrus Crockaert. He taught arts in the Dominican monastery of St. Jacques from 1512 to 1516, and theology from 1516 to 1523; in the latter year, he began to teach theology in the monastery of San Gregorio in Valladolid. He held the first professorship of theology at the university of Salamanca from 1526 to 1546. From 1540 onward, illness often prevented him from lecturing, and this led him to decline the invitation to take part in the Council of Trent.

Vitoria had his own vision of the societal function of theology. Whereas contemporary theologians almost exclusively studied the questions thrown up by humanism and the Reformation, he considered these topics of controversial theology as secondary when compared with the cosmological, theological, ethical, and legal questions generated by the new geopolitical situation. He insisted that it was necessary to elaborate fundamental principles in international law, economics, and philosophical anthropology, and it is in these theological boundary areas that his great achievements lay. The first question he studied (in 1535) was the contradiction between God's will that all human persons shall find salvation and the fact that the Christian revelation was not communicated to the New World for many centuries. Later, in 1537, he reacted to accounts of the natural state of life of the peoples discovered in Latin America and to their alleged cannibalism and human sacrifices. Finally, in his two lectures *De indis* and *De iure belli* (1539), he cast serious doubt on the rights of the Spanish crown in the New World. The politically explosive character of these topics delayed the publication of these lectures.

■ *LThK*[3] 10:830f. (unabridged version).

■ **Literature:** U. Horst, "Ekklesiologie und Reform. Voraussetzungen und Bedingungen der kirchlichen Erneuerung nach F. de V.," in *Revista de História das Ideias* 9 (Coimbra 1987) 117–60; F. Castilla Urbano, "F. de V.," in B. Ares et al., eds., *Humanismo y visión del otro en la España moderna* (Madrid, 1992) 13–135; A. Lamacchia, "Le 'Relectiones' di F. de V. e la innovazione filosofico-giuridica nell'università di Salamanca," in idem, ed., *La filosofia nel siglo de oro* (Bari, 1995) 17–118; R. Hernández, *F. de V. Vida y pensamiento internacionalista* (Madrid, 1995); F. Fernández Buey, *La gran perturbación* (Barcelona, 1995).

FERNANDO DOMÍNGUEZ

Vives, *Juan Luis.* Humanist, philosopher, born March 6, 1492 in Valencia, died May 6, 1540 in Bruges. His family had Jewish origins, and his parents fell victims to the Inquisition because of their alleged relapse into Judaism. After studies in Valencia and Paris, he worked as private tutor and scholar in Bruges from 1512 to 1516, at the royal court in Brussels in 1516, and in Louvain from 1518 onward. He taught Latin in Louvain from 1521 to 1523, and was lector at Corpus Christi College in Oxford from 1523 to 1525. He was tutor at the royal court in London from 1526 to 1528. He was in Bruges from 1528 to 1536, and worked from 1537 to 1539 as counselor to the duchess of Nassau, Mencía de Mendoza, in Breda.

He was a friend and admirer of → Erasmus of Rotterdam, who in turn saw Vives as the embodiment of the ideal of the Christian layman. This allows us to appreciate Vives's role as humanist: we may simplify by calling Erasmus the successful *publicist* of Christian humanism and Vives its *thinker*. The encyclopedic breadth and the eclectic and unsystematic character of his thinking make it difficult to get an overview of his writings. Dominant elements in his works are the criticism of philosophy (and of the way in which it was taught) and of common religious sentiments (without discussing the individual theological questions in detail), sketches of a political theory, and contributions to a concept of education. Vives saw the entire life of the human person as dependent on education, but he believed it was wrong to understand education in terms of moral goals, and he held that education should be controlled by the state, not by the church. As a pacifist, he had great hopes of → Charles V, whom he saw as the man who would create a new epoch. Vives was a thinker of genius, who anticipated philosophical postulates of the modern age in his inductive methodology, the way he looked at nature, his critical examination of traditional authorities, and his evaluation of classical sources, as well as in the anthropological and practical orientation of knowledge, which must take into account the continually changing needs of the human person. He looked on the Christian revelation as the source of an ethical code, rather than as a doctrine to be believed.

■ **Works:** *Opera omnia*, 2 vols., ed. N. Episcopius (Basle, 1555); *Opera omnia*, 8 vols., ed. G. Mayans y Siscar (Valencia, 1782–1790; reprint, London, 1964); *Opera omnia*, ed. A. Mestre, vols. 1ff. (Valencia, 1992ff.); *Selected Works of J. L. V.*, ed. C. Matheeussen et al., vols. 1ff. (Leiden, 1987ff.); *Über die Gründe des Verfalls der Künste/De causis corruptarum artium* (Latin-German ed.), ed. E. Hidalgo-Serna (Munich, 1990, with bibliography); *De ratione dicendi, lateinisch-deutsch,* trans. A. Ott (Marburg, 1993).

■ **Literature:** *Handbuch der Geschichte der Philosophie,* ed. W. Totok, vol. 3 (Frankfurt/Main, 1980) 492–99; *CEras* 3:409–13.—C. G. Noreña, *J. L. V.* (The Hague, 1970); A. Buck, ed., *J. L. V.* (Hamburg, 1981); E. González González, *J. L. V.* (Valencia, 1987); A. Fontán, *J. L. V.* (Valencia, 1992); M. Mourelle de Lema, ed., "J. L. V.," in *Actas del simposio* (Valencia, 1992; Madrid, 1993); Ch. Strosetzki, ed., *J. L. V. Sein Werk und seine Bedeutung für Spanien und Deutschland* (Frankfurt/Main, 1995); F. J. Fernández Nieto, A. Melero, and A. Mestre, eds., *L. V. y el humanismo europeo* (Valencia, 1998); J. A. Fernández-Santamaría, "The Theater of Man," *J. L. V. on Society* (Philadelphia, 1998); K. Reinhardt, *Bibelkommentare spanischer Autoren,* vol. 2 (Madrid, 1999) 411ff.

FERNANDO DOMÍNGUEZ

Volpe, *Giovanni Antonio.* Bishop of Como, nuncio in Switzerland, born December 30, 1513 in Como, where he died August 28, 1588. After studies in Pavia, he initially worked as a lawyer and poet. After his ordination, he became vicar general in Como. The pope appointed him bishop of this

see in 1559, and he retained it until his death. He took part in the Council of Trent and supported Catholic reform (education of the clergy, chapter conferences, synods, visitations). He was sent as nuncio to Switzerland (1560-1564, 1565, 1573-1574), where he persuaded the Catholic regions to send Melchior → Lussy and abbot Joachim Eichhorn to the third period of the Council of Trent, and to accept the conciliar decisions. Subsequently, he failed in his attempt to have the Reformed Christians expelled from the territories ruled by the federal government.

■ **Literature:** *Helvetia Sacra,* vol. I/1 (Berne, 1972) 41f.; I/6, 187f.; *BBKL* 12:1591–94.—K. Fry, *G. A. V. Seine erste Nuntiatur in der Schweiz 1560–64* (Basle and Freiburg, 1931); U. Fink, *Die Luzerner Nuntiatur 1586–1873* (Lucerne and Stuttgart, 1997) 37f.

MARKUS RIES

Vorst, *Peter van der.* Born before 1500 in Antwerp, died December 8, 1548 in Worms. He took his doctorate in civil and canon law in Louvain, and accompanied Hadrian of Utrecht (later Pope → Hadrian VI) to Spain and Rome. He was a member of the household of Cardinal Willem van Enkevoirt, canon in Emmerich, and provost of the collegiate church of St. Cassius in Bonn. He was appointed an auditor of the Roman Rota in 1526, and bishop of Acqui in 1534. He was sent as extraordinary nuncio to Germany in 1536-1537, with the aim of persuading the Germans to take part in the ecumenical council which → Paul III had convoked to meet in Mantua, but this invitation was rejected by the Protestant imperial princes in Schmalkalden.

■ **Sources:** F. X. de Ram, "Nonciature de P. V.," *Nouvaux Mémoires d'Académie Royale Belgique* 12 (1839); *CT* 4:42–141.

■ **Literature:** *NDB* I/2, passim; *HCMA* 3:113; L. von Pastor, *Geschichte der Päpste seit dem Ausgang des Mittelalters,* vol. 5 (Freiburg, 1909) 59–67; Jedin 1:255–62.

ALEXANDER KOLLER

W

Waldburg. Princely dynasty (ancestral seat near Ravensburg), which held the hereditary office of imperial high steward (German: *Truchsess*) from

1526 onward and therefore assumed the name "Truchsess von Waldburg."

(1) *Otto.* Cardinal (1544), bishop of Augsburg (hence also known as Otto of Augsburg), born February 25, 1514 in Scheer castle (Saulgau, Württemberg), died April 2, 1573 in Rome. He was a candidate for several canonries (1521 in Constance, 1526 in Augsburg, 1529 in Speyer). He studied in Tübingen, Dôle, Bologna, and Padua, and entered the diplomatic service of the curia in 1537. He served Emperor → Charles V and Pope → Paul III until 1543, *inter alia* at the imperial parliaments in Speyer and Nuremberg, and at the religious dialogues in → Hagenau, → Worms, and → Regensburg. On the recommendation both of the emperor and of the pope, he was elected bishop of Augsburg on March 10, 1543 and ordained priest and bishop in Dillingen at the end of September of that year; he became prince-provost of Ellwangen in 1552. His main goal was the restoration of church unity in the empire by means of a general council. In the Schmalkaldic War (1546-1547), Waldburg supported the emperor; he was rewarded at the imperial parliament in Augsburg in 1548, when Charles restored to him the ecclesiastical property and rights which the church had lost to the city of Augsburg in 1537. Although Waldburg himself disapproved of the → Augsburg Interim, he implemented it with rigor in his diocese. When his ecclesiastical territory was occupied for a time in 1552 during the War of the princes (→ Moritz of Saxony), Waldburg withdrew for a year to Rome. At the imperial parliament in Augsburg in 1555 (Religious Peace of → Augsburg), he protested vigorously against handing over Catholic rights and property.

From this time onward, under the influence of his close friend, Peter → Canisius, Waldburg devoted more attention to reforms within the church. He had already held diocesan synods in 1543 and 1548, and erected a *Collegium literarum* in Dillingen in 1549. He had set up a printing press in 1550 and supported the foundation of the German College in Rome in 1552. Now he appointed Canisius cathedral preacher in Augsburg (1559); in 1563, he entrusted to the Jesuits the faculty in Dillingen, which had been raised to the status of a university in 1551. In 1566, at the imperial parliament in Augsburg, he persuaded the Catholic Estates to reject the Protestant demands, which included a national council. In 1567, he convoked the first post-Tridentine synod on German soil in Dillingen, to adapt Tridentine reforms in the diocese and initiate reforms specific to Augsburg. In 1567, Waldburg was involved in setting up the *Congregatio Germanica,* which was meant to promote Catholic interests in the empire; he himself had become cardinal protector of the German nation in 1557.

He was essentially a Renaissance prince, who lived in great splendor in his court at Dillingen. He encouraged the arts, especially music, and was a patron of the sciences—so generous was his patronage that he incurred debts of 20,000 guilders on behalf of his ecclesiastical territory. These expenditures, as well as the loans he arranged (with the banking house of → Fugger and others), and the foundation of the university of Dillingen led to acute controversies with the cathedral chapter. This led Waldburg to settle in Rome in 1568, a move that did not improve the situation in Augsburg. After his death, he was buried on April 3, 1472 in the German national church of Santa Maria dell'Anima in Rome; his remains were brought to Dillingen in 1614 and interred in the university church there in 1643. Despite his luxurious lifestyle, Waldburg was a reforming bishop who halted the decline of the Catholic Church in the diocese of Augsburg and laid the foundations of the subsequent spiritual renewal in this area, not least by founding the university of Dillingen and entrusting it to the Society of Jesus.

■ **Literature:** *Handbuch der Bayerischen Kirchengeschichte,* ed. W. Brandmüller, vol. 2 (St. Ottilien, 1993).—F. Zoepfl, *Das Bistum Augsburg und seine Bischöfe im Reformationsjahrhundert* (Munich and Augsburg, 1969) 173–463; A. Layer, "Musikpflege am Hofe der Fürstbischöfe von Augsburg," *Jahrbuch des Vereins für Augsburger Bistumsgeschichte* 10 (1974) 201–8; M. B. Rössner, *Konrad Braun, ein katholischer Jurist . . . und Kirchenreformer im konfessionellen Zeitalter* (Münster, 1991); A. Schmid, "Humanistenbischöfe, Untersuchungen zum vortridentinischen Episkopat in Deutschland," *RQ* 87 (1992) 159–92; E. Gatz, ed., *Die Bischöfe des Heiligen Römischen Reiches 1448–1648* (Berlin, 1996) 707–10; J. Oswald and P. Rummel, eds., *Petrus Canisius, Reformer der Kirche* (Augsburg, 1996).

PETER RUMMEL

(2) *Gebhard.* Archbishop of Cologne, nephew of (1), born November 10, 1547 in Heiligenberg

(Baden) in the Trauchburg line of his family, died May 31, 1601 in Strasbourg. After studies in Dillingen, Ingolstadt, Louvain, and Perugia, he acquired several cathedral benefices (Augsburg, Cologne, Strasbourg). He was elected archbishop of Cologne, succeeding Salentin von Isenburg, who had retired in 1577; he narrowly defeated his rival, → Ernest of Bavaria, who was the imperial, Spanish, and papal favorite. Although he was a man who sought to mediate between the religious factions, he initially emphasized his Catholic convictions; he was ordained priest in 1578 and made the Tridentine profession of faith. Roughly at the same time as he received papal confirmation of his election, in 1580, Waldburg began an affair with Agnes von Mansfeld, a Protestant canoness whom he married in 1583, after he had publicly broken with the pope in 1582. The Protestant cathedral canons forced Waldburg to convert to Protestantism, and he then attempted to introduce the Reformation into Cologne and to secularize ecclesiastical property. This infringement of his electoral capitulation, of the → Ecclesiastical reservation, and of the agreements which regulated these matters in the Rhineland, prompted a reaction on the part of Bavaria, Spain, and the emperor, who feared that the Catholic party in the northwestern regions of the empire, which was already unstable, would now be exposed to grave danger. After Waldburg was deposed, excommunicated, and declared an outlaw (1583), Ernest of Bavaria was elected archbishop. The ensuing "War of Cologne," a lesser theater of war parallel to the war of liberation in the Netherlands, lasted six years, and inflicted terrible devastations on the ecclesiastical territory and on Westphalia, until Ernest succeeded in defeating Walburg and the troops of the electoral Palatinate and the Netherlands in 1589. His victory established a permanent Bavarian secundogeniture in the archbishopric of Cologne. Waldburg moved to Strasbourg, where he died as Protestant dean of the cathedral in 1601; it is probable that he died childless.

■ **Literature:** M. Lossen, *Der Kölnische Krieg*, 2 vols. (Gotha, 1882–97); idem, "Römische Nuntiaturberichte als Quellen zur Geschichte des Kölnischen Krieges," *Historische Zeitschrift* 75 (1895) 1–18; J. Hansen, "Der Informativprozess De vita et moribus des Kölner Erzbischofs G. Truchsess," *Mitteilungen des Kölner Stadtarchivs* 20 (1892) 39–66; G. von Lojewski, *Bayerns Weg nach Köln* (Bonn, 1962); B. Garbe, "Reformmassnahmen und Formen der katholischen Erneuerung

in der Erzdiözese Köln (1555–1648)," *Jahrbuch des Kölnischen Geschichtsvereins* 47 (1976) 136–77; A. Klein, "Die Kölner Kirche im Zeitalter der Glaubensspaltung und der katholischen Erneuerung," *Almanach für das Erzbistum Köln* 2 (1982) 334–406; B. Roberg, "Der Kölnische Krieg in der deutschen und europäischen Geschichte," *Godesberger Heimatblätter* 21 (1983) 37–50; K. Repgen, "Der Bischof zwischen Reformation, katholischer Reform und Konfessionsbildung," in *Der Bischof in seiner Zeit.* Festschrift J. Höffner (Cologne, 1986) 245–314; A. Schröer, *Die Kirche in Westfalen im Zeichen der Erneuerung (1555–1648),* vol. 1 (Münster, 1986) 220ff.; E. Gatz, ed., *Die Bischöfe des Heiligen Römischen Reiches 1448–1648* (Berlin, 1996) 705ff.

MATTHIAS ASCHE

■ **Additional Bibliography:** H. Wünsch, "Agnes von Mansfeld (1550–1615)," *Monatshefte für evangelische Kirchengeschichte des Rheinlandes* 47/48 (1998/99) 247–58.

Waldeck, *Count Franz von.* Born 1491, died July 15, 1533 in Wolbeck castle near Münster (tomb in Münster cathedral). He studied in Erfurt and Leipzig, and became a cathedral canon in Cologne in 1510, subsequently also acquiring canonries in Trier and Paderborn; he was a member of the collegiate chapter of St. Victor's in Mainz and provost of St. Alexander's in Einbeck. He became bishop of Minden in 1531. On July 1, 1532, he was elected bishop of Münster by the cathedral chapter; ten days later, he was also elected bishop of Osnabrück. He was ordained priest on December 28, 1540, and bishop on January 1, 1541.

Despite his Lutheran leanings, Waldeck accepted the obligation in his electoral capitulation with the cathedral chapter of Münster to protect the Catholic faith in this diocese and to suppress Lutheran teaching. Six months after he had received papal confirmation, he bowed to the influence of → Philip of Hessen and permitted the municipal council of Münster "to possess without disturbance the Word of God and to preach it in the six parish churches." In 1535, he allowed Hermann → Bonnus to introduce a Lutheran church order in Osnabrück too. In the same year, he freed Münster from the violent rule of the → Baptists and restored the churches of the city to Catholic worship. He received the Lutheran Lord's Supper before his death.

■ **Literature:** H. J. Behr, "F. von W.," *Westfälische Lebensbilder* 14 (1987) 38–62; A. Schröer, "Die Bischöfe von Münster," *Das Bistum Münster,* vol. 1, ed. W.

Thissen (Münster, 1993) 190ff.; E. Gatz, ed., *Die Bischöfe des Heiligen Römischen Reiches 1448–1648* (Berlin, 1996) 190ff.; H. J. Behr, *F. von W.*, 2 vols. (Münster, 1996–98).

ALOIS SCHRÖER

Walter, *Johann.* Cantor and composer, born 1496 in Kahla (Thuringia), died March 25, 1570 in Torgau (Elbe). He embraced Martin Luther's Reformation at an early age and became Luther's closest musical collaborator. From 1521 onward, he was a member of the court chapel of the elector of Saxony in Altenburg, and later in Torgau, where he was the first to found a secular city choir. He directed the music in the court chapel in Dresden from 1548 to 1554. His main achievement is the foundation and early consolidation of a body of Protestant German church music (→ Music and Reformation). He edited the *Geystliche gesangk Buchleyn,* with arrangements of Protestant hymns for several voices, which played a central role in this process; it had a foreword by Luther and went through many editions in Wittenberg between 1524 and 1551; a facsimile of the 1525 edition was published at Kassel in 1979. The history of the German Protestant settings of the passion begins with Walter.

■ **Works:** *Gesamtausgabe,* ed. O. Schröder et al., 6 vols. (Kassel, 1943–73).
■ **Literature:** *Die Musik in Geschichte und Gegenwart,* ed. F. Blume, vol. 14 (Kassel, 1968) 192–201; *The New Grove Dictionary of Music and Musicians,* ed. S. Sadie, vol. 20 (London, 1980) 188f.—H. Otto, "Luthers Kantor. Zum 500. Geburtstag von J. W.," *Lutherische Beiträge* 1 (1996) 228–33; J. Stalmann, "Musik beim Evangelium. Gedanke und Gestalt einer protestantischen Kirchenmusik im Leben und Schaffen von J. W.," *Musik und Kirche* 66 (1996) 356–61; A. Brinzing, "J. W. und der Streit um Luthers Erbe," *Musik und Kirche* 66:362–70; A. Schneiderheinze, *J. W. und die Musik der Reformation* (Torgau, 1996).

GÜNTHER MASSENKEIL

Wanner (Wannius, Vannius, Vanius), *Johannes.* Protestant theologian and Reformer, born in Kaufbeuren (?), died 1529 in Memmingen. His family probably came from Munderkingen. He registered at the university of Tübingen (?) in 1495. He was preacher in Kaufbeuren and parish priest in Mindelheim from 1520 to 1522; he was appointed preacher at the Minster in Constance on March 3, 1522, and soon became a supporter of the Reformation movement. He became acquainted with Huldrych Zwingli in Zurich in 1522; in 1524, he was dismissed from office by the bishop.—He was appointed preacher at St. Stephen's church, and married a former Cistercian nun in 1525. Wanner took part in disputations and preached in various towns in Swabia in 1525-1526. He received his final charge at Our Lady's church in Memmingen in 1527.

■ **Principal Works:** *Ministorium Verbi Apud Constanciam Ad P. Anthonium Pyrata, Vicarium Fratru Dominici caliu Epistola* (Basle, 1524, with J. Windner).
■ **Literature:** *BBKL* 13:329f.—F. Zoepfl, *Memminger Geschichtsblatt* 7 (1927) 9–14; K. Alt, *Reformation und Gegenreformation in der freien Reichsstadt Kaufbeuren* (Munich, 1932); B. Kroemer, *Die Einführung der Reformation in Memmingen* (Memmingen, 1981).

STEFAN SIEMONS

Warham, *William.* Archbishop of Canterbury, born c. 1456 in Church Oakley (Hampshire), died August 22, 1532 in Hackington near Canterbury. He was educated in Winchester and studied at New College in Oxford, becoming a fellow of his college in 1475. After taking his doctorate, he moved to London in 1488 and worked at the Court of Arches. He became principal of the School of Civil Law in Oxford (1490), precentor in Wells (1493), Master of the Rolls (1494), and archdeacon of Huntingdon (1496); he was appointed bishop of London in 1502, archbishop of Canterbury in 1503, and lord chancellor in 1504. From then onward, he played a leading role in all matters of national importance. He arranged a marriage between King Henry VII and Margaret of Savoy in 1506 (which however did not take place). He became chancellor of Oxford University in 1506. In 1509, Warham crowned → Henry VIII and Catharine of Aragon.

After Thomas → Wolsey was appointed papal legate in 1518, the two men clashed increasingly in public, although their personal relationship remained friendly. Wolsey drew on Warham's expertise in 1527, during his secret investigation of the validity of the king's marriage; subsequently, Warham was chairman of the legal advisers to the queen, but he did not give her any support. In 1530, he was a signatory to the petition which asked the pope to allow the king to divorce Catharine; it is possible that this signature was a response to the king's threat to destroy all the ecclesiastical authority in England if the clergy refused to follow his wishes. When the English clergy was compelled to acknowledge Henry as "head of the church" in 1531, Warham added the clause: "as far as the law of Christ allows." In 1532, he made a formal (but fruitless) protest against all the laws of parliament which undermined the authority of the pope. Warham was a generous patron, who gave support above all to scholars such as → Erasmus of Rotterdam; his attitude towards the Reformation was negative.

■ **Literature:** *DNB* 59:378–83; *LMA* 8:2048f.; *BBKL* 13:356ff.—*Archaeologica Cantiana* 1 (1858) 9–41; 2 (1859) 149–74, esp. 149–52; W. F. Hook, *Lives of the Archbishops of Canterbury*, vol. 6 (London, 1888) 155–421; F. R. H. Du Boulay, "Calendar of W.'s Canterbury demesne leases, 1503–32," in idem, ed., *Documents Illustrative of Medieval Kentish Society* (Maidstone, 1964) 266–97; K. L. Wood-Legh, *Kentish Visitations of Archbishop W. W. and his Deputies, 1511–12* (Maidstone, 1984); P. Gwyn, *The King's Cardinal. Rise and Fall of Thomas Wolsey* (London, 1992); F. L. Clark, *W. W.* (Otford, 1993); N. Tanner, *Kent Heresy Proceedings* (Maidstone, 1997).

CHARLES BURNS

Weigel, *Valentin.* Lutheran pastor and mystical-speculative thinker, born 1533 in Grossenhain near Meissen, died June 10, 1588 in Zschopau. In his numerous philosophical, theological, and homiletic writings (first published from 1609 onward), which have their foundations in Reformation theology, Weigel linked ideas of Renaissance humanism, influences from Neoplatonism and medieval mysticism, spiritualistic ideas, and cosmological speculations. The influence he exercised on the Rosicrucians, the Pietists, and German Idealism makes Weigel a key figure in the intellectual history of the early modern period.

■ **Editions:** *Sämtliche Schriften,* ed. W.-E. Peuckert and W. Zeller (Stuttgart and Bad Cannstatt, 1962–78); *Sämtliche Schriften, Neue Edition,* ed. H. Pfefferl (Stuttgart and Bad Cannstatt, 1996ff.).
■ **Literature:** W. Zeller, *Die Schriften V. W.s* (Berlin, 1940; new printing, Vaduz, 1965); H. Pfefferl, "Die Überlieferung der Schriften V. W.s," (dissertation [partial], Marburg, 1992); idem, "Das neue Bild V. W.s—Ketzer oder Kirchenmann?," *Herbergen der Christenheit* 18 (1993/94) 67–79; A. Weeks, *V. W. German Religious Dissenter, Speculative Theorist, and Advocat of Tolerance* (Albany, 2000).

HORST PFEFFERL

■ **Additional Literature:** *V. W.: Selected Spiritual Writings,* trans. and intro. A. Weeks, foreword by R. E. McLaughlin (Mahwah, 2003).

Westphal, *Joachim.* Lutheran theologian, born 1510 in Hamburg, where he died January 16, 1574. He began his studies under Martin Luther and Philipp Melanchthon in Wittenberg in 1529. He studied and lectured in Erfurt, Marburg, and Leipzig. In 1541, he was appointed principal pastor in St. Catharine's church in Hamburg. In 1562, he became temporary third superintendent in Hamburg, and this appointment was made definitive in 1571. He fought to preserve a pure Lutheran doctrine (→ Gnesiolutherans) against Melanchthon and the Philippists, against the emphasis by Georg → Major on the role of good works in the attainment of salvation, against Andreas → Osiander's doctrine of justification, and against the synergists. In the controversy about the descent of Christ to the underworld, he supported the first superintendent in Hamburg, Johannes Aepinus. In the so-called second → eucharistic controversy between the Lutheran and the Reformed parties, he opposed the Calvinists and affirmed the presence of Christ in the Lord's Supper. In his book *Farrago confuseanorum . . .* (1552), he warned against Calvinist and other non-Lutheran understandings of the doctrine of the Lord's Supper.

■ **Works:** *Teufelbücher in Auswahl,* ed. R. Starnbaugh, vol. 3: *J. W. Hoffahrtsteufel* (Berlin, 1973).
■ **Literature:** H. V. Schade, *J. W. und Peter Braubach* (Hamburg, 1981).

ROLF DECOT

■ **Additional Bibliography:** J. N. Tylenda, "Calvin and W.," in *Calvin's Books.* Festschrift P. De Klerk (Heerenveen, 1997) 9–21.

Widmanstetter (Latin: Vidmestadius), *Johann Albrecht von.* Orientalist, born 1506 in Nellingen, died March 28, 1557 in Regensburg (tomb in the cathedral). He studied classical philology, Arabic, Hebrew, and Syriac in Tübingen and above all in Italy. He became secretary of → Clement VII (whom he informed about the Copernican system) in 1533. From 1535 to 1537, he was secretary to Cardinal Nikolaus von → Schönberg. In 1539, he entered the diplomatic service of Duke Ludwig

X of Bavaria-Landshut, whose illegitimate daughter Anna he married in 1542. He worked primarily in Italy for his father-in-law, for Archbishop Ernst of Salzburg (1545-1546), and for Cardinal Otto Truchsess von → Waldburg (1546-1552). He became an honorary citizen of Rome in 1551. He was appointed imperial chancellor of Lower Austria in 1553, and reformed the university of Vienna. After the death of his wife, he became a member of the cathedral chapter in Regensburg in 1556, and was ordained priest in 1557. His achievements in the study of the Syriac language were outstanding: he produced the first edition of the Syriac New Testament (Vienna, 1555). His library forms the basic stock of today's Bavarian national library.

■ Literature: *BBKL* 14:1548ff.—M. Müller, *W.* (Bamberg, 1908); H. Bobzin, *Der Koran im Zeitalter der Reformation* (Stuttgart, 1995) 277–363; *Ausstellungskatalog "Prachtkorane aus tausend Jahren. Ausstellung der Bayerischen Staatsbibliothek"* (Munich, 1998).

MANFRED HEIM

Wied, (1) *Hermann von.* Archbishop (Hermann V) and electoral prince of Cologne (1515-1547), born January 14, 1477 in Wied, the fourth son of Agnes von Virneburg and Count Friedrich zu Wied, died August 15, 1552 in Wied. He was appointed prebendary of the cathedral in Cologne while a small child (1483), and was given a seat in the cathedral chapter on August 24, 1490. He was elected archbishop on March 14, 1515, receiving all the major orders subsequently; he was ordained bishop in 1518. The chapter in Paderborn postulated him as administrator of the diocese on June 13, 1532; at Wied's own wish, Adolf von → Schauenburg was appointed coadjutor in Cologne in 1533.

Wied had received an education in keeping with his aristocratic origins; its intellectual level was modest, and he had not studied theology. He proved one of the most important supporters of the Catholic Church in Germany until 1538. In 1526, he appointed two lawyers as his most important collaborators: Bernhard von Hagen as chancellor and Johann → Gropper as keeper of the Great Seal. His policies entailed important reforms in the regions under his rule, above all thanks to new legal structures. He also crushed the incipient Reformation movements which were active first in the city of Cologne. He gave his sup-

port to the Edict of Worms during the consultations at the imperial parliament in 1521. In 1529, after the imperial parliament in Speyer, the archiepiscopal high court in Cologne condemned Peter Fliedsteden and Adolf → Clarenbach for heresy and passed the death sentence. In 1536, a provincial council gave its approval to reforms proposed by Gropper; according to Franzen, these were the most important pre-Tridentine reforms anywhere in Europe.

After 1538, Wied gradually abandoned these reforming endeavors, and he was the first bishop in the German Roman empire who sought to introduce the Reformation. Initiatives in this direction acquired special force after the imperial resolution in favor of reform in 1541. While Martin → Bucer and the secular Estates in the archiepiscopal territory in the Rhineland supported these measures, they met with vigorous opposition from the cathedral chapter and the archiepiscopal curia, and especially from Gropper. In July 1543, Wied granted the → chalice for the laity. He helped Bucer and Philipp Melanchthon draw up the *Einfältige Bedenken* (Bonn, 1543), which set out a program for the Reformation in Cologne. Although the secular Estates gave their assent to this document, it did not become law in Wied's territory, since the cathedral chapter was allowed to examine it, and they replied at the end of 1543 in a completely negative memorandum penned by Gropper, the "contrary report" (published in Cologne at the beginning of 1544). Bucer replied in his *Bestendige Verantwortung,* and also helped compile the widely used *Bonnisch Gesangbüchlein* (Bonn, 1544).

The Reformation did not win the day in Cologne; both parties sometimes used the churches simultaneously. The controversy generated a flurry of polemical writings on both sides. The cathedral chapter, the clergy of Cologne, and the theologians at the university appealed to the pope and the emperor for support (October 9, 1544), and → Charles V and → Paul III took action to end the conflict. On November 11, 1544, Wied renounced his obedience to the papal jurisdiction. On June 27, 1545, the emperor formally accepted the appeal from Cologne and demanded in a mandate (January 26, 1546) that Wied abolish all his innovations, under penalty of losing his position as feudal ruler; the Roman proceedings ended on April 16, 1546 with Wied's excommunication and deposition (the decree was published on July 3 of that year). The administration of the archdiocese was entrusted to his coadjutor. Wied was informed of this Roman decision on November 3, and appealed on November 8 to a council or an imperial parliament. On December 21, imperial commissioners directed the cities to renounce allegiance to their territorial ruler and summoned a local parliament, which deposed Wied on January 24, 1547 and acknowledged Adolf von Schauenburg as his successor. Wied resigned the see of Cologne on January 25, and Paderborn one day later.

■ **Literature:** *BBKL* 2:756–59; *DHGE* 24:78–81; E. Gatz, ed., *Die Bischöfe des Heiligen Römischen Reiches 1448–1648* (Berlin, 1996) 755–58.—A. Franzen, *Bischof und Reformation* (Münster, 1971); J. F. G. Goeters, "Der katholische H. von W.," *Monatshefte für Evangelische Kirchengeschichte des Rheinlandes* 35 (1986) 1–17; M. B. Rössner, "Zur Entstehungsgeschichte der 'Gegenberichtung' in der Auseinandersetzung um den Reformationsversuch H.s von W.," *Jahrbuch des Kölnischen Geschichtsvereins* 64 (1993) 75–103; M. Wichelhausm "Die erzbischöfliche Denkschrift und der Gegenbericht des Domkapitels zur Kölnischen Reformation 1543," *Jahrbuch des Kölnischen Geschichtsvereins* 64:61–74; H. Molitor, "H. von W. als Reichsfürst und Reformer," in *Recht und Reich im Zeitalter der Reformation.* Festschrift H. Rabe (Frankfurt/Main, 1996) 295–308; K. Repgen, "Der Bischof zwischen Reformation, katholischer Reform und Konfessionsbildung," in idem, *Dreissigjähriger Krieg und Westfälischer Friede* (Paderborn, 1998) 183–259; R. Sommer, *H. von W.* (Cologne, 2000).

FRANZ BOSBACH

(2) *Friedrich von.* Archbishop and electoral prince (Friedrich IV) of Cologne (1562–1567), nephew of (1), born 1518, died December 23, 1568 in Cologne. He was appointed canon in 1537, *chorepiscopus* in 1548, and dean of the cathedral chapter of Cologne in 1558; he held other benefices in Bonn, at St. Gereon's church in Cologne, in Maastricht, and in Utrecht, but never received major orders. An imperial decree entrusted him with the feudal lordship and confirmed his secular jurisdiction in 1566. The pope withheld confirmation of the appointment, since the curia intended to implement the decrees of Trent consistently, and Wied refused to make the requisite profession of faith: he agreed with those imperial princes who considered the oath about questions of faith as an act of submission to the

pope. This fundamental conflict, in addition to disagreements with the cathedral chapter, led to Wied's resignation in 1567. His family background—his uncle Hermann (see [1], above) had been deposed as electoral prince and archbishop of Cologne in 1546 for confessional reasons, and his brother had introduced the Reformation in the county of Wied—and denunciations meant that he was for a time unjustly suspected of heresy. During his period in office, no synods or visitations were held. He was buried in the Dominican church in Cologne; his tomb was later destroyed.

■ **Sources:** *NBD* II vols. 4–6; J. Hansen, *Rheinische Akten zur Geschichte des Jesuitenordens* (Bonn, 1896).

■ **Literature:** *DHGE* 18,1160f.—E. Reimann, *Forschungen zur deutschen Geschichte*, 11:13–19; 13:351–71 (Göttingen, 1871/73); G. Wolf, *Aus Kurköln im 16.Jh.* (Berlin, 1905); R. Schwarz, *Personal- und Amtsdaten* (Cologne, 1914).

HANSGEORG MOLITOR

Wigand, *Johann.* Lutheran theologian, born 1523 in Mansfeld, died October 21, 1587 in Liebemühl (Prussia). He studied in Wittenberg, and was appointed pastor in Mansfeld (1538), then in Magdeburg (1533). He became professor in Jena in 1560, but was dismissed in the following year during the controversy about synergism. He worked as superintendent in Wismar from 1562 to 1568. He was restored to his professorship in the latter year and took part in the religious dialogue in → Altenburg, but was again dismissed from office in 1573. Thereafter, he became professor in Königsberg. He was appointed bishop of Pomesania in 1575, and additionally bishop of Samland in 1577. As a → Gnesiolutheran, he became involved in many theological controversies. He was one of the chief editors of the → Magdeburg Centuries.

■ **Works:** *VD 16* 22:2701–2911.

■ **Literature:** *OER* 4:272f.—H. Scheible, *Die Entstehung der Magdeburger Zenturien* (Gütersloh, 1966); R. Diener, "J. W.," in *Shapes of Religious Tradition in Germany, Switzerland, and Poland 1560–1600*, ed. J. Raitt (New Haven and London, 1981) 19–38.

BRUNO STEIMER

Wild (Ferus), *Johannes.* Franciscan Observant (c. 1515), preacher and exegete, born June 24, c. 1495 in Swabia, died September 8, 1554 in Mainz. He was appointed preacher at the cathedral in Mainz in 1528. He wrote biblical commentaries which were free of theological hair-splitting, and hence were very popular among preachers. His commentaries on John (Mainz, 1550; often reprinted) and on Matthew (Mainz, 1559; often reprinted) were placed on the Index in Paris in 1551 and 1559 respectively, because they allegedly spread Reformation ideas. Miguel de → Medina defended the commentary on John against the attacks by Domingo de → Soto, and published revised versions of Wild's works in Spain, where they became very influential. Although the university of Salamanca had allowed them to be published with only slight changes, they were placed on the Index in Spain and Portugal towards the close of the century. Finally, all of Wild's works were put on the Index in Rome in 1596.

■ **Literature:** N. Paulus, *J. W.* (Cologne, 1893); F. Domínguez Reboiras, *Gaspar de Grajal* (Münster, 1998) 496.

FERNANDO DOMÍNGUEZ

William IV of Bavaria (1508-1550). Born November 13, 1493 in Munich, where he died March 6, 1550. He was the eldest of the three sons of Albrecht IV. Despite the law of primogeniture which had been promulgated in 1506, all three sons demanded a share in government; Ludwig (died 1545) became coruler, in charge of the administration in Landshut, and Ernst became bishop of Passau (1516) and then of Salzburg (1540; died 1560). William married Jakobäa of Baden. His intellectual interests were slight, but his political ambitions were great, and he offered his counselors, especially Leonhard von Eck (who directed his politics), a considerable scope for independent action. Although William did not succeed in achieving his goals of gaining more territory and becoming an imperial elector, the decisions he took had great historical importance. He gave decisive support to the Catholic Church. He crushed Lutherans and → Baptists (religious mandates of 1522, 1524, and 1531) and demanded church reform. He supported the theologian Johannes → Eck, maintained contact with the Roman curia, intervened to help the Catholic confession in Baden, and invited the Jesuits to come to Bavaria (1549). A counterpoint to this position was his constant opposition to Emperor → Charles V and the Habsburgs, e.g., in clashes over

the elections to the crowns of Bohemia and Germany (1526-1531). William also formed political alliances with Protestants, ignoring the religious factor, and his politics led him to oppose the confessional reconciliation at which the emperor aimed. From 1534 onward (Treaty of Linz), and especially after his son married Anna of Austria in 1546, William was on good terms with the emperor and supported him in the Schmalkaldic War, but his opposition flared up again in 1548 (→ Augsburg Interim, imperial league). William's rule was of crucial importance to the survival of the Catholic faith in Germany.

■ **Literature:** *ADB* 42:705–17; *ARCEG* 1–6; *Handbuch der bayerischen Geschichte,* compiled by M. Spindler, ed. A. Kraus, vol. 2 (Munich, ²1988) 322ff.; *Handbuch der Bayerischen Kirchengeschichte,* ed. W. Brandmüller, vol. 2 (St. Ottilien, 1993) 11ff.—S. von Riezler, *Geschichte Bayerns,* vol. 4 (Gotha, 1899) 3ff.; E. Metzger, *Leonhard von Eck* (Munich, 1980); K. Kopfmann, *Die Religionsmandate der bayerischen Herzöge . . . in der frühen Reformationszeit* (Munich, 1999).

WALTER ZIEGLER

■ **Additional Bibliography:** M. Weitlauff, "Die bayerischen Herzöge W. IV. und Ludwig X. und ihre Stellung zur Reformation Martin Luthers," *Beiträge zur altbayerischen Kirchengeschichte* 45 (2000) 59–110.

William I of Orange. Count of Nassau, prince of Orange (1544), born April 24, 1533 in a Lutheran family in Dillenburg, murdered July 10, 1584 in Delft. In 1544, he inherited extensive territories in the Netherlands, but in order to take possession of this inheritance, he had to move to Breda or Brussels and convert to the Catholic faith. → Charles V appointed him commander-in-chief of the Maas army in 1555, and → Philip II made him a member of the council of state for the Netherlands in the same year. In 1559, he became governor of Holland, West Frisia, Seeland, and Utrecht. However, he joined other members of the high nobility in the Netherlands in opposing Philip's absolutist policies (which entailed the loss of ancient privileges on the part of the aristocracy). The fact that the Spanish rule was a foreign government increasingly gave a nationalist character to William's opposition. After the attack on images in 1566 (→ Art and Reformation), he recognized that mere reforms were not enough, and he resolved to take military action; however, he was forced to flee from Duke → Alba to Dillenburg in

1567. After William began to cooperate with the water-→ Geusen, he had his first military successes in 1572, so that he was able to maintain his position as governor. The Pacification of Geneva in 1576 allowed him to extend the revolt to all the provinces in the Netherlands. When the Union of Arras was formed to crush the rebels on January 6, 1579, the seven northern provinces reacted by forming the Union of Utrecht on January 23; this meant in practice that William accepted the division of the Low Countries, and the northern provinces declared their independence from the Spanish crown in 1581. Even after his conversion to → Calvinism in 1573, William consistently pursued a policy of religious tolerance, but this broke down because of the fanaticism of some Calvinists. After Philip II had called for the removal of William—as "a plague in Christendom"—he was assassinated by a fanatical Catholic.

■ **Literature:** *BBKL* 13:1260–64.—H. L. T. de Beaufort, *W. von Oranien* (Berlin, 1956); K. Vetter, *W. von Oranien* (Berlin, 1987); idem, *Am Hofe W.s von Oranien* (Leipzig, 1990); A. P. Bijl, "Een Prince van Oraengien," in *Portret van Willem van Oranje* (Kampen, 1995); H. Klink, *Opstand, politiek en religie bij Willem van Oranje 1559–68* (Heerenveen, 1997).

JENS GRÜHN

Wimpfeling, *Jakob.* Humanist, pedagogue, priest, born July 25, 1450 in Schlettstadt, where he died November 17, 1528. He was a pupil of Ludwig Dringenberg in Schlettstadt, and studied in Freiburg, Erfurt, and Heidelberg. He was rector in Heidelberg in 1481-1482, and took his licentiate in theology in 1496. From 1484 to 1490, he was a curate at the cathedral in Speyer. From 1498 to 1501, he was a humanistic teacher in Heidelberg, and then was mostly in Strasbourg until 1515; after that date, he lived in Schlettstadt. He was a central figure of humanism in the Upper Rhineland, a friend of Johannes → Geiler von Kaysersberg, Sebastian → Brant, Johann Trithemius, and → Erasmus of Rotterdam. He was a collaborator of Christoph von Utenheim (bishop of Basle), and the mentor of Jakob → Sturm. He engaged in debates with Thomas → Murner, Jakob Lochner, and the Augustinian Hermits. His writings on the humanistic reform of teaching (especially his *Adolescentia* [Strasbourg, 1500]) tended increasingly to envisage a reform of the secular clergy (*De integritate* [Strasbourg, 1505]) which united the ideas of John Gerson with humanistic concerns; the same aim is served by his liturgical works, his religious poetry, the *Catalogus episcoporum Argentinensium* (Strasbourg, 1508), and editions of the works of Gerson and of other texts. His history of Germany (*Epithoma rerum Germanicarum* [Strasbourg, 1505]) was a trail-blazing work in conceptual terms. He wrote a memorandum for Maximilian I on the → gravamina against the Roman church. Initially, he took a positive view of Martin Luther, but from 1523-1524 onward, he wrote polemically against him and against the Reformers in Upper Germany.

■ **Principal Works:** E. von Borries, *W. und Murner im Kampf um die ältere Geschichte des Elsasses* (Heidelberg, 1926 [Germania, Latin-German]); *J. W. Opera selecta,* vol. 1: *Adolescentia,* ed. O. Herding (Munich, 1965); vol. 2/1: *J. W.—Beatus Rhenanus, Das Leben des Johannes Geiler von Kaysersberg,* ed. idem (Munich, 1970); vol. 3/1–2: *Briefwechsel,* ed. idem and D. Mertens (Munich, 1990); *Stylpho,* ed. H. C. Schnur (Salzburg, 1971) (Latin-German); B. Singer, *Die Fürstenspiegel in Deutschland im Zeitalter des Humanismus und der Reformation* (Munich, 1981, Agatharchia); C. Sieber-Lehmann and T. Wilhelmi, *In Helvetios—wider die Kuhschweizer* (Berlin, 1998, Ad Helvetios).

■ **Literature:** *BBKL* 13:1358–61; *LMA* 9:222f.—Ch. Schmidt, *Histoire littéraire de l'Alsace,* 2 vols. (Paris, 1879, new printing, 1966); J. Knepper, *J. W.* (Freiburg, 1902, new printing, 1965); F. Rapp, *Réformes et Réformation à Strasbourg* (Strasbourg, 1974); R. Donner, *J. W.s Bemühungen um die Verbesserung der liturgischen Texte* (Mainz, 1976); U. Muhlack, *Geschichtswissenschaft im Humanismus und in der Aufklärung* (Munich, 1991); D. Mertens, "J. W.," in *Humanismus im deutschen Südwesten,* ed. P. G. Schmidt (Sigmaringen, 1993) 35–57; Th. A. Brady, "Protestant Politics," in *Jacob Sturm and the German Reformation* (Atlantic Highlands, N.J., 1995); M. Müller, *Die spätmittelalterliche Bistumsgeschichtsschreibung* (Cologne, 1998) 387–96.

DIETER MERTENS

Wimpina (real name: Koch), *Konrad.* Controversial theologian, born 1460 in Wimpfen, died June 16, 1531 in Amorbach. He began his studies in Leipzig in 1479, taking the degrees of master of arts in 1485 and doctor of theology in 1503. In 1505, he was appointed the first rector of the newly founded university of Frankfurt on the Oder, where he taught theology from 1506 onward. He was involved in the controversies about the Reformation, and especially about Martin Luther, from 1517 on. He was a convinced adherent of scholasticism, with no serious interest in humanism, and sought to defend the Roman Catholic position on the questions of the sacrifice of the Mass, free will, → justification, monastic vows, the priesthood, and the veneration of the → saints. He collaborated in 1530 on the *Confutatio* of the → Confessio Augustana.

■ **Catalogue of Works:** *VD 16* 10:520–23.

■ **Literature:** *KThR* 3:7–117.—J. Negwer, *K. W., ein katholischer Theologe der Reformationszeit* (Breslau, 1909); K. Honselmann, "*W.'s* Druck der Ablassthesen Martin Luthers 1528 (nach einem der 1517 von Luther herausgegebenen Texte) und Luthers frühe Aussagen zur Verbreitung seiner Ablassthesen," *ZKG* 97 (1986) 189–204; D. Fabricius, *Die theologischen Kontroversen in Lüneburg im Zusammenhang mit der Einführung der Reformation* (Lüneburg, 1988).

HERIBERT SMOLINSKY

Winkel (Winckel), *Heinrich.* Lutheran theologian, born 1493 in Wernigerode (Harz), died 1551 in Braunschweig. He became a canon regular in the monastery of Halberstadt in 1507. He began the study of arts in Leipzig in 1511, and returned to Halberstadt after taking his degree; he became prior in 1523. Shortly afterwards, at the request of the city council, he became parish priest of St. Martin's church. After Winkel embraced the Reformation, → Albrecht of Brandenburg deposed him from this office. After studies in Wittenberg and Jena, he was invited to come to Braunschweig in 1528, in order to reorganize church life there. From 1529 onward, he played a key role in the development of Protestant parish structures in Göttingen, Hanover, and Hildesheim. In 1543, he returned to Braunschweig, where he worked as visitor.

■ **Literature:** *ADB* 43:337–41.—E. Jacobs, *H. W. und die Reformation im südlichen Niedersachsen* (Halle, 1896); O. Mörke, *Rat und Bürger in der Reformation* (Hildesheim, 1983).

MICHAEL BECHT

Winzet, *Ninian.* Benedictine, born c. 1518 in Renfrew (Scotland), died September 21, 1592 in Regensburg. He studied theology at the university of Glasgow, and was ordained priest there in 1540. Thereafter, he taught at the grammar school in Linlithgow. When the Reformation was intro-duced into Scotland in 1560, he sought refuge at the court of → Mary Queen of Scots, whose father confessor he became. He attacked the Reformation in resolute and well-argued writings: the *Certane Tractatis for Reformatioun of Doctryne and Maneris* and *The Last Blast of the Trumpet of Godis Worde aganis the usurpit auctoritie of J. Knox* (both published at Edinburgh, 1562). After he escaped from the country in 1562, he continued his fight, first in Antwerp, and then in Paris from 1565 onward. He graduated from the Sorbonne, where he was procurator of the German nation (which included England and Scotland) from 1567 to 1570 and from 1571 to 1573. He spent a short period with the imprisoned Mary Queen of Scots in 1571. He took his master's degree and the licentiate in theology at → Douai, the university of the Catholic emigrants, in 1575-1576. He was a member of the group of English and Scottish emigrants in Rome in 1576-1577, and → Gregory XIII nominated him abbot of the Scottish monastery of St. James in Regensburg. He gave this monastery a new prestige, and continued his debates with the Reformers. His writings show that he was the ablest of John Knox' critics and the most prominent intellectual representative of the Catholic Church in Scotland.

■ **Works:** J. K. Hewison, ed., *Certain tractates,* 2 vols. (Edinburgh, 1888–90).

■ **Literature:** L. Hammermayer, "Deutsche Schottenklöster, schottische Reformation, katholische Reform und Gegenreformation in West- und Mitteleuropa," *Zeitschrift für bayerische Landesgeschichte* 26 (1963) 131–255; C. H. Kuipers, "Quintin Kennedy: Two Eucharistic Tracts" (dissertation, Nimwegen, 1964); M. Dilworth, "N. W. Some New Material," *Innes Review* 24 (1973) 125–32; idem, *The Scots in Franconia. A Century of Monastic Life* (Edinburgh, 1974) 23–31; E. Hochholzer, *Die Benediktinerabteien im Hochstift Würzburg in der Zeit der katholischen Reform 1550–1618* (Neustadt [Aisch], 1988) 168f., 209ff.; L. Hammermayer, "Die 'Schotten-Kongregation,'" *Germania Benedictina,* vol. 1 (Ottobeuren and St. Ottilien, 1999).

LUDWIG HAMMERMAYER

Winzler, *Johann.* Franciscan Observant (1494), born 1477/1478 in Horb (Neckar), died January 13, 1555 in Munich. He defended the Catholic doctrine against the Reformers in his activity as preacher in Weissenburg (Alsace), Lenzfried, Ulm, and other towns between 1520 and 1540. In 1537, he was present at the synod of Salzburg, and in 1540 at the religious dialogue in → Worms. He was a friend and companion of Kaspar → Schatzgeyer, and served as provincial of his Order from 1540 to 1543. Sermons and four controversial letters from his hand survive in manuscripts; Demuth has published some of this material.

■ **Literature:** M. Demuth, "J. W., ein Franziskaner aus der Reformationszeit," *Franziskanische Studien* 4 (1917) 254–94; *Analecta Franciscana*, vol. 8 (Quaracchi, 1946) 848.

LEONHARD LEHMANN

Wittenberg Concord (May 29, 1536). After several years of debates between the Lutherans in northern and central Germany and the southern (or Upper) German Protestant imperial cities, which were more strongly orientated to Huldrych Zwingli, the attempt was made in this profession of faith to establish a common basis for mutually divergent Protestant understandings of the Lord's Supper (→ eucharistic controversy). The Wittenberg Concord was motivated not only by a genuinely religious desire to find a unity in faith which would be faithful to the early church and have a Lutheran accent, but also by the wish of the Protestant imperial cities and sovereign princes to weld the Protestant party into a compact opposition, by forming a united front against the emperor (→ Schmalkaldic League). After it proved impossible to overcome the dissension between Martin Luther and Zwingli, the ablest promoters of Protestant unity, viz., Marquis → Philip of Hessen and the Strasbourg Reformer Martin → Bucer, attempted to persuade at least those Upper Germans who sympathized with Zwingli to unite with the Lutherans, and this was achieved by the Wittenberg Concord. Thanks to Bucer's persistence and to his willingness to make compromises on the disputed question of the Lord's Supper, the concord succeeded in uniting the Upper Germans with the central German Lutherans (the so-called "Wittenbergers") on the basis of a formula which was sufficiently elastic to do justice to the differing views of all the partners, who were able in good conscience to sign the text.

The controversy concerned the "eating" and the participation of "unbelievers" (*impii*) in the Lord's Supper. The final wording could be understood both in terms of a "spiritual eating" (as the Upper Germans held) and in terms of a "real eat-ing" of Christ under the form of bread. The Upper Germans objected to Luther's view that even unbelievers received the Lord in the sacrament (the *manducatio impiorum*), and the Wittenberg Concord toned this down by speaking instead of "unworthy" persons who received the Lord's Supper. This ambiguity did nothing to prevent the Upper German Protestants from being absorbed into Lutheranism over the course of the coming decades (and centuries). The historical importance of the Wittenberg Concord is precisely that it made this absorption possible.

■ **Sources:** M. Bucer, *Opera omnia, Deutsche Schriften*, vol. 6/1: *WK* (1536). *Schriften zur Wittenberger Konkordie* (1534–37) (Gütersloh, 1988).
■ **Literature:** *EKL*[3] 1:18f.; *RGG*[4] 1:24–28.—E. Bizer, "Martin Butzer und der Abendmahlsstreit," *ARG* 35 (1938) 203–37; 36 (1939) 68–87, 14–252. → Eucharistic controversy.

ERNST WALTER ZEEDEN

Witzel, *Georg*. Catholic reformer, born 1501 in Vacha, died February 16, 1573 in Mainz. He studied in Erfurt from 1516 to 1518, and studied briefly in Wittenberg, perhaps in 1520. He was ordained a priest, but after his marriage in 1523, he became a Protestant pastor in Wenigen-Lüpnitz (Thüringen), and later in Niemegk (Saxony). In 1531, he resigned from his parish and returned to Catholicism; in 1533, he was preacher in the Catholic Church of St. Andrew in Eisleben. In 1538, he became counselor to Duke → George of Saxony in Dresden; after the duke died and Saxony embraced Protestantism, Witzel fled. He was given employment by the prince-abbot of Fulda in 1541, and lived from 1554 onward in Mainz, where he wrote expert memoranda for King → Ferdinand.

Witzel saw himself as a pupil of → Erasmus of Rotterdam. Like all the Erasmians, he took a middle position (→ mediating theology) in the conflict between the confessions, and held that Martin Luther's concerns would best be met in a renewed Catholic Church. He formulated this view in memoranda on church unity, in books about the doctrine of justification, in aids for preachers, and in liturgical works; he also put this position forward in imperial parliaments and religious dialogues (Leipzig, 1539; → Regensburg, 1541; Speyer, 1542 [?], 1544; Augsburg, 1547; Regensburg, 1556). He agreed with Georg → Cassander that the decisions of the Council of Trent and the emergence of the Jesuits rendered such a position obsolete. Witzel held that the work of theological mediation between the confessions should look to the early church, and this view influenced both the Helmstedt theology (Georg Calixt) and Hugo Grotius.

■ **Literature:** *KThR* 1:125–32; *CEras* 3:458f.—M. B. Lukens. *G. W. and Sixteenth Century Catholic Reform* (Ann Arbor, 1980); Th. A. Thompson, *The Ecclesiology of G. W.* (Ann Arbor, 1980); Th. Witzel, "G. W. und seine Bemühungen um die Einheit der Kirche," *Fuldaer Geschichtsblätter* 62 (1986) 39–52; B. von Bundschuh, *Das Wormser Religionsgespräch von 1557* (Münster, 1988); M. B. Lukens, "W. and Erasmian Irenicism in the 1530s," *Journal of Theological Studies* n.s. 39 (1988) 134ff.; H. Gelhaus, *Der Streit um Luthers Bibelverdeutschung* (Tübingen, 1989) 57–97 158–67; W. Kathrein, "Ein Reformgutachten G. W.s für Herzog Georg den Bärtigen," *Archiv für mittelrheinische Kirchengeschichte* 44 (1992) 343–79; C. Augustijn, "Der Leipziger Reformationsentwurf (Januar 1539)," in *Martin Bucers deutsche Schriften,* vol. 9/1 (Gütersloh, 1995) 13–22; B. Henze, *Aus Liebe zur Kirche Reform. Die Bemühungen G. W.s um die Kircheneinheit* (Münster, 1995); idem, "Erasmianisch: Die 'Methode,' Konflikte zu lösen? Das Wirken W.s und Cassanders," in *Erasmianism: Idea and Reality,* ed. M. E. H. N. Mout et al. (Amsterdam, 1997) 155–68; idem, "Erwartungen eines Theologen an die Obrigkeit. Der 'Fuldaer' G. W. in seinen Widmungsvorreden," *Archiv für mittelrheinische Kirchengeschichte* 49 (1997) 79–97.

BARBARA HENZE

■ **Literature:** W. Kathrein, ed., *Im Dienst um die Einheit und die Reform der Kirche* (Frankfurt am Main, 2003).

Wolsey, *Thomas.* Cardinal and lord chancellor of England, born 1472/1474 in Ipswich in modest circumstances, died November 29, 1530 in Leicester. He studied in Oxford and was ordained priest in 1498. In 1501, he became domestic chaplain to the archbishop of Canterbury, and was appointed chaplain to Henry VII in 1507. Under his successor, → Henry VIII, Wolsey became a royal counselor (1511). He was appointed bishop of Lincoln and archbishop of York in 1514, cardinal and lord chancellor in 1515, and papal legate in 1518. His main interest was foreign policy. Here he often changed sides, skillfully playing off the empire and France against each other, with the aim of exploiting the balance of power to make England the leading power in Europe. Nevertheless, he was obliged to sign a secret treaty of alliance with Emperor → Charles V in 1521. He was regarded as *papabile* in the conclaves of 1521 and 1523.

The ruthless methods he employed to raise funds for the war against France, his arrogance, and his luxurious lifestyle cost him his popularity and made him many political enemies in England. Wolsey accepted only with reluctance Henry's request that he petition Rome to sanction his divorce from Catharine of Aragon. His lack of success both in this matter and in foreign politics—which became obvious when Charles V and → Francis I signed the Treaty of Cambrai—sealed his fate. In 1529, he confessed that he was guilty of infringing the *Praemunire* statute, since he had appealed to Rome and had accepted Roman decrees without the king's permission. He was then forced to relinquish all his offices, and his considerable fortune was confiscated to the royal treasury; all that remained to Wolsey was his archdiocese, to which he devoted the last months of his life. A denunciation by his Italian physician led to charges of high treason in November, 1530, but he died en route to his trial in London. Of the colleges founded by Wolsey, Cardinal's College (known today as Christ Church) in Oxford still survives. This had been founded out of the revenues from small monasteries which Wolsey had dissolved.

He was more a statesman than a churchman. His sometimes unscrupulous exploitation of his enormous powers was a very important factor in the extension of royal control of the church. In the ensuing period, this was to have fatal consequences for ecclesiastical life in England.

■ **Sources:** U. G. Cavendish, *The Life and Death of Cardinal W.* (1557, reprinted 1641), ed. R. S. Sylvester and D. P. Harding (New Haven, 1973).

■ **Literature:** Ch. W. Ferguson, *Naked to Mine Enemies. The Life of Cardinal W.,* 2 vols. (New York, 1965); N. Williams, *The Cardinal and the Secretary* (London, 1975); J. A. Guy, "The Cardinal's Court," in *The Impact of Th. W. in Star Chamber* (Hassocks [West Sussex], 1977); N. L. Harvey, *Th. Cardinal W.* (New York, 1980); J. Ridley, "Statesman and Saint," in *Cardinal W., Sir Thomas More, and the Politics of Henry VIII* (New York, 1983); P. Gwyn, *The King's Cardinal. The Rise and Fall of Th. W.* (London, 1990); S. J. Gunn and P. G. Lindley, eds., *Cardinal W.* (Cambridge, 1991).

CHARLES BURNS

■ **Additional Bibliography:** R. H. Britnell, "Penitence and Prophecy. George Cavendish on the Last State of Cardinal W.," *JEH* 48 (1997) 263–81.

Worms, religious dialogues

1. October 28, 1540–January 18, 1541.

The Hagenau Resolution of July 28, 1540 stipulated that the religious dialogue which had begun there (→ Hagenau, religious dialogue) was to be resumed in Worms on October 28, with eleven Catholic and eleven Protestant participants representing the imperial Estates, to discuss the → Confessio Augustana and its Apologia. It was only on November 25 that the imperial orator, Nicolas Perrenot de → Granvella, opened the dialogue, together with the four presidents (counselors of the archbishop of Mainz, of the electoral prince of the Palatinate, of the duke of Bavaria, and of the bishop of Strasbourg). The Protestants—Philipp Melanchthon, Andreas → Osiander, Erhard → Schnepf, Martin → Frecht, Johannes → Brenz, Jean Calvin, Wenzeslaus → Linck, Simon → Grynäus, Martin → Bucer, and Wolfgang → Capito—made use of the delay to clarify their position, which Wolfgang → Musculus noted in a memorandum. The Catholic participants included Johannes → Eck, Eberhard → Billick, Johannes → Cochlaeus, Johannes → Fabri, Johann → Gropper, and Friedrich → Nausea. When the memoranda on the Confessio Augustana presented by Brandenburg, the Palatinate, and Jülich took a position close to the Protestant doctrine of justification, and all that Eck managed to present was a majority vote of the other seven Catholic imperial Estates, Granvella organized secret negotiations (December 15-31) between Gropper and Gerhard Veltwyck (for the Catholics) and Bucer and Capito (for the Protestants). These drew up the "Book of Worms" (M. Bucer, *Opera omnia, Deutsche Schriften* 9/1 [Gütersloh, 1995] 328-483), which was based both on Gropper's *Enchiridion christianae religionis* (1538) and on Bucer's commentary on Romans, and served as the basis for the religious dialogue of → Regensburg in 1541. Melanchthon and Eck discussed → original sin (CA 2) from January 13 to 18, 1541. Thereafter, Granvella transferred the religious dialogue to Regensburg.

2. September 11–October 8, 1557.

This religious dialogue was suggested at the imperial parliament in Augsburg in 1555, and decided upon in Regensburg in 1556. The participants were Michael → Helding, Johann → Gropper, and Peter → Canisius (for the Catholics), and

Philipp Melanchthon, Johannes → Brenz, and Erhard → Schnepf (for the Protestants). They began by discussing the relationship between scripture and tradition. The debate broke down when Canisius demonstrated that the Protestants themselves did not agree on the doctrines of → original sin and → justification, and the Protestant theologians present in Worms were unable to resolve their disagreements.

■ **Literature:** *BDG* 4 nn. 538f.; W. H. Neuser, *Die Vorbereitung der Religionsgespräche von Worms und Regensburg 1540/41* (Neukirchen-Vluyn, 1974); M. Hollerbach, *Das Religionsgespräch als Mittel der konfessionellen und politischen Auseinandersetzung im Deutschland des 16.Jh.* (Frankfurt/Main, 1982); B. V. Bundschuh, *Das Wormser Religionsgespräch von 1557. Unter besonderer Berücksichtigung der Kaiserlichen Religionspolitik* (Münster, 1988); V. Ortmann, "Die Tätigkeit M. Bucers bei den Religionsgesprächen in Leipzig, Hagenau, Worms und Regensburg 1540/41" (dissertation, Bonn, 1997).

KARL-HEINZ ZUR MÜHLEN

Worship. On the basis of the doctrine of justification, the Reformation understands worship primarily as God's work for us by means of Word and sacrament, and only secondarily as our work of faith (the sacrifice of praise, thanksgiving, and prayer, and a daily life in accordance with the gospel; cf. Vajta). Martin Luther's definition indicates that the words spoken in worship have the character of a dialogue: "Our dear Lord himself speaks with us through his holy Word, and we then speak with him through prayer and songs of praise" (Torgau, 1544; WA 49:588).

In its principal act of Sunday worship, the Lutheran Reformation adheres to the Western tradition of the Mass, although the canon is radically reduced to the words of institution, followed by the Lord's Prayer and → communion. Matins and Vespers become parish acts of worship consisting primarily of readings, a sermon, and community hymns (*Deutsche Messe*, 1526; WA 19:72ff.).

In Upper Germany and the Reformed regions, the starting point for worship is the sermon-service of the late Middle Ages. The Lord's Supper is celebrated more rarely, but the tradition of the Mass can still be recognized in it.

The Anglican Reformation initially followed the regional Sarum rite in its celebration of the Eucharist (1549), but its structure was completely reshaped in 1552, in keeping with the praxis of Luther and Johannes → Bugenhagen: the words of institution are immediately followed by communion, with an anamnetic formula of administration. The *Book of* → *Common Prayer,* which includes all the acts of worship and rites, also makes Morning and Evening Prayer communal acts of parish → liturgy.

■ *LThK*³ 4:904 (unabridged version).

■ **Literature:** (G.=Gottesdienst, worship) V. Vajta, *Die Theologie des G. bei Luther* (Göttingen, 1952); *Leiturgia. Handbuch des evangelischen G.,* ed. K. F. Müller and W. Blankenburg, 5 vols. (Kassel, 1952–1970); *Handbuch der Liturgik,* ed. H.-Ch. Schmidt-Lauber and K.-H. Bieritz (Leipzig and Göttingen, 1995).

HANS-CHRISTOPH SCHMIDT-LAUBER

■ **Additional Bibliography:** *RGG*⁴ 3:1187–90.—W. Herbst, ed., *Evangelischer Gottesdienst* (Göttingen, ²1992); M. B. Aune, "'A Heart Moved': Philip Melanchthon's Forgotten Truth about Worship," *Lutheran Quarterly* 12 (1998) 395–418; R. M. Kingdon, "The Genevan Revolution in Public Worship," *Princeton Seminary Bulletin* 20 (1999) 264–80.

Wulffer (Wolfer), *Wolfgang.* One of Martin Luther's earliest opponents, born in Schneeberg, died after 1538. He began his studies in Leipzig in 1491, taking the bachelor's degree in civil and canon law. He became municipal secretary in Dresden in 1513. From 1519 onward, he was curate and notary at the castle chapel in Dresden. He was a member of the group of writers against the Reformation, whom Duke → George of Saxony gathered under the leadership of Hieronymus → Emser. Wulffer wrote against the Wittenberg theologians in German, using popular language.

■ **Works:** *Zwei Gedichte gegen Luthers Lehre (1520) und Heirat* (1525); *fünf Streitschriften gegen das allgemeine Priestertum* (1522), *Reformation* (1522), *Ehegebot* (1528), *Verdrehung der Bibel* (n.d.) *und den Eilenburger Schuster Schönichen* (1523); *VD 16* 23:4582ff.

■ **Literature:** *WA* 8:245; *ADB* 44:269.—*Akten und Briefe zur Kirchenpolitk Herzog Georgs von Sachsen,* ed. F. Gess, vol. 1 (Leipzig, 1905) 313; H. Smolinski, *Augustin von Alveldt und Hieronymus Emser* (Münster, 1983) 46, 337f., 344ff., 367ff., 416; *Flugschriften gegen die Reformation (1518–1524),* ed. A. Laube (Berlin, 1997) 28ff., 303.

OTTO SCHEIB

Würtzburg, *Veit* (II). Bishop of Bamberg, born June 15, 1519 in Rothenkirchen castle (Upper Franconia), died July 8, 1577 in Bamberg. He became a canon in the collegiate church of St. Burkard in Würzburg in 1532, in the cathedral of Bamberg in 1535, and in the cathedral of Würzburg in 1536. He studied civil and canon law from 1538 to 1544 at the universities of Heidelberg and Erfurt, which were influenced by the Reformation. He became master of the cathedral school in Bamberg in 1556 and cathedral provost in 1559. He was appointed prince bishop of Bamberg in 1561, and was ordained priest and bishop in 1566. Initially, his lifestyle was not exemplary; he lived in concubinate. However, under the influence of the curia, Würtzburg increasingly came to accept his responsibility as bishop, and became a pioneer of Catholic reform. He was the first bishop of Bamberg to hold visitations; however, his attempts to found a seminary came to nothing. In his capacity as ruler, he consolidated the finances and the administration of the episcopal territory, and built the Old Court.

■ **Literature:** W. Hotzelt, *V. II. von W.* (Freiburg, 1919); Ch. Grebner, *Kaspar Gropper (1514 bis 1594) und Nikolaus Elgard (ca. 1538 bis 1587)* (Münster, 1982); H. Schieber, "Die Vorgeschichte des Bamberger Priesterseminars," in *Seminarium Ernestinum* (Bamberg, 1986) 17–86; D. J. Weiss, "Reform und Modernisierung," *Berichte des Historischen Vereins Bamberg* 134 (1998) 165–87; idem, *Das exemte Bistum Bamberg* (Berlin and New York, 2000) 157–200; E. Gatz, ed., *Die Bischöfe des Heiligen Römischen Reiches 1448–1648* (Berlin, 1996) 764f.

WOLFGANG WEISS

Wyttenbach, *Thomas.* Reformer of Biel, born 1472 in Biel, where he died in 1526. He studied in Tübingen, where his professors included Konrad Summenhart and Paulus Scriptoris. He took the degrees of master of arts in 1500 and bachelor of biblical studies in 1504, and was lecturer on the *Sentences* at the university of Basle from 1505 to 1507. Here, he heard Huldrych Zwingli and Leo → Jud, who left a lasting impression on him. He was rector of the church in Biel from 1507 onward, and took his doctorate in theology in Basle in 1515. From 1515 to 1520, he was also custodian of the chapter of St. Vincent in Berne. His sermons taught the doctrine of Zwingli's Reformation no later than 1523; he lost his ecclesiastical office when he married in 1524. Very little is known about his own doctrine.

■ **Literature:** *RE* 21:574–77; *BBKL* 14:264f.—W. Bourquin, *Die Reformation in Biel: Gedenkschrift zur*

Vierhundertjahrfeier der Bernischen Kirchenreformation (Berne, 1928) 347–85; H. R. Guggisberg, "Jakob Würben von Biel," *Zwingliana* 13 (1969–73) 570–90; K. Tremp-Utz, "Die Chorherren des Kollegiatstifts St. Vinzenz in Bern," *Berner Zeitschrift für Geschichte und Heimatkunde* 46 (1984) 55–110.

ALFRED SCHINDLER

Z

Zanchi, *Girolamo.* Reformed theologian, born February 2, 1516 in Alano near Bergamo, died November 9, 1590 in Heidelberg. He lived as a canon regular in Bergamo from 1531 onward, and in Lucca from 1541. Under the influence of Pietro Martire → Vermigli, his prior in the latter monastery, who introduced him to the writings of Philipp Melanchthon, Heinrich → Bullinger, and Martin → Bucer, Zanchi came to hold Protestant views. After he fled from the Inquisition, he stayed in Graubünden and Geneva, and then taught philosophy and theology in Strasbourg from 1553 to 1563. There, he came into conflict with Johannes → Marbach about the doctrine of the Lord's Supper. After some years as pastor in Graubünden, Zanchi was appointed professor of theology in Heidelberg in 1568; he subsequently became professor in Neustadt (Haardt) in 1576. He was a disciple of Bucer, and is considered, along with Theodor → Beza, as the founder of Reformed orthodoxy.

■ **Works:** *Omnia opera theologica,* 8 vols. (Geneva, 1617–19); *Epistolarium libri duo* (Hannover, 1609).
■ **Literature:** *EKL*[3] 3:1883f.; *OER* 4:305f.; *BBKL* 14:339–43.—J. Moltmann, *Prädestination und Perseveranz* (Neukirchen-Vluyn, 1961) 72–109; O. Gründler, *Die Gotteslehre G. Z.s und ihre Bedeutung für seine Lehre von der Prädestination* (Neukirchen-Vluyn, 1965); W. Van't Spijker, "Bucer als Zeuge Z.s im Strassburger Prädestinationsstreit," *Zwingliana* 19 (1991/92) 327–42; J. L. Farthing, "Foedus evangelicum. Jerôme Z. on the Covenant," *Calvin Theological Journal* 29 (1994) 149–67.

WILLEM VAN'T SPIJKER

Zasius, *Ulrich.* Humanist lawyer, born 1461 in Constance, died November 24, 1535 in Freiburg. After working in his hometown and in Baden (Aargau), he spent most of his life as municipal secretary and professor at the faculty of jurisprudence in Freiburg. He is the main author of the new municipal law promulgated in Freiburg in 1520. Like the rest of his literary works, this bears the imprint of his endeavors to unite German legal tradition and Roman canon law in a practical and convenient way. He was a friend of → Erasmus of Rotterdam and Bonifatius → Amerbach. Initially, he sympathized with Martin Luther's Reformation, above all because this movement fought against scholasticism and ecclesiastical abuses; this is the reason why his writings were placed on the Index. However, he remained a member of the Catholic Church, emphatically acknowledging the papacy and the authority of canon law.

■ **Literature:** *Handwörterbuch zur deutschen Rechtsgeschichte,* vol. 5 (Berlin, 1991) 1612ff.; *BBKL* 14:357ff.—R. von Stintzing, *U. Z.* (Basle, 1857; new printing, Darmstadt, 1961); G. Kisch, *Erasmus und die Jurisprudenz seiner Zeit* (Basle, 1960); idem, *Z. und Reuchlin* (Constance and Stuttgart, 1961); E. Wolf, *Grosse Rechtsdenker der deutschen Geistesgeschichte* (Tübingen, [4]1963) 59–101; F. Wieacker, *Privatrechtsgeschichte der Neuzeit* (Göttingen, [2]1967); H. Thieme, *Ideengeschichte und Rechtsgeschichte. Gesammelte Schriften,* vol. 1 (Cologne and Vienna, 1986) 508–80; S. Rowan, *U. Z. A Jurist in the German Renaissance* (Frankfurt/Main, 1987); K.-F. Schröder, "U. Z.," *Juristische Schulung* 35 (1995) 97–102; G. Kleinheyer and J. Schröder, eds., *Deutsche und europäische Juristen aus neun Jahrhunderten* (Heidelberg, [4]1996) 445–59.

ALEXANDER HOLLERBACH

Zegenhagen (Ziegenhagen), *Johannes.* The first Lutheran chief pastor of Hamburg, born in Magdeburg, died January 17, 1531 in Hamburg. He was pastor of St. Catherine's in Magdeburg in 1524, and it is possible that he already held this position before the Reformation. The jurors of St. Catharine's church in Hamburg appointed him preacher in 1526. Here he at once preached the Reformation doctrine, and was the first in Hamburg to administer the sacrament under both kinds. When the municipal council threatened to forbid his ministry and to expel him from the city, this resulted in riots, and they were forced to yield on this issue. On September 20, 1526, Zegenhagen was elected chief pastor of St. Nicolas's church, where he now took a completely Protestant position on questions such as the Lord's Supper, confession, and priestly celibacy. Together with Stefan Kempe, he played a central role in the gradual introduction of the Reformation into Hamburg; he and others defended the movement successfully in two public disputations (1527, 1528). He followed the Wittenberg model and introduced the church treasury system in 1527. The Reformation in Hamburg was completed by means of Johannes → Bugenhagen's church order in 1529.

■ **Literature:** *BBKL* 14:1586f.—C. H. W. Sillem, *Die Einführung der Reformation in Hamburg* (Halle, 1886); R. Postel, *Die Reformation in Hamburg 1517–26* (Gütersloh, 1986).

ROLF DECOT

Zell, (1) *Matthäus* (Mathis). Protestant pastor, born September 21, 1477 in Kaysersberg, died January 9, 1548 in Strasbourg. He studied in Erfurt (1494), Ingolstadt (1495), and Freiburg (matriculation, 1502; master of arts, 1505; bachelor of the *Sentences,* 1511). He was appointed rector at St. Laurence in Strasbourg in 1517, and pastor of souls at the same church in the following year. He preached the ideas of Martin Luther from 1521 onward, and defended himself in his *Christliche Verantwortung* (printed 1523) against the accusation that he was inciting people to rebel against the church. In 1523, he married Katharina Schütz. He was a popular preacher and played a central role in establishing the Reformation in Strasbourg.

■ **Works:** *VD 16* 22:347–56.

■ **Literature:** *BBKL* 14:383ff.—M. Lienhard, "La percée du mouvement évangélique à Strasbourg: Le rôle et la figure de Matthieu Z. (1477–1548)," in *Strasbourg au cœur religieux du XVIᵉ siècle* (Strasbourg, 1977) 85–98; R. Bornert, *La réforme protestante du culte à Strasbourg au XVIᵉ siècle* (Leiden, 1981); M. Weyer, "Martin Bucer et les Z.: Une solidarité critique," in *Martin Bucer and Sixteenth Century Europe*, ed. Ch. Krieger and M. Lienhard, vol. 1 (Leiden, 1993) 275–95.

(2) *Katharina.* Née Schütz, Protestant theologian, born between July 15, 1497 and July 15, 1498 in Strasbourg, where she died September 5, 1562; wife of (1). She called herself "mother of the church." She received a good education in the house of her highly respected and wealthy parents. She married in 1523, and defended her own marriage and offered a biblical defense of priestly marriage (→ celibacy) in her *Entschuldigung Katharina Schützinn.* The municipal council forbade her to print theological works, and only the

following texts were published: a pamphlet of consolation to the wives of the men who had been expelled from Kenzingen for taking the side of Jakob → Otter; the address at her husband's funeral; and an exposition of Ps 51 with a paraphrase of the Lord's Prayer. She exchanged letters with the → Blarer brothers, Johannes → Brenz, Martin → Bucer, Martin Luther, and others. She compiled a collection of hymns taken from the hymnal of the → Bohemian Brethren. She defended Kaspar von → Schwenckfeld and the "left wing" of the Reformation. In addition to her work as pastor's wife, she took care of refugees, cared for those sick with the plague, and encouraged reforms in the "smallpox house." She defended herself against her husband's successor, Ludwig Rabus, in the autobiographical text *Ein Brieff an die gantze Burgerschafft der Statt Strassburg* (1557).

■ **Sources:** *VD 16* 20:342–46; *K. Schütz Z.*, vol. 2: *The Writings. A Critical Edition*, ed. E. A. McKee (Leiden, 1999).

■ **Literature:** *BiDi* 1:97–125; E. A. McKee, "The Defense of Schwenckfeld, Zwingli, and the Baptists, by K. Schütz Z.," in *Reformiertes Erbe*. Festschrift G. W. Locher, vol. 1 (Zurich, 1992) 245–64; U. Wiethaus, "Female Authority and Religiosity in the Letters of K. Z. and Caritas Pirckheimer," *Mystics Quarterly* 19 (1993) 123–35; E. A. McKee, "Reforming Popular Piety in Sixteenth-Century Strasbourg," in *K. Schütz Z. and Her Hymnbook* (Princeton, N.J., 1994); R. H. Bainton, "K. Z.," in idem, ed., *Frauen der Reformation . . .* (Gütersloh, 1995) 56–83; M. H. Jung, "K. Z. geborene Schütz (1497/98–1562). Eine 'Laientheologin' der Reformationszeit?," *ZKG* 107 (1996) 145–78; Th. Kaufmann, "Pfarrfrau und Publizistin—Das reformatorische 'Amt' der K. Z.," *ZHF* 23 (1996) 169–218; E. A. McKee, "Speaking Out: K. Schütz Z. and the Command to Love One's Neighbor as an Apologia for Defending the Truth," in *Ordenlich und fruchtbar*. Festschrift W. van't Spijker (Leiden, 1997) 9–22; A. Conrad, "'Ein männisch Abrahamisch gemuet,' K. Z. im Kontext der Strassburger Reformationsgeschichte," in *Geschlechterperspektiven. Forschungen zur Frühen Neuzeit*, ed. H. Wunder and G. Engel (Königstein [Taunus], 1998) 120–34; E. A. McKee, *K. Schütz Z.*, vol. 1: *The Life and Thought of a Sixteenth-Century Reformer* (Leiden, 1999).

BARBARA HENZE

■ **Additional Bibliography:** G. Hobbs, "Le cri d'une pierre. La prédication de K. Schuetz-Z. dans son contexte religieux," *Positions luthériennes* 47 (1999) 107–25; M. Obitz, "K. Z.," *Evangelische Theologie* 60 (2000) 371–88.

Zell, *Wilhelm von.* Protestant theologian, born c. 1470 possibly in Zell (near Kaufbeuren), died before September 15, 1541 in Constance. He was acquainted with everyone of importance in southern Germany, and was active in the transmission of information, especially from Huldrych Zwingli (from 1525 onward) and Kaspar von → Schwenckfeld (from c. 1534 on). One who made use of his services was Joachim → Vadian, who wished to refute Schwenckfeld's writings, and got hold of them *via* Johannes → Zwick, in whose house in Constance von Zell lived from July 1539 on. Von Zell took part in the colloquy held in Ulm between Schwenckfeld and Martin → Frecht and others in June, 1534.

■ **Sources:** *Corpus Schwenckfeldianorum,* vols. 4f. and 7 (Leipzig, 1914–26); CR 96:330.

■ **Literature:** B. Moeller, *Johannes Zwick und die Reformation in Konstanz* (Gütersloh, 1961); R. Emmet McLaughlin, *Caspar Schwenckfeld Reluctant Radical. His Life to 1540* (New Haven and London, 1986) 170f.

BARBARA HENZE

Ziegler, *Jakob.* Humanist and theologian, born c. 1470 in Landau (Isar), died 1549 in Passau. He studied in Ingolstadt under Conrad Celtis. While in Moravia, he wrote a treatise against the → Bohemian Brethren. He came to the court of → Leo X in Rome in 1521, but turned into a passionate enemy of the papacy. He embraced Reformation ideas and went to Strasbourg in 1531; however, he clashed with the preachers there and gradually returned to Catholicism. He was appointed professor of theology in Vienna in 1541, and was welcomed as a member of the humanist circle of Prince Bishop Wolfgang von Salm in Passau in 1543. All of Ziegler's numerous writings on mathematics, geography, astronomy, and philological exegesis were placed on the Index.

■ **Literature:** K. Schottenloher, *J. Z. aus Landau an der Isar* (Münster, 1910); K. Stadtwald, *Roman Popes and German Patriots* (Geneva, 1996) 105–36.

ALFRED SCHINDLER

Zobel von Giebelstadt, *Melchior.* Prince bishop of Würzburg (1544), born c. 1500, murdered April 15, 1558 in Würzburg. He studied in Wittenberg (1521), Leipzig, and Mainz (?). He was a candidate for a canonry in 1521, and became a member of

the cathedral chapter in 1532 and dean in 1540; he was ordained priest in 1541. He attempted in vain to re-establish the episcopal jurisdiction in the Protestant territories which belonged to his diocese. The War of the Princes (→ Moritz of Saxony) and the second Margravial War (1553-1554) prevented the Catholic reform measures which Zobel initiated (diocesan synod in 1548, visitations) from bearing lasting fruit.

■ **Literature:** A. Wendehorst, *Das Bistum Würzburg,* part 3 (Berlin and New York, 1978) 109–32; Ch. Bauer, *M. Z.* (Münster, 1998).

CHRISTOPH BAUER

Zúñiga (Stunica), *Diego López de.* Biblical philologist, born before 1490 in Extremadura, died 1530/1531 in Naples. He studied theology and the biblical languages in Salamanca, where his professors included Antonio de Nebrija. In Alcalá, he helped prepare the edition of the New Testament in the Complutensian Polyglot by comparing ancient Latin and Greek manuscripts, and he wrote his first polemical works against Jakob → Faber Stapulensis and → Erasmus of Rotterdam. He moved to Rome in 1522 and continued his campaign against Erasmus and other humanists.

■ **Works:** *Annotationes contra Iacobum Fabrum Stapulensem* (Alcalá, 1519, often reprinted); *Annotationes contra Erasmum Roterodamum in defensionem translationis Novi Testamenti* (Alcalá, 1520, often reprinted); *Erasmi Roterodami blasphemiae et impietates* (Rome, 1522); *Libellus trium illorum voluminum praecursor quibus Erasmicas impietates ac blasphemias redarguit* (Rome, 1522); *Conclusiones principaliter suspectae et scandalosae, quae reperiuntur in libris Erasmi Rot.* (Rome, 1523); *Assertio ecclesiasticae translationis Novi Testamenti a soloecismis quos illi Erasmus Rot. impegerat* (Rome, 1524).

■ **Literature:** *CEras* 3:140–43.—C. Gilly, *Spanien und der Basler Buchdruck bis 1600* (Basle, 1985); E. Rummel, *Erasmus and His Catholic Critics,* vol. 1 (Nieuwkoop, 1989) 144–77; A. Sáenz-Badillos, *La filología bíblica en los primeros helenistas de Alcalá* (Estella, 1992) 197–317; K. Reinhardt, *Bibelkommentare spanischer Autoren,* vol. 2 (Madrid, 1999) 426ff.

FERNANDO DOMÍNGUEZ

Zwick, *Johannes.* Reformer, born c. 1496 in a patrician family in Constance, died October 23, 1542 in Bischofszell. He studied jurisprudence in Freiburg, Bologna, and Basle. Initially, he was close to the humanist circle around → Erasmus of

345

Rotterdam, but he embraced the Reformation after reading Martin Luther, and preached the Protestant doctrine in a parish in Riedlingen from 1522 onward. After he was deposed from office in the aftermath of the → Peasants' War, Zwick returned to the imperial city of Constance, where he was the most important Reformer after Ambrosius → Blarer. His catechetical writings, like the numerous memoranda he composed on questions of theological controversy, reveal him as a pugnacious defender of the Upper German Reformation. He was also active in the work of visitation and preaching outside Constance, especially in Thurgau. As envoy of the city of Constance, he followed his instructions in refusing to sign the → Wittenberg Concord in 1536, although he himself looked favorably on the endeavors to restore church unity. He successfully fought against the membership of Constance in the Swiss alliance in 1539-1540, since he saw this as a threat to the link between Constance and the Schmalkaldic League.

■ **Literature:** B. Moeller, *J. Z. und die Reformation in Konstanz* (Gütersloh, 1961); K. J. Rüetschi, "J. Z. und Heinrich Bullinger in ihren Briefen," *Zwingliana* 18 (1989/91) 337–42.

FRANZ BRENDLE

Zwickau, prophets of. This name was coined by Martin Luther for the cloth-workers *Nikolaus Storch* and *Thomas Drechsel* and the student *Markus Thomae*, who came from the group around Thomas → Müntzer and preached a social revolution marked by religious → enthusiasm. They gave their support to a revolt by the cloth-working apprentices in Zwickau, and when this was crushed, they took part in the riots in Wittenberg at the end of 1521, until Luther put an end to their activities by means of his *Invocavit* sermons in 1522. The prophets of Zwickau rejected infant baptism and every external expression of worship, emphasizing the interior working of the Spirit. They proclaimed a "thousand years' reign of the elect" which would be purged both of priests and of the godless. They appealed to direct divine revelations, dreams, and visions, and conversations with God. Later historians wrongly identified the origins of the → Baptist movement in the milieu around the prophets of Zwickau.

■ **Literature:** *RGG*³ 6:1951; *LThK*² 10:1431.—S. Hoyer, "Radikale Prediger und soziales Umfeld. Bemerkungen zu Th. Müntzers Tätigkeit in Zwickau," in R. Postel, ed., *Reformation und Revolution* (Stuttgart, 1989) 155–69; H. J. Diekmannshenke, *Die Schlagwörter der Radikalen der Reformationszeit (1520–36). Spuren utopischen Bewusstseins* (Frankfurt/Main, 1994); G. Seebass, *Die Reformation und ihre Aussenseiter*, ed. I. Dingel (Göttingen, 1997).

PETER LÜNING

■ **Additional Literature:** O. Kuhr, "The Zwickau Prophets, the Wittenberg Disturbances, and Polemical Historiography," *Mennonite Quarterly Review* 70 (1996) 203–14.

Zwingli, *Huldrych,* theologian and Reformer
1. Life—2. Writings—3. Theology—4. Influence

1. Life

Zwingli was born January 1, 1484 in Wildhaus (Toggenburg) and died October 11, 1531 near Kappel. We have few sources for the period before he came to Zurich, and we know relatively little about his early years, his education, his first years as a priest, and his intellectual development. After studying at the universities of Vienna (1498-1502) and Basle (1502-1506), Zwingli worked as a priest in Glarus (1506-1516) and Einsiedeln (1516-1518). In this period, he devoted himself to the study of scholastic, patristic, and classical works, and came increasingly into contact with humanists. He accompanied mercenary soldiers from Glarus on their campaigns, received an annual pension from the pope, and took part in a pilgrimage to Aachen. His literary and personal encounter with → Erasmus of Rotterdam in 1516 marks a turning point in his biography.

His activity in Zurich is marked by the implementation and spread of the Reformation in the city and throughout Switzerland. On January 1, 1519, Zwingli began his work as pastor of souls at the Great Minster, and at once began to expound biblical texts in a *lectio continua,* presenting the life and work of Jesus as the model for Christians. Over a lengthy period, Zwingli was profoundly influenced by reading the Bible in the original languages, by his study of the church fathers (especially Augustine), and by the events surrounding Martin Luther; but it was only in 1522 that his emphasis on the Bible as the sole basis of doctrine and life in the church and in society (as opposed to the traditional constellation of authorities, viz., scripture, dogma, councils, and the papacy) emerged with full clarity, in the public conflict about fasting regulations, the veneration of the saints, and the monastic way of life. After he had justified his preaching by means of the sixty-seven theses he presented at the First Disputation of Zurich (January 29, 1523), the city council declared that his preaching was in conformity with scripture, and ordered all preachers to observe the same principle. After the Second Disputation about church ornaments and the Mass in October of that year, innovations were gradually introduced: church ornaments were removed (1524; → Art and Reformation), the celebration of the Lord's Supper was introduced (1525), a system of care for the poor and the sick was established (1525), and a court was set up to judge matrimonial cases and questions of morals (1526). Zwingli's followers increasingly questioned the competence of the municipal council in spiritual matters, and this ultimately led to the foundation of the → Baptist community in Zollikon.

Once the Reformation was firmly established in Zurich, Zwingli worked hard to spread it in Switzerland and southern Germany. Berne, Basle, and Schaffhausen accepted the Reformation in 1528-1529, but the introduction of the Reformation in the "common territories," which were subject to the authority of the Confederation as a whole, led to military clashes between the Catholic and the Reformed Estates. The troops from central Switzerland crushed the Zurich forces in the second skirmish, near Kappel, on October 11, 1531, and Zwingli himself died on the battlefield.

2. Writings

Zwingli's literary production spans more than twenty years, but most of his writings come from his Zurich period. He wrote poems, songs, letters, memoranda, and liturgical texts; he revised his sermons and gave them the form of theological treatises; and he justified and defended his faith in voluminous theological works. His early works, *Das Fabelgedicht von Ochsen* (1510) and *Der Labyrinth* (1514/1516), deal with the position of the Swiss confederation in the mercenary military alliances of that time. Many of his theological treatises were originally sermons, which he revised extensively before publication. *Von Erkiesen und Freiheit der Speisen* (1522) demonstrates that the fasting regulations observed in the church are of human origin, so that their validity is limited; *Von Klarheit und Gewissheit des Wortes Gottes* (1522) offers a summary of the fundamental scriptural principle; *Eine Predigt von der reinen Magd Maria* (1522) gives a strictly christological interpretation of the doctrine concerning the Virgin Mary; *Von göttlicher und menschlicher Gerechtigkeit* (1523) defines the relationship between divine and human legislation, and criticizes against this background the current praxis of interest and tithes; *Der Hirt* (1524) deals with the office of the pastor in his parish. *Sermonis de providentia anamnema* (1530), a long monograph in Latin on divine providence which is based on a sermon held at the religious dialogue in Marbach in the presence of Marquis → Philip of Hessen, is a trenchant discussion of central theological questions such as the doctrine of God, anthropology, soteriology, and the Lord's Supper; it maintains a position distinct both from Luther and from Erasmus's defense of the freedom of the human will.

Other theological writings too have their genesis in specific circumstances. The *Apologeticus Archeteles* (1522) is a justification of Zwingli's attitude on trading in the Lenten period, and rejects the authority of the bishop. In *Wer Ursache gebe zu Aufruhr* (1524), Zwingli attacks the peasants' revolts; in *Von der Taufe, von der Wiedertaufe und von der Kindertaufe* (1525), his polemic is directed against the Baptists; in *Eine klare Unterrichtung vom Nachtmahl Christi* (1526), he attacks the doctrine of the real presence and defends his own symbolic view of the sacrament.

His most important dogmatic writings include the *Auslegen und Gründe der Schlussreden* (1523), his lengthiest work, in which he sets out and justifies the sixty-seven theses he had composed for the First Zurich Disputation; the *De vera et falsa religione commentarius* (1525), which presents the foundations of his theology (part I) and the questions raised in controversial theology (part II); the *Fidei ratio* (1530) and the *Christianae fidei expositio* (1531), both of which follow the outline of the Apostles' Creed.

In comparison to Luther and Jean Calvin, only fragments of Zwingli's exegesis survive. The biblical commentaries and translations in the "Zurich Bible" have their origin in the "Prophezei," a circle of canons regular, pastors, and Latin pupils which met on a regular basis to hear the Zurich Reformers read the biblical books in the original languages and provide an exegesis in Latin; the fruits of these sessions were made available to the parishes through sermons in German. Only two of these commentaries (those on Isaiah and Jeremiah) were published by Zwingli himself.

He also wrote a large number of letters. His work as a whole is characterized by humanistic learning, an acute perception of the issues involved in the Reformation, and a clear theological profile.

3. Theology
(a) Dualism

One fundamental trait found throughout Zwingli's theological thinking is the strict distinction between creator and creature, heaven and earth, spirit and flesh, soul and body. This view, born of the influence of Erasmus of Rotterdam and Augustine, is confirmed by Zwingli's reading of relevant texts in the Old Testament (the prophets) and the New (Paul). The creature cannot ever be the bearer of divine salvation. The criterion supplied by this distinction leads Zwingli to offer a harsh criticism of the doctrine, life, and authorities of the traditional → church, which he sees as the work of human beings and indeed as the attribution to the creature of matters pertaining to the creator alone.

(b) Spirit and Word

Only the Word of God possesses authority. The biblical word itself cannot transmit faith: it is God himself who must draw the human person (Jn 6:44) and enlighten him internally by the Holy Spirit, so that he understands the biblical word to be the Word of God, and trusts this word. This means that God is the source of all true knowledge, both of God and of the human person.

(c) God

God is that Being on whom all that exists depends. God is that which is good, movement and life, wisdom, knowledge, and providence, kindness and generosity. Zwingli's emphasis on providence underlines God's sovereignty and the dependence of the human person on God; at the same time, it rejects the freedom of the human will and any merits on the part of the human person. As the highest good, God is perfection and righteousness, and this is what he demands of the human person too.

(d) The Human Person

As a sinner, the human person can never live up to what God demands. Zwingli defines "sin" as an incurable disease which is congenital to the human person after Adam's fall. It consists both in our self-love and in our transgression of the law. This disease of sin explains why we can know neither ourselves nor God, and why fellowship with God is impossible for us—a fact that must lead the human person to despair.

(e) The Event That Brings Salvation

God's address to the fallen Adam is the salvific event in which God bestows salvation on the human person, and the prelude to the salvation which the human race receives in Christ; at the same time, it is the origin and beginning of that "religion" whereby the human person endeavors to come to God.

(f) Jesus Christ

Jesus is the Son of God, who died for us and satisfied the demands of the righteousness of God. Zwingli's understanding of Christ's sacrificial death is marked by the doctrine of satisfaction proposed by Anselm of Canterbury. Zwingli emphasizes the divine nature of Christ, since it is this that guarantees our salvation. At the same time, under the influence of Erasmus, he underlines the role of Jesus as teacher and model.

(g) The Church

Christ is the head of the church, and the believers are its members. On the one hand, the church is catholic and universal, scattered over the whole world, visible to God but invisible to human beings. On the other hand, the church is local, made visible in the individual local community. The church is holy, to the extent that it remains in Christ, but at the same time "mixed," since it includes both believers and unbelievers. Zwingli emphasizes the unity of the church, which is guaranteed by the Holy Spirit. The members of the visible church confess their faith in Christ, participate in the sacraments, and lead a life in keeping with these realities.

(h) The Sacraments

The sacraments accomplish nothing, since salvation depends on God alone. It is God who bestows faith, and external means are not necessary, although God does make use of them.

(i) Baptism

Baptism is the sign of the covenant of grace which God made with Adam, Abraham, and the people of Israel; essentially, this covenant is not different from the covenant in Christ. Baptism gives admittance to this covenant and makes one a member of the ecclesial fellowship, obligating one to lead a Christian life.

(j) The Lord's Supper

In the Lord's Supper, believers recall the one sacrifice of Christ. They give thanks (*eucharistia*) for the redemption he accomplished, bear witness to their fellowship with Christ, and obligate each other to lead worthy lives. The basic reality here is faith in Christ as the Son of God, who is present according to his divine nature, but sits at the right hand of God according to his human nature. Zwingli rejects the bodily presence or the bodily eating of Christ, since "It is the Spirit who makes alive, the flesh is of no avail" (Jn 6:63). He understands the words of institution—"This is my body"—as meaning: "This signifies my body"; the expression to "eat" Christ (Jn 6) means to believe in Christ.

(k) Church and Society

These are virtually identical, since both aim to live in accordance with the will of God. The secular authorities administer human justice, which maintains the external social order, while the church acts in keeping with the interior, divine justice which is in agreement with God's law; human justice finds its criterion in the divine justice. As far as the church is concerned, the secular authorities are competent only in external religious matters. They submit to the Word of God, request the consent of the church, regulate the external course of life in Zurich in keeping with the law of God, and support the preaching of the gospel. Church and society are not two juxtaposed spheres, but one single sphere under the one lordship of God.

■ **Works:** *Sämtliche Werke*, ed. E. Egli et al., 14 vols. (CR 88–101; Berlin, 1905–91); German trans., *Schriften* (selection), ed. Th. Brunnschweiler and S. Lutz, 4 vols. (Zurich, 1995).

■ **Literature:** *Bibliographies*: G. Finsler, *Z.-Bibliographie* (Zurich, 1897); U. Gäbler, *H. Z. im 20.Jh.* (Zurich, 1975)

(bibliography 1897–1972); *Zwingliana* 1–26 (1897–1999) with index 1897–1996 (1997) (annual bibliographies from 1972).—G. W. Locher, *Die Zwinglische Reformation im Rahmen der europäischen Kirchengeschichte* (Göttingen and Zurich, 1979); U. Gäbler, *H. Z. Eine Einführung in sein Leben und sein Werk* (Munich, 1983); W. P. Stephens, *The Theology of H. Z.* (Oxford, 1986); J. V. Pollet, *H. Z. et le zwinglianisme* (Paris, 1988); [W.] P. Stephens, *Z. Einführung in sein Denken* (Zurich, 1997); M. Sallmann, *Zwischen Gott und Mensch. H. Z.s theologischer Denkweg im De vera et falsa religione commentarius (1525)* (Tübingen, 1999); *Die Zürcher Reformation. Ausstrahlungen und Rückwirkungen*, ed. A. Schindler and H. Stickelberger, with the collaboration of M. Sallmann (Berne, 2001).

MARTIN SALLMANN

Zwinglianism. Alongside → Calvinism, Zwinglianism is one of the main roots of the → Reformed tradition. A number of factors determine how this phenomenon is to be described.

1. Problems of Definition

The conflict about fasting regulations, the veneration of the saints, and the monastic way of life led Huldrych → Zwingli, pastor of souls at the Great Minster in Zurich, to break publicly with the Roman church in 1522. In the First Zurich Disputation (January, 1523), the city council judged that Zwingli's work as a preacher was in accordance with scripture, and laid down that all must preach in keeping with the Bible. As a Reformer, Zwingli had to contend with two kinds of opponents. On the one hand, the Catholics disputed his view of the authority and the religious praxis of the traditional church; on the other hand, the → Baptists held different views of baptism and of the authority of the secular rulers, and Martin Luther had a different understanding of the Lord's Supper. All the important writings from Zwingli's pen come from this combative phase of his life, and have therefore an apologetic character. His activity came to an abrupt end when he died a violent death on the battlefield near Kappel in 1531. This was a serious setback to the spread of the Reformation under the leadership of Zurich; the movement which he had begun remained basically limited to the four municipal states of Zurich, Berne, Basle, and Schaffhausen.

Heinrich → Bullinger (1504-1575) had embraced the Reformation independently of Zwingli; he became his friend and theological discussion partner in 1523, and succeeded him at the Great Minster, where he worked for over forty years. Although he supported his predecessor unconditionally, the demands of changing historical circumstances led him to interpret and reshape the inheritance he had accepted from Zwingli.

The definition of the precise substance of "Zwinglianism" depends on our evaluation both of Zwingli and of Bullinger, and of the importance we attach to what each did. Scholars have not yet reached definitive conclusions about the complex transformation process of Zwinglianism during Bullinger's ministry; one sign of this hesitation is the alternative descriptions of the period after Zwingli's death as "late Zwinglianism" (Locher), or as "Bullingerianism" (Staedtke).

Despite these reservations, we can point to characteristic divergences between Lutheranism, Calvinism, and Zwinglianism on four doctrinal issues, viz., the Lord's Supper, predestination, church discipline, and the covenant. The concept of "Zwinglianism" (as is so often the case with party labels) was coined by opponents. For example, Luther applied the term "Zwinglians" in 1528 to those who tended to take a symbolic view of the Lord's Supper; the abstract noun "Zwinglianism" is found as early as the 1540s.

2. Phases

The history of Zwinglianism can be divided into three phases. The relevance of the four doctrinal points mentioned above varied in the course of historical developments.

(a) First Phase (1525-1550)

In his *De vera et falsa religione* (1525), Zwingli offered the first systematic presentation of his Reformed theology. Subsequently, in the conflict with the Baptists, he discovered that God's covenant with Israel essentially corresponded to his covenant with Christians: the unity of God's action drew together the people of God and the church of Christ, the Old Testament and the New, circumcision and baptism, Passover and Lord's Supper. At the same time, in his public controversy with Luther, Zwingli defended his symbolic understanding of the Lord's Supper. The mediation of salvation does not depend on the sacramental elements, but only on God, who bestows

faith in Christ as the Son of God. In terms of his divine nature, Christ is present in the sacrament; in terms of his human nature, he sits at the right hand of God. Zwingli understands the words of institution—"This is my body"—to mean: "This signifies my body"; the expression to "eat" Christ (Jn 6) means to believe in Christ. The religious dialogue in Marburg in 1529 between Zwingli and Luther broke down because of their divergent views of the presence of Christ in the Lord's Supper. The *Confessio Helvetica prior* of 1536 (→ confessional documents), a text which owes much to Bullinger, its co-author, was accepted by the Protestant Estates in Switzerland, and basically confirms the symbolic understanding of the Lord's Supper. In the same year, Bullinger rejected the Wittenberg Concord, which Martin → Bucer, the Reformer of Strasbourg, had envisaged as a basis for unity with the Lutherans. Lengthy negotiations between Bullinger and Jean Calvin, the Reformer of Geneva, led in 1549 to the → *Consensus Tigurinus* ("Agreement of Zurich"), in which both theologians retreated from their original sacramental doctrine. Bullinger conceded that the external reception of the Lord's Supper confirms the internal working of the Holy Spirit. This agreement created a distance between Calvin and the Lutherans, and integrated Calvin into Swiss Protestantism.

(b) Second Phase (1550-1585)

The *Consensus Tigurinus* covered sacramental doctrine, but left open essential questions such as predestination and church discipline. In his conflict with the Baptists, Zwingli had used election as an argument against linking salvation to baptism. Over against Calvin, whose starting point was a double divine decree of election and damnation, Bullinger insisted on election by divine grace. Predestination continually provoked vehement controversies, and remained a matter of dispute until the synod of Dordrecht (see below).

Johannes → Oecolampadius, the Reformer of Basle, envisaged the creation of a specific organ with responsibility for church discipline, but Zwingli (after some hesitation) rejected this idea for Zurich, where the magistrates were charged with this task. In Geneva, Calvin followed the Basle model; in Berne, the Zurich model was adopted. In Heidelberg, Thomas → Erastus championed the Zurich model, with the civil authorities exercising church discipline, and received the active support of Heinrich Bullinger in his disputes with Caspar → Olevian. The same debate raged in the Netherlands too, where the national synod confirmed the autonomy of the church vis-à-vis the secular authorities in 1578, while Caspar Coolhaes (1536-1615) appealed to the works of Bullinger, Rudolf Gwalther, and Wolfgang → Musculus, and joined the magistrates of Leiden in defending the Zurich model. Coolhaes lost this battle, and was finally excommunicated.

Bullinger exercised restraint in his treatment of the matters on which Zurich and Geneva disagreed, but he remained unyielding vis-à-vis Lutheranism. At the request of the Palatinate count → Frederick III, Bullinger published in 1566 the *Confessio Helvetica posterior,* which was signed by the Protestant Estates in the Swiss confederation and by Geneva (Basle did not sign this document until 1644). This confession won wide acceptance: it was translated in France, the Netherlands, and England, and was signed by the churches in Scotland, Hungary, and Poland.

(c) Third Phase (1585-1620)

The Genevan concept of church discipline was further elaborated by Theodor → Beza, and Walter Travers and Thomas Cartwright propagated it in England in the early 1570s. They were opposed by John Whitgift and Richard Hooker, who appealed to Erastus (see above) in defense of the system of church discipline by the secular authorities. Subsequently, the Zurich model prevailed in England throughout the 17th century.

Bullinger adopted Zwingli's teaching on the covenant (see above) and elaborated it into a logical system in a monograph published in 1534. This was to prove fundamental for the development of Reformed → covenant theology, which had a profound impact in England and Scotland.

The theology of predestination which Beza had further developed in Geneva came increasingly under attack in Basle (Amandus Polanus), Berne (Abraham Musculus), and Zurich (Johannes Stucki). At the synod of Dordrecht (1618-1619), the teachings of the Arminians were condemned and the Calvinist understanding of predestination was confirmed. Since the Arminians had appealed (not without reason) to Bullinger, Johann Jakob Breitinger, the church president in Zurich, was obliged to defend Bullinger and to affirm that his theology had in reality been in agreement with Calvin. This fact alone shows that in this third phase, Calvinism had won the day over Zwinglianism.

■ Literature: *OER* 4:323–27.—*Heinrich Bullinger 1504–75. Gesammelte Aufsätze zum 400. Todestag,* vols. 1–2, ed. U. Gäbler and E. Herkenrath (Zurich, 1975); G. W. Locher, *Die Zwinglische Reformation im Rahmen der europäischen Kirchengeschichte* (Göttingen and Zurich, 1979); J. Staedtke, *Bullingers Theologie—eine Fortsetzung der zwinglischen? Bullinger-Tagung 1975. Vorträge,* ed. U. Gäbler and E. Zsindely (Zurich, 1982) 87–98; J. V. Pollet, *Huldrych Zwingli et le Zwinglianisme* (Paris, 1988); *Die Zürcher Reformation. Ausstrahlungen und Rückwirkungen,* ed. A. Schindler and H. Stickelberger, with the collaboration of M. Sallmann (Berne, 2001).

MARTIN SALLMANN

■ **Additional Literature:** B. Gordon, *The Swiss Reformation* (Manchester, 2002); U. Gäbler, *H. Z., Leben und Werk* (Zürich [2]2004).

Time Line

SECULAR HISTORY		CHURCH HISTORY	

1509-47	Henry VIII of England		
		1512-17	Fifth Lateran Council
		1513-21	Leo X
1515-47	Francis I of France		
		1516	Concordat of Bourges
		1517	95 Theses of Martin Luther
1519-56	Charles V (1530 Emperor)	1519	Leipzig Disputation
		1520	Papal Bull *Exsurge Domine* and Threatened Excommunication of Martin Luther
1521	Imperial Parliament at Worms	1521	Papal Bull *Decet Romanum Pontificem* Excommunicating Martin Luther
1521-26	War of Charles I against Francis I	1521/22	Luther at Wartburg
1522/23	Feud of Sickingen	1522/23	Hadrian VI
1522-24	Imperial Parliament at Nuremberg		
		1523-34	Clement VII
1524-25	Peasants' War		
1525	League of Dessau		
1526	Imperial Parliament at Speyer		
1526	League of Torgau		
1527	Sack of Rome		
1527-29	War of Charles V against Francis I		
1529	Imperial Parliament at Speyer Protest of Speyer	1529	Marburg Religious Dialogue
1529	Turks before Vienna		
1530	Imperial Parliament at Augsburg	1530	*Confessio Augustana, Confutatio*
1531-47	Schmalkaldic League	1531	Death of Zwingli
1532	Peace of Nuremberg		
1534	Act of Supremacy	1534	Act of Supremacy
		1534/35	Rule of the Baptists in Münster
		1534-49	Paul III
1536-38	War of Charles V against Francis I	1536	Wittenberg Concord
		1536/37	Schmalkaldic Articles
		1537	Convocation of the Council at Mantua
1539	Peace of Frankfurt		
		1540	Hagenau Religious Dialogue
		1541	Regensburg Religious Dialogue
		1541/42	Worms Religious Dialogue
1542-44	War of Charles V against Francis I		
		1545-48	Council of Trent, First Session
1546/47	Schmalkaldic War	1546	Death of Luther

Time Line

SECULAR HISTORY		CHURCH HISTORY	
		1546	Regensburg Religious Dialogue
1547-53	Edward VI of England		
1547-59	Henry II of France		
1548	Augsburg Interim		
		1549	Book of Common Prayer
		1549	Consensus Tigurinus
		1550-55	Julius III
		1551/52	Council of Trent, Second Session
1552	Treaty of Passau		
1552/53	War of the Princes		
1553-58	Mary I of England (Bloody Mary)		
1555		1555	Marcellus II
		1555-59	Paul IV
1556-64	Ferdinand I		
1556-98	Philip II of Spain		
		1557	Worms Religious Dialogue
1558-1603	Elizabeth I of England	1558	Frankfurt Recess
1559/60	Francis II of France	1559-65	Pius IV
1560-74	Charles IX of France	1560	Death of Melanchthon
1561	Naumburg Assembly of Princes		
1562-98	War of Religion in France	1562/63	Council of Trent, Third Session
		1563	Anglican Articles
1564-76	Maximilian II	1564	Death of Calvin
		1566-72	Pius V
		1566	*Catechismus Romanus*
		1568/69	Altenburg Religious Dialogue
1572	St. Bartholomew's Night	1572-85	Gregory XIII
1574-89	Henry III of France	1574	Swabian Concord
		1575	Death of Bullinger
		1576	Assembly in Torgau
		1577	Formula of Concord
		1579	Socinians in Poland
		1580	Book of Concord
1581	Separation of The Netherlands from Spain		
		1582	Gregorian Calendar
		1582-89	War of Cologne
		1585-90	Sixtus V
1589-1610	Henry IV of France		
		1590	Urban VII
		1590/91	Gregory XIV
1598	Edict of Nantes		

LIST OF ENTRIES AND CROSS-REFERENCES

All the entries in the *Dictionary of the Reformation* are listed below. Entries following "see also" indicate cross-references (identified by an arrow → in the *Dictionary*), where additional information can be found on a subject.

Acontius, Jacobus. *See also* Fundamental Articles

Adelmann von Adelmannsfelden. *See also* Eyb, Gabriel von

Adiaphora controversy. *See also* Flacius, Matthias; Frankfurt, Recess of; Gallus, Nikolaus; Gnesiolutherans and Philippists; Moritz of Saxony

Agricola, Johann. *See also* Antinomian controversy; Augsburg Interim; Confessio Augustana; Luther, Martin

Agricola, Mikael

Agricola (K[C]astenbauer, also called Boius)

Alba, Fernando Álvarez de Toledo. *See also* Calvinism; Paul IV; Philip II of Spain; Rythovius, Balduinus Martinus; William I of Orange

Alber, Matthäus

Albrecht V of Bavaria. *See also* Chalice for laity; Franck, Kaspar; Porcia, Count Bartolomeo

Albrecht of Brandenburg. *See also* Aurifaber, Andreas; Hutten, Ulrich von; Joachim I Nestor of Brandenburg; Luther, Martin; Rauch, Petrus; Tetzel, Johann; Vehe, Michael; Winkel, Heinrich. *See also under* Albrecht of Brandenburg-Ansbach the Elder

Albrecht of Brandenburg-Ansbach the Elder. *See also* Aurifaber, Andreas; Briesmann, Johannes; Crotus Rubeanus; Dessau, League of; Doppenn, Bernhard; Łaski, Jan; Luther, Martin; Mörlin, Joachim; Osiander, Andreas; Polentz, Georg von; Speratus, Paul; Tetzel, Johann; Vehe, Michael; Winkel, Heinrich

Aleander, Hieronymus. *See also* Badia, Tommaso; Campeggi, Lorenzo; Eck, Johannes; *Exsurge Domine;* Massarelli, Angelo

Allen, William. *See also* Douai

Altenburg Religious Dialogue. *See also* Concord, Formula and Book; Religious dialogues; Wigand, Johann

Altham(m)er, Andreas

Alveldt, Augustin von. *See also* Controversial theology; Fritzhans, Johannes; George III of Saxony

Ambrosius Catharinus Politus. *See also* Cajetan, Thomas; Controversial theology; Original sin

Amerbach, Bonifatius. *See also* Łaski, Jan; Zasius, Ulrich

Amerbach (Amerpachius; real name: Trolmann), Veit

Amman (Ammon), Kaspar

Amsdorf, Nikolaus von. *See also* Adiaphora controversy; Concord, Formula and Book; Enthusiasts; Frankfurt, Recess of; Gnesiolutherans and Philippists; Major, Georg; Pflug, Julius; Schnepf(f), Erhard

Andersson, Lars

Andreae, Jakob. *See also* Concord, Formula and Book; Flacius, Matthias; Franck, Kaspar; Haydlauf, Sebastian; Toussain, Peter

Anglican Articles. *See also* Common Prayer, Book of; Confessional documents; Edward VI of England; Elizabeth I of England; England, Church of; Parker, Matthew; Sacraments

Antinomian controversy. *See also* Agricola, Johann; Gnesiolutherans and Philippists; Law and Gospel; Luther, Martin

Antitrinitarians. *See also* Biandrata, Giorgio; Calvin, Jean; Concord, Formula and Book; Dudith, András; Hätzer, Ludwig; Servet, Michael; Socinians; Stancaro, Francesco

Arcimboldi, Giovannangelo. *See also* Tetzel, Johann

Armagnac, Georges d'

Arnold of Tongern

Arnoldi, Bartholomäus. *See also* Confessio Augustana

Arnoldi, Franz

Art and Reformation. *See also* Adiaphora controversy; Controversial theology; Eck, Johannes; Emser, Hieronymus; Enthusiasts; Frecht, Martin; Hätzer, Ludwig; Karlstadt, Andreas von; Oecolampad(ius), Johannes; Pelargus, Ambrosius; Reformed churches; Saints, veneration; Trent, council; William I of Orange; Zwingli, Huldrych

Articulus stantis et cadentis ecclesiae ("article of faith by which the church stands or falls"). *See also* Justification

Auger, Edmond

Augsburg Interim. *See also* Adiaphora controversy; Agricola, Johann; Alber, Matthäus; Amsdorf, Nikolaus von; Andreae, Jakob; Billick, Eberhard; Braun, Konrad; Brenz, Johannes; Bucer, Martin; Chalice for laity; Charles V; Christopher of Württemberg; Confessio Virtembirgica; Corvinus, Antonius; Dietrich, Veit; Flacius, Matthias; Frankfurt, Recess of; Frecht, Martin; Gallus, Nikolaus; Gnesiolutherans and Philippists; Heerbrand, Jakob; Helding, Michael; Joachim II Hector of Brandenburg; Major, Georg; Malvenda, Pedro de; Moritz of Saxony; Mörlin, Joachim; Musculus, Andreas; Osiander, Andreas; Pamphlets; Paul III; Pfeffinger, Johannes; Pflug, Julius; Reformation; Schauenburg, Count Adolf III von; Schnepf(f), Erhard; Timann, Johannes; Ulrich of Württemberg; Waldburg, Otto; William IV of Bavaria

Augsburg, Religious Peace of. *See also* Augsburg Interim; Billick, Eberhard; Camerarius, Joachim; Charles V; Confessio Augustana; Counter-Reformation; Ecclesiastical reservation; Ferdinand I; Ius reformandi; Landeskirchentum; Maximilian II; Moritz of Saxony; Ottheinrich of the Palatinate; Passau, Treaty of; Paul IV; Pius V; Reformation; Schmalkaldic League; Waldburg, Otto

Augustine of Piedmont. *See also* Badia, Tommaso

Aurifaber, (1) Andreas

Aurifaber, (2) Johann

Aurifaber (Goldschmied), Johann

Aurogallus (Goldhahn), Matthäus

Avenarius (Habermann), Johannes

Aventinus (Turmair), Johannes. *See also* Adelmann von Adelmannsfelden;

Baden Disputation. *See also* Ber(us), Ludwig; Bürki, Barnabas; Eck, Johannes; Fabri, Johannes; Haller, Berchtold; Kretz, Matthias;

Müller, Gallus; Murner, Thomas; Oecolampad(ius), Johannes; Oswald, Wendelin; Religious dialogues; Treger, Konrad

Badia, Tommaso

Bajus (De Bay), Michael. *See also* Granvella, Antoine Perrenot de; Gregory XIII; Hessels, Jan; Pius V; Ravesteyn, Josse; Soto, Pedro de; Stapleton, Thomas; Tapper, Ruard; Toledo, Francisco de; Villavicencio, Lorenzo de

Baptists. *See also* Antitrinitarians; Art and Reformation; Augsburg, Religious Peace of; Brès, Guy de; Bucer, Martin; Bullinger, Heinrich; Campanus, Johannes; Concord, Formula and Book; Confessio Augustana; Eck, Johannes; Enthusiasts; Grebel, Konrad; Hätzer, Ludwig; Hubmaier, Balthasar; Hutterite Brethren; Joris, David; Kessler, Johannes; Landeskirchentum; Land(t)sperger, Johannes; Lang, Matthäus; Luther, Martin; Marpeck, Pilgram; Menno Simons; Ministry, church; Oecolampad(ius), Johannes; Osiander, Andreas; Pelargus, Ambrosius; Philip I of Hessen; Reformation; Reublin, Wilhelm; Rothmann, Bernhard; Sattler, Michael; Schwenckfeld, Kaspar von; Stadion, Christoph von; Vadian, Joachim; Waldeck, Count Franz von; William IV of Bavaria; Zwickau, prophets of; Zwingli, Huldrych; Zwinglianism

Barlow, William

Barnes, Robert. *See also* Bilney, Thomas; Coverdale, Miles

Bartholomew, Night of, Saint. *See also* Charles IX; Coligny, Gaspard; Duplessis-Mornay, Philippe; Gonzaga, Ludovico; Gregory VIII; Guise, sons of François; Henry III of France; Henry IV of France; Huguenots; Medici, Catharine de'; Pithou, Pierre; Toussain, Daniel

Bauduin (Balduin), François. *See also* Mediating theology

Beatus Rhenanus (Beat Bild). *See also* Pirckheimer, Willibald

Beccadelli, Ludovico. *See also* Pole, Reginald

Beda, Noel. *See also* Berquin, Louis de

Bembo, Pietro. *See also* Paleario, Aonio; Pole, Reginald

Benedictus Deus

Berquin, Louis de

Bertano, Pietro. *See also* Gonzaga, Ercole

Berthold of Chiemsee

Ber(us) (Bär), Ludwig

Beza (de Bèze), Theodor. *See also* Bauduin,

François; Bolsec, Jérôme; Calvinism; Castellio, Sebastian; Corro, Antonio del; Huguenot Psalter; Pérez de Pineda, Juan; Poissy, religious dialogue; Vermigli, Pietro Martire; Zanchi, Girolamo; Zwinglianism

Biandrata (Blandrata), Giorgio

Bibliander (Buchmann), Theodor. *See also* Vermigli, Pietro Martire

Biel, Gabriel. *See also* Confessio Augustana; Luther, Martin; *Simul iustus et peccator*

Billicanus (Gerlacher), Theobald (Diepold)

Billick (Steinberger, Lapicida), Eberhard. *See also* Augsburg Interim; Regensburg, religious dialogues; Trent, council; Worms, religious dialogues

Bilney, Thomas. *See also* Latimer, Hugh

Blankenfeld, Johannes. *See also* Joachim I Nestor of Brandenburg

Blarer, (1) Ambrosius. *See also* Enzinas, Francisco de; Frecht, Martin; Oecolampad(ius), Johannes; Otter, Jakob; Schnepf(f), Erhard; Ulrich of Württemberg; Zell, Katharina; Zwick, Johannes

Blarer, (2) Thomas. *See also* Zell, Katharina

Blomevenna, Peter. *See also* Arnold of Tongern

Bohemian Brethren (Unitas Fratrum). *See also* Crypto-Protestantism; Dungershei(y)m, Hieronymus; Eucharistic controversy; Luke of Prague; Zell, Katharina; Ziegler, Jakob

Bolsec, Jérôme. *See also* Beza, Theodor; Calvin, Jean

Bonner, Edmund. *See also* John of Feckenham

Bonnus, Hermann. *See also* Waldeck, Count Franz von

Bora, Katharina von. *See also* Luther, Martin

Borrhaus (Bur[r]ess, Cellarius), Martin

Borromeo, Charles. *See also Catechismus Romanus;* Counter-Reformation; Gregory XIV; Lussy, Melchior; Paleotti, Gabriele; Pius IV; Pius V; Porcia, Count Bartolomeo; Reform, Catholic; Sirleto, Guglielmo; Visitation

Botzhelm (Botzemus, Abstemius), Johann von

Brant, Sebastian. *See also* Geiler von Kaysersberg, Johannes; Murner, Thomas; Wimpfeling, Jakob

Braun, Konrad

Bredenbach (Brempke, Breidbach), Matthias

Brendel von Homburg, Daniel

Brenz, Johannes. *See also* Alber, Matthäus; Andreae, Jakob; Christopher of Württemberg; Church order; Confessio Virtembirgica; Frecht, Martin; Guise, Charles;

Hosius, Stanislaus; Lutheranism; Oecolampad(ius), Johannes; Petri, Laurentius; Regensburg, religious dialogues; Schnepf(f), Erhard; Timann, Johannes; Vermigli, Pietro Martire; Worms, religious dialogues; Zell, Katharina

Brès, Guy de (Guido de Bray). *See also* Calvinism

Briçonnet, Guillaume. *See also* Calvin, Jean; Faber Stapulensis, Jakob; Louise of Savoy

Briesmann, Johannes. *See also* Giese, Tiedemann; Polentz, Georg von

Brück, Gregor

Brus von Müglitz, Anton

Bucer (Butzer), Martin. *See also* Billick, Eberhard; Bohemian Brethren; Calvin, Jean; Calvinism; Capito, Wolfgang; Church order; Confessio Scotica; Confirmation; Diaz, Juan; England, Church of; Enzinas, Francisco de; Frecht, Martin; Geneva Catechism; Gerbel, Nikolaus; Gropper, Johann; Hardenberg, Albert; Hoen, Cornelis Henricxzoon; Latomus, Bartholomäus; Lutheranism; Malvenda, Pedro de; Marbach, Johannes; Megander, Kaspar; Melander, Dionysius the Elder; Ministry, church; Murner, Thomas; Musculus, Wolfgang; Oecolampad(ius), Johannes; Pigge, Albert; Reformed churches; Regensburg Book; Regensburg, religious dialogues; Servet, Michael; Sickingen, Franz von; Sleidan(us), Johannes; Sturm, Jakob; Timann, Johannes; Wied, Hermann von; Wittenberg Concord; Worms, religious dialogues; Zanchi, Girolamo; Zell, Katharina; Zwinglianism

Buchstab, Johannes

Budé (Budaeus), Guillaume

Bugenhagen (Pomeranus), Johannes. *See also* Agricola, Stephan; Bonnus, Hermann; Christian III of Denmark; Church order; Eber, Paul; Landeskirchentum; Liturgy; Lutheranism; More, Sir Thomas; Tausen, Hans Andreas; Worship; Zegenhagen, Johannes

Bullinger, Heinrich. *See also* Calvin, Jean; Calvinism; Confessio Scotica; Consensus Tigurinus; Covenant theology; Enzinas, Francisco de; Erastus, Thomas; Hardenberg, Albert; Jud, Leo; Melander, Dionysius the Elder; Olevian, Caspar; Sim(m)ler, Josias; Truber, Primus; Zanchi, Girolamo; Zwinglianism

Bürki (also Steiger), Barnabas

Buschius (von Büschen, von dem Busche; Pasiphilus), Hermannus

Confessio Virtembirgica (Württemberg Confession; CV). *See also* Brenz, Johannes; Confessional documents; Heerbrand, Jakob; Soto, Pedro de

Confessional documents. *See also* Capito, Wolfgang; Church; Confessio Virtembirgica; Controversial theology; *Corpus doctrinae*; Geneva Catechism; Marbach, Johannes; Primacy; Reformed churches; Zwinglianism

Confessionalization. *See also* Counter-Reformation; Humanism; Mediating theology; Reform, Catholic

Confirmation. *See also* Bucer, Martin

Consensus Tigurinus. *See also* Bullinger, Heinrich; Calvin, Jean; Crypto-Calvinism; Zwinglianism

Contarini, Gasparo. *See also* Aleander, Hieronymus; Ambrosius Catharinus Politus; Badia, Tommaso; Beccadelli, Ludovico; Bembo, Pietro; Cortese, Gregorio; Counter-Reformation; Evangelism; Gonzaga, Ercole; Morone, Giovanni; Paul III; Pius V; Pole, Reginald; Reform, Catholic; Regensburg Book; Regensburg, religious dialogues; Vermigli, Pietro Martire

Controversial theology. *See also* Humanism

Cordatus (Hertz), Conrad. *See also* Cruciger, Caspar the Elder

Corpus doctrinae. See also Concord, Formula and Book; Confessional documents; Lutheranism; Major, Georg

Corro, Antonio del. *See also* Gil, Juan; Valera, Cipriano de

Cortese, Gregorio. *See also* Paul III; Pole, Reginald

Corvinus (Rabe), Antonius. *See also* Church order

Coster, Frans

Counter-Reformation (CR). *See also* Antitrinitarians; Confessionalization; Gregory XIII; Paul III; Religious dialogues

Covenant theology. *See also* Calvinism; Ursinus, Zacharias; Zwinglianism

Coverdale, Miles

Cranmer, Thomas. *See also* Anglican Articles; Common Prayer, Book of; Cromwell, Thomas; Edward VI of England; England, Church of; Henry VIII of England; John of Feckenham; Łaski, Jan; Latimer, Hugh; Mary I of England; Supremacy, Act of

Crespin, Jean

Cromwell, Thomas. *See also* Henry VIII of England; Latimer, Hugh

Crotus Rubeanus. *See also* Camerarius, Joachim; Hess, Johann; Mutianus Rufus, Conradus; Obscure Men, Letters of; Pflug, Julius

Cruciger, (1) Caspar the Elder. *See also* Altenburg Religious Dialogue; Cordatus, Conrad; George III of Anhalt-Dessau

Cruciger, (2) Caspar the Younger. *See also* Altenburg Religious Dialogue; Cordatus, Conrad; George III of Anhalt-Dessau

Crypto-Calvinism. *See also* Cruciger, Caspar the Younger; Gnesiolutherans and Philippists; Hemmingsen, Niels; Krell, Nikolaus; Melanchthon, Philipp; Peucer, Caspar; Pezel, Christoph; Ursinus, Zacharias

Crypto-Protestantism

Cuius regio, eius religio. See also Augsburg, Religious Peace of; Bohemian Brethren; *Ius reformandi*; Landeskirchentum; Reformation

Daneau, Lambert

Decet Romanum Pontificem. See also Leo X; Reformation

Delfino (Dolfino), Zaccaria

Delphius (Delfius, Delphinus; real name: Brants), Johannes

Denck, Hans. *See also* Hätzer, Ludwig; Müntzer, Thomas

Dessau, League of. *See also* Albrecht of Brandenburg; Counter-Reformation; Joachim I Nestor of Brandenburg; Reformation

Devotio moderna. See also Biel, Gabriel

Diaz, Juan. *See also* Malvenda, Pedro de

Dick (Dickius; in the Greek form, Pachis), Leopold

Dietenberger, Johannes. *See also* Confessio Augustana

Dietrich, Veit. *See also* Truber, Primus

Doppenn (Doppen, Dappen), Bernhard

Doré, Pierre

Douai. *See also* Allen, William; Bajus, Michael; Granvella, Antoine Perrenot de; Stapleton, Thomas; Winzet, Ninian

Draconites (Drach), Johannes

Drašković de Trakošćan, Juraj

Driedo(ens), Johannes (Johan Nys). *See also* Church; Controversial theology; Latomus, Jacobus

Du Bellay, Guillaume. *See also* Sleidan(us), Johannes

Dudith (Dudich), András

Dumoulin, Charles

Dungershei(y)m (Ochsenfart), Hieronymus

Duplessis-Mornay, Philippe

Duprat (Du Prat), Antoine-Bohier

chism; Luther, Martin; Lutheranism; Schmalkaldic Articles; *Simul iustus et peccator*

Leib, Kilian. *See also* Adelmann von Adelmannsfelden; Eyb, Gabriel von; Hutten, Moritz von

Leipzig Disputation. *See also* Controversial theology; Eck, Johannes; Emser, Hieronymus; George III of Saxony; Hutten, Ulrich von; Karlstadt, Andreas von; Luther, Martin; Melanchthon, Philipp; Mosellanus, Petrus; Pfeffinger, Johannes; Poliander, Johann; Reformation

Leisentrit(t) von Julisberg, Johann. *See also* Paracelsus

Lemnius, Simon

Leo X, Pope. *See also* Bembo, Pietro; Charles V; Clement VII; Duprat, Antoine-Bohier; Francis I of France; Giberti, Gian Matteo; Hadrian VI; Henry VIII of England; Hoogstraeten, Jacob; Indulgences; Luther, Martin; Sadoleto, Jacopo; Schiner, Matthäus; Ziegler, Jakob

Linck (Link), Wenzeslaus. *See also* Worms, religious dialogues

Lindanus (van der Lindt), Wilhelmus Damasus. *See also* Cassander, Georg; Soto, Pedro de

Lippomani (Lip[p]omano, Lipomanus), Luigi. *See also* Surius, Laurentius; Trent, council

Lipsius, Justus. *See also* Scaliger, Joseph Justus

Liturgy. *See also* Music and the Reformation; Reformation; Uniformity, Acts of

Loher, Dietrich

Lord's Supper, → Communion/Lord's Supper.

Lorichius, Gerhard

Lotzer, Sebastian. *See also* Peasants' War

Louise of Savoy

Luke of Prague. *See also* Bohemian Brethren

Lussy, Melchior. *See also* Volpe, Giovanni Antonio

Luther, Martin

Lutheranism. *See also* Antinomian controversy; Augsburg, Religious Peace of; Controversial theology; Counter-Reformation; Crypto-Calvinism; Protestantism; Reformation

Luther's Bible. *See also* Luther, Martin

Madruzzo, (1) Cristoforo. *See also* Acontius; Prée, Laurent de la

Madruzzo, (2) Ludovico

Magdeburg Centuriators. *See also* Braun, Konrad; Canisius, Peter; Flacius, Matthias; Medina, Miguel de; Wigand, Johann

Magni, Petrus. *See also* Petri, Laurentius

Magnus, (1) Johannes

Magnus, (2) Olaus

Major (Meier), Georg. *See also* Adiaphora controversy; Amsdorf, Nikolaus von; Frankfurt, Recess of; Gnesiolutherans and Philippists; Regensburg, religious dialogues; Schnepf(f), Erhard; Westphal, Joachim

Malvenda, Pedro de. *See also* Regensburg, religious dialogues

Marbach, Johannes. *See also* Concord, Formula and Book; Pappus, Johannes; Vermigli, Pietro Martire; Zanchi, Girolamo

Marburg, religious dialogue. *See also* Confessio Augustana; Dietrich, Veit; Eucharistic controversy; Luther, Martin; Menius, Justus; Myconius, Friedrich; Oecolampad(ius), Johannes; Philip I of Hessen; Reformation; Schmalkaldic League; Schwabach Articles

Marcello, Cristoforo

Marcellus II, Pope. *See also* Beccadelli, Ludovico; Hervet, Gentien; Massarelli, Angelo; Reform, Catholic; Sirleto, Guglielmo; Trent, council

Margaret of Parma. *See also* Geusen

Marius (real name: Mair, Mayr), Wolfgang

Marpeck (Marbeck), Pilgram. *See also* Schwenckfeld, Kaspar von

Marriage. *See also* Latomus, Jacobus; Regensburg Book; Trent, council

Marschalk, Nikolaus

Mary I of England. *See also* Bonner, Edmund; Edward VI of England; Gardiner, Stephen; Jewel, John; Julius III; Knox, John; Łaski, Jan; Latimer, Hugh; Ochino, Bernardino; Parker, Matthew; Phiip II of Spain; Pole, Reginald; Sotomaior, Luiz de; Supremacy, Act of

Mary Queen of Scots. *See also* Hamilton, John; John of Feckenham; Sixtus V; Winzet, Ninian

Massarelli, Angelo

Mathesius, Johannes

Maximilian II. *See also* Camerarius, Joachim; Gerstmann, Martin von; Pius IV; Sittard, Matthias

Mediating theology. *See also* Humanism; Moritz of Saxony; Witzel, Georg

Medici, Catharine de'. *See also* Bartholomew, Night of Saint; Charles IX; Gonzaga, Ludovico; Henry II of France; Huguenots; Poissy, religious dialogue; Tournon, François de

Medina, Miguel de. *See also* Wild, Johannes

Megander (real name: Grossmann), Kaspar

de; Charles V; Douai; Granvella, Antoine
Perrenot de; Gregory XIII; Hessels, Jan;
Margaret of Parma; Mary I of England;
Orozco, Alonso de; Panvini(o), Onofrio;
Pius IV; Pius V; Pole, Reginald; Sixtus V;
Sonnius, Franciscus; Villavicencio, Lorenzo
de; William I of Orange

Pigge (Pighius), Albert. *See also* Church; Controversial theology; Mediating theology; Original sin;

Pirckheimer, (1) C(h)aritas. *See also* Scheurl,
Christoph

Pirckheimer, (2) Willibald. *See also* Adelmann
von Adelmannsfelden; Haner, Johannes;
Leib, Kilian; Pflug, Julius; Spengler, Lazarus

Pithou, Pierre

Pius IV, Pope. *See also* Borromeo, Charles;
Campeggi, Tommaso; *Catechismus
Romanus;* Chalice for laity; Counter-
Reformation; Granvella, Antoine Perrenot
de; Morone, Giovanni; Naumburg, assembly
of princes; Panvini(o), Onofrio; Paul IV;
Philip II of Spain; Schlegel, Theodul; Simo-
netta, Ludovico; Sirleto, Guglielmo; Trent,
council; Tschudi, Aegidius; Vargas y Mexía,
Francisco de

Pius V, Pope. *See also* Canisius, Peter; Carne-
secchi, Pietro; *Catechismus Romanus;*
Counter-Reformation; Elizabeth I of Eng-
land; Maximilian II; Medina, Miguel de;
Philip II of Spain; Sirleto, Guglielmo;
Tridentine liturgy

Plettenberg, Wolter von. *See also* Blankenfeld,
Johannes

Poissy, religious dialogue. *See also* Cassander,
Georg; Espence, Claude d'; Guise, Charles;
Huguenots; Laínez, Diego; Religious dia-
logues; Trent, council; Vermigli, Pietro
Martire

Pole, Reginald. *See also* Beccadelli, Ludovico;
Carnesecchi, Pietro; Contarini, Gasparo;
Cortese, Gregorio; Counter-Reformation;
Dudith, András; Evangelism; Gonzaga,
Ercole; Gonzaga, Giulia; Mary I of England;
Morone, Giovanni; Paul III; Paul IV; Pius V;
Reform, Catholic; Trent, council; Vermigli,
Pietro Martire

Polentz, Georg von. *See also* Albrecht of Brandenburg

Poliander (real name: Gramann or Graumann),
Johann

Ponce de la Fuente, Constantino. *See also* Gil,
Juan; Pérez de Pineda, Juan

Porcia, Count Bartolomeo

Predestination. *See also* Calvinism; Toledo, Francisco de

Prée (Pratanus), Laurent de la

Prierias (real name: Mazzolini), Sylvester. *See also*
Controversial theology; Reformation;
R(h)adinus, Thomas

Primacy. *See also* Latomus, Jacobus; Leipzig Dis-
putation; Luther, Martin; Orzechowski,
Stanislaw; Pius IV; Schmalkaldic Articles;
Trent, council; Trent, council

Protestantism. *See also* Reformation

Puritans. *See also* Calvinism; Parker, Matthew

Rab, Hermann

Rauch (von Ansbach), (1) Bartholomäus

Rauch (2) Petrus

Ravesteyn, Josse. *See also* Bajus, Michael; Tapper,
Ruard; Villavicencio, Lorenzo de

Reform, Catholic. *See also* Confessionalization;
Counter-Reformation; Gregory XIII;
Humanism; Ignatius of Loyola; Lang,
Matthäus; Liturgy; Morone, Giovanni;
Pfyffer, Ludwig; Regensburg Convent and
League

Reformation. *See also* Aleander, Hieronymus;
Controversial theology; Counter-Reformation; Peasants' War; Protestantism; Religious
dialogues

Reformed churches. *See also* Calvinism;
Zwinglianism

Regensburg Book. *See also* Bucer, Martin; Calvin,
Jean; Corvinus, Antonius; Regensburg, religious dialogues

Regensburg Convent and League. *See also*
Counter-Reformation; Dessau, League of;
Fabri, Johannes; Nausea, Friedrich

Regensburg, religious dialogues. *See also* Bembo,
Pietro; Billick, Eberhard; Candidus, Alexan-
der; Cochlaeus, Johannes; Cruciger, Caspar
the Elder; Diaz, Juan; Dietrich, Veit; Eck,
Johannes; Frecht, Martin; Gropper, Johann;
Hagenau, religious dialogue; Hutten, Moritz
von; Joachim II Hector of Brandenburg;
Johann Friedrich of Saxony; Leib, Kilian;
Luther, Martin; Major, Georg; Malvenda,
Pedro de; Mensing, Johannes; Morone,
Giovanni; Musculus, Wolfgang; Paul III;
Pigge, Albert; Reform, Catholic; Reforma-
tion; Regensburg Book; Religious dialogues;
Schnepf(f), Erhard; Sleidan(us), Johannes;
Timann, Johannes; Trent, council; Vergerio,
Pietro Paolo the Younger; Waldburg, Otto;
Witzel, Georg; Worms, religious dialogues

ENCYCLOPEDIA OF THEOLOGY AND CHURCH
Dictionary of the Popes and the Papacy
Bruno Steimer and Michael Parker, Editors

The definitive reference work on the history of the popes!

Under the editorial direction of Walter Cardinal Kasper, a large body of international scholars and special advisors have created the third edition of the *Lexikon für Theologie und Kirche*. The *LTHK* forms the basis for the English series, the *Encyclopedia of Theology and Church*.

This first installment of the new multi-volume library of theological dictionaries makes available for the first time in English the wealth of information from the internationally acclaimed *Lexikon für Theologie und Kirche*. Edited by Karl Rahner in the completely reworked, revised, and updated third edition, the *Lexikon für Theologie und Kirche* is the most authoritative starting point for information on a wide variety of theological topics. Used around the world by scholars and students of theology, church history, art history, history, sociology, and other areas of interest, these accessible articles offer comprehensive information as well as maps, drawings, and a wealth of bibliographic data, completely updated and adapted for English-language publication.

The *Dictionary* is two dictionaries in one. Part One includes concise biographical entries on the pontificates of all popes and antipopes of historical record; Part Two contains entries on the institutional, canonical, and theological aspects of the papacy. Articles of contemporary interest such as the Holy (Jubilee) Year are also included.

"Gratitude to the editors of this impressive volume and to its many contributors. It contains a wealth of information about the papacy. No other work like it exists in English. Highly recommended."
— Patrick Granfield, The Catholic University of America

0-8245-1918-3, $50.00 hardcover

crossroad

Walter Cardinal Kasper
LEADERSHIP IN THE CHURCH
How Traditional Roles Can Serve the Christian Community Today

A sense of urgency pervades the Catholic Church. On questions as diverse as the nature of ordination, the role of deacons, the priestly and episcopal offices, and the objectives of canon law, as well as the relations between universal and local churches and the progress of ecumenism, there is a widespread conviction that the Church has arrived at a crossroad in its great history.

In *Leadership in the Church,* Cardinal Kasper writes on a variety of the most pressing questions facing leadership within the Catholic Church today and its faithful pursuit of service to the Christian community. On each point, he reminds us of the resources available from the tradition, indicates the pressing nature of the current debate, and proclaims the authentically Christian hope for the future.

0-8245-1977-9, $24.95 hardcover

Siegmar Doepp and Wilhelm Geerlings, Editors
DICTIONARY OF EARLY CHRISTIAN LITERATURE

An easily accessible overview of the literature of early Christianity

The long-awaited successor to Berthold Altaner's *Patrologie* handbook, the *Dictionary of Early Christian Literature* presents the life and work of Christian authors up to the eighth century and an assessment of their lasting influence on the Christian tradition. The *Dictionary* offers compact and precise information as well as an updated bibliography in an easy-to-use alphabetical arrangement. Articles on authors provide a brief description of their lives, a presentation of their works, and an assessment of their influence on the Christian tradition.

"I would recommend this work highly to specialists and non-specialists alike who have an interest in the period of early Christianity."
— Thomas F. Martin, O.S.A., Ph.D., Villanova University

0-8245-1805-5, $75.00 hardcover

Please support your local bookstore,
or call 1-800-707-0670 for Customer Service.

For a free catalog, write us at

THE CROSSROAD PUBLISHING COMPANY
481 Eighth Avenue, Suite 1550
New York, NY 10001

Visit our website at
www.crossroadpublishing.com
All prices subject to change.

crossroad